Toyota

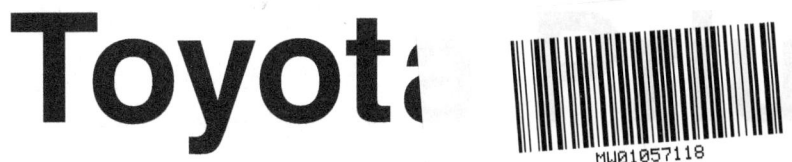

Repair and Maintenance Manual

2004, 2005, 2006, 2007, 2008

B BentleyPublishers®
.com

Table of Contents

1 Familiarization

General
Background and development
What is a hybrid
Toyota hybrid system II (THS II)

Prius operating modes
Suspension, brakes, steering
Body
Dashboard layout

2 Prius Hybrid System

Toyota hybrid system
Gasoline engine
Engine emission controls
Hybrid transaxle

High voltage (HV) system
  components
Electric A/C compressor
Electric power steering
  (EPS)

Regenerative braking
  system
Tire pressure warning
  system (TPWS)

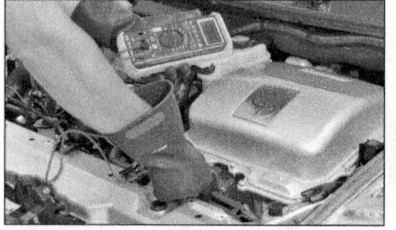

3 Safety

General
Warnings
Cautions
High voltage precautions

Before working on your Prius
Testing for high voltage
Emergency procedures
Jump starting and towing

4 Service and Repair Fundamentals

General
Jacking and lifting
Preliminary service advice

Fasteners
Buying parts
Tools

Using Toyota TIS
Maintenance schedules

5 Engine

General
Engine compartment covers
Engine oil service
Engine air filter

Serpentine belt
Ignition coils and spark plugs
Valve clearance
Cooling system

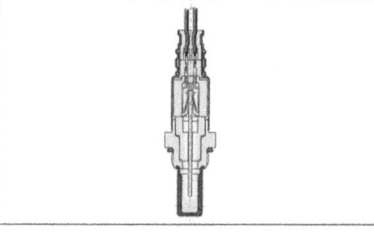

6 Emission Controls

General
Positive crankcase ventilation (PCV)
  valve

Air-fuel ratio and oxygen sensors
Evaporative emission control (EVAP)
  system

7 Hybrid Transaxle

General
Transaxle / inverter coolant service

Transaxle fluid service

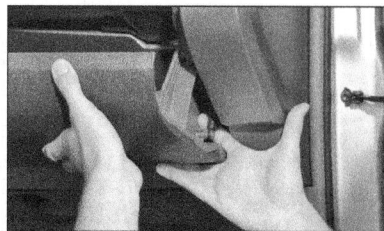

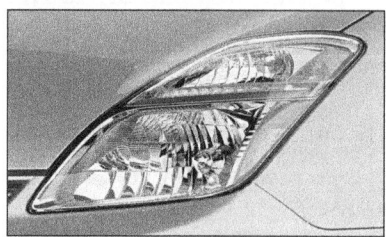

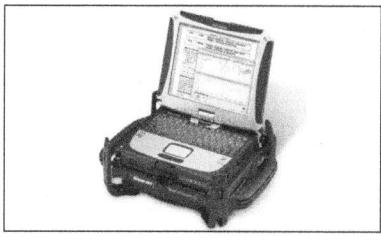

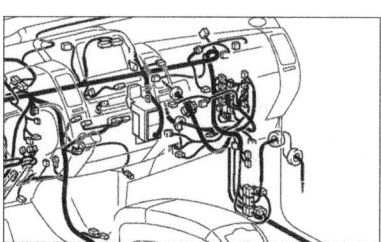

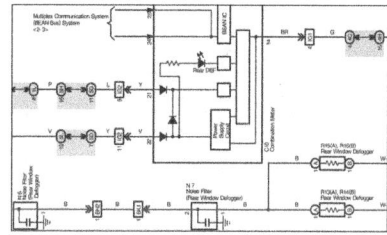

BENTLEY PUBLISHERS® | Automotive Reference™

Bentley Publishers, a division of Robert Bentley, Inc.
1734 Massachusetts Avenue
Cambridge, MA 02138 USA
800-423-4595 / 617-547-4170

Information that makes
the difference®

BentleyPublishers®
.com

Technical contact information

We welcome your feedback. Please submit corrections and additions to our Toyota technical discussion forum at:

http://www.BentleyPublishers.com

Updates and corrections

We will evaluate submissions and post appropriate editorial changes online as updates or tech discussion. Appropriate updates and corrections will be added to the book in future printings. Check for updates and corrections for this book before beginning work on your vehicle. See the following web address for additional information:

http://www.BentleyPublishers.com/updates/

This manual is prepared, published and distributed by Bentley Publishers, 1734 Massachusetts Avenue, Cambridge, Massachusetts 02138 USA. All information contained in this manual is based on the information available to the publisher at the time of editorial closing. Toyota has not reviewed and does not vouch for the accuracy or completeness of the technical specifications and work procedures described and given in this manual.

ISBN 978-0-8376-1766-4   **Job code: TP08-05**   *Editorial closing 01 / 2008

Library of Congress Cataloging-in-Publication Data for 2008 edition
Toyota Prius : repair and maintenance manual : 2004, 2005, 2006, 2007, 2008.
   p. cm.
  Includes index.
  ISBN 978-0-8376-1553-0 (alk. paper)
  1. Prius automobile--Maintenance and repair--Handbooks, manuals, etc.

  TL215.P78T68 2008
  629.28'722--dc22

          2008005890

Manufactured in the United States of America

201904R001

Foreword

For the Toyota owner with automotive mechanical skills, and for independent service professionals, this book includes maintenance and repair procedures the Prius is likely to need during its service life, including many procedures and specifications that were available in an authorized Toyota dealer service department at the time this manual was prepared. The Toyota owner with no intention of working on his or her car will find that owning and referring to this book will make it possible to be better informed and to more knowledgeably discuss repairs with a professional automotive technician.

For those intending to do maintenance and repair on the Prius, it is essential that high voltage safety equipment be used and safety precautions observed when working around high voltage. A minimum equipment list includes insulated lineman's gloves, eye protection, and a fire extinguisher (Class C or Class D). Please read **3 Prius Safety** for more information on safety equipment. A selection of good quality hand tools is also needed. This includes a torque wrench to ensure that fasteners are tightened in accordance with specifications. Additional information on tools is in **4 Service and Repair Fundamentals**.

Disclaimer

We have endeavored to ensure the accuracy of the information in this book. When the vast array of data presented in the book is taken into account, however, no claim to infallibility can be made. We therefore cannot be responsible for the result of any errors that may have crept into the text. Please also read the **WARNING–important safety notice** on the copyright page.

A thorough prereading of each procedure, the **WARNINGS** and **CAUTIONS** found in **3 Prius Safety,** and any **WARNING** or **CAUTION** that accompanies the procedure is essential. Reading a procedure before beginning work helps you determine in advance the need for specific skills, identify hazards, prepare for appropriate capture and handling of hazardous materials and the need for particular tools and replacement parts such as gaskets.

Bentley Publishers encourages comments from the readers of this book with regard to errors, and/or suggestions for improvement of our product. These communications have been and will be carefully considered in the preparation of this and other books. If you identify inconsistencies in the book, you may have found an error. Please contact the publisher and we will endeavor to post applicable corrections on our website. Posted corrections (errata) should be reviewed before beginning work. Please see the following web address:

http://www.BentleyPublishers.com/updates/

Toyota continues to issue service information and parts retrofits after the editorial closing of this book. Some of this updated information may apply to procedures and specifications in this book. For the latest information, please see the following web address:

https://techinfo.toyota.com

Toyota offers extensive warranties, especially on components of the fuel delivery and emission control systems. Therefore, before deciding to repair a Toyota that may be covered wholly or in part by any warranties issued by Toyota Motor Sales (TMS) USA, Inc., consult your authorized Toyota dealer. You may find that the dealer can make the repair either free or at minimum cost. Regardless of its age, or whether it is under warranty, your Toyota is both an easy car to service and an easy car to get serviced. So if at any time a repair is needed that you feel is too difficult to do yourself, a trained Toyota technician is ready to do the job for you.

Bentley Publishers

Vehicle Identification
VIN decoder

Some of the information in this manual applies only to cars of a particular model year or range of years. For example, 2006 refers to the 2006 model year but does not necessarily match the calendar year in which the car was manufactured or sold. To be sure of the model year of a particular car, check the vehicle identification number (VIN) on the car.

The VIN is a unique sequence of 17 characters assigned by Toyota to identify each individual car. When decoded, the VIN tells the country and year of manufacture; make, model and serial number; assembly plant and even some equipment specifications.

The Toyota VIN is placed at various positions on the vehicle, including a plate mounted on the top of the dashboard, on the driver's side where the number can be seen through the windshield. The 10th character is the model year code. The letters I, O, Q, U, Z and the number 0 are not used for model year designation. Examples: Y for 2000, 1 for 2001, etc. The table below explains some of the codes in the VIN for 2004 through 2008 Toyota Prius vehicles covered by this manual.

Sample VIN: JTD KB20U X 6 0 999999
position   1 2 3   4 5 6 7 8   9 10 11   12-17

VIN position	Description	Decoding information	
1 - 3	World manufacturer indentifier	J T D	Japan Toyota Passenger vehicle
4	Body / drive type	K	5-door sedan, 2-wheel drive, hatchback
5	Engine family	B	1NZ-FXE +3CM
6	Series	2	NHW20 (Prius)
7	Restraint system	0 2 6 7 8	Manual belts, 2 airbags, side airbags, side curtain shield airbags Manual belts, 2 airbags Manual belts, 2 airbags, side airbags, side curtain shield airbags and knee airbags (driver seat) Manual belts, 2 airbags and knee airbags (driver seat) Manual belts, 2 airbags and side airbags
8	Car line	U	Prius
9	Check digit	0 - 9 or X	Calculated by NHTSA
10	Model year	4 5 6 7 8	2004 2005 2006 2007 2008
11	Assembly plant	0 - 9, K, J	Toyota Motor Corporation
12 - 17	Serial number	999999	Serial number

1

Familiarization

Hybrid Synergy Drive: environmentally responsible power and performance

Familiarization

Courtesy Toyota Motor Sales (TMS) USA, Inc.

GENERAL

The information included in this chapter is based on introductory and preliminary sales information for the 2004 - 2008 second generation Toyota Prius (Toyota sales designation: NHW20) sold in the USA or Canada. The content provided is intended as a product familiarization guide and is subject to change.

> **WARNING—**
> *Check the Toyota Technical Information System (TIS) at https://techinfo.toyota.com and the publisher's website at http://www.bentleypublishers.com for information that may supersede any information included in this section.*

NOTE—
- *This product familiarization chapter describes the complete Prius automobile, including some basic information about the Toyota Hybrid System II (THS II). In-depth hybrid system information is in* **2 Prius Hybrid System.**

**2000 Prius
(1st generation)**

TP0801014

Courtesy Toyota Motor Sales (TMS) USA, Inc.

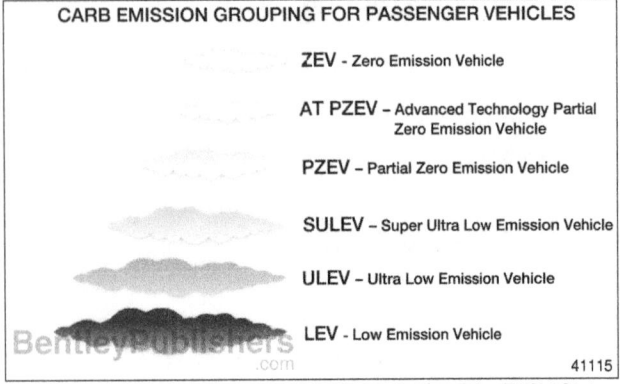

CARB EMISSION GROUPING FOR PASSENGER VEHICLES

ZEV - Zero Emission Vehicle

AT PZEV – Advanced Technology Partial
Zero Emission Vehicle

PZEV – Partial Zero Emission Vehicle

SULEV – Super Ultra Low Emission Vehicle

ULEV – Ultra Low Emission Vehicle

LEV - Low Emission Vehicle

41115

Courtesy Toyota Motor Sales (TMS) USA, Inc.

41248

Courtesy Toyota Motor Sales (TMS) USA, Inc.

BACKGROUND AND DEVELOPMENT

Prius development began in the early 1990s, when Toyota established the G21 committee. G21 stands for "globe" and "21st century." The committees's goal was to develop vehicles with low emissions. Late in 1994, a year after the committee was formed, a concept vehicle was developed called the "Prius," taken from the Latin word for "before", as in "ahead."

First sold exclusively in Japan starting in 1997, the Prius entered the worldwide market in model year 2001 (launched August 2000 in the U.S. with an MSRP of $19,999). By the end of 2003, nearly 160,000 units had been produced for sale in Japan, Europe and North America. As of April 2006, combined first and second generation Prius sales hit the 500,000 mark.

The 2001 - 2003 Prius was certified as a Super Ultra Low Emission Vehicle (SULEV) by the California Air Resources Board (CARB).

Points of interest

- The Prius has won numerous awards including Car of the Year awards for Europe, Japan and North America.
- Prius drivers (and other hybrid engine automobiles) are allowed to drive by themselves in carpool (high occupancy vehicle) lanes in some US states, including Virginia (requires a special Clean Fuel Vehicle license plate), California (requires a small one-time fee for a decal, 85k limit), Florida (requires a decal), and New York.
- Los Angeles and San Jose, California allow free parking at meters for hybrid vehicles within the posted time limits.
- Prius drivers in London, UK, are exempt from the £8 ($16) daily London congestion charge (congestion charge requires £10 per year registration).
- The NHW20 Prius fuel tank holds 45 liters (11.9 US gal), although the internal bladder in North American models limits the fill, giving a range of up to 600 miles.
- Starting with the 2004 model, Toyota began producing the Prius on a standard mass production assembly line, resulting in one being produced every minute instead of one every 8 to 10 minutes.
- The high voltage battery pack of the 2004 Prius is guaranteed for 100,000 miles or 8 years (Toyota has stated that they expect it to last 15 years). The warranty is extended to 150,000 miles or 10 years for Prius in California and several other states that adopted the Californian emission control standards.

NHW20 Prius (2nd generation)

Toyota has sold more Prius cars than all other hybrid vehicles combined, and for good reasons. Since the debut of the second generation Prius in the 2004 model year, the midsize hatchback has racked up award after award and continues to sell in record numbers.

The 2004 model was a complete redesign of the previous generation of Prius and certified as an Advanced Technology Partial Zero Emission Vehicle (AT-PZEV).

Courtesy Toyota Motor Sales (TMS) USA, Inc.

Courtesy Toyota Motor Sales (TMS) USA, Inc.

The new model is powered by Hybrid Synergy Drive (also called Toyota Hybrid System II), replacing the earlier Toyota Hybrid System (THS) technology.

The four-door hatchback can seat up to five people. The powertrain features a small gasoline-fueled engine in conjunction with two electric motor / generators and a planetary gear set that functions as a continuously variable transmission.

The result is adequate power, high fuel economy and reduced tailpipe emissions. The gas engine produces 76 horsepower and 82 lb-ft of torque, while the electric motors generate the equivalent of 67 hp and 295 lb-ft of torque.

Under the hood is a 1.5-liter Atkinson cycle engine that works with a 50-kW electric motor. Fuel efficiency is rated in the mid-50 miles-per-gallon range. And it is comparatively quick: 0 to 60 mph in 10.1 seconds.

With a smaller and lower voltage NiMH battery and a boost converter to step the voltage up to 500 V, the 2004 model was more powerful (2 seconds faster in 0 to 60 kph acceleration) and is 15% more fuel efficient than the previous generation Prius.

For comparison, the first generation (1997 - 2003) Prius could not operate air-conditioning unless the engine was running. The 2004 model introduced an all-electric A/C compressor for cooling. This not only allowed the use of air-conditioning without the engine running, it also allowed more use of electric-motor-only mode.

Under full acceleration, both electric and gasoline power sources work together to provide maximum power, but under lighter load conditions, such as stop-and-go traffic, the Prius alternates between the two, often running on battery power alone.

A regenerative braking system converts energy normally lost as heat into electricity to charge the high-voltage battery pack. Regenerative braking was greatly improved, relying so little upon the friction-type brakes (except for panic stops) that the original brake pads could potentially last for the life of the car.

The drag coefficient (C_d) of 0.26 was the second lowest in the industry, after the smaller Honda Insight at 0.25. EPA ratings improved up to 60 mpg and efficiency was improved 37%.

Prius dimensions and weight

- Overall height .... 58.1 in. (1475 mm)
- Track
  Front .... 59.3 in (1506 mm)
  Rear .... 58.3 in (1481 mm)
- Overall width .... 67.9 in (1725 mm)
- Wheelbase .... 106.2 in (2700 mm)
- Overall length .... 175.0 in (4445 mm)
- Ground clearance .... 4.9 in (124 mm)
- Turning circle .... 34.1 ft (10.4 m)
- Curb weight ....2932 lb (1330 kg)
- Passenger volume .... 96.2. ft^3 (2.7 m^3)
- Cargo volume .... 16.1 ft^3 (0.45 m^3)

Familiarization

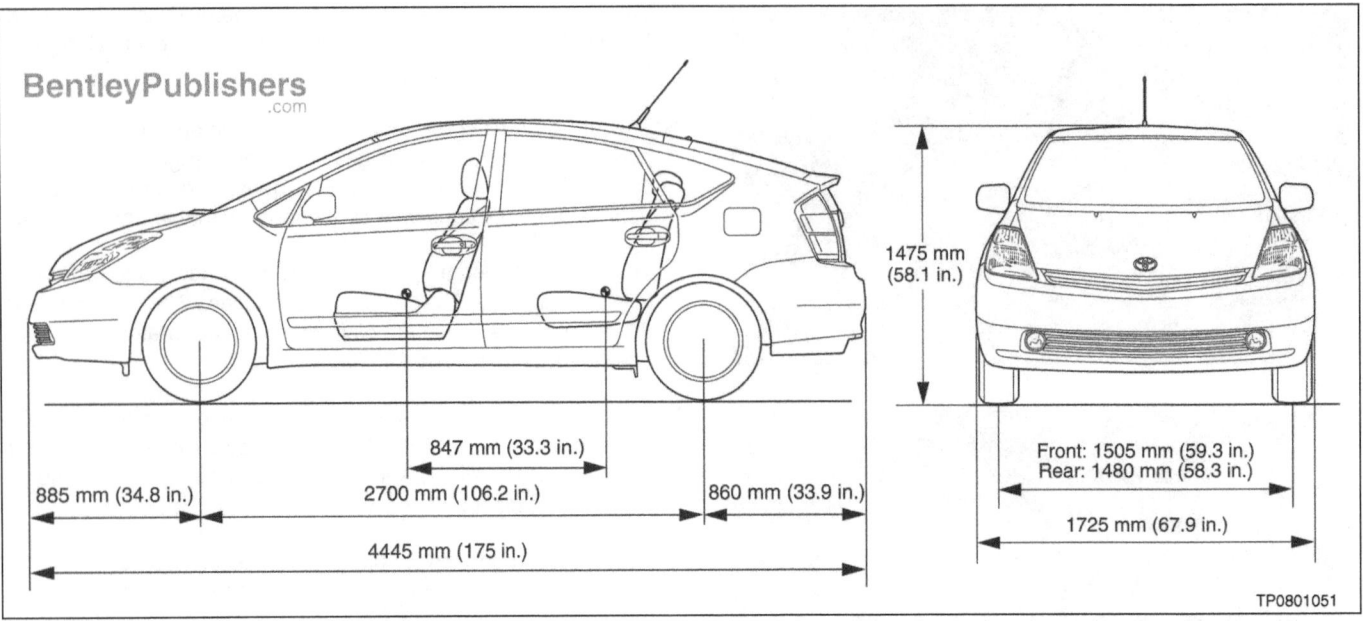

Courtesy Toyota Motor Sales (TMS) USA, Inc.

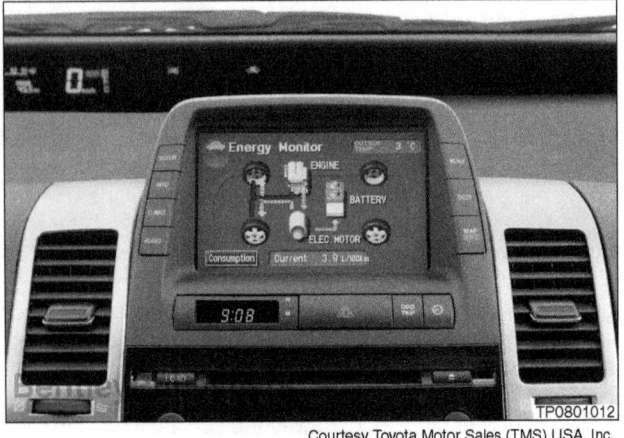

Courtesy Toyota Motor Sales (TMS) USA, Inc.

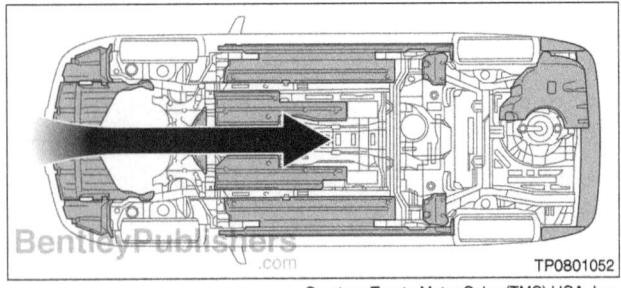

Courtesy Toyota Motor Sales (TMS) USA, Inc.

Standard equipment list (2006 model)

- 1.5L inline-4 cylinder VVT-i gasoline engine with 76 horsepower and 82 lb-ft of torque
- 500 volt electric motors with 67 horsepower and 295 lb-ft of torque
- Nickel metal hydride (NiMH) battery technology pack with a maximum output of 30 kW
- Continuously variable transmission
- Automatic climate control that can run with gasoline engine OFF
- Electrically assisted rack-and-pinion steering
- Traction control, brake assist
- Split-folding rear seat
- Remote entry
- Push button starting
- Liquid crystal multi-information display panel with energy monitoring, climate control, outside temperature and audio status modes
- Driver's instrument display with digital speedometer, fuel gauge, shift-lever indicator and odometer with twin trip odometers and warning lights
- Use of wheel spats and underbody pans resulting in a low coefficient of aerodynamic drag (C_d) of 0.26
- AM / FM radio and CD player with six speakers

Package #1 -GY- $650
Includes driver and front passenger front seat-mounted side and front and rear side curtain airbags.

Package #2 -HE- $825
Includes AM / FM radio and CD player with six speakers, auxiliary audio jack and MP3/WMA playback capability, Smart Key System, and backup camera.

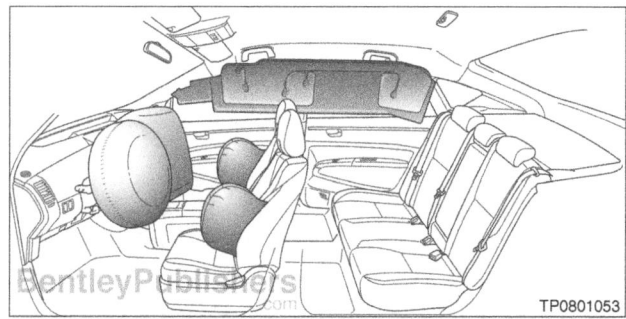

Courtesy Toyota Motor Sales (TMS) USA, Inc.

Smart key door handle

Courtesy Toyota Motor Sales (TMS) USA, Inc.

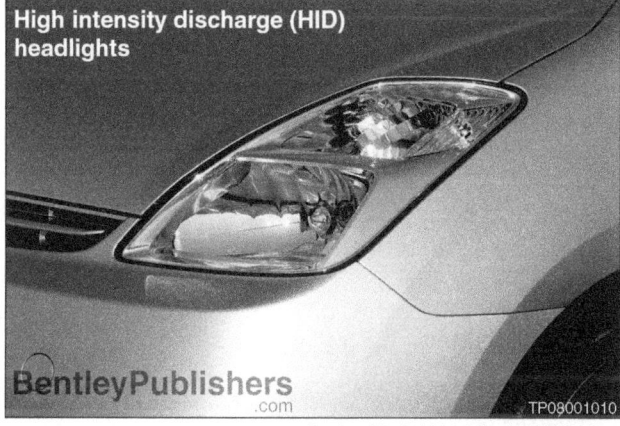

High intensity discharge (HID) headlights

Courtesy Toyota Motor Sales (TMS) USA, Inc.

Package #3 -HF- $1,475
Includes driver and front passenger front seat-mounted side and front and rear side curtain airbags, AM / FM radio and CD player with six speakers, auxiliary audio jack and MP3/WMA playback capability, Smart Key system, and backup camera.

Package #4 -HG- $1,825
Includes driver and front passenger front seat-mounted side and front and rear side curtain airbags, AM / FM radio and CD player with six speakers, auxiliary audio jack and MP3 / WMA playback capability, Smart Key system, backup camera and Vehicle Stability Control (VSC).

Package #5 -HI- $3,205
Includes driver and front passenger front seat-mounted side and front and rear side curtain airbags, anti-theft system and auto-dimming rearview mirror with HomeLink® universal transceiver, Smart Key system, backup camera, Vehicle Stability Control (VSC), and JBL® AM / FM radio and 6-disc in-dash CD changer with nine speakers in seven locations, auxiliary audio jack, MP3 / WMA playback capability and hands-free phone capability via Bluetooth® wireless technology.

Package #6 -HK- $3,830
Includes driver and front passenger front seat-mounted side and front and rear side curtain airbags, anti-theft system and auto-dimming rearview mirror with HomeLink® universal transceiver, Smart Key system, backup camera, Vehicle Stability Control (VSC), xenon (HID) headlights and integrated foglights, and JBL® AM / FM 6-disc in-dash CD changer with nine speakers in seven locations, auxiliary audio jack, MP3 / WMA playback capability and hands-free phone capability via Bluetooth® wireless technology.

Package #7 -NL- $5,730
Includes driver and front passenger front seat-mounted side and front and rear side curtain airbags, anti-theft system and auto-dimming rearview mirror with HomeLink® universal transceiver, Smart Key system, backup camera, Vehicle Stability Control (VSC), xenon (HID) head lights and integrated foglights, JBL® AM / FM 6-disc in-dash CD changer with nine speakers in seven locations, auxiliary audio jack, MP3 / WMA playback capability and hands-free phone capability via Bluetooth® wireless technology, and voice-activated DVD navigation system.

Package #8 -NW- $6,890
Includes driver and front passenger front seat-mounted side and front and rear side curtain airbags, anti-theft system and auto-dimming rearview mirror with HomeLink® universal transceiver, Smart Key system, backup camera, Vehicle Stability Control (VSC), xenon (HID) head lights and integrated foglights, JBL® AM / FM 6-disc in-dash CD changer with nine speakers in seven locations, auxiliary audio jack, MP3 / WMA playback capability and hands-free phone capability via Bluetooth® wireless technology, voice-activated DVD navigation system, and leather-trimmed seats and steering wheel.

Courtesy Toyota Motor Sales (TMS) USA, Inc.

41226

WHAT IS A HYBRID?

◄ A simple definition of a hybrid automobile is: "a vehicle that uses more than one energy source for propulsion." The most common hybrid vehicle built today unites an internal combustion gasoline engine with power from an electric motor. The Prius is configured in this way. Energy sources are stored in two ways: chemical energy is stored in the gasoline, and electrical energy is stored in a high voltage (HV) battery pack.

In addition to providing motive force, the engine runs a generator that recharges the high voltage battery while the vehicle is driven. You never need to "plug in" to charge the battery. The combination of a gasoline engine and an electric motor allow the engine to run as close as possible to a constant-speed-constant-load mode of operation. This can permit a gasoline engine to run very efficiently.

By combining two complementary sources of power, hybrid vehicles can realize increased efficiency, improved performance and reduced harmful emissions.

Types of hybrids

There are two types of hybrid systems in common use:
• Series hybrid
• Parallel hybrid

The Prius is a parallel hybrid.

Series hybrid

◄ In a series hybrid vehicle, a gasoline engine directly drives a generator instead of the wheels. Electrical energy from the generator is stored in a high voltage battery, and an electric motor drives the wheels. The gasoline engine is not connected to the wheels and the wheels are driven only by the electric motor. This arrangement can be described as an electric vehicle with an onboard engine-driven generator. Diesel-electric railroad locomotives are configured in this way.

Series hybrid systems can permit the engine to run in a very efficient constant-speed / constant-load mode of operation.

Parallel hybrid

◄ A parallel hybrid vehicle is configured so that either the engine or an electric motor can provide power to drive the wheels. Complex electronic controls manage the contribution from both the engine and the electric motor. The engine also directly drives a generator to recharge the high voltage battery.

Parallel hybrid systems can be more flexible and provide better performance than series hybrids. Also, a smaller high voltage battery pack can be used in a parallel hybrid since the vehicle relies less on stored electrical energy.

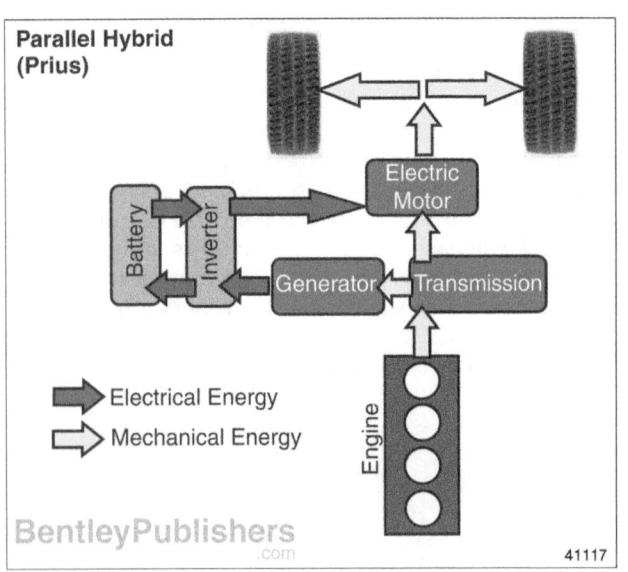

Series Hybrid

➡ Electrical Energy
⇨ Mechanical Energy

41116

Parallel Hybrid (Prius)

➡ Electrical Energy
⇨ Mechanical Energy

41117

Types of parallel hybrids

There are two types of parallel hybrid vehicles:
- Mild parallel hybrid
- Full parallel hybrid

The Prius is a full parallel hybrid.

Mild parallel hybrids

Mild parallel hybrid vehicles derive most of their driving force from the engine. Mild hybrids are essentially conventionally-powered vehicles with a more powerful electric starter motor / generator.

The electric motor may provide some additional torque when starting off to reduce demands on the engine, but this torque contribution is small. "Engine-off-at-stop" capability is the major benefit of a mild hybrid. The electric motor can also be configured to function as the generator to recharge the high voltage battery pack. While overall benefits are less impressive than the benefits of full hybrid vehicles, mild hybrids are typically less expensive to manufacture than full parallel hybrids.

Full parallel hybrids

Full parallel hybrid vehicles have the ability to move with power from either the engine, the electric motor, or a combination of both. The amount of torque and power supplied from each motive source depends on system design. The engine can directly drive the wheels or drive a generator, which can recharge the high voltage battery and can also supply power to an electric drive motor to drive the wheels. Full parallel hybrids combine the best characteristics of both series and parallel hybrids.

TOYOTA HYBRID SYSTEM II (THS II)

 Toyota Hybrid System II (THS II), also called Hybrid Synergy Drive (HSD) is a refinement of the original Toyota Hybrid System (THS) used in the 1997 – 2003 Toyota Prius.

THS II has the following features and advantages:
- Gasoline engine is switched OFF when the vehicle comes to a stop (unless commanded ON for some reason, such as the need to charge the high voltage battery).
- A portion of the vehicle's kinetic energy (the energy of motion) that is normally lost to heat when the brakes are used to slow or stop the vehicle is recovered and stored as electrical energy.
- Overall efficiency and fuel mileage is improved.
- Total of polluting emissions are reduced, including great reduction in carbon dioxide (CO_2) emissions.
- New vehicle purchase may be eligible for an IRS tax credit applied to vehicles powered by clean-burning fuels.
- Use of HOV commuter lanes may be permitted.

For more detailed information on THS II, see **2 Prius Hybrid System**.

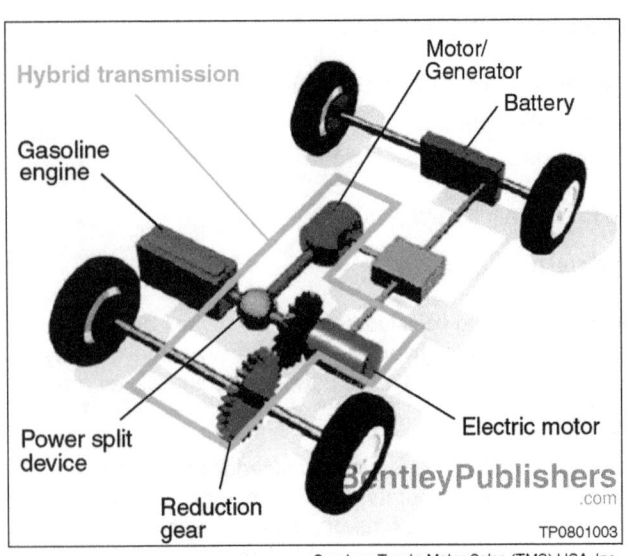

Courtesy Toyota Motor Sales (TMS) USA, Inc.

◄ The main components of THS II are:

- High voltage (HV) battery
- High output electric motor / generators
- Power control unit (inverter assembly)
- Hybrid continuously variable transaxle
- Gasoline engine.

THS II is a drive-by-wire system with no direct mechanical connection between the engine and the engine controls: both the gas pedal / accelerator and the gearshift lever send electrical signals to a control computer.

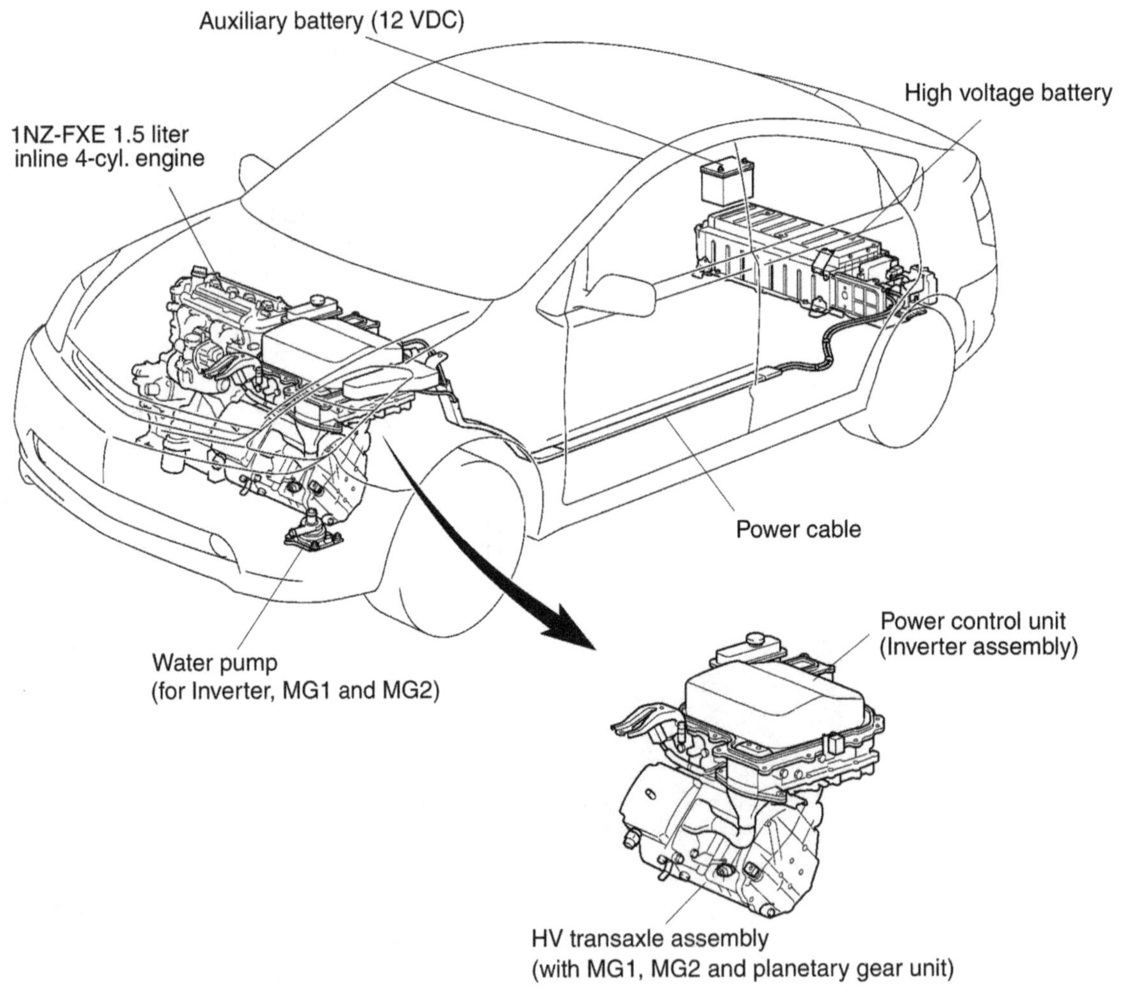

Auxiliary battery (12 VDC)

High voltage battery

1NZ-FXE 1.5 liter inline 4-cyl. engine

Power cable

Water pump (for Inverter, MG1 and MG2)

Power control unit (Inverter assembly)

HV transaxle assembly (with MG1, MG2 and planetary gear unit)

TP0801024

Courtesy Toyota Motor Sales (TMS) USA, Inc.

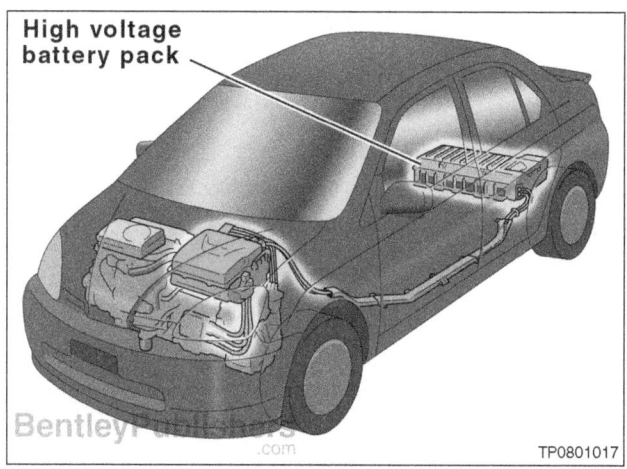

High voltage
battery pack

TP0801017

Courtesy Toyota Motor Sales (TMS) USA, Inc.

High voltage battery

◀ In addition to being light-weight and long-lived, the nickel metal hydride (NiMH) battery provides a high power output in relation to its weight. The 200 volt (nominal voltage of 201.6 volts) battery delivers approximately 540 watts per kg, one of the highest input / output to weight ratios of its type.

THS II maintains the battery charge by monitoring and computing the amount of discharge under acceleration, and recharging by regenerative braking or with surplus power under normal running conditions. Avoiding excessive battery draining / recharging contributes to the long life of the battery.

High output electric motor / generators

There are two motor / generators installed in the HV transaxle unit: MG1 and MG2. These units efficiently produce good torque up into the high rpm ranges and also provide control for torque and speed.

Power control unit (inverter assembly)

◀ The power control unit is a direct current (DC) / alternating current (AC) inverter as well as a voltage-boosting converter.

The inverter converts DC voltage supplied by the high voltage (HV) battery to AC voltage to turn the electric motors. It also converts AC voltage generated by the generator into DC voltage to recharge the HV battery.

The voltage-boosting converter increases the normal 201.6 volt DC supply voltage to a maximum of 500 volts to supply the electric motors and the generators as required. This means more power can be generated from a small current to obtain better performance from the high output motors, enhancing overall system efficiency. It also means that the inverter can be smaller and lighter.

The DC / DC converter steps down the 201.6 volt supply voltage from the battery to 12 V, to be used by ancillary systems and electronic devices like electronic control units (ECUs).

TP0801030

Courtesy Toyota Motor Sales (TMS) USA, Inc.

Familiarization

Hybrid transaxle with MG1, MG2 and planetary gear set

The hybrid transaxle contains:

• Motor / generator 1 (MG1) - generates electrical power.

• Motor / generator 2 (MG2) - drives the vehicle.

• A planetary gear unit - provides continuously variable gear ratios and serves as a power splitting device.

• A silent chain.

• Counter gears - transfer power to the final drive.

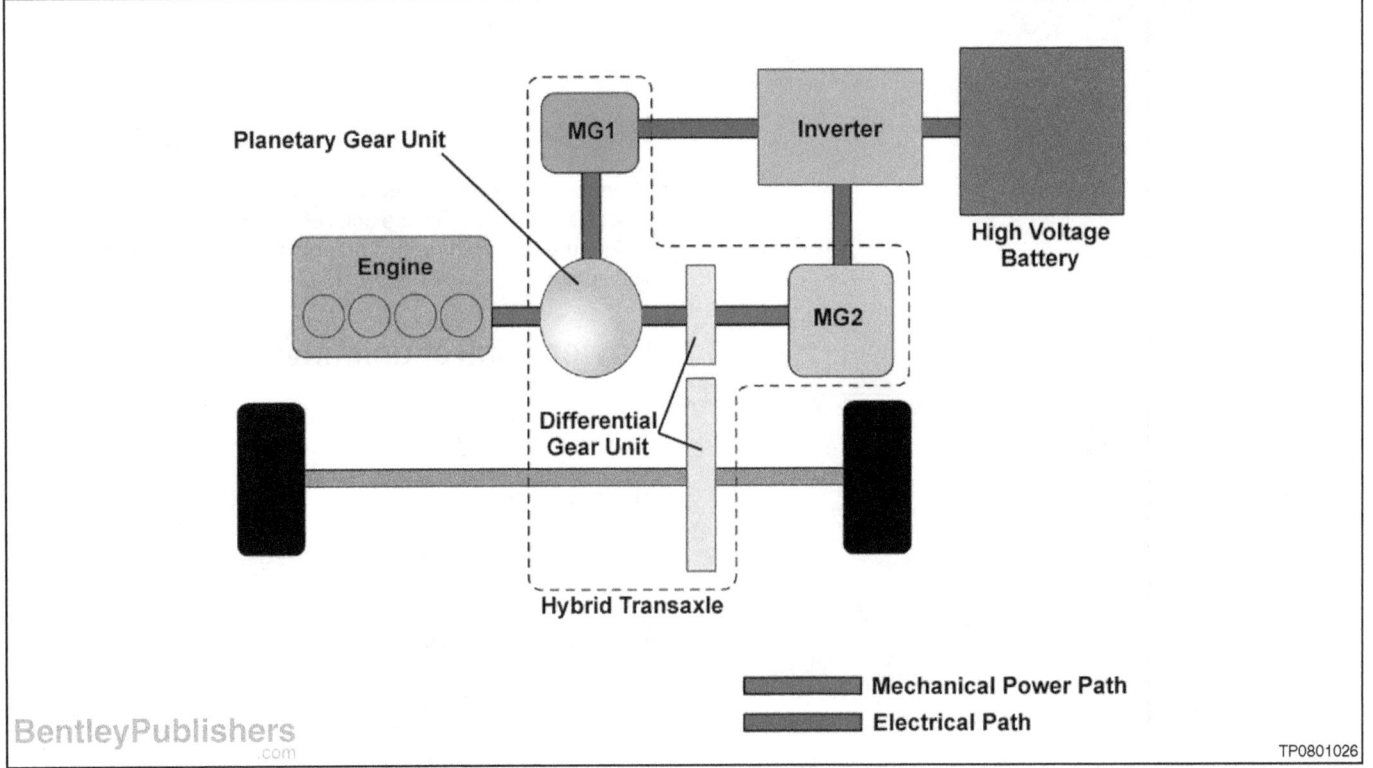

Mechanical Power Path
Electrical Path

TP0801026

Courtesy Toyota Motor Sales (TMS) USA, Inc.

1NZ-FXE engine

TP0801008

Courtesy Toyota Motor Sales (TMS) USA, Inc.

◁ The Prius uses the 1NZ-FXE, a 1.5-liter gasoline engine, specifically developed for hybrid system application. It is an inline 4-cylinder, chain-driven 4-valve (2 intake and 2 exhaust valves per cylinder) dual-overhead-camshaft (DOHC) engine.

This engine uses the VVT-i (Variable Valve Timing-intelligent) system, high-expansion ratio Atkinson cycle, offset crankshaft, and two oxygen sensors. Weight reduction and low-friction measures have been implemented to achieve extremely low fuel consumption, low exhaust emissions, a compact shape, low vibrations, and low noise levels.

One unique feature is the coolant heat storage system that recovers hot coolant from the engine and stores it in an insulated tank where it stays hot for up to three days. An electric pump pre-circulates the hot coolant through the engine to reduce HC emissions normally associated with a cold start.

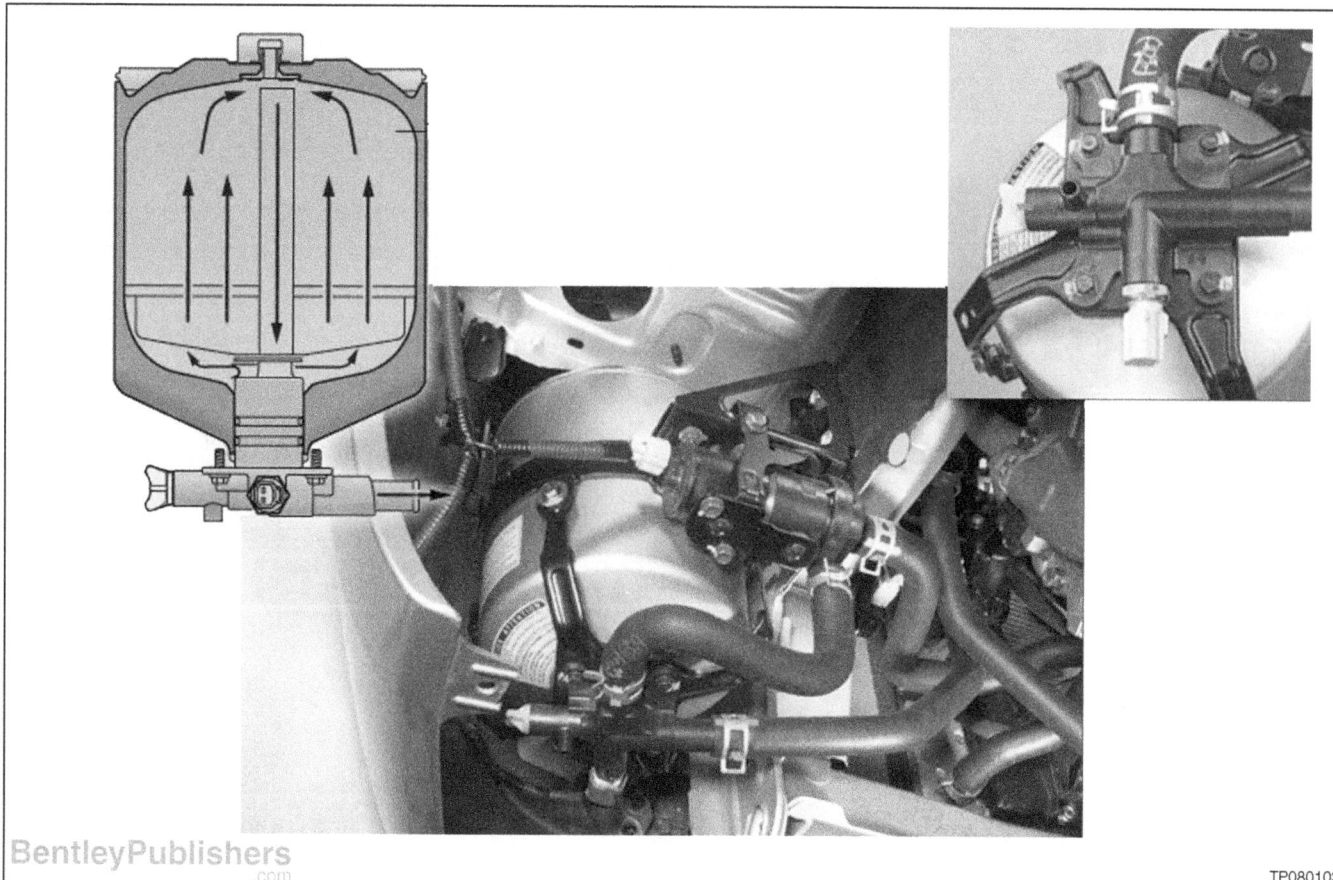

TP0801031

Courtesy Toyota Motor Sales (TMS) USA, Inc.

PRIUS OPERATING MODES

The main parts of the Prius THS II hybrid system are:

- Internal combustion gasoline engine.
- Two electric motor / generators: MG1 and MG2.
- Planetary gear set that links gasoline engine, MG1 and MG2.
- Electronic controls to manage system operation.
- Final drive gearing to transmit power from planetary gears to differential and front wheels.

On the next page is a simplified diagram of the main parts of the Prius drivetrain. Refer to it when you read the descriptions of the operating modes that follow.

Both MG1 and MG2 can function as electric motors, and also as high voltage generators.

MG1 can run as an electric motor to start the gasoline engine, or it can be driven by the gasoline engine as a generator.

MG2 is geared directly to the front wheels and can drive the wheels as an electric motor, or it can be driven by the front wheels as a generator. Whenever the front wheels turn, MG2 also turns. The planetary gear set links the engine, MG1, MG2 and the front wheels.

Prius hybrid system

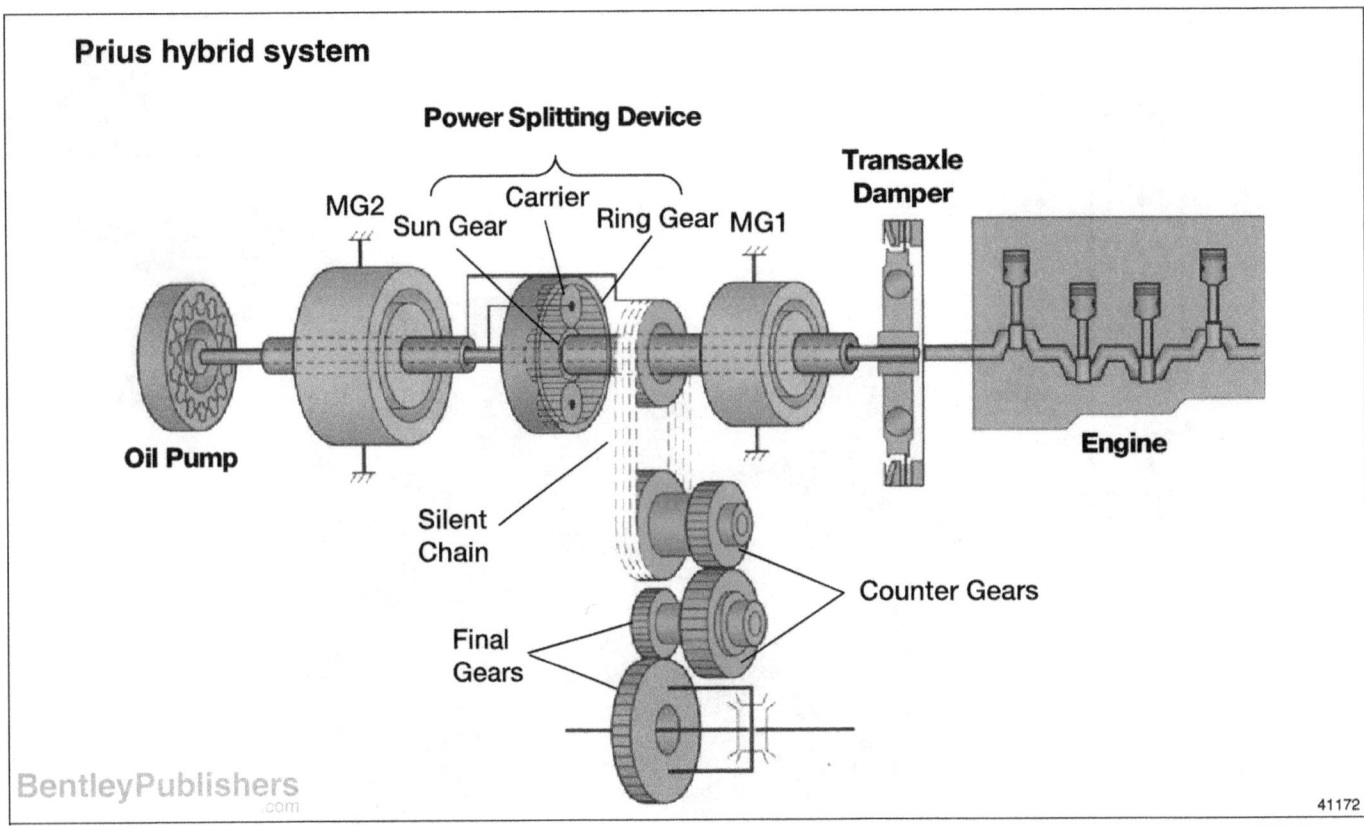

Courtesy Toyota Motor Sales (TMS) USA, Inc.

41172

Courtesy Toyota Motor Sales (TMS) USA, Inc.

41120

> **WARNING—**
> • *When towing a Prius, do not allow the front wheels to rotate. The front wheels are directly connected to motor / generator 2 (MG2), and when the front wheels are turning MG2 also turns. This may generate high voltage, create a shock hazard, and cause damage to the inverter or the high voltage battery. See* **3 Safety** *for more information.*

Depending on the driving situation, the Prius THS II system functions in the following operating modes:

• Starting

• Low speed

• Full throttle and high speed

• Deceleration and braking

• Reverse

Starting

When a Prius starts to move with light pressure on the accelerator pedal, the power train is under light load. MG2 supplies power to the front wheels, and the vehicle moves under electric power only. MG2 runs as an electric motor and receives power from the HV battery.

In this mode, MG1 rotates backwards and just idles; it does not generate electricity and does not charge the HV battery.

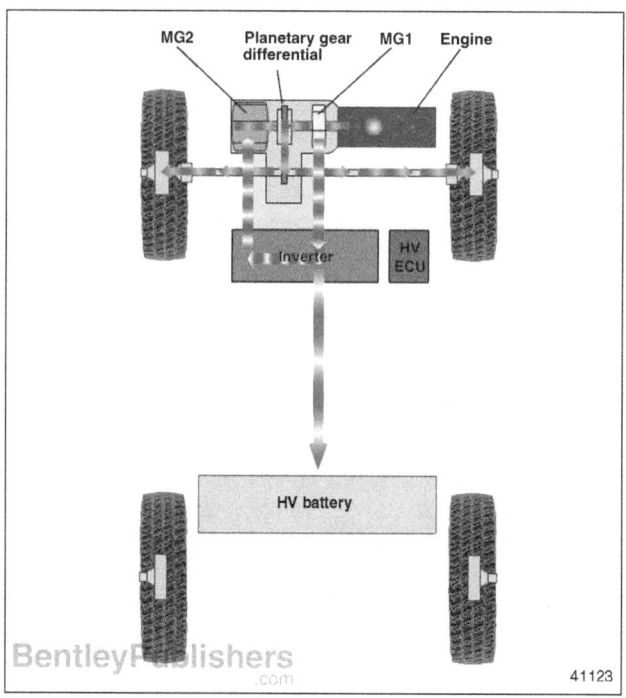

Courtesy Toyota Motor Sales (TMS) USA, Inc.

The engine may not run when the vehicle is in this mode. The engine, however, starts and runs automatically if the HV battery requires charging.

Low speed

As vehicle speed increases, the hybrid system starts the engine using MG1, which functions as a starting motor. To perform this function, MG1 receives power from the HV battery and runs as an electric motor.

The vehicle is driven by the engine and also by MG2 which runs as an electric motor to provide additional torque to the front wheels.

MG2 receives power from MG1 which is rotated by the engine as a generator. Power from MG1 can also charge the HV battery when necessary.

Full throttle and high speed

For full throttle acceleration and for high speed driving, both MG2 and the engine provide power to the front wheels.

Power from MG1 drives MG2 as an electric motor.

Engine power is split to drive the front wheels and also drive MG1 as a generator. Power from MG2 can be further increased with additional current supplied by the HV battery.

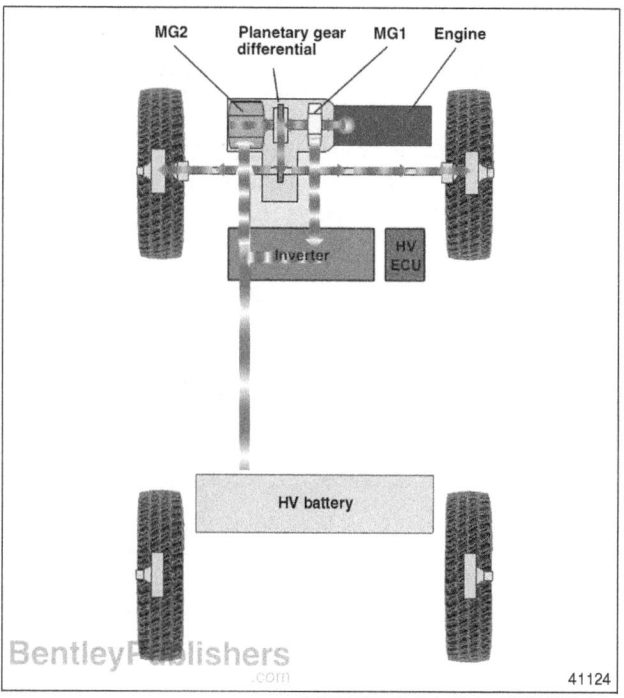

Courtesy Toyota Motor Sales (TMS) USA, Inc.

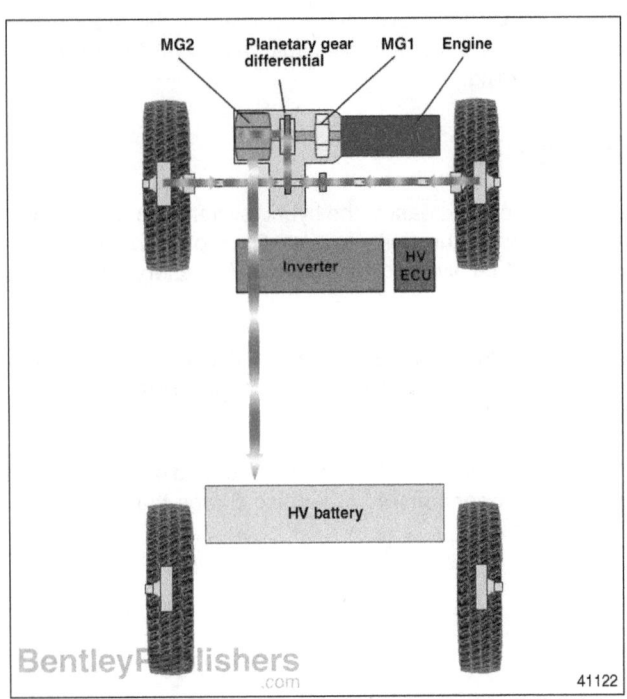

Courtesy Toyota Motor Sales (TMS) USA, Inc.

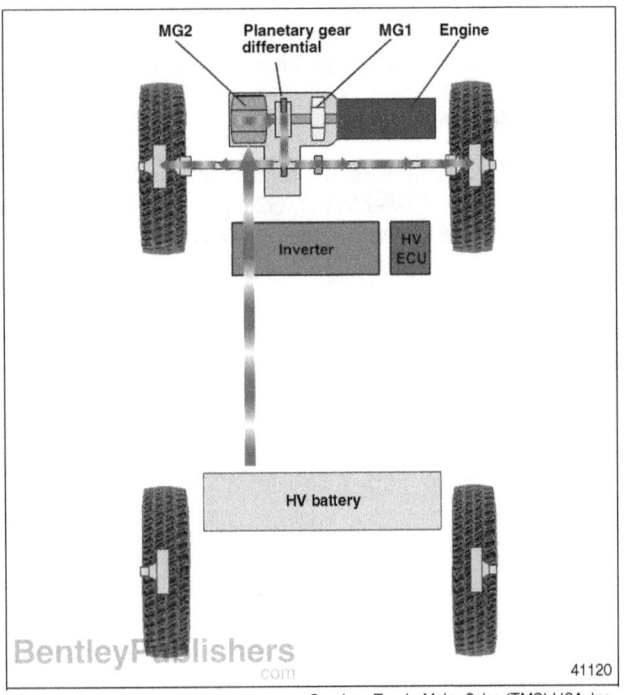

Courtesy Toyota Motor Sales (TMS) USA, Inc.

Deceleration and braking

◀ As soon as the accelerator pedal is released, the hybrid system causes MG2 to function as a generator. MG2 generates electricity to recharge the HV battery as it is turned by the front wheels.

In a conventional vehicle, when you release the accelerator and close the engine throttle, engine compression slows the vehicle. This is called engine braking. In the Prius, the drag of MG2 acting as a generator also slows the vehicle and is programmed to feel like engine braking.

As the vehicle decelerates, the engine may stop running, and MG1 turns backwards to maintain the desired gear ratio.

When the brake pedal is depressed, most of the initial braking force comes from MG2 being driven as a generator. This is called regenerative braking. Conventional hydraulic disc and drum brakes supplement regenerative braking and provide more of the braking force as the vehicle slows. At very low speeds, all braking is done by conventional hydraulic brakes.

Reverse

◀ The only gears in the Prius transmission are the planetary gear set (plus transfer gears to get the power to the differential and wheels). There is no reverse gear as in a conventional vehicle, so another method must be used to move a Prius in reverse.

Since the engine does not run backwards, MG2 rotates in the reverse direction as an electric motor to move a Prius in reverse. MG2 is powered by the HV battery to run in reverse and turns the front wheels in the reverse direction.

In this mode, the gasoline engine does not run unless the HV battery requires charging.

MG1 rotates forward and just idles; it does not generate electricity and does not charge the HV battery.

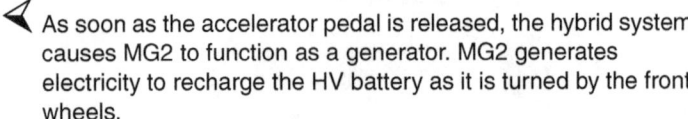

SUSPENSION, BRAKES, STEERING

Front and rear suspension

◀ Many light weight aluminum components are used, including the front steering knuckle and the brake calipers.

The Prius running gear incorporates MacPherson struts and lower wishbones on the front axle. The rear suspension is a torsion beam and trailing arm design with built-in stabilizer bar. It is designed to maximize available interior room.

This suspension package results in maximum steering precision and clearly defined handling with excellent cornering stability.

Prius running gear

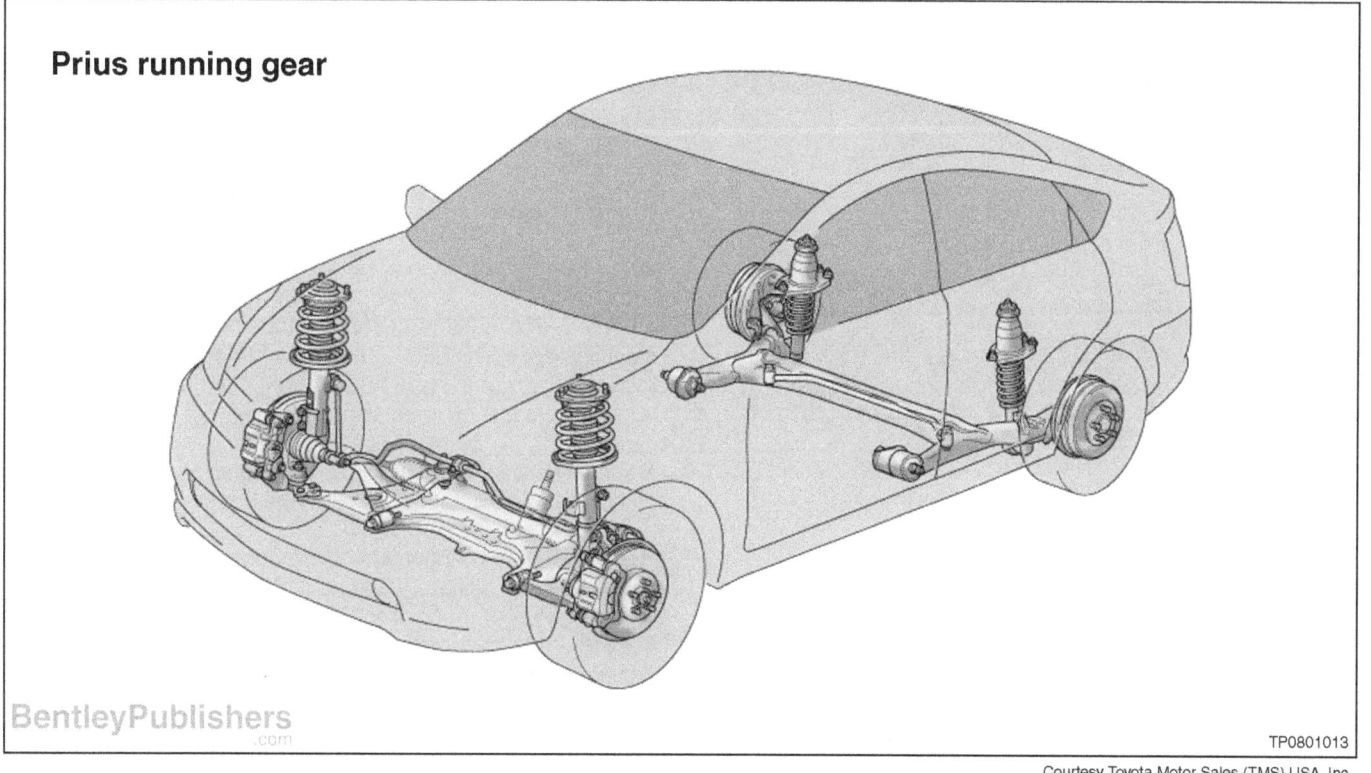

TP0801013

Brake system

The hybrid vehicle brake system with ABS includes both hydraulic brakes and a unique regenerative braking system that uses vehicle momentum to recharge the HV battery.

Ventilated disc brakes are used in the front and leading-trailing-shoe drum brakes are used in the rear.

Familiarization

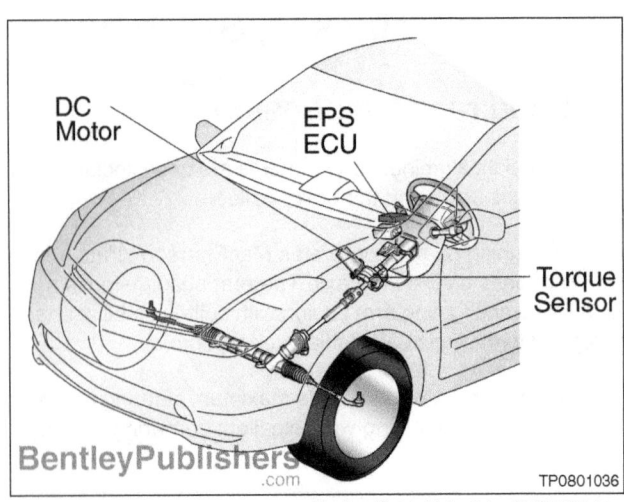

Courtesy Toyota Motor Sales (TMS) USA, Inc.

Electric power steering (EPS)

◄ Electric power steering (EPS) allows power assist to steering even when the vehicle is being driven by the electric motor alone. It also improves fuel economy because the system consumes energy only when it is being used.

If the EPS ECU detects a malfunction in the EPS system, a warning light illuminates to alert the driver. The EPS ECU stores DTCs, the system powers down, and the vehicle reverts to manual steering.

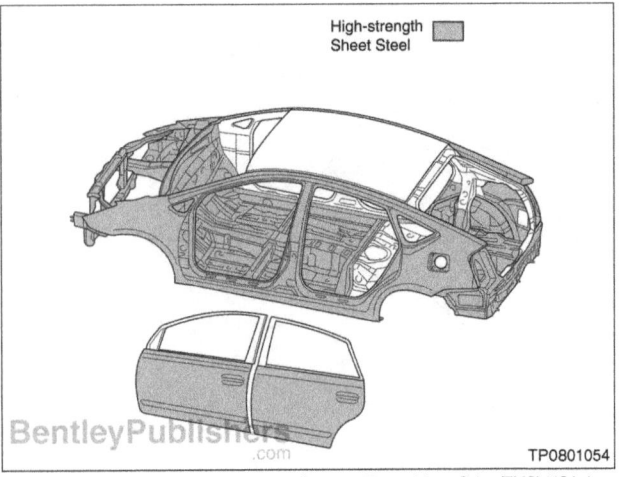

Courtesy Toyota Motor Sales (TMS) USA, Inc.

BODY

Body exterior

◄ The Prius body is lightweight and very rigid, employing high strength sheet steel.

Ultra high-strength sheet steel and hot-stamp material are used in the center pillar reinforcements and roof cross members in order to realize a lightweight body. Ultra high-strength sheet steel has approximately 1.6 times the strength of conventional high-strength sheet steel. Furthermore, the hot-stamp material is approximately 2.5 times stronger. Therefore, to provide the same strength of high-strength sheet steel, a weight reduction of approximately 40% can be realized with ultra high-strength sheet steel, and approximately 60% with the hot-stamp material.

Rust-resistance is enhanced by extensive use of anti-corrosion sheet steel, as well as by an anti-corrosion treatment, which includes the application of anti-rust wax, sealer and anti-chipping paint to easily corroded parts such as the doors and rocker panels.

◄ To improve aerodynamic performance, the following steps were taken:

• Rear spoiler integrated with back door.

• Bumper spoiler provided under the rear bumper.

• Engine under cover and front fender liner designed to an aerodynamically optimum shape.

• Spats and front spoiler smooth out airflow around tires and reduce air resistance.

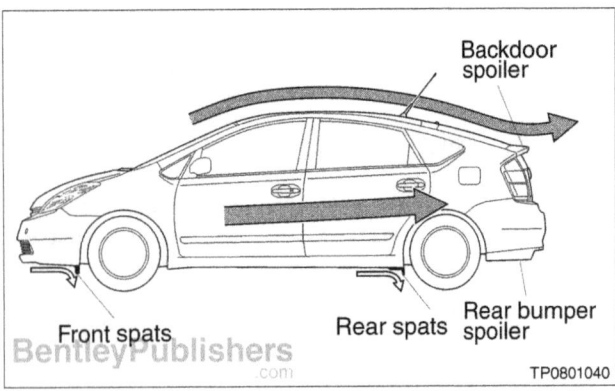

Courtesy Toyota Motor Sales (TMS) USA, Inc.

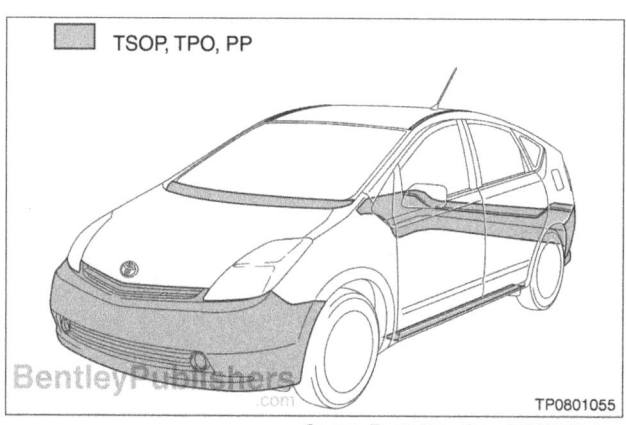

TSOP, TPO, PP

TP0801055

Courtesy Toyota Motor Sales (TMS) USA, Inc.

◀ TSOP (Toyota Super Olefin Polymer), TPO (Thermoplastic Olefin) and PP (Polypropylene), with superior recyclable properties, are utilized while the use of chlorine is reduced as much as possible.

Body interior

The interior of the Prius is ample with room for 5 adults.

◀ Storage spaces with large capacity have been effectively allocated in the center console, which also serves as an armrest.

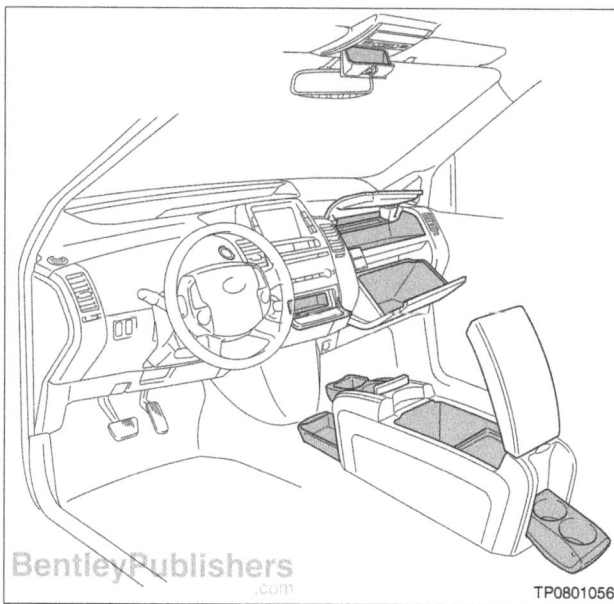

TP0801056

Courtesy Toyota Motor Sales (TMS) USA, Inc.

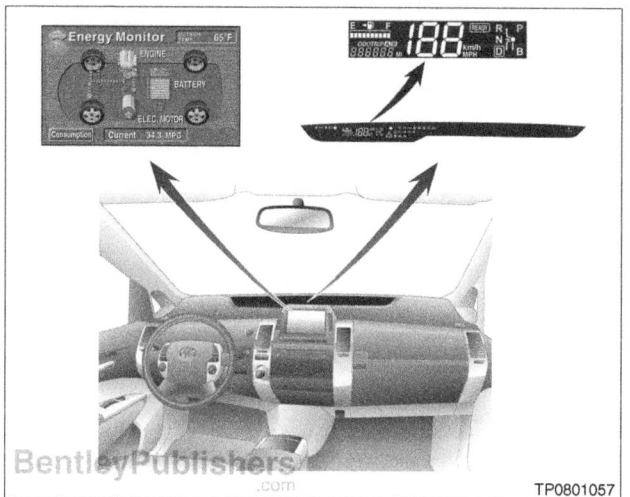

TP0801057

Courtesy Toyota Motor Sales (TMS) USA, Inc.

◀ Four vertical bands with a metallic look accentuate dashboard design and emphasize a futuristic look.

• The center of the dashboard has adopted a sophisticated design through the combination of a multi-display and a black-smoke motif audio unit.

• The instrument cluster, which consists of center meters that require a minimal amount of eye movement and a VFD (Vacuum Fluorescent Display) for the display panel.

• Airbag door for front passenger has been made invisible for a streamlined look.

Familiarization

DASHBOARD LAYOUT

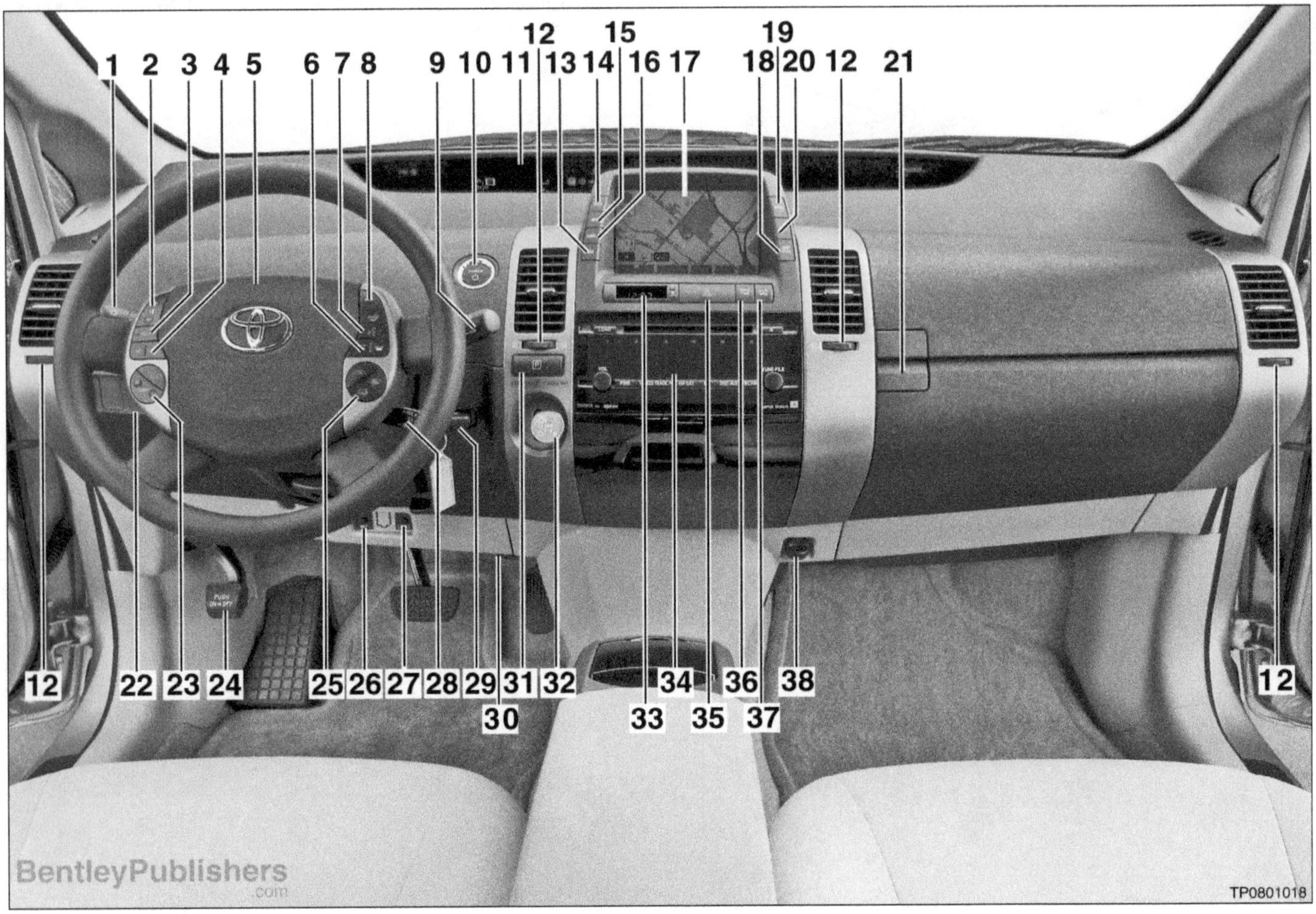

TP0801018

1. Headlight, turn signal, front foglight switch
2. Audio volume control
3. Audio mode control
4. Radio station control or CD track control
5. Horn button and driver airbag
6. Telephone controls
7. Phone book display control
8. Telephone volume
9. Wipers and washers switch
10. Power push button
11. Instrument cluster
12. Dashboard vent control
13. Audio control switch
14. Multi-information display switch
15. Multi-information info switch
16. Climate control switch
17. Multi-information touchscreen
18. Navigation system menu
19. Destination
20. Map control
21. Glove compartment latch button

22. Instruments light control
23. A/C control
24. Parking brake
25. Heating and ventilation control
26. Smart Key cancel switch
27. Tire Pressure Warning System reset
28. Cruise control switch
29. Ignition key slot
30. OBD II plug
31. PARK button
32. Shift lever
33. Digital clock
34. Radio
35. Hazard warning switch
36. Trip odometer reset
37. Mph or kph switch
38. 12 volt power outlet

Courtesy Toyota Motor Sales (TMS) USA, Inc.

2

Prius Hybrid System

Hybrid system technical details

Prius Hybrid System

TP0803011

Courtesy Toyota Motor Sales (TMS) USA, Inc.

TOYOTA HYBRID SYSTEM

◀ The Toyota Hybrid System (THS) is a powertrain management system that controls the operation of the gasoline engine, two high voltage electric motor / generators, a high voltage battery, the hybrid transaxle, and all related systems.

The 2001 - 2003 model Prius was the first Toyota hybrid model to be sold in North America with the Toyota Hybrid System. THS was an innovative, clean-sheet-of-paper design that provided a significant increase in vehicle operating economy and reduced emissions.

The 2004 - 2008 model Prius has an improved version of the Toyota Hybrid System known as THS II (also known as Hybrid Synergy Drive). THS II has been re-engineered to improve performance and economy over the version found in the previous generation Prius.

NOTE—

• *Two generations of the Prius have been sold in North America (Toyota models NHW11 and NHW20). An earlier model (Toyota model NHW10) was built in small numbers from 1997 to 2001 and sold only in Japan. The NHW10 model looks much like the first Prius sold in the USA, although there are some differences in the hybrid system. Therefore, the two Prius models that have been imported and sold in North America are more correctly called second- and third- generation Prius models.*

This chapter includes a detailed look at many of the innovative and unique features of THS II on the 2004 - 2008 Prius.

GASOLINE ENGINE

The gasoline engine used in the Prius is an in-line 1.5 liter 4-cylinder engine. The Toyota engine code is 1NZ-FXE. This is a modern dual overhead camshaft 16-valve engine that has been modified to work efficiently with the hybrid system. As used in this vehicle, the engine performs two functions:

• Provides power to drive the front wheels (along with motor / generator 2 (MG2).

• Turns motor / generator 1 (MG1) as a generator to recharge the high voltage battery.

The Prius engine has low-tension piston rings, light valve springs, and a low maximum rpm to help reduce friction and optimize midrange torque and economy. The engine also has several modifications and features expressly developed to optimize engine operation with the hybrid system.

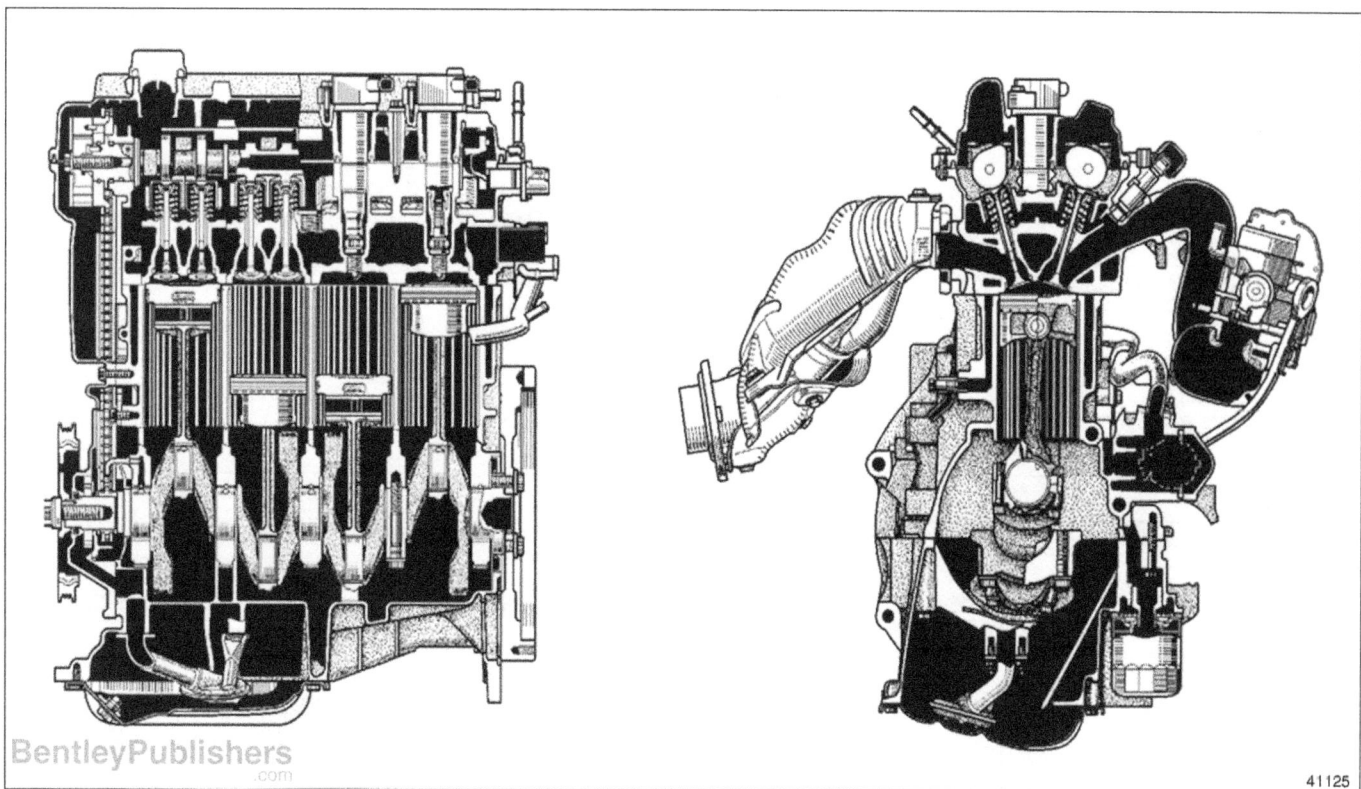

41125

Courtesy Toyota Motor Sales (TMS) USA, Inc.

Engine evolution and specifications

The engine design helps the Prius to achieve very low tailpipe emissions. An earlier version of the 1NZ-FXE engine was used in the 2001 - 2003 model Prius to help that car meet stringent Super Ultra Low Emission Vehicle (SULEV) tailpipe emissions standards. Vehicles that meet this standard will emit less than 1 pound of hydrocarbons (HC) in 100,000 miles. That represents approximately 1 pint of gasoline.

The current engine, as used in the 2004 - 2008 model Prius, meets even tighter emissions standards. This vehicle complies with SULEV tailpipe emissions standards, and also Advanced Technology Partial Zero Emission Vehicle (AT-PZEV) evaporative emissions standards. Vehicles that meet this standard produce zero emissions during at least part of their driving cycle.

Differences from the previous generation engine include:
- Increased engine horsepower
- Piston design changes
- Engine coolant heat storage tank added
- Charcoal HC trap added to engine air filter housing
- Fuel system and evaporative emissions (EVAP) system changes
- Heated oxygen (O2) sensor (Bank 1 Sensor 1) changed to heated air / fuel ratio (A/F) sensor (Bank 1 Sensor 1)
- Hydrocarbon adsorption catalyst (HCAC) system eliminated

Prius Hybrid System

• Engine control module (ECM) changed from 16-bit to 32-bit processor
• Controller area network (CAN) communications network added allowing ECM to communicate with other control modules.

Table a. lists the 1NZ-FXE engine specifications for the current generation Prius and differences (if any) from the previous generation Prius.

Table a. Prius gasoline engine specification		
Model	**2001 - 2003 (NHW11)**	**2004 - 2008 (NHW20)**
Engine type	---	1NZ-FXE
No. of cylinders and cylinder arrangement	---	4-cylinder, in-line
Valve mechanism	---	16 valve DOHC, chain drive with VVT-i
Combustion chamber	---	Pentroof type
Manifolds	---	Cross-flow
Fuel system	---	SFI
Displacement	---	1497 cc (91.3 cu in)
Bore x stroke	---	75.0 x 84.7 mm (2.95 x 3.33 in)
Compression ratio	---	13.0 : 1
Max. output (SAE-Net)	52 kw @ 4500 rpm (70 hp @ 4500 rpm)	57 kw @ 5000 rpm (76 hp @ 5000 rpm)
Max. torque (SAE-Net)	---	111 Nm @ 4200 rpm (82 ft-lb @ 4200 rpm)
Intake valve open	18° to approx. -25° BTDC	18° to approx. -15° BTDC
Intake valve close	72° to approx. 115° ABDC	72° to approx. 105° ABDC
Exhaust valve open	---	34° BBDC
Exhaust valve close	---	2° ATDC
Firing order	---	1-3-4-2
Research octane number	---	91 or higher
Pump octane rating	---	87 or higher
Engine service mass* (reference)	86.6 kg (190.9 lb)	86.1 kg (189.8 lb)
Oil grade	API SH, SJ, EC or ILSAC	API SJ, SL, EC or ILSAC
Tailpipe emissions regulation	---	SULEV
Evaporative emission regulation	LEV-II ORVR	AT-PZEV, ORVR
*: Weight shows the figure with the oil and engine coolant fully filled		

Atkinson cycle

In a conventional 4-stroke cycle gasoline engine, intake and exhaust valve timing, which determines when the intake and exhaust valves open and close, are set to make the engine compression ratio and expansion ratio approximately equal. The compression ratio indicates how much the intake air / fuel charge is compressed as the piston goes up in the cylinder before the power stroke begins. The expansion ratio indicates how much the burning gases expand as the piston goes down in the cylinder during the power stroke.

◀ At times during operation, the Prius engine changes from the conventional 4-stroke cycle to the Atkinson cycle. Atkinson cycle engines have compression and expansion ratios that can be separately set and the two ratios can be very different. The Prius 1NZ-FXE engine has a very long stroke, and a high expansion ratio. This means that more energy from the power stroke is converted to mechanical motion. During the intake stroke, however, the intake valves can be made to close very late, causing the compression stroke to begin later. This effectively reduces the engine's compression ratio to a more appropriate number as the rising piston pushes a small amount of the intake charge back into the intake manifold. This also effectively reduces engine displacement.

The increased stroke, lower compression and late closing of the intake valves tends to reduce maximum power, but can improve engine torque, efficiency and economy. For more information, see **Variable valve timing (VVT-i)** in this chapter.

NOTE—

• *The Atkinson cycle was defined by an English engineer named James Atkinson in 1882. His concept enables the engine compression ratio and expansion ratio to be set independently, allowing these ratios to be different.*

Offset crankshaft

◀ The centerline of the engine crankshaft is offset 12 mm (0.47 in) relative to the cylinder bore centerline in the engine block. This reduces side loads on the pistons when they are near top dead center (TDC) at the beginning of the power stroke.

Courtesy Toyota Motor Sales (TMS) USA, Inc.

Courtesy Toyota Motor Sales (TMS) USA, Inc.

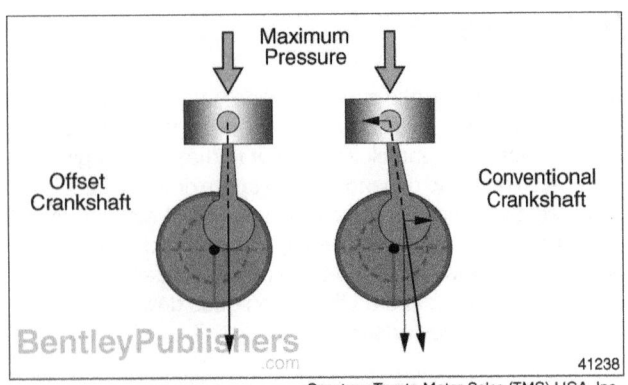

Courtesy Toyota Motor Sales (TMS) USA, Inc.

The offset crankshaft also improves piston-to-crankshaft geometry and mechanical advantage. Piston-to-cylinder wall friction is reduced and more torque is transmitted to the crankshaft for more efficiency and improved economy.

Variable valve timing (VVT-i)

The Prius engine has two overhead camshafts. One camshaft actuates the intake valves, and the other camshaft actuates the exhaust valves. Toyota Variable Valve Timing with Intelligence (VVT-i) can vary intake valve timing as much as 33° relative to the crankshaft.

An oil control valve varies intake valve timing by modulating engine lubricating oil pressure to the camshaft timing assembly.

The exhaust valve timing on the Prius engine is fixed.

Courtesy Toyota Motor Sales (TMS) USA, Inc.

Courtesy Toyota Motor Sales (TMS) USA, Inc.

The VVT-i feature varies intake valve timing and changes the engine mode from the conventional 4-stroke cycle to the Atkinson cycle. For more information, see **Atkinson cycle** in this chapter.

41164
Courtesy Toyota Motor Sales (TMS) USA, Inc.

Intake manifold

◁ The intake manifold on the Prius engine is configured with a large integral plenum or surge tank. This extra manifold volume accommodates the intake charge that the piston pushes back into the intake manifold during Atkinson Cycle operation.

Electronic throttle control system (ETCS-i)

◁ There is no throttle cable connecting the accelerator pedal with the throttle plate on the Prius engine. Instead, throttle opening is controlled electronically by the engine control module (ECM). Toyota calls this the Electronic Throttle Control System with Intelligence (ETCS-i).

41148
Courtesy Toyota Motor Sales (TMS) USA, Inc.

◁ The ETCS-i accelerator pedal assembly has an accelerator pedal position sensor which sends a signal in proportion to pedal position to the HV ECU and to the ECM. The ECM combines information from this input and other inputs to determine the optimum throttle opening and engine speed.

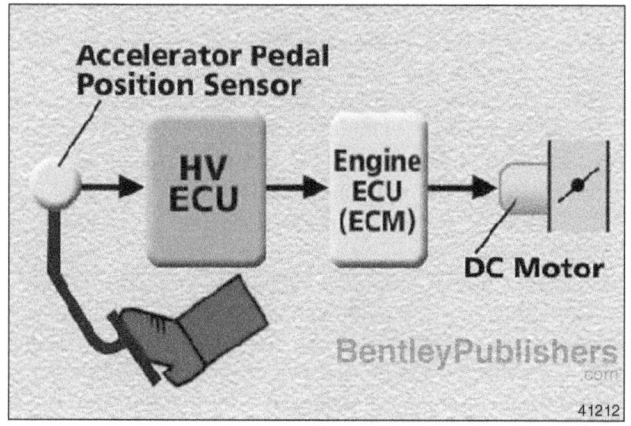

41212
Courtesy Toyota Motor Sales (TMS) USA, Inc.

Prius Hybrid System

ENGINE EMISSION CONTROLS

The function of the engine management system is to control fuel delivery, spark timing, and other engine functions so that the engine runs smoothly, has good drivability, and provides low exhaust emissions. The Prius engine and its engine management system have some unique features that make the engine better suited for its tasks as part of the hybrid system.

Engine air filter

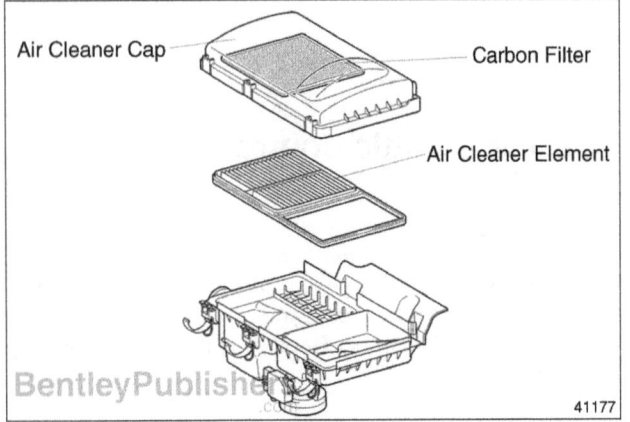

Air Cleaner Cap — Carbon Filter

Air Cleaner Element

BentleyPublisher

41177

Courtesy Toyota Motor Sales (TMS) USA, Inc.

◄ 2004 - 2008 Prius models have a carbon filter in the engine air filter housing. The carbon filter absorbs and holds unburned fuel vapors (unburned hydrocarbons or HC) that accumulate in the intake system when the engine is stopped. This carbon filter is one of the additional devices that help the 2004 - 2008 Prius to meet Advanced Technology Partial Zero Emission Vehicle (AT-PZEV) evaporative emissions standards. The carbon filter is integral with the air filter housing cover, does not require periodic maintenance, and is not serviced separately.

Mass air flow meter

◄ The mass air flow meter measures the amount of air flowing into the intake manifold. This component provides one of the main inputs into the engine management system.

The mass air flow meter is located between the air filter housing and the throttle body where it measures incoming air flow with a heated platinum wire. An electric current heats the platinum wire, and air flow tends to cool the wire. The electric current is varied to maintain the wire at a constant temperature. As airflow increases, the current flow must also increase to keep the wire hot. The ECM knows how much current is required to maintain the temperature of the wire and can therefore calculate the volume of intake air flowing into the engine.

NOTE—

• *Any air leaking into the engine intake system that is not first measured by the mass air flow meter is not measured air and is unknown to the ECM. This can upset the air / fuel ratio and engine drivability, performance and economy. Check intake air system joints carefully, especially the clamp that attaches the air filter housing to the throttle body.*

41149

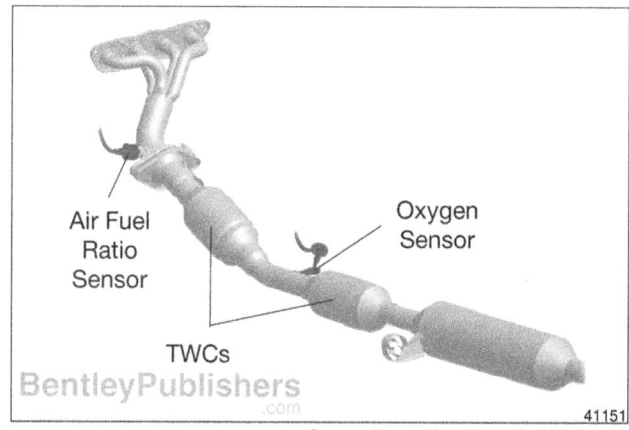

Air Fuel Ratio Sensor

Oxygen Sensor

TWCs

41151

Courtesy Toyota Motor Sales (TMS) USA, Inc.

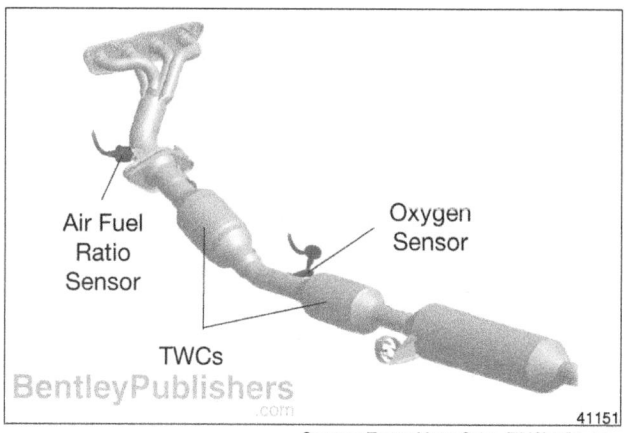

Air Fuel Ratio Sensor

Oxygen Sensor

TWCs

41151

Courtesy Toyota Motor Sales (TMS) USA, Inc.

Catalytic converters

 The 2004 - 2008 Prius uses two three-way catalyst (TWC) catalytic converters in the exhaust system.

Oxidation and reduction reactions within the catalysts greatly reduce amounts of unburned hydrocarbons, carbon monoxide, and oxides of nitrogen in the exhaust, creating mostly water vapor and carbon dioxide.

Oxygen sensors and air / fuel ratio (A/F) sensors

 The 2004 - 2008 Prius uses one heated air / fuel ratio (A/F) sensor and one heated oxygen (O2) sensor:

• Heated air / fuel ratio (A/F) sensor (Bank 1 Sensor 1): is located ahead of the catalytic converter where it measures oxygen content in the exhaust leaving the engine. The ECM uses this input to adjust fuel mixture. The A/F sensor responds to a wider range of air / fuel ratios when compared to conventional heated oxygen (O2) sensors. This allows the ECM to make more precise fuel trim adjustments. The A/F sensor design allows it to heat faster and provide a usable signal to the ECM sooner.

• Heated oxygen (O2) sensor (Bank 1 Sensor 2): is located after the catalytic converter. The ECM compares the signal from Sensor 2 with the signal from Sensor 1 to determine the efficiency and condition of the catalytic converter.

Fuel system

The Prius fuel system is a non-return type, with one fuel line to the engine and no return line to the fuel tank. The in-tank fuel pump pushes fuel to the engine's fuel injectors as needed at a standard pressure of 304 - 343 kPa (44 - 50 psi). Since fuel is not returned to the tank from the engine, as in return-loop-type fuel systems, fuel temperature in the tank is kept as low as possible. This reduces fuel evaporation.

The fuel pump, fuel filter, pressure regulator, and fuel level sensor are all located in the fuel tank. None of these components can be replaced individually.

The Prius fuel tank is designed to greatly reduce evaporative fuel emissions. Inside the steel outer tank is a semi-flexible plastic inner bladder. All fuel is contained within the plastic bladder, which expands and contracts as fuel is added and used. The changes in bladder shape minimizes the amount of vapor space above the liquid fuel, reducing the space for fuel evaporation.

Prius Hybrid System

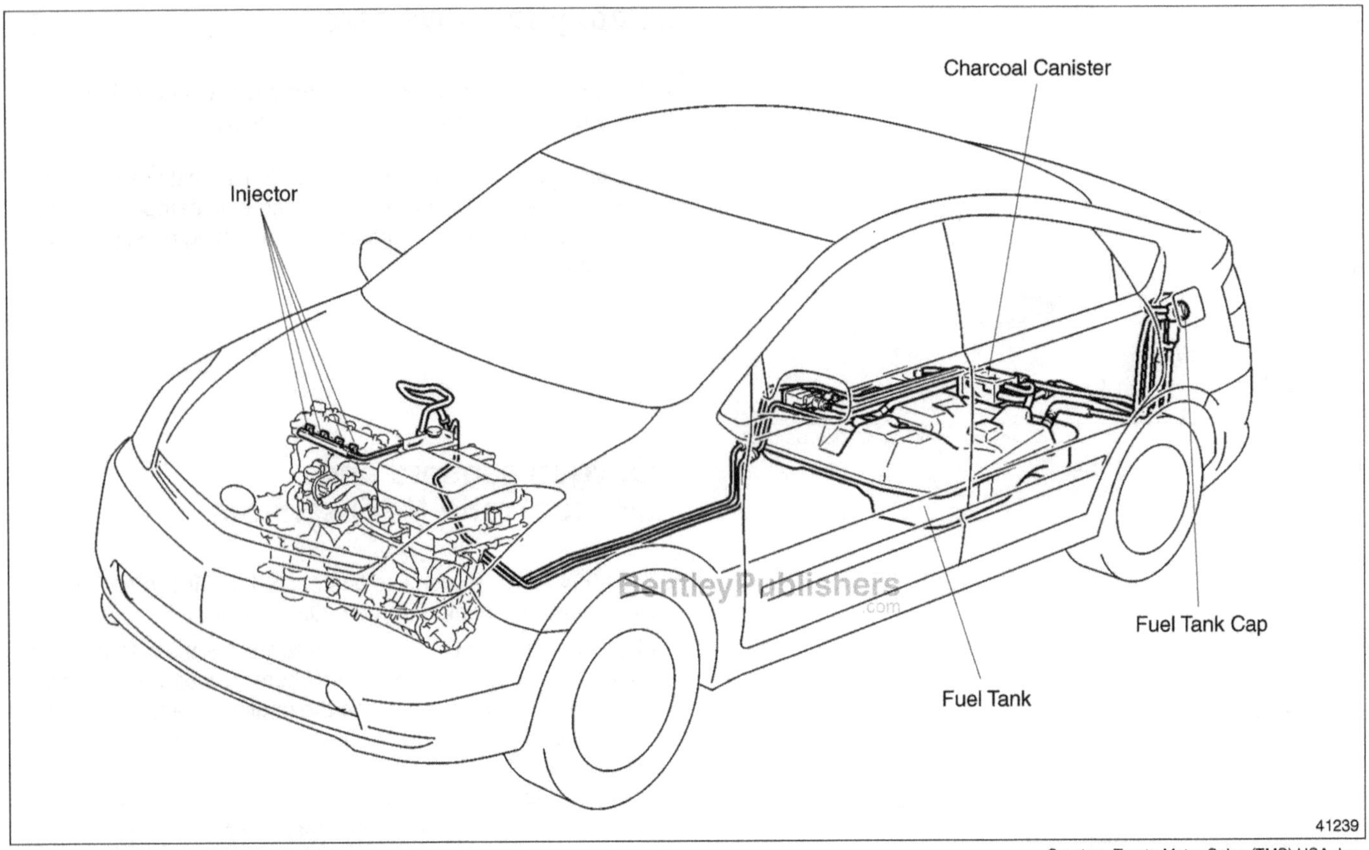

Charcoal Canister

Injector

Fuel Tank Cap

Fuel Tank

41239

Courtesy Toyota Motor Sales (TMS) USA, Inc.

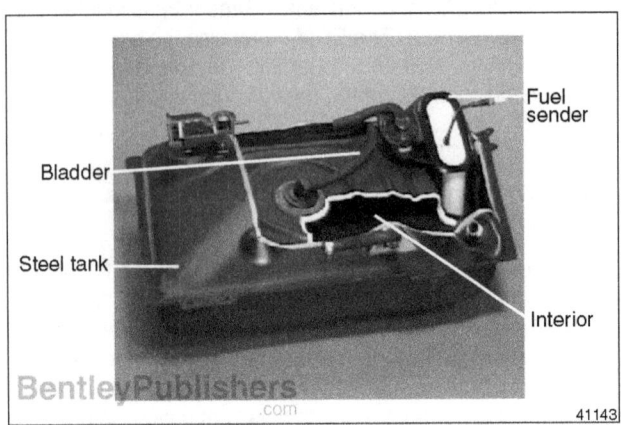

Fuel sender

Bladder

Steel tank

Interior

41143

Courtesy Toyota Motor Sales (TMS) USA, Inc.

◄ Only air should be present in the space between the bladder and steel fuel tank. The Prius evaporative emissions control (EVAP) system checks this space for the presence of fuel vapors.

Because of the unique design of the fuel tank, fuel capacity may vary for several reasons:

• Changes in ambient temperature – Low ambient temperatures cause the plastic bladder to stiffen and the bladder may not fully expand when filling. For example, when the ambient temperature is 14° F, tank capacity is reduced by approximately 10%.

• Fit of fuel nozzle in filler neck – The bladder fuel tank uses pressure created by the fuel discharging from the gas pump nozzle to help expand the bladder when refueling. There is a rubber seal ring in the fuel filler neck on the vehicle to create a tight seal between the fuel nozzle and the filler neck. If the fit is poor because of a damaged nozzle or rubber seal ring, fuel tank capacity may be reduced.

CAUTION—
• *Do not overfill or "top off" the Prius fuel tank. Overfilling pushes excess fuel into the evaporative emission control (EVAP) system and may require replacement of some EVAP system components.*

• *Use only regular grade fuel (87 pump octane) in the Prius. Use of premium grade fuel may cause engine starting problems.*

Evaporative emission control (EVAP) system

The evaporative emission control (EVAP) system performs several important functions which reduce hydrocarbon (HC) emissions from evaporating fuel:

EVAP system vapor storage

Charcoal in the EVAP charcoal canister absorbs and stores fuel vapors (HC) that are normally created in the fuel system. This reduces HC emissions to the atmosphere.

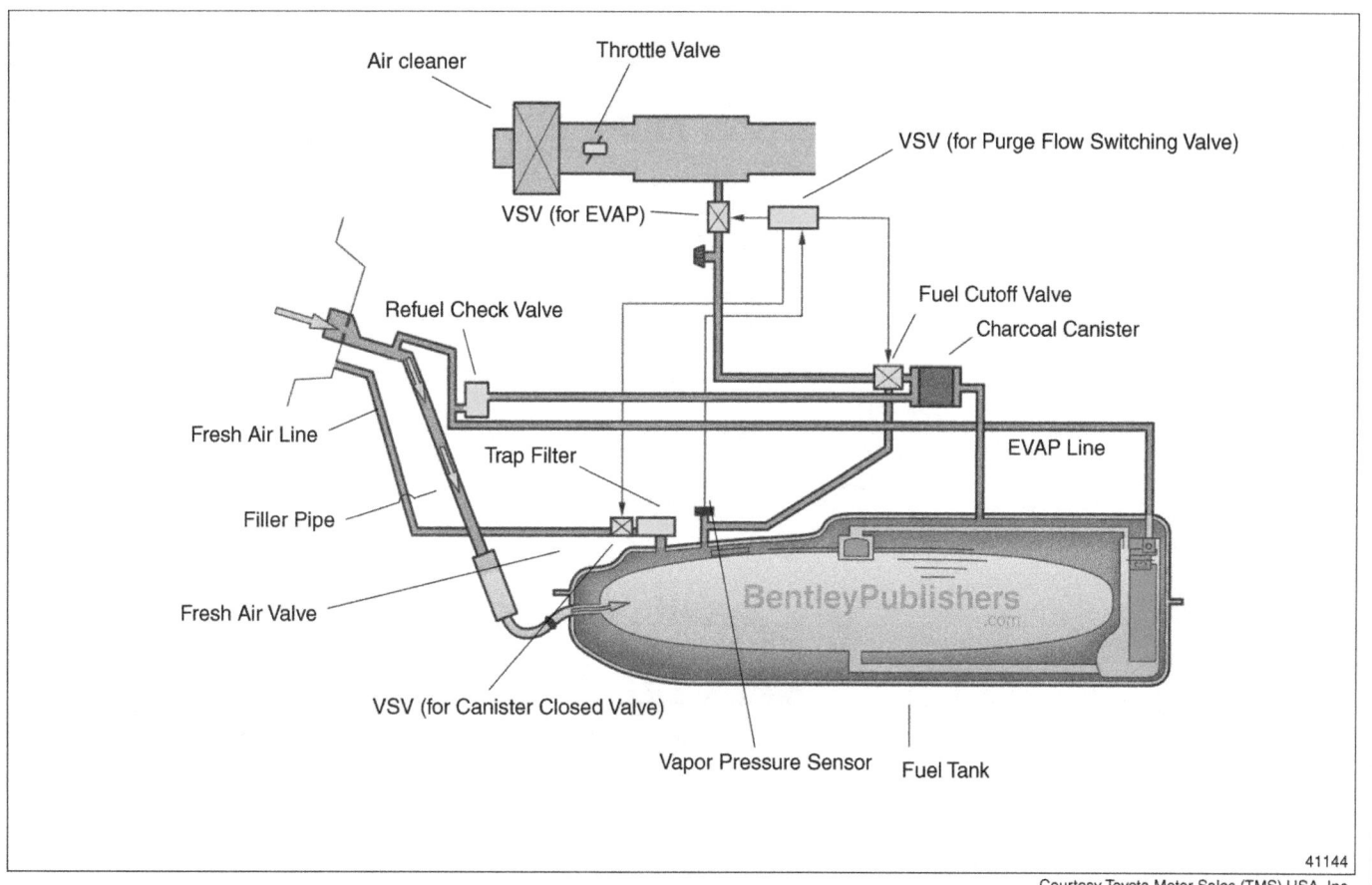

41144

Courtesy Toyota Motor Sales (TMS) USA, Inc.

EVAP system purging

When the engine runs, and when conditions are favorable, the EVAP system purges stored fuel vapors (HC) from charcoal canister. Engine intake manifold vacuum creates flow. Fresh air is pulled through charcoal canister, and air / fuel vapor mixture is metered into intake manifold as part of engine intake air flow. The flow rate is controlled by the vacuum switching valve (VSV) for EVAP, which receives commands from the ECM.

PURGING

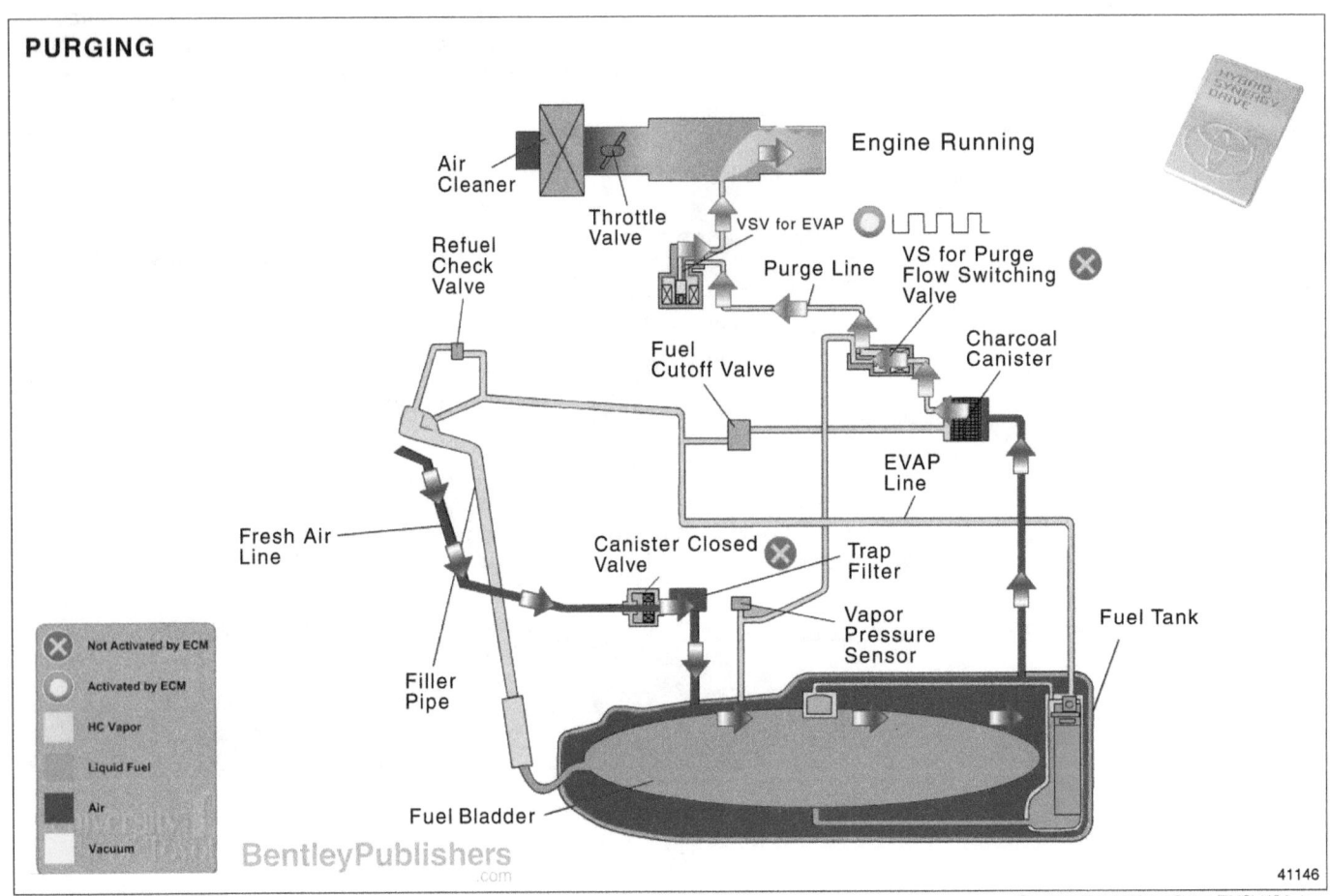

Air Cleaner
Throttle Valve
Refuel Check Valve
VSV for EVAP
Engine Running
Purge Line
VS for Purge Flow Switching Valve
Fuel Cutoff Valve
Charcoal Canister
EVAP Line
Fresh Air Line
Canister Closed Valve
Trap Filter
Vapor Pressure Sensor
Fuel Tank
Filler Pipe
Fuel Bladder

Not Activated by ECM
Activated by ECM
HC Vapor
Liquid Fuel
Air
Vacuum

41146

Courtesy Toyota Motor Sales (TMS) USA, Inc.

EVAP system vapor recovery

The Prius is equipped with an on-board refueling vapor recovery (ORVR) system. ORVR helps prevent the escape of fuel vapors resulting from refueling. The incoming flow of fuel, and the rubber seal ring in the fuel filler neck, cause fuel vapors to flow into the charcoal canister, where they are held until purged. This reduces fuel vapor (HC) emissions during refueling.

ORVR REFUELING

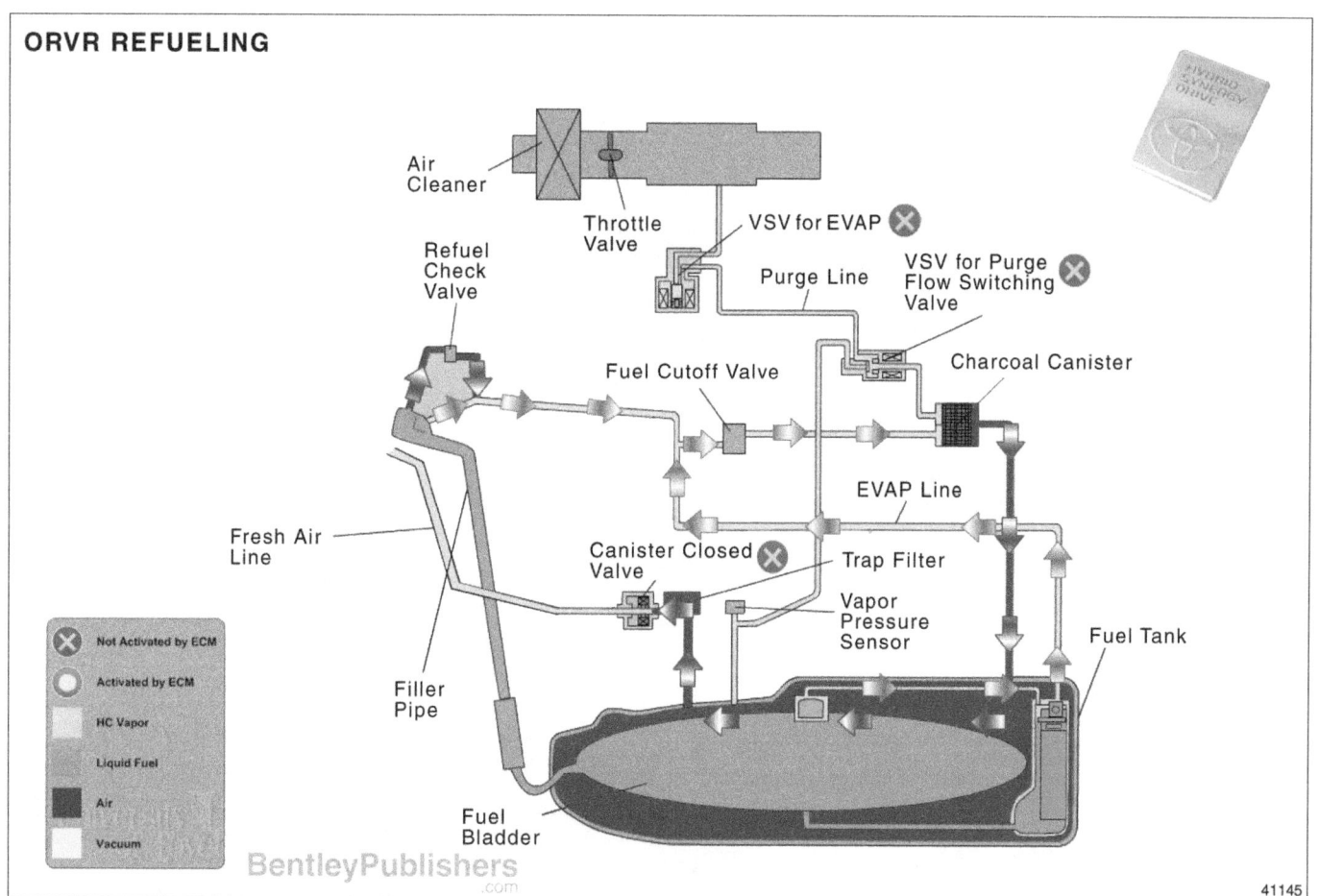

Courtesy Toyota Motor Sales (TMS) USA, Inc.

41145

Prius Hybrid System

EVAP system leak check

The EVAP system checks fuel and EVAP system lines, components, and the fuel tank plastic bladder for leaks. The leak check is performed with the engine running. Engine intake manifold vacuum is used to reduce pressure (to create a partial vacuum) in the EVAP system. The system is then closed and monitored for changes in pressure. A rapid rise in pressure (loss of vacuum) can indicate a leak.

When a leak is detected, the ECM will set a diagnostic trouble code (DTC) and will illuminate the check engine lamp (malfunction indicator lamp or MIL). A common source of leak check failures is a fuel filler cap that is not properly tightened, or a defective fuel filler cap gasket. Leaks can also be caused by leaking hoses and hose connections.

LEAK CHECK-COMPLETE SYSTEM

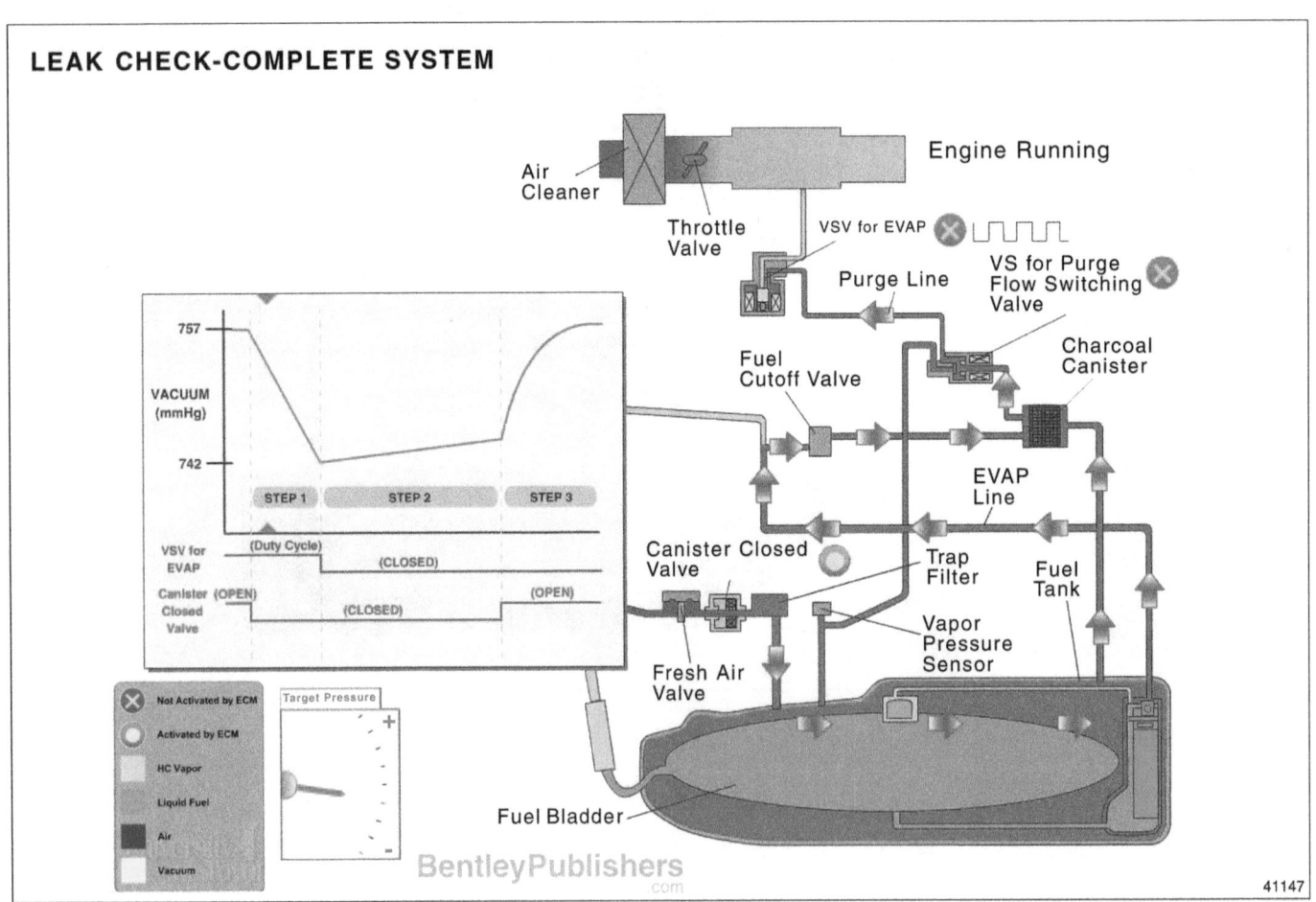

Courtesy Toyota Motor Sales (TMS) USA, Inc.

ENGINE COOLING SYSTEM

The engine cooling system in all Prius models is a conventional pressurized system with a thermostat and a belt-driven coolant pump.

The engine cooling system is completely separate from the transaxle / inverter cooling system. Each of these systems has its own coolant reservoir, radiator, coolant supply, and circulation pump. See **Transaxle / inverter cooling system** in this chapter.

The 2004 - 2008 Prius has a coolant heat storage tank which can store hot coolant for up to three days. See below.

Periodic engine coolant replacement is recommended by Toyota. See **4 Service and Repair Fundamentals** for recommended engine coolant service intervals.

Toyota specifies Toyota Super Long Life Coolant (SLLC) for the 2004 - 2008 Prius. See **5 Engine**, for engine coolant checking, drain, and refill procedures.

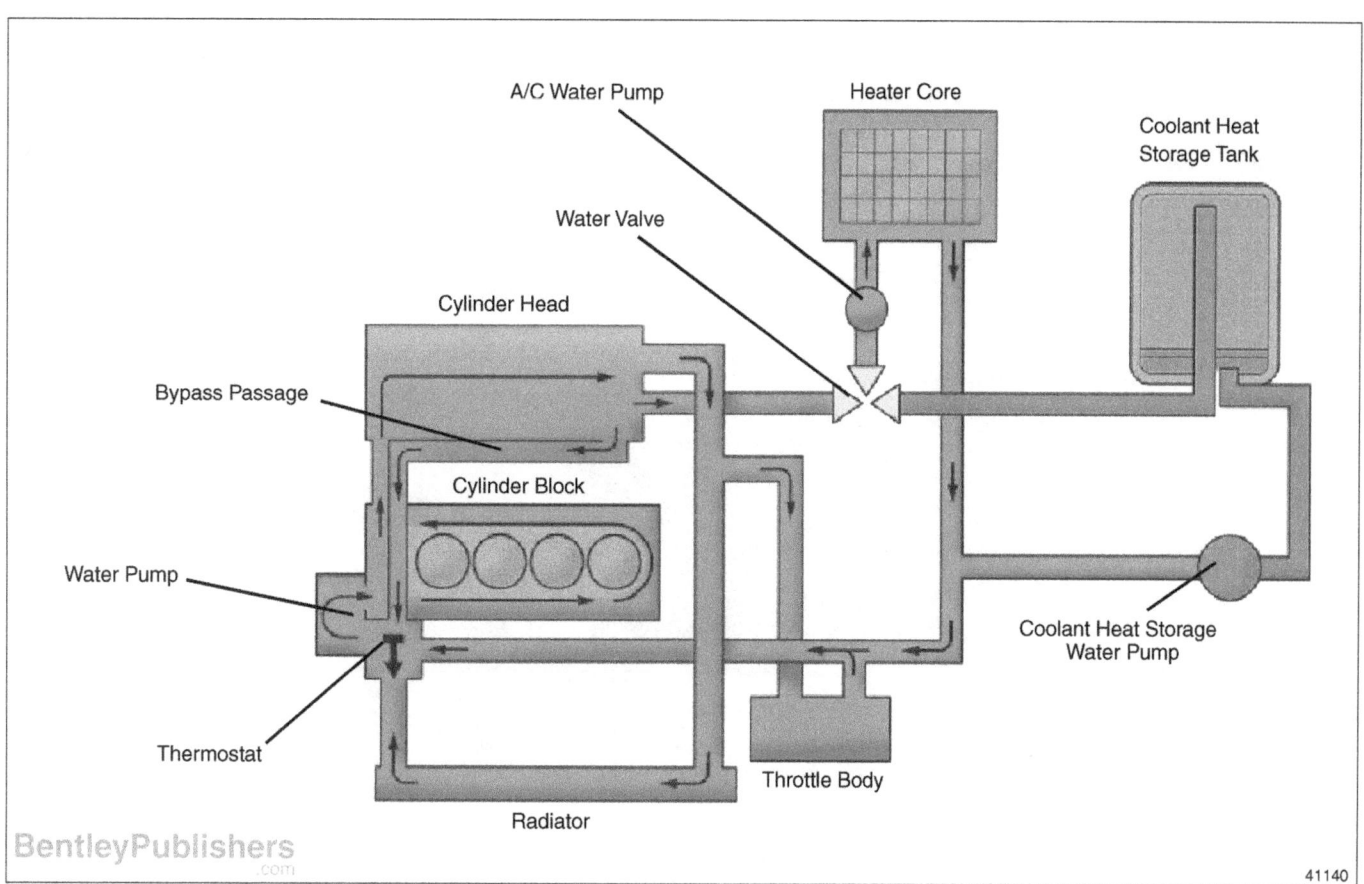

41140

Courtesy Toyota Motor Sales (TMS) USA, Inc.

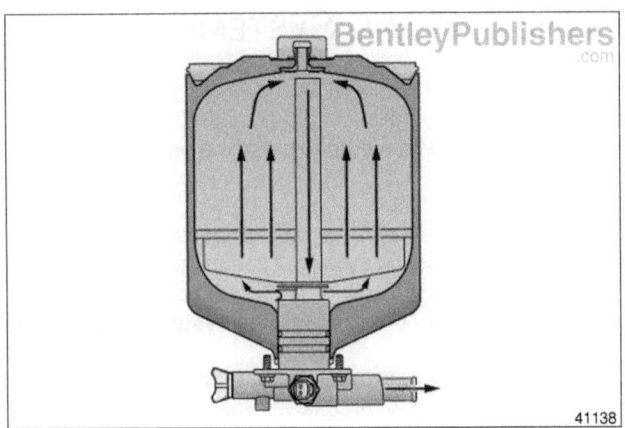

41138

Courtesy Toyota Motor Sales (TMS) USA, Inc.

Engine coolant heat storage tank

◄ The engine cooling system on 2004 - 2008 Prius models includes a unique stainless steel coolant heat storage tank. The tank is fabricated with double-walled construction similar to a vacuum bottle (Thermos® bottle). The partial vacuum between the inner and outer walls effectively insulates the hot coolant stored in the tank.

When the engine is running, hot coolant from the engine is circulated through the coolant heat storage tank. When the vehicle is turned OFF, the insulating properties of the tank allow coolant in the tank to remain hot (as high as 176°F) for as long as 3 days.

When the vehicle is started and the engine is cold, a dedicated electric pump on the coolant heat storage tank circulates the stored hot coolant through the engine and intake manifold. This speeds engine warm-up, improves fuel vaporization in the intake, and reduces hydrocarbon (HC) and carbon monoxide (CO) emissions.

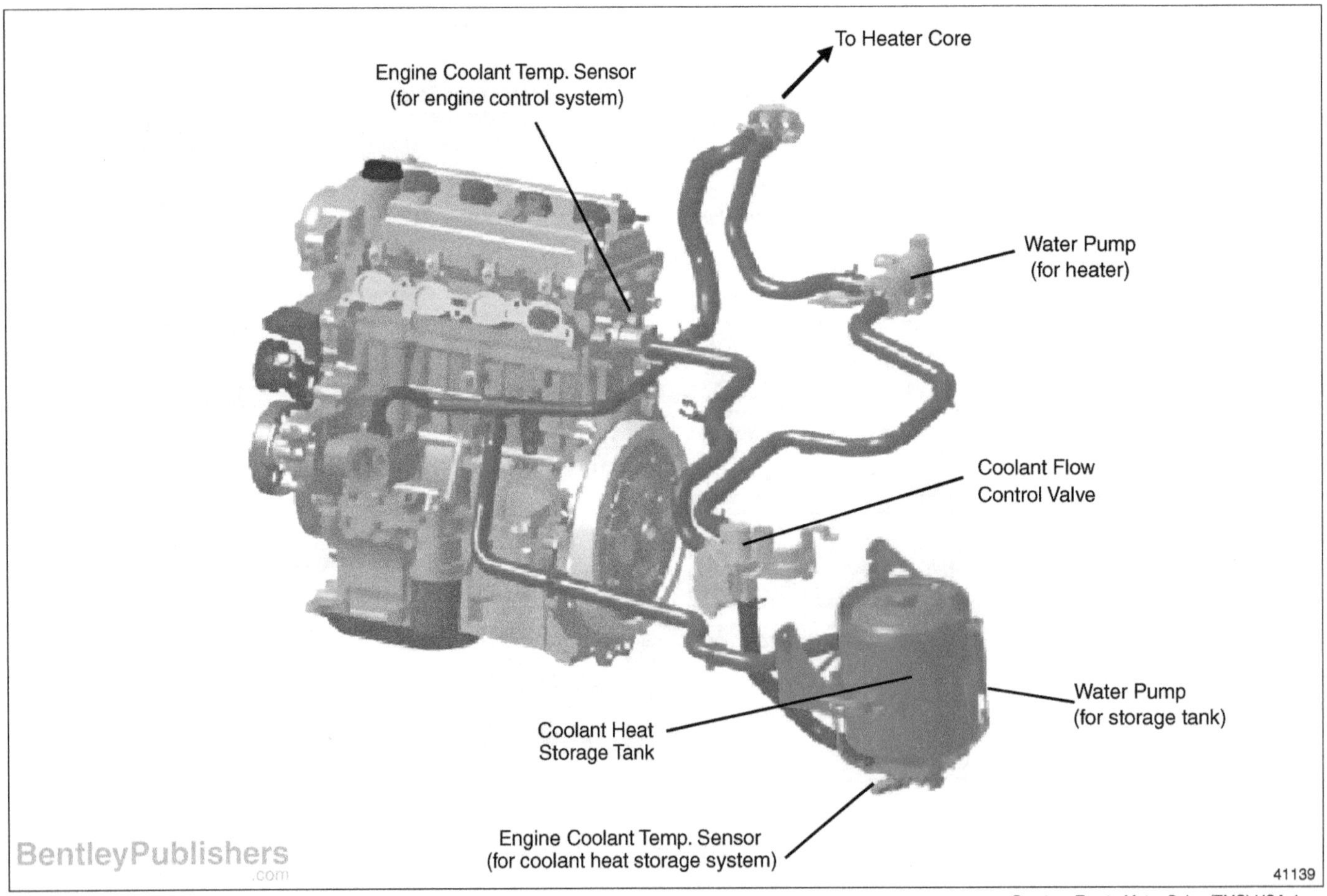

To Heater Core

Engine Coolant Temp. Sensor
(for engine control system)

Water Pump
(for heater)

Coolant Flow
Control Valve

Water Pump
(for storage tank)

Coolant Heat
Storage Tank

Engine Coolant Temp. Sensor
(for coolant heat storage system)

41139

Courtesy Toyota Motor Sales (TMS) USA, Inc.

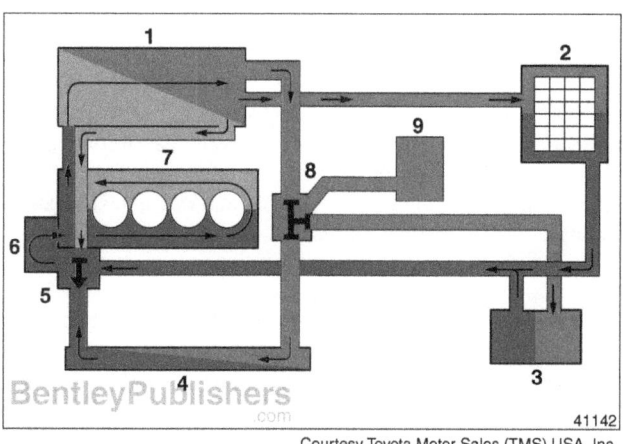

Courtesy Toyota Motor Sales (TMS) USA, Inc.

◄ A 3-way coolant flow control rotary valve switches between 3 positions to control the flow of coolant in and out of the coolant heat storage tank.

1. Cylinder head
2. Heater core
3. Intake manifold
4. Radiator
5. Thermostat
6. Water pump
7. Cylinder block
8. 3-way valve
9. Heat storage

The coolant heat storage tank (**arrow**) is located in the left front fender, ahead of the front wheel.

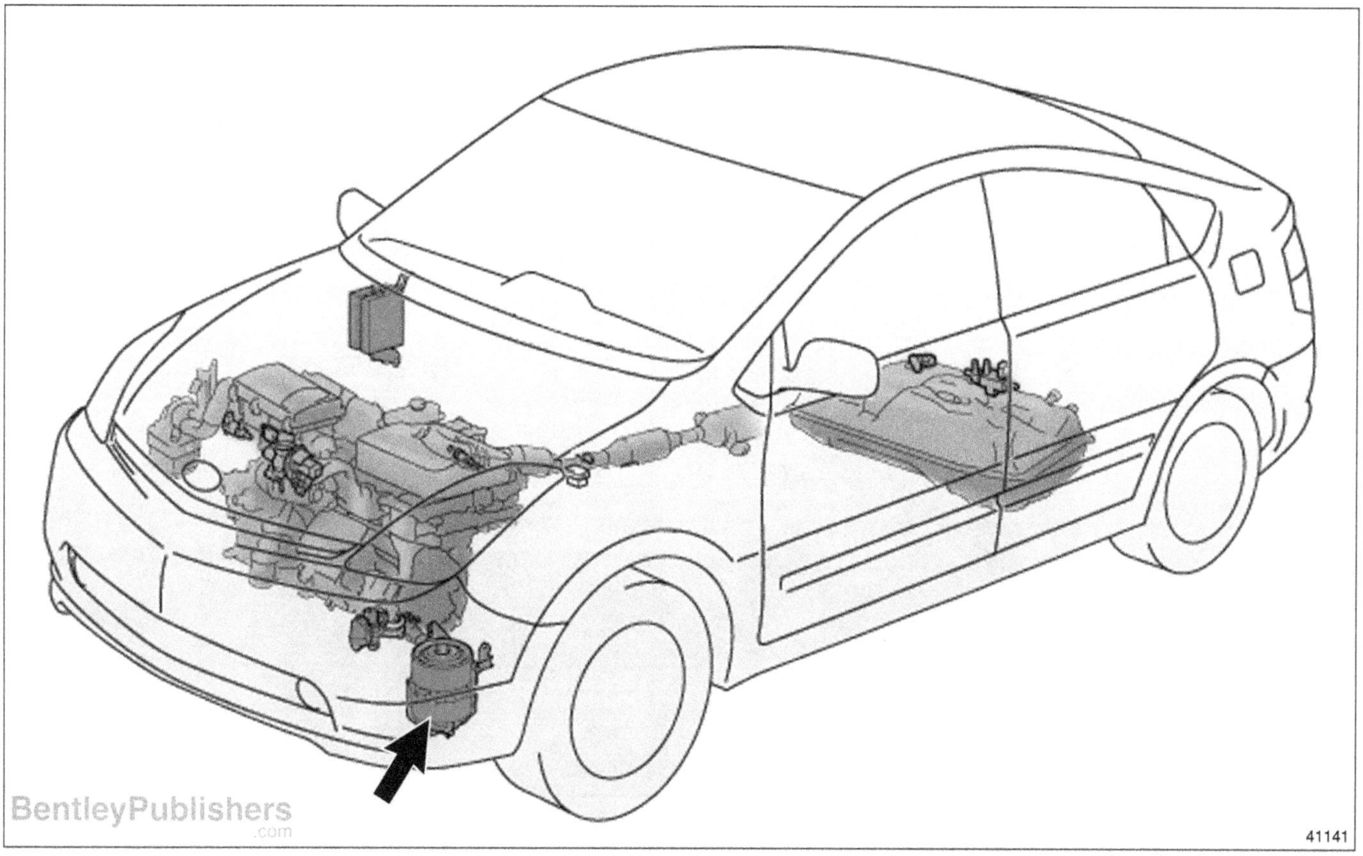

Courtesy Toyota Motor Sales (TMS) USA, Inc.

Prius Hybrid System

WARNING—

- *Coolant stored in the coolant heat storage tank can remain hot (as high as 176°F) for as long as 3 days. A tank malfunction may cause the surface of the coolant heat storage tank to become very hot. Use caution when working around the coolant heat storage tank. See* **5 Engine**.

HYBRID TRANSAXLE

The Prius hybrid transaxle is an elegant design with a very simple gear train. The transaxle has only one planetary gear set, similar to gears in many automatic transmissions. This simple gear set allows the transaxle to function in a way that is similar to a continuously variable transmission (CVT). Like a CVT, it can provide a wide range of virtual gear ratios that allow the engine to run at optimum rpm for any road speed and load. The transaxle also makes the Prius a **parallel hybrid**, as it acts as a power splitting device between the gasoline engine and electric motor / generator 2 (MG2). For more information, see **1 Familiarization**.

Major hybrid transaxle components include:

- Motor / generator 1 (MG1)
- Motor / generator 2 (MG2)
- Planetary gear unit (power splitting device)
- Power transfer unit with silent chain and gears – transmits power from planetary gears to differential
- Differential – transaxle output to axle shafts and front wheels
- Hybrid system high voltage components, including the inverter and DC-DC converter, mounted on top of the transaxle.

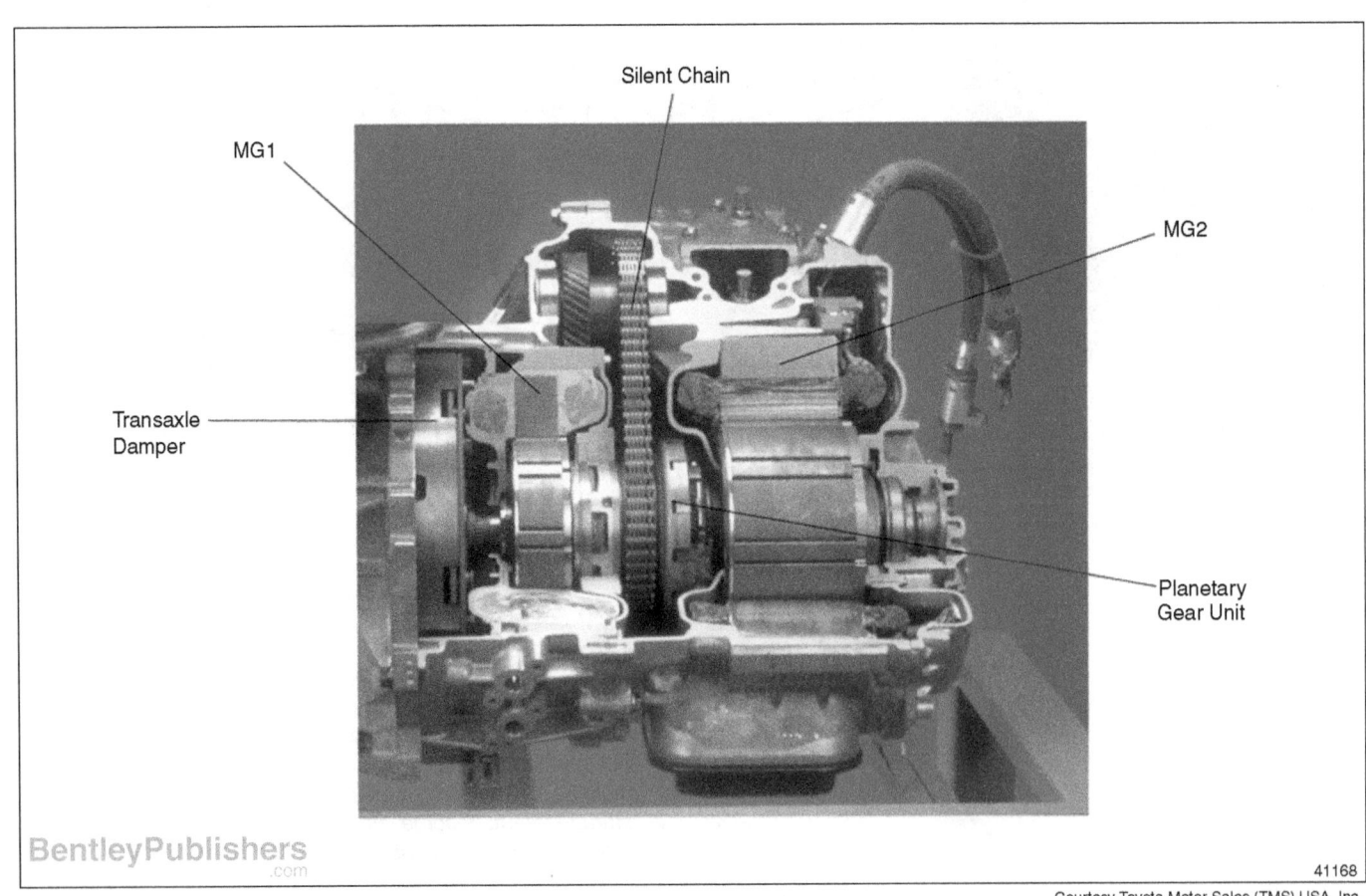

41168

Courtesy Toyota Motor Sales (TMS) USA, Inc.

A dedicated liquid cooling system, separate from the engine cooling system, is used to cool MG1, MG2, the inverter, and other transaxle components. See **Transaxle / inverter cooling system** in this chapter.

Transaxle evolution and specifications

The 2004 - 2008 Prius uses the type P112 transaxle, which is an improved version of the type P111 transaxle used on the 2001 - 2003 Prius. The basic layout and components are similar for both types. Improvements in the P112 transaxle include:

- MG1 and MG2 have higher torque and higher rpm capability
- V-shaped permanent magnets in MG1 and MG2 rotors
- Differential gear ratio changed
- New lubricating oil specified

Table b. Prius hybrid transaxle specifications

Model		2001 - 2003 (NHW11)	2004 - 2008 (NHW20)
Transaxle type		P111	P112
Planetary Gear	Ring gear teeth	---	78
	Pinion gear teeth	---	23
	Sun gear teeth	---	30
Differential gear ratio		3.905	4.113
Chain	Links	74	72
	Drive sprocket teeth	39	36
	Driven sprocket teeth	36	35
Counter gear	Drive gear teeth	---	30
	Driven gear teeth	---	44
Final gear	Drive gear teeth	---	26
	Driven gear teeth	---	75
Fluid capacity		4.6 L (4.0 qts)	3.8 L (4.0 qts)
Fluid type		ATF type T-IV or equivalent	ATF WS or equivalent
Weight (reference)*		---	107 kg (236 lbs)
* Weight with fluid fully filled			

Prius Hybrid System

Motor / generators

The Prius uses two powerful motor / generators (MG1 and MG2), which are connected by a power splitting device.

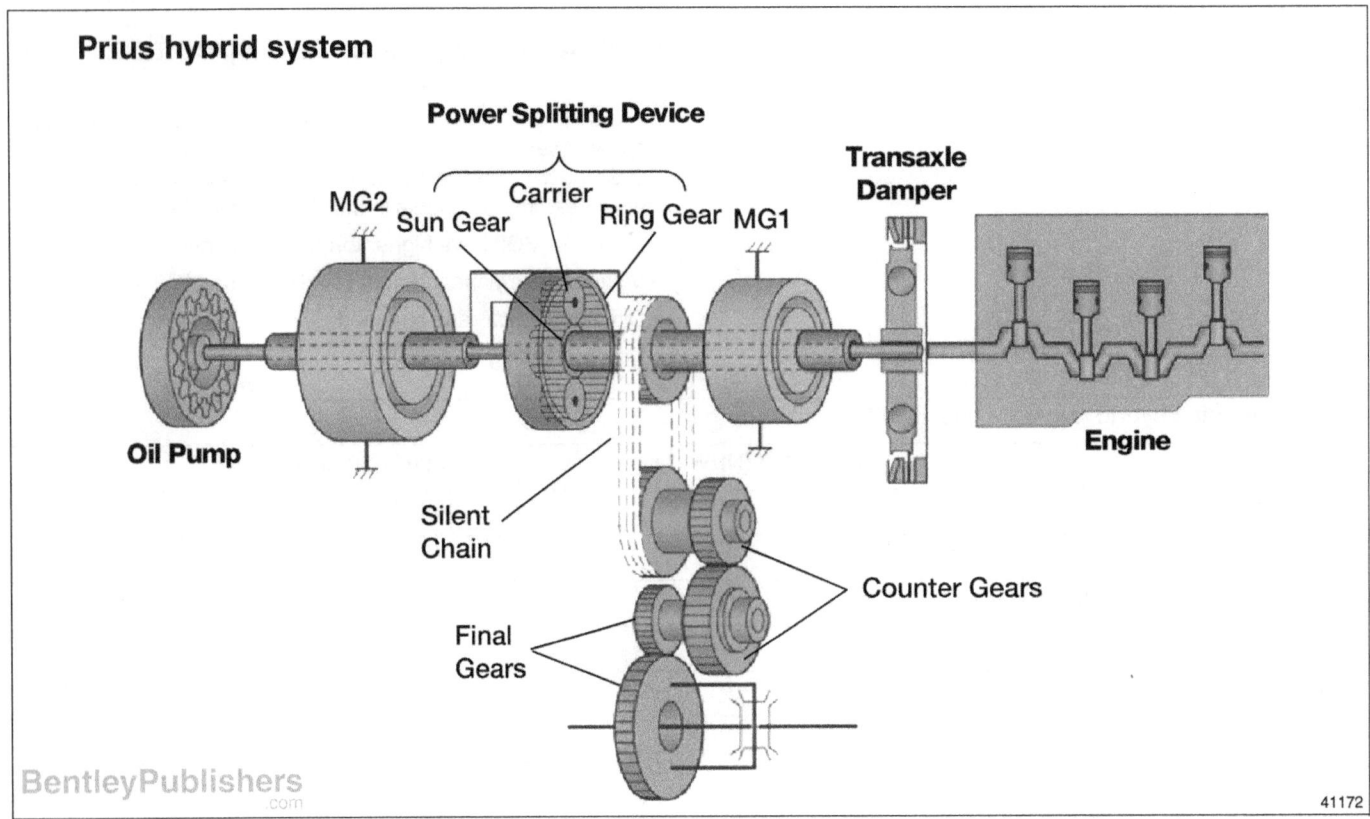

Prius hybrid system

Courtesy Toyota Motor Sales (TMS) USA, Inc.

Courtesy Toyota Motor Sales (TMS) USA, Inc.

Motor / generator 1 (MG1)

◄ Motor / generator 1 (MG1) (**arrow**) is a brushless three-phase synchronous alternating current (AC) motor / generator with very strong permanent magnets. MG1 performs these functions in the Prius hybrid transaxle:

- When driven as a generator by the engine, MG1 recharges the high voltage battery and supplies electrical power to MG2

- When run as an electric motor, MG1 acts as the starter motor for the gasoline engine

- When regulated by THS II, MG1 acts as the transaxle power split control element which helps to determine rpm and power contribution from gasoline engine.

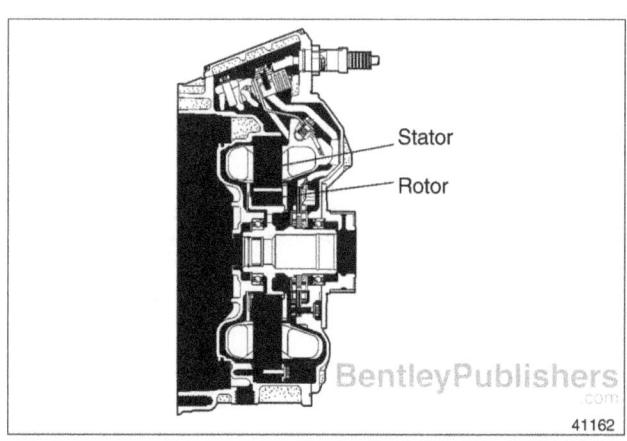

Stator

Rotor

41162
Courtesy Toyota Motor Sales (TMS) USA, Inc.

◄ The three-phase stator coils in MG1 operate on voltages up to 500 volts AC.

A dedicated liquid cooling system, separate from the engine cooling system, is used to cool MG1 and other transaxle components. See **Transaxle / inverter cooling system** in this chapter.

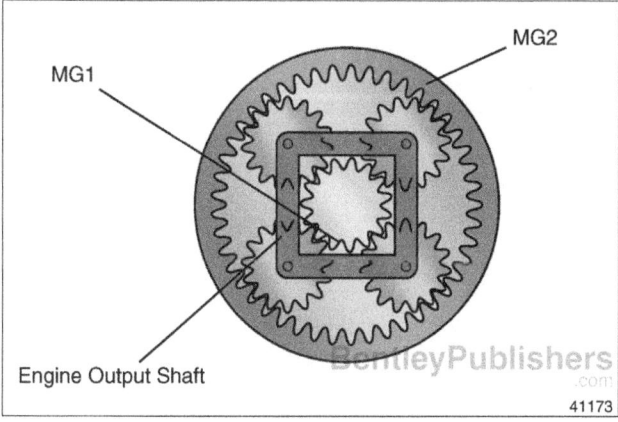

MG2

MG1

Engine Output Shaft

41173
Courtesy Toyota Motor Sales (TMS) USA, Inc.

◄ MG1 is directly connected to the sun gear in the planetary gear set.

Item	Connection
Sun gear	MG1
Ring gear	MG2
Carrier	Engine output shaft

For an explanation of the operation of this type of electric motor, see **Permanent magnet motors** in this chapter.

Motor / generator 2 (MG2)

TP0803013
Courtesy Toyota Motor Sales (TMS) USA, Inc.

◄ Motor / generator 2 (MG2) (**arrow**) is a brushless three-phase synchronous alternating current (AC) motor / generator with very strong magnets. MG2 is similar to, but larger than, MG1. MG2 performs these functions in the Prius hybrid transaxle:

• MG2 is geared directly to the front wheels. Whenever the front wheels turn, MG2 also turns.

• When driven as an electric motor, MG2 drives the vehicle. Power from MG2 supplements power from the gasoline engine.

• When coasting and when brakes are applied, MG2 is driven by the front wheels as a generator. Electromechanical drag in the generator drag slows the vehicle, and vehicle kinetic energy is converted to electrical energy which is stored in the high voltage battery.

Prius Hybrid System

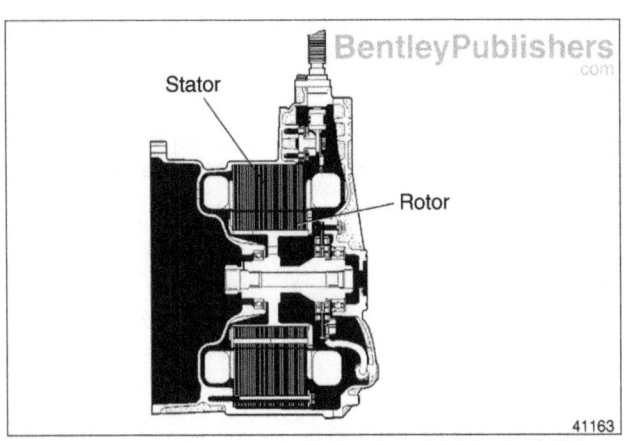

Courtesy Toyota Motor Sales (TMS) USA, Inc.

◄ The three-phase stator coils in MG2 operate on voltages up to 500 volts AC.

- Maximum output: 50 kw (67 hp) @ 1200 - 1540 rpm
- Maximum torque: 400 Nm (295 lb-ft.) @ 1 - 1200 rpm

A dedicated liquid cooling system, separate from the engine cooling system, is used to cool MG2 and other transaxle components. See **Transaxle / inverter cooling system** in this chapter.

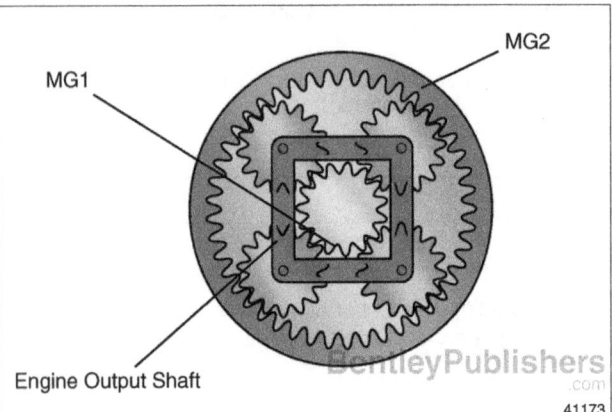

Courtesy Toyota Motor Sales (TMS) USA, Inc.

◄ MG2 is directly connected to the ring gear in the planetary gear set, which is geared directly to the front wheels.

Item	Connection
Sun gear	MG1
Ring gear	MG2
Carrier	Engine output shaft

WARNING —

- *When towing a Prius, do not allow the front wheels to rotate. The front wheels are directly connected to motor / generator 2 (MG2). When the front wheels are turning MG2 also turns. This may generate high voltage and create a shock hazard, and may also cause inverter and / or high voltage battery damage. See **3 Safety**.*

For an explanation of the operation of this type of electric motor, see **Permanent magnet motors** in this chapter.

Permanent magnet motors

◄ Both MG1 and MG2 are brushless permanent magnet three-phase synchronous alternating current (AC) motor / generators. The rotating component (the rotor) has very strong permanent magnets. The stationary component (the stator) has three separate windings.

When a three-phase high voltage alternating current is passed through the three-phase stator windings (U, V, and W in the schematic shown), a magnetic field is created in the stator that causes the rotor to turn. By controlling and changing the direction of current through the stator windings according to rotor position and speed, the permanent magnets in the rotor are attracted to a particular region of the stator and repelled from another region of the stator. This generates a rotational torque which causes the rotor to turn. Current through the stator windings is controlled by the inverter.

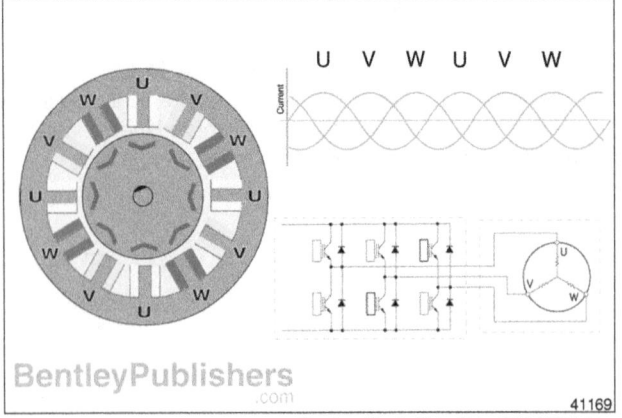

Courtesy Toyota Motor Sales (TMS) USA, Inc.

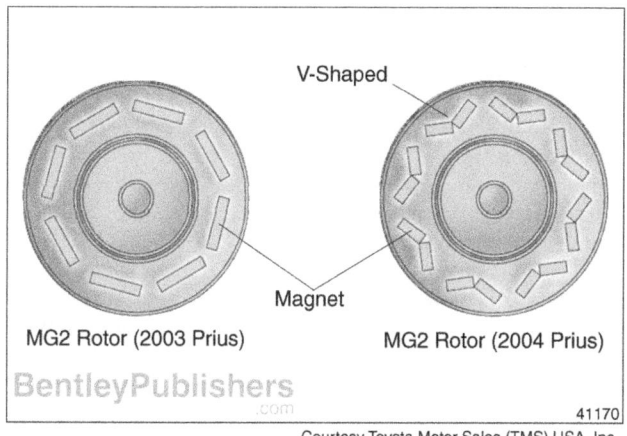

MG2 Rotor (2003 Prius)   MG2 Rotor (2004 Prius)

41170

Courtesy Toyota Motor Sales (TMS) USA, Inc.

Motor rotational torque is approximately proportional to the magnitude of the electric current flow in the stator windings. Rotor speed is controlled by the frequency of the alternating current in the stator windings. This type of motor can produce high torque at high speeds by properly controlling the magnetic field in the stator.

◀ In 2004 - 2008 Prius models, the permanent magnets in the rotors in both MG1 and MG2 have been revised. The permanent magnets are now configured in a V-shaped arrangement. The result is much higher motor torque and higher rpm capability when compared with the design of the previous generation Prius.

Speed sensor (resolver)

In order to precisely control rotor speed and torque in MG1 and MG2, instantaneous rotor position and speed must be accurately measured. The sensor that accomplishes this is called the speed sensor or resolver.

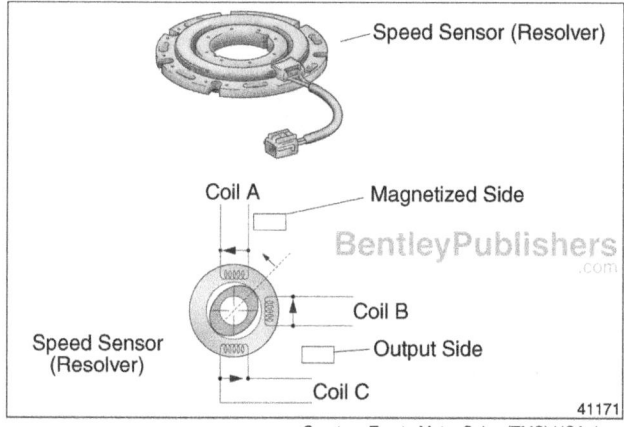

41171

Courtesy Toyota Motor Sales (TMS) USA, Inc.

◀ The resolver precisely detects rotor position. The resolver rotor turns with its motor / generator rotor. The resolver stator has 3 coils arranged as shown. Since the resolver rotor is oval in shape, the air gap between the stator coils and rotor varies with rotor rotation.

An alternating input current is passed through coil A. Output currents are induced in coils B and C that vary with rotor position. The rate of change of signals from coils B and C is used to calculate motor / generator rotor rpm. The HV-ECU uses these input signals to determine rotor absolute position and rpm.

Planetary gear unit

◀ The planetary gear unit is a very simple set of gears that permits the transaxle to split and control the power from MG1, MG2 and the gasoline engine. The planetary gear unit is composed of three parts. Each part of the planetary gear unit is directly connected to one of the power sources.

Item	Connection
Sun gear	MG1
Ring gear	MG2
Carrier	Engine output shaft

Engine Output Shaft

41173

Courtesy Toyota Motor Sales (TMS) USA, Inc.

Courtesy Toyota Motor Sales (TMS) USA, Inc.

The pinion gears on the planet carrier mesh with both the sun gear and the ring gear (an internal gear with teeth on the inner circumference). In its simplest application, a planetary gear unit will transmit power when one of the three gears is the input, one gear is held (the reaction gear), and the third is gear is the output. For example, if the planet carrier is the input (driven by the engine), the ring gear is the output (driving the front wheels), and the sun gear is held (MG1 rotor is not turning), then the engine can drive the wheels.

The planetary gear unit can provide an infinite range of gear ratios, depending upon which gears are the input, output, and reaction gears. In the Prius, MG1 can be made to turn at varying speeds and in either direction to control power split, gear ratio, and speed.

MG2 drives the ring gear in the planetary gear set, which is geared directly to the final drive, differential gears, and the vehicle's front wheels by means of a silent chain drive.

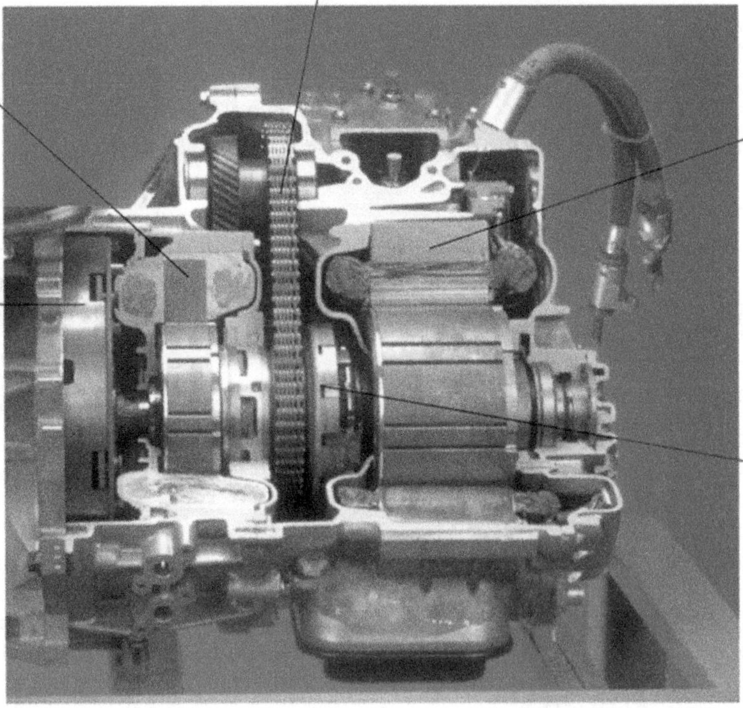

Silent Chain

MG1

MG2

Transaxle Damper

Planetary Gear Unit

41168

Courtesy Toyota Motor Sales (TMS) USA, Inc.

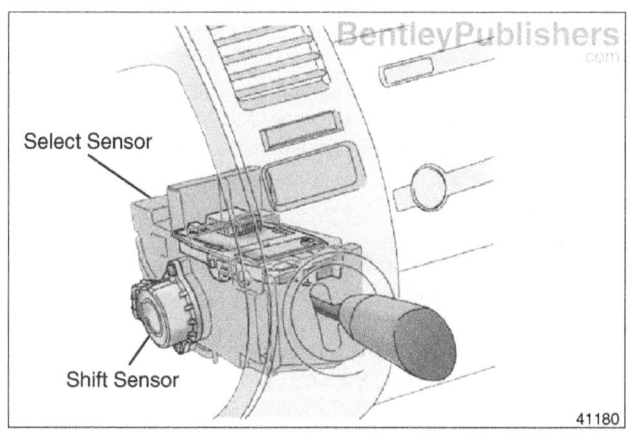

Select Sensor

Shift Sensor

41180

Courtesy Toyota Motor Sales (TMS) USA, Inc.

Transaxle shift control system

◄ The Prius gear selector is a shift-by-wire system. There is no mechanical connection between the gear selector and the transaxle.

As the driver selects the desired gear, the gear selector outputs unique voltage signal to the HV-ECU. Hall-effect sensors in the gear selector send a signal to the HV-ECU for each gear selector position. The HV-ECU then places the transaxle in the desired gear.

NOTE—

• *The transaxle gearshift and park lock systems are electronic and use the 12-volt auxiliary battery for power. If this battery is discharged or is disconnected, the vehicle cannot be started or shifted out of park.*

• *If a 2004 - 2008 Prius cannot be placed in PARK, there may be a malfunction in the gear selector that is preventing the transaxle from engaging the park lock. It may also not be possible to turn the vehicle OFF with the power button. If this occurs, stop the vehicle and apply the parking brake. This will bypass the fault and permit shutdown of the hybrid system. The vehicle will then not restart until the fault is corrected. See* **11 Diagnostics***.*

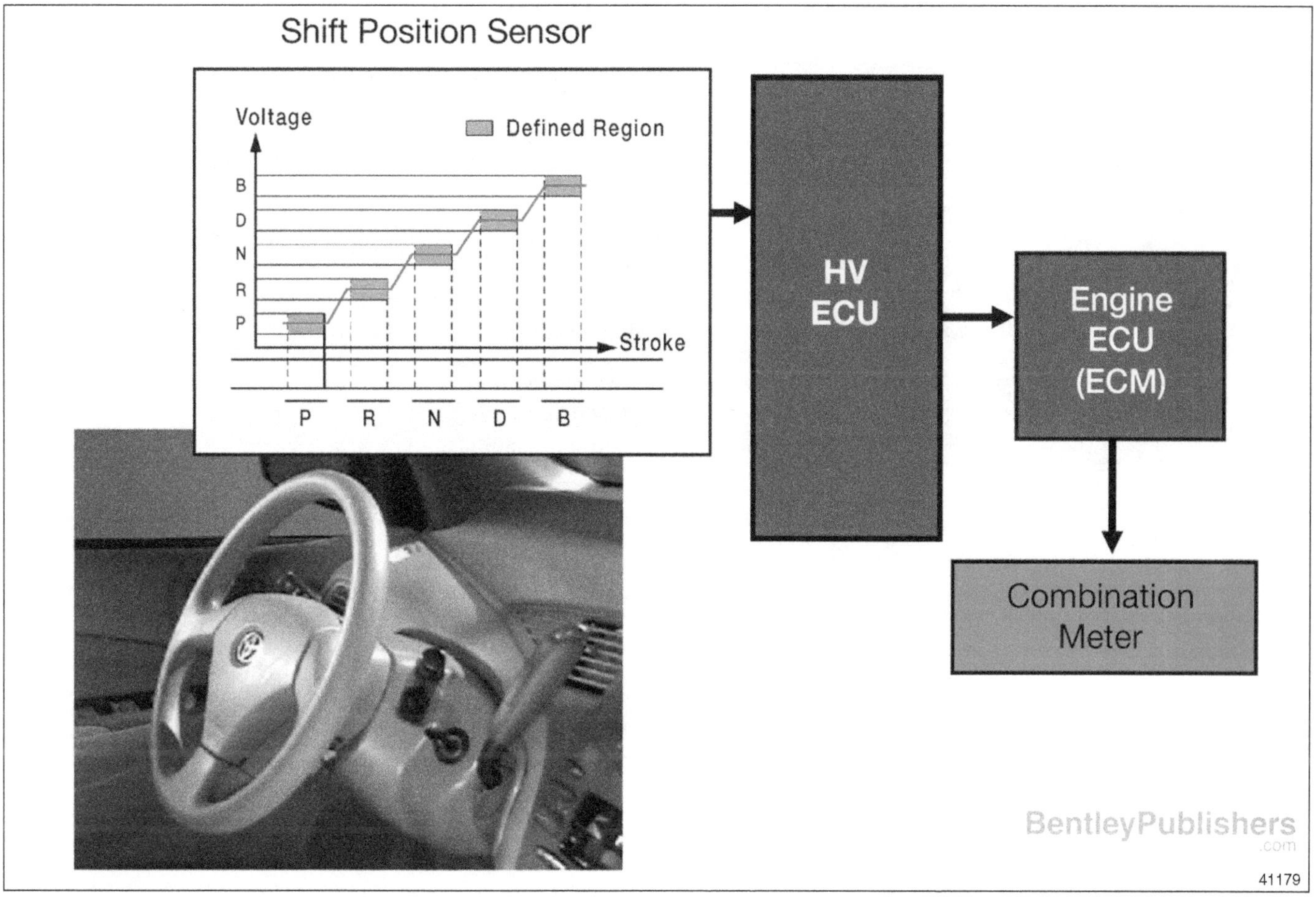

Prius Hybrid System

Shift Position Sensor

Voltage

☐ Defined Region

B
D
N
R
P

→ Stroke

P   R   N   D   B

HV
ECU

→

Engine
ECU
(ECM)

↓

Combination
Meter

41179

Courtesy Toyota Motor Sales (TMS) USA, Inc.

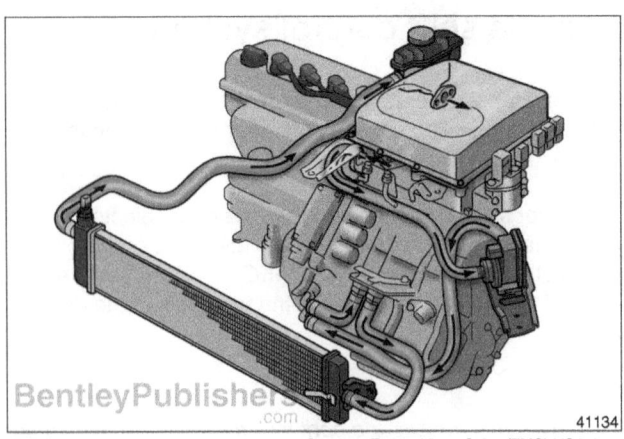

Courtesy Toyota Motor Sales (TMS) USA, Inc.

Transaxle / inverter cooling system

◄ A dedicated liquid cooling system completely separate from the engine cooling system is used to cool the inverter, MG1, MG2, and other transaxle components. The transaxle / inverter cooling system has its own coolant reservoir, radiator, coolant supply, and electric pump.

The transaxle / inverter cooling system electric pump runs whenever the ignition is ON.

The transaxle / inverter cooling system is drained and filled separately from the engine cooling system. Periodic transaxle / inverter coolant replacement is recommended by Toyota. See **4 Service and Repair Fundamentals** for recommended transaxle / inverter coolant service intervals.

Toyota specifies Toyota Super Long Life Coolant (SLLC) for the 2004 - 2008 Prius. See **7 Hybrid Transaxle**, for transaxle / inverter coolant checking, drain, and refill procedures.

HIGH VOLTAGE (HV) SYSTEM COMPONENTS

Inverter

◄ The inverter is an electrical device that changes high-voltage direct current (DC) from the HV battery to three-phase alternating current (AC) to power MG1 and MG2 as electric motors. When MG1 and MG2 function as generators, then the inverter rectifies three-phase alternating current generator output to direct current which is sent to the HV battery.

The inverter circuit contains two three-phase bridge circuits with six power transistors each for MG1 and MG2. The power transistors are controlled by the HV-ECU.

The inverter is located in the engine compartment on top of the hybrid transaxle.

Courtesy Toyota Motor Sales (TMS) USA, Inc.

Boost converter

On the 2004 - 2008 Prius, HV battery voltage (201.6 volts) is increased by the boost converter to approximately 500 volts to drive MG1 and MG2 as electric motors.

When MG1 and MG2 run as generators, the boost converter reduces the 500 volt generator output down to HV battery voltage (201.6 volts).

The ability to increase HV battery voltage at MG1 and MG2 is one reason why voltage and size of the HV battery pack has been reduced in the 2004 - 2008 Prius when compared with the HV battery pack in the 2001 - 2003 Prius.

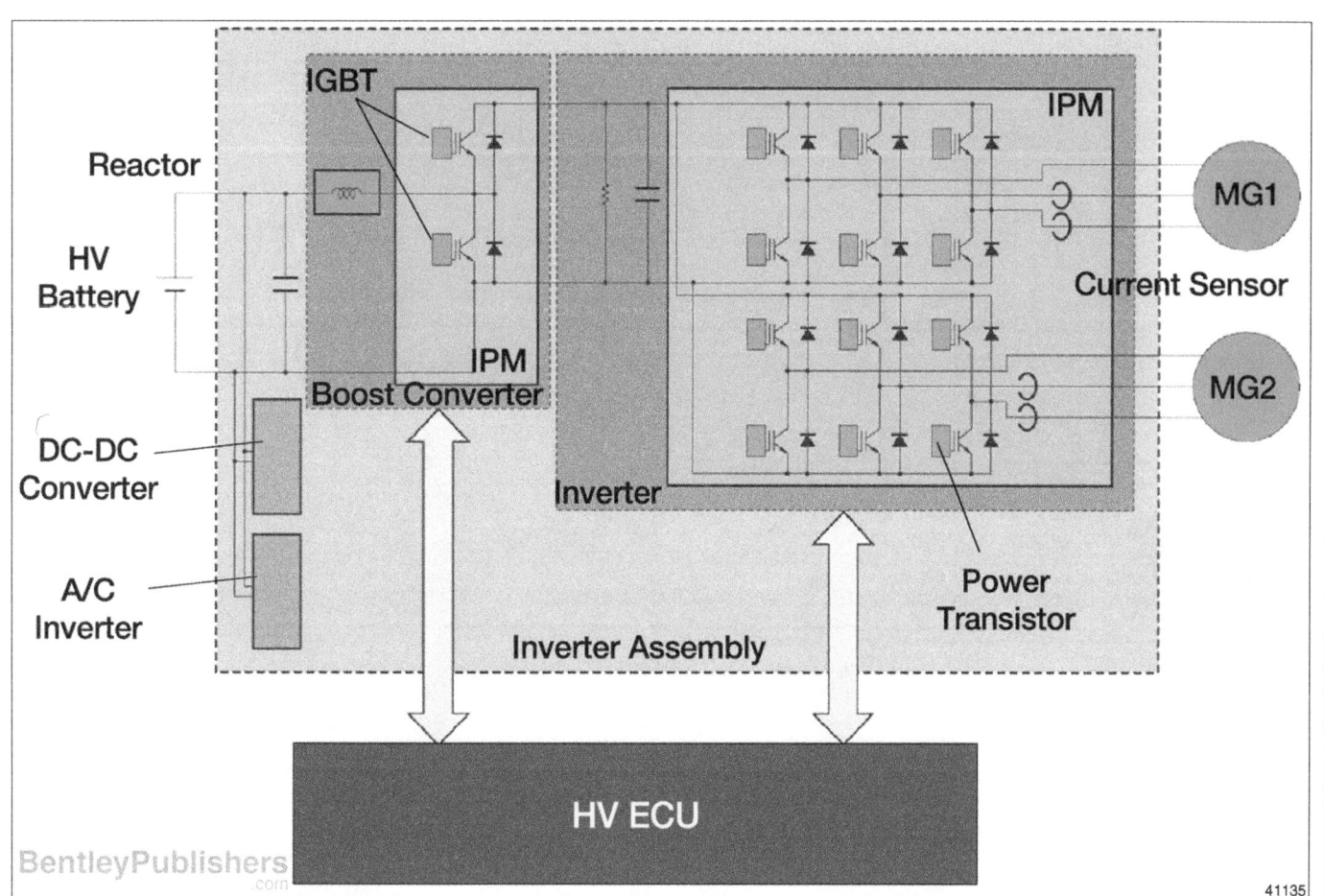

Courtesy Toyota Motor Sales (TMS) USA, Inc.

41135

Prius Hybrid System

Air-conditioning (A/C) inverter

On the 2004 - 2008 Prius, the air-conditioning (A/C) compressor is driven by a high voltage electric motor, and not by an engine belt in the conventional manner. There is a separate A/C inverter within the hybrid system inverter housing to supply power to the air-conditioning compressor motor. The A/C inverter changes HV battery DC output into three-phase AC to run the compressor electric motor. Voltage to the motor is approximately the same as HV battery voltage (201.6 volts).

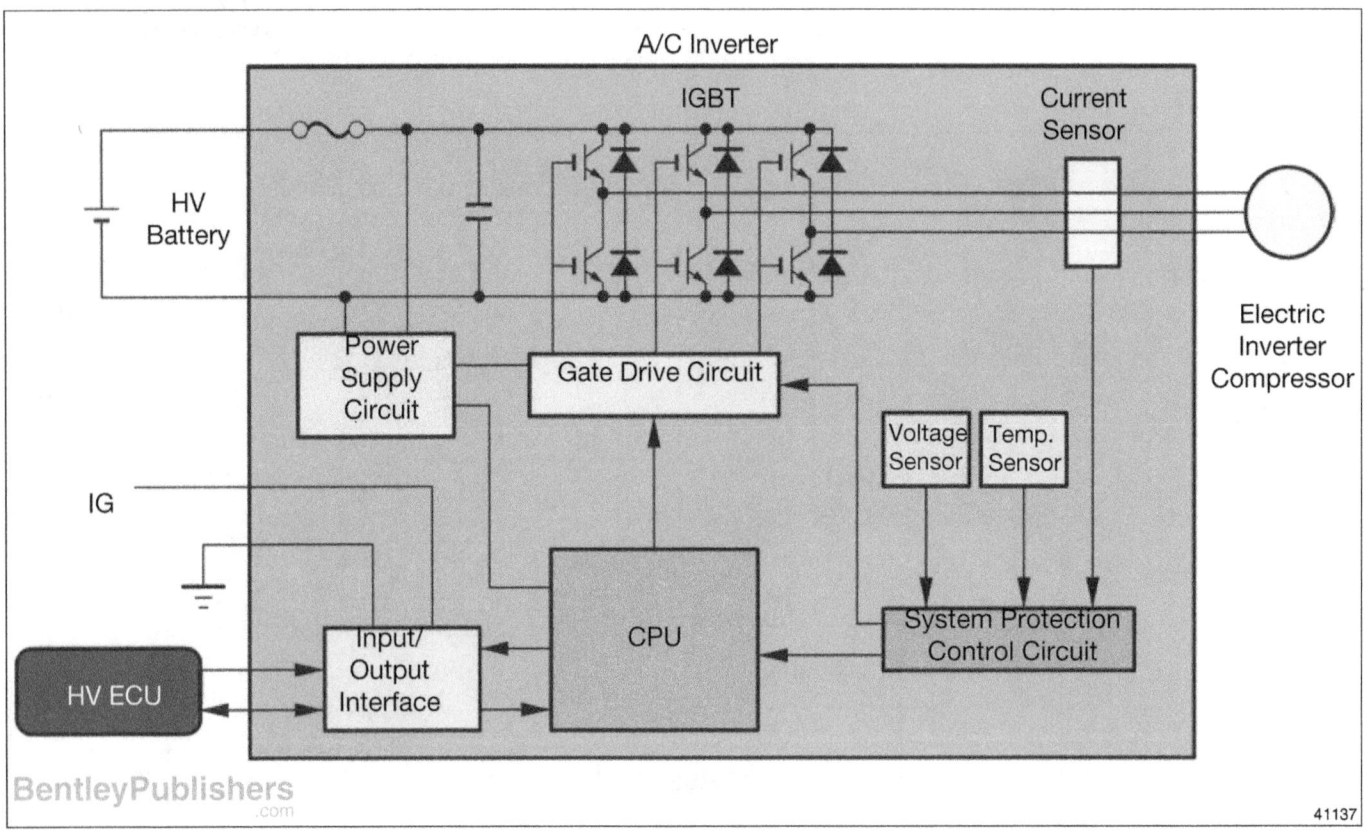

41137

Courtesy Toyota Motor Sales (TMS) USA, Inc.

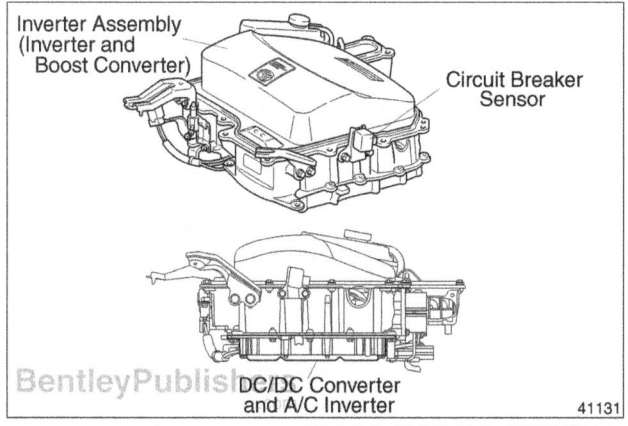

Inverter Assembly
(Inverter and
Boost Converter)

Circuit Breaker
Sensor

DC/DC Converter
and A/C Inverter

41131

Courtesy Toyota Motor Sales (TMS) USA, Inc.

DC-DC converter

◀ Auxiliary electrical equipment and electronic devices on the
Prius, such as lights, radiator fans, the audio system, and
electronic control units, all require nominal 12-volt DC power.
Power to these devices is supplied by the DC-DC converter.

The DC-DC converter reduces HV battery output (201.6 volts) to
approximately 12 volts DC to power these devices, and also to
charge the 12-volt auxiliary battery.

The DC-DC converter is located under the inverter in the engine
compartment. The inverter / converter assembly is mounted on
top of the transaxle.

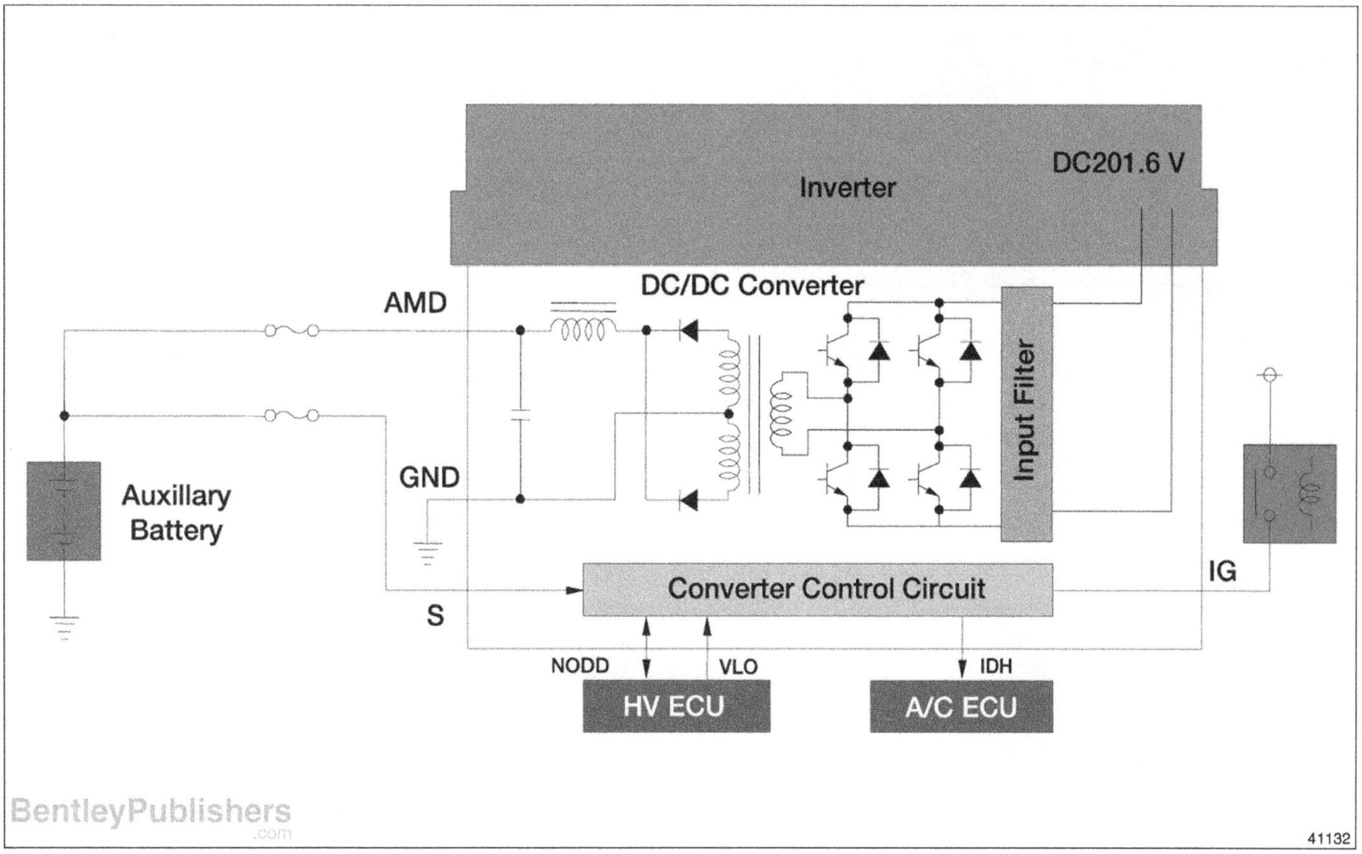

Prius Hybrid System

Inverter

DC201.6 V

DC/DC Converter

AMD

Input Filter

Auxillary
Battery

GND

IG

Converter Control Circuit

S

NODD   VLO   IDH

HV ECU   A/C ECU

41132

Courtesy Toyota Motor Sales (TMS) USA, Inc.

High voltage (HV) battery

Electrical power for the high voltage hybrid system is stored in a high voltage (HV) battery pack. The HV battery provides power to MG1 and MG2 when they operate as electric motors. The HV battery also provides power to the electric air-conditioning compressor on the 2004 - 2008 Prius. HV battery voltage is also stepped-down by the DC-DC converter to power 12-volt systems and components. See **Air-conditioning (A/C) inverter**, and **DC-DC converter** in this chapter.

When in use, the HV battery is continuously charged and discharged. The HV battery is charged when either MG1 or MG2 operate as generators. The hybrid system controls battery state-of-charge (SOC), and the HV battery never needs to be "plugged in" or charged with an external charger when the system operates normally. See **Battery ECU** in this chapter.

◀ The high voltage battery pack is located in the cargo area in the rear of the vehicle. The entire HV battery pack assembly is contained within a protective sheet metal housing that is bolted to the vehicle floor.

◀ The HV battery is modular in construction, with 168 individual nickel metal hydride (NiMH) battery cells. Each battery cell generates 1.2 volts. Six cells are connected in series to make each battery module which generates 7.2 volts. The HV battery has 28 battery modules which are connected in series to produce 201.6 volts. The complete HV battery weighs 39 kg (86 lb).

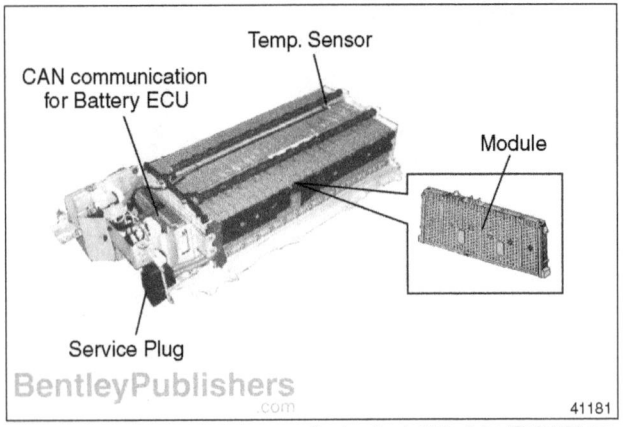

Temp. Sensor

CAN communication
for Battery ECU

Module

Service Plug

Courtesy Toyota Motor Sales (TMS) USA, Inc.

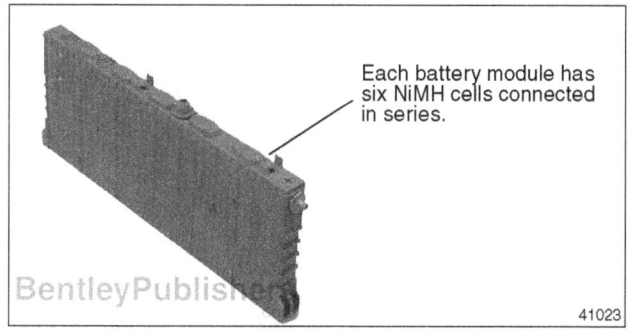

Each battery module has six NiMH cells connected in series.

41023

Courtesy Toyota Motor Sales (TMS) USA, Inc.

◁ Each battery module has six NiMH cells connected in series. The active materials in each battery cell are contained within a molded hard plastic housing. Cell electrodes are made of porous nickel and metal hydride alloy. Battery electrolyte contains potassium hydroxide and sodium hydroxide. The electrolyte is a paste, and leaks are unlikely; however, the electrolyte is a very caustic alkaline substance with a very high pH of 13.5. Never touch the electrolyte! See **3 Safety**, for HV battery safety information.

2004 - 2008 Prius high voltage (HV) battery	
Number of NiMH cells	168
Number of NiMH modules	28
NiMH module voltage	7.2v
HV battery voltage	201.6v
Weight of complete HV battery pack	39 kg (86 lb)

Other high voltage system components located with the high voltage battery pack include:

- Service plug
- Battery ECU
- System main relay (SMR)

Service plug

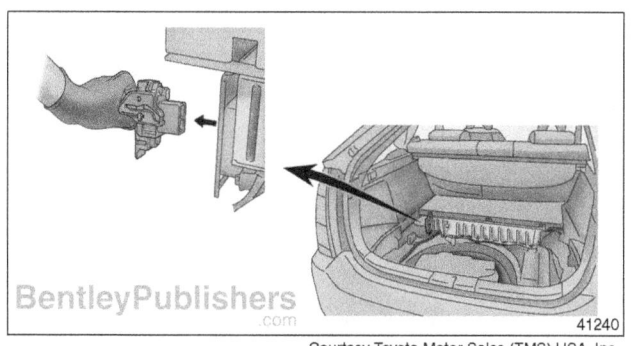

41240

Courtesy Toyota Motor Sales (TMS) USA, Inc.

◁ The service plug provides a manual method to isolate the HV battery and to remove high voltage from hybrid system components. The service plug assembly contains a pair of heavy load-carrying main contacts and the high voltage circuit fuse (rated for 125 amps).

41184

◁ The service plug also has a separate pair of small safety interlock switch contacts. The safety interlock circuit is complete only when the service plug is fully installed, and with the latch in the locked position. The HV-ECU will turn the system main relay ON only when the safety interlock circuit is complete. When the service plug latch is lifted, the safety interlock circuit is opened. In this condition, the HV-ECU will not turn ON the system main relay or the hybrid system.

NOTE—

- *The service plug must be removed before working on any Prius components that are connected to the hybrid high voltage system. Always wear lineman's gloves when removing the service plug, and whenever high voltage may be present. See* **3 Safety**.

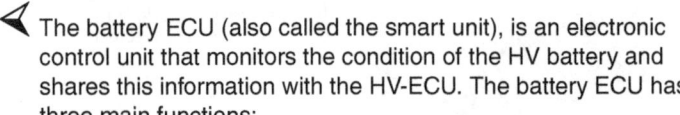

Courtesy Toyota Motor Sales (TMS) USA, Inc.

Battery ECU

◄ The battery ECU (also called the smart unit), is an electronic control unit that monitors the condition of the HV battery and shares this information with the HV-ECU. The battery ECU has three main functions:

- Manages and regulates HV battery state-of-charge (SOC): The battery ECU estimates how much current flows into and out of the HV battery and sends HV battery charging and discharging requests to the HV-ECU to maintain HV battery SOC at or near the target level.

- Regulates the HV battery cooling fan: The battery ECU estimates the amount of heat generated in the HV battery during charging and discharging and regulates cooling fan speed to maintain HV battery temperature within the acceptable range.

- Protects the HV battery: The battery ECU monitors HV battery voltage, temperature, and electrical leakage, and is capable of restricting or even stopping charging and discharging to protect the HV battery.

The HV battery is never fully charged or fully discharged when in use. The hybrid system manages HV battery charging and discharging so that the state-of-charge (SOC) is kept within the predetermined range: 40-80% charge, with the target SOC equal to 60%.

The HV battery is repetitively charged and discharged when in use. The battery ECU monitors HV battery SOC, and sends this information to the HV-ECU. When the HV battery SOC drops below the green control region, the HV-ECU signals the engine control module (ECM) to increase engine power to drive MG1 as a generator and increase the charging rate.

NOTE—

- *A severely undercharged HV battery may not be capable of recovery and may require replacement.*

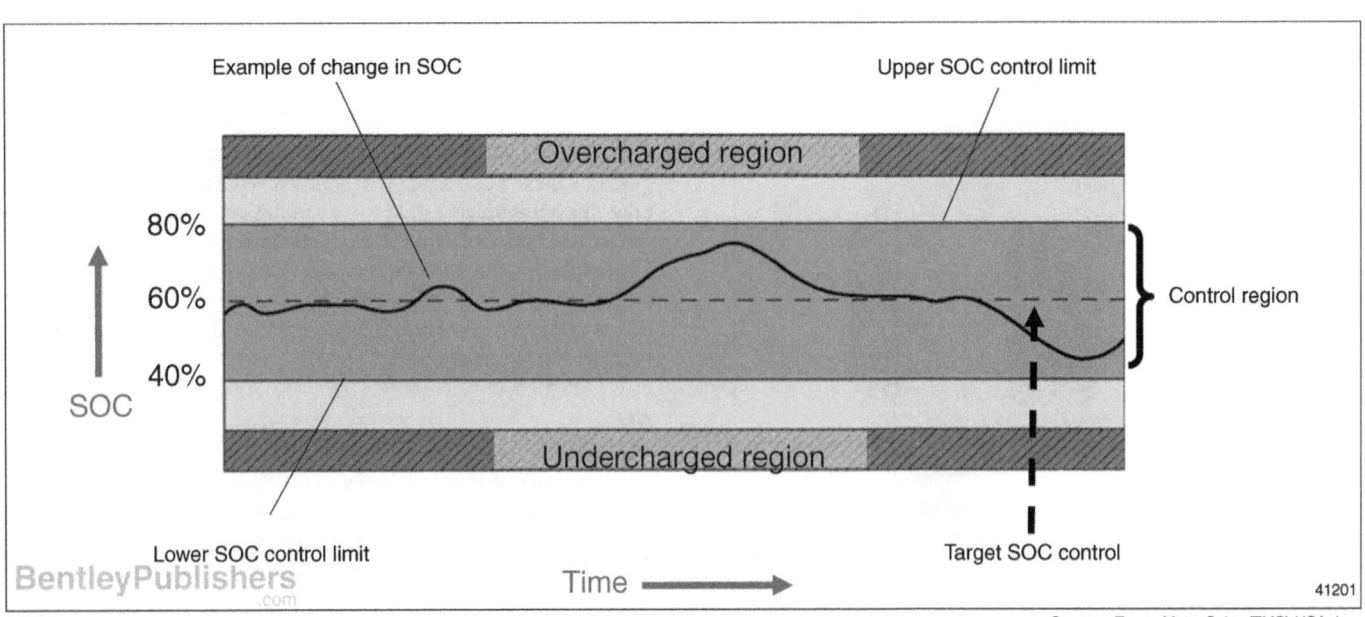

Courtesy Toyota Motor Sales (TMS) USA, Inc.

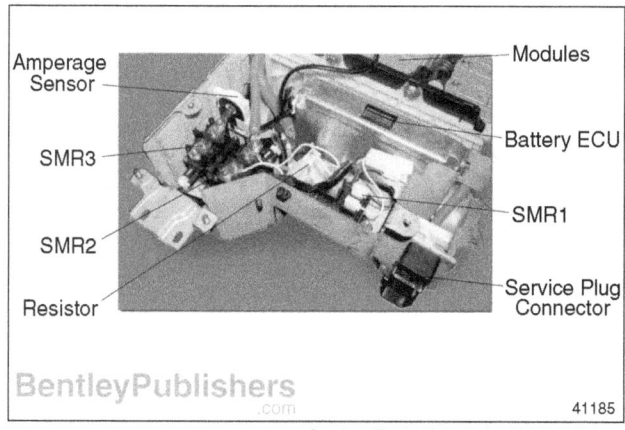

Amperage Sensor — SMR3 — SMR2 — Resistor — Modules — Battery ECU — SMR1 — Service Plug Connector

41185

Courtesy Toyota Motor Sales (TMS) USA, Inc.

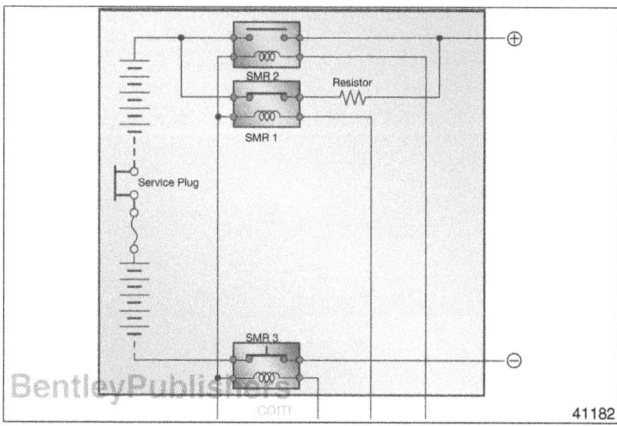

41182

Courtesy Toyota Motor Sales (TMS) USA, Inc.

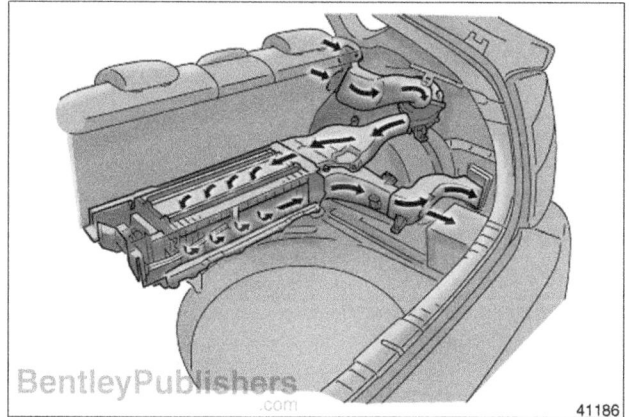

41186

Courtesy Toyota Motor Sales (TMS) USA, Inc.

System main relay (SMR)

◄ The system main relay (SMR) connects and disconnects high voltage battery power to high voltage hybrid circuits on commands from the HV-ECU. Three relays operate in a specific sequence to connect or disconnect high voltage power. Two of the relays are on the positive (+) side of the high voltage circuit, and one relay is on the negative (-) side of the high voltage circuit.

◄ When the hybrid system is turned ON, the HV-ECU turns ON relays SMR1 and SMR3. The SMR1 circuit has a resistor in series which protects the system from excessive initial inrush current. Next, relay SMR2 turns ON, bypassing the resistor and allowing full current flow. Finally, SMR1 turns OFF. High voltage battery power is then connected to high voltage hybrid circuits.

When the hybrid system is turned OFF, the HV-ECU first turns OFF relay SMR2, then turns OFF relay SMR3. This disconnects high voltage battery power from high voltage hybrid circuits.

The service plug is another protective device in the high voltage circuit. When the service plug is manually removed, this also disconnects high voltage battery power from the high voltage hybrid circuits, just like the system main relay. As you can see in the illustration, removing the service plug effectively splits the high voltage battery pack in two. See **Service plug** in this chapter for further information.

HV battery cooling system

When the vehicle is in operation, charging and discharging the HV battery generates heat and the battery must be cooled. The battery ECU monitors HV battery temperature and also the temperature of cooling intake air with battery pack temperature sensors. The battery ECU controls the operation and speed of the HV battery cooling fan in order to keep the temperature of the HV battery within the predetermined range.

◄ The air intake for HV battery cooling is located in the passenger compartment on the right side of the rear seat back.

Be sure that the HV battery cooling air intake is not obstructed by clothing or other objects in the vehicle interior. A reduction in cooling air flow may allow the HV battery to overheat. This may cause a diagnostic trouble code to set and a warning light to illuminate.

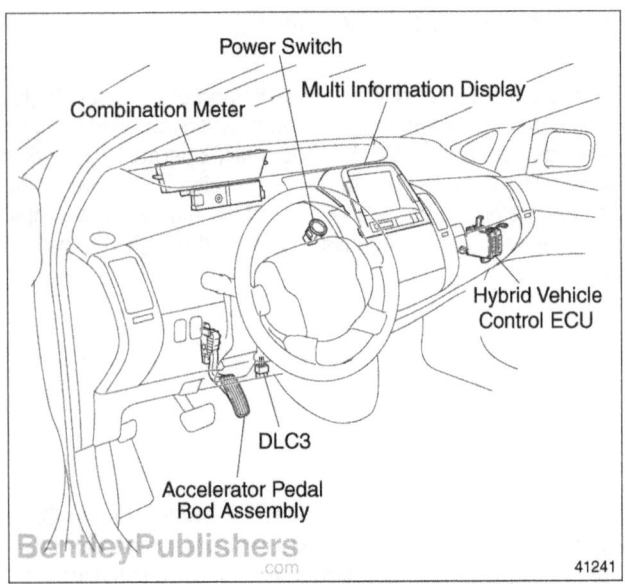

Courtesy Toyota Motor Sales (TMS) USA, Inc.

Hybrid vehicle electronic control unit (HV-ECU)

◄ The hybrid vehicle electronic control unit (HV-ECU) controls the overall operation of the hybrid transaxle and the gasoline engine. The HV-ECU receives inputs (information) from the driver's torque request (accelerator pedal position), regenerative braking (brake pedal position), vehicle speed, shifter position, and state-of-charge (SOC) of the high voltage battery.

To perform the required tasks, the HV-ECU communicates with the engine control module (ECM), the skid control ECU (brake control module), the inverter, and other control modules, sensors, and components.

THS II block diagram for the 2004 - 2008 Prius:

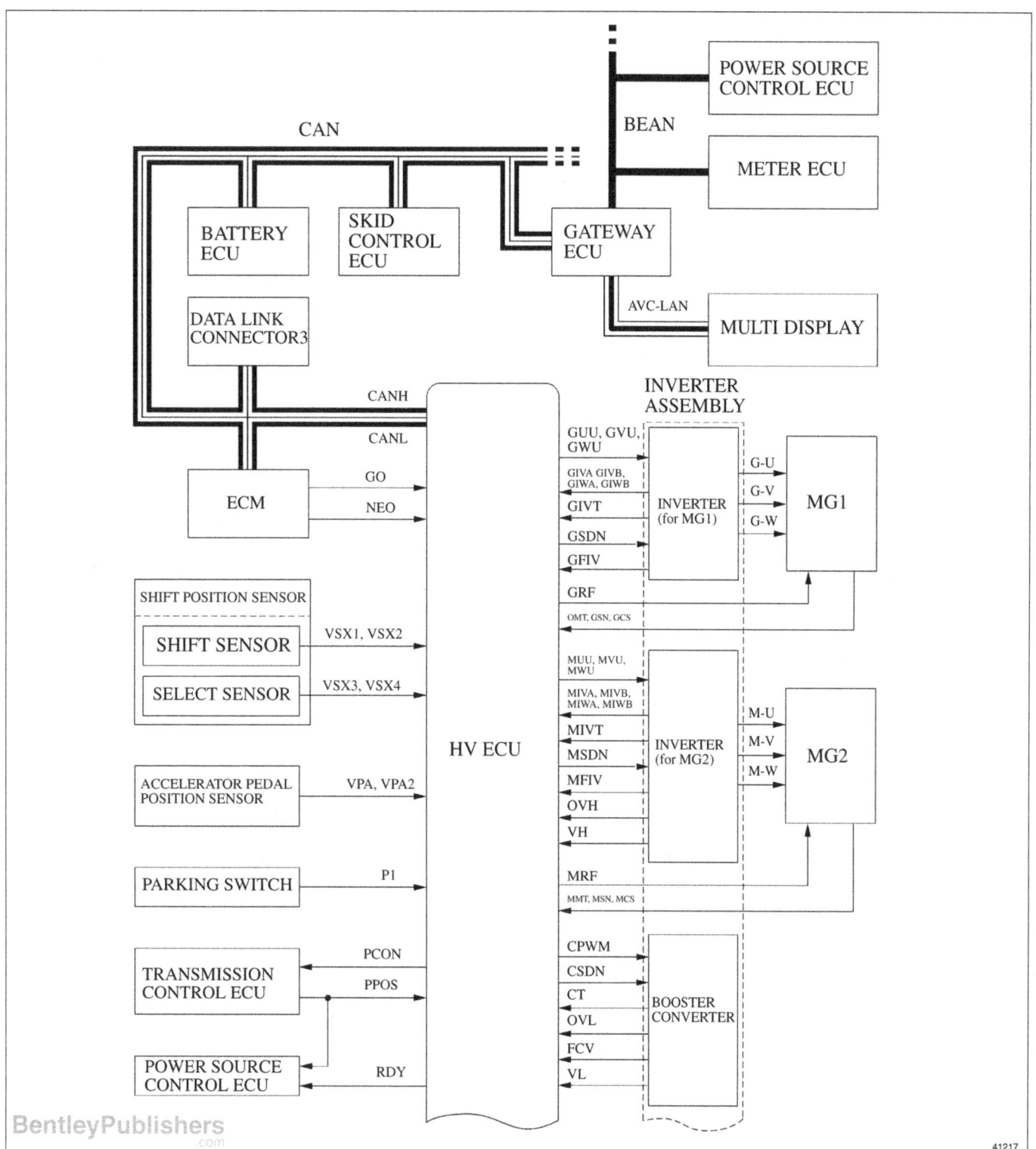

Courtesy Toyota Motor Sales (TMS) USA, Inc.

41217

Prius Hybrid System

**THS II block diagram for the 2004 - 2008 Prius
(continued):**

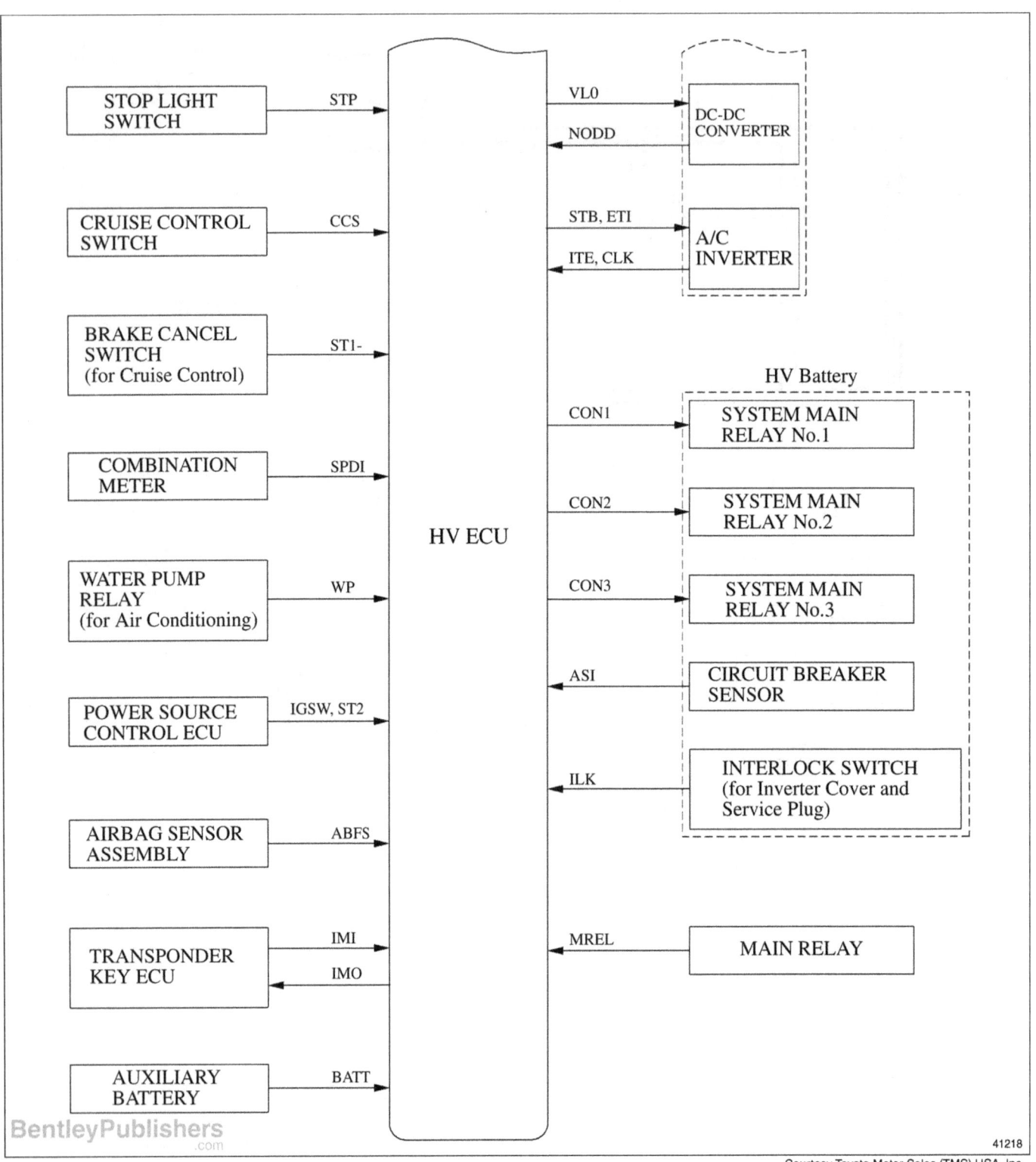

41218

Courtesy Toyota Motor Sales (TMS) USA, Inc.

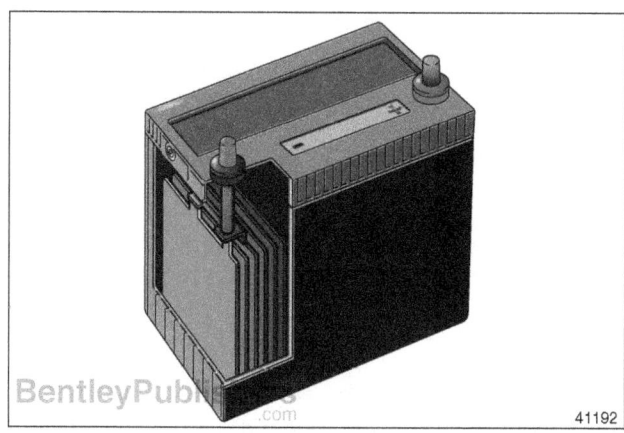

41192

Courtesy Toyota Motor Sales (TMS) USA, Inc.

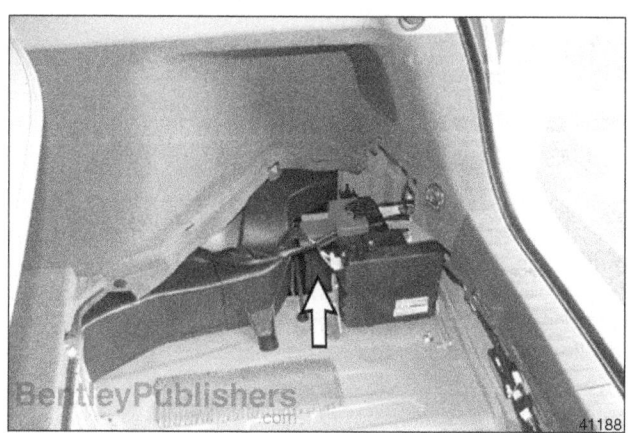

41188

12-volt auxiliary battery

◄ The 12-volt auxiliary battery provides power to electronic control units during startup, and continuous power to maintain control unit memory when the hybrid system is turned OFF. The vehicle will not start if 12-volt auxiliary battery voltage is too low because the battery is defective or needs charging.

The 12-volt auxiliary battery is a sealed maintenance-free low current capacity absorbed-glass-mat (AGM) type lead-acid battery. There is very little electrolyte fluid contained in this type of battery when compared with a typical flooded-cell lead-acid battery. The battery is the valve-regulated type, and there is little out gassing of hydrogen and oxygen when the battery is charging, so there is no need to check electrolyte level in normal service.

◄ The 12-volt auxiliary battery (**arrow**) is located in the trunk / cargo area, on the right side in the 2004 - 2008 model Prius.

Since the battery is located in an area that is open to the passenger compartment, the battery is vented outside the body to ambient air with a small diameter flexible hose.

> **WARNING—**
> • *Always replace the 12-volt auxiliary battery with a new battery of similar type. Do not substitute a conventional flooded-cell lead-acid battery.*

This table lists part numbers for Prius 12-volt auxiliary batteries:

12-volt auxiliary battery	Toyota part no.
Standard vehicles	S34B20R
Vehicles with smart key / navigation	S46D24R

ELECTRIC AIR-CONDITIONING (A/C) COMPRESSOR

◄ The 2004 - 2008 Prius has an air-conditioning compressor that is driven by an internal high voltage electric motor. Since the compressor is not driven by a conventional engine-driven belt, compressor operation is possible even when the engine is not running. Air-conditioning system performance is not affected by engine operation.

41190

Courtesy Toyota Motor Sales (TMS) USA, Inc.

Prius Hybrid System

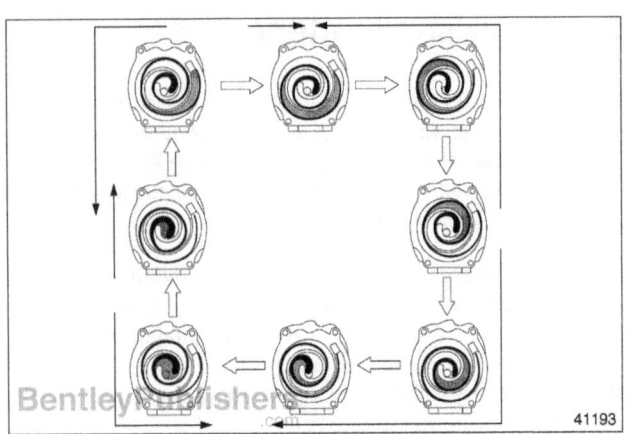

41193

Courtesy Toyota Motor Sales (TMS) USA, Inc.

◄ All Prius models use a scroll-type A/C compressor, regardless of how the A/C compressor is driven. This type of compressor is compact, efficient, and has few moving parts.

In scroll-type compressors, there are two spiral scrolls. One scroll is fixed and does not move. The second scroll does not rotate, but is made to oscillate by the electric motor. Clearance between the two scrolls is so small that refrigerant is captured in spaces formed between the two scrolls and is pumped as the movable scroll oscillates. As refrigerant gas is pumped from the outer region toward the center, it is compressed and its pressure is increased.

The speed of the electric motor can be varied to control refrigerant rate-of-flow.

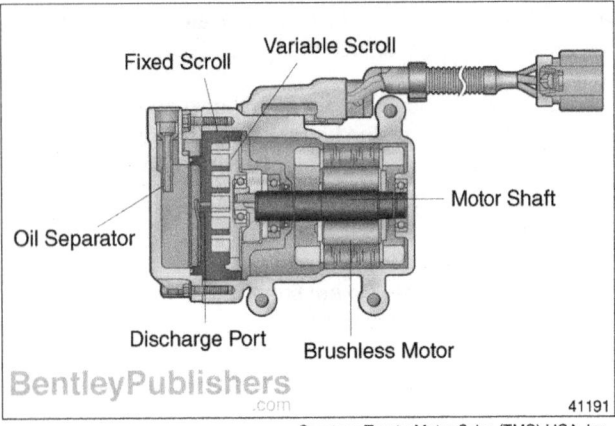

Variable Scroll
Fixed Scroll
Oil Separator
Motor Shaft
Discharge Port
Brushless Motor

41191

Courtesy Toyota Motor Sales (TMS) USA, Inc.

◄ Components within the electric A/C compressor include:
- Fixed and movable compressor scrolls
- Brushless three-phase AC high-voltage electric motor
- Refrigerant oil separator

A separate A/C inverter located within the hybrid system inverter supplies power to the air-conditioning compressor. The A/C inverter changes HV battery DC output into three-phase AC to power the compressor electric motor. Voltage to the motor is approximately HV battery voltage (201.6 volts). See **Air-conditioning (A/C) inverter** in this chapter.

> **WARNING** —
> - *The A/C compressor is a high voltage component. Use the same high voltage safety procedures that you would use when working on high voltage hybrid system components. See* **3 Safety**, *for additional safety and service information.*

TP0803010

◄ The high voltage electric motor in the electric A/C compressor is a "wet-type" motor. The rotating motor armature is bathed in A/C refrigerant and refrigerant oil for cooling. For this reason, ONLY special high-dielectric (high insulation) refrigerant oil (type ND-OIL 11) must be used. Do not use any other specification refrigerant oil other than type ND-OIL 11.

If conventional refrigerant oil is added to the A/C system, the inferior dielectric properties of the incorrect refrigerant oil will reduce system performance. The reduced insulation creates a potential safety hazard. Since refrigerant oil travels with the refrigerant throughout the A/C system, purging and cleaning incorrect refrigerant oil from a system can be difficult and expensive.

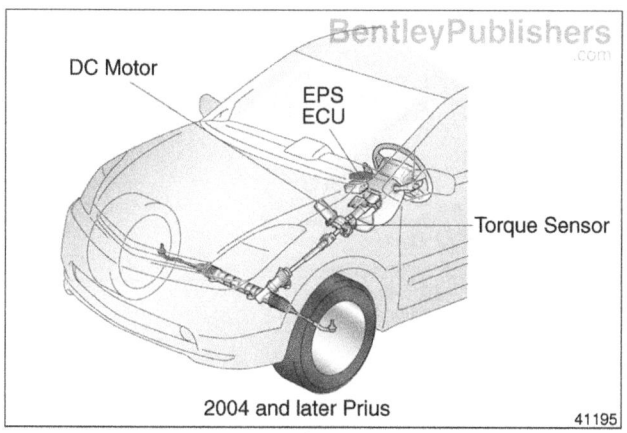

2004 and later Prius

41195

Courtesy Toyota Motor Sales (TMS) USA, Inc.

ELECTRIC POWER STEERING (EPS)

◀ Prius models use an electric power steering (EPS) system. Unlike conventional power steering which is powered by an engine-driven hydraulic pump, the Prius EPS system uses a steering-column-mounted electric motor for power assist. With EPS, steering assist is available even when the engine is not running, and there is no difference in steering feel as the engine starts and stops. EPS also improves fuel economy because the system consumes energy only when power assist is required.

Main EPS components include:

• Steering rack (rack and pinion type)

• Steering torque sensor (measures steering effort)

• 12-volt DC electric steering assist motor

• Electric power steering electronic control unit (EPS ECU)

The electric steering assist motor and torque sensor are located high on the steering column behind the instrument panel. The 12-volt electric steering assist motor receives power from the EPS ECU.

The steering rack is a simple mechanical rack-and-pinion mechanism.

◀ Steering effort or torque is measured by a torque sensor located high on the steering column behind the instrument panel. A torsion bar in the torque sensor twists an amount in proportion to steering effort. When the torsion bar twists, the torque sensor detection rings rotate in relation to one another. The detection coil senses a change in inductance that is proportional to the amount of torque applied.

The torque sensor sends a voltage signal to the EPS ECU reporting the amount of twist in the torsion bar. The EPS ECU uses the torque sensor signal input and other information such as vehicle speed to determine the amount of assist required. The EPS ECU controls voltage and current to the EPS electric motor to provide steering assist.

If the EPS ECU detects a malfunction in the EPS system, it stores a diagnostic trouble code (DTC), illuminates a warning light and powers down the system. The vehicle reverts to manual steering.

41198

Courtesy Toyota Motor Sales (TMS) USA, Inc.

Prius Hybrid System

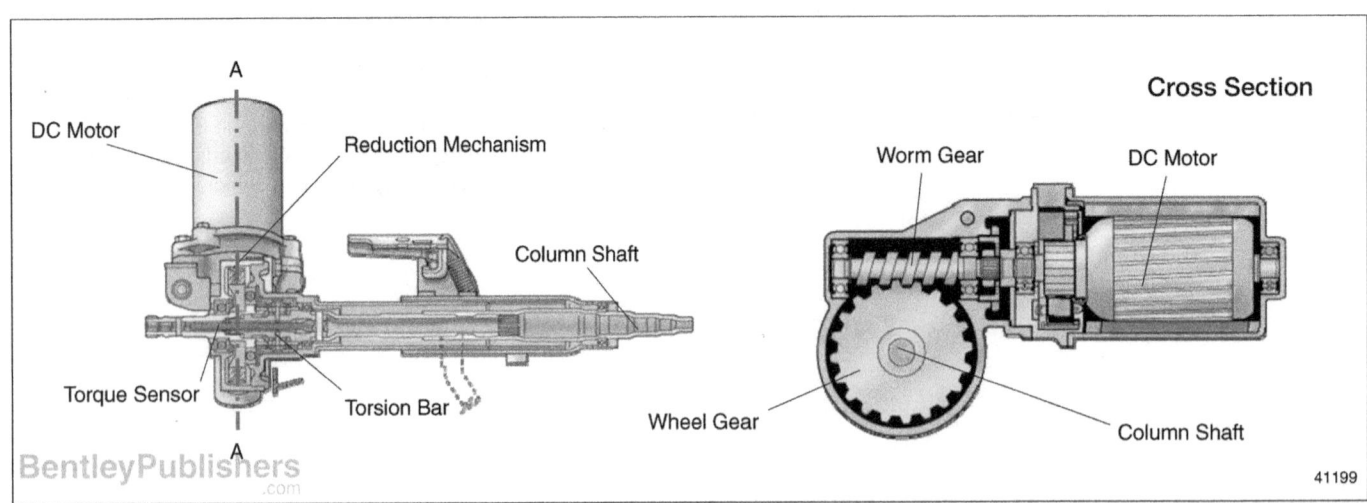

Courtesy Toyota Motor Sales (TMS) USA, Inc.

The EPS electric motor transmits power for steering assist to the steering shaft with worm and pinion drive gears. Whenever any of the following components are removed or replaced, carry out Zero Point Calibration procedure to reset steering sensor, yaw rate sensor and deceleration sensor calibration:

• Steering column assembly

• EPS ECU

• Steering wheel

• Steering gear (rack-and-pinion) assembly

• Whenever there is a difference in feel or effort between steering left and steering right

Courtesy Toyota Motor Sales (TMS) USA, Inc.

See **8 Brakes, Suspension and Steering**.

REGENERATIVE BRAKING SYSTEM

The braking system on all Prius models includes both conventional hydraulic disc / drum brakes and also a regenerative braking system. The regenerative braking system uses the momentum (kinetic energy) of the vehicle to recharge the hybrid system HV battery.

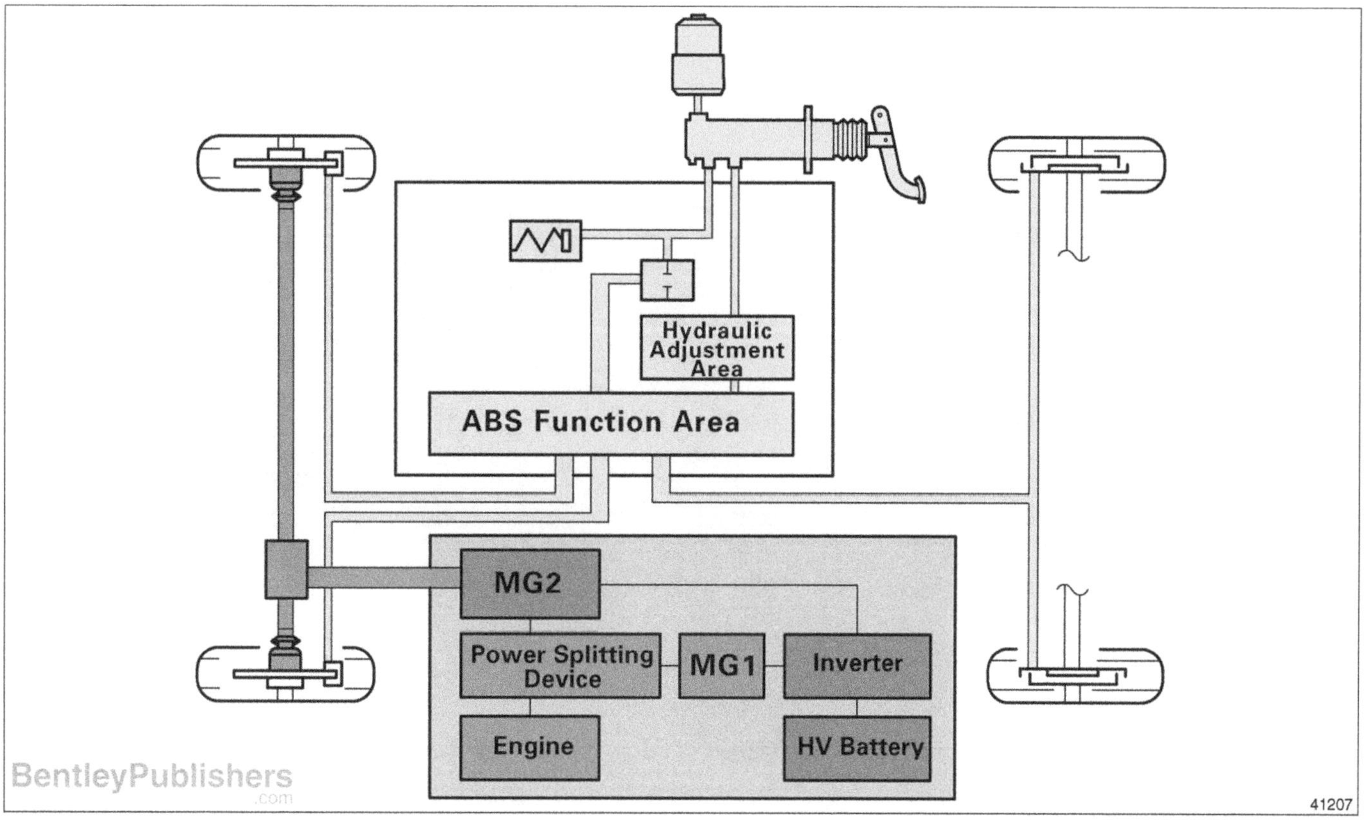

Courtesy Toyota Motor Sales (TMS) USA, Inc.

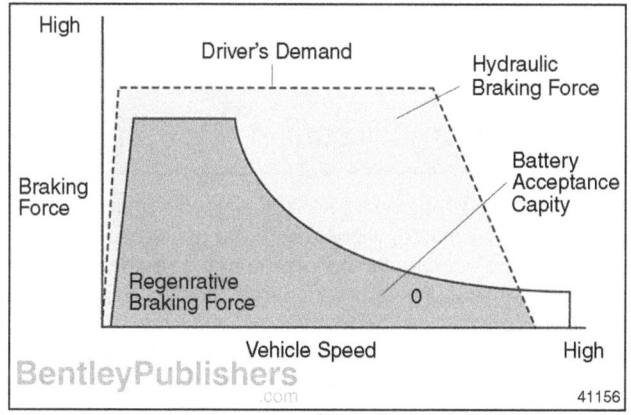

Courtesy Toyota Motor Sales (TMS) USA, Inc.

◄ Whenever the vehicle is moving, as soon as the accelerator pedal is released, MG2 is configured to operate as a generator. The energy required to turn MG2 as a generator contributes to slowing the vehicle. This process also recharges the HV battery. The hydraulic brakes do not take part in this first phase of braking.

As braking continues, the proportion of overall braking contributed by conventional hydraulic disc / drum brakes and by regenerative braking is continuously monitored and adjusted by the skid control ECU.

The hydraulic brakes do much of the braking during rapid stops, and during the last phase of braking when the vehicle is moving slowly.

In the 2004 - 2008 Prius, the skid control ECU controls the following brake system functions:

- Control of normal braking
- Antilock brake system (ABS) control
- Electronic brake distribution (EBD) control
- Brake assist
- Enhanced vehicle stability control (VSC)
- Regenerative braking control

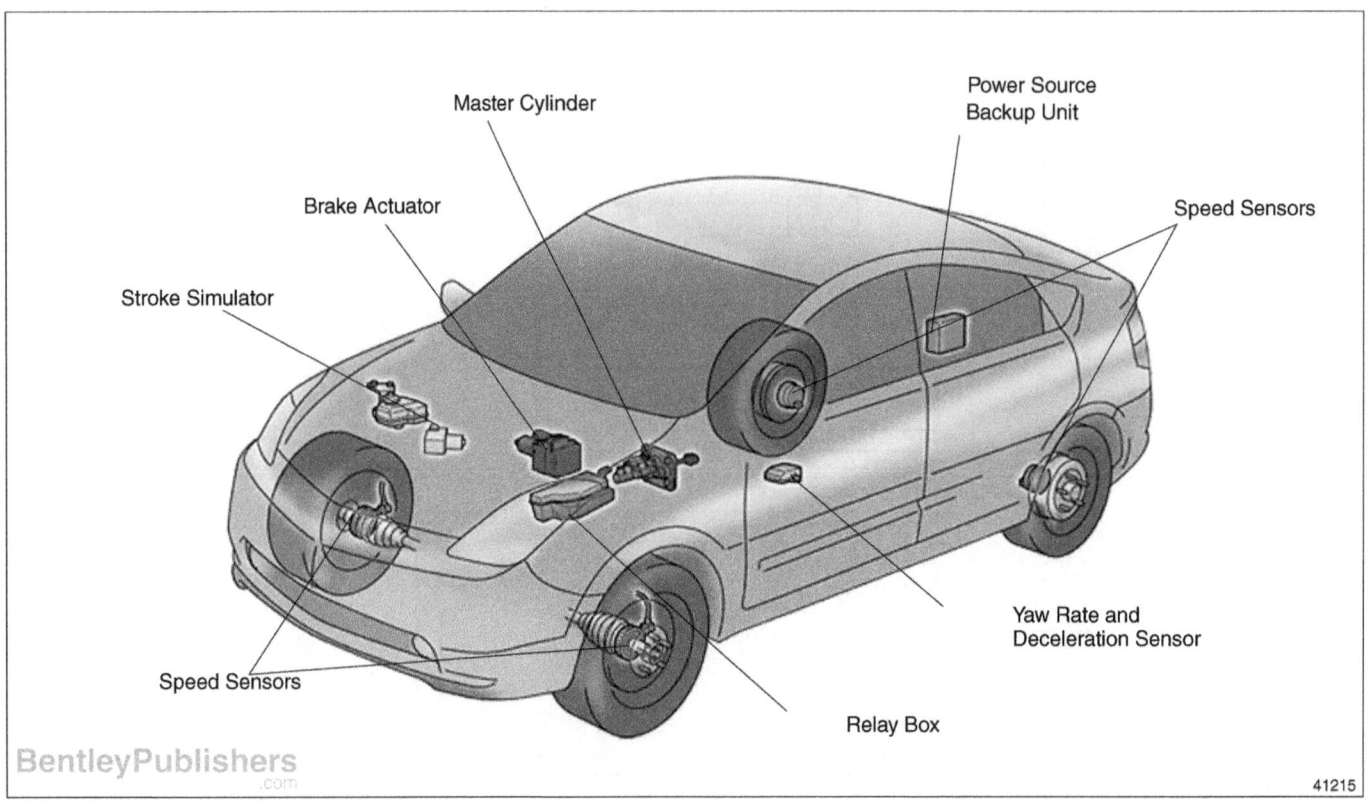

Courtesy Toyota Motor Sales (TMS) USA, Inc.

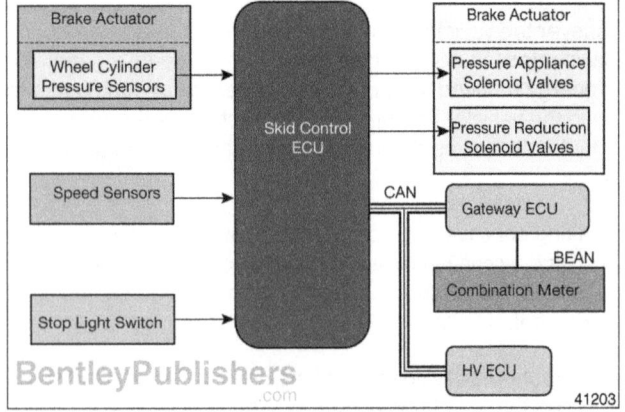

Courtesy Toyota Motor Sales (TMS) USA, Inc.

The skid control ECU shares sensor input information with the EPS ECU and the HV-ECU.

Brake system operation

During normal braking, the brake fluid hydraulic pressure generated in the master cylinder when the brake pedal is depressed does not directly actuate the brakes at the wheels as it does with conventional brakes. Instead, the hydraulic pressure generated in the master cylinder serves as a pressure signal. The actual control pressure which is used to directly actuate the brakes at the wheels comes from regulated fluid pressure from the brake actuator.

The skid control ECU uses input from the master cylinder pressure sensor and brake pedal stroke sensor to calculate the target hydraulic line pressure for each wheel. Actual hydraulic line pressure is then compared with target line pressure. The diagrams that follows show how the skid control ECU reacts to differences in target and actual hydraulic line pressure.

Brake system operation – increasing line pressure

When actual hydraulic line pressure is lower than the target pressure, then the skid control ECU opens solenoid valves to feed fluid pressure from the accumulator to the wheels.

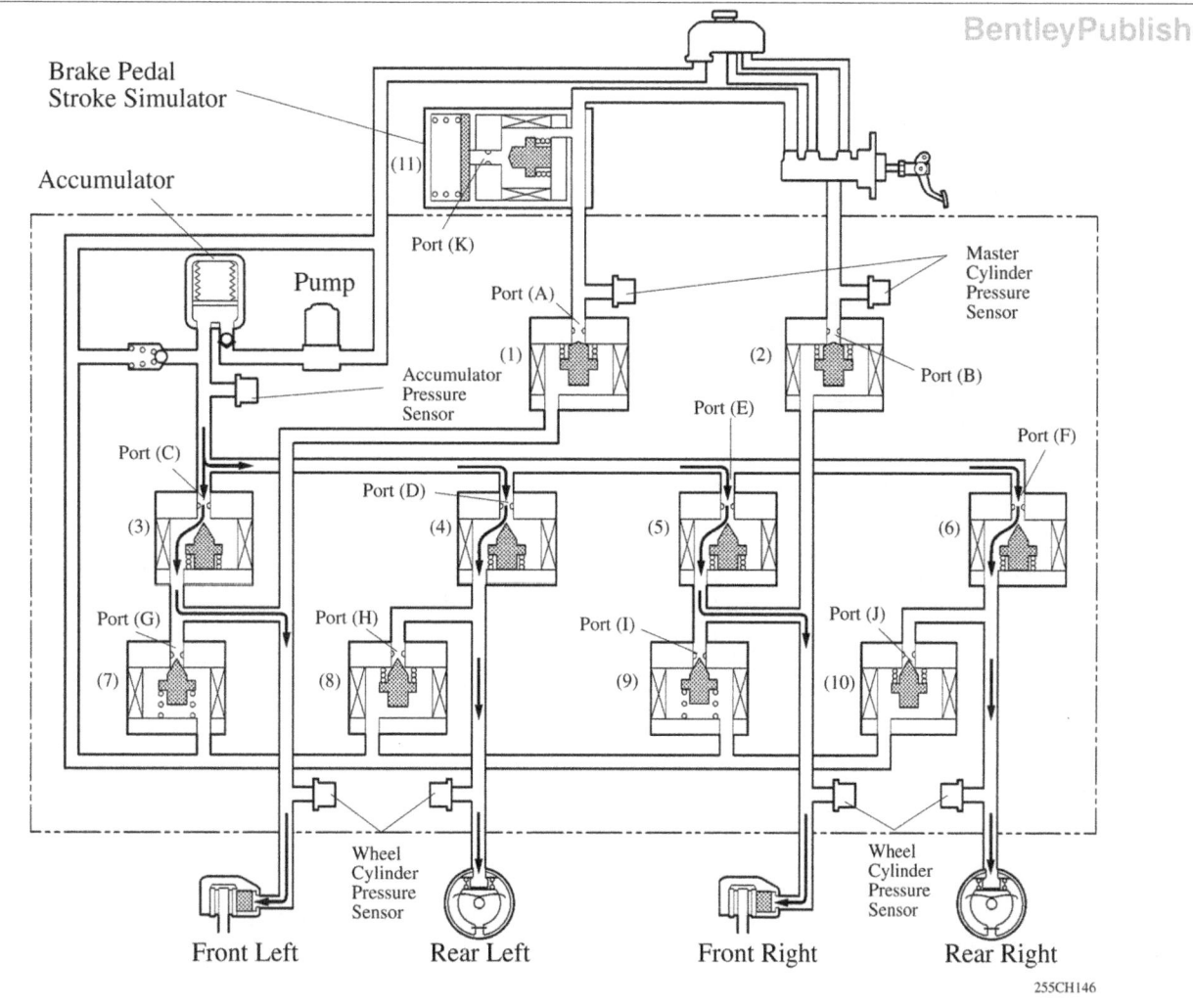

255CH146

Item		Normal Braking Increase Mode
(1), (2)	Master Cylinder Cut Solenoid Valve	ON (Close)
	Port: (A), (B)	
(3), (4), (5), (6)	Pressure Appliance Solenoid Valve	ON (Half-Open*)
	Port: (C), (D), (E), (F)	
(7), (9)	Pressure Reduction Solenoid Valve	OFF (Close)
	Port: (G), (I)	
(8), (10)	Pressure Reduction Solenoid Valve	ON (Close)
	Port: (H), (J)	
(11)	Stroke Simulator Cut Solenoid Valve	ON (Open)
	Port: (K)	

*: The solenoid valve constantly regulates the amount of opening of the port in accordance with the use conditions in order to control the fluid pressure.

41208

Courtesy Toyota Motor Sales (TMS) USA, Inc.

Brake system operation – holding line pressure

When actual hydraulic line pressure at each wheel equals the calculated (desired) target line pressure, then the skid control ECU closes all solenoid valves to hold and maintain hydraulic line pressure at each wheel at current values.

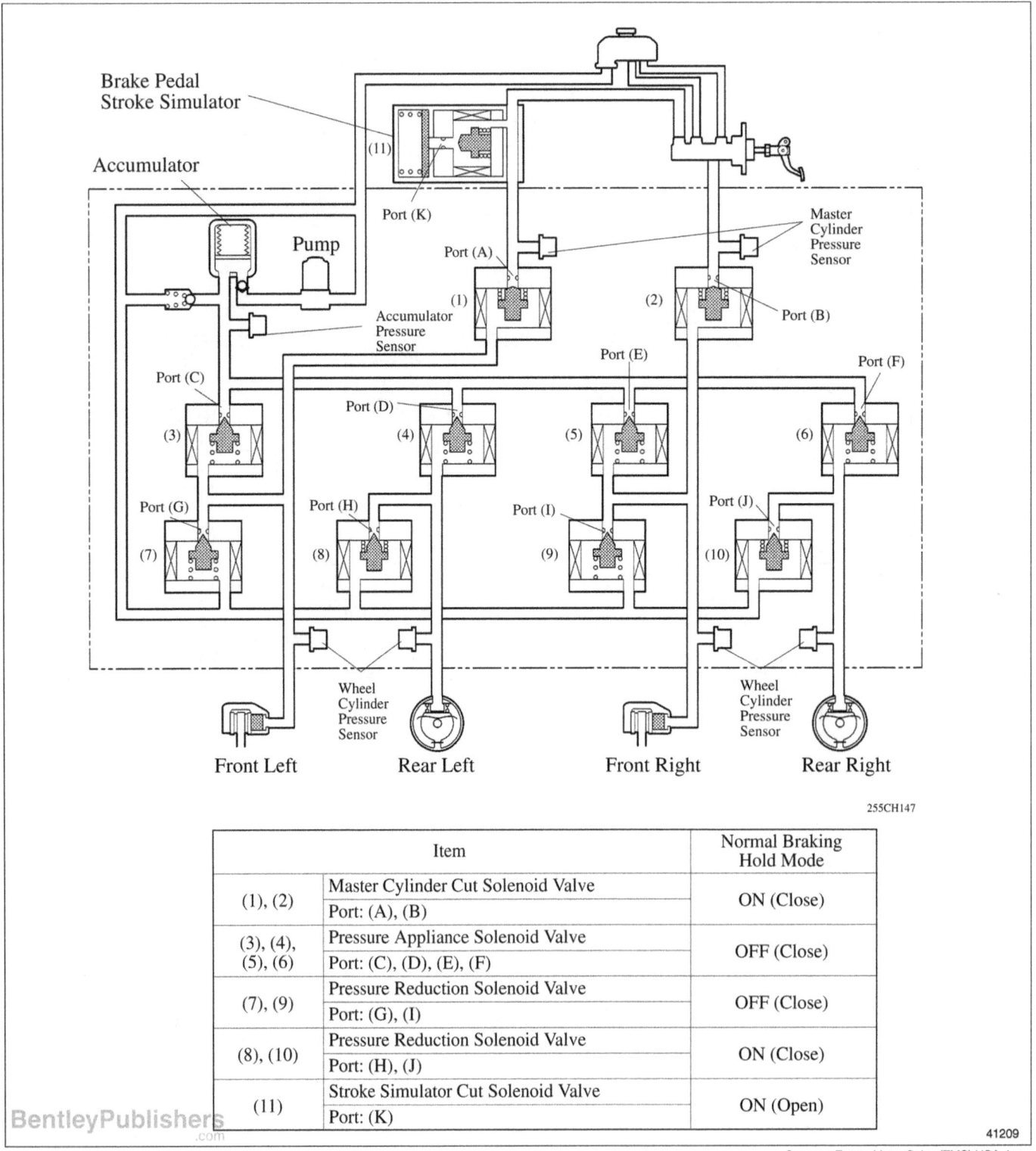

255CH147

	Item		Normal Braking Hold Mode
(1), (2)	Master Cylinder Cut Solenoid Valve		ON (Close)
	Port: (A), (B)		
(3), (4), (5), (6)	Pressure Appliance Solenoid Valve		OFF (Close)
	Port: (C), (D), (E), (F)		
(7), (9)	Pressure Reduction Solenoid Valve		OFF (Close)
	Port: (G), (I)		
(8), (10)	Pressure Reduction Solenoid Valve		ON (Close)
	Port: (H), (J)		
(11)	Stroke Simulator Cut Solenoid Valve		ON (Open)
	Port: (K)		

41209

Courtesy Toyota Motor Sales (TMS) USA, Inc.

Brake system operation – decreasing line pressure

When actual hydraulic line pressure at each wheel is greater than the calculated (desired) target line pressure, then the skid control ECU opens the pressure reduction solenoid valves to reduce hydraulic line pressure at each wheel.

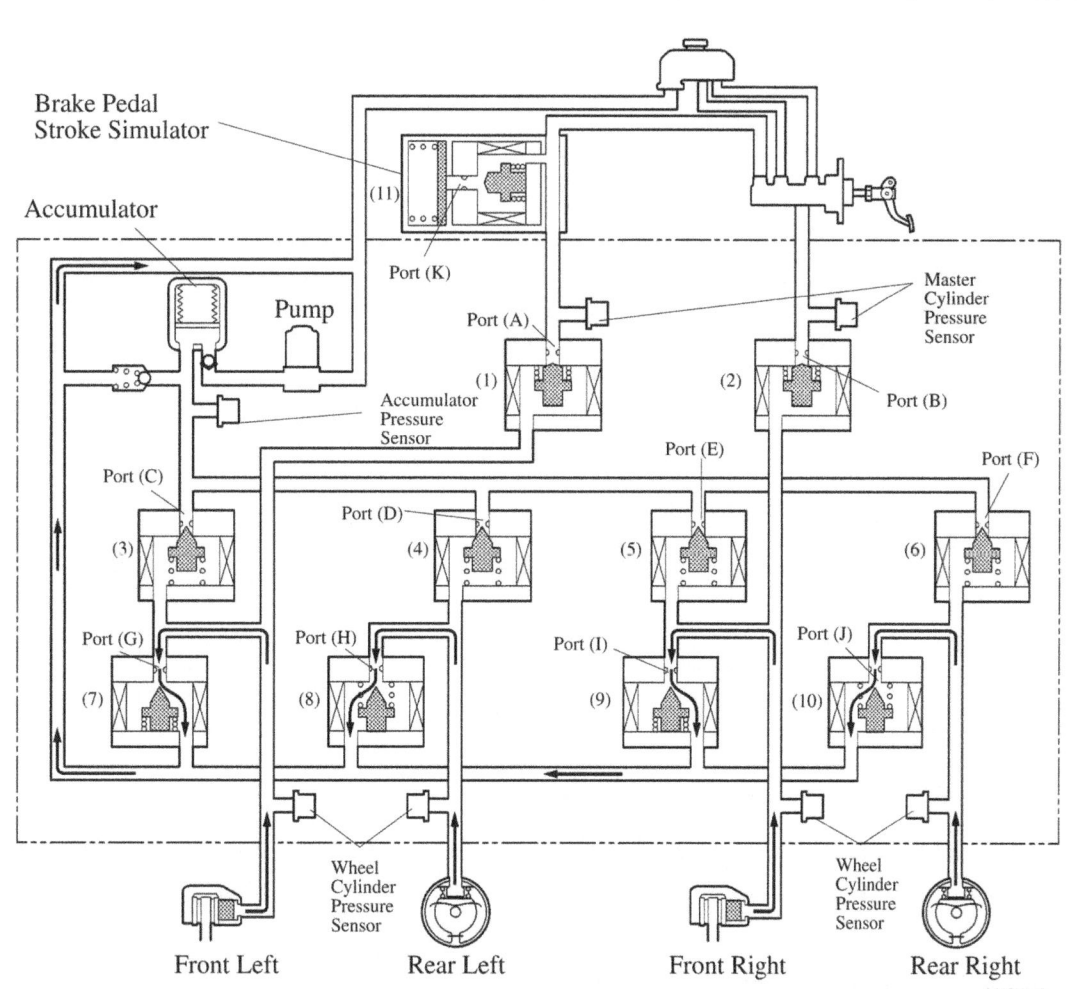

255CH148

	Item		Normal Braking Reduce Mode
(1), (2)	Master Cylinder Cut Solenoid Valve		ON (Close)
	Port: (A), (B)		
(3), (4), (5), (6)	Pressure Appliance Solenoid Valve		OFF (Close)
	Port: (C), (D), (E), (F)		
(7), (9)	Pressure Reduction Solenoid Valve		ON (Half-Open*)
	Port: (G), (I)		
(8), (10)	Pressure Reduction Solenoid Valve		ON (Half-Open*)
	Port: (H), (J)		
(11)	Stroke Simulator Cut Solenoid Valve		ON (Open)
	Port: (K)		

*: The solenoid valve constantly regulates the amount of opening of the port in accordance with the use conditions in order to control the fluid pressure.

41210

Brake system operation – malfunction

If a failure occurs in either the regenerative or hydraulic brakes, the remaining system still functions. However, the brake pedal have a harder feel, stopping distances increases, and the brake system warning light illuminates.

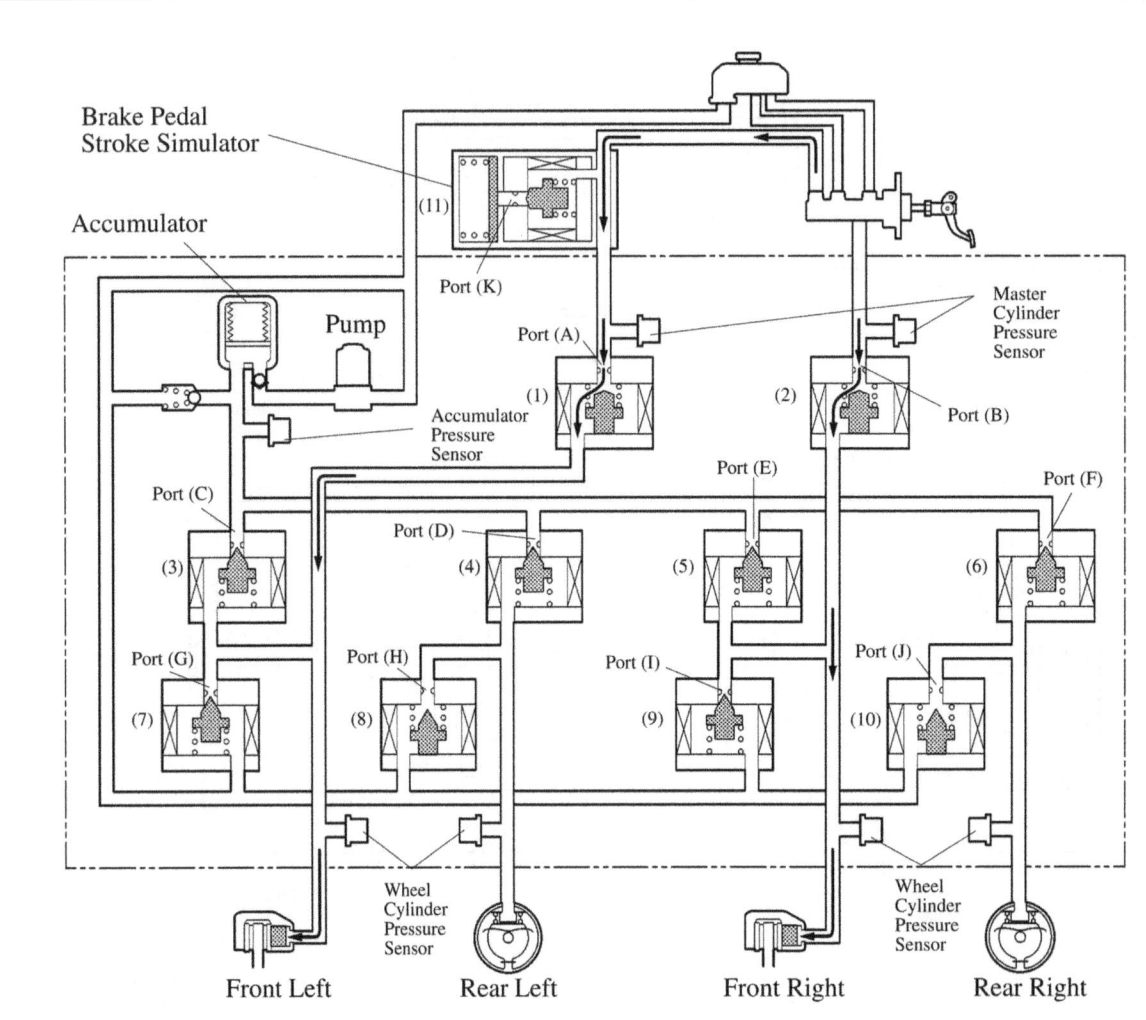

255CH149

	Item	System OFF & Fail-Safe Mode
(1), (2)	Master Cylinder Cut Solenoid Valve	OFF (Open)
	Port: (A), (B)	
(3), (4), (5), (6)	Pressure Appliance Solenoid Valve	OFF (Close)
	Port: (C), (D), (E), (F)	
(7), (9)	Pressure Reduction Solenoid Valve	OFF (Close)
	Port: (G), (I)	
(8), (10)	Pressure Reduction Solenoid Valve	OFF (Open)
	Port: (H), (J)	
(11)	Stroke Simulator Cut Solenoid Valve	OFF (Close)
	Port: (K)	

41211

Courtesy Toyota Motor Sales (TMS) USA, Inc.

Fail-safe mode

When a failure in the brake system is detected, the skid control ECU reverts to fail-safe mode. In this mode, the master cylinder cut solenoid valves are opened (they are normally-open valves, so whenever power is OFF, they are open). This opens lines from the brake master cylinder to the front wheel brakes. In this mode, depressing the brake pedal sends fluid to the front wheel brakes similar to vehicles with conventional brakes.

NOTE—

• *In fail-safe mode, only the front brakes are actuated, and the rear brakes do not function.*

Power brake backup unit

The brake system in the 2004 - 2008 Prius has a power backup unit that enables the vehicle to make repeated stops even after primary power is interrupted.

◁ The power backup unit contains 28 capacitors that store a 12-volt electrical charge. The capacitors are charged every time the vehicle is driven. The capacitors discharge within 5 minutes when the ignition is turned OFF.

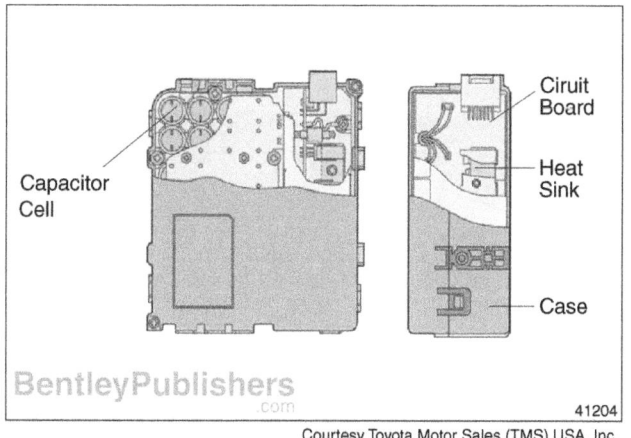

Capacitor Cell — Ciruit Board — Heat Sink — Case

41204

Courtesy Toyota Motor Sales (TMS) USA, Inc.

◁ The power backup unit is located next to the 12-volt auxiliary battery in the rear cargo area.

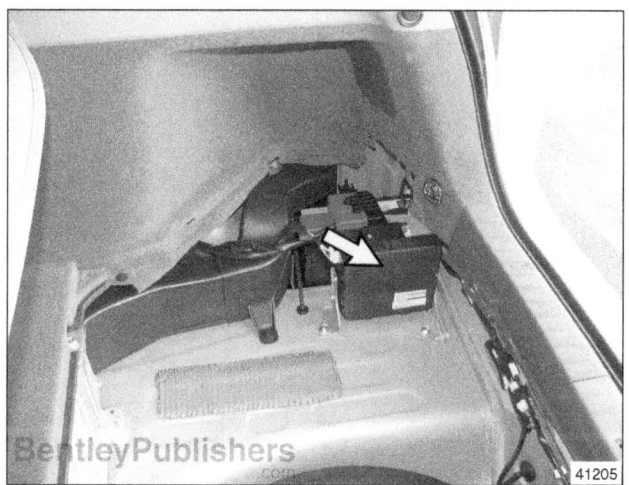

41205

Prius Hybrid System

TIRE PRESSURE WARNING SYSTEM (TPWS)

Beginning with the 2006 model year, Prius vehicles for sale in the United States are equipped with a tire pressure warning system (TPWS). The system is a direct pressure-sensing type, with built-in electronic circuits to directly measuring tire inflation pressure, and a wireless transmitter to send pressure data and sensor identification data (ID code) to the tire pressure warning ECU.

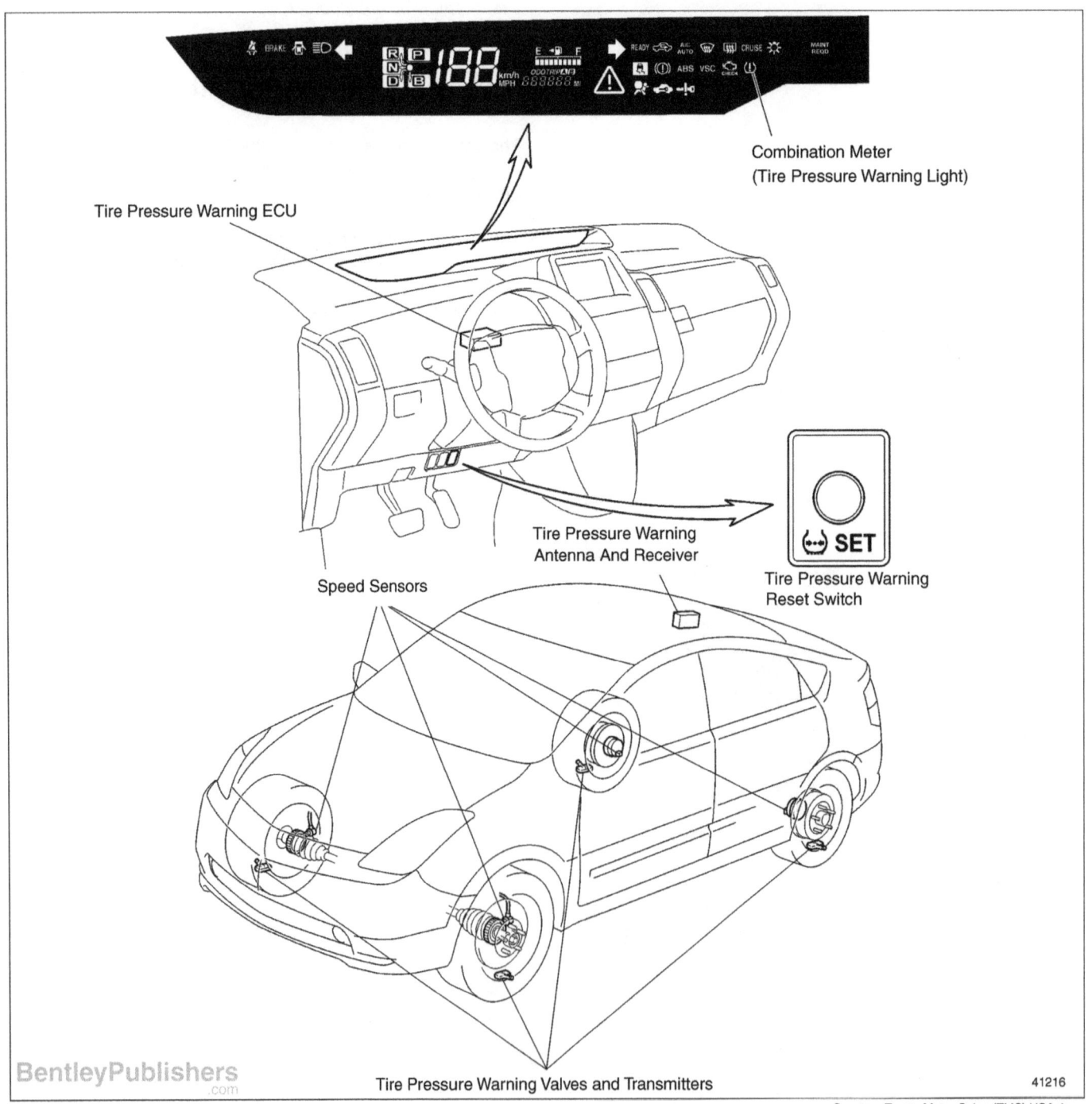

Combination Meter
(Tire Pressure Warning Light)

Tire Pressure Warning ECU

Tire Pressure Warning
Antenna And Receiver

Tire Pressure Warning
Reset Switch

Speed Sensors

Tire Pressure Warning Valves and Transmitters

41216

Courtesy Toyota Motor Sales (TMS) USA, Inc.

◀ Each of the four road wheels has a tire pressure sensor / transmitter fitted to the tire valve (**arrow**). The Prius temporary spare wheel is not fitted with a TPWS sensor / transmitter.

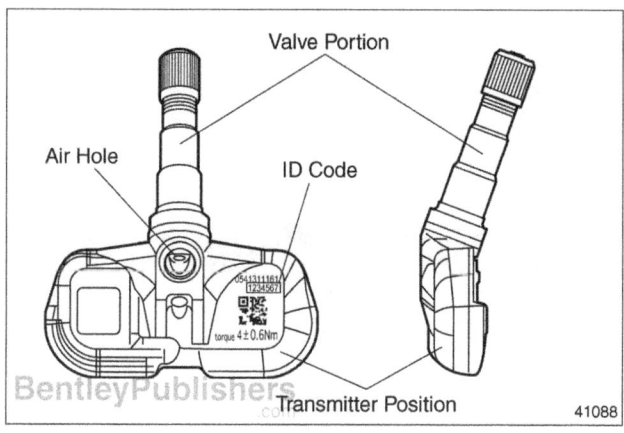

Courtesy Toyota Motor Sales (TMS) USA, Inc.

◀ The tire pressure sensor / transmitter is integral with the tire inflation air valve. The tire pressure sensor / transmitter is mounted to the alloy wheel through the conventional air valve hole. The tire pressure sensor / transmitter valve stem is sealed and retained by a rubber grommet and threaded nut.

The tire pressure sensor / transmitter is powered by a non-replaceable lithium battery with an expected life of approximately 10 years. When battery voltage begins to drop, the tire pressure warning ECU stores a diagnostic trouble code (DTC) in memory. When battery voltage drops further, the transmitter will stop working, a DTC will be stored in memory, and the instrument panel tire pressure warning lamp will illuminate to alert the driver.

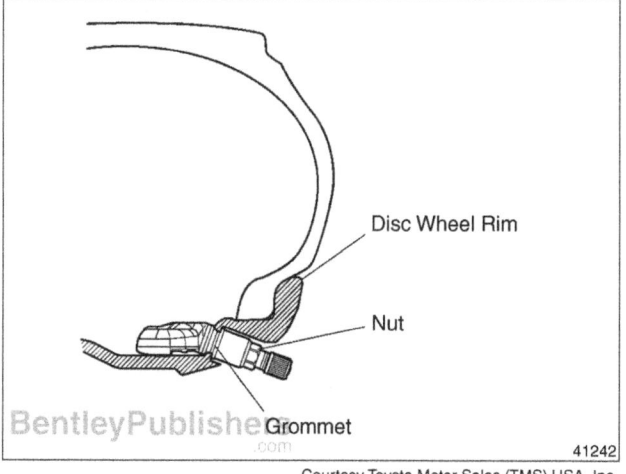

Courtesy Toyota Motor Sales (TMS) USA, Inc.

◀ Each tire pressure sensor / transmitter has a unique ID code that is registered (recorded) in the tire pressure warning ECU. The unique ID codes permit the tire pressure warning ECU to know that the pressure data received is in fact from sensor / transmitters mounted on this vehicle, and not from another nearby sensor / transmitter on another car.

NOTE—

- *When dismounting and mounting a tire with TPWS, the tire pressure sensor / transmitter can be easily damaged by the tire bead, tire machine, or tools. Special procedures are required when replacing tire pressure sensor / transmitters. Also, when new tire pressure sensor / transmitters are installed, their unique ID codes must be registered in the tire pressure warning ECU. See* **8 Brakes, Suspension and Steering**.

If the TPWS warning light blinks or is illuminated with IG-ON, then there is a fault or malfunction in the system.
See **11 Diagnostics** for possible causes.

Prius Hybrid System

VALET INSTRUCTIONS

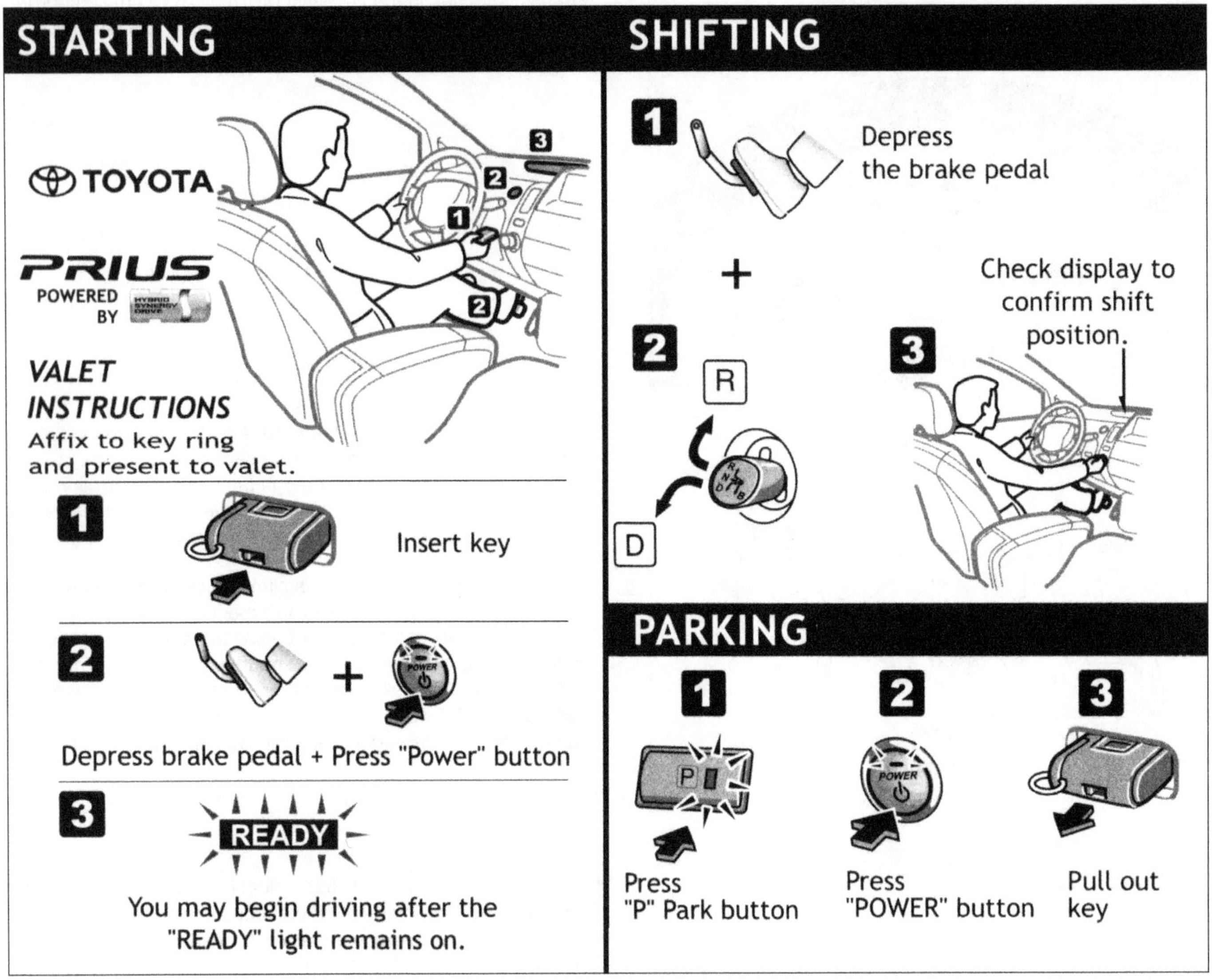

STARTING

TOYOTA

PRIUS
POWERED BY HYBRID SYNERGY DRIVE

VALET INSTRUCTIONS
Affix to key ring and present to valet.

1 Insert key

2 Depress brake pedal + Press "Power" button

3 READY

You may begin driving after the "READY" light remains on.

SHIFTING

1 Depress the brake pedal

+

2 R / D

Check display to confirm shift position.

3

PARKING

1 Press "P" Park button

2 Press "POWER" button

3 Pull out key

3

Safety

Recommendations for working on the Prius

Safety

WARNING—

• *This chapter discusses practices and procedures that are intended to prevent electrical shock and injury posed by the hazards of high voltage circuits. Your common sense, sound reasoning and good judgement are crucial to safe service work. Before attempting any work on your Toyota Prius, read* **WARNINGS** *and* **CAUTIONS** *in this chapter, as well as any WARNINGS and CAUTIONS that accompany a procedure in this book.*

GENERAL

High voltage circuits in hybrid vehicles are designed with occupant and technician safety in mind. However, there are inherent dangers when working around electricity.

Most hybrid vehicles manufactured today have high voltage electric motor / generators, electrical circuits, wiring, and other potentially dangerous high voltage components. Voltages in hybrid circuits can range from 144 volts to as high as 650 volts (AC or DC), depending upon the vehicle manufacturer.

The high voltage battery in the Prius supplies 201.6 volts, but system voltage to the electric motor/generators can reach levels as high as 500 volts for increased performance.

This chapter attempts to explain how to recognize which components are part of the Prius high voltage hybrid system, how to safely disable the system, and how to be sure that high voltages are no longer present in any components that you are working on.

Safety

WARNINGS—

- Read the **important safety notice** on the copyright page at the beginning of the book.

- Thoroughly read each procedure and the **WARNINGS** and **CAUTIONS** that accompany the procedure. Also review posted corrections at **www.BentleyPublishers.com/errata/** before beginning work.

- Be sure that the hybrid system is OFF (READY indicator not illuminated) before beginning any repair procedure. Remove the ignition key or Smart Key (if equipped) from the vehicle. Store Smart Key in a safe place at least 15 feet away from the vehicle. For added safety, switch the Smart Key function (if equipped) OFF by depressing the cancel switch under the steering column.

- The Prius hybrid system has circuits with voltages as high as 500 volts. Voltages over 60 volts DC and 25 volts (rms) AC are a shock hazard. Wear lineman's gloves when removing the service plug, and whenever high voltage may be present.

- Wait at least five minutes after removing the service plug to allow high voltage capacitors to discharge before servicing the vehicle.

- After removing the service plug, test high voltage components for residual voltage to ensure that high voltage has dissipated before beginning work. Wear lineman's gloves until you are sure that high voltage is not present.

- Disconnect the 12-volt auxiliary battery negative (-) terminal whenever you work on the fuel system or the electrical system.

- If any procedure, tightening torque, wear limit, specification or data presented in this manual does not appear to be appropriate for a specific application, contact the publisher or the vehicle manufacturer for clarification before using the information in question.

- Do not reuse worn or deformed fasteners. Many fasteners are designed to be used only once and become unreliable and may fail when used a second time. This includes, but is not limited to, nuts, bolts, washers, self-locking nuts or bolts, snap rings and cotter pins. Replace these fasteners with new parts.

- When towing a Prius, do not allow the front wheels to rotate. Tow the vehicle with the front wheels on a towing dolly or transport on a flatbed. The front wheels are directly connected to motor / generator 2 (MG2). When the front wheels are turning MG2 also turns. This may generate high voltage and create a shock hazard, and also cause damage to the inverter or high voltage battery.

- Do not work under a lifted car unless it is solidly supported on stands designed for the purpose. Do not support a car on cinder blocks, hollow tiles, bricks, or other props that may crumble under continuous load. Do not work under a car that is supported solely by a jack. Do not work under the car while the engine is running.

- If you are going to work under a car on the ground, make sure that the ground is level. Block the wheels to keep the car from rolling. Disconnect the 12-volt auxiliary battery negative (-) terminal to prevent anyone from starting the car while you are under it.

- Place jack stands only at locations specified by the manufacturer. The vehicle lifting jack supplied with the vehicle is intended for tire changes only. Use a heavy duty floor jack to lift vehicle before installing jack stands.

- Do not run the engine unless the work area is well ventilated. Carbon monoxide kills.

- Remove rings, bracelets and other jewelry so that they cannot cause electrical shorts, get caught in running machinery, or be crushed by heavy parts.

- Tie long hair behind your head. Do not wear a necktie or scarf, loose clothing or a necklace when you work near machine tools or running engine. If your hair, clothing, or jewelry were to get caught in the machinery, severe injury could result.

- Do not attempt to work on your car if you do not feel well. You increase the danger of injury to yourself and others if you are tired, upset or have taken medication or any other substance that may keep you from being fully alert.

- Illuminate your work area adequately but safely. Use a portable safety light for working inside or under the car. Make sure that the bulb is enclosed in a wire cage. The hot filament of an accidentally broken bulb can ignite spilled fuel, vapors or oil.

- When draining fuel, oil, coolant or brake fluid, collect in suitable containers. Do not use food or beverage containers that might mislead someone into drinking from them. Store flammable fluids away from fire hazards. Wipe up spills at once, but do not store oily rags, which can ignite and burn spontaneously.

- Greases, lubricants and other automotive chemicals contain toxic substances, many of which are absorbed directly through the skin. Read the manufacturer's instructions and warnings carefully. Use hand and eye protection. Avoid prolonged direct skin contact.

- Many solvents used for parts cleaning contain hazardous, toxic chemicals, and are highly flammable, especially in aerosol form. Use with extreme care in well ventilated areas. Do not smoke. Do not use these products near sources of heat, sparks or flame. Read label warnings.

- Observe good workshop practices. Wear goggles when you operate machine tools or work with battery acid. Wear gloves or other protective clothing whenever the job requires working with harmful substances.

- Do not remove engine radiator pressure cap when engine is hot. Hot coolant may spray under pressure and cause severe burns.

- Coolant stored in the coolant heat storage tank can remain hot (as high as 176°F) for as long as 3 days. A malfunction may cause the surface of the coolant heat storage tank to become very hot. Use extreme caution when working around the coolant heat storage tank.

- Use extreme care when draining engine coolant. Even when the engine is cold, the coolant heat storage tank maintains coolant at high temperature. Hot engine coolant can cause severe burns.

- Allow transaxle to cool before checking or draining transaxle fluid. Hot transaxle fluid can cause severe burns.

- Bleeding the brake hydraulic system or changing brake fluid without using the Toyota hand-held tester or equivalent tool is not recommended. Air may remain trapped in lines or components, creating a hazardous condition.

- Do not smoke or work near heaters or other fire hazards. Keep an approved fire extinguisher handy.

- Use and wear appropriate safety equipment while performing services and repairs.

- Lead-acid batteries give off explosive hydrogen gas during charging. Keep sparks, lighted matches and open flames away from the top of the battery. If escaping hydrogen gas is ignited, the flame may travel into the cells and cause the battery to explode.

WARNINGS (continued)—

- Battery acid (electrolyte) in the 12-volt auxiliary lead-acid battery can cause severe burns. Flush contact area with water, then seek medical attention.

- Replace the 12-volt auxiliary battery with a new battery of similar type. Do not substitute a conventional flooded-cell lead-acid battery.

- Nickel metal hydride battery cells in the high voltage battery pack contain a very caustic alkaline electrolyte which can cause severe burns. Seek medical attention immediately when exposed.

- The air-conditioning system is filled with chemical refrigerant which is hazardous. Make sure the system is serviced only by a trained technician using approved refrigerant recovery / recycling equipment, trained in related safety precautions, and familiar with regulations governing the discharging and disposal of automotive chemical refrigerants.

- Do not expose any part of the A/C system to high temperatures such as an open flame. Excessive heat increases system pressure and may cause the system to burst.

- Friction materials (such as brake pads and shoes) contain asbestos fibers or other similar materials. Do not create dust by grinding, sanding, or by cleaning with compressed air. Avoid breathing dust. Breathing any friction material dust can cause serious diseases and may result in death.

- Some aerosol tire inflators are highly flammable. Be extremely cautious when repairing a tire that may have been inflated using an aerosol tire inflator. Keep sparks, open flame or other sources of ignition away from the tire repair area. Inflate and deflate the tire at least four times before breaking the bead from the rim. Completely remove the tire from the rim before attempting any repair.

- Aerosol tire inflators are not recommended for use on vehicles with tire pressure monitoring systems.

- Vehicles covered by this manual are equipped with a supplemental restraint system (SRS) that automatically deploys airbags and pyrotechnic seat belt tensioners in case of a frontal or side impact. These are explosive devices. Handled improperly or without adequate safeguards, they can be accidentally activated and can cause serious injury.

- The ignition system produces high voltages that can be fatal. Avoid contact with exposed terminals and use extreme care when working on a vehicle with the engine running or the ignition in READY mode.

- Aerosol cleaners and solvents may contain hazardous or deadly vapors and are highly flammable. Use only in a well ventilated area. Do not use on hot surfaces (engines, brakes, etc.).

CAUTIONS—

- If you lack the skills, tools and equipment, or a suitable workshop for any procedure described in this manual, leave such repairs to an authorized Toyota dealer or other qualified shop.

- Toyota is constantly improving its cars and sometimes these changes, both in parts and specifications, are made applicable to earlier models. Any part numbers listed in this manual are for reference only. Check with your authorized Toyota dealer parts department for the latest information.

- Before starting a job, be sure that you have the necessary tools and parts on hand. Read all the instructions thoroughly, and do not attempt shortcuts. Use tools appropriate to the work and use only replacement parts meeting Toyota specifications.

- Use pneumatic and electric tools only to loosen threaded parts and fasteners. Do not use these tools to tighten fasteners, especially on light alloy parts. Use a torque wrench to tighten fasteners to the tightening torque specification listed.

- Be mindful of the environment and ecology. Before you drain engine or transaxle lubricants, learn the proper way to dispose of the oil. Do not pour oil onto the ground, down a drain, or into a stream, pond or lake. Dispose of waste in accordance with federal, state and local laws.

- The control module for the anti-lock brake system (ABS) cannot withstand temperatures from a paint-drying booth or a heat lamp in excess of 203°F (95°C). Do not subject to temperatures in excess of 185°F (85°C) for more than two hours.

- Before doing any electrical welding on cars equipped with ABS, disconnect the 12-volt auxiliary battery negative (-) terminal (ground strap) and the ABS control module connector.

- Be sure that the hybrid system is OFF (READY indicator not illuminated) before disconnecting the 12-volt auxiliary battery.

- Do not depress the POWER button when the Service Plug is removed from the vehicle. Damage to electronic control units (ECUs) may occur.

- Do not charge the 12-volt auxiliary battery with a fast charger. This battery is an absorbed glass mat (AGM) type battery, and must be charged at a low rate not to exceed 3.5 amps. Disconnect the battery from the vehicle before charging.

- Connect and disconnect a battery charger only with the battery charger switched OFF.

- Do not drive a Prius when in inspection mode. Transaxle damage may occur.

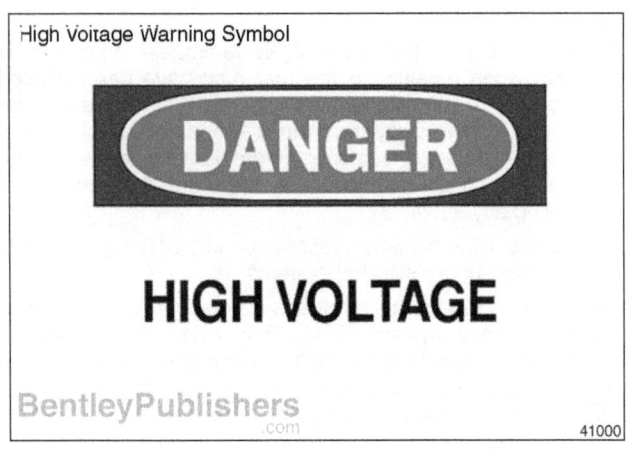

High Voltage Warning Symbol

41000

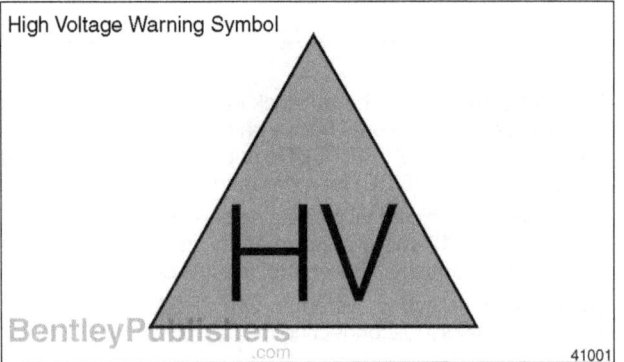

High Voltage Warning Symbol

41001

HIGH VOLTAGE PRECAUTIONS

Voltage, current and the human body

 Voltage is the measure of the electrical pressure or "push" that makes an electric **current** flow in a circuit. The unit of measurement for voltage is the **volt**.

Current is the actual flow of electricity (flow of electrons) in the wire or circuit. The unit of measurement for current flow is the **amp** or **ampere**.

Resistance is the measure of how easily current can pass through a material. The unit of measure for electrical resistance is the **ohm**.

When your skin is dry, it has high electrical resistance (tens of thousands of ohms). When your skin is wet, the resistance value drops to only a few thousand ohms, so it is a better conductor of electricity. It is much easier to sustain an electrical shock with wet skin. Your interior body tissues are an even better conductor of electricity (typically around a few hundred ohms). If the skin is broken, the risk of electric shock is even greater.

When your body is exposed to a live electrical circuit, the circuit voltage can cause an electric current to pass through your body (a shock). Major factors that affect the severity of the shock received when your body is part of an electrical circuit are:

- The magnitude or amount of current flowing through the body. Higher voltages "push" with greater force and make more electric current flow.
- The path of the current through the body.
- The length of time that the body is part of the circuit and is exposed to the current.

Other factors that may effect the severity of a shock are:

- The voltage applied to the circuit. Voltages above 60 volts DC (direct current) can push enough current through the body to be dangerous. The effects of AC (alternating current) voltages can be 3 to 5 times as great as DC voltages, only 25 volts (rms) AC can be a hazard.
- The level of moisture or humidity in the surrounding environment.
- The phase of the human heart cycle when the shock occurs.
- The general health and condition of the person experiencing the shock.

Effects on the body from an electrical shock can range from a barely perceptible tingle to severe burns and immediate cardiac arrest. Also, involuntary reactions to a shock may cause additional injuries from striking nearby objects.

It is not possible to list exact injuries that would result from exposure to a given amperage, but it is possible to draw general conclusions. **Table a** shows the effects of increasing electric currents on the body. The table assumes a shock of 1 second duration from an AC 60-cycle voltage (mA = current in milliamps; A = current in amps).

Table a. Probable effects of electric currents on the human body

Current level	Probable effects
1 mA	Perception level. Slight tingling sensation. Still dangerous under certain conditions, especially wet conditions.*
5 mA	Slight shock felt, not painful but disturbing. Average person can let go. However, strong involuntary reactions to shocks in this range can lead to injury.
6 to 30 mA	Painful shock, muscular control is lost.
50 to 150 mA	Extreme pain, respiratory arrest, severe muscular contractions. Individual cannot let go. Can be fatal.**
1 to 4.3 A	Ventricular fibrillation: the rhythmic pumping action of the heart ceases. Muscular contraction and nerve damage occur. Fatal injuries likely.***
10 A	Cardiac arrest, severe burns. Death probable.

(Courtesy OSHA, www.osha.gov)

* Wet conditions contribute to low-voltage electrocutions. Dry skin has high electrical resistance, but wet skin has much lower electrical resistance.

Dry skin: current = volts/ohms = 120/100,000 = 1 mA (this is a barely perceptible current level).

Wet skin: current = volts/ohms = 120/1,000 = 120 mA (this current level is sufficient to cause ventricular fibrillation).

** When muscular contractions caused by electrical stimulation (shock) do not allow the victim to let go, even relatively low voltages can be dangerous. The degree of injury increases with the length of time that the body is exposed to the current.

100 mA for 3 seconds is equivalent to 900 mA for 0.03 seconds. Both levels can cause ventricular fibrillation.

*** High voltage electrical energy greatly reduces the body's resistance by quickly breaking down and puncturing human skin. Once the skin is punctured, electrical resistance is greatly reduced, resulting in massive current flow.

Conditions that create shock hazards

When working on a hybrid vehicle, here are a few conditions to keep in mind that can create a shock hazard. Exercise care and avoid the following to reduce your risk:

• Contact with both positive and negative high voltage wiring uninsulated terminals at the same time.

• Contact with an uninsulated positive high voltage terminal and ground, when a short to ground is present.

• Contact with an uninsulated positive high voltage terminal and a component, when a short to the component case is present.

It is critical that all high voltage components have good ground circuits or ground straps with low resistance.

Safety equipment

Safety precautions must kept in mind when working on hybrid vehicles, The possibility of injuries caused by electricity, splashed chemicals, foreign objects, and fire can be reduced by using the following safety equipment.

> **WARNING—**
> • *Always use and wear appropriate safety equipment while performing services and repairs.*

NOTE—
• *For general automotive advice see* **4 Service and Repair Fundamentals**.

Eye protection

◀ Wear safety goggles when working near the high voltage battery and the 12-volt auxiliary battery.

41026

◀ Wear safety glasses while performing all other services and repairs.

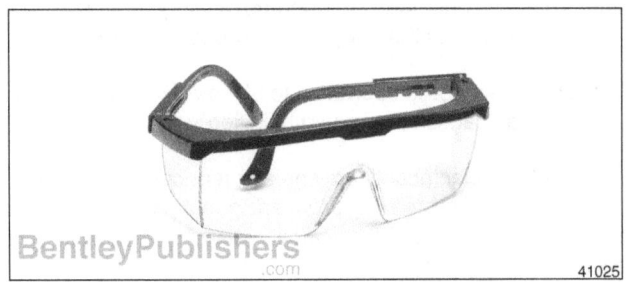

41025

High voltage lineman's gloves

◀ Wear rubber high voltage lineman's gloves whenever high voltage is present. Always wear the insulated gloves when removing the service plug, when testing high voltage system components, and whenever high voltage may be present and you are not certain about the safety of the high voltage system.

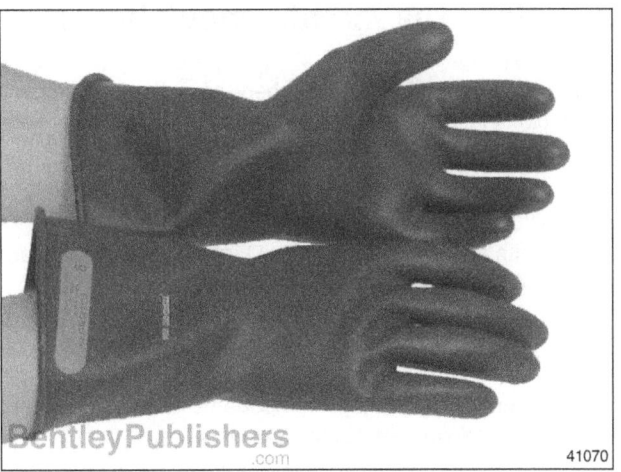

41070

Use lineman's gloves that meet or exceed ANSI/ASTM Class 0 (1,000 volt AC) insulation specifications.

Before use, inspect gloves for cuts and punctures by blowing into the open end and holding like a balloon. If you suspect a leak, hold the inflated glove under water and look for bubbles. Even a small pinhole can be dangerous. Dry gloves before use.

Store lineman's gloves in a cool, dry place and protect from direct sunlight, heat, oil, and ozone. Do not fold or store inside-out, as this may cause the rubber to stress and crack. Before working on a vehicle, remove all jewelry such as watches, rings, chains, and bracelets.

41027

Fire extinguishers

◄ Use Class C or Class D fire extinguisher for fires caused by either electricity or battery chemicals. The extinguishing agent in Class C extinguishers is non-conductive and is therefore the best choice for electrical fires. Class D fire extinguishers are designed for use on flammable metals. If a Class C or Class D extinguisher is unavailable, water is a suitable alternative.

Identifying high voltage wiring

For easy identification, the insulation and protective jackets on all high voltage wiring cables are colored orange. This is an industry-standard practice that is currently used on all hybrid vehicles with high voltage systems.

41008

Courtesy Toyota Motor Sales (TMS) USA, Inc.

◄ High voltage power cables run from the high voltage battery in the rear, underneath the vehicle, to the inverter in the engine compartment. Where necessary, the cables are protected by flexible or rigid plastic covers. Use caution when jacking a vehicle, or working on or around these high voltage cables. Avoid piercing, cutting, crushing, or damaging the insulation and cable, or otherwise creating a hazardous condition. See **4 Service and Repair Fundamentals**.

◄ Orange high voltage cables and connectors (**arrows**) located in engine compartment.

41003

◄ Orange high voltage cables (**arrows**) located under white protective plastic cover under vehicle.

41004

Prius high voltage safety systems

All high voltage hybrid system components on the Prius are well insulated and well protected from damage from road hazards, accidents and abuse. These systems and components protect occupants from high voltage:

High voltage fuse (1) provides protection from short circuits to the high voltage battery.

Positive and negative high voltage cables (2) connect the high voltage battery and inverter through 12-volt normally open (NO) high voltage relays **(3)**. When the hybrid system is OFF and not in READY mode, the high voltage relays open the circuit between the high voltage battery and inverter. The high voltage cables are isolated from the metal body, so you cannot receive a shock by touching the vehicle body. Voltage in the high voltage cables is 0 volts when the hybrid system is OFF (not in READY mode).

Ground fault monitor (4): While the hybrid system is ON and in READY mode, a ground fault monitor continuously monitors for high voltage leakage to the vehicle body. If a fault is detected, the computer **(5)** will illuminate the master warning and the hybrid system warning indicators in the instrument cluster. The system will also open the high voltage relays to interrupt power and shut down the system. This action is similar to the way a ground fault circuit interrupter (GFCI) works in home wiring.

The diagram below shows the hybrid system OFF (READY indicator not illuminated). Voltage in the high voltage cables is 0 volts.

— Master Warning

— Hybrid System Warning

TP0805001

Courtesy Toyota Motor Sales (TMS) USA, Inc.

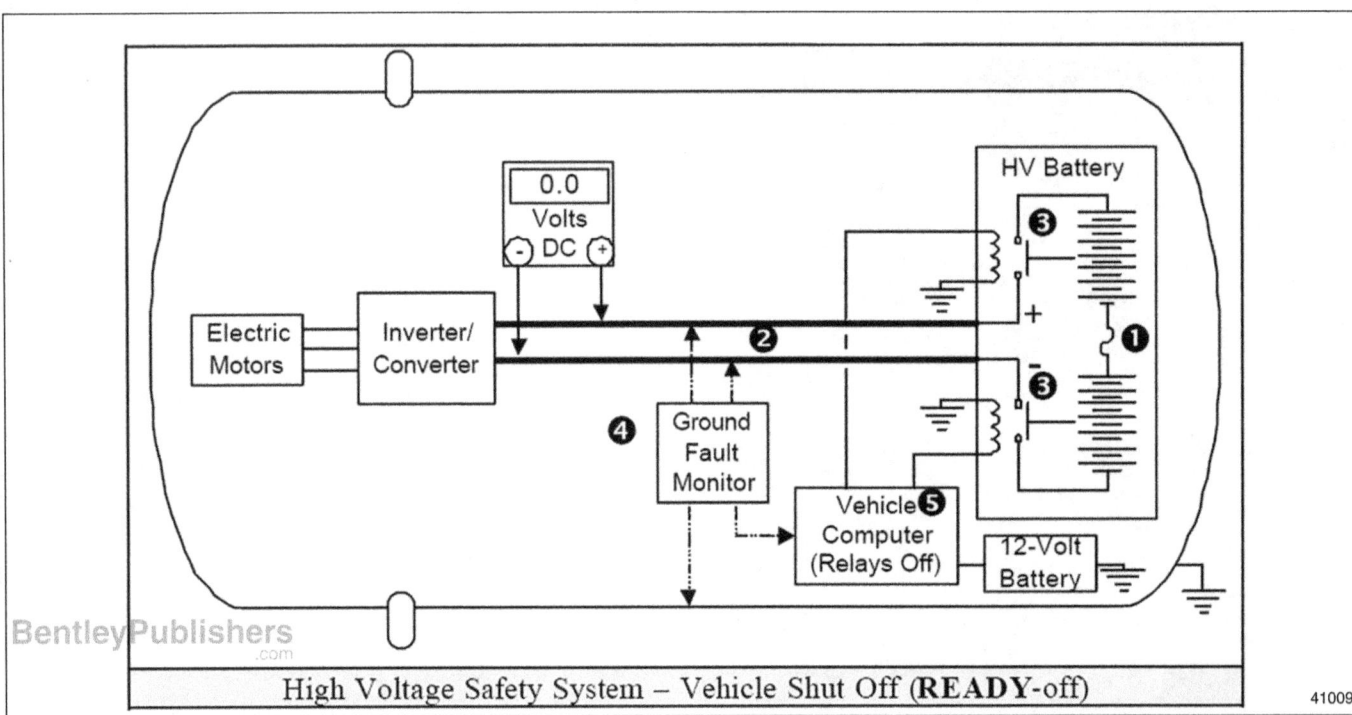

High Voltage Safety System – Vehicle Shut Off (**READY**-off)

41009

Courtesy Toyota Motor Sales (TMS) USA, Inc.

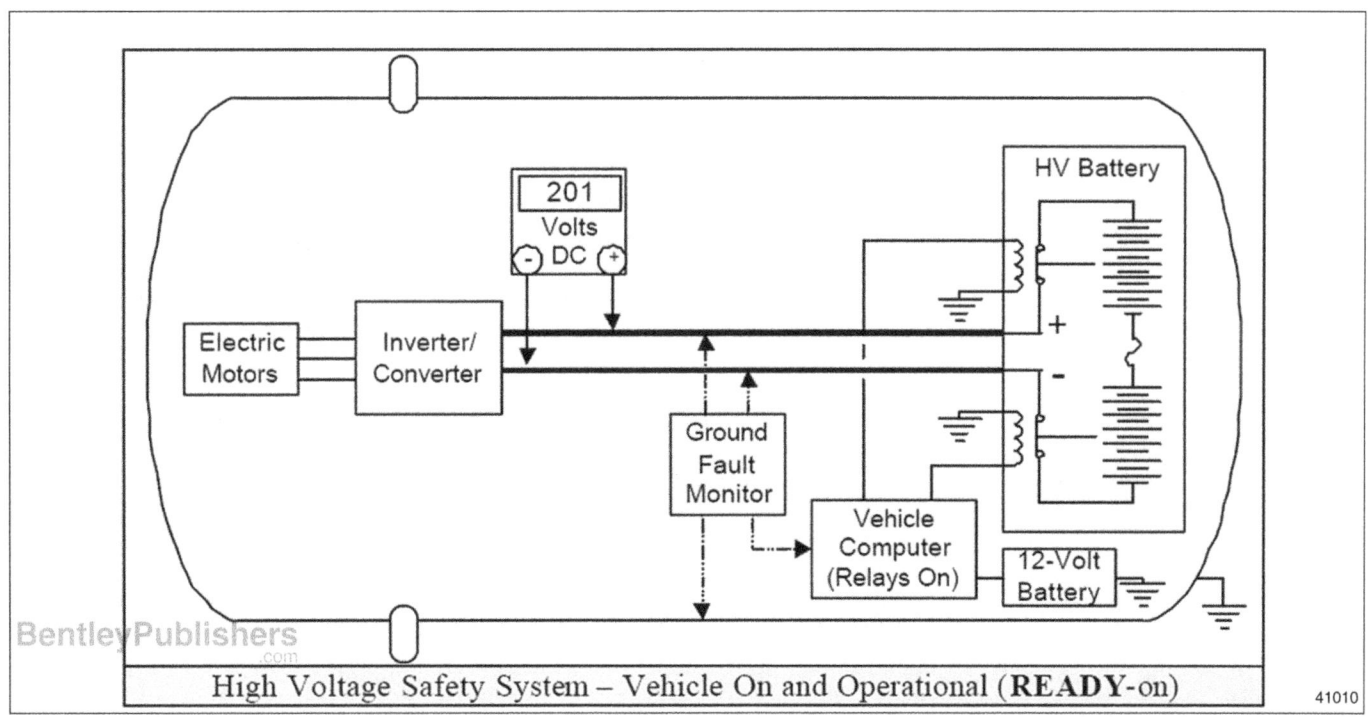

High Voltage Safety System – Vehicle On and Operational (**READY**-on)

41010

The diagram above shows the hybrid system ON (READY indicator illuminated). The high voltage relays are now closed and voltage in the high voltage cables is now approximately 201 volts.

BEFORE WORKING ON YOUR PRIUS

Before working on your Prius it is essential that you:

1. Turn OFF the hybrid system. See **Servicing systems without high voltage components** and **Switching hybrid system OFF** in this chapter.

2. Determine whether the service or repair work will expose you to high voltage components. See **Servicing systems with high voltage components** and **Disabling high voltage system by removing service plug** in this chapter.

Servicing systems without high voltage components

Before performing any service, maintenance or repair procedures on Prius systems without high voltage components, turn OFF the hybrid system. This includes nearly all service, maintenance or repair tasks. Perform this crucial step even when doing something simple, such as checking engine oil level.

If you are unsure if the work you intend to perform will expose you to high voltage, see **Identifying high voltage wiring** in this chapter. For a table of repair procedures that involve high voltage components, see **4 Service and Repair Fundamentals**.

When the hybrid system is ON, engine operation is controlled by the hybrid vehicle electronic control unit (HV-ECU), which may cause the engine to start at any time. The engine may be started to charge the high voltage battery, for example. An unexpected engine start can be extremely dangerous. Always turn the hybrid system OFF before working on your Prius. See **Switching hybrid system OFF** in this chapter.

Before performing any service, maintenance or repair on Prius systems with high voltage components, disable the high voltage system. See **Servicing systems without high voltage components** in this chapter.

Switching hybrid system OFF

Switch hybrid system OFF before performing any service, maintenance or repair procedure on your Prius.

◀ Check to see if READY indicator (**arrow**) is illuminated. READY indicator is located on instrument panel warning display.

NOTE—

• *Location of READY indicator shown for 2004-2005 models. Location is slightly different on 2006-2008 models.*

41031

◀ If the READY indicator is illuminated, depress the brake pedal, and push and release the POWER button until the READY indicator goes out.

– Remove the ignition key or smart key (if equipped).

◀ Models with smart key: Turn OFF smart key function.

– Working under steering column, turn OFF the smart key function by depressing the smart key cancel switch button. The button will latch in the depressed position.

– Check that smart key Function is OFF:
  • Make sure smart key is not inserted in key slot.
  • Depress brake pedal, and push and release the POWER button.
  • Make sure READY indicator does not illuminate.
  • If the READY indicator does illuminate, depress the smart key cancel switch again and repeat steps to verify smart key function is OFF.

All models: The hybrid system is now OFF and not in the READY mode. When work is completed, remember to turn the smart key function ON (if equipped) by depressing the smart key switch.

Servicing systems with high voltage components

Before working on any Prius components that are connected to the hybrid high voltage system, you must first disable the hybrid system. This will disconnect the high voltage battery from the vehicle.

If you are unsure if the work you intend to perform will cause exposure to high voltage, see **Identifying high voltage wiring** in this chapter. For a table of repair procedures that involve high voltage components, see **4 Service and Repair Fundamentals**.

Safety

Before servicing systems with high voltage components, read and understand the warnings and cautions below and see **Disabling high voltage system by removing service plug** in this chapter.

> *WARNING —*
> - *Prius hybrid system has circuits with voltages as high as 500 volts. Voltages over 60 volts DC and 25 volts (rms) AC are a shock hazard. Wear lineman's gloves when removing the service plug, and whenever high voltage may be present.*

> *CAUTION—*
> - *On Prius models, disconnecting the 12-volt auxiliary battery is part of the service plug removal procedure. The 12-volt auxiliary battery provides power to various electronic control units during start-up and maintains control unit memory at all times. Disconnecting the 12-volt auxiliary battery erases preset radio station selections and stored destinations and other settings in the GPS navigation system (if equipped). Record station selections and other desired information before disconnecting the 12-volt auxiliary battery.*
> - *Reinitialize the power window control system whenever 12-volt auxiliary battery power is interrupted. If the power window control system is not reinitialized, AUTO UP/DOWN operation, and jam protection do not function. See* **10 Electrical System, Lights**.
> - *Always check for diagnostic trouble codes (DTCs) that may be stored in control unit memory before removing the service plug. service plug removal may erase any stored DTCs. If DTCs are present, retrieve and record them before removing the service plug. See* **11 Diagnostics**.
> - *Be sure that the hybrid system is OFF and not in READY mode (READY indicator not illuminated).*

Disabling high voltage system by removing service plug

This procedure disconnects the high voltage battery from the hybrid system. Complete these steps before servicing any Prius system that is part of the high voltage system.

> *WARNING —*
> - *Prius hybrid system has circuits with voltages as high as 500 volts. Voltages over 60 volts DC and 25 volts (rms) AC are a shock hazard. Wear lineman's gloves when removing the service plug, and whenever high voltage may be present.*
> - *After removing the service plug, test high voltage components for residual voltage to ensure that all high voltage has dissipated. See* **Testing for High Voltage** *in this chapter.*

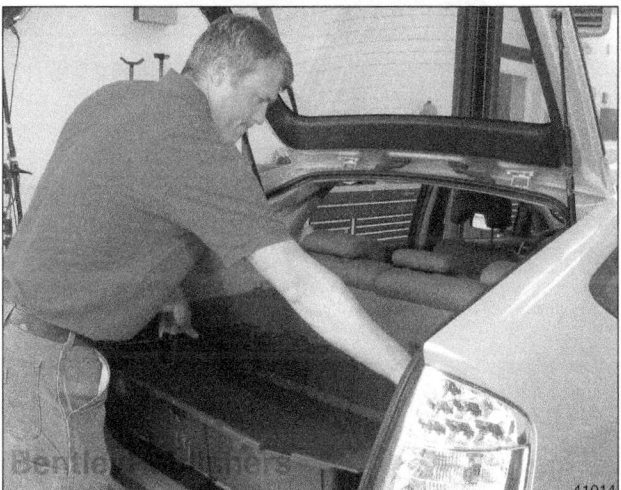

> **CAUTION—**
>
> • *Removing the service plug may erase diagnostic trouble codes (DTCs) that are stored in control unit memory. If DTCs are present, retrieve and record DTCs before removing the service plug. See* **11 Diagnostics***.*
>
> • *Do not depress the POWER button when service plug is removed from the vehicle. Damage to electronic control units (ECUs) may occur.*
>
> • *Disconnecting the 12-volt auxiliary battery erases preset radio station selections and stored destinations and other settings in the GPS navigation system (if equipped). Record station selections and other desired information before disconnecting the 12-volt auxiliary battery.*
>
> • *Disconnecting the 12-volt auxiliary battery requires reinitialization of the power window control system. If the power window control system is not reinitialized, AUTO UP/DOWN operation and jam protection do not function. To reinitialize the power window control system, see* **10 Electrical System, Lights***.*

– Switch hybrid system OFF. See **Switching hybrid system OFF** in this chapter.

◄ Working in the cargo compartment, disconnect the 12-volt auxiliary battery. To access the auxiliary battery, rotate two release knobs on rear no. 2 floor board.

◄ Lift and remove rear no. 2 floor board.

◄ Remove rear floor box.

Safety

Safety

◀ Using a trim tool or equivalent, release 4 retention claws, and remove rear no. 3 floor board.

> **CAUTION—**
> - *Record radio presets and GPS destinations (if equipped) before disconnecting the 12-volt auxiliary battery.*
> - *Reinitialized power windows whenever 12-volt auxiliary battery is disconnected. See* **10 Electrical System, Lights**.

◀ Disconnect 12-volt auxiliary battery negative (ground) cable (**arrow**). Wrap cable connector with insulating tape to avoid accidental reconnection.

◀ Service plug is located in the cargo compartment at front left, ahead of previously removed rear floor box.

> **WARNING—**
> - *Always wear lineman's gloves when removing the service plug, and whenever high voltage may be present.*

> **CAUTION—**
> - *Removing the service plug may erase diagnostic trouble codes (DTCs) that are stored in control unit memory. If DTCs are present, retrieve and record DTCs before removing the service plug. See* **11 Diagnostics**.

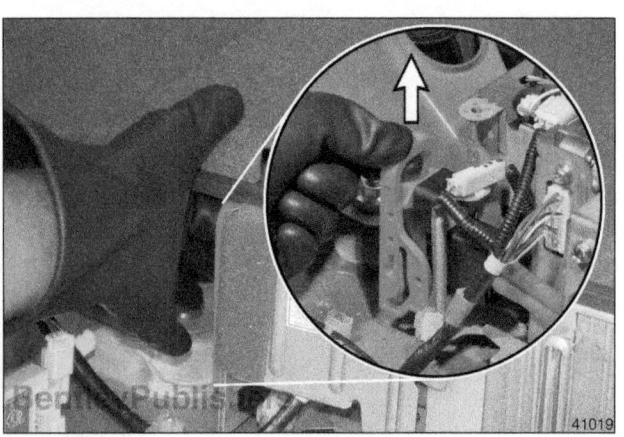

◀ Wearing lineman's gloves, pull service plug latch straight upward (**arrow**).

> **NOTE—**
> - *For clarity,* **insets** *in photos illustrate service plug with high voltage battery compartment cover removed. It is not necessary to remove these covers to gain access to the service plug.*

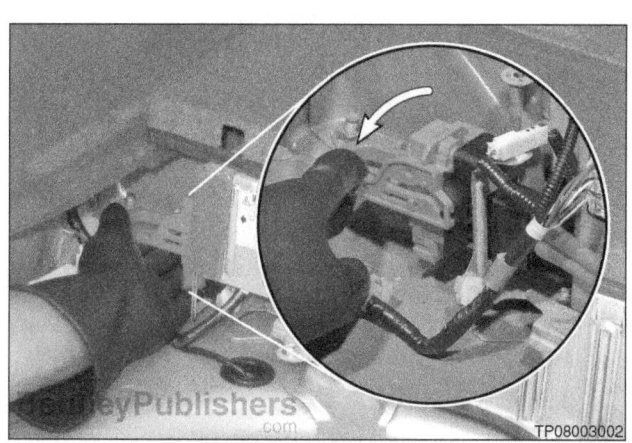

◀ Rotate latch 90° downward (to left).

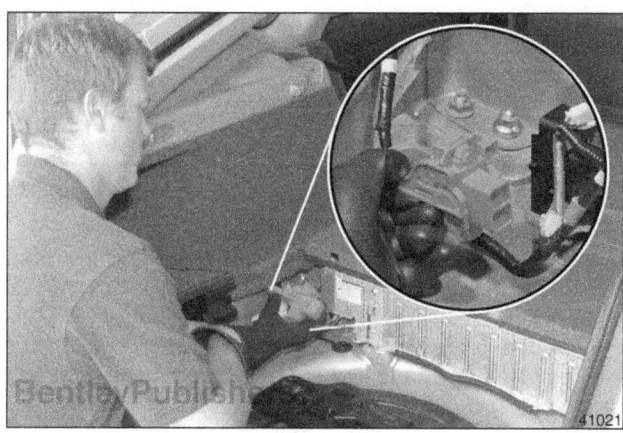

◀ Pull service plug to left and remove from high voltage battery connector. Hybrid system components are disconnected from high voltage battery.

> **CAUTION—**
> • *Do not press the POWER button when service plug is removed from the vehicle. Damage to electronic control units (ECUs) may occur.*

— Store service plug in your pocket or in a safe place away from vehicle.

— Test system for high voltage. See **Switching hybrid system OFF** in this chapter.

> **WARNING—**
> • *High voltage may be present in the hybrid system for up to five minutes after service plug is removed. Always wait at least five minutes after removing service plug to allow high voltage capacitors to discharge before servicing the vehicle.*
> • *After removing service plug, always test high voltage components for residual voltage to ensure that all high voltage has dissipated. Wear lineman's gloves until you are sure that high voltage is not present. See* **Switching hybrid system OFF** *in this chapter.*

◀ Installation is reverse of removal, noting the following:

• When reinstalling service plug, begin with locking latch in open position (**A**). Insert plug fully into service plug socket.

• Rotate latch up 90° (**B**).

• Push latch downward fully to lock service plug in place (**C**).

• Tighten 12-volt auxiliary battery negative (ground) cable clamp nut to specification.

• Reinitialize power windows. See **10 Electrical System, Lights**.

• Reenter radio station selections (presets) and GPS navigation destinations (if equipped).

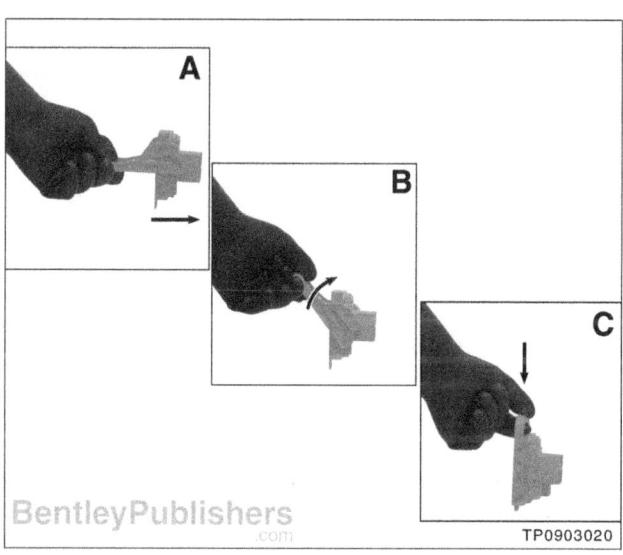

Tightening torque	
12-volt auxiliary battery negative (ground) cable clamp nut	6 Nm (53 in-lb)

TESTING FOR HIGH VOLTAGE

Always test for high voltage before working on any Prius system that has high voltage and each time you disable the Prius high voltage system. See **Disabling high voltage system by removing service plug** in this chapter.

Perform the following tests to be sure that high voltage capacitors have discharged, and that high voltage is not present in systems that you will be working on. Remember, poor electrical connections and unwanted resistance can prevent residual high voltage from dissipating and can create a shock hazard.

> **WARNING—**
> • *Always wear lineman's gloves until you are sure that high voltage is not present.*

Voltage tests

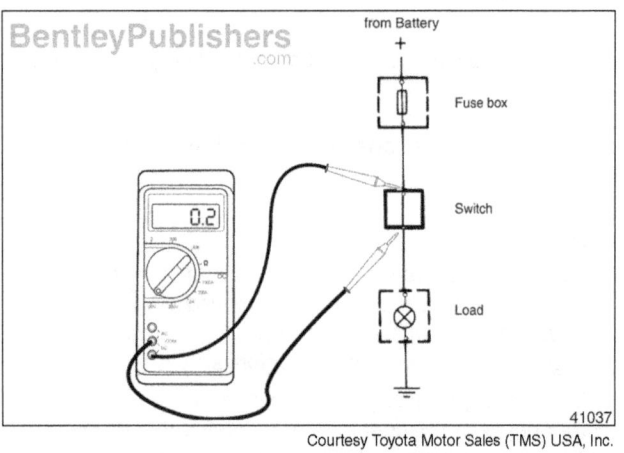

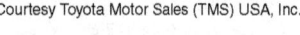

Courtesy Toyota Motor Sales (TMS) USA, Inc.

◀ One way to ensure that high voltage is not present in any hybrid system components is to measure voltage between any two high voltage components, and also between high voltage components and ground. Poor connections, poor grounds, and unwanted resistance can affect the dissipation of stored voltage in capacitors and can cause a shock hazard. This test will help confirm that high voltage is not present and that it is safe to work on high voltage system components.

– Using a digital multimeter, set the meter to test voltage. If the meter does not have an auto-range feature (and does not automatically select a range appropriate for the voltage measured), then manually set the meter for a high range (at least 200 volts).

◀ Measure voltage between high voltage components. For this test, place test probes on the case for each HV component. Test between the transaxle, inverter, and electric A/C compressor.

Readings near 0 volts indicate that dangerous high voltage is not present.

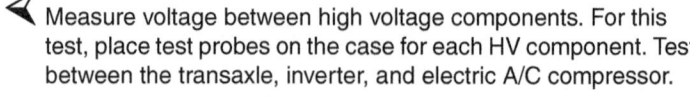

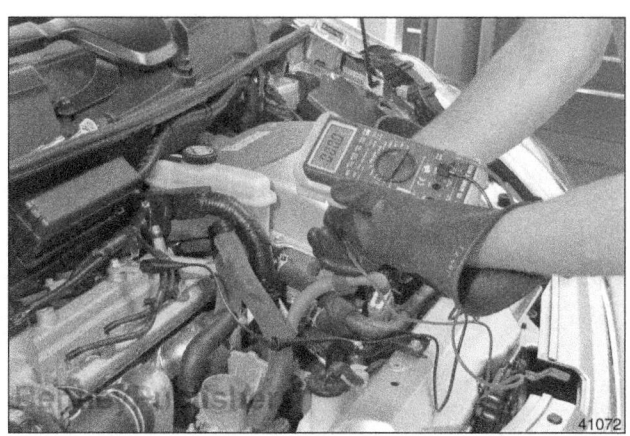

◄ Now measure voltage between all high voltage components and chassis ground. For this test, place one probe on the case for each HV component, and the other probe to a good ground. Test the transaxle, inverter, electric air-conditioning compressor, and HV battery.

Again, readings near 0 volts indicate that dangerous high voltage is not present.

Potential equalization tests

Potential equalization tests are another method to verify that excessive resistance does not exist between high voltage components. A specialized tester is required, such as the Fluke model 1520 MegOhmMeter. This tester has a very low resistance (Ohms) scale, and an accuracy of +/- 50 milliohms.

Follow all instructions provided by the meter manufacturer to perform potential equalization tests. Test between all HV components, and also between HV components and ground.

Insulation resistance tests

Insulation resistance tests can locate insulation failures within MG1 and MG2. These tests can also verify the integrity of insulation in other high voltage circuits and components by applying approximately 500 volts to the circuits being tested. A specialized tester is required, such as the Fluke model 1520 MegOhmMeter.

Follow all instructions provided by the meter manufacturer to perform insulation resistance tests.

EMERGENCY PROCEDURES

The following procedures can be used in an emergency. For the complete Toyota Emergency Response Guide see **15 Toyota Emergency Response Guide**.

Switching hybrid system OFF in emergency

If you are unable to switch hybrid system OFF (see **Switching hybrid system OFF** in this chapter), perform the following emergency procedures:

◀ Disconnect 12-volt auxiliary battery negative (ground) cable (**arrow**). Wrap cable connector with insulating tape to avoid accidental reconnection.

◀ Remove HEV fuse (20 amp yellow fuse) from engine compartment junction block. If unsure, remove all fuses from this junction block. See **12 Electrical Component Locations**.

High voltage battery handling

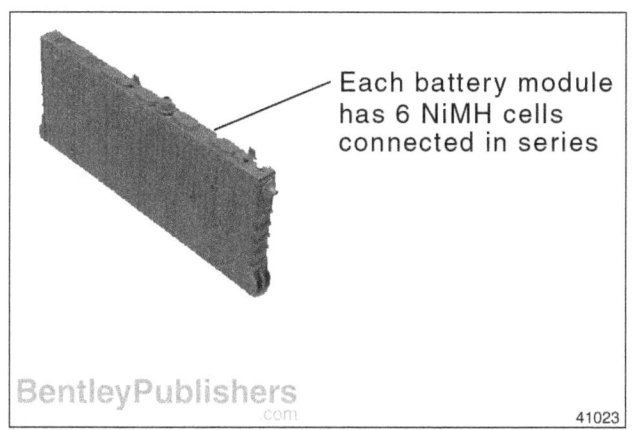

Each battery module has 6 NiMH cells connected in series

BentleyPublishers
.com

41023

Courtesy Toyota Motor Sales (TMS) USA, Inc.

The high voltage battery in the Prius contains a large number of individual nickel metal hydride (NiMH) battery cells. Each cell has a hard plastic housing and generates 1.2 volts. Six cells are connected in series to make a battery module that generates 7.2 volts.

In all there are 168 individual battery cells grouped in 28 modules. The complete battery produces 201.6 volts.

The electrolyte in each cell contains potassium hydroxide and sodium hydroxide. This electrolyte is a paste and leaks are unlikely; however, the electrolyte is a very caustic alkaline substance with a very high pH of 13.5. Never touch the electrolyte.

Neutralizing NiMH battery electrolyte spills

If a high voltage battery is damaged and an electrolyte spill occurs, the spilled electrolyte must be contained and neutralized as soon as possible. Hazmat containment and cleanup products are available from many suppliers.

Acceptable neutralizers are a dilute boric acid solution or vinegar. (Boric acid solution: 800 g boric acid to 20 liters water, or 5.5 oz boric acid to 1 gallon water).

Safety

WARNING—
- *Nickel metal hydride battery cells in the high voltage battery pack contain a very caustic alkaline electrolyte which can cause severe burns. Flush contact area with water, then seek medical attention.*

TP0804001

25-foot jumper cables

TP0804002

JUMP STARTING AND TOWING

Jump starting

The Prius does not start if 12-volt auxiliary battery is discharged.

◄ Boost (jump start) discharged 12-volt battery using a good 12-volt battery.

CAUTION—
- *Before attempting to jump start, be sure the no-start condition is caused by a discharged auxiliary battery. One indication of this is an instrument display that is dim or not illuminated with ignition in IG-ON position.*
- *Make sure the booster battery is 12 volts. Do not jump start auxiliary battery unless jumper battery is correct. For best results, charge booster battery first by running engine of booster vehicle for several minutes.*
- *Jump starting another vehicle from the Prius auxiliary battery is not recommended. The Prius 12-volt system delivers significantly fewer amps than most automotive 12-volt starter motors consume. Jump starting another car is likely to cause the Prius master fuse to overload or other electrical system damage.*
- *If the 12-volt battery is discharged with transaxle in PARK, the vehicle cannot be moved unless front wheels are raised. The front wheels are locked by means of the parking lock mechanism.*

◄ A set of long high-quality jumper cables may work when the vehicles can not be parked nose to nose.

The 12-volt auxiliary battery is located on the right side of the cargo area. But the rear hatch cannot be opened if the 12-volt battery is discharged. Use the jump starting terminal in the engine compartment, as described below.

WARNING—
- *To avoid serious personal injury and damage to your vehicle which might result from battery explosion, acid burns, electrical burns, or damaged electronic components, follow these instructions precisely.*
- *Take care to keep battery acid from contacting eyes, skin, or clothing. Wear eye protection. Do not smoke and do not work near any open flames.*

– Apply parking brake. Switch OFF headlights, interior lights and other unnecessary lights and accessories.

– Switch hybrid system OFF (READY indicator not illuminated).

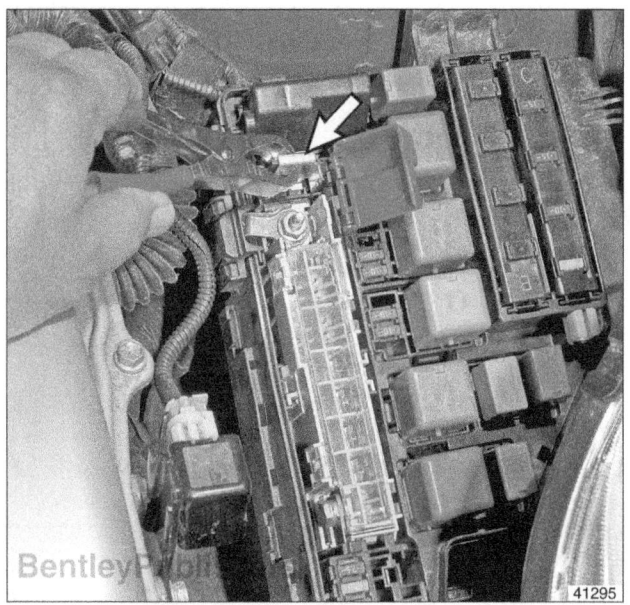

– Open hood. Remove junction block / relay block cover on left side of engine compartment. Flip open red cover to expose jump starting positive (+) terminal.

NOTE —

• *If booster battery is installed in another vehicle, make sure vehicles are not touching.*

– If applicable, remove booster battery vent plugs. Lay a cloth over open vents. (This helps reduce explosion hazard, personal injuries and burns.)

◄ Connect clamp of positive (red) jumper cable to jump starting positive (+) terminal (**arrow**).

◄ Connect clamp at other end of positive (red) jumper cable to positive (+) terminal on booster battery.

◄ Connect clamp of negative (black) jumper cable to negative (–) terminal on booster battery.

TP0804005

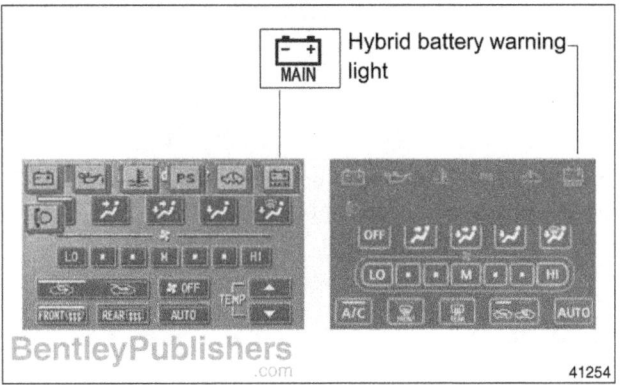

Hybrid battery warning light

41254

Courtesy Toyota Motor Sales (TMS) USA, Inc.

◄ Connect clamp at other end of negative (black) jumper cable to solid, stationary, unpainted, metal ground point of Prius with discharged battery.

– Charge discharged battery with jumper cables connected for approx. 5 minutes. If applicable, run engine in vehicle with booster battery at about 2000 rpm with accelerator pedal lightly depressed.

– Start hybrid system. Make sure READY light is ON.

NOTE—

• *If the hybrid battery warning light comes on in the multi-information display, the high-voltage hybrid battery is also discharged. The high voltage battery cannot be jump started under normal conditions. Contact your Toyota dealer.*

– Carefully disconnect cables in exact reverse order: Negative cable first, then positive cable.

– Carefully dispose of battery cover cloths which may be contaminated with sulfuric acid. Replace battery vent plugs, if applicable.

– If first jump start attempt is not successful, check that clamps on jumper cables are tight. Recharge discharged battery with jumper cables connected for several minutes and restart hybrid system in normal way. If another attempt is not successful, the battery may be depleted. Have it checked at your Toyota dealer.

If the cause of your 12-volt battery discharging is not apparent (for example, lights left on), have it checked at your Toyota dealer.

Towing

WARNING—

• *When towing a Prius, do not allow the front wheels to rotate. The front wheels are directly connected to motor / generator 2 (MG2), and when the front wheels are turning MG2 also turns. This may generate high voltage, create a shock hazard, and cause damage to the inverter or the high voltage battery.*

◄ Prius front wheels are directly connected to motor / generator 2 (MG2) through drive axles and the differential. Tow with the front wheels lifted on a towing dolly, or on a flatbed truck.

NOTE—

• *If the 12-volt battery is discharged with transaxle in PARK, the vehicle cannot be moved unless front wheels are raised. The front wheels are locked by means of the parking lock mechanism.*

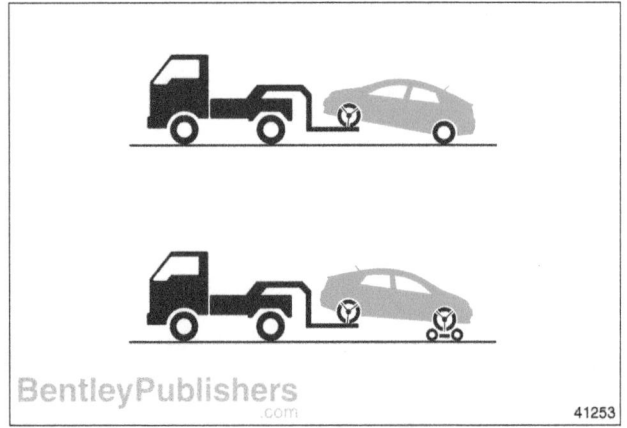

41253

Courtesy Toyota Motor Sales (TMS) USA, Inc.

4

Service and Repair Fundamentals

Basic information to know before working on the Prius

GENERAL

This chapter is intended to help the Prius owner and the automotive service professional get started with basic service and maintenance on the Prius.

◄ The repair and maintenance tasks included throughout book can mostly be done with common hand tools. With care, a little planning, and cautious respect for high voltage, you can safely and successfully maintain and repair your Prius.

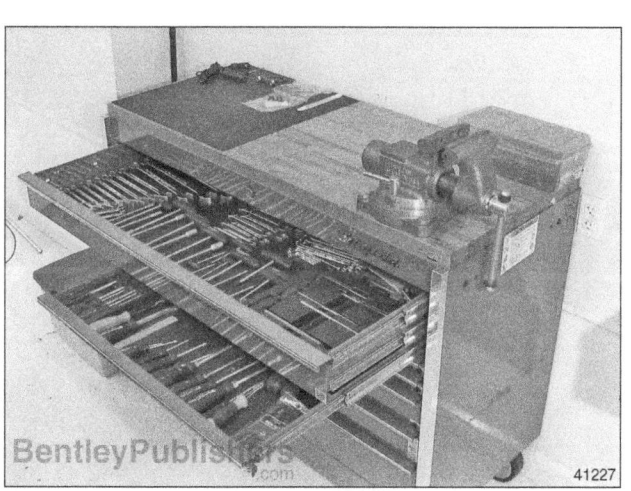

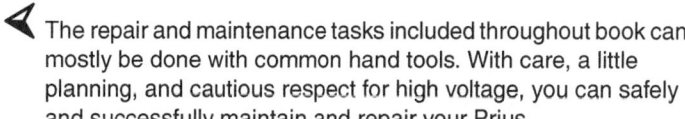

Hybrid safety

Working on a vehicle creates some unavoidable hazards, but common sense and quality tools can reduce the risks. Accidents often happen because of carelessness. Read and observe the **Warnings**, **Cautions** and recommended work procedures in **3 Safety**.

The gasoline engine-electric hybrid power plant in the Prius uses high voltage components, including a high voltage battery and two electric motor / generators that operate at up to 500 volts. Orange-colored cables carry lethal high voltage. Use extreme care when working near high voltage cables and components.

> *WARNING—*
> * *Risk of electrocution! Avoid touching orange-colored high voltage wiring and high voltage components unless you are certain that high voltage is not present.*
> * *The Prius hybrid system has voltages as high as 500 volts. Voltages over 60 volts DC and 25 volts AC are a shock hazard.*

The Prius engine may start at any time if the hybrid system is in **READY** mode. See **3 Safety** for instructions on turning OFF the hybrid system.

> *WARNING—*
> * *Be sure hybrid system is OFF when servicing vehicle (READY indicator not illuminated). Failure to switch the hybrid system OFF could result in engine start at any time.*

JACKING AND LIFTING

– Switch hybrid system OFF (READY indicator not illuminated). See **3 Safety**.

> *WARNING—*
> • *Failure to switch the hybrid system OFF could result in engine start at any time without warning.*

◄ Some repair or maintenance procedures require lifting the car for access to components underneath. A hydraulic floor jack can be used to lift one end or one corner of the car high enough to insert jack stands for some repair and service procedures, such as changing oil or working on brakes.

For other procedures, a professional lift is needed to raise the vehicle higher for more access. While jacks and jack stands can be used to raise both ends of the car evenly (some procedures require you to keep the car level), raising the car with a lift accomplishes this more easily. To avoid damage to the vehicle, always lift on specified underbody "hard" points as shown on the following pages.

> *WARNING—*
> • *Use the jack supplied with the vehicle only for changing a tire. Do not work under a vehicle supported only by the factory-supplied jack. Follow instructions in the vehicle owner's manual.*

Courtesy Toyota Motor Sales (TMS) USA, Inc.

◄ The Prius has limited underbody ground clearance. The height of many floor jacks is too great to allow the jack to roll under the car without interference. This is especially true at the front end of the vehicle. One solution is to raise the front by first driving on two boards. In this example, two 2 x 12 boards are used. The actual measurements of the boards are 1.5 in x 11 in x 14 in. The additional 1.5 in height adds sufficient clearance for most jacks.

◄ For your safety, use a hydraulic jack only for lifting. Do not rely on the jack (or any hydraulic device) for holding and steady support. Hydraulic devices can fail suddenly and without warning.

Use a positive method of support, such as jack stands, before getting under a vehicle.

See diagrams on the following pages to locate suitable "hard" points on the Prius body for jacking or lifting.

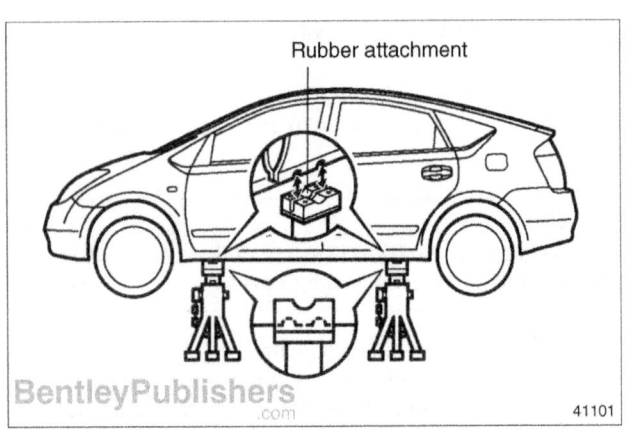

Rubber attachment

41101

Courtesy Toyota Motor Sales (TMS) USA, Inc.

◀ When possible, use blocks or hard rubber between jack or jack stands and vehicle lift points. This spreads load over a greater area and can reduce underbody deformation.

> **WARNING—**
> • *Do not use concrete blocks, bricks, or other brittle materials to support a vehicle in place of jack stands. These materials can break and collapse without warning.*

Jacking and lifting points

See the following illustrations for suitable "hard" points for jacking or lifting the 2004 - 2008 Prius.

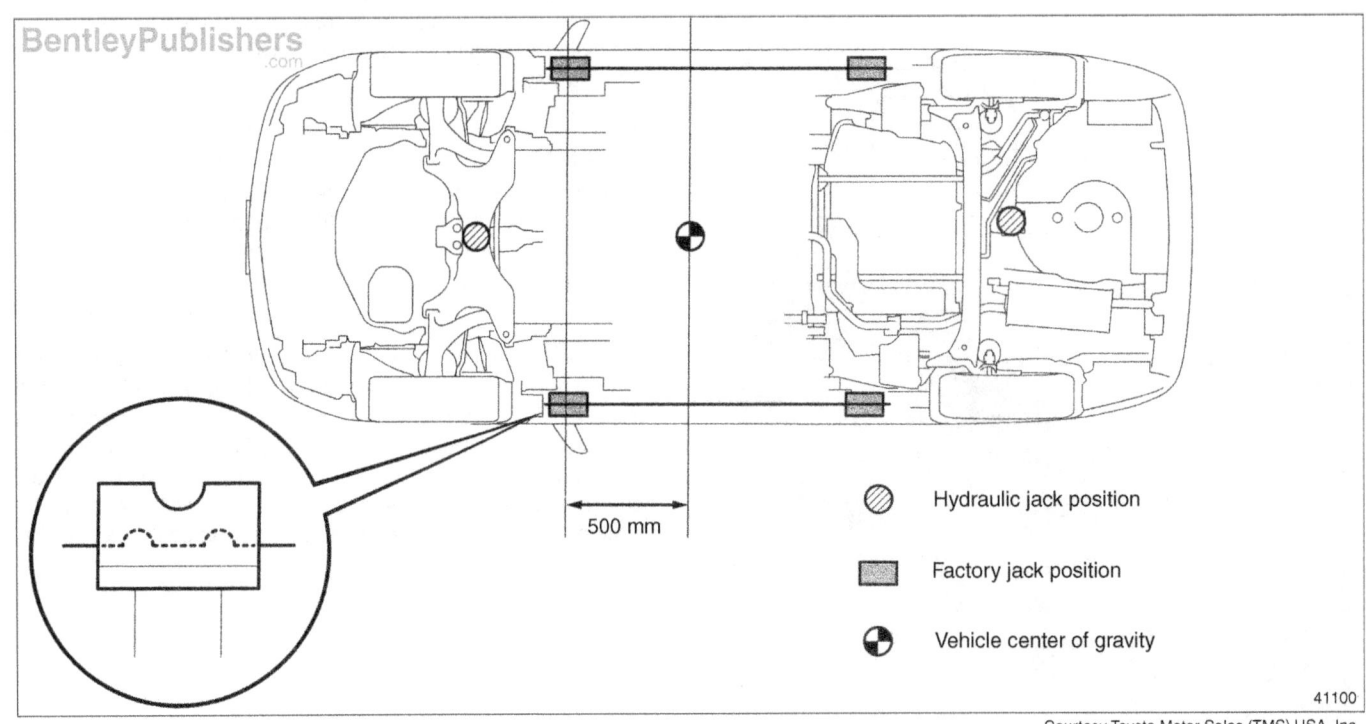

500 mm

⊘ Hydraulic jack position

▧ Factory jack position

◉ Vehicle center of gravity

41100

Courtesy Toyota Motor Sales (TMS) USA, Inc.

The illustration below shows suitable "hard" points when using a lift to raise a 2004 - 2008 Prius.

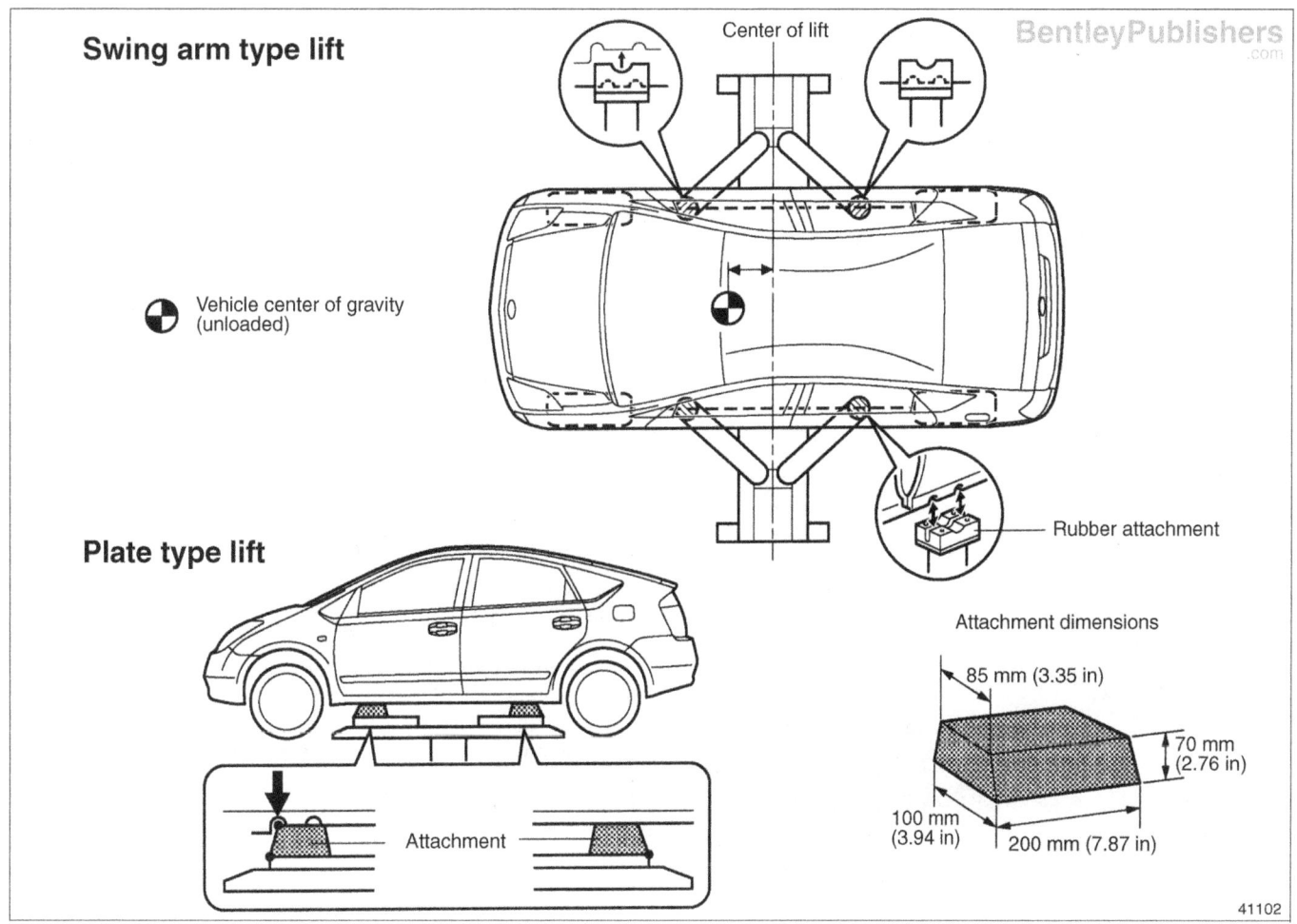

Swing arm type lift

Center of lift

Vehicle center of gravity
(unloaded)

Rubber attachment

Plate type lift

Attachment dimensions

Attachment

85 mm (3.35 in)

70 mm
(2.76 in)

100 mm
(3.94 in)

200 mm (7.87 in)

41102

Courtesy Toyota Motor Sales (TMS) USA, Inc.

Jacking the Prius

— Switch hybrid system OFF (READY indicator not illuminated). See **3 Safety**.

> **WARNING—**
> • *Failure to switch the hybrid system OFF could result in engine start at any time without warning.*

— Follow jack manufacturer's recommendations and instructions.

— Park vehicle on a flat, level, hard surface.

— Unload vehicle before jacking. Remove heavy items from trunk and passenger compartment.

— Use wheel chocks to prevent movement of wheels on ground.

— Use blocks of hard rubber between jack and vehicle lift points.

◀ Lift only on specified underbody "hard" points. Check to be sure that jack does not contact high voltage wiring. See **3 Safety**.

— If jacking vehicle at front, release parking brake and place chocks only behind rear wheels.

— If jacking vehicle at rear, place chocks only in front of front wheels.

— Once vehicle is lifted to desired height, place chocks on both sides of wheels on ground.

— Slide jack stands under vehicle edge "hard" points. Use blocks of hard rubber between jack stands and vehicle. Lower vehicle carefully on jack stands. Check to be sure that jack stands do not contact high voltage wiring. See **3 Safety**.

— Lower jack slightly so that vehicle is supported only by jack stands. Carefully shake vehicle to check for stability.

— When satisfied that vehicle is stable, lower and remove jack.

Lifting the Prius

— Switch hybrid system OFF (READY indicator not illuminated). See **3 Safety**.

> **WARNING—**
> • *Failure to switch the hybrid system OFF could result in engine start at any time without warning.*

— Follow lift manufacturer's recommendations and instructions.

— When positioning lift swing arms, check that arms stabilize vehicle. Vehicle center of gravity should be as close as possible to lift center.

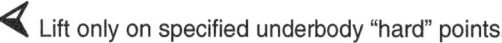 Lift only on specified underbody "hard" points.

• Use rubber pads on lift swing arms. Check to be sure that lift does not contact high voltage wiring. See **3 Safety**.

• Check that lift arms are locked in position while lifting.

— Raise vehicle so that tires are a few inches above floor. Carefully shake vehicle to check for stability.

— When you are sure that vehicle is stable, lift to desired height.

— Check that lift mechanical safety locks engage.

41229

PRELIMINARY SERVICE ADVICE

The following tips are general advice to help the do-it-yourself Prius owner perform maintenance and repair procedures more easily and safely.

Planning ahead

Most maintenance and repair procedures described in this book can be completed successfully by anyone with basic tools and abilities. Read and understand procedures completely before starting work to avoid surprises. This allows you to gather necessary parts and special tools.

Cleanliness

Keep your work area, workbench, tools, components, and vehicle organized, neat, and clean. This is essential for quality work and for your safety.

Try to anticipate fluid discharges from vehicle systems that you are working on. Drain fluids into suitable containers. Clean up spills promptly. Lubricants, coolants, and other fluids can create slippery conditions.

When working under the hood, use fender covers to protect painted finish. Be sure that vehicle is clean before using fender covers. Vehicle finish may be scratched by dirt under a fender cover.

Clean the parts that you plan to reuse. This will improve the quality of your work. For cleaning old parts, there are many environmentally friendly solvents and parts cleaners available.

WARNING—
- *Many solvents used for parts cleaning contain hazardous, toxic chemicals, and are highly flammable, especially in aerosol form. Use with extreme care in well ventilated areas. Do not smoke. Do not use these products near sources of heat, sparks, or flame. Read all label warnings.*

Allow solvents and cleaning products to dry completely. Low pressure compressed air, if available, can be used to speed drying. Use only lint-free shop towels for cleaning and drying.

Brake fluid can damage paint. Clean and remove any brake fluid spills from painted surfaces immediately.

Keep rubber parts such as belts and hoses free from oil and gasoline, which can cause premature softening and failure.

FASTENERS

Tightening fasteners

When installing a component with bolts or nuts, tighten fasteners gradually and evenly.

- This can help avoid component misalignment or overstressing.
- For components that are sealed with a gasket, this procedure helps ensure that the gasket seals evenly and properly.

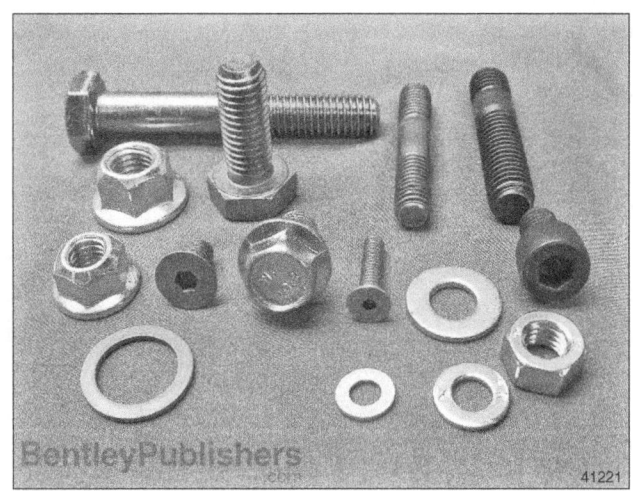

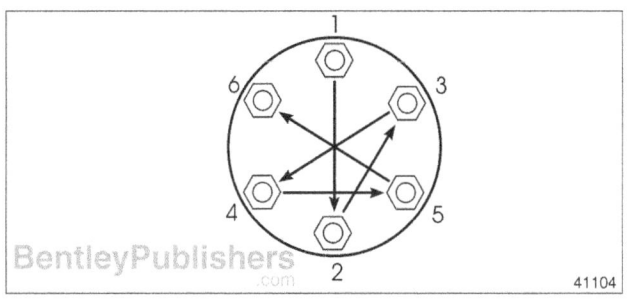

◄ When there are several fasteners holding a component, tighten fasteners in a sequence alternating between opposite sides of component, such as the one shown here.

Some repairs require a specific tightening sequence, or a particular order of assembly. These special conditions are noted in the text, and the required sequence is illustrated.

When a fastener must be tightened to a specific torque value, the torque specification is provided. Torque specifications are listed with both metric and English measurements.

Here is an example of a torque specification provided in the maintenance and repair information:

Tightening torque	
Ground cable to auxiliary battery	6 Nm (53 in-lb)

Tightening torques: standard bolts

When no tightening torque specification is available, use values from this standard torque table.

NOTE—

* *This table is for general reference only. The values are not intended to be used as a substitute for specific torque specifications.*

Class	Diameter mm	Pitch mm	Specified torque					
			Hexagon head bolt			Hexagon flange bolt		
			N·m	kgf·cm	ft·lbf	N·m	kgf·cm	ft·lbf
4T	6	1	5	55	48 in.·lbf	6	60	52 in.·lbf
	8	1.25	12.5	130	9	14	145	10
	10	1.25	26	260	19	29	290	21
	12	1.25	47	480	35	53	540	39
	14	1.5	74	760	55	84	850	61
	16	1.5	115	1,150	83	-	-	-
5T	6	1	6.5	65	56 in.·lbf	7.5	75	65 in.·lbf
	8	1.25	15.5	160	12	17.5	175	13
	10	1.25	32	330	24	36	360	26
	12	1.25	59	600	43	65	670	48
	14	1.5	91	930	67	100	1,050	76
	16	1.5	140	1,400	101	-	-	-
6T	6	1	8	80	69 in.·lbf	9	90	78 in.·lbf
	8	1.25	19	195	14	21	210	15
	10	1.25	39	400	29	44	440	32
	12	1.25	71	730	53	80	810	59
	14	1.5	110	1,100	80	125	1,250	90
	16	1.5	170	1,750	127	-	-	-
7T	6	1	10.5	110	8	12	120	9
	8	1.25	25	260	19	28	290	21
	10	1.25	52	530	38	58	590	43
	12	1.25	95	970	70	105	1,050	76
	14	1.5	145	1,500	108	165	1,700	123
	16	1.5	230	2,300	166	-	-	-
8T	8	1.25	29	300	22	33	330	24
	10	1.25	61	620	45	68	690	50
	12	1.25	110	1,100	80	120	1,250	90
9T	8	1.25	34	340	25	37	380	27
	10	1.25	70	710	51	78	790	57
	12	1.25	125	1,300	94	140	1,450	105
10T	8	1.25	38	390	28	42	430	31
	10	1.25	78	800	58	88	890	64
	12	1.25	140	1,450	105	155	1,600	116
11T	8	1.25	42	430	31	47	480	35
	10	1.25	87	890	64	97	990	72
	12	1.25	155	1,600	116	175	1,800	130

Courtesy Toyota Motor Sales (TMS) USA, Inc.

Non-reusable fasteners

Some fasteners are designed to be used once and are replaced once they are removed. One-time-use fasteners can include (but are not limited to): bolts, nuts (self-locking, nylock, etc.), cotter pins, studs, brake fittings and hardware, roll pins, clips, and washers. Replace one-time-use fasteners with genuine Toyota replacement parts intended for the purpose.

Bolts stretch when tightened. Some bolts are designed to stretch beyond their elastic limit and are permanently deformed when properly tightened. These bolts are classified as torque-to-yield fasteners. Replace fasteners if instructed to do so. Failure to replace these fasteners can result in vehicle damage and personal injury. Replace torque-to-yield fasteners with genuine Toyota replacement parts intended for the purpose.

Over the life of the vehicle, fasteners can be subjected to conditions that promote corrosion, rust, and other types of wear. Replace worn or rusty fasteners.

Gaskets and seals

Mating surfaces on smooth metal parts still have imperfections that may allow fluids to leak. To prevent leakage at critical joints, formed-in-place liquid gasket (FIPG) compounds, or gaskets made from soft, conformable material are used.

To be effective, gaskets are designed to crush and become thinner as the mating parts are bolted together. Once a gasket has been used, it is unlikely that it can be reused without leaking. Plan to use new gaskets when reassembling components. This is also true for other types of seals such as O-rings and copper washers.

Some gaskets, such as head gaskets, are directional and must be oriented correctly. Be sure to install directional gaskets with correct orientation.

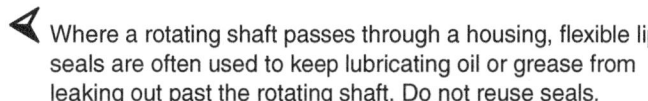Where a rotating shaft passes through a housing, flexible lip seals are often used to keep lubricating oil or grease from leaking out past the rotating shaft. Do not reuse seals.

When removing a seal, take care to avoid damaging, scratching or scoring housing bore or shaft surfaces. Even minor damage to sealing surfaces can cause leaks and premature wear.

When installing a seal, coat seal circumference with oil. Also coat lip with oil so that it does not run dry on rotating shaft. It is important to install the seal straight (not cocked), and without damage. Use a seal driver that is almost equal to seal outside diameter. A socket of appropriate size can also be used.

Be sure that seal lip faces correct direction. Some seals are directional, and special installation instructions apply. Usually, lip faces inward, or toward fluid that it is retaining. Note orientation of old seal before removal.

BUYING PARTS

Most maintenance and repair procedures described in this book require the installation of new parts, lubricants, coolant, and other supplies. Plan to have the necessary tools, new parts and supplies on hand before beginning work. Some maintenance and repair procedures, such as engine valve adjustment, require partial disassembly in order to determine specific parts needs. Read the procedure carefully, and make arrangements to obtain needed parts while your vehicle is disassembled.

Genuine Toyota parts

◀ Genuine Toyota replacement parts from an authorized Toyota dealer are designed and manufactured to the same high standards as original parts. Often, replacement parts incorporate improvements and actually perform better than original parts. Genuine Toyota replacement parts have the correct materials, are manufactured to the same specifications and are guaranteed to fit and work. Genuine replacement parts may also include a limited warranty.

Many independent repair shops use genuine Toyota parts. Even though these parts are sometimes more expensive, the shop knows that they may be taking unnecessary risks with third-party components.

Non-returnable parts

Some purchased parts cannot be returned for credit or refund, even if they are not the correct part for the car. Frequently, electrical parts cannot be returned, for example, because they can easily sustain internal damage.

Buy all parts, and especially electrical parts carefully. Be sure that replacements are needed for all of the components that you are buying. Seek assistance from a dealer, independent shop, or other expert to verify your diagnosis before purchasing parts that cannot be returned.

Information needed to purchase parts

Model: In general, it is important to know the correct model designation for your vehicle. This is less important with the Prius, since there have been only two US models sold to date:

• 2001 - 2003: NHW11 model

• 2004 - 2008: NHW20 model

◀ **Model year** and the vehicle year of manufacture may or may not be the same. An early 2007 model may have actually been manufactured late in 2006, for example. Prius model year information is listed on the manufacturing label on the driver's door B-pillar.

Date of manufacture can be helpful when ordering replacement parts, and when determining if any recalls are applicable to your vehicle. Sometimes, changes are made to vehicle components partway through a model year. The month and year of manufacture is listed on the manufacturing label on the driver's door B-pillar.

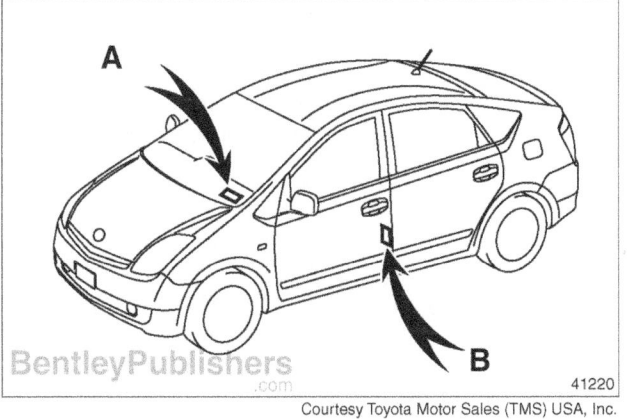

Courtesy Toyota Motor Sales (TMS) USA, Inc.

◀ **Vehicle identification number (VIN)** is a 17-digit combination of letters and numbers unique to each vehicle. The VIN appears on the registration documents, and on the vehicle in several places. By law the VIN must be clearly visible on the lower left corner of the windshield. For anti-theft purposes, the VIN must also appear on major body parts. See page viii for VIN decoder.

TOOLS

Most maintenance and repair procedures can be accomplished with a good selection of basic hand tools. Hand tools are readily available from a large number of sources and retail outlets, and vary widely in quality and cost.

Avoid purchasing the cheapest tools for several reasons. Some are so weak that they are likely to break with the first use. Personal injury and damage to the vehicle can result. It is not difficult to find high quality tools that are similar to the most expensive for less money, and often with a lifetime guarantee.

Some repair procedures described in this book require the use of special tools, such as a spring compressor or specialized electronic tester. These special tools are named, and where possible, the Toyota Special Service Tool number (SST) is provided. These special tools can be purchased at an authorized Toyota dealer or on this internet site: **http://toyota.spx.com**. Available alternatives to Toyota special tools are also provided where possible.

Required basic tools

Basic hand tools recommended for the maintenance and repair procedures in this book are described here.

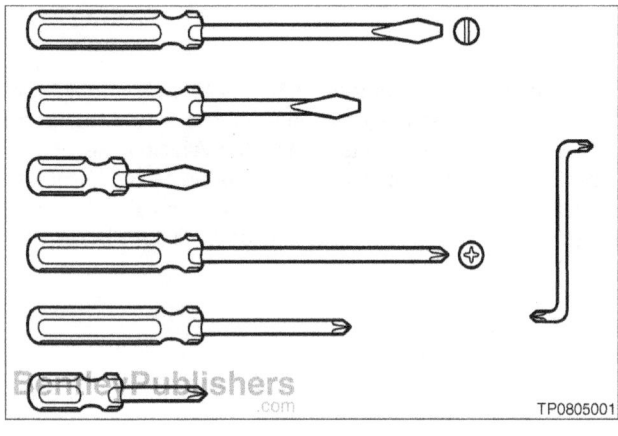

◄ **Screwdrivers.** Fasteners accepting three different types of screwdrivers can be found on Prius models. A selection of different sizes and shank lengths is required for these types of screwdrivers:

- Flat blade
- Phillips
- Torx®

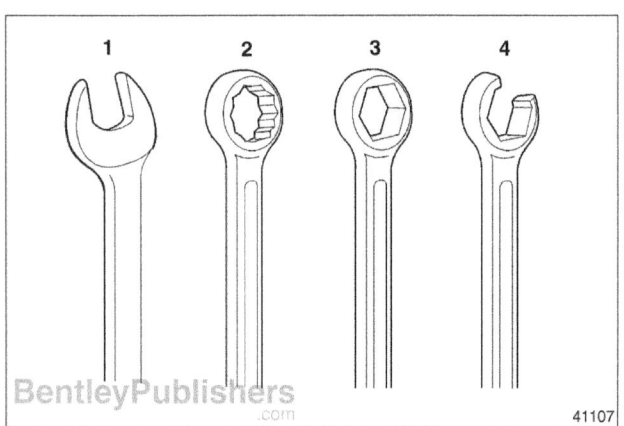

◄ **Wrenches** are made in different forms for different uses.

1. Open-end wrench can be used in limited spaces, but you cannot exert maximum torque because the wrench grips the hex head of the fastener on only two sides.

2. Box-end wrench can be used to exert the greatest torque on a fastener, since the wrench grips the hex head of the fastener on all sides. Box-end wrenches are available in 6-point and 12-point varieties. A 12-point box-end wrench is better where there is limited space to "swing" the wrench.

3. 6-point box-end wrench can be used to exert more torque.

4. For hex fasteners on fluid lines such as brake lines or fuel lines, a flare-nut wrench is the best choice. A flare-nut wrench provides the advantages of a box-wrench, but has an opening permitting the wrench to be slipped over the line or hose to be disconnected.

Combination wrenches are open-end wrenches on one end, and box-end wrenches on the other. They are popular and can be a cost-effective choice. As with all wrench types, various shank lengths are available.

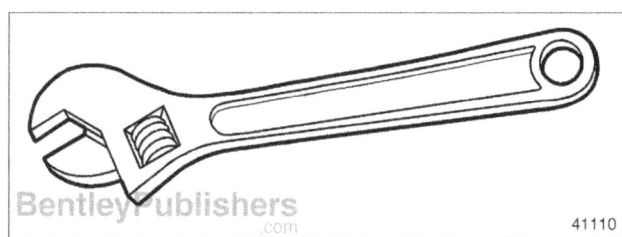

41110

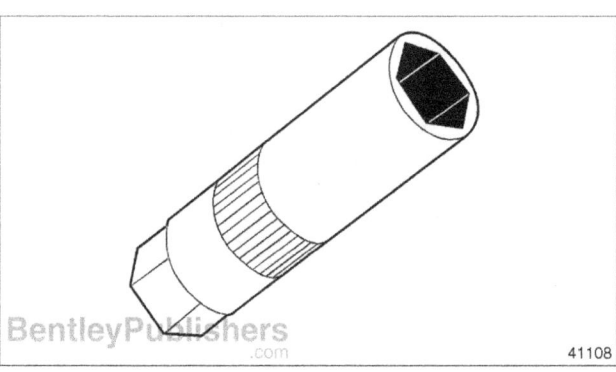

41108

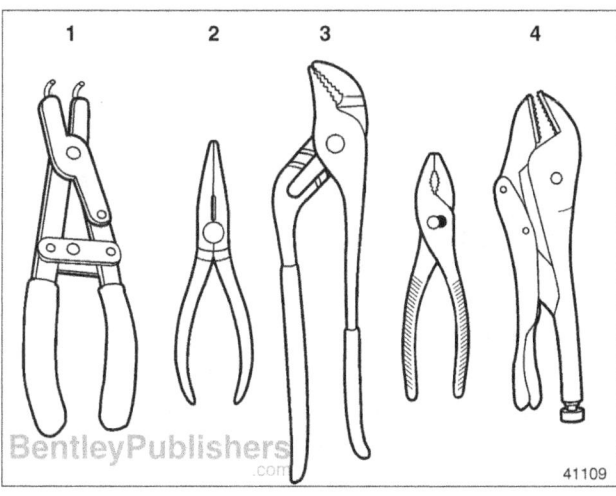

41109

◄ **Adjustable wrench** is a useful tool, but do not rely on it to exert high torque. Use extra care when using an adjustable wrench, as it can loosen, slip, and damage the fastener.

◄ **Sockets** used with ratchet handles perform the same tasks as box-end wrenches, but with greater flexibility. Extensions and universal joints allow fasteners with limited access to be reached more easily.

The square hole at one end of the socket is the drive. Sockets are available with three common drive sizes: ¼ in, ³/₈ in, and ½ in.

Sockets are available in standard (short) and deep (long) lengths, and with 6-point or 12-point internal flutes. As with box-end wrenches, a 6-point socket can be used to exert more torque on a fastener.

A special socket is available for spark plug removal and installation. This socket is deep and has a rubber insert to grip the spark plug ceramic insulator for protection and removal.

◄ **Pliers:** Many types of pliers are available and useful for a variety of tasks. Pliers can be used for holding irregular objects, bending, crimping, cutting, and removing special fasteners such as snap rings.

1. Snap-ring and circlip pliers have special tips and jaws which make the removal and installation of these fasteners easier.

2. Needle nose pliers are used for wiring work, gripping small objects and objects in difficult places.

3. The jaws of Channel-lock®, water-pump, and other adjustable-jaw pliers can be easily changed to grip a wide range of objects. The geometry and long handles of adjustable-jaw pliers allow great leverage and a strong grip.

4. Locking pliers such as Vise-Grip® pliers are useful for tightly gripping parts with one hand.

Torque wrench is used to tighten fasteners precisely to a predetermined specification. Many maintenance and repair procedures in this book require fasteners to be tightened with a torque wrench.

Torque wrenches with ranges of 0 - 200 in-lb (inch-pounds), and 0 - 200 ft-lb (foot-pounds) are specified in this book. Use the smaller torque wrench with the 0 - 200 in-lbf range when the torque specification is 10 Nm or less.

Torque unit conversion	
1 ft-lb	12 in-lb
1 ft-lb	1.4 Nm
1 Nm	0.7 ft-lb
1 Nm	8.9 in-lb

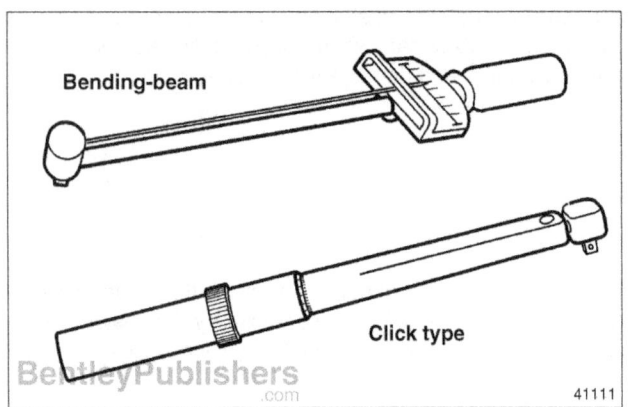

Bending-beam

Click type

41111

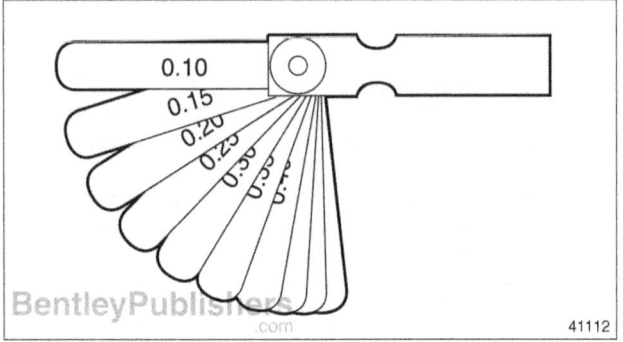

0.10
0.15
0.20
0.25
0.30

41112

41230

Several types of torque wrench are available, and features vary. The illustration shows two common types of torque wrench: the bending-beam type, and the click type.

The bending-beam type torque wrench is usually the least expensive but also the least accurate. The main beam of the tool bends as torque is increased. A pointer, which does not bend with the beam, indicates torque value on a scale. Since the scale is quite small, and since the user must do two things at once (apply torque and read the scale), this type of torque wrench is usually not very precise.

Click type torque wrenches resemble ratchet handles. Usually, the handle grip can be screwed in and out to preset the desired torque value on a micrometer-type scale. When the fastener is tightened to the preset torque value, this type of tool gives an audible click, and the handle "breaks away" or moves noticeably. This feedback tells you that the desired torque value has been reached.

Typically (but not always), torque specifications assume that fastener threads have been lightly lubricated. Be aware that torque values and actual clamping force created by the tightened fastener can vary tremendously depending upon cleanliness, condition, and lubrication. Fastener threads must be in good condition. Follow the manufacturer's recommendations.

Feeler gauges are precisely made thin metal strips that are used to measure small clearances. Normally, feeler gauges are supplied as a set in a holder or housing, although feeler gauge strips are also available individually. Each strip or leaf has its thickness marked.

Jacks and jack stands

Jacks can be used to lift your Prius, but do not rely on the jack to hold the vehicle. Jacks and other hydraulic devices are temporary lifting devices. Use for lifting purposes only. Support the vehicle on jack stands made for the purpose before working under the vehicle. Use only quality equipment that you can trust.

Jack stands: Use strong jack stands with a load rating more than sufficient to support the vehicle. Use jack stands that are designed for this purpose. Do not use blocks of wood, concrete blocks, bricks, etc. These may fail suddenly under load and are not suitable substitutes.

Select jack stands with a wide base for stability, and a positive method for locking the raised support.

See **Jacking and Lifting** in this chapter.

Digital multimeter (DMM)

Digital multimeter (DMM): Sensitive electrical components in microprocessors or integrated circuits may be damaged if tested with an analog multimeter. Analog meters with sweep needle displays have relatively low impedance. This can allow excessive current to flow in the circuit being tested and can damage sensitive electronics. Use only certified high impedance equipment such as a digital multimeter (DMM) for such tests.

The DMM can be used to measure voltage, resistance, and current in circuits.

> **CAUTION—**
> * Do not use a 12-volt test light, analog multimeter or other high current test device when testing sensitive circuits that have microprocessors and integrated circuits. Excessive current can damage the circuit being tested.

USING TOYOTA TIS

The Toyota technical information system (TIS) provides service and maintenance information in an electronic format over an internet connection. TIS is a comprehensive and easy-to-navigate database that includes service information for most Toyota, Lexus, and Scion brand models from 1990 onward. Included are:

* Repair manuals
* Technical service bulletins (TSBs)
* Service campaign
* Wiring diagrams.

There are hot links which provide quick navigation to related topics, and pages can be downloaded, saved and printed. A keyword search feature is also included. TIS is a good resource for technical information beyond the scope of this book. Access requires a subscription fee. The Toyota TIS internet address is **https://techinfo.toyota.com**.

MAINTENANCE SCHEDULES

Service recommendations

Toyota recommends servicing the 2004 - 2008 Prius every 5,000 miles or 6 months, whichever comes first. In general, Toyota service requirements are approximately equivalent to the maintenance requirements that other automobile manufacturers specify.

Oil change service tasks are listed in **Table a**.

15,000 mile inspection tasks are listed in **Table b**. These include oil change service tasks plus additional ones.

30,000 mile inspection tasks are listed in **Table c**. These include 15,000 mile service tasks plus additional ones.

Finally, long-interval additional service is listed in **Table d**.

Toyota may update recommended maintenance procedures and requirements. The information contained here is as accurate as possible at the time of publication. If necessary, consult an authorized Toyota dealer for the latest information on factory-recommended maintenance.

Except where noted, maintenance tasks apply to all models and model years covered by this manual. The "repair information in" column refers to the chapter in this manual where the relevant repair information can be found.

In addition to regular maintenance items listed, additional services are recommended when the vehicle is operated under special or severe service conditions, consisting of driving on unpaved dirt or dusty roads.

Table a. Oil service (every 5000 miles or 6 months)	Tools required	New parts required	Warm engine required	Repair information in chapter
Service under normal conditions				
Engine oil and oil filter, change	*	*	*	4
Tires, rotate	*			8
Brake pads, rotors, shoes, drums, inspect				8
Service under special or severe conditions				
Ball joints and rubber boots, inspect				8
Axle shaft rubber boots, inspect				8
Engine air filter, inspect				5
Steering linkage and rubber boots, inspect				8
Chassis fasteners, inspect and tighten	*			8

Table b. Major service 1 (every 15,000 miles or 18 months)	Tools required	New parts required	Warm engine required	Repair information in
Service under normal conditions				
Engine oil and oil filter, change	*	*	*	5
Tires, rotate	*			8
Brake pads, rotors, shoes, drums, inspect				8
Brake lines and hoses, inspect				8
Ball joints and rubber boots, inspect				8
Axle shaft rubber boots, inspect				8
Engine and transaxle / inverter coolant, inspect				5, 7
Radiator, condenser, inspect				5
Exhaust system and mounts, inspect				
Steering linkage and rubber boots, inspect				8
Transaxle lubricant, inspect				7
Service under special or severe conditions				
Engine air filter, inspect				5
Chassis fasteners, inspect and tighten	*			8

Table c. Major service 2 (every 30,000 miles or 36 months)	Tools required	New parts required	Warm engine required	Repair information in chapter
Service under normal conditions				
Engine oil and oil filter, change	∗	∗	∗	5
Tires, rotate	∗			8
Cabin air filter, replace		∗		9
Engine air filter, replace		∗		5
Brake pads, rotors, shoes, drums, inspect				8
Brake lines and hoses, inspect				8
Ball joints and rubber boots, inspect				8
Axle shaft rubber boots, inspect				8
Engine and transaxle / inverter coolant, inspect				5, 7
Radiator, condenser, inspect				5
Exhaust system and mounts, inspect				
Fuel lines and connections, fuel tank strap, fuel tank vapor and vent system hoses, inspect				6
Fuel filler cap gasket, inspect				6
Steering linkage and rubber boots, inspect				8
Service under special or severe conditions				
Chassis fasteners, inspect and tighten	∗			8

Table d. Additional service requirements	Tools required	New parts required	Warm engine required	Repair information in chapter
Every 60,000 miles or 72 months				
Engine drive belt, inspect				5
Engine valve clearance, inspect	∗			5
Every 75,000 miles or 90 months				
Engine drive belt, inspect				5
Every 100,000 miles or 120 months				
Engine and transaxle / inverter coolant, replace	∗	∗		5, 7
Every 105,000 miles or 126 months				
Engine drive belt, inspect				5
Every 120,000 miles or 144 months				
Spark plugs, replace PZEV vehicles sold in CA, MA, ME, NY, VT: Replace spark plugs at 150,000 miles	∗	∗		5

TP08005002
Courtesy Toyota Motor Sales (TMS) USA, Inc.

5

Engine

Overview, preventative maintenance and repairs

GENERAL

This chapter covers high frequency engine maintenance and service procedures for the Prius. A selection of hand tools is required for most of these procedures. Special tools may also be required. Be sure to read **4 Service and Repair Fundamentals** before starting work.

Hybrid safety

In addition to the safety warnings given here, always read and observe the **Warnings**, **Cautions** and safety procedures in **3 Safety** before working on vehicle. Orange-colored cables carry lethal high voltage. Use extreme care when working near high voltage cables and components.

> **WARNING—**
> - *Risk of electrocution! Avoid touching orange-colored high voltage wiring and high voltage components unless you are certain that high voltage is not present.*
> - *The Prius hybrid system has voltages as high as 500 volts. Voltages over 60 volts DC and 25 volts AC are a shock hazard.*

The Prius engine may start at any time if the hybrid system is in **READY** mode. See **3 Safety** for instructions on turning OFF the hybrid system.

> **WARNING—**
> - *Be sure hybrid system is OFF when servicing vehicle (READY indicator not illuminated). Failure to switch the hybrid system OFF could result in engine start at any time.*

Table a is a listing of repair procedures in this chapter and the hybrid safety requirements for each.

Table a. Hybrid safety requirements for repair procedures			
Procedure	Switch hybrid system OFF	Disconnect 12-volt battery	Remove service plug
Engine compartment cover removal	✓		
Engine oil service	✓		
Engine air filter service	✓		
Serpentine belt service	✓		
Ignition coils and spark plug replacement	✓	✓	
Valve clearance adjustment	✓	✓	
Engine coolant service	✓		
Coolant pump replacement	✓		
Coolant thermostat replacement	✓		
Engine cooling fan replacement	✓	✓	
Radiator replacement	✓	✓	

Warnings and Cautions

> **WARNING—**
> - *When draining automotive fluids, collect in suitable containers. Do not use food or beverage containers that might mislead someone into drinking from them.*
> - *Store flammable fluids away from fire hazards.*
> - *Wipe up spills at once, but do not store oily towels which can ignite and burn spontaneously.*

> **CAUTION—**
> - *Some procedures require that you disconnect the 12-volt auxiliary battery. This causes loss of radio and navigation system presets and power window initialization. Record radio and navigation system presets before disconnecting battery. Reinitialize windows after reconnecting battery. See* **10 Electrical System, Lights**.

5

ENGINE COMPARTMENT COVERS

Radiator cover, removing

– Switch hybrid system OFF (READY indicator not illuminated). See **3 Safety**.

> **WARNING—**
> • *Be sure hybrid system is OFF when servicing vehicle (READY indicator not illuminated). Failure to switch the hybrid system OFF could result in engine start at any time.*

◄ Remove 6 retainers (**arrows**) on radiator cover.

◄ To remove retainers:
- Turn center pin ¼ turn with Phillips screwdriver until center pin lifts.
- Use small flat-blade screwdriver to gently pry out pin and retainer.

– Remove radiator cover.

Engine splash shields, removing

– Switch hybrid system OFF (READY indicator not illuminated). See **3 Safety**.

> **WARNING—**
> • *Be sure hybrid system is OFF when servicing vehicle (READY indicator not illuminated). Failure to switch the hybrid system OFF could result in engine start at any time.*

– Raise vehicle and support safely. See **4 Service and Repair Fundamentals**.

> **WARNING—**
> • *Make sure the vehicle is stable and well supported at all times. Use a professional automotive lift or jack stands designed for the purpose. A floor jack is not adequate support.*

◀ Remove lower front splash shield (9 fasteners). Pull shield out toward rear of car.

◀ Remove left or right engine splash shield mounting fasteners. Remove splash shield(s) as necessary.

> **NOTE—**
> • *Right splash shield fasteners show. Left shield is retained in similar way.*

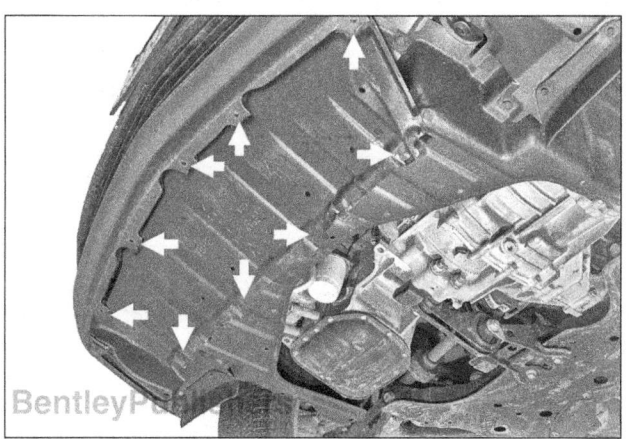

Right splash shield

Left splash shield

TP08006017

Courtesy Toyota Motor Sales (TMS) USA, Inc.

ENGINE OIL SERVICE

Engine oil, checking level

> **WARNING—**
> • *Greases, lubricants and other automotive chemicals contain toxic substances, many of which are absorbed directly through the skin. When checking or changing engine oil, use hand and eye protection and avoid prolonged direct skin contact.*

– Switch hybrid system OFF (READY indicator not illuminated). See **3 Safety**.

> **WARNING—**
> • *Be sure hybrid system is OFF when servicing vehicle (READY indicator not illuminated). Failure to switch the hybrid system OFF could result in engine start at any time.*

– Check oil level with car on level surface, engine warm and after engine has stopped for a few minutes.

◄ Check oil level by pulling out dipstick and wiping it clean. Reinsert dipstick fully, then withdraw again.

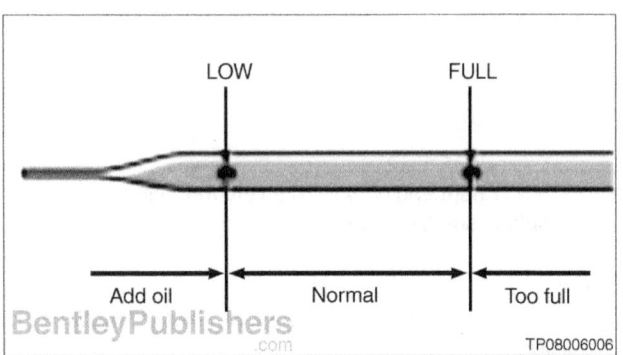

Courtesy Toyota Motor Sales (TMS) USA, Inc.

◄ Engine oil level is correct when between two marks at end of dipstick.

– If oil level is low, check for leaks, then add correct specification oil.

Prius engine oil specifications	
API grade	SL energy conserving (ILSAC)
Viscosity	5W - 30 SAE

◄ Remove oil filler cap (**arrow**) on top of cylinder head cover.

– Add only amount of oil required to bring level up to FULL mark on dipstick.

– Reinstall dipstick and oil filler cap.

Engine oil and filter, changing

See maintenance schedules in **4 Service and Repair Fundamentals** for recommended engine oil and filter service intervals.

The following items will be required to complete this job:

- oil filter
- oil filter wrench (Toyota special tool SST 09228-06501 or equivalent), drain plug wrench
- oil drain plug sealing washer
- oil drain pan

> **WARNING** —
> - *Hot oil scalds. Wear protective clothing and gloves.*
> - *Greases, lubricants and other automotive chemicals contain toxic substances. When checking or changing engine oil, use hand and eye protection and avoid prolonged direct skin contact. Wear protective clothing and gloves.*
> - *Wash your skin thoroughly with soap and water, or use a water-less hand cleaner to remove any engine oil. Do not use gasoline, thinners or solvents.*

– Begin procedure with engine cold, run engine for a few minutes, just enough to warm engine oil. Switch hybrid system ON (READY indicator illuminated) until engine starts, or run engine in inspection mode. See **11 Diagnostics**.

– Switch hybrid system OFF (READY indicator not illuminated). See **3 Safety**.

> **WARNING** —
> - *Be sure hybrid system is OFF when servicing vehicle (READY indicator not illuminated). Failure to switch the hybrid system OFF could result in engine start at any time.*

◄ Remove oil filler cap (**arrow**) on top of cylinder head cover.

– Raise vehicle and support safely. See **4 Service and Repair Fundamentals**.

> **WARNING** —
> - *Make sure the vehicle is stable and well supported at all times. Use a professional automotive lift or jack stands designed for the purpose. A floor jack is not adequate support.*

– Place suitable oil drain pan beneath engine.

◄ Remove oil drain plug (**arrow**) and allow oil to drain.

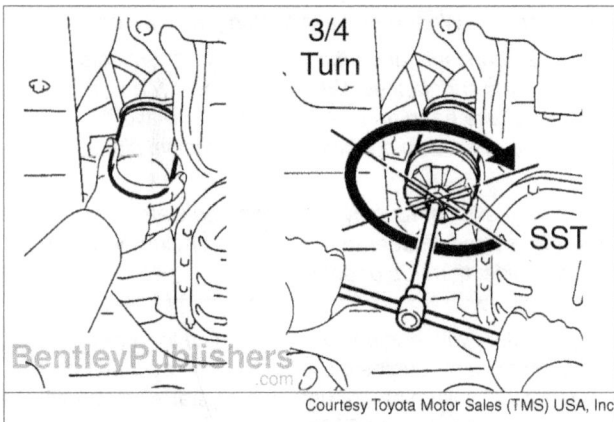

Courtesy Toyota Motor Sales (TMS) USA, Inc.

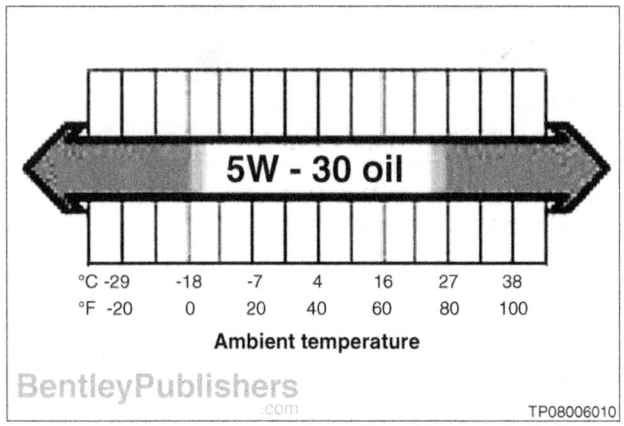

Courtesy Toyota Motor Sales (TMS) USA, Inc.

◄ Use oil filter wrench (Toyota special tool SST 09228-06501 or equivalent) to remove oil filter (**arrow**).

- Be prepared for dripping oil.
- Allow filter to drain into oil drain pan.

> **CAUTION—**
> - *Dispose of waste oil and filters in an environmentally responsible manner.*

– Inspect and wipe clean oil filter mounting flange.

– Apply film of oil to seal ring on new filter.

◄ Install filter until seal contacts mounting flange, then turn additional amount as recommended by filter manufacturer, typically ¾ turn. Use oil filter wrench to tighten filter if necessary.

– Inspect and clean oil drain plug.

– Replace oil drain plug gasket.

– Install oil drain plug and tighten to specification.

Tightening torque	
Oil drain plug to engine oil sump	38 Nm (28 ft-lb)

◄ Specified oil viscosity is suitable for a wide range of ambient temperatures.

Prius engine oil specifications	
API grade	SL energy conserving (ILSAC)
Viscosity	5W - 30 SAE
Oil capacity • with filter change • without filter change • dry fill	3.7 liters (3.9 US qt) 3.4 liters (3.6 US qt) 4.1 liters (4.3 US qt)

– Install oil filler cap.

– Switch hybrid system ON (READY indicator illuminated) until engine starts, or run engine in inspection Mode. See **11 Diagnostics**.

– Check for oil leaks.

– Switch hybrid system OFF (READY indicator not illuminated) and recheck oil level.

– Lower vehicle.

TP08006048

Courtesy Toyota Motor Sales (TMS) USA, Inc.

Engine oil change reminder, resetting

◄ The USA model Prius instrument panel is equipped with a MAINT REQD indicator (**arrow**) which serves as an engine oil change reminder. The indicator is a two stage reminder:

- Approx. 7,200 km (4,500 mi) since last reset:
  With IG-ON, indicator illuminates for approx. 3 seconds, then flashes for approx. 12 seconds, then switches OFF.

- Approx. 8,000 km (5,000 mi) since last reset:
  With IG-ON, indicator illuminates continuously.

After changing engine oil, reset indicator as follows:

— With brake pedal *not* depressed, push and release POWER button twice to select IG-ON. Check that odometer is displayed (not trip odometer).

— Push and release POWER button to turn hybrid system OFF (READY indicator not illuminated).

— While depressing and holding trip meter reset button, and with brake pedal *not* depressed, push and release POWER button twice to select IG-ON.

— Continue to depress trip meter reset button for at least 5 seconds. Odometer reads 000000 and indicator light switches OFF.

— Release trip meter reset button and push POWER button to turn hybrid system OFF (READY indicator not illuminated).

If reset procedure is not successful, oil change reminder indicator continues to flash. If this occurs, repeat reset procedure.

5

DRAIN 19mm
22 ft-lb
FILTER 32mm
18 ft-lb

ENGINE AIR FILTER

Air filter, removing and installing

See maintenance schedules in **4 Service and Repair Fundamentals** for recommended air filter service intervals.

– Switch hybrid system OFF (READY indicator not illuminated). See **3 Safety**.

> **WARNING—**
> • Be sure hybrid system is OFF when servicing vehicle (READY indicator not illuminated). Failure to switch the hybrid system OFF could result in engine start at any time.

◀ Unclip 4 spring latches (**arrows**) on air filter housing cover.

◀ Lift up air filter housing cover and remove air filter element.

– Installation is reverse of removal.

Air filter, checking and cleaning

– Switch hybrid system OFF (READY indicator not illuminated). See **3 Safety**.

> **WARNING—**
> • Be sure hybrid system is OFF when servicing vehicle (READY indicator not illuminated). Failure to switch the hybrid system OFF could result in engine start at any time.

– Remove air filter element. See **Air filter, removing and installing** in this chapter.

– Inspect condition of engine air filter element. Clean or replace element.

◀ If element is not extremely dirty, clean with compressed air.

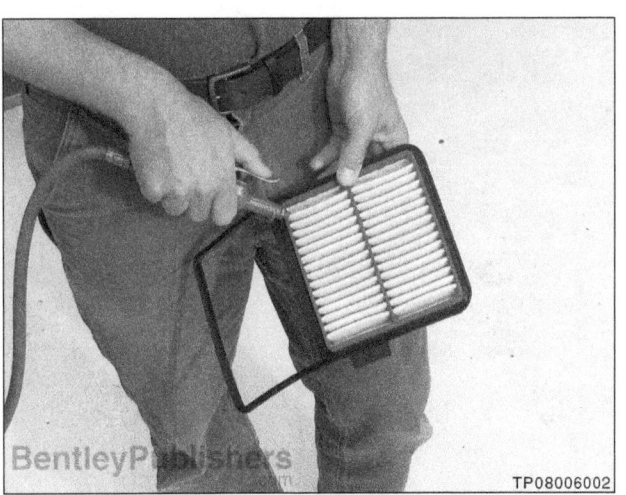

— Clean inside of air filter housing if necessary.

NOTE—

- *Oil on air filter element or in housing may indicate a stuck positive crankcase ventilation (PCV) valve. See* **6 Emission Controls**.

— Reinstall air filter element.

Air filter housing, removing and installing

— Switch hybrid system OFF (READY indicator not illuminated). See **3 Safety**.

WARNING—

- *Be sure hybrid system is OFF when servicing vehicle (READY indicator not illuminated). Failure to switch the hybrid system OFF could result in engine start at any time.*

◀ Working at air filter housing:

- Loosen air inlet hose clamp (**A**) and detach air inlet hose.
- Loosen throttle body hose clamp (**B**).
- Disconnect mass air flow sensor connector (**C**).

◀ Remove 2 air filter housing bolts (**arrows**).

— Lift and remove air filter housing assembly.

— Installation is reverse of removal. Replace hose clamps if necessary.

Tightening torque	
Air filter housing to bracket	7 Nm (62 in-lb)
Air inlet hose clamp	3 Nm (27 in-lb)

SERPENTINE BELT

Serpentine belt, inspecting and adjusting

The engine serpentine belt is a flat multi-ribbed belt with a long service life. The belt is at the front of the engine on the right side and is driven by the crankshaft. The serpentine belt drives the engine coolant pump only. The air-conditioning compressor is driven by an electric motor.

– Switch hybrid system OFF (READY indicator not illuminated). See **3 Safety**.

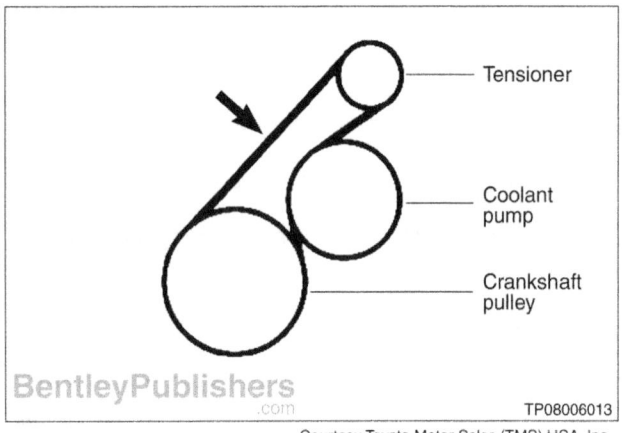

Small cracks   Missing piece   Frayed

BentleyPublishers
.com   TP08006011

Courtesy Toyota Motor Sales (TMS) USA, Inc.

WARNING —
• *Be sure hybrid system is OFF when servicing vehicle (READY indicator not illuminated). Failure to switch the hybrid system OFF could result in engine start at any time.*

◄ Visually check serpentine belt condition.

• Small cracks on ribbed side are acceptable.

• Replace belt if excessively worn, frayed, cracked, or if pieces of belt are missing. See **Serpentine belt, removing and installing** in this chapter.

◄ Measure serpentine belt tension: Apply approx. 22 lb force at point shown (**arrow**).

Serpentine belt tension (manual method)	
Belt deflection with 22 lb force	
• New belt (< 5 min. running time)	9 - 12 mm (0.35 - 0.47 in)
• Used belt (> 5 min. running time)	11 - 15 mm (0.43 - 0.59 in)

Tensioner

Coolant pump

Crankshaft pulley

BentleyPublishers
.com   TP08006013

Courtesy Toyota Motor Sales (TMS) USA, Inc.

◄ Alternatively, use Denso BTG-20 (Toyota special tool SST 95506-00020), Borroughs BT-33-73F, or equivalent belt tension gauge to measure belt tension.

Serpentine belt tension (belt tension gauge method)	
Belt tension using tool	
• New belt (< 5 min. running time)	99 - 121 lb
• Used belt (> 5 min. running time)	55 - 77 lb

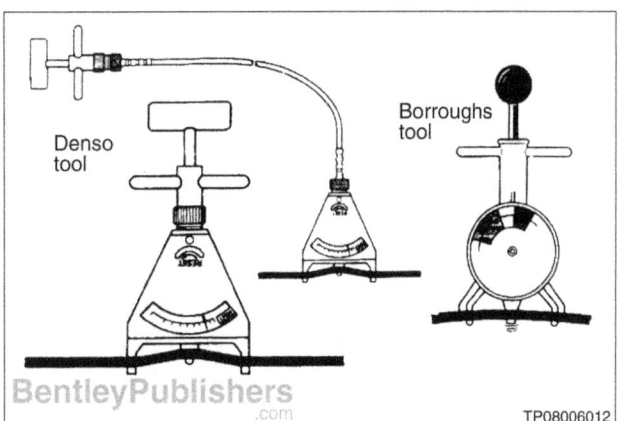

Denso tool

Borroughs tool

BentleyPublishers
.com   TP08006012

Courtesy Toyota Motor Sales (TMS) USA, Inc.

Loosen air filter housing inlet air duct clamp (**arrow**) and remove duct.

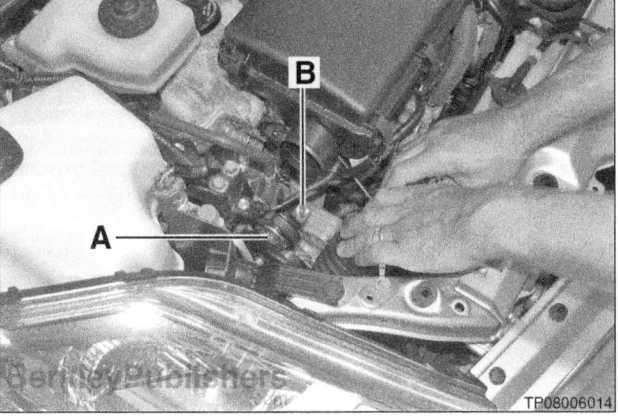

If belt tension is not within specifications, adjust belt tension.
  • Loosen tensioner lock nut (**A**).
  • Loosen or tighten tensioner adjusting bolt (**B**) as necessary.

– Using socket wrench on crankshaft pulley bolt, turn crankshaft at least 2 revolutions before rechecking belt tension.

– Tighten tensioner lock nut to specification.

Tightening torque	
Belt tensioner lock nut to tensioner pulley	40 Nm (30 ft-lb)

Serpentine belt, removing and installing

See maintenance schedules in **4 Service and Repair Fundamentals** for recommended belt service intervals.

– Switch hybrid system OFF (READY indicator not illuminated). See **3 Safety**.

> *WARNING*—
> • *Be sure hybrid system is OFF when servicing vehicle (READY indicator not illuminated). Failure to switch the hybrid system OFF could result in engine start at any time.*

– Raise vehicle and support safely. See **4 Service and Repair Fundamentals**.

> *WARNING*—
> • *Make sure the vehicle is stable and well supported at all times. Use a professional automotive lift or jack stands designed for the purpose. A floor jack is not adequate support.*

– Remove right side splash shield underneath engine. See **Engine splash shields, removing** in this chapter.

Loosen air filter housing inlet air duct clamp (**arrow**) and remove duct.

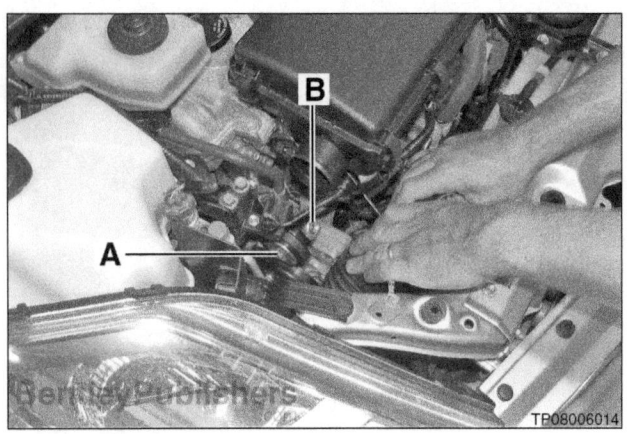

TP08006014

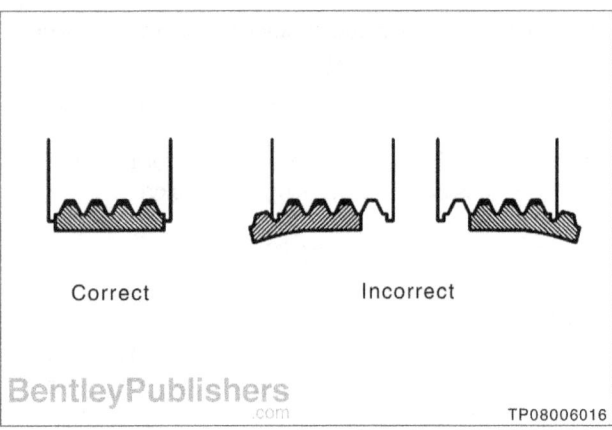

Correct   Incorrect

TP08006016

Courtesy Toyota Motor Sales (TMS) USA, Inc.

◀ Working at serpentine belt tensioner:

- Loosen tensioner lock nut (**A**).
- Loosen tensioner adjusting bolt (**B**) to slacken belt tension until belt can be removed.

◀ When reinstalling, make sure serpentine belt ribs are in pulley grooves.

– Adjust belt tension. See **Serpentine belt, inspecting and adjusting** in this chapter.

– When a new belt is installed, run engine for at least 5 minutes, then recheck belt tension. Use "used belt" specification when rechecking tension.

– Switch hybrid system ON (READY indicator illuminated) until engine starts, or run engine in inspection mode. See **11 Diagnostics**. Check for abnormal belt noises.

– Switch hybrid system OFF (READY indicator not illuminated). See **3 Safety**.

– Install engine splash shields and lower vehicle.

IGNITION COILS AND SPARK PLUGS

Ignition coils, removing and installing

The Prius engine uses a coil-on-spark-plug direct ignition system. Individual ignition coils are mounted on top of each spark plug.

> **WARNING**—
> • *To avoid personal injury, be sure the engine is cold before beginning this procedure.*

– Switch hybrid system OFF (READY indicator not illuminated). See **3 Safety**.

> **WARNING**—
> • *Be sure hybrid system is OFF when servicing vehicle (READY indicator not illuminated). Failure to switch the hybrid system OFF could result in engine start at any time.*

– Disconnect 12-volt auxiliary battery. See **3 Safety**.

> **CAUTION**—
> • *Auxiliary battery disconnection causes loss of radio and navigation system presets. Record presets before disconnecting battery.*

◀ Remove engine compartment relay block 2 mounting bolts (**arrows**). Move relay block to one side.

◀ Working at ignition coils:
• Unplug ignition coil electrical connectors (**A**).
• Remove ignition coil hold-down bolts (**B**).

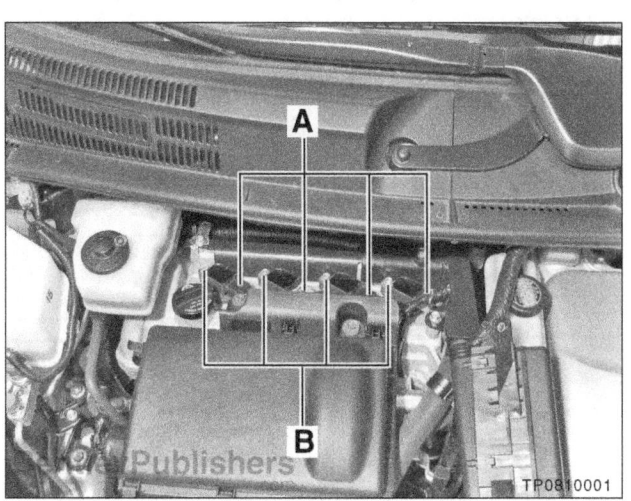

◀ Pull ignition coil straight upward to remove.

– Installation is reverse of removal, noting the following:

Tightening torques	
Ignition coil to cylinder head cover	9 Nm (80 in-lb)
Negative cable to 12-volt auxiliary battery	6 Nm (53 in-lb)
Relay block to cowl bulkhead	8.4 Nm (74 in-lb)

– Reconnect auxiliary battery and switch hybrid system ON (READY indicator illuminated) until engine starts, or run engine in inspection mode. See **11 Diagnostics**. Check engine operation.

– Reinitialize power windows. See **10 Electrical System, Lights**.

– Reprogram radio and navigation system presets (if applicable).

Spark plugs, removing and installing

The plugs are in deep wells between the camshafts on top of the engine below the ignition coils.

Toyota specifies iridium-tipped replacement spark plugs for long service life and consistently reliable spark.

> **WARNING—**
> • *To avoid personal injury, be sure the engine is cold before beginning this procedure.*

– Switch hybrid system OFF (READY indicator not illuminated). See **3 Safety**.

> **WARNING—**
> • *Be sure hybrid system is OFF when servicing vehicle (READY indicator not illuminated). Failure to switch the hybrid system OFF could result in engine start at any time.*

– Disconnect 12-volt auxiliary battery. See **3 Safety**.

> **CAUTION—**
> • *Auxiliary battery disconnection causes loss of radio and navigation system presets. Record presets before disconnecting battery.*

– Remove ignition coils. See **Ignition coils, removing and installing** in this chapter.

◀ Remove spark plugs using 16 mm (⅝ in) spark plug socket and extension.

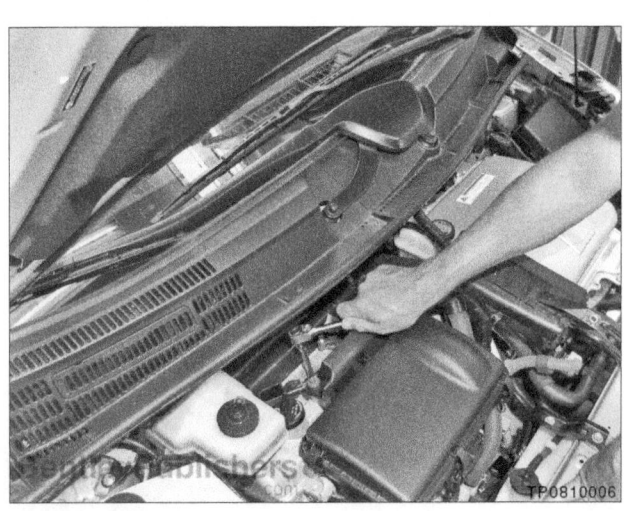

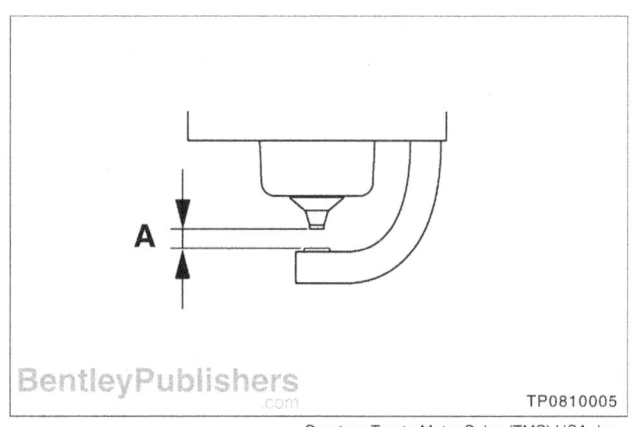

BentleyPublishers
.com

TP0810005

Courtesy Toyota Motor Sales (TMS) USA, Inc.

◀ Inspect spark plug condition.

- Check condition of threads and insulator.

- Check electrode gap **A**. If gap exceeds maximum specification, replace spark plugs.

Spark plug recommendation	
2004 - 2008 Prius	
• Denso	SK16R11
• NGK	IFR5A11

Spark plug gap	
Gap **A**	
• New spark plug	1.0 - 1.1 mm (0.039 - 0.043 in)
• Maximum	1.3 mm (0.051 in)

– Installation is reverse of removal. Lightly coat spark plug threads with anti-seize compound.

Tightening torques	
Ignition coil to cylinder head cover	9 Nm (80 in-lb)
Negative cable to 12-volt auxiliary battery	6 Nm (53 in-lb)
Spark plug to cylinder head	18 Nm (13 ft-lb)

– Reconnect 12-volt auxiliary battery and switch hybrid system ON (READY indicator illuminated) until engine starts, or run engine in inspection mode. See **11 Diagnostics**. Check engine operation.

– Reinitialize power windows. See **10 Electrical System, Lights**.

– Reprogram radio and navigation system presets (if applicable).

5

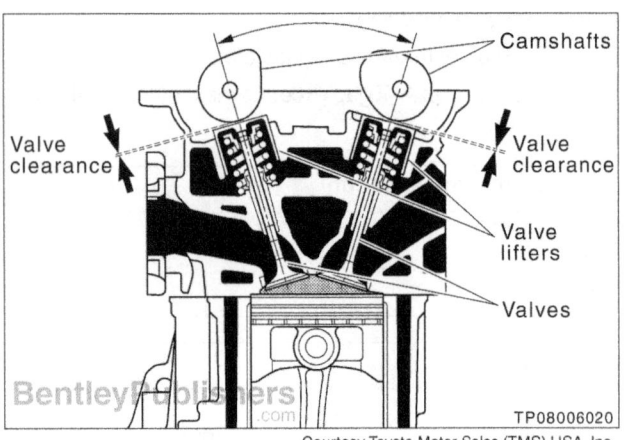

Valve clearance

Camshafts

Valve clearance

Valve lifters

Valves

TP08006020

Courtesy Toyota Motor Sales (TMS) USA, Inc.

VALVE CLEARANCE

Valve clearance, checking and adjusting

> **WARNING—**
> • *To avoid personal injury, be sure the engine is cold before beginning this procedure.*

◀ The Prius 1NZ-FXE engine has dual overhead camshafts (DOHC), and variable valve timing for the intake valves. Both intake and exhaust camshafts act directly on the valves through bucket-style valve lifters. The valve lifters are one-piece selective-fit with no separate adjustment shims.

Valve clearance is set as follows:

• Measure clearances.

• Remove camshafts.

• Remove and replace lifters. Lifters are available in 35 thicknesses varying in increments of 0.020 mm (0.0008 in), from 5.060 mm (0.1992 in) to 5.740 mm (0.2260 in).

— Checking and resetting valve clearance is a complicated job requiring special tools. Read the complete procedure before starting work.

— Switch hybrid system OFF (READY indicator not illuminated). See **3 Safety**.

> **WARNING—**
> • *Be sure hybrid system is OFF when servicing vehicle (READY indicator not illuminated). Failure to switch the hybrid system OFF could result in engine start at any time.*

— Disconnect 12-volt auxiliary battery. See **3 Safety**.

> **CAUTION—**
> • *Auxiliary battery disconnection causes loss of radio and navigation system presets. Record presets before disconnecting battery.*

— Raise vehicle and support safely. See **4 Service and Repair Fundamentals**.

> **WARNING—**
> • *Make sure the vehicle is stable and well supported at all times. Use a professional automotive lift or jack stands designed for the purpose. A floor jack is not adequate support.*

— Remove left and right engine splash shields. See **Engine splash shields, removing** in this chapter.

— Remove wiper arms, cowl cover and wiper assembly with wiper motor. See **9 Body** and **10 Electrical System, Lights**.

- Remove engine compartment upper rear bulkhead (cowl-top panel). See **9 Body**.

- Remove radiator cover. See **Radiator cover, removing** in this chapter.

- Remove air filter housing. See **Air filter housing, removing and installing** in this chapter.

◄ Working at brake master cylinder fluid reservoir:
- Detach electrical connector.
- Remove reservoir mounting bolts (**arrows**).
- Disengage reservoir retention claw (**inset**).

- Raise and suspend brake master cylinder reservoir with wire or string to create clearance for cylinder head cover removal.

> **CAUTION—**
> • *Keep brake master cylinder reservoir as level as possible to avoid brake fluid spills and to prevent air from entering brake fluid lines.*

Courtesy Toyota Motor Sales (TMS) USA, Inc.

◄ Working at brake master cylinder fluid reservoir:
- Disconnect hose and wire harness clamp from reservoir bracket (**arrows**).
- Remove bracket bolt (**inset**).
- Remove bracket.

- Remove windshield washer fluid reservoir. See **11 Electrical System, Lights**.

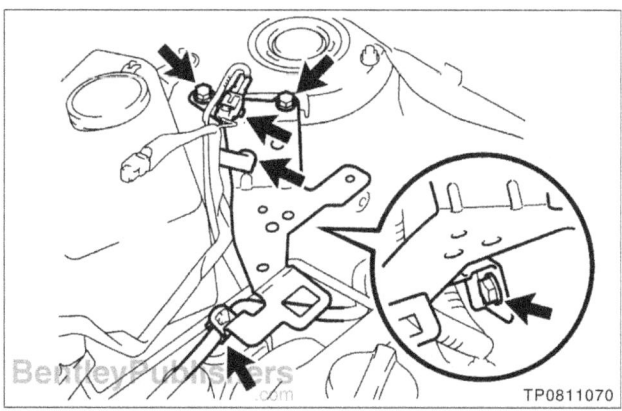

Courtesy Toyota Motor Sales (TMS) USA, Inc.

◄ Detach fuel injector and ignition electrical connectors (**arrows**).

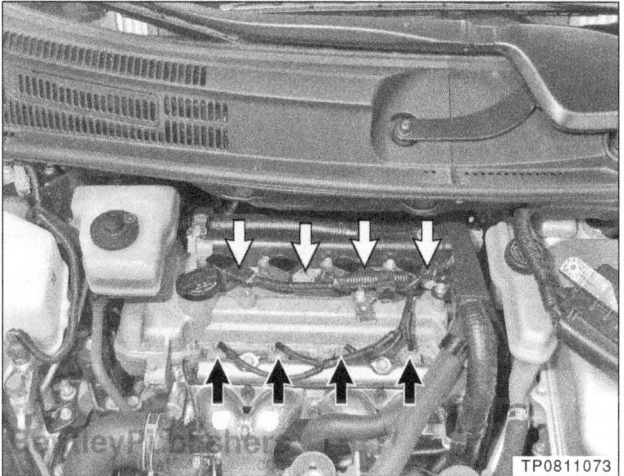

◀ Remove ignition coil and fuel injector wire loom clamp bolts (**arrows**). Tie loom to side.

– Remove brake master cylinder plastic shield.

– Disconnect cylinder head cover vent hoses.

– Remove ignition coils. See **Ignition coils, removing and installing** in this chapter.

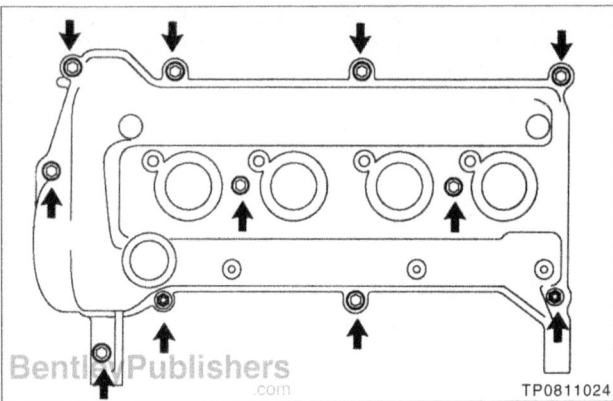

Courtesy Toyota Motor Sales (TMS) USA, Inc.

◀ Remove cylinder head cover fasteners (**arrows**) and lift off cover.

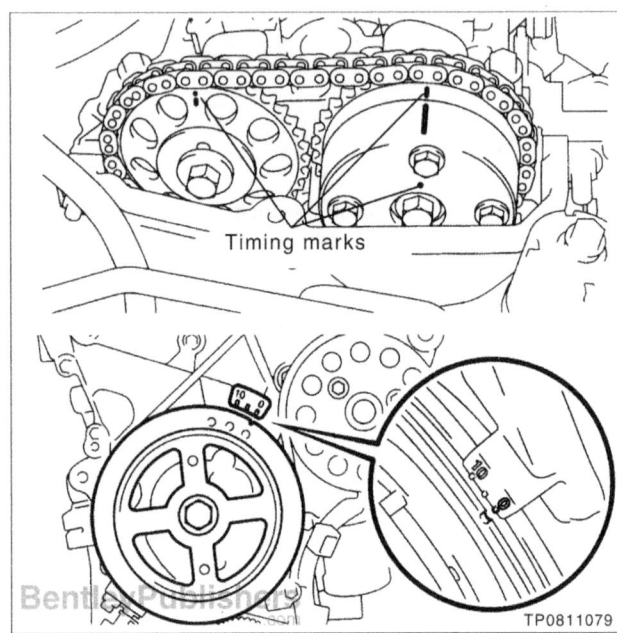

Timing marks

Courtesy Toyota Motor Sales (TMS) USA, Inc.

◀ To inspect valve clearance, set cylinder 1 to TDC compression stoke:

• Using a wrench on crankshaft pulley bolt, rotate crankshaft clockwise.

• Align crankshaft pulley timing mark notch with 0 timing mark (**inset**).

• Make sure camshaft sprocket timing marks are at 12 o'clock position as shown. If not, rotate crankshaft 1 revolution and align timing marks as shown.

• This indicates cylinder 1 TDC compression.

Cylinder 1 at TDC compression

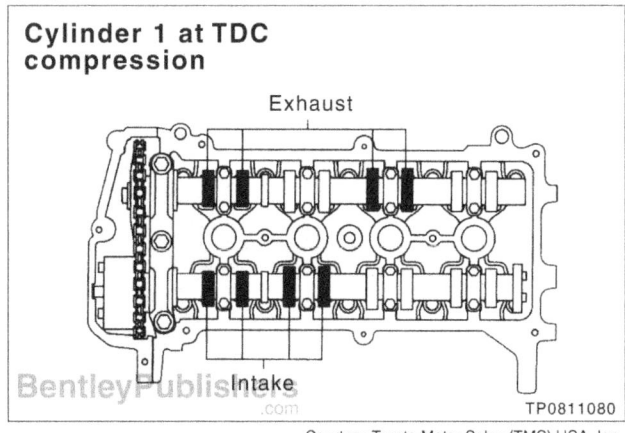

TP0811080

Cylinder 4 at TDC compression

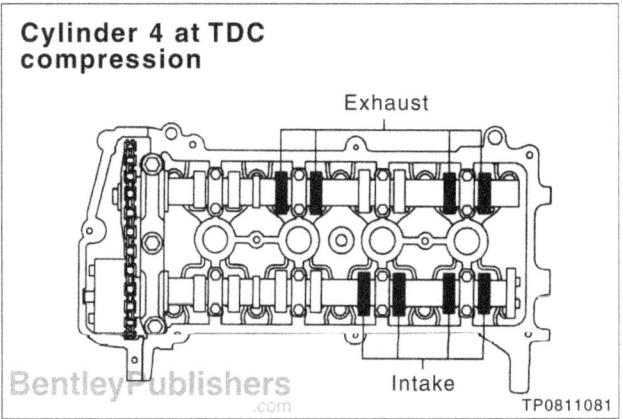

TP0811081

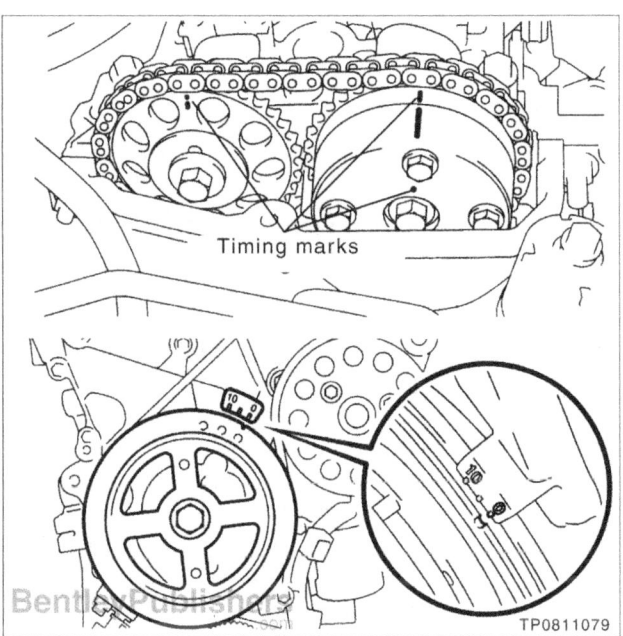

Timing marks

TP0811079

◄ Measure valve clearance for valves indicated by cam lobes shown black.

- Be sure engine is cold when measuring valve clearance.
- Use feeler gauge to measure clearance.
- Record measurements and compare with specifications in **Table b**.

– Rotate crankshaft clockwise 1 complete revolution and again make sure crankshaft pulley timing mark aligns with 0 timing mark.

- Make sure camshaft sprocket timing marks are *not* visible at top.
- This indicates cylinder 4 TDC compression.

◄ Measure valve clearance for valves indicated by cam lobes shown black.

- Be sure engine is cold when measuring valve clearance.
- Use feeler gauge to measure clearance.
- Record measurements and compare with specifications in **Table b**.

Table b. Prius valve clearance	
Intake valve	0.17 – 0.23 mm (0.007 – 0.009 in)
Exhaust valve	0.27 – 0.33 mm (0.011 – 0.013 in)

– If measurements are not within specifications, adjust valve clearance.

◄ To begin, set cylinder 1 to TDC compression stoke:

- Using a wrench on crankshaft pulley bolt, rotate crankshaft clockwise.
- Align crankshaft pulley timing mark notch with 0 timing mark (**inset**).
- Make sure camshaft sprocket timing marks are at 12 o'clock position as shown. If not, rotate crankshaft 1 revolution and align timing marks as shown.
- This indicates cylinder 1 TDC compression.

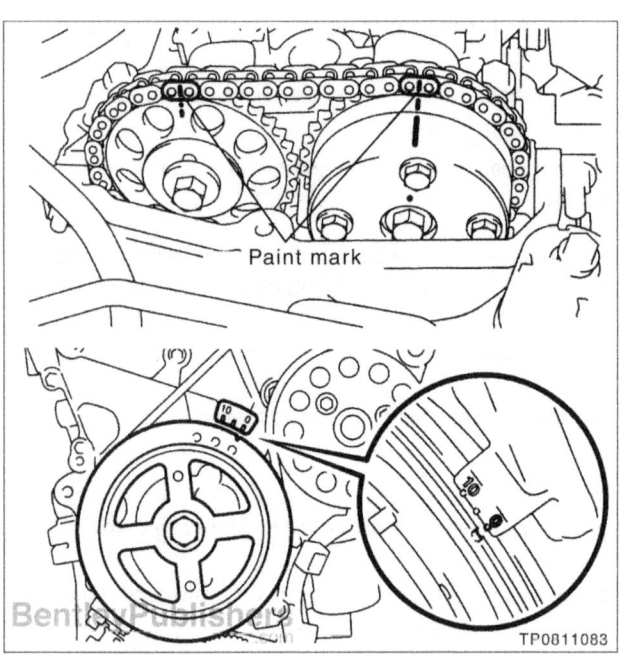

Paint mark

TP0811083

Courtesy Toyota Motor Sales (TMS) USA, Inc.

◀ Place paint marks on timing chain links to align with camshaft sprocket timing marks.

NOTE—

• *Wipe oil from timing chain links so that paint adheres.*

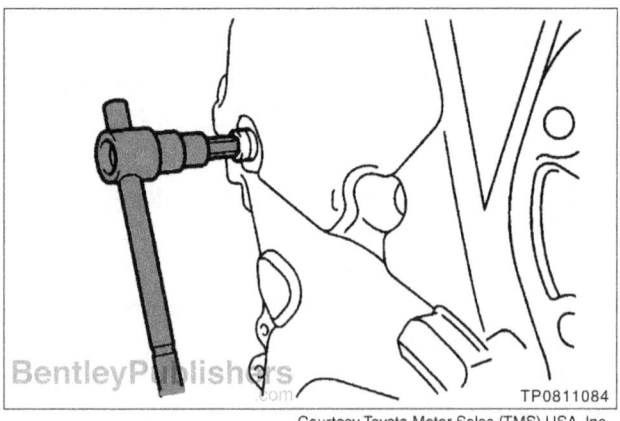

TP0811084

Courtesy Toyota Motor Sales (TMS) USA, Inc.

◀ Using 8 mm Allen wrench, remove service hole plug from engine timing cover.

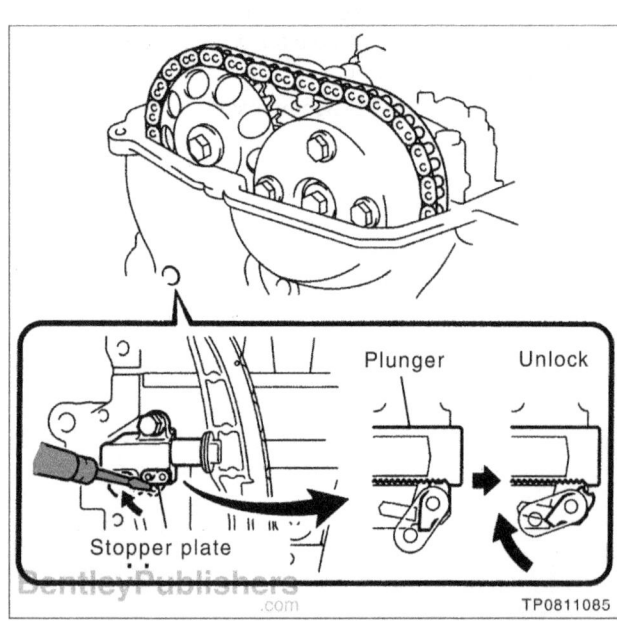

Plunger   Unlock

Stopper plate

TP0811085

Courtesy Toyota Motor Sales (TMS) USA, Inc.

◀ Use screwdriver inserted into service hole to lift and hold chain tensioner stopper plate as shown.

NOTE—

• *Lifting up on the chain tensioner stopper plate unlocks the chain tensioner plunger.*

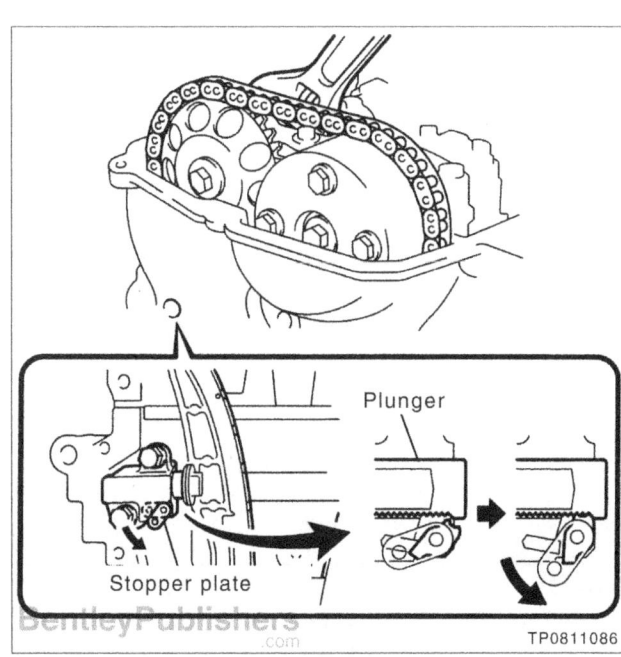

Plunger

Stopper plate

TP0811086

Courtesy Toyota Motor Sales (TMS) USA, Inc.

◀ Continue to lift and hold chain tensioner stopper plate,

- Place adjustable wrench on exhaust camshaft hex lobes (just behind camshaft sprocket).
- Rotate camshaft slightly clockwise. This retracts chain tensioner plunger.
- Remove screwdriver from chain tensioner, allowing tensioner to drop. This locks chain tensioner plunger in retracted position.

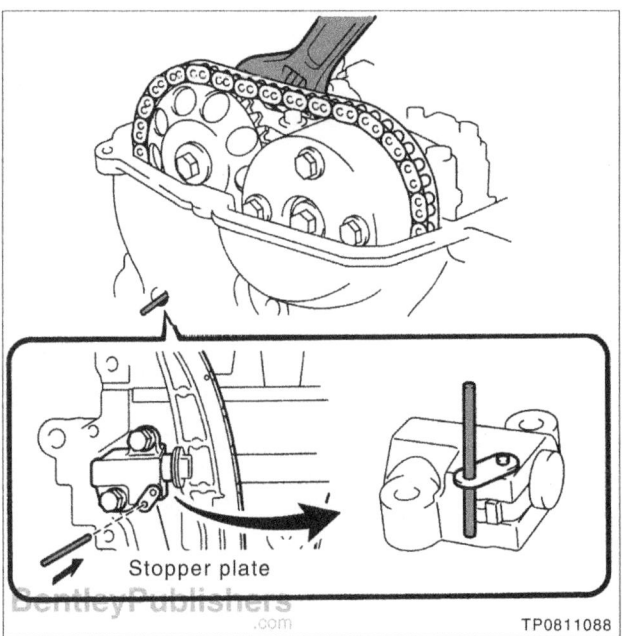

Stopper plate

TP0811088

Courtesy Toyota Motor Sales (TMS) USA, Inc.

◀ Insert 3.0 mm (0.118 in) dia. 3-inch-long pin or drill bit into chain tensioner stopper plate hole. This holds chain tensioner stopper plate in the DOWN and LOCKED position.

- If necessary, slightly rotate exhaust camshaft back and forth while inserting pin or drill bit.
- Use duct tape or equivalent to hold pin or drill bit in position.

SST
09023-38401

TP0811089

Courtesy Toyota Motor Sales (TMS) USA, Inc.

◀ While holding exhaust camshaft with adjustable wrench, use camshaft bolt wrench (Toyota special tool SST 09023-38401 or equivalent) to loosen exhaust camshaft bolt.

- Do not remove exhaust camshaft bolt at this time.

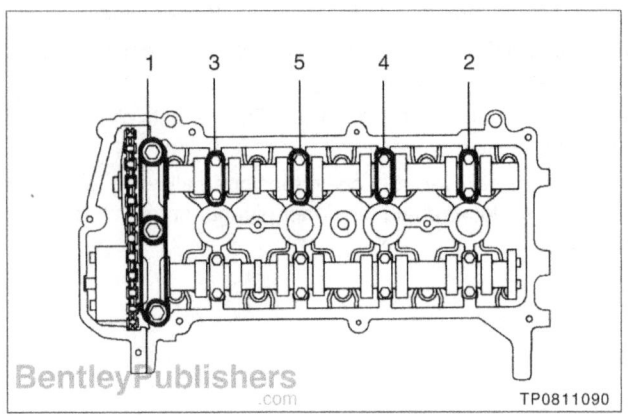

Courtesy Toyota Motor Sales (TMS) USA, Inc.

◄ Remove 5 exhaust camshaft bearing caps in order shown.

> **CAUTION—**
> • *Loosen bearing cap bolts evenly in several steps.*

> **NOTE—**
> • *Bearing cap 1 is a double cap for both exhaust and intake camshafts.*

— Remove exhaust camshaft sprocket bolt. Detach sprocket from camshaft.

— Remove exhaust camshaft from cylinder head.

— Disengage sprocket from timing chain and remove.

◄ Remove 4 intake camshaft bearing caps in order shown.

> **CAUTION—**
> • *Loosen bearing cap bolts evenly in several steps.*

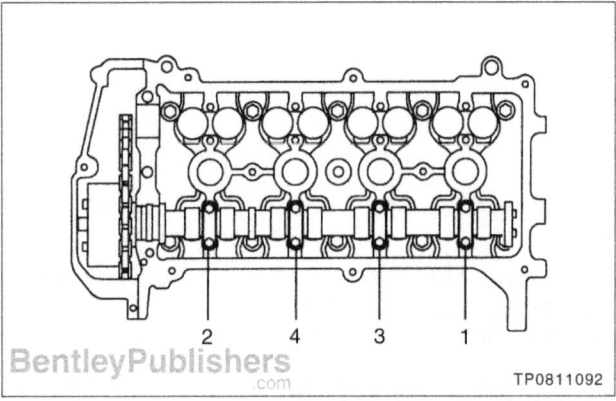

Courtesy Toyota Motor Sales (TMS) USA, Inc.

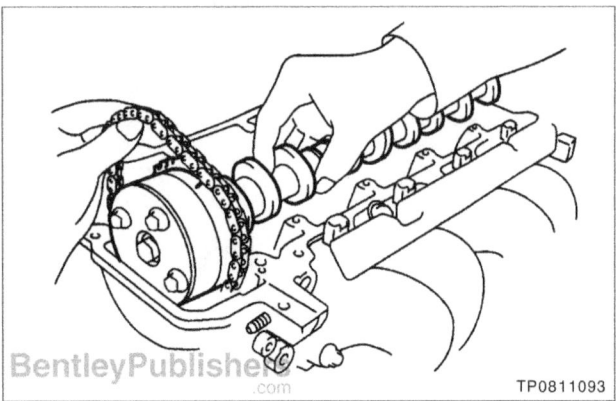

Courtesy Toyota Motor Sales (TMS) USA, Inc.

◄ Hold timing chain and lift out intake camshaft and timing sprocket.

> **CAUTION—**
> • *Do not allow chain to drop into engine. Keep timing chain under tension.*

◄ Secure timing chain with string or wire so it does not drop into engine.

> **CAUTION—**
> • *Cover opening in engine to prevent foreign objects from dropping into timing chain cover.*

Courtesy Toyota Motor Sales (TMS) USA, Inc.

— Referring to valve clearance measurement notes made previously, remove first lifter requiring clearance adjustment.

> **CAUTION—**
> - *Remove lifters one at a time.*
> - *Keep lifters in original locations. Do not exchange or mix up lifters. Do not remove lifters with correct clearance.*

◀ Using a micrometer, measure lifter thickness as shown.

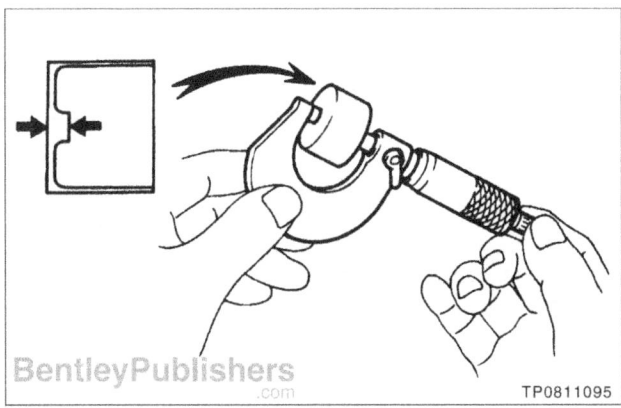

TP0811095

Courtesy Toyota Motor Sales (TMS) USA, Inc.

— Use this formula to calculate thickness of new lifter needed for correct valve clearance:
Intake lifter A = B + [C − 0.20 mm (0.008 in)]
Exhaust lifter A = B + [C − 0.30 mm (0.012 in)]
A = Thickness of new lifter
B = Thickness of used lifter
C = Measured valve clearance

Example (using metric measurements):
Measured clearance for intake valve (C) = 0.40 mm
Measured thickness of used lifter (B) = 5.25 mm
A = B + (C − 0.20 mm)
A = 5.25 mm + (0.40 mm − 0.20 mm)
A = 5.45 mm
Obtain new lifter as close as possible to calculated 5.45 mm thickness.

Example (using English measurements):
Measured clearance for intake valve (C) = 0.0158 in
Measured thickness of used lifter (B) = 0.2067 in
A = B + (C − 0.008 in)
A = 0.2067 in + (0.0158 in − 0.008 in)
A = 0.2146 in
Obtain new lifter as close as possible to calculated 0.2146 in thickness.

35 lifter sizes are available with thicknesses varying in increments of 0.020 mm (0.0008 in), from 5.060 mm (0.1992 in) to 5.740 mm (0.2260 in).

— Lightly oil lifter when reinstalling.

— Continue to adjust valve clearances as necessary. Remove and install lifters one at a time to make sure they are kept in order.

◀ Hold timing chain as shown. Install intake camshaft and timing sprocket so that paint mark on timing chain aligns with timing mark on sprocket.

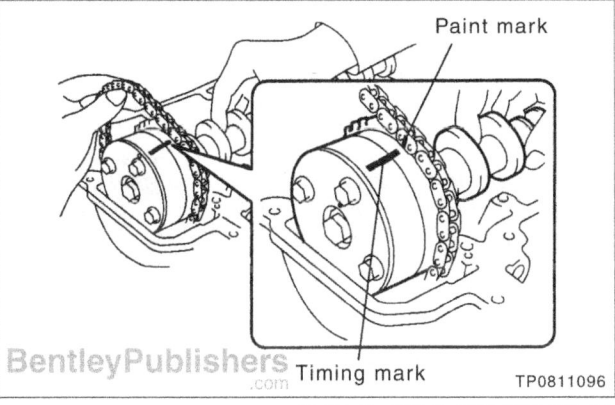

Paint mark

Timing mark

TP0811096

Courtesy Toyota Motor Sales (TMS) USA, Inc.

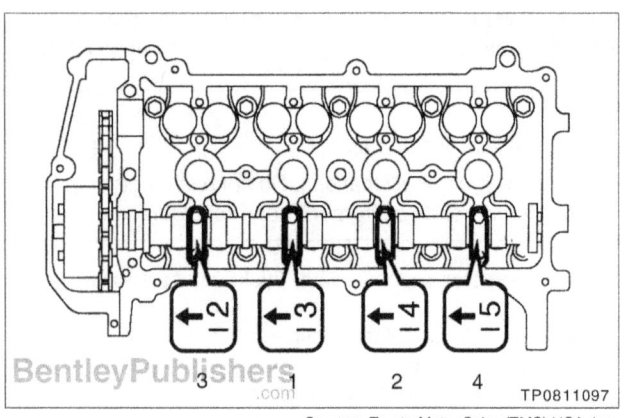

TP0811097

Courtesy Toyota Motor Sales (TMS) USA, Inc.

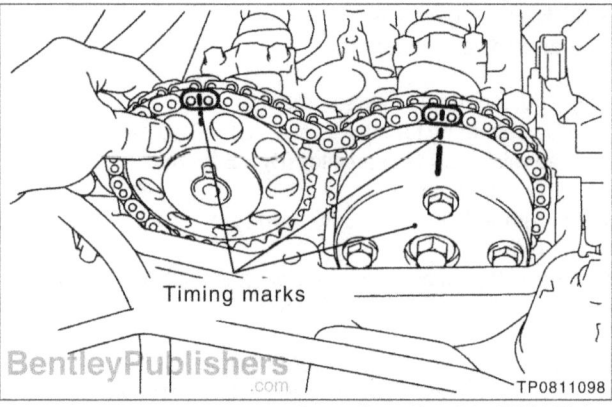

Timing marks

TP0811098

Courtesy Toyota Motor Sales (TMS) USA, Inc.

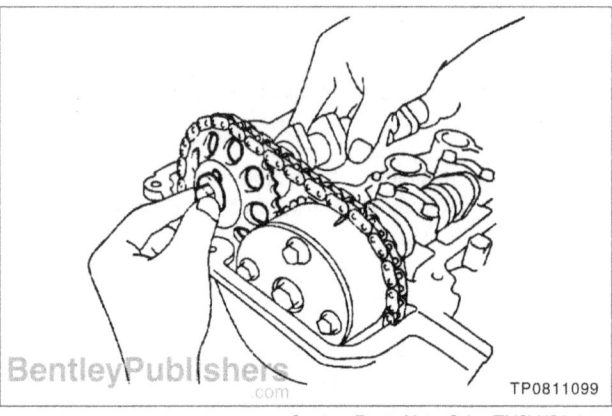

TP0811099

Courtesy Toyota Motor Sales (TMS) USA, Inc.

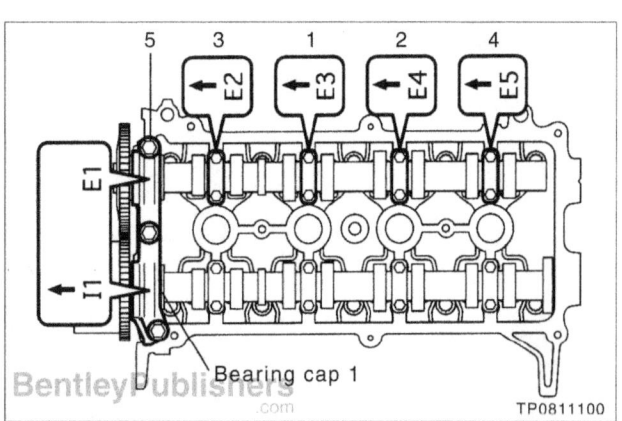

Bearing cap 1

TP0811100

Courtesy Toyota Motor Sales (TMS) USA, Inc.

◀ Install intake camshaft bearing caps. Check to be sure that you have correct camshaft bearing caps and in correct order.

NOTE—

- *Bearing caps are marked to indicate bearing number, intake (I) or exhaust (E) camshaft, and orientation (arrow points toward sprockets).*

– Tighten intake camshaft bearing cap bolts in order shown.

> *CAUTION—*
> - *Tighten bearing cap bolts evenly in several steps.*

Tightening torque	
Camshaft bearing cap to cylinder head	13 Nm (9.6 ft-lb)

◀ Install exhaust camshaft timing sprocket so that paint mark on chain aligns with timing mark on sprocket.

– Place exhaust camshaft on cylinder head. Align pin on exhaust camshaft with sprocket groove.

◀ Install exhaust camshaft sprocket bolt finger-tight.

- Do not tighten or torque bolt at this time.

– Install exhaust camshaft bearing caps. Check to be sure that you have correct camshaft bearing caps and in correct order.

NOTE—

- *Bearing caps are marked to indicate bearing number, intake (I) or exhaust (E) camshaft, and orientation (arrow points toward sprockets).*

◀ Tighten exhaust camshaft bearing cap bolts in order shown. Tighten to specification.

> *CAUTION—*
> - *Tighten bearing cap bolts evenly in several steps.*

Tightening torque	
Camshaft bearing cap to cylinder head	13 Nm (9.6 ft-lb)

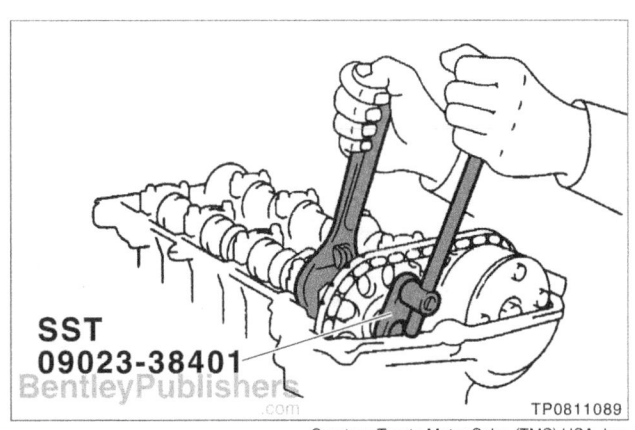

SST
09023-38401

TP0811089
Courtesy Toyota Motor Sales (TMS) USA, Inc.

◄ While holding exhaust camshaft with adjustable wrench, use camshaft bolt wrench (Toyota special tool SST 09023-38401 or equivalent) to tighten exhaust camshaft sprocket bolt.

Tightening torque	
Camshaft sprocket to camshaft	64 Nm (47 ft-lb)

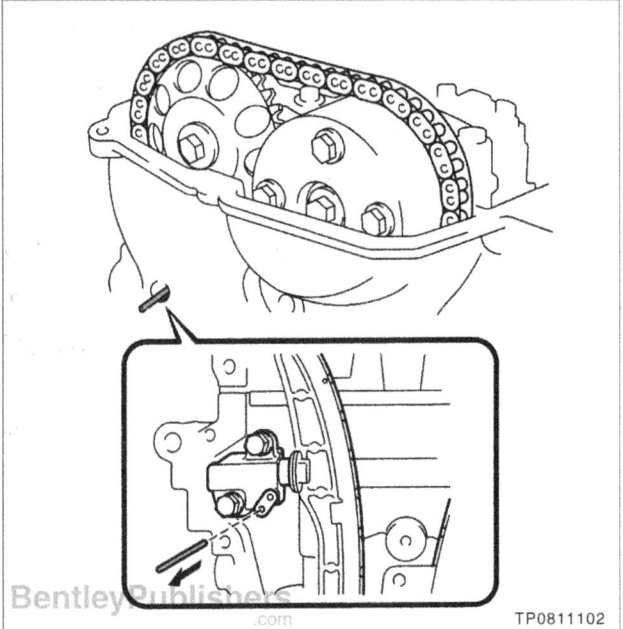

TP0811102
Courtesy Toyota Motor Sales (TMS) USA, Inc.

◄ Remove 3.0 mm (0.118 in) dia. pin or drill bit from chain tensioner stopper plate hole.

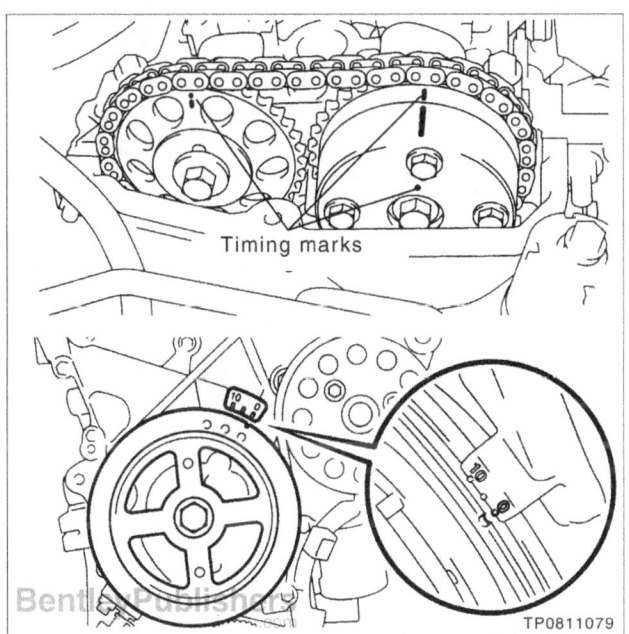

Timing marks

TP0811079
Courtesy Toyota Motor Sales (TMS) USA, Inc.

◄ Using a wrench on crankshaft pulley bolt, rotate crankshaft clockwise.

 • Align crankshaft pulley timing mark notch with 0 timing mark (**inset**).

 • Make sure camshaft sprocket timing marks are at 12 o'clock position as shown.

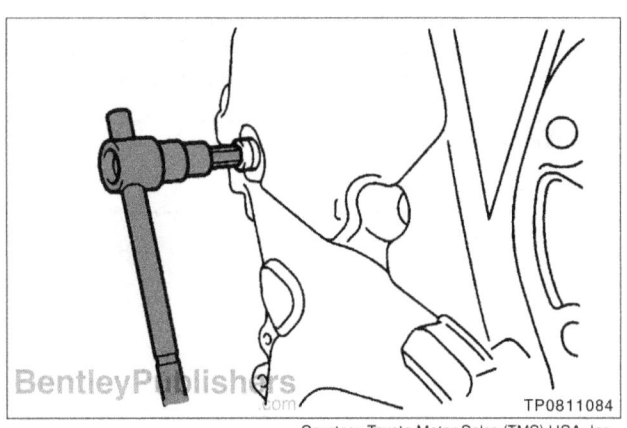

TP0811084

Courtesy Toyota Motor Sales (TMS) USA, Inc.

◄ Working at front timing chain cover:

- Clean oil from threads in service hole and on service hole plug.
- Apply thread-locking compound (Toyota part no. 08833-00070; 3-Bond part no.1324, or equivalent) to service hole plug threads.
- Install service hole plug.

Tightening torque	
Service hole plug to timing chain cover	15 Nm (11 ft-lb)

— Apply formed-in-place gasket (FIPG) compound (Toyota part no. 08826-00080 or equivalent self-forming gasket) to seal timing chain cover to engine block joint area.

> **CAUTION—**
> - Be sure to assemble parts within 3 minutes of sealant application.

◄ Install cylinder head cover. Tighten cylinder head cover nuts and bolts uniformly in several steps in sequence shown.

Tightening torque	
Cylinder head cover to cylinder head	10 Nm (7.4 ft-lb)

— Remainder of assembly is reverse of disassembly. Clean wiper pivot serrations when reinstalling wiper arms.

Tightening torque	
Brake fluid reservoir bracket to brake master cylinder	8.5 Nm (75 in-lb)
Brake fluid reservoir to bracket	8.5 Nm (75 in-lb)
Cowl cover to cowl	6.4 Nm (57 in-lb)
Negative cable to 12-volt auxiliary battery	6 Nm (53 in-lb)
Relay block to cowl	8.4 Nm (74 in-lb)
Wiper assembly to body	5.5 Nm (49 in-lb)

— Reconnect 12-volt auxiliary battery and switch hybrid system ON (READY indicator illuminated) until engine starts, or run engine in inspection mode. See **11 Diagnostics**. Check engine operation.

— Adjust wiper arm position. See **10 Electrical System, Lights**.

— Reinitialize power windows. See **10 Electrical System, Lights**.

— Reprogram radio and navigation system presets (if applicable).

TP0811106

Courtesy Toyota Motor Sales (TMS) USA, Inc.

COOLING SYSTEM

The Prius engine cooling system is a conventional pressurized type. The engine coolant pump is driven by the engine serpentine belt.

There is an electric circulation pump for the passenger compartment heating system, and a coolant heat storage tank with its own electric circulation pump to decrease cold engine warm-up time.

Toyota recommends periodic coolant replacement. See maintenance schedules in **4 Service and Repair Fundamentals** for engine coolant service intervals.

Properly bleeding the engine cooling system after cooling system work requires special tools, including Toyota scan tool or equivalent. Be sure that you have the necessary skills. Read the complete procedure before starting work.

Engine coolant level, checking

— Switch hybrid system OFF (READY indicator not illuminated). See **3 Safety**.

WARNING—
• *Make sure hybrid system is OFF when servicing vehicle (READY indicator not illuminated). Failure to switch the hybrid system OFF could result in engine start at any time.*

◄ Engine coolant reservoir cap (**arrow**) is at front of engine compartment, near radiator.

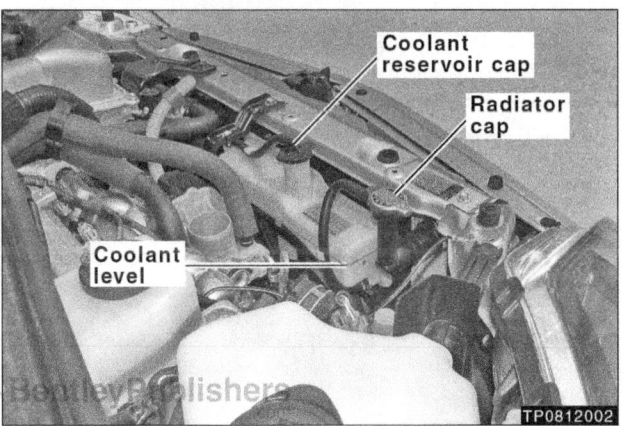

◄ Engine coolant level is visible through translucent plastic reservoir. (Plastic radiator cover removed for photo clarity.)

— Check engine coolant level when engine is cold.
• Make sure coolant level in reservoir is between LOW and FULL marks on reservoir.
• Make sure radiator is full.

WARNING—
• *Do not remove radiator pressure cap when engine is hot. Hot coolant may spray under pressure and cause severe burns.*

— If engine coolant level is low, check engine cooling system for leaks.

— Check condition of coolant, reservoir, radiator and radiator pressure cap.

- If there is rust or scale deposits around cap or filler opening, flush cooling system and refill.
- If there is oil in coolant, have cylinder head and head gasket tested for leaks.

— Add recommended coolant as required.

> *CAUTION—*
> - *Do not use alcohol-type coolant or plain water alone. Using incorrect coolant may damage the engine cooling system.*

Prius engine coolant specification	
Recommended coolant	Toyota super long life coolant (SLLC) or equivalent

> *NOTE—*
> - *Toyota specifies high-quality nonsilicate, nonamine, nonborate ethylene glycol coolant with long-life hybrid organic acid technology. Toyota super long life coolant (SLLC) meets these requirements.*
> - *Toyota SLLC is premixed with water in the correct ratio.*

— Reinstall radiator pressure cap and reservoir cap.

Cooling system pressure testing

A cooling system pressure test is a good way to check for leaks if a visual inspection is inconclusive. Inspect the underside of the engine as well as in the engine compartment for dried anti-freeze or traces of wet coolant.

Be sure to pressure test radiator cap as well.

> *WARNING—*
> - *To avoid personal injury, be sure the engine is cold before beginning this procedure.*

— Switch hybrid system OFF (READY indicator not illuminated). See **3 Safety**.

> *WARNING—*
> - *Make sure hybrid system is OFF when servicing vehicle (READY indicator not illuminated). Failure to switch the hybrid system OFF could result in engine start at any time.*

— Remove radiator cover. See **Radiator cover, removing** in this chapter.

— Remove radiator cap and top off radiator and coolant reservoir, if necessary.

◄ Attach cooling system pressure tester to top of radiator.

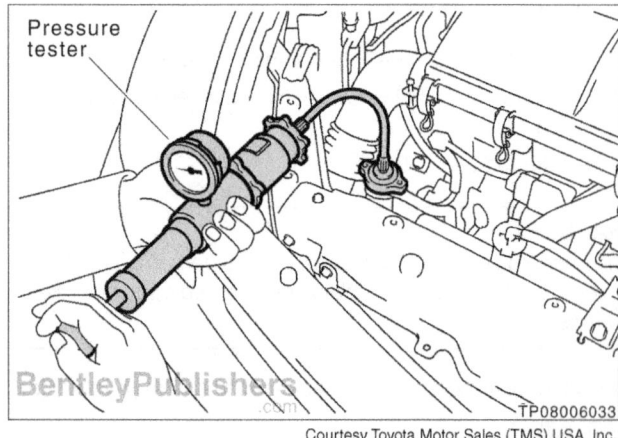

Pressure tester

TP08006033

Courtesy Toyota Motor Sales (TMS) USA, Inc.

− Run engine in inspection mode. See **11 Diagnostics**. Warm engine until thermostat opens (radiator becomes hot).

− Use pressure tester to increase cooling system to specification listed. Check that pressure does not drop.

Cooling system - pressure test specifications	
System test pressure (max.)	177 kPa (25.6 psi)

− If pressure drops, check hoses, radiator and coolant pump for leaks. If no external leaks are found, check engine block and cylinder head.

◀ Inspect pressure cap gaskets (**arrows**).

- Clean debris and dried antifreeze off gaskets using water.
- Make sure gasket are not deformed, cracked or swollen.
- Check that there is gap between smallest gasket and cap body and that gasket is not stuck to cap.

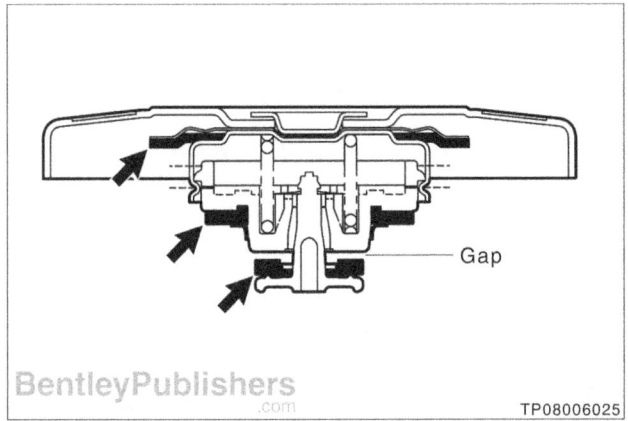

Gap

TP08006025
Courtesy Toyota Motor Sales (TMS) USA, Inc.

◀ Pressure test radiator cap.

- Wet cap gaskets with coolant before attaching to tester.
- Keep tester at an angle of 30° or more above horizontal.
- Pump tester several times at a rate of about 1 pump / second and check for maximum cap pressure. Replace cap if it does not meet specifications.

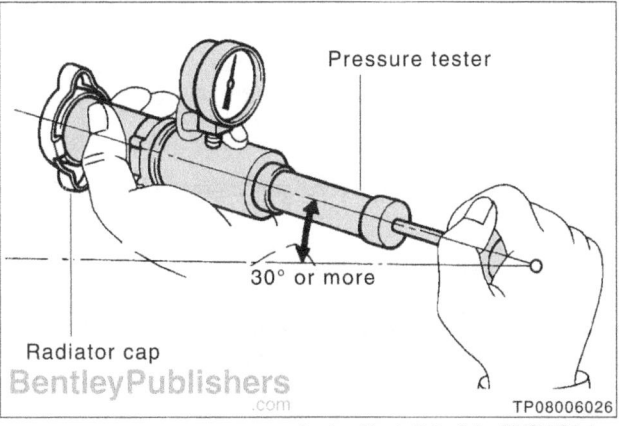

Pressure tester

30° or more

Radiator cap

TP08006026
Courtesy Toyota Motor Sales (TMS) USA, Inc.

Radiator cap - pressure test specifications	
Cap pressure (2004 -2005) • Standard (new cap) • Minimum (used cap)	74 - 103 kPa (10.7 - 14.9 psi) 59 kPa (8.5 psi)
Cap pressure (2006 -2008) • Standard (new cap) • Minimum (used cap)	93.3 - 122.7 kPa (15.5 - 17.8 psi) 78.5 kPa (11.4 psi)

Engine coolant, draining and refilling (without cooling system bleed tool)

The following procedure is based on Toyota repair information and requires the use of the Toyota scan tool or equivalent.

A critical part of draining and filling the cooling system is bleeding air from the system after the refill. This is a time consuming procedure. Be sure to read the complete procedure before starting work.

NOTE—

- *Why is bleeding necessary after refilling the cooling system? The intricate design of the Prius cooling system may cause air to become trapped during refilling. Trapped air prevents proper coolant flow, possibly causing overheating and setting DTCs.*

- *For automotive professionals, an additional approach to filling and bleeding the system is given under* **Engine coolant, draining and refilling (with cooling system bleed tool)** *in this chapter. The procedure requires a special cooling system bleed tool and a source of compressed air.*

> **WARNING—**
> - *To avoid personal injury, be sure the engine is cold before beginning this procedure.*

- Switch hybrid system OFF (READY indicator not illuminated). See **3 Safety**.

> **WARNING—**
> - *Make sure hybrid system is OFF when servicing vehicle (READY indicator not illuminated). Failure to switch the hybrid system OFF could result in engine start at any time.*

- Remove radiator cover. See **Radiator cover, removing** in this chapter.

- Loosen left front wheel lug nuts slightly before lifting vehicle.

- Raise vehicle and support safely. Make sure vehicle is level. See **4 Service and Repair Fundamentals**.

> **WARNING—**
> - *Make sure the vehicle is stable and well supported at all times. Use a professional automotive lift or jack stands designed for the purpose.*

- Remove left front wheel.

- Remove left and right engine splash shields. See **Engine splash shields, removing** in this chapter.

◄ Remove screws (**arrows**) and detach forward part of left front fender liner. It is not necessary to remove entire front fender liner.

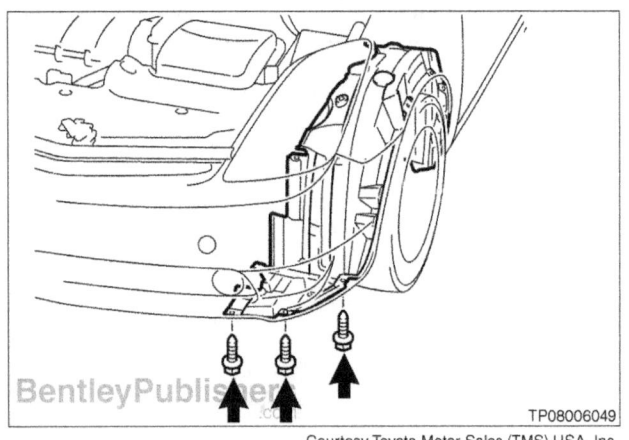

TP08006049

Courtesy Toyota Motor Sales (TMS) USA, Inc.

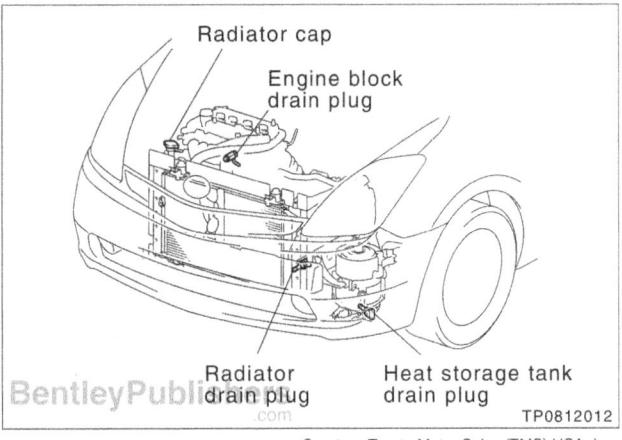

Radiator cap

Engine block
drain plug

Radiator
drain plug

Heat storage tank
drain plug

TP0812012

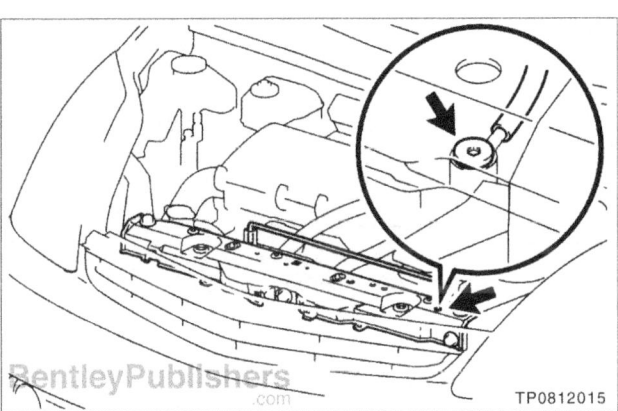

TP0812015

‒ Remove radiator pressure cap.

> **WARNING**—
> • Do not remove radiator pressure cap when engine is hot. Hot coolant may spray under pressure and cause severe burns.

◄ Disconnect connector from pump on coolant heat storage tank pump (**arrow**).

> **NOTE**—
> • Disconnecting the pump connector may cause the ECM to set diagnostic trouble codes P1151 or P2601 and illuminate the malfunction indicator lamp (MIL). Clear DTCs after completing the engine coolant drain and refill procedure. See **11 Diagnostics**.

> **WARNING**—
> • The coolant heat storage tank can remain hot (as high as 176°F) for as long as 3 days. Use extreme caution when working around the coolant heat storage tank.

‒ Place coolant drain pan underneath engine.

◄ Open engine block, radiator and coolant heat storage tank drain plugs and allow coolant to drain.

> **WARNING**—
> • Use extreme care when draining engine coolant. Even when the engine is cold, the coolant heat storage tank maintains coolant at high temperature. Hot engine coolant can cause severe burns.
> • Automotive antifreeze is poisonous and lethal, specially to pets. Clean up spills immediately and rinse area with water.
> • Dispose of coolant in an environmentally safe manner.

‒ Close and tighten drain plugs.

Tightening torque	
Drain plug to engine block	13 Nm (10 ft-lb)

◄ Connect transparent plastic hose to engine radiator bleeder plug (**arrow**) at top left of radiator.

◄ Place other end of transparent hose into open engine coolant reservoir.

– Open radiator bleeder plug.

– Remove radiator fill cap and fill engine with recommended coolant slowly.

CAUTION—
• *Do not use alcohol-type coolant or plain water alone. Using incorrect coolant may damage the engine cooling system.*

Prius engine coolant specification	
Recommended coolant	Toyota super long life coolant (SLLC) or equivalent
Coolant capacity	8.6 liters (9.0 US qt)

NOTE—
• *Toyota specifies high-quality nonsilicate, nonamine, nonborate ethylene glycol coolant with long-life hybrid organic acid technology. Toyota super long life coolant (SLLC) meets these requirements.*
• *Toyota SLLC is premixed with water in the correct ratio.*

– Squeeze and release radiator inlet and outlet hoses. If coolant level in reservoir drops, add more coolant.

– Close and tighten radiator bleeder plug.

Tightening torque	
Bleeder plug to radiator	1.5 Nm (13 in-lb)

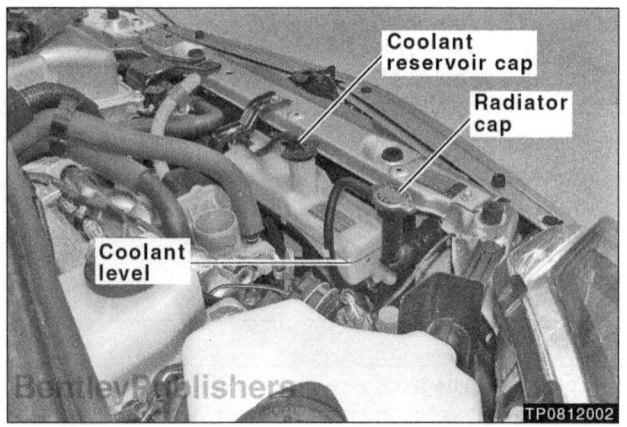

◄ Check coolant level in reservoir and in radiator.
• Make sure coolant level in reservoir is between LOW and FULL.
• Make sure radiator is full.
• If coolant level is low, add coolant.
• Reinstall radiator pressure cap.
• Reconnect coolant heat storage pump connector.

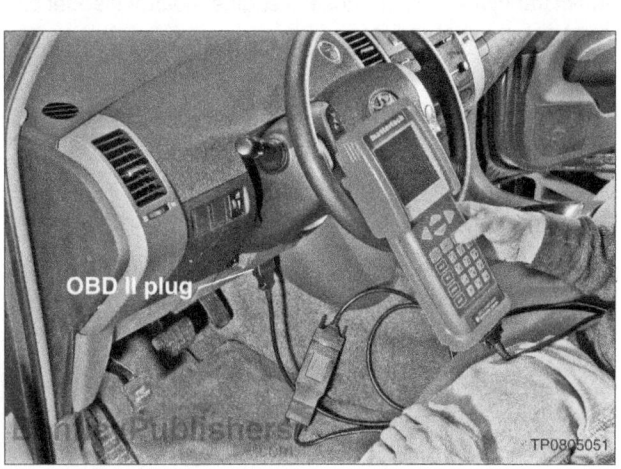

◄ Connect Toyota scan tool or equivalent to OBD II plug underneath dashboard.
• Use tester in ACTIVE TEST mode to run electric coolant pump. Follow on-screen instructions. ACTIVE TEST mode operates coolant pump for approximately 30 seconds.

CAUTION—
• *Fill cooling system before beginning ACTIVE TEST mode.*

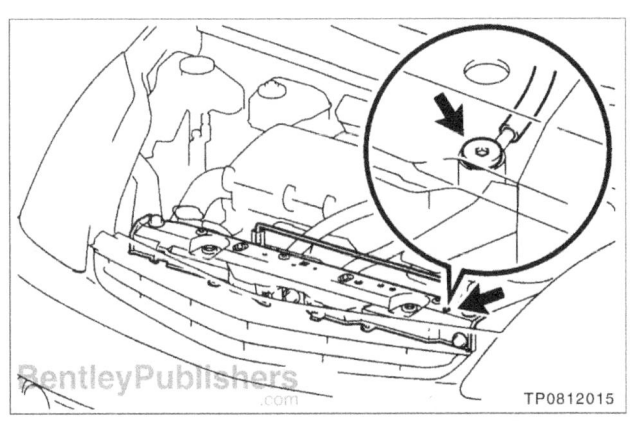

Courtesy Toyota Motor Sales (TMS) USA, Inc.

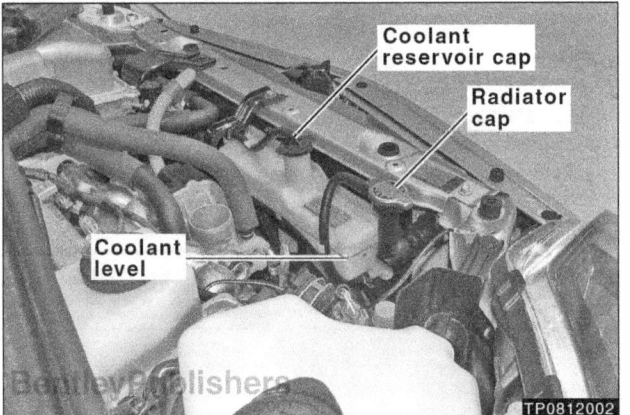

◄ Open radiator bleeder plug.

– Remove engine radiator pressure cap and fill radiator with coolant up to rim of filler.

– Squeeze and release radiator inlet and outlet hoses. If coolant level in reservoir drops, add more coolant.

– Close and tighten engine radiator bleeder plug.

Tightening torque	
Bleeder plug to radiator	1.5 Nm (13 in-lb)

– Reinstall engine radiator pressure cap.

– Repeat ACTIVE TEST procedure to run electric coolant pump until coolant level no longer drops when pump runs. Detach scan tool.

– Remove transparent plastic hose from engine radiator bleeder plug and engine coolant reservoir.

◄ Final coolant bleeding steps:
• Run engine in inspection mode. See **11 Diagnostics**.
• Warm engine until thermostat opens (radiator becomes hot).
• Press POWER button to switch engine and hybrid system OFF and exit inspection mode.
• Allow engine to cool below 50°C (122°F).
• Remove engine radiator pressure cap and fill radiator.
• Make sure coolant level in reservoir is between LOW and FULL marks on reservoir.
• Make sure radiator is full.
• If coolant level is low, add coolant.
• Reinstall radiator pressure cap and coolant reservoir cap.

– If coolant was added in previous step, run engine in inspection mode and repeat previous steps. Engine cooling system is bled when coolant level no longer drops.

– Check for coolant leaks.

– Reassemble engine compartment and front fender liner. Reinstall left front wheel.

Tightening torque	
Wheel to wheel hub	103 Nm (76 ft-lb)

– Clear any diagnostic trouble codes set. See **11 Diagnostics**.

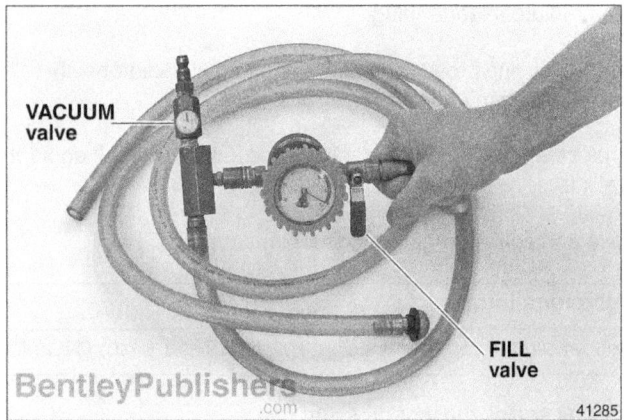

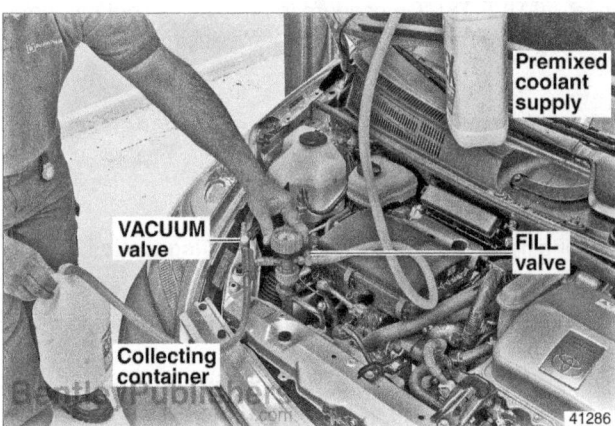

Engine coolant, draining and refilling (with cooling system bleed tool)

◄ The following procedure uses of a compressed-air-operated cooling system bleed tool. This procedure does not require the use of the factory scan tool, but an OBD II scan tool may be necessary to clear any DTCs set during the draining procedure. Be sure to read the complete procedure before starting work.

NOTE—

- *Why is bleeding necessary after refilling the cooling system? The intricate design of the Prius cooling system may cause air to become trapped during refilling. Trapped air prevents proper coolant flow, possibly causing overheating and setting DTCs.*

◄ The cooling system bleed tool works as follows: Starting with a drained cooling system, the tool uses compressed air to create a partial vacuum in the cooling system. Once the cooling system is placed under vacuum, the VACUUM valve on the tool is closed and the FILL valve is opened. Premixed coolant (such as Toyota SLLC) is pushed by atmospheric pressure up a hose inserted into the bottom of a coolant supply container, through the cooling system bleed tool and into the cooling system.

The process (draw vacuum, fill, draw vacuum, fill, etc.) may need to be repeated several times to remove all air from the system (although some technicians say once is enough). Coolant hoses may collapse during the procedure.

> ***WARNING—***
> - *To avoid personal injury, be sure the engine is cold before beginning this procedure.*

— Switch hybrid system OFF (READY indicator not illuminated). See **3 Safety**.

> ***WARNING—***
> - *Make sure hybrid system is OFF when servicing vehicle (READY indicator not illuminated). Failure to switch the hybrid system OFF could result in engine start at any time.*

— Remove radiator cover. See **Radiator cover, removing** in this chapter.

— Loosen left front wheel lug nuts slightly before lifting vehicle. This makes removing wheel and tire easier when vehicle is raised.

— Raise vehicle and support safely. Make sure vehicle is level. See **4 Service and Repair Fundamentals**.

> ***WARNING—***
> - *Make sure the vehicle is stable and well supported at all times. Use a professional automotive lift or jack stands designed for the purpose. A floor jack is not adequate support.*

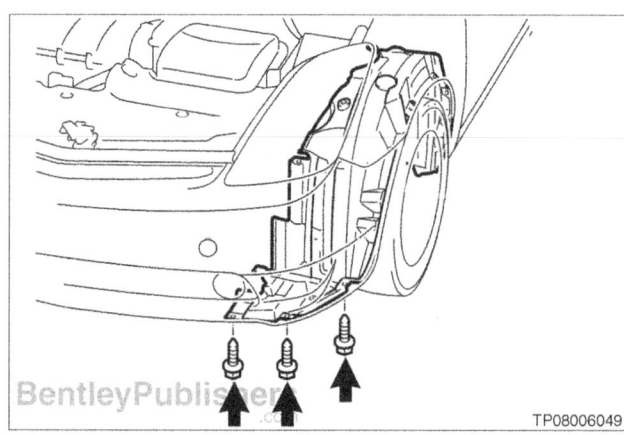

TP08006049

Courtesy Toyota Motor Sales (TMS) USA, Inc.

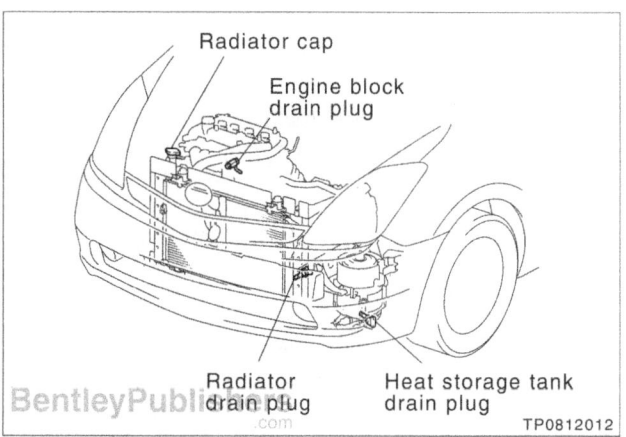

Radiator cap

Engine block
drain plug

Radiator   Heat storage tank
drain plug   drain plug

TP0812012

Courtesy Toyota Motor Sales (TMS) USA, Inc.

— Remove left front wheel.

— Remove left side engine splash shield. See **Engine splash
shields, removing** in this chapter.

◀ Remove screws (**arrows**) and detach forward part of left front
fender liner. It is not necessary to remove entire front fender
liner.

— Remove radiator pressure cap.

> **WARNING—**
> • *Do not remove radiator pressure cap when engine is hot.
> Hot coolant may spray under pressure and cause severe
> burns.*

◀ Disconnect coolant heat storage pump electrical connector
(**arrow**).

> **NOTE—**
> • *Disconnecting the pump connector may cause the ECM to set
> diagnostic trouble codes P1151 or P2601 and illuminate the
> malfunction indicator lamp (MIL). Clear DTCs after completing
> the engine coolant drain and refill procedure. See* **11
> Diagnostics**.

> **WARNING—**
> • *The coolant heat storage tank stores engine coolant. The
> tank can remain hot (as high as 176°F) for as long as 3
> days. A malfunction may cause the surface of the tank to
> become very hot. Use extreme caution when working
> around the coolant heat storage tank.*

— Place coolant drain pan underneath engine.

◀ Open engine block, radiator and coolant heat storage tank drain
plugs and allow coolant to drain.

> **WARNING—**
> • *Hot engine coolant can cause severe burns.*
> • *Automotive antifreeze is poisonous and lethal, specially to
> pets. Clean up spills immediately and rinse area with water.*
> • *Dispose of coolant in an environmentally safe manner.*

— Close and tighten drain plugs.

Tightening torque	
Drain plug to engine block	13 Nm (10 ft-lb)

— Reconnect coolant heat storage pump electrical connector.

— Reassemble front fender liner. Reinstall left front wheel.

Tightening torque	
Wheel to wheel hub	103 Nm (76 ft-lb)

— Lower vehicle.

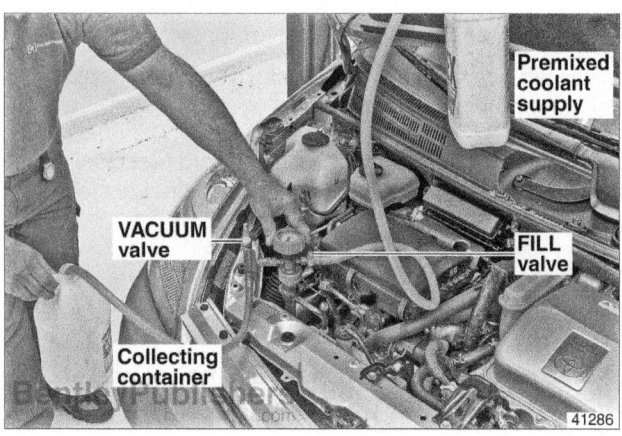

◄ Install cooling system bleed tool on radiator filler neck per manufacturer's instructions.

– Attach compressed air supply hose to cooling system bleed tool.

NOTE—

- *Cooling system bleed tool typically requires approx. 90 psi line pressure.*

– Place cooling system bleed tool suction hose (coolant supply hose) into container of premixed coolant. Suction hose should go to bottom of container. Place container so that bottom of container is higher than radiator cap to aid siphon action when refilling.

Engine coolant specification	
Recommended coolant	Toyota super long life coolant (SLLC) or equivalent
Coolant capacity	8.6 liters (9.0 US qt)

NOTE—

- *Toyota specifies high-quality nonsilicate, nonamine, nonborate ethylene glycol coolant with long-life hybrid organic acid technology. Toyota super long life coolant (SLLC) meets these requirements.*

- *Toyota SLLC is premixed with water in the correct ratio.*

- *Be sure to have sufficient quantity of approved coolant available.*

– Place tool vent hose into an empty container to collect any liquid that may discharge with exhaust air.

– Turn compressed air supply ON and open VACUUM valve on tool to begin evacuating cooling system. Continue until level of vacuum on gauge reaches manufacturer's recommended value.

NOTE—

- *Some technicians begin by purging air from suction hose (coolant supply hose) before evacuating cooling system. As soon as air supply is turned ON and a low vacuum exists in the system, crack open coolant supply (FILL) valve on tool to draw coolant up tube, then close coolant supply valve.*

– When desired level of vacuum is reached, close VACUUM valve and open FILL valve on tool. Coolant is drawn from container of premixed coolant into cooling system. When container is nearly empty, close FILL valve and refill container. Keep end of pickup tube submerged in coolant. Again open FILL valve on tool. Continue filling system until reading on vacuum gauge drops to zero.

– Remove cooling system bleed tool from radiator filler neck. If coolant level is near top of filler neck, system is full. Make sure coolant level in reservoir is between LOW and FULL marks on reservoir.

– If coolant level is low, reattach cooling system bleed tool and repeat air bleeding procedure.

- Switch hybrid system ON (READY indicator illuminated) until engine starts, or run engine in inspection mode. See **11 Diagnostics**. Run engine and switch heater ON to purge air from heater core, a high point in cooling system. Run engine until radiator cooling fan(s) operate.

- Press POWER button to switch engine and hybrid system OFF and exit inspection mode.

- Allow engine to cool below 50°C (122°F).

- Remove engine radiator pressure cap and check coolant level.

> **WARNING —**
> • *Do not remove radiator pressure cap when engine is hot. Hot coolant may spray under pressure and cause severe burns.*

- Make sure coolant level in coolant reservoir is between LOW and FULL marks on reservoir.

- Reinstall radiator pressure cap and coolant reservoir cap.

- Reinstall radiator cover.

- Check for coolant leaks.

- Clear any diagnostic trouble codes set. See **11 Diagnostics**.

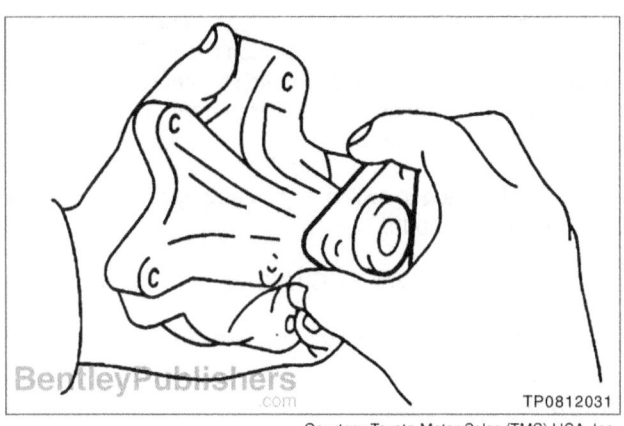

TP0812031

Courtesy Toyota Motor Sales (TMS) USA, Inc.

Coolant pump, removing and installing

◀ The Prius engine coolant pump is a conventional centrifugal impeller type pump driven by the engine and the serpentine belt. The coolant pump is on the front of the engine near the right inner fender.

After pump replacement, fill and bleed air out of cooling system. See **Engine coolant, draining and refilling (without cooling system bleed tool)** in this chapter.

> **WARNING—**
> • *To avoid personal injury, be sure the engine is cold before beginning this procedure.*

— Switch hybrid system OFF (READY indicator not illuminated). See **3 Safety**.

> **WARNING—**
> • *Make sure hybrid system is OFF when servicing vehicle (READY indicator not illuminated). Failure to switch the hybrid system OFF could result in engine start at any time.*

— Remove radiator cover. See **Radiator cover, removing** in this chapter.

— Raise vehicle and support safely. Make sure vehicle is level. See **4 Service and Repair Fundamentals**.

> **WARNING—**
> • *Make sure the vehicle is stable and well supported at all times. Use a professional automotive lift or jack stands designed for the purpose. A floor jack is not adequate support.*

— Remove left and right engine splash shields. See **Engine splash shields, removing** in this chapter.

— Drain engine coolant. See **Engine coolant, draining and refilling (without cooling system bleed tool)** in this chapter.

> **WARNING—**
> • *Automotive antifreeze is poisonous and lethal, specially to pets. Clean up spills immediately and rinse area with water.*
> • *Dispose of coolant in an environmentally safe manner.*

— Remove air filter housing. See **Air filter housing, removing and installing** in this chapter.

— Remove serpentine belt. See **Serpentine belt, removing and installing** in this chapter.

◀ Using Toyota special tool SST 09960-10010 or equivalent, hold engine coolant pump pulley.

• Remove 3 engine coolant pump pulley bolts.

• Remove engine coolant pump pulley.

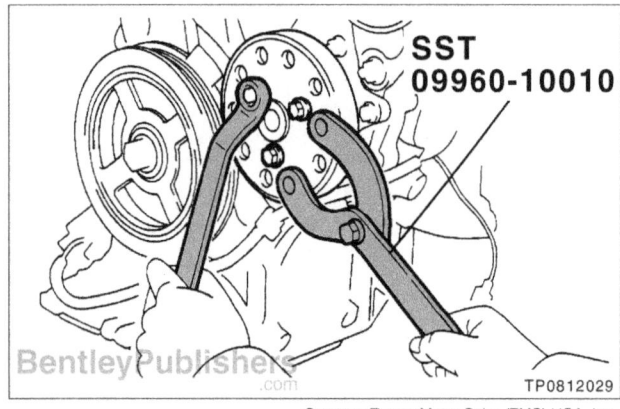

SST
09960-10010

TP0812029

Courtesy Toyota Motor Sales (TMS) USA, Inc.

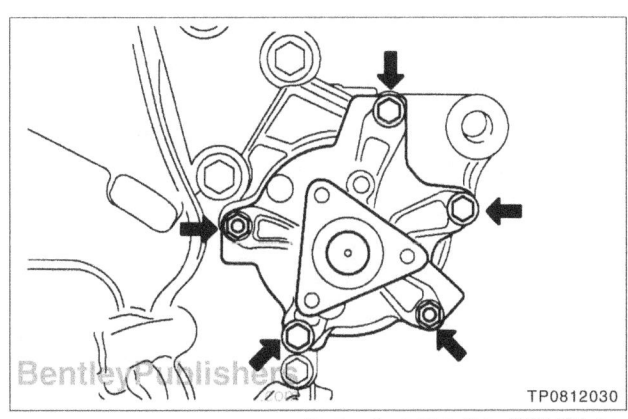

TP0812030

Courtesy Toyota Motor Sales (TMS) USA, Inc.

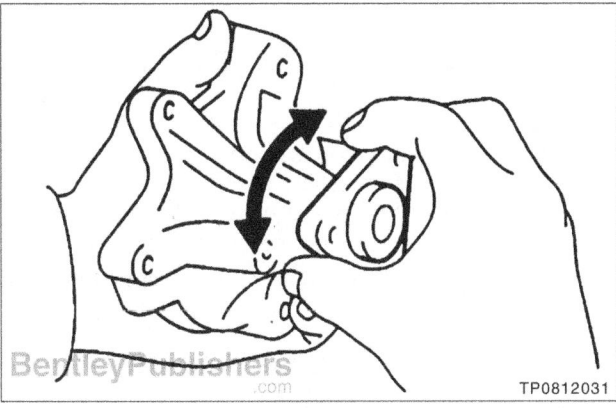

TP0812031

Courtesy Toyota Motor Sales (TMS) USA, Inc.

◀ Remove coolant pump mounting fasteners (**arrows**).

– Remove coolant pump and gasket.

– Visually check engine coolant pump drain hole for coolant leakage.

◀ Rotate engine coolant pump shaft to check bearing for roughness or free play.

– Replace engine coolant pump if leakage or bearing defects are present.

– Installation is reverse of removal, noting the following:
  • Use new coolant pump gasket.
  • Fill and bleed cooling system. See **Engine coolant, draining and refilling (without cooling system bleed tool)** in this chapter.
  • Check for coolant leaks.

Tightening torques	
Coolant pump to engine	11 Nm (8 ft-lb)
Pulley to coolant pump	15 Nm (11 ft-lb)

Coolant thermostat, removing and installing

The engine cooling system thermostat is located on the radiator side of the engine and is easily replaced.

After thermostat replacement, fill and bleed air out of cooling system. See **Engine coolant, draining and refilling (without cooling system bleed tool)** in this chapter.

> **WARNING** —
> • *To avoid personal injury, be sure the engine is cold before beginning this procedure.*

— Switch hybrid system OFF (READY indicator not illuminated). See **3 Safety**.

> **WARNING** —
> • *Make sure hybrid system is OFF when servicing vehicle (READY indicator not illuminated). Failure to switch the hybrid system OFF could result in engine start at any time.*

— Remove radiator cover. See **Radiator cover, removing** in this chapter.

— Raise vehicle and support safely. Make sure vehicle is level. See **4 Service and Repair Fundamentals**.

> **WARNING** —
> • *Make sure the vehicle is stable and well supported at all times. Use a professional automotive lift or jack stands designed for the purpose. A floor jack is not adequate support.*

— Remove left and right engine splash shields. See **Engine splash shields, removing** in this chapter.

— Drain engine coolant. See **Engine coolant, draining and refilling (without cooling system bleed tool)** in this chapter.

> **WARNING** —
> • *Automotive antifreeze is poisonous and lethal, specially to pets. Clean up spills immediately and rinse area with water.*
> • *Dispose of coolant in an environmentally safe manner.*

◄ Working at right side of engine compartment:
- Remove thermostat flange mounting fasteners (**arrows**).
- Remove thermostat flange from engine block.
- Remove thermostat and gasket from engine block.

TP0812040

TP0812041

Courtesy Toyota Motor Sales (TMS) USA, Inc.

TP0812042

Courtesy Toyota Motor Sales (TMS) USA, Inc.

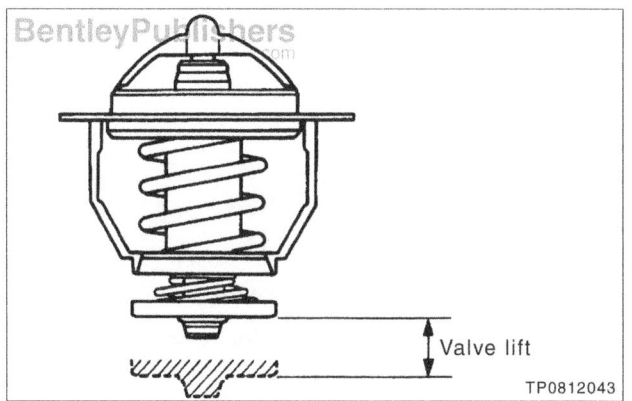

Valve lift

TP0812043

Courtesy Toyota Motor Sales (TMS) USA, Inc.

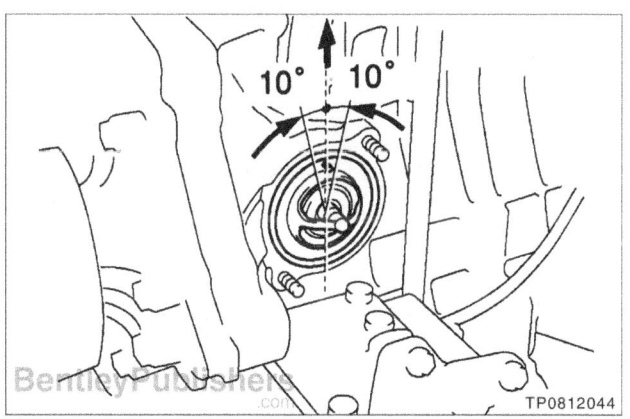

TP0812044

Courtesy Toyota Motor Sales (TMS) USA, Inc.

◀ Thermostat is stamped with opening temperature.

◀ To check thermostat, immerse in cold water and gradually heat water. Thermostat is calibrated to open at specified temperature.

Thermostat calibration	
Opening temperature • Nominal opening temperature • Permissible range	82°C (180°F) 80° - 84°C (176° - 183°F)

◀ Check that thermostat valve is fully closed at specified low temperature, and valve lift is correct at specified high temperature.

Thermostat calibration	
Valve lift • at 93°C (199°F) • below 40°C (104°F)	8.5 mm (0.345 in) fully closed

− Replace thermostat if it does not meet specifications.

◀ Installation is reverse of removal, noting the following:
- Use new thermostat gasket.
- Install thermostat in engine cylinder block with jiggle valve upward, and within 10° of 12 o'clock position as shown.
- Fill and bleed cooling system. See **Engine coolant, draining and refilling (without cooling system bleed tool)** in this chapter.
- Check for coolant leaks.

Tightening torques	
Thermostat flange to engine block	9 Nm (80 in-lb)

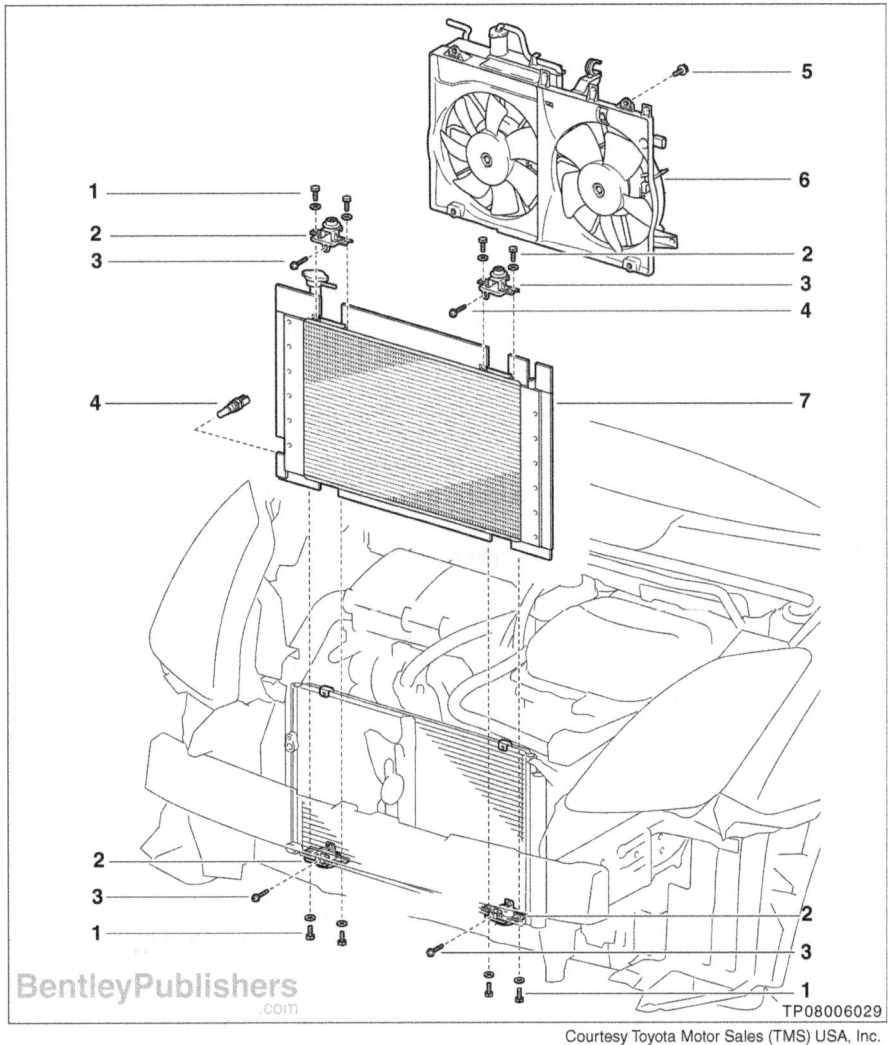

TP08006029

Courtesy Toyota Motor Sales (TMS) USA, Inc.

Radiator and cooling fan assembly

1. **Screw**
   - tighten to 5 Nm (44 in-lb)
2. **Radiator mount**
3. **Screw**
   - tighten to 3.9 Nm (35 in-lb)
4. **Fan switch**
   - tighten to 7 Nm (62 in-lb)
5. **Screw**
   - tighten to 7.5 Nm (66 in-lb)
6. **Cooling fan assembly**
7. **Radiator**

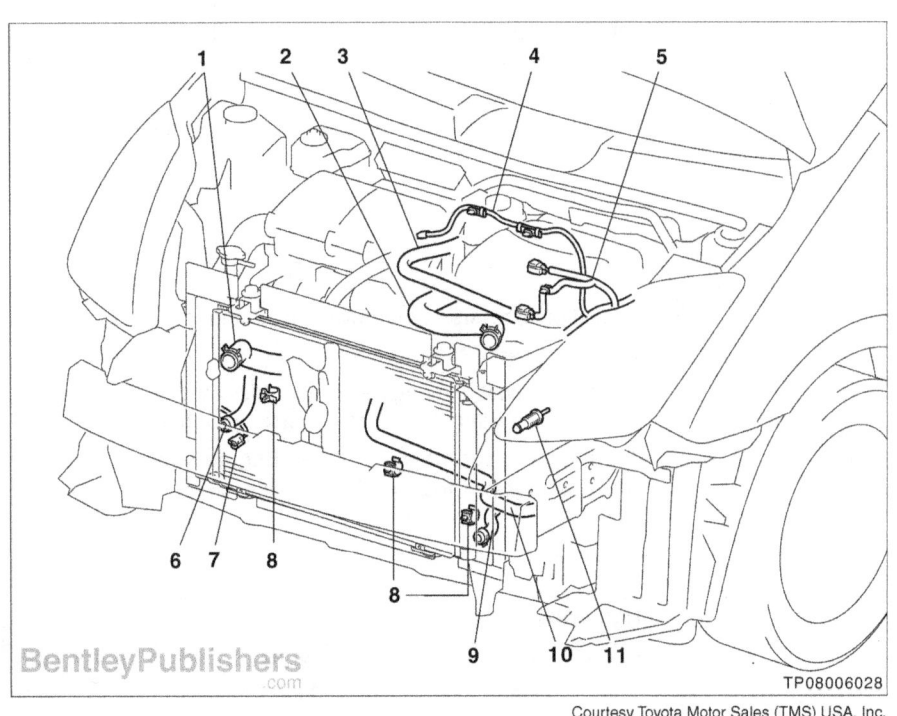

TP08006028

Courtesy Toyota Motor Sales (TMS) USA, Inc.

Coolant hoses

1. **Radiator outlet hose**
2. **Radiator inlet hose**
3. **Inverter cooling hose 2**
4. **Wiring harness**
5. **Cooling fan electrical harness**
6. **Inverter cooling hose 1**
7. **Fan switch electrical connector**
8. **Hose bracket**
9. **Inverter cooling hose 5**
10. **Heat storage tank bypass hose 1**
11. **Radiator drain plug**

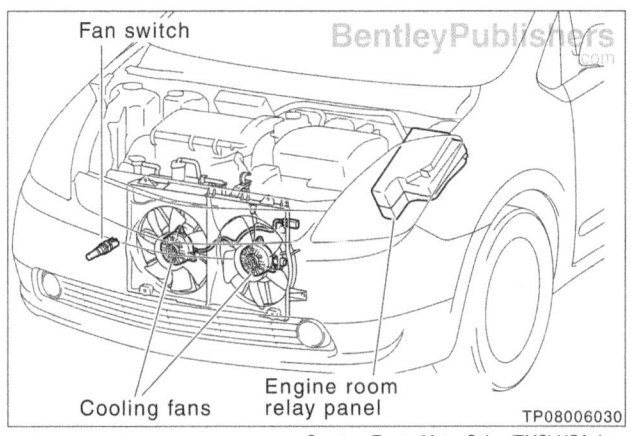

Fan switch

Engine room
relay panel

Cooling fans

TP08006030

Courtesy Toyota Motor Sales (TMS) USA, Inc.

Engine cooling fan control

◄ The dual engine cooling fan assembly is attached to the rear of the radiator.

The fan switch is screwed in the right lower corner of the radiator and detects coolant temperature.

Power to the fan assembly is provided by relays in the engine room relay panel.

See also **12 Electrical Component Locations** and **13 Electrical Wiring Diagrams**.

Engine cooling fan assembly, removing and installing

For coolant hose layout, see **Coolant hoses** in this chapter.

> *WARNING*—
> • *To avoid personal injury, be sure the engine is cold before beginning this procedure.*

– Switch hybrid system OFF (READY indicator not illuminated). See **3 Safety**.

> *WARNING*—
> • *Make sure hybrid system is OFF when servicing vehicle (READY indicator not illuminated). Failure to switch the hybrid system OFF could result in engine start at any time.*

– Disconnect 12-volt auxiliary battery. See **3 Safety**.

– Remove radiator cover. See **Radiator cover, removing** in this chapter.

– Raise vehicle and support safely. See **4 Service and Repair Fundamentals**.

> *WARNING*—
> • *Make sure the vehicle is stable and well supported at all times. Use a professional automotive lift or jack stands designed for the purpose. A floor jack is not adequate support.*

– Remove left and right engine splash shields. See **Engine splash shields, removing** in this chapter.

– Drain engine coolant. See **Engine coolant, draining and refilling (without cooling system bleed tool)** in this chapter. After draining coolant, remove radiator drain plug.

– Drain transaxle cooling system. See **7 Hybrid Transaxle**.

– Remove front bumper cover. See **9 Body**.

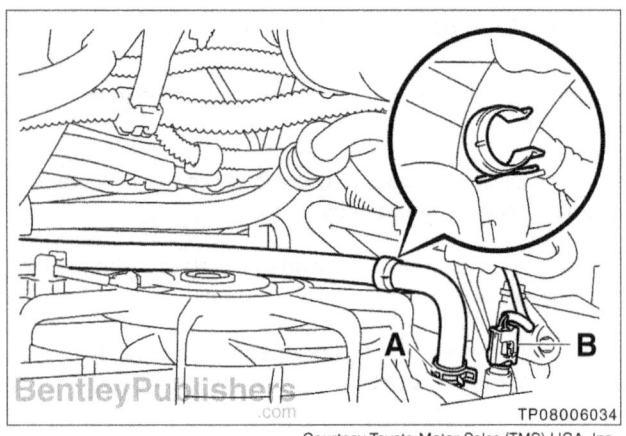

TP08006034

Courtesy Toyota Motor Sales (TMS) USA, Inc.

> **WARNING—**
> • *Automotive antifreeze is poisonous and lethal, specially to pets. Clean up spills immediately and rinse area with water.*
> • *Dispose of coolant in an environmentally safe manner.*

◀ Working underneath right side of radiator:

• Loosen clamp (**A**) and detach inverter cooling hose 1.

• Detach radiator fan switch electrical connector (**B**).

• Unhook hose from bracket (**inset**).

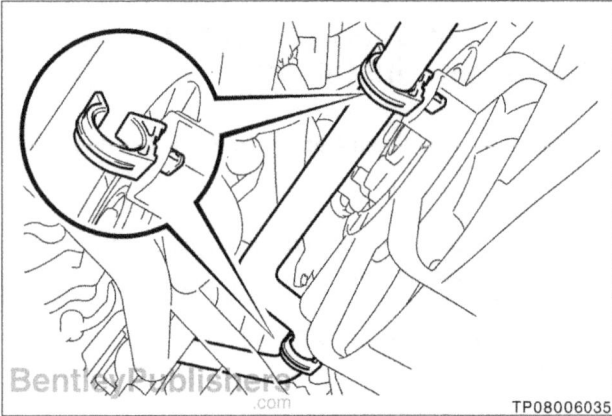

TP08006035

Courtesy Toyota Motor Sales (TMS) USA, Inc.

◀ Loosen hose clamps and detach cross-hose. Unhook from brackets (**inset**).

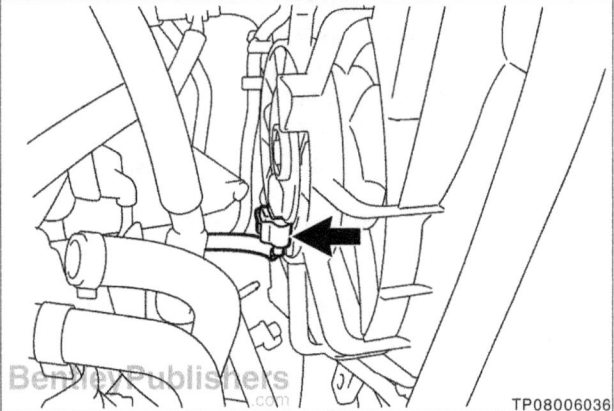

TP08006036

Courtesy Toyota Motor Sales (TMS) USA, Inc.

◀ Detach cooling fans electrical connector (**arrow**).

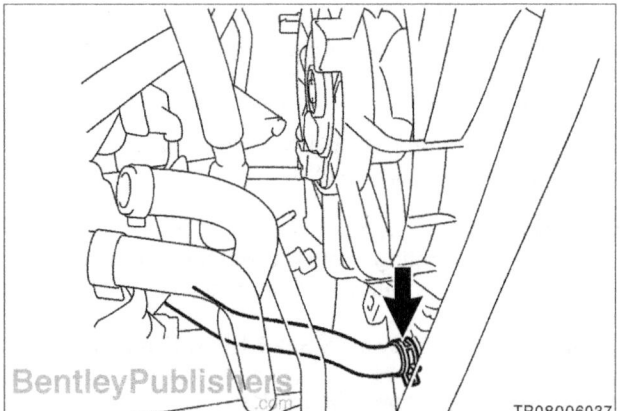

TP08006037

Courtesy Toyota Motor Sales (TMS) USA, Inc.

◀ Working under left side of radiator, loosen hose clamp (**arrow**) and detach inverter cooling hose.

◄ Working at top right of radiator, loosen hose clamps (**arrows**) and detach radiator outlet hose and coolant reservoir hose.

◄ Unhook inverter reservoir hose from brackets (**arrows**).

◄ Working at top left of radiator:
- Loosen hose clamps (**arrows**) and detach radiator inlet hose.
- Detach electrical connector (**inset**) under hose.

◄ Remove inverter mounting bracket and coolant reservoir bracket fasteners (**arrows**).
- Lift off brackets.
- Remove coolant reservoir.

◄ Working at upper right front of radiator, detach horn connector (**arrow**).

◄ Working at engine hood latch:
- Detach hood latch cable.
- Remove hood latch mounting bolts (**arrows**) and lift off latch.

◄ Remove radiator support mounting bolts (**arrows**). Detach hood release cable and lift off radiator support.

◄ Unhook wire harness from brackets (**arrows**).

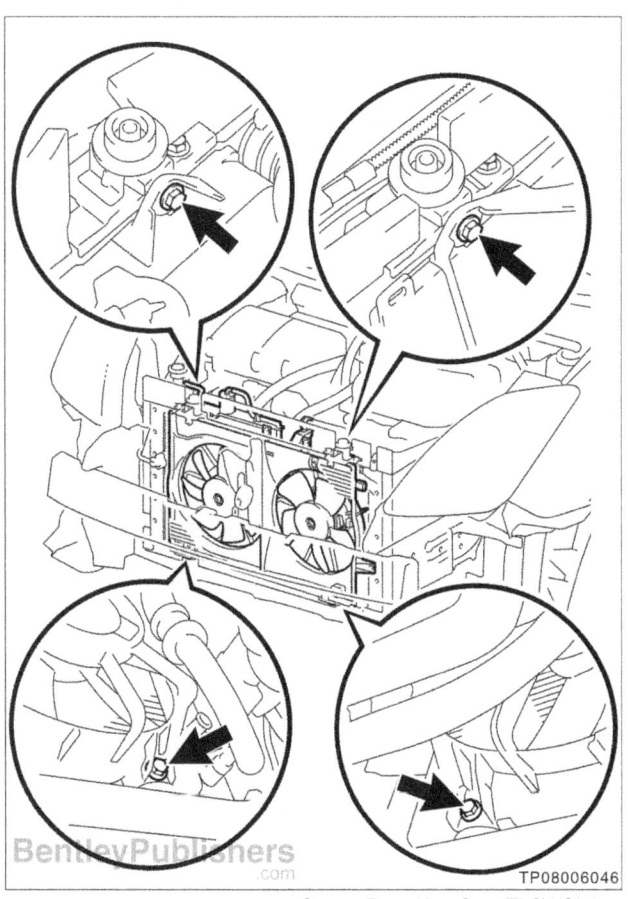

Courtesy Toyota Motor Sales (TMS) USA, Inc.

◄ Remove fan assembly mounting bolts (**arrows**). Lift fans out of engine compartment.

– Installation is reverse of removal. Use new hose clamps as needed.

- Fill and bleed engine cooling system. See **Engine coolant, draining and refilling (without cooling system bleed tool)** in this chapter.
- Fill and bleed transaxle cooling system. See **7 Hybrid Transaxle**.
- Check for coolant leaks.

Tightening torques	
Coolant reservoir bracket bolts: • Bracket to radiator support • Bracket to reservoir	20 Nm (15 ft-lb) 8.5 Nm (75 in-lb)
Fan assembly to radiator	7.5 Nm (66 in-lb)
Inverter bracket bolts: • Bracket to radiator support • Bracket to inverter	21 Nm (16 ft-lb) 25 Nm (18 ft-lb)
Radiator support to radiator	5 Nm (44 in-lb)

– Reinitialize power windows. See **10 Electrical System, Lights**.

– Reprogram radio and navigation system presets (if applicable).

Radiator, removing and installing

> **WARNING—**
> • To avoid personal injury, be sure the engine is cold before beginning this procedure.

– Switch hybrid system OFF (READY indicator not illuminated). See **3 Safety**.

> **WARNING—**
> • Make sure hybrid system is OFF when servicing vehicle (READY indicator not illuminated). Failure to switch the hybrid system OFF could result in engine start at any time.

– Disconnect 12-volt auxiliary battery. See **3 Safety**.

– Remove radiator cover. See **Radiator cover, removing** in this chapter.

– Raise vehicle and support safely. See **4 Service and Repair Fundamentals**.

> **WARNING—**
> • Make sure the vehicle is stable and well supported at all times. Use a professional automotive lift or jack stands designed for the purpose. A floor jack is not adequate support.

– Remove engine splash shields. See **Engine splash shields, removing** in this chapter.

– Drain engine coolant. See **Engine coolant, draining and refilling (without cooling system bleed tool)** in this chapter. After draining coolant, remove radiator drain plug.

> **WARNING—**
> • Automotive antifreeze is poisonous and lethal, specially to pets. Clean up spills immediately and rinse area with water.
> • Dispose of coolant in an environmentally safe manner.

– Drain transaxle cooling system. See **7 Hybrid Transaxle**.

– Remove front bumper cover. See **9 Body**.

– Remove cooling fan assembly. See **Engine cooling fan assembly, removing and installing** in this chapter.

◄ Remove radiator mount screws (**arrows**). Lift radiator out of engine compartment.

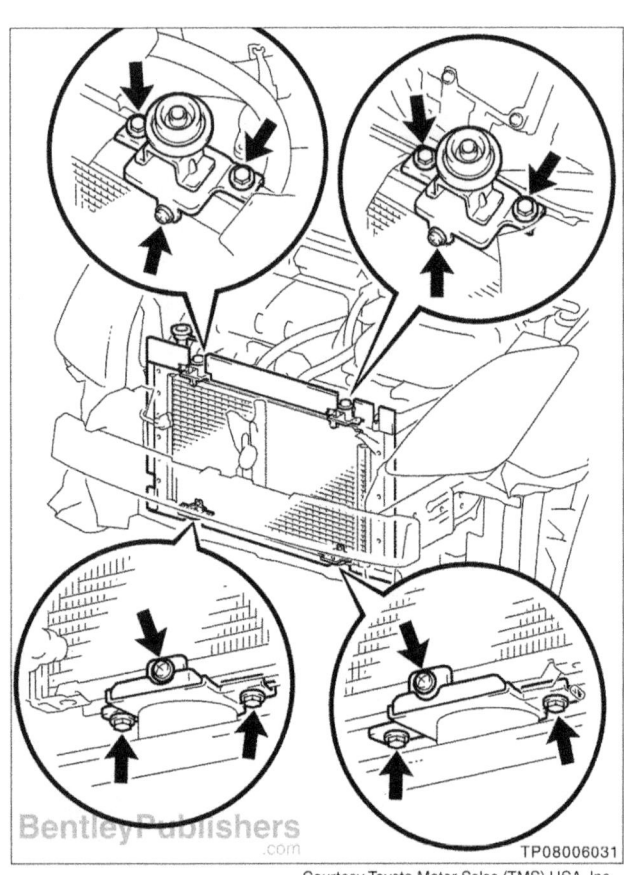

TP08006031

Courtesy Toyota Motor Sales (TMS) USA, Inc.

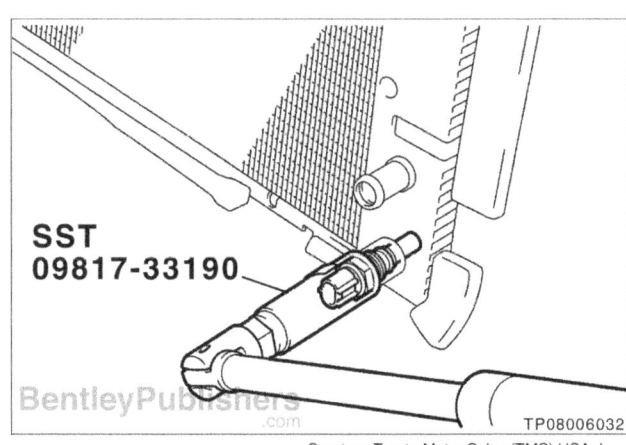

SST
09817-33190

TP08006032

Courtesy Toyota Motor Sales (TMS) USA, Inc.

◄ Use long socket (Toyota special tool SST 09817-33190 or equivalent) to remove radiator fan switch.

– Installation is reverse of removal. Use new hose clamps.

• Fill and bleed engine and transaxle cooling systems. See **Engine coolant, draining and refilling (without cooling system bleed tool)** in this chapter and **7 Hybrid Transaxle**.

• Check for coolant leaks.

Tightening torques	
Coolant reservoir bracket bolts:	
• Bracket to radiator support	20 Nm (15 ft-lb)
• Bracket to reservoir	8.5 Nm (75 in-lb)
Fan assembly to radiator	7.5 Nm (66 in-lb)
Fan switch to radiator	7 Nm (62 in-lb)
Inverter bracket bolts:	
• Bracket to radiator support	21 Nm (16 ft-lb)
• Bracket to inverter	25 Nm (18 ft-lb)
Radiator support to radiator	5 Nm (44 in-lb)

– Reinitialize power windows. See **10 Electrical System, Lights**.

– Reprogram radio and navigation system presets (if applicable).

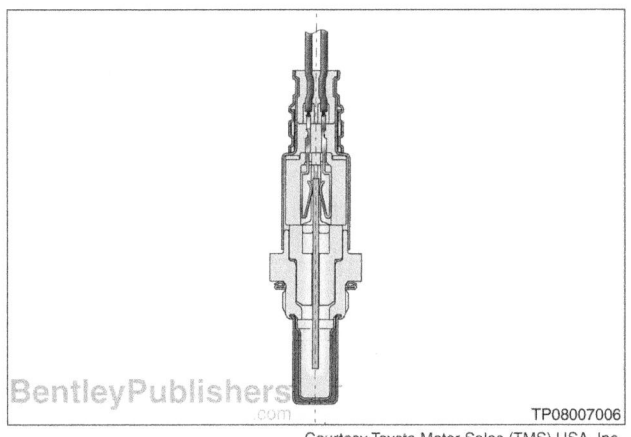

TP08007006

Courtesy Toyota Motor Sales (TMS) USA, Inc.

6

Emission Controls

Emission control functions and components

GENERAL

This chapter covers repairs to emission control components. Prius engine controls are described in **2 Prius Hybrid System**.

Hybrid safety

In addition to the safety warnings given here, always read and observe the **Warnings**, **Cautions** and safety procedures in **3 Safety** before working on vehicle. Orange-colored cables carry lethal high voltage. Use extreme care when working near high voltage cables and components.

> **WARNING—**
> • *Risk of electrocution! Avoid touching orange-colored high voltage wiring and high voltage components unless you are certain that high voltage is not present.*
>
> • *The Prius hybrid system has voltages as high as 500 volts. Voltages over 60 volts DC and 25 volts AC are a shock hazard.*

The Prius engine may start at any time if the hybrid system is in **READY** mode. See **3 Safety** for instructions on switching the hybrid system OFF.

WARNING—

• *Be sure hybrid system is OFF when servicing vehicle (READY indicator not illuminated). Failure to switch the hybrid system OFF could result in engine start at any time.*

Table a is a listing of repair procedures in this chapter and the hybrid safety requirements for each.

Table a. Hybrid safety requirements for repair procedures			
Procedure	Switch hybrid system OFF	Disconnect 12-volt battery	Remove service plug
PCV valve, servicing and replacing	✓		
Oxygen sensor, testing	✓		
Air / fuel ratio sensor, accessing	✓	✓	✓
Oxygen sensor, replacing	✓	✓	

Cautions

CAUTION—

• *Some procedures require that you disconnect the 12-volt auxiliary battery. This causes loss of radio and navigation system presets and power window initialization. Record radio and navigation system presets before disconnecting battery. Reinitialize windows after reconnecting battery. See* **10 Electrical System, Lights**.

• *Overfilling or topping off the fuel tank may cause fuel to enter the evaporative emissions (EVAP) system. This may cause a diagnostic trouble code (DTC) to set and may illuminate a warning in the instrument cluster. Overfilling may also cause fuel to enter and damage EVAP system components.*

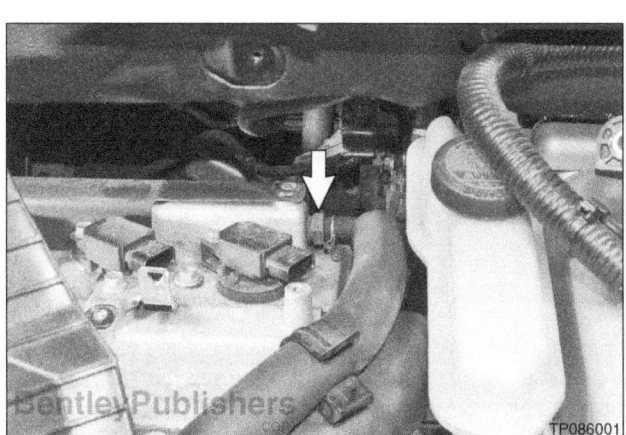

POSITIVE CRANKCASE VENTILATION (PCV) VALVE

◀ The positive crankcase ventilation (PCV) valve is located in the cylinder head cover at the left rear (transaxle side) of the engine. The PCV valve controls the flow of blowby gases from the engine crankcase to the air intake system. Oil on the air filter element may indicate a stuck PCV valve. (Photo shows PCV valve location with engine left side harness moved aside.

PCV valve, servicing and replacing

– Switch hybrid system OFF (READY indicator not illuminated). See **3 Safety**.

> **WARNING—**
> • *Be sure hybrid system is OFF when servicing vehicle (READY indicator not illuminated). Failure to switch the hybrid system OFF could result in engine start at any time.*

◀ Remove engine left side harness bracket mounting bolts (**arrows**). Tie harness aside.

◀ Disconnect hose from PCV valve and unscrew valve (**arrow**) from cylinder head cover.

– Inspect PCV valve condition.

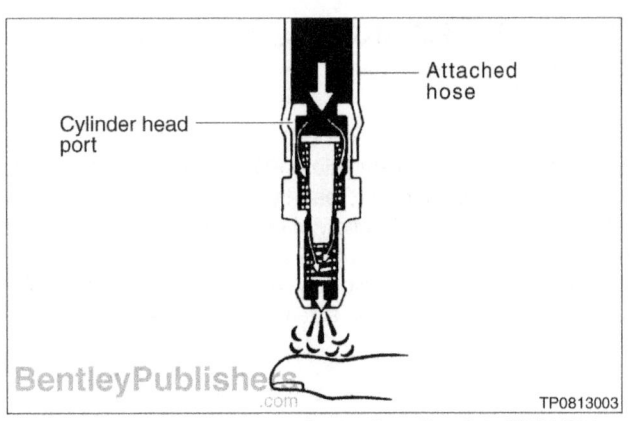

Courtesy Toyota Motor Sales (TMS) USA, Inc.

◀ Attach clean hose to cylinder head port of PCV valve. Blow low-pressure air through valve and check to see that air passes through valve.

> **WARNING—**
> • *Do not suck air through PCV valve with your mouth. Hydrocarbon deposits in valve are harmful.*

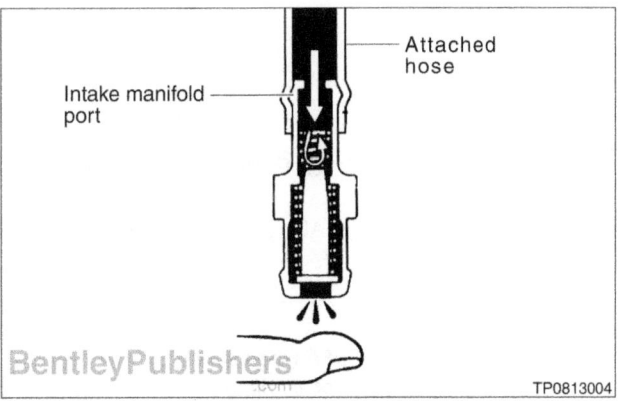

Courtesy Toyota Motor Sales (TMS) USA, Inc.

◀ Attach clean hose to intake manifold port of PCV valve. Blow low-pressure air through valve. Check to see that very little air passes through valve.

> **WARNING—**
> • *Do not suck air through PCV valve with your mouth. Hydrocarbon deposits in valve are harmful.*

– Replace PCV valve if it is stuck, clogged, or does not pass above test procedures.

Courtesy Toyota Motor Sales (TMS) USA, Inc.

◀ Inspect hoses, connections and gaskets (**arrows**) for damage or leaks.

– Installation is reverse of removal. Reconnect hose to PCV valve.

Tightening torque	
PCV valve to cylinder head cover	27 Nm (20 ft-lb)

AIR / FUEL RATIO AND OXYGEN SENSORS

The Prius is equipped with pre- and post- catalyst sensors in the exhaust system. The sensors are electronic probes positioned in the exhaust stream that function to reduce vehicle emissions.

The front (precatalyst) sensor is a heated air / fuel ratio sensor (Bank 1 Sensor 1). It is a wide-band type sensor with feedback loop circuitry. It provides the ECM with precise information about the proportions of air and fuel entering the engine allowing quick and accurate adjustments to air / fuel ratio.

At the rear (post-catalyst) location is a conventional zirconia-type heated oxygen sensor (Bank 1 Sensor 2) which monitors catalytic converter condition.

Air / fuel ratio sensor or oxygen sensor, checking for faults

Faults in sensor circuit or sensor heater circuit typically set one or more diagnostic trouble codes (DTCs) and illuminate the malfunction indicator light (MIL). Some of the DTCs that may indicate sensor failure are shown in **Table b**.

 To view fault codes, connect Toyota scan tool or equivalent to OBD II connector underneath dashboard. Be sure to use a CAN-bus compatible scan tool.

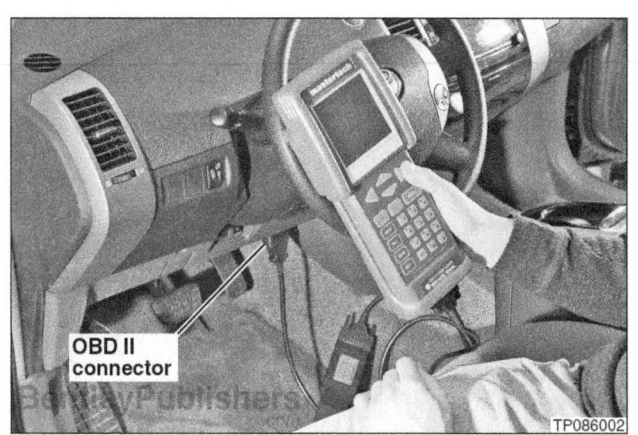

OBD II connector

TP086002

Table b. Oxygen sensor DTCs	
DTC	Possible fault
Air / fuel ratio sensor (precatalyst)	
P0031	Heater control circuit low
P0032	Heater control circuit high
P2195	Signal remains lean
P2196	Signal remains rich
P2238	Pumping current circuit low
P2239	Pumping current circuit high
P2252	Reference ground circuit low
P2253	Reference ground circuit high
P2A00	Slow response
Oxygen sensor (post-catalyst)	
P0037	Heater control circuit low
P0038	Heater control circuit high
P0136	Circuit malfunction
P0137	Circuit low voltage
P0138	Circuit high voltage

If one or more of the DTCs listed above are stored, it may be necessary to replace the corresponding sensor. There are other possible causes for these DTCs however, including:

• Open or short in sensor wiring harness or connectors

• EFI M relay (integration relay) fault

• ECM fault

• Air intake system fault

• Fuel system fault

• PCV system fault

Use a digital multimeter (DMM) to test the resistance at the sensor electrical connectors. See **Air / fuel ratio sensor or oxygen sensor circuit, testing** in this chapter.

Sensor replacement is covered in **Air / fuel ratio sensor, replacing** or **Oxygen sensor, replacing**.

Air / fuel ratio sensor or oxygen sensor circuit, testing

The connector for the precatalyst air / fuel ratio sensor is located under the inverter. See **Air / fuel ratio sensor, replacing** in this chapter.

The connector for the post-catalyst oxygen sensor is located under the carpet in passenger compartment near the console on right side. See **Oxygen sensor connector, accessing** in this chapter.

 Using digital multimeter (DMM) as an ohmmeter, measure resistance between sensor connector terminals on sensor harness (not vehicle wiring harness).

Sensor terminal resistance	
Air fuel ratio sensor connector: • Between **1** and **2**	1.8 - 3.4 Ω at 20°C (68°F)
Oxygen sensor connector: • Between **1** and **2** • Between **1** and **4**	11 - 16 Ω at 20°C (68°F) 10 kΩ min.

If resistance values are not within specifications, replace sensor. See **Air / fuel ratio sensor, replacing** or **Oxygen sensor, replacing** in this chapter.

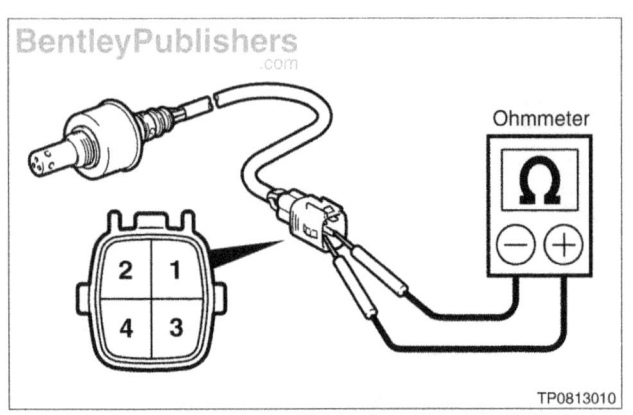

Ohmmeter

Ω

⊖ ⊕

2 1

4 3

TP0813010

Courtesy Toyota Motor Sales (TMS) USA, Inc.

Air / fuel ratio sensor, replacing

Gaining access to precatalyst air / fuel ratio sensor and its connector is an involved procedure that includes draining transaxle coolant, disconnecting high voltage power cables to motor / generators, inverter and A/C compressor, and removing inverter.

High voltage safety precautions apply and special tools and equipment are required to refill / bleed the transaxle cooling system. Be sure to read the procedure completely before starting the job.

> **WARNING—**
> • *To avoid personal injury, be sure the engine is cold before beginning this procedure.*

– Switch hybrid system OFF (READY indicator not illuminated). See **3 Safety**.

> **WARNING—**
> • *Be sure hybrid system is OFF when servicing vehicle (READY indicator not illuminated). Failure to switch the hybrid system OFF could result in engine start at any time.*

– Disconnect 12-volt auxiliary battery. See **3 Safety**.

> **CAUTION—**
> • *Disconnecting 12-volt auxiliary battery causes loss of radio and navigation system presets. Record presets before disconnecting battery.*

– Wearing insulated lineman's gloves, remove high voltage **service plug** as described in **3 Safety**.

> **WARNING—**
> • *Risk of electrocution! The Prius hybrid system has voltages as high as 500 volts. Avoid touching orange-colored high voltage wiring and high voltage components unless you are certain that high voltage is not present.*

– Remove radiator cover. See **5 Engine**.

– Raise vehicle and support safely. Make sure vehicle is level. See **4 Service and Repair Fundamentals**.

> **WARNING—**
> • *Make sure the vehicle is stable and well supported at all times. Use a professional automotive lift or jack stands designed for the purpose. A floor jack is not adequate support.*

– Remove left and right engine splash shields. See **5 Engine**.

– Drain transaxle coolant. See **7 Hybrid Transaxle**.

– Remove wiper arms, cowl cover and wiper assembly with wiper motor. See **9 Body** and **10 Electrical System, Lights**.

— Remove engine compartment upper rear bulkhead (cowl-top panel). See **9 Body**.

◄ Wearing insulated lineman's gloves, remove inverter cover fasteners (**arrows**).

- Note location of T30 Torx bolt.

- Remove inverter cover.

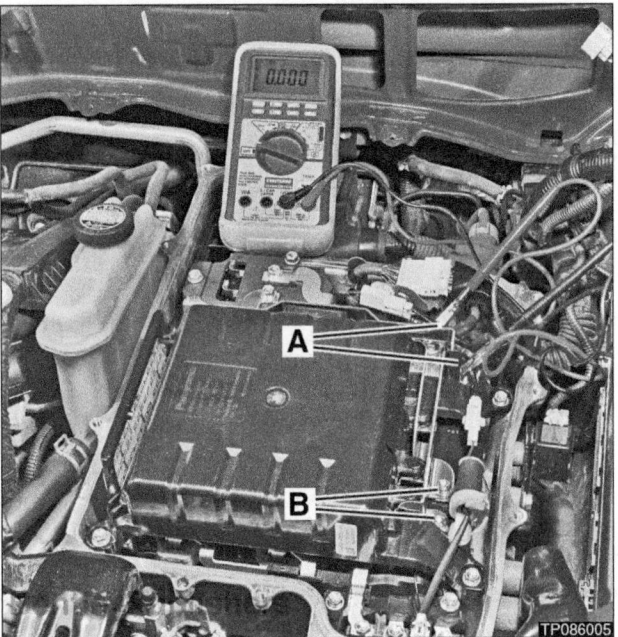

◄ Wearing insulated lineman's gloves, verify that voltage in inverter is 0 volts.

- Using a digital multimeter (DMM), measure high voltage terminals at pairs of terminals **A** and **B**. Be sure meter is set to 400 volts DC or higher.

- Measured voltage should be near 0 volts.

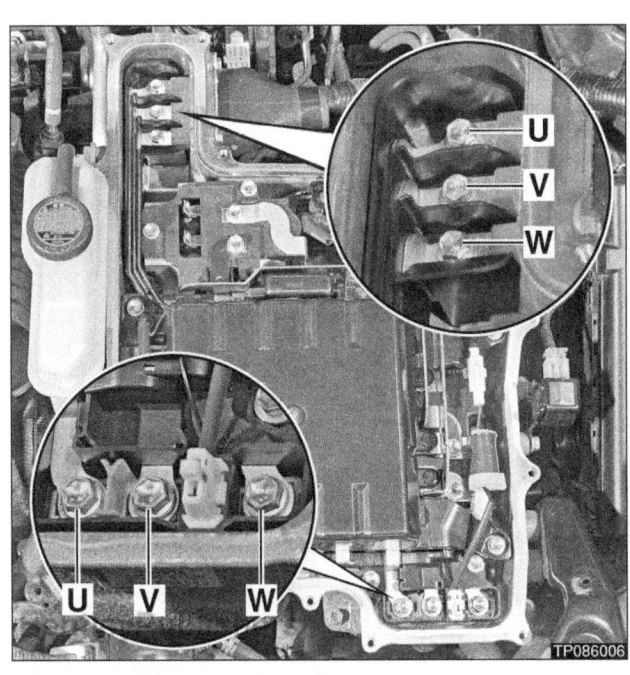

◄ Wearing insulated lineman's gloves, measure voltage between terminals of three-phase connectors (**insets**).

• Measure voltage for all combinations (**U** - **V**, **V** - **W**, **U** - **W**) at each connector. Be sure meter is set to 400 volts DC or higher.

• Measured voltage should be near 0 volts.

◄ Loosen hose clamp (**arrow**) and detach inverter cooling hose no. 2.

◄ Loosen hose clamp (**arrow**) and detach inverter cooling hose no. 1.

◄ Loosen hose clamp (**arrow**) and detach inverter cooling hose no. 6.

◄ Wearing insulated lineman's gloves, disconnect wiring harness from front airbag sensor LH (**arrow**).

◄ Wearing insulated lineman's gloves, press in locking clips (**arrows**) to detach 2 high voltage connectors from inverter assembly. Once removed, insulate connector contacts with electrical tape.

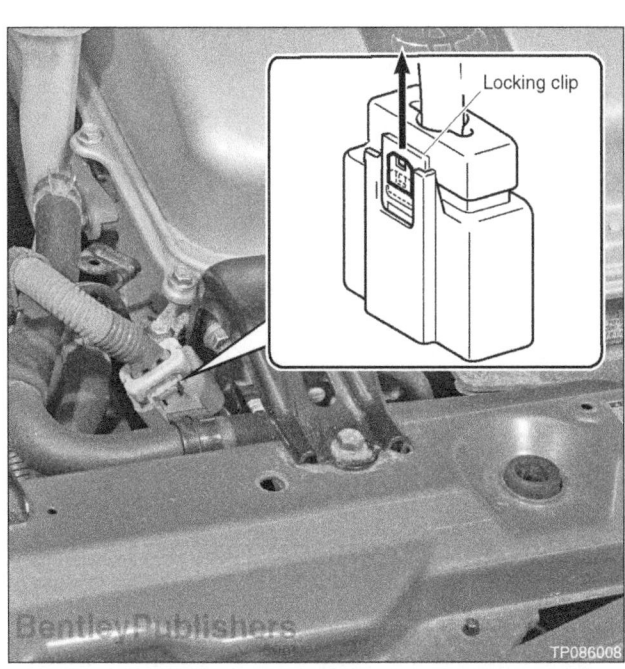

Locking clip

◀ Wearing insulated lineman's gloves:

• Use a small screwdriver to lift green locking clip (**arrow**) on A/C compressor inverter connector.

• Detach connector.

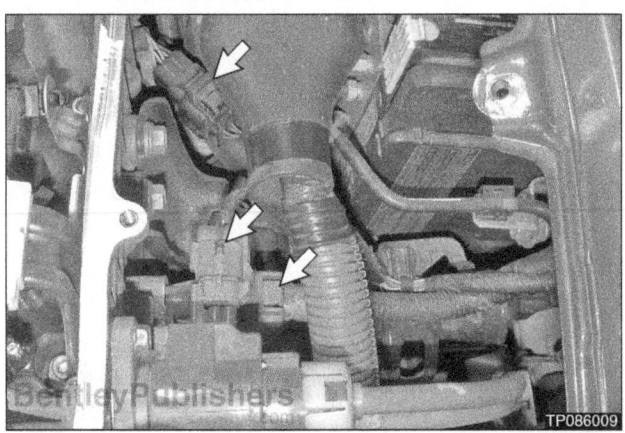

◀ Wearing insulated lineman's gloves, disconnect 3 electrical connectors (**arrows**) behind inverter housing.

◀ Wearing insulated lineman's gloves, disconnect 3 electrical connectors (**arrows**) in inverter housing.

6

◣ Wearing insulated lineman's gloves:

- Remove motor / generator power cable fasteners (**arrows**) and detach cables.
- Insulate cable connector contacts with electrical tape.

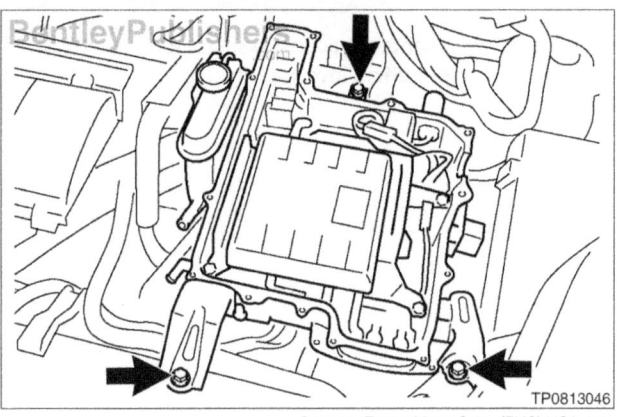

Courtesy Toyota Motor Sales (TMS) USA, Inc.

◣ Remove 3 inverter bolts (**arrows**) and lift out inverter.

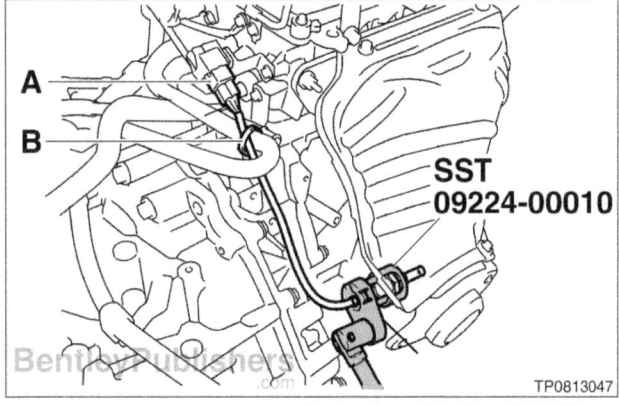

Courtesy Toyota Motor Sales (TMS) USA, Inc.

◣ Working under inverter housing:

- Detach air / fuel ratio sensor connector (**A**).
- Cut wire tie (**B**).
- Use oxygen sensor wrench (Toyota special tool SST 09224-00010 or equivalent) to remove sensor from exhaust system.

6

- Installation is reverse of removal, noting the following:
  - Apply anti-seize compound to oxygen sensor threads.
  - Wear insulated lineman's gloves when reattaching motor / generator, inverter and A/C compressor power cables.
  - Make sure electrical harnesses are not twisted and not near hot exhaust system components.
  - Make sure engine main wiring harness grommet inserts into U-shaped opening in inverter housing.
  - Use new hose clamps and wire ties as needed.
  - Wear insulated lineman's gloves when installing inverter.
  - Wear insulated lineman's gloves when installing service plug. See **3 Safety**.
  - Reconnect 12-volt auxiliary battery.
  - Fill and bleed transaxle cooling system. See **7 Hybrid Transaxle**.
  - Check for coolant leaks.

Tightening torques	
Air fuel ratio sensor to exhaust system	44 Nm (32.5 ft-lb)
Cowl cover to cowl	6.4 Nm (57 in-lb)
Inverter cover to inverter (T30 Torx bolts)	11 Nm (8 ft-lb)
Inverter to chassis	21 Nm (15.5 ft-lb)
Negative cable to 12-volt auxiliary battery	6 Nm (53 in-lb)
Power cable to motor / generator	8 Nm (71 in-lb)
Relay block to cowl	8.4 Nm (74 in-lb)
Wiper assembly to body	5.5 Nm (49 in-lb)

- Switch hybrid system ON (READY indicator illuminated) until engine starts, or run engine in inspection mode. See **11 Diagnostics**. Check engine operation.

- Adjust wiper arm position. See **10 Electrical System, Lights**.

- Reinitialize power windows. See **10 Electrical System, Lights**.

- Reenter radio and navigation system presets (if applicable).

- Road test vehicle.

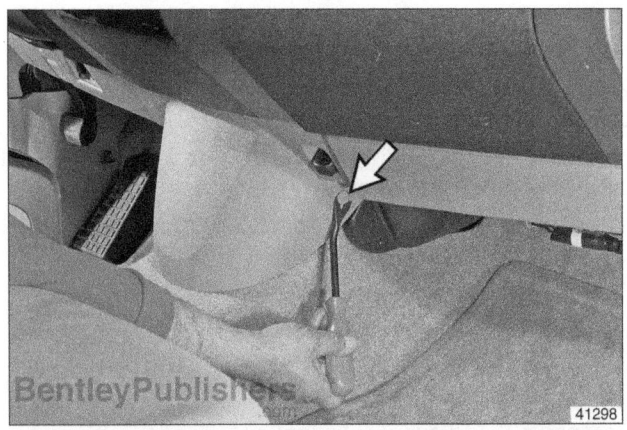

Oxygen sensor connector, accessing

The electrical connector for the post-catalyst oxygen sensor is located under the carpet in the passenger compartment on the right side of the center tunnel near the lower center finish panel.

◀ Remove clip (**arrow**) on right side of lower center finish panel.

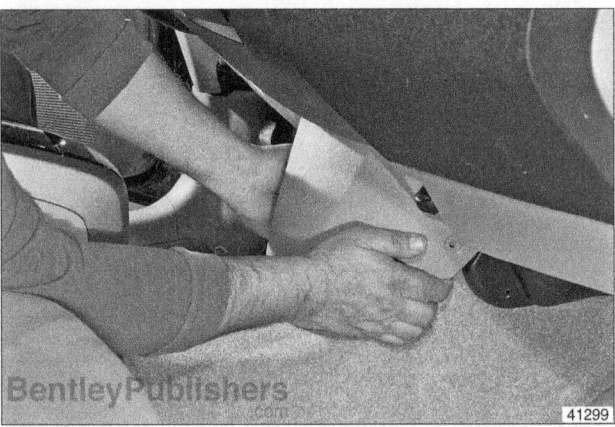

◀ Remove lower center finish panel by pulling rearward.

– Disconnect connector from 12-volt power socket.

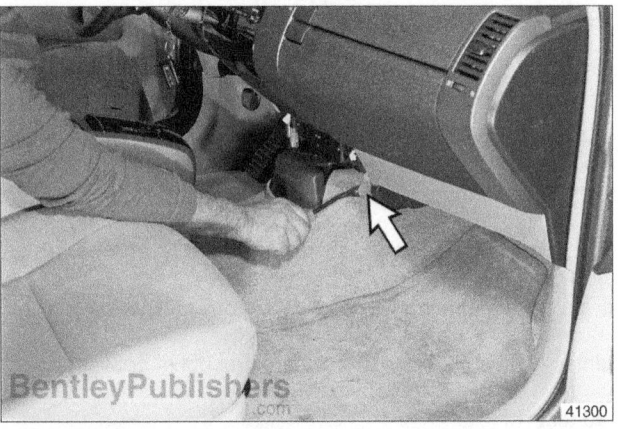

◀ Remove carpet clip (**arrow**).

◀ Pull back carpet on right side near console. Post-catalyst oxygen sensor connector (**arrow**) is now accessible.

Oxygen sensor, replacing

This procedure describes replacing the rear (post-catalyst) oxygen sensor.

> **WARNING—**
> • To avoid personal injury, be sure the engine is cold before beginning this procedure.

— Switch hybrid system OFF (READY indicator not illuminated). See **3 Safety**.

> **WARNING—**
> • Be sure hybrid system is OFF when servicing vehicle (READY indicator not illuminated). Failure to switch the hybrid system OFF could result in engine start at any time.

— Disconnect 12-volt auxiliary battery. See **3 Safety.**

> **CAUTION—**
> • Auxiliary battery disconnection causes loss of radio and navigation system presets. Record presets before disconnecting battery.

— Working in passenger compartment, pull back carpet on right side near console. Disconnect post-catalyst oxygen sensor connector. See **Oxygen sensor connector, accessing** in this chapter.

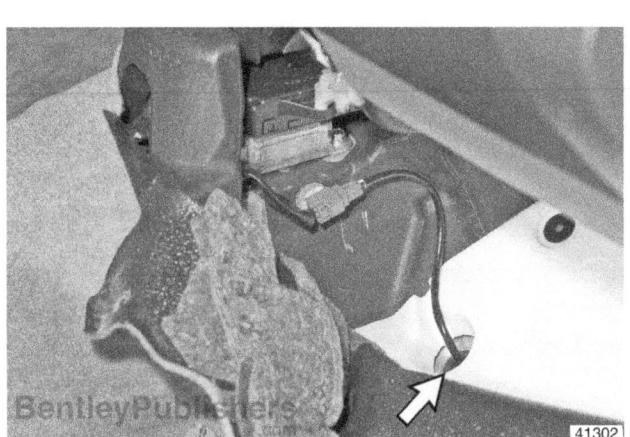

◄ Feed oxygen sensor harness connector and grommet through hole in body (**arrow**).

— Raise vehicle and support safely. See **4 Service and Repair Fundamentals**.

> **WARNING—**
> • Make sure the vehicle is stable and well supported at all times. Use a professional automotive lift or jack stands designed for the purpose. A floor jack is not adequate support.

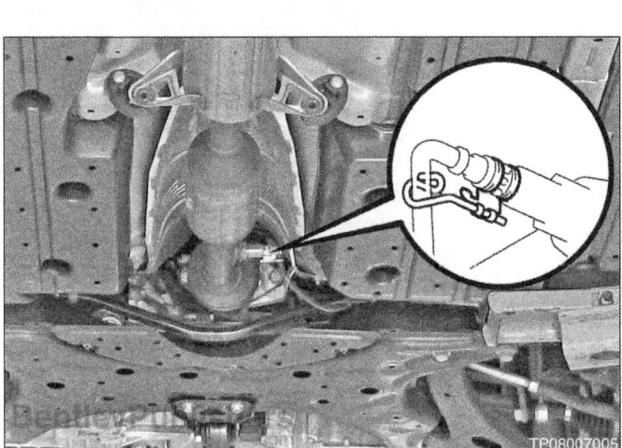

◄ Working underneath vehicle at exhaust system:
- Detach wiring harness clip (**inset**) from post-catalyst oxygen sensor.
- Use oxygen sensor wrench (Toyota special tool SST 09224-00010 or equivalent) to remove sensor from exhaust system.

— Installation is reverse of removal, noting the following:
- Apply anti-seize compound to oxygen sensor threads.
- Make sure oxygen sensor harness is not twisted and not near hot exhaust system components.
- Reconnect 12-volt auxiliary battery.

Tightening torques	
Negative cable to 12-volt auxiliary battery	6 Nm (53 in-lb)
Oxygen sensor to exhaust system	44 Nm (32.5 ft-lb)

— Switch hybrid system ON (READY indicator illuminated) until engine starts, or run engine in inspection mode.
See **11 Diagnostics**. Check engine operation.

— Reinitialize power windows. See **10 Electrical System, Lights**.

— Reprogram radio and navigation system presets (if applicable).

— Road test vehicle.

EVAPORATIVE EMISSION CONTROL (EVAP) SYSTEM

The evaporative emission control (EVAP) system stores and purges fuel vapors (hydrocarbons or HC) which normally occur within the fuel system. To prevent HC from escaping to the atmosphere, the EVAP system uses a canister filled with charcoal granules which absorb and store the HC. When operating conditions are appropriate, the system purges HC from the charcoal canister to the engine intake manifold.

Inspect fuel and EVAP system components, vacuum lines and hoses to make sure they are free of leaks and in good condition. Leaks anywhere in the fuel and EVAP systems may cause diagnostic trouble codes (DTCs) to be set and the malfunction indicator light (MIL) to illuminate.

Very small EVAP system leaks can be difficult to locate. They may require the use of specialized equipment to locate and repair. Such procedures are beyond the scope of this manual.

Fuel filler cap gasket, checking

The fuel filler cap is an EVAP system component. Check to make sure that it is tight when vehicle is in use. A loose fuel filler cap or defective cap gasket (**arrow**) are common causes for DTCs indicating EVAP leaks.

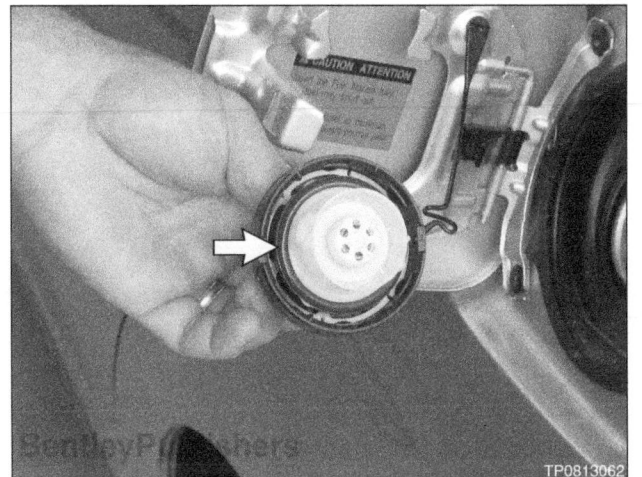

– Inspect filler cap for cracks or damage.

– Inspect filler cap gasket for tears or defects. Also inspect gasket seating surface in fuel filler pipe.

– If DTCs are present indicating an EVAP system leak, see **11 Diagnostics**.

TP0813062

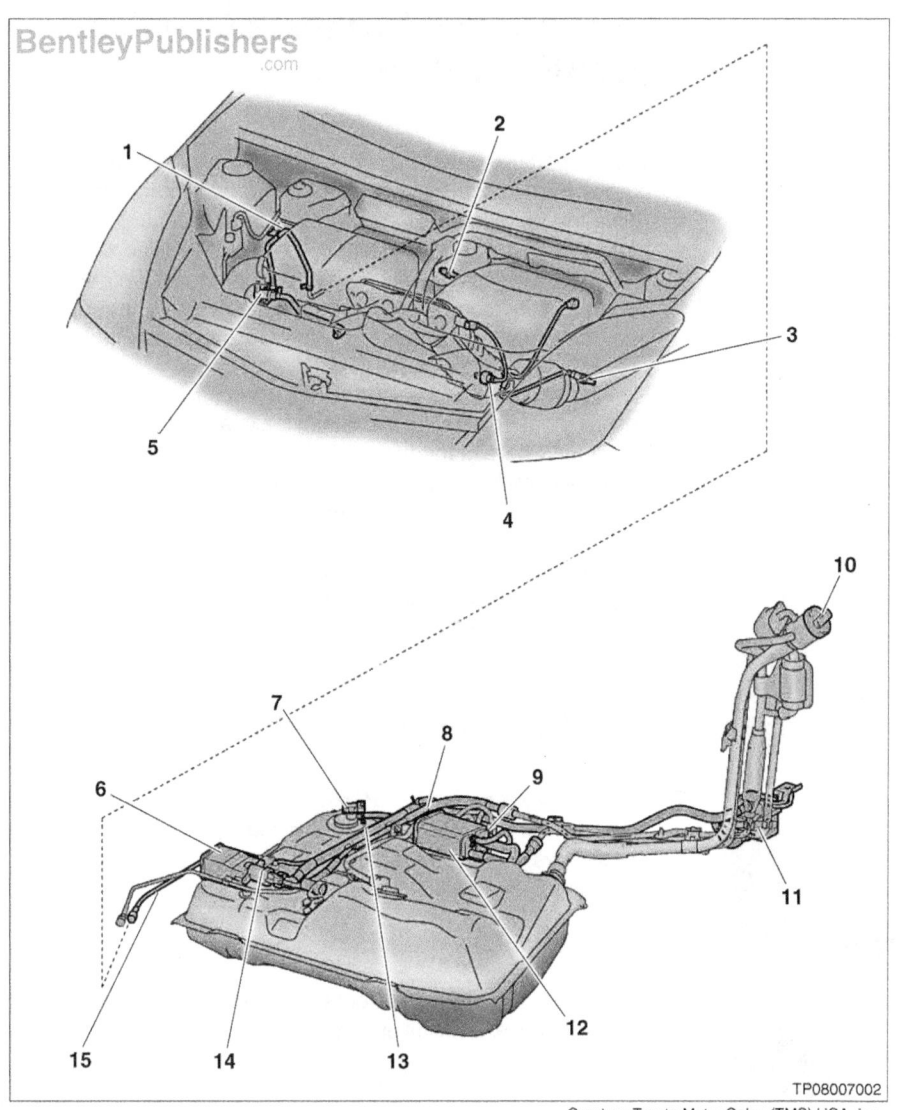

TP08007002
Courtesy Toyota Motor Sales (TMS) USA, Inc.

EVAP system components

1. Purge port
2. Ventilation valve assembly
3. Post-catalyst oxygen sensor
4. Precatalyst oxygen sensor (air / fuel ratio sensor)
5. EVAP vacuum valve 2
6. Canister outlet valve
7. Vapor pressure sensor
8. Air inlet line
9. Vacuum switching valve (purge flow valve)
10. Fuel filler cap
11. Charcoal canister filter
12. Charcoal canister
13. EVAP lines
14. Canister closed valve
15. Purge lines

TP08008010

7

Hybrid Transaxle

Transaxle fluid service

GENERAL

This chapter covers transaxle coolant and lubricant service.

See maintenance schedules in **4 Service and Repair Fundamentals** for recommended transaxle coolant and lubricant service intervals.

Hybrid safety

In addition to the safety warnings given here, always read and observe the **Warnings**, **Cautions** and safety procedures in **3 Safety** before working on vehicle. Orange-colored cables carry lethal high voltage. Use extreme care when working near high voltage cables and components.

WARNING—

- *Risk of electrocution! Avoid touching orange-colored high voltage wiring and high voltage components unless you are certain that high voltage is not present.*

- *The Prius hybrid system has voltages as high as 500 volts. Voltages over 60 volts DC and 25 volts AC are a shock hazard.*

The Prius engine may start at any time if the hybrid system is in **READY** mode. See **3 Safety** for instructions on turning OFF the hybrid system.

WARNING—

• *Be sure hybrid system is OFF when servicing vehicle (READY indicator not illuminated). Failure to switch the hybrid system OFF could result in engine start at any time.*

Table a is a listing of repair procedures in this chapter and the hybrid safety requirements for each.

Table a. Hybrid safety requirements for repair procedures			
Procedure	Switch hybrid system OFF	Disconnect 12-volt battery	Remove service plug
Transaxle coolant, checking level	✓		
Transaxle coolant, draining and filling	✓		
Transaxle lubricant, checking level	✓		
Transaxle lubricant, changing	✓		

Warnings and Cautions

WARNING—

• *When draining automotive fluids, collect in suitable containers. Do not use food or beverage containers that might mislead someone into drinking from them.*

• *Greases, lubricants and other automotive chemicals contain toxic substances, many of which are absorbed directly through the skin. Read the manufacturer's instructions and warnings carefully. Use hand and eye protection. Avoid prolonged direct skin contact.*

• *Store flammable fluids away from fire hazards.*

• *Wipe up spills at once, but do not store oily towels which can ignite and burn spontaneously.*

CAUTION—

• *Some procedures require that you disconnect the 12-volt auxiliary battery. This causes loss of radio and navigation system presets and power window initialization. Record radio and navigation system presets before disconnecting battery. Reinitialize windows after reconnecting battery. See* **10 Electrical System, Lights**.

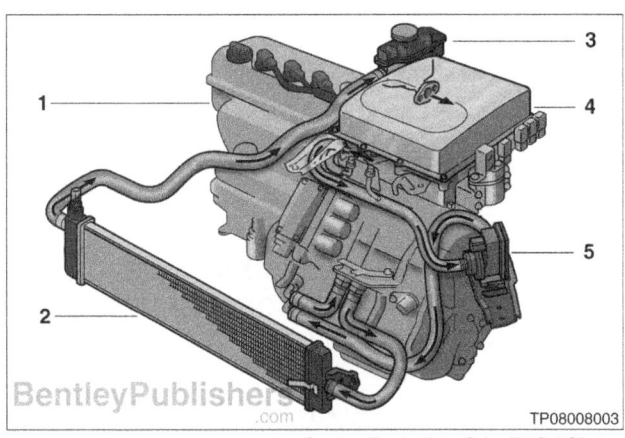

Courtesy Toyota Motor Sales (TMS) USA, Inc.

TP08008003

TRANSAXLE / INVERTER COOLANT SERVICE

◄ The Prius transaxle / inverter assembly is cooled by a dedicated liquid cooling system that is separate from the engine cooling system, with its own radiator, coolant supply, reservoir, and electric pump.

1. Engine

2. Transaxle / inverter coolant radiator

3. Transaxle / inverter coolant reservoir

4. Transaxle / inverter assembly

5. Transaxle / inverter coolant electric pump

Toyota recommends periodic coolant replacement. See maintenance schedules in **4 Service and Repair Fundamentals**.

Transaxle / inverter coolant, checking level

◄ Transaxle / inverter coolant reservoir (**arrow**) is in engine compartment rear, near cowl. Check coolant level with engine cold.

> **WARNING—**
> • *Allow transaxle to cool before checking coolant. Hot coolant can cause severe burns.*

– Switch hybrid system OFF (READY indicator not illuminated). See **3 Safety**.

> **WARNING—**
> • *Make sure hybrid system is OFF when servicing vehicle (READY indicator not illuminated). Failure to switch the hybrid system OFF could result in engine start at any time.*

◄ Coolant level is visible through translucent plastic reservoir.

• Make sure coolant level is near FULL mark on reservoir.

• If level is low, check cooling system for leaks.

• Remove reservoir cap and add coolant as required.

> **CAUTION—**
> • *Do not use alcohol-type coolant or plain water alone. Using incorrect coolant may damage the cooling system.*

Transaxle / inverter coolant specification	
Recommended coolant	Toyota super long life coolant (SLLC) or equivalent

TP08008001a

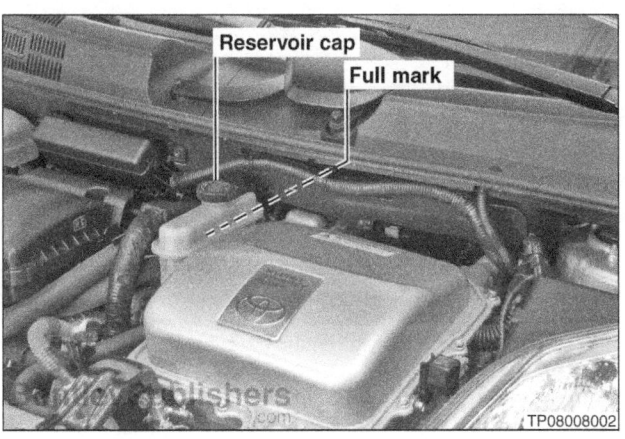

Reservoir cap

Full mark

TP08008002

NOTE—

- *Toyota specifies high-quality nonsilicate, nonamine, nonborate ethylene glycol coolant with long-life hybrid organic acid technology. Toyota super long life coolant (SLLC) meets these requirements.*
- *Toyota SLLC is premixed with water in the correct ratio.*

— Reinstall coolant reservoir cap.

Transaxle / inverter coolant, draining and refilling (without cooling system bleed tool)

The following procedure is based on Toyota repair information. A critical part of draining and filling the cooling system is bleeding air from the system after the refill. This is a time consuming procedure. Be sure to read the complete procedure before starting work.

NOTE—

- *Why is bleeding necessary after refilling the cooling system? The intricate design of the Prius cooling system may cause air to become trapped during refilling. Trapped air prevents proper coolant flow, possibly causing overheating and setting DTCs.*
- *For automotive professionals, an additional approach to filling and bleeding the system is given under* **Transaxle / inverter coolant, draining and refilling (with cooling system bleed tool)** *in this chapter. The procedure requires a special cooling system bleed tool and a source of compressed air.*

> *WARNING—*
> - *To avoid personal injury, be sure the engine is cold before beginning this procedure.*

— Switch hybrid system OFF (READY indicator not illuminated). See **3 Safety**.

> *WARNING—*
> - *Make sure hybrid system is OFF when servicing vehicle (READY indicator not illuminated). Failure to switch the hybrid system OFF could result in engine start at any time.*

◄ Remove coolant reservoir cap (**arrow**).

— Remove radiator cover. See **5 Engine**.

— Raise vehicle and support safely. Make sure vehicle is level. See **4 Service and Repair Fundamentals**.

> *WARNING—*
> - *Make sure the vehicle is stable and well supported at all times. Use a professional automotive lift or jack stands designed for the purpose. A floor jack is not adequate support.*

TP08008001

– Place coolant drain pan underneath transaxle.

◀ Remove transaxle / inverter coolant drain plug and allow coolant to drain.

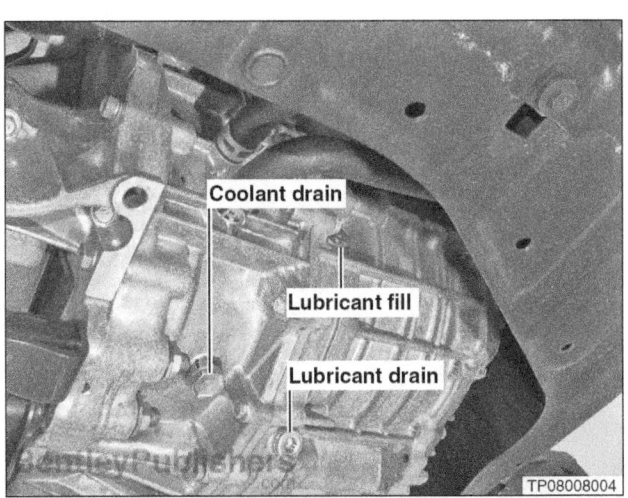

> **CAUTION—**
> • *Be sure to remove correct drain plug.*
> • *Automotive antifreeze is poisonous and lethal, especially to pets. Clean up spills immediately and rinse area with water.*
> • *Dispose of coolant in an environmentally safe manner.*

– Inspect and clean coolant drain plug. Replace drain plug seal.

– Install drain plug and tighten to specification.

Tightening torque	
Coolant drain plug to transaxle housing	39 Nm (29 ft-lb)

◀ Loosen bleeder plug (**arrow**) at front of transaxle / inverter assembly.

◀ Working at transaxle / inverter coolant reservoir:

• Remove reservoir cap.

• Connect length of transparent plastic hose (¼ inch inside diameter, 30 inches long) to bleeder plug and place other end of hose into coolant reservoir as shown.

• Cover coolant reservoir with shop towel to prevent coolant from splashing.

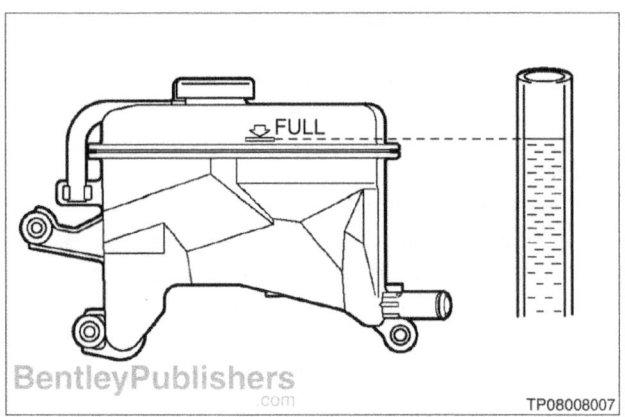

TP08008007

Courtesy Toyota Motor Sales (TMS) USA, Inc.

◀ Add coolant to reservoir until level of coolant in hose reaches same level as FULL mark on reservoir. Close bleeder.

Transaxle / inverter coolant specification	
Recommended coolant	Toyota super long life coolant (SLLC) or equivalent

NOTE—

- *Toyota specifies high-quality nonsilicate, nonamine, nonborate ethylene glycol coolant with long-life hybrid organic acid technology. Toyota super long life coolant (SLLC) meets these requirements.*
- *Toyota SLLC is premixed with water in the correct ratio.*

— Switch ignition ON:
  - Press and release POWER switch twice.
  - Do not depress brake pedal.

— Allow transaxle coolant pump to run for approximately 20 seconds. Press and release POWER switch again to turn ignition OFF.

— Loosen bleeder plug and bleed air from cooling system. Again add coolant to reservoir until level of coolant in hose reaches same level as FULL mark on reservoir.

— Close bleeder again. Switch ignition ON and allow transaxle coolant pump to run for 20 seconds. Turn ignition OFF.

— Repeat bleeding steps, each time adding more coolant, until sound from transaxle coolant pump becomes lower in pitch and more muffled, and coolant in reservoir flows faster.

— Switch ignition ON and allow coolant pump to run for approximately 5 minutes after completing air bleeding.

— Make sure bleeder plug is closed and tightened.

— Add coolant until reservoir is full. Reinstall coolant reservoir cap.

Transaxle / inverter coolant capacity	
P112 transaxle / inverter assembly	2.7 liters (2.9 US qt)

— Reinstall radiator cover.

— Run engine and check for coolant leaks.

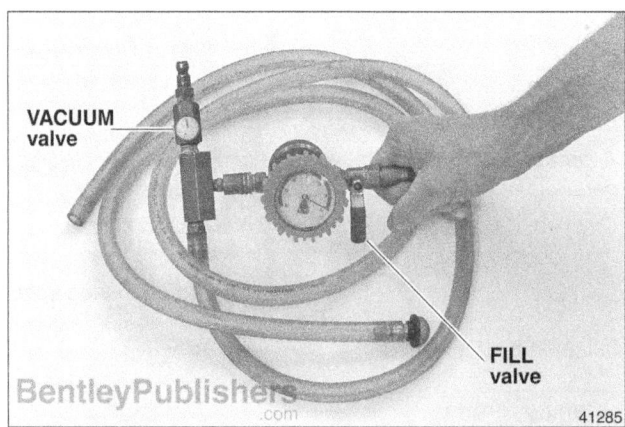

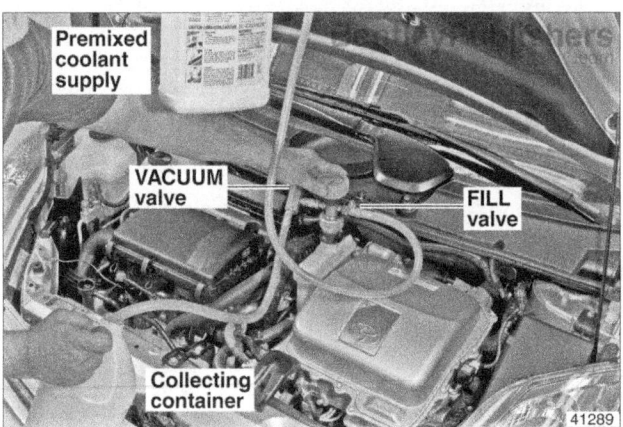

Transaxle / inverter coolant, draining and refilling (with cooling system bleed tool)

◄ The following procedure uses a compressed-air-operated cooling system bleed tool. This procedure does not require the use of the factory scan tool, but an OBD II scan tool may be necessary to clear any DTCs set during the draining procedure. Be sure to read the complete procedure before starting work.

NOTE—

• Why is bleeding necessary after refilling the cooling system? The intricate design of the Prius transaxle / inverter cooling system may cause air to become trapped during refilling. Trapped air prevents proper coolant flow, possibly causing overheating and setting DTCs.

◄ The cooling system bleed tool works as follows: Starting with a drained cooling system, the tool uses compressed air to create a partial vacuum in the cooling system. Once the cooling system is placed under vacuum, the VACUUM valve on the tool is closed and the FILL valve is opened. Premixed coolant (such as Toyota SLLC) is pushed by atmospheric pressure up a hose inserted into the bottom of a coolant supply container, through the cooling system bleed tool and into the cooling system.

The process (draw vacuum, fill, draw vacuum, fill, etc.) may need to be repeated several times to remove all air from the system. Coolant hoses may collapse during the procedure.

WARNING—

• To avoid personal injury, be sure the engine and transaxle are cold before beginning this procedure.

– Switch hybrid system OFF (READY indicator not illuminated). See **3 Safety**.

WARNING—

• Make sure hybrid system is OFF when servicing vehicle (READY indicator not illuminated). Failure to switch the hybrid system OFF could result in engine start at any time.

– Raise vehicle and support safely. Make sure vehicle is level. See **4 Service and Repair Fundamentals**.

WARNING—

• Make sure the vehicle is stable and well supported at all times. Use a professional automotive lift or jack stands designed for the purpose. A floor jack is not adequate support.

◄ Remove transaxle / inverter coolant reservoir cap (**arrow**)..

WARNING—

• Do not remove reservoir cap when transaxle is hot. Hot coolant may spray under pressure and cause severe burns.

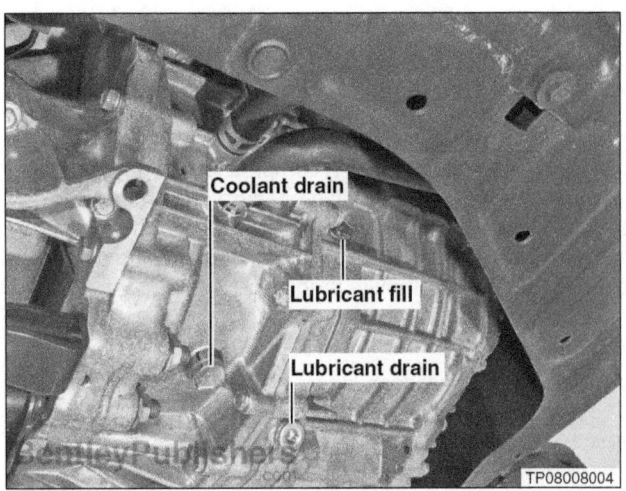

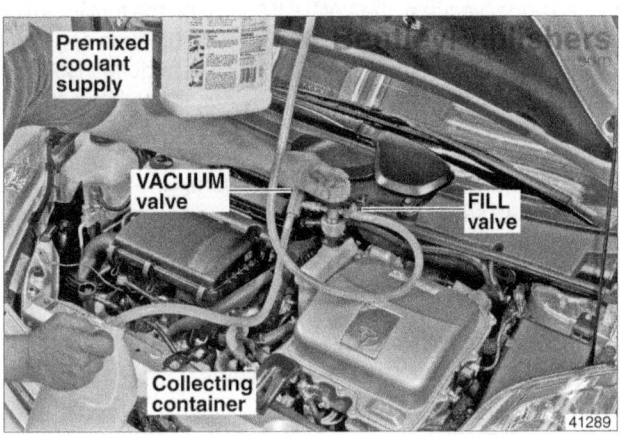

– Place coolant drain pan underneath transaxle.

◄ Remove transaxle / inverter coolant drain plug and allow coolant to drain.

> **CAUTION—**
> - *Be sure to remove correct drain plug.*
> - *Automotive antifreeze is poisonous and lethal, especially to pets. Clean up spills immediately and rinse area with water.*
> - *Dispose of coolant in an environmentally safe manner.*

– Inspect and clean coolant drain plug. Replace drain plug seal.

– Install drain plug and tighten to specification.

Tightening torque	
Coolant drain plug to transaxle housing	39 Nm (29 ft-lb)

– Lower vehicle.

◄ Install cooling system bleed tool on transaxle / inverter coolant reservoir filler neck per manufacturer's instructions.

– Attach compressed air supply hose to cooling system bleed tool.

> **NOTE—**
> - *Cooling system bleed tool typically requires approx. 90 psi line pressure.*

– Place cooling system bleed tool suction hose (coolant supply hose) into container of premixed coolant. Suction hose should go to bottom of container. Place container so that bottom of container is higher than coolant reservoir filler neck to aid siphon action when refilling.

> **CAUTION—**
> - *Do not use alcohol-type coolant or plain water alone. Using incorrect coolant may damage the transaxle / inverter cooling system.*

Transaxle / inverter coolant specification	
Recommended coolant	Toyota super long life coolant (SLLC) or equivalent
Coolant capacity	2.7 liters (2.9 US qt)

> **NOTE—**
> - *Toyota specifies high-quality nonsilicate, nonamine, nonborate ethylene glycol coolant with long-life hybrid organic acid technology. Toyota super long life coolant (SLLC) meets these requirements.*
> - *Toyota SLLC is premixed with water in the correct ratio.*
> - *Be sure to have sufficient quantity of approved coolant available.*

– Place cooling system bleed tool vent hose into an empty container to collect any liquid that may discharge.

— Turn compressed air supply ON and open VACUUM valve on tool to begin evacuating cooling system. Continue until level of vacuum on gauge reaches manufacturer's recommended value.

NOTE—

- *Some technicians begin by purging air from suction hose (coolant supply hose) before evacuating cooling system. As soon as air supply is turned ON and a low vacuum exists in the system, crack open coolant supply (FILL) valve on tool to draw coolant up tube, then close coolant supply valve.*

— When desired level of vacuum is reached, close VACUUM valve and open FILL valve on tool. Coolant is drawn from container of premixed coolant into cooling system. When container is nearly empty, close FILL valve and refill container. Keep end of pickup tube submerged in coolant. Again open FILL valve on tool. Continue filling system until reading on vacuum gauge drops to zero.

— Remove cooling system bleed tool from reservoir filler neck. Make sure coolant level in reservoir is between LOW and FULL marks on reservoir.

— If coolant level is low, reattach cooling system bleed tool and repeat air bleeding procedure.

— Switch ignition ON:
   - Press and release POWER switch twice.
   - Do not depress brake pedal.

— Allow transaxle coolant pump to run for approximately 5 minutes. Sound from transaxle coolant pump should be low in pitch and muffled, and you can see coolant flowing through reservoir.

— Press and release POWER switch to turn ignition OFF.

— Add coolant to reservoir up to FULL mark. Reinstall coolant reservoir cap.

— Check for coolant leaks.

— Clear any diagnostic trouble codes set. See **11 Diagnostics**.

TRANSAXLE LUBRICANT SERVICE

The 2004 - 2008 Prius is equipped with the P112 hybrid transaxle. Be sure to use the correct lubricant when topping off or changing transaxle fluid.

> **CAUTION—**
> • Using an incorrect fluid type, or insufficient or excessive quantities of fluid in the transaxle can cause serious failures.

See **4 Service and Repair Fundamentals** for recommended transaxle fluid service intervals.

Transaxle lubricant, checking level

> **WARNING—**
> • Allow transaxle to cool before checking or draining lubricant. Hot transaxle lubricant can cause severe burns.

− Switch hybrid system OFF (READY indicator not illuminated). See **3 Safety**.

> **WARNING—**
> • Make sure hybrid system is OFF when servicing vehicle (READY indicator not illuminated). Failure to switch the hybrid system OFF could result in engine start at any time.

− Raise vehicle and support safely. Make sure vehicle is level. See **4 Service and Repair Fundamentals**.

> **WARNING—**
> • Make sure the vehicle is stable and well supported at all times. Use a professional automotive lift or jack stands designed for the purpose. A floor jack is not adequate support.

◄ Remove transaxle lubricant fill plug. Be prepared to catch dripping fluid.

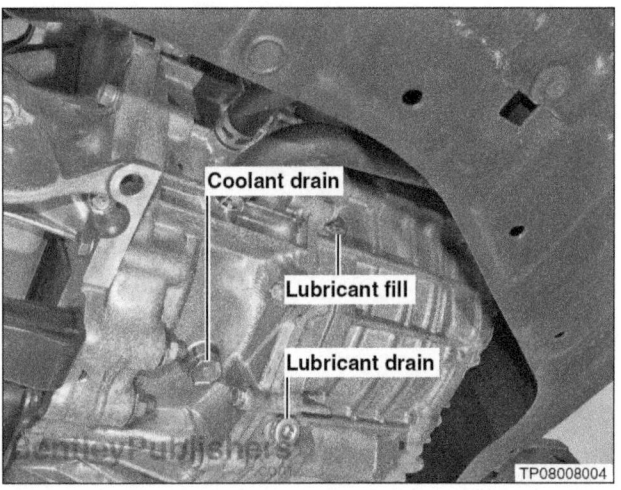

Coolant drain
Lubricant fill
Lubricant drain

TP08008004

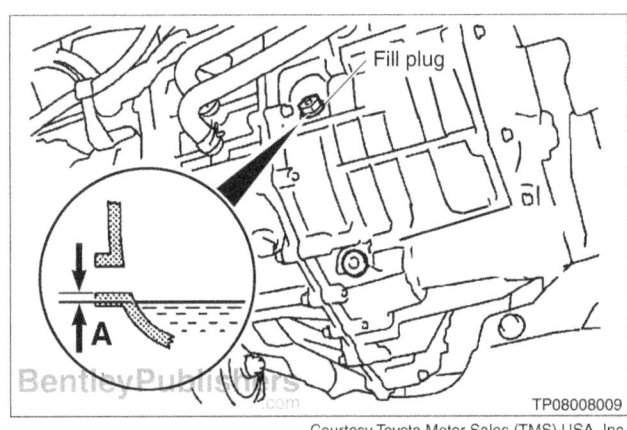

Fill plug

TP08008009

Courtesy Toyota Motor Sales (TMS) USA, Inc.

◀ Use suction gun or squeeze bottle to add fluid if needed.

- Correct fluid level (**A**) is 0 - 5 mm (0 - 0.2 in) from lower edge of filler hole. Do not overfill.
- If fluid is low, check transaxle for leaks.
- Add recommended type of fluid only.

Recommended transaxle lubricant	
P112 transaxle	ATF type WS

– Inspect and clean fill plug. Replace fill plug seal and reinstall to specifications.

Tightening torque	
Fill plug to transaxle housing	39 Nm (29 ft-lb)

Transaxle lubricant, changing

WARNING—
- *Allow transaxle to cool before checking or draining lubricant. Hot transaxle lubricant can cause severe burns.*

– Switch hybrid system OFF (READY indicator not illuminated). See **3 Safety**.

WARNING—
- *Make sure hybrid system is OFF when servicing vehicle (READY indicator not illuminated). Failure to switch the hybrid system OFF could result in engine start at any time.*

– Raise vehicle and support safely. Make sure vehicle is level. See **4 Service and Repair Fundamentals**.

WARNING—
- *Make sure the vehicle is stable and well supported at all times. Use a professional automotive lift or jack stands designed for the purpose. A floor jack is not adequate support.*

◀ Remove transaxle lubricant drain plug and allow fluid to drain.

CAUTION—
- *Be sure to remove correct drain plug.*
- *Dispose of used fluids in an environmentally safe manner.*

– Inspect and clean lubricant drain plug. Replace drain plug seal.

– Install drain plug and tighten to specification.

Tightening torque	
Drain plug to transaxle housing	39 Nm (29 ft-lb)

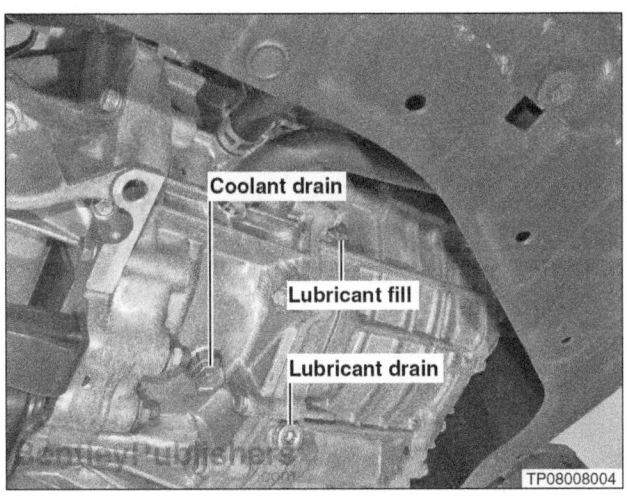

Coolant drain

Lubricant fill

Lubricant drain

TP08008004

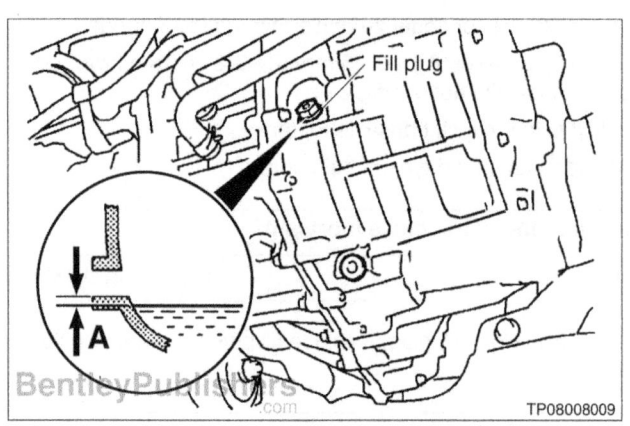

TP08008009

Courtesy Toyota Motor Sales (TMS) USA, Inc.

◄ Remove lubricant fill plug. Use suction gun or squeeze bottle to add fluid.

- Correct fluid level (**A**) is 0 - 5 mm (0 - 0.2 in) from lower edge of filler hole. Do not overfill.
- Add recommended type of fluid only.

Transaxle lubricant specifications	
Lubricant	ATF type WS
Fill capacity	3.8 liters (4.0 US qt)

– Inspect and clean lubricant fill plug. Replace fill plug seal and reinstall. Tighten to specification.

Tightening torque	
Fill plug to transaxle housing	39 Nm (29 ft-lb)

– Recheck fluid level after vehicle is driven.

TP0809017

8

Brakes, Suspension and Steering

Common underbody service and repairs

GENERAL

This chapter covers brake, suspension and steering repairs. Basic hand tools and some special tools are required. Read procedures through before beginning work.

See **4 Service and Repair Fundamentals** for maintenance advice and for recommended brake, suspension and steering system service intervals.

Hybrid safety

In addition to the safety warnings given here, always read and observe the **Warnings**, **Cautions** and safety procedures in **3 Safety** before working on vehicle. Orange-colored cables carry lethal high voltage. Use extreme care when working near high voltage cables and components.

> **WARNING—**
> • *Risk of electrocution! Avoid touching orange-colored high voltage wiring and high voltage components unless you are certain that high voltage is not present.*
> • *The Prius hybrid system has voltages as high as 500 volts. Voltages over 60 volts DC and 25 volts AC are a shock hazard.*

The Prius engine may start at any time if the hybrid system is in **READY** mode. See **3 Safety** for instructions on turning off the hybrid system.

> **WARNING—**
> • *Be sure hybrid system is OFF when servicing vehicle (READY indicator not illuminated). Failure to switch the hybrid system OFF could result in engine start at any time.*

Table a is a listing of repair procedures in this chapter and the hybrid safety requirements for each.

Table a. Hybrid safety requirements for repair procedures			
Procedure	Switch hybrid system OFF	Disconnect 12-volt battery	Remove service plug
Brakes repairs	✓		
Front suspension repairs	✓		
Rear suspension repairs	✓		
Driver airbag removal	✓	✓	✓
Steering wheel removal	✓	✓	✓
Wheel and tire repairs	✓		

Warnings and Cautions

> **WARNING**—
> - *Brake system bleeding must be performed using a Toyota scan tool or equivalent. See* **Brake fluid, bleeding** *in this chapter.*
> - *Semimetallic and metallic brake friction materials in brake pads or shoes produce dangerous dust. Treat all brake dust as a hazardous material. Do not create dust by grinding, sanding or cleaning brake friction surfaces with compressed air.*
> - *Brake fluid is poisonous, corrosive and dangerous to the environment. Wear safety glasses and rubber gloves when working with brake fluid. Do not siphon brake fluid with your mouth. Dispose of brake fluid properly.*
> - *A car with electronic stability control is still subject to normal physical laws. Avoid excessive speeds for the road conditions encountered.*
> - *The airbag mounted in the steering wheel is an explosive device. Treat it with extreme caution.*
> - *Serious injury may result if airbag system service is attempted by persons unfamiliar with the Toyota SRS and its approved service procedures.*
> - *Improper handling of the airbag could cause serious injury. Store the airbag with the horn pad facing up. If stored facing down, accidental deployment could propel airbag violently into the air, causing injury.*
> - *Before performing any work involving airbags, disconnect the negative (-) battery cable. See* **3 Safety***.*
> - *Toyota airbags are equipped with a back-up power supply inside the airbag control module. Observe a 90 second waiting period after disconnecting the battery cable to allow the reserve power supply to discharge.*
> - *Do not reuse self-locking nuts. They are designed to be used only once and may fail if reused. Replace with new.*
> - *Do not install bolts and nuts coated with undercoating wax, as correct tightening torque cannot be assured. Clean the threads with solvent before installation, or install new parts.*
> - *Do not attempt to weld or straighten steering components. Replace damaged parts.*
> - *When working on brake and steering components, maintain absolute cleanliness to ensure proper operation of the hydraulic system.*

> **CAUTION**—
> - *Some procedures require that you disconnect the 12-volt auxiliary battery. This causes loss of radio and navigation system presets, and power window initialization. Record radio and navigation presets before disconnecting battery. Reinitialize windows after reconnecting battery. See* **10 Electrical System, Lights***.*
> - *Brake fluid damages paint. Immediately clean brake fluid spilled on painted surfaces and wash with water.*
> - *Use new brake fluid from a fresh, unopened container. Brake fluid absorbs moisture from the air. This can lead to corrosion in the brake system and lower fluid boiling point.*

BRAKES

Prius models are equipped with front disc and rear drum brakes. The front brakes have ventilated discs, and the rear brakes use leading-trailing shoes. Both front and rear brakes are auto-adjusting. A pedal-type mechanical parking brake acts on the rear drum brake shoes.

On Prius models with the electronically controlled brake (ECB) system, procedures such as retracting caliper pistons, installing new brake pads, replacing brake rotors, or bleeding the brakes may cause diagnostic trouble codes (DTCs) to set and brake warning light to illuminate when the brake pedal is depressed after the repair is completed. See **11 Diagnostics** for service procedures to extinguish the malfunction indicator light (MIL) if DTCs occur.

See **4 Service and Repair Fundamentals** for recommended brake system service intervals.

NOTE—

• *Some procedures in this section require the use of a Toyota scan tool, or equivalent.*

Front brake components

1. **Slide pin bolt**
   • Tighten to 34 Nm (25 ft-lb)

2. **Antisqueal shim**

3. **Inner antisqueal shim**
   • Apply disc brake grease to both sides (**arrows**) when installing

4. **Inner pad**

5. **Outer pad**

6. **Pad support plates**

7. **Brake caliper**

8. **Pad carrier**

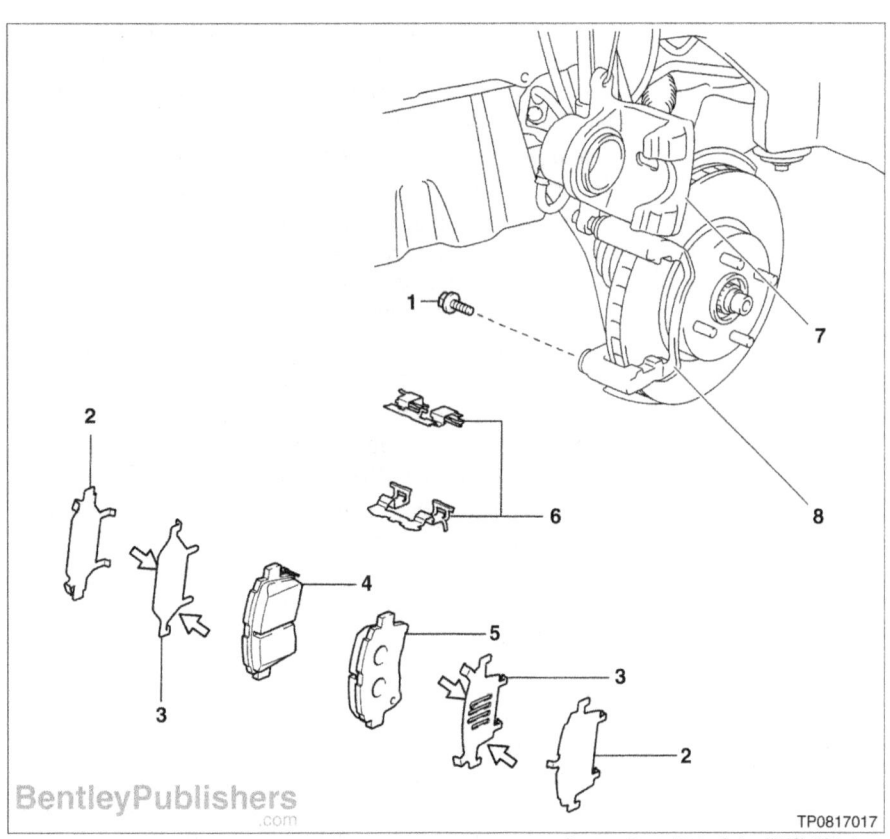

TP0817017

Courtesy Toyota Motor Sales (TMS) USA, Inc.

Front brake pads, checking

– Switch hybrid system OFF (READY indicator not illuminated). See **3 Safety**.

> **WARNING—**
> • *Make sure hybrid system is OFF when servicing vehicle (READY indicator not illuminated). Failure to switch the hybrid system OFF could result in engine start at any time.*

– Raise vehicle and support safely. See **4 Service and Repair Fundamentals**.

> **WARNING—**
> • *Make sure the vehicle is stable and well supported at all times. Use a professional automotive lift or jack stands designed for the purpose. A floor jack is not adequate support.*

– Remove front wheels.

◀ Measure front disc brake pad lining thickness through the brake caliper inspection hole (**arrow**).

– Compare your measurements with specifications below.

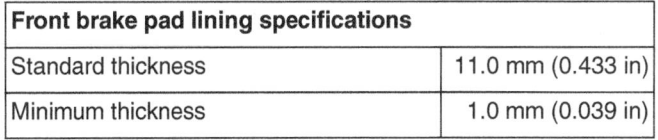

Front brake pad lining specifications	
Standard thickness	11.0 mm (0.433 in)
Minimum thickness	1.0 mm (0.039 in)

– To inspect front disc brake pad linings more thoroughly, unbolt and swing disc brake caliper away from brake rotor.

◀ Hold lower slide pin with wrench.

– Remove lower caliper slide pin bolt.

> **NOTE—**
> • *Do not disconnect flexible brake hydraulic hose to caliper.*

◀ Swing caliper upward. Caliper pivots on upper slide pin.

– Tie caliper securely in this position with strong wire or string. Caliper can be tied to front suspension coil spring.

– Remove inner and outer brake pads, 2 brake pad support plates, and 4 antisqueal shims.

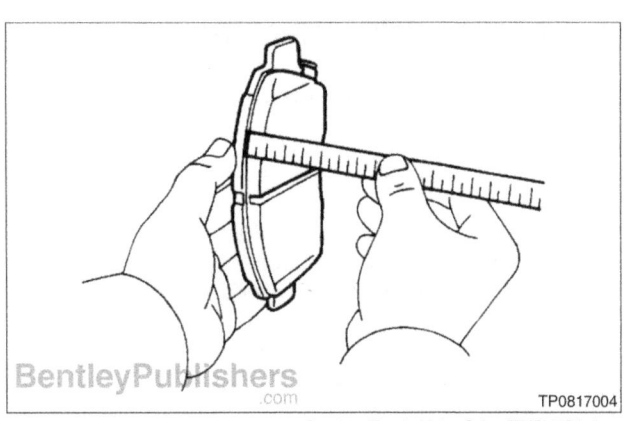

TP0817004

Courtesy Toyota Motor Sales (TMS) USA, Inc.

◀ Measure brake pad lining thickness with scale or ruler.

− Compare your measurements with specifications below.

Front brake pad lining specifications	
Standard thickness	11.0 mm (0.433 in)
Minimum thickness	1.0 mm (0.039 in)

− Replace front brake pads if lining is worn to minimum thickness, if wear is severe or uneven, or if pad lining is contaminated with oil or grease. See **Front brake pads, removing and installing** in this chapter.

− Remainder of installation is the reverse of removal, noting the following:

• Brake pad support plates can be reused if not excessively worn.

• Be sure that upper and lower brake pad support plates are not reversed.

• Install 2 antisqueal shims behind each brake pad.

• Install inner pad with pad wear indicator tab facing upward.

• Tighten caliper slide pin bolt to specification.

• Install front wheels.

• Tighten wheel lug nuts to specification.

• After brakes are reassembled, depress brake pedal several times to seat brake pads and ensure that clearances between pads and disc are correct. If this is not done, brake pedal travel may be excessive and brakes may not hold when first applied.

• Lower vehicle.

• Test drive vehicle.

Tightening torques	
Caliper slide pin bolt	34 Nm (25 ft-lb)
Wheel to wheel hub	103 Nm (76 ft-lb)

Front brake discs, checking

– Switch hybrid system OFF (READY indicator not illuminated). See **3 Safety**.

> **WARNING—**
> • Make sure hybrid system is OFF when servicing vehicle (READY indicator not illuminated). Failure to switch the hybrid system OFF could result in engine start at any time.

– Raise vehicle and support safely. See **4 Service and Repair Fundamentals**.

> **WARNING—**
> • Make sure the vehicle is stable and well supported at all times. Use a professional automotive lift or jack stands designed for the purpose. A floor jack is not adequate support.

– Remove front wheels.

◄ Hold lower slide pin with wrench.

– Remove lower caliper slide pin bolt.

> **NOTE—**
> • Do not disconnect flexible brake hydraulic hose to caliper.

◄ Swing caliper upward. Caliper pivots on upper slide pin.

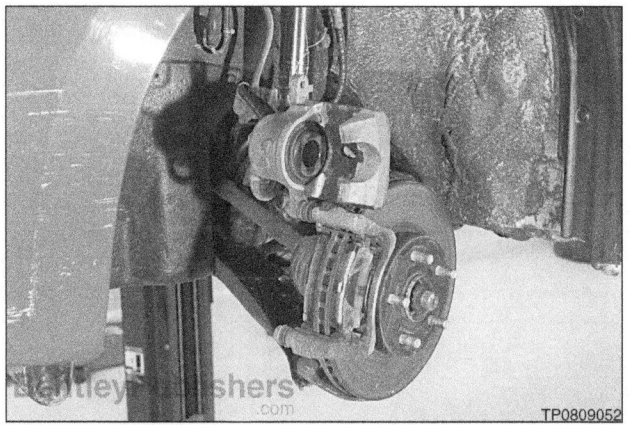

– Tie caliper securely in this position with strong wire or string. Caliper can be tied to front suspension coil spring.

– Remove brake pads.

◄ Using 0 - 1 inch micrometer, measure front brake disc thickness.

– Compare your measurements with specifications below.

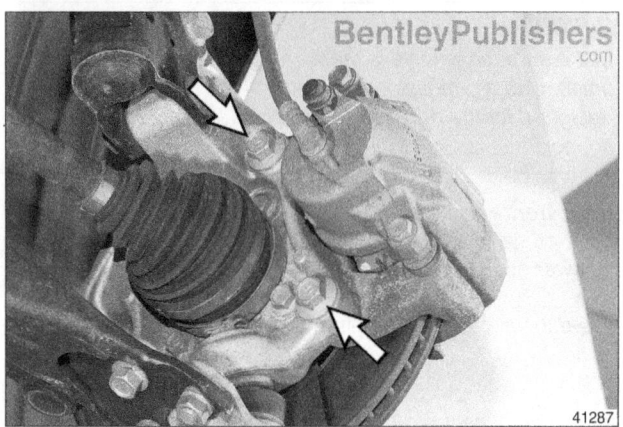

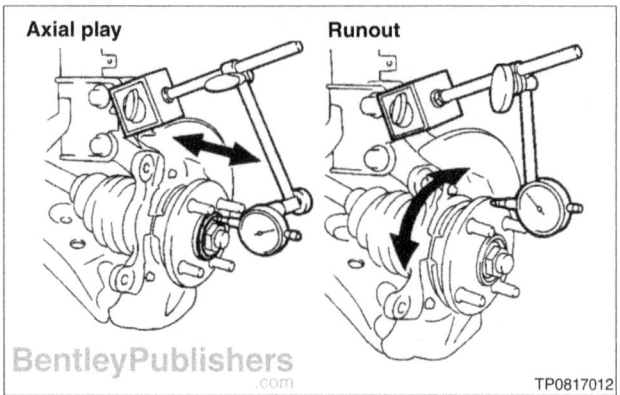

Courtesy Toyota Motor Sales (TMS) USA, Inc.

◀ Using dial indicator, measure front brake disc runout:

- Thread two wheel lug nuts or equivalent nuts on two opposite wheel studs.
- Tighten nuts to hold brake disc in place on hub.
- Measure runout approximately 10 mm (0.39 in) in from disc edge. Compare measurements with specifications.

Front brake disc specifications	
Standard thickness	22.0 mm (0.866 in)
Minimum thickness	20.0 mm (0.787 in)
Maximum runout	0.05 mm (0.0020 in)

– If disc runout is excessive, also check wheel bearing play and hub runout.

◀ To check wheel bearing play and hub runout, remove 2 caliper-to-steering-knuckle bolts (**arrows**).

– Remove caliper from disc.

NOTE—

- *Do not disconnect flexible brake hydraulic hose to caliper.*

– Tie caliper securely with strong wire or string. Caliper can be tied to front suspension coil spring.

– Mark orientation of brake disk relative to wheel hub and remove brake disc.

◀ Using dial indicator, measure wheel bearing axial play. Compare measurements with specifications below.

– Using dial indicator, measure hub flange runout. Compare measurements with specifications below.

Front wheel hub specifications	
Wheel bearing axial play (max.)	0.05 mm (0.0020 in)
Hub flange runout (max.)	0.07 mm (0.0028 in)

– If wheel bearing axial play exceeds specifications, replace the wheel bearing.

– If hub flange runout exceeds specifications, replace the axle hub.

– If wheel bearing axial play and hub flange runout are within specifications, attempt to bring disc runout within specifications by relocating disc on hub:

- Remove disc from hub and rotate ¼ turn, noting your previous orientation marks.
- Thread two wheel lug nuts or equivalent nuts on two opposite wheel studs. Tighten nuts to hold brake disc in place on hub as you did previously.

◀ Again measure runout approximately 10 mm (0.39 in) in from disc edge. Compare your measurements with specifications.

– If disc runout is within specifications, leave disc in this position on hub.

— If disc runout is still excessive, again remove disc from hub and rotate ¼ turn, noting your previous orientation marks.

— If necessary, try all 4 disc positions on hub.

— Replace front brake disc if disc is worn to minimum thickness, if disc wear is severe or uneven, if disc is severely scored, or if disc runout is excessive. For brake disc replacement procedure, see **Front brake discs, removing and installing** in this chapter.

— Installation is reverse of removal. Tighten fasteners to specifications.

Tightening torques	
Caliper to pad carrier	34 Nm (25 ft-lb)
Pad carrier to steering-knuckle	107 Nm (79 ft-lb)
Wheel to wheel hub	103 Nm (76 ft-lb)

Front brake pads, removing and installing

— Switch hybrid system OFF (READY indicator not illuminated). See **3 Safety**.

> **WARNING—**
> • *Make sure hybrid system is OFF when servicing vehicle (READY indicator not illuminated). Failure to switch the hybrid system OFF could result in engine start at any time.*

— Raise vehicle and support safely. See **4 Service and Repair Fundamentals**.

> **WARNING—**
> • *Make sure the vehicle is stable and well supported at all times. Use a professional automotive lift or jack stands designed for the purpose. A floor jack is not adequate support.*

— Remove front wheels.

— Measure front disc brake pad lining thickness. See **Front brake pads, checking** in this chapter.

— Replace front brake pads if lining is worn to minimum thickness, if wear is severe or uneven, or if pad lining is contaminated with oil or grease.

◄ To replace brake pads, unbolt and swing disc brake caliper away from brake rotor.

— Counterhold lower slide pin with wrench and remove lower caliper slide pin bolt.

TP0809051

TP0809052

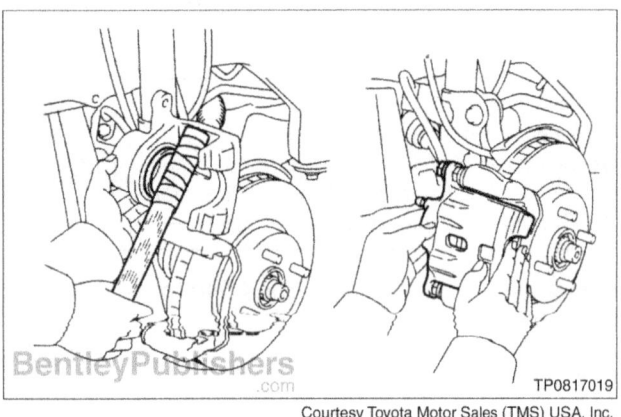

TP0817019

Courtesy Toyota Motor Sales (TMS) USA, Inc.

◄ Swing caliper upward. Caliper pivots on upper slide pin. Do not disconnect flexible brake hydraulic hose to caliper.

— Tie caliper securely in this position with strong wire or string. Caliper can be tied to front suspension coil spring.

— Remove inner and outer brake pads, 2 brake pad support plates, and 4 antisqueal shims. See **Front brake components** in this chapter.

— Measure front brake disc thickness and runout. See **Front brake pads, checking** in this chapter.

— Replace brake discs if required. See **Front brake discs, removing and installing** in this chapter.

— Note brake fluid level in reservoir. If level in reservoir is high, remove enough fluid so that it will not overflow when caliper piston is retracted. Use suction bulb for this purpose.

> **WARNING—**
> • *Avoid prolonged direct skin contact with brake fluid.*
> • *Collect brake fluid in a suitable container. Dispose of brake fluid as hazardous waste.*

◄ Using a hammer handle wrapped with tape, pry or push caliper piston back into caliper.
  • If piston is difficult to push, loosen bleed screw on caliper so that brake fluid can escape while piston is pushed.
  • Open bleed screw only when piston is being pushed so that air does not enter brake system.
  • Connect a bleeder hose onto the bleed screw and collect expelled brake fluid in a suitable container.

> **WARNING—**
> • *Dispose of brake fluid as hazardous waste.*

— Install 2 pad support plates.
  • Support plates can be reused if they have sufficient spring, and have no deformation, cracks, or wear.
  • Clean support plates thoroughly before installation.
  • Be sure that upper and lower support plates are not reversed.

  − Install new brake pads with new antisqueal shims, noting the following:

  • When new brake pads are installed, install new antisqueal shims also.

  • Apply disc brake grease to both sides of inner antisqueal shim. See **Front brake components** in this chapter.

  • Install 2 antisqueal shims with each brake pad.

  • Install inner brake pad with wear indicator tab facing upward.

  • Tighten caliper slide pin bolt to specification.

CAUTION—
• *Make sure brake pads and discs are not contaminated with oil or grease.*

Tightening torque	
Caliper to pad carrier	34 Nm (25 ft-lb)

  − Install front wheels and tighten wheel lug nuts to specification.

Tightening torque	
Wheel to wheel hub	103 Nm (76 ft-lb)

  − After brakes are reassembled, depress brake pedal several times to seat brake pads and ensure that clearances between pads and disc are correct. If this is not done, brake pedal travel may be excessive and brakes may not hold when first applied.

  − Vehicle with electronically controlled brake (ECB) system: procedures such as retracting caliper pistons, installing new brake pads, replacing brake rotors, or bleeding the brakes may cause diagnostic trouble codes (DTCs) to set and brake warning light to illuminate when brake pedal is depressed after repair is completed. If this condition occurs, see **11 Diagnostics**.

  − Lower and test drive vehicle.

Front brake discs, removing and installing

– Switch hybrid system OFF (READY indicator not illuminated). See **3 Safety**.

> **WARNING—**
> • *Make sure hybrid system is OFF when servicing vehicle (READY indicator not illuminated). Failure to switch the hybrid system OFF could result in engine start at any time.*

– Raise vehicle and support safely. See **4 Service and Repair Fundamentals**.

> **WARNING—**
> • *Make sure the vehicle is stable and well supported at all times. Use a professional automotive lift or jack stands designed for the purpose. A floor jack is not adequate support.*

– Remove front wheels.

◄ Remove pad carrier (caliper) mounting bolts (**arrows**).

– Remove caliper assembly with pad carrier from disc.

> **NOTE—**
> • *Do not disconnect flexible brake hose to caliper.*

> **CAUTION—**
> • *Do not twist flexible brake hose.*

– Hang caliper securely with strong wire or string. Caliper can be tied to front suspension coil spring.

– Measure front brake disc thickness and runout. Replace front brake disc if disc is worn to minimum thickness, if disc wear is severe or uneven, if disc is severely scored, or if disc runout is excessive. See **Front brake discs, checking** in this chapter.

◄ If brake disc will be reused, mark orientation of disk relative to wheel hub (**arrow**) and remove disc from hub.

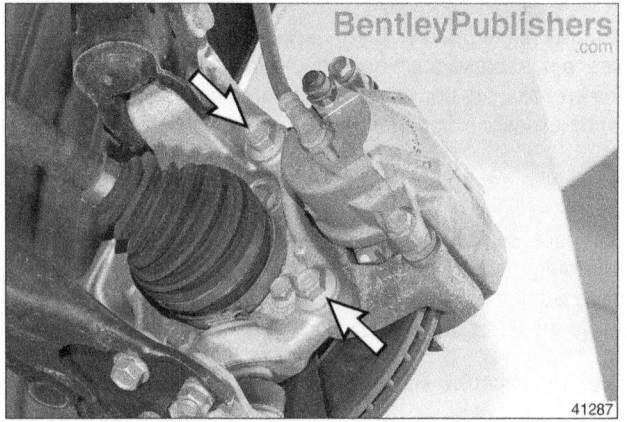

– Installation is reverse of removal, noting the following:

  • To reduce possibility of disc runout problems, be sure that hub flange is clean and flat. If necessary, use sandpaper or a file to remove rust or deposits.

  • Tighten fasteners to specifications.

  • Install front wheels and tighten wheel lug nuts to specification.

Tightening torque	
Pad carrier to steering knuckle	107 Nm (79 ft-lb)
Wheel to wheel hub	103 Nm (76 ft-lb)

– After brakes are reassembled, depress brake pedal several times to seat brake pads and ensure that clearances between pads and disc are correct. If this is not done, brake pedal travel may be excessive and brakes may not hold when first applied.

– Vehicle with electronically controlled brake (ECB) system: Procedures such as retracting caliper pistons, installing new brake pads, replacing brake rotors, or bleeding the brakes may cause diagnostic trouble codes (DTCs) to set and brake warning light to illuminate when brake pedal is depressed after repair is completed. If necessary, see **11 Diagnostics**.

– Lower and test drive vehicle.

8

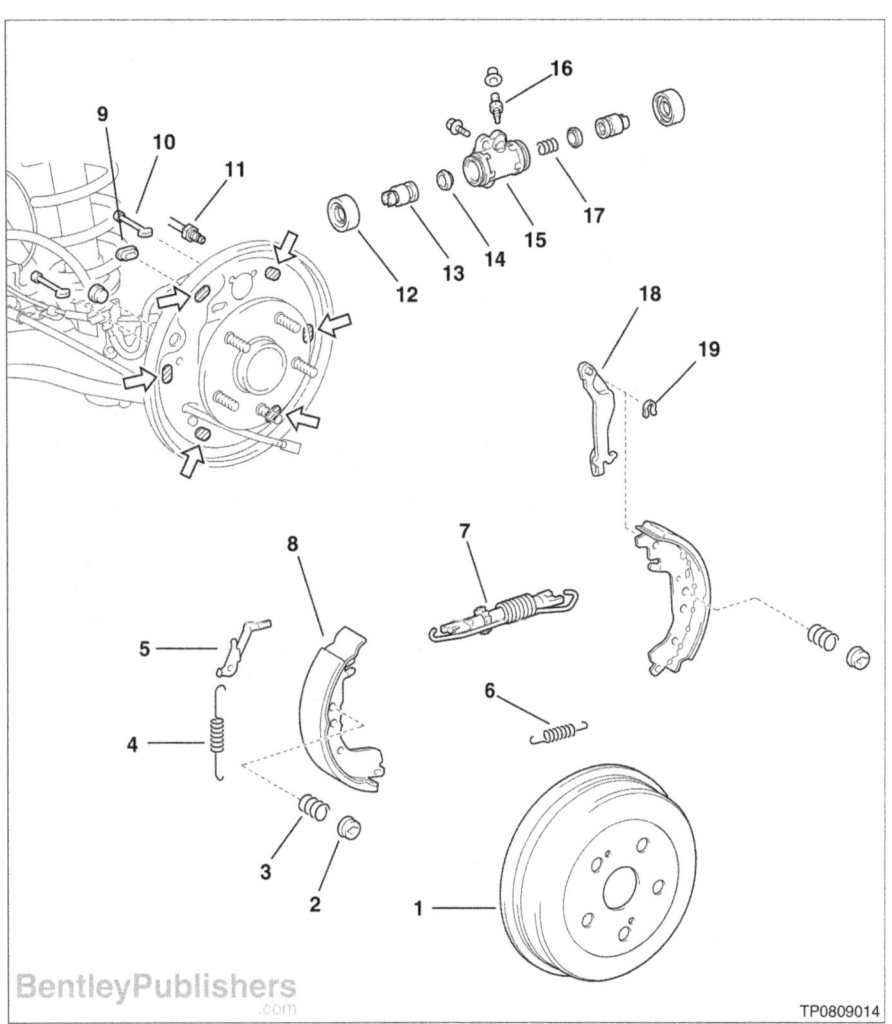

TP0809014

Courtesy Toyota Motor Sales (TMS) USA, Inc.

Rear drum brake components

1. Brake drum
2. Hold down spring cup
3. Hold down spring
4. Adjustment lever tensioning spring
5. Adjustment lever
6. Tension spring
7. Shoe strut set
8. Brake shoe
9. Hole plug
10. Hold down spring pin
11. Hydraulic line
12. Cylinder dust boot
13. Piston
14. Cylinder cup
15. Brake cylinder
16. Bleeder screw
17. Compression spring
18. Parking brake lever
19. C-washer

Rear brake shoes and drums, checking

– Switch hybrid system OFF (READY indicator not illuminated). See **3 Safety**.

> **WARNING—**
> • *Make sure hybrid system is OFF when servicing vehicle (READY indicator not illuminated). Failure to switch the hybrid system OFF could result in engine start at any time.*

– Raise vehicle and support safely. See **4 Service and Repair Fundamentals**.

> **WARNING—**
> • *Make sure the vehicle is stable and well supported at all times. Use a professional automotive lift or jack stands designed for the purpose. A floor jack is not adequate support.*

– Remove rear wheels.

◀ A round inspection hole is provided in the backing plate for a quick evaluation of rear brake shoe lining thickness.

> **NOTE—**
> • *The round inspection hole location allows inspecting only the front brake shoe.*

– Remove plug from round inspection hole in backing plate and check brake shoe lining thickness through hole. Compare your measurements with specification.

Rear brake shoe lining specifications	
Standard thickness	4.0 mm (0.157 in)
Minimum thickness	1.0 mm (0.039 in)

◀ To inspect brake shoe linings more thoroughly:

• Mark orientation of brake drum relative to the wheel hub (**arrows**).

• Remove brake drum. Be sure parking brake is released.

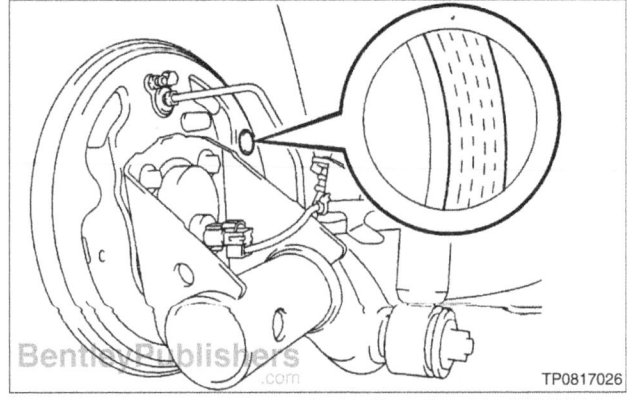

TP0817026

Courtesy Toyota Motor Sales (TMS) USA, Inc.

TP0809016

◄ If brake drum is stuck, remove rust from hub with emery cloth or sandpaper.

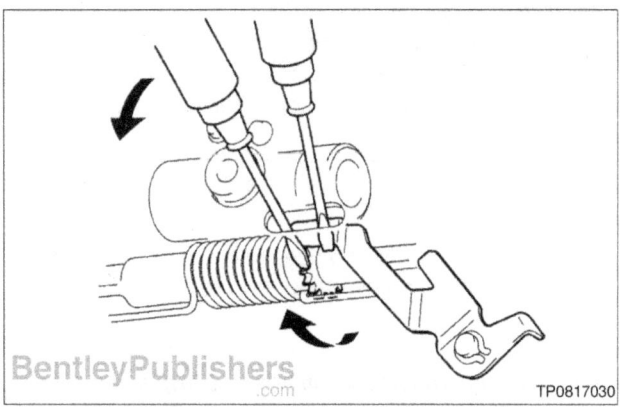

TP0817030

Courtesy Toyota Motor Sales (TMS) USA, Inc.

◄ If brake shoes are preventing brake drum removal, adjust brake shoes away from drum:

- Remove plug from elongated hole in backing plate.
- Insert two screwdrivers into elongated hole.
- Use one screwdriver to hold adjusting lever away from star wheel adjuster.
- Use second screwdriver to rotate star wheel adjuster in direction shown to adjust brake shoes away from drum.

TP0809017

◄ If drum is still stuck on hub:

- Screw two M8 x 1.25 x 30 mm bolts (**arrows**) into threaded holes in brake drum.
- Using a wrench, tighten screws evenly and carefully to force brake drum from hub.
- After removing brake drum, clean rust from hub and drum mating surfaces.

◄ Using ruler or scale, check brake shoe lining thickness and condition.

— Compare your measurements with specification..

Rear brake shoe lining specifications	
Standard thickness	4.0 mm (0.157 in)
Minimum thickness	1.0 mm (0.039 in)

— Replace rear brake shoes if lining is worn to minimum thickness, if wear is severe or uneven, or if lining is contaminated with oil or grease. Replace brake shoes as a set.

TP0817032

Courtesy Toyota Motor Sales (TMS) USA, Inc.

- For brake shoe replacement and adjustment procedure, see **Rear brake shoes, removing and installing** in this chapter.

- Examine brake drum friction surface for excessive or uneven wear, scoring, discoloration or hot spots. Replace if necessary.

◄ Using a brake drum and shoe gauge (KD Tools P/N KDS3377 or equivalent), measure inside diameter of brake drum friction surface.

- Compare your measurements with specification below.

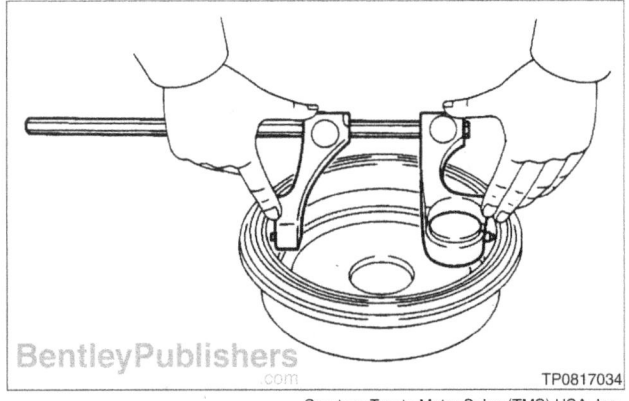

TP0817034

Courtesy Toyota Motor Sales (TMS) USA, Inc.

Rear brake drum specifications	
Standard inside diameter	200.0 mm (7.874 in)
Maximum inside diameter	201.0 mm (7.913 in)

- A worn or scored drum may be machined on a brake lathe up to the maximum inside diameter.

- Replace rear brake drums if friction surface is excessively or unevenly worn, or if scoring, discoloration or hot spots are present.

- For brake shoe replacement and adjustment procedure, see **Rear brake shoes, removing and installing** in this chapter.

- Installation is reverse of removal. If brake drum is replaced or machined, readjust brake shoes. See **Rear brake shoes, removing and installing** in this chapter.

- Install rear wheels and tighten wheel lug nuts to specification.

Tightening torque	
Wheel to wheel hub	103 Nm (76 ft-lb)

- Lower and test drive vehicle.

Rear brake shoes, removing and installing

Brake shoes, removing

— Switch hybrid system OFF (READY indicator not illuminated). See **3 Safety**.

> **WARNING**—
> • *Make sure hybrid system is OFF when servicing vehicle (READY indicator not illuminated). Failure to switch the hybrid system OFF could result in engine start at any time.*

— Raise vehicle and support safely. See **4 Service and Repair Fundamentals**.

> **WARNING**—
> • *Make sure the vehicle is stable and well supported at all times. Use a professional automotive lift or jack stands designed for the purpose. A floor jack is not adequate support.*

— Remove rear wheels and brake drums. See **Rear brake shoes and drums, checking** in this chapter.

— Measure rear brake shoe lining thickness. Replace rear brake shoes if lining is worn to minimum thickness, if wear is severe or uneven, or if lining is contaminated with oil or grease. Replace brake shoes as a set.

— Replace rear brake drums if friction surface is excessively or unevenly worn, or if scoring, discoloration or hot spots are present.

◄ Remove forward brake shoe:

 • Using brake return spring tool (Toyota special tool SST 09703-30010 or equivalent), disconnect return spring from rear brake shoe.

 • Using needle-nose pliers, disconnect tension spring.

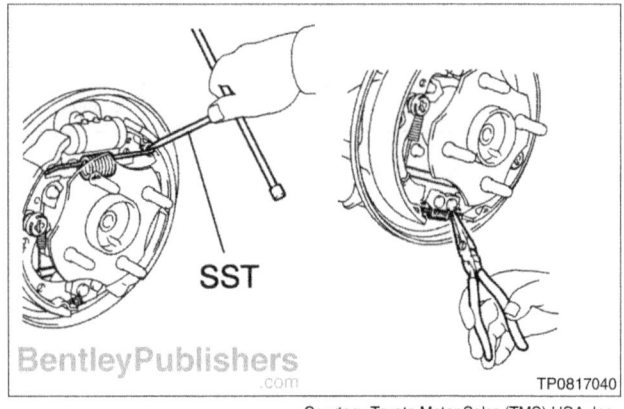

SST

TP0817040

Courtesy Toyota Motor Sales (TMS) USA, Inc.

◄ Using brake hold-down spring tool (Toyota special tool SST 09718-00010 or equivalent), remove hold-down spring, pin, and cup for forward brake shoe.

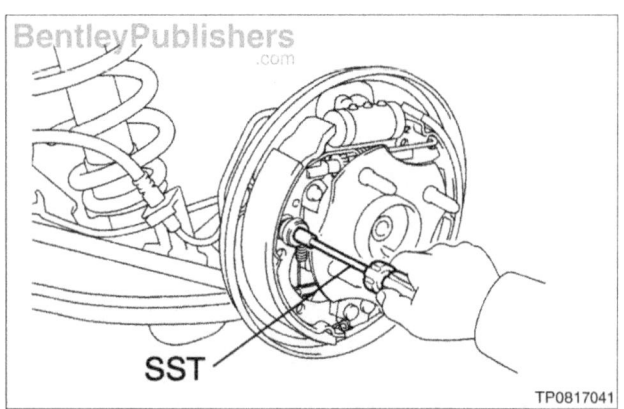

SST

TP0817041

Courtesy Toyota Motor Sales (TMS) USA, Inc.

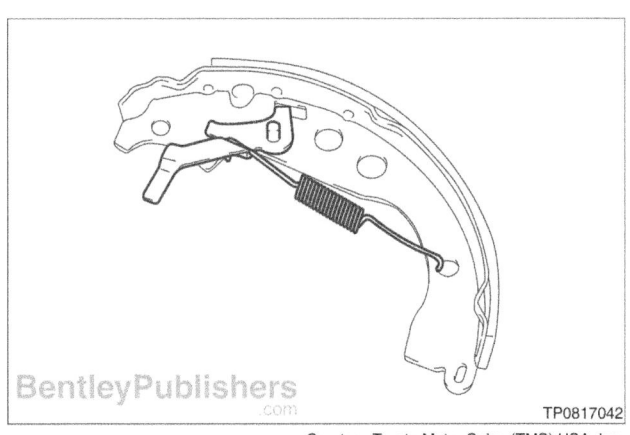

TP0817042

Courtesy Toyota Motor Sales (TMS) USA, Inc.

◀ Remove forward brake shoe, adjusting lever, and adjusting lever spring.

– Using needle-nose pliers, remove adjusting lever spring.

– Remove adjusting lever from forward brake shoe.

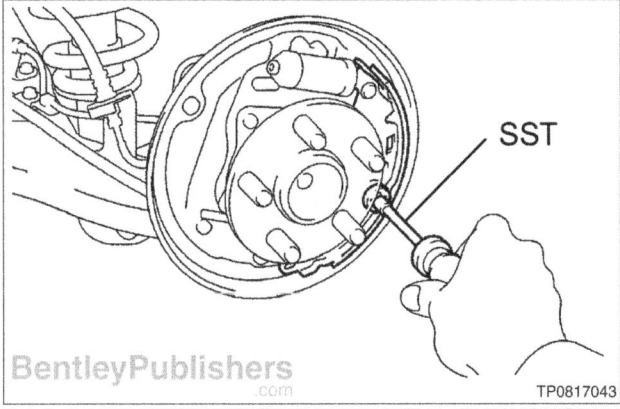

SST

TP0817043

Courtesy Toyota Motor Sales (TMS) USA, Inc.

◀ Using brake hold-down spring tool (SST 09718-00010 or equivalent), remove hold-down spring, pin, and cup for rear brake shoe.

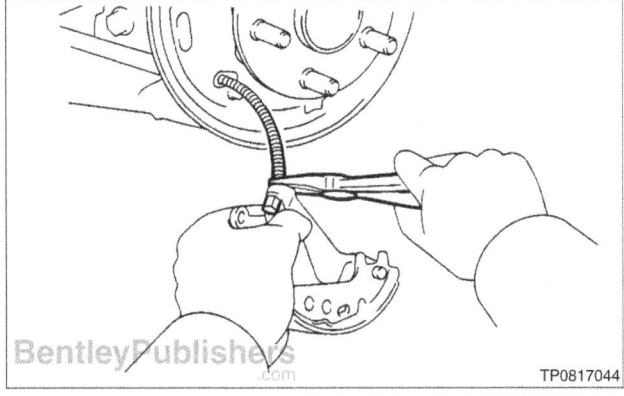

TP0817044

Courtesy Toyota Motor Sales (TMS) USA, Inc.

◀ Using needle-nose pliers, disconnect parking brake cable from parking brake lever.

– Remove rear brake shoe.

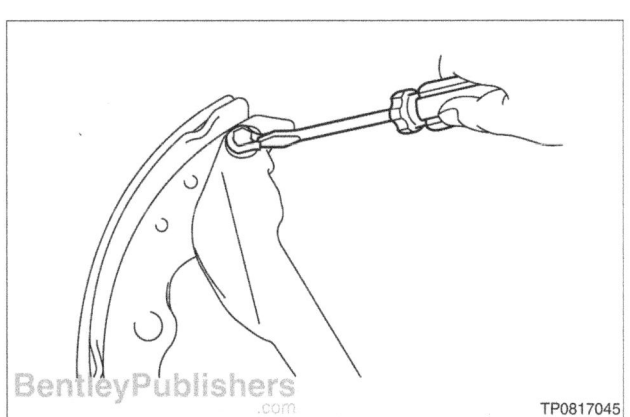

TP0817045

Courtesy Toyota Motor Sales (TMS) USA, Inc.

◀ Remove C-washer and remove parking brake lever from rear brake shoe.

– For brake shoe and brake drum inspection procedure, see **Rear brake shoes and drums, checking** in this chapter.

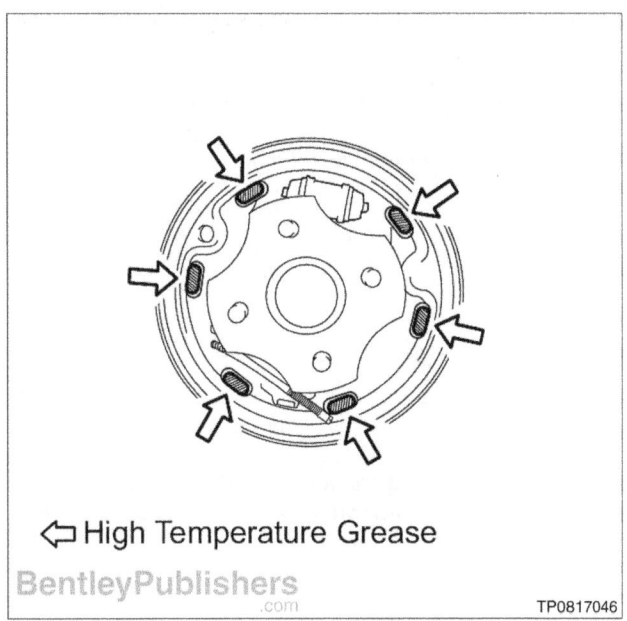

⇐ High Temperature Grease

TP0817046
Courtesy Toyota Motor Sales (TMS) USA, Inc.

Brake shoes, installing

◄ Clean brake backing plate. Apply lithium grease or high temperature grease to points indicated (**arrows**).

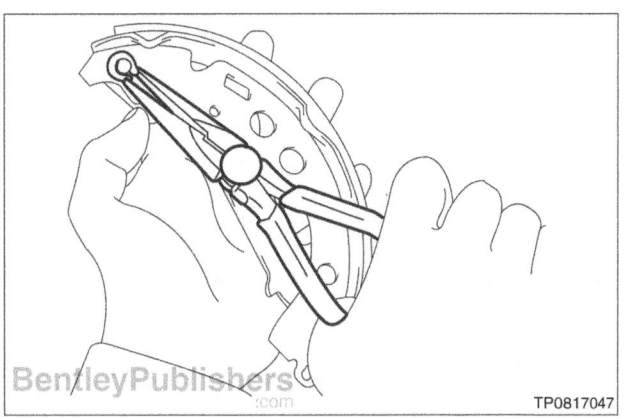

TP0817047
Courtesy Toyota Motor Sales (TMS) USA, Inc.

◄ Using needle-nose pliers, install C-washer and parking brake lever on rear brake shoe.

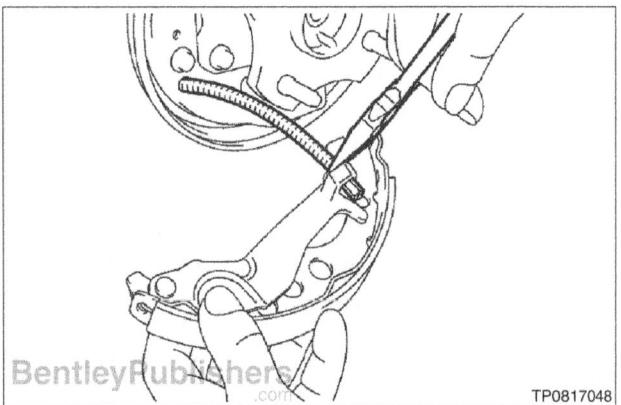

TP0817048
Courtesy Toyota Motor Sales (TMS) USA, Inc.

◄ Using needle-nose pliers, connect parking brake cable to parking brake lever on rear brake shoe.

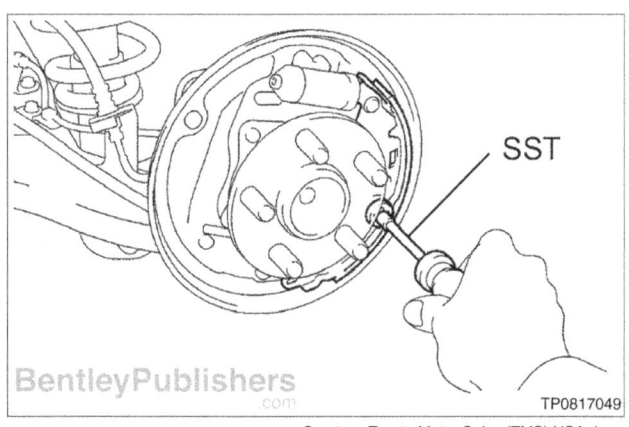

◄ Using brake hold-down spring tool (Toyota special tool SST 09718-00010 or equivalent), install hold-down spring, pin, and cup for rear brake shoe.

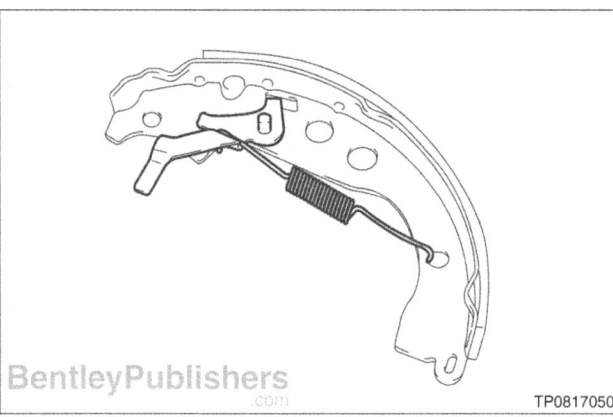

◄ Install adjusting lever and spring on forward brake shoe.

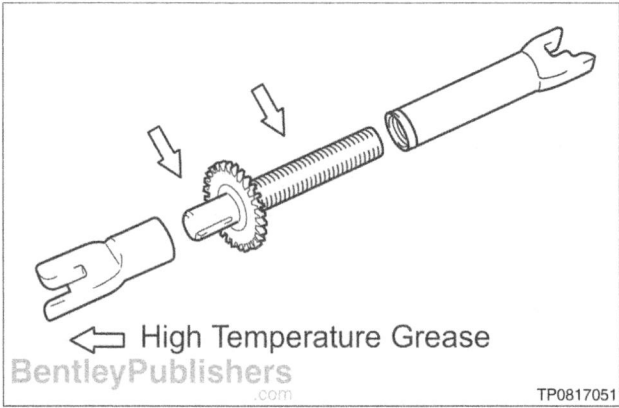

High Temperature Grease

◄ Apply high temperature grease to adjuster assembly (**arrows**).

– Assemble adjuster components. Fully thread star wheel into adjuster.

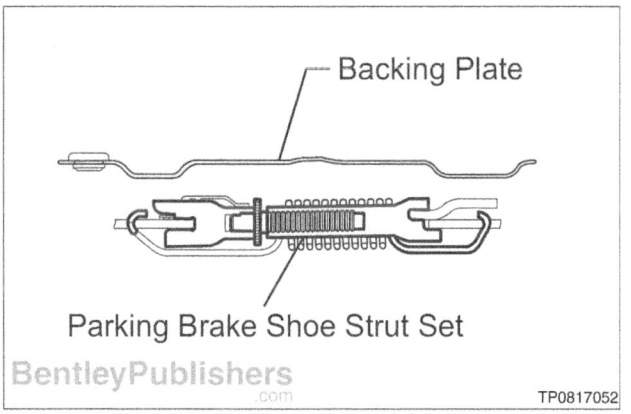

– **Backing Plate**

Parking Brake Shoe Strut Set

◄ Install shoe return spring on adjuster assembly.

– Install adjuster assembly onto brake backing plate and rear brake shoe.

TP0817053

Courtesy Toyota Motor Sales (TMS) USA, Inc.

◀ Connect tension spring to front and rear brake shoes.

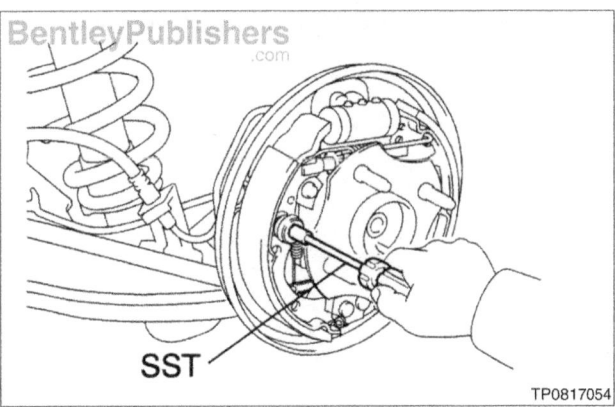

SST

TP0817054

Courtesy Toyota Motor Sales (TMS) USA, Inc.

◀ Using brake hold-down spring tool (Toyota special tool SST 09718-00010 or equivalent), install hold-down spring, pin and cup for forward brake shoe.

– Using brake return spring tool (Toyota special tool SST 09703-30010 or equivalent), connect shoe return spring on adjuster assembly to forward and rear brake shoes.

> **CAUTION—**
> • *Do not damage rubber boot on wheel cylinder.*

– Move parking brake lever on rear brake shoe back and forth and be sure that adjusting lever rotates star wheel adjuster.

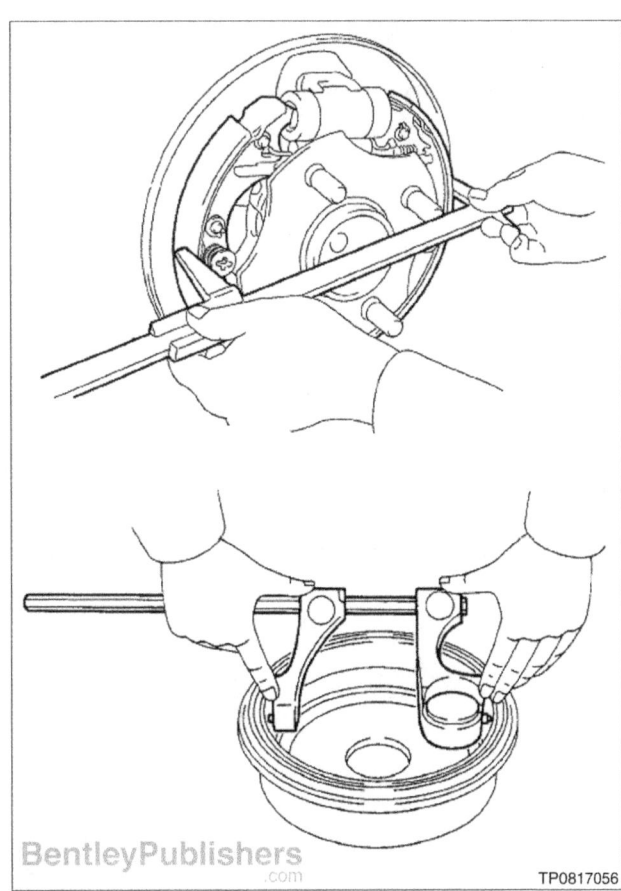

TP0817056

Courtesy Toyota Motor Sales (TMS) USA, Inc.

◀ Adjust initial brake-shoe-to-drum clearance:

• Using vernier caliper, or a brake drum and shoe gauge (KD Tools P/N KDS3377 or equivalent), measure outside diameter of brake shoes.

• Using brake drum and shoe gauge (KD Tools P/N KDS3377 or equivalent), measure inside diameter of brake drum.

• Turn star wheel adjuster to set brake-shoe-to-drum clearance per specification.

> **CAUTION—**
> • *Make sure brake shoes and drums are not contaminated with oil or grease.*

Tightening torque	
Shoe-to-drum clearance	0.6 mm (0.024 in)

– To reduce possibility of drum runout problems, be sure that hub flange is clean and flat. If necessary, use sandpaper or file to remove rust or deposits.

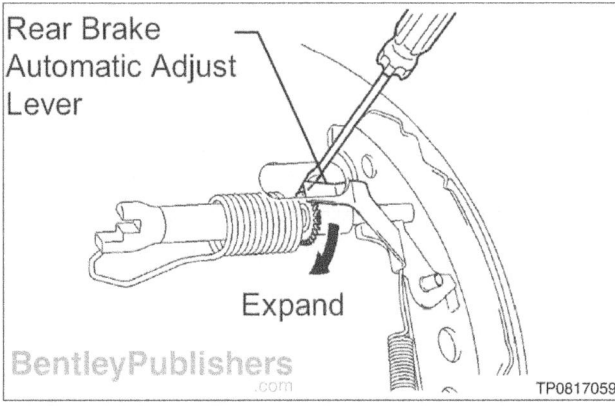

Courtesy Toyota Motor Sales (TMS) USA, Inc.

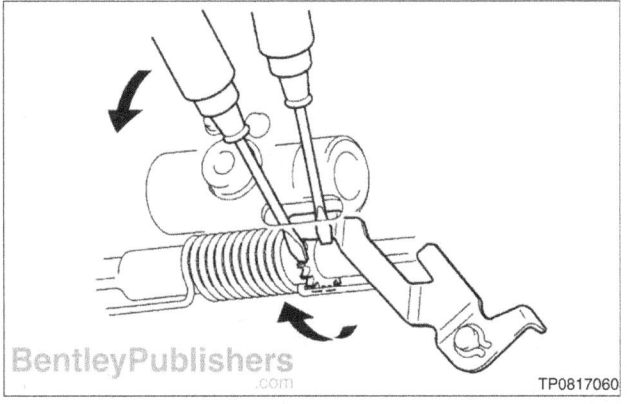

Courtesy Toyota Motor Sales (TMS) USA, Inc.

◄ Install brake drum. If used brake drum is being reinstalled, align orientation marks (**arrows**).

◄ Adjust final brake-shoe-to-drum clearance.

– Temporarily thread two wheel lug nuts or equivalent nuts onto two opposite wheel studs. Tighten nuts to hold brake drum in place on hub.

– Remove plug from elongated hole in backing plate.

– Insert screwdriver into elongated hole.

– Use screwdriver to rotate star wheel adjuster in direction shown to adjust brake shoes toward drum until drum cannot be turned.

◄ Insert a second screwdriver into elongated hole.

– Use second screwdriver to hold adjusting lever away from star wheel adjuster.

– Use first screwdriver to rotate star wheel adjuster 8 notches in direction shown to adjust brake shoes away from drum.

– Be sure that drum can turn freely without brake shoe drag.

– Reinstall plug in elongated hole in backing plate.

– Check parking brake pedal travel. See **Parking brake, adjusting** in this chapter.

– Remove temporary wheel lug nuts or equivalent nuts and install wheel.

– Tighten wheel lug nuts to specification.

Tightening torque	
Wheel to wheel hub	103 Nm (76 ft-lb)

– Lower and test drive vehicle.

Brake fluid, bleeding

> **WARNING—**
> • *Bleeding the brake hydraulic system or changing brake fluid requires a Toyota scan tool or equivalent.*

The hydraulic lines in the brake system must be free of air for brakes to function properly. Whenever brake lines have been open, or you suspect air in the lines, the system must be bled. When bleeding brakes, always ensure that the level of brake fluid in the fluid reservoir is between MIN and MAX level marks. If excessive amounts of air enter the system because of low fluid level in the reservoir, bleeding the system can be extremely difficult.

> **NOTE—**
> • *This procedure requires the use of a Toyota scan tool, or equivalent.*
> • *Do not step on brake pedal when brake fluid reservoir cap is not in place. Brake fluid may overflow or splash out of reservoir.*
> • *Remove brake fluid from painted surfaces immediately.*
> • *Diagnostic trouble codes (DTCs) may be stored in vehicle control units during bleeding procedures. Any DTCs that have been set will be cleared at the end. See* **11 Diagnostics** *for more information on DTCs.*

– Switch hybrid system OFF (READY indicator not illuminated). See **3 Safety**.

> **WARNING—**
> • *Make sure hybrid system is OFF when servicing vehicle (READY indicator not illuminated). Failure to switch the hybrid system OFF could result in engine start at any time.*

◄ Fill reservoir with specified brake fluid to MAX level mark.

> **NOTE—**
> • *While bleeding, check brake fluid level periodically so level remains between MIN and MAX marks.*

Brake fluid specifications	
Brake fluid	SAI J1703 or FMVSS no. 116 DOT3

– Raise vehicle and support safely. See **4 Service and Repair Fundamentals**.

> **WARNING—**
> • *Make sure the vehicle is stable and well supported at all times. Use a professional automotive lift or jack stands designed for the purpose. A floor jack is not adequate support.*

– Remove wheels and tires to provide easier access to brake bleeders.

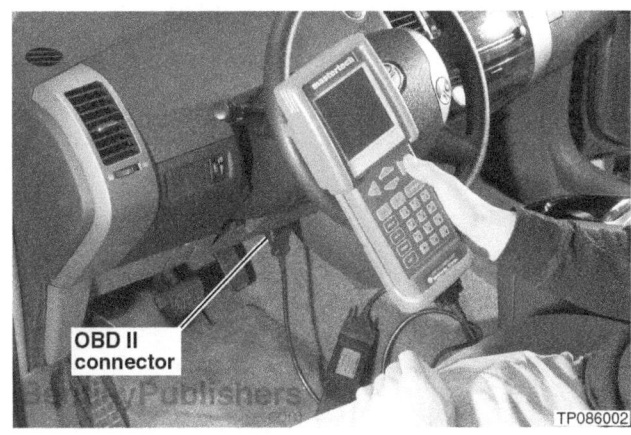

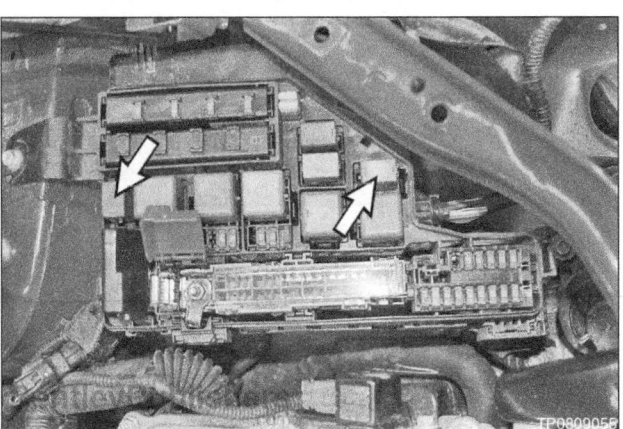

— Depress PARK button and apply parking brake.

◄ Connect Toyota scan tool or equivalent to OBD II connector (DLC3) and switch tester ON.

NOTE—

• *Be sure to use a scan tool with CAN interface.*

— With brake pedal *not* depressed, push POWER button twice. This switches hybrid system to IG-ON position (POWER button amber, READY indicator not illuminated, engine will not start).

— Using the Toyota scan tool or equivalent, follow on-screen instructions to begin brake bleeding sequence.

WARNING—

• *Read and understand the manufacturer's instructions before initiating the brake bleeding sequence. Incomplete bleeding could result in brake failure.*

◄ When instructed by scan tool, turn hybrid system OFF and remove ABS motor relays 1 and 2 (**arrows**) located in engine compartment junction and relay block.

CAUTION—

• *Be sure that the hybrid system is OFF (READY indicator not illuminated) before removing relays.*

— After successfully following scan tool preliminary procedures, perform the following steps to bleed air from brakes for right front wheel when instructed by scan tool:

• With brake pedal *not* depressed, push POWER button twice (IG-ON position).

• Remove bleeder cap and attach transparent bleeder hose.

• Depress brake pedal several times.

• With brake pedal depressed, open right front wheel bleeder. Allow brake fluid to drain into suitable container.

WARNING—

• *Avoid prolonged direct skin contact with brake fluid.*

• *Collect brake fluid in a suitable container. Dispose of brake fluid as hazardous waste.*

— When brake fluid stops flowing out of bleeder, close bleeder and release brake pedal.

— Repeat until no air bubbles are present in bleeder hose.

NOTE—

• *During bleeding procedures, do not pump brake pedal. Hold brake pedal depressed when bleeding air and fluid.*

• *During bleeding procedures, a buzzer may sound because of a drop in brake system accumulator pressure. Do not interrupt bleeding procedures.*

— Tighten bleeder to specification and reinstall cap.

Tightening torque	
Brake bleeder to caliper	8.4 Nm (74 in-lb)

— Repeat above steps for left front left wheel.

— When finished bleeding front wheels, turn hybrid system OFF (READY indicator not illuminated).

— Reinstall ABS motor relays 1 and 2.

CAUTION—
- *Be sure that the hybrid system OFF (READY indicator not illuminated*

— Perform the following steps to bleed air from brakes for left rear wheel:
- With brake pedal *not* depressed, push POWER button twice (IG-ON position).
- Remove bleeder cap and attach transparent bleeder hose.
- Depress brake pedal several times.
- With brake pedal depressed, open left rear wheel bleeder. Allow brake fluid to drain into suitable container.

WARNING—
- *Avoid prolonged direct skin contact with brake fluid.*
- *Collect brake fluid in a suitable container. Dispose of brake fluid as hazardous waste.*

— When brake fluid stops flowing out of bleeder, close bleeder and release brake pedal.

— Repeat until no air bubbles are present in bleeder hose.

NOTE—
- *During bleeding procedures, do not pump brake pedal. Hold brake pedal depressed when bleeding air and fluid.*
- *During bleeding procedures, a buzzer may sound because of a drop in brake system accumulator pressure. Do not interrupt bleeding procedures.*

— Tighten bleeder to specification and reinstall cap.

Tightening torque	
Brake bleeder to wheel cylinder	8.4 Nm (74 in-lb)

— Repeat above steps for right rear wheel.

— Scan tool indicates when bleeding procedure is complete.

WARNING—
- *Continue brake bleeding until scan tool indicates that procedure is complete. Incomplete bleeding could result in brake failure.*

— Switch hybrid system OFF (READY indicator not illuminated).

— Switch OFF and disconnect Toyota scan tool from the OBD II connector (DLC3).

— Clear any diagnostic trouble codes (DTCs). See **11 Diagnostics**.

— Check brake fluid level in reservoir. If necessary, fill reservoir with specified brake fluid to MAX level mark.

— Install wheels and tighten wheel lug nuts to specification.

Tightening torque	
Wheel to wheel hub	103 Nm (76 ft-lb)

— Vehicle with electronically controlled brake (ECB) system: Procedures such as retracting caliper pistons, installing new brake pads, replacing brake rotors, or bleeding the brakes may cause diagnostic trouble codes (DTCs) to set and brake warning light to illuminate when brake pedal is depressed after repair is completed. If this condition occurs, see **11 Diagnostics**.

— Lower and test drive vehicle.

8

Parking brake, adjusting

– Switch hybrid system OFF (READY indicator not illuminated). See **3 Safety**.

> **WARNING**—
> • *Make sure hybrid system is OFF when servicing vehicle (READY indicator not illuminated). Failure to switch the hybrid system OFF could result in engine start at any time.*

◄ Depress parking brake pedal fully with specified force and count clicks.

– Compare number of clicks you counted with specification.

Parking brake adjustment specifications	
Pedal application force	300 N (67.4 lb)
Number of clicks	6 - 9

– If parking brake requires adjustment, first verify correct rear brake shoe adjustment. See **Rear brake shoes, removing and installing** in this chapter.

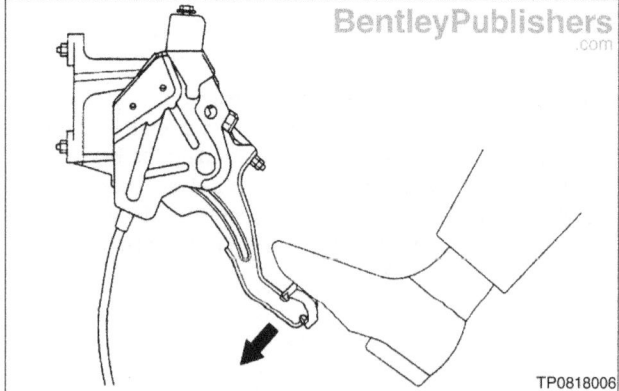

Courtesy Toyota Motor Sales (TMS) USA, Inc.

◄ To adjust parking brake, remove center console upper subassembly:

• Pull console upper subassembly upward in direction of (**arrow**).

• Remove console upper subassembly.

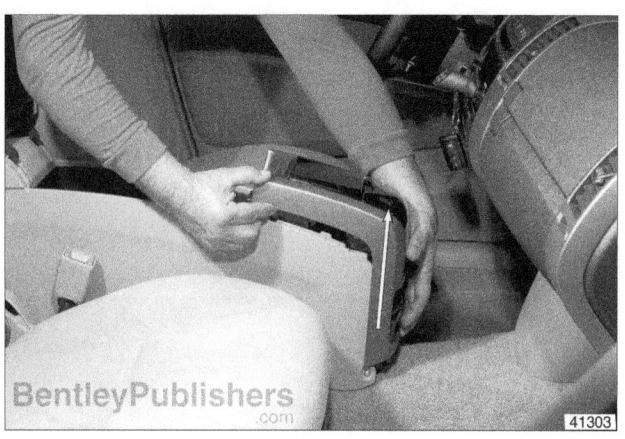

◄ Remove 2 screws from lower front of console box.

– Remove console storage box carpet.

– Remove 2 bolts from console storage box.

– Pull up on front of console box and pivot console box rearward (**curved arrow**) to expose parking brake intermediate lever and parking brake adjuster.

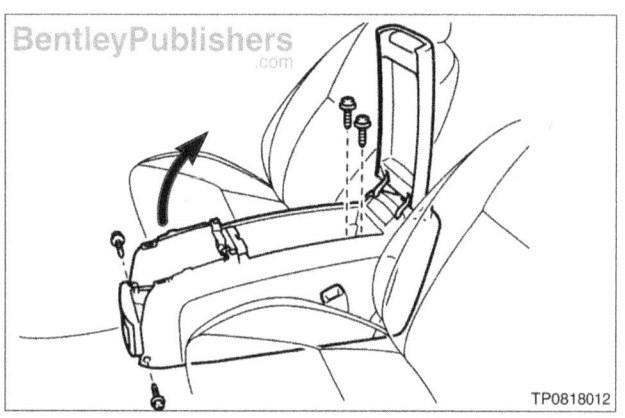

Courtesy Toyota Motor Sales (TMS) USA, Inc.

◀ Using screwdriver, slide plastic cover on parking brake intermediate lever subassembly to rear (**arrow**).

– Depress parking brake pedal 5 clicks.

◀ Hold parking brake adjusting nut with wrench and loosen lock nut.

– Release parking brake pedal.

– Turn parking brake adjusting nut to adjust parking brake pedal travel.

– To check parking brake pedal travel, depress and release parking brake pedal 3 – 4 times, then depress pedal fully with specified force and count clicks.

– Compare number of clicks you counted with specification.

Parking brake adjustment specifications	
Pedal application force	300 N (67.4 lb)
Number of clicks	6 - 9

– Verify that parking brake does not drag when released.

– Verify that parking brake indicator light illuminates when parking brake is applied.

– Tighten lock nut to specification.

Tightening torque	
Lock nut for parking brake adjusting nut	12.5 Nm (9 ft-lb)

– Remainder of installation is the reverse of removal.

Tightening torque	
Front floor crossmember reinforcement left side subassembly bolts	18 Nm (13 ft-lb)

SUSPENSION AND STEERING

Suspension and steering overview

The Prius front suspension is a conventional design with struts, integral shock absorbers and concentric coil springs. One lower suspension arm per side locates the lower end of the strut and steering knuckle.

The rear suspension includes a pivoting transverse beam axle, and strut-type shock absorbers with concentric coil springs.

The steering rack is a simple manual rack. The electric steering assist motor is mounted high on the steering column behind the steering wheel and instrument panel.

See **4 Service and Repair Fundamentals** for recommended suspension and steering system service intervals.

***NOTE*—**

• *Some procedures in this section require the use of a Toyota scan tool, or equivalent.*

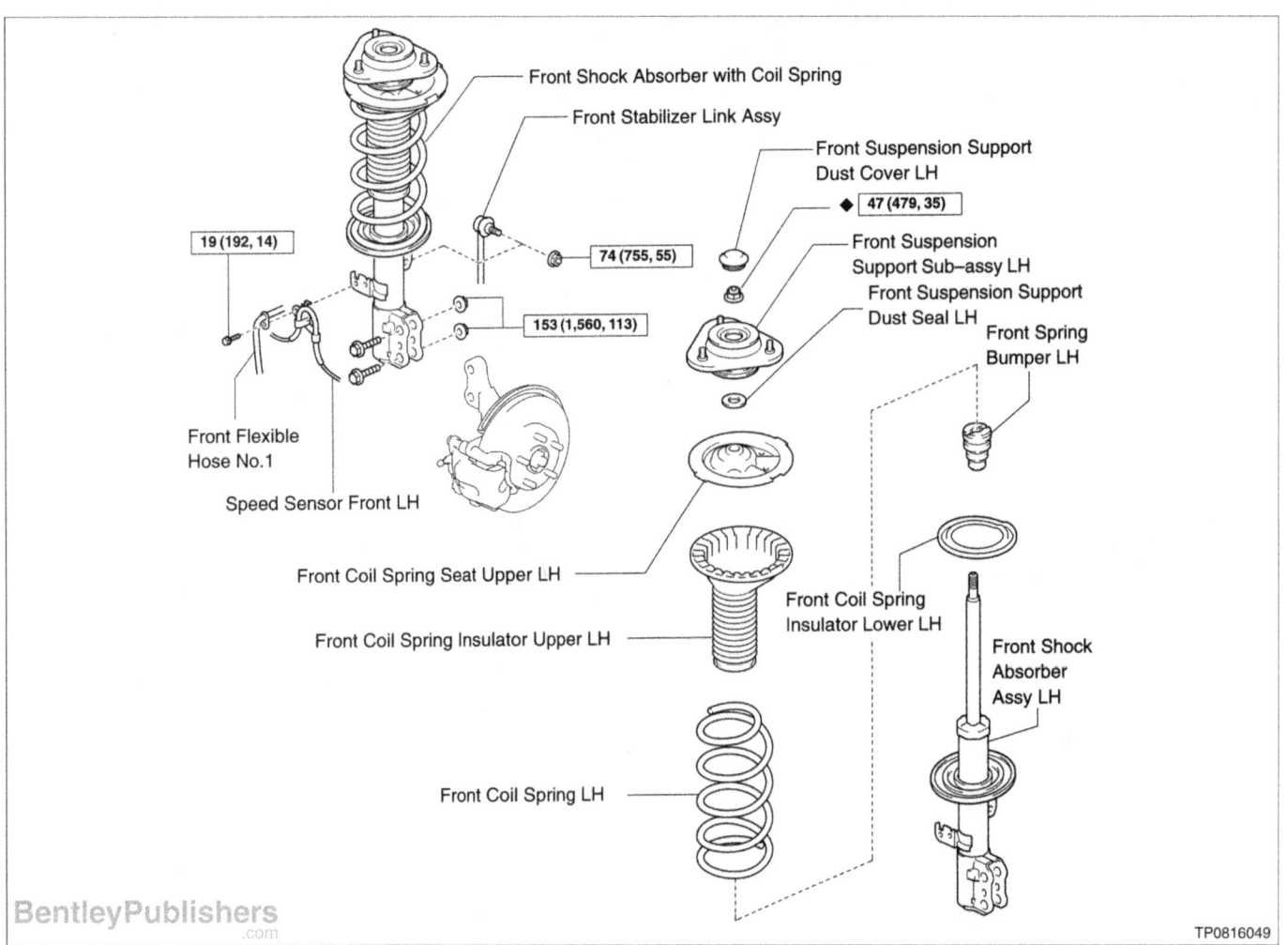

- Front Shock Absorber with Coil Spring
- Front Stabilizer Link Assy
- Front Suspension Support Dust Cover LH
  - ◆ 47 (479, 35)
- Front Suspension Support Sub-assy LH
- Front Suspension Support Dust Seal LH
- Front Spring Bumper LH
- 19 (192, 14)
- 74 (755, 55)
- 153 (1,560, 113)
- Front Flexible Hose No.1
- Speed Sensor Front LH
- Front Coil Spring Seat Upper LH
- Front Coil Spring Insulator Lower LH
- Front Shock Absorber Assy LH
- Front Coil Spring Insulator Upper LH
- Front Coil Spring LH

TP0816049

Courtesy Toyota Motor Sales (TMS) USA, Inc.

Suspension problems and symptoms

Use **Table b** to help determine the cause of suspension problems.

Table b. Suspension problems and symptoms	
Problem or symptoms	**Cause**
Vehicle unstable	• Tires worn or incorrect inflation pressures • Wheel alignment incorrect • Wheel bearing faulty • Shock absorbers worn or faulty
Vehicle bottoms on bumps	• Vehicle overloaded • Shock absorbers worn or faulty
Vehicle sways and/or pitches	• Tires worn or incorrect inflation pressures • Front stabilizer bar faulty • Shock absorbers worn or faulty
Vehicle pulls to one side	• Tires worn or incorrect inflation pressures • Wheel alignment incorrect • Brakes dragging • Steering not centered
Tires worn abnormally	• Tires worn or incorrect inflation pressures • Wheel alignment incorrect • Wheels not correctly balanced
Front wheels shimmy	• Tires worn or incorrect inflation pressures • Wheel alignment incorrect • Wheels not correctly balanced • Wheel bearing faulty • Front shock absorbers worn or faulty • Ball joint worn or faulty • Front lower suspension arm or bushing worn, faulty or damaged
Noise (front)	• Tires worn or incorrect inflation pressures • Wheel bearing faulty • Front shock absorbers worn or faulty • Ball joint worn or faulty • Drive axle assembly worn or faulty
Noise (rear)	• Wheel bearing faulty • Rear shock absorbers worn or faulty

8

Ball joints and boots, checking

— Switch hybrid system OFF (READY indicator not illuminated). See **3 Safety**.

> **WARNING—**
> • *Make sure hybrid system is OFF when servicing vehicle (READY indicator not illuminated). Failure to switch the hybrid system OFF could result in engine start at any time.*

— Raise front of vehicle and support safely. Make sure front wheels are off the ground. See **4 Service and Repair Fundamentals**.

> **WARNING—**
> • *Make sure the vehicle is stable and well supported at all times. Use a professional automotive lift or jack stands designed for the purpose.*

◀ For a quick check of ball joint condition, use a jack:

• Gently lift upward on ball joint to check for ball joint play. Use a block of wood on jack to protect suspension arm and ball joint bolts.

• Release jack, raise again, and observe movement (**arrow**) between ball joint and steering knuckle.

• There should be no play or looseness between ball joint and steering knuckle.

— Check condition of rubber boot on ball joint. Boot should be free of cracks, tears, and no grease should leak.

— Replace ball joint if play is excessive, or if rubber boot is damaged or leaking grease.

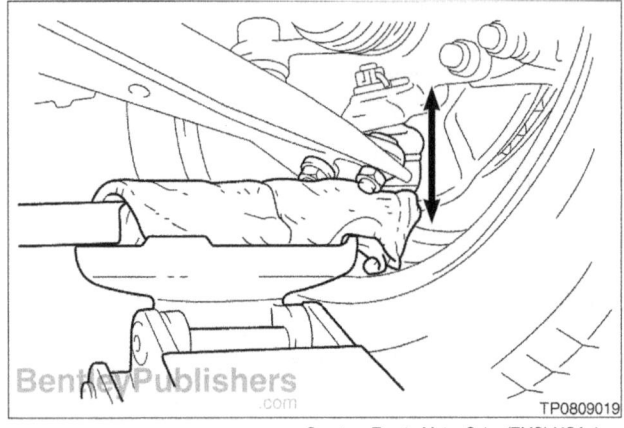

TP0809019
Courtesy Toyota Motor Sales (TMS) USA, Inc.

Drive axle joints and boots, checking

— Switch hybrid system OFF (READY indicator not illuminated). See **3 Safety**.

> **WARNING—**
> • *Make sure hybrid system is OFF when servicing vehicle (READY indicator not illuminated). Failure to switch the hybrid system OFF could result in engine start at any time.*

— Raise vehicle and support safely. See **4 Service and Repair Fundamentals**.

> **WARNING—**
> • *Make sure the vehicle is stable and well supported at all times. Use a professional automotive lift or jack stands designed for the purpose. A floor jack is not adequate support.*

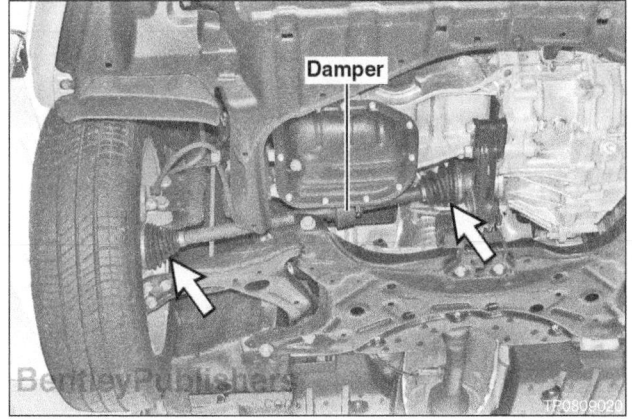

Damper

◀ Inspect rubber boots (**arrows**) for both inner and outer drive axle joints on left and right axles. Make sure boots are free of cracks, tears and grease leaks.

> **NOTE—**
> • *The inner joint is referred to as a tripod joint*
> • *The outer joint is referred to as a constant velocity or CV joint.*
> • *Rubber boots for both joints are similar.*

— Check condition of damper on right side drive axle. Make sure it is not damaged or loose on shaft.

— If rhythmic noises are heard from front of vehicle while driving, diagnose and replace drive axles as necessary.

— Replace drive axle if rubber boots are damaged or leaking.

Steering joints and boots, checking

— Switch hybrid system OFF (READY indicator not illuminated). See **3 Safety**.

> **WARNING—**
> • *Make sure hybrid system is OFF when servicing vehicle (READY indicator not illuminated). Failure to switch the hybrid system OFF could result in engine start at any time.*

— Raise vehicle and support safely. See **4 Service and Repair Fundamentals**.

> **WARNING—**
> • *Make sure the vehicle is stable and well supported at all times. Use a professional automotive lift or jack stands designed for the purpose. A floor jack is not adequate support.*

— Inspect both left and right side steering rack boots. Boot should be free of cracks, tears, and no grease should leak.

— For a quick check of tie rod end condition, try to detect play by moving tie rod end upward and downward. Also rotate tie rod end ball joint.

   • Tie rod end ball joint should rotate smoothly, and there should be no play or looseness between tie rod ball joint and steering knuckle arm.

— Inspect both left and right side tie rod ends.

— Check condition of rubber boot on tie rod ball joint. Boot should be free of cracks, tears, and no grease should leak.

— Replace tie rod end if play is excessive, or if rubber boot is damaged or leaking grease.

— Replace steering rack boot when rubber boot is damaged or leaking.

Shock absorbers and springs, checking

– Switch hybrid system OFF (READY indicator not illuminated). See **3 Safety**.

> **WARNING** —
> • *Make sure hybrid system is OFF when servicing vehicle (READY indicator not illuminated). Failure to switch the hybrid system OFF could result in engine start at any time.*

– Raise vehicle and support safely. See **4 Service and Repair Fundamentals**.

> **WARNING** —
> • *Make sure the vehicle is stable and well supported at all times. Use a professional automotive lift or jack stands designed for the purpose.*

– Remove wheels.

– Inspect front and rear shock absorbers.

– The following two graphics are from a Toyota Technical Service Bulletin that defines acceptable and unacceptable amounts of oil leakage from shock absorbers.

Strut Type:

	LEVEL 5	LEVEL 4	LEVEL 3	LEVEL 2	LEVEL 1
OIL LEAK CRITERIA	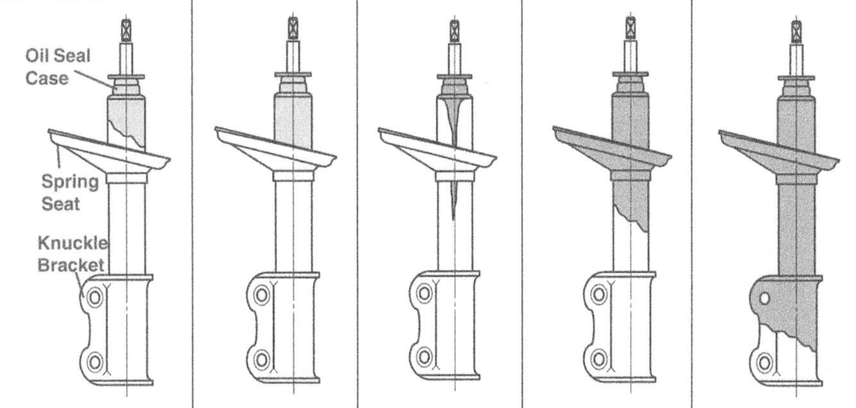 Oil Seal Case / Spring Seat / Knuckle Bracket				
CONDITION	Slight oil seepage from oil seal case	Moderate oil seepage from oil seal case	Oil leak/drip on the seal case, extending below the spring seat	Oil leak, covering top, spring seat, and part of strut body	Oil leak, covering entire strut body, spring seat, and knuckle bracket
ACTION	Normal oil evaporation — NOT necessary to replace the shock absorber	Normal oil evaporation — NOT necessary to replace the shock absorber	Abnormal oil leak — Replace the shock absorber	Abnormal oil leak — Replace the shock absorber	Abnormal oil leak — Replace the shock absorber

TP0816006

Courtesy Toyota Motor Sales (TMS) USA, Inc.

Shock Absorber Type with Spring Seat:

	LEVEL 5	LEVEL 4	LEVEL 3	LEVEL 2	LEVEL 1
OIL LEAK CRITERIA	Oil Seal Case / Lower Bushing / Lower Bracket	1/3 L / L			
CONDITION	Slight oil seepage from oil seal case	Moderate oil seepage from oil seal case	Oil leak/drip on the seal case, extending below the spring seat	Oil leak, covering top, spring seat, and part of shock body	Oil leak, covering entire shock body and spring seat, and extending to lower bushing
ACTION	Normal oil evaporation — NOT necessary to replace the shock absorber	Normal oil evaporation — NOT necessary to replace the shock absorber	Abnormal oil leak — Replace the shock absorber	Abnormal oil leak — Replace the shock absorber	Abnormal oil leak — Replace the shock absorber

TP0816007

Courtesy Toyota Motor Sales (TMS) USA, Inc.

- Springs should be in good condition and not broken.

- Shock absorbers should not be dented, bent or damaged, and not leaking large quantities of oil.

- Check rubber bushings on rear shock absorbers. Bushings should be in place and not torn, loose, or cracked.

- Replace shock absorbers or springs if damaged, broken, or leaking. For a list of problems that can be caused by faulty shock absorbers, see **Table b** in this chapter.

- For front shock absorber and spring replacement procedure, see **Front shock absorbers and springs, removing and installing** in this chapter.

- For rear shock absorber and spring replacement procedure, see **Rear shock absorbers and springs, removing and installing** in this chapter.

- Install wheels and tighten wheel lug nuts to specification.

Tightening torque	
Wheel to wheel hub	103 Nm (76 ft-lb)

- Lower vehicle.

Front strut assembly, removing and installing

— Switch hybrid system OFF (READY indicator not illuminated). See **3 Safety**.

> **WARNING** —
> • *Make sure hybrid system is OFF when servicing vehicle (READY indicator not illuminated). Failure to switch the hybrid system OFF could result in engine start at any time.*

> **NOTE** —
> • *This procedure requires the use of a Toyota scan tool or equivalent.*

— Remove windshield wiper arms. See **10 Electrical System, Lights**.

— Remove windshield cowl cover. See **9 Body**.

— Remove windshield wiper motor assembly. See **10 Electrical System, Lights**.

— Remove engine compartment upper bulkhead. See **9 Body**.

— Loosen front wheel lug nuts slightly before lifting vehicle. This makes removing wheels and tires easier when vehicle is raised.

— Raise vehicle and support safely. See **4 Service and Repair Fundamentals**.

> **WARNING** —
> • *Make sure the vehicle is stable and well supported at all times. Use a professional automotive lift or jack stands designed for the purpose. A floor jack is not adequate support.*

— Remove front wheels.

◄ Using a jack, gently lift upward on suspension arm. Use a block of wood on jack to protect suspension arm and ball joint bolts.

— Remove front stabilizer bar link nut.

— Disconnect front stabilizer bar link from shock absorber.

> **NOTE** —
> • *If stabilizer link ball joint turns when removing nut, hold ball joint stud with 6 mm Allen wrench.*

◄ Remove bolt and disconnect ABS speed sensor harness and flexible brake hose from shock absorber assembly.

> **NOTE** —
> • *Be sure that ABS speed sensor harness is completely disconnected from shock absorber assembly.*

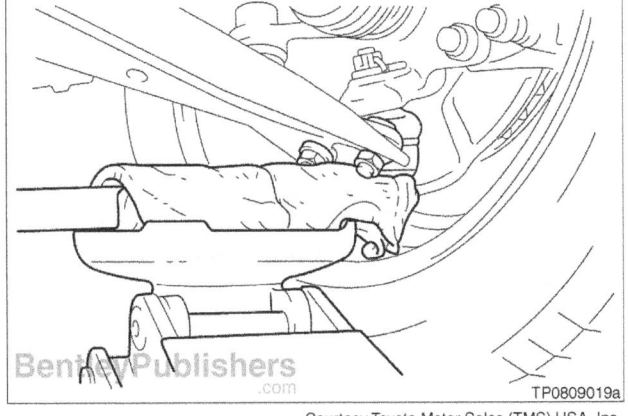

TP0809019a

Courtesy Toyota Motor Sales (TMS) USA, Inc.

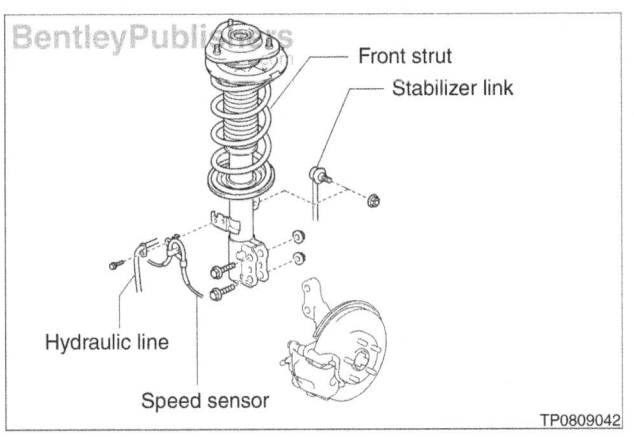

Front strut
Stabilizer link
Hydraulic line
Speed sensor

TP0809042

Courtesy Toyota Motor Sales (TMS) USA, Inc.

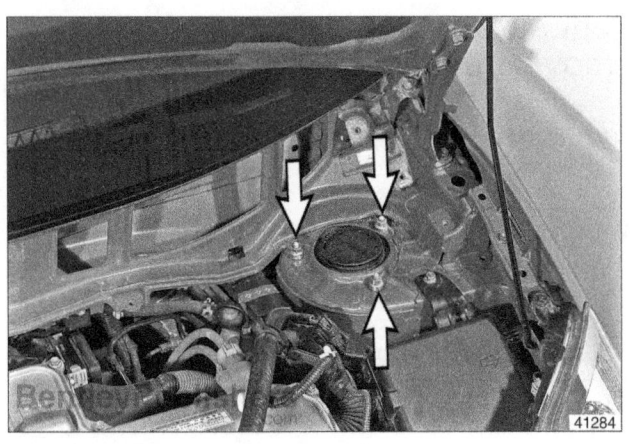

41284

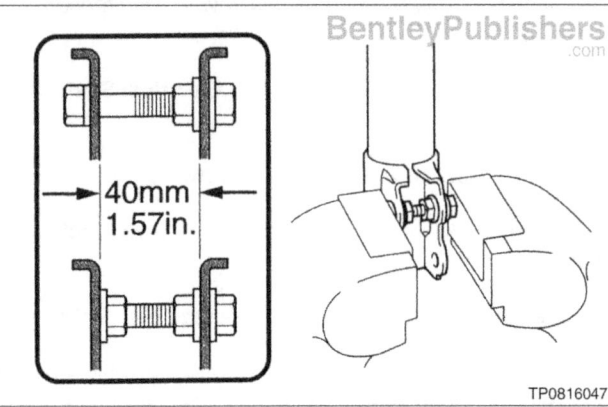

40mm
1.57in.

TP0816047
Courtesy Toyota Motor Sales (TMS) USA, Inc.

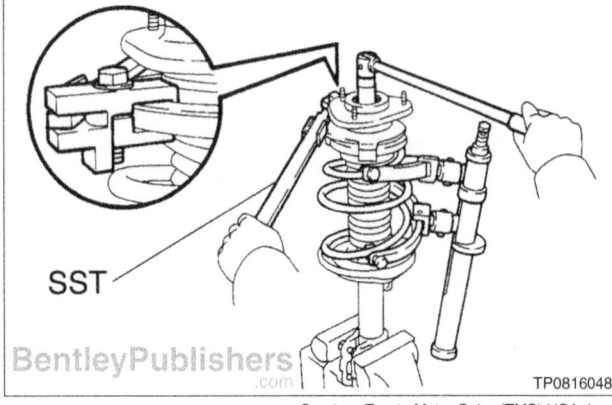

SST

TP0816048
Courtesy Toyota Motor Sales (TMS) USA, Inc.

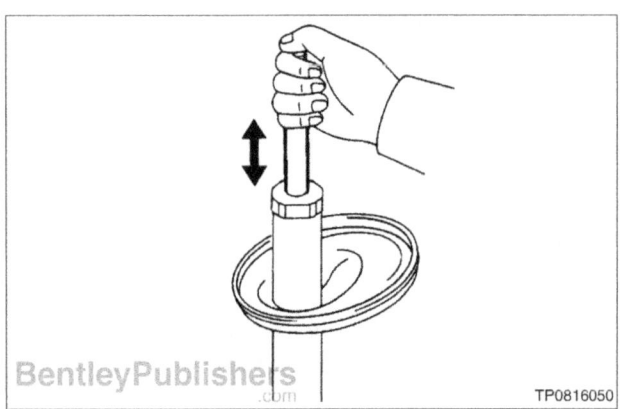

TP0816050
Courtesy Toyota Motor Sales (TMS) USA, Inc.

– Loosen and remove 2 nuts clamping shock absorber bracket to steering knuckle at lower end of shock absorber. Do not remove bolts at this time.

◄ Remove upper shock absorber mount nuts (**arrows**) in engine compartment.

– Lower jack slowly and remove shock absorber assembly from vehicle.

– Support shock absorber assembly while removing 2 steering knuckle bolts.

– Remove shock absorber assembly downward.

◄ Temporarily install bolt with 2 nuts in top bolt hole of bracket at lower end of shock absorber (**inset**). This prevents bracket from being crushed or bent when shock absorber is clamped in a vise.

– Hold shock absorber in a vise by clamping on temporary bolt with 2 nuts.

– Use spring compressor tool (Toyota special tool SST 09727-30021 or equivalent) to fully compress coil spring.

> **WARNING—**
> • Much energy is stored in a compressed spring. Be sure to follow tool manufacturer's instructions and use all tool safety features. Always stand to the side of the compressed spring.

> **CAUTION—**
> • Do not use an impact wrench to compress or extend the spring compressor.

– Remove dust cap from top of upper shock absorber mount.

◄ Hold upper spring seat with holding tool (Toyota special tool SST 09729-22031 or equivalent) and remove upper shock absorber mount nut.

> **CAUTION—**
> • Do not use an impact wrench to remove upper mount nut.

– Remove upper shock absorber mount, dust seal, upper spring seat, upper insulator, coil spring, spring bumper, and lower insulator.

◄ To inspect shock absorber, compress and extend shock absorber piston rod at least 4 times.

– Note any roughness, excessive resistance, excessive play, noise, or excess fluid leakage.

– Replace shock absorber if any defects are found.

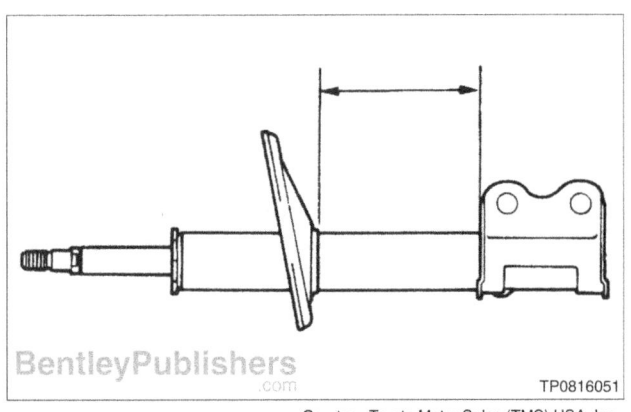

Courtesy Toyota Motor Sales (TMS) USA, Inc.

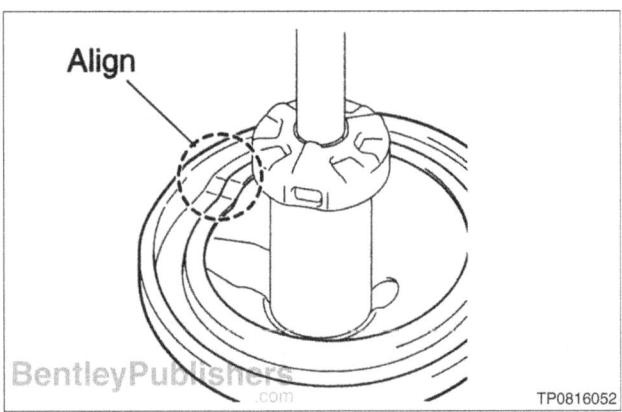

Align

Courtesy Toyota Motor Sales (TMS) USA, Inc.

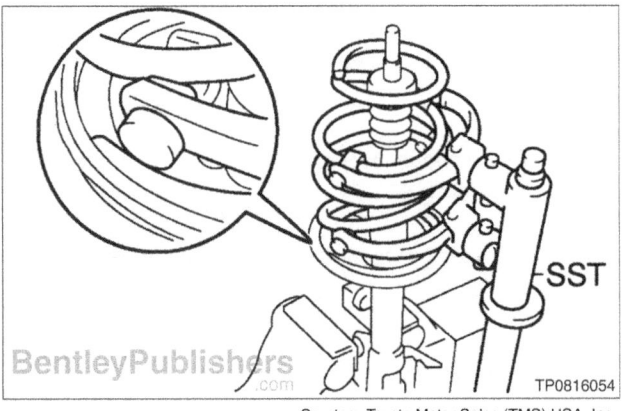

SST

Courtesy Toyota Motor Sales (TMS) USA, Inc.

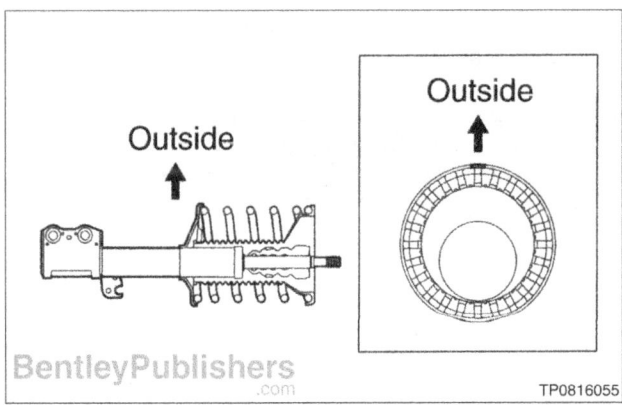

Outside

Outside

Outside

Courtesy Toyota Motor Sales (TMS) USA, Inc.

◀ To release gas pressure in the pressurized shock absorber before disposal, fully extend shock absorber piston rod.

> **WARNING—**
> • *The procedure to release gas pressure in shock absorbers requires drilling. Escaping gas is not harmful but may carry debris and metal chips. Always wear safety goggles.*

— Drill hole approx. 3 mm (0.125 in) dia. in area shown to release gas pressure.

◀ When reinstalling, install lower insulator on shock absorber. Be sure that step in insulator aligns with step on lower spring seat.

— Install spring bumper on shock absorber piston rod.

— Clamp shock absorber in vise, using bolt with 2 nuts to prevent crushing of strut bracket, as before.

◀ Use spring compressor tool (Toyota special tool SST 09727-30021 or equivalent), to compress coil spring.

> **WARNING—**
> • *Much energy is stored in a compressed spring. Be sure to follow tool manufacturer's instructions and use all tool safety features. Always stand to the side of the compressed spring.*

> **CAUTION—**
> • *Do not use an impact wrench to compress or extend the spring compressor.*

— Install compressed coil spring on shock absorber with smaller spring diameter is at top.

— Fit lower end of spring into mating recess in shock absorber lower spring seat.

◀ Install upper insulator on shock absorber piston rod.

— Be sure that upper insulator is oriented as shown.

8

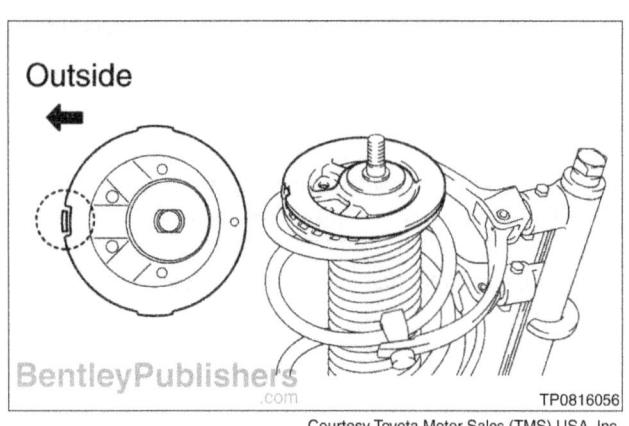

Outside

TP0816056
Courtesy Toyota Motor Sales (TMS) USA, Inc.

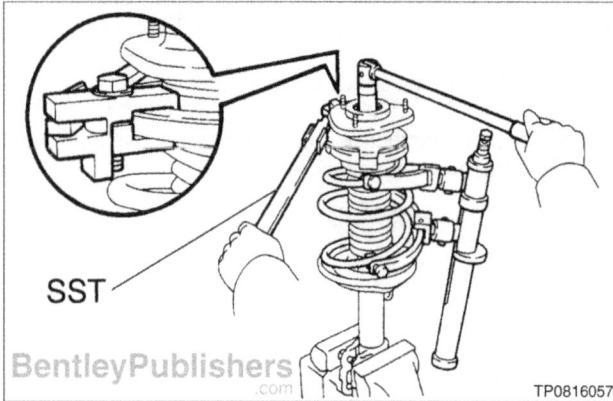

SST

TP0816057
Courtesy Toyota Motor Sales (TMS) USA, Inc.

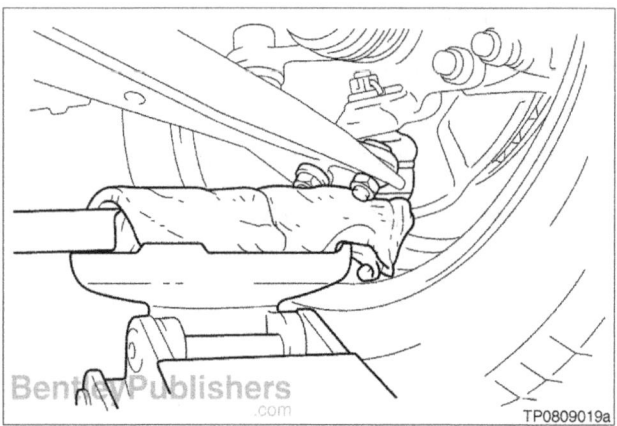

MP Grease No.2

TP0816058
Courtesy Toyota Motor Sales (TMS) USA, Inc.

◄ Install upper spring seat on shock absorber piston rod with notch facing outside of vehicle. Engage tab on upper insulator (**inset**) with notch on upper spring seat.

— Be sure that hole in upper spring seat is fully engaged with flats on shock absorber piston rod.

— Install dust seal and suspension support on shock absorber piston rod.

◄ Hold upper spring seat with holding tool (Toyota special tool SST 09729-22031 or equivalent). Install new upper shock absorber mount nut and tighten to specification.

> **CAUTION—**
> • *Do not reuse upper shock absorber mount nut. Replace with new nut.*
> • *Do not use an impact wrench to tighten upper mount nut.*

Tightening torque	
Upper shock absorber mount to shock absorber	47 Nm (35 ft-lb)

— Slowly remove spring compressor tool from coil spring while being sure to align upper and lower spring ends with steps in upper and lower spring seats.

> **CAUTION—**
> • *Do not use an impact wrench to compress or extend the spring compressor.*

◄ Apply multi-purpose grease to shock absorber upper mount bearing where shown. Do not apply grease to rubber part of upper mount.

— Install dust cap on top of upper mount.

— Install shock absorber assembly on steering knuckle.

— Install 2 bolts through bracket and steering knuckle at lower end of shock absorber assembly. Do not install nuts at this time.

◄ Using a jack, gently lift upward on suspension arm. Use a block of wood on jack to protect suspension arm and ball joint bolts. Slowly raise jack until 3 studs for shock absorber upper mount are through holes in strut tower in engine compartment.

TP0809019a
Courtesy Toyota Motor Sales (TMS) USA, Inc.

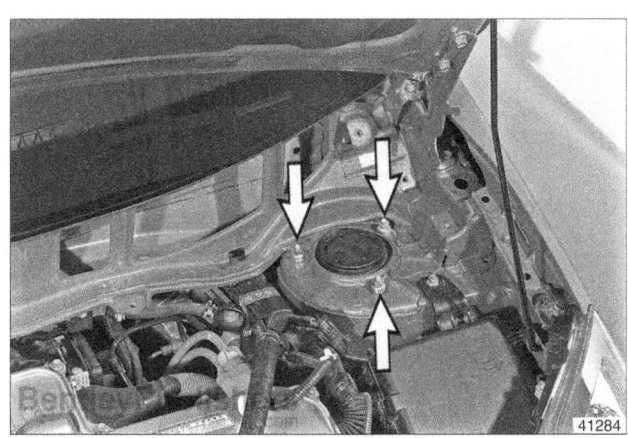

◀ Lubricate studs, then install shock absorber upper mount nuts (**arrows**). Tighten to specification.

Tightening torque	
Upper shock absorber mount to strut tower	39 Nm (29 ft-lb)

– Install 2 nuts on bolts clamping shock absorber bracket to steering knuckle at lower end of shock absorber. Tighten nuts to specification.

Tightening torque	
Front shock absorber lower bracket nut	153 Nm (113 ft-lb)

– Install ABS speed sensor harness clamp and flexible brake hose to shock absorber assembly. Tighten bolt to specification.

> *CAUTION—*
> • *Do not twist ABS speed sensor wire harness when installing.*

Tightening torque	
ABS speed sensor harness and brake hose to shock absorber	19 Nm (14 ft-lb)

– Reconnect front stabilizer bar link to shock absorber. Tighten stabilizer bar link nut to specification.

Tightening torque	
Front stabilizer bar link to shock absorber	74 Nm (55 ft-lb)

> *NOTE—*
> • *If stabilizer link ball joint turns when removing nut, hold ball joint stud with 6 mm Allen wrench.*

– Reinstall engine compartment upper bulkhead, windshield wiper assembly, windshield cowl cover and windshield wiper arms. See **9 Body** and **10 Electrical System, Lights**.

– Install front wheels and tighten wheel lug nuts to specification.

Tightening torque	
Wheel to wheel hub	103 Nm (76 ft-lb)

– Lower vehicle.

– Have vehicle professionally aligned.

– Perform steering torque sensor zero point setting. See **Torque sensor, setting zero point** in this chapter.

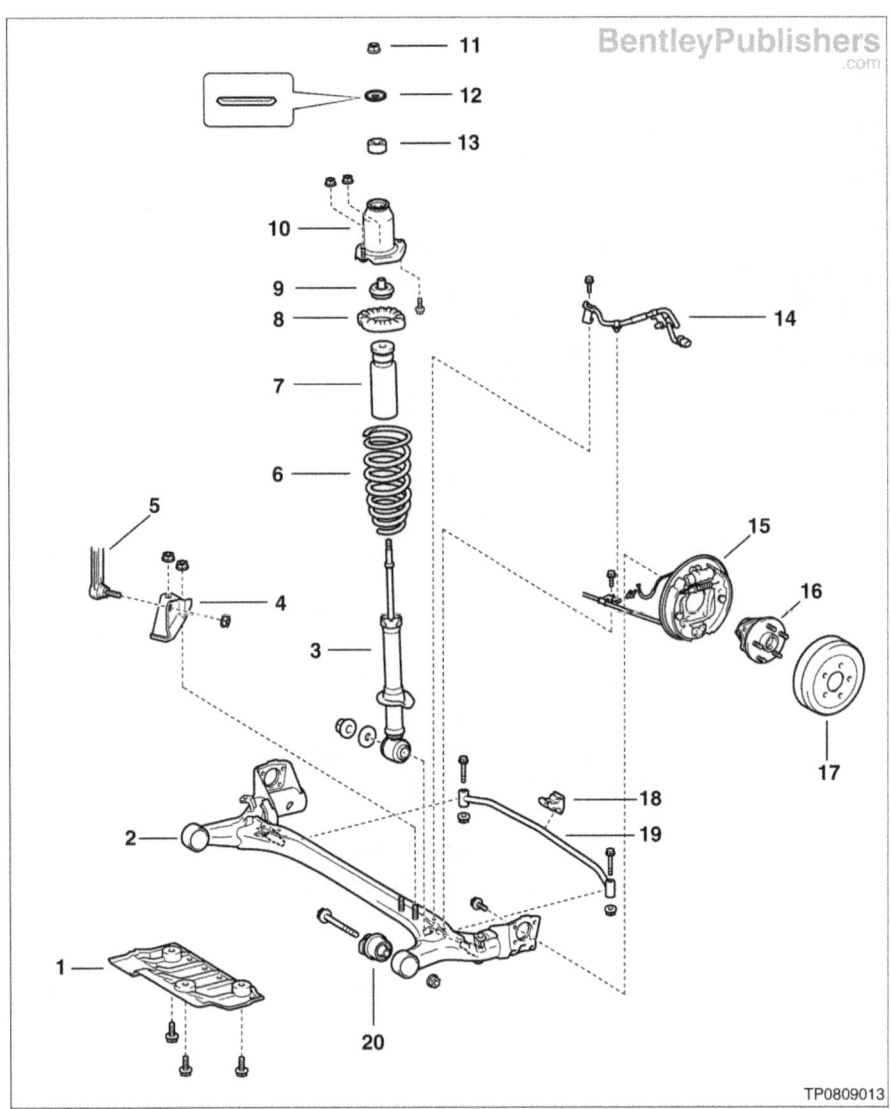

TP0809013

Courtesy Toyota Motor Sales (TMS) USA, Inc.

Rear suspension components

1. Floor panel side plate
2. Rear axle beam assembly
3. Shock absorber
4. Level sensor bracket
5. Level sensor arm
6. Coil spring
7. Spring bumper
8. Spring insulator
9. Bushing
10. Upper mount
11. Upper mount nut
12. Cushion washer
13. Cushion
14. Stability control harness
15. Brake assembly
16. Brake drum hub
17. Brake drum
18. Axle damper
19. Stabilizer bar
20. Axle carrier bushing

Rear shock absorbers and springs, removing and installing

The rear suspension includes a pivoting transverse beam axle and shock absorbers with concentric coil springs. See **Rear suspension components** in this chapter.

– Switch hybrid system OFF (READY indicator not illuminated). See **3 Safety**.

> **WARNING**—
> • *Make sure hybrid system is OFF when servicing vehicle (READY indicator not illuminated). Failure to switch the hybrid system OFF could result in engine start at any time.*

– Remove tonneau cover assembly (if equipped).

◄ Rotate 2 release knobs on rear no. 2 floor board.

◄ Lift and remove rear no. 2 floor board.

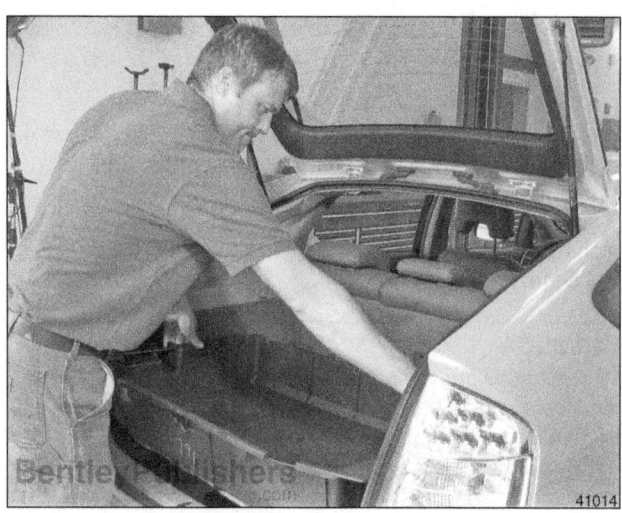

◄ Remove rear floor box from vehicle.

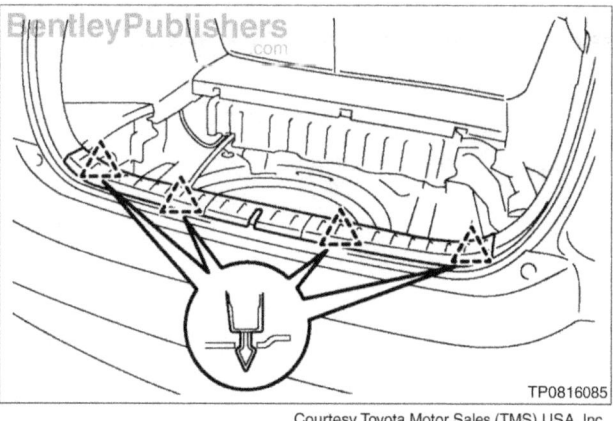

Courtesy Toyota Motor Sales (TMS) USA, Inc.

◄ Remove rear deck trim cover by prying off clips (**inset**).

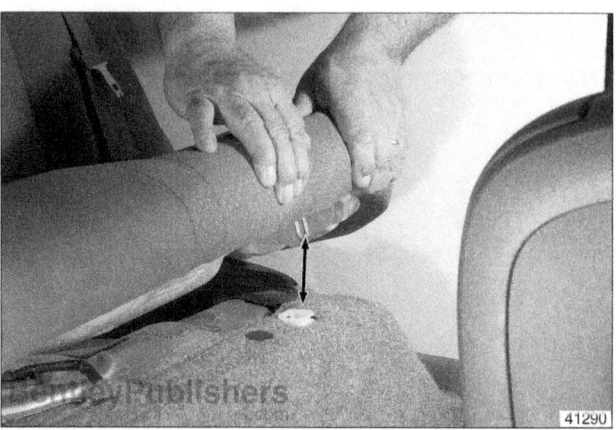

◄ Remove rear seat for access to rear shock absorber upper
mount fasteners. Pull upward on front edge of rear seat cushion
to release 2 latches (**arrow**).

> **WARNING—**
> • *The underside of seat cushions can have sharp features
> and may cause injury.*

> **CAUTION—**
> • *Seat cushion frame is easily deformed. To prevent damage,
> place your hands on either side of one of the seat cushion
> latches as shown and pull upward. Repeat for other side.*

— Push downward on rear center of rear seat cushion and pull
toward front of vehicle to release seat hook and remove cushion.

— Remove rear seat belt floor anchor bolt.

— Raise front part of rear no. 1 floor board.

– Right rear seat back:
  • Fold seat back assembly fully forward.
  • Remove 2 seat back assembly bolts.
  • Remove seat back assembly.

– Repeat steps for left rear seat back.

◄ Remove right rear side seat back frame bolt.
  • Using trim tool or screwdriver, detach 4 retention claws (**insets**).
  • Remove right rear side seat back frame.

> **CAUTION—**
> • *If using a screwdriver to remove trim, wrap with tape to protect finish of interior components.*

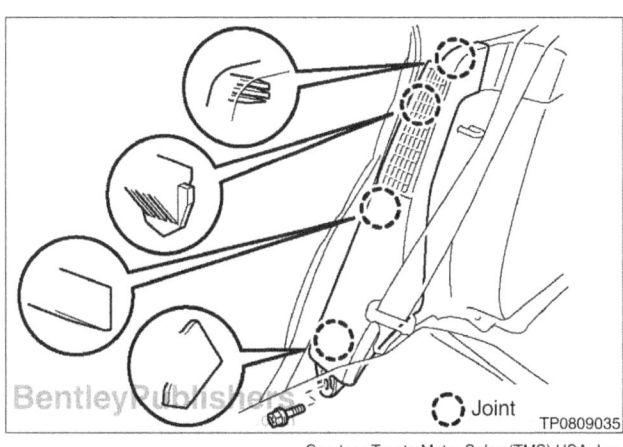

Courtesy Toyota Motor Sales (TMS) USA, Inc.

◄ Remove left rear side seat back frame bolt.
  • Using trim tool or screwdriver, detach 3 retention claws (**insets**).
  • Remove left rear side seat back frame.

> **CAUTION—**
> • *If using a screwdriver to remove trim, wrap with tape to protect finish of interior components.*

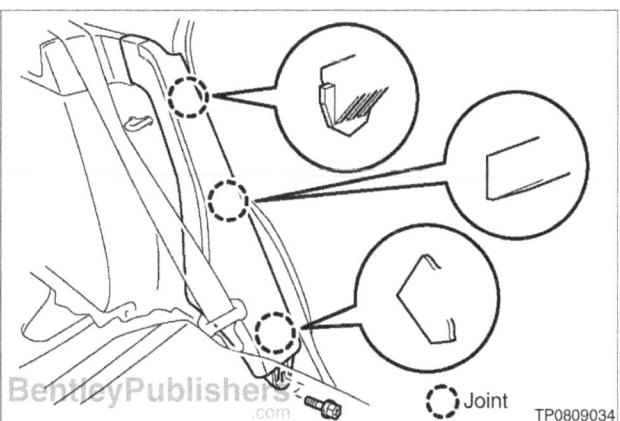

Courtesy Toyota Motor Sales (TMS) USA, Inc.

◄ Remove rear no. 1 floor board.
  • Remove 2 luggage tie down bolts and 2 luggage tie downs (**inset**).
  • Using trim tool or screwdriver, detach 5 clips and remove rear no.1 floor board.

– Working on right side of luggage compartment (above 12-volt battery), use trim tool or screwdriver to detach 4 retention claws and remove rear no. 3 floor board.

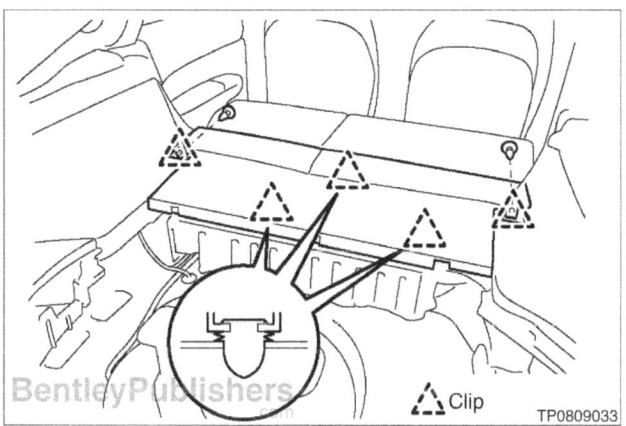

Courtesy Toyota Motor Sales (TMS) USA, Inc.

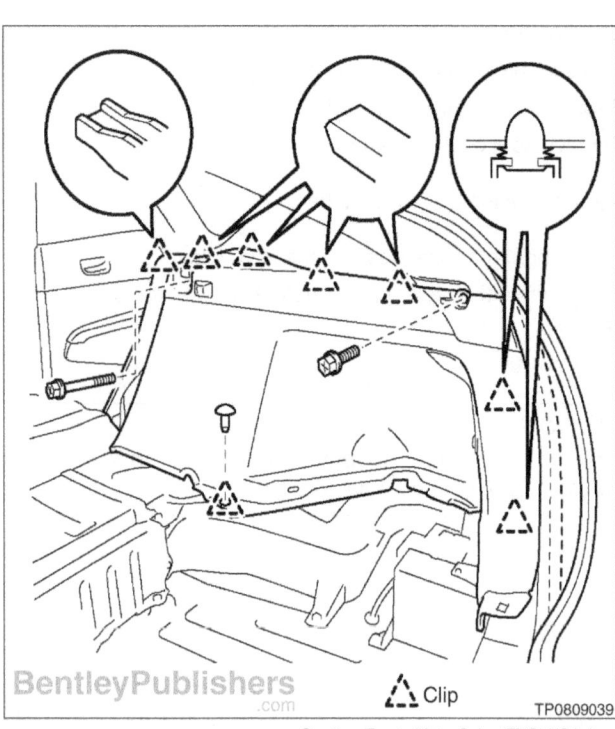

Clip

TP0809039

Courtesy Toyota Motor Sales (TMS) USA, Inc.

◀ Remove 2 bolts from right deck trim side panel assembly.
- Using trim tool or screwdriver, remove clip.
- Using trim tool or screwdriver, detach retention claws and 2 remaining clips (**insets**).

– Remove right deck trim side panel assembly.

41294

◀ Pull tab (**arrow**) and remove rear No. 4 floor board.

41291

◀ Using trim tool or screwdriver, remove clip (**arrow**) and remove left deck floor box.

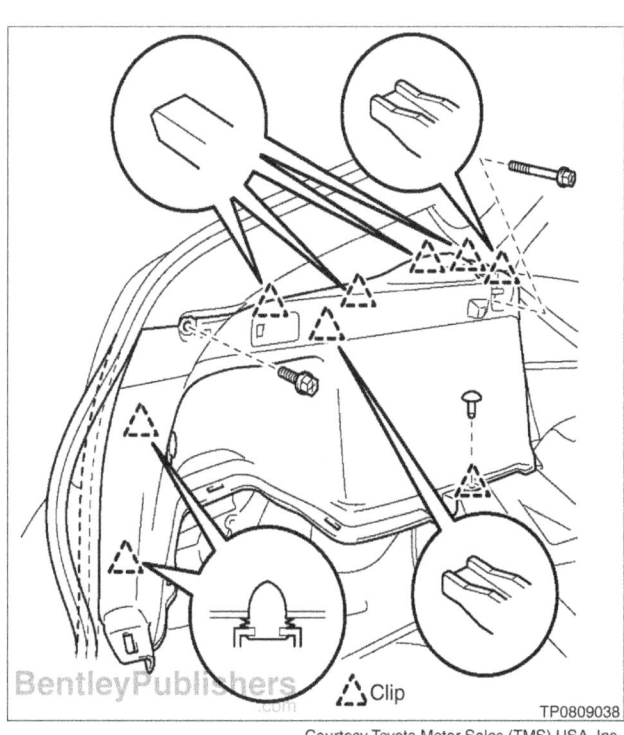

△ Clip

TP0809038

Courtesy Toyota Motor Sales (TMS) USA, Inc.

◀ Remove 2 bolts from left deck trim side panel assembly.
- Remove 1 screw.
- Using trim tool or screwdriver, remove clip.
- Using trim tool or screwdriver, detach retention claws and 3 remaining clips (**insets**).
- Remove left deck trim side panel assembly.

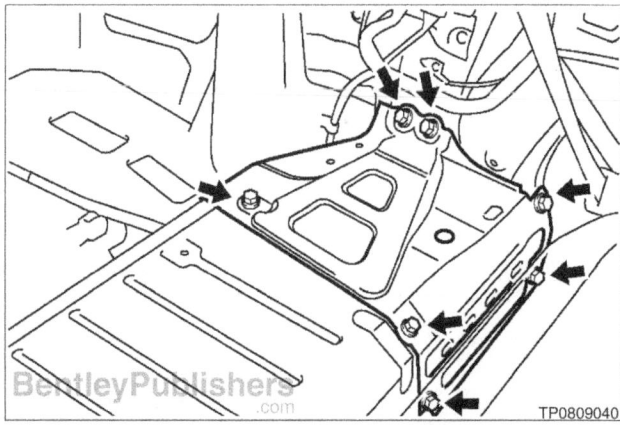

TP0809040

Courtesy Toyota Motor Sales (TMS) USA, Inc.

◀ Remove 7 high voltage battery carrier bracket bolts (**arrows**).

– Remove high voltage battery carrier bracket.

– Raise vehicle and support safely. See **4 Service and Repair Fundamentals**.

> **WARNING—**
> - *Make sure the vehicle is stable and well supported at all times. Use a professional automotive lift or jack stands designed for the purpose. A floor jack is not adequate support.*

– Remove rear wheels.

◀ If necessary, disconnect battery blower relay electrical connector and remove high voltage battery vent duct fasteners (**arrows**). Lift off vent duct.

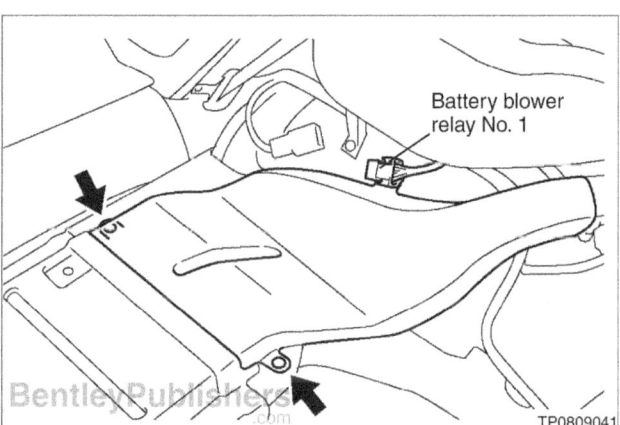

Battery blower relay No. 1

TP0809041

Courtesy Toyota Motor Sales (TMS) USA, Inc.

8

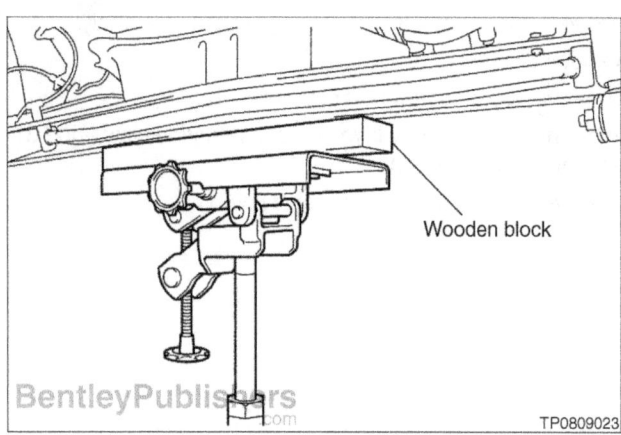

Courtesy Toyota Motor Sales (TMS) USA, Inc.

◀ Support rear axle beam as shown with jack and block of wood.

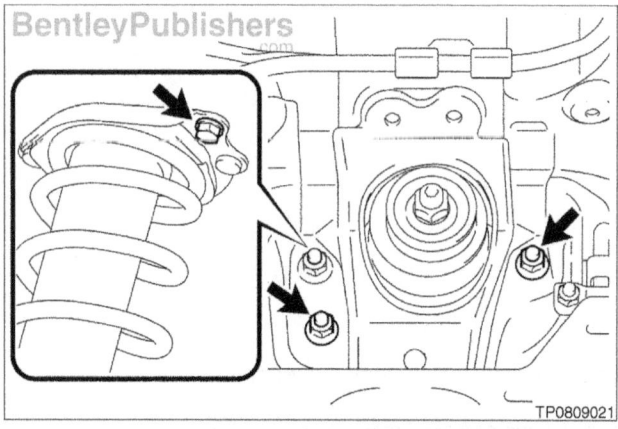

Courtesy Toyota Motor Sales (TMS) USA, Inc.

◀ Remove 2 nuts (**arrows**) at top of upper shock mount and 1 bolt (**inset**) on underside of rear shock absorber assembly.

◀ Remove nut and washer (**arrow**) at lower end of rear shock absorber assembly and remove rear shock absorber assembly.

– If more clearance is required to remove shock absorber assembly, lower jack slowly.

> **CAUTION—**
> • *When removing only one shock absorber assembly, lower jack carefully so remaining shock absorber and xenon (HID) headlight height control sensor linkage (if equipped) are not stressed.*

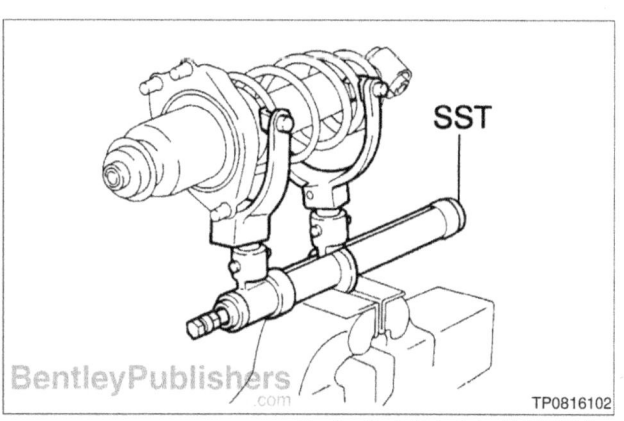

Courtesy Toyota Motor Sales (TMS) USA, Inc.

◀ Remove coil spring from shock absorber:
   • Use spring compressor tool (Toyota special tool SST 09727-30021 or equivalent) to fully compress coil spring.
   • Hold shock absorber in vise by clamping on spring compressor.

> **WARNING—**
> • *Much energy is stored in a compressed spring. Be sure to follow tool manufacturer's instructions and use all tool safety features. Always stand to the side of the compressed spring.*

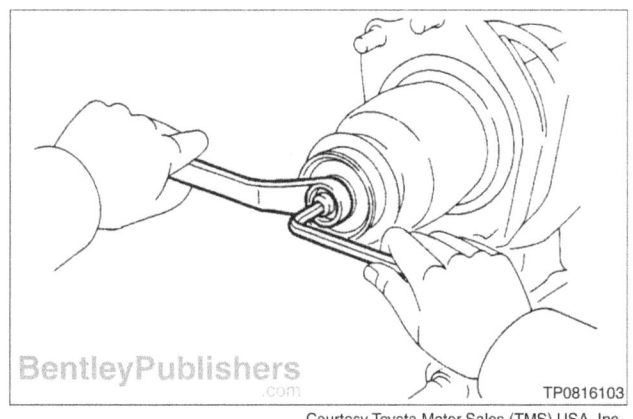

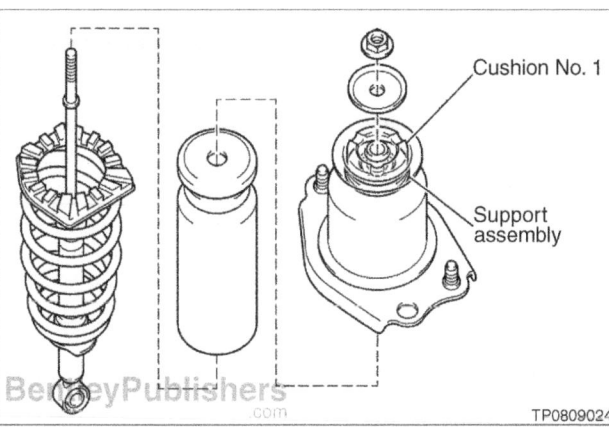

Cushion No. 1

Support
assembly

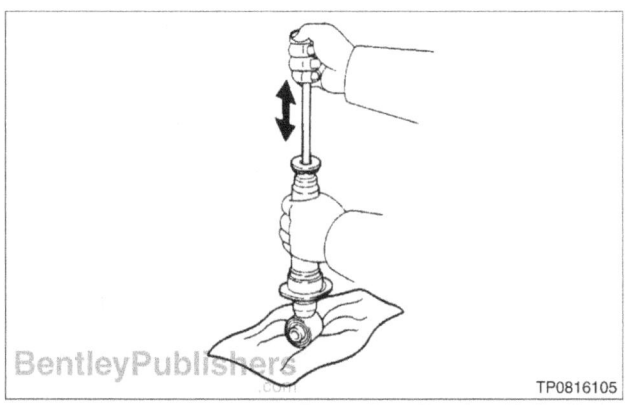

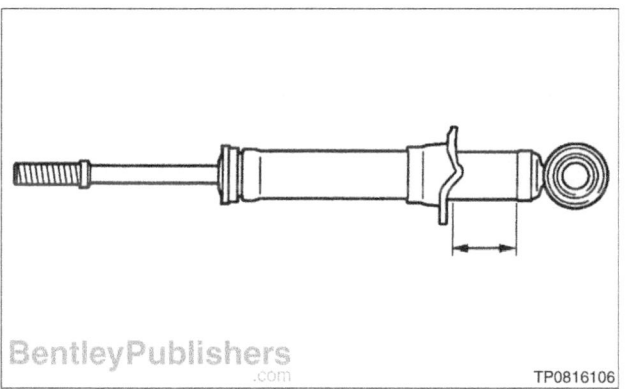

CAUTION—
• *Do not use an impact wrench to compress or extend the spring compressor.*

◄ With spring compressed, hold shock absorber piston rod with 6 mm Allen wrench. Remove piston rod center nut.

CAUTION—
• *Do not use an impact wrench to remove shock absorber piston rod center nut. Be sure that hex wrench is fully inserted into piston rod.*

◄ Remove cushion washer no. 1, rear spring front bracket subassembly, rear coil spring upper insulator, and rear spring bumper no. 1.

◄ To inspect shock absorber, compress and extend shock absorber piston rod at least 4 times.
• Note any roughness, excessive resistance, excessive play, noise, or excess fluid leakage.
• Replace shock absorber if any defects are found.

◄ To release gas pressure in pressurized shock absorber prior to disposal:
• Fully extend shock absorber piston rod.
• Drill hole approx. 3 mm (0.125 in) dia. in area shown to release gas pressure.

WARNING—
• *The procedure to release gas pressure in shock absorbers requires drilling. Escaping gas is not harmful but may carry debris and metal chips. Wear safety goggles.*

8

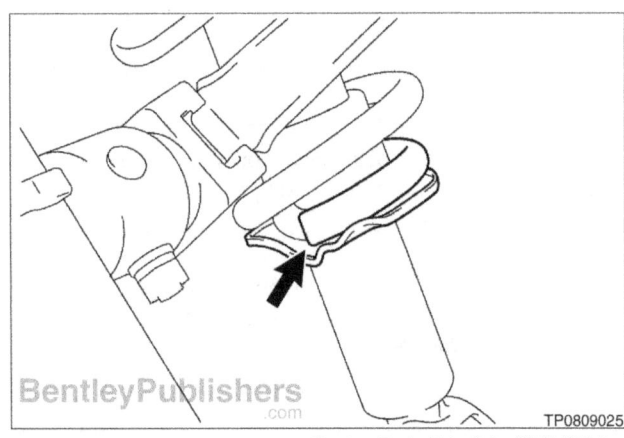

TP0809025

Courtesy Toyota Motor Sales (TMS) USA, Inc.

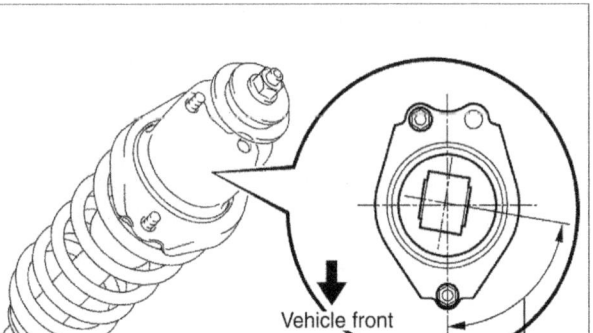

Vehicle front

80.6°

TP0809026

Courtesy Toyota Motor Sales (TMS) USA, Inc.

- Installation is reverse of removal. Use spring compressor tool (Toyota special tool SST 09727-30021 or equivalent) to compress coil spring.

- Insert shock absorber into compressed coil spring, making sure that spring smaller diameter is at bottom.

◀ Fit lower end of spring (**arrow**) into mating recess in shock absorber lower spring seat.

- Install rear coil spring upper insulator, rear spring bumper no. 1, rear spring front bracket subassembly, and cushion washer no. 1.

- Be sure that piston rod center nut is threaded fully onto piston rod.

◀ Install rear shock absorber upper mount with orientation as shown.

- Install cushion washer no.1 with protrusion facing downward.

- Install and temporarily tighten piston rod center nut.

> **WARNING—**
> • Be sure that piston rod center nut is threaded fully on piston rod

- Remove spring compressor and recheck orientation of spring bracket.

- Tighten piston rod center nut to specification.

Tightening torque	
Upper shock absorber mount to piston rod	56 Nm (41 ft-lb)

> **CAUTION—**
> • Do not use an impact wrench to tighten piston rod center nut. Be sure that hex wrench is fully inserted into piston rod.

- With rear axle beam supported with jack and block of wood, install shock absorber assembly.

  • Install lower end of rear shock absorber assembly on stud on rear axle.

  • Temporarily install nut and washer at lower end of rear shock absorber assembly. Do not tighten nut and washer at lower end of rear shock absorber assembly at this time.

- Raise jack and guide 2 studs on upper shock absorber mount through holes in body.

> **CAUTION—**
> • Do not raise rear axle more than necessary. Raise jack carefully so remaining shock absorber and xenon (HID) headlight height control sensor linkage are not damaged.

— Lubricate threads with oil before installing nuts, then install 2 nuts and 1 bolt at shock absorber upper mount assembly. Tighten fasteners to specification.

Tightening torque	
Rear shock absorber upper mount to chassis	80 Nm (59 ft-lb)

— Install interior components and rear seat. Tighten rear seat back assembly bolts to specification.

Tightening torque	
Rear seat back assembly to chassis	37 Nm (27 ft-lb)

— Install rear wheels and tighten wheel lug nuts to specification.

Tightening torque	
Wheel to wheel hub	103 Nm (76 ft-lb)

— Lower vehicle and bounce rear of vehicle to be sure suspension components stabilized at ride height.

— With vehicle at proper ride-height, tighten nut at lower end of rear shock absorber assembly to specification.

Tightening torque	
Rear shock absorber to axle beam	80 Nm (59 ft-lb)

— Test drive vehicle and check for abnormal noises.

— Models with xenon (HID) headlights:

• Perform headlight leveling ECU initialization and check headlight aim. See **10 Electrical System, Lights**.

8

Driver airbag / horn assembly, removing and installing

– Switch hybrid system OFF (READY indicator not illuminated). See **3 Safety**.

> **WARNING —**
> • *Make sure hybrid system is OFF when servicing vehicle (READY indicator not illuminated). Failure to switch the hybrid system OFF could result in engine start at any time.*

– Disconnect 12-volt auxiliary battery negative (-) terminal. See **3 Safety**.

> **WARNING —**
> • *After disconnecting 12-volt auxiliary battery, wait 90 seconds before beginning work on airbag components.*

– Center steering wheel in straight ahead position.

◄ Working at steering wheel, use a plastic prying tool or screwdriver with tip wrapped with tape to pry off steering wheel lower covers (**2** and **3**) to reveal Torx screws (**arrows**).

– Using a T30 Torx wrench, loosen 2 Torx screws until groove along screw circumference catches on screw case.

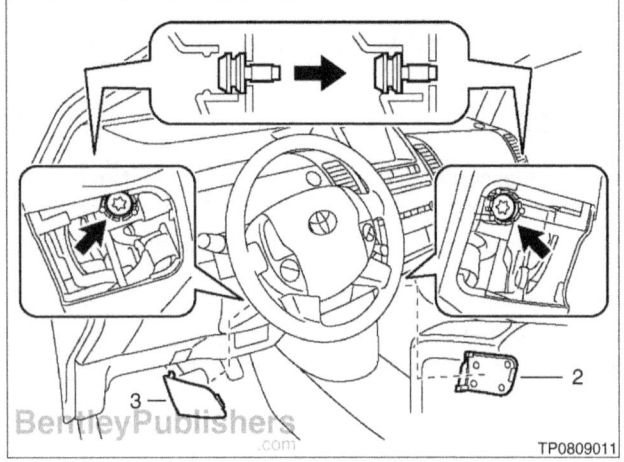

Courtesy Toyota Motor Sales (TMS) USA, Inc.

◄ Carefully release airbag / horn assembly from steering wheel and hold in one hand. Do not strain or damage wiring harness.

– Release electrical connectors and remove airbag / horn assembly (**arrows**).

> **WARNING —**
> • *Store the removed airbag unit with the horn pad facing up. If stored facing down, accidental deployment could propel airbag violently into the air, causing injury.*
> • *Once an airbag is removed, do not drive the car.*
> • *Do not reconnect the 12-volt auxiliary battery with the airbag disconnected. A fault code will be stored and the airbag warning light will illuminate*

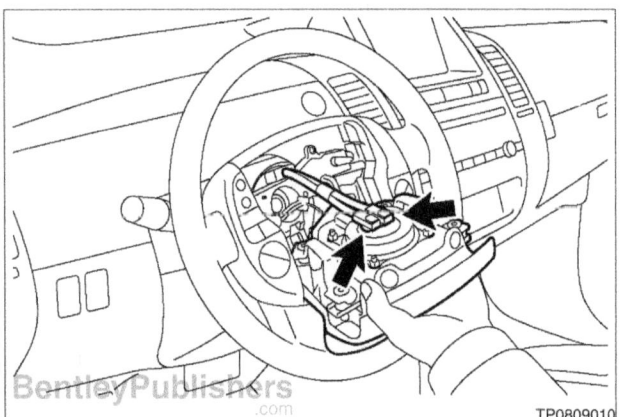

Courtesy Toyota Motor Sales (TMS) USA, Inc.

‒ Installation is reverse of removal. Remember to:

• Inspect wiring harness for damage and reconnect electrical connectors.

• Check that Torx screws remain in place and tighten to specification.

Tightening torque	
Airbag / horn assembly to steering wheel	8.8 Nm (78 in-lb)

‒ Connect 12-volt auxiliary battery. See **3 Safety**.

‒ Reinitialize power windows. See **10 Electrical System, Lights**.

> **WARNING—**
> • *Once the airbag unit is installed and all other service procedures are completed, start the engine and check that the airbag warning light goes out. If the warning light stays on, the airbag system will not function as designed. Have the system diagnosed and repaired by an authorized Toyota dealer.*

Steering wheel, removing and installing

‒ Switch hybrid system OFF (READY indicator not illuminated). See **3 Safety**.

> **WARNING—**
> • *Make sure hybrid system is OFF when servicing vehicle (READY indicator not illuminated). Failure to switch the hybrid system OFF could result in engine start at any time.*

‒ Disconnect 12-volt auxiliary battery negative (-) terminal. See **3 Safety**.

> **WARNING—**
> • *After disconnecting 12 volt auxiliary battery, wait 90 seconds before beginning work on airbag components.*

‒ Center steering wheel in straight ahead position.

‒ Remove driver airbag / horn assembly. See **Driver airbag / horn assembly, removing and installing** in this chapter.

‒ Remove steering wheel center nut.

◀ Place match marks on steering wheel and steering shaft (**inset**).

‒ Using Toyota special service tool or equivalent puller, remove steering wheel.

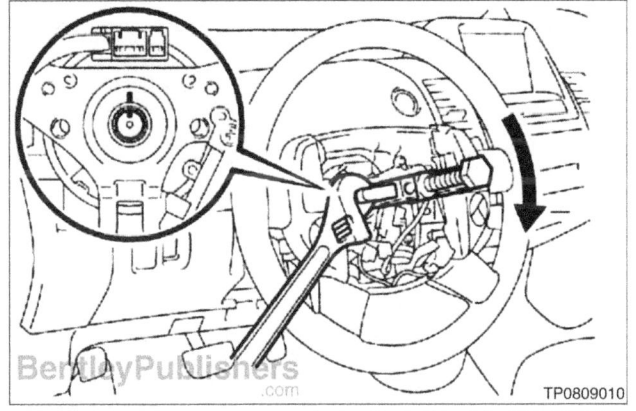

TP0809010

Courtesy Toyota Motor Sales (TMS) USA, Inc.

— Installation is reverse of removal. Remember to:

  • Align match marks on steering wheel and steering shaft

  • Tighten steering wheel center nut to specification.

Tightening torque	
Steering wheel to steering shaft	50 Nm (37 ft-lb)

— Replace airbag / horn assembly.

— Connect 12-volt auxiliary battery. See **3 Safety**.

— Initialize power windows. See **10 Electrical System, Lights**.

> **WARNING—**
> • *Once the airbag unit is installed and all other service procedures are completed, start the engine and check that the airbag warning light goes out. If the warning light stays on, the airgbag system will not function as designed. Have the system diagnosed and repaired by an authorized Toyota dealer.*

Torque sensor, setting zero point

This procedure can only be performed using the Toyota scan tool or equivalent.

Perform steering torque sensor zero point setting after any of the following occur:

- Replacement of steering column assembly (including torque sensor)
- Replacement of power steering ECU
- Replacement of steering wheel
- Whenever steering pulls to one side, or there is a difference in steering effort between left and right
- Whenever front suspension components are replaced and vehicle wheel alignment is adjusted

— Park vehicle on level surface.

— Turn steering wheel to straight-ahead position. Do not turn steering from straight-ahead position.

— Switch hybrid system OFF (READY indicator not illuminated). See **3 Safety**.

> **WARNING—**
> • *Make sure hybrid system is OFF when servicing vehicle (READY indicator not illuminated). Failure to switch the hybrid system OFF could result in engine start at any time.*

◄ Connect Toyota scan tool or equivalent to OBD II connector and switch tester ON.

> **NOTE—**
> • *Be sure to use a scan tool with CAN interface.*
> • *While performing torque sensor zero point setting, keep the vehicle stationary and on a level surface.*

— Switch hybrid system ON (IG-ON, READY indicator not illuminated).

— Operate tester to perform torque sensor zero point setting procedure. Refer to tester on-screen instructions.

— Erase any DTCs present.

— Switch hybrid system OFF (READY indicator not illuminated).

— Switch OFF hand-held tester and disconnect from the OBD II connector.

— Test drive vehicle and check for normal steering.

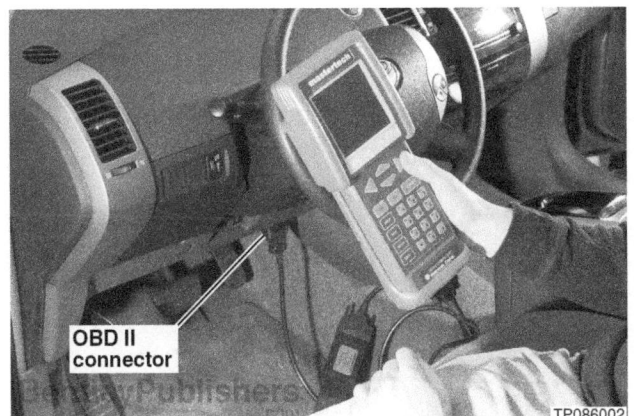

OBD II connector

TP086002

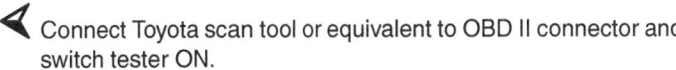

WHEEL AND TIRES

Toyota recommends that tires be replaced preferably in sets of four, and at least in pairs for each axle. Spare tires are space-saver wheels and tires and are for temporary use only.

Snow tires are permitted and if used, a full set of four are recommended. Select snow tires with size, construction, and load rating similar to the original tires.

Wheel and tire specifications

Table c. Wheel and tire specifications			
Type	Wheel size	Tire size	Inflation pressure (cold)
Standard road wheel	15 x 6 JJ	P185 / 65R15 86S	Front: 240 kPa (35 psi) Rear: 230 kPa (33 psi)
Optional road wheel	16 x 6 JJ	P195 / 55R16 86V	Front: 240 kPa (35 psi) Rear: 230 kPa (33 psi)
Temporary space-saver spare	16 x 4T	T125 / 70D16 96M	420 kPa (60 psi)

◄ Tire size, capacity, and inflation information are listed in the owner's manual, and on a label (**arrow**) on the driver's door B-pillar.

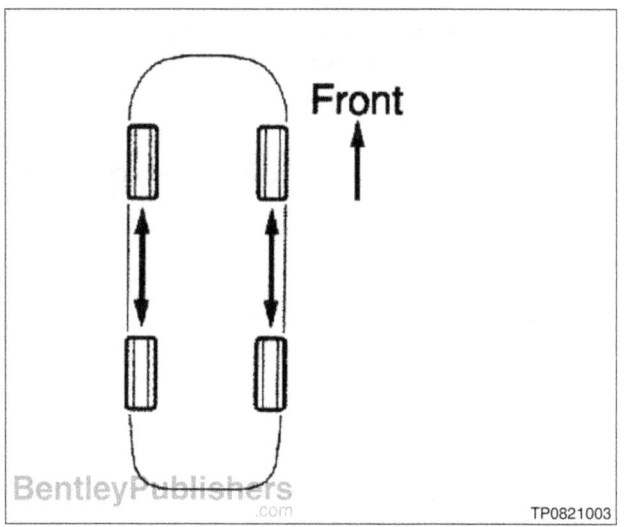

Front

◄ Rotate tires as shown. See **4 Service and Repair Fundamentals**, for recommended tire rotation intervals.

– Recheck wheel lug nut torque on alloy wheels after vehicle has been driven 1600 km (1000 miles).

Tightening torque	
Wheel to wheel hub	103 Nm (76 ft-lb)

Courtesy Toyota Motor Sales (TMS) USA, Inc.

Tire pressure warning system (TPWS)

Beginning with the 2006 model year, Prius vehicles for sale in the US are equipped with a tire pressure warning system (TPWS). The system is a direct-sensing type, with built-in wheel sensors to directly measure tire inflation pressure, and a wireless transmitter to send pressure data and sensor identification data (ID code). Each tire pressure sensor / transmitter on the car has a unique ID code that is recognized by the tire pressure warning ECU.

Each of the four road wheels, but not the temporary spare wheel, has a tire pressure sensor / transmitter.

◀ The tire pressure sensor / transmitter is integral with the tire inflation air valve (**arrow**). The tire pressure sensor/transmitter attaches to the alloy wheel through the conventional air valve mounting hole, and is sealed and retained by a rubber grommet and threaded nut.

TPWS service tips

The TPWS includes sensitive components that can be easily damaged. Here are a few suggested cautions and tips:

When dismounting and mounting a tire, position the wheel so that the tire pressure sensor/transmitter is not damaged by the tire bead, tire machine, or tools. See **Dismounting and mounting tires with TPWS** in this chapter.

Check condition of tire pressure sensor/transmitter air valve rubber grommet, washer, and mounting nut. If leaking air, replace rubber grommet, washer and nut. Tighten mounting nut to specification.

Be sure that tire pressure sensor/transmitter, rubber grommet, washer, mounting nut, and wheel are clean when installing parts.

Use the manufacturer-supplied air valve cap.

After completing tire mounting and re-installing tire and wheel on vehicle, release air from tire rapidly to reduce tire pressure by at least 6 psi within 30 seconds. Check that the instrument panel tire pressure warning light illuminates. Reinflate tire to correct pressure.

Tire pressure sensor / transmitter is powered by a non-replaceable lithium battery with an expected life of approx. 10 years. When battery voltage begins to drop, the tire pressure warning ECU stores a diagnostic trouble code (DTC) in memory. When battery voltage drops further, the transmitter stops working, a DTC is stored in memory and the instrument panel tire pressure warning lamp illuminates to alert the driver.

When replacing a tire pressure sensor / transmitter, be sure that the new unit has an ID code that is different from the others on the vehicle. The ID code for the new tire pressure sensor / transmitter must be registered in the tire pressure warning ECU. See **Registering TPWS sensor / transmitters** in this chapter.

To prolong shelf life, a newly purchased tire pressure sensor / transmitter is in sleep mode. Sleep mode is canceled when the tire is inflated to the specified pressure.

Dismounting and mounting tires with TPWS

When dismounting and mounting a tire with TPWS, the tire pressure sensor/transmitter can be easily damaged by the tire bead, tire machine, or tools. Follow these procedures to minimize possible damage.

Dismounting tire

— Switch hybrid system OFF (READY indicator not illuminated). See **3 Safety**.

> **WARNING —**
> • *Make sure hybrid system is OFF when servicing vehicle (READY indicator not illuminated). Failure to switch the hybrid system OFF could result in engine start at any time.*

— Raise vehicle and support safely. See **4 Service and Repair Fundamentals**.

> **WARNING —**
> • *Make sure the vehicle is stable and well supported at all times. Use a professional automotive lift or jack stands designed for the purpose. A floor jack is not adequate support.*

— Remove air valve cap and valve core to release air from tire.

— When air is released from tire, loosen and remove nut and washer from air valve. Push on air valve to drop tire pressure sensor/transmitter inside tire.

— Using tire machine, disengage upper tire bead from wheel. Do not pinch tire pressure sensor / transmitter between tire beads.

— Using tire machine, remove upper tire bead from wheel.

— Remove tire pressure sensor / transmitter from tire.

— Using tire machine, remove lower tire bead from wheel.

— Check condition of tire pressure sensor / transmitter air valve, rubber grommet, washer, and mounting nut. If damaged, replace components.

Mounting tire

− Check to be sure that the sensor, wheel rim surface and mounting hole are clean with no damage.

− Check to be sure that no oil, water, or other lubricant is present on wheel, mounting hole, or tire pressure sensor/transmitter components.

◄ When installing a new tire pressure sensor/ transmitter, record 7-digit ID code that is printed on new unit. ID code number must be registered (recorded) in tire pressure warning ECU. See **Registering TPWS sensor / transmitters** in this chapter.

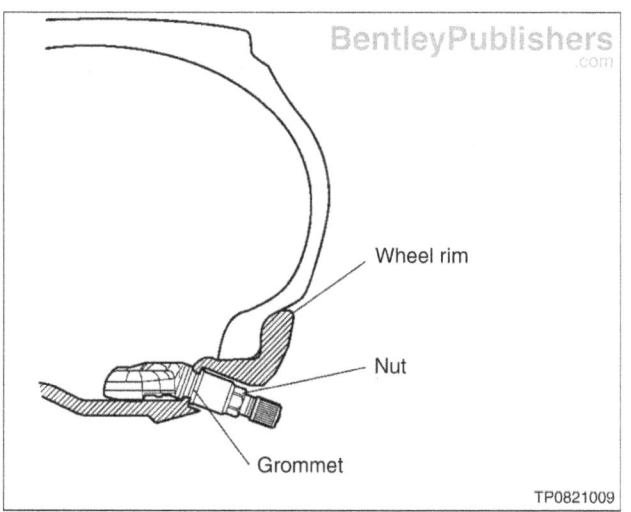

ID code

05413111161
1234567
torque 4±0.6Nm

TP0821008

◄ Insert tire pressure sensor / transmitter into mounting hole on wheel. Check to be sure that rubber grommet is in place on air valve.

− Insert sensor/transmitter so that printing on sensor is away from wheel and can be seen.

− Install washer and mounting nut. Tighten mounting nut to specification.

Tightening torque	
Tire pressure sensor mounting nut to rim	4.0 Nm (35 in-lb)

Wheel rim

Nut

Grommet

TP0821009

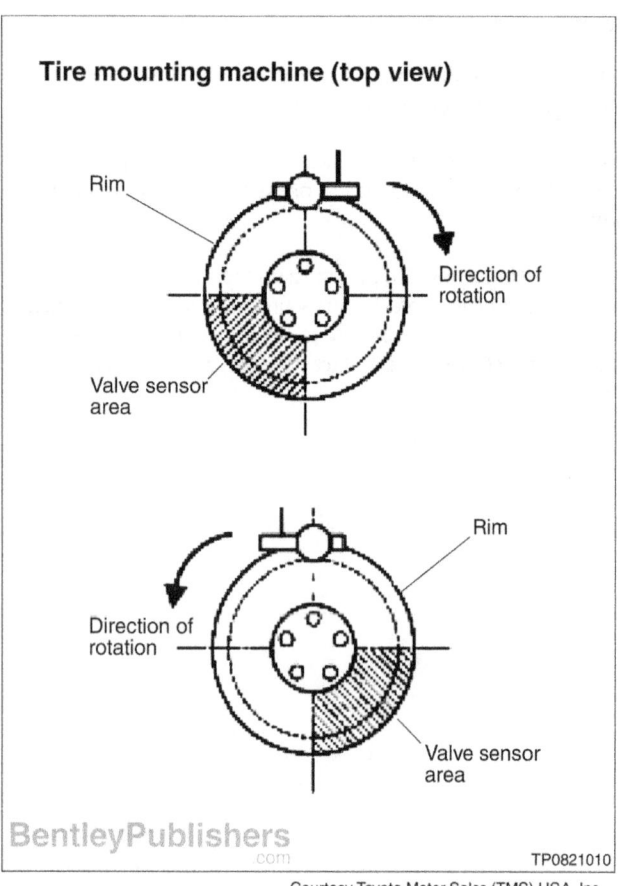

Tire mounting machine (top view)

Rim

Direction of rotation

Valve sensor area

Rim

Direction of rotation

Valve sensor area

TP0821010

Courtesy Toyota Motor Sales (TMS) USA, Inc.

◄ Using tire machine, mount tire. Locate sensor as shown in the illustration to minimize possibility of damage to sensor / transmitter.

— Inflate tire to correct pressure.

Tire inflation pressure	
Tire pressure (cold): • Front • Rear	 240 kPa (35 psi) 230 kPa (33 psi)

— Mounting nut may loosen when the tire is inflated. Retorque mounting nut, then check for leaks with soapy water.

— Install wheels on vehicle and tighten wheel lug nuts to specification.

Tightening torque	
Wheel to wheel hub	103 Nm (76 ft-lb)

— Lower vehicle.

— When a new tire pressure sensor/transmitter is installed, register sensor ID code. See **Registering TPWS sensor / transmitters** in this chapter.

TPWS initialization

Initializing the TPWS system records the current tire inflation pressures from each wheel sensor/transmitter as the standard pressure value into the tire pressure warning ECU. The ECU compares these stored standard pressure values with actual tire pressures. The ECU then illuminates the TPWS warning light when pressure in a tire decreases by a predetermined amount.

Initializing the TPWS system ensures that the tire pressure warning ECU is comparing actual tire pressures with stored standard values that are correct for the size and type of tire fitted to the vehicle.

Initialize TPWS system whenever any of the following conditions occur:

• Tires rotated front-to-back

• Tire pressure changed

• Tire size changed

• Tires replaced

• TPWS sensor / transmitter replaced

◄ Use tire pressure warning system (TPWS) reset switch (**arrow**) under steering column to initialize system:

- Check and adjust pressures in all tires to correct pressure. Use an accurate tire pressure gauge.

- Adjust tire pressures when tires are cold and have not run for more than a few miles.

- With brake pedal *not* depressed, press POWER button twice to switch hybrid system to IG-ON. (READY indicator not illuminated, the engine will not start).

- Depress and hold TPWS reset switch for at least 3 seconds, then release and wait. During initialization, tire pressure warning ECU records pressure signal from each wheel sensor / transmitter at rate of approx. one per minute. Initialization is complete when signals from all 4 wheels is recorded. This can take approx. 4 minutes.

- Make sure vehicle is not moving when TPWS reset switch is depressed.

- When the system is initialized, TPWS warning light blinks 3 times at ½ second intervals.

- If warning light does not blink 3 times as described, repeat initialization procedure.

Registering TPWS sensor / transmitters

Each tire pressure sensor / transmitter on the car has a unique ID code that is registered (recorded) in the tire pressure warning ECU. The unique ID codes permit the tire pressure warning ECU to know that the pressure data received is in fact from sensor / transmitters mounted on this vehicle, and not from another nearby sensor/transmitter on another car.

◄ 7-digit ID code is printed on the sensor / transmitter. Be sure to record this number before installing a new sensor / transmitter.

NOTE—

- *You must record all 4 sensor / transmitter ID code numbers before beginning the registration process. During registration, all previously registered ID codes are deleted. Even when replacing only 1 sensor / transmitter, be sure to write down all 4 ID code numbers.*

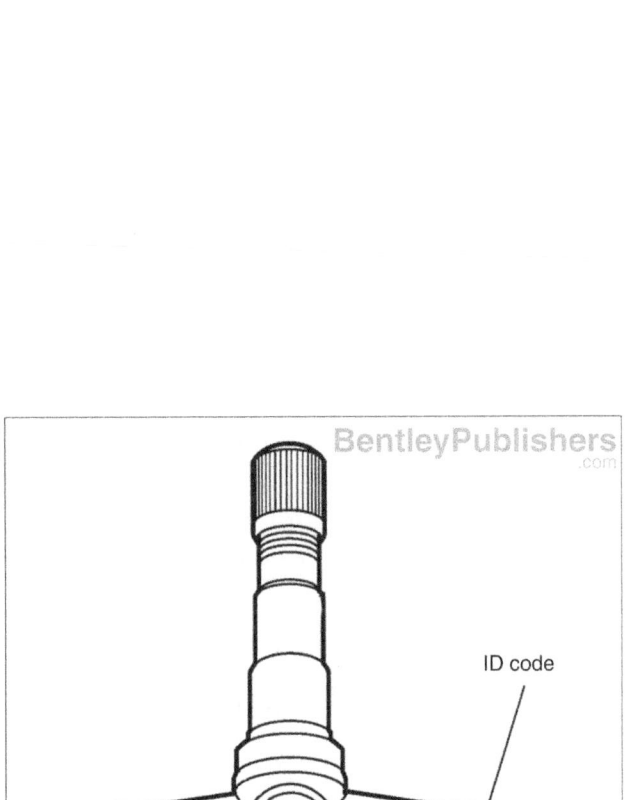

ID code

torque 4±0.6Nm

Courtesy Toyota Motor Sales (TMS) USA, Inc.

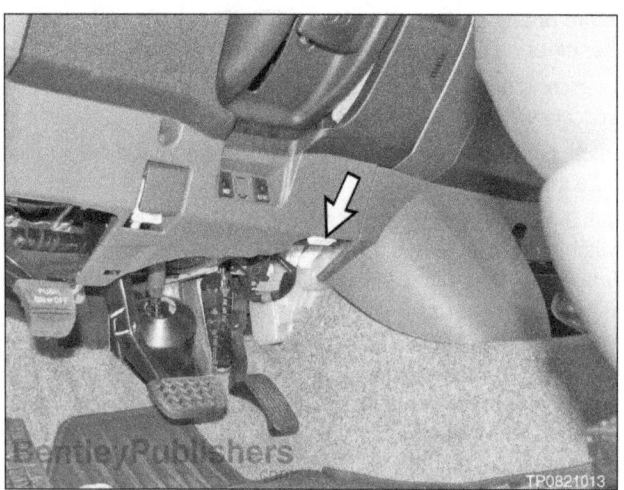

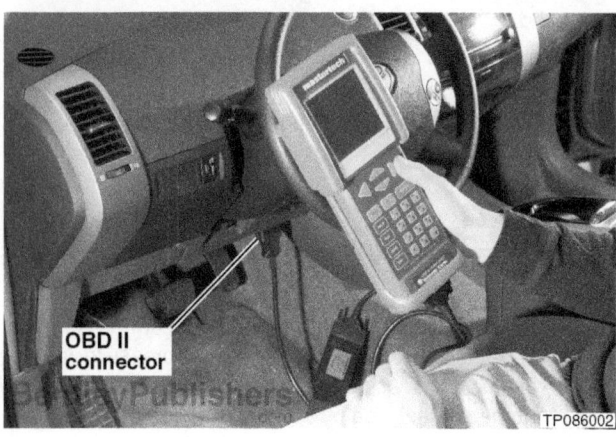

◀ Locate OBDII (DLC3) connector (**arrow**) under dash on driver's side.

◀ Connect Toyota scan tool or equivalent to OBD II connector (DLC3) and switch tester ON.

NOTE—
- *Use a scan tool with CAN interface.*

− With brake pedal *not* depressed, press POWER button twice to switch hybrid system to IG-ON. (READY indicator not illuminated, the engine will not start).

− Read DATA LIST and record ID code numbers (ID1 through ID4) than are currently in ECU memory.

NOTE—
- *You must record all 4 sensor / transmitter ID code numbers before beginning the registration process. During registration, all previously registered ID codes are deleted.*

− Follow on-screen instructions and input 4 TPWS ID codes.

− Complete registration process within 5 minutes.

− Check to be sure that successful registration is acknowledged by scan tool.

− Check to be sure that TPWS warning light is OFF.

− To complete procedure, perform TPWS initialization. See **TPWS initialization** in this chapter.

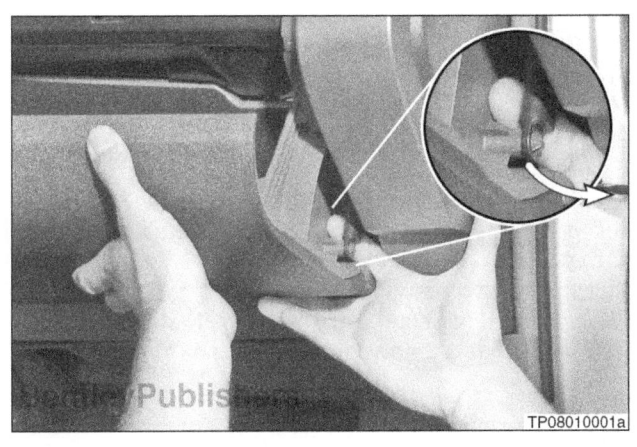

TP08010001a

9

Body

Interior and exterior repairs

GENERAL

This chapter covers repairs to exterior and interior body components.

See also **5 Engine** for engine covers removal.

Hybrid safety

In addition to the safety warnings given here, always read and observe the **Warnings**, **Cautions** and safety procedures in **3 Safety** before working on vehicle. Orange-colored cables carry lethal high voltage. Use extreme care when working near high voltage cables and components.

WARNING—

- *Risk of electrocution! Avoid touching orange-colored high voltage wiring and high voltage components unless you are certain that high voltage is not present.*
- *The Prius hybrid system has voltages as high as 500 volts. Voltages over 60 volts DC and 25 volts AC are a shock hazard.*

The Prius engine may start at any time if the hybrid system is in **READY** mode. See **3 Safety** for instructions on turning OFF the hybrid system.

WARNING—

- *Be sure hybrid system is OFF when servicing vehicle (READY indicator not illuminated). Failure to switch the hybrid system OFF could result in engine start at any time.*

Table a is a listing of repair procedures in this chapter and the hybrid safety requirements for each.

Table a. Hybrid safety requirements for repair procedures

Procedure	Disconnect 12-volt battery	Switch hybrid system OFF	Remove service plug
Front bumper removal		✓	
Cabin air filter replacement		✓	
Windshield cowl cover removal		✓	
Engine compartment upper bulkhead removal		✓	
Door panel removal		✓	
Window glass removal		✓	
Window regulator removal		✓	
Outside mirror removal		✓	
Front seat removal	✓	✓	

Warnings and Cautions

> **WARNING—**
>
> - *The airbag is a vehicle safety system. Serious injury may result if system service is attempted by persons unfamiliar with approved Toyota airbag system service procedures.*
> - *Prior to working on airbag system components, disconnect the 12-volt auxiliary battery and wait 90 seconds before beginning work. The airbag system is equipped with a backup power source. If work is started within 90 seconds after disconnecting the battery, the airbag may deploy.*

> **CAUTION—**
>
> - *Some procedures require that you disconnect the 12-volt auxiliary battery. This causes loss of radio and navigation system presets and power window initialization. Record radio and navigation system presets before disconnecting battery. Reinitialize windows after reconnecting battery. See* **10 Electrical System, Lights**.
> - *To avoid damaging vehicle trim, use a plastic prying tool or a screwdriver with the tip wrapped with masking tape.*
> - *Interior trim fasteners are easily damaged. Have spare fasteners on hand before beginning job.*

9

BUMPERS

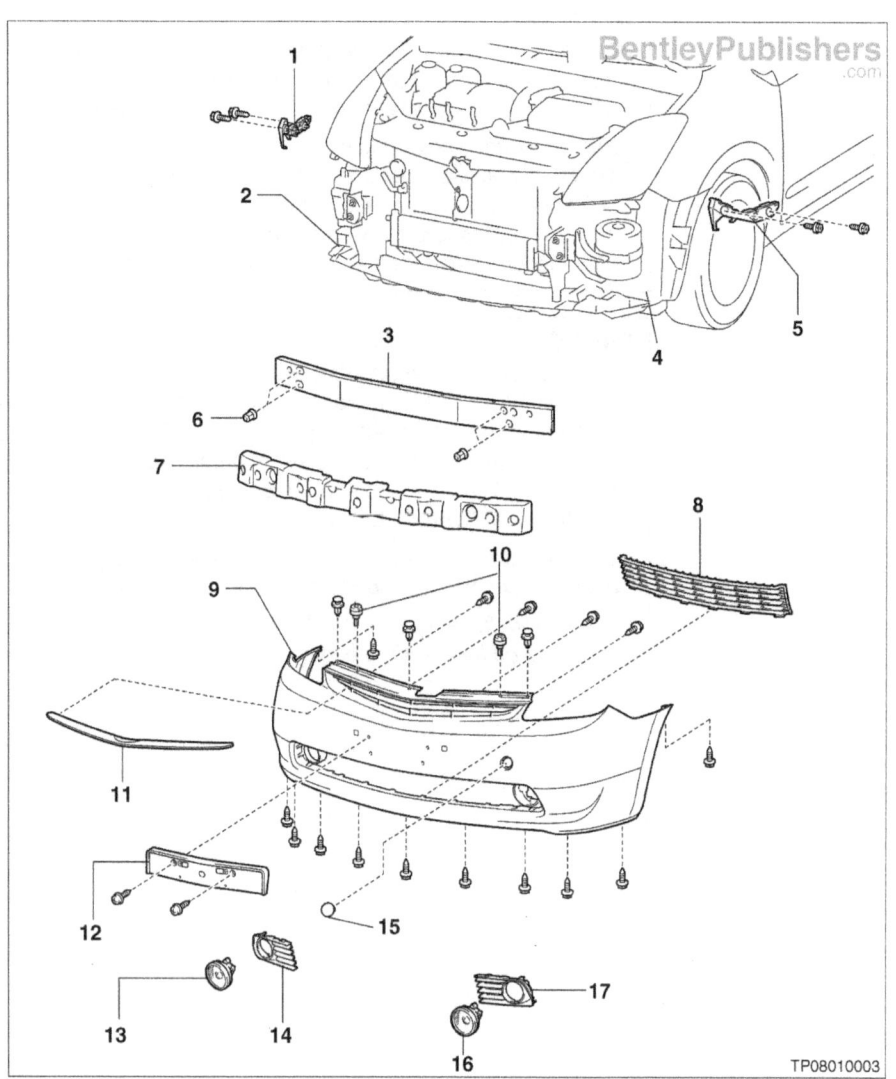

TP08010003
Courtesy Toyota Motor Sales (TMS) USA, Inc.

Front bumper assembly

1. **Bumper right side support**
2. **Right front fender liner**
3. **Bumper reinforcement**
4. **Left front fender liner**
5. **Bumper left side support**
6. **Bolt**
   - Tighten to 13 Nm (10 ft-lb)
7. **Bumper energy absorber**
8. **Radiator grille**
9. **Bumper cover**
10. **Radiator grille protector**
    - Tighten to 5 Nm (44 in-lb)
11. **Molding**
12. **Bumper extension mounting bracket**
13. **Right front foglight**
14. **Right lower grille**
15. **Tow hook opening cover**
16. **Left front foglight**
17. **Left lower grille**

Front bumper, removing and installing

– Switch hybrid system OFF (READY indicator not illuminated). See **3 Safety**.

> **WARNING—**
> • *Make sure hybrid system is OFF when servicing vehicle (READY indicator not illuminated). Failure to switch the hybrid system OFF could result in engine start at any time.*

– Raise front of vehicle and support safely. See **4 Service and Repair Fundamentals**.

> **WARNING—**
> • *Make sure the vehicle is stable and well supported at all times. Use a professional automotive lift or jack stands designed for the purpose. A floor jack is not adequate support.*

– Remove left and right engine splash shields. See **5 Engine**.

◄ Remove screws (**arrows**) and detach front of left front fender liner. It is not necessary to remove entire front fender liner.

– Similarly, detach front of right front fender liner.

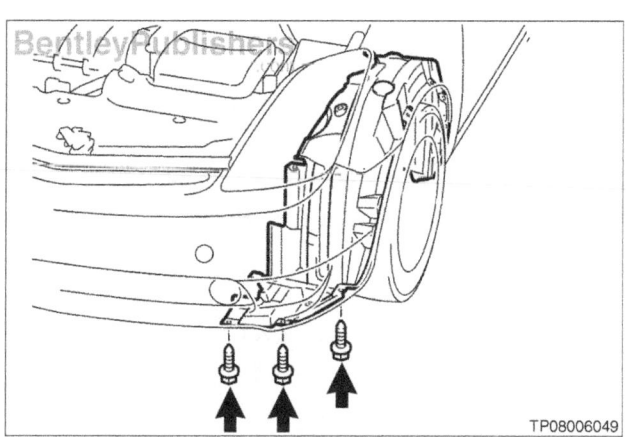

TP08006049

Courtesy Toyota Motor Sales (TMS) USA, Inc.

◄ Working at front bumper:

- • Place protective tape under front fender. Use clip remover to remove 3 plastic rivets.
- • Remove 2 radiator grille protectors and 5 screws.
- • Flex fender liner to access upper fastener.
- • Use screwdriver to disengage 8 claws (4 on either side) at sides of bumper. To protect vehicle finish, tape screwdriver tip before use.
- • Vehicle with foglights: Disconnect 2 foglight connectors.

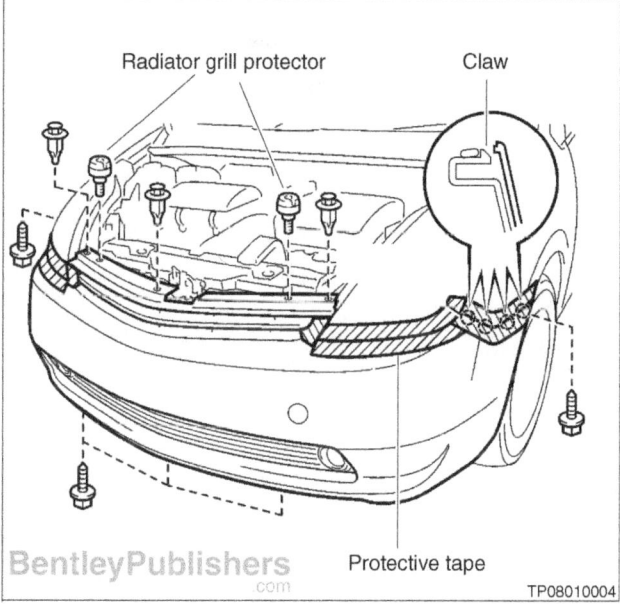

Radiator grill protector   Claw

BentleyPublishers
.com   Protective tape

TP08010004

Courtesy Toyota Motor Sales (TMS) USA, Inc.

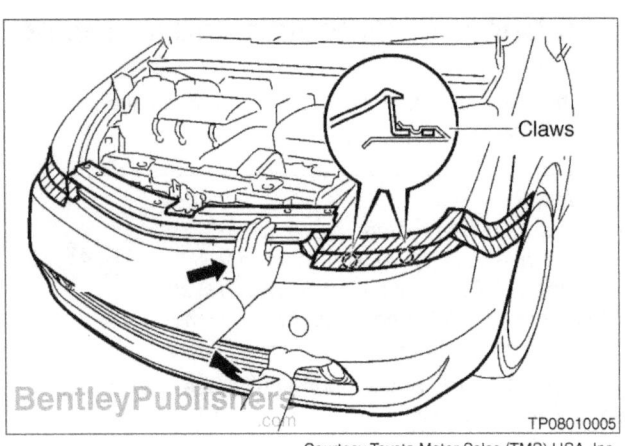

— Claws

TP08010005

Courtesy Toyota Motor Sales (TMS) USA, Inc.

◄ To remove bumper cover, tilt cover up by grasping lower edge and pulling up while securely holding upper edge in place.

> **CAUTION—**
> • *Do not forcibly pull bumper straight off. Bumper disengages from 4 front claws when it is tilted as described. Otherwise, claws may deform or break.*

— Remove bumper energy absorber and reinforcement.

— Use plastic prying tool or taped screwdriver to pry off grille and foglight assemblies.

— Installation is reverse of removal. Use new plastic clips for assembly, as necessary.

Tightening torques	
Bumper reinforcement to body	13 Nm (10 ft-lb)
Radiator grille protectors to bumper	5 Nm (44 in-lb)

Rear bumper assembly

1. **Bumper reinforcement**
2. **Bumper reinforcement right side mount**
3. **Bumper right side support**
4. **Bumper reinforcement left side mount**
5. **Bumper left side support**
6. **Bumper cover**
7. **Bumper center support**
8. **Spacer**
9. **Bumper energy absorber**
10. **Left spoiler**
11. **Center spoiler**
12. **Right spoiler**

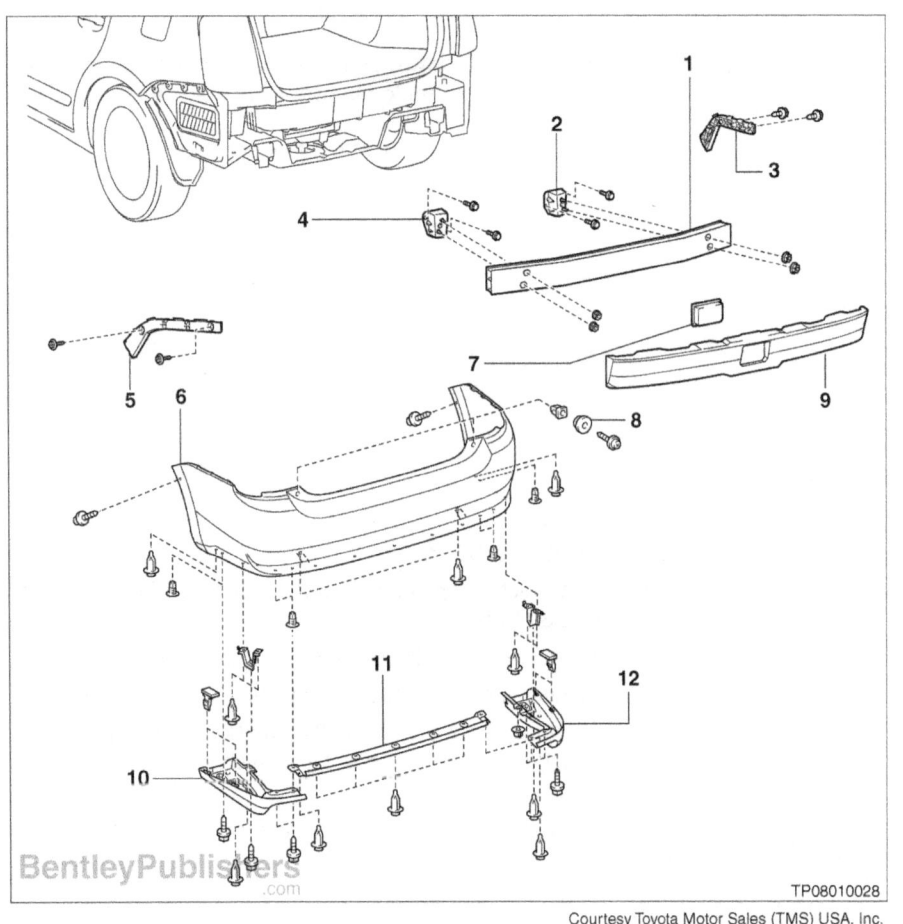

TP08010028

Courtesy Toyota Motor Sales (TMS) USA, Inc.

CABIN AIR FILTER

Cabin air filter, removing and installing

To remove dust and dirt from outside air before it enters the passenger compartment, the Prius is equipped with a cabin air filter built into the air-conditioning system. The filter may clog over time. Inspect and replace periodically to maintain proper air flow and performance.

The cabin air filter is located behind the glove compartment.

− Switch hybrid system OFF (READY indicator not illuminated). See **3 Safety**.

> **WARNING**—
> • *Make sure hybrid system is OFF when servicing vehicle (READY indicator not illuminated). Failure to switch the hybrid system OFF could result in engine start at any time.*

◄ Open glove compartment and slide off damper linkage (**curved arrow**).

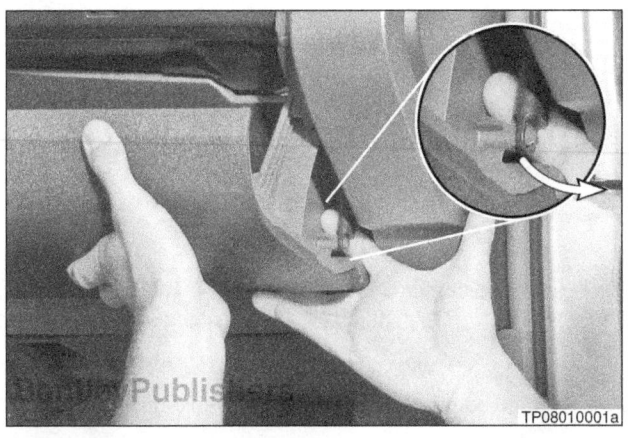

◄ Push in both sides of glove compartment (**arrows**) to disconnect latches. Allow glove compartment to rotate downward.

◄ Pull cabin air filter carrier rearward to remove from blower housing.

◄ Remove filter from filter carrier and discard. Clean filter carrier.

– When installing, be sure that flat side of filter is toward filter carrier and ribbed side of filter is up.

◄ Slide in filter and carrier under retention tabs in blower housing. Be sure filter carrier is installed with UP marking (**circle**) pointing upward.

– Reinstall glove compartment and damper linkage.

COWL COVERS

Remove plastic covers at the rear of the engine compartment to gain access to a number of components including wiper components, front strut tower fasteners and cylinder head cover.

Windshield cowl cover, removing

– Switch hybrid system OFF (READY indicator not illuminated). See **3 Safety**.

> **WARNING**—
> • *Make sure hybrid system is OFF when servicing vehicle (READY indicator not illuminated). Failure to switch the hybrid system OFF could result in engine start at any time.*

– With engine hood open, remove 3 wiper arm nuts and lift off wiper arms. See **10 Electrical System, Lights**.

◄ Disengage 8 clips and remove hood-to-cowl top seal.

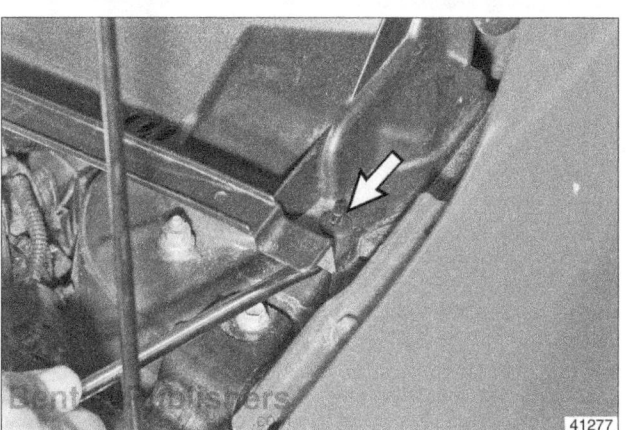

◄ Using flat screwdriver, push upward on plastic rivet pin on left cowl top ventilation louver.

– Remove plastic rivet.

◄ To remove left cowl top ventilation louver, lift front edge upward and gently pull forward.

◀ Remove plastic rivet pin on right cowl top ventilation louver. Lift front edge upward and gently pull forward to remove.

Engine compartment upper bulkhead, removing

– Switch hybrid system OFF (READY indicator not illuminated). See **3 Safety**.

> **WARNING—**
> • *Make sure hybrid system is OFF when servicing vehicle (READY indicator not illuminated). Failure to switch the hybrid system OFF could result in engine start at any time.*
>
>

– With engine hood open, remove 3 wiper arm nuts and lift off wiper arms. See **10 Electrical System, Lights**.

– Remove cowl covers. See **Windshield cowl cover, removing** in this chapter.

◀ Remove wiper assembly mounting bolts (**arrows**) and lift out complete wiper assembly. Detach wiper motor electrical connector.

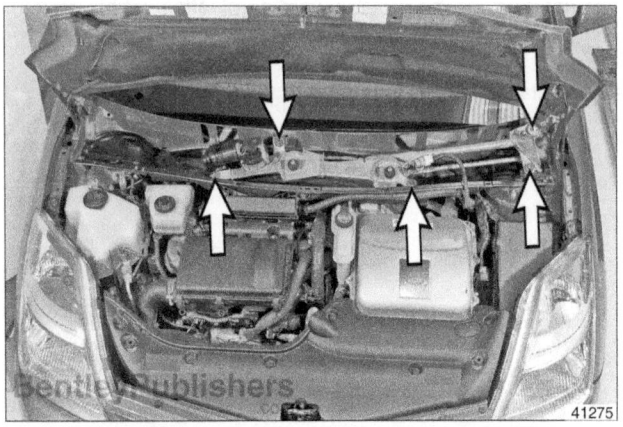

◀ Remove engine compartment relay block mounting bolts (**arrows**). Move relay block to one side.

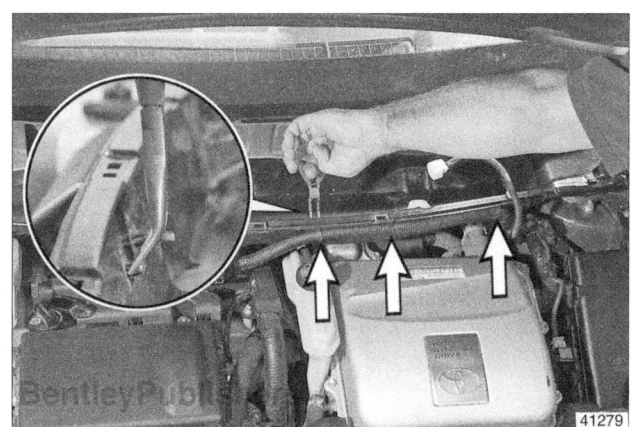

◀ Use pliers to remove 3 plastic clamps (**arrows**) from bulkhead to free wiring harness. See **inset**.

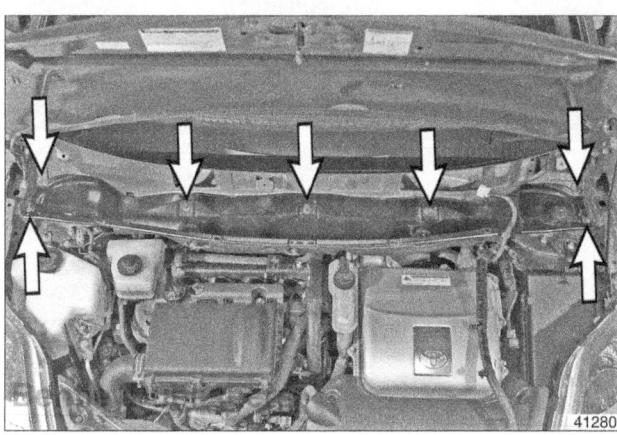

◀ Remove bulkhead mounting bolts (**arrows**) and remove bulkhead.

DOORS AND WINDOWS

The left front door is illustrated in this section. Other door assemblies are similar.

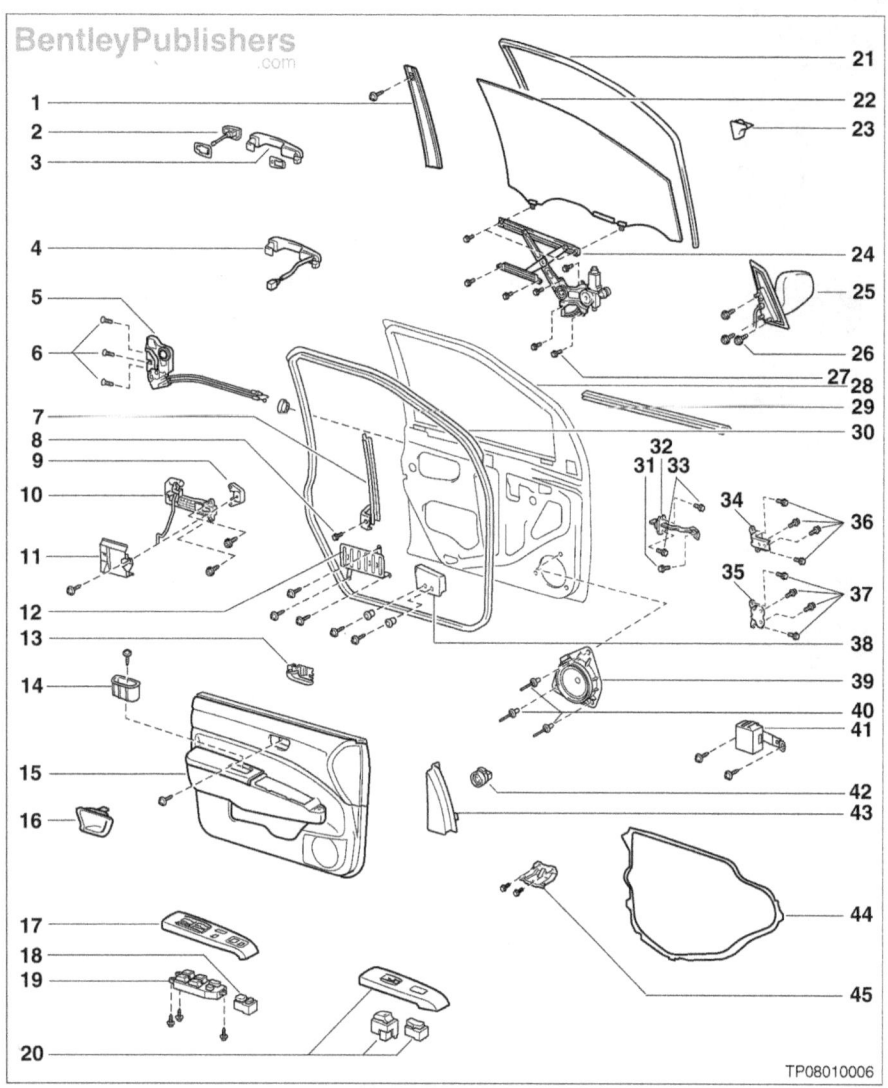

TP08010006

Courtesy Toyota Motor Sales (TMS) USA, Inc.

Front door assembly

1. **Window rear frame molding**

2. **Key cylinder**

3. **Outside door handle**

4. **Smart entry system outside handle**

5. **Lock assembly**

6. **Bolt**
   - Replace or use Locktite® when reassembling
   - Tighten to 5.5 Nm (49 in-lb)

7. **Window glass rear lower track**

8. **Bolt**
   - Tighten to 8 Nm (71 in-lb)

9. **Outside handle retainer**

10. **Outside handle inner assembly**

11. **Lock reinforcement**

12. **Service hole cover**

13. **Inside door opener handle**

14. **Door pull-handle**

15. **Door panel**

16. **Inside door opener handle bezel**

17. **Door switch assembly bezel**

18. **Outside mirror switch**

19. **Door switch assembly (left door)**

20. **Door switch assembly (right door)**

21. **Window glass upper track**

22. **Door glass**

23. **Door frame trim**

24. **Power window regulator and motor assembly**

25. **Outside rear view mirror**

26. **Mirror fasteners**
   - Bolts: tighten to 5.5 Nm (49 in-lb)
   - Nuts: tighten to 8 Nm (71 in-lb)

27. **Bolt**
   - Tighten to 8 Nm (71 in-lb)

28. **Door skin**

29. **Lower window frame molding**

30. **Weather-strip**

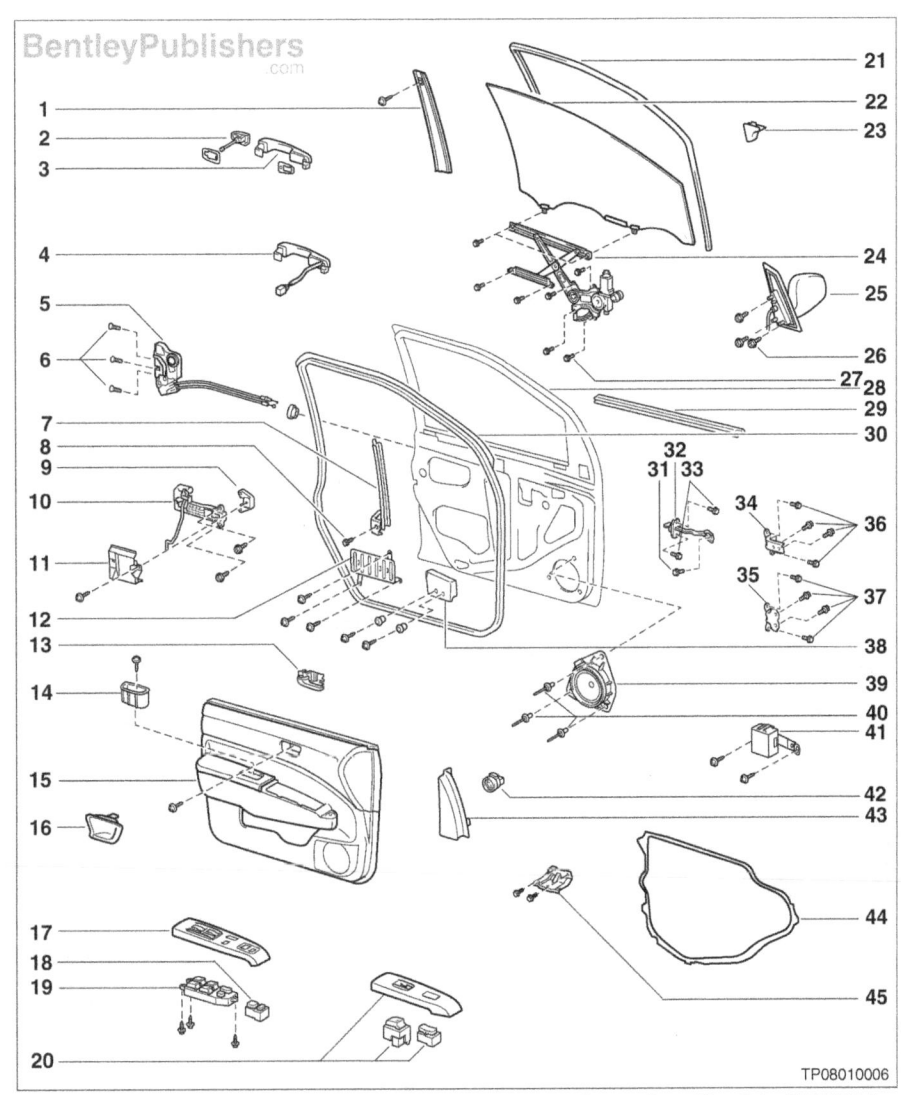

TP08010006

Courtesy Toyota Motor Sales (TMS) USA, Inc.

Front door assembly *(cont.)*

31. Bolts
  • Tighten to 26 Nm (19 ft-lb)

32. Door check

33. Screw
  • Tighten to 8.5 Nm (75 in-lb)

34. Upper door hinge

35. Lower door hinge

36. Bolts
  • Tighten to 26 Nm (19 ft-lb)

37. Bolts
  • Tighten to 26 Nm (19 ft-lb)

38. Door stiffener

39. Midrange speaker

40. Rivets

41. Door control module

42. Tweeter (high-range speaker)

43. Speaker trim

44. Service hole cover (vapor barrier)
  • Replace with new when reassembling

45. Trim bracket

Door panel, removing and installing

Left front door panel removal is described in this procedure. Other door assemblies are similar.

Use plastic prying tool or screwdriver tip wrapped with tape to pry off plastic parts.

— Switch hybrid system OFF (READY indicator not illuminated). See **3 Safety**.

> **WARNING —**
> • *Make sure hybrid system is OFF when servicing vehicle (READY indicator not illuminated). Failure to switch the hybrid system OFF could result in engine start at any time.*

◄ Working at front window corner speaker enclosure:

• Use plastic prying tool to pry top of enclosure.

• Once plastic clip at top is released, slide enclosure up to remove (**curved arrow**).

• Disconnect speaker wire harness connector.

◄ Remove inside door pull-handle mounting screw and lift off handle.

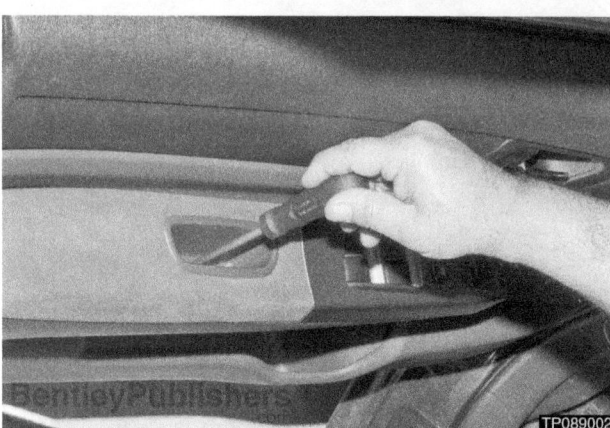

◄ Use plastic prying tool to pry off inside door release handle trim bezel.

— Remove door switch assembly. See **10 Electrical System, Lights**.

— Pry off courtesy light at bottom of door panel, if equipped, and detach electrical connector.

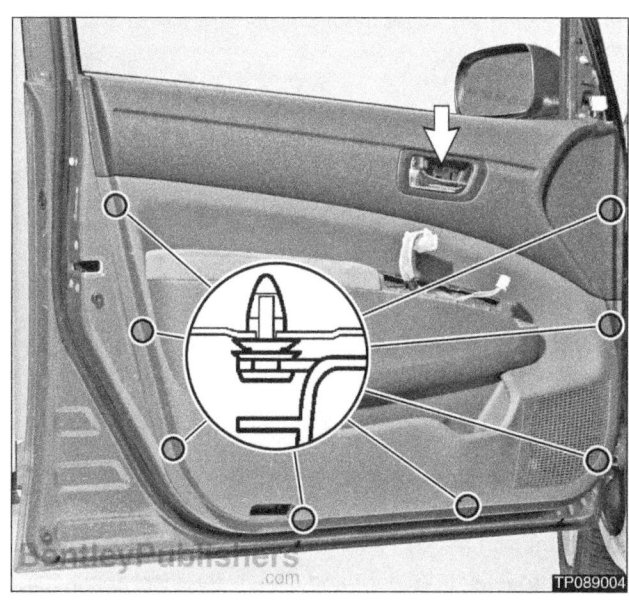

◀ Working at inside door panel:

- Remove panel mounting screw (**arrow**).
- Pry or pull on panel to disengage mounting clips (**inset**) from door.

– Installation is reverse of removal.

Door window glass, removing and installing

Left front door window removal is described in this procedure. Other door assemblies are similar.

– Switch hybrid system OFF (READY indicator not illuminated). See **3 Safety**.

> **WARNING—**
> • *Make sure hybrid system is OFF when servicing vehicle (READY indicator not illuminated). Failure to switch the hybrid system OFF could result in engine start at any time.*

– Remove door switch assembly. See **10 Electrical System, Lights**.

– Remove inner door panel. See **Door panel, removing and installing** in this chapter.

◀ Working at inside door release handle:

- Use plastic prying tool to pull off clip.
- Slide handle rearward and tilt out of door (**curved arrow**).
- Disengage door lock release cables from plastic clip on door (**arrow**).

– Remove outside rear view mirror. See **Outside rear-view mirror, removing and installing** in this chapter.

◀ To remove door vapor barrier:

- Unplug door lock electrical connector (**A**).
- Remove inside door pull-handle support bracket mounting bolts (**B**) and remove bracket.
- Peel off vapor barrier, threading electrical harnesses and door lock cables through openings as necessary.

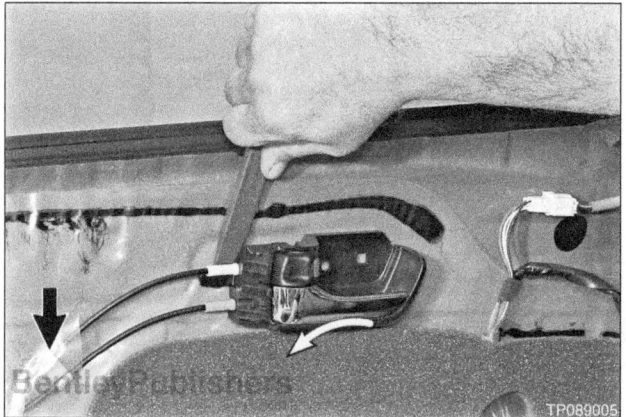

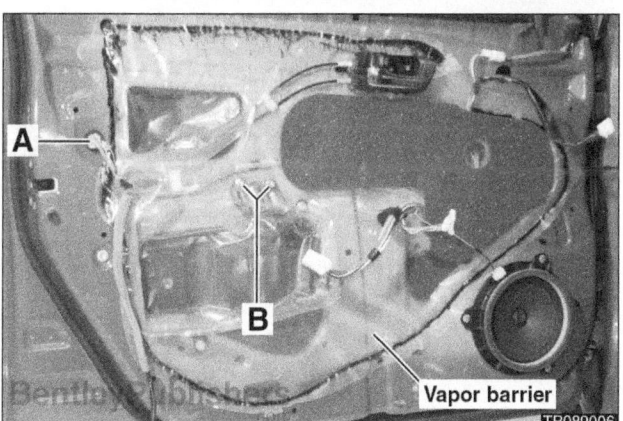

Vapor barrier

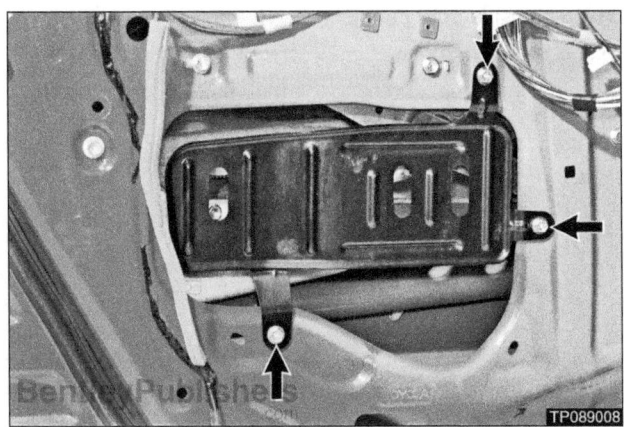

◄ Remove door cavity cover mounting bolts (**arrows**) and lift off cover.

◄ Use 4 mm ($\frac{5}{32}$ in) or smaller drill bit to drill out speaker mounting rivets (**arrows**).

- Make sure rivet remnants are completely drilled out of door.
- Remove speaker from door and detach electrical connector.
- Use vacuum cleaner to clean out rivet remnants from inside door cavity.

> **WARNING—**
> • *Freshly drilled out rivets are hot.*

> **CAUTION—**
> • *To avoid damaging speaker and door rivet holes, be sure to drill out rivets by holding drill perpendicular to door.*

◄ Remove lower window frame outside molding:

- Tape door under molding to prevent paint damage.
- Use molding remover tool to pry out molding. Tape tool tip to prevent paint damage.

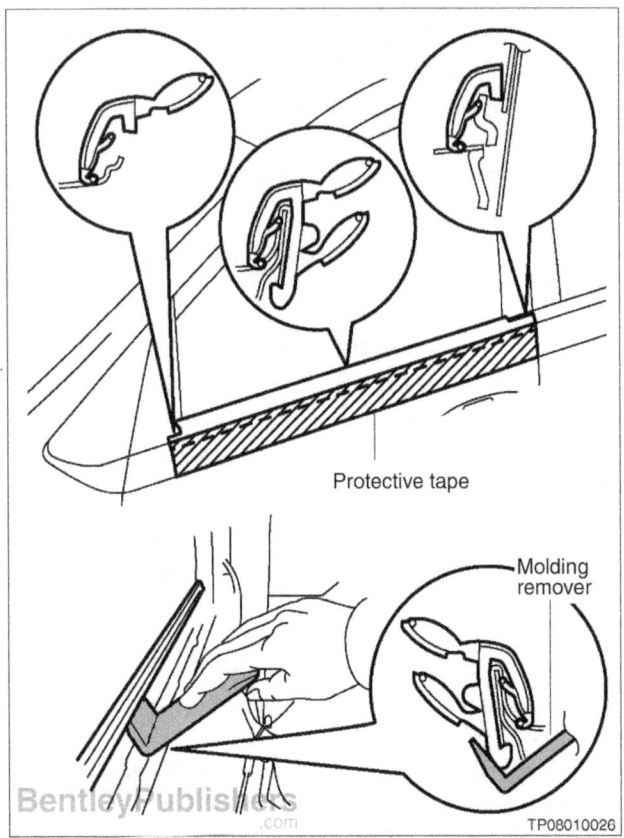

Protective tape

Molding remover

Courtesy Toyota Motor Sales (TMS) USA, Inc.

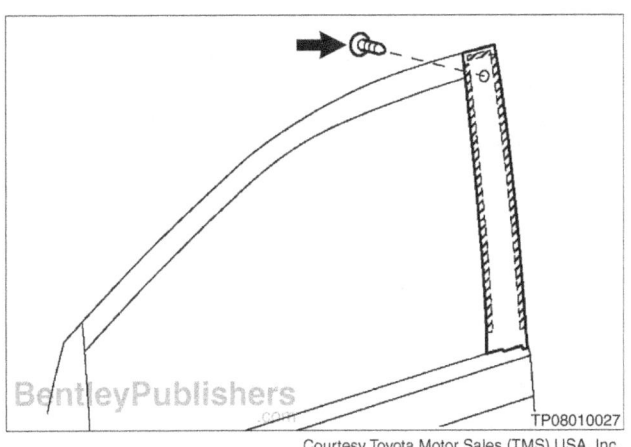

TP08010027
Courtesy Toyota Motor Sales (TMS) USA, Inc.

◀ Working at window rear frame molding:

- Remove mounting screw (**arrow**).
- Heat molding using heat gun to soften adhesive and remove molding from door.

> **CAUTION—**
> • *Make sure you do not exceed the following heat limits:*
>   *-Body: 40° - 60°C (104° - 140°F)*
>   *-Molding: 20° - 30°C (68° - 86°F)*

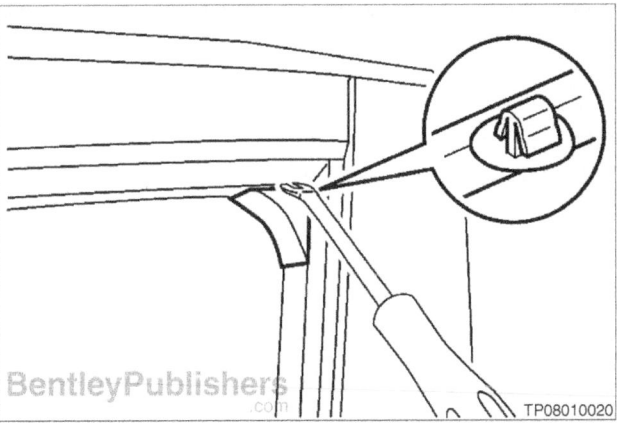

TP08010020
Courtesy Toyota Motor Sales (TMS) USA, Inc.

◀ Using forked clip remover, remove window frame corner reinforcement.

TP089009

◀ Working inside door cavity:

- Place cushioning material inside door to prevent door glass damage.
- Reconnect window switch assembly and raise or lower window until glass mounting bolt heads (**arrows**) become visible in service holes.
- Remove bolts.

> **CAUTION—**
> • *Support glass to prevent breakage.*

◀ Tilt glass (**arrow**) and lift out of door cavity.

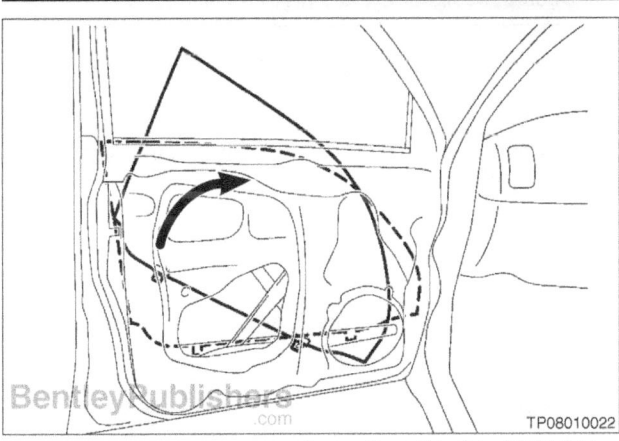

TP08010022
Courtesy Toyota Motor Sales (TMS) USA, Inc.

— When reinstalling glass:

• Make sure glass is fitted correctly to window tracks in door.

• If necessary, reattach window switch assembly and raise or lower glass support bracket until glass mounting bolt holes become visible in service holes.

• Make sure glass support bracket and window glass are parallel to each other.

Tightening torque	
Glass to glass support bracket	8 Nm (71 in-lb)

— Remainder of installation is reverse of removal. Keep in mind the following:

• Clean old sealing material from rear window molding. Apply double-sided tape to molding and adhere in place using heat gun.

• Rivet speaker firmly to door.

• Use butyl tape to attach new vapor barrier to door opening. Make sure wires, connectors and cables are routed correctly. Also make sure vapor barrier is smooth, without folds and wrinkles.

Tightening torques	
Outside mirror to door • Bolts • Nuts	 5.5 Nm (49 in-lb) 8 Nm (71 in-lb)

Window regulator, removing and installing

Left front window regulator removal is described in this procedure. Other door assemblies are similar.

— Switch hybrid system OFF (READY indicator not illuminated). See **3 Safety**.

> **WARNING—**
> • *Make sure hybrid system is OFF when servicing vehicle (READY indicator not illuminated). Failure to switch the hybrid system OFF could result in engine start at any time.*

— Remove door switch assembly. See **10 Electrical System, Lights**.

— Remove inner door panel. See **Door panel, removing and installing** in this chapter.

— Remove outside rear view mirror. See **Outside rear-view mirror, removing and installing** in this chapter.

— Remove window glass. See **Door window glass, removing and installing** in this chapter.

— After removing window glass, disconnect window switch again.

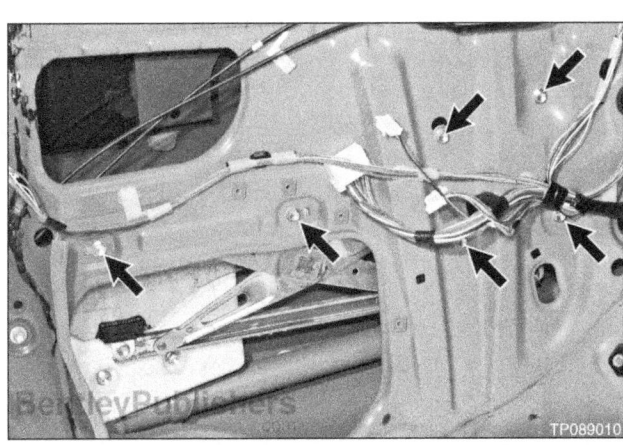

TP089010

◄ Working inside door cavity:

- Detach window regulator electrical connector.
- While supporting regulator, remove regulator mounting bolts (**arrows**) and slide regulator out of door cavity.

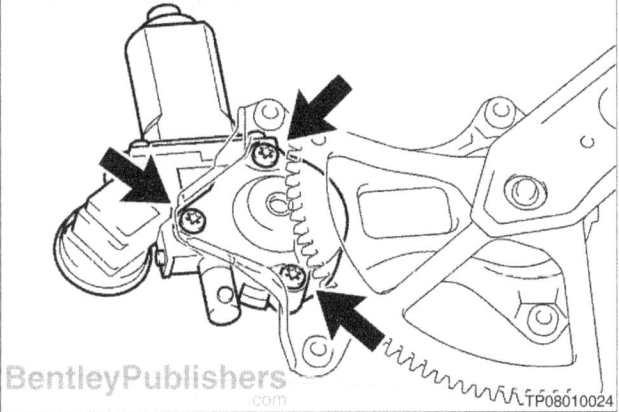

TP08010024

Courtesy Toyota Motor Sales (TMS) USA, Inc.

◄ If necessary, use T25 Torx driver to remove 3 screws (**arrows**) and detach electric motor from window regulator.

Tightening torque	
Motor to window regulator (T25 Torx)	5.4 Nm (48 in-lb)

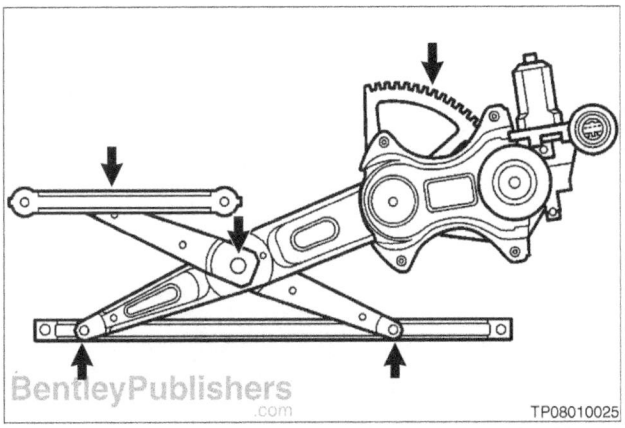

TP08010025

Courtesy Toyota Motor Sales (TMS) USA, Inc.

◄ Prior to reinstallation, lightly grease sliding and rotating window regulator joints (**arrows**).

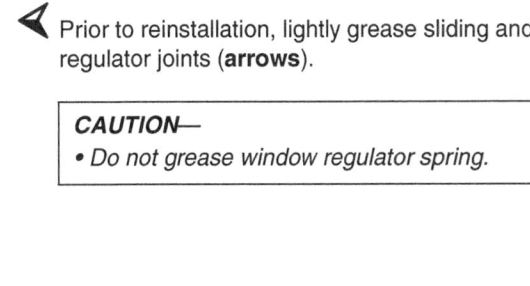

CAUTION—
• Do not grease window regulator spring.

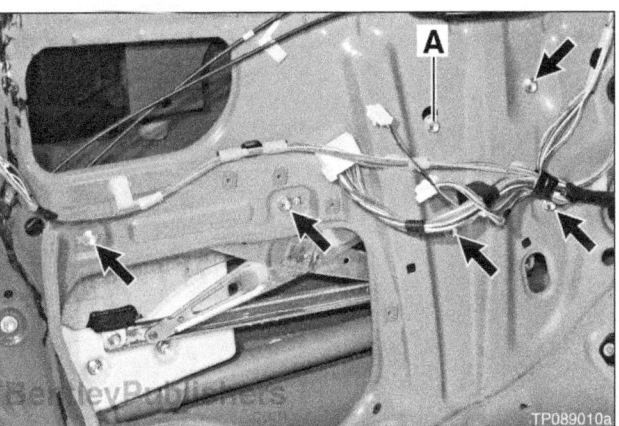

TP089010a

◄ When installing:

- Hang window regulator inside door cavity by attaching bolt **A** finger tight.
- Install remainder of bolts and reattach connector.

Tightening torque	
Window regulator to door assembly	8 Nm (71 in-lb)

9

— When installing door glass to regulator:

- Reattach window switch assembly and raise or lower glass support bracket until glass mounting bolt holes become visible.

- Make sure glass support bracket and window glass are parallel to each other.

Tightening torque	
Glass to glass support bracket	8 Nm (71 in-lb)

— Remainder of installation is reverse of removal. Remember to:

- Use butyl tape to attach new vapor barrier to door cavity.

- Make sure wires, connectors and cables are routed correctly.

Tightening torques	
Outside mirror to door • Bolts • Nuts	 5.5 Nm (49 in-lb) 8 Nm (71 in-lb)

— Reinitialize power windows. See **10 Electrical System, Lights**.

MIRRORS

Outside rear-view mirror, removing and installing

Left outside mirror removal is described in this procedure. Right outside mirror is similar.

– Switch hybrid system OFF (READY indicator not illuminated). See **3 Safety**.

> **WARNING**—
> • Make sure hybrid system is OFF when servicing vehicle (READY indicator not illuminated). Failure to switch the hybrid system OFF could result in engine start at any time.

– Remove inner door panel. See **Door panel, removing and installing** in this chapter.

◄ Working at front corner of window frame:
  • Detach mirror electrical connector.
  • Remove 3 mounting fasteners (**arrows**) and detach mirror.

> **CAUTION**—
> • While removing fasteners, support mirror to prevent it from falling off the door and breaking.

– Installation is reverse of removal.

Tightening torque	
Outside mirror to door	
• Bolts	5.5 Nm (49 in-lb)
• Nuts	8 Nm (71 in-lb)

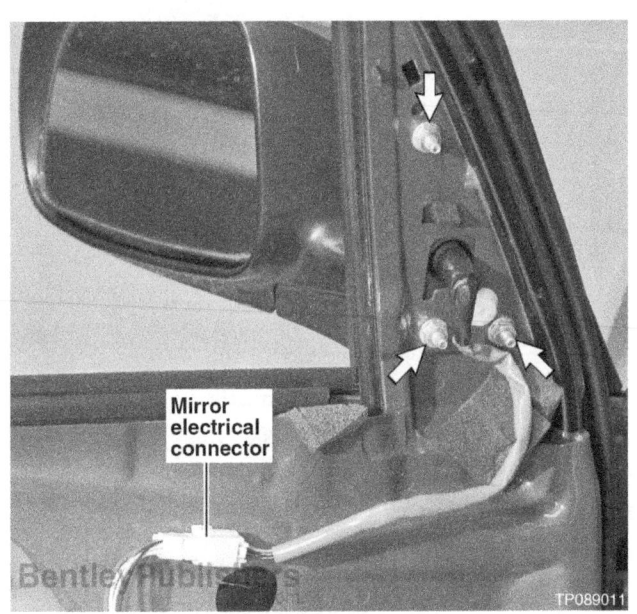

Mirror electrical connector

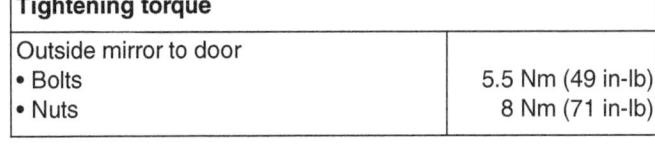

SEATS

In some Prius models the front seat backrests are equipped with side bolster airbags. Be sure to read the airbag warnings in **Warnings and Cautions** in this chapter before beginning work.

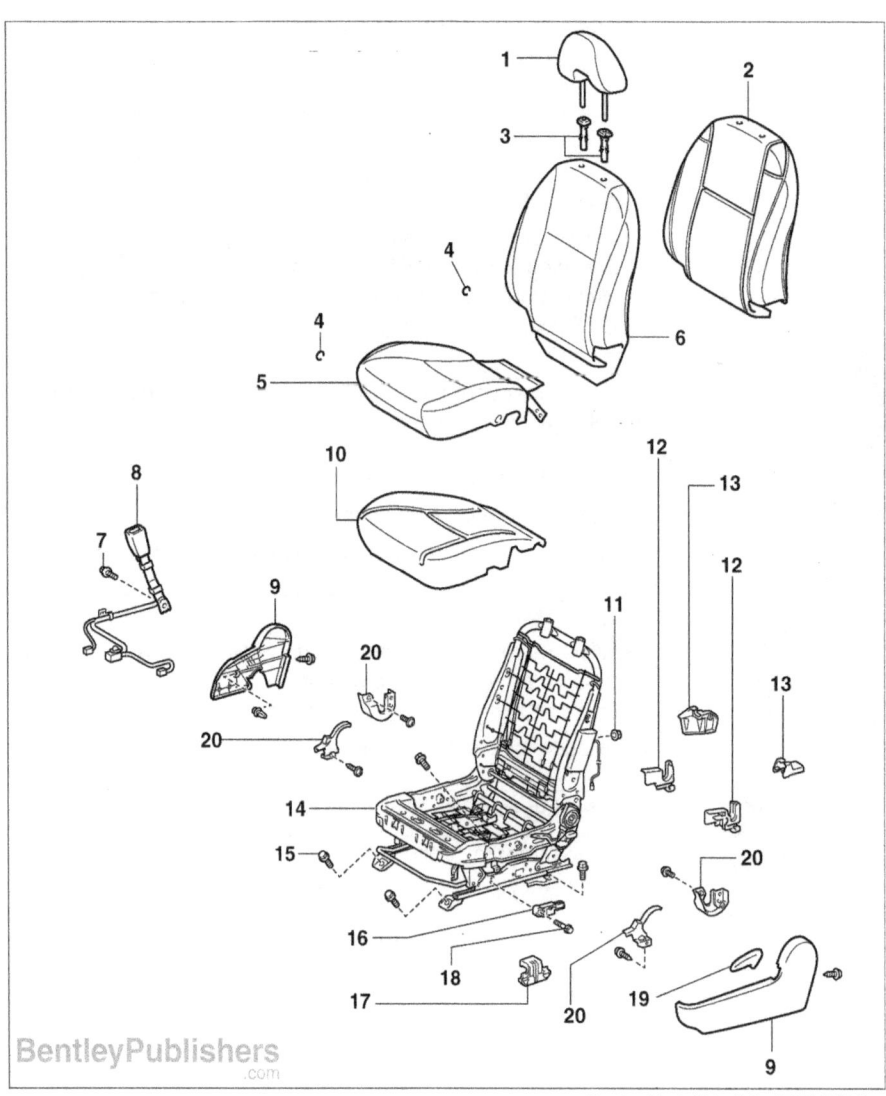

Courtesy Toyota Motor Sales (TMS) USA, Inc.

BentleyPublishers.com

Front seat assembly (left seat)

1. **Headrest**
2. **Backrest pad**
3. **Headrest support bushings**
4. **Hog ring (upholstery clip)**
   - Do not reuse
5. **Seat cushion cover**
6. **Backrest cover**
7. **Bolt**
   - Tighten to 42 Nm (31 ft-lb)
8. **Seat belt latch assembly**
9. **Plastic trim**
10. **Seat cushion pad**
11. **Nut**
    - Tighten to 5.5 Nm (49 ft-lb)
12. **Lower seat cushion shield**
13. **Seat track trim cover**
14. **Seat frame**
15. **Bolt**
    - Tighten to 37 Nm (27 ft-lb)
16. **Airbag seat position sensor**
17. **Seat position sensor protector**
18. **Bolt**
    - Tighten to 8 Nm (71 in-lb)
19. **Recliner handle**
20. **Reclining adjuster components**

Front seat, removing and installing

> **WARNING—**
> • *Wear protective gloves. Sharp edges on seat tracks may cause hand injuries.*

The left front seat is illustrated in this section. Right front seat assembly is similar.

— Switch hybrid system OFF (READY indicator not illuminated). See **3 Safety**.

> **WARNING—**
> • *Be sure hybrid system is OFF when servicing vehicle (READY indicator not illuminated). Failure to switch the hybrid system OFF could result in engine start at any time.*
>
>

— Disconnect 12-volt auxiliary battery. See **3 Safety**.

> **WARNING—**
> • *Vehicle with side-bolster airbags: After disconnecting battery, wait at least 90 seconds before starting work on seat.*

> **CAUTION—**
> • *Disconnecting 12-volt auxiliary battery causes loss of radio and navigation system presets. Record presets before disconnecting battery.*

◄ Use plastic prying tool to disengage mounting clips (**inserts**) on trim cover at rear of outer seat track. Detach trim cover.

TP08010014

Courtesy Toyota Motor Sales (TMS) USA, Inc.

◄ Similarly, disengage mounting clips (**inserts**) on trim cover at rear of inner seat track and detach trim cover.

— Pull off seat headrest.

— Slide seat to rearmost position. Remove front seat track mounting bolts.

— Slide seat to frontmost position. Remove rear seat track mounting bolts.

— Tip seat back and disconnect electrical connector under seat.

— Remove seat.

> **CAUTION—**
> • *To avoid damaging door sill trim, cover with padding or blanket.*

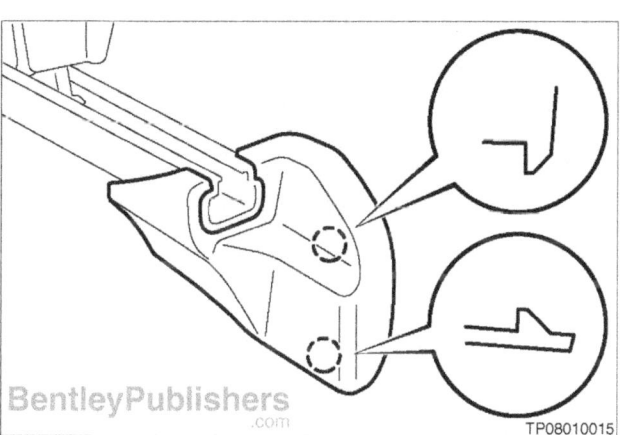

TP08010015

Courtesy Toyota Motor Sales (TMS) USA, Inc.

— Installation is reverse of removal, bearing in mind the following:

- Reattach electrical connector before installing mounting bolts.
- Tighten front seat mounting bolts first.

Tightening torque	
Front seat to vehicle floor	37 nm (27 ft-lb)

— Reconnect 12-volt auxiliary battery and reinitialize power windows. See **10 Electrical System, Lights**.

— Reprogram radio and navigation system presets (if applicable).

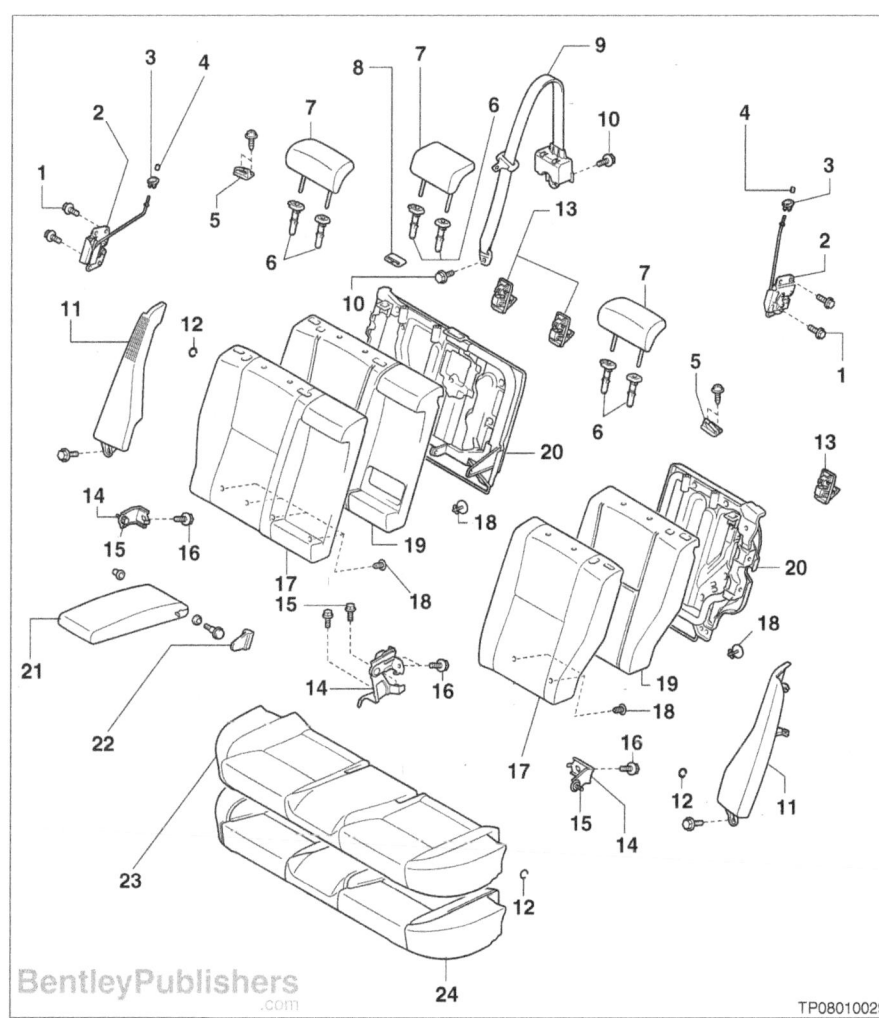

TP08010029
Courtesy Toyota Motor Sales (TMS) USA, Inc.

Rear seat assembly

1. **Bolt**
   • Tighten to 18 Nm (13 ft-lb)
2. **Backrest lock**
3. **Grommet**
4. **Release button**
5. **Shoulder belt guide**
6. **Headrest support bushings**
7. **Headrest**
8. **Shoulder belt trim**
9. **Shoulder belt**
10. **Bolt**
    • Tighten to 42 Nm (31 ft-lb)
11. **Side bolster**
12. **Hog ring (upholstery clip)**
    • Do not reuse
13. **Child seat anchors**
14. **Backrest hinge**
15. **Bolt**
    • Tighten to 18 Nm (13 ft-lb)
16. **Bolt**
    • Tighten to 36.8 Nm (27 ft-lb)
17. **Backrest cover**
18. **Clip**
19. **Backrest padding**
20. **Backrest frame**
21. **Armrest**
22. **Hinge cover**
23. **Seat cushion cover**
24. **Seat cushion pad**

TP08011041

10

Electrical System, Lights

Repairs for common electrical problems

GENERAL

This chapter covers service and maintenance information for the 12-volt auxiliary battery, lights, horns, wipers, and electrical switches. Also covered here is power window reinitialization.

Additional related service and repairs may be found in:
- **3 Safety**
- **4 Service and Repair Fundamentals**
- **11 Diagnostics**
- **12 Electrical Component Locations**
- **13 Electrical Wiring Diagrams**

Hybrid safety

In addition to the safety warnings given here, always read and observe the **Warnings**, **Cautions** and safety procedures in **3 Safety** before working on vehicle. Orange-colored cables carry lethal high voltage. Use extreme care when working near high voltage cables and components.

WARNING—

- *Risk of electrocution! Avoid touching orange-colored high voltage wiring and high voltage components unless you are certain that high voltage is not present.*

- *The Prius hybrid system has voltages as high as 500 volts. Voltages over 60 volts DC and 25 volts AC are a shock hazard.*

The Prius engine may start at any time if the hybrid system is in **READY** mode. See **3 Safety** for instructions on turning OFF the hybrid system.

WARNING—

- *Be sure hybrid system is OFF when servicing vehicle (READY indicator not illuminated). Failure to switch the hybrid system OFF could result in engine start at any time.*

Table a is a listing of repair procedures in this chapter and the hybrid safety requirements for each.

Procedure	Switch hybrid system OFF	Disconnect 12-volt battery	Remove service plug
12-volt auxiliary battery, charging, disconnecting, removing	✓	✓	
Headlight aim control, reinitializing	✓		
Headlight aim, checking and adjusting	✓		
Headlight bulbs, replacing	✓		
Front foglight aim, adjusting	✓		
Front foglight, removing and installing	✓		
Taillight housing, removing and installing	✓		
Center brake light, replacing	✓		
License plate light bulb, replacing	✓		
Interior light service	✓		
Brake light switch, replacing	✓		
Door switch assembly, removing	✓		
Hazard warning light switch, removing	✓	✓	
Steering column stalk switches, removing	✓	✓	
Windshield wiper arms, removing	✓		
Windshield wiper assembly, removing	✓		

Table a. Hybrid safety requirements for repair procedures

Window control system, reinitializing

Reinitialize power window control system whenever 12-volt auxiliary battery power is interrupted. If window control system is not reinitialized, AUTO UP / DOWN and anti-trap protection do not function.

1. Turn hybrid system ON (READY indicator illuminated).

2. Open driver door window halfway by depressing power window switch.

3. Fully close driver door window by holding window switch in full-up position. Once window is closed, continue holding switch in full-up position for at least 1 second.

4. Try AUTO UP / DOWN functions on driver door window. If functions operate normally, reset is complete. If operation is not normal, continue with steps below:

   • Disconnect negative cable from 12-volt auxiliary battery for at least 10 seconds, then reconnect cable. See **12-volt auxiliary battery, disconnecting** in this chapter.

   • Repeat steps 1 – 4.

Warnings and Cautions

WARNING—
• *The airbag is a vehicle safety system. Serious injury may result if system service is attempted by persons unfamiliar with approved Toyota airbag system service procedures.*

• *Prior to working on airbag system components, disconnect the 12-volt auxiliary battery and wait 90 seconds before beginning work. The airbag system is equipped with a backup power source. If work is started within 90 seconds after disconnecting the battery, the airbag may deploy.*

CAUTION—
• *Some repair procedures require that you disconnect the 12-volt auxiliary battery. This causes loss of radio and navigation system presets and power window initialization. Record radio and navigation system presets before disconnecting battery. Reinitialize windows after reconnecting battery.*

• *If the Prius cannot be switched OFF with the power button, there may be a fault in the shift control actuator that prevents the transaxle from engaging PARK. Stop the vehicle and apply the parking brake. This bypasses the fault and permits shutdown of the hybrid system.*

• *To avoid damaging vehicle trim, use a plastic prying tool or a screwdriver with the tip wrapped with masking tape.*

• *Use a digital multimeter with high impedance for troubleshooting electrical circuits.*

10

12-Volt Auxiliary Battery

> **CAUTION—**
> - *Record radio presets and GPS destinations (if equipped) before disconnecting the 12-volt auxiliary battery.*
> - *Do not leave the ignition in the ACC or IG-ON positions with the hybrid system OFF (READY indicator not illuminated) for an extended period of time. The 12-volt auxiliary battery discharges quickly.*
> - *Disconnect the 12-volt auxiliary battery if the vehicle is not to be used for approximately one month or more.*
> - *Do not let the vehicle sit in NEUTRAL with the READY indicator illuminated. The high voltage battery is not charged when in NEUTRAL.*
> - *Do not charge the 12-volt auxiliary battery at a high rate with a regular battery charger. Use a pulse-type charger and charge at a rate no higher than 3.5 amps.*
> - *When parking the Prius for more than a few days, disable the Smart Key system (if equipped) to reduce drain on the 12-volt auxiliary battery. The Smart Key switch is under the steering column.*
> - *The transaxle gearshift and park lock systems are electronic and use the 12-volt auxiliary battery for power. If this battery is discharged or is disconnected, the vehicle cannot be started or shifted out of PARK.*
> - *When the warning light is illuminated or the battery has been disconnected and reconnected, pressing the power switch may not start the vehicle on the first try. If so, press the power switch again.*

The 12-volt auxiliary battery is a sealed, maintenance-free low-current-capacity absorbed-glass-mat (AGM) lead-acid unit located in the cargo compartment, underneath the right rear floorboard.

The auxiliary battery provides power to control units during startup, and continuous power to maintain control unit memory when the hybrid system is switched OFF. The vehicle does not start if auxiliary battery voltage is too low due to discharging or a defect.

12-volt auxiliary battery, charging

If you suspect that the 12-volt auxiliary battery is discharged, check battery voltage.

- If hybrid system has been OFF (READY indicator not illuminated) for at least 20 minutes, battery voltage may be measured immediately.

- If hybrid system has been ON (READY indicator illuminated) within 20 minutes, switch ignition, headlights, high blower speed and rear window defogger ON for 1 minute to remove battery surface charge before measuring battery voltage.

– Switch hybrid system OFF (READY indicator not illuminated). See **3 Safety**.

> **WARNING—**
> - *Be sure hybrid system is OFF when servicing vehicle (READY indicator not illuminated). Failure to switch the hybrid system OFF could result in engine start at any time.*

– Gain access to auxiliary battery terminals. See **12-volt auxiliary battery, disconnecting** in this chapter.

– Measure auxiliary battery voltage.
- Place digital multimeter probes on positive and negative battery terminals of 12-volt auxiliary battery.
- Compare your measurements with specifications below.

12-volt auxiliary battery	
Normal voltage at 20°C (68°F)	12.5 - 12.9 v

 If voltage is below specifications, charge battery:
- Disconnect cable (**arrow**) from battery negative terminal.
- Use pulse-type charger to charge battery.

> **CAUTION—**
> - *Do not charge the absorbed-glass-mat (AGM) 12-volt auxiliary battery at a high rate with a regular battery charger. Use a pulse-type charger and charge at a rate no higher than 3.5 amps.*
> - *Connect and disconnect battery charger cable with the charger switched OFF. Follow battery charger manufacturer's instructions.*
> - *Record radio presets and GPS destinations (if equipped) before disconnecting the 12-volt auxiliary battery.*

– When finished charging, reconnect negative cable.

Tightening torque	
Negative battery cable clamp nut	6 Nm (53 in-lb)

– Once battery is reconnected, reset radio and navigation system (if equipped) presets. Be sure to reinitialize windows. See **Window control system, reinitializing** in this chapter

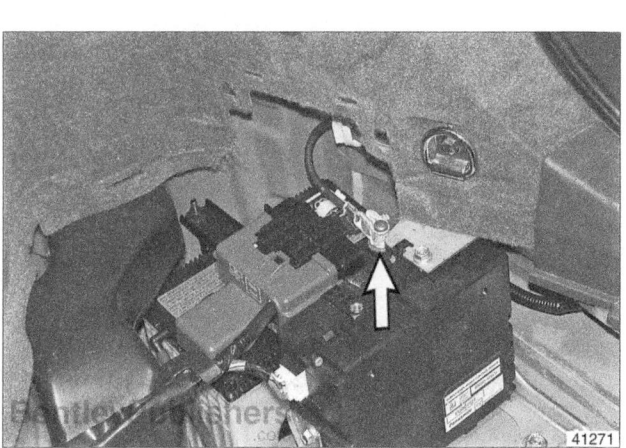

10

12-volt auxiliary battery, disconnecting

– Switch hybrid system OFF (READY indicator not illuminated).
See **3 Safety**.

> **WARNING—**
> • *Be sure hybrid system is OFF when servicing
> vehicle (READY indicator not illuminated).
> Failure to switch the hybrid system OFF could
> result in engine start at any time.*

◀ Working in cargo compartment, rotate two release knobs on rear
floor board.

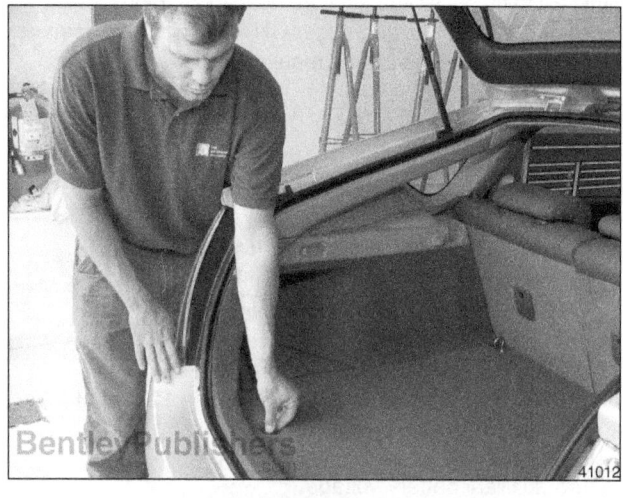

◀ Lift and remove rear floor board.

◀ Remove rear floor storage box.

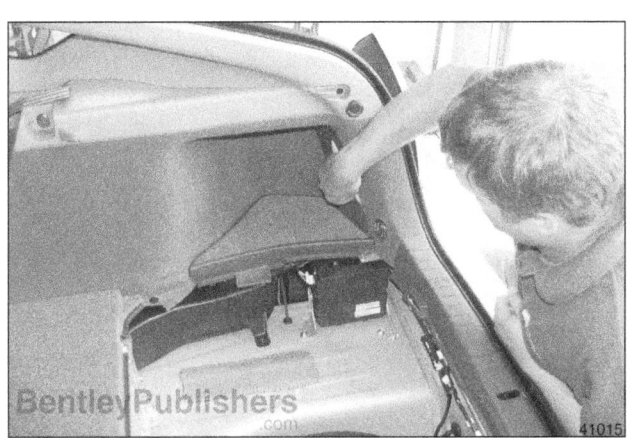

◀ Using plastic trim tool, release 4 retaining claws and remove right rear floor board.

◀ Disconnect 12-volt auxiliary battery negative (ground) cable (**arrow**) from battery terminal.

> **CAUTION—**
> • *Record radio presets and GPS destinations (if equipped) before disconnecting the 12-volt auxiliary battery.*

– Wrap negative (ground) cable connector with insulating tape to avoid accidental contact with battery terminal.

– Once battery is reconnected, reset radio and navigation system (if equipped) presets.

– Be sure to reinitialize windows. See **Window control system, reinitializing** in this chapter.

12-volt auxiliary battery, removing and installing

– Switch hybrid system OFF (READY indicator not illuminated). See **3 Safety**.

> **WARNING—**
> • *Be sure hybrid system is OFF when servicing vehicle (READY indicator not illuminated). Failure to switch the hybrid system OFF could result in engine start at any time.*

– Disconnect 12-volt auxiliary battery. See **12-volt auxiliary battery, disconnecting** in this chapter.

> **CAUTION—**
> • *Record radio presets and GPS destinations (if equipped) before disconnecting the 12-volt auxiliary battery.*

◀ Detach 3 retaining claws (**insets**) and remove connector cover from auxiliary battery positive terminal.

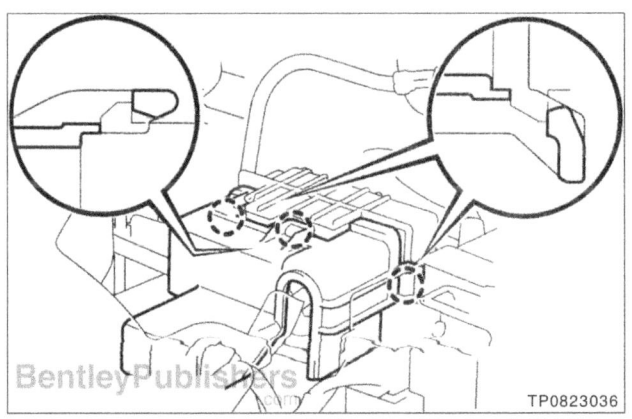

◀ Working at top of 12-volt auxiliary battery:

- Disconnect brake control power supply connector (**A**) and 2 fusible link block connectors (**B**).
- Detach wire harness (**C**) from right rear vent duct.

◀ Working at right rear vent duct, remove mounting bolts (**arrows**) and pull off duct.

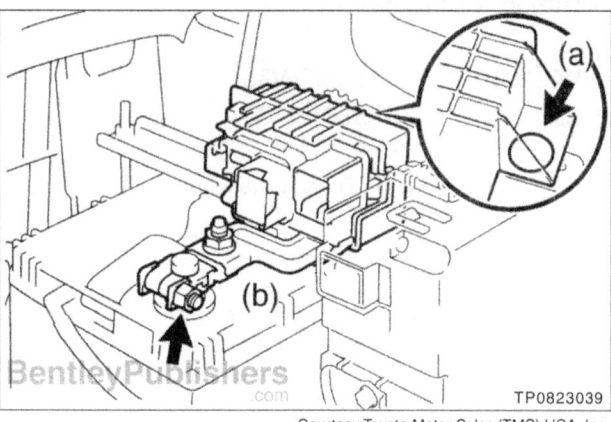

Courtesy Toyota Motor Sales (TMS) USA, Inc.

◀ Working at top of battery:

- Remove clip (**a**) from fusible link block assembly.
- Loosen positive terminal clamp nut (**b**) and remove fusible link block assembly from battery.

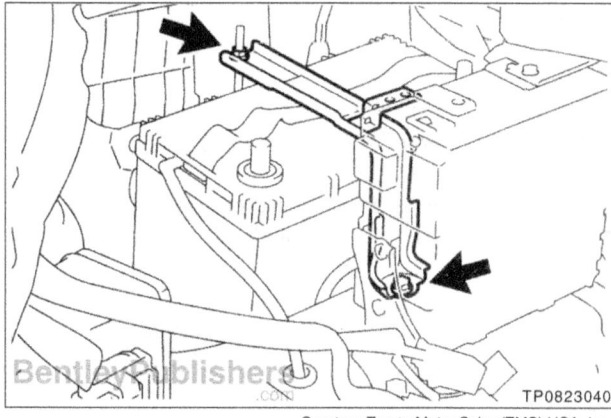

Courtesy Toyota Motor Sales (TMS) USA, Inc.

◀ Remove battery hold-down bracket fasteners (**arrows**). Remove battery hold-down bracket.

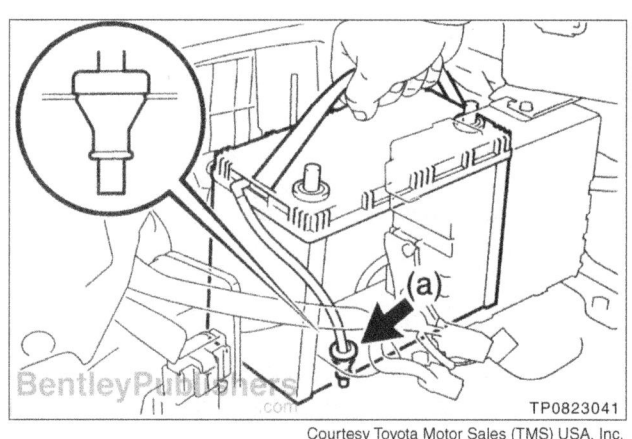

TP0823041

Courtesy Toyota Motor Sales (TMS) USA, Inc.

◀ Detach battery vent hose grommet (**a**) from vehicle and lift out battery.

– Installation is reverse of removal.

Tightening torques	
Battery hold-down bracket to chassis	5.4 Nm (48 in-lb)
Negative battery cable clamp nut	6 Nm (53 in-lb)
Positive battery clamp nut (fusible link assembly)	6 Nm (53 in-lb)
Vent duct to chassis	4.0 Nm (35 in-lb)

– Once battery is reconnected, reset radio and navigation system (if equipped) presets.

– Be sure to reinitialize windows. See **Window control system, reinitializing** in this chapter.

HORNS

In order to replace either low-range or high-range horn, remove front bumper cover. See **9 Body**.

Horn components

1. **Low range horn**
2. **Bolt**
   • Tighten to 20 Nm (15 ft-lb)
3. **High range horn**
4. **Front bumper cover**

10

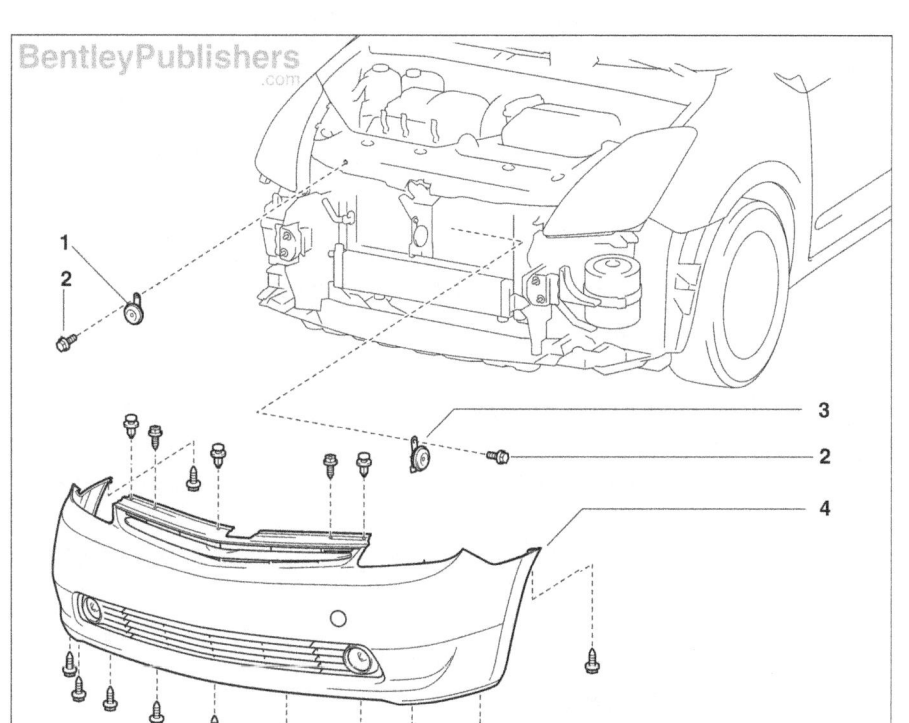

TP08011026

Courtesy Toyota Motor Sales (TMS) USA, Inc.

LIGHTS

> **WARNING—**
> • *There is high pressure inside a halogen or xenon (HID) headlight bulb. Bulb temperature may exceed 700°C. Wear safety glasses and gloves when removing and installing a headlight bulb.*
> • *Do not look directly at an operating xenon bulb. The UV emissions are approximately 2.5 times that of a comparable halogen bulb.*
> • *Do not connect a tester to headlight xenon bulb high voltage socket as high voltage may lead to serious injury.*
> • *When replacing a xenon bulb, keep it away from water including rain, turn the light switch off, and disconnect the auxiliary battery terminal and the connector of the light control ECU in advance to avoid electric shock. See* **12 Electrical Component Locations**.

> **CAUTION—**
> • *When working with xenon (HID) electronic components, use an antistatic mat and work with caution.*
> • *Do not apply power to the xenon control module unless a bulb is connected.*
> • *Do not handle bulb glass with bare fingers. Dirt and skin oils cause a bulb to fail prematurely. If necessary, wipe bulb using a clean cloth dampened with rubbing alcohol.*

Headlight aim control, reinitializing

Prius models with optional xenon (high-intensity discharge or HID) headlights are equipped with a headlight leveling system. This system uses a suspension height sensor on the rear axle beam to control headlight aim.

Whenever rear suspension components are disassembled or replaced, reinitialize headlight leveling ECU and check aim of headlights.

Prior to headlight aim control reinitialization, prepare the vehicle as follows:

• Fuel quantity in tank: approx. 10 liters (2.6 gal.) (2 bars on fuel level indicator)

• No luggage or cargo

• Driver only, no passenger

• Headlights OFF

With brake pedal *not* depressed, push POWER button twice. This switches hybrid system to IG-ON position (READY indicator not illuminated, engine will not start).

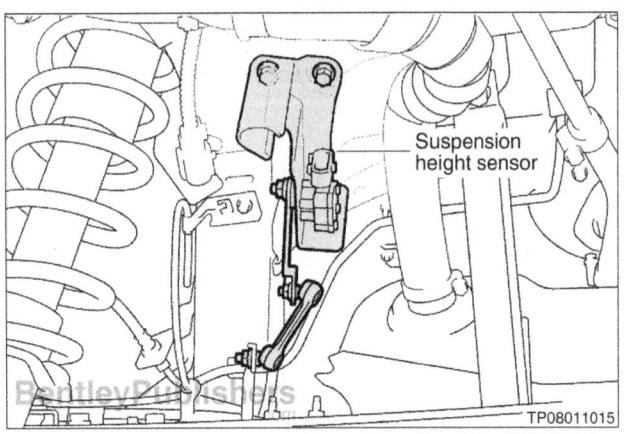

Suspension height sensor

TP08011015

Courtesy Toyota Motor Sales (TMS) USA, Inc.

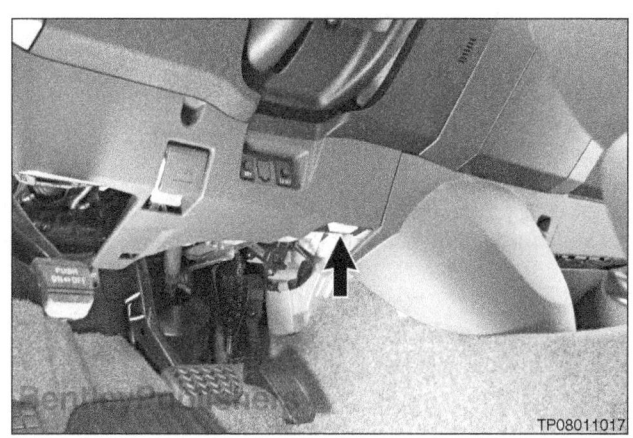

◀ Locate OBD II connector (**arrow**) under dashboard on driver side.

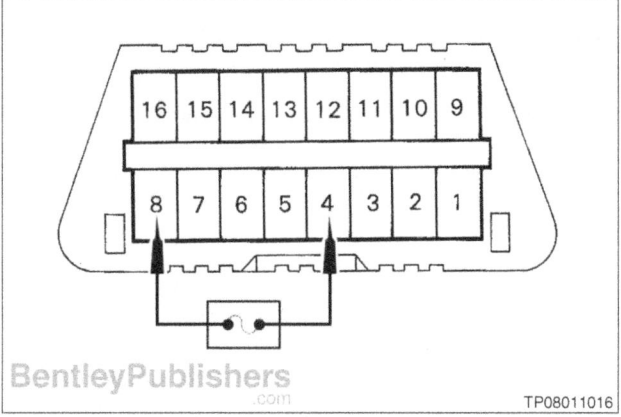

Courtesy Toyota Motor Sales (TMS) USA, Inc.

◀ Using jumper wire, connect terminals 4 and 8 in OBD II connector.

> **CAUTION—**
> • *Avoid spreading or deforming female terminals in OBD II connector. Use an appropriate jumper wire gauge and do not force jumper wire into terminals.*

◀ Using headlight flasher / dimmer switch, flash headlights 3 or more times.

 • Each time hold headlight flasher ON (**arrow**) for approx. 1 second.

 • Complete at least 3 flashes within 20 seconds.

– Headlight aim control is reinitialized if both master warning light and automatic headlight leveling system warning light illuminate, then switch OFF.

– If warning lights remain illuminated, repeat initialization procedure.

– Remove jumper wire from OBD II connector.

– Check and adjust headlight aim. See **Headlight aim, checking and adjusting** in this chapter.

10

Headlight aim, checking and adjusting

The following procedure to check and adjust headlight aim applies to Prius models with either halogen or xenon (HID) headlights.

Adjust headlight aim on low-beam setting. Be sure that headlight units and surrounding bodywork are not damaged or deformed.

Prior to headlight aim adjustment, prepare vehicle as follows:
• Fuel quantity in tank: full
• Engine oil level: full
• Engine coolant level: full
• Inverter / transaxle coolant level: full
• Tire pressures: correct
• Spare tire, tools, and jack in place
• No luggage or cargo
• Driver only, no passenger. Driver weight approx. 68 kg (150 lb).

— With brake pedal *not* depressed, push POWER button twice to switch hybrid system to IG-ON (READY indicator not illuminated; engine will not start).

— Switch headlights ON and switch to low-beams.

◄ Adjust headlight aim by rotating aiming screw (**inset**):
• Rotate screw **clockwise** to adjust headlight aim **downward**
• Rotate screw **counter-clockwise** to adjust headlight aim **upward**.

NOTE—
• *Make final adjusting screw rotation clockwise.*
• *If adjusting screw is over-tightened, loosen once and retighten to adjust headlight aim.*

— When finished, switch headlights OFF.

— Push POWER button to switch hybrid system OFF.

TP08011003
Courtesy Toyota Motor Sales (TMS) USA, Inc.

Headlight bulbs, replacing

— Switch hybrid system OFF (READY indicator not illuminated). See **3 Safety**.

WARNING—
• *Be sure hybrid system is OFF when servicing vehicle (READY indicator not illuminated). Failure to switch the hybrid system OFF could result in engine start at any time.*

◄ Remove 6 retainers (**arrows**) on radiator cover:
• Turn center pin ¼ turn with Phillips screwdriver until center pin lifts (**inset**).
• Use small flat-blade screwdriver to gently pry out pin and retainer.

TP08006019

– Remove radiator cover.Left side bulb:

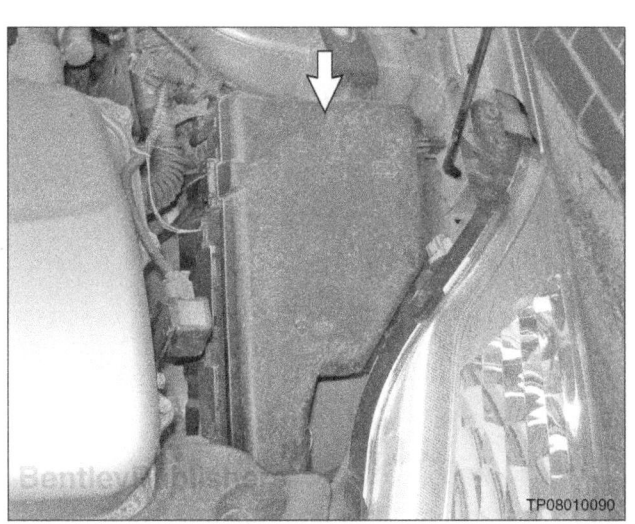 Remove fuse panel cover (**arrow**).

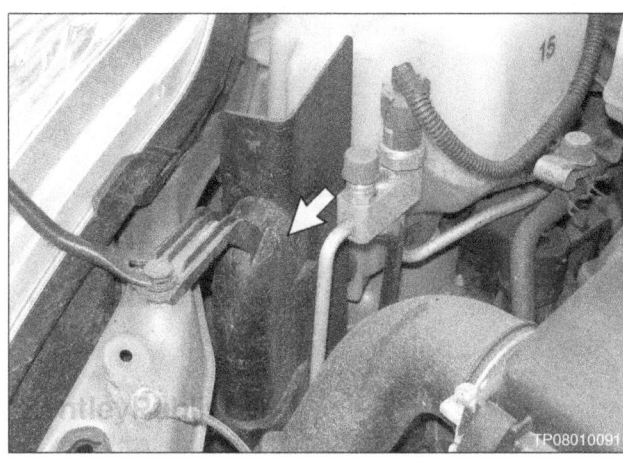 **Right side bulb**: Remove air intake duct (**arrow**).

Halogen headlight bulb, replacing

 Disconnect electrical connector (**arrow**) from bulb.

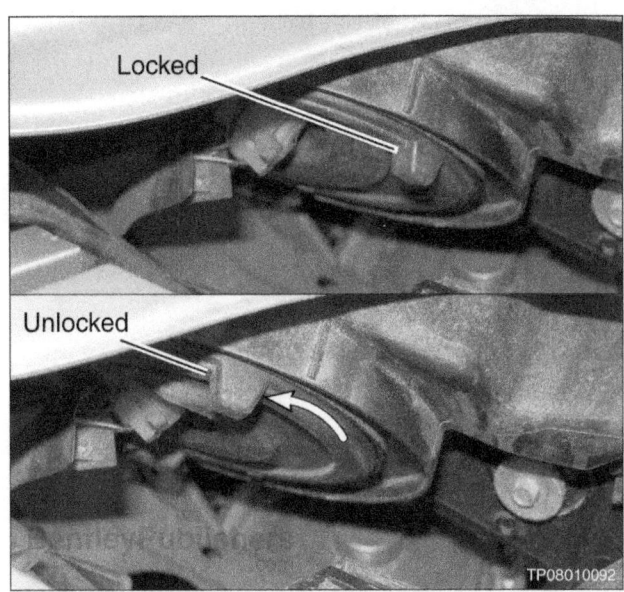

◀ Rotate headlight bulb cover counter clockwise (**arrow**) to unlock and remove.

NOTE—

• *Heat from headlight bulb may cause rubber cover to harden and stick to base of bulb. Insert small screwdriver or similar tool between rubber cover and bulb base to loosen before attempting to remove.*

◀ Disengage set spring (**arrow**) then remove headlight bulb. Do not touch bulb glass with your fingers.

– Installation is reverse of removal.

Xenon (HID) headlight bulb, replacing

◀ Rotate headlight bulb cover (**arrow**) and remove.

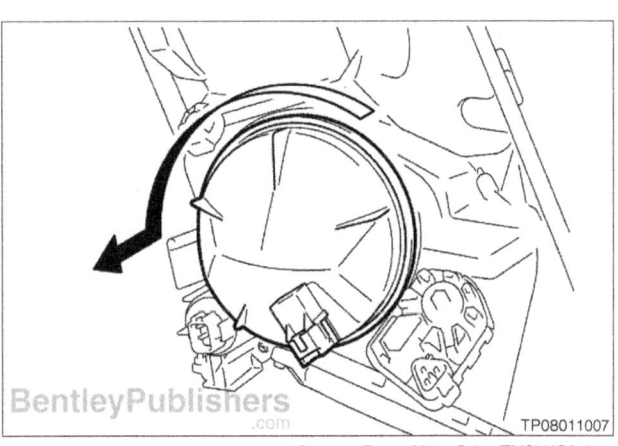

Courtesy Toyota Motor Sales (TMS) USA, Inc.

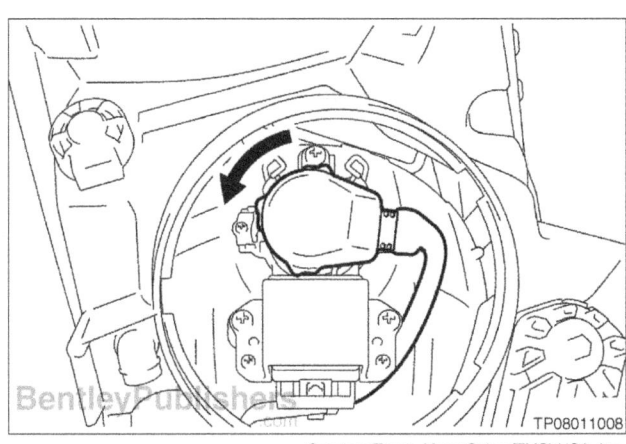

Courtesy Toyota Motor Sales (TMS) USA, Inc.

◄ Rotate xenon (HID) headlight control module socket (**arrow**) to disengage from bulb.

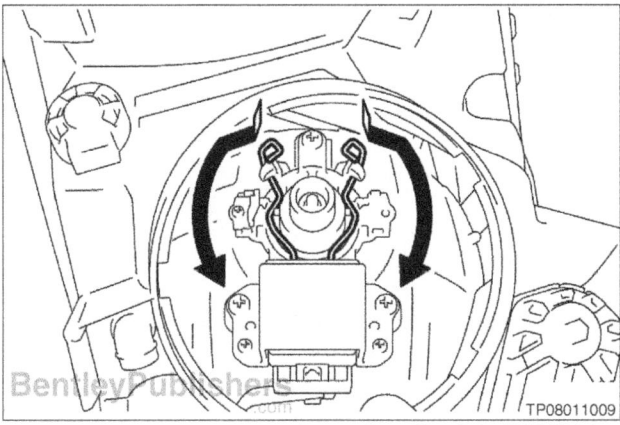

Courtesy Toyota Motor Sales (TMS) USA, Inc.

◄ Disengage set spring (**arrow**) to remove headlight bulb. Do not touch bulb glass with your fingers.

– Installation is reverse of removal.

Headlight assembly, removing

> **CAUTION—**
> • *Do not touch bulb glass with your fingers.*
> • *If a bulb is dirty or has been handled by the glass end, clean it with soft, lint-free cloth and rubbing alcohol. Any oils or dirt drastically reduces bulb life span.*

◄ Halogen headlight components, left side:

1. Repair brackets
2. Turn signal bulb socket
3. Turn signal bulb
4. Running light bulb
5. Running light bulb socket
6. Bulb cover
7. Halogen headlight bulb
8. Headlight housing

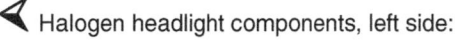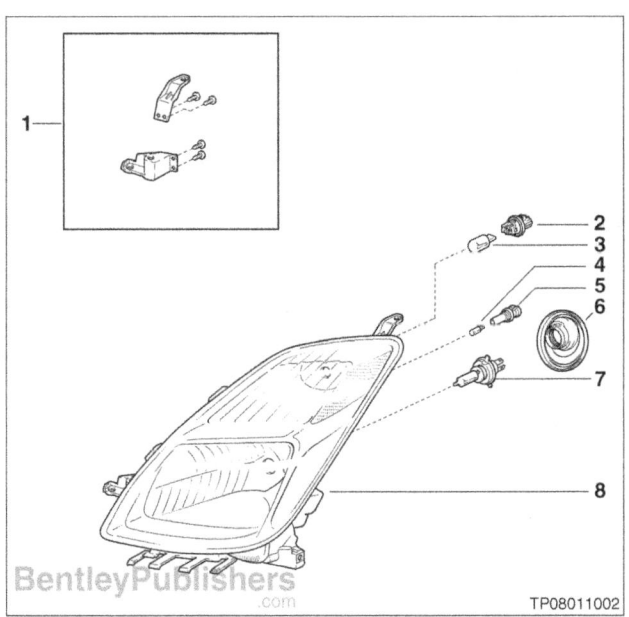

Courtesy Toyota Motor Sales (TMS) USA, Inc.

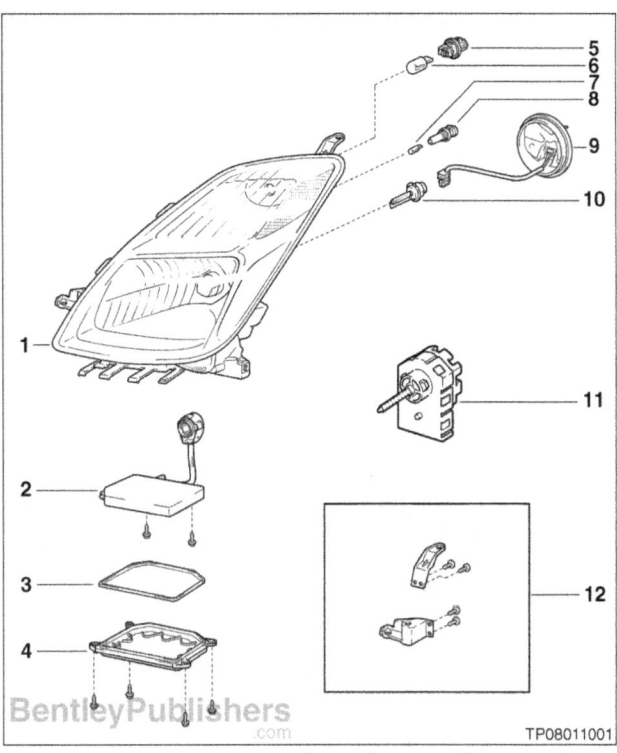

Courtesy Toyota Motor Sales (TMS) USA, Inc.

TP08011001

◄ Xenon (HID) headlight components, left side:

1. Headlight housing
2. Xenon (HID) headlight control module
3. Gasket
4. Cover
5. Turn signal bulb socket
6. Turn signal bulb
7. Running light bulb
8. Running light bulb socket
9. Bulb cover
10. Xenon (HID) bulb
11. Headlight leveling motor
12. Repair brackets

— Switch hybrid system OFF (READY indicator not illuminated). See **3 Safety**.

> **WARNING—**
> • *Be sure hybrid system is OFF when servicing vehicle (READY indicator not illuminated). Failure to switch the hybrid system OFF could result in engine start at any time.*

— Raise vehicle and support safely. See **4 Service and Repair Fundamentals**.

> **WARNING—**
> • *Make sure vehicle is stable and well supported at all times. Use a professional automotive lift or jack stands. A floor jack is not adequate support.*

— Remove left and right engine splash shields. See **5 Engine**.

◄ Remove screws (**arrows**) and detach forward part of front fender liners. It is not necessary to remove entire front fender liners.

— Remove front bumper cover. See **9 Body**.

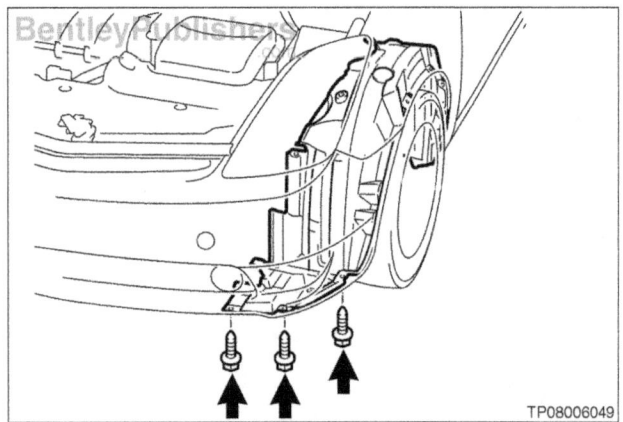

Courtesy Toyota Motor Sales (TMS) USA, Inc.

TP08006049

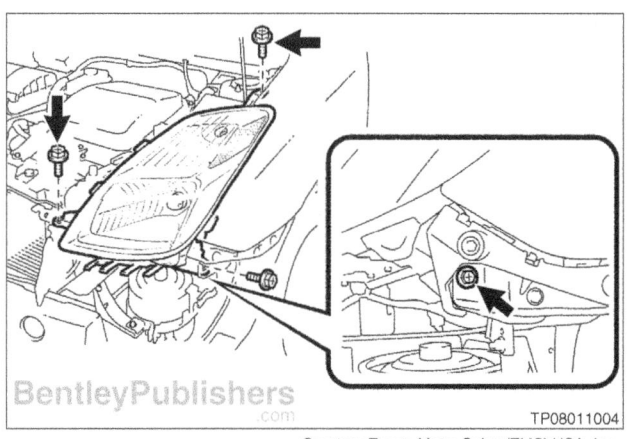

TP08011004

Courtesy Toyota Motor Sales (TMS) USA, Inc.

◀ Remove headlight housing:

- Remove 3 mounting screws (**arrows**).

- Pull headlight housing forward, disconnect electrical connectors and remove headlight housing.

Front running light bulb, replacing

– Switch hybrid system OFF (READY indicator not illuminated). See **3 Safety**.

> **WARNING—**
>
> - *Be sure hybrid system is OFF when servicing vehicle (READY indicator not illuminated). Failure to switch the hybrid system OFF could result in engine start at any time.*

– Open engine hood.

◀ Working at top rear of headlight assembly:

- Detach electrical connector from running light bulb socket (**arrow**).

- Rotate running light bulb socket and remove.

– Replace bulb in socket, then install socket in housing. Do not touch bulb glass with your fingers.

– Reconnect electrical connector.

41264

10

Front turn signal bulb, replacing

– Switch hybrid system OFF (READY indicator not illuminated). See **3 Safety**.

> **WARNING—**
> • *Be sure hybrid system is OFF when servicing vehicle (READY indicator not illuminated). Failure to switch the hybrid system OFF could result in engine start at any time.*

– Open engine hood.

◄ Working at top rear of headlight assembly:

  • Detach electrical connector from turn signal bulb socket (**arrow**).

  • Rotate turn signal bulb socket and remove.

– Replace bulb in socket, then install socket in housing. Do not touch bulb glass with your fingers.

– Reconnect electrical connector.

41265

Front foglight aim, adjusting

Be sure that foglight units and surrounding bodywork are not damaged or deformed.

Prior to foglight aim adjustment, prepare vehicle as follows:

• Fuel quantity in tank: full

• Engine oil level: full

• Engine coolant level: full

• Inverter / transaxle coolant level: full

• Tire pressures: correct

• Spare tire, tools, and jack in place

• No luggage or cargo

• Driver only, no passenger. Driver weight approx. 68 kg (150 lb).

– Turn hybrid system ON (READY indicator illuminated). Be sure to depress PARK button and set parking brake.

◄ Working underneath front bumper:

  • Insert screwdriver into front fender liner foglight service hole.

  • Rotate screw to adjust foglight.
    Clockwise: Foglight beam aims higher.
    Counterclockwise: Beam aims lower.

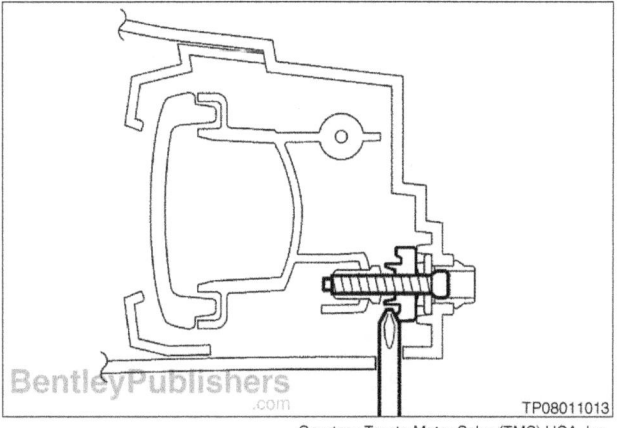

TP08011013

Courtesy Toyota Motor Sales (TMS) USA, Inc.

Front foglight, removing and installing

— Switch hybrid system OFF (READY indicator not illuminated). See **3 Safety**.

> **WARNING**—
> • Be sure hybrid system is OFF when servicing vehicle (READY indicator not illuminated). Failure to switch the hybrid system OFF could result in engine start at any time.

— Raise vehicle and support safely. See **4 Service and Repair Fundamentals**.

> **WARNING**—
> • Make sure the vehicle is stable and well supported at all times. Use a professional automotive lift or jack stands designed for the purpose. A floor jack is not adequate support.

— Remove left and right engine splash shields. See **5 Engine**.

◀ Remove screws (**arrows**) and detach forward part of front fender liners. It is not necessary to remove entire front fender liners.

— Remove front bumper cover. See **9 Body**.

— Unclip lower radiator clips from bumper cover.

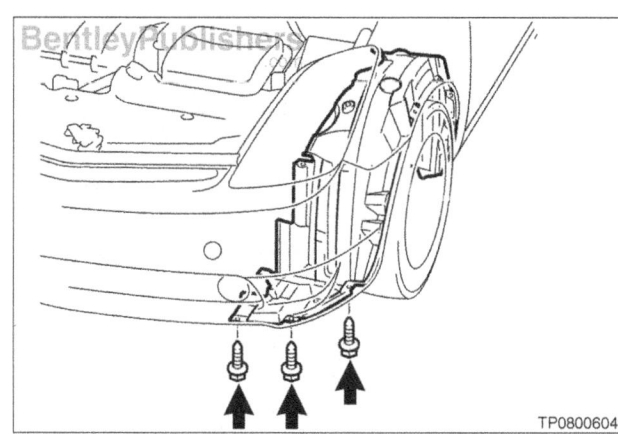

TP08006049
Courtesy Toyota Motor Sales (TMS) USA, Inc.

◀ Working at foglight:
   • Disengage 3 claws (**inset**) and press foglight housing forward to disengage.
   • Detach foglight electrical connector.
   • Twist bulb socket to remove from back of foglight housing. Do not touch bulb glass with your fingers.

— Installation is reverse of removal.

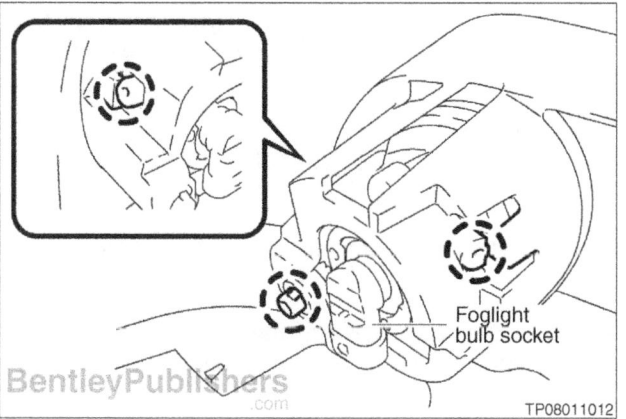

Foglight
bulb socket

TP08011012
Courtesy Toyota Motor Sales (TMS) USA, Inc.

10

Taillight housing, removing and installing

— Switch hybrid system OFF (READY indicator not illuminated). See **3 Safety**.

> **WARNING—**
> • *Be sure hybrid system is OFF when servicing vehicle (READY indicator not illuminated). Failure to switch the hybrid system OFF could result in engine start at any time.*

— Working in cargo compartment, remove taillight housing service cover.

◀ Working in cargo compartment at taillight housing:

- Remove 2 mounting nuts (**arrows**).
- Gently pry housing to disengage pins from vehicle.
- Detach electrical connector.
- Replace bulbs as necessary. Do not touch bulb glass with your fingers.

— Installation is reverse of removal.

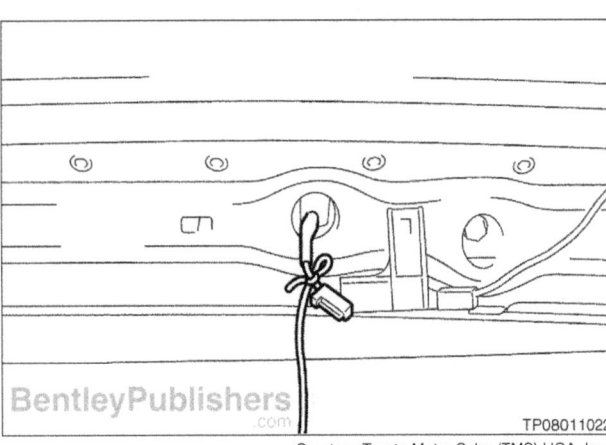

Courtesy Toyota Motor Sales (TMS) USA, Inc.

Center brake light, replacing

— Switch hybrid system OFF (READY indicator not illuminated). See **3 Safety**.

> **WARNING—**
> • *Be sure hybrid system is OFF when servicing vehicle (READY indicator not illuminated). Failure to switch the hybrid system OFF could result in engine start at any time.*

— Remove tailgate trim panel.

◀ Before removing center brake light assembly, detach electrical connector and tie a string around connector harness attached to light assembly.

Courtesy Toyota Motor Sales (TMS) USA, Inc.

◀ Remove 2 screws (**arrows**) and lift off center brake light assembly.

— Detach string from connector harness but do not pull string fully out of tailgate.

— Tie string hanging inside tailgate around new center brake light connector harness. Use string to pull connector harness into tailgate.

— Attach center brake light assembly with 2 screws. Remove string and reconnect connector. Reassemble trim panel.

Courtesy Toyota Motor Sales (TMS) USA, Inc.

License plate light bulb, replacing

– Switch hybrid system OFF (READY indicator not illuminated). See **3 Safety**.

WARNING—

• *Be sure hybrid system is OFF when servicing vehicle (READY indicator not illuminated). Failure to switch the hybrid system OFF could result in engine start at any time.*

– Remove tailgate trim panel.

◄ Working at license plate light socket:

    1. Push socket in direction indicated by **arrow**.

    2. Tilt socket to remove (**curved arrow**).

– Detach electrical connector.

– Remove license plate light lens and replace bulb. Do not touch bulb glass with your fingers.

– Installation is reverse of removal.

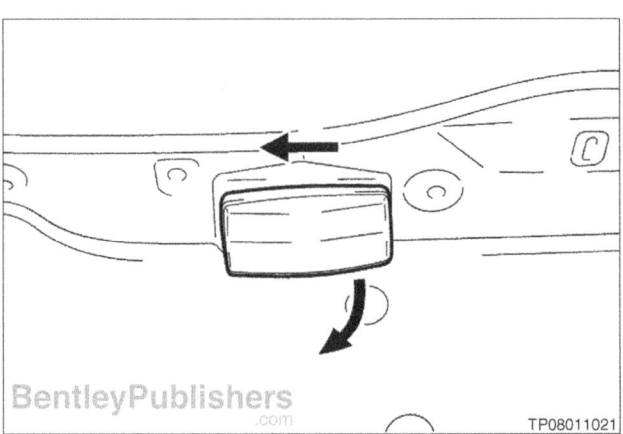

TP08011021

Courtesy Toyota Motor Sales (TMS) USA, Inc.

Interior light service

Map light bulb, accessing

◄ Working at map light housing and sunglasses compartment overhead:

• Open sunglasses compartment cover (**curved arrow**).

• Remove mounting screws (**arrow**).

• Use plastic prying tool to disengage clips (**insets**) and pull down map light housing.

– Detach electrical connector.

– Replace bulbs as necessary. Do not touch bulb glass with your fingers.

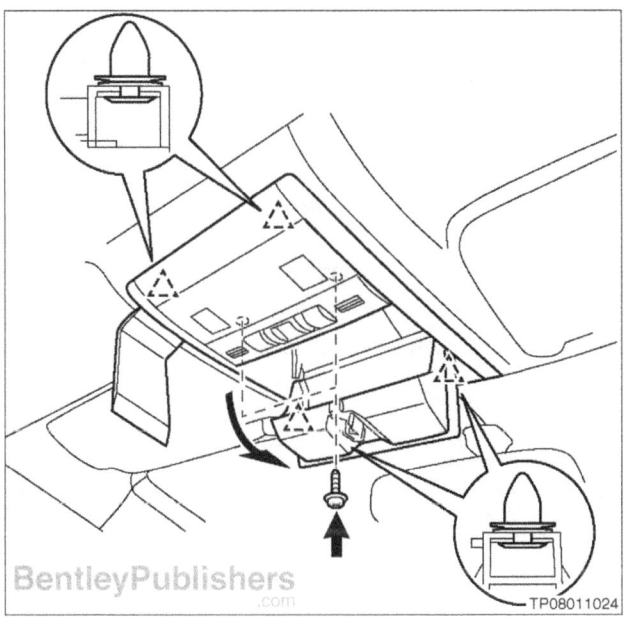

TP08011024

Courtesy Toyota Motor Sales (TMS) USA, Inc.

10

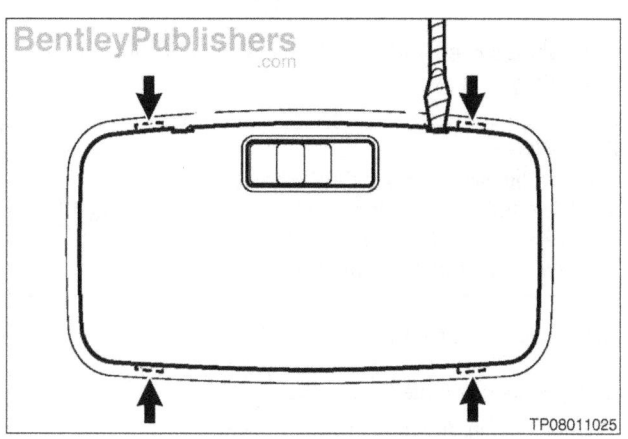

TP08011025

Courtesy Toyota Motor Sales (TMS) USA, Inc.

Dome light bulb, accessing

◀ Use plastic prying tool or screwdriver with tape-wrapped tip to pry off 4 claws (**arrows**) and remove dome light lens.

– Replace bulb as necessary. Do not touch bulb glass with your fingers.

SWITCHES

Back-up light control

Back-up lights are powered ON via a relay integrated in the engine compartment junction and relay block. Back-up light switching is via shift lever position sensor circuits.

Brake light switch, replacing

The brake light switch is under left side of dashboard above the brake pedal.

– Switch hybrid system OFF (READY indicator not illuminated). See **3 Safety**.

> **WARNING —**
> • *Be sure hybrid system is OFF when servicing vehicle (READY indicator not illuminated). Failure to switch the hybrid system OFF could result in engine start at any time.*

◀ Working above brake pedal underneath dashboard:
   • Detach switch electrical connector.
   • Loosen switch lock nut, then unscrew switch from bracket.

– Installation is reverse of removal.

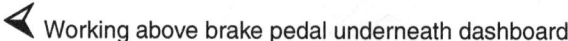

Tightening torque	
Lock nut to brake light switch bracket	26 Nm (19 ft-lb)

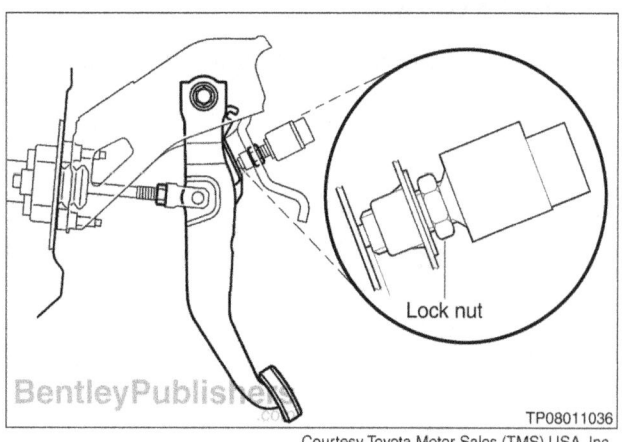

Lock nut

TP08011036

Courtesy Toyota Motor Sales (TMS) USA, Inc.

Door switch assembly, removing

The left front door armrest houses the following switches:

• Control switches for all four door windows

• Door lock master switch

• Outside mirror control switch

The right front door armrest houses the following:

• Right front window switch

• Door lock master switch

Left front door switch assembly is illustrated here. Right door switch is similar.

– Switch hybrid system OFF (READY indicator not illuminated). See **3 Safety**.

> **WARNING—**
> • *Be sure hybrid system is OFF when servicing vehicle (READY indicator not illuminated). Failure to switch the hybrid system OFF could result in engine start at any time.*

◄ Working at door switch assembly:

• Disengage 2 clips and 4 claws using a plastic prying tool.

• Lift off armrest and switch assembly.

• Detach switch electrical connector.

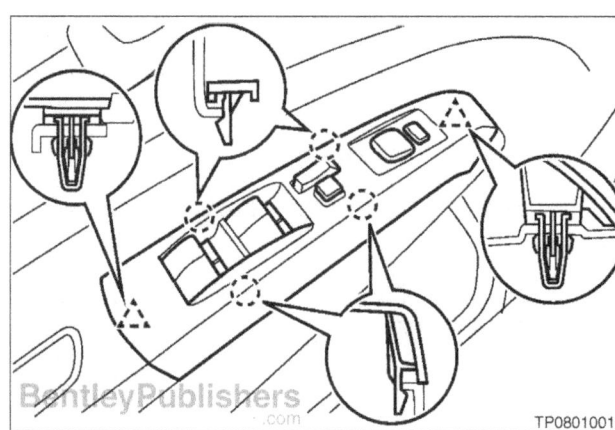

TP08010010

Courtesy Toyota Motor Sales (TMS) USA, Inc.

Hazard warning light switch, removing and installing

– Switch hybrid system OFF (READY indicator not illuminated). See **3 Safety**.

> **WARNING—**
> • Be sure hybrid system is OFF when servicing vehicle (READY indicator not illuminated). Failure to switch the hybrid system OFF could result in engine start at any time.

– Disconnect 12-volt auxiliary battery. See **3 Safety**.

> **WARNING—**
> • After disconnecting battery, wait at least 90 seconds before starting work on dashboard components.

> **CAUTION—**
> • Disconnecting 12-volt auxiliary battery causes loss of radio and navigation system presets. Record presets before disconnecting battery.

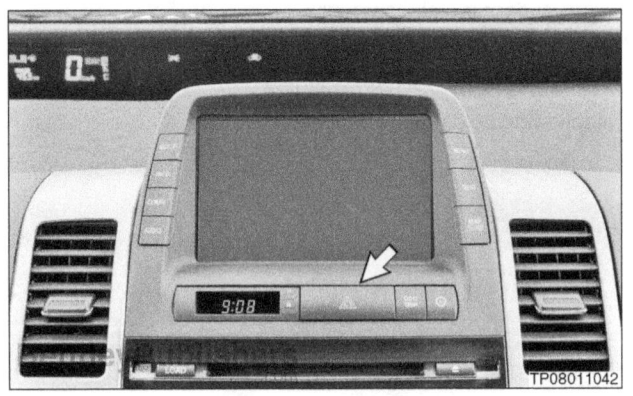

◄ Use plastic prying tool or tape-wrapped screwdriver tip to pry out hazard warning switch (**arrow**) from center of dashboard. Detach electrical connector.

– Installation is reverse of removal.

– Once battery is reconnected, reset radio and navigation system (if equipped) presets.

– Be sure to reinitialize windows. See **Window control system, reinitializing** in this chapter.

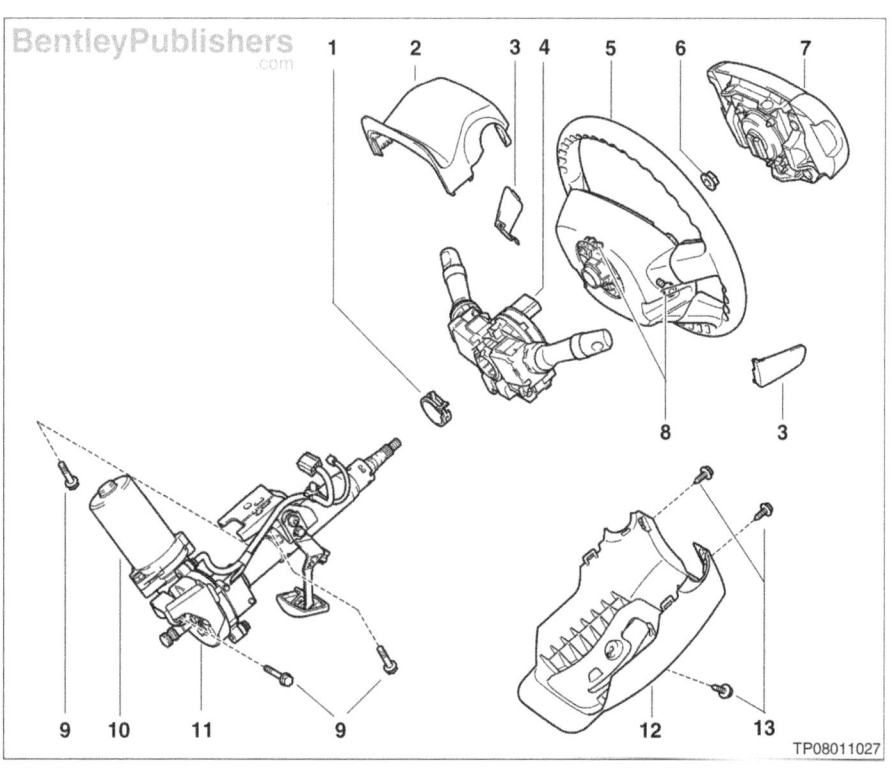

TP08011027

Courtesy Toyota Motor Sales (TMS) USA, Inc.

Steering column components

1. **Clamp**

2. **Upper cover**

3. **Steering wheel side cover**

4. **Stalk switch assembly**

5. **Steering wheel**

6. **Steering wheel mounting nut**
   • Tighten to 50 Nm (37 ft-lb)

7. **Horn button and airbag**

8. **Airbag mounting bolt**
   • Tighten to 8.8 Nm (78 in-lb)

9. **Steering column mounting bolt**
   • Tighten to 25 Nm (18 ft-lb)

10. **Power steering motor**

11. **Steering column, upper, with tilt control handle**

12. **Lower cover**

13. **Trim screws**

Steering column stalk switches, removing and installing

The stalk switch assembly includes switches for the following functions:

• Foglights

• Headlights, side marker lights, taillights, front running lights

• Headlight dimmer

• Turn signals

• Wipers and washers (front and rear)

To replace any of these switches, remove the horn button, driver airbag and steering wheel. Be sure to read the airbag warnings in **Warnings and Cautions** in this chapter before beginning work.

— Switch hybrid system OFF (READY indicator not illuminated). See **3 Safety**.

> **WARNING —**
> • *Be sure hybrid system is OFF when servicing vehicle (READY indicator not illuminated). Failure to switch the hybrid system OFF could result in engine start at any time.*

— Disconnect 12-volt auxiliary battery. See **3 Safety**.

— Place steering wheel in straight-ahead position, then remove horn button, driver airbag and steering wheel. See **8 Brakes, Suspension and Steering**.

◀ Working underneath steering column, remove tilt control handle mounting screws (**arrows**).

Courtesy Toyota Motor Sales (TMS) USA, Inc.

◀ Remove steering column cover screws (**arrows**). Lift covers off column.

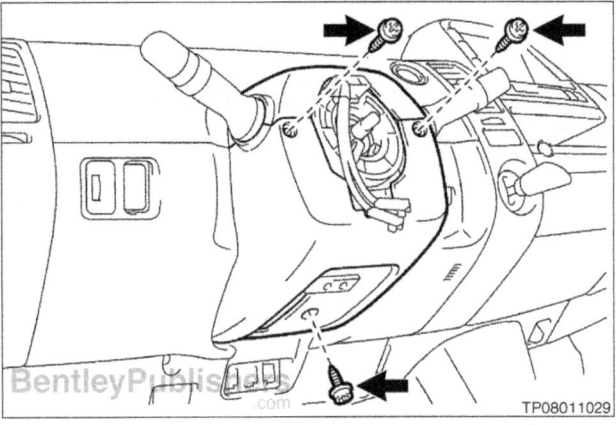

Courtesy Toyota Motor Sales (TMS) USA, Inc.

◀ Working at top of steering column:
• Detach connectors from airbag spiral contact (spring contact ring).
• Disengage 3 claws (**broken circles**) and remove spiral contact assembly.

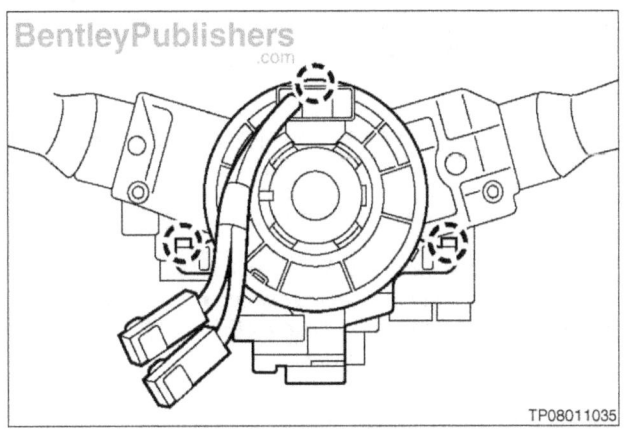

Courtesy Toyota Motor Sales (TMS) USA, Inc.

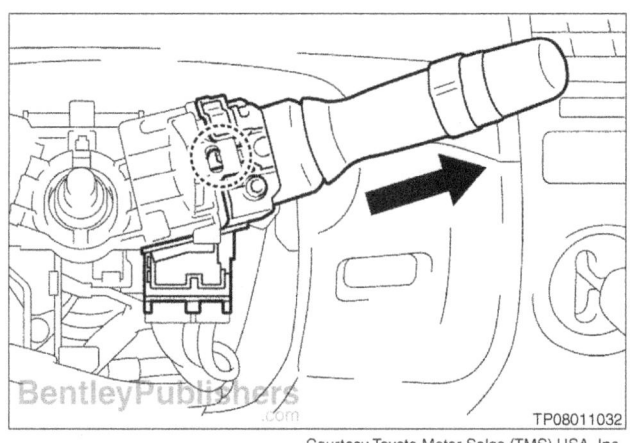

TP08011032

Courtesy Toyota Motor Sales (TMS) USA, Inc.

Wiper and washer switch, removing

◀ Working at wiper and washer switch:
- Detach electrical connector.
- Push on claw (**broken circle**) to disengage and remove switch (**arrow**).

> **CAUTION—**
> • *Claw breaks if pressed too hard.*

– Installation is reverse of removal.

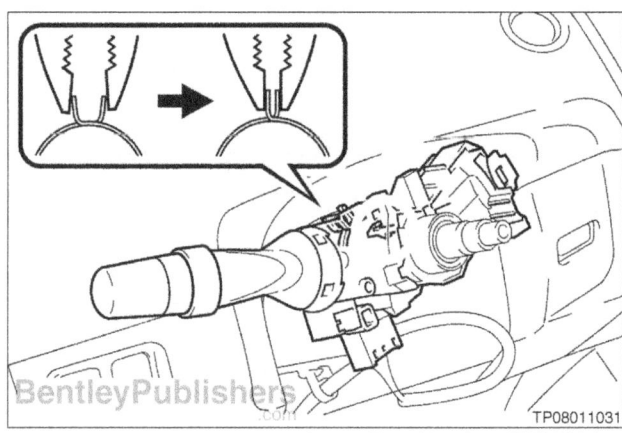

TP08011031

Courtesy Toyota Motor Sales (TMS) USA, Inc.

Turn signal, exterior lights and headlight dimmer switch, removing

◀ Working at turn signal switch:
- Detach electrical connectors.
- Remove band clamp (**inset**).

◀ Disengage mounting claws (**insets**) and remove switch assembly (**arrow**).

– When installing, check to see that tab in switch matches recess in rotating stopper.

> **CAUTION—**
> • *Make sure turn signal switch is in the neutral position or switch pin may snap off.*

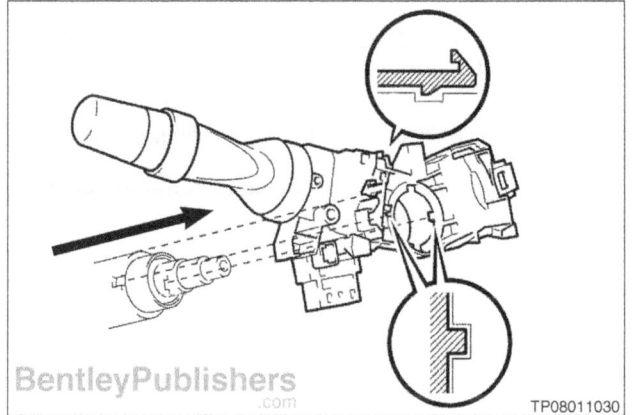

TP08011030

Courtesy Toyota Motor Sales (TMS) USA, Inc.

10

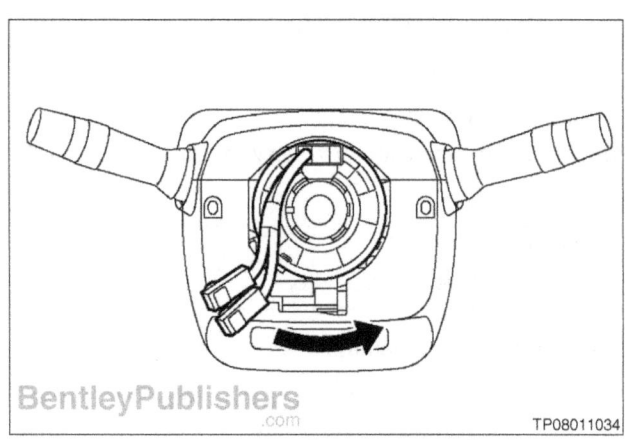

TP08011034
Courtesy Toyota Motor Sales (TMS) USA, Inc.

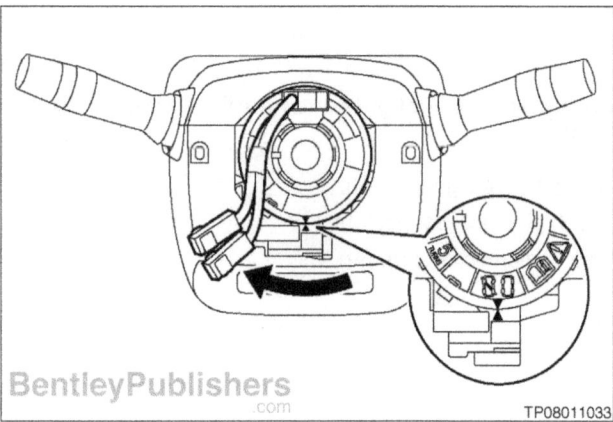

TP08011033
Courtesy Toyota Motor Sales (TMS) USA, Inc.

◄ Installing airbag spiral contact:

- Place assembly on steering column. Press firmly to lock in place.
- Reconnect harness connectors.
- Rotate spiral contact counterclockwise (**arrow**) to stop.

◄ Rotate spiral contact clockwise (**arrow**) approx. 2½ turns to line up marks (**inset**).

***NOTE*—**

- *Spiral contact rotates approx. 2½ turns to both left and right of center position.*

– If replacing spiral contact assembly with new, remove lock pin before installing steering wheel.

– Install steering wheel, horn button and driver airbag.

> ***CAUTION*—**
> - *Do not pinch airbag harness.*

Tightening torques	
Airbag and horn button to steering wheel	8.8 Nm (78 in-lb)
Steering wheel to steering shaft	50 Nm (37 ft-lb)

– Once 12-volt auxiliary battery is reconnected:

- Check horn function.
- Switch ignition ON and monitor SRS warning light. SRS self-test lasts about 6 seconds, after which warning light switches OFF.
- Reset radio and navigation system (if equipped) presets.

– Be sure to reinitialize windows. See **Window control system, reinitializing** in this chapter.

WIPERS AND WASHERS

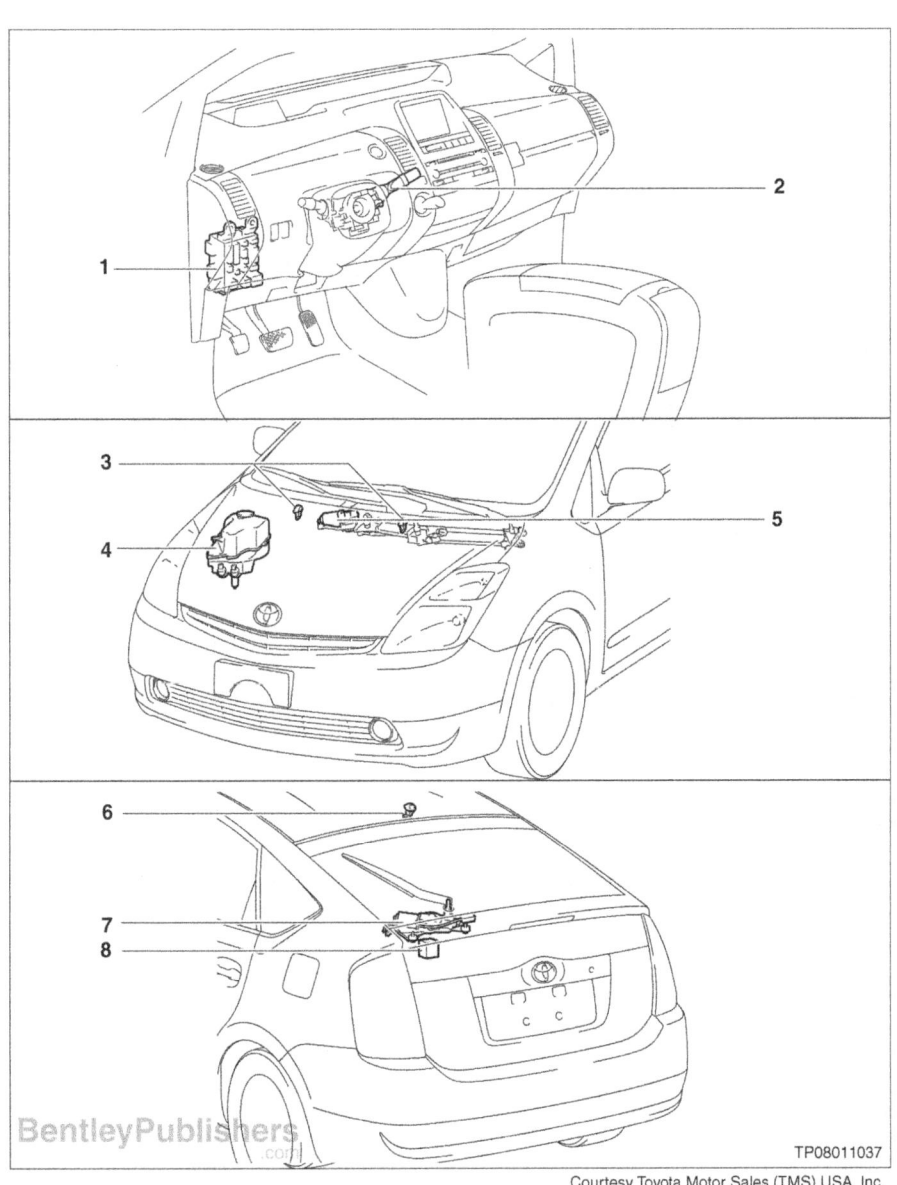

TP08011037

Courtesy Toyota Motor Sales (TMS) USA, Inc.

Wiper and washer system components

1. **Power supply components in driver side junction block under left end of dashboard:**
   IG1 relay
   WSH fuse
   WIP fuse
   - See **12 Electrical Component Locations**

2. **Wiper and washer switch**
   - See **Steering column stalk switches, removing and installing** in this chapter

3. **Windshield washer nozzles**

4. **Washer fluid reservoir and pump**

5. **Windshield wiper motor assembly**
   - See **Windshield wiper motor assembly, removing and installing** in this chapter

6. **Rear window washer nozzle**

7. **Rear window wiper motor**

8. **Rear window wiper relay**

10

Windshield wiper arms, removing and installing

– Before removing wiper arms, make sure wipers are in PARK position.

– Switch hybrid system OFF (READY indicator not illuminated). See **3 Safety**.

> **WARNING** —
> • *Be sure hybrid system is OFF when servicing vehicle (READY indicator not illuminated). Failure to switch the hybrid system OFF could result in engine start at any time.*

◄ With engine hood open, remove wiper arm mounting nut trim cap.

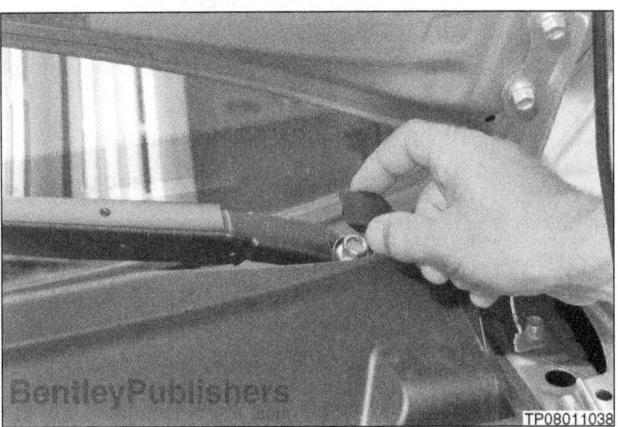

◄ Remove wiper arm mounting nuts (**arrows**).

– Remove wiper arms.

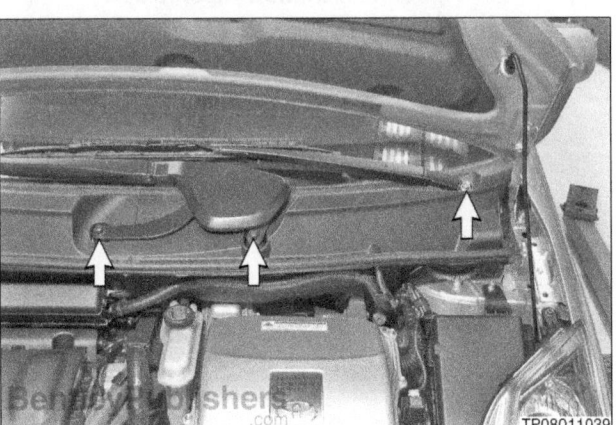

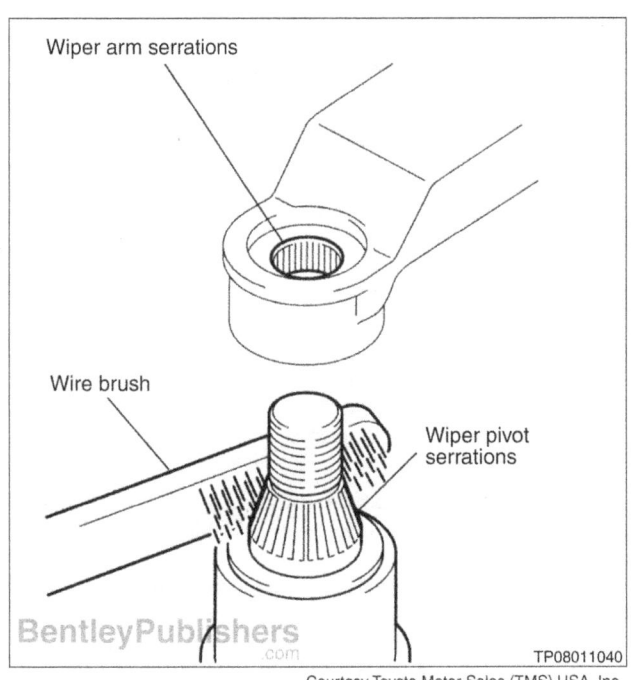

Courtesy Toyota Motor Sales (TMS) USA, Inc.

◀ Before reinstallation, use wire brush to clean wiper arm and wiper pivot serrations.

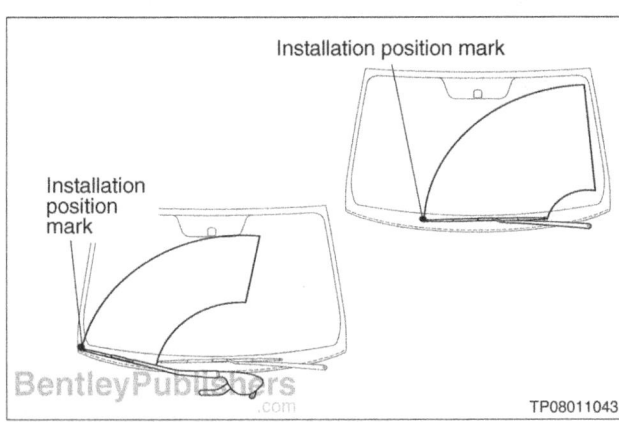

Courtesy Toyota Motor Sales (TMS) USA, Inc.

◀ When installing, align wiper blades with installation position marks at base of windshield. Push down on wiper arm hinge in order to start wiper arm mounting nut(s).

Tightening torque	
Wiper arm to wiper pivot	21 Nm (15 ft-lb)

10

Windshield wiper motor assembly, removing and installing

– Before removing wiper arms, make sure wipers are in PARK position.

– Switch hybrid system OFF (READY indicator not illuminated). See **3 Safety**.

> **WARNING —**
> • *Be sure hybrid system is OFF when servicing vehicle (READY indicator not illuminated). Failure to switch the hybrid system OFF could result in engine start at any time.*

– With engine hood open, remove wiper arms. See **Windshield wiper arms, removing and installing** in this chapter.

– Remove windshield cowl cover and cowl top ventilation louvers on right and left. See **9 Body**.

◀ Remove wiper assembly mounting bolts (**arrows**) and lift out complete wiper assembly. Detach wiper motor electrical connector.

– Installation is reverse of removal. Reconnect electrical connector.

Tightening torques	
Wiper arm to wiper pivot	21 Nm (15 ft-lb)
Wiper assembly to cowl	5.5 Nm (49 in-lb)

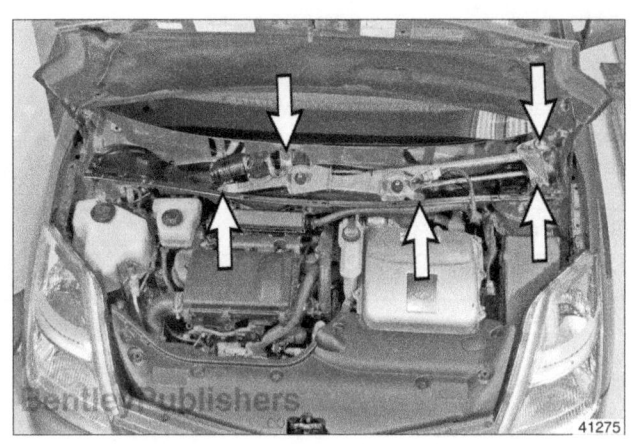

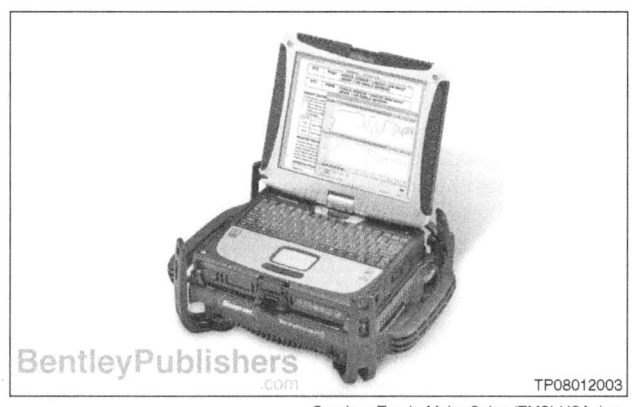

TP08012003

Courtesy Toyota Motor Sales (TMS) USA, Inc.

11

Diagnostics

Troubleshooting, DTC tables

11

GENERAL

This chapter covers Prius inspection mode, on-board diagnostics, diagnostic scan tools, diagnostic tips for specific Prius problems, and diagnostic trouble codes and information codes.

Prius safety precautions

In addition to the safety warnings given here, always read and observe the **Warnings**, **Cautions** and safety procedures in **3 Safety** before working on vehicle. Orange-colored cables carry lethal high voltage. Use extreme care when working near high voltage cables and components.

> **WARNING—**
> • *Risk of electrocution! Avoid touching orange-colored high voltage wiring and high voltage components unless you are certain that high voltage is not present.*
> • *The Prius hybrid system has voltages as high as 500 volts. Voltages over 60 volts DC and 25 volts AC are a shock hazard.*

The Prius engine may start at any time if the hybrid system is in **READY** mode. See **3 Safety** for instructions on turning OFF the hybrid system.

> **WARNING—**
> • *Be sure hybrid system is OFF when servicing vehicle (READY indicator not illuminated). Failure to switch the hybrid system OFF could result in engine start at any time.*

PRIUS INSPECTION MODE

Prius inspection mode is a method Toyota has provided to allow the gasoline engine to run continuously for inspection purposes, testing and diagnosis, or other reasons.

During normal operation, the Prius gasoline engine is controlled by the hybrid system. The hybrid vehicle electronic control unit (HV ECU) determines whether the engine must run or not. The engine does not run continuously and may stop running at any time when the HV ECU determines that engine power is not needed to move the vehicle, recharge the high voltage battery, or for any other purpose.

State inspection procedures or other diagnostic procedures may require the use of inspection mode. Prius inspection mode can be entered using a Toyota scan tool (or equivalent), or manually without a scan tool.

Entering inspection mode (with scan tool)

◄ Enter inspection mode using a Toyota scan tool (or equivalent):

1. Be sure hybrid system is OFF (READY indicator not illuminated).
2. Connect Toyota scan tool or equivalent tool to the OBD II connector (DLC3). Scan tool must be CAN-compatible, see **Diagnostic Scan Tools** in this chapter.
3. Turn the hybrid system ON (READY indicator illuminated).
4. Turn the tester ON.
5. Follow tester instructions for this ACTIVE TEST function.
6. The hybrid system warning on the multi-function display should flash.
7. The engine should start and run continuously.

— When in inspection mode, engine speed depends upon accelerator pedal position. See **Table a**.

— To exit inspection mode, turn the hybrid system OFF.

OBD II connector

TP086002

> **CAUTION—**
> • When entering inspection mode, any stored diagnostic trouble codes (DTCs) will cause the master warning light, and possibly other warnings, to illuminate. If this occurs, exit inspection mode and diagnose the DTCs.

11

Entering inspection mode (without scan tool)

Enter inspection mode without a scan tool:

1. Check to be sure air-conditioning is OFF, parking brake is set, gear selector is in P position.

2. Check to be sure that the engine is warm. Turn the hybrid system ON (READY indicator illuminated). The engine should stop within several seconds after starting.

3. Turn the hybrid system OFF (READY indicator not illuminated).

4. Perform the following steps within 60 seconds.

5. Turn the hybrid system from OFF to IG-ON position (do not depress brake pedal, and depress and release POWER button twice).

6. With the shift lever in P position, fully depress and release the accelerator pedal 2 times.

7. Depress brake pedal and move gear selector to N position. Fully depress and release the accelerator pedal 2 times.

8. Depress brake pedal and move gear selector to P position. Fully depress and release the accelerator pedal 2 times.

9. The hybrid system warning on the multi-function display should flash.

10. Turn the hybrid system ON (READY indicator illuminated). The engine should start and run continuously in inspection mode.

— When in inspection mode, engine speed depends upon accelerator pedal position. See **Table a**.

— To exit inspection mode, turn the hybrid system OFF.

> *CAUTION—*
> * *When entering inspection mode, any stored diagnostic trouble codes (DTCs) will cause the master warning light, and possibly other warnings, to illuminate. If this occurs, exit inspection mode and diagnose the DTCs.*

Table a. Engine speed in inspection mode

Accelerator pedal position	Engine speed
Accelerator pedal not depressed	idle (approx. 1000 rpm)
Accelerator pedal depressed > 60%	approx. 1500 rpm
Accelerator pedal depressed < 60%	approx. 2250 rpm

NOTE—
* *There is another way to force the Prius gasoline engine to run continuously, although this method does not permit the engine to idle. With the hybrid system ON (READY indicator illuminated) and gear selector in PARK, simply depress the accelerator. Engine speed corresponds to accelerator pedal position as shown in **Table a**, and the engine runs as long as the accelerator is depressed. Release the accelerator to stop the engine.*

ON-BOARD DIAGNOSTICS II (OBD II)

On-board diagnostics II (OBD II) standards were developed by the SAE (Society of Automotive Engineers) and CARB (California Air Resources Board) as way to reduce harmful emissions from passenger vehicles. OBD II represents the second generation of on-board self-diagnostic equipment requirements. In simple terms, OBD II adds self-monitoring and self-diagnostic capabilities to vehicle engine management systems.

OBD II standards were originally mandated for California vehicles. Since 1996 they have been required for all passenger vehicles sold in the United States.

On-board diagnostic capabilities are incorporated into the hardware and software of the engine control module (ECM) to monitor virtually every engine and powertrain component that can affect vehicle emissions. OBD II capabilities include:

- Monitoring the performance and condition of emissions-related components and systems (see **Monitors** in this chapter).

- When a fault is detected, stores diagnostic trouble codes (DTCs) which supply information about the fault (see **Diagnostic trouble codes (DTCs)** in this chapter).

- When a fault is detected, informs the driver by illuminating a warning lamp (see **Malfunction indicator lamp (MIL)** in this chapter).

- Storing information about whether or not the self-diagnostic software is ready to monitor the systems and components (see **Readiness codes** in this chapter).

Monitors

Emissions-related components and systems are checked by diagnostic software routines called monitors that are stored in electronic control units and modules (ECUs and ECMs). Monitors verify proper functioning by running tests and checks on specific emission control sensors, circuits, components, and system functions.

OBD II regulations require that the software be capable of monitoring the following engine management emissions-related systems:

- Air / fuel ratio and oxygen sensors
- Catalyst efficiency
- Engine misfire
- A comprehensive list of components (emission-related sensors and other components)
- Evaporative emissions (EVAP) control system
- Fuel trim (rich / lean or air / fuel ratio control)
- Secondary air injection (Prius not equipped)
- Exhaust gas recirculation (EGR) (Prius not equipped)

Emission control systems vary by vehicle model, year, and options. For example, 2004-2008 Prius vehicles are not equipped with secondary air injection or EGR, so monitors for these emission control systems are not required.

Monitors check sensor circuits for these electrical conditions:

• Circuit open

• Circuit shorted

• Circuit grounded

• Circuit rationality (whether the signal from a sensor makes sense when compared with other sensors and vehicle operating conditions at that moment)

When a fault is detected, the OBD II system has the ability to store diagnostic trouble codes (DTCs) and to inform the driver by illuminating a warning lamp. See **Diagnostic trouble codes (DTCs)** and **Malfunction indicator lamp (MIL)** in this chapter.

Drive cycles

Monitors usually check specified systems while the vehicle is driven (although sometimes EVAP monitors perform their checks when the vehicle is OFF and parked). Typically, most monitors will run their tests during normal driving, but Toyota and other manufacturers specify drive cycles to ensure that all monitors can run.

A drive cycle very specifically defines how to drive the vehicle. Some drive cycles vary conditions enough to allow all monitors to run. Sometimes, the manufacturer specifies different drive cycles for each monitor. The latter is the approach that Toyota has used for the Prius.

A drive cycle usually begins with a cold start, and the vehicle is allowed to be brought up to operating temperature. For example, the Prius drive cycle for the catalyst monitor states that engine coolant temperature must reach at least 80°C (176°F). Sometimes, a maximum starting temperature is specified, and manufacturer's specifications can vary. A drive cycle is complete when the specified diagnostic monitors have run their tests without interruption and have set readiness codes. Readiness codes are a "flag" which indicate whether the OBD II system is actually ready to monitor the various emission control systems on the vehicle. See **Readiness codes** in this chapter.

Below is shown a graph for a typical drive cycle. This is the drive cycle for the Prius air / fuel sensor and oxygen sensor monitors. This graph, and enabling conditions that must be met for the monitor to run, are shown in the Toyota technical information system (TIS). To access TIS, see **4 Service and Repair Fundamentals**.

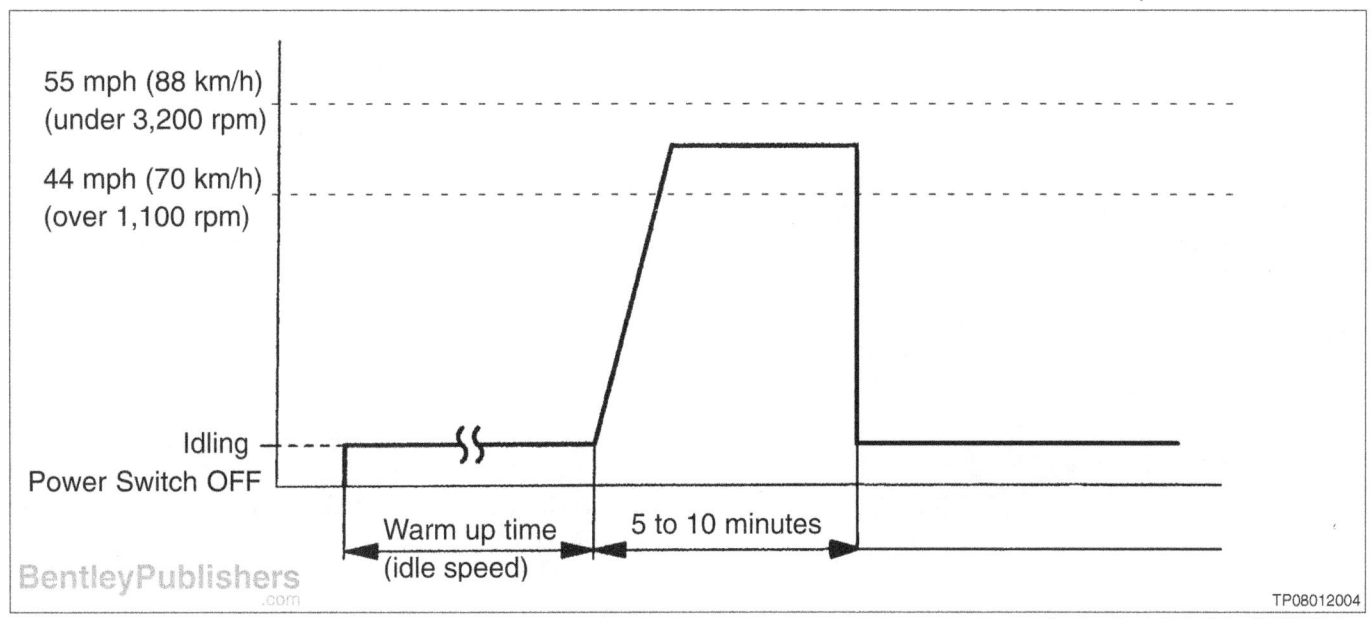

55 mph (88 km/h)
(under 3,200 rpm)

44 mph (70 km/h)
(over 1,100 rpm)

Idling
Power Switch OFF

Warm up time
(idle speed)

5 to 10 minutes

TP08012004

Courtesy Toyota Motor Sales (TMS) USA, Inc.

Readiness codes

Readiness codes are a mandated Inspection / maintenance (I/M) requirement of OBD II. A readiness code is stored in the ECM after a monitor completes its diagnostic check of specified components and systems. Readiness codes indicate whether the OBD II system is actually ready to monitor the various emission control systems on the vehicle. The vehicle must complete a drive cycle to set all readiness codes to the "ready" state. The readiness code is binary:

• 0 for ready

• 1 for not ready

When all zeros are displayed on a scan tool, the system has established readiness. Readiness codes can be displayed using Toyota and equivalent scan tools.

Readiness codes are set to 1 (not ready) when:

• The 12-volt auxiliary battery or ECM is disconnected.

• DTCs are erased after completion of repairs and a drive cycle is not completed.

The readiness code function was designed to prevent manipulating an I/M emission test procedure by clearing fault codes or by disconnecting the ECM or battery.

Courtesy Toyota Motor Sales (TMS) USA, Inc.

Malfunction indicator lamp (MIL)

◀ OBD II regulations require that the malfunction indicator lamp (MIL or CHECK ENGINE lamp) on the instrument panel illuminate whenever the OBD II software detects a fault that may cause vehicle emissions levels to increase more than 1.5 times the Federal standards.

The MIL illuminates under the following conditions:

• Engine management system fault is detected during two consecutive OBD II drive cycles. See **Drive cycles** in this chapter.

• Catalyst damaging fault detected (MIL begins to flash immediately when detected).

• Component malfunction may cause emissions to exceed 1.5 times OBD II standards.

• Manufacturer-defined specifications for components, circuit, or system are exceeded.

• Implausible input signal from sensor.

• Engine misfire detected.

• Evaporative emission (EVAP) system leak or purge flow fault.

• ECM fails to enter closed-loop operation within specified time.

If the malfunction does not recur during 3 consecutive trips, the MIL is turned OFF but the DTCs remain recorded in the ECM memory.

Erasing the OBD II fault memory and extinguishing the MIL can only be accomplished using a scan tool. Removing ECM connectors or disconnecting the 12-volt auxiliary battery does not erase fault memory.

Diagnostic trouble codes (DTCs)

Whenever the OBD II software detects a fault that may cause vehicle emissions levels to increase more than 1.5 times the Federal standards, in addition to illuminating the MIL, the OBD II system also stores diagnostic trouble codes (DTCs) in ECM memory. DTCs are a 5-digit alphanumeric codes that contain information about the detected fault so that a technician can accurately find and fix the problem.

Some DTCs and their definitions are standardized by Society of Automotive Engineers (SAE) standard J2012. These are known as generic DTCs. All manufacturers are required to apply the SAE definitions to these generic DTCs. Here are examples of SAE generic DTCs:

P0120 Throttle/Pedal Position Sensor/ Switch "A" Circuit

P0441 Evaporative Emission Control System Incorrect Purge Flow

Manufacturers can also create their own proprietary (manufacturer-specific) DTCs with their own definitions. Here is an example of a proprietary DTC created by Toyota for the Prius:

P2239 Oxygen Sensor Pumping Current Circuit High (for A/F sensor Bank 1 sensor 1)

While another manufacturer may also use the DTC "P2239", the definition of the code can be whatever the manufacturer wishes and is likely to be different than Toyota's definition.

The following table explains the meaning of each DTC digit:

Table b. DTC digits	
1st digit P B C U	powertrain body chassis Communication / networking
2nd digit 0 1 - 3	SAE (standardized DTCs) Toyota (mfg-specific DTCs)
3rd digit 0 1 2 3 4 5 6 7 8, 9, A - F	total system air / fuel induction fuel injection ignition system or misfire auxiliary emission control vehicle speed & idle control ECM inputs / outputs transmission Toyota (mfg-specific DTCs)
4th - 5th digits 0 - 9, A - F	individual circuits or components

11

For a listing of Prius DTCs and their definitions, see **Diagnostic Trouble Code (DTC) and Information Code Tables** in this chapter.

DTC detection logic

When a fault is detected for the first time in a system being checked, applicable DTCs are stored in ECM memory. However, the MIL does not illuminate after this first occurrence of the DTC (exception: severe engine misfire will cause the MIL to illuminate and flash immediately).

DTCs stored after the first occurrence are sometimes called pending DTCs. DTCs are stored in memory only after a completed drive cycle.

If the same fault is again detected during the **next consecutive** drive cycle, then the MIL will illuminate and the DTC will be stored as a mature or hard code. Two complete and consecutive drive cycles with the fault present are required to illuminate the MIL. This is called two-trip logic. Most faults use two-trip logic to set DTCs.

If the monitor was unable to check the fault because the second drive cycle was not completed, then the ECM counts the third drive cycle as the next consecutive drive cycle. The MIL illuminates if the fault is still present when the system is checked.

Once the MIL is illuminated, it remains illuminated until the vehicle completes three consecutive drive cycles without detecting the fault. However, even after the MIL is extinguished, the DTC remains in memory. The fault code is cleared from memory automatically when the vehicle completes 40 consecutive drive cycles without the fault being detected.

There are exceptions to two-trip logic. Some faults are considered so serious that a DTC will set immediately after the first occurrence. Severe engine misfire is an example.

Information codes (INFs)

In order to increase the amount of stored diagnostic information, Toyota has appended a numeric suffix (1 -3 digits) to some 5-digit DTCs. This additional code is called an **information code**. Information codes permit Toyota to define a DTC more precisely. A single DTC may have many possible information codes, each with a slightly different definition or fault description. Here are two examples of the same DTC with two different information codes, and their definitions:

P0705-572 Transmission Range Sensor Circuit (+B short in shift main sensor circuit)

P0705-573 Transmission Range Sensor Circuit (Open or ground in shift sub sensor circuit)

Not all systems are assigned information codes. Available information codes are shown in the DTC tables. See **Diagnostic Trouble Code (DTC) and Information Code Tables** in this chapter.

Freeze frame data

When a DTC is recorded in memory, the ECM also records data about engine and operating conditions that were present when the DTC occurred. This information, called freeze frame data, is a "snapshot" of information from various sensors at the moment that the DTC was recorded. Typical freeze frame data includes vehicle speed, engine speed, engine temperature, fuel trim, throttle position, ignition timing, and other parameters. When diagnosing a problem, freeze frame data can help determine conditions and what was happening when the fault occurred.

OBD II connector

◀ DTCs and other OBD II data can be accessed and retrieved from ECM fault memory with specialized scan tool equipment. The scan tool is connected to the vehicle at the OBD II connector. All passenger vehicles sold in the United States since 1996 have a standardized 16-pin OBD II connector under the dashboard.

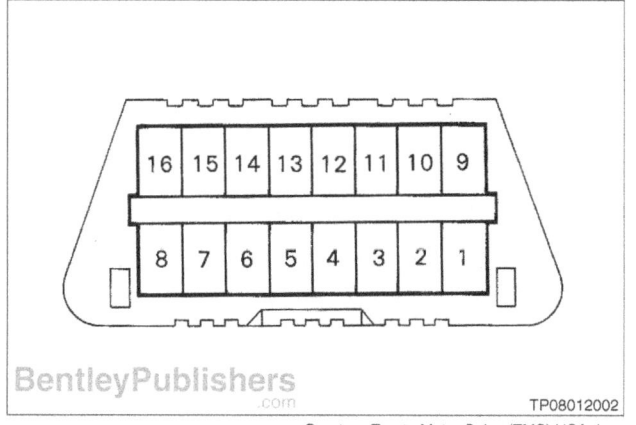

TP08012002

Courtesy Toyota Motor Sales (TMS) USA, Inc.

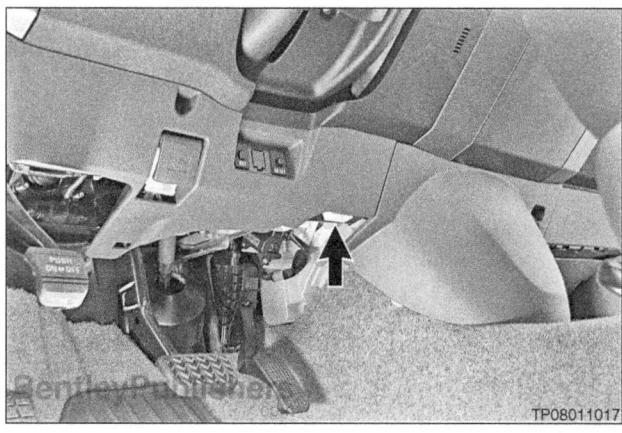

TP08011017

◀ This is the OBD II connector location on the 2004-2008 Prius.

For more information on the use of scan tools for retrieving OBD II data and other diagnostic information, see **Diagnostic Scan Tools** in this chapter.

11

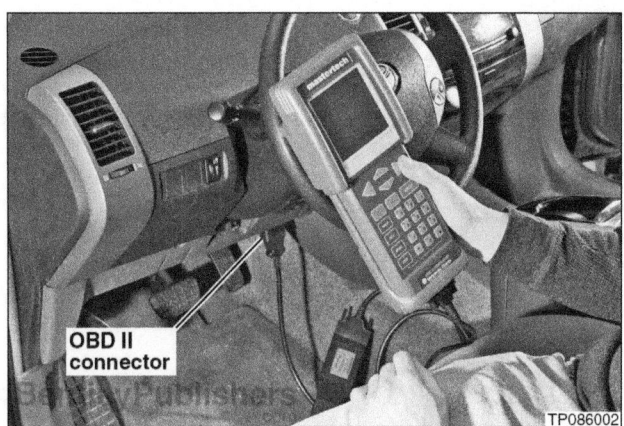

OBD II
connector

TP086002

DIAGNOSTIC SCAN TOOLS

A scan tool is an electronic diagnostic tool that can be connected to a vehicle to retrieve information stored in on-board electronic control units (ECUs). The Prius, like all vehicles in production today, is equipped with many ECUs that control and manage various functions and systems.

◀ A scan tool can be easily connected to the 16-pin OBD II connector in a vehicle. This connector is present on all vehicles sold in the United States since 1996. Since the 2004-2008 Prius wiring system includes a controller area network (CAN), the scan tool must be CAN-enabled. Some older scan tools, such as the Toyota Mastertech hand-held tester, require an external CAN interface module. Newer scan tools have built-in CAN compatibility and do not require this external module.

Manufacturer-specific scan tools

Scan tools with full capability are available from vehicle manufacturers such as Toyota. Aftermarket scan tools from third-party suppliers with similar functionality are also available.

Manufacturer-specific scan tools typically have most or all of these capabilities:

- Display both generic and manufacturer-specific diagnostic trouble codes (DTCs) for ECM-controlled powertrain faults
- Display both generic and manufacturer-specific diagnostic trouble codes (DTCs) for other vehicle systems such as brakes, climate control, audio system, etc.
- Display freeze frame data for stored DTCs
- Display monitor readiness data
- Display live data from various vehicle sensors and systems
- Ability to control and turn components and systems ON and OFF with the ACTIVE TEST mode.
- Log vehicle sensor data while driving
- Wireless communication capability between vehicle and scan tool
- Diagnostic oscilloscope function
- Diagnostic testing functions such as multimeter and noise-vibration-harshness (NVH) tests
- Manufacturer-specific functions such as immobilizer key registration
- Ability to reprogram ECUs (when connected to factory service network)
- Ability to access manufacturer's service information such as TIS (when connected to factory service network)

Scan tools are built into either an application-specific housing or the software is installed on an existing available PC computer (usually a laptop).

41293

◀ The Toyota Mastertech hand-held tester is a scan tool that is built into an application-specific housing. Toyota started phasing-out this tester in 2007.

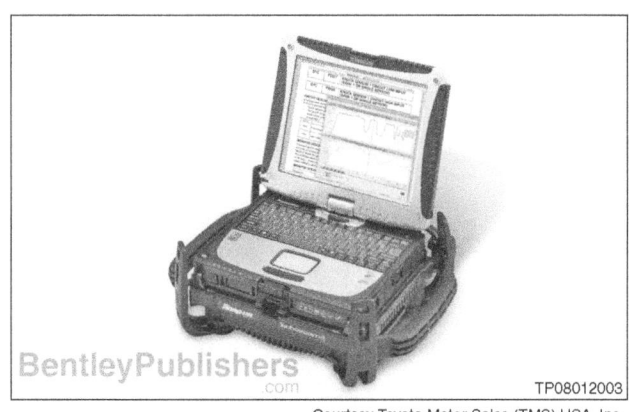

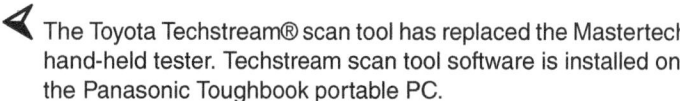
TP08012003

Courtesy Toyota Motor Sales (TMS) USA, Inc.

◀ The Toyota Techstream® scan tool has replaced the Mastertech hand-held tester. Techstream scan tool software is installed on the Panasonic Toughbook portable PC.

NOTE —

• *Third-party manufacturers such as AutoEnginuity and others sell scan tools and scan tool software that emulates some or all of the capabilities of the factory tools.*

Generic scan tools

TP08012007

◀ Generic scan tools can display SAE-mandated generic DTCs and other information. Generic scan tools are available from many third-part suppliers and their capabilities vary. These tools can access the SAE-mandated generic information on any OBD II compatible vehicle. Typical generic scan tools have these capabilities:

• Display generic diagnostic trouble codes (DTCs) for ECM-controlled powertrain faults

• Display freeze frame data for stored DTCs

• Display monitor readiness data

• Display live data from various vehicle sensors and systems

11

PRIUS HINTS AND DIAGNOSTIC TIPS

Below are hints and diagnostic tips to help you deal with several known conditions that may occur on the 2004-2008 Prius.

Audible reverse warning ON/OFF

The audible warning that sounds when reverse is selected can be toggled ON and OFF with this procedure:

1. Turn hybrid system ON (READY indicator illuminated).
2. Set the Trip / ODO display to ODO (Odometer). If it is already on ODO and you have a 2005 - 2008 model, go to step 5. On 2004 models, you may still have to cycle through Trip A, Trip B then back to ODO.
3. Turn hybrid system OFF (READY indicator not illuminated).
4. Depress brake and again turn hybrid system ON (READY indicator illuminated). Keep brake pedal depressed.
5. As soon as the "Ready" light illuminates, press and hold the Trip / ODO button for at least 10 seconds.
6. While still holding the Trip / ODO button, shift the gear selector from P to R and back to P.
7. Release the Trip / ODO button.
8. The Trip / ODO display should now read "b on" or "b off". Use the Trip / ODO button to toggle between the two options. "b on" = the audible reverse beep is on. "b off" = the audible reverse beep is off.
9. Turn hybrid system OFF (READY indicator not illuminated).

MIL ON and DTC set after engine coolant drain and refill

Disconnecting the coolant heat storage pump connector may cause the ECM to set diagnostic trouble codes (P1151 or P2601) in memory and to illuminate the malfunction indicator lamp (MIL). The Prius ECM will periodically actuate the electric coolant heat storage pump when the hybrid system is in the OFF position to verify that the coolant heat storage system is functioning properly. If the ECM attempts to actuate the the pump with the electrical connector disconnected a DTC may be set. Disconnecting the coolant heat storage pump connector is a required to drain and refill engine coolant. Use a Toyota scan tool or equivalent to clear DTCs after completing the engine coolant drain and refill procedure. See **5 Engine** for more information.

Tire pressure warning system (TPWS) warning lamp ON

In addition to indicating low tire pressure, a flashing or illuminated Tire Pressure Warning System (TPWS) warning lamp can indicate a fault or malfunction in the TPWS system. Possible causes include:

• Tire pressure sensor/transmitter battery failure

• Wheels not equipped with tire pressure sensor/transmitters

• ID codes of tire pressure sensor/transmitters not registered (recorded) in tire pressure warning ECU

• Other electronic device with similar radio frequency in use

• Window tint installed that affects transmission of radio frequency signals

• Large amount of snow or ice in wheel housings

• Aftermarket wheels or tires installed

• Tire chains installed

• Extremely high tire pressure - greater than 500 kPa (72.5 psi)

Check TPWS and use a Toyota scan tool or equivalent to clear DTCs. See **8 Brakes, Suspension and Steering** for more information.

Evaporative emission control (EVAP) system DTC set

Overfilling or topping off a Prius fuel tank may cause fuel to enter the evaporative emissions (EVAP) system. This may cause a diagnostic trouble code (DTC) to set and may illuminate a warning in the instrument cluster. Overfilling the fuel tank may also cause fuel to enter and damage the EVAP system charcoal canister. If this occurs, the charcoal canister must be replaced. See **6 Emission Controls**.

Transaxle PARK function failure, turning vehicle OFF

The Prius transaxle gear selector and park lock systems are electronic and use the 12-volt auxiliary battery for power. If the 12-volt auxiliary battery is discharged or is disconnected, the vehicle cannot be started or shifted out of park.

If Prius cannot be placed in PARK, there may be a gear selector malfunction that is preventing the transaxle from engaging the park lock. This condition may also prevent you from turning the vehicle OFF with the POWER button. If these symptoms occur, stop the vehicle and apply the parking brake. This will bypass the fault and permit shutdown of the hybrid system. Note that it will not be possible to restart the vehicle until the fault is corrected.

11

MIL ON after brake pad replacement

The 2004-2008 Prius is equipped with the electronically controlled brake (ECB) system. Repair and maintenance procedures such as retracting brake caliper pistons, installing new brake pads, replacing brake rotors, and bleeding the brakes may cause DTCs to set when the brake pedal is depressed after the repair is completed. Perform the following procedure to extinguish the MIL lamp if this occurs.

NOTE—
- *This procedure requires the use of a Toyota scan tool or equivalent.*

— Switch hybrid system OFF (READY indicator not illuminated). See **3 Safety**.

WARNING—
- *Make sure hybrid system is OFF when servicing vehicle (READY indicator not illuminated). Failure to switch the hybrid system OFF could result in engine start at any time.*

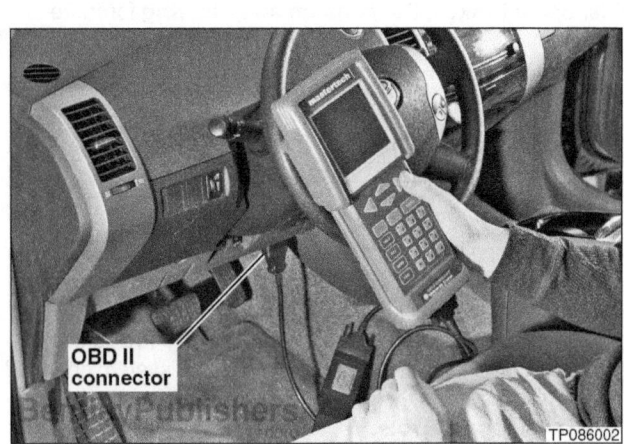

OBD II connector

TP086002

◄ Connect Toyota scan tool or equivalent to the OBD II connector (DLC3). When connecting the Toyota hand-held tester to a 2004-2008 Prius, you must also use a CAN interface module.

— Turn hybrid system ON (IG-ON or READY indicator illuminated). Turn tester ON.

— Read DTCs. If DTC listed in table below is present, continue with following steps. If DTC other than ones listed in table is present, you must first diagnose that DTC before continuing.

DTC	Description
C1341	Front Hydraulic System RH Malfunction
C1342	Front Hydraulic System LH Malfunction
C1343	Rear Hydraulic System RH Malfunction
C1344	Rear Hydraulic System LH Malfunction

— Delete DTC.

— Test drive the vehicle.

— If DTC does not return, the repair is complete.

— If DTC returns, additional diagnosis is required. The following conditions may cause DTCs to occur:
- Brake fluid leaks
- Brake vibration caused by uneven brake rotor wear
- Foreign matter in brake system solenoid valve
- Brake system line pressure drop during bleeding
- Brake pad or rotor replacement

See **4 Service and Repair Fundamentals** and **8 Brakes, Suspension and Steering** for more information. Additional diagnostic and repair information is available from the Toyota Technical Information System (TIS) website.

DIAGNOSTIC TROUBLE CODE (DTC) AND INFORMATION CODE TABLES

The following pages have tables listing diagnostic trouble codes (DTCs) and Toyota information codes (INFs) for various Prius systems. Table contents are provided by Toyota Motor Corporation. Introductory information for each system explains the code structure, code definitions, and how to retrieve codes.

Air-conditioning system

The table(s) in this section contain Air-conditioning system DTCs, Toyota INF codes, code definitions and likely trouble areas.

Retrieving DTCs

Air-conditioning system DTCs and information codes can be retrieved by using Toyota scan tool or equivalent. See **Diagnostic Scan Tools** in this chapter.

Clearing DTCs

Clear air-conditioning DTCs with Toyota scan tool or equivalent.

— Connect scan tool to OBD II connector.

— Turn hybrid system ON (IG-ON, READY indicator not illuminated).

— Operate tester to clear DTCs. Refer to tester operating instructions.

Table c. Air-Conditioning

DTC	INF Code	Definition	Trouble Area
B1400		Normal operation	
B1411		Open or short in room temperature sensor circuit	• A/C room temperature sensor • Harness or connector between cooler A/C room temperature sensor and A/C amplifier • A/C amplifier
B1412		Open or short in ambient temperature sensor circuit	• A/C ambient temperature sensor • Harness or connector between A/C ambient temperature sensor and ECM • ECM • Multiplex communication circuit • A/C amplifier
B1413		Open or short in evaporator temperature sensor circuit	• A/C evaporator temperature sensor (A/C thermistor) • Harness or connector between A/C evaporator temperature sensor and A/C amplifier • A/C amplifier
B1421		Open or short in solar sensor circuit. (If the check is performed in a dark place, DTC B1421 may be displayed.)	• A/C solar sensor • Harness or connector between A/C solar sensor and A/C amplifier or body ECU • A/C amplifier

Table c. Air-Conditioning

DTC	INF Code	Definition	Trouble Area
B1423		Pressure Switch Circuit	• Pressure switch • Harness or connector between pressure switch and body ground • Multiplex communication circuit • Refrigerant pipe line • A/C amplifier
B1431		Air Mix Damper Position Sensor Circuit (Passenger Side)	• Air mix control servomotor (air mix damper position sensor) • Harness or connector between Air mix control servomotor and A/C amplifier • A/C amplifier
B1432		Air Inlet Damper Position Sensor Circuit	• Air inlet control servomotor (air inlet damper position sensor) • Harness or connector between air inlet control servomotor and A/C amplifier • A/C amplifier
B1433		Air Outlet Damper Position Sensor Circuit	• Air outlet control servomotor (air outlet damper position sensor) • Harness or connector between air outlet control servomotor and A/C amplifier • A/C amplifier
B1441		Air Mix Damper Control Servo Motor Circuit (Passenger Side)	• Air mix control servomotor • Harness or connector between air mix control servomotor and A/C amplifier • A/C amplifier
B1442		Air Inlet Damper Control Servo Motor Circuit	• Air inlet control servomotor • Harness or connector between air inlet control servomotor and A/C amplifier • A/C amplifier
B1443		Air Outlet Damper Control Servo Motor Circuit	• Air outlet control servomotor • Harness or connector between air outlet control servomotor and A/C amplifier • A/C amplifier
B1462		Room Humidity Sensor Circuit	• A/C room humidity sensor (A/C room temperature sensor) • Harness or connector between A/C room humidity sensor (A/C room temperature sensor) and A/C amplifier • A/C amplifier
B1471		A/C Inverter High Voltage Power Resource System Malfunction	• Hybrid control ECU • A/C inverter (inverter with converter) • A/C inverter (w/converter inverter assy)
B1472		A/C Inverter High Voltage Output System Malfunction	• Hybrid control ECU • Electric inverter compressor (w/motor compressor assy) • A/C inverter (w/converter inverter assy)
B1473		A/C Inverter Start-up Signal System Malfunction	• Harness or connector between hybrid control ECU and w/converter inverter assy • A/C inverter (w/converter inverter assy) • Hybrid control ECU
B1474		A/C Inverter (w/converter inverter assy) Malfunction	A/C inverter (w/converter inverter assy)

Table c. Air-Conditioning

DTC	INF Code	Definition	Trouble Area
B1475		A/C Inverter Cooling / Heating System Malfunction	A/C inverter (w/converter inverter assy)
B1476		A/C Inverter Load System Malfunction	• Volume of refrigerant • Electric inverter compressor (w/motor compressor assy) • Cooling fan circuit
B1477		A/C Inverter Low Voltage Power Resource System Malfunction	A/C inverter (w/converter inverter assy)
B1498		Communication Malfunction (A/C Inverter Local)	• Harness or connector between hybrid control ECU and A/C inverter (w/converter inverter assy) • Hybrid control ECU • A/C inverter (w/converter inverter assy)
B1499		Multiplex Communication Circuit	Open in multiplex communication circuit
P0AA6	611	Hybrid Battery Voltage System Isolation Fault	• Electric inverter compressor (w/motor compressor) • A/C inverter (inverter with converter) • Compressor oil
P3009	611	High Voltage System Insulation Malfunction	• Electric inverter compressor (w/motor compressor assy) • A/C inverter (w/converter inverter assy) • Compressor oil

11

Audio system

The table(s) in this section contain audio system DTCs, code definitions and likely diagnosis.

The first 2 digits (before dash) are the device logical address. The second 2 digits (after dash) are the 2-digit DTC.

Retrieving DTCs

◀ Audio system DTCs can be retrieved on multifunction display (touch screen) in center of instrument panel. Multifunction display must be in diagnostic mode to display DTCs. Additional fault information may also be onscreen. See **Multifunction Display**.

Clearing DTCs

— Audio system DTCs can be cleared on multifunction display. See **Multifunction Display**.

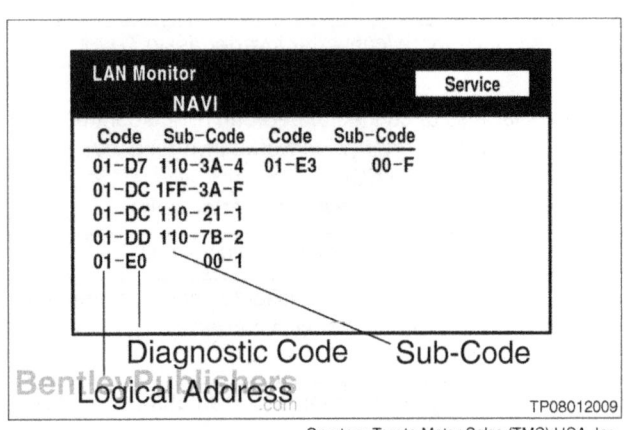

Diagnostic Code   Sub-Code
Logical Address

TP08012009

Courtesy Toyota Motor Sales (TMS) USA, Inc.

Table d. Audio - Bluetooth		
DTC	**Definition**	**Diagnosis**
57-47	Bluetooth module initialization failed	

Table e. Audio - Gateway ECU		
DTC	**Definition**	**Diagnosis**
01-D4	Regulator communication error	The device whose code is recorded is separated when the power switch is in ON (or ACC) position. When the code is recorded, the multi-display is disconnected.

Table f. Audio - Multi-display		
DTC	**Definition**	**Diagnosis**
01-21	ROM error	ROM is detected.
01-22	RAM error	Abnormal condition of RAM
01-D5	Registered component is missed	Component in which this code is recorded is or was disconnected from the system when power switch is in ACC (ON).
01-D8	No response for connection check	The device indicated by the sub code is (was) disconnected from the system after engine start.
01-D9	Last mode error	The device (for audio visual system) that had functioned before the engine stopped is (was) disconnected from the system when the power switch is (was) in the ACC or ON state.
01-DA	No response against ON/OFF command	No response is identified when changing mode (audio and visual mode change). Detected when sound and image do not change by switch operation

Table f. Audio - Multi-display

DTC	Definition	Diagnosis
01-DB	Mode status error	This code detects a dual alarm.
01-DC	Failure in transmission	This code indicates a transmission failure to the device indicated by the sub code. NOTE: This DTC may have no direct relationship with the malfunction.
01-DE	Slave reset	This code is stored when a slave device has been disconnected after engine start.
21-10 23-10 24-10 25-10	Panel SW failure	Panel SW detection circuit

Table g. Audio - Radio Receiver Assy

DTC	Definition	Diagnosis
01-D5	Registered component is missed	Component in which this code is recorded is or was disconnected from the system when power switch is in ACC (ON).
01-D6	Absence of master unit	Component in which this code is recorded was disconnected from system or master component with ignition switch in ACC or ON.
01-D7	Connection check error	Component in which this code is recorded is (was) disconnected from system after engine start. Either that, or radio receiver assy was disconnected when this code was recorded.
01-D8	No response for connection check	The device indicated by the sub code is (was) disconnected from the system after engine start.
01-D9	Last mode error	The device (for audio visual system) that had functioned before the engine stopped is (was) disconnected from the system when the power switch is (was) in the ACC or ON state.
01-DA	No response against ON/OFF command	No response is identified when changing mode (audio and visual mode change). Detected when sound and image do not change by switch operation.
01-DB	Mode status error	This code detects a dual alarm.
01-DC	Failure in transmission	This code indicates a transmission failure to the device indicated by the sub code. NOTE: This DTC may have no direct relationship with the malfunction.
01-DD	Master reset	After the power switch ON (READY), master component was disconnected from system.
01-DE	Slave reset	This code is stored when a slave device has been disconnected after engine start.
01-DF	Master error	Due to defective cognition of component with a display, master function is switched to audio equipment. Error occurs in communication between sub-master (audio) and master component.
01-E0	Registration complete indication error	"Registration complete" command from the master device cannot be received. NOTE: This DTC may not be directly related to the problem.
01-E1	Voice processing device ON error	The AMP device records that the AMP output does not function even while the source device operates.

11

Table g. Audio - Radio Receiver Assy

DTC	Definition	Diagnosis
01-E2	ON/OFF indication parameter error	The command for ON/OFF control from the master device has a problem.
01-E3	Registration demand transmission	The registration demand command from the slave device is output, or the registration demand command is output by receiving connection confirmation command from the sub master device. NOTE: This DTC may not be directly related to the problem.
01-E4	Multiple frame incomplete	The multiple frame transmission ends incomplete. NOTE: This DTC may not be directly related to the problem.
60-10	AM turner PLL does not lock	The PULL circuit in the AM tuner is abnormal.
60-11	FM tuner PLL does not lock	The PULL circuit in the FM tuner is abnormal.
60-40	Antenna not connection	Antenna is disconnected.
60-41	Antenna power source error	A malfunction is detected in the antenna power supply system.
60-42	Tuner power source error	The power source of the tuner is abnormal.
60-43	AM tuner error	The AM tuner is abnormal.
60-44	FM tuner error	The FM tuner is abnormal.
60-45	SW tuner error	The SW tuner is abnormal.
60-50	Malfunction in Internal IC	Radio receiver
61-10	Belt cut	The inside belt is cut or come off.
61-40	Mechanical error of media	A malfunction due to mechanical problem, cassette tape is cut or entangled.
61-41	EJECT error	A malfunction due to mechanical problem.
61-42	Tape tangling	Cassette tape is tangled
61-43	Head dirt	Head is dirty
61-44	Device power supply problem	A short or open in the power circuit
62-10	CD player mechanical error	A mechanical error in the CD player is detected while the CD is not being inserted or ejected.
62-11	CD insertion & eject error	CD insertion or ejection is failed.
62-12	CD reading abnormal	CD read problem occurs.
62-40	No disc	No disc is inserted.
62-41	Wrong disc	An unsuitable disc is inserted.
62-42	Disc cannot be read	The disc cannot be read.
62-43	CD-ROM abnormal	CD-ROM operation is abnormal.
62-44	CD abnormal	Operation error in the CD mechanism (except for code 10).
62-45	EJECT error	The magazine cannot be ejected.
62-46	CD has scratches or upside down	CD has dirt or scratches on the surface or is up-side down.
62-47	CD temperature is high	The sensor detects that the CD unit temperature is high.
62-48	Over-current detection	Over-current flows in to the CD changer.
62-50	Tray insertion/ejection error	The tray insertion/ejection error occurs in the CD changer.
62-51	Elevator error	Elevator error occurs in the CD changer.
62-52	Clamp error	Clamp error occurs in the CD changer.

Table g. Audio - Radio Receiver Assy

DTC	Definition	Diagnosis
62-78	DSP error	Radio receiver
62-7D	Disc cannot be played	• CD • Radio receiver
62-7E	No playable files	• CD • Radio receiver
62-7F	Copyright protection error	• CD • Radio receiver
63-10	CD player mechanical error	A mechanical error in the CD player is detected while the CD is not being inserted or ejected.
63-11	CD insertion & eject error	CD insertion or ejection is failed.
63-12	CD reading abnormal	CD read problem occurs.
63-40	No disc	No disc is inserted.
63-41	Wrong disc	An unsuitable disc is inserted.
63-42	Disc cannot be read	The disc cannot be read.
63-43	CD-ROM abnormal	CD-ROM operation is abnormal.
63-44	CD abnormal	Operation error in the CD mechanism (except for code 10).
63-45	EJECT error	The magazine cannot be ejected.
63-46	CD has scratches or upside down	CD has dirt or scratches on the surface or is up-side down.
63-47	CD temperature is high	The sensor detects that the CD unit temperature is high.
63-48	Over-current detection	Over-current flows in to the CD changer.
63-50	Tray insertion/ejection error	The tray insertion/ejection error occurs in the CD changer.
63-51	Elevator error	Elevator error occurs in the CD changer.
63-52	Clamp error	Clamp error occurs in the CD changer.
63-78	DSP Error	Radio receiver
63-7D	Disc cannot be played	• CD • Radio receiver
63-7E	No playable files	• CD • Radio receiver
63-7F	Copyright protection error	• CD • Radio receiver

Table h. Audio - Stereo Component Amplifier Assy

DTC	Definition	Diagnosis
01-D6	Absence of master unit	Component in which this code is recorded was disconnected from system or master component with ignition switch in ACC or ON.
01-D7	Connection check error	Component in which this code is recorded is (was) disconnected from system after engine start. Either that, or radio receiver assy was disconnected when this code was recorded.
01-DC	Failure in transmission	This code indicates a transmission failure to the device indicated by the sub code. NOTE: This DTC may have no direct relationship with the malfunction.

11

Table h. Audio - Stereo Component Amplifier Assy

DTC	Definition	Diagnosis
01-DD	Master reset	After the power switch ON (READY), master component was disconnected from system.
01-DF	Master error	Due to defective cognition of component with a display, master function is switched to audio equipment. Error occurs in communication between sub-master (audio) and master component.
01-E0	Registration complete indication error	"Registration complete" command from the master device cannot be received. NOTE: This DTC may not be directly related to the problem.
01-E1	Voice processing device ON error	The AMP device records that the AMP output does not function even while the source device operates.
01-E2	ON/OFF indication parameter error	The command for ON/OFF control from the master device has a problem.
01-E3	Registration demand transmission	The registration demand command from the slave device is output, or the registration demand command is output by receiving connection confirmation command from the sub master device. NOTE: This DTC may not be directly related to the problem.
01-E4	Multiple frame incomplete	The multiple frame transmission ends incomplete. NOTE: This DTC may not be directly related to the problem.
74-40	Short in speaker circuit	Wire harness Speaker Stereo component amplifier

Brake system

The table(s) in this section contain brake system DTCs, Toyota INF codes, code definitions and likely trouble areas.

5-digit DTCs and 2-digit blink codes are separated by slash (example: **C0200/31**).

Retrieving DTCs

Brake system DTCs and information codes can be retrieved two ways:

- Toyota scan tool or equivalent (retrieves 5-digit DTCs and 1 - 3 digit information codes)
- Warning light blinking pattern (retrieves 2-digit blink codes)

To retrieve 5-digit DTCs and 1 - 3 digit information codes using Toyota scan tool or equivalent, see **Diagnostic Scan Tools** in this chapter.

- To retrieve 2-digit blink codes, perform the following procedure:

- Be sure hybrid system is OFF (READY indicator not illuminated).

> **WARNING—**
> - Be sure hybrid system is OFF when servicing vehicle (READY indicator not illuminated). Failure to switch the hybrid system OFF could result in engine start at any time.

◀ Using jumper wire, connect terminals 4 (CG) and 13 (TC) in OBD II connector.

> **CAUTION—**
> - Avoid spreading or deforming female terminals in OBD II connector. Use an appropriate jumper wire gauge and do not force jumper wire into terminals.

◀ Turn hybrid system ON (IG-ON, READY indicator not illuminated). One of three brake system warning lights will blink (flash), depending on which part of brake system has fault.

TC

| 16 | 15 | 14 | 13 | 12 | 11 | 10 | 9 |
| 8 | 7 | 6 | 5 | 4 | 3 | 2 | 1 |

CG

TP08012008

Brake Control Warning Light

ABS Warning Light

USA: **ABS**

Canada:

VSC Warning Light

VSC

TP08012011

Table i. Brake system warning lights

Warning light flashing	System with DTC
Brake control	ECB system
ABS	ABS system
VSC	VSC system

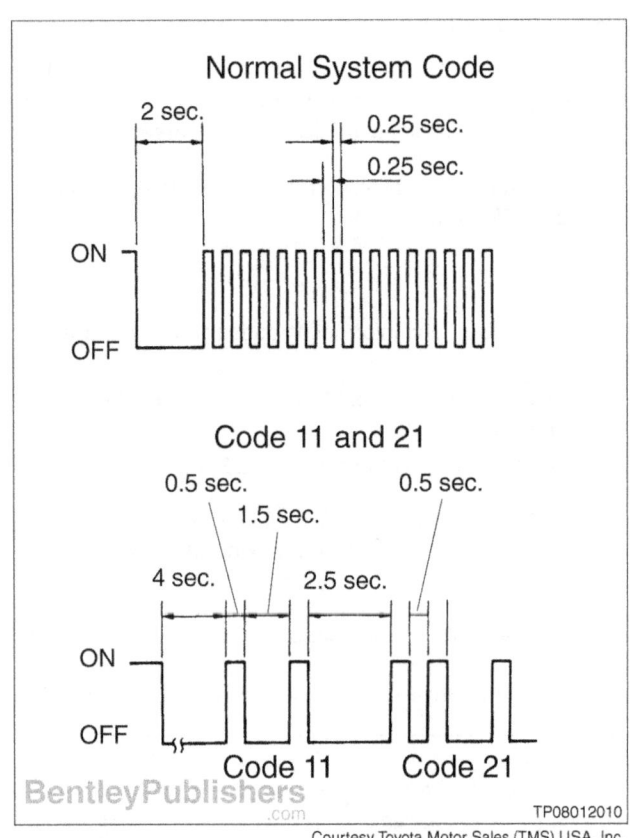

Courtesy Toyota Motor Sales (TMS) USA, Inc.

◀ Warning light blinks in pattern as shown on left to display 2-digit DTCs.

— Warning light will repeat blink pattern until turned OFF.

— If more than one DTC is stored, warning light will blink each DTC in ascending order.

— When check is complete, remove jumper from OBD II connector.

Clearing DTCs

Brake system DTCs can be cleared two ways:
• Toyota scan tool or equivalent
• OBD II connector jumper / brake pedal procedure

To clear DTCs with Toyota scan tool or equivalent:

— Connect scan tool to OBD II connector.

— Turn hybrid system ON (IG-ON, READY indicator not illuminated). Turn tester ON.

— Operate tester to clear DTCs. Refer to tester operating instructions.

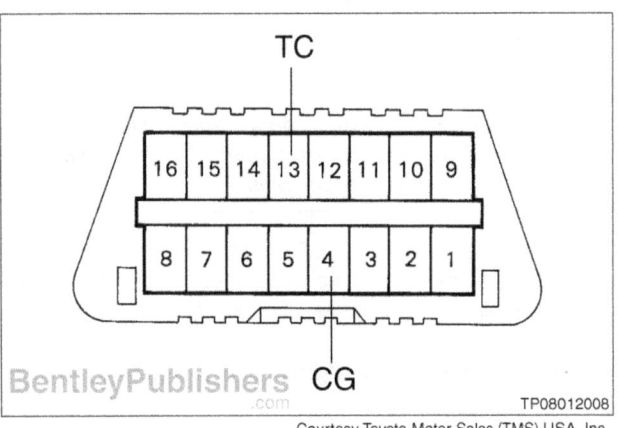

Courtesy Toyota Motor Sales (TMS) USA, Inc.

To clear DTCs with OBD II connector jumper / brake pedal procedure:

◀ Using jumper wire, connect terminals 4 (CG) and 13 (TC) in OBD II connector.

> **CAUTION—**
> • Avoid spreading or deforming female terminals in OBD II connector. Use an appropriate jumper wire gauge and do not force jumper wire into terminals.

— Turn hybrid system ON (IG-ON, READY indicator not illuminated).

— Depress and release brake pedal at least 8 times within 5 seconds.

— Remove jumper from OBD II connector.

> **NOTE—**
> • Disconnecting the 12-volt auxiliary battery or removing the ECU-IG fuse will not clear DTCs.

Table j. Brake

DTC	INF Code	Definition	Trouble Area
C0200/31	251 252 253 254 255 256 257 258 259 260 261 262	Right front wheel speed sensor signal malfunction	• Right front speed sensor • Speed sensor circuit • Sensor rotor • Sensor installation
C0205/32	264 265 266 267 268 269 270 271 272 273 274 275	Left front wheel speed sensor signal malfunction	• Left front speed sensor • Speed sensor circuit • Sensor rotor • Sensor installation
C0210/33	277 278 279 280 281 282 283 284 285 286 287 288	Right rear wheel speed sensor signal malfunction	• Right rear speed sensor • Speed sensor circuit • Sensor rotor • Sensor installation
C0215/34	290 291 292 293 294 295 296 297 298 299 300 301	Left rear wheel speed sensor signal malfunction	• Left rear speed sensor • Speed sensor circuit • Sensor rotor • Sensor installation
C1235/35	302	Metal stuck to speed sensor (FR)	• Right front speed sensor • Speed sensor circuit • Sensor installation
C1236/36	303	Metal stuck to speed sensor (FL)	• Left front speed sensor • Speed sensor circuit • Sensor installation

11

Table j. Brake

DTC	INF Code	Definition	Trouble Area
C1238/38	304	Metal stuck to speed sensor (RR)	• Right rear speed sensor • Speed sensor circuit • Sensor installation
C1239/39	305	Metal stuck to speed sensor (RL)	• Left rear speed sensor • Speed sensor circuit • Sensor installation
C1243/43	317	Malfunction in deceleration sensor (constant output)	• Yaw rate (deceleration) sensor • Skid control ECU
C1244/44	314	Open or short circuit in deceleration sensor circuit	• Yaw rate (deceleration) sensor • Yaw rate (deceleration) sensor installation • Zero point calibration not done • Skid control ECU
C1245/45	313	Malfunction in deceleration sensor	• Yaw rate (deceleration) sensor • Zero point calibration not done • Skid control ECU
C1381/97	315	Malfunction in power supply voltage of yaw / deceleration sensor	• Yaw rate (deceleration) sensor circuit • Harness and connector • Skid control ECU

Table k. Brake - ECB

DTC	INF Code	Definition	Trouble Area
C1202/68	511 512	Brake fluid level low / open circuit in brake fluid level warning switch circuit	• Brake fluid level • Brake fluid level warning switch • Harness and connector • Skid control ECU
C1203/95		Engine control system communication circuit malfunction	Skid control ECU
C1241/41	81 82 83 84	Low battery positive voltage or abnormally high battery positive voltage	• ABS No.1 relay • ABS No.2 relay • Harness and connector • Skid control power supply circuit • Brake control power supply assy • Hybrid control system
C1242/42	87 88	Open circuit in IG2 circuit	• ABS No.1 relay • ABS No.2 relay • Harness and connector • Skid control power supply circuit • Brake control power supply assy • Hybrid control system
C1246/46	191 192 194 195 197 198 199 200 201 202 205	Malfunction in master cylinder pressure sensor	• Brake actuator assy • Skid control ECU • Harness and connector

Table k. Brake - ECB

DTC	INF Code	Definition	Trouble Area
C1247/47	171 172 173 174 175 176 177 179 180	Malfunction in stroke sensor	• Brake pedal stroke sensor • Skid control ECU • Harness and connector
C1249/49	520	Open circuit in stop light switch circuit	• Stop lamp switch • Stop lamp switch circuit • Stop lamp bulb
C1252/52	130	Hydro-booster pump motor malfunction	Brake actuator assy
C1253/53	132 133 134 136 137 138 140	Hydro-booster pump motor relay malfunction	• ABS MTR relay • ABS MTR2 relay • Harness and connector • Brake actuator assy
C1256/57	141 143	Accumulator low pressure malfunction	Brake actuator assy (accumulator pressure, accumulator pressure sensor, pump motor)
C1259/58	150	HV system regenerative malfunction	Hybrid control system
C1300		Malfunction in ECU	Skid control ECU
C1311/11	1	Open circuit in main relay 1	• ABS No.1 relay • Skid control ECU • Harness and connector
C1312/12	3	Short circuit in main relay 1	• ABS No.1 relay • Skid control ECU • Harness and connector
C1313/13	4	Open circuit in main relay 2	• ABS No.2 relay • Skid control ECU • Harness and connector
C1314/14	6	Short circuit in main relay 2	• ABS No.2 relay • Skid control ECU • Harness and connector
C1315/31	61 62 63 64	Changeover solenoid malfunction (SMC1)	• Brake actuator assy (SMC1) • Skid control ECU • Harness and connector
C1316/32	66 67 68 69	Changeover solenoid malfunction (SMC2)	• Brake actuator assy (SMC2) • Skid control ECU • Harness and connector
C1319/35	71 72 73 74	Changeover solenoid malfunction (SCSS)	• Stroke simulator • Skid control ECU • Harness and connector

11

Table k. Brake - ECB

DTC	INF Code	Definition	Trouble Area
C1341/62	551 552 553 554 555	Malfunction in hydraulic system(FR)	• Fluid leakage • Brake actuator assy • Disc rotor
C1342/63	561 562 563 564 565	Malfunction in hydraulic system(FL)	• Fluid leakage • Brake actuator assy • Disc rotor
C1343/64	571 572 573 574 575	Malfunction in hydraulic system(RR)	• Fluid leakage • Brake actuator assy • Disc rotor
C1344/65	581 582 583 584 585	Malfunction in hydraulic system(RL)	• Fluid leakage • Brake actuator assy • Disc rotor
C1345/66	501 502 503 504	Not learning linear valve offset abnormality	Initialization of linear solenoid valve and calibration undone
C1352/21	11 12 13 14	Increasing pressure solenoid malfunction (FR)	• Brake actuator assy • Skid control ECU • Harness and connector
C1353/23	21 22 23 24	Increasing pressure solenoid malfunction (FL)	• Brake actuator assy • Skid control ECU • Harness and connector
C1354/25	31 32 33 34	Increasing pressure solenoid malfunction (RR)	• Brake actuator assy • Skid control ECU • Harness and connector
C1355/27	41 42 43 44	Increasing pressure solenoid malfunction (RL)	• Brake actuator assy • Skid control ECU • Harness and connector
C1356/22	16 17 18 19	Decreasing pressure solenoid malfunction (FR)	• Brake actuator assy • Skid control ECU • Harness and connector
C1357/24	26 27 28 29	Decreasing pressure solenoid malfunction (FL)	• Brake actuator assy • Skid control ECU • Harness and connector
C1358/26	36 37 38 39	Decreasing pressure solenoid malfunction (RR)	• Brake actuator assy • Skid control ECU • Harness and connector

Table k. Brake - ECB

DTC	INF Code	Definition	Trouble Area
C1359/28	46 47 48 49	Decreasing pressure solenoid malfunction (RL)	• Brake actuator assy • Skid control ECU • Harness and connector
C1364/61	221 222 224 225 226 227 228 230 231 232 233 234 236 237 238 239 240 242 243 244	Malfunction in W/C pressure sensor	• Brake actuator assy • Skid control ECU • Harness and connector
C1365/54	211 212 214 215 216	Malfunction in ACC pressure sensor	• Brake actuator assy (accumulator pressure sensor) • Skid control ECU
C1368/67	505	Linear valve offset malfunction	• Initialization of linear solenoid valve and calibration undone • Skid control ECU
C1377/43	101 102 103 105 106 108 109 110 113	Capacitor malfunction	• Brake control power supply • Harness and connector • ABS No.1 fuse • ABS No.2 fuse • ABS No.3 fuse • Apply high voltage
C1378/44	112	Capacitor communication circuit malfunction	• Harness and connector • Skid control ECU
C1391/69	591	Abnormal leak of ACC PRESS	• Fluid leakage • Brake actuator assy
C1392/48		Un-correction of zero point of stroke sensor	• Brake pedal stroke sensor zero point calibration undone (initialization of linear solenoid valve and calibration undone) • Skid control ECU

11

Table I. Brake - Enhanced VSC

DTC	INF Code	Definition	Trouble Area
C1210/36	336	Zero point calibration of yaw rate sensor undone	Zero point calibration undone (Perform zero point calibration and check DTC. If DTC is not output again, the sensor is normal.)
C1231/31	341 342 343 344 345 346 347 348 349	Malfunction in steering angle sensor	• Steering angle sensor • Skid control ECU
C1232/32	311 312	Malfunction in deceleration sensor	• Yaw rate (deceleration) sensor • Skid control ECU
C1234/34	331 332 333 334 335 337	Malfunction in yaw rate sensor	Yaw rate (deceleration) sensor
C1310/51	156	Malfunction in HV system	Hybrid control system (Enhanced VSC, TRAC system)
C1336/39	318	Zero point calibration of deceleration sensor undone	Zero point calibration undone (Perform zero point calibration and check DTC. If DTC is not output again, the sensor is normal.)

Table m. Brake - Test Mode

DTC	Definition	Trouble Area
C0371/71	Yaw Rate Sensor (Test Mode DTC)	Yaw rate sensor (Deceleration sensor)
C1271/71	Low Output Signal of Front Speed Sensor RH	• Right front speed sensor • Speed sensor circuit • Sensor installation • Sensor rotor
C1272/72	Low Output Signal of Front Speed Sensor LH	• Left front speed sensor • Speed sensor circuit • Sensor installation • Sensor rotor
C1273/73	Low Output Signal of Rear Speed Sensor RH	• Right rear speed sensor • Speed sensor circuit • Sensor installation • Sensor rotor
C1274/74	Low Output Signal of Rear Speed Sensor LH	• Left rear speed sensor • Speed sensor circuit • Sensor installation • Sensor rotor
C1275/75	Abnormal Change in Output Signal of Front Speed Sensor RH	• Right front speed sensor • Speed sensor circuit • Sensor installation

Table m. Brake - Test Mode

DTC	Definition	Trouble Area
C1276/76	Abnormal Change in Output Signal of Front Speed Sensor LH	• Left front speed sensor • Speed sensor circuit • Sensor installation
C1277/77	Abnormal Change in Output Signal of Rear Speed Sensor RH	• Right rear speed sensor • Speed sensor circuit • Sensor installation
C1278/78	Abnormal Change in Output Signal of Rear Speed Sensor LH	• Left rear speed sensor • Speed sensor circuit • Sensor installation
C1279/79	Acceleration Sensor Output Voltage Malfunction	• Yaw rate (deceleration) sensor • Yaw rate (deceleration) sensor circuit
C1281/81	Master Cylinder Pressure Sensor Output Malfunction	• Brake actuator assembly • Skid control ECU

11

Controller area network (CAN)

The table(s) in this section contain controller area network (CAN) DTCs, Toyota INF codes, code definitions and likely trouble areas.

Retrieving DTCs

CAN DTCs and information codes can be retrieved by using Toyota scan tool or equivalent. See **Diagnostic Scan Tools** in this chapter.

Clearing DTCs

Clear CAN DTCs with Toyota scan tool or equivalent.

— Connect scan tool to OBD II connector.

— Turn hybrid system ON (IG-ON, READY indicator not illuminated). Turn tester ON.

— Operate tester to clear DTCs. Refer to tester operating instructions.

Table n. CAN - Battery ECU

DTC	Definition	Trouble Area
U0100	Lost Communication With ECM/PCM "A"	
U0293	Lost Communication With Hybrid Vehicle Control System	

Table o. CAN - ECM

DTC	Definition	Trouble Area
U0293	Lost Communication With Hybrid Vehicle Control System	

Table p. CAN - Hybrid Vehicle Control ECU

DTC	INF Code	Definition	Trouble Area
P3108	594	Lost Communication With A/C System Control Module	
U0100	211 212 530	Lost Communication With ECM/PCM "A"	
U0111	208 531	Lost Communication With Battery Energy Control Module "A"	
U0129	220 222 528 529	Lost Communication With Brake System Control Module	
U0131	433 434	Lost Communication With Power Steering Control Module	

Table p. CAN - Hybrid Vehicle Control ECU

DTC	INF Code	Definition	Trouble Area
U0146	435	Lost Communication With Gateway "A"	

Table q. CAN - Power Steering ECU

DTC	Definition	Trouble Area
U0073	Control Module Communication Bus Off	
U0121	Lost Communication With Anti-Lock Brake System (ABS) Control Module	

Table r. CAN - Skid Control ECU

DTC	INF Code	Definition	Trouble Area
U0073	360	Control Module Communication Bus Off	
U0123		Lost Communication With Yaw Rate Sensor Module	
U0124		Lost Communication With Lateral Acceleration Sensor Module	
U0126		Lost Communication With Steering Angle Sensor Module	
U0293	152 153 154	Lost Communication With Hybrid Vehicle Control System	

11

Cruise control system

The table(s) in this section contain cruise control DTCs, code definitions and likely trouble areas.

Retrieving DTCs

Cruise control system DTCs can be retrieved by using Toyota scan tool or equivalent. See **Diagnostic Scan Tools** in this chapter.

Clearing DTCs

Clear cruise control system DTCs with Toyota scan tool or equivalent.

— Connect scan tool to OBD II connector.

— Turn hybrid system ON (IG-ON, READY indicator not illuminated). Turn tester ON.

— Operate tester to clear DTCs. Refer to tester operating instructions.

Table s. Cruise Control		
DTC	**Definition**	**Trouble Area**
P0500	Vehicle Speed Sensor "A"	• Vehicle speed sensor • Vehicle speed sensor circuit • Combination meter • Hybrid vehicle control ECU
P0571	Brake Switch "A" Circuit	• Stop lamp switch • Stop lamp switch circuit • Hybrid vehicle control ECU
P0607	Control Module Performance	• Stop lamp switch • Hybrid vehicle control ECU

Door locks

The table(s) in this section contain door lock DTCs, code definitions and likely trouble areas.

Retrieving DTCs

Door lock system DTCs can be retrieved by using Toyota scan tool or equivalent. See **Diagnostic Scan Tools** in this chapter.

Clearing DTCs

Clear door lock system DTCs with Toyota scan tool or equivalent.

− Connect scan tool to OBD II connector.

− Turn hybrid system ON (IG-ON, READY indicator not illuminated). Turn tester ON.

− Operate tester to clear DTCs. Refer to tester operating instructions.

Table t. Door Locks

DTC	Definition	Trouble Area
B1241	Door Control Switch Circuit Diagnosis	• Power window regulator master switch assy (Door control switch) • Door control switch assy • Wire harness • Instrument panel J/B assy (Multiplex network body ECU)

Table u. Door Locks, Wireless Control

DTC	Definition	Trouble Area
B1242	Wireless Door Lock Tuner Circuit Malfunction	• Wire harness • Door control receiver • Smart key ECU assy (when equipped) • Instrument panel J/B assy (Multiplex network body ECU)

11

Electric power steering (EPS) system

The table(s) in this section contain electric power steering (EPS) DTCs, code definitions and likely trouble areas.

Retrieving DTCs

EPS DTCs can be retrieved by using Toyota scan tool or equivalent. See **Diagnostic Scan Tools** in this chapter.

Clearing DTCs

Clear EPS DTCs with Toyota scan tool or equivalent.

— Connect scan tool to OBD II connector.

— Turn hybrid system ON (IG-ON, READY indicator not illuminated). Turn tester ON.

— Operate tester to clear DTCs. Refer to tester operating instructions.

Table v. Electric Power Steering (EPS)

DTC	Definition	Trouble Area
C1511 C1512 C1513	Torque sensor abnormal	• Steering column assy (Torque sensor) • Power steering ECU assy
C1514	Torque sensor power supply abnormal	• Steering column assy (Torque sensor) • Power steering ECU assy
C1515	Torque sensor zero point adjustment undone	• Torque sensor zero point calibration • Steering column
C1516	Torque sensor zero point adjustment incomplete	• Torque sensor zero point calibration • Steering column
C1517	Torque hold abnormal	• Steering column assy (Torque sensor) • Power steering ECU assy
C1524	Motor abnormal	• Power steering motor • Power steering ECU assy
C1531 C1532 C1533 C1534	ECU abnormal	Power steering ECU assy
C1551	IG power source voltage abnormal	• ECU-IG fuse • IG power source circuit • Power steering ECU assy
C1552	PIG power supply voltage abnormal	• EPS fuse • PIG power source circuit • Power steering ECU assy
C1554	Power supply relay failure	• EPS fuse • PIG power source circuit • Power steering ECU assy
C1555	Motor relay welding failure	• EPS fuse • PIG power source circuit • Power steering ECU assy
C1581	Assist map number un-writing	Power steering ECU assy

Table v. Electric Power Steering (EPS)

DTC	Definition	Trouble Area
U0073	Control module communication bus off	Can communication system
U0121	Lost communication with anti-lock brake system (ABS) Control Module	• Can communication system • Skid control ECU

Engine immobilizer

The table(s) in this section contain engine immobilizer DTCs, Toyota INF codes, code definitions and likely trouble areas.

Retrieving DTCs

Engine immobilizer DTCs and information codes can be retrieved by using Toyota scan tool or equivalent. See **Diagnostic Scan Tools** in this chapter.

Clearing DTCs

Clear engine immobilizer DTCs with Toyota scan tool or equivalent.

— Connect scan tool to OBD II connector.

— Turn hybrid system ON (IG-ON, READY indicator not illuminated). Turn tester ON.

— Operate tester to clear DTCs. Refer to tester operating instructions.

Table w. Engine Immobilizer w/ or w/o Smart Entry - HV ECU

DTC	INF Code	Definition	Trouble Area
B2799	539 540 541 542 543 544	Engine Immobilizer System Malfunction	• Wire harness • Hybrid vehicle control ECU

Table x. Engine Immobilizer w/ Smart Entry - Transponder Key ECU

DTC	Definition	Trouble Area
B2775	Interior Verification Abnormal (To Theft Deterrent ECU)	• Transponder key ECU assy • Smart ECU
B2784	Antenna Coil Open / Short	• Wire harness • Key slot • Transponder key ECU assy
B2785	Ignition Switch ON Malfunction	• Wire harness • Transponder key ECU assy • Power source control ECU
B2793	Transponder Chip Malfunction	Smart key (Door control transmitter)
B2794	Unmatched Encryption Code	Smart key (Door control transmitter)
B2795	Unmatched Key Code	Smart key (Door control transmitter)
B2796	No Communication in Immobilizer System	• Smart key (Door control transmitter) • Key slot • Wire harness
B2797	Communication Malfunction No. 1	• Smart key (Door control transmitter) • Key slot • Wire harness

Table x. Engine Immobilizer w/ Smart Entry - Transponder Key ECU

DTC	Definition	Trouble Area
B2798	Communication Malfunction No. 2	Smart key (Door control transmitter)

Table y. Engine Immobilizer w/o Smart Entry - Transponder Key ECU

DTC	Definition	Trouble Area
B2784	Antenna Coil Open / Short	• Wire harness • Key slot • Transponder key ECU assy
B2785	Ignition Switch ON Malfunction	• Wire harness • Key slot • Transponder key ECU assy • Power source control ECU
B2793	Transponder Chip Malfunction	Key (Door control transmitter)
B2794	Unmatched Encryption Code	Key (Door control transmitter)
B2795	Unmatched Key Code	Key (Door control transmitter)
B2796	No Communication in Immobilizer System	• Key (Door control transmitter) • Key slot • Wire harness
B2797	Communication Malfunction No. 1	• Key (Door control transmitter) • Wire harness • Key slot
B2798	Communication Malfunction No. 2	Key (Door control transmitter)

11

Engine management system

The table(s) in this section contain engine management system DTCs, code definitions and likely trouble areas.

Retrieving DTCs

Engine management system DTCs can be retrieved by using Toyota scan tool or equivalent. See **Diagnostic Scan Tools** in this chapter.

Clearing DTCs

Clear engine management DTCs with Toyota scan tool or equivalent.

— Connect scan tool to OBD II connector.

— Turn hybrid system ON (IG-ON, READY indicator not illuminated). Turn tester ON.

— Operate tester to clear DTCs. Refer to tester operating instructions.

Table z. Engine Management System

DTC	Definition	Trouble Area
P0010	Camshaft Position "A" Actuator Circuit (Bank 1)	• Open or short in oil control valve circuit • Oil control valve • ECM
P0011	Camshaft Position "A" Timing Over-Advanced or System Performance (Bank 1)	• Valve timing • Oil control valve • Camshaft timing gear assembly • ECM
P0012	Camshaft Position "A" -Timing Over- Retarded (Bank 1)	Same as DTC P0011
P0016	Crankshaft Position -Camshaft Position Correlation (Bank 1Sensor A)	• Mechanical system (timing chain has jumped a tooth, chain stretched) • ECM
P0031	Oxygen (A/F) Sensor Heater Control Circuit Low (Bank 1 Sensor 1)	• Open or short in heater circuit of A/F sensor • A/F sensor heater • EFI M relay (integration relay) • ECM
P0032	Oxygen (A/F) Sensor Heater Control Circuit High (Bank 1 Sensor 1)	• Short in heater circuit of A/F sensor • A/F sensor heater • EFI M relay (integration relay) • ECM
P0037	Oxygen Sensor Heater Control Circuit Low (Bank 1 Sensor 2)	• Open or short in heater circuit of the heated oxygen sensor • Heated oxygen sensor heater • EFI M relay (integration relay) • ECM
P0038	Oxygen Sensor Heater Control Circuit High (Bank 1 Sensor 2)	• Short in heater circuit of the heated oxygen sensor • Heated oxygen sensor heater • EFI M relay (integration relay) • ECM

Table z. Engine Management System

DTC	Definition	Trouble Area
P0100	Mass or Volume Air Flow Circuit	• Open or short in mass air flow meter circuit • Mass air flow meter • ECM
P0101	Mass or Volume Air Flow Circuit Range/Performance Problem	Mass air flow meter
P0102	Mass or Volume Air Flow Circuit Low Input	• Open in mass air flow meter circuit • Mass air flow meter • ECM
P0103	Mass or Volume Air Flow Circuit High Input	• Short in mass air flow meter circuit • Mass air flow meter • ECM
P0110	Intake Air Temperature Circuit	• Open or short in intake air temperature sensor circuit • Intake air temperature sensor (built in mass air flow meter) • ECM
P0112	Intake Air Temperature Circuit Low Input	• Short in intake air temperature sensor circuit • Intake air temperature sensor (built in mass air flow meter) • ECM
P0113	Intake Air Temperature Circuit High Input	• Open in intake air temperature sensor circuit • Intake air temperature sensor (built in mass air flow meter) • ECM
P0115	Engine Coolant Temperature Circuit	• Open or short in engine coolant temperature sensor circuit • Engine coolant temperature sensor • ECM
P0116	Engine Coolant Temperature Circuit Range/Performance Problem	Engine coolant temperature sensor
P0117	Engine Coolant Temperature Circuit Low Input	• Short in engine coolant temperature sensor circuit • Engine coolant temperature sensor • ECM
P0118	Engine Coolant Temperature Circuit High Input	• Open in engine coolant temperature sensor circuit • Engine coolant temperature sensor • ECM
P0120	Throttle/Pedal Position Sensor/ Switch "A" Circuit	• Open or short in throttle position sensor circuit • Throttle position sensor (built in throttle body) • ECM
P0121	Throttle/Pedal Position Sensor/ Switch "A" Circuit Range/Performance Problem	Throttle position sensor (built in throttle body)
P0122	Throttle/Pedal Position Sensor/ Switch "A" Circuit Low Input	• Throttle position sensor • Open in VTA1 circuit • Open in VC circuit (when the VC circuit is open, DTCs P0222 and P2135 are also output simultaneously) • ECM
P0123	Throttle/Pedal Position Sensor/ Switch "A" Circuit High Input	• Throttle position sensor (built in throttle body) • Open in VTA circuit • Open in E2 circuit • VC and VTA circuits are short-circuited • ECM
P0125	Insufficient Coolant Temperature for Closed Loop Fuel Control	• Cooling system • Engine coolant temperature sensor • Thermostat

Table z. Engine Management System

DTC	Definition	Trouble Area
P0128	Coolant Thermostat (Coolant Temperature Below Thermostat Regulating Temperature)	• Thermostat • Cooling system • Engine coolant temperature sensor • ECM
P0136	Oxygen Sensor Circuit Malfunction (Bank 1 Sensor 2)	• Heated oxygen sensor (bank 1 sensor 2) circuit • Heated oxygen sensor (bank 1 sensor 2) • Heated oxygen sensor heater (bank 1 sensor 2) • A/F sensor (bank 1 sensor 1) • A/F sensor heater
P0137	Oxygen Sensor Circuit Low Voltage (Bank 1 Sensor 2)	• Heated oxygen sensor (bank 1 sensor 2) circuit • Heated oxygen sensor (bank 1 sensor 2) • Heated oxygen sensor heater (bank 1 sensor 2) • A/F sensor (bank 1 sensor 1) • A/F sensor heater
P0138	Oxygen Sensor Circuit High Voltage (Bank 1 Sensor 2)	• Heated oxygen sensor (bank 1 sensor 2) circuit • Heated oxygen sensor (bank 1 sensor 2) • Heated oxygen sensor heater (bank 1 sensor 2) • A/F sensor (bank 1 sensor 1) • A/F sensor heater
P0171	System Too Lean (Bank 1)	• Air induction system • Injector has blockage • Mass air flow meter • Engine coolant temperature sensor • Fuel pressure • Gas leakage in exhaust system • Open or short in A/F sensor (bank 1 sensor 1) circuit • A/F sensor (bank 1 sensor 1) • A/F sensor heater (bank 1 sensor 1) • EFI M relay (integration relay) • PCV valve and hose • PCV hose connection • ECM
P0172	System Too Rich (Bank 1)	• Injector has leakage or blockage • Mass air flow mete • Engine coolant temperature sensor • Ignition system • Fuel pressure • Gas leakage in exhaust system • Open or short in A/F sensor (bank 1 sensor 1) circuit • A/F sensor (bank 1 sensor 1) • A/F sensor heater (bank 1 sensor 1) • EFI M relay (integration relay) • ECM
P0220	Throttle/Pedal Position Sensor / Switch "B" Circuit	• Open or short in throttle position sensor circuit • Throttle position sensor • ECM
P0222	Throttle/Pedal Position Sensor / Switch "B" Circuit Low Input	• Throttle position sensor • Open in VTA2 circuit • Open in VC circuit (when the VC circuit is open, DTCs P0122 and P2135 are also output simultaneously)
P0223	Throttle/Pedal Position Sensor / Switch "B" Circuit High Input	Throttle position sensor

Table z. Engine Management System		
DTC	**Definition**	**Trouble Area**
P0300	Random / Multiple Cylinder Misfire Detected	• Open or short in engine wire harness • Connector connection • Vacuum hose connection • Ignition system • Injector • Fuel pressure • Mass air flow meter • Engine coolant temperature sensor • Compression pressure • Valve clearance • Valve timing • PCV hose connection • PCV hose • ECM
P0301	Cylinder 1 Misfire Detected	Same as DTC P0300
P0302	Cylinder 2 Misfire Detected	Same as DTC P0300
P0303	Cylinder 3 Misfire Detected	Same as DTC P0300
P0304	Cylinder 4 Misfire Detected	Same as DTC P0300
P0325	Knock Sensor 1 Circuit (Bank 1 or Single Sensor)	• Open or short in knock sensor circuit • Knock sensor (looseness) • ECM
P0327	Knock Sensor 1 Circuit Low Input (Bank 1 or Single Sensor)	• Short in knock sensor circuit • Knock sensor • ECM
P0328	Knock Sensor 1 Circuit High Input (Bank 1 or Single Sensor)	• Open in knock sensor circuit • Knock sensor • ECM
P0335	Crankshaft Position Sensor "A" Circuit	• Open or short in crankshaft position sensor circuit • Crankshaft position sensor • Signal plate (crankshaft) • ECM
P0340	Camshaft Position Sensor "A" Circuit (Bank 1 or Single Sensor)	• Open or short in camshaft position sensor circuit • Camshaft position sensor • Camshaft timing pulley • Timing chain has jumped a tooth • ECM
P0341	Camshaft Position Sensor "A" Circuit Range/Performance (Bank 1 or Single Sensor)	Same as DTC P0340
P0351	Ignition Coil "A" Primary / Secondary Circuit	• Ignition system • Open or short in IGF or IGT1 circuit between ignition coil with igniter and ECM • No.1 ignition coil with igniter • ECM
P0352	Ignition Coil "B" Primary / Secondary Circuit	• Ignition system • Open or short in IGF or IGT2 circuit between ignition coil with igniter and ECM • No.2 ignition coil with igniter • ECM

11

Table z. Engine Management System

DTC	Definition	Trouble Area
P0353	Ignition Coil "C" Primary / Secondary Circuit	• Ignition system • Open or short in IGF or IGT3 circuit between ignition coil with igniter and ECM • No.3 ignition coil with igniter • ECM
P0354	Ignition Coil "D" Primary / Secondary Circuit	• Ignition system • Open or short in IGF or IGT4 circuit between ignition coil with igniter and ECM • No.4 ignition coil with igniter • ECM
P0420	Catalyst System Efficiency Below Threshold (Bank 1)	• Gas leakage in exhaust system • A/F sensor (bank 1 sensor 1) • Heated oxygen sensor (bank 1 sensor 2) • Three-way catalytic converter (exhaust manifold)
P043E	Evaporative Emission System Reference Orifice Clog Up	• Canister pump module (Reference orifice, leak detection pump, vent valve) • Connector/wire harness (Canister pump module-ECM) • EVAP system hose (pipe from air inlet port to canister pump module, canister filter, fuel tank vent hose) • ECM
P043F	Evaporative Emission System Reference Orifice High Flow	Same as DTC P043E
P0441	Evaporative Emission Control System Incorrect Purge Flow	• Fuel tank cap is incorrectly installed • Fuel tank cap is cracked or damaged • Vacuum hose is cracked, blocked, damaged or disconnected ((1), (2), (3), (4), (5), (6) and (7) in Fig. 1) • Open or short in vapor pressure sensor circuit • Vapor pressure sensor • Open or short in VSV circuit for EVAP • VSV for EVAP • Open or short in VSV circuit for CCV • VSV for CCV • Open or short in VSV circuit for pressure switching valve • VSV for pressure switching valve • Fuel tank is cracked or damaged • Charcoal canister is cracked or damaged • Fuel tank over fill check valve is cracked or damaged • ECM
P0442	Evaporative Emission Control System Leak Detected (small leak)	• Fuel tank cap is incorrectly installed • Fuel tank cap is cracked or damaged • Vacuum hose cracks is blocked, damaged or disconnected ((1), (2), (3), (4), (5), (6) and (7) in Fig. 1 of the circuit description • Open or short in vapor pressure sensor circuit • Vapor pressure sensor • Open or short in VSV circuit for EVAP • VSV for EVAP • Open or short in VSV circuit for CCV • VSV for CCV • Open or short in VSV circuit for pressure switching valve • VSV for pressure switching valve • Fuel tank is cracked or damaged • Charcoal canister is cracked or damaged • Fuel tank over fill check valve is cracked or damaged • ECM

Table z. Engine Management System

DTC	Definition	Trouble Area
P0446	Evaporative Emission Control System Vent Control Circuit	Same as DTC P0441
P0450	Evaporative Emission Control System Pressure Sensor Malfunction	• Canister pump module • EVAP system hose (pipe from air inlet port to canister pump module, canister filter, fuel tank vent hose) • Connector / wire harness (Canister pump module ECM) • ECM
P0451	Evaporative Emission Control System Pressure Sensor/Switch Range/Performance	• Open or short in vapor pressure sensor circuit • Vapor pressure sensor • ECM
P0452	Evaporative Emission Control System Pressure Sensor/Switch Low Input	Same as DTC P0451
P0453	Evaporative Emission Control System Pressure Sensor/Switch High Input	Same as DTC P0451
P0455	Evaporative Emission Control System Leak Detected (gross leak)	Same as DTC P0442
P0456	Evaporative Emission Control System Leak Detected (very small leak)	Same as DTC P0442
P0505	Idle Air Control System	• Open or short in idle speed control (ISC) valve circuit • Idle speed control (ISC) valve has stuck closed • ECM • Air induction system • PCV valve and hose
P0560	System Voltage	• Open in back up power source circuit • ECM
P0604	Internal Control Module Random Access Memory (RAM) Error	ECM
P0606	ECM/PCM Processor	ECM
P0607	Control Module Performance	ECM
P0630	Vin Not Programmed or Mismatch - ECM/PCM	ECM
P0657	Actuator Supply Voltage Circuit/ Open	ECM
P1115	Coolant Temperature Sensor Circuit For Coolant Heat Storage System	• Coolant heat storage tank outlet temperature sensor • Open or short in temperature sensor circuit • ECM
P1116	Coolant Temperature Sensor Circuit Stuck For Coolant Heat Storage System	• Coolant heat storage tank outlet temperature sensor • Cooling system (clogging)
P1117	Coolant Temperature Sensor Circuit Low For Coolant Heat Storage System	• Coolant heat storage tank outlet temperature sensor • Short in temperature sensor circuit • ECM
P1118	Coolant Temperature Sensor Circuit High For Coolant Heat Storage System	• Coolant heat storage tank outlet temperature sensor • Open in temperature sensor circuit • ECM
P1120	Coolant Flow Control Valve Position Sensor Circuit	• Open or short in water valve position sensor circuit • Water valve (coolant flow control valve) • ECM
P1121	Coolant Flow Control Valve Position Sensor Circuit Stuck	• Water valve (coolant flow control valve) • Cooling system (clogging)

11

Table z. Engine Management System

DTC	Definition	Trouble Area
P1122	Coolant Flow Control Valve Position Sensor Circuit Low	• Water valve (coolant flow control valve) • Short in WBAD (valve position signal) circuit • Open in VC circuit • ECM
P1123	Coolant Flow Control Valve Position Sensor Circuit High	• Water valve (coolant flow control valve) • Open in E2 circuit • VC and WBAD circuits are short-circuited • Open in WBAD circuit • ECM
P1150	Coolant Path Clog Up For Coolant Heat Storage System	• Coolant heat storage tank outlet temperature sensor • Water valve (coolant flow control valve) • Cooling system (clogging) • Heat storage tank • ECM
P1151	Coolant Heat Storage Tank	Heat storage tank
P1450	Fuel Tank Pressure Sensor	• Fuel tank pressure sensor • Connector/wire harness (Fuel tank pressure sensor-ECM) • ECM
P1451	Fuel Tank Pressure Sensor Range/Performance	• Fuel tank pressure sensor • Connector/wire harness (Fuel tank pressure sensor-ECM) • ECM
P1452	Fuel Tank Pressure Sensor Low Input	• Fuel tank pressure sensor • Connector/wire harness (Fuel tank pressure sensor-ECM) • ECM
P1453	Fuel Tank Pressure Sensor High Input	• Fuel tank pressure sensor • Connector/wire harness (Fuel tank pressure sensor-ECM) • ECM
P1455	Vapor Reducing Fuel Tank System Malfunction	Fuel Tank
P2102	Throttle Actuator Control Motor Circuit Low	• Open or short in throttle control motor circuit • Throttle control motor • ECM
P2103	Throttle Actuator Control Motor Circuit High	• Short in throttle control motor circuit • Throttle control motor • Throttle valve • Throttle body assembly • ECM
P2111	Throttle Actuator Control System Stuck Open	• Throttle control motor circuit • Throttle control motor • Throttle body • Throttle valve
P2112	Throttle Actuator Control System Stuck Closed	• Throttle control motor circuit • Throttle control motor • Throttle body • Throttle valve
P2118	Throttle Actuator Control Motor Current Range / Performance	• Open in ETCS power source circuit • ETCS fuse • ECM
P2119	Throttle Actuator Control Throttle Body Range / Performance	• Electric throttle control system • ECM

Table z. Engine Management System

DTC	Definition	Trouble Area
P2135	Throttle / Pedal Position Sensor / Switch "A"/"B" Voltage Correlation	• VTA and VTA2 circuits are short-circuited • Open in VC circuit • Throttle position sensor
P2195	Oxygen (A/F) Sensor Signal Stuck Lean (Bank 1 Sensor 1)	• Open or short in A/F sensor (bank 1 sensor 1) circuit • A/F sensor (bank 1 sensor 1) • A/F sensor heater • Integration relay • A/F sensor heater and relay circuit • Air induction system • Fuel pressure • Injector • PCV hose connection • ECM
P2196	Oxygen (A/F) Sensor Signal Stuck Rich (Bank 1 Sensor 1)	Same as DTC P2195
P2237	Oxygen (A/F) Sensor Pumping Current Circuit / Open (Bank 1 Sensor 1)	• Open or short in A/F sensor (sensor 1) circuit • A/F sensor (sensor 1) circuit • ECM
P2238	Oxygen Sensor Pumping Current Circuit Low (for A/F sensor Bank 1 Sensor 1)	• Open or short in A/F sensor (bank 1 sensor 1) • A/F sensor (bank 1 sensor 1) • A/F sensor heater • EFI M relay (integration relay) • A/F sensor heater and relay circuit • ECM
P2239	Oxygen Sensor Pumping Current Circuit High (for A/F sensor Bank 1 Sensor 1)	Same as DTC P2238
P2252	Oxygen Sensor Reference Ground Circuit Low (for A/F sensor Bank 1 Sensor1)	Same as DTC P2238
P2253	Oxygen Sensor Reference Ground Circuit High (for A/F sensor Bank 1 Sensor1)	Same as DTC P2238
P2401	Evaporative Emission Leak Detection Pump Stuck OFF	Same as DTC P043E
P2402	Evaporative Emission Leak Detection Pump Stuck ON	Same as DTC P043E
P2419	Evaporative Emission Switching Valve Stuck ON	Same as DTC P043E
P2420	Evaporative Emission Switching Valve Stuck OFF	• Pump module (0.02 inch orifice, vacuum pump, vent valve) • Connector/wire harness (Pump module ECM) • ECM
P2601	Coolant Pump Control Circuit Range/Performance	• CHS water pump • CHS water pump relay • Open or short in CHS water pump circuit • ECM
P2610	ECM/PCM Internal Engine Off Timer Performance	ECM

11

Table z. Engine Management System

DTC	Definition	Trouble Area
P2A00	A/F Sensor Circuit Slow Response (Bank 1 Sensor 1)	• Open or short in A/F sensor (bank 1 sensor 1) circuit • A/F sensor (bank 1 sensor 1) • A/F sensor heater • EFI M relay (integration relay) • A/F sensor heater and relay circuit • Air induction system • Fuel pressure • Injector • PCV hose connection • ECM
P3190	Poor Engine Power	• Air induction system • Throttle body • Fuel pressure • Engine • Air flow meter • Lack of fuel • Engine coolant temperature sensor • Crankshaft position sensor • Camshaft position sensor • ECM
P3191	Engine Does Not Start	• Air induction system • Throttle body • Fuel pressure • Engine • Air flow meter • Lack of fuel • Crankshaft position sensor • Camshaft position sensor • ECM
P3193	Fuel Run Out	• Lack of fuel • ECM
U0293	Lost Communication With HV ECU	• Wire harness • HV ECU • ECM

Hybrid battery system

The table(s) in this section contain hybrid battery system DTCs, code definitions and likely trouble areas.

Retrieving DTCs

Hybrid battery system DTCs can be retrieved by using Toyota scan tool or equivalent. See **Diagnostic Scan Tools** in this chapter.

Clearing DTCs

Clear hybrid battery system DTCs with Toyota scan tool or equivalent.

- Connect scan tool to OBD II connector.

- Turn hybrid system ON (IG-ON, READY indicator not illuminated). Turn tester ON.

- Operate tester to clear DTCs. Refer to tester operating instructions.

Table aa. Hybrid Battery

DTC	Definition	Trouble Area
P0560	System Voltage	• Wire harness or connector • HEV fuse • Battery ECU
P0A1F	Battery Energy Control Module	Battery ECU
P0A7F	Hybrid Battery Pack Deterioration	• HV battery assembly • Battery ECU
P0A80	Replace Hybrid Battery Pack	• HV battery assembly • Battery ECU
P0A81	Hybrid Battery Pack Cooling Fan 1	• Quarter vent duct (blower motor controller) • Battery ECU
P0A82	Hybrid Battery Pack Cooling Fan 1	• Quarter vent duct • Quarter vent duct No. 2 • Quarter vent duct inner No. 2 • Ventilator inner duct • Battery blower assembly • Battery ECU
P0A84	Hybrid Battery Pack Cooling Fan 1 Control Circuit Low	• Wire harness or connector • BATT FAN fuse • Battery blower relay No. 1 • Battery blower assembly • Quarter vent duct (blower motor controller) • Battery ECU
P0A85	Hybrid Battery Pack Cooling Fan 1	• Wire harness or connector • BATT FAN fuse • Battery blower relay No. 1 • Battery blower assembly • Quarter vent duct (blower motor controller) • Battery ECU

11

Table aa. Hybrid Battery

DTC	Definition	Trouble Area
P0A95	High Voltage Fuse	• High voltage fuse • Service plug grip • Battery plug • Battery ECU
P0A9C	Hybrid Battery Temperature Sensor "A" Range/Performance	• HV battery assembly (battery temperature sensor) • Battery ECU
P0A9D	Hybrid Battery Temperature Sensor "A" Circuit Low	• HV battery assembly (battery temperature sensor) • Battery ECU
P0A9E	Hybrid Battery Temperature Sensor "A" Circuit High	• HV battery assembly (battery temperature sensor) • Battery ECU
P0AAC	Hybrid Battery Pack Air Temperature Sensor "A" Circuit	• HV battery assembly (intake air temperature sensor) • Battery ECU
P0ABF	Hybrid Battery Pack Current Sensor Circuit	• HV battery assembly (wire harness or connector) • Battery current sensor • Battery ECU
P0AC0	Hybrid Battery Pack Current Sensor Circuit Range/Performance	• HV battery assembly (wire harness or connector) • Battery current sensor • Battery ECU
P0AC1	Hybrid Battery Pack Current Sensor Circuit Low	• HV battery assembly (wire harness or connector) • Battery current sensor • Battery ECU
P0AC2	Hybrid Battery Pack Current Sensor Circuit High	• HV battery assembly (wire harness or connector) • Battery current sensor • Battery ECU
P0AFA	Hybrid Battery System Voltage Low	• Junction block assembly (busbar module) • No. 2 frame wire (busbar and wire harness) • Battery ECU
P3011	Battery Block 1 Weak	• HV battery assembly • Battery ECU
P3012	Battery Block 2 Weak	• HV battery assembly • Battery ECU
P3013	Battery Block 3 Weak	• HV battery assembly • Battery ECU
P3014	Battery Block 4 Weak	• HV battery assembly • Battery ECU
P3015	Battery Block 5 Weak	• HV battery assembly • Battery ECU
P3016	Battery Block 6 Weak	• HV battery assembly • Battery ECU
P3017	Battery Block 7 Weak	• HV battery assembly • Battery ECU
P3018	Battery Block 8 Weak	• HV battery assembly • Battery ECU
P3019	Battery Block 9 Weak	• HV battery assembly • Battery ECU
P3020	Battery Block 10 Weak	• HV battery assembly • Battery ECU

Table aa. Hybrid Battery

DTC	Definition	Trouble Area
P3021	Battery Block 11 Weak	• HV battery assembly • Battery ECU
P3022	Battery Block 12 Weak	• HV battery assembly • Battery ECU
P3023	Battery Block 13 Weak	• HV battery assembly • Battery ECU
P3024	Battery Block 14 Weak	• HV battery assembly • Battery ECU
P3030	Disconnection between Battery and ECU	• Junction block assembly (busbar module) • Frame wire No. 2 (busbar and wire harness) • Battery ECU
U0100	Lost Communication with ECM / PCM "A"	CAN communication system
U0293	Lost Communication with Hybrid Vehicle Control System	CAN communication system

11

Hybrid control system

The table(s) in this section contain hybrid control system DTCs, Toyota INF codes, code definitions, detection condition, and likely trouble areas.

Retrieving DTCs

Hybrid control system DTCs and information codes can be retrieved by using Toyota scan tool or equivalent. See **Diagnostic Scan Tools** in this chapter.

Clearing DTCs

Clear hybrid control system DTCs with Toyota scan tool or equivalent.

– Connect scan tool to OBD II connector.

– Turn hybrid system ON (IG-ON, READY indicator not illuminated). Turn tester ON.

– Operate tester to clear DTCs. Refer to tester operating instructions.

Table ab. Hybrid Control System

DTC	INF Code	Definition	Detection Condition	Trouble Area
B2799	539 540 541 542 543 544	Immobilizer Malfunction	Immobilizer malfunction	Immobilizer system
P0336	137	Crankshaft Position Sensor "A" Circuit Range/Performance	Engine speed sensor deviation malfunction (CAN communication)	• Wire harness or connector • Crankshaft position sensor • Camshaft position sensor • HV control ECU
P0338	600	Crankshaft Position Sensor "A" Circuit High Input	NEO signal circuit malfunction	• Wire harness or connector • HV control ECU
P0340	532	Camshaft Position Sensor "A" Circuit	Engine speed sensor deviation malfunction (pulse signal)	• Wire harness or connector • Crankshaft position sensor • Camshaft position sensor • HV control ECU
P0343	601	Camshaft Position Sensor "A" Circuit High Input	GO signal circuit malfunction	• Wire harness or connector • HV control ECU
P0500	352	Vehicle Speed Sensor "A"	No input of vehicle speed signal during cruise control driving	Cruise control system
P0560	117	System Voltage	HV control ECU back-up power source circuit malfunction	• Wire harness or connector • HEV fuse
P0571	115	Brake Switch "A" Circuit	Open or short in stop lamp switch circuit	Cruise control system
P0607	116	Control Module Performance	When STP signal of HV control ECU is inconsistent with that of skid control ECU, with cruise control indicator ON	Cruise control system

Table ab. Hybrid Control System

DTC	INF Code	Definition	Detection Condition	Trouble Area
P0630	804	Vin Not Programmed or Mismatch - ECM/PCM		ECM
P0705	571	Transmission Range Sensor Circuit	Open or GND short in shift main sensor circuit	• Wire harness or connector • Selector lever • HV control ECU
P0705	572	Transmission Range Sensor Circuit	+B short in shift main sensor circuit	• Wire harness or connector • Selector lever • HV control ECU
P0705	573	Transmission Range Sensor Circuit	Open or GND short in shift sub sensor circuit	• Wire harness or connector • Selector lever • HV control ECU
P0705	574	Transmission Range Sensor Circuit	+B short in shift sub sensor circuit	• Wire harness or connector • Selector lever • HV control ECU
P0705	575	Transmission Range Sensor Circuit	Open or GND short in select main sensor circuit	• Wire harness or connector • Selector lever • HV control ECU
P0705	576	Transmission Range Sensor Circuit	+B short in select main sensor circuit	• Wire harness or connector • Selector lever • HV control ECU
P0705	577	Transmission Range Sensor Circuit	Open or GND short in select sub sensor circuit	• Wire harness or connector • Selector lever • HV control ECU
P0705	578	Transmission Range Sensor Circuit	+B short in select sub sensor circuit	• Wire harness or connector • Selector lever • HV control ECU
P0705	595	Transmission Range Sensor Circuit	Difference between shift main sensor value and shift sub sensor value is large	• Wire harness or connector • Selector lever • HV control ECU
P0705	596	Transmission Range Sensor Circuit	Difference between select main sensor value and select sub sensor value is large	• Wire harness or connector • Selector lever • HV control ECU
P0851	579	Park/Neutral Switch Input Circuit Low	GND short in P position switch circuit	• Wire harness or connector • P position switch • HV control ECU
P0852	580	Park/Neutral Switch Input Circuit High	Open or +B short in P position switch circuit	• Wire harness or connector • P position switch • HV control ECU

11

Table ab. Hybrid Control System

DTC	INF Code	Definition	Detection Condition	Trouble Area
P0A08	264	DC/DC Converter Status Circuit	DC/DC converter malfunction	• Auxiliary battery • FL block • HV control ECU • Fuse (for 12 V electrical equipment) • Engine room R/B • Inverter cooling hose • Water w/ motor and bracket pump assy • Cooling fan motor • Cooling fan motor No.2 • Wire harness or connector • Converter inverter assembly (DC/DC converter)
P0A09	265	DC/DC Converter Status Circuit Low Input	Open or GND short in NODD signal circuit of DC/DC converter	• Wire harness or connector • Converter inverter assembly
P0A09	591	DC/DC Converter Status Circuit Low Input	Open or GND short in VLO signal circuit of DC/DC converter	• Wire harness or connector • Converter inverter assembly
P0A0D	350	High Voltage System Interlock Circuit	Operating safety devices with vehicle stopped (ILK signal is ON)	• Service plug grip installation • Inverter cover installation
P0A0D	351	High Voltage System Interlock Circuit	Open in interlock signal Circuit while vehicle is running	• Wire harness or connector • Battery plug (interlock switch No. 2) • Converter inverter assembly (interlock switch No. 1)
P0A0F	204	Engine Failed to Start	Abnormal signal input from ECM (abnormal engine output)	• ECM • SFI system
P0A0F	205	Engine Failed to Start	Abnormal signal input from ECM (engine is unable to start)	• ECM • SFI system
P0A0F	238	Engine Failed to Start	Engine does not start even though cranking it (transaxle input malfunction [engine system])	• Engine assembly • HV transaxle assembly (shaft or gear) • Transmission input damper • Wire harness or connector • HV control ECU
P0A0F	533	Engine Failed to Start	Abnormal signal input from ECM (abnormal engine output by running out of fuel)	• ECM • SFI system
P0A0F	534	Engine Failed to Start	Abnormal signal input from ECM (engine is unable to start by running out of fuel)	• ECM • SFI system
P0A10	263	DC/DC Converter Status Circuit High Input	+B short in NODD signal circuit of DC/DC converter	• Wire harness or connector • Converter inverter assembly
P0A10	592	DC/DC Converter Status Circuit High Input	+B short in VLO signal Circuit of DC/DC converter	• Wire harness or connector • Converter inverter assembly
P0A1D	134 135 139 140 141	Hybrid Powertrain Control Module	HV control ECU internal error	HV control ECU

Table ab. Hybrid Control System

DTC	INF Code	Definition	Detection Condition	Trouble Area
P0A1D	142	Hybrid Powertrain Control Module	ST signal of HV control ECU is ON with power switch OFF	• Wire harness or connector • Power source control ECU
P0A1D	143 144 145 148 149 150 151 152 155 156	Hybrid Powertrain Control Module	HV control ECU internal error	HV control ECU
P0A1D	158 159 160 163 164 165 166 167 168 177	Hybrid Powertrain Control Module	HV control ECU internal error	HV control ECU
P0A1D	178 180 181 182 183 184 185 186 187 188	Hybrid Powertrain Control Module	HV control ECU internal error	HV control ECU
P0A1D	189 192 193 195 196 197 198 199 200	Hybrid Powertrain Control Module	HV control ECU internal error	HV control ECU
P0A1D	390	Hybrid Powertrain Control Module	Charge control malfunction	HV control ECU
P0A1D	392 393 511 512 564 565 567 568 569 570 615	Hybrid Powertrain Control Module	HV control ECU internal error	HV control ECU

11

Table ab. Hybrid Control System

DTC	INF Code	Definition	Detection Condition	Trouble Area
P0A1F	123	Battery Energy Control Module	Abnormal signal input from battery ECU (ROMRAM malfunction)	HV battery system Battery ECU
P0A1F	129	Battery Energy Control Module	HV battery voltage circuit malfunction	• HV battery voltage circuit • Service plug grip • High voltage fuse • Battery plug • Battery ECU
P0A1F	593	Battery Energy Control Module	IG2 signal circuit of battery ECU malfunction	• Wire harness or connector • Battery ECU
P0A2B	248	Drive Motor "A" Temperature Sensor Circuit Range/Performance	Motor temperature sensor No. 1 malfunction	Hybrid vehicle motor
P0A2B	250	Drive Motor "A" Temperature Sensor Circuit Range/Performance	Motor temperature sensor No. 1 performance problem	Hybrid vehicle motor
P0A2C	247	Drive Motor "A" Temperature Sensor Circuit Low	GND short in motor temperature sensor No. 1 circuit	• Wire harness or connector • Hybrid vehicle motor • HV control ECU
P0A2D	249	Drive Motor "A" Temperature Sensor Circuit High	Open or +B short in motor temperature sensor No. 1 circuit	• Wire harness or connector • Hybrid vehicle motor • HV control ECU
P0A37	258	Generator Temperature Sensor Circuit Range / Performance	Motor temperature sensor No. 2 malfunction	Hybrid vehicle motor
P0A37	260	Generator Temperature Sensor Circuit Range / Performance	Motor temperature sensor No. 2 performance problem	• Hybrid vehicle motor • Transaxle fluid leakage • HV transaxle assembly
P0A38	257	Generator Temperature Sensor Circuit Low	GND short in motor temperature sensor No. 2 circuit	• Wire harness or connector • Hybrid vehicle motor • HV control ECU
P0A39	259	Generator Temperature Sensor Circuit High	Open or +B short in motor temperature sensor No. 2 circuit	• Wire harness or connector • Hybrid vehicle motor • HV control ECU
P0A3F	243	Drive Motor "A" Position Sensor Circuit	Interphase short in motor resolver circuit	• Wire harness or connector • Hybrid vehicle motor • HV control ECU
P0A40	500	Drive Motor "A" Position Sensor Circuit Range / Performance	Motor resolver output is out of normal range	• Wire harness or connector • Hybrid vehicle motor • HV control ECU
P0A41	245	Drive Motor "A" Position Sensor Circuit Low	Open or short in motor resolver circuit	• Wire harness or connector • Hybrid vehicle motor • HV control ECU
P0A4B	253	Generator Position Sensor Circuit	Interphase short in generator resolver circuit	• Wire harness or connector • Hybrid vehicle motor • HV control ECU
P0A4C	513	Generator Position Sensor Circuit Range / Performance	Generator resolver output is out of normal range	• Wire harness or connector • Hybrid vehicle motor • HV control ECU

Table ab. Hybrid Control System

DTC	INF Code	Definition	Detection Condition	Trouble Area
P0A4D	255	Generator Position Sensor Circuit Low	Open or short in generator resolver circuit	• Wire harness or connector • Hybrid vehicle motor • HV control ECU
P0A51	174	Drive Motor "A" Current Sensor Circuit	HV control ECU internal error	HV control ECU
P0A60	288	Drive Motor "A" Phase V Current	Phase V current sub sensor of motor inverter current sensor malfunction	• Wire harness or connector • Converter inverter assembly
P0A60	289	Drive Motor "A" Phase V Current	Open in phase V current sub sensor circuit of motor inverter current sensor	• Wire harness or connector • Converter inverter assembly
P0A60	290	Drive Motor "A" Phase V Current	Phase V current main Sensor of motor inverter current sensor malfunction	• Wire harness or connector • Converter inverter assembly
P0A60	292	Drive Motor "A" Phase V Current	Open in phase V current main sensor circuit of motor inverter current sensor	• Wire harness or connector • Converter inverter assembly
P0A60	294	Drive Motor "A" Phase V Current	Phase V current main and sub sensors of motor inverter current sensor performance problem	• Wire harness or connector • Converter inverter assembly
P0A60	501	Drive Motor "A" Phase V Current	Phase V current main and sub sensors of motor Inverter current sensor offset malfunction	• Wire harness or connector • Converter inverter assembly
P0A63	296	Drive Motor "A" Phase W Current	Phase W current sub sensor of motor inverter current sensor malfunction	• Wire harness or connector • Converter inverter assembly
P0A63	297	Drive Motor "A" Phase W Current	Open in phase W current sub sensor circuit of motor inverter current sensor	• Wire harness or connector • Converter inverter assembly
P0A63	298	Drive Motor "A" Phase W Current	Phase W current main sensor of motor inverter current sensor malfunction	• Wire harness or connector • Converter inverter assembly
P0A63	300	Drive Motor "A" Phase W Current	Open in phase W current main sensor circuit of motor inverter current sensor	• Wire harness or connector • Converter inverter assembly
P0A63	302	Drive Motor "A" Phase W Current	Phase W current main and sub sensors of motor inverter current sensor performance problem	• Wire harness or connector • Converter inverter assembly
P0A63	502	Drive Motor "A" Phase W Current	Phase W current main and sub sensors of motor inverter current sensor offset malfunction	• Wire harness or connector • Converter inverter assembly
P0A72	326	Generator Phase V Current	Phase V current sub sensor of generator inverter current sensor malfunction	• Wire harness or connector • Converter inverter assembly
P0A72	327	Generator Phase V Current	Open in phase V current sub sensor circuit of generator inverter current sensor	• Wire harness or connector • Converter inverter assembly

11

Table ab. Hybrid Control System

DTC	INF Code	Definition	Detection Condition	Trouble Area
P0A72	328	Generator Phase V Current	Phase V current main sensor of generator inverter current sensor malfunction	• Wire harness or connector • Converter inverter assembly
P0A72	330	Generator Phase V Current	Open in phase V current main sensor circuit of generator inverter current sensor	• Wire harness or connector • Converter inverter assembly
P0A72	333	Generator Phase V Current	Phase V current main and sub sensors of generator inverter current sensor performance problem	• Wire harness or connector • Converter inverter assembly
P0A72	515	Generator Phase V Current	Phase V current main and sub sensors of generator inverter current sensor offset malfunction	• Wire harness or connector • Converter inverter assembly
P0A75	334	Generator Phase W Current	Phase W current sub sensor of generator inverter current sensor malfunction	• Wire harness or connector • Converter inverter assembly
P0A75	335	Generator Phase W Current	Open in phase W current sub sensor circuit of generator inverter current sensor	• Wire harness or connector • Converter inverter assembly
P0A75	336	Generator Phase W Current	Phase W current main sensor of generator inverter current sensor malfunction	• Wire harness or connector • Converter inverter assembly
P0A75	338	Generator Phase W Current	Open in phase W current main sensor circuit of generator inverter current sensor	• Wire harness or connector • Converter inverter assembly
P0A75	341	Generator Phase W Current	Phase W current main and sub sensors of generator inverter current sensor performance problem	• Wire harness or connector • Converter inverter assembly
P0A75	516	Generator Phase W Current	Phase W current main and sub sensors of generator inverter current sensor offset malfunction	• Wire harness or connector • Converter inverter assembly
P0A78	266	Drive Motor "A" Inverter Performance	Open or GND short in inverter voltage (VH) signal circuit	• Wire harness or connector • Converter inverter assembly • HV control ECU
P0A78	267	Drive Motor "A" Inverter Performance	+B short in inverter voltage (VH) signal circuit	• Wire harness or connector • Converter inverter assembly • HV control ECU
P0A78	272	Drive Motor "A" Inverter Performance	Abnormality in motor PWM circuit	• Wire harness or connector • Converter inverter assembly
P0A78	278	Drive Motor "A" Inverter Performance	+B short in motor inverter over-voltage (OVH) signal circuit	• Wire harness or connector • Converter inverter assembly
P0A78	279	Drive Motor "A" Inverter Performance	Motor inverter over voltage (OVH) signal detection (over voltage by inverter assembly malfunction)	• Wire harness or connector • HV transaxle assembly • Hybrid vehicle motor • Hybrid vehicle generator • HV control ECU • Converter inverter assembly

Table ab. Hybrid Control System

DTC	INF Code	Definition	Detection Condition	Trouble Area
P0A78	280	Drive Motor "A" Inverter Performance	Open or GND short in motor inverter over-voltage (OVH) signal circuit	• Wire harness or connector • Converter inverter assembly
P0A78	282	Drive Motor "A" Inverter Performance	Motor inverter over voltage (OVH) signal detection (Circuit malfunction)	• Wire harness or connector • Converter inverter assembly
P0A78	283	Drive Motor "A" Inverter Performance	+B short in motor inverter fail (MFIV) signal circuit	• Wire harness or connector • Converter inverter assembly
P0A78	284	Drive Motor "A" Inverter Performance	Motor inverter fail (MFIV) signal detection (inverter overheating)	• Wire harness or connector • Inverter cooling system • Water w/ motor & bracket pump assembly • Cooling fan motor • Cooling fan motor No. 2 • HV transaxle assembly • Hybrid vehicle motor • HV control ECU • Converter inverter assembly
P0A78	285	Drive Motor "A" Inverter Performance	Open or GND short in motor inverter fail (MFIV) signal circuit	• Wire harness or connector • Converter inverter assembly
P0A78	286	Drive Motor "A" Inverter Performance	Motor inverter fail (MFIV) signal detection (circuit Malfunction)	• Wire harness or connector • Converter inverter assembly
P0A78	287	Drive Motor "A" Inverter Performance	Motor inverter fail (MFIV) signal detection (over current by inverter assembly malfunction)	• Wire harness or connector • HV transaxle assembly • Hybrid vehicle motor • HV control ECU • Converter inverter assembly
P0A78	304	Drive Motor "A" Inverter Performance	Open or +B short in motor gate shutdown (MSDN) signal circuit	• Wire harness or connector • Converter inverter assembly
P0A78	305	Drive Motor "A" Inverter Performance	GND short in motor gate shutdown (MSDN) signal circuit	• Wire harness or connector • Converter inverter assembly
P0A78	306	Drive Motor "A" Inverter Performance	Failure in monitoring MG2 torque performance	• Hybrid vehicle motor • Converter inverter assembly
P0A78	308	Drive Motor "A" Inverter Performance	Collision signal input from airbag ECU or circuit breaker sensor No. 1	• Supplemental restraint system • Circuit breaker sensor No. 1
P0A78	503	Drive Motor "A" Inverter Performance	Motor inverter over voltage (OVH) signal detection (over voltage by HV control ECU malfunction)	• Wire harness or connector • HV transaxle assembly • Hybrid vehicle motor • Hybrid vehicle generator • HV control ECU • Converter inverter assembly
P0A78	504	Drive Motor "A" Inverter Performance	Motor inverter over voltage (OVH) signal detection (over voltage by HV transaxle assembly malfunction)	• Wire harness or connector • HV transaxle assembly • Hybrid vehicle motor • Hybrid vehicle generator • HV control ECU • Converter inverter assembly

11

Table ab. Hybrid Control System

DTC	INF Code	Definition	Detection Condition	Trouble Area
P0A78	505	Drive Motor "A" Inverter Performance	Motor inverter fail (MFIV) signal detection (over current by HV control ECU malfunction)	• Wire harness or connector • HV transaxle assembly • Hybrid vehicle motor • HV control ECU • Converter inverter assembly
P0A78	506	Drive Motor "A" Inverter Performance	Motor inverter fail (MFIV) signal detection (over current by HV transaxle assembly malfunction)	• Wire harness or connector • HV transaxle assembly • Hybrid vehicle motor • HV control ECU • Converter inverter assembly
P0A78	507	Drive Motor "A" Inverter Performance	Open in motor gate shutdown (MSDN) signal circuit	• Wire harness or connector • Converter inverter assembly
P0A78	508	Drive Motor "A" Inverter Performance	Motor gate shutdown (MSDN) signal malfunction	• Wire harness or connector • HV control ECU
P0A78	510	Drive Motor "A" Inverter Performance	Motor inverter gate malfunction	• Wire harness or connector • Converter inverter assembly
P0A78	523	Drive Motor "A" Inverter Performance	Inverter voltage (VH) sensor offset malfunction	• System main relay • Converter inverter assembly
P0A78	586	Drive Motor "A" Inverter Performance	Inverter voltage (VH) sensor performance problem	• Wire harness or connector • Converter inverter assembly
P0A7A	309	Generator Inverter Performance	Abnormality in generator PWM circuit	• Wire harness or connector • Converter inverter assembly
P0A7A	321	Generator Inverter Performance	+B short in generator Inverter fail (GFIV) signal circuit	• Wire harness or connector • Converter inverter assembly
P0A7A	322	Generator Inverter Performance	Generator inverter fail (GFIV) signal detection (Inverter overheating)	• Wire harness or connector • Inverter cooling system • Water w/ motor & bracket pump assembly • Cooling fan motor • Cooling fan motor No. 2 • HV transaxle assembly • Hybrid vehicle generator • HV control ECU • Converter inverter assembly
P0A7A	323	Generator Inverter Performance	Open or GND short in generator inverter fail (GFIV) signal circuit	• Wire harness or connector • Converter inverter assembly
P0A7A	324	Generator Inverter Performance	Generator inverter fail (GFIV) signal detection (Circuit malfunction)	• Wire harness or connector • Converter inverter assembly
P0A7A	325	Generator Inverter Performance	Generator inverter fail (GFIV) signal detection (over current by inverter assembly malfunction)	• Wire harness or connector • HV transaxle assembly • Hybrid vehicle generator • HV control ECU • Converter inverter assembly
P0A7A	342	Generator Inverter Performance	Open or +B short in generator gate shutdown (GSDN) signal circuit	• Wire harness or connector • Converter inverter assembly
P0A7A	343	Generator Inverter Performance	GND short in generator gate shutdown (GSDN) signal circuit	• Wire harness or connector • Converter inverter assembly
P0A7A	344	Generator Inverter Performance	Failure in monitoring MG1 torque performance	• Hybrid vehicle generator • Converter inverter assembly

Table ab. Hybrid Control System

DTC	INF Code	Definition	Detection Condition	Trouble Area
P0A7A	517	Generator Inverter Performance	Generator inverter fail (GFIV) signal detection (over current by HV control ECU malfunction)	• Wire harness or connector • HV transaxle assembly • Hybrid vehicle generator • HV control ECU • Converter inverter assembly
P0A7A	518	Generator Inverter Performance	Generator inverter fail (GFIV) signal detection (over current by HV transaxle assembly malfunction)	• Wire harness or connector • HV transaxle assembly • Hybrid vehicle generator • HV control ECU • Converter inverter assembly
P0A7A	519	Generator Inverter Performance	Open in generator gate shutdown (GSDN) signal circuit	• Wire harness or connector • Converter inverter assembly
P0A7A	520	Generator Inverter Performance	Generator gate shutdown (GSDN) signal malfunction	• Wire harness or connector • HV control ECU
P0A7A	522	Generator Inverter Performance	Generator inverter gate malfunction	• Wire harness or connector • Converter inverter assembly
P0A90	239	Drive Motor "A" Performance	HV transaxle input malfunction (shaft damaged)	• Engine assembly • HV transaxle assembly (shaft or gear) • Transmission input damper • Wire harness or connector • HV control ECU
P0A90	240	Drive Motor "A" Performance	Generator locked	Hybrid vehicle generator
P0A90	241	Drive Motor "A" Performance	HV transaxle input malfunction (torque limiter slipping)	• Engine assembly • HV transaxle assembly (shaft or gear) • Transmission input damper • Wire harness or connector • HV control ECU
P0A90	242	Drive Motor "A" Performance	Planetary gear locked	HV transaxle assembly
P0A90	251	Drive Motor "A" Performance	MG2 magnetic force deterioration or same phase short circuit	Hybrid vehicle motor
P0A90	509	Drive Motor "A" Performance	MG2 system malfunction	• Hybrid vehicle motor • Converter inverter assembly
P0A90	602	Drive Motor "A" Performance	HV transaxle output malfunction	• Engine assembly • HV transaxle assembly (shaft or gear) • Transmission input damper • Wire harness or connector • HV control ECU
P0A90	604	Drive Motor "A" Performance	MG2 power balance malfunction (small power balance)	• Battery current sensor • Hybrid vehicle motor
P0A90	605	Drive Motor "A" Performance	MG2 power balance malfunction (large power balance)	• Battery current sensor • Hybrid vehicle motor
P0A92	261	Hybrid Generator Performance	MG1 magnetic force deterioration or same phase short circuit	Hybrid vehicle generator
P0A92	521	Hybrid Generator Performance	MG1 system malfunction	• Hybrid vehicle generator • Converter inverter assembly

Table ab. Hybrid Control System

DTC	INF Code	Definition	Detection Condition	Trouble Area
P0A92	606	Hybrid Generator Performance	MG1 power balance malfunction (small power balance)	• Battery current sensor • Hybrid vehicle generator
P0A92	607	Hybrid Generator Performance	MG1 power balance malfunction (large power balance)	• Battery current sensor • Hybrid vehicle generator
P0A93	346	Inverter Cooling System Performance	Inverter cooling system Malfunction (water pump system malfunction)	• Wire harness or connector • Inverter cooling system • Water w/ motor & bracket pump assembly • Cooling fan motor • Cooling fan motor No. 2 • Converter inverter assembly
P0A93	347	Inverter Cooling System Performance	Inverter cooling system Malfunction (electric cooling fan system malfunction)	• Wire harness or connector • Inverter cooling system • Water w/ motor & bracket pump assembly • Cooling fan motor • Cooling fan motor No. 2 • w/ converter inverter assembly
P0A94	442	DC/DC Converter Performance	Abnormal voltage execution value	Converter inverter assembly
P0A94	545	DC/DC Converter Performance	Open or GND short in boost converter over voltage (OVL) signal circuit	• Wire harness or connector • Converter inverter assembly
P0A94	546	DC/DC Converter Performance	+B short in boost converter over-voltage (OVL) signal circuit	• Wire harness or connector • Converter inverter assembly
P0A94	547	DC/DC Converter Performance	Boost converter over voltage (OVL) signal detection (over voltage by HV control ECU malfunction)	• Wire harness or connector • HV transaxle assembly • Hybrid vehicle motor • Hybrid vehicle generator • HV control ECU • Converter inverter assembly
P0A94	548	DC/DC Converter Performance	Boost converter over voltage (OVL) signal detection (over voltage by inverter assembly malfunction)	• Wire harness or connector • HV transaxle assembly • Hybrid vehicle motor • Hybrid vehicle generator • HV control ECU • Converter inverter assembly
P0A94	549	DC/DC Converter Performance	Boost converter over voltage (OVL) signal detection (over voltage by HV transaxle assembly malfunction)	• Wire harness or connector • HV transaxle assembly • Hybrid vehicle motor • Hybrid vehicle generator • HV control ECU • Converter inverter assembly
P0A94	550	DC/DC Converter Performance	Boost converter over voltage (OVL) signal detection (circuit malfunction)	• Wire harness or connector • Converter inverter assembly
P0A94	551	DC/DC Converter Performance	Open or GND short in boost converter fail (FCV) signal circuit	• Wire harness or connector • Converter inverter assembly
P0A94	552	DC/DC Converter Performance	+B short in boost converter fail (FCV) signal circuit	• Wire harness or connector • Converter inverter assembly

Table ab. Hybrid Control System

DTC	INF Code	Definition	Detection Condition	Trouble Area
P0A94	553	DC/DC Converter Performance	Boost converter fail (FCV) signal detection (boost converter overheating)	• Wire harness or connector • Inverter cooling system • Water w/ motor & bracket pump assembly • Cooling fan motor • Cooling fan motor No. 2 • HV transaxle assembly • Hybrid vehicle motor • Hybrid vehicle generator • HV control ECU • Converter inverter assembly
P0A94	554	DC/DC Converter Performance	Boost converter fail (FCV) signal detection (over current by HV control ECU malfunction)	• Wire harness or connector • HV transaxle assembly • Hybrid vehicle motor • Hybrid vehicle generator • HV control ECU • Converter inverter assembly
P0A94	555	DC/DC Converter Performance	Boost converter fail (FCV) signal detection (over current by inverter assembly malfunction)	• Wire harness or connector • HV transaxle assembly • Hybrid vehicle motor • Hybrid vehicle generator • HV control ECU • Converter inverter assembly
P0A94	556	DC/DC Converter Performance	Boost converter fail (FCV) signal detection (over current by HV transaxle as-sembly malfunction)	• Wire harness or connector • HV transaxle assembly • Hybrid vehicle motor • Hybrid vehicle generator • HV control ECU • Converter inverter assembly
P0A94	557	DC/DC Converter Performance	Boost converter fail (FCV) signal detection (circuit Malfunction)	• Wire harness or connector • Converter inverter assembly
P0A94	558	DC/DC Converter Performance	GND short in boost converter gate shutdown (CSDN) signal circuit	• Wire harness or connector • Converter inverter assembly
P0A94	559	DC/DC Converter Performance	Open or +B short in boost converter gate shutdown (CSDN) signal circuit	• Wire harness or connector • Converter inverter assembly
P0A94	560	DC/DC Converter Performance	Open in boost converter gate shutdown (CSDN) signal circuit	• Wire harness or connector • Converter inverter assembly
P0A94	561	DC/DC Converter Performance	Abnormal boost converter gate shutdown (CSDN) signal	• Wire harness or connector • HV control ECU
P0A94	583	DC/DC Converter Performance	Open or GND short in boost converter temperature Sensor circuit	• Wire harness or connector • Converter inverter assembly • HV control ECU
P0A94	584	DC/DC Converter Performance	+B short in boost converter temperature sensor circuit	• Wire harness or connector • Converter inverter assembly • HV control ECU
P0A94	585	DC/DC Converter Performance	Boost converter voltage (VL) sensor performance problem	• Wire harness or connector • Converter inverter assembly

11

Table ab. Hybrid Control System

DTC	INF Code	Definition	Detection Condition	Trouble Area
P0A94	587	DC/DC Converter Performance	Difference between voltages from HV battery voltage (VB) sensor and boost converter voltage (VL) sensor is large	• Wire harness or connector • Converter inverter assembly • Service plug grip • High voltage fuse • Battery ECU
P0A94	588	DC/DC Converter Performance	Abnormality in boost converter PWM circuit	• Wire harness or connector • Converter inverter assembly
P0A94	589	DC/DC Converter Performance	Open or GND short in boost converter voltage (VL) signal circuit	• Wire harness or connector • Converter inverter assembly • HV control ECU
P0A94	590	DC/DC Converter Performance	+B short in boost converter voltage (VL) signal circuit	• Wire harness or connector • Converter inverter assembly • HV control ECU
P0AA1	224	Hybrid Battery Positive Contactor Circuit Stuck Closed	Open or +B short in system main relay No. 1 circuit	• Wire harness or connector • System main relay No. 1 • HV control ECU
P0AA1	226	Hybrid Battery Positive Contactor Circuit Stuck Closed	Open or +B short in system main relay No. 2 circuit	• Wire harness or connector • System main relay No. 2 • HV control ECU
P0AA1	231	Hybrid Battery Positive Contactor Circuit Stuck Closed	System main relay terminal of HV battery positive side stuck closed	• System main relay No. 1 • System main relay No. 2
P0AA1	233	Hybrid Battery Positive Contactor Circuit Stuck Closed	System main relay terminals of HV battery positive and negative sides stuck closed	• System main relay No. 1 • System main relay No. 2 • System main relay No. 3
P0AA2	225	Hybrid Battery Positive Contactor Circuit Stuck Open	GND short in system main relay No. 1 circuit	• Wire harness or connector • System main relay No. 1 • HV control ECU
P0AA2	227	Hybrid Battery Positive Contactor Circuit Stuck Open	GND short in system main relay No. 2 circuit	• Wire harness or connector • System main relay No. 2 • HV control ECU
P0AA4	228	Hybrid Battery Negative Contactor Circuit Stuck Closed	Open or +B short in system main relay No. 3 circuit	• Wire harness or connector • System main relay No. 3 • HV control ECU
P0AA4	232	Hybrid Battery Negative Contactor Circuit Stuck Closed	System main relay terminal of HV battery negative side stuck closed	• System main relay No. 3
P0AA5	229	Hybrid Battery Negative Contactor Circuit Stuck Open	GND short in system main relay No. 3 circuit	• Wire harness or connector • System main relay No. 3 • HV control ECU
P0AA6	526	Hybrid Battery Voltage System Isolation Fault	Insulation resistance of high voltage circuit and body is low	• Frame wire • System main relay • System main resistor • HV battery assembly • Motor compressor assembly • Battery ECU • HV transaxle assembly • Converter inverter assembly • Main battery cable • Main battery cable No. 2 • Battery plug • Frame wire No. 2 • Junction block assembly

Table ab. Hybrid Control System

DTC	INF Code	Definition	Detection Condition	Trouble Area
P0AA6	611	Hybrid Battery Voltage System Isolation Fault	Insulation resistance of A/C compressor motor or A/C Inverter is low	• Motor compressor assembly • Converter inverter assembly
P0AA6	612	Hybrid Battery Voltage System Isolation Fault	Insulation resistance of HV battery, battery ECU, System main relay, or system main resistor is low	• HV battery assembly • Battery ECU • System main relay • System main resistor • Main battery cable • Main battery cable No. 2 • Battery plug • Frame wire No. 2 • Junction block assembly
P0AA6	613	Hybrid Battery Voltage System Isolation Fault	Insulation resistance of HV transaxle or motor and generator inverters is low	• HV transaxle assembly • Converter inverter assembly
P0AA6	614	Hybrid Battery Voltage System Isolation Fault	Insulation resistance of motor and generator inverters, A/C inverter, system main relay, system main resistor, or frame wire is low	• Frame wire • System main relay • System main resistor • HV battery assembly • Converter inverter assembly • Main battery cable • Main battery cable No. 2 • Battery plug • Frame wire No. 2 • Junction block assembly
P0ADB-227		Hybrid Battery Positive Contactor Control Circuit Low	GND short in No. 2 system main relay circuit	• Wire harness or connector • No. 2 system main relay • HV control ECU
P0ADC-226		Hybrid Battery Positive Contactor Control Circuit High	Open or +B short in No. 2 system main relay circuit	• Wire harness or connector • No. 2 system main relay • HV control ECU
P0ADF-229		Hybrid Battery Negative Contactor Control Circuit Low	GND short in No. 3 system main relay circuit	• Wire harness or connector • No. 3 system main relay • HV control ECU
P0AE0	274	Drive Motor Inverter Temperature Sensor "A" High	+B short in motor inverter temperature sensor circuit	• Wire harness or connector • Converter inverter assembly • HV control ECU
P0AE0-228		Hybrid Battery Negative Contactor Control Circuit High	Open or +B short in No. 3 system main relay circuit	• Wire harness or connector • No. 3 system main relay • HV control ECU
P0AE6-225		Hybrid Battery Precharge Contactor Control Circuit Low	GND short in No. 1 system main relay circuit	• Wire harness or connector • No. 1 system main relay • HV control ECU
P0AE7-224		Hybrid Battery Precharge Contactor Control Circuit High	Open or +B short in No. 1 system main relay circuit	• Wire harness or connector • No. 1 system main relay • HV control ECU

Table ab. Hybrid Control System

DTC	INF Code	Definition	Detection Condition	Trouble Area
P0AEE	276	Drive Motor Inverter Temperature Sensor "A" Circuit Range/Performance	Sudden change in motor Inverter temperature sensor output	• Wire harness or connector • Inverter cooling system • Water w/ motor & bracket pump assembly • Cooling fan motor • Cooling fan motor No. 2 • Converter inverter assembly
P0AEE	277	Drive Motor Inverter Temperature Sensor "A" Circuit Range/Performance	Motor inverter temperature sensor output deviation	• Wire harness or connector • Inverter cooling system • Water w/ motor & bracket pump assembly • Cooling fan motor • Cooling fan motor No. 2 • Converter inverter assembly
P0AEF	275	Drive Motor Inverter Temperature Sensor "A" Low	Open or GND short in motor inverter temperature sensor circuit	• Wire harness or connector • Converter inverter assembly • HV control ECU
P2120	111	Throttle/Pedal Position Sensor/Switch "D" Circuit	Accelerator pedal position main sensor value does not change while its sub sensor value changes	Accelerator pedal rod assembly
P2121	106	Throttle/Pedal Position Sensor/Switch "D" Circuit Range/Performance	Internal error of accelerator pedal position main sensor	Accelerator pedal rod assembly
P2121	114	Throttle/Pedal Position Sensor/Switch "D" Circuit Range/Performance	Accelerator pedal not smoothly returning to its original position	Accelerator pedal rod assembly
P2122	104	Throttle/Pedal Position Sensor/Switch "D" Circuit Low Input	Open or GND short in accelerator pedal position main sensor circuit	• Wire harness or connector • Converter inverter assembly • HV control ECU
P2123	105	Throttle/Pedal Position Sensor/Switch "D" Circuit High Input	+B short in accelerator pedal position main sensor circuit	• Wire harness or connector • Converter inverter assembly • HV control ECU
P2125	112	Throttle/Pedal Position Sensor/Switch "E" Circuit	Accelerator pedal position sub sensor value does not change while its main Sensor value changes	Accelerator pedal rod assembly
P2126	109	Throttle/Pedal Position Sensor/Switch "E" Circuit Range/Performance	Internal error of accelerator pedal position sub sensor	Accelerator pedal rod assembly
P2127	107	Throttle/Pedal Position Sensor/Switch "E" Circuit Low Input	Open or GND short in accelerator pedal position sub sensor circuit	• Wire harness or connector • Accelerator pedal rod assembly • HV control ECU
P2128	108	Throttle/Pedal Position Sensor/Switch "E" Circuit High Input	+B short in accelerator pedal position sub sensor circuit	• Wire harness or connector • Accelerator pedal rod assembly • HV control ECU
P2138	110	Throttle/Pedal Position Sensor/Switch "D"/"E" Voltage Correlation	Difference between main sensor value and sub Sensor value is large	Accelerator pedal rod assembly
P3000	123	Battery Control System Malfunction	Abnormal signal input from battery ECU (HV battery system malfunction)	• HV battery system • Battery ECU

Table ab. Hybrid Control System

DTC	INF Code	Definition	Detection Condition	Trouble Area
P3000	125	Battery Control System Malfunction	Abnormal signal input from battery ECU (High voltage fuse blown out)	• HV battery system • Battery ECU
P3000	388	Battery Control System Malfunction	Abnormal signal input from battery ECU (discharge inhibition control malfunction)	• HV control system • Fuel shortage • HV battery assembly
P3000	389	Battery Control System Malfunction	Abnormal signal input from battery ECU (drop of high voltage)	• HV control system • HV battery assembly
P3000	603	Battery Control System Malfunction	Abnormal signal input from battery ECU (HV battery cooling system malfunction)	• HV battery system • Battery ECU
P3004	131	High Voltage Power Resource Malfunction	High voltage fuse has blown out, service plug grip is disconnected or limiter resistance is cut off	• HV battery system • System main resistor • System main relay No. 1 • System main relay No. 3 • Main battery cable • Main battery cable No. 2 • Frame wire • Converter inverter assembly • HV control ECU
P3004	132	High Voltage Power Resource Malfunction	Inverter voltage sensor Malfunction, or limiter resistance increases	• HV control system • System main resistor • System main relay No. 1 • System main relay No. 3 • Main battery cable • Main battery cable No. 2 • Frame wire • Converter inverter assembly • HV control ECU
P3004	133	High Voltage Power Resource Malfunction	Abnormal signal input from battery ECU	• HV battery system • Battery ECU
P3102	524	Transmission Control ECU Malfunction	BEAN communication problem of transmission control ECU	• Wire harness or connector • Transmission control ECU • HV control ECU • Power source control ECU
P3102	525	Transmission Control ECU Malfunction	Transmission control ECU IG OFF command Malfunction	• Wire harness or connector • Transmission control ECU • HV control ECU • Power source control ECU
P3102	581	Transmission Control ECU Malfunction	Transmission control ECU malfunction	• Wire harness or connector • Transmission control ECU • HV control ECU • Power source control ECU
P3102	582	Transmission Control ECU Malfunction	P position (PPOS) signal is logically inconsistent	• Wire harness or connector • Transmission control ECU • HV control ECU • Power source control ECU
P3102	597	Transmission Control ECU Malfunction	GND short in P position (PPOS) signal circuit	• Wire harness or connector • Transmission control ECU • HV control ECU • Power source control ECU

11

Table ab. Hybrid Control System

DTC	INF Code	Definition	Detection Condition	Trouble Area
P3102	598	Transmission Control ECU Malfunction	+B short in P position (PPOS) signal circuit	• Wire harness or connector • Transmission control ECU • HV control ECU • Power source control ECU
P3102	599	Transmission Control ECU Malfunction	P position (PPOS) signal malfunction (output pulse is abnormal)	• Wire harness or connector • Transmission control ECU • HV control ECU • Power source control ECU
P3107	213	Lost Communication with Airbag System Control Module	GND short in Communication circuit between airbag ECU and HV control ECU	• Wire harness or connector • Airbag ECU
P3107	214	Lost Communication with Airbag System Control Module	Open or +B short in communication circuit between airbag ECU and HV control ECU	• Wire harness or connector • Airbag ECU
P3107	215	Lost Communication with Airbag System Control Module	Abnormal communication signals between airbag ECU and HV control ECU	• Wire harness or connector • Airbag ECU
P3108	535	Lost Communication with A/C System Control Module	Serial communication malfunction	• Wire harness or connector • Converter inverter assembly
P3108	536	Lost Communication with A/C System Control Module	A/C inverter malfunction	• Wire harness or connector • Converter inverter assembly
P3108	537	Lost Communication with A/C System Control Module	A/C amplifier malfunction	A/C amplifier
P3108	538	Lost Communication with A/C System Control Module	Open in STB signal circuit	• Wire harness or connector • Converter inverter assembly
P3108	594	Lost Communication with A/C System Control Module	CAN communication malfunction	CAN communication system
P3110	223	HV Main Relay Malfunction	IGCT relay is always closed	• Wire harness or connector • Integration relay (IGCT relay)
P3110	527	HV Main Relay Malfunction	IG2 logical inconsistency	• Wire harness or connector • Integration relay (IG2 relay)
P3137	348	Collision Sensor Low Input	GND short in circuit breaker sensor No. 1 circuit	• Wire harness or connector • Circuit breaker sensor No. 1
P3138	349	Collision Sensor High Input	Open or +B short in circuit breaker sensor No. 1 circuit	• Wire harness or connector • Circuit breaker sensor No. 2
P3221	314	Generator Inverter Temperature Sensor Circuit Range/Performance	Sudden change in generator inverter temperature sensor output	• Wire harness or connector • Inverter cooling system • Water w/ motor & bracket pump assembly • Cooling fan motor • Cooling fan motor No. 2 • Converter inverter assembly
P3221	315	Generator Inverter Temperature Sensor Circuit Range/Performance	Generator inverter temperature sensor output deviation	• Wire harness or connector • Inverter cooling system • Water w/ motor & bracket pump assembly • Cooling fan motor • Cooling fan motor No. 2 • Converter inverter assembly

Table ab. Hybrid Control System

DTC	INF Code	Definition	Detection Condition	Trouble Area
P3222	313	Generator Inverter Temperature Sensor Circuit High/Low	Open or GND short in generator inverter temperature sensor circuit	• Wire harness or connector • Converter inverter assembly • HV control ECU
P3223	312	Generator Inverter Temperature Sensor Circuit High	+B short in generator inverter temperature sensor circuit	• Wire harness or connector • Converter inverter assembly • HV control ECU
P3226	562	DC/DC (Boost) Converter Temperature Sensor Malfunction	Sudden change in boost converter temperature sensor output	• Wire harness or connector • Inverter cooling system • Water w/ motor & bracket pump assembly • Cooling fan motor • Cooling fan motor No. 2 • Converter inverter assembly
P3226	563	DC/DC (Boost) Converter Temperature Sensor Malfunction	Boost converter temperature sensor output deviation	• Wire harness or connector • Inverter cooling system • Water w/ motor & bracket pump assembly • Cooling fan motor • Cooling fan motor No. 2 • Converter inverter assembly
U0100	211	Lost Communication with ECM/PCM "A"	CAN communication problem between ECM and HV control ECU (no signal in-put)	CAN communication system
U0100	212	Lost Communication with ECM/PCM "A"	CAN communication problem between ECM and HV control ECU (transmission error)	CAN communication system
U0100	530	Lost Communication with ECM/PCM "A"	CAN communication problem between ECM and HV control ECU (CAN communication system malfunction)	CAN communication system
U0111	208	Lost Communication with Battery Energy Control Module "A"	CAN communication problem between battery ECU and HV control ECU (no signal input)	CAN communication system
U0111	531	Lost Communication with Battery Energy Control Module "A"	CAN communication problem between battery ECU and HV control ECU (CAN communication system Malfunction)	CAN communication system
U0129	220	Lost Communication with Brake System Control Module	CAN communication problem between skid control ECU and HV control ECU (no signal input)	CAN communication system
U0129	222	Lost Communication with Brake System Control Module	CAN communication problem between skid control ECU and HV control ECU (CAN communication System malfunction)	CAN communication system
U0129	528	Lost Communication with Brake System Control Module	CAN communication problem between skid control ECU and HV control ECU (transmission error)	CAN communication system
U0129	529	Lost Communication with Brake System Control Module	CAN communication problem between skid control ECU and HV control ECU (regenerative torque Malfunction)	CAN communication system

11

Table ab. Hybrid Control System

DTC	INF Code	Definition	Detection Condition	Trouble Area
U0131	433	Lost Communication with Power Steering Control Module	CAN communication problem between power steering ECU and HV control ECU (no signal input)	CAN communication system
U0131	434	Lost Communication with Power Steering Control Module	CAN communication problem between power steering ECU and HV control ECU (CAN communication System malfunction)	CAN communication system
U0146	435	Lost Communication with Gateway "A"	CAN communication problem between gateway ECU and HV control ECU (no signal input)	CAN communication system

Lighting system

The table(s) in this section contain lighting system DTCs, code detection item and likely trouble areas.

Retrieving DTCs

Lighting system DTCs can be retrieved by using Toyota scan tool or equivalent. See **Diagnostic Scan Tools** in this chapter.

Clearing DTCs

Clear lighting system DTCs with Toyota scan tool or equivalent.

– Connect scan tool to OBD II connector.

– Turn hybrid system ON (IG-ON, READY indicator not illuminated). Turn tester ON.

– Operate tester to clear DTCs. Refer to tester operating instructions.

Table ac. Lighting

DTC	Detection Item	Trouble Area
B1244	Light Sensor Circuit Malfunction	• Automatic light control sensor • Wire harness • Main body ECU

Multiplex (MUX) communications

The table(s) in this section contain multiplex (MUX) communications DTCs, code definitions and likely trouble areas.

Retrieving DTCs

MUX DTCs can be retrieved by using Toyota scan tool or equivalent. See **Diagnostic Scan Tools** in this chapter.

Clearing DTCs

Clear MUX DTCs with Toyota scan tool or equivalent.

— Connect scan tool to OBD II connector.

— Turn hybrid system ON (IG-ON, READY indicator not illuminated). Turn tester ON.

— Operate tester to clear DTCs. Refer to tester operating instructions.

Table ad. Multiplex (MUX) Communications

DTC	Definition	Trouble Area
B1200	Body ECU communication stop	• Wire harness • Instrument panel J/B assy • Multiplex network (Body ECU)
B1207	Smart ECU communication stop	• Wire harness • Smart ECU
B1210	Power source control ECU communication stop	• Wire harness • Power source control ECU
B1214	Short to B+ in Door System Communication Bus Malfunction	• Wire harness and connector in BEAN • A/C ECU • Certification ECU • Combination meter • Driver side junction block • Gateway ECU • Power source control ECU • Tire pressure monitor ECU • Transmission control ECU • Transponder key ECU
B1215	Short to GND in Door System Communication Bus Malfunction	• Wire harness and connector in BEAN • A/C ECU • Certification ECU • Combination meter • Driver side junction block • Gateway ECU • Power source control ECU • Tire pressure monitor ECU • Transmission control ECU • Transponder key ECU
B1247	Tire Pressure Monitor Receiver Communication Stop	• Wire harness • Tire pressure warning ECU
B1248	AVC-LAN communication impossible	• Wire harness • ECU (AVC-LAN system bus)

Table ad. Multiplex (MUX) Communications

DTC	Definition	Trouble Area
B1260	Transmission control ECU communication stop	• Wire harness • Transmission control ECU
B1262	A/C ECU communication stop	• Wire harness • A/C ECU
B1271	Combination meter ECU communication stop	• Wire harness • Meter ECU
B1294	Immobilizer ECU communication stop	• Wire harness • Transponder key ECU assy

11

Navigation system

The table(s) in this section contain navigation system DTCs, code definitions, likely trouble areas, and verification information.

The first 2 digits (before dash) are the device logical address. The second 2 digits (after dash) are the 2-digit DTC

Retrieving DTCs

◀ Navigation system DTCs can be retrieved on multifunction display (touch screen) in center of instrument panel. Multifunction display must be in diagnostic mode to display DTCs, and additional fault information may also be onscreen. See **Multifunction Display**.

Clearing DTCs

– Navigation system DTCs can be cleared on multifunction display. See **Multifunction Display**.

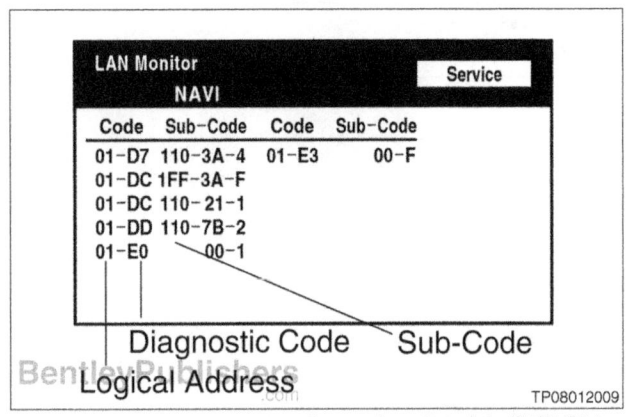

Diagnostic Code   Sub-Code

Logical Address

TP08012009

Courtesy Toyota Motor Sales (TMS) USA, Inc.

Table ae. Navigation - ECU			
DTC	**Definition**	**Trouble Area**	**Verification**
01-D6	No master	• When either the following condition meets. • The device that stores (stored) the code has (had) been disconnected when the power switch is in ON (ACC) or ON (ON) position. • The master device has (had) been disconnected when this code is stored.	• Power source circuit (multi-display) • AVC-LAN circuit (navigation ECU-multi-display) • Power source circuit (navigation ECU) • Replace multi-display • Replace navigation ECU
01-D7	Connection check error	• When either the following condition meets. • The device that stored this code has (had) been disconnected after the system starts (started). • The master device has (had) been disconnected when this code is (was) stored.	• Power source circuit (multi-display) • AVC-LAN circuit (navigation ECU-multi-display) • Power source circuit (navigation ECU) • Replace multi-display • Replace navigation ECU
01-DC	Transmission error	The device stores the fact that transmission to the device indicated by the sub code has failed.	Inspection for the device indicated by the sub code. (Refer to the inspection list for the device indicated by the sub code.)
01-DD	Master reset	When the device that should be the master has been disconnected after system starts.	• Power source circuit (multi-display) • AVC-LAN circuit (navigation ECU-multi-display) • Replace multi-display
01-DF	Master error	When the device with a display fails and the master is switched to the audio device. Also when a communication error between sub master (audio) and master occurs, this code is stored.	• Power source circuit (multi-display) • AVC-LAN circuit (navigation ECU-multi-display) • Replace multi-display
01-E0	Registration complete indication error	When "Registration complete" command from the master device cannot be received.	This code will be detected when signal receiving time is delayed.

Table ae. Navigation - ECU

DTC	Definition	Trouble Area	Verification
01-E1	Voice processing device ON error	When the AMP device records that the AMP output does not function even while the source device operates.	• Power source circuit (multi-display) • AVC-LAN circuit (navigation ECU-multi-display) • Replace multi-display
01-E2	ON/OFF indication parameter error	When the command for ON/OFF control from the master device has a problem.	Replace multi-display
01-E3	Registration demand transmission	When the registration demand command from the slave device is output, or when the registration demand command is output by receiving connection confirmation command from the sub master device.	
01-E4	Multiple frame incomplete	When the multiple frame transmission ends incomplete.	
58-10	Gyro error	Ground short, power supply short, or open circuit in the gyro signal, gyro failure.	• Inspect the gyro error • Replace GPS antenna • Replace navigation ECU
58-11	GPS receiver error	RTC, ROM, and RAM of the GPS receiver and TCXO errors. GPS receiver is failed.	Replace navigation ECU
58-40	GPS antenna error	GPS antenna error	Replace GPS antenna Replace navigation ECU
58-41	GPS antenna power source error	Error of the power source to the GPS antenna	Replace GPS antenna Replace navigation ECU
58-42	Map disc read error	Player error. A scratch or dirt on the disc. Access to an invalid address due to software error.	• Inspect map disc read error • Replace map disc • Replace navigation ECU
58-43	SPD signal error	The difference between the GPS speed and SPD pulse is detected.	• Inspect speed signal error • Speed signal circuit • Replace navigation ECU
58-44	Player Error	Navigation ECU	
58-45	High Temperature	Navigation ECU	
5C-40	Camera Picture Error	• Wire harness • Television camera assembly • Multi-display	
80-10	Gyro error	Ground short, power supply short, or open circuit in the gyro signal, gyro failure.	• Inspect the gyro error • Replace GPS antenna • Replace navigation ECU
80-11	GPS receiver error	RTC, ROM, and RAM of the GPS receiver and TCXO errors. GPS receiver is failed.	Replace navigation ECU
80-40	GPS antenna error	GPS antenna error	Replace GPS antenna Replace navigation ECU
80-41	GPS antenna power source error	Error of the power source to the GPS antenna	Replace GPS antenna Replace navigation ECU
80-42	Map disc read error	Player error. A scratch or dirt on the disc. Access to an invalid address due to software error.	• Inspect map disc read error • Replace map disc • Replace navigation ECU
80-43	SPD signal error	The difference between the GPS speed and SPD pulse is detected.	• Inspect speed signal error • Speed signal circuit • Replace navigation ECU

11

Table ae. Navigation - ECU

DTC	Definition	Trouble Area	Verification
80-45	High Temperature	Navigation ECU	

Table af. Navigation - Gateway ECU

DTC	Definition	Trouble Area
01-D4	Regular Communication Error	Component in which this code is recorded has been disconnected from system with power in the ACC or ON position. Either that, or the multi-display was disconnected when this code was recorded.

Table ag. Navigation - Multi-display

DTC	Definition	Trouble Area	Verification
01-21	ROM error	This code is output when a malfunction exists in ROM.	Replace multi-display
01-22	RAM error	This code is output when a malfunction exists in RAM.	Replace multi-display
01-D5	Absence of registration unit	A device that the sub code shows is (was) disconnected from the system when turning the power switch to the ON (ACC) or ON (ON) position. The communication condition with the device that the code shows cannot be obtained when the system starts.	Inspection for the device indicated by the sub code. (Refer to the inspection list for the device indicated by the sub code.)
01-D8	No response for connection check	The device indicated by the sub code is (was) disconnected from the system after system start.	Inspection for the device indicated by the sub code. (Refer to the inspection list for the device indicated by the sub code.)
01-D9	Last mode error	The device (for audio visual system) that had functioned before the system stopped is (was) disconnected from the system when the power switch is (was) in the ON (ACC) or ON (ON) position.	Inspection for the device indicated by the sub code. (Refer to the inspection list for the device indicated by the sub code.)
01-DA	No response against ON/OFF command	No response is identified when changing mode (audio and visual mode change). Detected when sound and image do not change by switch operation.	Inspection for the device indicated by the sub code. (Refer to the inspection list for the device indicated by the sub code.)
01-DB	Mode status error	This code detects a dual alarm.	Inspection for the device indicated by the sub code. (Refer to the inspection list for the device indicated by the sub code.)
01-DC	Failure in transmission	This code indicates a transmission failure to the device indicated by the sub code. NOTE: This DTC may have no direct relationship with the malfunction.	Inspection for the device indicated by the sub code. (Refer to the inspection list for the device indicated by the sub code.)
01-DE	Slave reset	This code is stored when a slave device has been disconnected after system start.	Inspection for the device indicated by the sub code. (Refer to the inspection list for the device indicated by the sub code.)
21-10	Panel switch error	The panel SW detection circuit has a failure.	Replace multi-display
21-11	Touch switch error	Multi-display	
23-10	Panel switch error	The panel SW detection circuit has a failure.	Replace multi-display

Table ag. Navigation - Multi-display

DTC	Definition	Trouble Area	Verification
23-11	Touch switch error	Multi-display	
24-10	Panel switch error	The panel SW detection circuit has a failure.	Replace multi-display
24-11	Touch switch error	Multi-display	
25-10	Panel switch error	The panel SW detection circuit has a failure.	Replace multi-display
25-11	Touch switch error	Multi-display	
34-10	Error in Picture Circuit	Multi-display	
34-11	No Current in Back-light Error	Multi-display	
34-12	Excess Current in Back-light Error	Multi-display	
57-47	Bluetooth Module Initialization Failed	Multi-display	

Table ah. Navigation - Radio Receiver Assy

DTC	Definition	Trouble Area	Verification
01-D5	Absence of registration unit	A device that the sub code shows is (was) disconnected from the system when turning the power switch to the ON (ACC) or ON (ON) position. The communication condition with the device that the code shows cannot be obtained when the system starts.	Inspection for the device indicated by the sub code. (Refer to the inspection list for the device indicated by the sub code.)
01-D6	No master	• When either the following condition meets. • The device that stores (stored) the code has (had) been disconnected when the power switch is in ON (ACC) or ON (ON) position. • The master device has (had) been disconnected when this code is stored.	• Power source circuit (multi-display) • AVC-LAN circuit (multi-display -radio receiver assy) • Power source circuit (radio receiver assy) • Replace multi-display • Replace radio receiver assy
01-D7	Connection check error	• When either the following condition meets. • The device that stored this code has (had) been disconnected after the system starts (started). • The master device has (had) been disconnected when this code is (was) stored.	• Power source circuit (multi-display) • AVC-LAN circuit (multi-display -radio receiver assy) • Power source circuit (radio re-ceiver assy) • Replace multi-display • Replace radio receiver assy
01-D8	No response for connection check	The device indicated by the sub code is (was) disconnected from the system after system start	Inspection for the device indicated by the sub code. (Refer to the inspection list for the device indicated by the sub code.)
01-D9	Last mode error	The device (for audio visual system) that had functioned before the system stopped is (was) disconnected from the system when the power switch is (was) in the ACC or ON position.	Inspection for the device indicated by the sub code. (Refer to the inspection list for the device indicated by the sub code.)
01-DA	No response to ON/OFF command	No response is identified when changing mode (audio and visual mode change). Detected when sound and image do not change by switch operation.	Inspection for the device indicated by the sub code. (Refer to the inspection list for the device indicated by the sub code.)

11

Table ah. Navigation - Radio Receiver Assy

DTC	Definition	Trouble Area	Verification
01-DB	Mode status error	This code detects a dual alarm.	Inspection for the device indicated by the sub code. (Refer to the inspection list for the device indicated by the sub code.)
01-DC	Failure in transmission	This code indicates a transmission failure to the device indicated by the sub code. NOTE: This DTC may have no direct relationship with the malfunction.	Inspection for the device indicated by the sub code. (Refer to the inspection list for the device indicated by the sub code.)
01-DD	Master reset	When the device that should be the master has been disconnected after system starts.	• Power source circuit (multi-display) • AVC-LAN circuit (multi-display -radio receiver assy) • Replace multi-display
01-DE	Slave reset	This code is stored when a slave device has been disconnected after system start.	Inspection for the device indicated by the sub code. (Refer to the inspection list for the device indicated by the sub code.)
01-DF	Master error	When the device with a display fails and the master is switched to the audio device. Also when a communication error between sub master (audio) and master occurs, this code is stored.	• Power source circuit (multi-display) • AVC-LAN circuit (multi-display -radio receiver assy) • Replace multi-display
01-E0	Registration complete indication error	When "Registration complete" command from the master device cannot be received.	This code will be detected when signal receiving time is delayed.
01-E1	Voice processing device ON error	When the AMP device records that the AMP output does not function even while the source device operates.	• Power source circuit (multi-display) • AVC-LAN circuit (multi-display -radio receiver assy) • Replace multi-display
01-E2	ON/OFF indication parameter error	When the command for ON/OFF control from the master device has a problem.	Replace multi-display
01-E3	Registration demand transmission	When the registration demand command from the slave device is output, or when the registration demand command is output by receiving connection confirmation command from the sub master device.	
01-E4	Multiple frame incomplete	When the multiple frame transmission ends incomplete	
60-10	AM tuner PLL does not lock	The PLL circuit in the AM tuner is abnormal.	• After clearing the DTC, check the antenna wiring. • If the same code is detected, replace the radio receiver assy.
60-11	FM tuner PLL does not lock	The PLL circuit in the FM tuner is abnormal.	• After clearing the DTC, check the antenna wiring. • If the same code is detected, replace the radio receiver assy.
60-40	Antenna is not connected	The antenna is disconnected.	• After clearing the DTC, check the antenna wiring. • If the same code is detected, replace the radio receiver assy.
60-41	Antenna power source error	The power source system of the antenna is abnormal.	• After clearing the DTC, check the antenna wiring. • If the same code is detected, replace the radio receiver assy.

Table ah. Navigation - Radio Receiver Assy

DTC	Definition	Trouble Area	Verification
60-42	Tuner power source error	The power source of the tuner is abnormal.	• Power source circuit (radio receiver assy) • Replace radio receiver assy
60-43	AM tuner error	The AM tuner is abnormal.	Replace radio receiver assy
60-44	FM tuner error	The FM tuner is abnormal.	Replace radio receiver assy
60-45	SW tuner error	The SW tuner is abnormal.	Replace radio receiver assy
61-10	Belt cut	The inside belt is cut or come off.	Replace radio receiver assy
61-40	Mechanical error of media	A malfunction due to mechanical problem, cassette tape is cut or entangled.	• Replace the cassette tape and recheck the symptom. • If the same code is detected, replace the radio receiver assy
61-41	EJECT error	A malfunction due to mechanical problem.	Replace radio receiver assy
61-42	Tape tangling	Cassette tape is tangled.	Replace radio receiver assy
61-43	Head dirt	Head is dirty.	• Clean the head and recheck the symptom. • If the same code is detected, replace the radio receiver assy
61-44	Device power supply problem	A short or open in the power circuit.	• Power source circuit (radio receiver assy) • Replace radio receiver assy
62-10	CD player mechanical error	A mechanical error in the CD player is detected while the CD is not being inserted or ejected.	Replace radio receiver assy
62-11	CD insertion & eject error	CD insertion or ejection is failed.	Replace radio receiver assy
62-12	CD reading abnormal	CD read problem occurs.	Replace radio receiver assy
62-40	No disc	No disc is inserted.	• Check whether the CD is inserted or not. If the CD is inserted, check whether it can be ejected or not. If it cannot be ejected, replace radio receiver assy. • Inspect CD. • If the same code is detected, replace the radio receiver assy
62-41	Wrong disc	An unsuitable disc is inserted.	• Inspect CD. • If the same code is detected, replace the radio receiver assy
62-42	Disc cannot be read	The disc cannot be read.	• Inspect CD. • If the same code is detected, replace the radio receiver assy
62-43	CD-ROM abnormal	CD-ROM operation is abnormal.	Replace radio receiver assy
62-44	CD abnormal	Operation error in the CD mechanism (except for code 10).	• After clearing the DTC, check the malfunction symptom. • If the same code is detected, replace the radio receiver assy
62-45	EJECT error	Magazine cannot be ejected	Replace radio receiver assy
62-46	Disc has scratches in the re-verse surface	CD has a dirt or scratches in the reverse side	• Inspect CD. • If the same code is detected, replace the radio receiver assy

11

Table ah. Navigation - Radio Receiver Assy

DTC	Definition	Trouble Area	Verification
62-47	CD temperature is high	The sensor detects that the CD unit temperature is high.	• Park the vehicle in a cool place. Turn the system off. After checking that the temperature of the radio and navigation assy becomes sufficiently low, turn the system on in order to verify the malfunction symptom. • If the same code is detected, replace the radio receiver assy
62-48	Excess current	Excess current is applied to the disc player changer	Replace radio receiver assy
62-50	Tray insertion/ejection error	Malfunction insertion/ejection system	Replace radio receiver assy
62-51	Elevator error	Mechanical error occurred during elevator operation	Replace radio receiver assy
62-52	Clamp error	Clamp unusually generating	Replace radio receiver assy
63-10	CD player mechanical error	A mechanical error in the CD player is detected while the CD is not being inserted or ejected.	Replace radio receiver assy
63-11	CD insertion & eject error	CD insertion or ejection is failed.	Replace radio receiver assy
63-12	CD reading abnormal	CD read problem occurs.	Replace radio receiver assy
63-40	No disc	No disc is inserted.	• Check whether the CD is inserted or not. If the CD is inserted, check whether it can be ejected or not. If it cannot be ejected, replace radio receiver assy. • Inspect CD. • If the same code is detected, replace the radio receiver assy
63-41	Wrong disc	An unsuitable disc is inserted.	• Inspect CD. • If the same code is detected, replace the radio receiver assy
63-42	Disc cannot be read	The disc cannot be read.	• Inspect CD. • If the same code is detected, replace the radio receiver assy
63-43	CD-ROM abnormal	CD-ROM operation is abnormal.	Replace radio receiver assy
63-44	CD abnormal	Operation error in the CD mechanism (except for code 10).	• After clearing the DTC, check the malfunction symptom. • If the same code is detected, replace the radio receiver assy
63-45	EJECT error	Magazine cannot be ejected	Replace radio receiver assy
63-46	Disc has scratches in the re-verse surface	CD has a dirt or scratches in the reverse side	• Inspect CD. • If the same code is detected, replace the radio receiver assy
63-47	CD temperature is high	The sensor detects that the CD unit temperature is high.	• Park the vehicle in a cool place. Turn the system off. After checking that the temperature of the radio and navigation assy becomes sufficiently low, turn the system on in order to verify the malfunction symptom. • If the same code is detected, replace the radio receiver assy

Table ah. Navigation - Radio Receiver Assy

DTC	Definition	Trouble Area	Verification
63-48	Excess current	Excess current is applied to the disc player changer	Replace radio receiver assy
63-50	Tray insertion / ejection error	Malfunction insertion / ejection system	Replace radio receiver assy
63-51	Elevator error	Mechanical error occurred during elevator operation	Replace radio receiver assy
63-52	Clamp error	Clamp unusually generating	Replace radio receiver assy

Table ai. Navigation - Stereo Component Amplifier Assy

DTC	Definition	Trouble Area	Verification
01-D6	No master	• When either the following condition meets. • The device that stores (stored) the code has (had) been disconnected when the power switch is in ON (ACC) or ON (ON) position. • The master device has (had) been disconnected when this code is stored.	• Power source circuit (multi-dis-play) • AVC-LAN circuit (multi-display -radio receiver assy) • Power source circuit (stereo component amplifier assy) • AVC-LAN circuit (radio receiver assy - stereo component amplifier assy) • Replace multi-display • Replace stereo component amplifier assy
01-D7	Connection check error	• When either the following condition meets. • The device that stored this code has (had) been disconnected after the system starts (started). • The master device has (had) been disconnected when this code is (was) stored.	• Power source circuit (multi-display) • AVC-LAN circuit (multi-display -radio receiver assy) • Power source circuit (stereo component amplifier assy) • AVC-LAN circuit (radio receiver assy - stereo component amplifier assy) • Replace multi-display • Replace stereo component amplifier assy
01-DC	Transmission error	The device stores the fact that transmission to the device indicated by the sub code has failed.	Inspection for the device indicated by the sub code. (Refer to the inspection list for the device indicated by the sub code.)
01-DD	Master reset	When the device that should be the master has been disconnected after system starts.	• Power source circuit (multi-dis-play) • AVC-LAN circuit (multi-display -radio receiver assy) • Replace multi-display
01-DF	Master error	When the device with a display fails and the master is switched to the audio device. Also when a communication error between sub master (audio) and master occurs, this code is stored.	• Power source circuit (multi-dis-play) • AVC-LAN circuit (multi-display -radio receiver assy) • Replace multi-display
01-E0	Registration complete indication error	When "Registration complete" command from the master device cannot be received.	This code will be detected when signal receiving time is delayed.
01-E1	Voice processing device ON error	When the AMP device records that the AMP output does not function even while the source device operates.	• Power source circuit (multi-display) • AVC-LAN circuit (multi-display -radio receiver assy) • Replace multi-display
01-E2	ON/OFF indication parameter error	When the command for ON/OFF control from the master device has a problem.	Replace multi-display

11

Table ai. Navigation - Stereo Component Amplifier Assy

DTC	Definition	Trouble Area	Verification
01-E3	Registration demand transmission	When the registration demand command from the slave device is output, or when the registration demand command is output by receiving connection confirmation command from the sub master device.	
01-E4	Multiple frame incomplete	When the multiple frame transmission ends incomplete	

Pushbutton start system

The table(s) in this section contain pushbutton start system DTCs, code definitions and likely trouble areas.

Retrieving DTCs

Pushbutton start system DTCs can be retrieved by using Toyota scan tool or equivalent. See **Diagnostic Scan Tools** in this chapter.

Clearing DTCs

Clear pushbutton start system DTCs with Toyota scan tool or equivalent.

— Connect scan tool to OBD II connector.

— Turn hybrid system ON (IG-ON, READY indicator not illuminated). Turn tester ON.

— Operate tester to clear DTCs. Refer to tester operating instructions.

Table aj. Pushbutton Start

DTC	Definition	Trouble Area
B2271	Ignition Hold Monitor Malfunction	• Power source control ECU • AM1 fuse • AM2 fuse • Wire harness
B2272	Ignition 1 Monitor Malfunction	• Power source control ECU • IG1 relay • Wire harness
B2273	Ignition 2 Monitor Malfunction	• Power source control ECU • Wire harness
B2274	ACC Monitor Malfunction	• Power source control ECU • ACC relay • Wire harness
B2275	STSW Monitor Malfunction	• Power source control ECU • Hybrid vehicle control ECU • Wire harness
B2277	Detection Vehicle Submersion	Power source control ECU
B2278	Main Switch (Power switch) Malfunction (starter switch 1 signal does not match to starter switch 2 signal)	• Power source control ECU • Power switch • Wire harness
B2281	P Signal Malfunction (cable information does not match BEAN information)	• Power source control ECU • Transmission control ECU • Wire harness
B2282	Vehicle Speed Signal Malfunction (cable information does not match BEAN information)	• Power source control ECU • Combination meter • Wire harness
B2284	Brake Signal Malfunction (cable information does not match BEAN information)	• Power source control ECU • Stop lamp switch • Wire harness

11

Table aj. Pushbutton Start

DTC	Definition	Trouble Area
B2286	READY Signal Malfunction	• Power source control ECU • Hybrid vehicle control ECU • Wire harness
B2287	LIN Communication Master Malfunction	• Power source control ECU • Transponder key ECU • Wire harness
B2289	Key Collation Waiting Time Over	• Power source control ECU • Engine immobilizer system • Wire harness

Shift control system

The table(s) in this section contain shift control system DTCs, code definitions, likely trouble areas, and light condition information.

Retrieving DTCs

Shift control system DTCs can be retrieved by using Toyota scan tool or equivalent. See **Diagnostic Scan Tools** in this chapter.

Clearing DTCs

Clear shift control system DTCs with Toyota scan tool or equivalent.

— Connect scan tool to OBD II connector.

— Turn hybrid system ON (IG-ON, READY indicator not illuminated). Turn tester ON.

— Operate tester to clear DTCs. Refer to tester operating instructions.

Table ak. Shift Control

DTC	Definition	Trouble Area	P Position Switch Indicator Light Condition
C2300	ACT System Malfunction	• Shift control actuator assy • Transaxle parking lock control relay • Transmission control ECU assy • Wire harness or connector	Blinks slowly
C2301	Shift Changing Time Malfunction	• Shift control actuator assy • Transmission control ECU assy	Blinks slowly
C2303	Relay Malfunction (+B Short)	• Transaxle parking lock control relay • Transmission control ECU assy • Wire harness or connector	Normal
C2304	Open or Short Circuit in U Phase	• Shift control actuator assy • Transmission control ECU assy • Transaxle parking lock control relay • Wire harness or connector	Blinks slowly
C2305	Open or Short Circuit in V Phase	• Shift control actuator assy • Transmission control ECU assy • Transaxle parking lock control relay • Wire harness or connector	Blinks slowly
C2306	Open or Short Circuit in W Phase	• Shift control actuator assy • Transmission control ECU assy • Transaxle parking lock control relay • Wire harness or connector	Blinks slowly
C2307	Power Source Malfunction	• Transmission control ECU assy • Wire harness or connector • Parking lock motor (Shift control actuator assy)	Blinks slowly
C2310	Open or Short Circuit in BATT	• P CON MAIN fuse • Transmission control ECU assy • Wire harness or connector	Normal

11

Table ak. Shift Control

DTC	Definition	Trouble Area	P Position Switch Indicator Light Condition
C2311	HV Communication Line Malfunction	• Transmission control ECU assy • Hybrid vehicle control ECU • Wire harness or connector	Blinks slowly
C2312	Power Source Control ECU Communication Line Malfunction	• Transmission control ECU assy • Power source control ECU	Normal
C2315	HV System Malfunction	• Hybrid vehicle control ECU • P position switch • Transmission control ECU assy • Wire harness or connector	Normal
C2318	Low Voltage Error (Power Supply Malfunction)	• HEV fuse • IGCT relay • Wire harness or connector • Auxiliary battery	Normal

Supplemental restraint system (SRS)

The table(s) in this section contain supplemental restraint system (SRS) DTCs, blink codes, code definitions and likely trouble areas. 5-digit DTCs and 2-digit blink codes are separated by slash.

Retrieving DTCs

SRS DTCs can be retrieved two ways:

• Toyota scan tool or equivalent (retrieves 5-digit DTCs)

• Warning light blinking pattern (retrieves 2-digit blink codes)

To retrieve 5-digit DTCs using Toyota scan tool or equivalent, see **Diagnostic Scan Tools** in this chapter.

— To retrieve 2-digit blink codes, perform the following procedure:

— Be sure hybrid system is OFF (READY indicator not illuminated).

> **WARNING—**
> • *Be sure hybrid system is OFF when servicing vehicle (READY indicator not illuminated). Failure to switch the hybrid system OFF could result in engine start at any time.*

Using jumper wire, connect terminals 4 (CG) and 13 (TC) in OBD II connector.

> **CAUTION—**
> • *Avoid spreading or deforming female terminals in OBD II connector. Use an appropriate jumper wire gauge and do not force jumper wire into terminals.*
> • *Connecting incorrect terminals may damage vehicle.*

— Turn hybrid system ON (IG-ON, READY indicator not illuminated). Wait approx. 60 seconds.

SRS warning light will blink (flash).

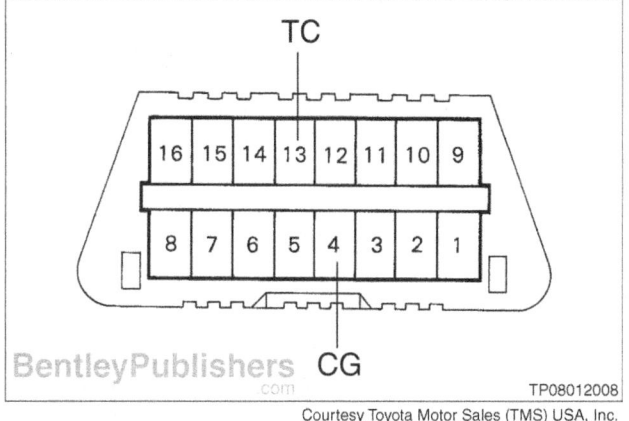

TC

| 16 | 15 | 14 | 13 | 12 | 11 | 10 | 9 |

| 8 | 7 | 6 | 5 | 4 | 3 | 2 | 1 |

CG

TP08012008

Courtesy Toyota Motor Sales (TMS) USA, Inc.

SRS Warning Light

TP08012013

11

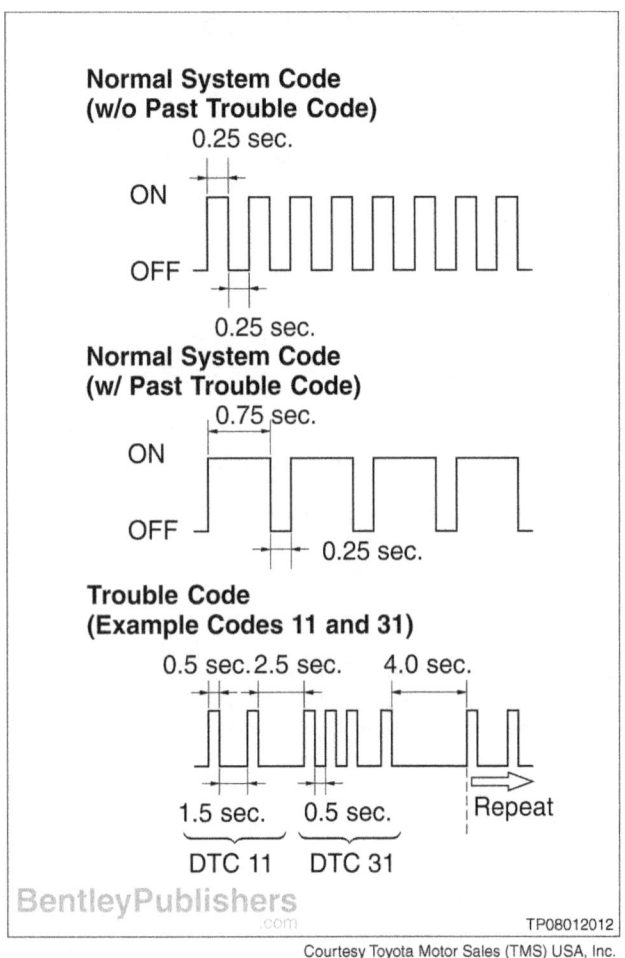

**Normal System Code
(w/o Past Trouble Code)**

0.25 sec.

ON

OFF

0.25 sec.

**Normal System Code
(w/ Past Trouble Code)**

0.75 sec.

ON

OFF

0.25 sec.

**Trouble Code
(Example Codes 11 and 31)**

0.5 sec. 2.5 sec.   4.0 sec.

1.5 sec.   0.5 sec.   Repeat

DTC 11   DTC 31

BentleyPublishers.com

TP08012012

Courtesy Toyota Motor Sales (TMS) USA, Inc.

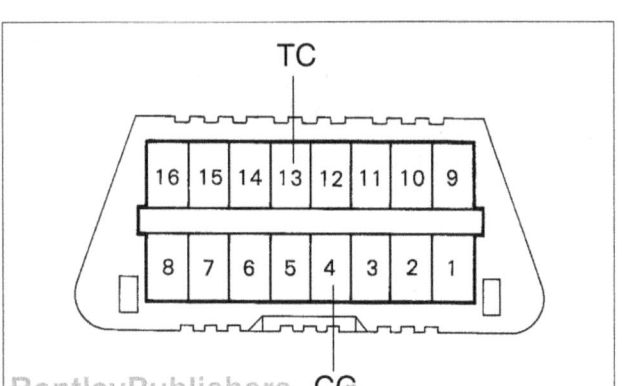

TC

| 16 | 15 | 14 | 13 | 12 | 11 | 10 | 9 |

| 8 | 7 | 6 | 5 | 4 | 3 | 2 | 1 |

BentleyPublishers.com   CG

TP08012008

Courtesy Toyota Motor Sales (TMS) USA, Inc.

◄ SRS warning light blinks in pattern as shown on left to display 2-digit DTCs.

— Warning light will repeat blink pattern until turned OFF.

— If more than one DTC is stored, warning light will blink each DTC in ascending order.

— When check is complete, remove jumper from OBD II connector.

Clearing DTCs

SRS system DTCs can be cleared two ways:
• Toyota scan tool or equivalent
• OBD II connector jumper / brake pedal procedure

To clear DTCs with Toyota scan tool or equivalent:

— Connect scan tool to OBD II connector.

— Turn hybrid system ON (IG-ON, READY indicator not illuminated). Turn tester ON.

— Operate tester to clear DTCs. Refer to tester operating instructions.

To clear DTCs using OBD II connector jumper wire:

◄ Using jumper wire, connect terminals 4 (CG) and 13 (TC) in OBD II connector.

> *CAUTION—*
> • *Avoid spreading or deforming female terminals in OBD II connector. Use an appropriate jumper wire gauge and do not force jumper wire into terminals.*
> • *Connecting incorrect terminals may damage vehicle.*

— Turn hybrid system ON (READY indicator illuminated).

— Disconnect jumper from terminal TC of OBD II connector within 3 to 10 seconds after the DTCs are output, and check if the SRS warning light turns ON after 3 seconds.

— Within 2 to 4 seconds after the SRS warning light turns ON, reconnect jumper to terminal TC. The SRS warning light should turn OFF within 2 to 4 seconds after connecting terminals TC and CG.

— Disconnect jumper from terminal TC within 2 to 4 seconds after the SRS warning light turns OFF. The SRS warning light turns ON again within 2 to 4 seconds after disconnecting terminal TC.

— Reconnect terminals TC and CG within 2 to 4 seconds after the SRS warning light turns ON. Check if the SRS warning light goes off 2 to 4 seconds after connecting terminals TC and CG.

— Check if the normal system code is output within 1 second after the SRS warning light goes off.

— Repeat this procedure until the codes are cleared.

— Remove jumper from OBD II connector.

Table al. Supplemental Restraint - Airbag System

DTC	Definition	Trouble Area
B1000/31	Airbag ECU assy malfunction	Airbag ECU assy
B1610/13	Front airbag sensor RH circuit malfunction	• Airbag front RH sensor • Airbag ECU assy • Instrument panel wire • Engine room main wire
B1615/14	Front airbag sensor LH circuit malfunction	• Airbag sensor front LH • Airbag ECU assy • Instrument panel wire • Engine room main wire
B1620/21	Side airbag sensor assembly (D seat side) malfunction	• Side airbag sensor assy LH • Airbag ECU assy • Floor wire
B1625/22	Side airbag sensor assembly (P seat side) malfunction	• Side airbag sensor assy RH • Airbag ECU assy • Floor wire No.2
B1630/23	Curtain shield airbag sensor (D seat side) malfunction	• Airbag sensor rear RH • Airbag ECU assy • Floor wire
B1635/24	Curtain shield airbag sensor (P seat side) malfunction	• Airbag sensor rear LH • Airbag ECU assy • Floor wire No.2
B1650/32	Occupant classification system malfunction	
B1653/35	Seat position sensor assembly malfunction	• Seat position airbag sensor • Airbag ECU assy • Floor wire
B1655/37	Seat belt buckle switch (D seat side) malfunction	• Front seat inner belt assy RH • Airbag ECU assy • Floor wire
B1660/43	Passenger Airbag ON / OFF indicator circuit malfunction	
B1800/51	Short in D squib circuit	• Horn button assy (D squib) • Spiral cable sub-assy • Airbag ECU assy • Instrument panel wire
B1801/51	Open in D squib circuit	• Horn button assy (D squib) • Spiral cable sub-assy • Airbag ECU assy • Instrument panel wire

11

Table al. Supplemental Restraint - Airbag System

DTC	Definition	Trouble Area
B1802/51	Short in D squib circuit (to ground)	• Horn button assy (D squib) • Spiral cable sub-assy • Airbag ECU assy • Instrument panel wire
B1803/51	Short in D squib circuit (to B+)	• Horn button assy (D squib) • Spiral cable sub-assy • Airbag ECU assy • Instrument panel wire
B1805/52	Short in P squib circuit	• Front passenger airbag assy (P squib) • Airbag ECU assy • Instrument panel wire • Instrument panel wire No.2
B1806/52	Open in P squib circuit	• Front passenger airbag assy (P squib) • Airbag ECU assy • Instrument panel wire • Instrument panel wire No.3
B1807/52	Short in P squib circuit (to ground)	• Front passenger airbag assy (P squib) • Airbag ECU assy • Instrument panel wire • Instrument panel wire No.4
B1808/52	Short in P squib circuit (to B+)	• Front passenger airbag assy (P squib) • Airbag ECU assy • Instrument panel wire • Instrument panel wire No.5
B1810/53	Short in D squib (Dual stage -2nd step) circuit	• Horn button assy (D squib, Dual stage - 2nd step) • Spiral cable sub-assy • Airbag ECU assy • Instrument panel wire
B1811/53	Open in D squib (Dual stage -2nd step) circuit	• Horn button assy (D squib, Dual stage - 2nd step) • Spiral cable sub-assy • Airbag ECU assy • Instrument panel wire
B1812/53	Short in D squib (Dual stage -2nd step) circuit (to ground)	• Horn button assy (D squib, Dual stage - 2nd step) • Spiral cable sub-assy • Airbag ECU assy • Instrument panel wire
B1813/53	Short in D squib (Dual stage -2nd step) circuit (to B+)	• Horn button assy (D squib, Dual stage - 2nd step) • Spiral cable sub-assy • Airbag ECU assy • Instrument panel wire
B1815/54	Short in P squib (Dual stage -2nd step) circuit	• Front passenger airbag assy (P squib, Dual stage - 2nd step) • Airbag ECU assy • Instrument panel wire • Instrument panel wire No.2
B1816/54	Open in P squib (Dual stage -2nd step) circuit	• Front passenger airbag assy (P squib, Dual stage - 2nd step) • Airbag ECU assy • Instrument panel wire • Instrument panel wire No.3

Table al. Supplemental Restraint - Airbag System

DTC	Definition	Trouble Area
B1817/54	Short in P squib (Dual stage -2nd step) circuit (to ground)	• Front passenger airbag assy (P squib, Dual stage - 2nd step) • Airbag ECU assy • Instrument panel wire • Instrument panel wire No.4
B1818/54	Short in P squib (Dual stage -2nd step) circuit (to B+)	• Front passenger airbag assy (P squib, Dual stage - 2nd step) • Airbag ECU assy • Instrument panel wire • Instrument panel wire No.5
B1820/55	Short in side squib (D seat side) circuit	• Front seat airbag assy LH (Side squib (D seat side)) • Airbag ECU assy • Floor wire • Seat airbag No.1 wire
B1821/55	Open in side squib (D seat side) circuit	• Front seat airbag assy LH (Side squib (D seat side)) • Airbag ECU assy • Floor wire • Seat airbag No.1 wire
B1822/55	Short in side squib (D seat side) circuit (to ground)	• Front seat airbag assy LH (Side squib (D seat side)) • Airbag ECU assy • Floor wire • Seat airbag No.1 wire
B1823/55	Short in side squib (D seat side) circuit (to B+)	• Front seat airbag assy LH (Side squib (D seat side)) • Airbag ECU assy • Floor wire • Seat airbag No.1 wire
B1825/56	Short in side squib (P seat side) circuit	• Front seat airbag assy RH (Side squib (P seat side)) • Airbag ECU assy • Floor wire No.2 • Seat airbag No.2 wire
B1826/56	Open in side squib (P seat side) circuit	• Front seat airbag assy RH (Side squib (P seat side)) • Airbag ECU assy • Floor wire No.2 • Seat airbag No.2 wire
B1827/56	Short in side squib (P seat side) circuit (to ground)	• Front seat airbag assy RH (Side squib (P seat side)) • Airbag ECU assy • Floor wire No.2 • Seat airbag No.2 wire
B1828/56	Short in side squib (P seat side) circuit (to B+)	• Front seat airbag assy RH (Side squib (P seat side)) • Airbag ECU assy • Floor wire No.2 • Seat airbag No.2 wire
B1830/57	Short in curtain shield airbag (D seat side) squib circuit	• Curtain shield airbag assy LH (curtain shield airbag (D seat side) squib) • Airbag ECU assy • Floor wire
B1831/57	Open in curtain shield airbag (D seat side) squib circuit	• Curtain shield airbag assy LH (curtain shield airbag (D seat side) squib) • Airbag ECU assy • Floor wire

11

Table al. Supplemental Restraint - Airbag System

DTC	Definition	Trouble Area
B1832/57	Short in curtain shield airbag (D seat side) squib circuit (to ground)	• Curtain shield airbag assy LH (curtain shield airbag (D seat side) squib) • Airbag ECU assy • Floor wire
B1833/57	Short in curtain shield airbag (D seat side) squib circuit (to B+)	• Curtain shield airbag assy LH (curtain shield airbag (D seat side) squib) • Airbag ECU assy • Floor wire
B1835/58	Short in curtain shield airbag (P seat side) squib circuit	• Curtain shield airbag assy RH (curtain shield airbag (P seat side) squib) • Airbag ECU assy • Floor wire No.2
B1836/58	Open in curtain shield airbag (P seat side) squib circuit	• Curtain shield airbag assy RH (curtain shield airbag (P seat side) squib) • Airbag ECU assy • Floor wire No.2
B1837/58	Short in curtain shield airbag (P seat side) squib circuit (to ground)	• Curtain shield airbag assy RH (curtain shield airbag (P seat side) squib) • Airbag ECU assy • Floor wire No.3
B1838/58	Short in curtain shield airbag (P seat side) squib circuit (to B+)	• Curtain shield airbag assy RH (curtain shield airbag (P seat side) squib) • Airbag ECU assy • Floor wire No.4
B1900/73	Short in P/T squib (D seat side) circuit	• Front seat outer belt assy LH (P/T squib (D seat side)) • Airbag ECU assy • Floor wire
B1901/73	Open in P/T squib (D seat side) circuit	• Front seat outer belt assy LH (P/T squib (D seat side)) • Airbag ECU assy • Floor wire
B1902/73	Short in P/T squib (D seat side) circuit (to ground)	• Front seat outer belt assy LH (P/T squib (D seat side)) • Airbag ECU assy • Floor wire
B1903/73	Short in P/T squib (D seat side) circuit (to B+)	• Front seat outer belt assy LH (P/T squib (D seat side)) • Airbag ECU assy • Floor wire
B1905/74	Short in P/T squib (P seat side) circuit	• Front seat outer belt assy RH (P/T squib (P seat side)) • Airbag ECU assy • Floor wire No.2
B1906/74	Open in P/T squib (P seat side) circuit	• Front seat outer belt assy RH (P/T squib (P seat side)) • Airbag ECU assy • Floor wire No.3
B1907/74	Short in P/T squib (P seat side) circuit (to ground)	• Front seat outer belt assy RH (P/T squib (P seat side)) • Airbag ECU assy • Floor wire No.4
B1908/74	Short in P/T squib (P seat side) circuit (to B+)	• Front seat outer belt assy RH (P/T squib (P seat side)) • Airbag ECU assy • Floor wire No.5

Table am. Supplemental Restraint - Occupant Classification System

DTC	Definition	Trouble Area
B1771	Passenger Side Buckle Switch Circuit Malfunction	• Floor wire • Front seat inner belt assembly (Buckle switch RH) • Occupant classification ECU
B1780	Front Occupant Classification Sensor LH Circuit Malfunction	• Front seat wire RH • Front seat assembly RH (Front occupant classification sensor RH) • Occupant classification ECU
B1781	Front Occupant Classification Sensor RH Circuit Malfunction	• Front seat wire RH • Front seat assembly RH (Front occupant classification sensor RH) • Occupant classification ECU
B1782	Rear Occupant Classification Sensor LH Circuit Malfunction	• Front seat wire RH • Front seat assembly RH (Front occupant classification sensor LH) • Occupant classification ECU
B1783	Rear Occupant Classification Sensor RH Circuit Malfunction	• Front seat wire RH • Front seat assembly RH (Front occupant classification sensor RH) • Occupant classification ECU
B1785	Front Occupant Classification Sensor LH Collision Detection	• Front seat wire RH • Front seat assembly RH (Front occupant classification sensor LH) • Occupant classification ECU
B1786	Front Occupant Classification Sensor RH Collision Detection	• Front seat wire RH • Front seat assembly RH (Front occupant classification sensor RH) • Occupant classification ECU
B1787	Rear Occupant Classification Sensor LH Collision Detection	• Front seat wire RH • Front seat assembly RH (Front occupant classification sensor LH) • Occupant classification ECU
B1788	Rear Occupant Classification Sensor RH Collision Detection	• Front seat wire RH • Front seat assembly RH (Front occupant classification sensor RH) • Occupant classification ECU
B1790	Center Airbag Sensor Assembly Communication Circuit Malfunction	• Floor wire No. 2 • Occupant classification ECU • Center airbag sensor assembly
B1793	Occupant Classification Sensor Power Supply Circuit Malfunction	• Front seat wire RH • Front seat assembly RH (Occupant classification sensors) • Occupant classification ECU
B1794	Open in Occupant Classification ECU Battery Positive Line	• Wire harness • Occupant classification ECU
B1795	Occupant Classification ECU Malfunction	• Battery • ECU-B Fuse • Floor wire No. 2 • Front seat inner belt RH • Occupant classification ECU
B1796	Sleep Operation Failure of Occupant Classification ECU	Occupant classification ECU

11

Tire pressure warning system (TPWS)

The table(s) in this section contain tire pressure warning system (TPWS) DTCs, blink codes, code definitions and likely trouble areas. 5-digit DTCs and 2-digit blink codes are separated by slash.

Retrieving DTCs

TPWS DTCs can be retrieved two ways:

- Toyota scan tool or equivalent (retrieves 5-digit DTCs)
- Warning light blinking pattern (retrieves 2-digit blink codes)

To retrieve 5-digit DTCs using Toyota scan tool or equivalent, see **Diagnostic Scan Tools** in this chapter.

– To retrieve 2-digit blink codes, perform the following procedure:

– Be sure hybrid system is OFF (READY indicator not illuminated).

> **WARNING—**
> - *Be sure hybrid system is OFF when servicing vehicle (READY indicator not illuminated). Failure to switch the hybrid system OFF could result in engine start at any time.*

◀ Using jumper wire, connect terminals 4 (CG) and 13 (TC) in OBD II connector.

> **CAUTION—**
> - *Avoid spreading or deforming female terminals in OBD II connector. Use an appropriate jumper wire gauge and do not force jumper wire into terminals.*
> - *Connecting incorrect terminals may damage vehicle.*

– Turn hybrid system ON (IG-ON, READY indicator not illuminated).

◀ TPWS warning light will blink (flash).

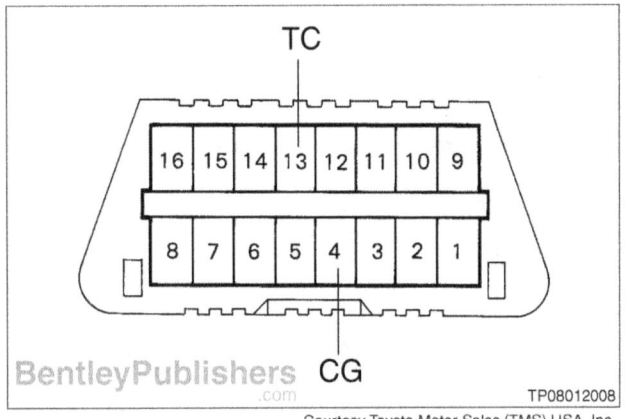

TP08012008

Courtesy Toyota Motor Sales (TMS) USA, Inc.

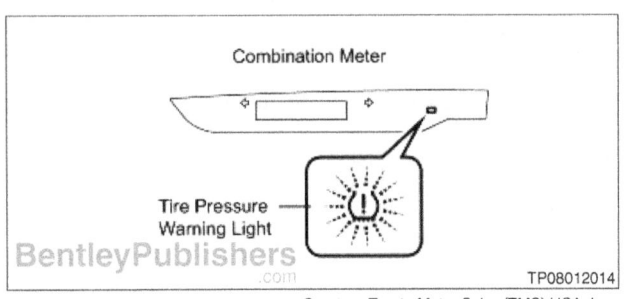

Combination Meter

Tire Pressure Warning Light

TP08012014

Courtesy Toyota Motor Sales (TMS) USA, Inc.

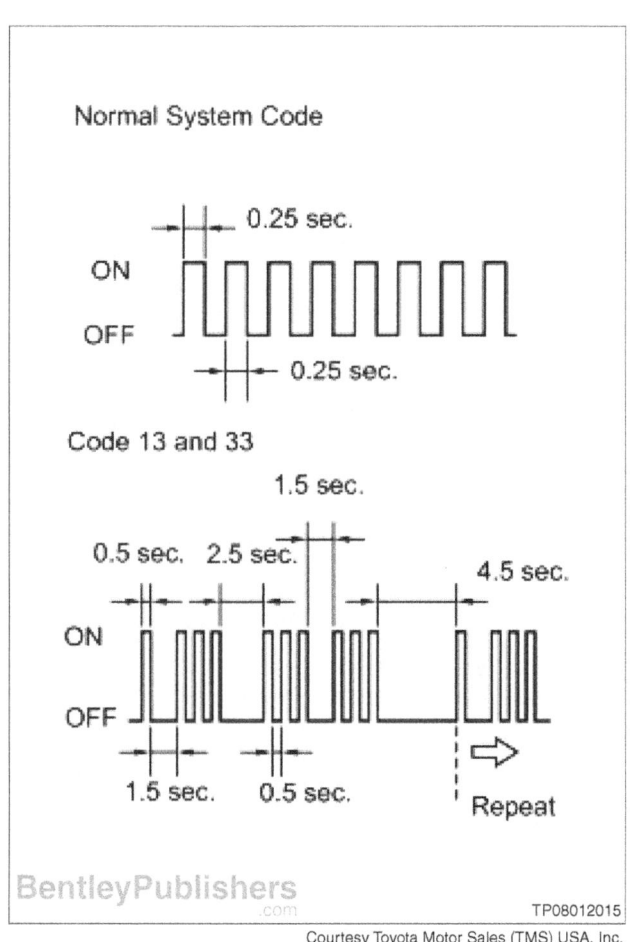

Normal System Code

0.25 sec.

Code 13 and 33

1.5 sec.

0.5 sec. 2.5 sec.

4.5 sec.

1.5 sec.   0.5 sec.   Repeat

BentleyPublishers.com

TP08012015

Courtesy Toyota Motor Sales (TMS) USA, Inc.

◀ Warning light blinks in pattern as shown on left to display 2-digit DTCs.

– Warning light will repeat blink pattern until turned OFF.

– If more than one DTC is stored, warning light will blink each DTC in ascending order.

– When check is complete, remove jumper from OBD II connector.

Clearing DTCs

Clear TPWS DTCs with Toyota scan tool or equivalent.

– Connect scan tool to OBD II connector.

– Turn hybrid system ON (IG-ON, READY indicator not illuminated).

– Operate tester to clear DTCs. Refer to tester operating instructions.

Table an. Tire Pressure Warning System (TPWS)

DTC	Definition	Trouble Area
C2111/11	Transmitter ID1 Operation Stop	• Tire pressure warning valve and transmitter • Tire pressure warning ECU
C2112/12	Transmitter ID2 Operation Stop	• Tire pressure warning valve and transmitter • Tire pressure warning ECU
C2113/13	Transmitter ID3 Operation Stop	• Tire pressure warning valve and transmitter • Tire pressure warning ECU
C2114/14	Transmitter ID4 Operation Stop	• Tire pressure warning valve and transmitter • Tire pressure warning ECU
C2121/21	No Signal from Transmitter ID1 in Main Mode	• Tire pressure warning valve and transmitter • Tire pressure warning antenna and receiver • Tire pressure warning ECU • Wire harness
C2122/22	No Signal from Transmitter ID2 in Main Mode	• Tire pressure warning valve and transmitter • Tire pressure warning antenna and receiver • Tire pressure warning ECU • Wire harness
C2123/23	No Signal from Transmitter ID3 in Main Mode	• Tire pressure warning valve and transmitter • Tire pressure warning antenna and receiver • Tire pressure warning ECU • Wire harness

11

Table an. Tire Pressure Warning System (TPWS)

DTC	Definition	Trouble Area
C2124/24	No Signal from Transmitter ID4 in Main Mode	• Tire pressure warning valve and transmitter • Tire pressure warning antenna and receiver • Tire pressure warning ECU • Wire harness
C2141/41	Transmitter ID1 Error	Tire pressure warning valve and transmitter
C2142/42	Transmitter ID2 Error	Tire pressure warning valve and transmitter
C2143/43	Transmitter ID3 Error	Tire pressure warning valve and transmitter
C2144/44	Transmitter ID4 Error	Tire pressure warning valve and transmitter
C2165/65	Abnormal Temperature Inside ID1 Tire	• Tire pressure warning valve and transmitter • Tire pressure warning antenna and receiver
C2166/66	Abnormal Temperature Inside ID2 Tire	• Tire pressure warning valve and transmitter • Tire pressure warning antenna and receiver
C2167/67	Abnormal Temperature Inside ID3 Tire	• Tire pressure warning valve and transmitter • Tire pressure warning antenna and receiver
C2168/68	Abnormal Temperature Inside ID4 Tire	• Tire pressure warning valve and transmitter • Tire pressure warning antenna and receiver
C2171/71	Transmitter ID not Registered in Main Mode	Tire pressure warning ECU
C2176/76	Receiver Error	• Tire pressure warning antenna and receiver • Tire pressure warning ECU • Wire harness
C2177/77	Initialization not Completed	• Tire pressure warning valve and transmitter • Tire pressure warning ECU
C2181/81	Transmitter ID1 not Received (Test Mode DTC)	• Tire pressure warning valve and transmitter • Each tire pressure warning valve and transmitter • Tire pressure warning ECU • Wire harness
C2182/82	Transmitter ID2 not Received (Test Mode DTC)	• Tire pressure warning valve and transmitter • Each tire pressure warning valve and transmitter • Tire pressure warning ECU • Wire harness
C2183/83	Transmitter ID3 not Received (Test Mode DTC)	• Tire pressure warning valve and transmitter • Each tire pressure warning valve and transmitter • Tire pressure warning ECU • Wire harness
C2184/84	Transmitter ID4 not Received (Test Mode DTC)	• Tire pressure warning valve and transmitter • Each tire pressure warning valve and transmitter • Tire pressure warning ECU • Wire harness
C2191/91	Vehicle Speed Signal Error (Test Mode DTC)	• Vehicle speed sensor • Tire pressure warning ECU • Combination meter • Wire harness

MULTIFUNCTION DISPLAY

Starting diagnostic mode, clearing DTCs

The following pages are from the Toyota Technical Information System (TIS). The pages explain how to place the multifunction display (touch screen) in the diagnostic mode, and how to retrieve and clear diagnostic trouble codes (DTCs).

11

05-1887

DIAGNOSTICS   -   NAVIGATION SYSTEM

DIAGNOSTIC START-UP/FINISH

06GGD-01

HINT:
- Illustrations may differ from the actual vehicle depending on the device settings and options. Therefore, some detailed areas may not be shown exactly the same as on the actual vehicle.
- After the power switch is ON (ACC), check that the map is displayed before starting the diagnostic mode. Otherwise, some items cannot be checked.

1. **There are 2 methods to start diagnostic mode. Start the mode by using one of them.**

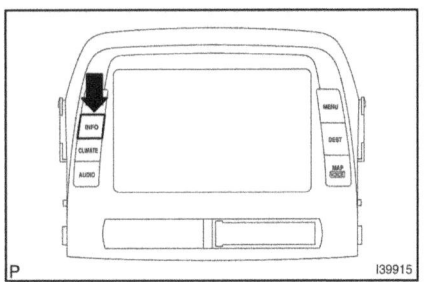

2. **Method 1**
(a) Start the HV system.
(b) While pressing and holding "INFO" switch, operate light control switch, OFF → TAIL → OFF → TAIL → OFF → TAIL → OFF.
(c) The diagnostic mode starts and the service check screen ("System Check Mode") will be displayed. Service inspection starts automatically and the result will be displayed.

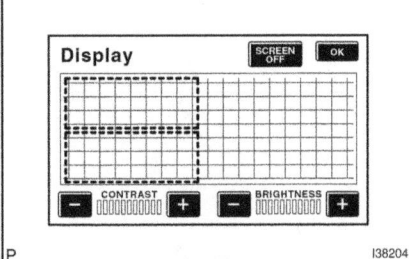

3. **Method 2**
(a) Start the HV system.
(b) Switch to the "Display Check" screen.
(c) From the display adjustment screen, touch the corners of the screen in the following order: upper left → lower left →upper left → lower left → upper left → lower left.
(d) The diagnostic mode starts and "Service Check" screen will be displayed. Service inspection starts automatically and the result will be displayed.

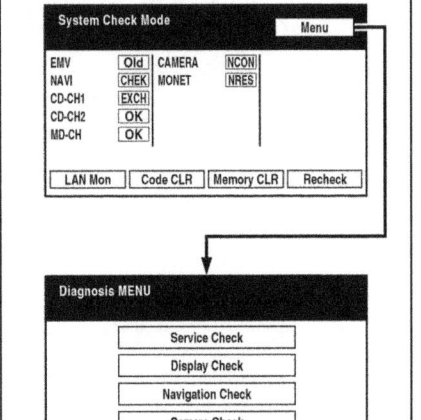

4. **Diagnosis MENU**
(a) Diagnostic screen will be displayed by pressing the menu switch on the service check screen.

5. **There are 2 methods to exit. Use one of them.**
(a) Turn the power switch off.
(b) Press the "DISPLAY" switch for 3 seconds.

05-1889

DIAGNOSTICS   -   NAVIGATION SYSTEM

SYSTEM CHECK MODE (DTC CHECK)

05GGE-01

HINT:

Illustrations may differ from the actual vehicle depending on the device settings and options. Therefore, some detailed areas may not be shown exactly the same as on the actual vehicle.

1.   **Start the diagnostic mode (see page 05-1887).**

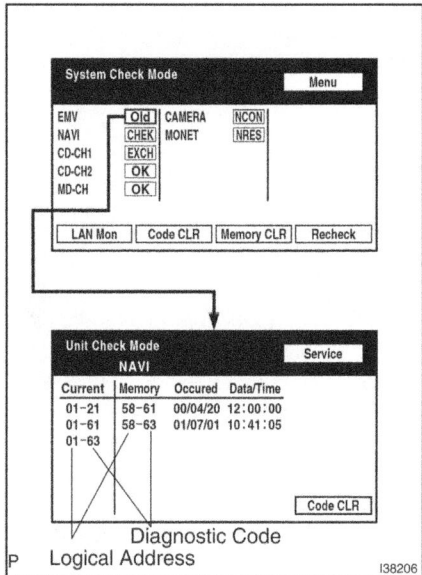

2.   **Read the system check result.**

(a)   If all check results of other devices are "EXCH," "CHEK" or "Old," touch the display to check the contents on the "Unit Check Mode" screen and record them on the customer problem analysis check sheet.

HINT:

-   If all check results are "OK," go to communication DTC check (go to step 3).
-   If a device name is not known, its physical address is displayed.

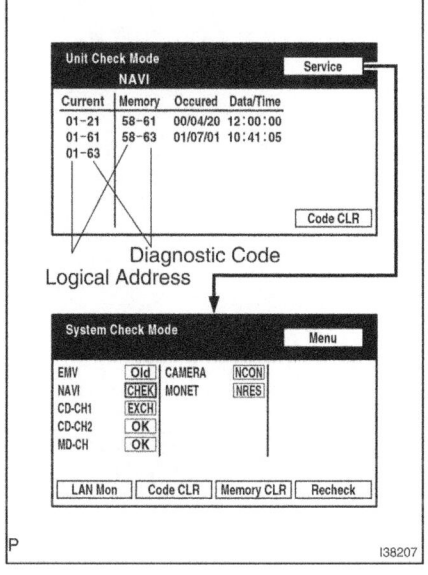

HINT:

If "EXCH", "CHEK" and "Old" as well as "OK" exist, press the service switch to return to the "System Check Mode". Then, check the "Unit Check Mode" screen and record them on the customer problem analysis check sheet.

05-1890

DIAGNOSTICS - NAVIGATION SYSTEM

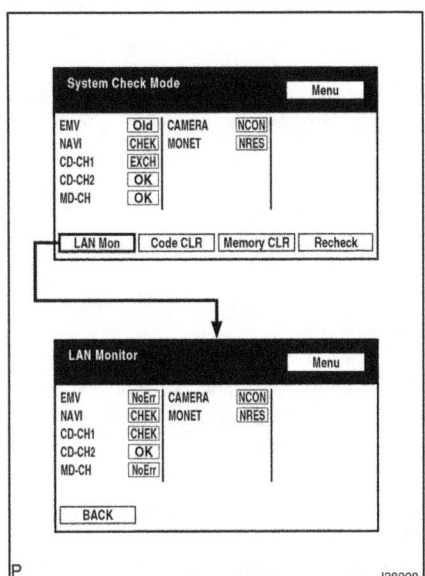

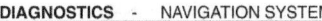

3. Read the communication diagnostic check result.

(a) Return to the "System Check Mode", and press "LAN Mon" switch to enter the LAN monitor screen.

(b) If the result is "CHEK" or "Old," touch the result switch to check the contents on the individual communication diagnostic screen and record them on the customer problem analysis check sheet.

HINT:

- If all check results are "No Err," the system judges that no DTC exists.
- The sub-code (relevant device) will be indicated by its physical address.

05-1891

DIAGNOSTICS - NAVIGATION SYSTEM

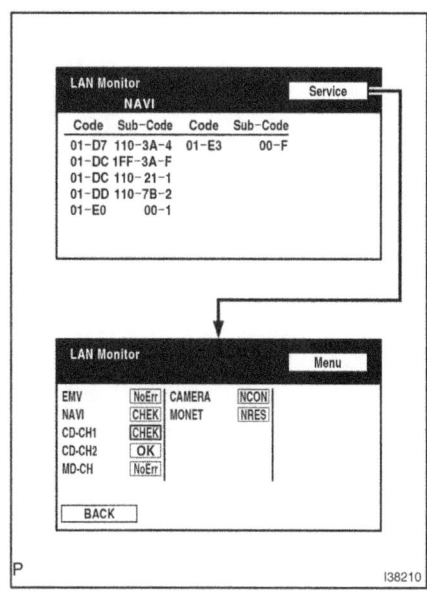

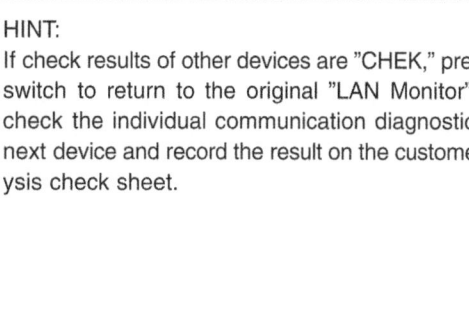

HINT:
If check results of other devices are "CHEK," press the "Service" switch to return to the original "LAN Monitor" screen. Then, check the individual communication diagnostic screen for the next device and record the result on the customer problem analysis check sheet.

05-1892

DIAGNOSTICS - NAVIGATION SYSTEM

SYSTEM CHECK MODE (DTC CLEAR/RECHECK)

05GGF-01

HINT:

Illustrations may differ from the actual vehicle depending on the device settings and options. Therefore, some detailed areas may not be shown exactly the same as on the actual vehicle.

1. **Enter the diagnostic mode (see page 05-1887).**

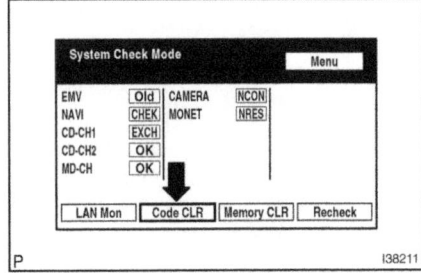

2. **Clear DTC**
(a) Press the "Code CLR" switch for 3 seconds.

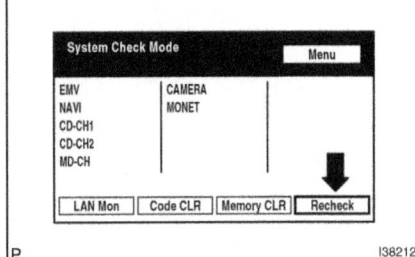

(b) Check result is cleared.
3. **Recheck**
(a) Press the "Recheck" switch.

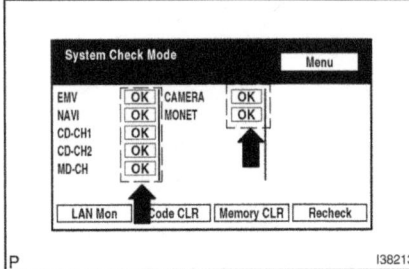

(b) Confirm that all diagnostic codes are "OK" when the check results are displayed.
If a code other than "OK" is displayed, troubleshoot again.

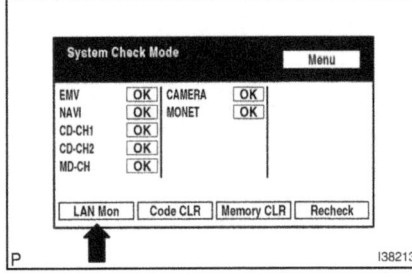

(c) Press the "LAN Mon" switch to change to "LAN Monitor" mode.

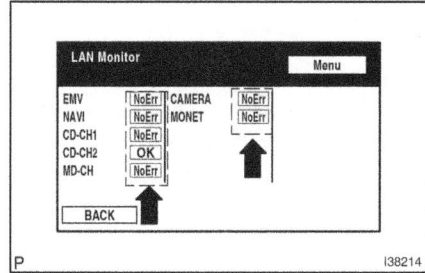

(d)   Confirm that all diagnostic codes are "No Err".
If a code other than "No Err" is displayed, troubleshoot again.

05-1869

DIAGNOSTICS - NAVIGATION SYSTEM

05GHM-01

DIAGNOSIS DISPLAY DETAILED DESCRIPTION

HINT:

- This section contains a detailed description of displays within diagnostic mode.
- Illustrations may differ from the actual vehicle depending on the device settings and options. Therefore, some detailed areas may not be shown exactly the same as on the actual vehicle.

1. System Check

(a) System Check Mode Display

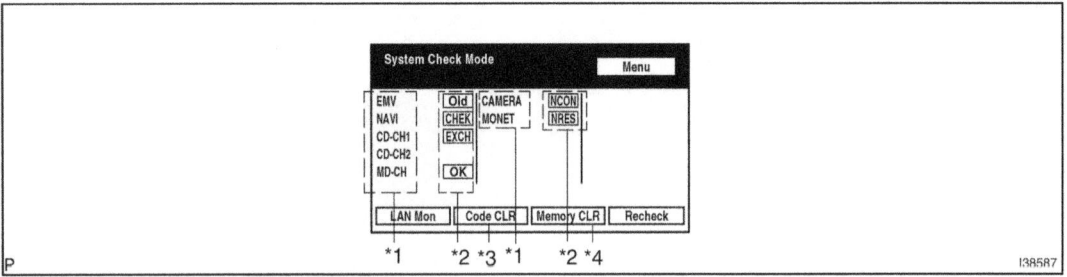

Device Names and hardware Address/*1

HINT:

- Registered device names are displayed below.
- If a device name is unknown to the system, its physical address is shown instead.

Address No.	Name	Address No.	Name
110	EMV	120	AVX
128	1DIN TV	140	AVN
144	G-BOOK	178	NAVI
17C	MONET	190	AUDIO H/U
1AC	CAMERA-C	1B0	Rr-TV
1C0	Rr-CONT	1C2	TV-TUNER2
1C4	PANEL	1C6	G/W
1C8	FM-M-LCD	1D8	CONT-SW
1EC	Body	1F0	RADIO TUNER
1F1	XM	1F2	SIRIUS
230	TV-TUNER	240	CD-CH2
250	DVD-CH	280	CAMERA
360	CD-CH1	3A0	MD-CH
17D	TEL	440	DSP-AMP
530	ETC	5C8	MAYDAY
1A0	DVD-P	1C6	CLOCK
1F4	RSA	1F6	RSE
480	AMP	-	-

05-1870

Check Result/*2

HINT:

Result codes for all devices are shown below.

Result	Meaning	Action
OK	The device did not respond with a DTC (excluding communication DTCs from the AVC-LAN).	-
EXCH	The device responds with a "replace"-type DTC.	Look up the DTC in "Unit Check Mode" and replace the device.
CHEK	The device responds with a "check"-type DTC.	Look up the DTC in "Unit Check Mode".
NCON	The device was previously present, but does not respond in diagnostic mode.	1. Check power supply wire harness of the device. 2. Check the AVC-LAN of the device.
Old	The device responds with an "old"-type DTC.	Look up the DTC in "Unit Check Mode".
NRES	The device responds in diagnostic mode, but gives no DTC information.	1. Check power supply wire harness of the device. 2. Check the AVC-LAN of the device.

Code Clear/*3

Present DTCs are cleared.

Memory Clear/*4

Present and past DTCs and registered connected device names are cleared.

(b)   Diagnosis MENU Display

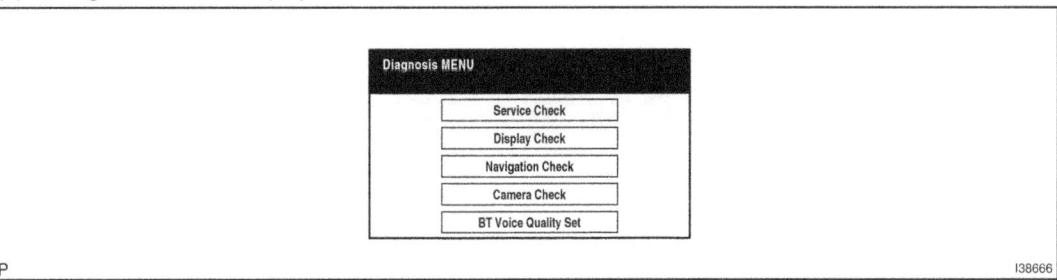

P   I38666

HINT:

Each item is grayed out or not displayed based on the device settings.

11

05-1871

DIAGNOSTICS - NAVIGATION SYSTEM

(c) Unit Check Mode Screen

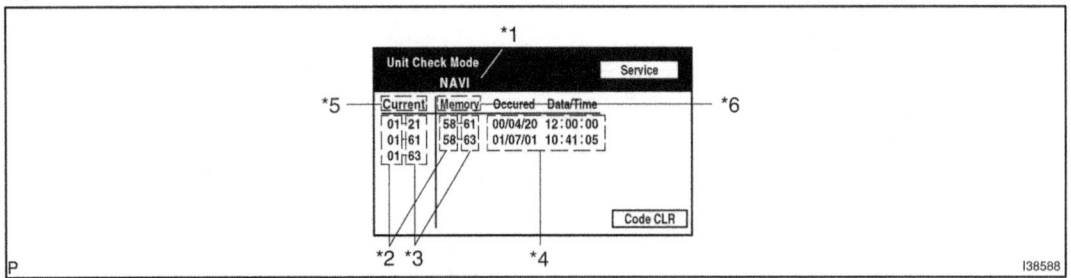

Screen Description

Display	Contents
Device name/*1	Target Device
Segment/*2	Target Device Logical address
DTC/*3	DTC (Diagnostic Trouble Code)
Timestamp/*4	The time and date of past DTCs displayed. (The year is displayed in 2 digit format.)
Present Code/*5	The DTC output at the service check is displayed.
Past Code/*6	Diagnostic memory results and recorded DTCs are displayed.

(d) LAN Monitor (Original) Screen

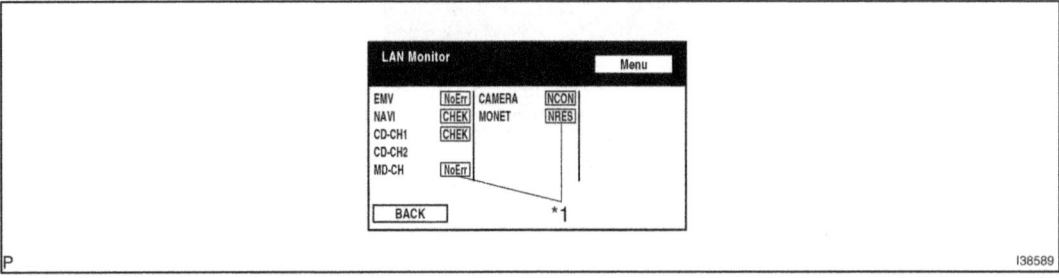

Check result
HINT:
Check results of all the devices are displayed.

Result	Meaning	Action
No Err (OK)	There are no communication DTCs.	-
CHEK	The device responds with a "check"-type DTC.	Look up the DTC in "Unit Check Mode".
NCON	The device was previously present, but does not respond in diagnostic mode.	1. Check power supply wire harness of the device. 2. Check the AVC-LAN of the device.
Old	The device responded with an old-type DTC.	Look up the DTC in "Unit Check Mode".
NRES	Device responds in diagnostic mode, but gives no DTC information.	1. Check power supply wire harness of the device. 2. Check the AVC-LAN of the device.

05-1872

DIAGNOSTICS - NAVIGATION SYSTEM

(e)   LAN Monitor (Individual) Screen

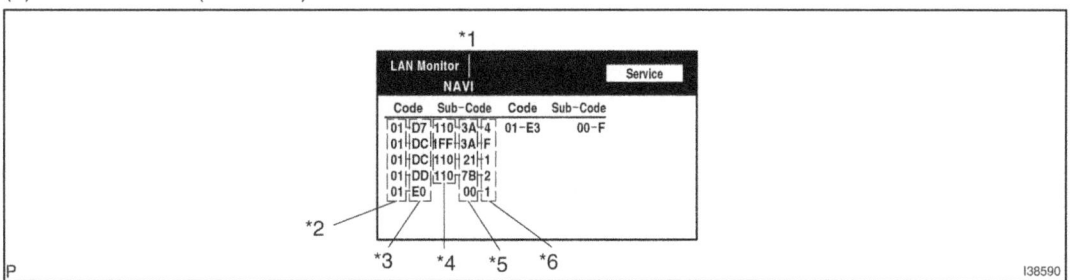

Screen Description

Display	Contents
Device name/*1	Target device
Segment/*2	Target logical address
DTC/*3	DTC (Diagnostic Trouble Code)
Sub-Code (device address)/*4	Physical address stored with DTC. (If there is no address, nothing is displayed.)
Connection check No./*5	Connection check number stored with DTC.
DTC occurrence/*6	Number of times the same DTC has been recorded.

2.   **DISPLAY CHECK**

(a)   Vehicle Signal Check Mode Screen

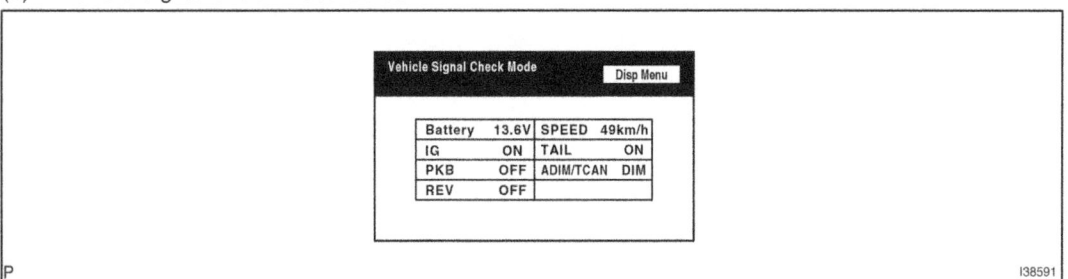

Screen Description

Name	Contents
Battery	Battery voltage is displayed.
PKB	Parking brake ON/OFF state is displayed.
REV	Reverse signal ON/OFF state is displayed.
IG	Power switch ON/OFF state is displayed.
ADIM/TCAN	Brightness state DIM (with)/ BRIGHT (without) is displayed.
SPEED	The vehicle speed, displayed in km/h.
TAIL	TAIL signal (Head lamp dimmer switch) ON/OFF state is displayed.

HINT:
- Only items sending a vehicle signal will be displayed.
- This screen is updated once per second when input signals to the vehicle are changed.

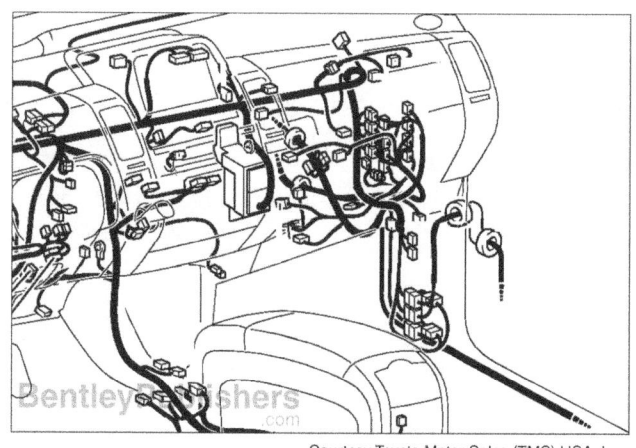

Courtesy Toyota Motor Sales (TMS) USA, Inc.

12

Electrical Component Locations

Fuses, relays and grounds

GENERAL

This chapter illustrates the electrical components, including fuses, relays, connectors, and ground points for the 2004 through 2008 Toyota Prius.

Prius safety precautions

In addition to the safety warnings given here, always read and observe the **Warnings**, **Cautions** and safety procedures in **3 Safety** before working on vehicle. Orange-colored cables carry lethal high voltage. Use extreme care when working near high voltage cables and components.

The Prius engine may start at any time if the hybrid system is in **READY** mode. See **3 Safety** for instructions on turning OFF the hybrid system.

WARNING—

- *Risk of electrocution! Avoid touching orange-colored high voltage wiring and high voltage components unless you are certain that high voltage is not present.*

- *The Prius hybrid system has voltages as high as 500 volts. Voltages over 60 volts DC and 25 volts AC are a shock hazard.*

WARNING—

- *Be sure hybrid system is OFF when servicing vehicle (READY indicator not illuminated). Failure to switch the hybrid system OFF could result in engine start at any time.*

WARNING—

- *Airbags and pyrotechnic seat belt tensioners utilize explosive devices. Handle with extreme care.*

- *Keep hands, clothing and other objects clear of the electric radiator cooling fan when working on a warm engine. The fan may start at any time.*

CAUTION—

- *Relay and fuse positions are subject to change. If questions arise, an authorized Toyota dealer is the best source for the most accurate and up-to-date information.*

- *Use a digital multimeter for electrical tests. Switch multimeter to appropriate function and range before making test connections.*

- *Many control modules are static sensitive. Static discharge damages them permanently. Handle the modules using proper static prevention equipment and techniques.*

- *To avoid damaging harness connectors or relay panel sockets, use jumper wires with flat-blade connectors that are the same size as the connector or relay terminals.*

- *Choose test equipment carefully. Use a digital multimeter with at least 10 MΩ input impedance, or an LED test light. An analog meter (swing-needle) or a test light with a normal incandescent bulb may draw enough current to damage sensitive electronic components.*

- *Do not use an ohmmeter to measure resistance on solid state components such as control modules.*

- *Disconnect the power supply before making resistance (ohm) measurements on a circuit.*

Abbreviations and acronyms

The following table lists common Toyota electrical system abbreviations and acronyms used throughout this chapter.

Table a. Electrical system abbreviations and acronyms	
AC	Alternating current (see DC)
A/C	Air-conditioning
ACC	Accessory
AMP	Amplifier
AVC-LAN	Audio visual communication - local area network
BA	Brake assist
BAT	Battery
BEAN	Body electronics area network
BK/UP	Back-up (light)
CAN	Controller area network
CDS	Condenser (air-conditioning)
CHS	Coolant heat storage
C/OPN	Circuit opening (relay)
DC	Direct current (see AC)
DEF	Defroster
DIM	Dimmer (headlights)
DLC	Data link connector
DLC3	Data link connector (OBD-II diagnostic connector)
DRL	Daytime running lights
EB	Electrical brake
EBD	Electric brake force distribution
ECM	Engine control module
ECU	Electronic control unit
EFI	Electronic fuel injection
EPS	Electric power steering
ETCS	Electronic throttle control system
EVAP	Evaporative emission
FR	Front
F/P	Fuel pump
GND	Ground
GPS	Global positioning system
HAZ	Hazard
HEV	Hybrid electric vehicle
HID	High intensity discharge (headlights)

H-LP	Headlight power
HTR	Heater
HV	Hybrid vehicle
IG	Ignition
IGN	Ignition
INV	Inverter
J/B	Junction block
LAN	Local area network
LCD	Liquid crystal display
LED	Light emitting diode
LH	Left hand
LP	Lamp or light
M/HTR	Mirror heater
MIL	Malfunction indicator lamp
MPX	Multiplex
MTR	Motor
OBD	On-board diagnostics
ODO	Odometer
P CON	Powertrain control
P/I	Power (ignition and hybrid system)
PS HTR	Electric heater in footwell duct
PTC HTR	Positive temperature coefficient (electric heater in heater core)
PWR	Power
R/B	Relay block
RDI	Radiator (cooling fans)
RH	Right hand
SFI	Sequential multiport fuel injection, *see also* EFI
SRS	Supplemental restraint system
SW	Switch
TEMP	Temperature
T-LP	Taillight and illumination power
TRAC	Traction control
VFD	Vacuum fluorescent display
VSC	Vehicle stability control
VSV	Vacuum switching valve
VVT-i	Variable valve timing - intelligent
WIP	Wiper (windshield)
W/P	Water pump
WSH	Washer (windshield)

12

FUSE, RELAY, AND ECU LOCATIONS

Relays and ECUs are located throughout the vehicle.

Fuses can be found in two places:

- in the left rear corner of the engine compartment,
- in the lower left side of the dashboard in the passenger compartment.

Fuse identification tables immediately follow the fuse block illustrations.

Engine compartment, overview

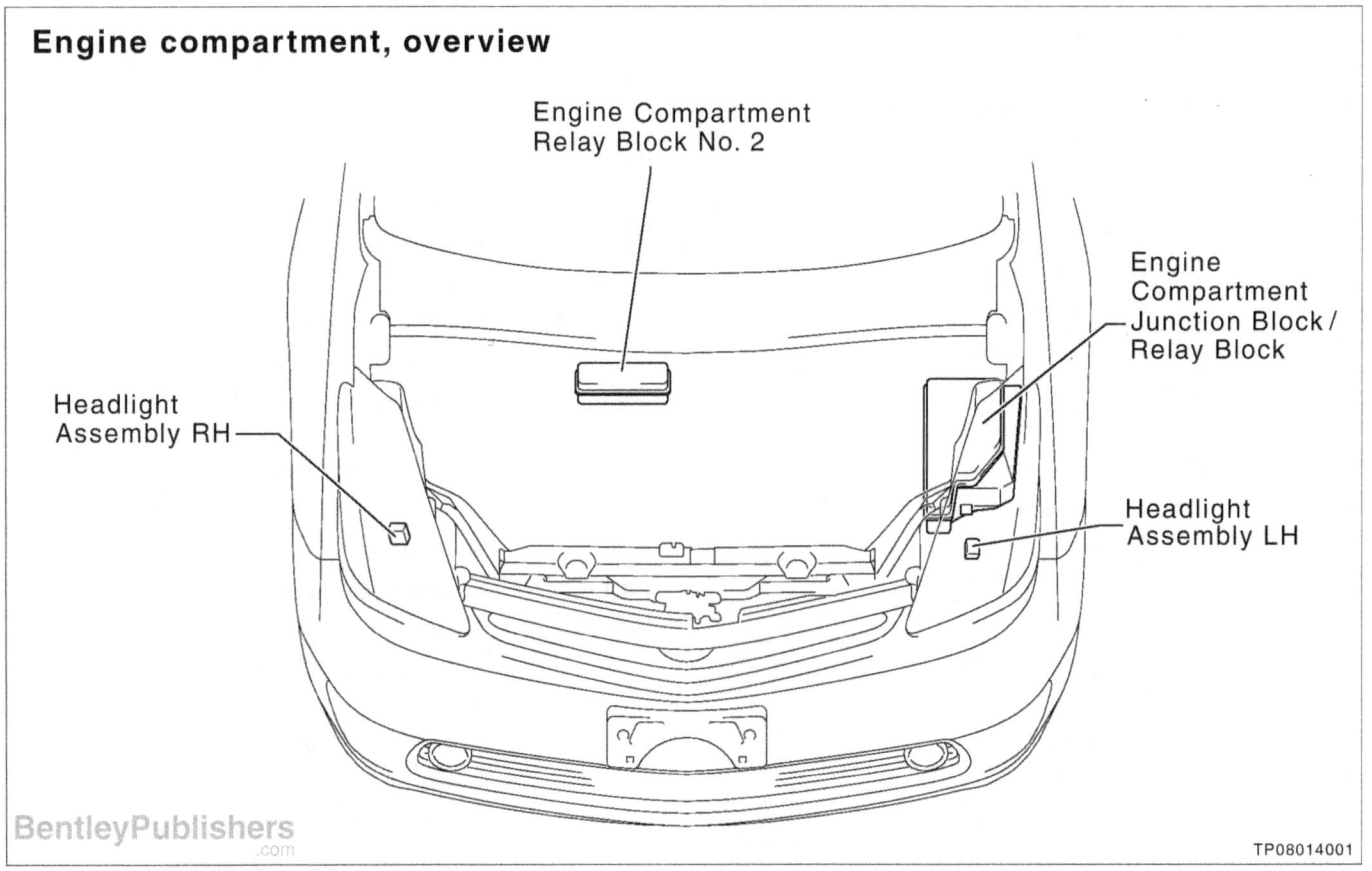

Engine Compartment
Relay Block No. 2

Engine
Compartment
Junction Block /
Relay Block

Headlight
Assembly RH

Headlight
Assembly LH

BentleyPublishers.com

TP08014001

Courtesy Toyota Motor Sales (TMS) USA, Inc.

Engine compartment junction block / relay block

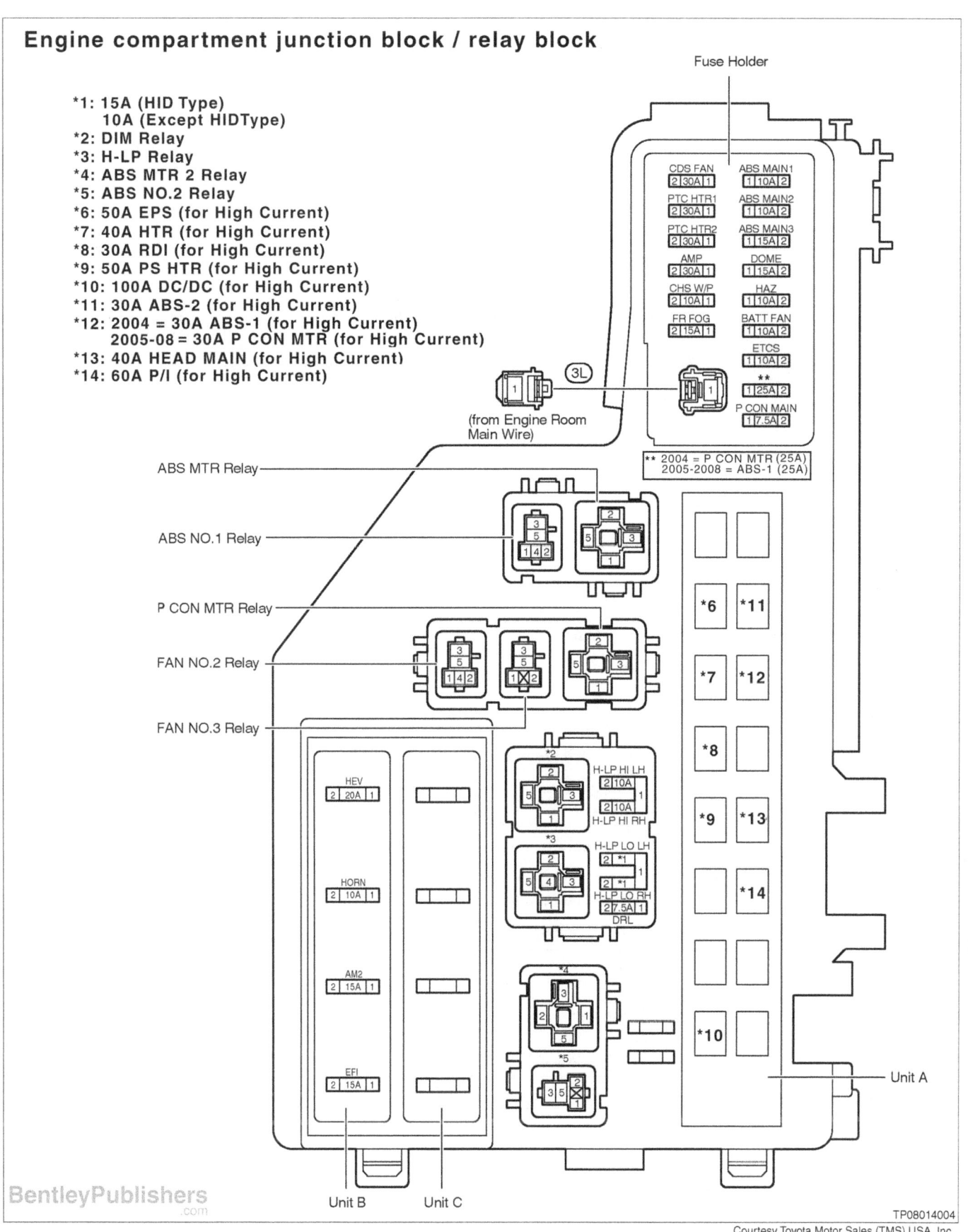

*1: 15A (HID Type)
    10A (Except HIDType)
*2: DIM Relay
*3: H-LP Relay
*4: ABS MTR 2 Relay
*5: ABS NO.2 Relay
*6: 50A EPS (for High Current)
*7: 40A HTR (for High Current)
*8: 30A RDI (for High Current)
*9: 50A PS HTR (for High Current)
*10: 100A DC/DC (for High Current)
*11: 30A ABS-2 (for High Current)
*12: 2004 = 30A ABS-1 (for High Current)
     2005-08 = 30A P CON MTR (for High Current)
*13: 40A HEAD MAIN (for High Current)
*14: 60A P/I (for High Current)

Fuse Holder

CDS FAN 2 30A 1   ABS MAIN1 1 10A 2
PTC HTR1 2 30A 1   ABS MAIN2 1 10A 2
PTC HTR2 2 30A 1   ABS MAIN3 1 15A 2
AMP 2 30A 1   DOME 1 15A 2
CHS W/P 2 10A 1   HAZ 1 10A 2
FR FOG 2 15A 1   BATT FAN 1 10A 2
                     ETCS 1 10A 2
(3L)   ** 1 25A 2
                     P CON MAIN 1 7.5A 2

(from Engine Room Main Wire)

** 2004 = P CON MTR (25A)
   2005-2008 = ABS-1 (25A)

ABS MTR Relay

ABS NO.1 Relay

P CON MTR Relay

FAN NO.2 Relay

FAN NO.3 Relay

HEV 2 20A 1

HORN 2 10A 1

AM2 2 15A 1

EFI 2 15A 1

H-LP HI LH 2 10A 1
H-LP HI RH 2 10A 1

H-LP LO LH 2 *1 1
H-LP LO RH 2 *1 1
DRL 2 7.5A 1

*6 *11
*7 *12
*8
*9 *13
    *14
*10

Unit A

Unit B   Unit C

TP08014004

Courtesy Toyota Motor Sales (TMS) USA, Inc.

12

Engine compartment relay block no. 2

(engine compartment, rear, on cowl)

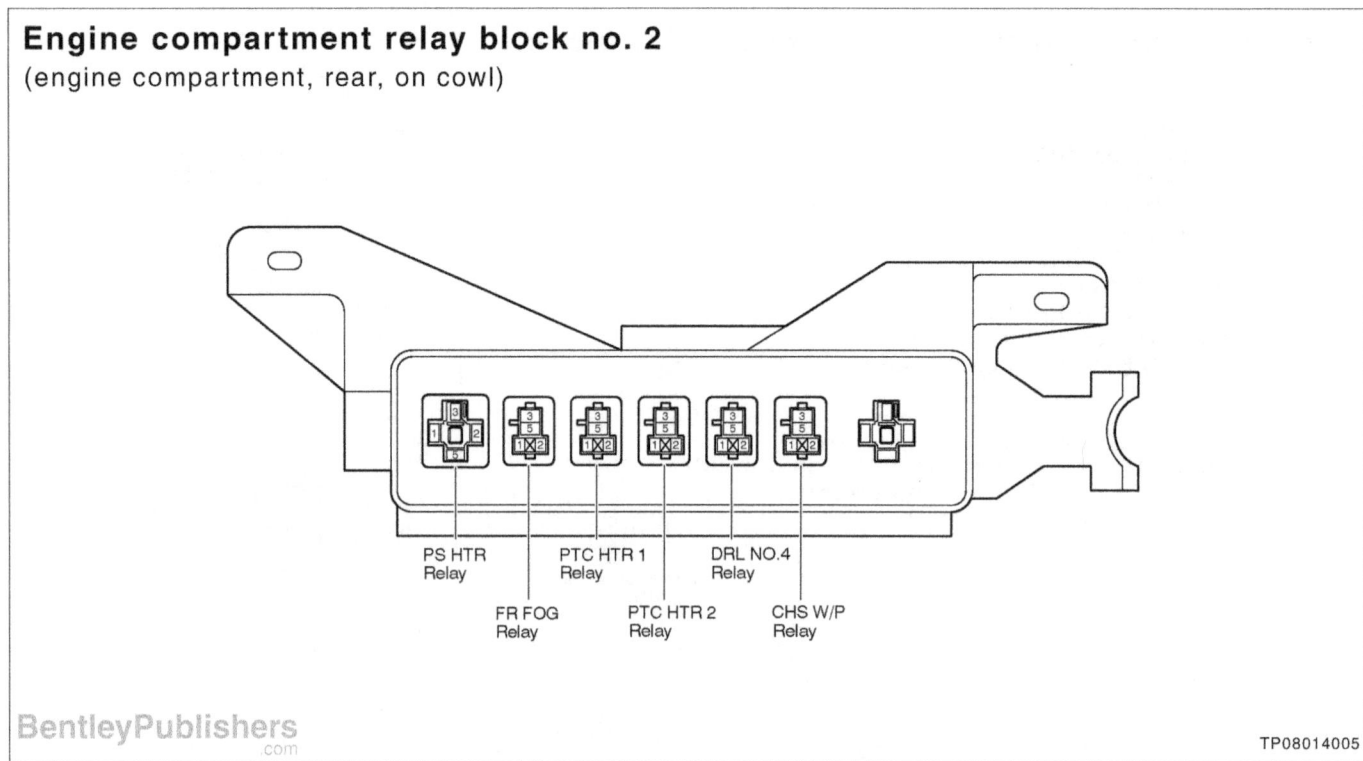

TP08014005

Courtesy Toyota Motor Sales (TMS) USA, Inc.

Table b. Fuse details - engine compartment, junction block / relay block

Fuse rating	Fuse ID	System
7.5A	DRL	Headlight
7.5A	P CON MAIN	Push button start system and hybrid vehicle immobilizer system Shift control system Smart entry system and wireless door lock control (w/ Smart entry system)
10 A	ABS MAIN 1	Brake control system Toyota hybrid system
10A	ABS MAIN 2	Brake control system Toyota hybrid system
10A	BATT FAN	Toyota hybrid system
10A	CHS W/P	Air conditioner Engine control
10A	ETCS	Cruise control Engine control Toyota hybrid system
10A	HAZ	Turn signal and hazard warning light
10A	H-LP HI LH	Headlight
10A	H-LP HI RH	Headlight
10A	H-LP LO LH (w/o HID)	Headlight
10A	H-LP LO RH (w/o HID)	Headlight

Fuse rating	Fuse ID	System
Table b. Fuse details - engine compartment, junction block / relay block		
Fuse rating	Fuse ID	System
10A	HORN	Horn Smart entry system and wireless door lock control (w/ Smart entry system) Theft deterrent Wireless door lock control (w/o smart entry system)
15A	ABS MAIN3	Brake control system
15A	AM2	Engine control Ignition Interior light Push button start system and hybrid vehicle immobilizer system Shift control system Toyota hybrid system
15A	DOME	Air conditioner Automatic glare-resistant electro-chromic mirror Automatic light control Back-up light Brake control system Clock Combination meter Cruise control Door lock control Engine control EPS Garage door opener Headlight Headlight beam level control Interior light Key reminder Light auto turn off system
15A	DOME	Luggage compartment door opener Multi-display and audio system (built-in amplifier) Multi-display and audio system (separate amplifier) Power window Push button start system and hybrid vehicle immobilizer system Rear window defogger and mirror heater Seat belt warning Shift control system Smart entry system and wireless door lock control (w/ smart entry system) SRS Taillight and illumination Theft deterrent Toyota hybrid system Wireless door lock control (w/o smart entry system)
15A	EFI	Cruise control Engine control Toyota hybrid system
15A	FR FOG	Front fog light
15A	H-LP LO LH (w/ HID)	Headlight
15A	H-LP LO RH (w/HID)	Headlight

12

Table b. Fuse details - engine compartment, junction block / relay block		
Fuse rating	**Fuse ID**	**System**
20A	HEV	Cruise control Push button start system and hybrid vehicle immobilizer system Shift control system Toyota hybrid system
30A	ABS-1	Brake control system Toyota hybrid system
30A	ABS-2	Brake control system Toyota hybrid system
30A	AMP	Multi-display and audio system (separate amplifier)
30A	CDS FAN	Radiator fan and condenser fan
30A	P CON MTR	Push button start system and hybrid vehicle immobilizer system Shift control system
30A	PTC HTR1	Air conditioner
30A	PTC HTR2	Air conditioner
30A	RDI	Engine control Radiator fan and condenser fan Toyota hybrid system
40A	HEAD MAIN	Automatic light control Headlight Headlight beam level control Light auto turn off system Smart entry system and wireless door lock control (w/ smart entry system) Theft deterrent Wireless door lock control (w/o smart entry system)
40A	HTR	Air conditioner Toyota hybrid system
50A	EPS	EPS
50A	PS HTR	Air conditioner
60A	P/I	Engine control Ignition Interior light
100A	DC/DC	Automatic light control Interior light Light auto turn off system Power window Push button start system and hybrid vehicle immobilizer system Smart entry system and wireless door lock control (w/ smart entry system) Taillight and illumination Theft deterrent Toyota hybrid system Wireless door lock control (w/o smart entry system)

Instrument panel, overview

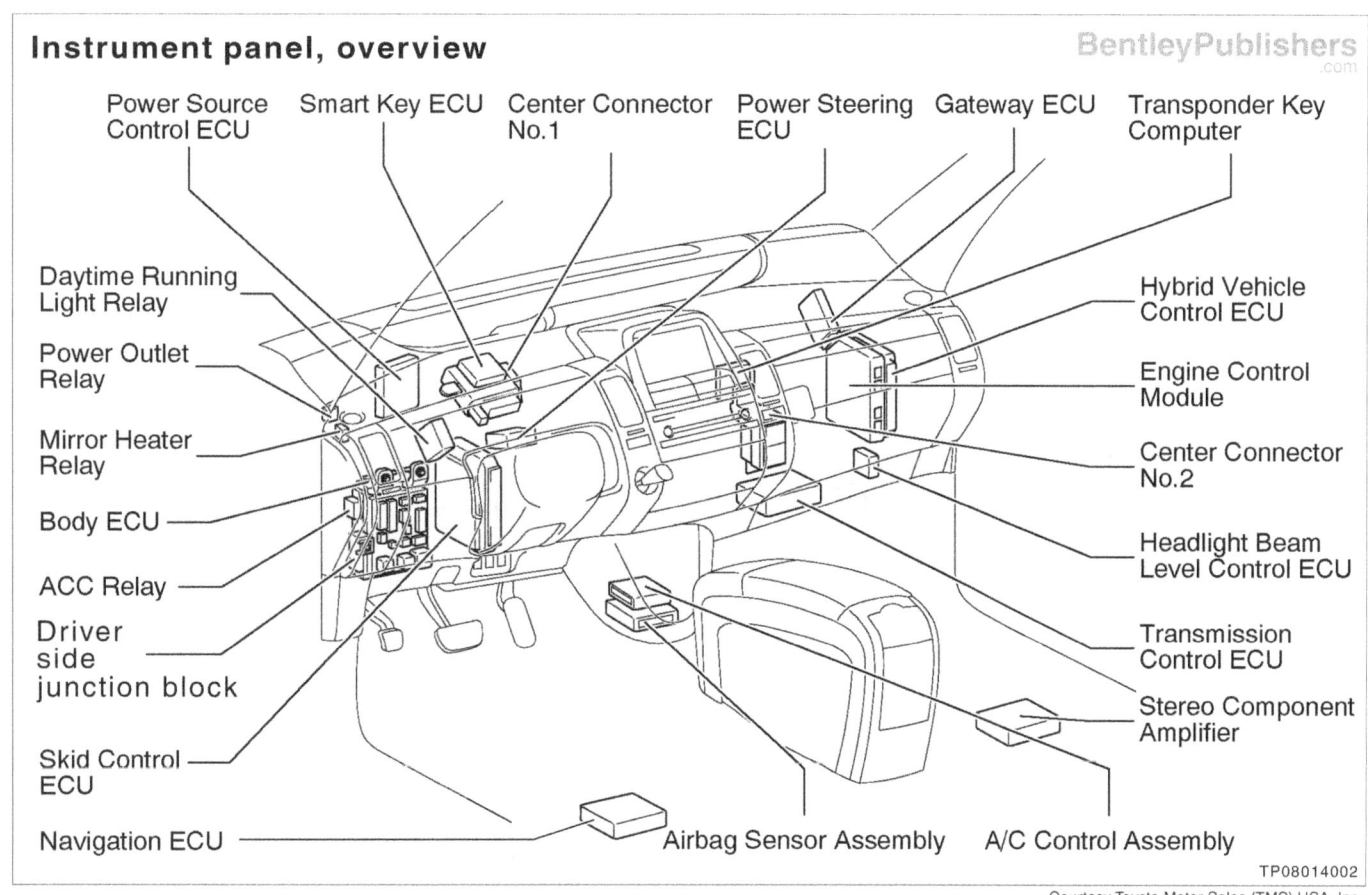

Power Source Control ECU　Smart Key ECU　Center Connector No.1　Power Steering ECU　Gateway ECU　Transponder Key Computer

Daytime Running Light Relay

Power Outlet Relay

Mirror Heater Relay

Body ECU

ACC Relay

Driver side junction block

Skid Control ECU

Navigation ECU

Hybrid Vehicle Control ECU

Engine Control Module

Center Connector No.2

Headlight Beam Level Control ECU

Transmission Control ECU

Stereo Component Amplifier

Airbag Sensor Assembly　A/C Control Assembly

TP08014002

Table c. Fuse details - driver's side junction block

Fuse rating	Fuse ID	System
7.5A	ACC	Clock Interior light, Light auto turn off system Key reminder Multi-display and audio system (built-in amplifier / separate amplifier) Multiplex communication system (AVC-LAN bus / BEAN bus / CAN bus) Power window Push button start system and hybrid vehicle immobilizer system Remote control mirror Shift control system Smart entry system and wireless door lock control Theft deterrent
7.5A	AM1	Interior light Push button start system and hybrid vehicle immobilizer system Shift control system Toyota hybrid system

12

Driver side junction block - fuse positions

(fuses located on under side of driver's side junction block)

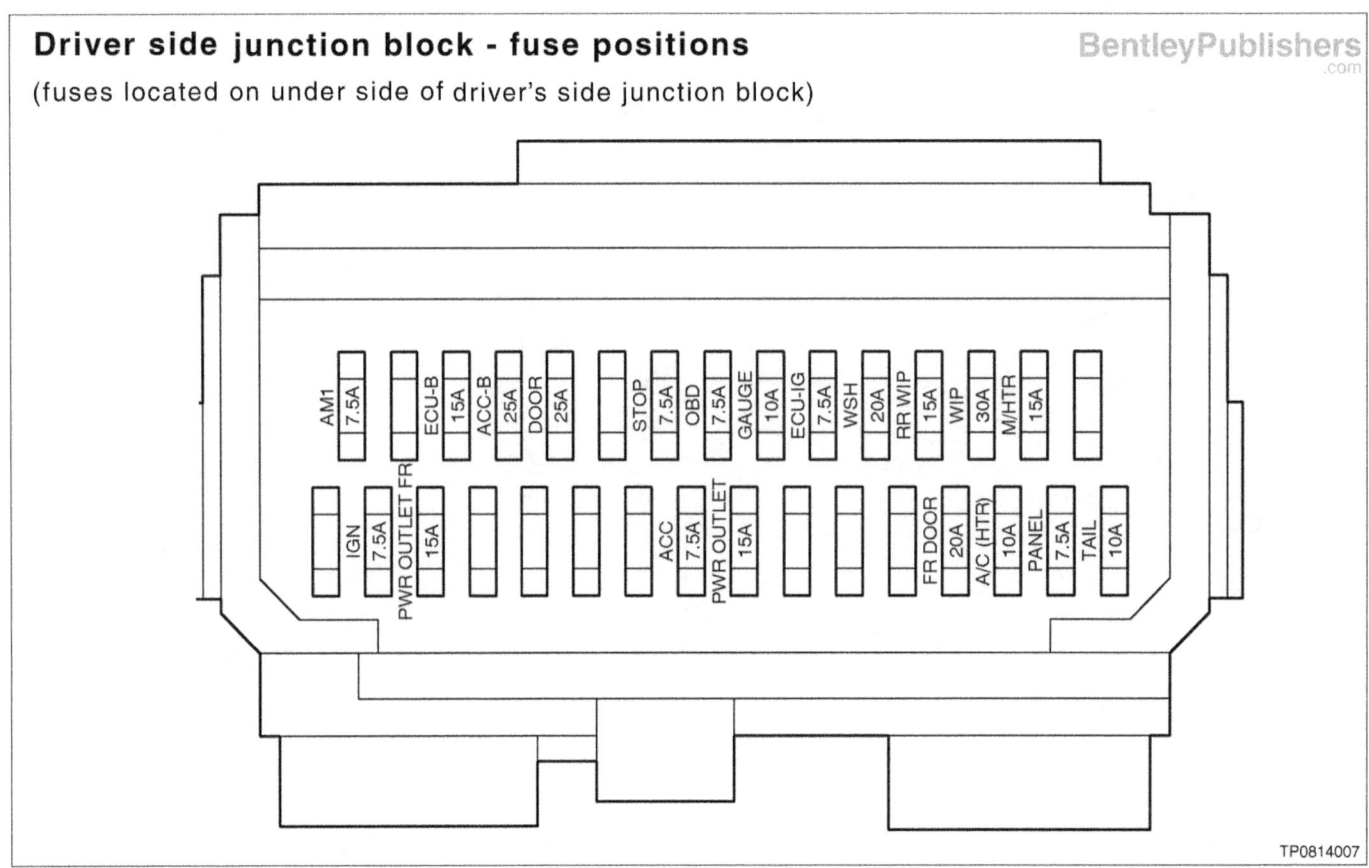

TP0814007

Courtesy Toyota Motor Sales (TMS) USA, Inc.

Table c. Fuse details - driver's side junction block

Fuse rating	Fuse ID	System
7.5A	ECU-IG	Automatic glare-resistant electro-chromic mirror Automatic light control Brake control system Door lock control Engine control EPS Garage door opener Headlight Interior light, Light auto turn off system Key reminder Luggage compartment door opener Multi-display and audio system (built-in amplifier / separate amplifier) Multiplex communication system (AVC-LAN bus / BEAN bus / CAN bus) Power window Push Button start system and hybrid vehicle immobilizer system Radiator fan and condenser fan Shift control system Smart entry system and wireless door lock control Theft deterrent Toyota hybrid system Wireless door lock control (w/o smart entry system)

Fuse rating	Fuse ID	System
Table c. Fuse details - driver's side junction block		
7.5A	IGN	Brake control system Combination meter Cruise control Engine control EPS Push button start system and hybrid vehicle immobilizer system Shift control system SRS Toyota hybrid system
7.5A	OBD	Engine control Toyota hybrid system
7.5A	PANEL	Clock Taillight and illumination
15A	ECU-B	Air conditioning Headlight Multi-display and audio system (built-in amplifier) Multi-display and audio system (separate amplifier) Multiplex communication system (AVC-LAN bus / BEAN Bus / CAN Bus) Rear window defogger and mirror heater Theft deterrent
7.5A	STOP	Brake control system Cruise control EPS Push button start system and hybrid vehicle immobilizer system Shift control system Smart entry system and wireless door lock control Stop light Toyota hybrid system
10A	A/C(HTR)	Air conditioning Rear window defogger and mirror heater
10A	GAUGE	Air conditioning Back-up light Brake control system Combination meter Cruise control Engine control EPS Headlight Headlight beam level control Key reminder Luggage compartment door opener Multi-display and audio system (built-in amplifier) Multi-display and audio system (separate amplifier) Power window Push button start system and hybrid vehicle immobilizer system Rear window defogger and mirror heater Seat belt warning Shift control system Smart entry system and wireless door lock control (w/ smart entry system) SRS Taillight and illumination Toyota hybrid system Turn signal and hazard warning light
10 A	TAIL	Front fog light Taillight and illumination

12

Table c. Fuse details - driver's side junction block

Fuse rating	Fuse ID	System
15A	M/HTR	Rear window defogger and mirror heater
15A	PWR OUTLET	Power outlet
15A	PWR OUTLET FR	Power outlet
15A	RR WIP	Rear wiper and washer
20A	FR DOOR	Power window
20A	WSH	Front and rear wiper and washer
25A	ACC-B	Push button start system and hybrid vehicle immobilizer system
25A	DOOR	Door lock control Luggage compartment door opener Smart entry system and wireless door lock control Theft deterrent Wireless door lock control (w/o smart entry system)
30A	POWER	Power window
30A	WIP	Front wiper and washer
40A	DEF	Rear window defogger and mirror heater

Additional relay and ECU locations

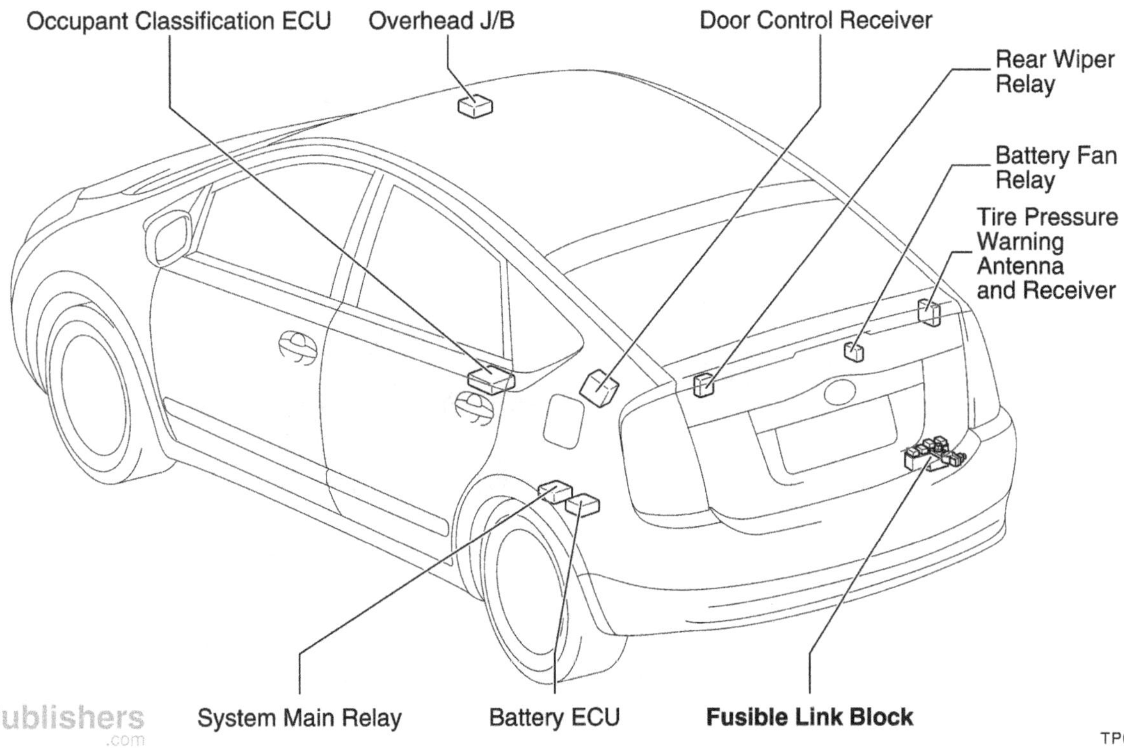

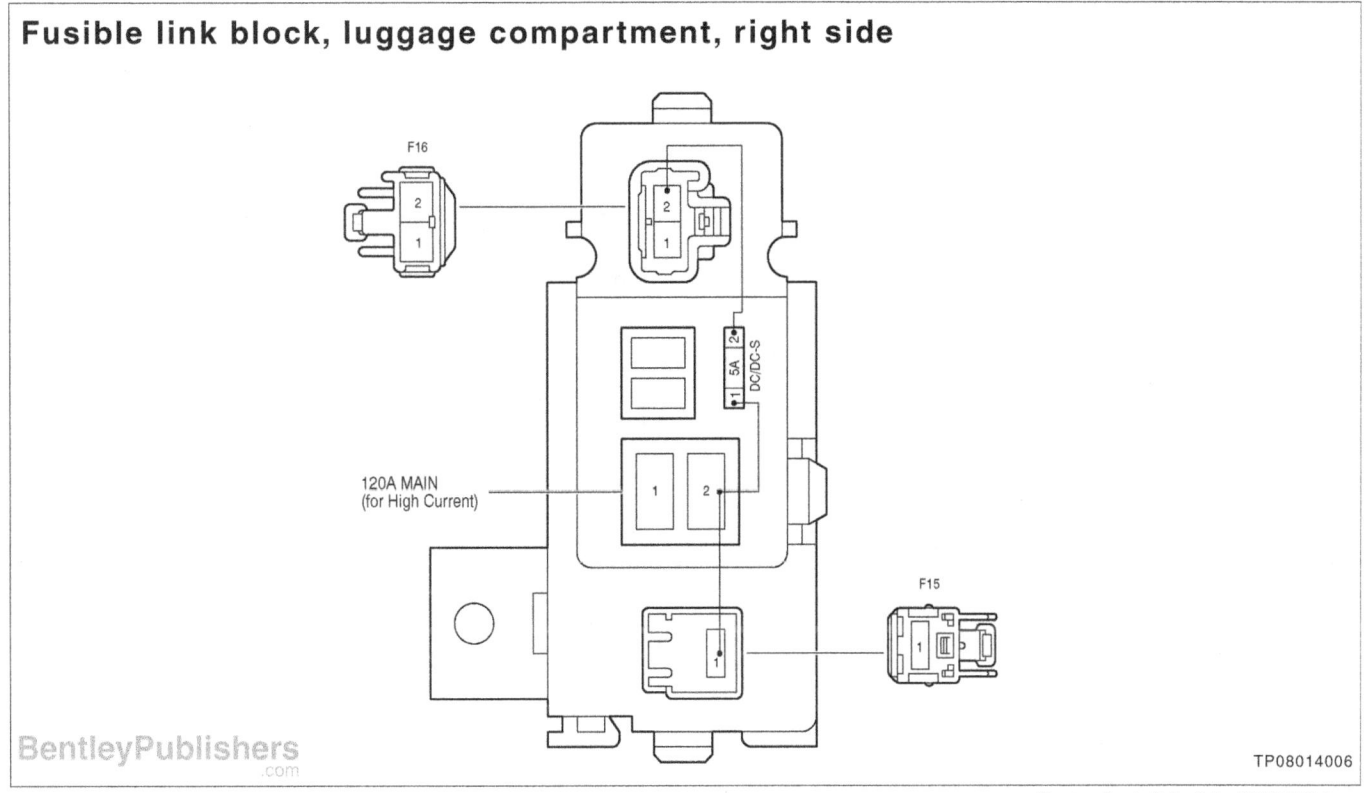

Occupant Classification ECU   Overhead J/B   Door Control Receiver

Rear Wiper Relay

Battery Fan Relay

Tire Pressure Warning Antenna and Receiver

System Main Relay   Battery ECU   **Fusible Link Block**

TP08014003

Courtesy Toyota Motor Sales (TMS) USA, Inc.

Fusible link block, luggage compartment, right side

F16

2

1

DC/DC-S
2
5A
1

120A MAIN
(for High Current)

1   2

F15

1

TP08014006

Courtesy Toyota Motor Sales (TMS) USA, Inc.

12

ELECTRICAL COMPONENT LOCATIONS

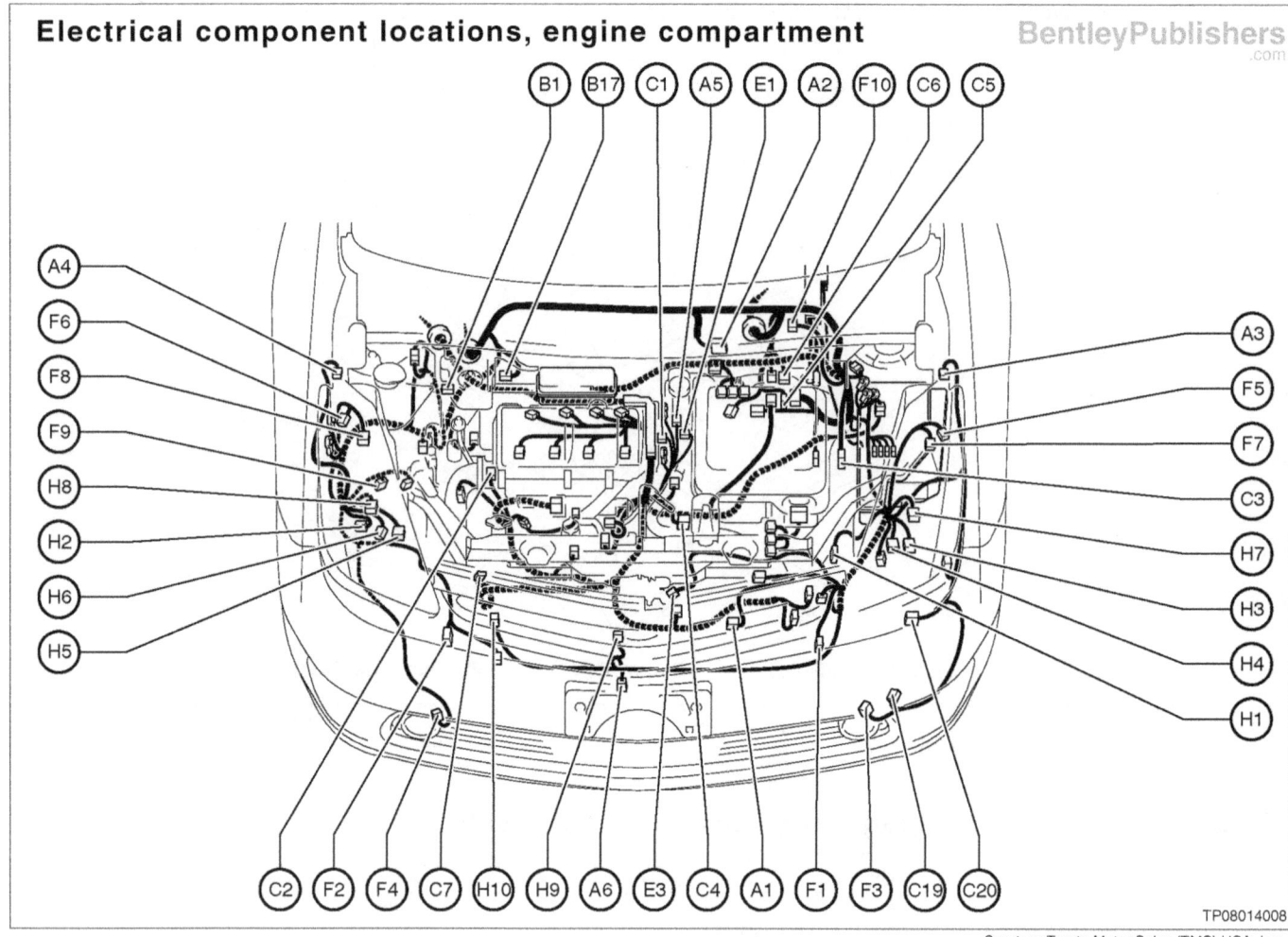

Electrical component locations, engine compartment

BentleyPublishers.com

TP08014008

Courtesy Toyota Motor Sales (TMS) USA, Inc.

A 1 A/C Condenser Fan Motor
A 2 ABS & BA & TRAC & VSC Actuator
A 3 ABS Speed Sensor Front LH
A 4 ABS Speed Sensor Front RH
A 5 Air Fuel Ratio Sensor (Bank 1 Sensor 1)
A 6 Ambient Temp. Sensor

B 1 Brake Fluid Level Warning SW
B17 Brake Master Stroke Simulator Cylinder Assembly

C 1 Camshaft Position Sensor
C 2 Camshaft Timing Oil Control Valve
C 3 Circuit Breaker Sensor
C 4 Compressor Assembly (Motor)
C 5 Converter
C 6 Converter
C 7 Crankshaft Position Sensor
C19 Coolant Heat Storage Tank Outlet Temp. Sensor
C20 Coolant Heat Storage Water Pump

E 1 Engine Coolant Temp. Sensor
E 3 Engine Hood Courtesy SW

F 1 Front Airbag Sensor LH
F 2 Front Airbag Sensor RH
F 3 Front Fog Light LH
F 4 Front Fog Light RH
F 5 Front Side Marker Light LH
F 6 Front Side Marker Light RH
F 7 Front Turn Signal Light LH
F 8 Front Turn Signal Light RH
F 9 Front Washer Motor
F 10 Front Wiper Motor

H 1 Headlight Beam Level Control Actuator LH
H 2 Headlight Beam Level Control Actuator RH
H 3 Headlight Assembly LH
H 4 Headlight Assembly LH
H 5 Headlight Assembly RH
H 6 Headlight Assembly RH
H 7 Headlight LH
H 8 Headlight RH
H 9 Horn (High)
H10 Horn (Lo)

Electrical component locations, engine compartment

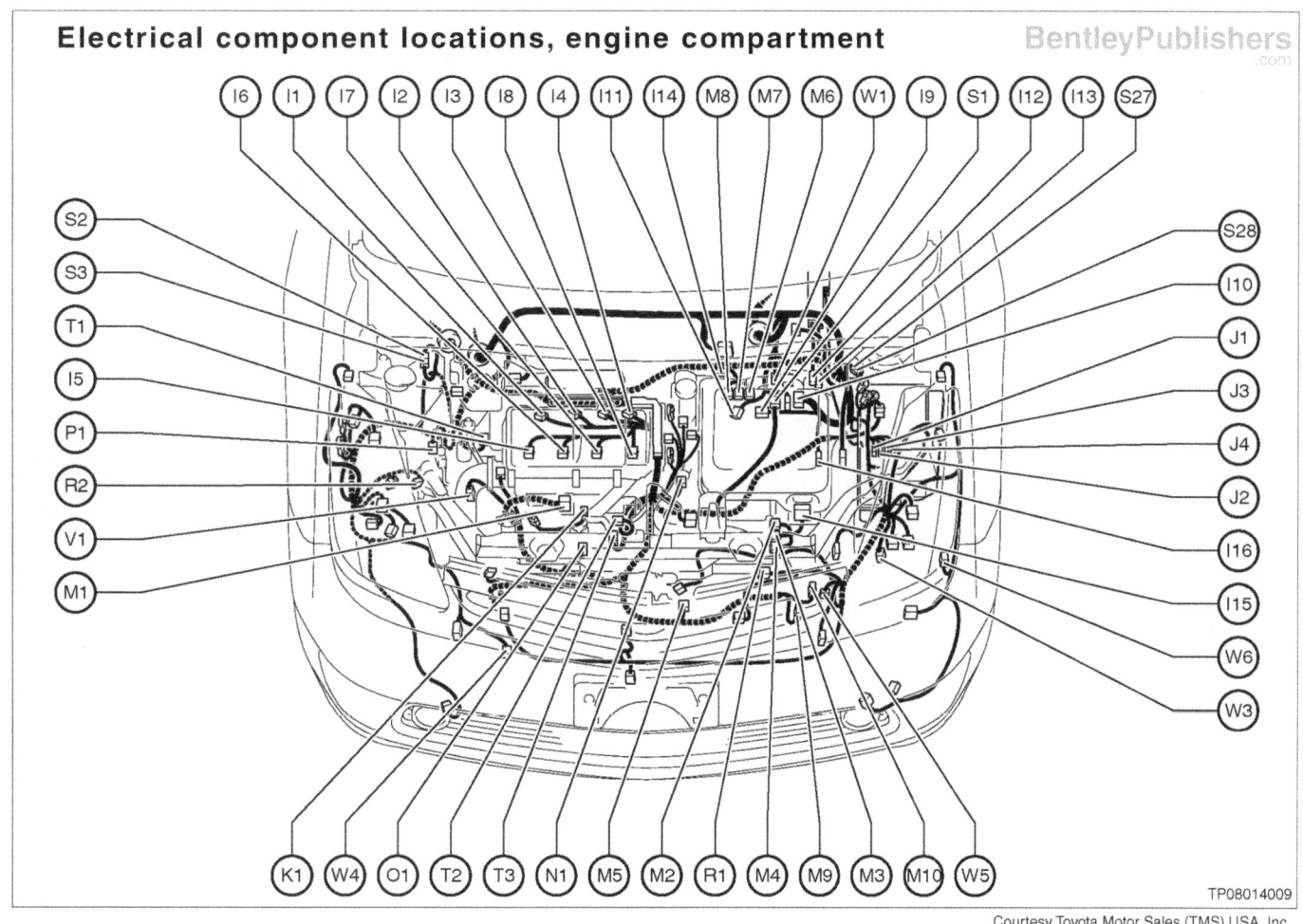

TP08014009

I 1 Ignition Coil and Igniter No.1
I 2 Ignition Coil and Igniter No.2
I 3 Ignition Coil and Igniter No.3
I 4 Ignition Coil and Igniter No.4
I 5 Injector No.1
I 6 Injector No.2
I 7 Injector No.3
I 8 Injector No.4
I 9 Inverter
I 10 Inverter
I 11 Inverter
I 12 Inverter
I 13 Inverter
I 14 Inverter
I 15 Inverter
I 16 Inverter
J 1 Junction Connector
J 2 Junction Connector
J 3 Junction Connector
J 4 Junction Connector
K 1 Knock Sensor
M 1 Mass Air Flow Meter
M 2 Motor Generator No.1
M 3 Motor Generator No.1
M 4 Motor Generator No.1

M 5 Motor Generator No.1
M 6 Motor Generator No.2
M 7 Motor Generator No.2
M 8 Motor Generator No.2
M 9 Motor Generator No.2
M10 Motor Generator No.2
N 1 Noise Filter (Ignition)
O 1 Oil Pressure SW
P 1 Pressure SW
R 1 Radiator Fan Motor
R 2 Rear Washer Motor
S 1 Shift Control Actuator
S 2 Short Connector
S 3 Short Connector
S27 Short Connector (Water Pump)
S28 Short Connector (Water Pump)
T 1 Theft Deterrent Horn
T 2 Throttle Control Motor
T 3 Throttle Position Sensor
V 1 VSV (EVAP)
W 1 Water Pump Motor (A/C)
W 3 Water Pump Motor (Inverter)
W 4 Water Temp. SW
W 5 Water Valve
W 6 Wireless Door Lock Buzzer

12

Electrical component locations, instrument panel

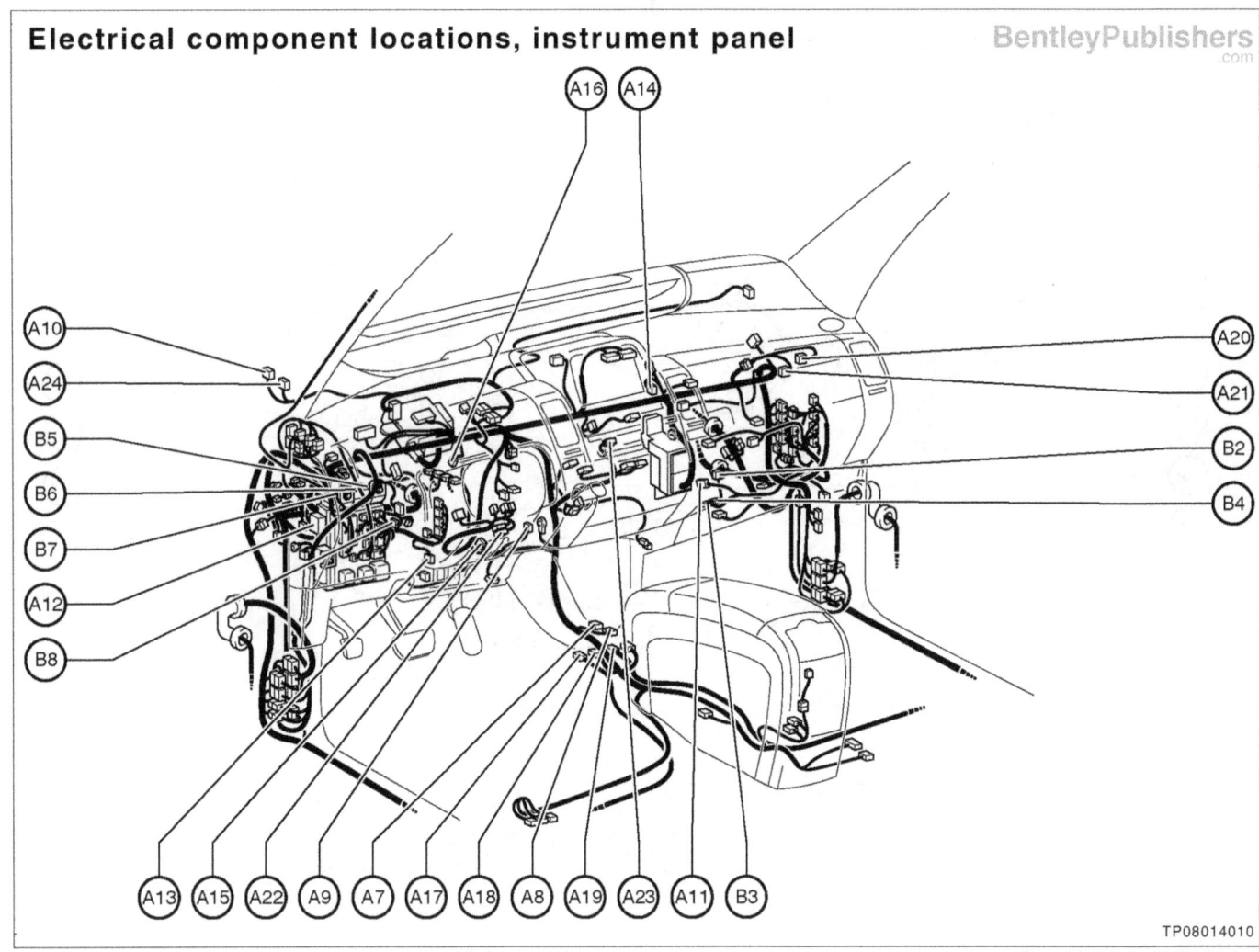

TP08014010

Courtesy Toyota Motor Sales (TMS) USA, Inc.

A 7 A/C Control Assembly
A 8 A/C Control Assembly
A 9 A/C Room Temp. Sensor
A10 A/C Solar Sensor
A 11 A/C Thermistor
A12 ACC Relay
A13 Accelerator Position Sensor
A14 Air Inlet Control Servo Motor
A15 Air Mix Control Servo Motor
A16 Air Vent Mode Control Servo Motor
A17 Airbag Sensor Assembly
A18 Airbag Sensor Assembly
A19 Airbag Sensor Assembly
A20 Airbag Squib (Front Passenger Airbag Assembly No.1)
A21 Airbag Squib (Front Passenger Airbag Assembly No.2)
A22 Airbag Squib (Steering Wheel Pad)
A23 Antenna Amplifier
A24 Automatic Light Control Sensor

B 2 Blower Motor
B 3 Blower Motor Controller
B 4 Blower Motor Controller
B 5 Body ECU
B 6 Body ECU
B 7 Body ECU
B 8 Brake Pedal Stroke Sensor

Electrical component locations, instrument panel

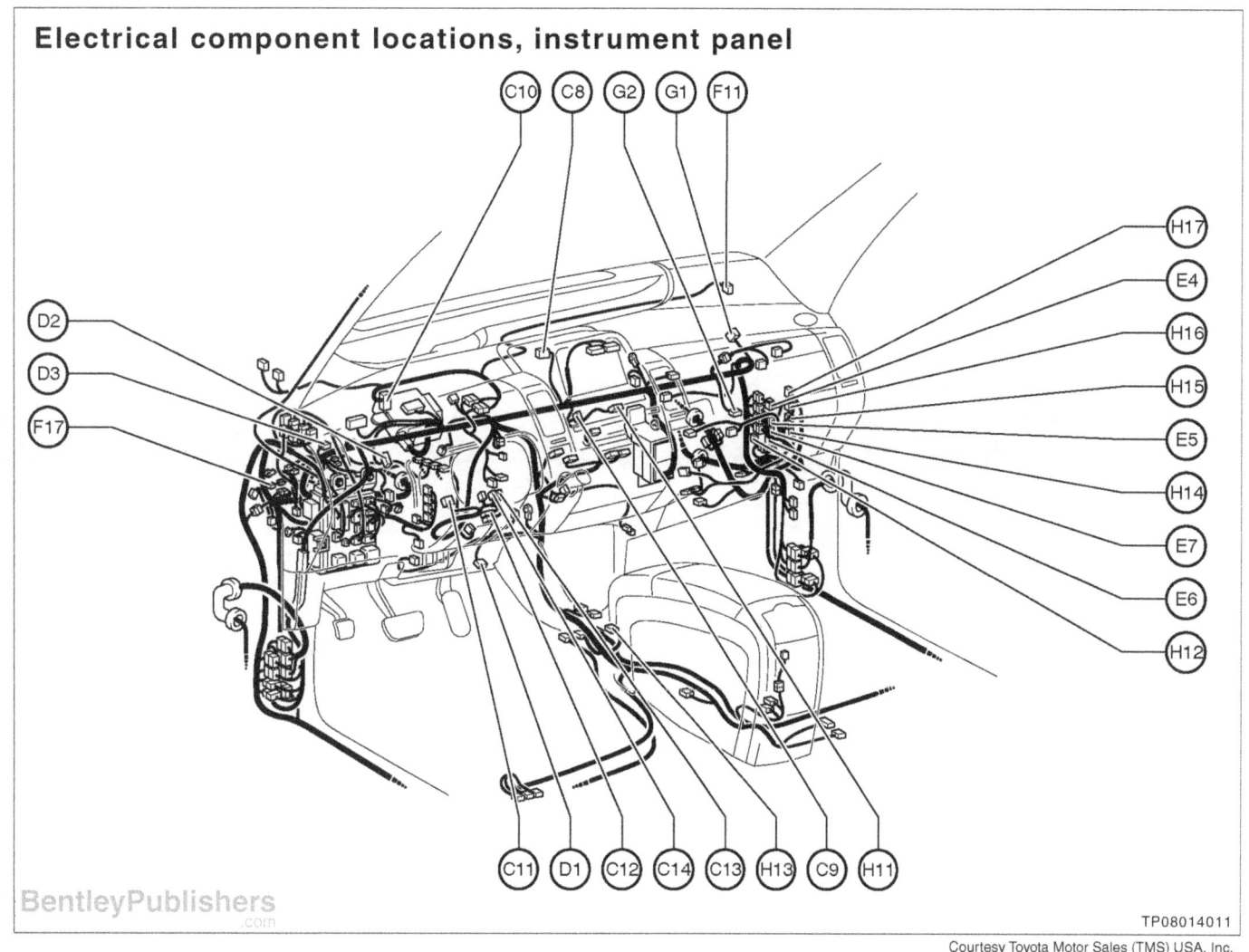

TP08014011

Courtesy Toyota Motor Sales (TMS) USA, Inc.

C 8 Center Speaker
C 9 Clock
C10 Combination Meter
C11 Combination SW
C12 Combination SW
C13 Combination SW
C14 Combination SW

D 1 Data Link Connector 3
D 2 Daytime Running Light Relay
D 3 Diode (Daytime Running Light)

E 4 Engine Control Module
E 5 Engine Control Module
E 6 Engine Control Module
E 7 Engine Control Module

F 11 Front Passenger Seat Belt Warning Light
F 17 Fuse Holder

G 1 Gateway ECU
G 2 Glove Box Light

H11 Hazard SW
     ODO/TRIP SW
H12 Headlight Beam Level Control ECU
H13 Heated Oxygen Sensor (Bank 1 Sensor 2)
H14 Hybrid Vehicle Control ECU
H15 Hybrid Vehicle Control ECU
H16 Hybrid Vehicle Control ECU
H17 Hybrid Vehicle Control ECU

12

Electrical component locations, instrument panel

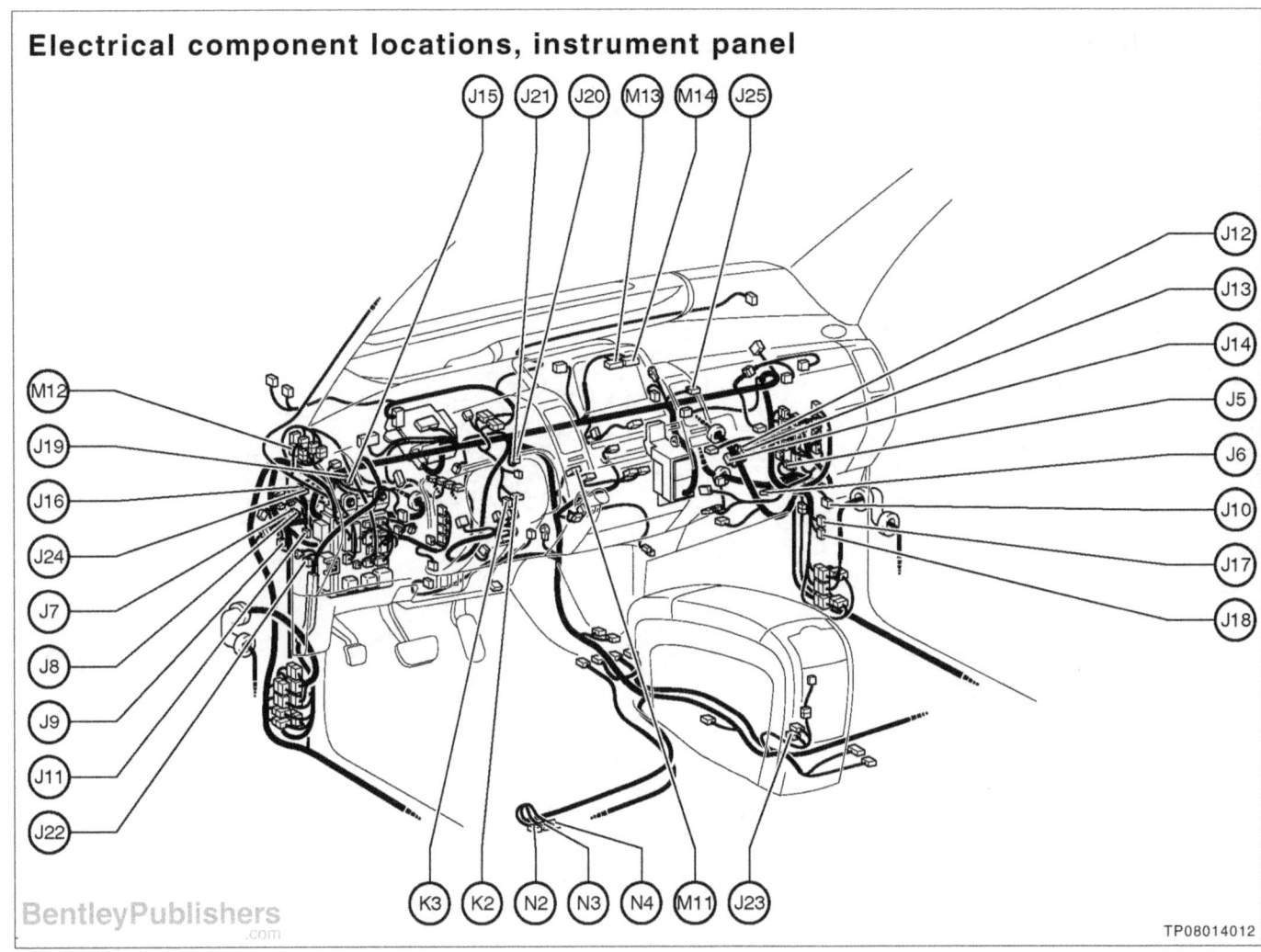

TP08014012

Courtesy Toyota Motor Sales (TMS) USA, Inc.

J 5 Junction Connector
J 6 Junction Connector
J 7 Junction Connector
J 8 Junction Connector
J 9 Junction Connector
J 10 Junction Connector
J 11 Junction Connector
J 12 Junction Connector
J 13 Junction Connector
J 14 Junction Connector
J 15 Junction Connector
J 16 Junction Connector
J 17 Junction Connector
J 18 Junction Connector
J 19 Junction Connector
J 20 Junction Connector
J 21 Junction Connector
J 22 Junction Connector

J 23 Junction Connector
J 24 Junction Connector
J 25 Junction Connector

K 2 Key Slot
K 3 Key Slot

M11 Main SW
M12 Mirror Heater Relay
M13 Multi-Display
M14 Multi-Display

N 2 Navigation ECU
N 3 Navigation ECU
N 4 Navigation ECU

Electrical component locations, instrument panel

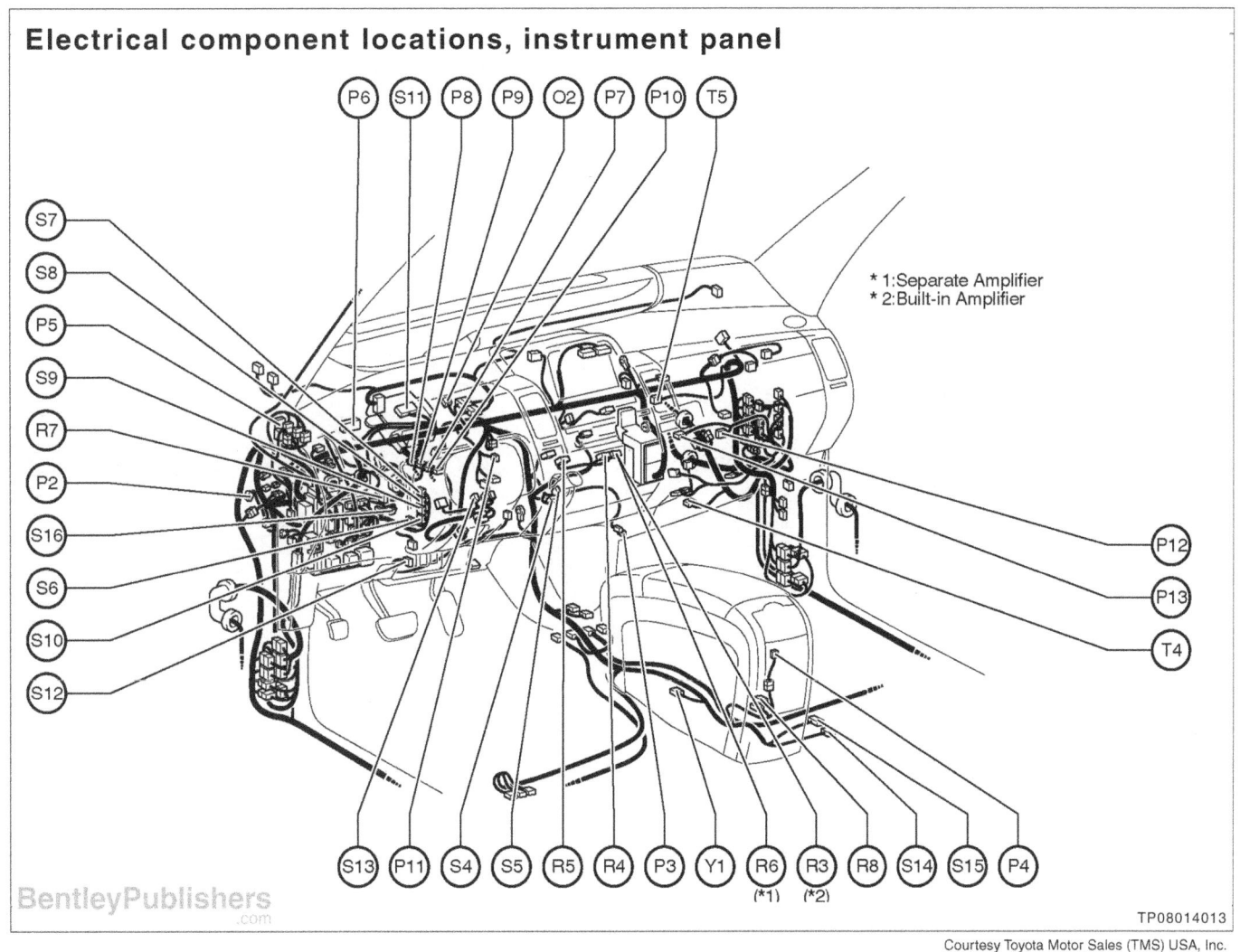

* 1:Separate Amplifier
* 2:Built-in Amplifier

TP08014013

Courtesy Toyota Motor Sales (TMS) USA, Inc.

O 2 Option Connector (Glass Breakage Sensor)

P 2 Parking Brake SW
P 3 Power Outlet No.1
P 4 Power Outlet No.2
P 5 Power Outlet Relay
P 6 Power Source Control ECU
P 7 Power Steering ECU
P 8 Power Steering ECU
P 9 Power Steering Motor
P10 Power Steering Torque Sensor
P 11 Power SW
P12 PTC Heater
P13 PTC Heater

R 3 Radio and Player
R 4 Radio and Player
R 5 Radio and Player
R 6 Radio and Player
R 7 Rheostat
R 8 Room Oscillator

S 4 Shift Lever Position Sensor
S 5 Shift Lever Position Sensor
S 6 Skid Control Buzzer
S 7 Skid Control ECU
S 8 Skid Control ECU
S 9 Skid Control ECU
S10 Skid Control ECU
S 11 Smart Key ECU
S12 Smart Key System Cancel SW
S13 Steering Sensor
S14 Stereo Component Amplifier
S15 Stereo Component Amplifier
S16 Stop Light SW

T 4 Transmission Control ECU
T 5 Transponder Key Computer

Y 1 Yaw Rate Sensor

12

Electrical component locations, body

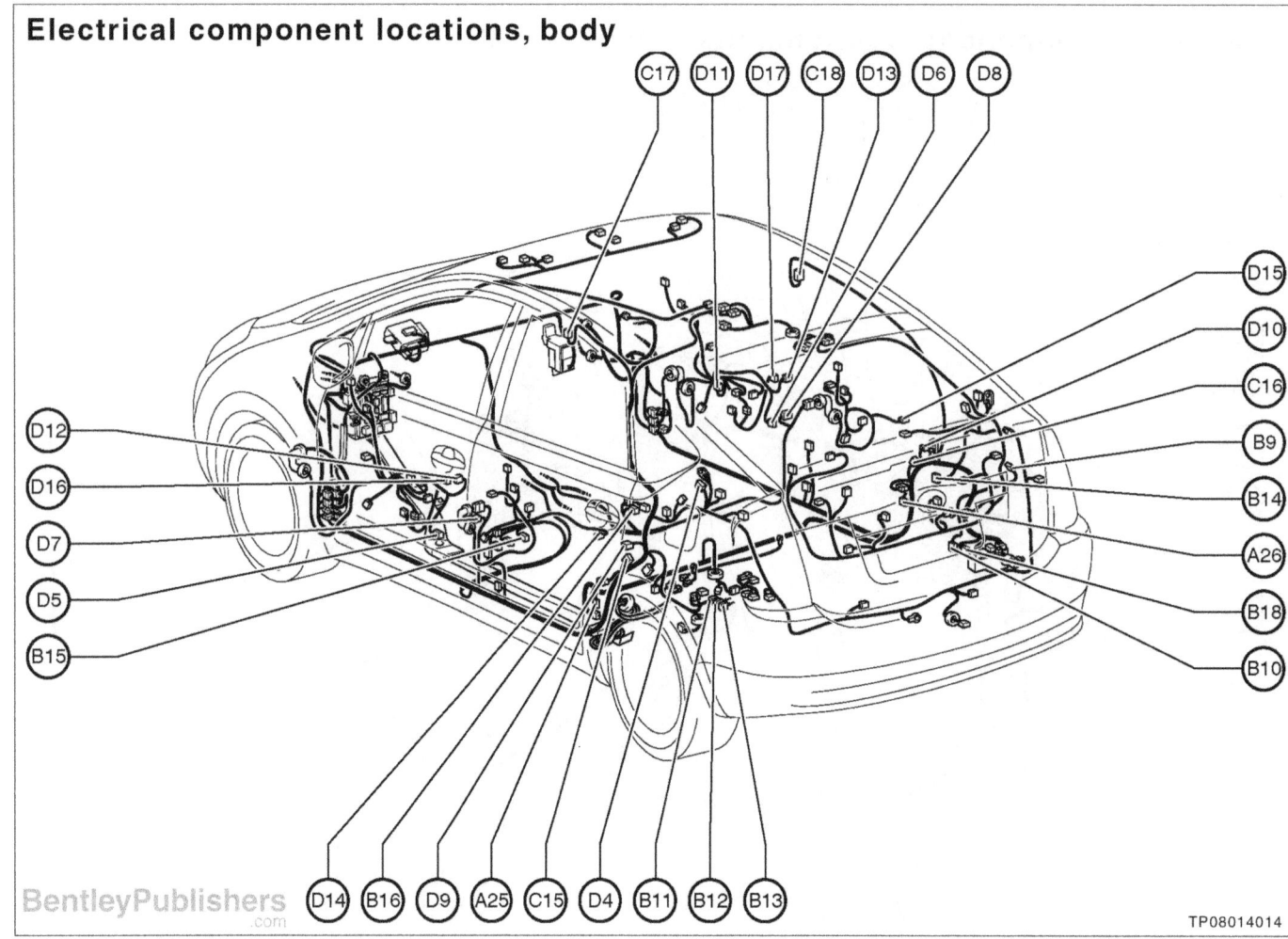

BentleyPublishers.com

TP08014014

Courtesy Toyota Motor Sales (TMS) USA, Inc.

A25 ABS Speed Sensor Rear LH
A26 ABS Speed Sensor Rear RH

B 9 Battery Blower Motor
B10 Battery Blower Motor Controller
B 11 Battery ECU
B12 Battery ECU
B13 Battery ECU
B14 Battery Fan Relay
B15 Buckle SW Front LH
B16 Buckle SW Front RH
B18 Brake Control Power Supply

C15 Curtain Shield Airbag Sensor LH
C16 Curtain Shield Airbag Sensor RH
C17 Curtain Shield Airbag Squib LH
C18 Curtain Shield Airbag Squib RH

D 4 Door Control Receiver
D 5 Door Courtesy Light Front LH
D 6 Door Courtesy Light Front RH
D 7 Door Courtesy SW Front LH
D 8 Door Courtesy SW Front RH
D 9 Door Courtesy SW Rear LH
D10 Door Courtesy SW Rear RH
D11 Door Lock Control SW Front RH
D12 Door Lock Motor Front LH
     Door Unlock Detection SW Front LH
D13 Door Lock Motor Front RH
     Door Unlock Detection SW Front RH
D14 Door Lock Motor Rear LH
     Door Unlock Detection SW Rear LH
D15 Door Lock Motor Rear RH
     Door Unlock Detection SW Rear RH
D16 Door Oscillator Front LH (w/ Sensor)
D17 Door Oscillator Front RH (w/ Sensor)

Electrical component locations, body

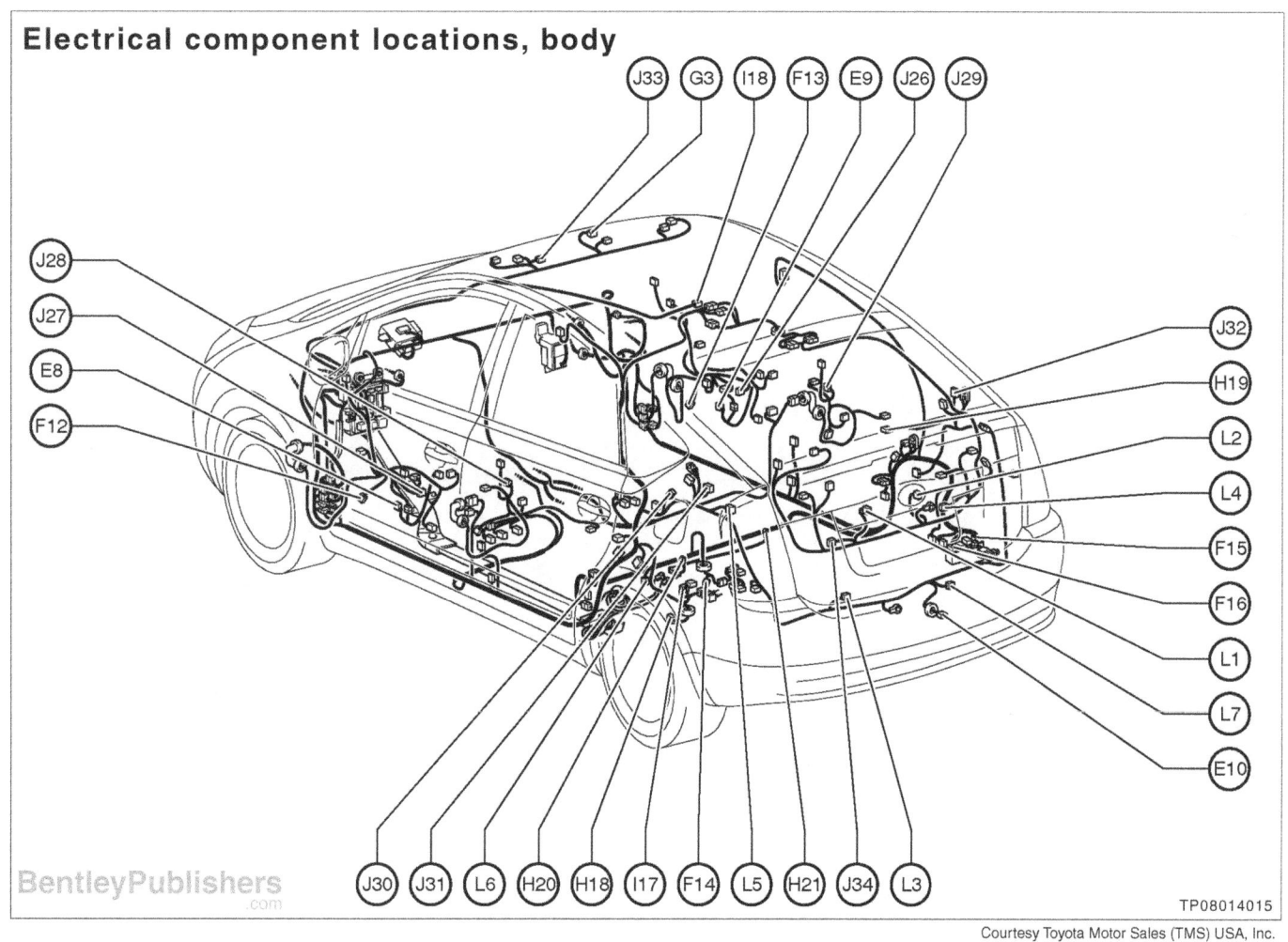

TP08014015

E 8 Electrical Key Antenna (Driver's Side)
E 9 Electrical Key Antenna (Front Passenger's Side)
E10 Electrical Key Antenna (Luggage Compartment Door)

F 12 Front Door Speaker LH
F 13 Front Door Speaker RH
F 14 Fuel Pump
    Fuel Sender
F 15 Fusible Link Block
F 16 Fusible Link Block

G 3 Garage Door Opener
    Inner Mirror

H18 Height Control Sensor
H19 High Mounted Stop Light
H20 Hybrid Vehicle Battery
H21 Hybrid Vehicle Battery

I 17 Inter Lock SW
I 18 Interior Light

J 26 Junction Connector
J 27 Junction Connector
J 28 Junction Connector
J 29 Junction Connector
J 30 Junction Connector
J 31 Junction Connector
J 32 Junction Connector
J 33 Junction Connector
J 34 Junction Connector

L 1 License Plate Light LH
L 2 License Plate Light RH
L 3 Luggage Compartment Courtesy SW
    Luggage Compartment Door Opener Motor
L 4 Luggage Compartment Door Lock SW
    Luggage Compartment Door Opener SW
L 5 Luggage Compartment Light
L 6 Luggage Oscillator (Inner)
L 7 Luggage Oscillator (Outer)

12

Electrical component locations, body

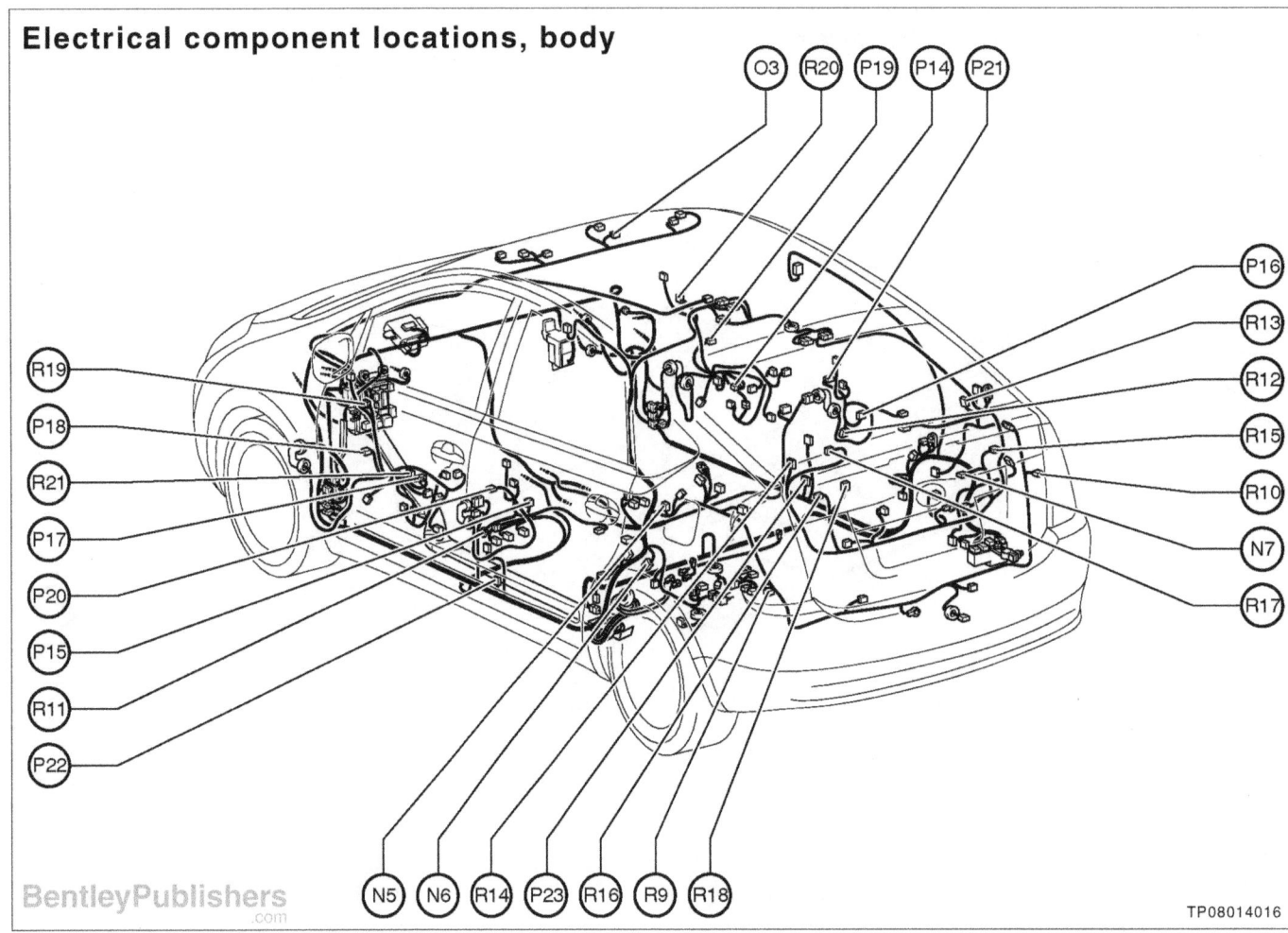

TP08014016

Courtesy Toyota Motor Sales (TMS) USA, Inc.

N 5 Noise Filter (High Mounted Stop Light)
N 6 Noise Filter (Rear Window Defogger)
N 7 Noise Filter (Rear Window Defogger)

O 3 Overhead J/B

P14 Power Window Control SW Front RH
P15 Power Window Control SW Rear LH
P16 Power Window Control SW Rear RH
P17 Power Window Master SW
P18 Power Window Motor Front LH
P19 Power Window Motor Front RH
P20 Power Window Motor Rear LH
P21 Power Window Motor Rear RH
P22 Pretensioner LH
P23 Pretensioner RH

R 9 Rear Combination Light LH
R10 Rear Combination Light RH
R11 Rear Door Speaker LH
R12 Rear Door Speaker RH
R13 Rear Window Defogger
R14 Rear Window Defogger
R15 Rear Window Defogger
R16 Rear Window Defogger
R17 Rear Wiper Motor
R18 Rear Wiper Relay
R19 Mirror Heater LH
    Remote Control Mirror LH
R20 Mirror Heater RH
    Remote Control Mirror RH
R21 Remote Control Mirror SW

Electrical component locations, body

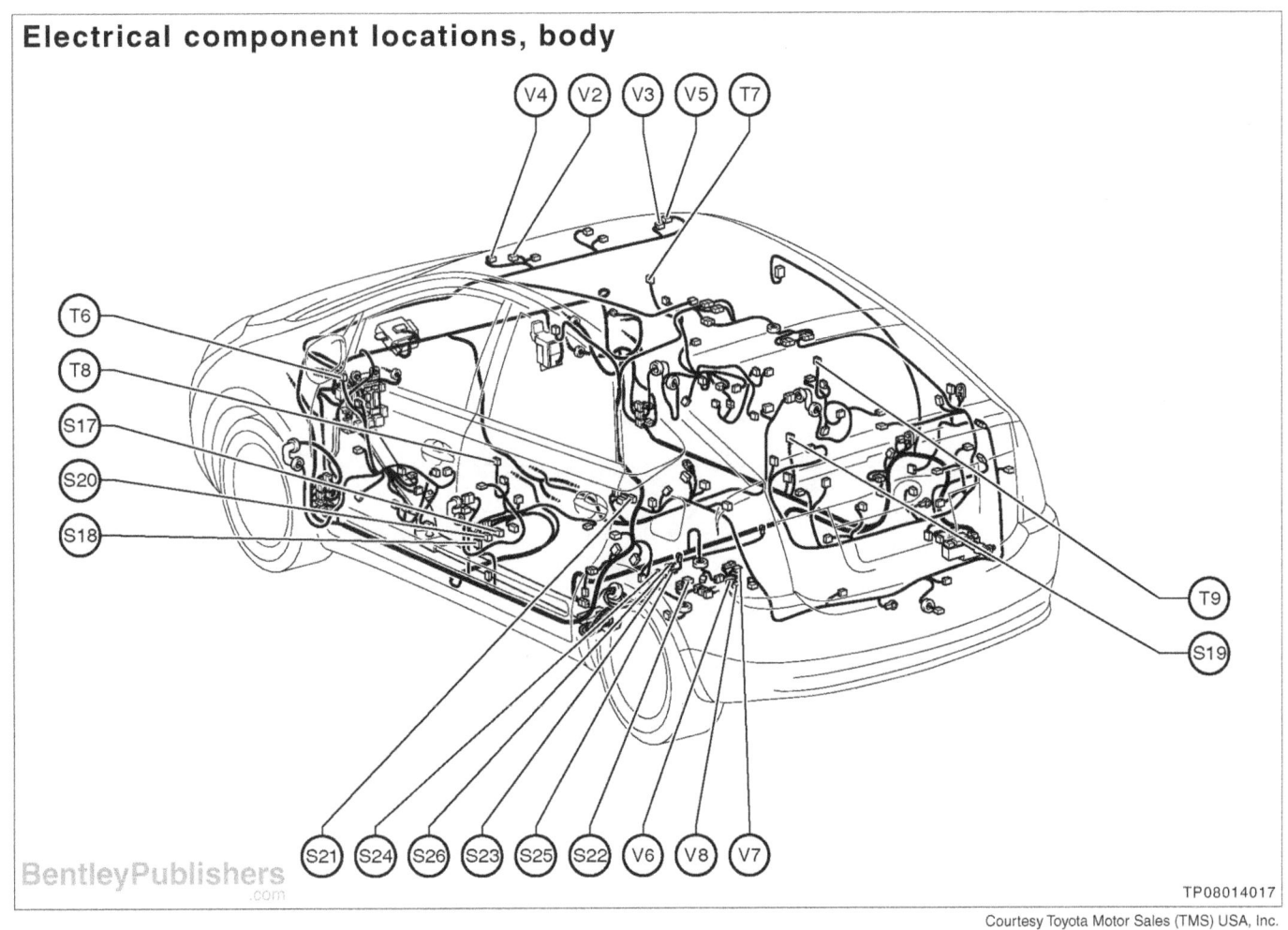

TP08014017

Courtesy Toyota Motor Sales (TMS) USA, Inc.

S17 Seat Position Airbag Sensor
S18 Side Airbag Sensor LH
S19 Side Airbag Sensor RH
S20 Side Airbag Squib LH
S21 Side Airbag Squib RH
S22 System Main Relay
S23 System Main Relay
S24 System Main Relay
S25 System Main Relay
S26 System Main Relay

T 6 Tweeter Front LH
T 7 Tweeter Front RH
T 8 Tweeter Rear LH
T 9 Tweeter Rear RH

V 2 Vanity Light LH
V 3 Vanity Light RH
V 4 Vanity Light SW LH
V 5 Vanity Light SW RH
V 6 Vapor Pressure Sensor
V 7 VSV (Canister Closed Valve)
V 8 VSV (Purge Flow Switching Valve)

12

CONNECTOR AND GROUND POINTS

Connector and ground points, engine compartment

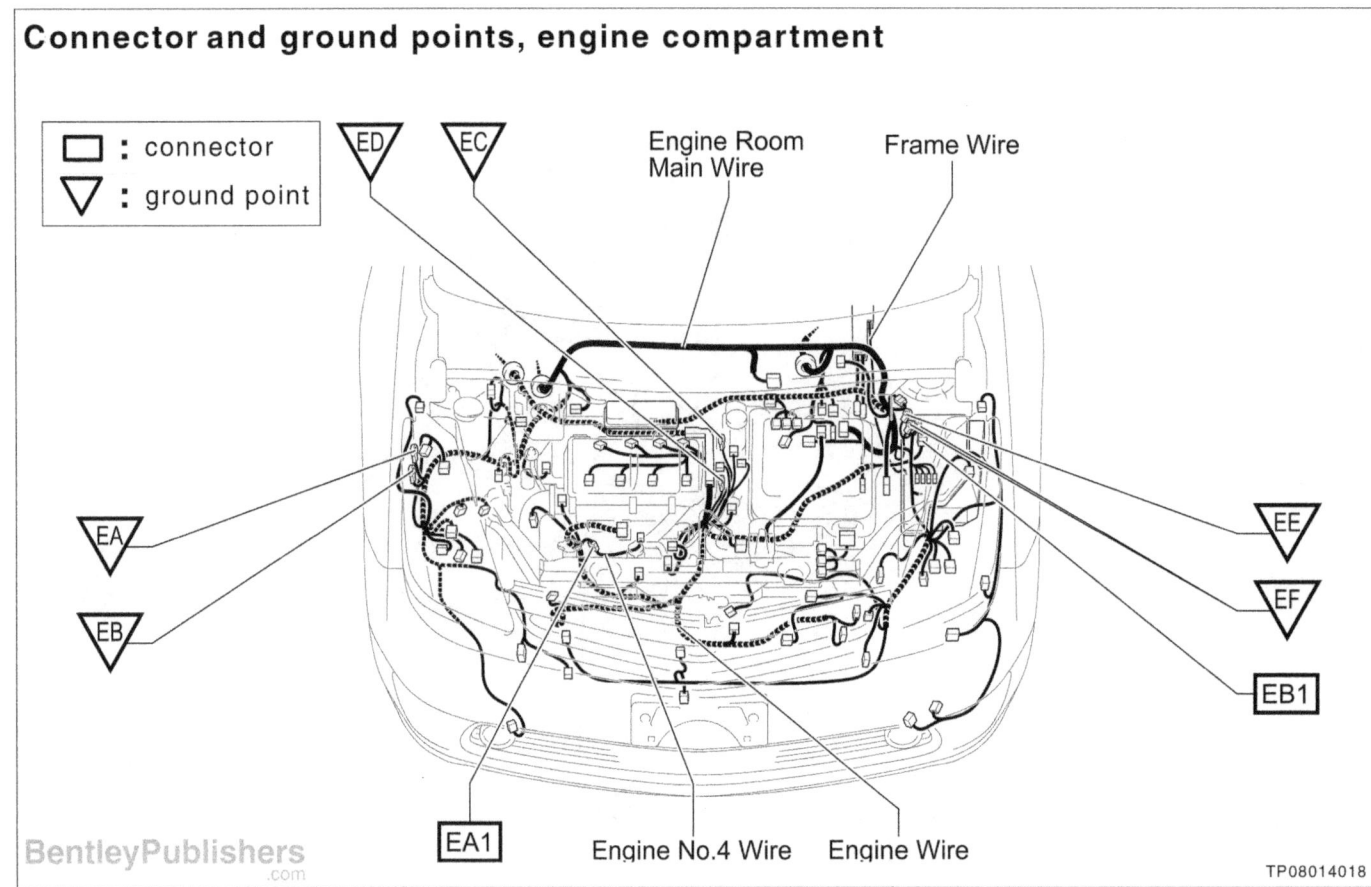

: connector

: ground point

Engine Room Main Wire

Frame Wire

ED EC EA EB EE EF EB1 EA1

Engine No.4 Wire   Engine Wire

TP08014018

Courtesy Toyota Motor Sales (TMS) USA, Inc.

Connector and ground points, instrument panel

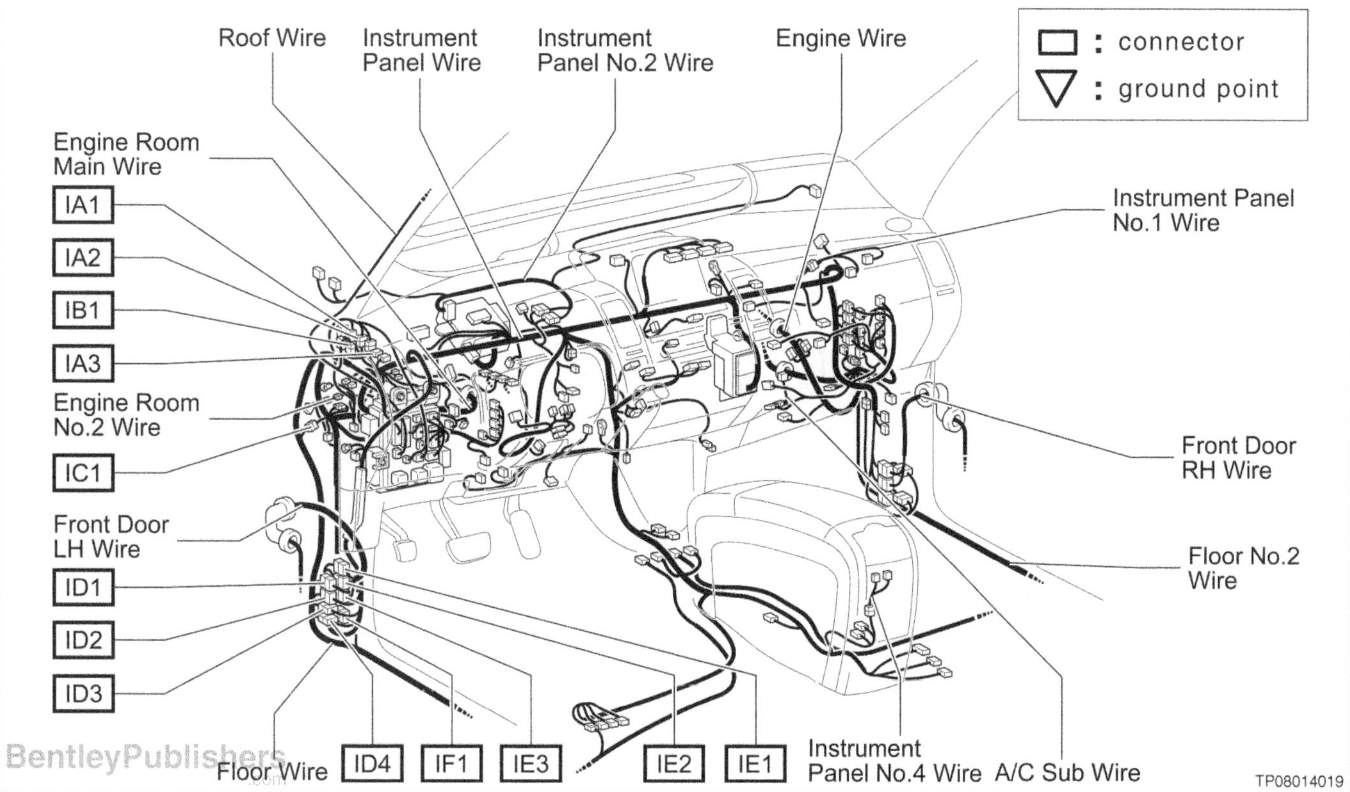

Roof Wire   Instrument   Instrument   Engine Wire
Panel Wire   Panel No.2 Wire

☐ : connector

▽ : ground point

Engine Room
Main Wire

IA1

IA2

IB1

IA3

Engine Room
No.2 Wire

IC1

Front Door
LH Wire

ID1

ID2

ID3

Instrument Panel
No.1 Wire

Front Door
RH Wire

Floor No.2
Wire

Floor Wire   ID4   IF1   IE3   IE2   IE1   Instrument   A/C Sub Wire
Panel No.4 Wire

BentleyPublishers

TP08014019

Courtesy Toyota Motor Sales (TMS) USA, Inc.

Connector and ground points, instrument panel

☐ : connector

▽ : ground point

IJ

IG

IH

II   IK

TP08014020

Courtesy Toyota Motor Sales (TMS) USA, Inc.

12

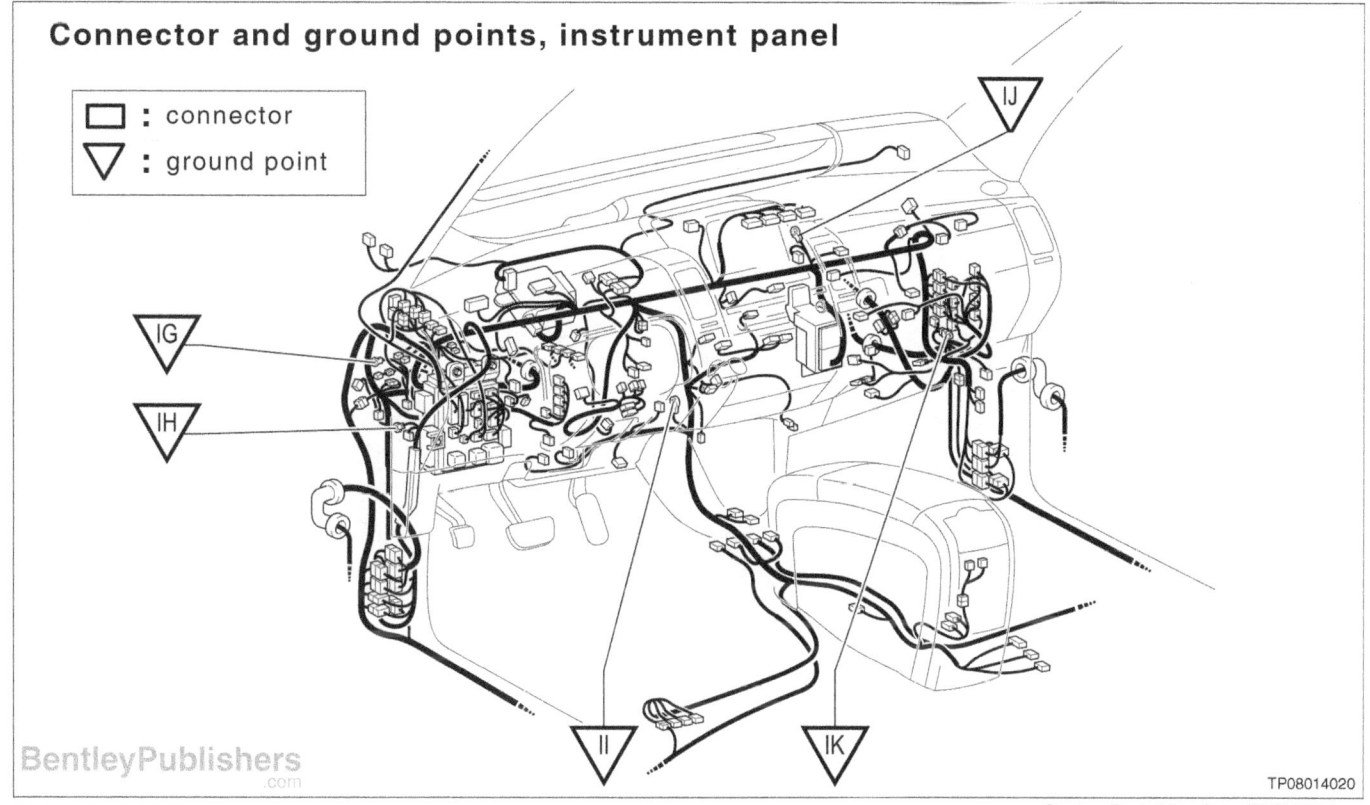

Connector and ground points, instrument panel

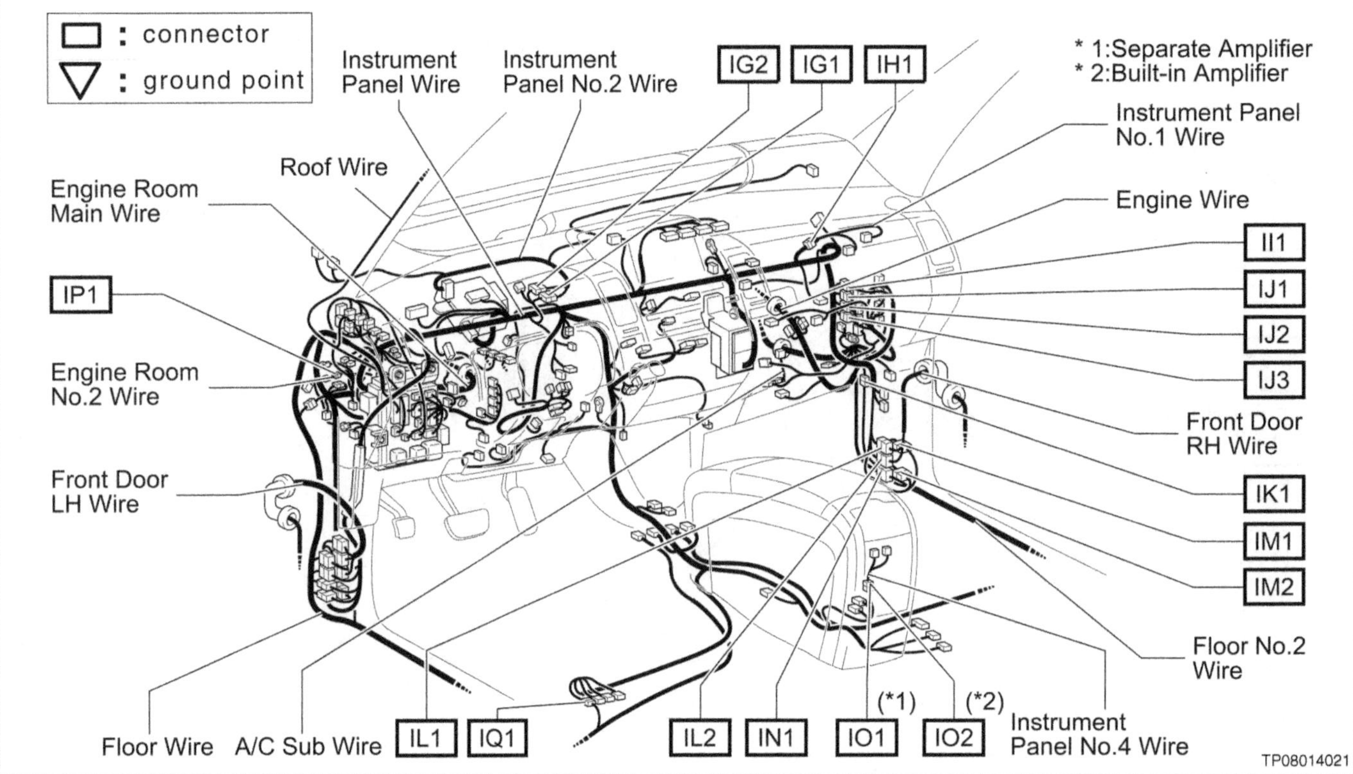

☐ : connector

▽ : ground point

Instrument Panel Wire

Instrument Panel No.2 Wire

IG2 IG1 IH1

* 1:Separate Amplifier
* 2:Built-in Amplifier

Instrument Panel No.1 Wire

Roof Wire

Engine Room Main Wire

Engine Wire

IP1

II1

IJ1

IJ2

IJ3

Engine Room No.2 Wire

Front Door RH Wire

IK1

Front Door LH Wire

IM1

IM2

Floor No.2 Wire

(*1) (*2)

Instrument Panel No.4 Wire

Floor Wire   A/C Sub Wire   IL1   IQ1   IL2   IN1   IO1   IO2

TP08014021

Courtesy Toyota Motor Sales (TMS) USA, Inc.

Connector and ground points, body

☐ : connector

▽ : ground point

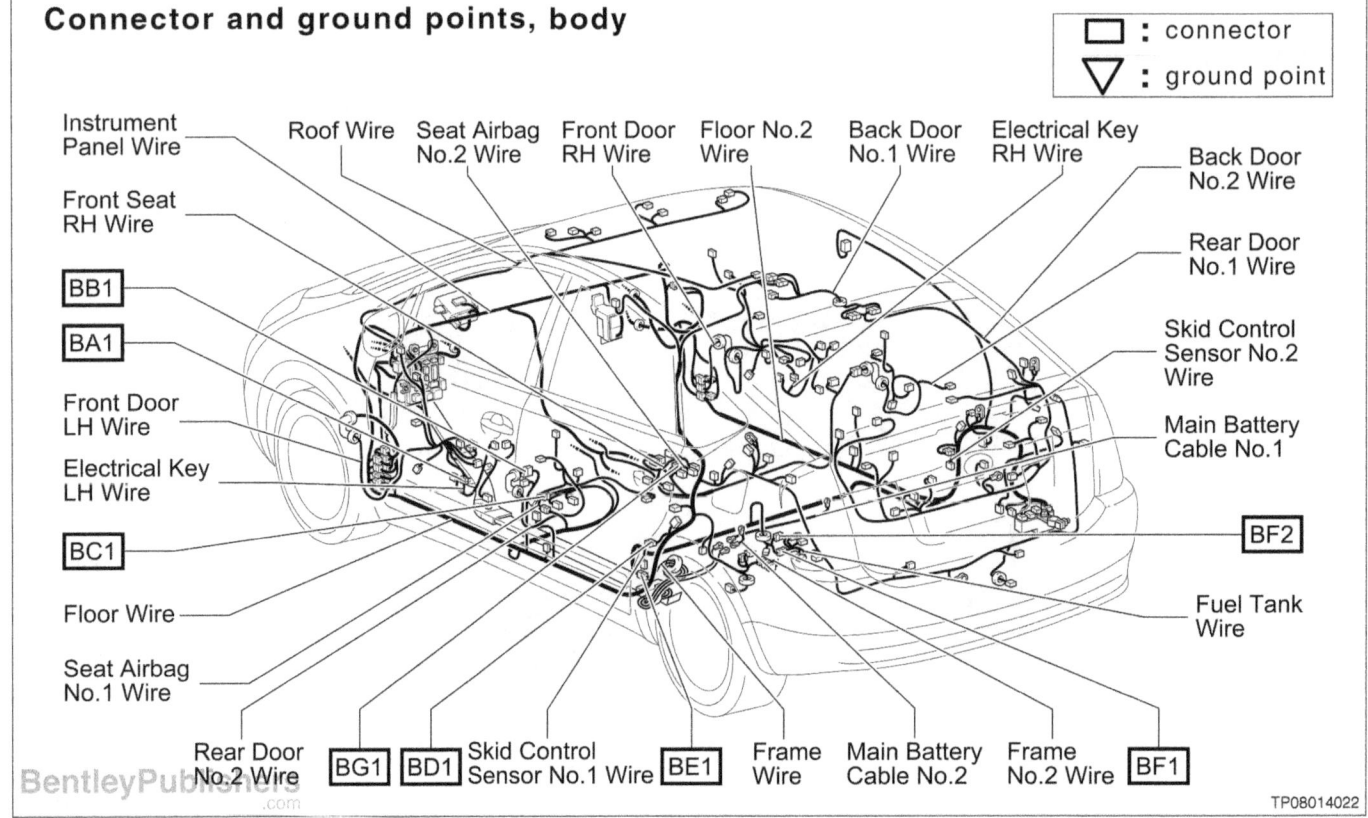

Instrument Panel Wire

Roof Wire   Seat Airbag No.2 Wire   Front Door RH Wire   Floor No.2 Wire   Back Door No.1 Wire   Electrical Key RH Wire

Back Door No.2 Wire

Front Seat RH Wire

Rear Door No.1 Wire

BB1

BA1

Skid Control Sensor No.2 Wire

Front Door LH Wire

Main Battery Cable No.1

Electrical Key LH Wire

BC1

BF2

Floor Wire

Fuel Tank Wire

Seat Airbag No.1 Wire

Rear Door No.2 Wire   BG1   BD1   Skid Control Sensor No.1 Wire   BE1   Frame Wire   Main Battery Cable No.2   Frame No.2 Wire   BF1

TP08014022

Courtesy Toyota Motor Sales (TMS) USA, Inc.

Connector and ground points, body

☐	: connector
▽	: ground point

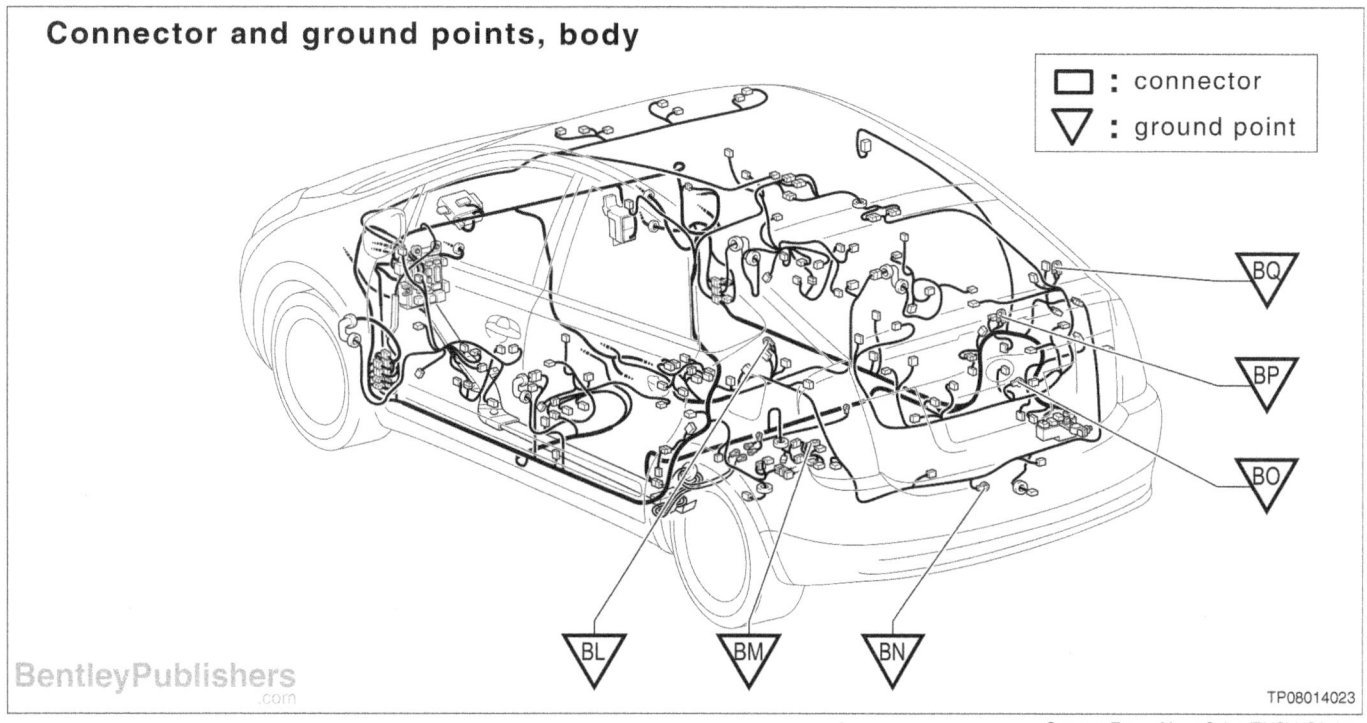

TP08014023

Courtesy Toyota Motor Sales (TMS) USA, Inc.

Connector and ground points, body

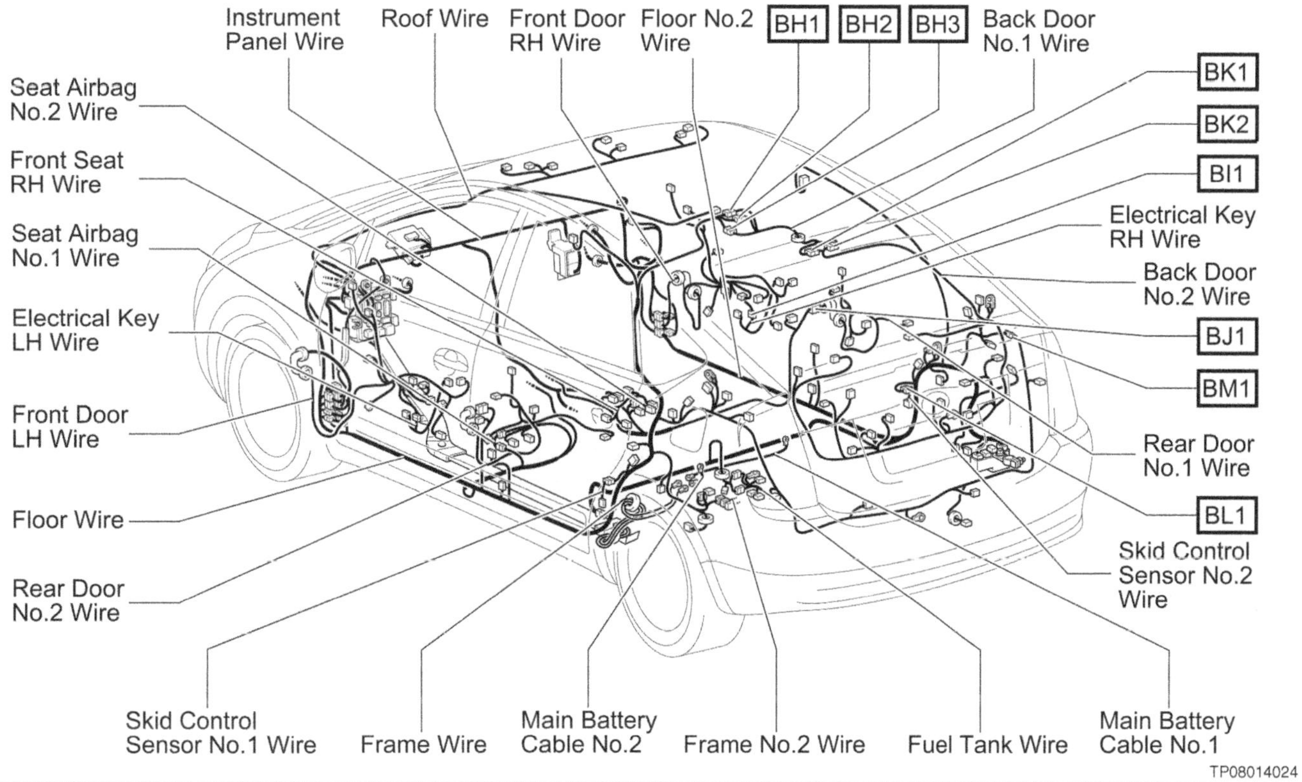

Instrument Panel Wire

Roof Wire

Front Door RH Wire

Floor No.2 Wire

BH1 BH2 BH3

Back Door No.1 Wire

Seat Airbag No.2 Wire

Front Seat RH Wire

Seat Airbag No.1 Wire

Electrical Key LH Wire

Front Door LH Wire

Floor Wire

Rear Door No.2 Wire

BK1

BK2

BI1

Electrical Key RH Wire

Back Door No.2 Wire

BJ1

BM1

Rear Door No.1 Wire

BL1

Skid Control Sensor No.2 Wire

Skid Control Sensor No.1 Wire

Frame Wire

Main Battery Cable No.2

Frame No.2 Wire

Fuel Tank Wire

Main Battery Cable No.1

TP08014024

Courtesy Toyota Motor Sales (TMS) USA, Inc.

12

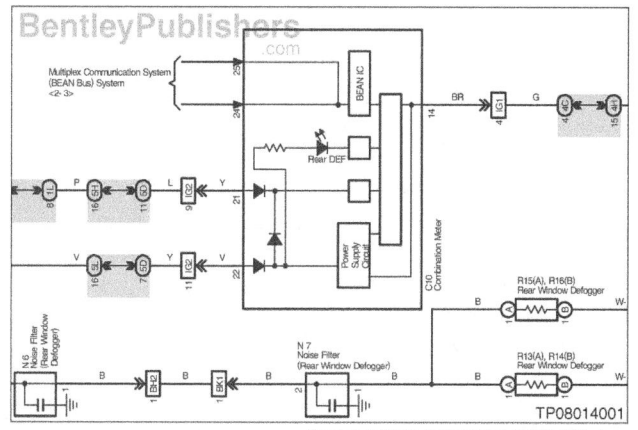

Courtesy Toyota Motor Sales (TMS) USA, Inc.

13

Electrical Wiring Diagrams

2004 and 2007 complete wiring schematics

GENERAL

This chapter contains electrical wiring diagrams for 2004 and 2007 Prius vehicles. The diagrams are provided by Toyota Motor Corporation. The publisher cannot vouch for the accuracy of these diagrams.

For a list of fuses and relays, and electrical component locations, see **12 Electrical Component Locations**.

Prius safety precautions

In addition to the safety warnings given here, always read and observe the **Warnings**, **Cautions** and safety procedures in **3 Safety** before working on vehicle. Use extreme care when working near high voltage cables and components.

> **WARNING—**
> - *Risk of electrocution! Avoid touching orange-colored high voltage wiring and high voltage components unless you are certain that high voltage is not present.*
> - *The Prius hybrid system has voltages as high as 500 volts. Voltages over 60 volts DC and 25 volts AC are a shock hazard.*

The Prius engine may start at any time if the hybrid system is in **READY** mode. See **3 Safety** for instructions on turning off the hybrid system.

> **WARNING—**
> - *Be sure hybrid system is OFF when servicing vehicle (READY indicator not illuminated). Failure to switch the hybrid system OFF could result in engine start at any time.*

Voltage and polarity

The Prius negative ground electrical system operates on two sources of voltage:

- Auxiliary 12-volt absorbed-glass-mat (AGM) lead-acid battery
- Hybrid system 201.6-volt nickel-metal-hydride (NiMH) battery

See **2 Prius Hybrid System** for details.

Warnings and Cautions

> **WARNING—**
> - *Airbags and pyrotechnic seat belt tensioners utilize explosive devices. Handle with extreme care.*
> - *Keep hands, clothing and other objects clear of the electric radiator cooling fan when working on a warm engine. The fan may start at any time, even when the ignition is switched OFF.*

> **CAUTION—**
> - *Relay and fuse positions are subject to change and may vary from car to car. If questions arise, an authorized Toyota dealer is the best source for the most accurate and up-to-date information.*
> - *Use a digital multimeter for electrical tests. Switch multimeter to appropriate function and range before making test connections.*
> - *Many control modules are static sensitive. Static discharge may damage them permanently. Handle modules using proper static prevention equipment and techniques.*
> - *To avoid damaging harness connectors or relay panel sockets, use jumper wires with flat-blade connectors that are the same size as the connector or relay terminals.*
> - *Choose test equipment carefully. Use a digital multimeter with at least 10 MΩ input impedance or an LED test light. An analog meter (swing-needle) or a test light with a normal incandescent bulb may draw enough current to damage sensitive electronic components.*
> - *Do not use an ohmmeter to measure resistance on solid state components such as control modules.*
> - *Disconnect the power supply before making resistance (ohm) measurements on a circuit.*

13

Abbreviations and acronyms

The following table lists common Toyota electrical system abbreviations and acronyms used throughout this manual.

Table a. Electrical system abbreviations and acronyms

AC	Alternating current
A/C	Air-conditioning
ACC	Accessory
AMP	Amplifier
AVC-LAN	Audio visual communication - local area network
BA	Brake assist
BAT	Battery
BEAN	Body electronics area network
BK/UP	Back-up (light)
CAN	Controller area network
CDS	Condenser (air-conditioning)
CHS	Coolant heat storage
C/OPN	Circuit opening (relay)
DC	Direct current
DEF	Defroster
DIM	Dimmer (headlights)
DLC	Data link connector
DLC3	OBD-II diagnostic connector
DRL	Daytime running lights
EB	Electrical brake
EBD	Electric brake force distribution
ECM	Engine control module
ECU	Electronic control unit
EFI	Electronic fuel injection
EPS	Electric power steering
ETCS	Electronic throttle control system
EVAP	Evaporative emission control
FR	Front
F/P	Fuel pump
GND	Ground
GPS	Global positioning system
HAZ	Hazard
HEV	Hybrid electric vehicle
HID	High intensity discharge (headlights)
H-LP	Headlight power

HTR	Heater
HV	Hybrid vehicle
IG	Ignition
IGN	Ignition
INV	Inverter
J/B	Junction block
LAN	Local area network
LCD	Liquid crystal display
LED	Light emitting diode
LH	Left hand
LP	Lamp or light
M/HTR	Mirror heater
MIL	Malfunction indicator lamp
MPX	Multiplex
MTR	Motor
OBD	On-board diagnostics
ODO	Odometer
P CON	Powertrain control
P/I	Power (ignition and hybrid system)
PS HTR	Electric heater in footwell duct
PTC HTR	Positive temperature coefficient (electric heater in heater core)
PWR	Power
R/B	Relay block
RDI	Radiator (cooling fans)
RH	Right hand
SFI	Sequential multiport fuel injection, *see also* EFI
SRS	Supplemental restraint system (airbags)
SW	Switch
TEMP	Temperature
T-LP	Taillight and illumination power
TRAC	Traction control
VFD	Vacuum fluorescent display
VSC	Vehicle stability control
VSV	Vacuum switching valve
VVT-i	Variable valve timing - intelligent
WIP	Wiper (windshield)
W/P	Water pump
WSH	Washer (windshield)

HOW TO READ WIRING DIAGRAMS

Wiring diagram details

Capital letters below and in the small diagrams correspond to details in the full-page sample wiring diagram.

A. System title

B. Wiring color.

B = black	L = blue
R = red	P = pink
W = white	V = violet
G = green	Y = yellow
BR = brown	SB = sky blue
LG = light green	GR = gray
O = orange	

C. Position of parts and wire routing

D. Connector pin number. Note that numbering system is different for female and male connectors.

E. Relay block. No shading distinguishes it from shaded junction block.

B (example):

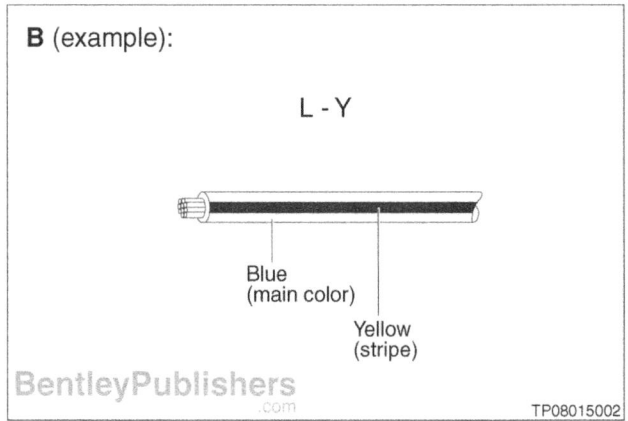

D (example):

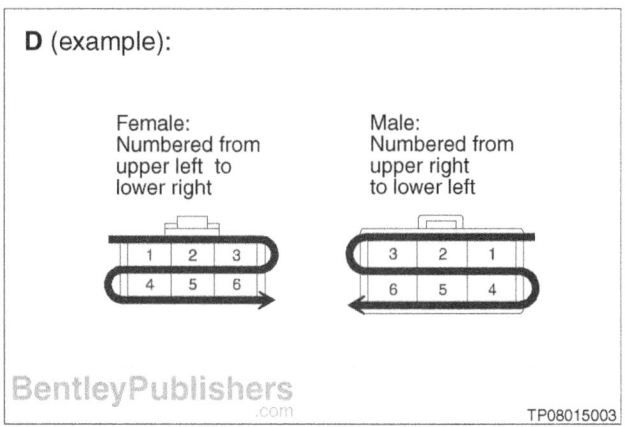

F. Junction block (J/B). J/B in circle with connector code next to it. Junction blocks shaded to clearly separate them from other parts.

G. Indicates related system.

F (example):

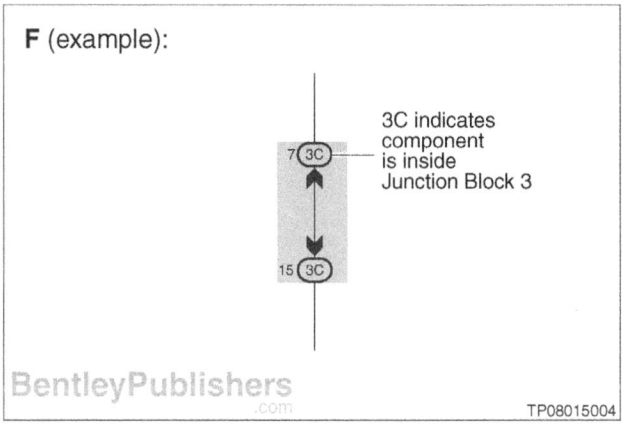

13

H (example):

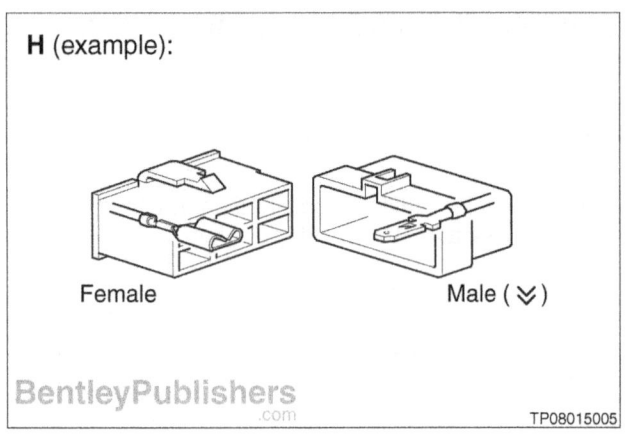

Female   Male (⩔)

BentleyPublishers
.com

TP08015005

H. Wiring harness connector. Male terminal shown with double arrows. Outside numerals are pin numbers.

I. Information in parenthesis ( ) indicates varying wiring, connectors, etc. with different models.

J (example):

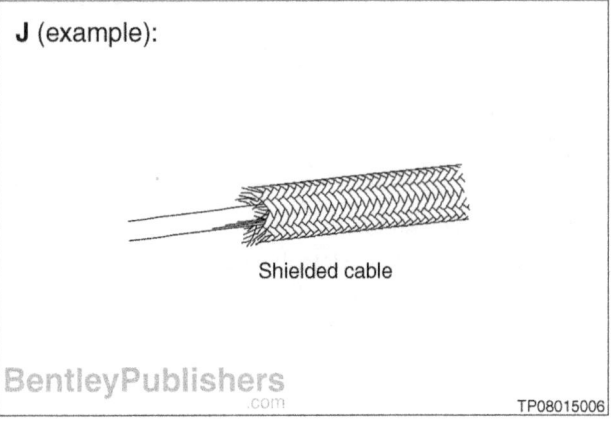

Shielded cable

BentleyPublishers
.com

TP08015006

J. Shielded cable

K. Ground point

L. Wiring diagram continues to next page (follow letters across pages).

Sample diagram

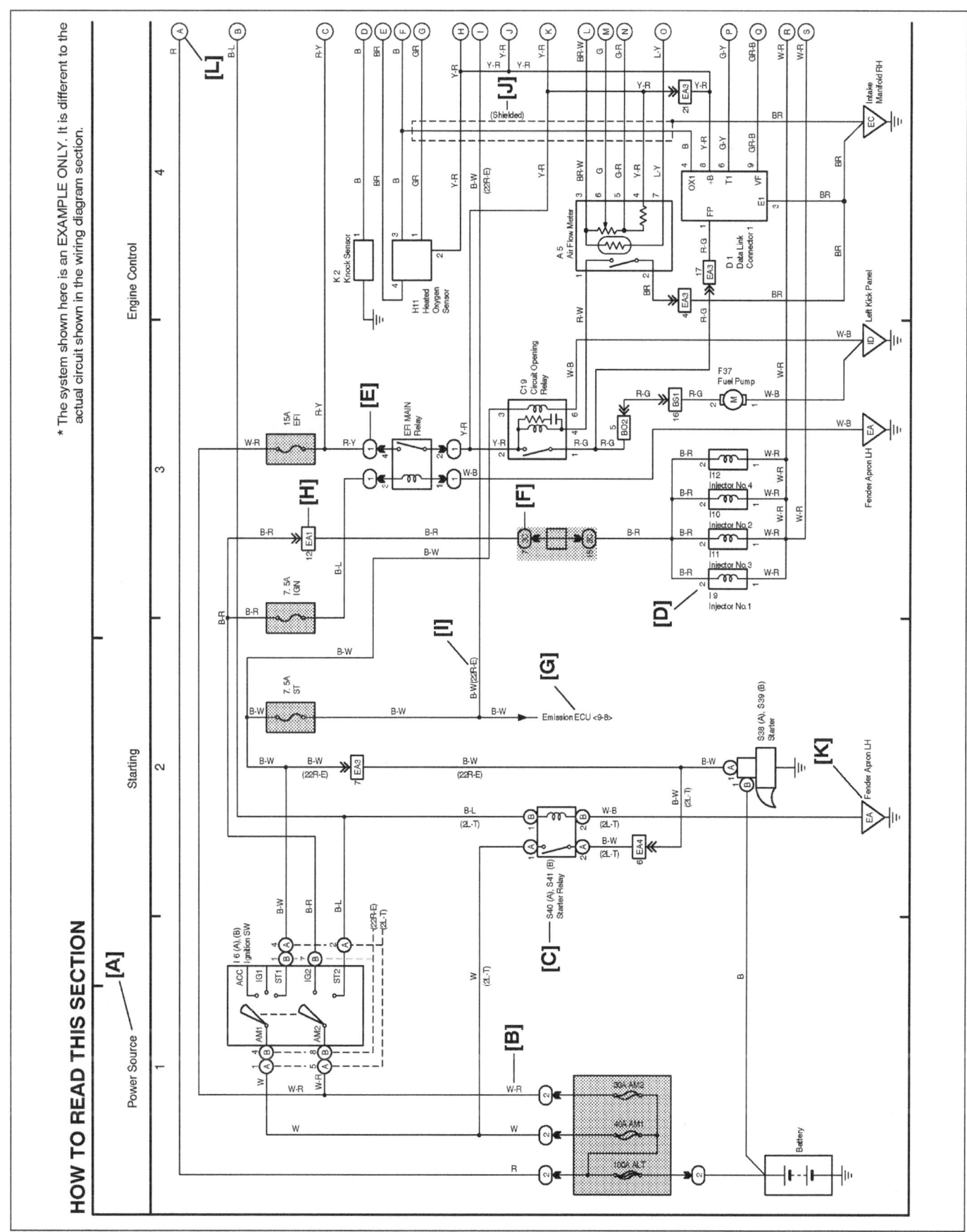

ELECTRICAL TROUBLESHOOTING

Most electrical troubleshooting calls for measuring voltage, current or resistance using a digital multimeter. A digital meter is preferred for precise measurements and for electronics work because it is generally more accurate than an analog meter (swing-needle). An analog meter may draw enough current to damage sensitive electronic components.

An LED test light is a safe, inexpensive tool that can be used to perform many simple electrical tests that would otherwise require a digital multimeter. The LED indicates when voltage is present between any two test-points in a circuit.

The integrated safety, comfort, security and handling systems on Toyota Prius vehicles are designed with self-diagnostic capabilities. The quickest way to diagnose many problems is to start with a scan tool read-out of diagnostic trouble codes (DTCs). See **11 Diagnostics**.

Electrical troubleshooting basics

Four things are required for current to flow in any electrical circuit:

• Voltage source.
• Wires or connections making a complete circuit for current to flow.
• Load or device that uses electricity.
• Connection to ground.

Most problems can be found using a digital multimeter (volt / ohm / ammeter) to check the following:

• Voltage supply.
• Breaks in the wiring (infinite resistance / no continuity).
• A path to ground that completes the circuit.

Electric current is logical in its flow, always moving from the voltage source toward ground. Electrical faults can usually be located through a process of elimination. When troubleshooting a complex circuit, separate the circuit into smaller parts. General tests outlined below may be helpful in finding electrical problems. The information is most helpful when used with wiring diagrams.

Be sure to analyze the problem. Use wiring diagrams to determine the most likely cause. Understand how the circuit works by following the circuit from ground back to the power source.

When making test connections at connectors and components, use care to avoid spreading or damaging connectors or terminals. Some tests may require jumper wires to bypass components or connections in the wiring harness. When connecting jumper wires, use blade connectors at the wire ends that match the size of the terminal being tested. The small internal contacts are easily spread apart, and this can cause intermittent or faulty connections that can lead to more problems.

Voltage and voltage drop

Wires, connectors, and switches that carry current are designed with very low resistance so that current flows with a minimum loss of voltage. A voltage drop is caused by higher than normal resistance in a circuit. This additional resistance actually decreases or stops the flow of current. Excessive voltage drop can be noticed by problems ranging from dim headlights to sluggish wipers. Some common sources of voltage drops are corroded or dirty switches, dirty or corroded connections or contacts, and loose or corroded ground wires and ground connections.

A voltage drop test is a good test to perform if current is flowing through the circuit but the circuit is not operating correctly. A voltage drop test helps pinpoint a corroded ground strap or a faulty switch. Normally, there should be less than 1 volt drop across most wires or closed switches. A voltage drop across a connector or short cable should not exceed 0.5 volt.

A voltage drop test is generally more accurate than a simple resistance check because the resistances involved are often too small to measure with most ohmmeters. For example, a resistance as small as 0.02 Ω results in a 3 volt drop in a typical 150 amp starter circuit. (150 amps x 0.02 Ω = 3 volts).

Keep in mind that voltage with ignition key ON and voltage with engine running are not the same. With ignition ON and engine OFF, fully charged battery voltage is approximately 12.6 volts. With engine running (charging voltage), normal voltage is approximately 14.0 volts. Measure voltage at battery with ignition ON and then with engine running to get exact measurements.

Voltage, measuring

◀ Connect digital multimeter negative lead to a reliable ground point on vehicle.

NOTE—

• *The negative (-) battery terminal is always a good ground point.*

– Connect digital multimeter positive lead to point in circuit you wish to measure.

– Check that voltage reading does not deviate more than 1 volt from voltage at battery. If voltage drop is more than this, check for a corroded connector or loose ground wire.

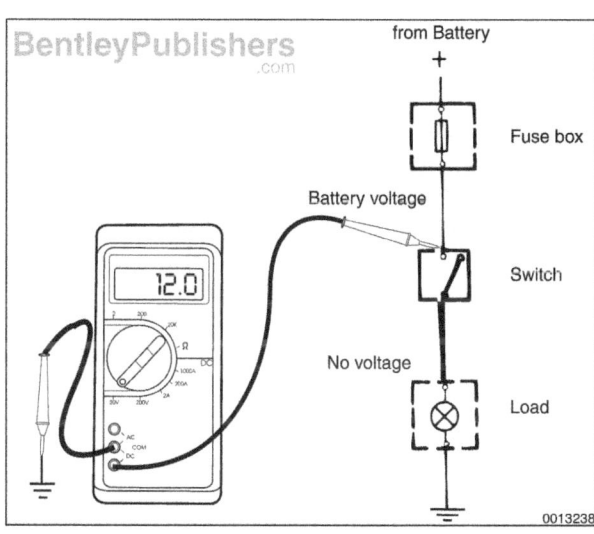

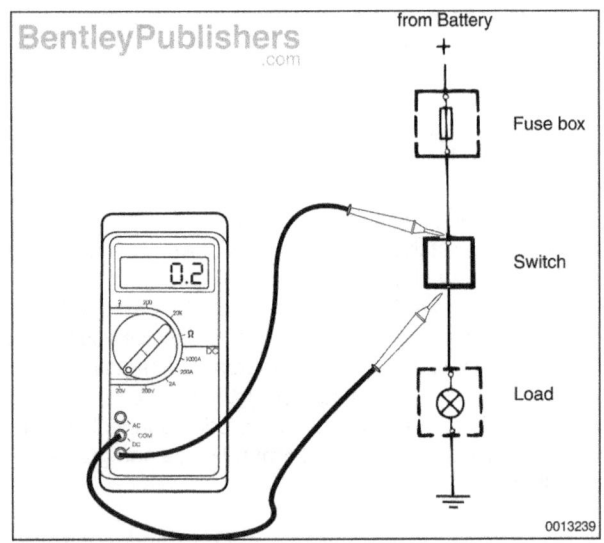

Voltage drop, testing

Check voltage drop only when there is a load on the circuit, such as headlights switched ON. Use a digital multimeter to ensure accurate readings.

◄ Connect digital multimeter positive lead to positive (+) battery terminal or a positive power supply close to battery source.

– Connect digital multimeter negative lead to other end of cable or switch being tested.

– With power switched ON and circuit working, meter shows voltage drop (difference between two points). This value should not exceed 1 volt.

– Maximum voltage drop in an automotive circuit, as recommended by the Society of Automotive Engineers (SAE), is as follows:

• 0 volt for small wire connections

• 0.1 volt for high current connections

• 0.2 volt for high current cables

• 0.3 volt for switch or solenoid contacts

– On longer wires or cables, the drop may be slightly higher. In any case, a voltage drop of more than 1.0 volt usually indicates a problem.

Continuity, checking

Use continuity test to check a circuit or switch. Because most automotive circuits are designed to have little or no resistance, a circuit or part of a circuit can be easily checked for faults using an ohmmeter. An open circuit or a circuit with high resistance does not allow current to flow. A circuit with little or no resistance allows current to flow easily.

When checking continuity, switch ignition OFF. On circuits that are powered at all times, disconnect battery. Using the appropriate wiring diagram, test circuit for faulty connections, wires, switches, relays and engine sensors by checking for continuity.

◄ Example: Test brake light switch for continuity:

• With brake pedal in rest position (switch open) there is no continuity (infinite Ω).

• With pedal depressed (switch closed) there is continuity (0 Ω).

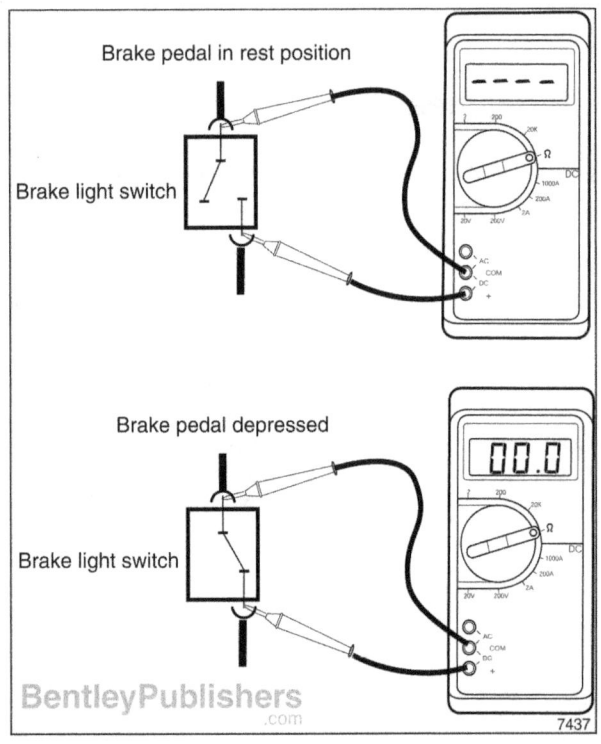

Short circuits, testing

Short circuits are exactly what the name implies. Current in the circuit takes a shorter path than it was designed to take. The most common short that causes problems is a short to ground where the insulation on a positive (+) wire wears away and the metal wire is exposed. When the wire rubs against a metal part of the vehicle or other ground source, the circuit is shorted to ground. If the exposed wire is live (positive battery voltage), a fuse blows and the circuit may be damaged.

Short circuits vary in nature and are often difficult to locate. They can be found using a logical approach based on knowledge of the current path.

Use a digital multimeter to locate short circuits.

> **CAUTION—**
> • *In circuits protected with high rating fuses (25 amp and greater), wires or circuit components may be damaged before the fuse blows. Check for wiring damage before replacing fuses of this rating. Also, check for correct fuse rating.*

Testing with ohmmeter

— Remove blown fuse from circuit and disconnect cables from battery. Disconnect harness connector from circuit load or consumer.

◄ Using an ohmmeter, connect one test lead to load side of fuse terminal (terminal leading to circuit) and other test lead to ground.

— If there is continuity to ground, there is a short to ground.

— If there is no continuity, work from wire harness nearest to fuse and relay panel and move or wiggle wires while observing meter. Continue to move down harness until meter displays a reading. This is the location of the short to ground.

— Visually inspect wire harness at this point for any faults. If no faults are visible, carefully slice open harness cover or wire insulation for further inspection. Repair any faults found.

Testing with voltmeter

— Remove blown fuse from circuit. Disconnect harness connector from circuit load or consumer.

> **NOTE—**
> • *Most fuses power more than one consumer. Be sure all consumers are disconnected when checking for a short circuit.*

◄ Using a digital multimeter, connect test leads across fuse terminals. Make sure power is present in circuit. If necessary switch ignition ON.

— If voltage is present at voltmeter, there is a short to ground.

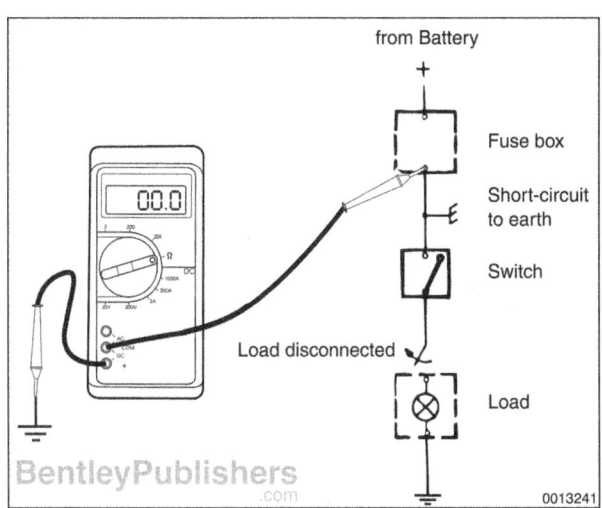

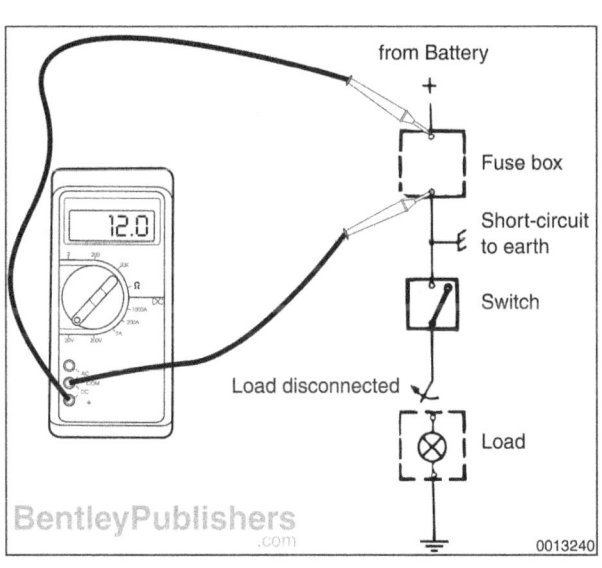

- If voltage is not present, work from wire harness nearest to fuse and relay panel and move or wiggle wires while observing meter. Continue to move down harness until meter displays a reading. This is the location of the short to ground.

- Visually inspect wire harness at this point for any faults. If no faults are visible, carefully slice open harness cover or wire insulation for further inspection. Repair any faults found.

ELECTRICAL WIRING DIAGRAMS

Electrical wiring diagrams for 2004 and 2007 model years have been selected from original source material provided by the vehicle manufacturer.

Major electrical components and systems are indexed separately for each model year:

- 2004 wiring index is on page 14-11. Wiring schematics begin on page 14-12.

- 2007 wiring index is on page 14-70. Wiring schematics begin on page 14-71.

Component	Page

MODEL YEAR 2004

2004 electrical wiring diagrams index

Component	Page

13

Model Year 2004

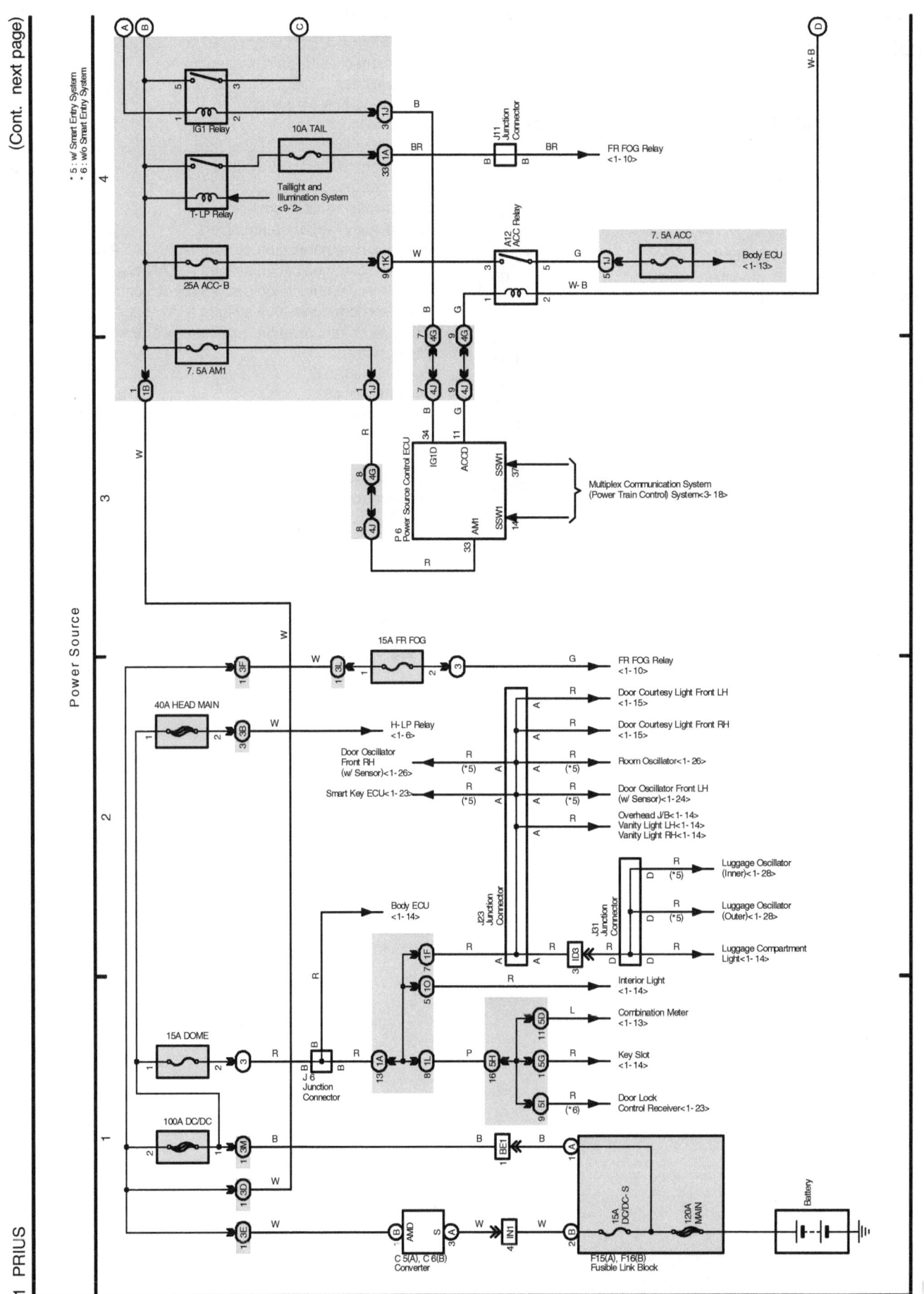

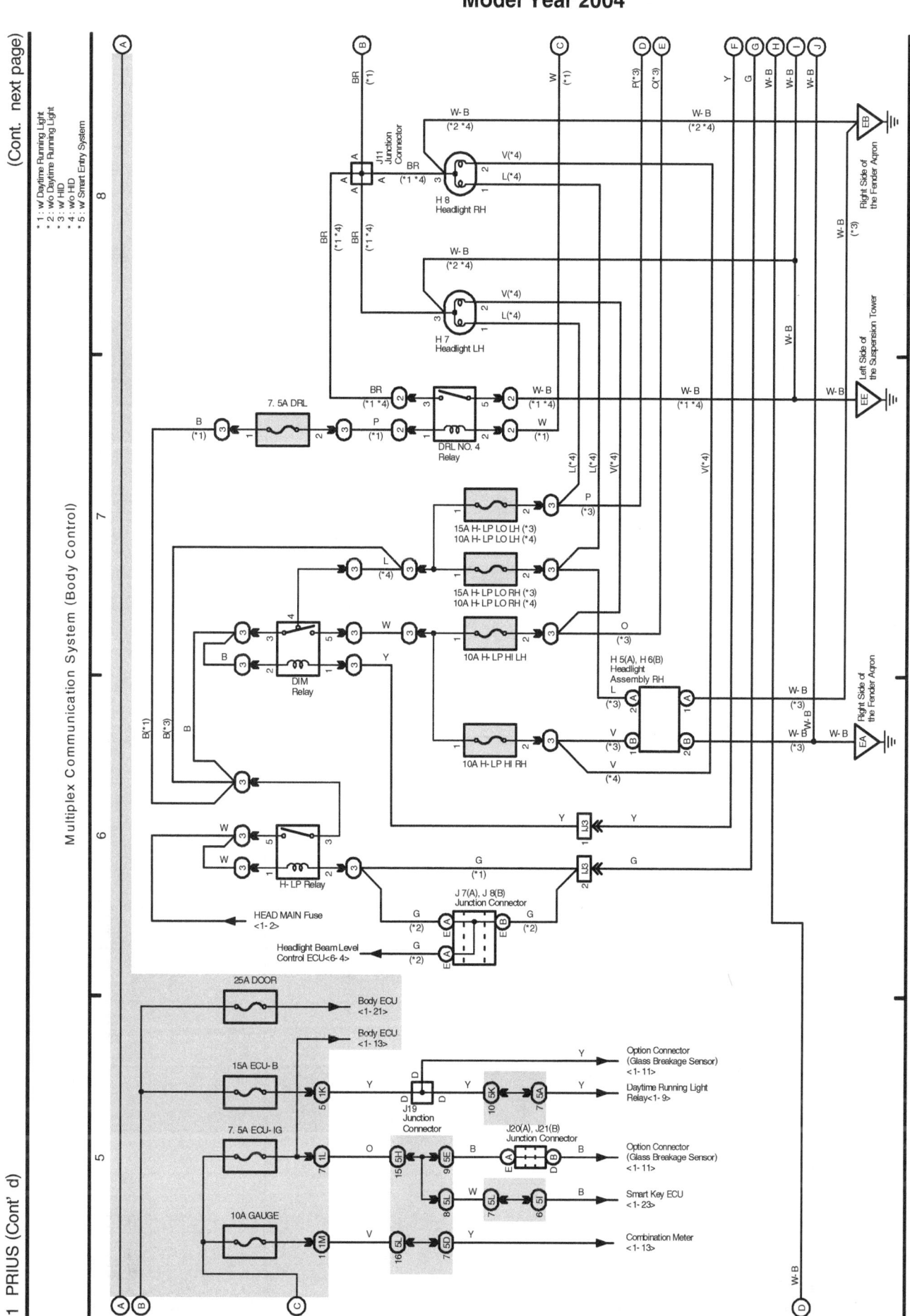

Model Year 2004

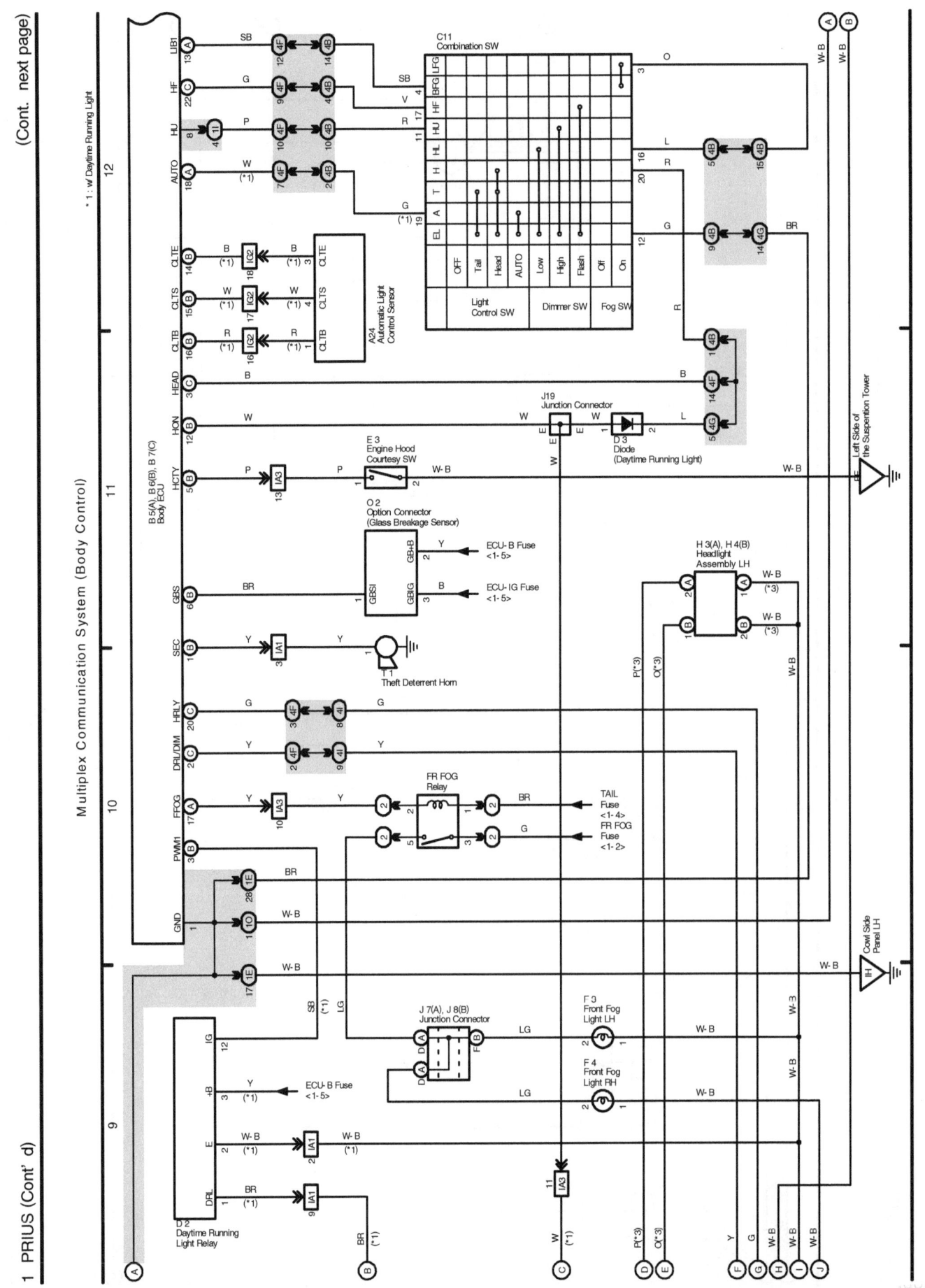

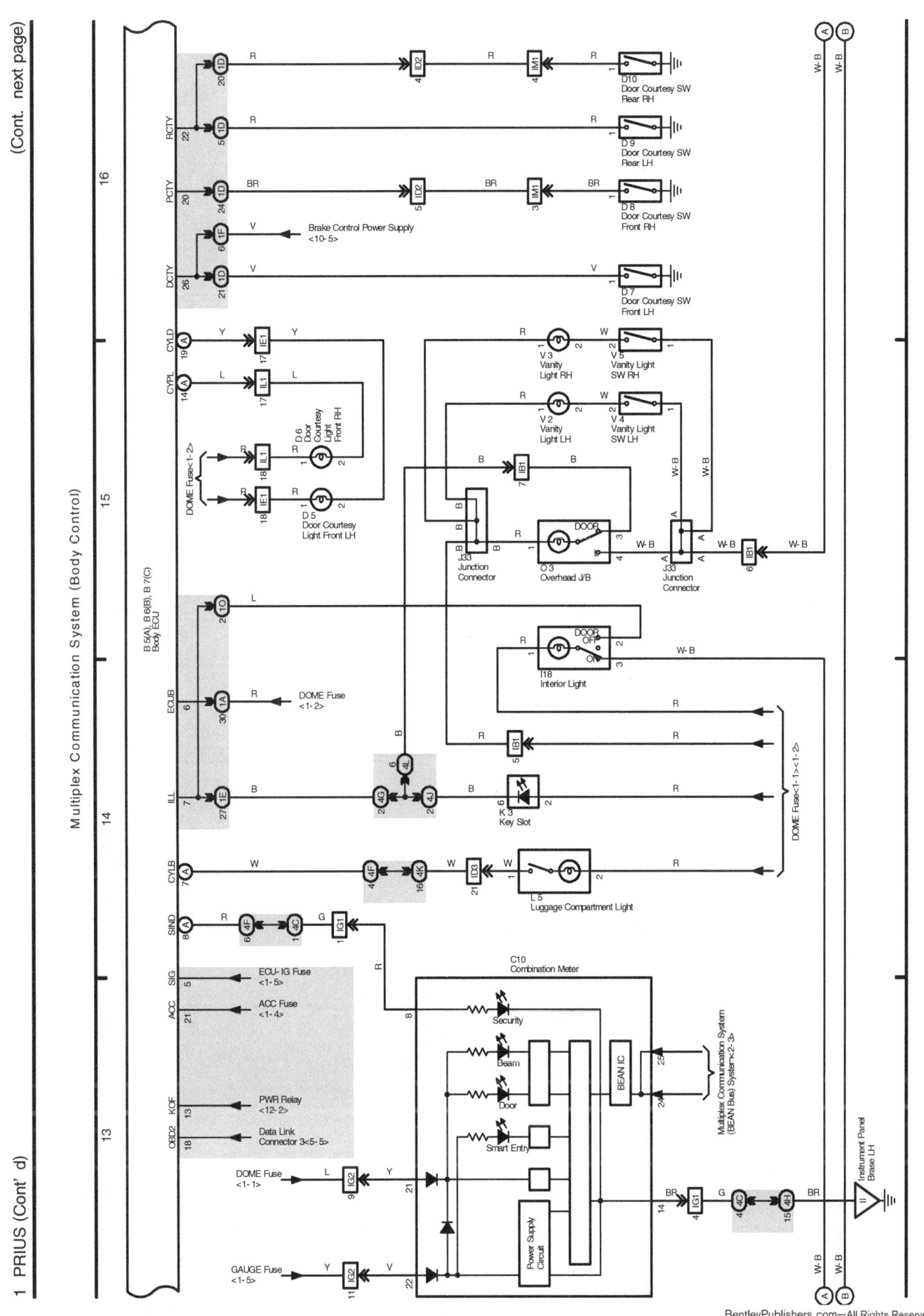

Model Year 2004

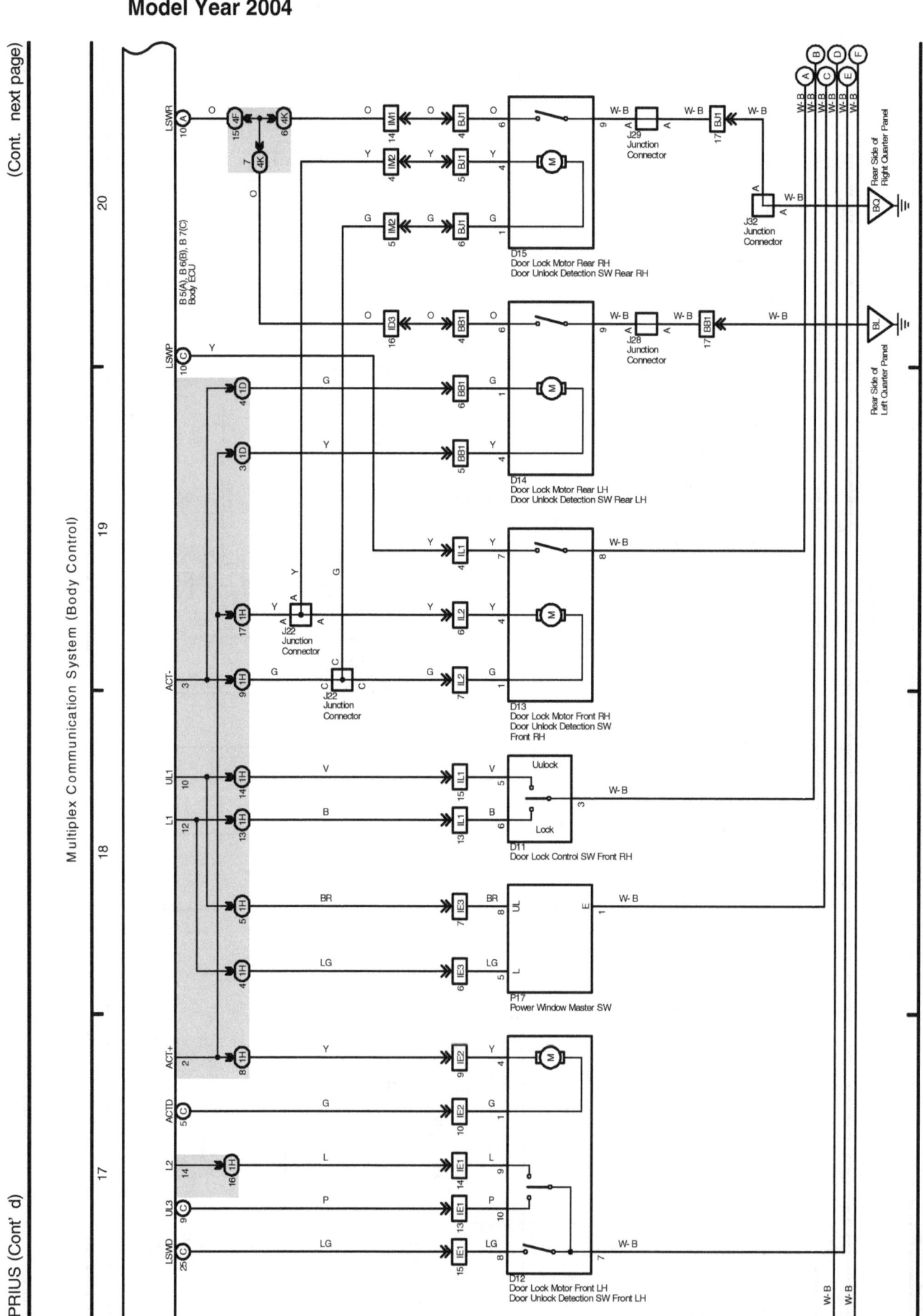

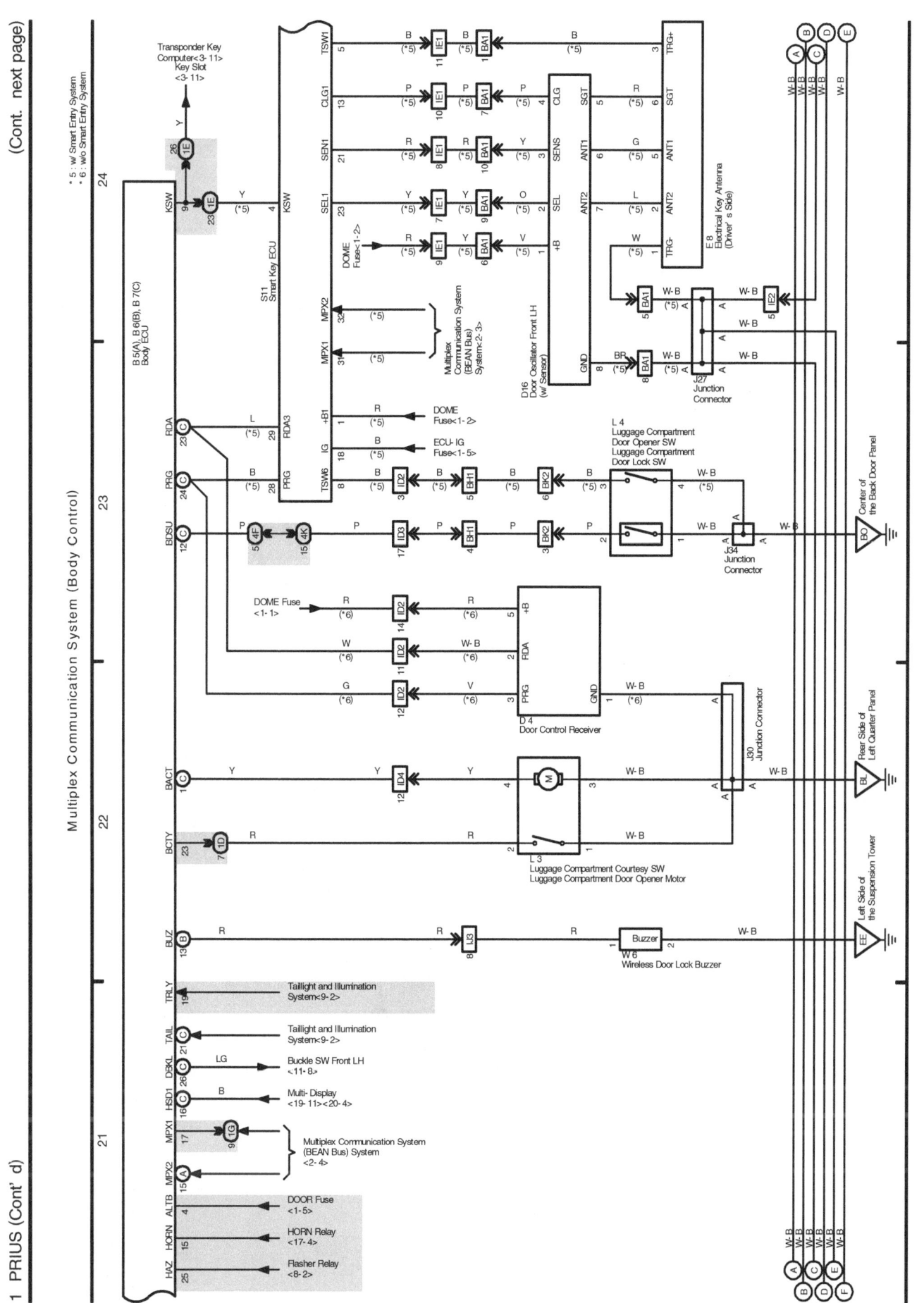

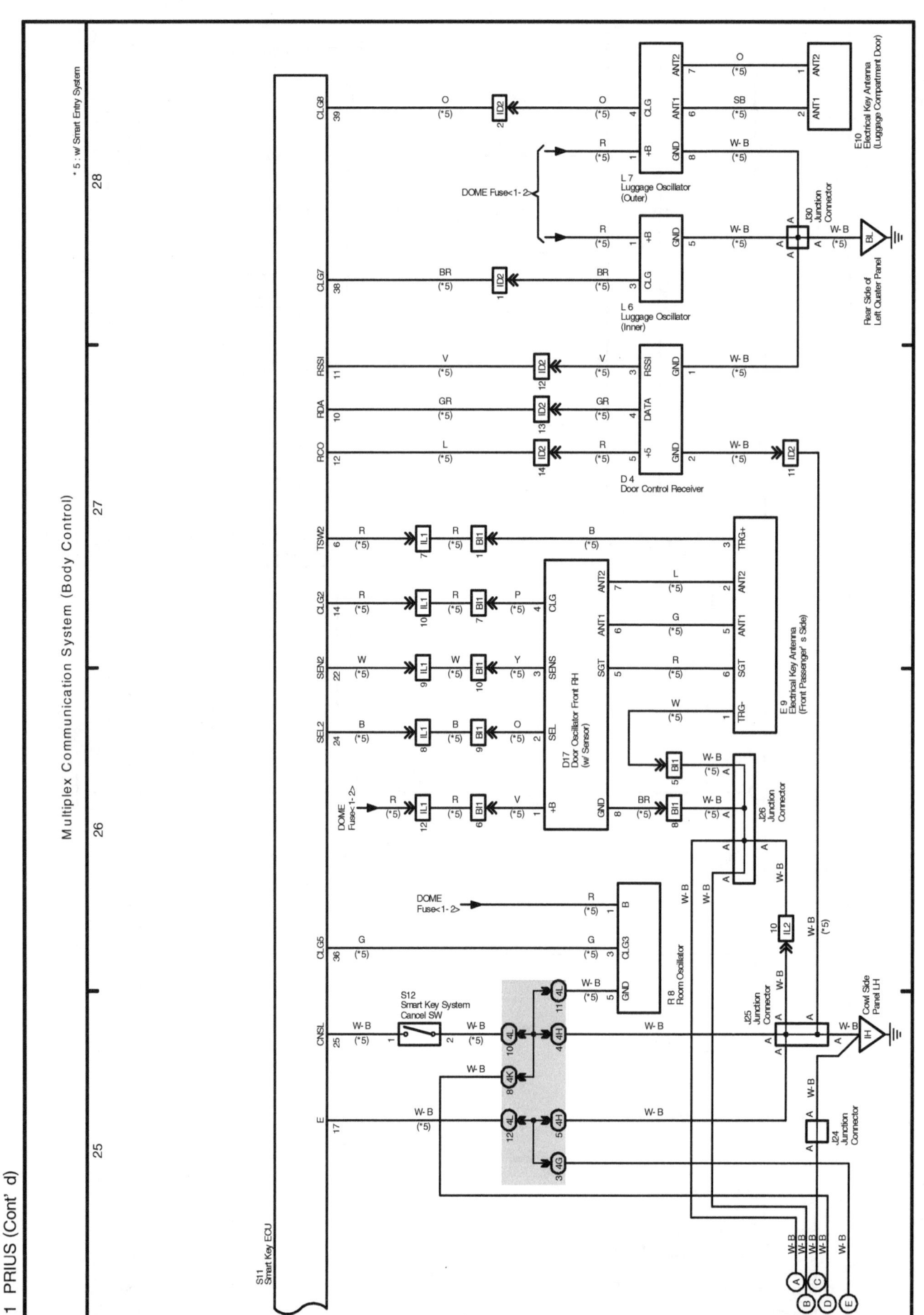

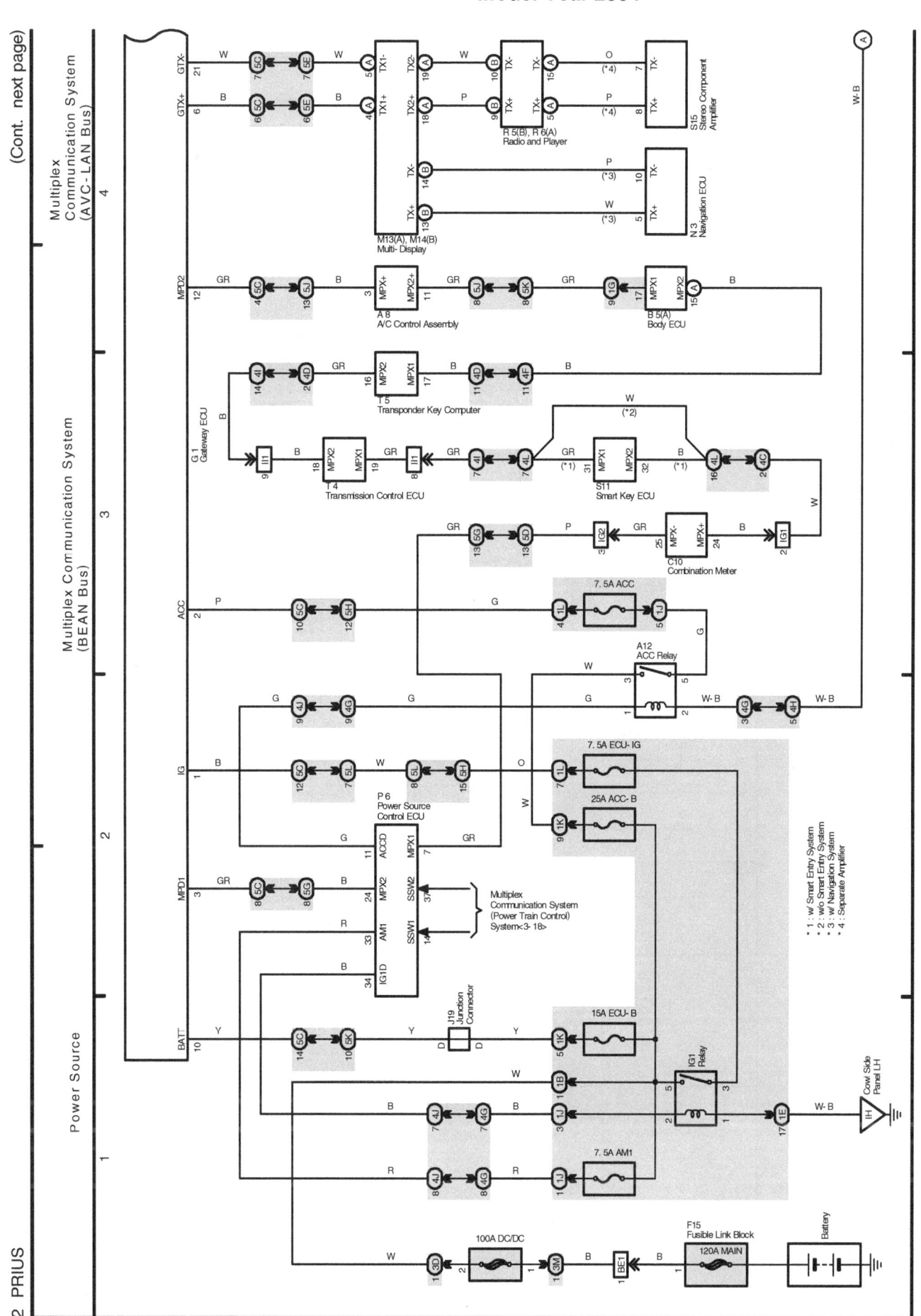

Model Year 2004

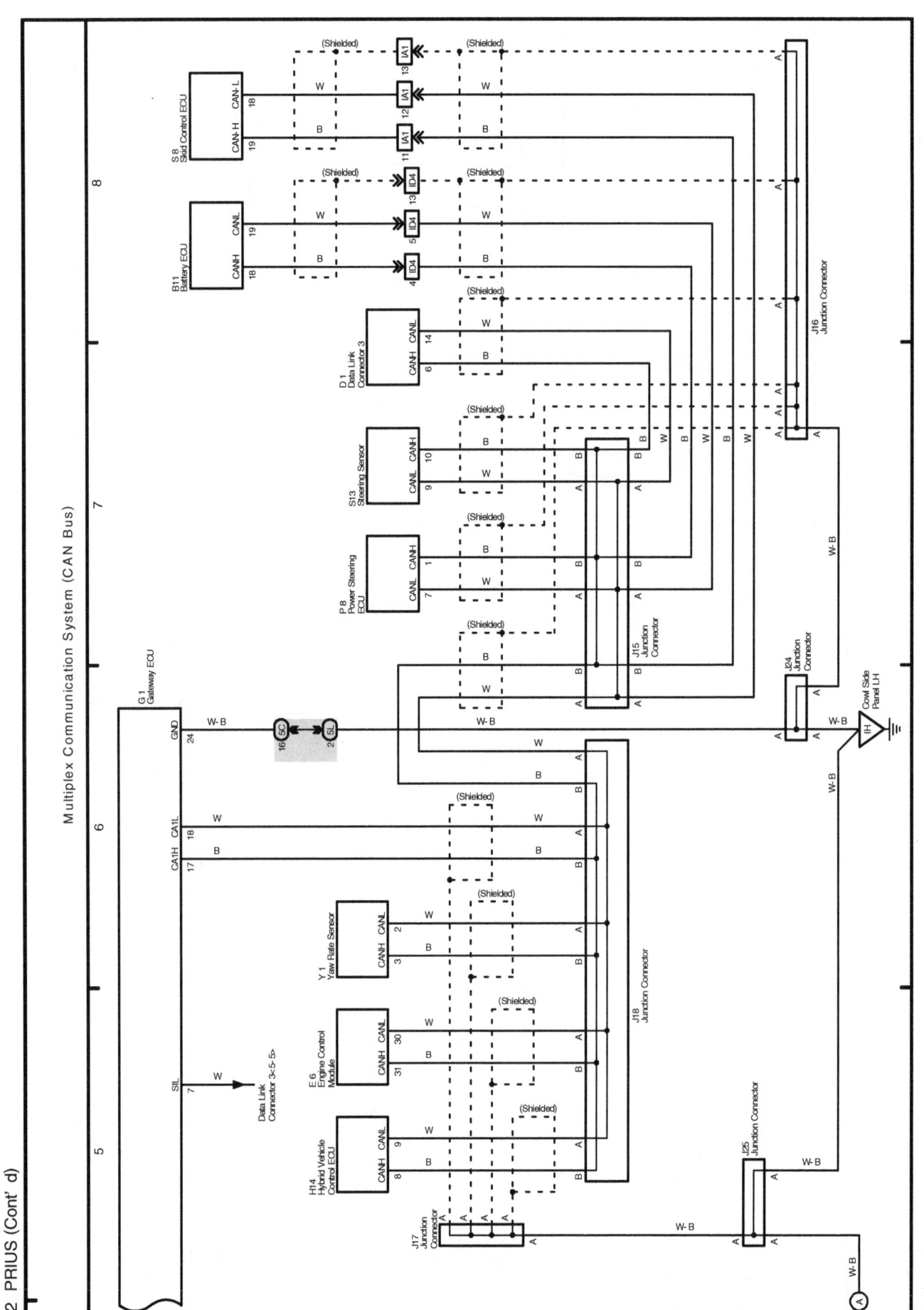

Multiplex Communication System (CAN Bus)

2 PRIUS (Cont' d)

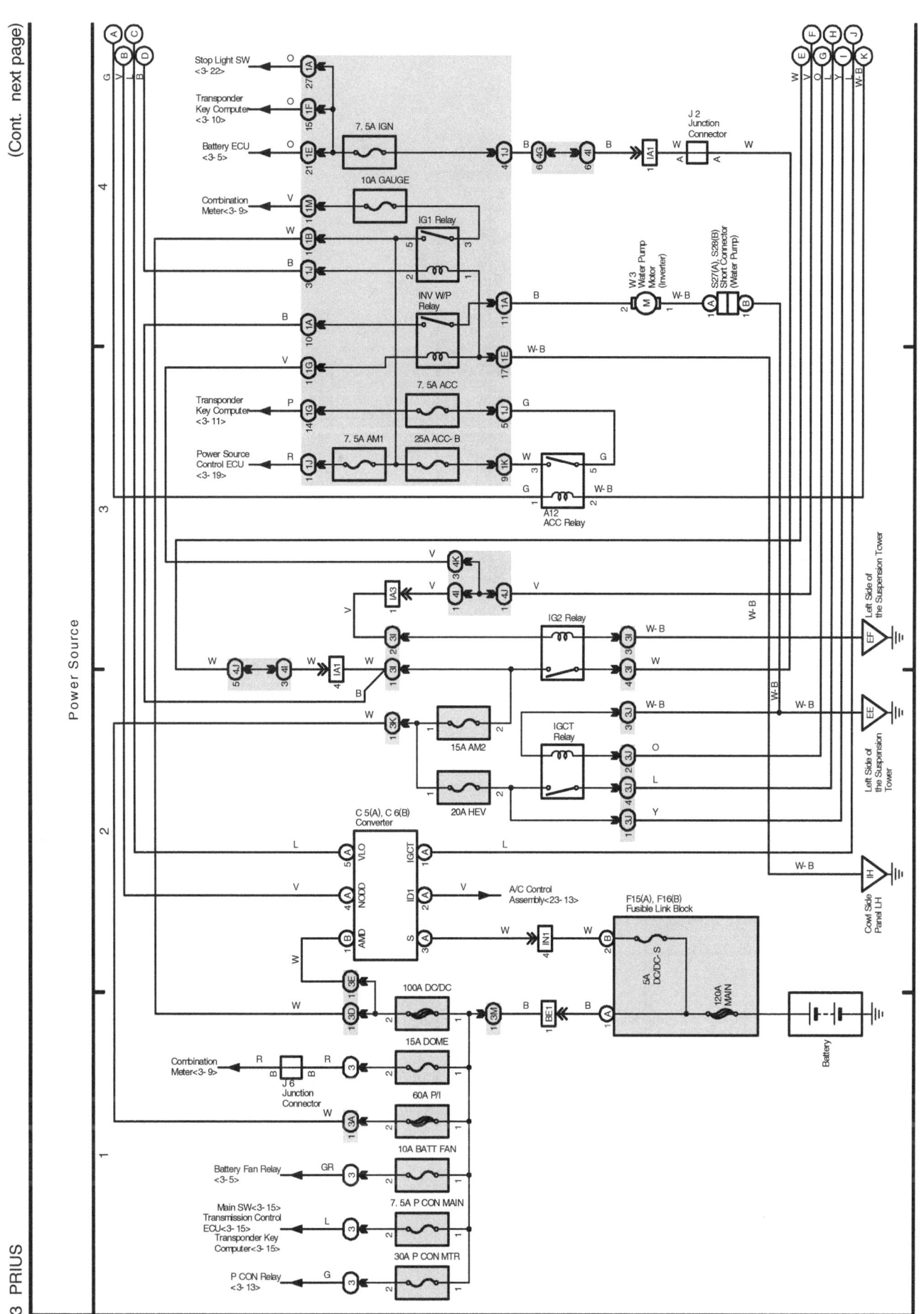

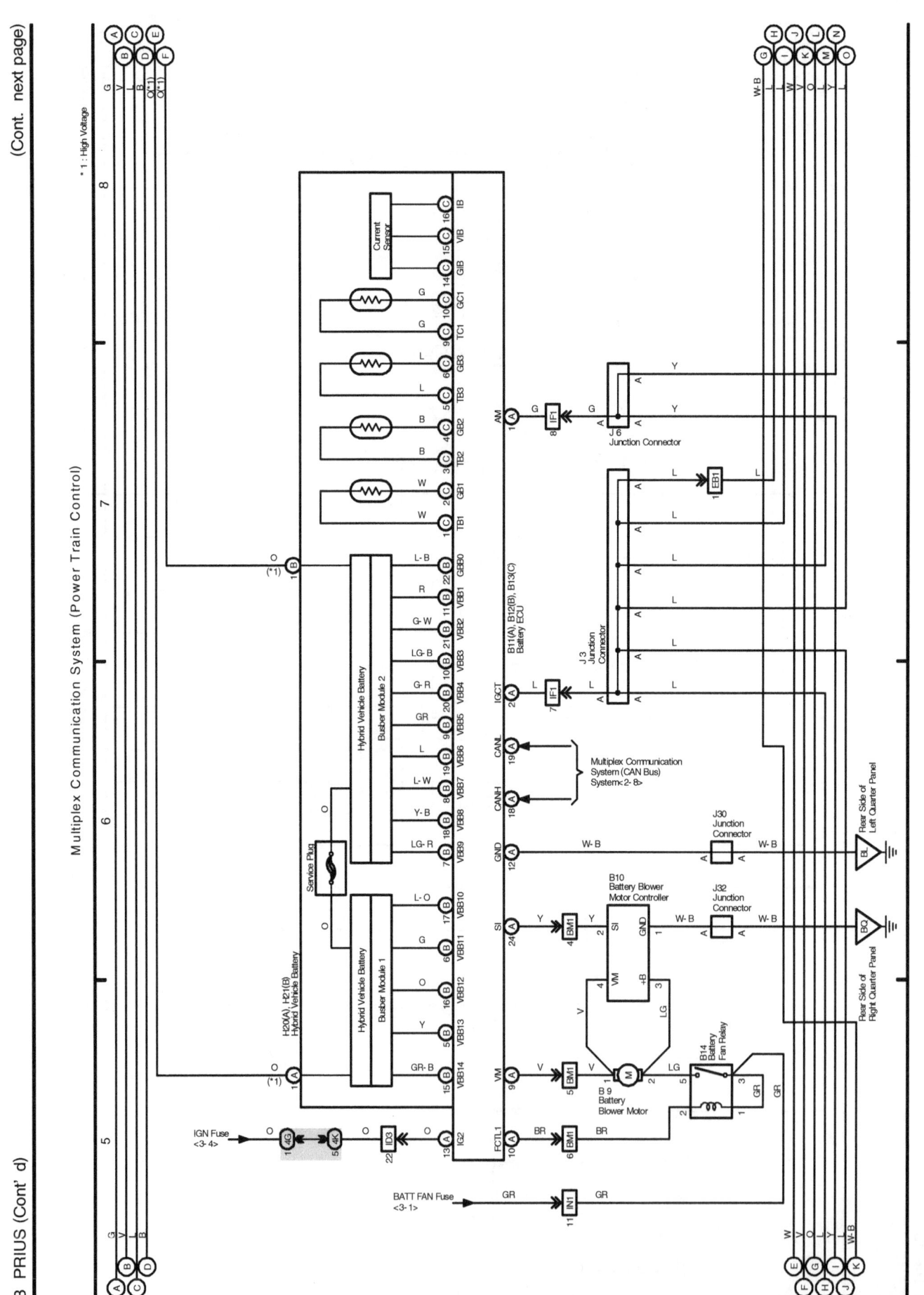

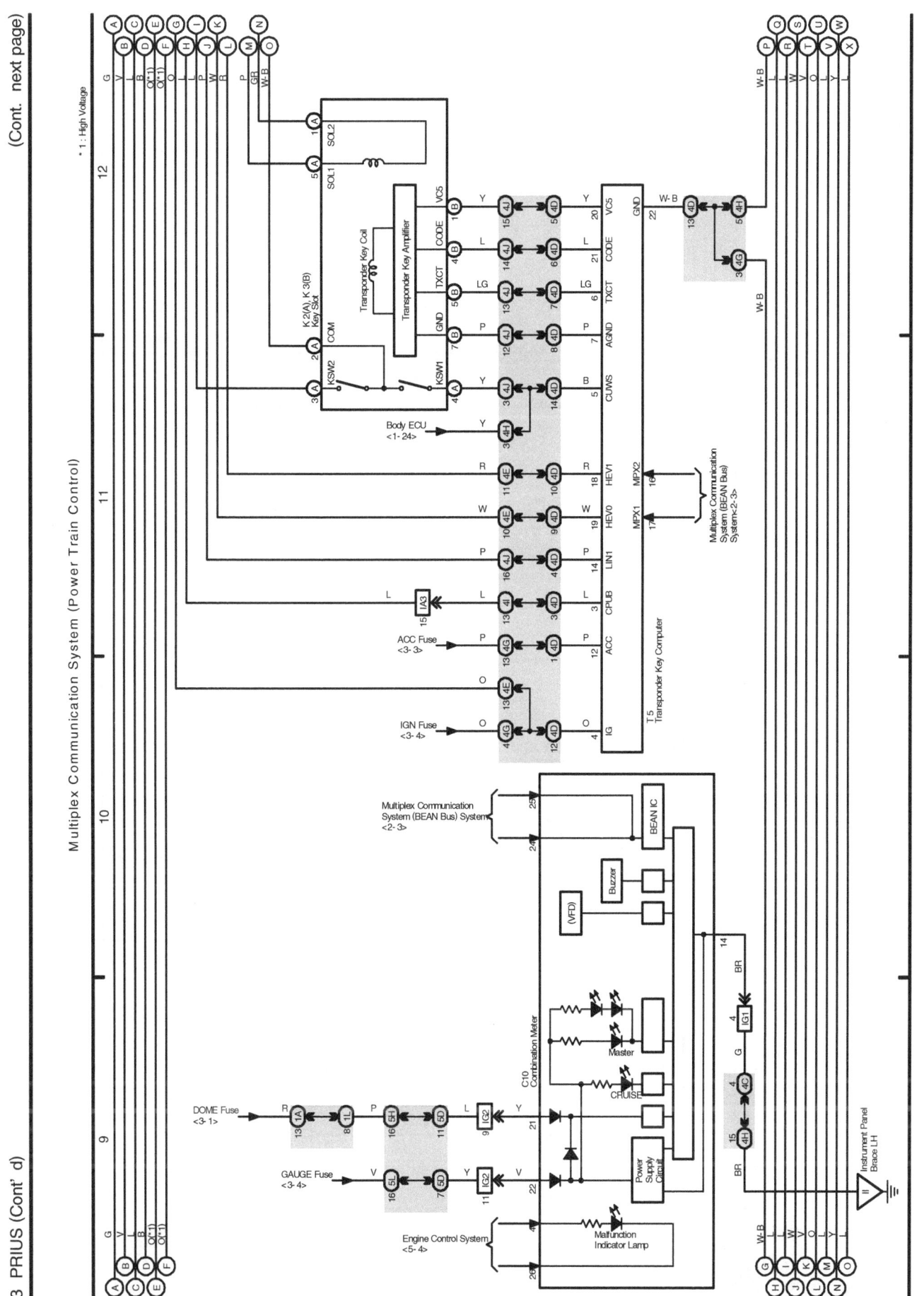

Model Year 2004

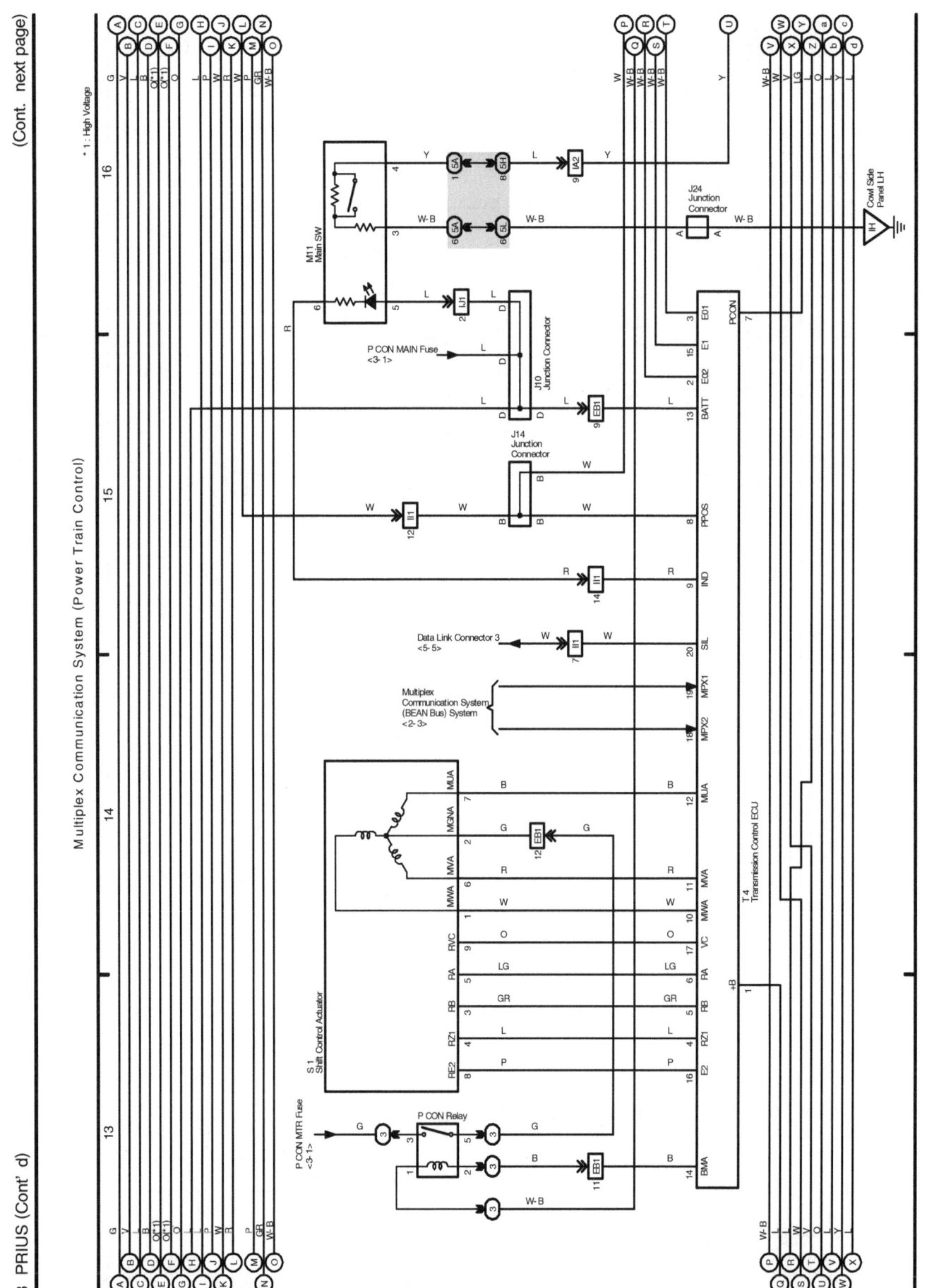

Model Year 2004

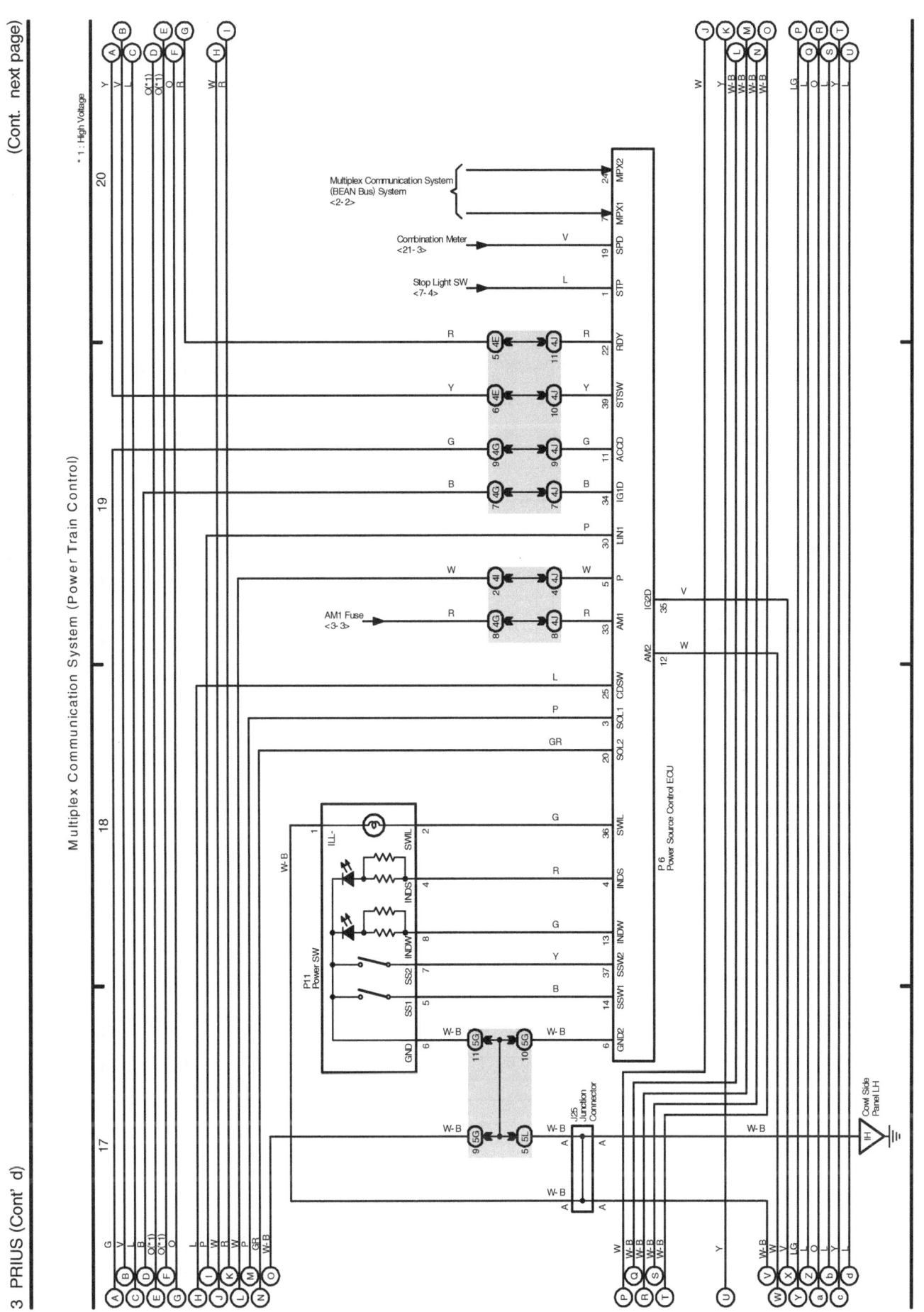

Model Year 2004

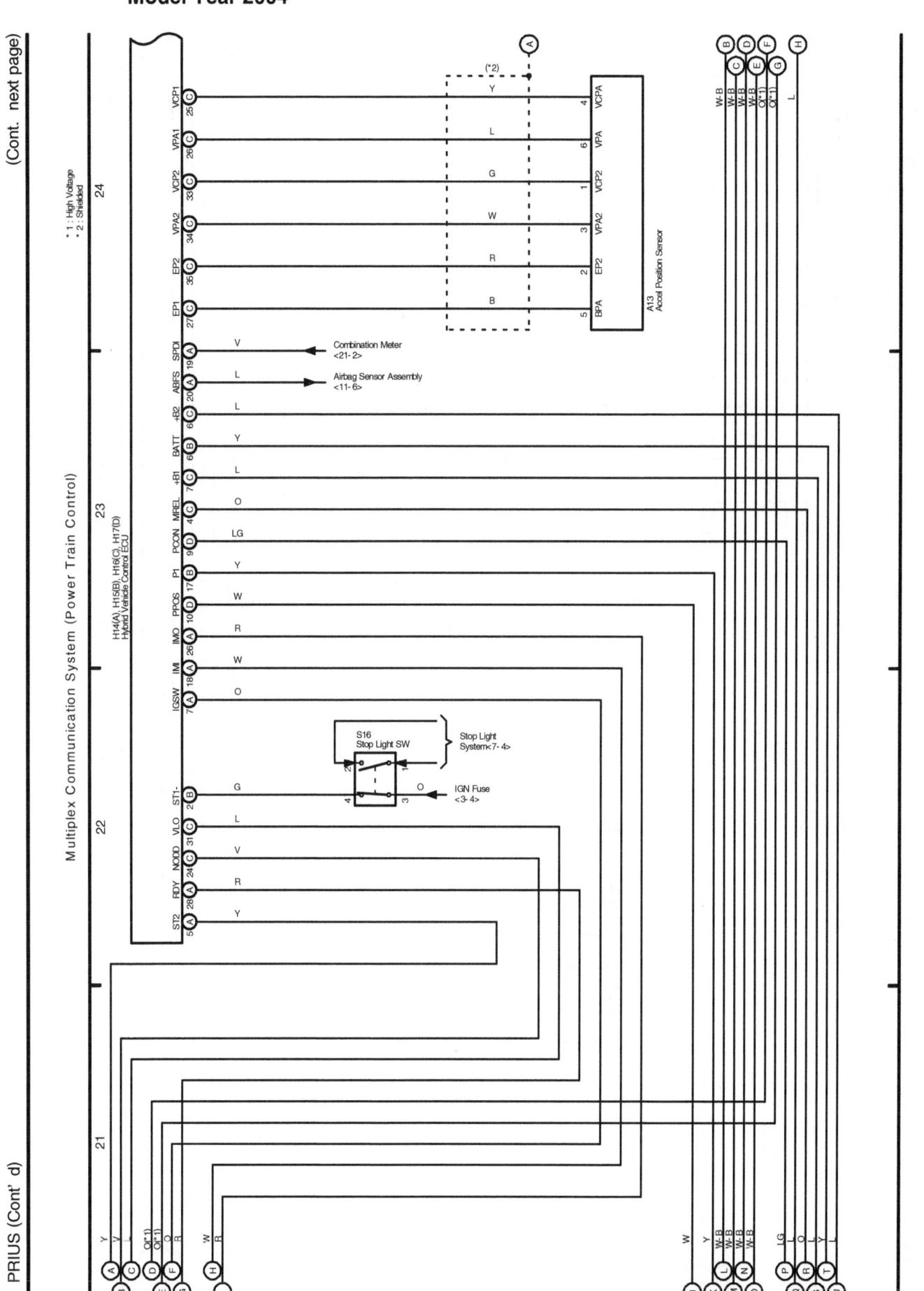

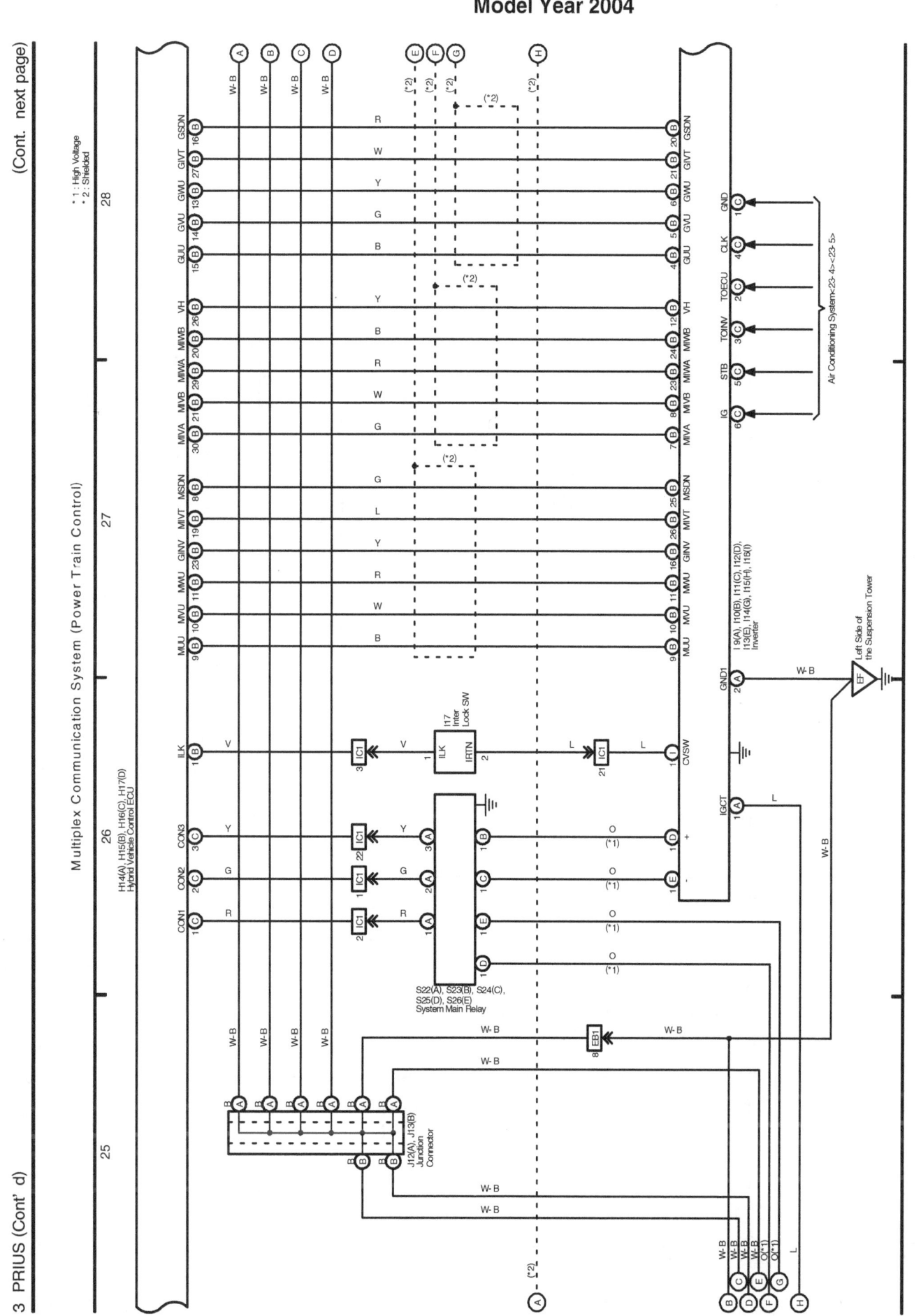

Model Year 2004

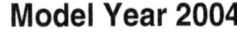

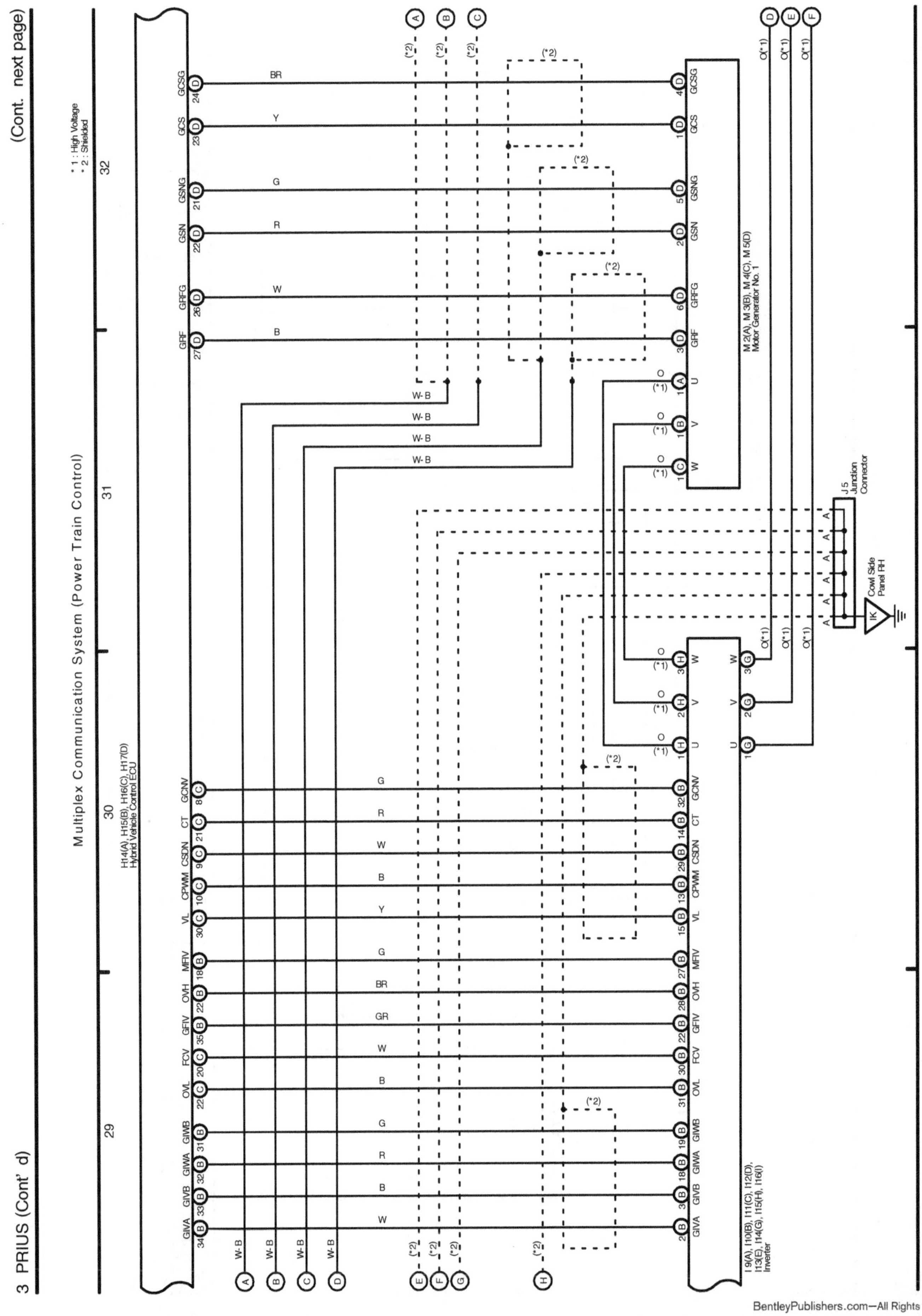
3 PRIUS (Cont' d)
(Cont. next page)
Multiplex Communication System (Power Train Control)
* 1 : High Voltage
* 2 : Shielded
H14(A), H15(B), H16(C), H17(D)
Hybrid Vehicle Control ECU
M 2(A), M 3(B), M 4(C), M 5(D)
Motor Generator No. 1
J 5
Junction Connector
IK
Cowl Side Panel RH
I 9(A), I10(B), I11(C), I12(D), I13(E), I14(G), I15(H), I16(I)
Inverter
GCSG
GCS
GSNG
GSN
GRFG
GRF
GCNV
CT
CSDN
CPWM
VL
MFIV
OVH
GFIV
FCV
OVL
GIWB
GIWA
GIVB
GIVA
W-B
(*2)
(*1)
29
30
31
32

Model Year 2004

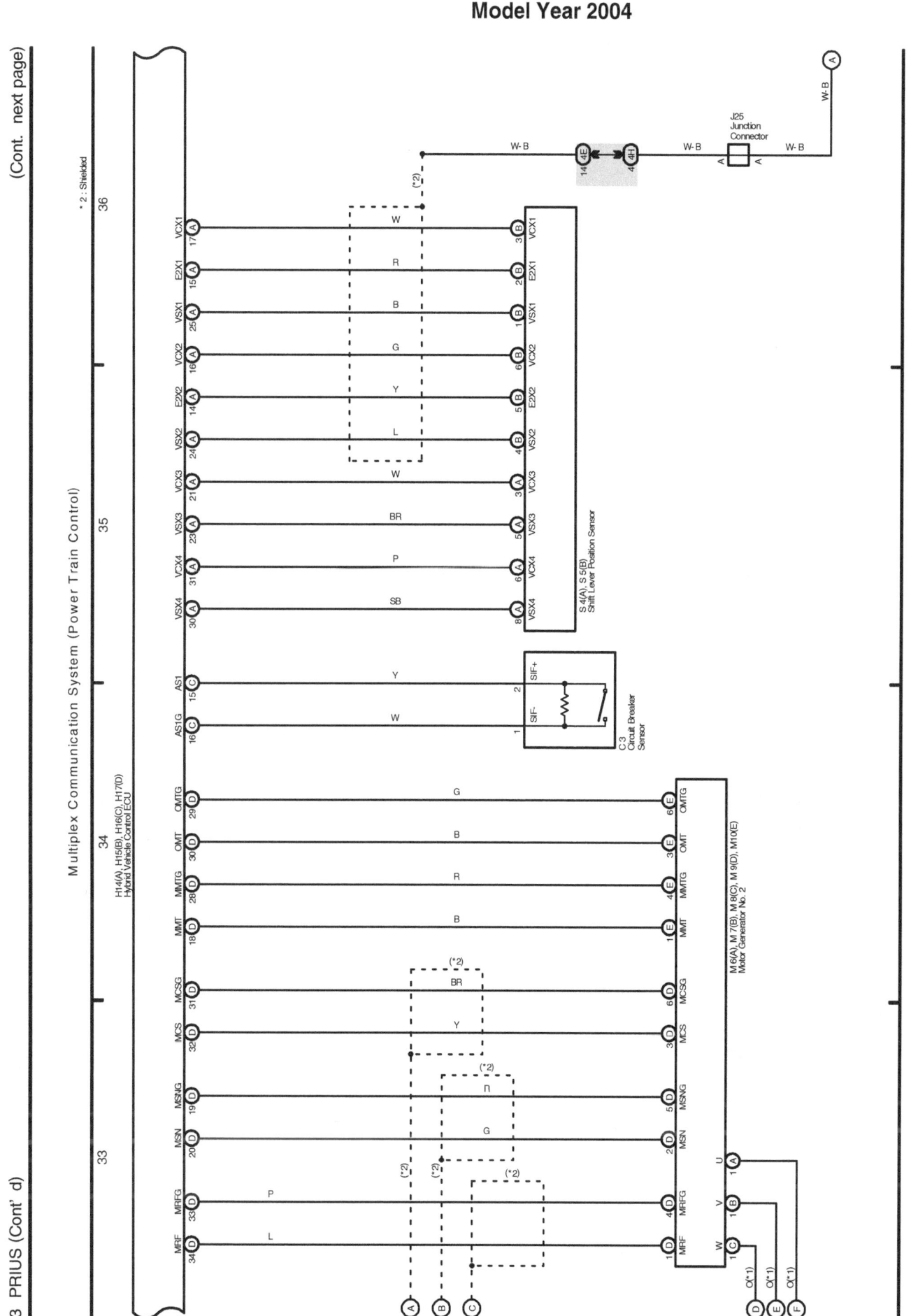

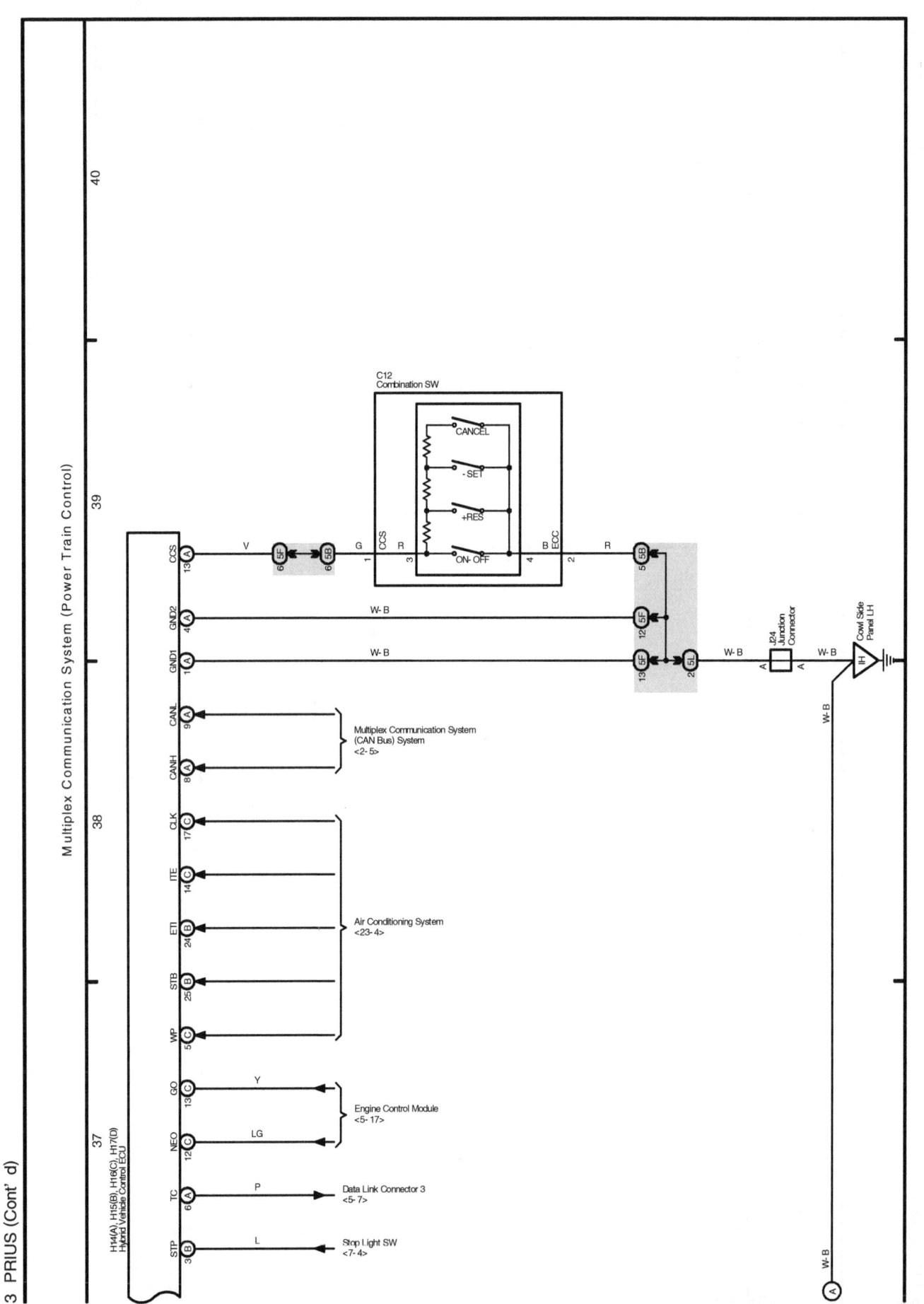

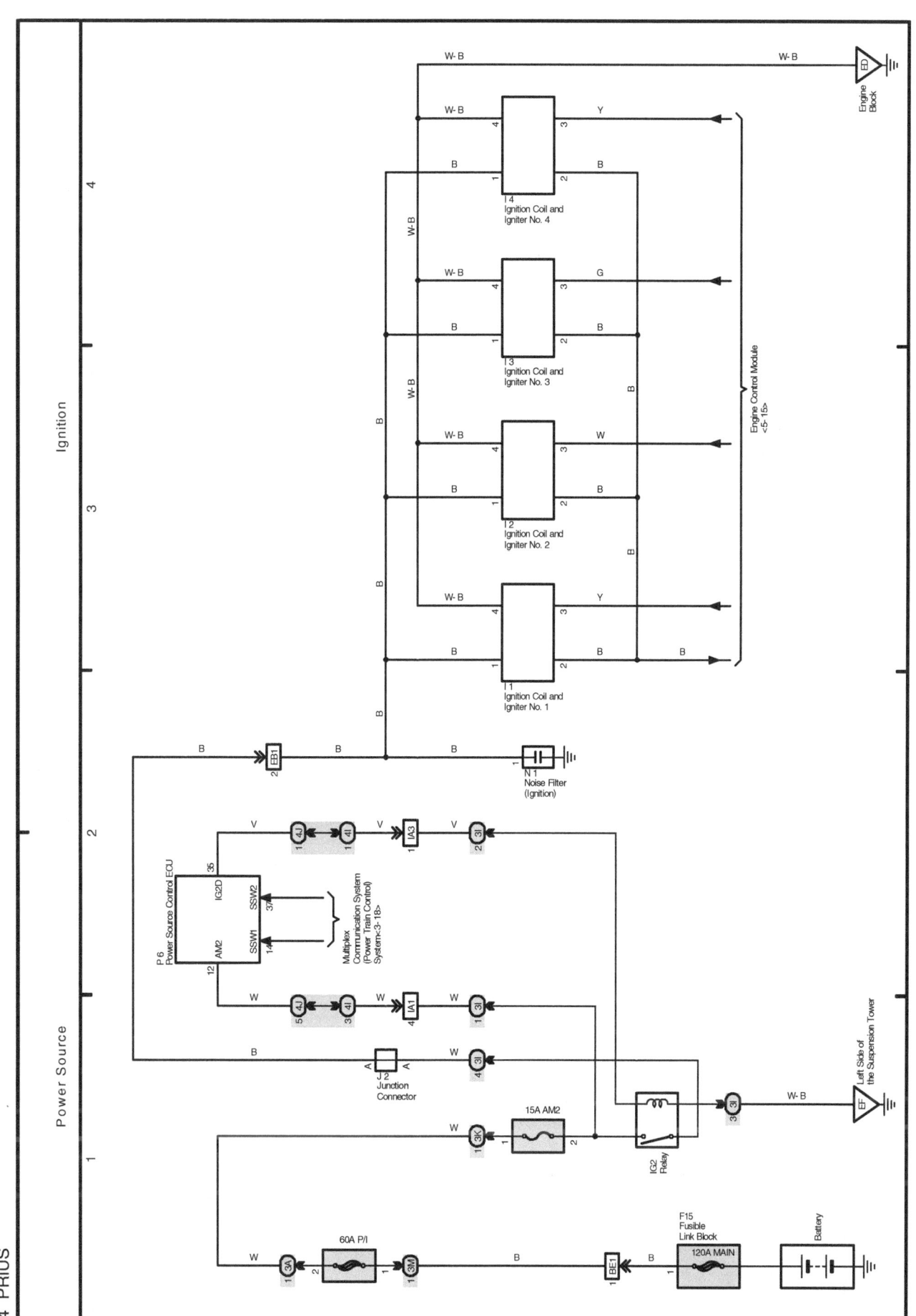

Model Year 2004

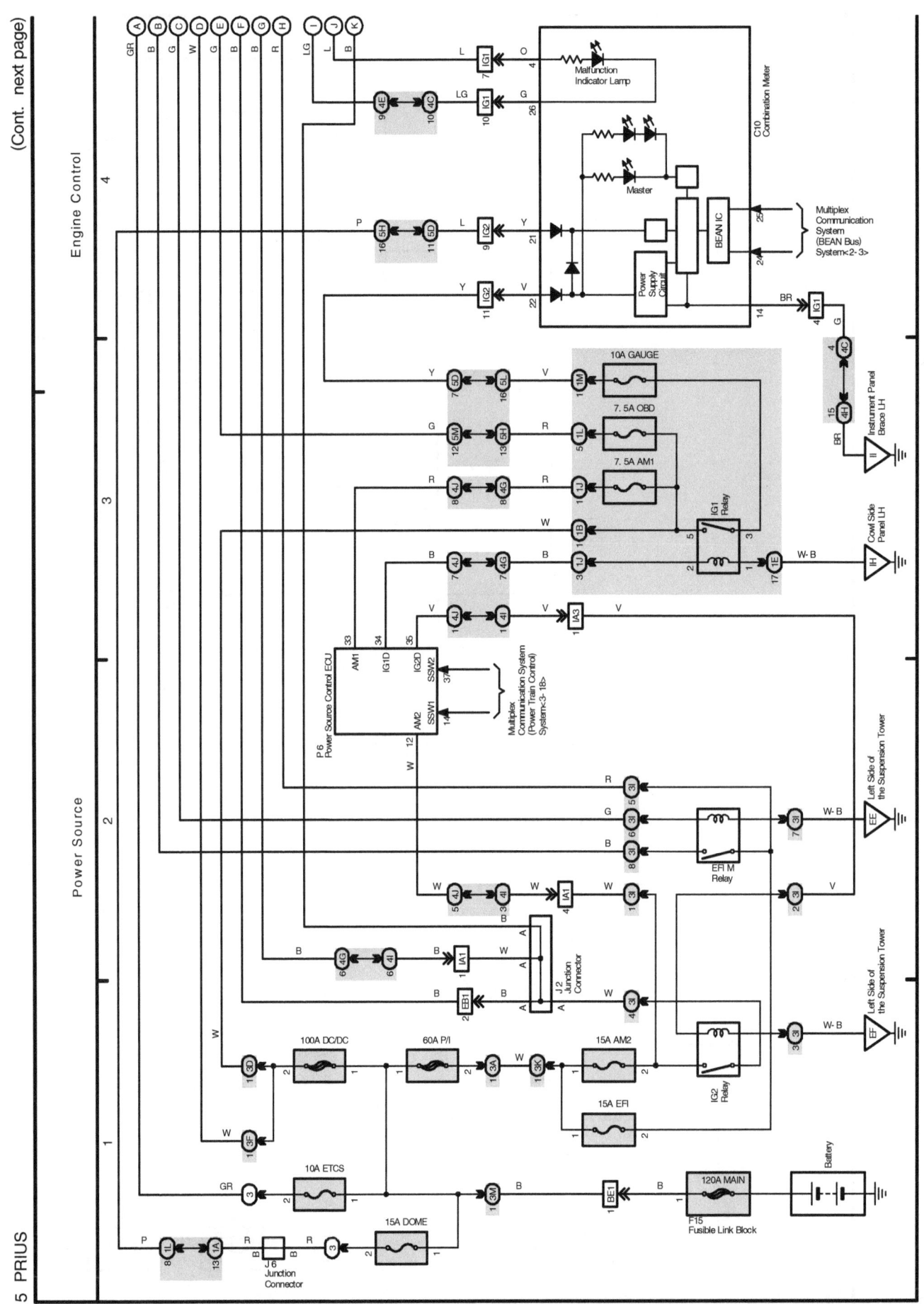

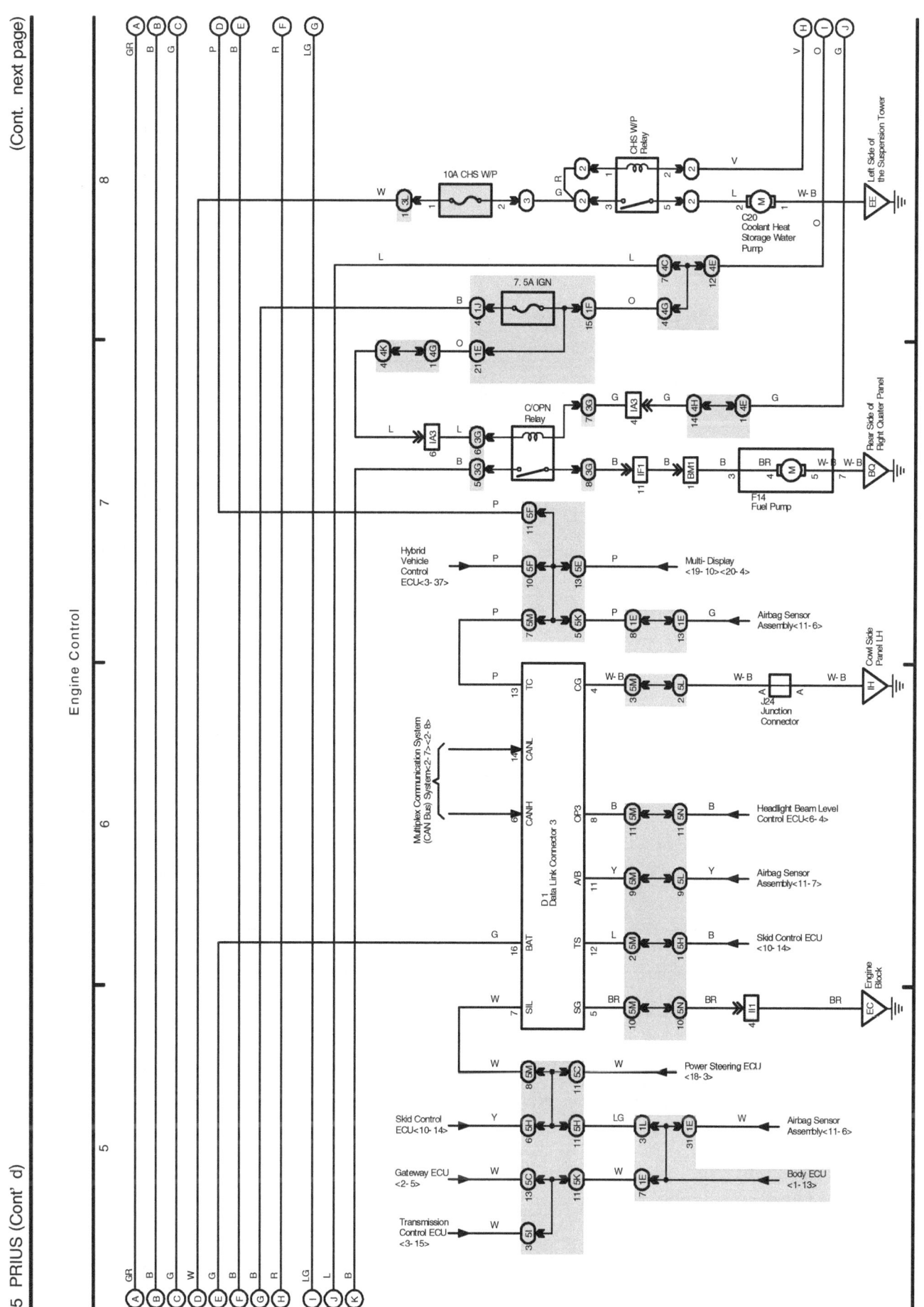

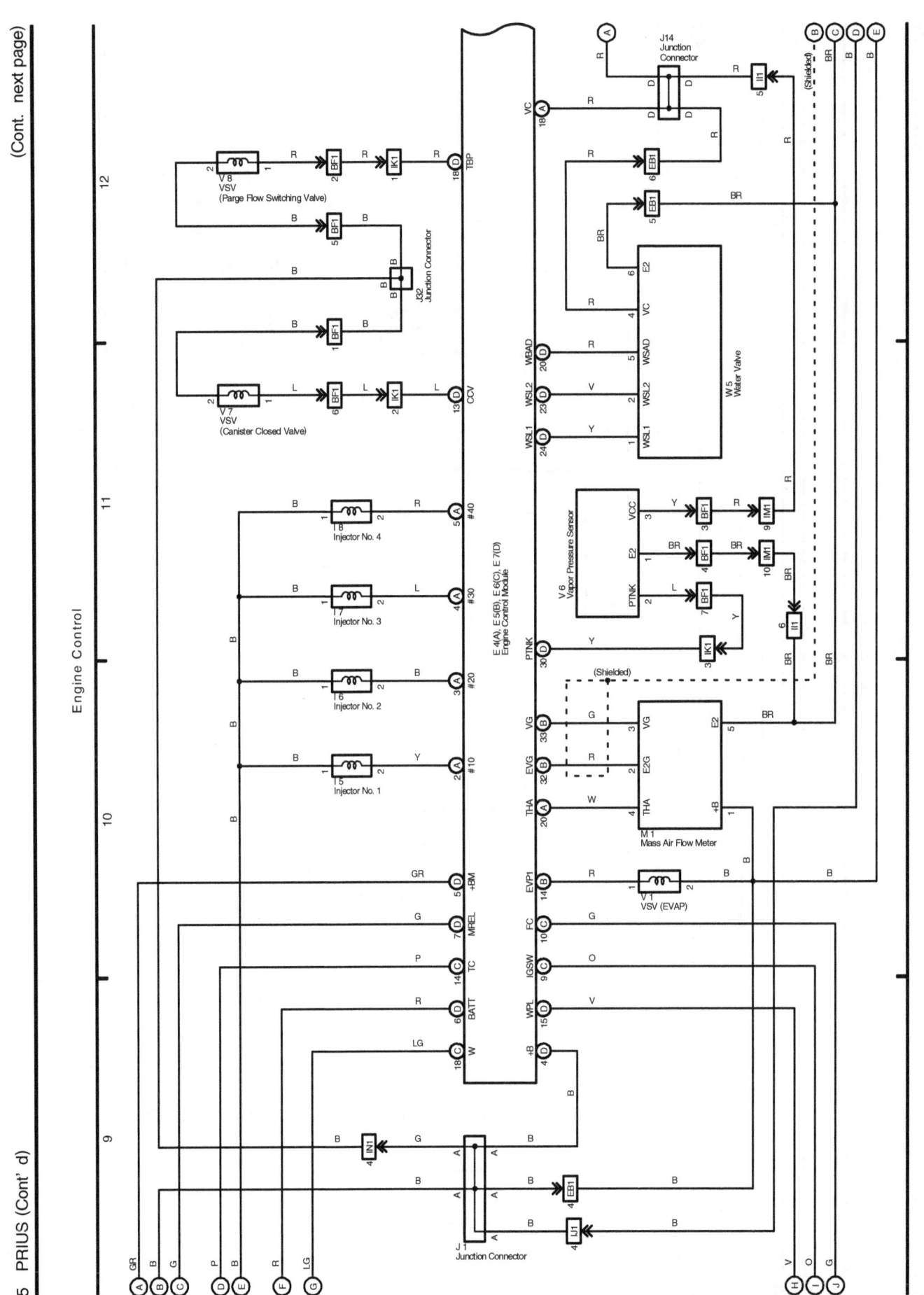

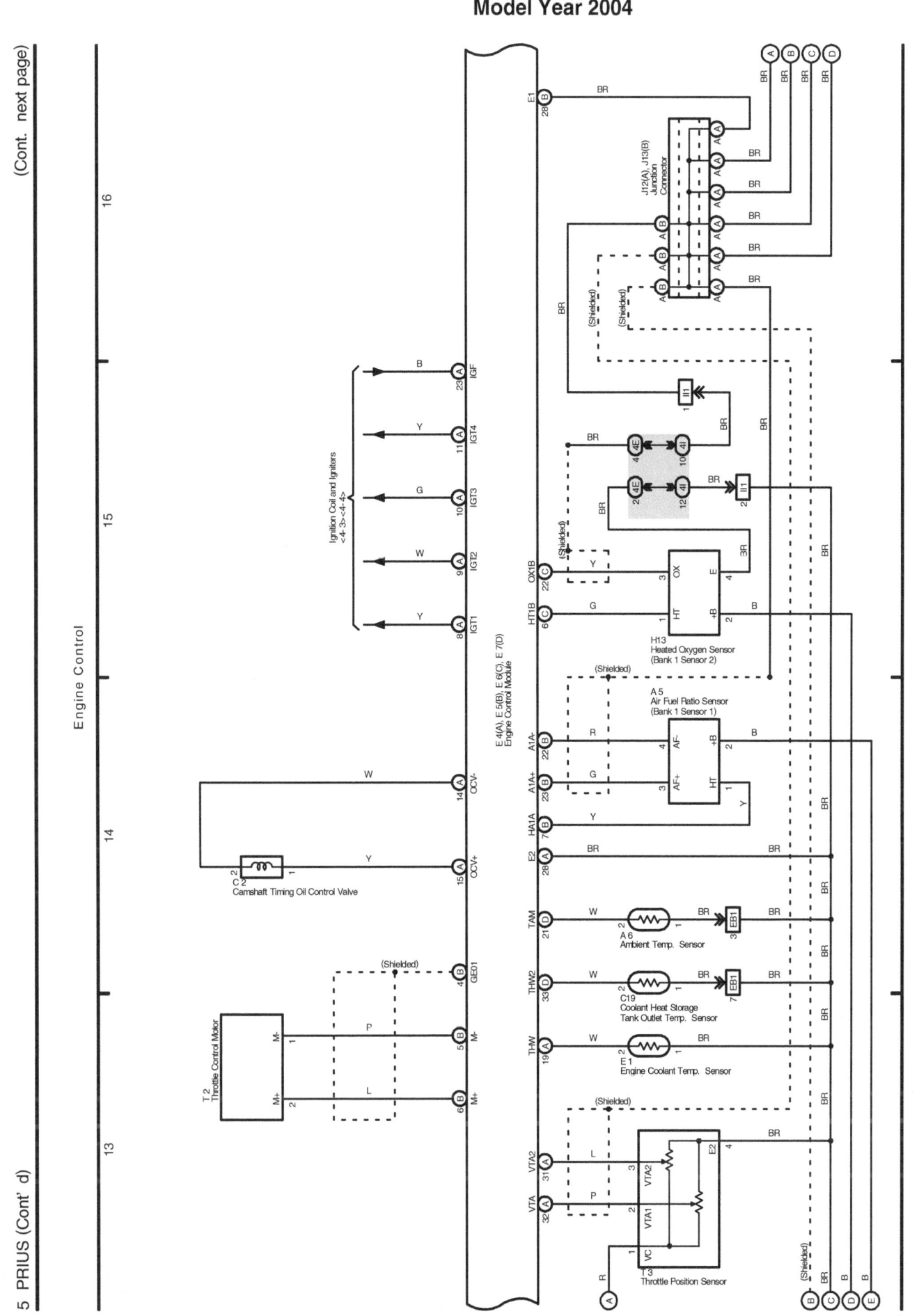

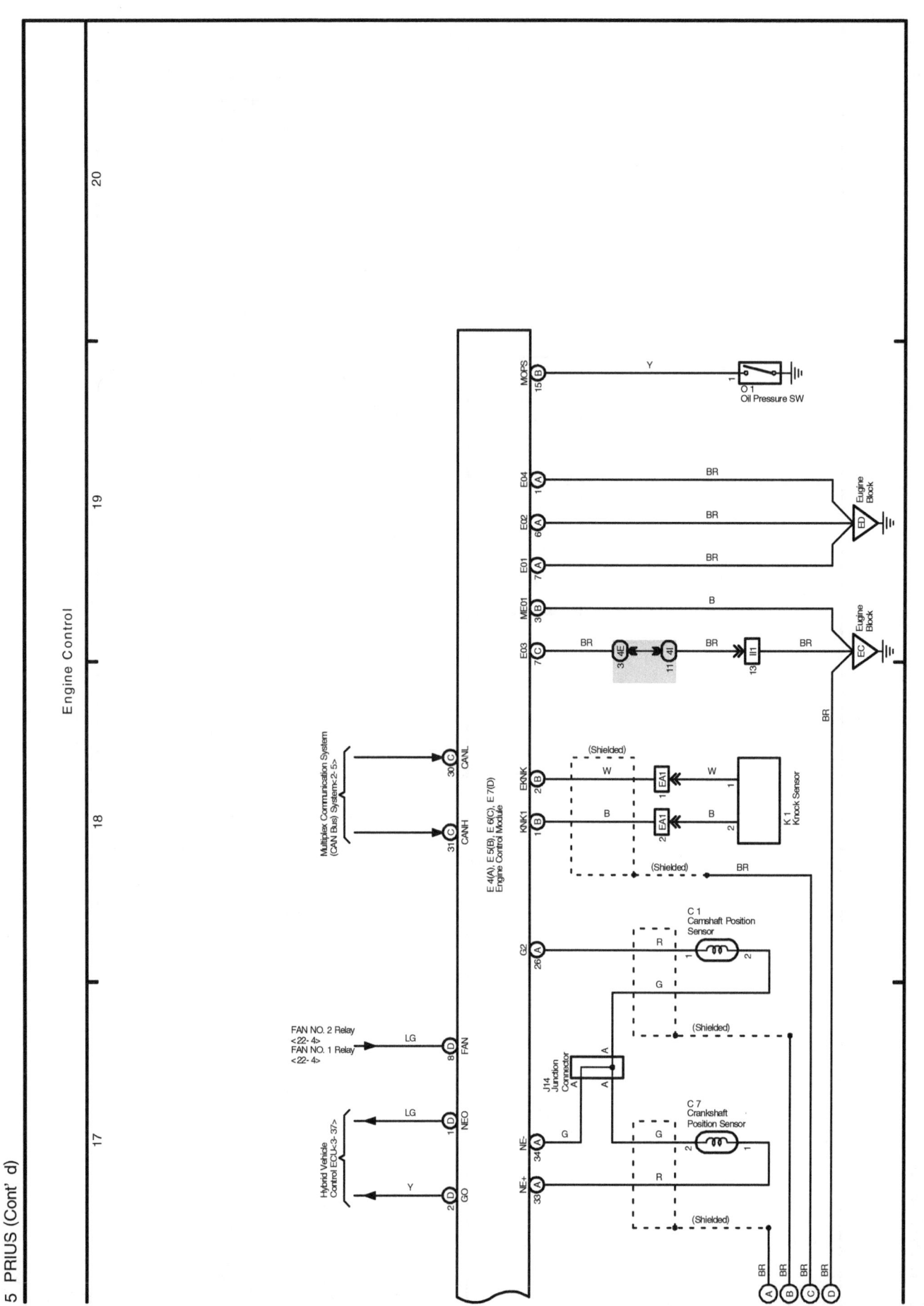

5 PRIUS (Cont' d)

Engine Control

(Cont. next page)

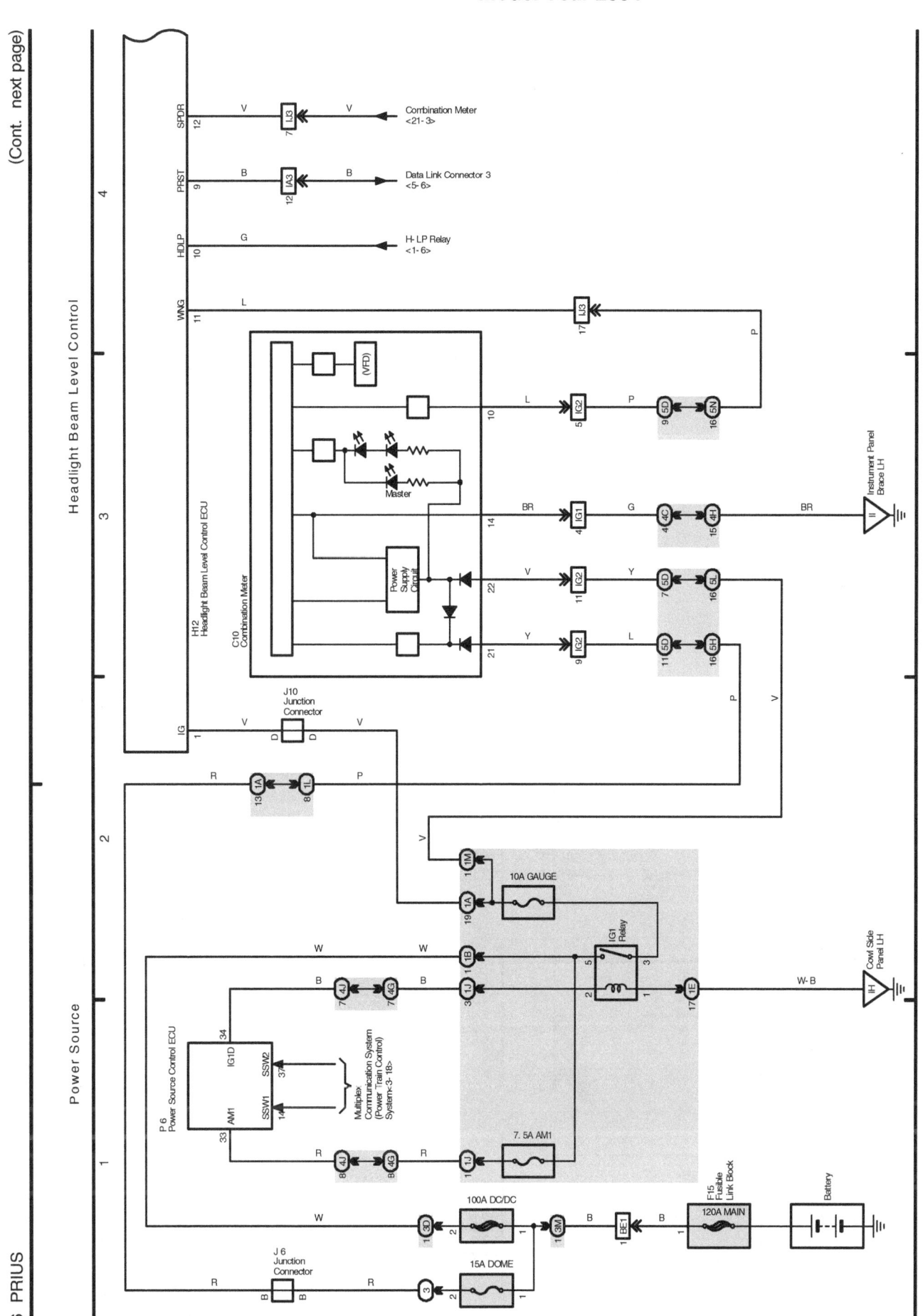

Headlight Beam Level Control

Power Source

6 PRIUS

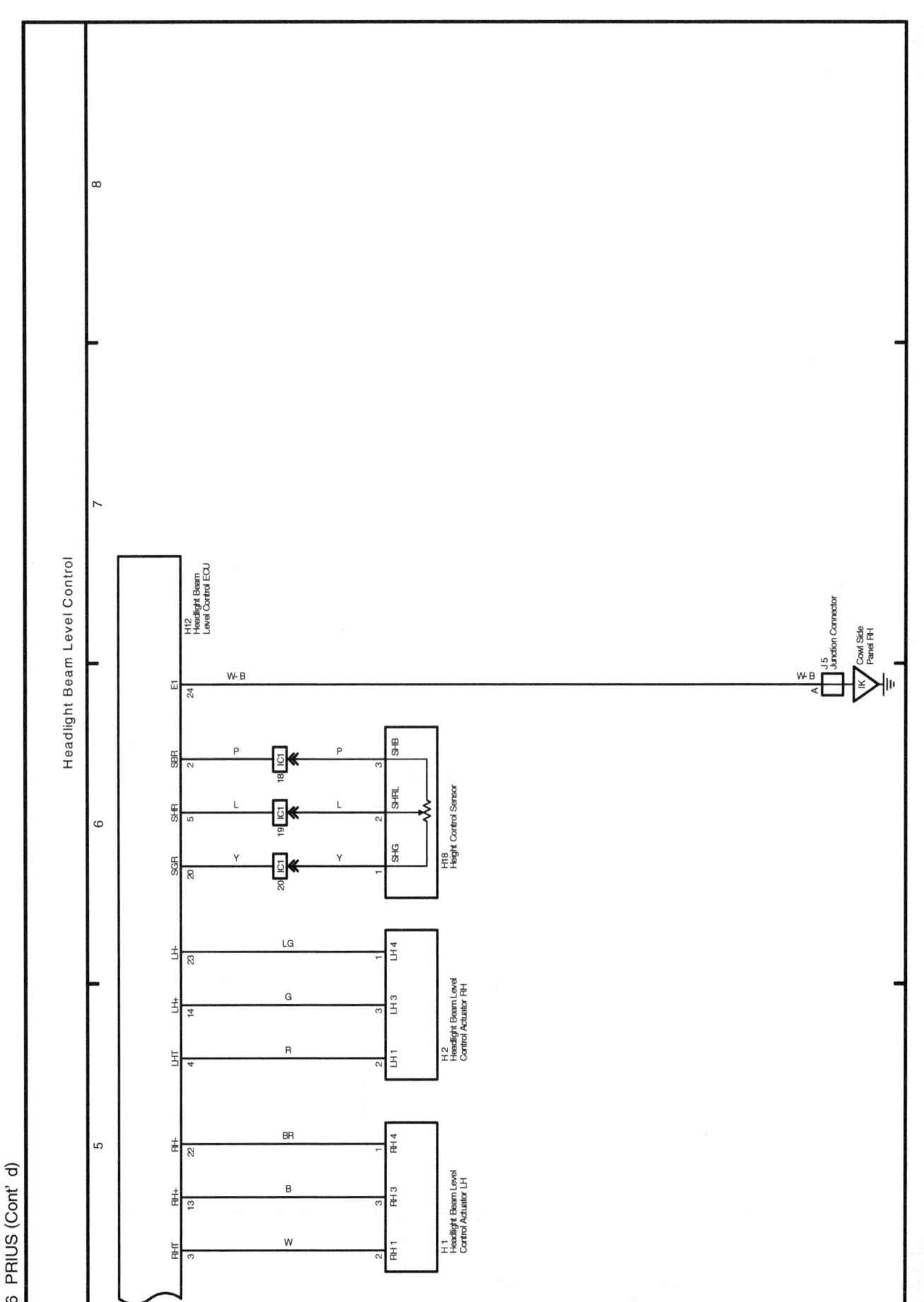

6 PRIUS (Cont' d)

Headlight Beam Level Control

H12
Headlight Beam
Level Control ECU

E1 24 W- B .... W- B A J5 Junction Connector IK Cowl Side Panel RH

SBR 2 P IC1 18 P 3 SHB
SHR 5 L IC1 19 L 2 SHRL H18 Height Control Sensor
SGR 20 Y IC1 20 Y 1 SHG

LH+ 23 LG 1 LH 4
LH+ 14 G 3 LH 3 H 2 Headlight Beam Level Control Actuator RH
LHT 4 R 2 LH 1

RH+ 22 BR 1 RH 4
RH+ 13 B 3 RH 3 H 1 Headlight Beam Level Control Actuator LH
RHT 3 W 2 RH 1

Model Year 2004

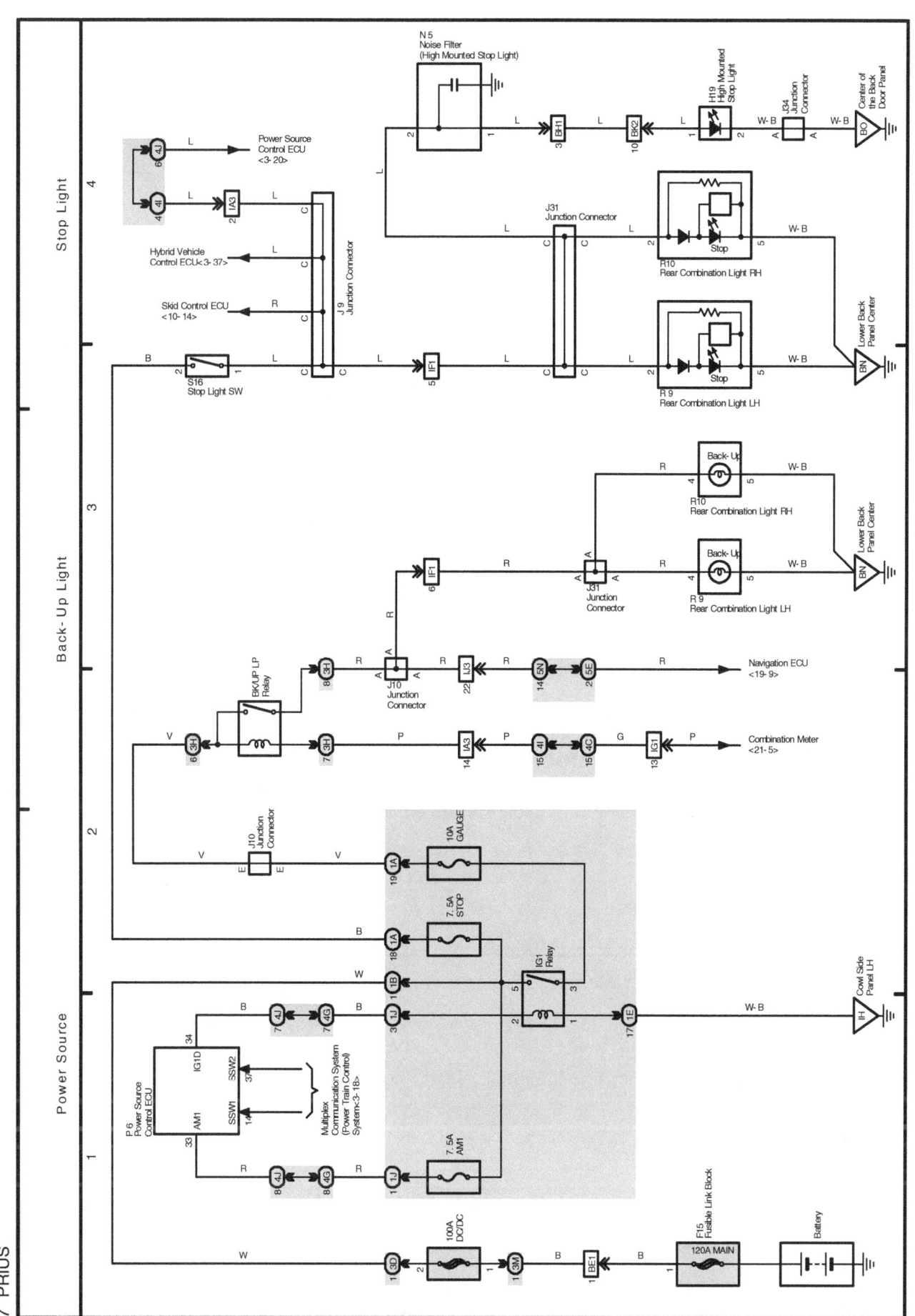

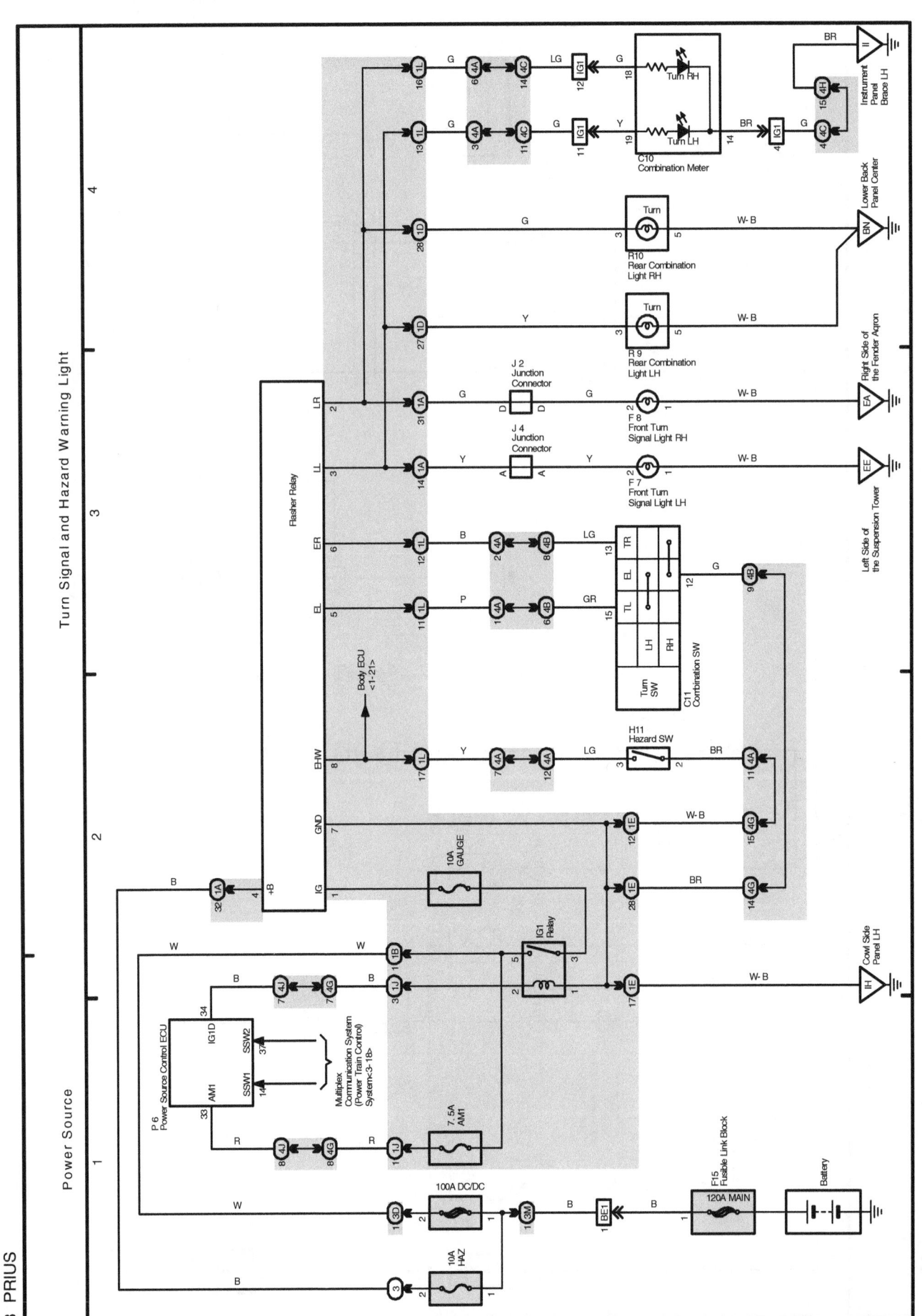

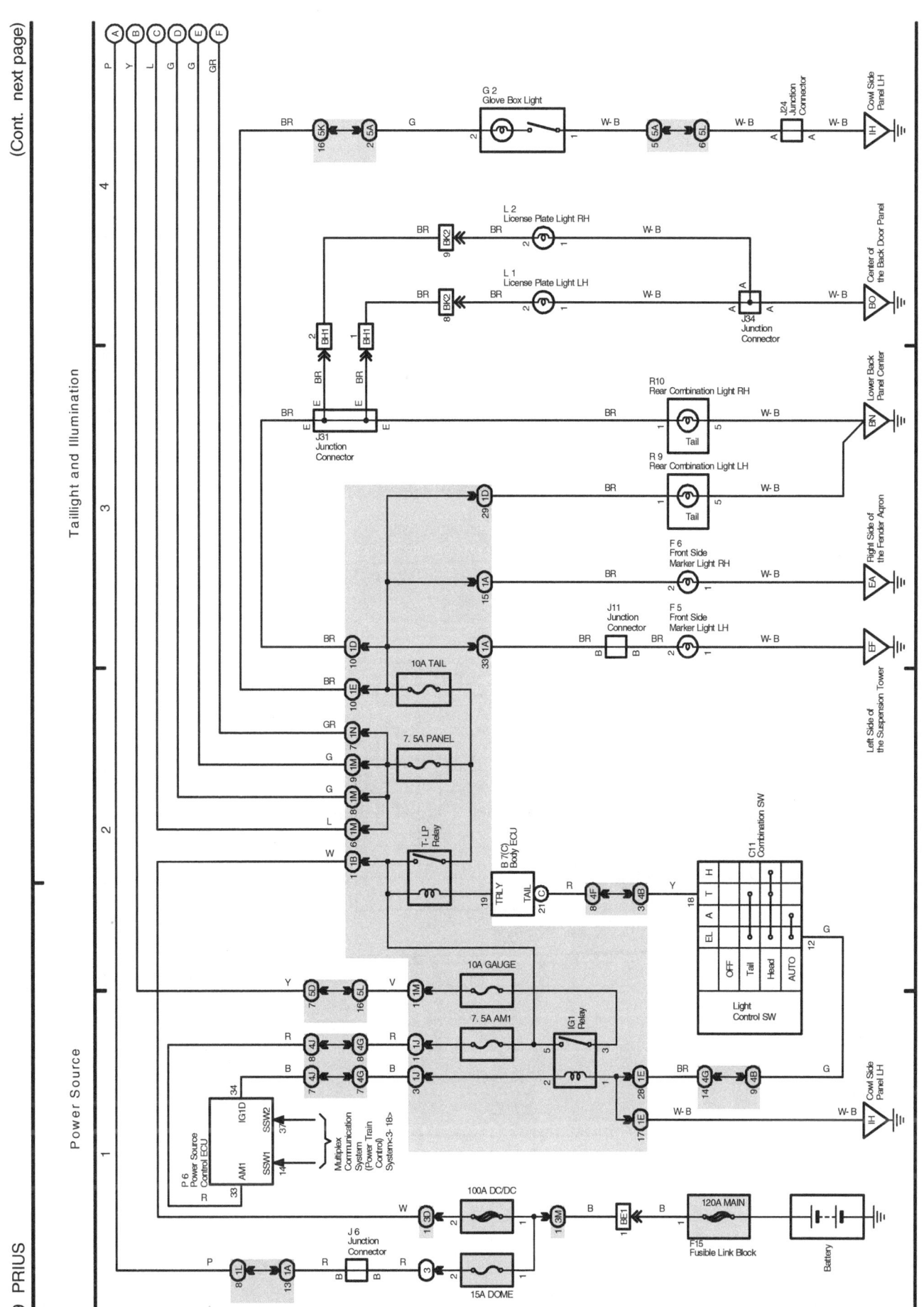

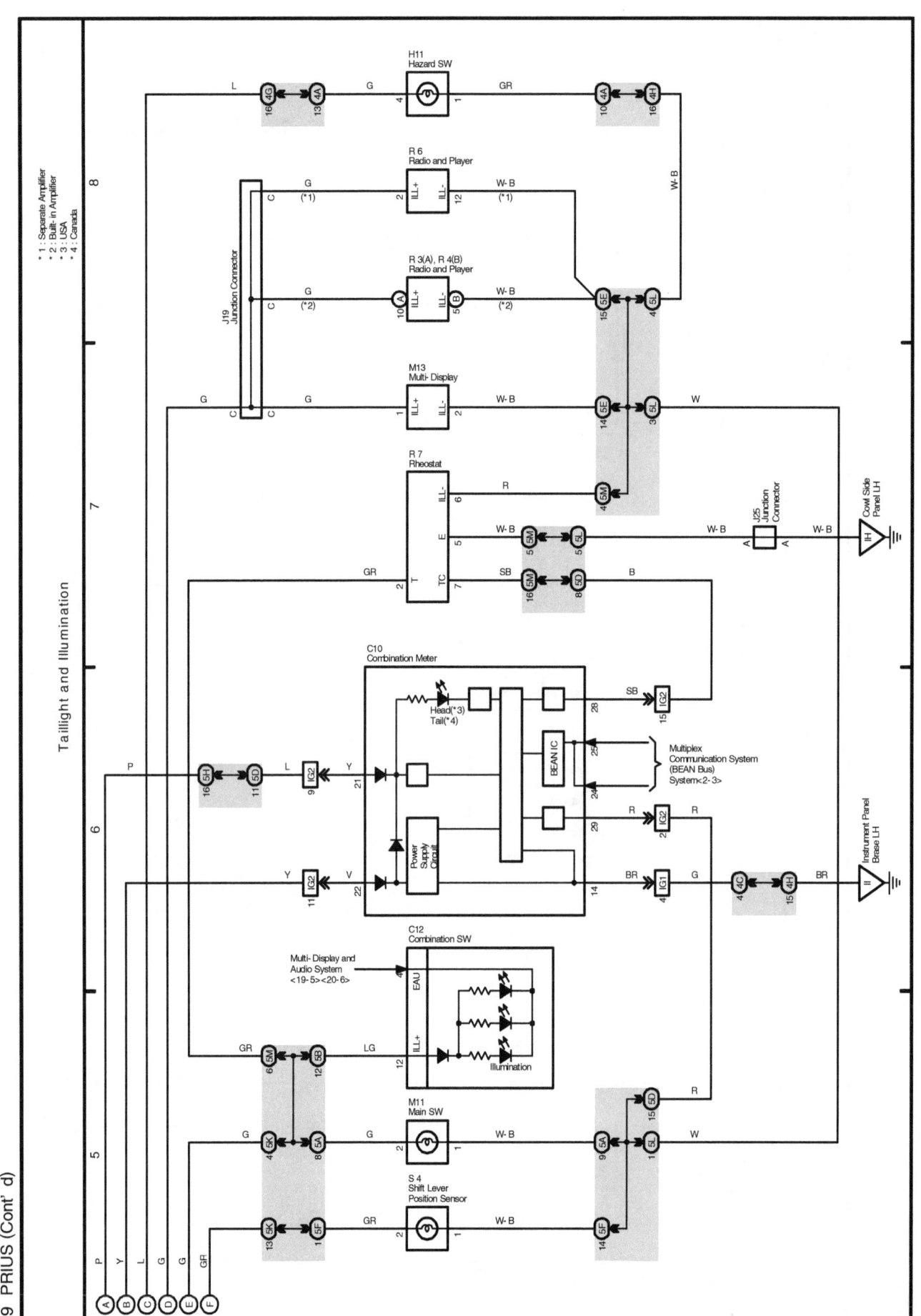

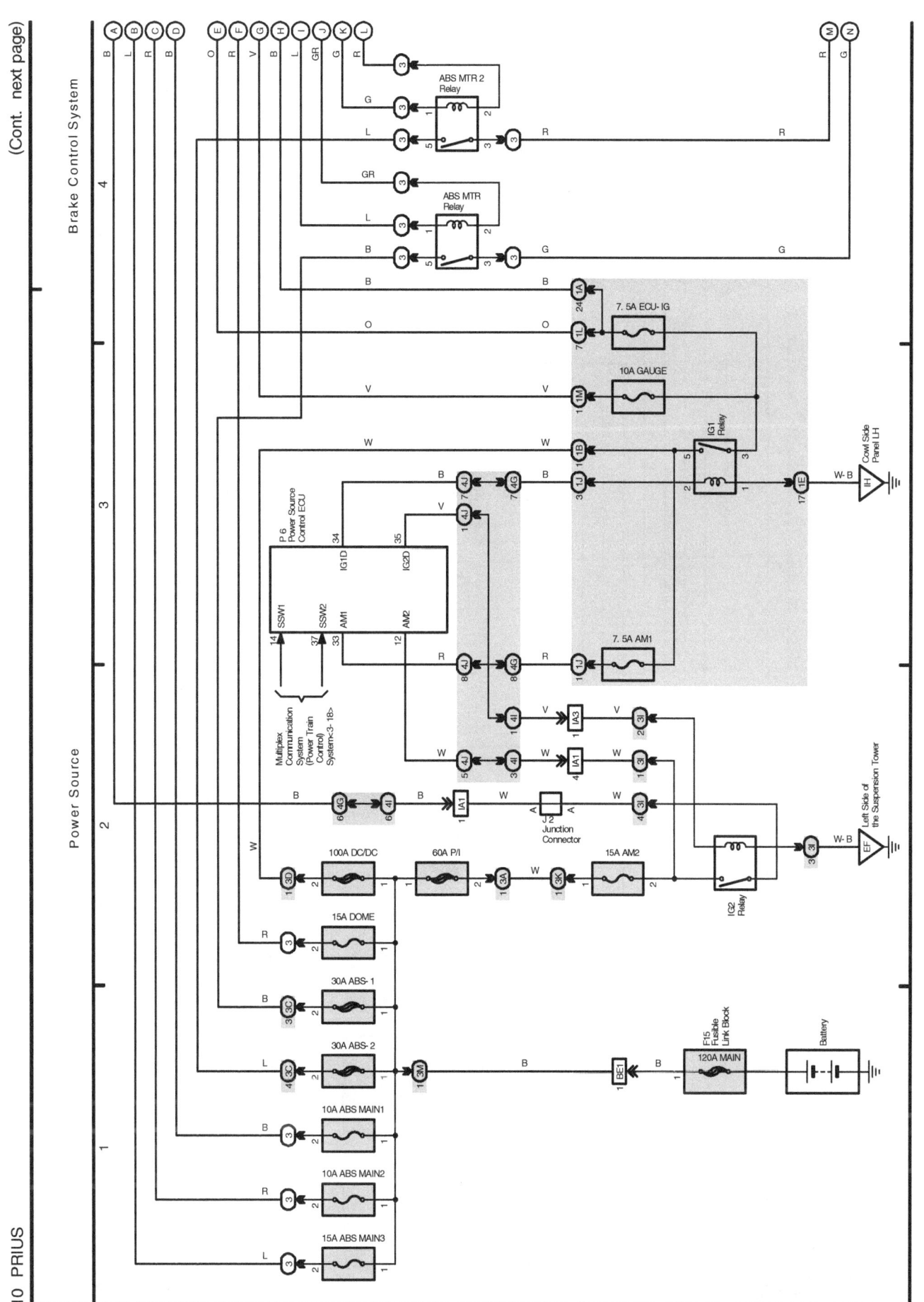

Model Year 2004

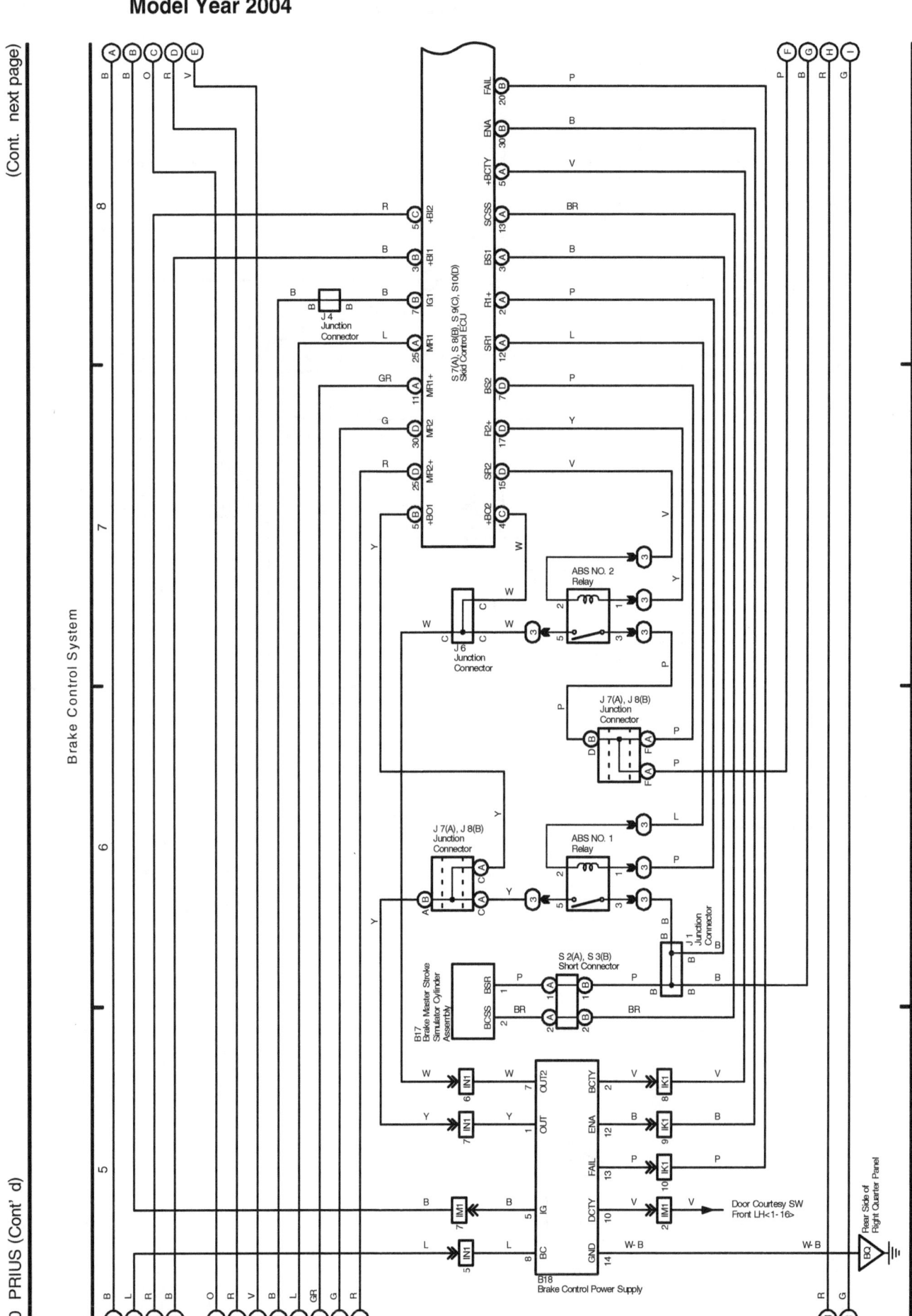

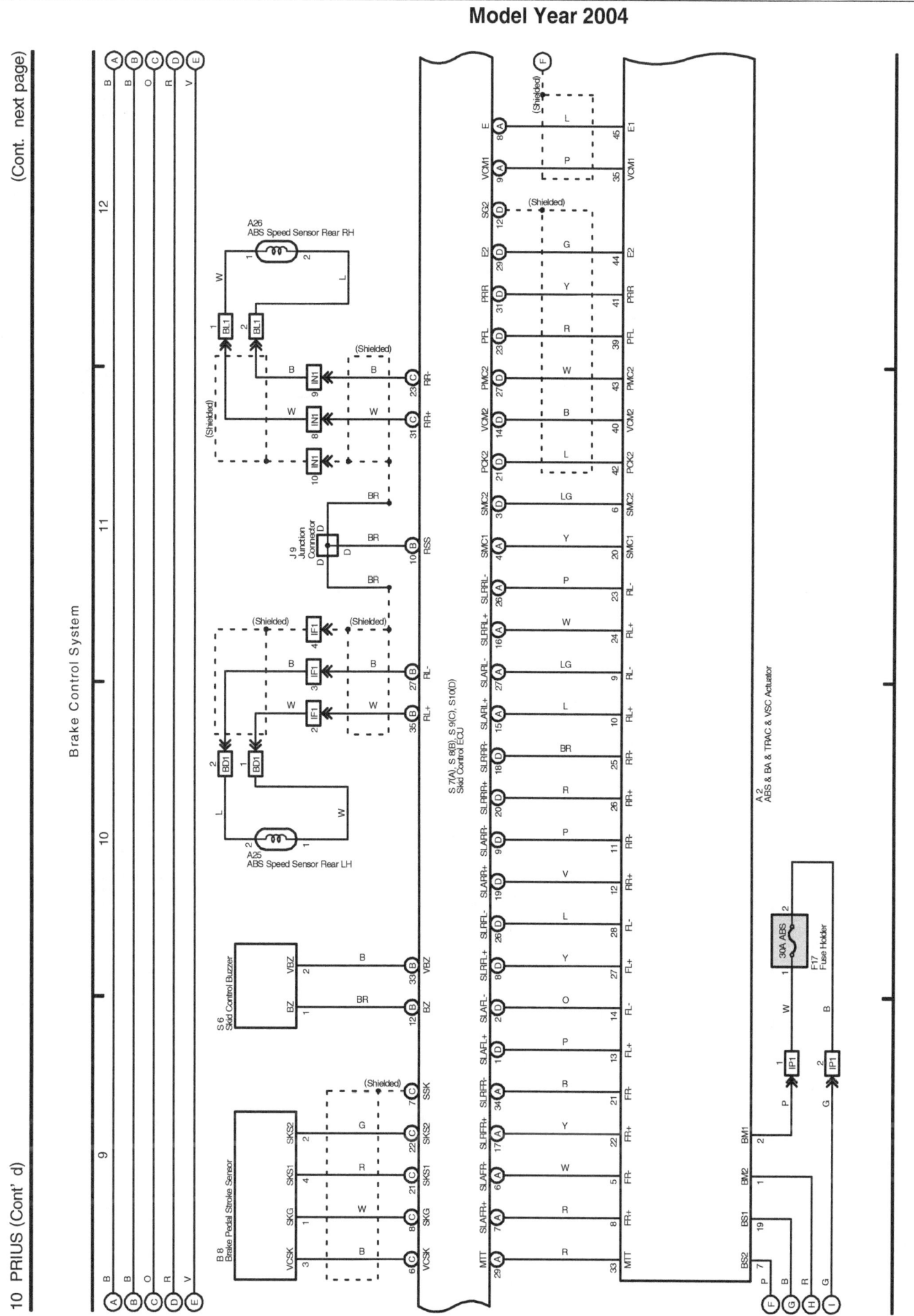

Brake Control System

(Cont. next page)

10 PRIUS (Cont' d)

S 7(A), S 8(B), S 9(C), S10(D)
Skid Control ECU

A 2
ABS & BA & TRAC & VSC Actuator

A26
ABS Speed Sensor Rear RH

A25
ABS Speed Sensor Rear LH

J 9
Junction Connector

S6
Skid Control Buzzer

B 8
Brake Pedal Stroke Sensor

F17
Fuse Holder

30A ABS

Model Year 2004

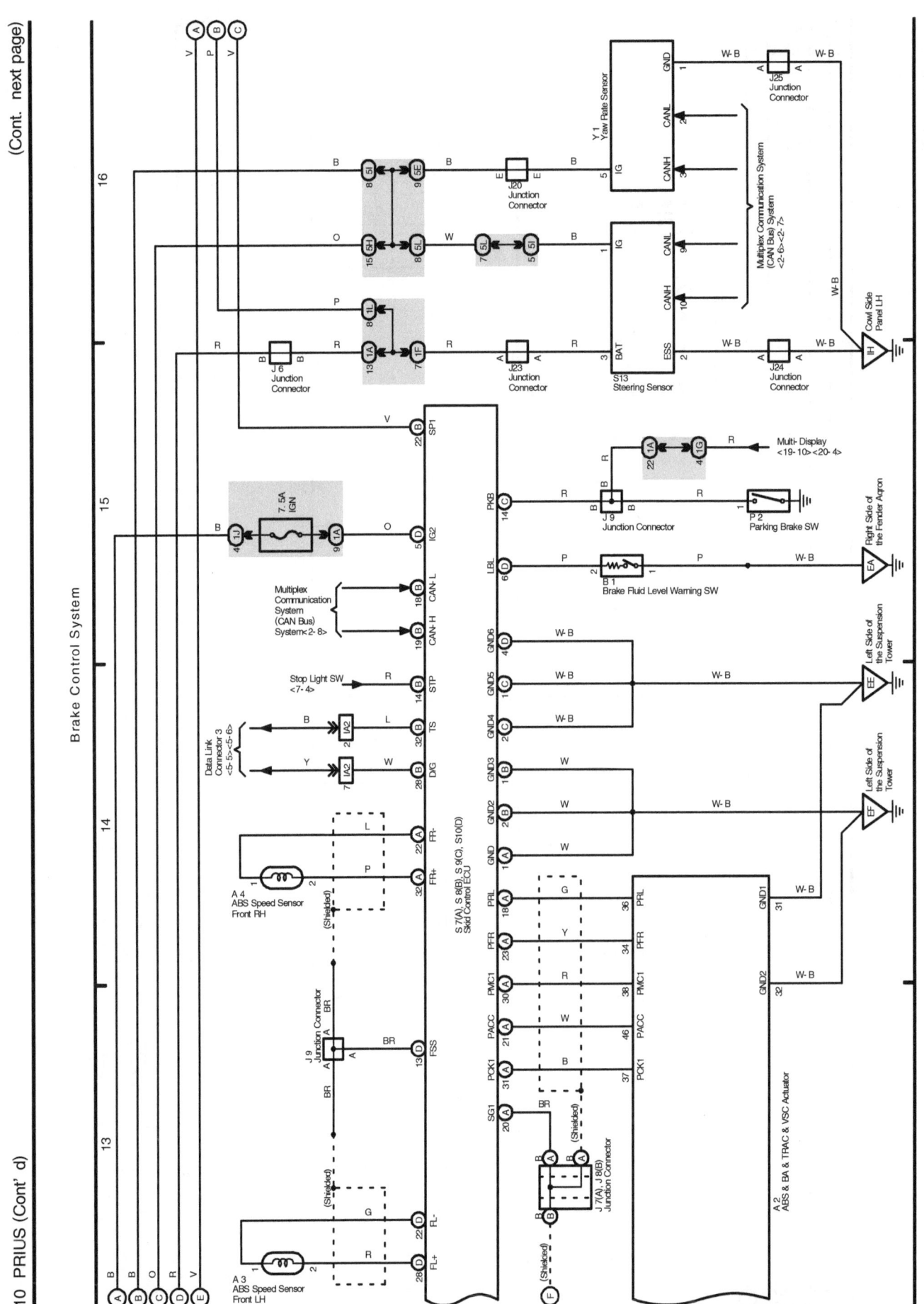

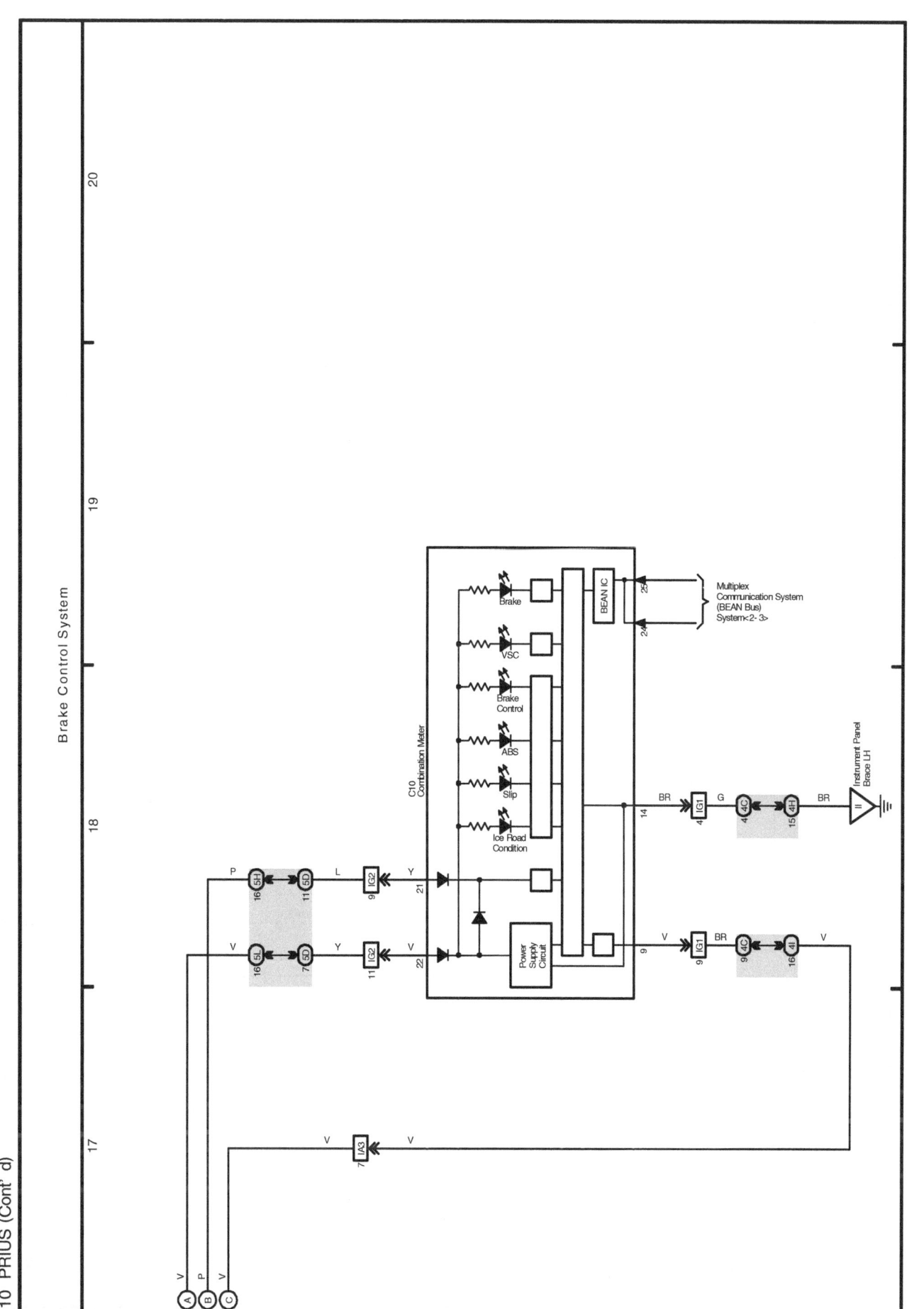

10 PRIUS (Cont' d)

Brake Control System

Model Year 2004

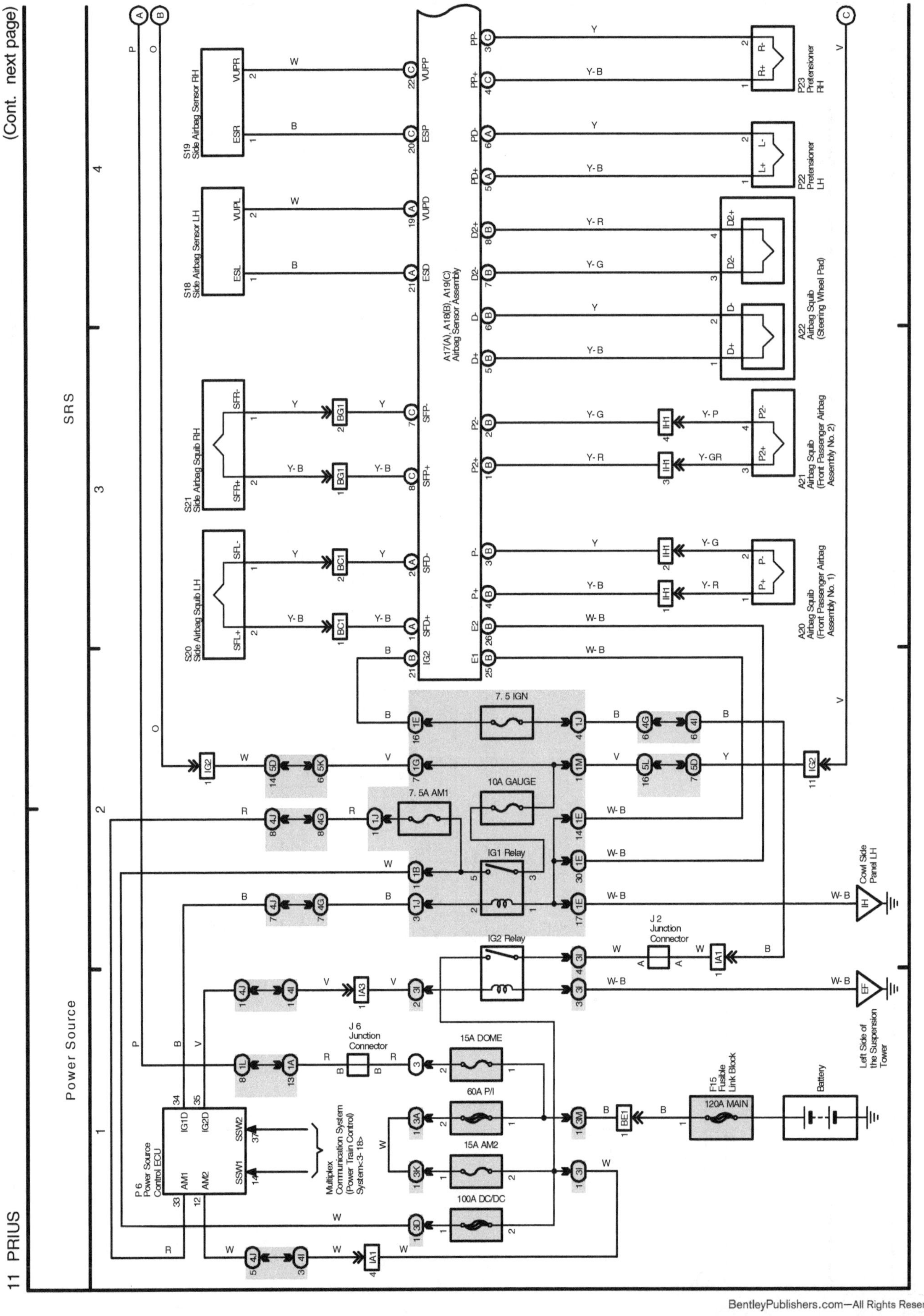

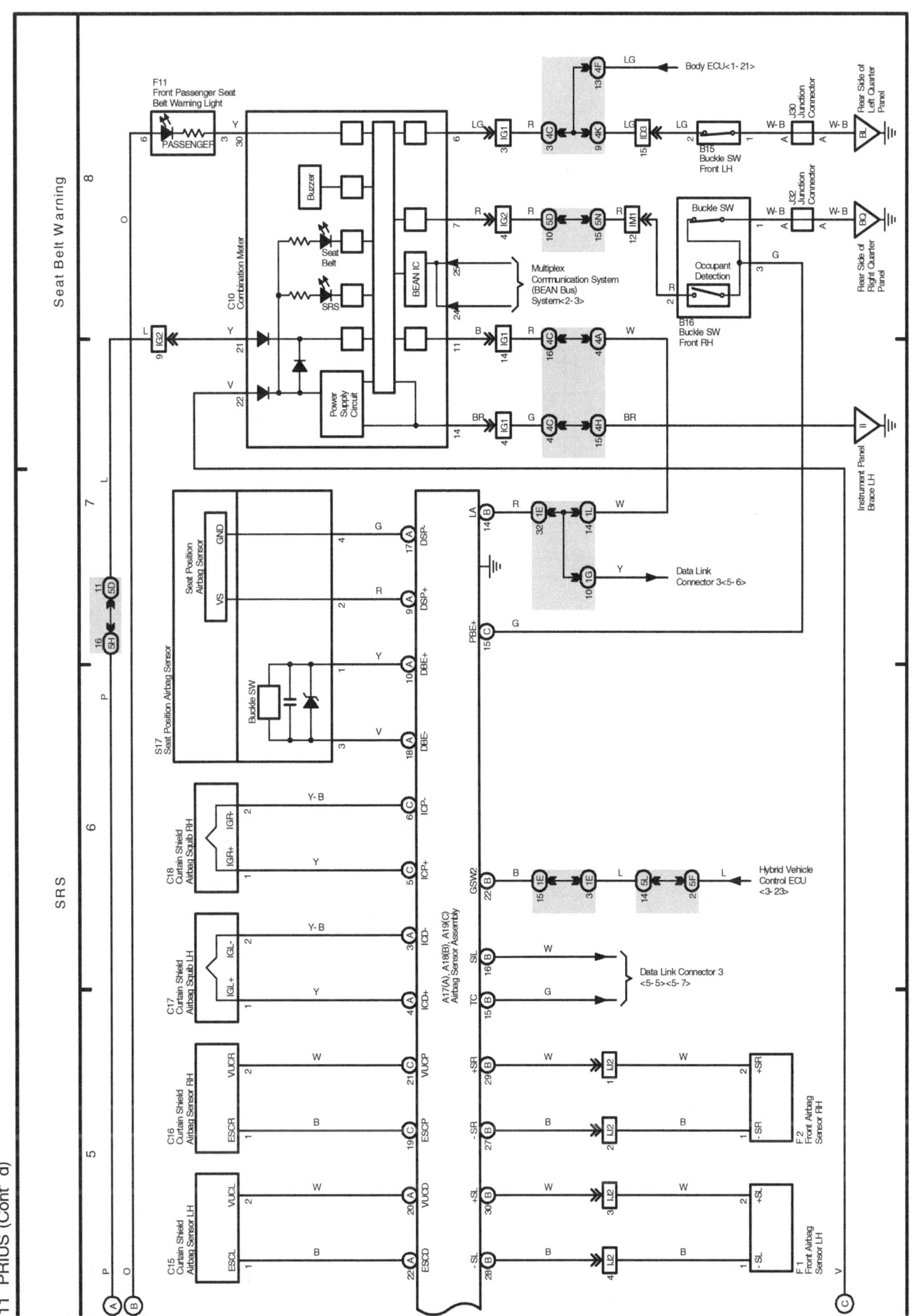

Model Year 2004

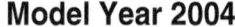

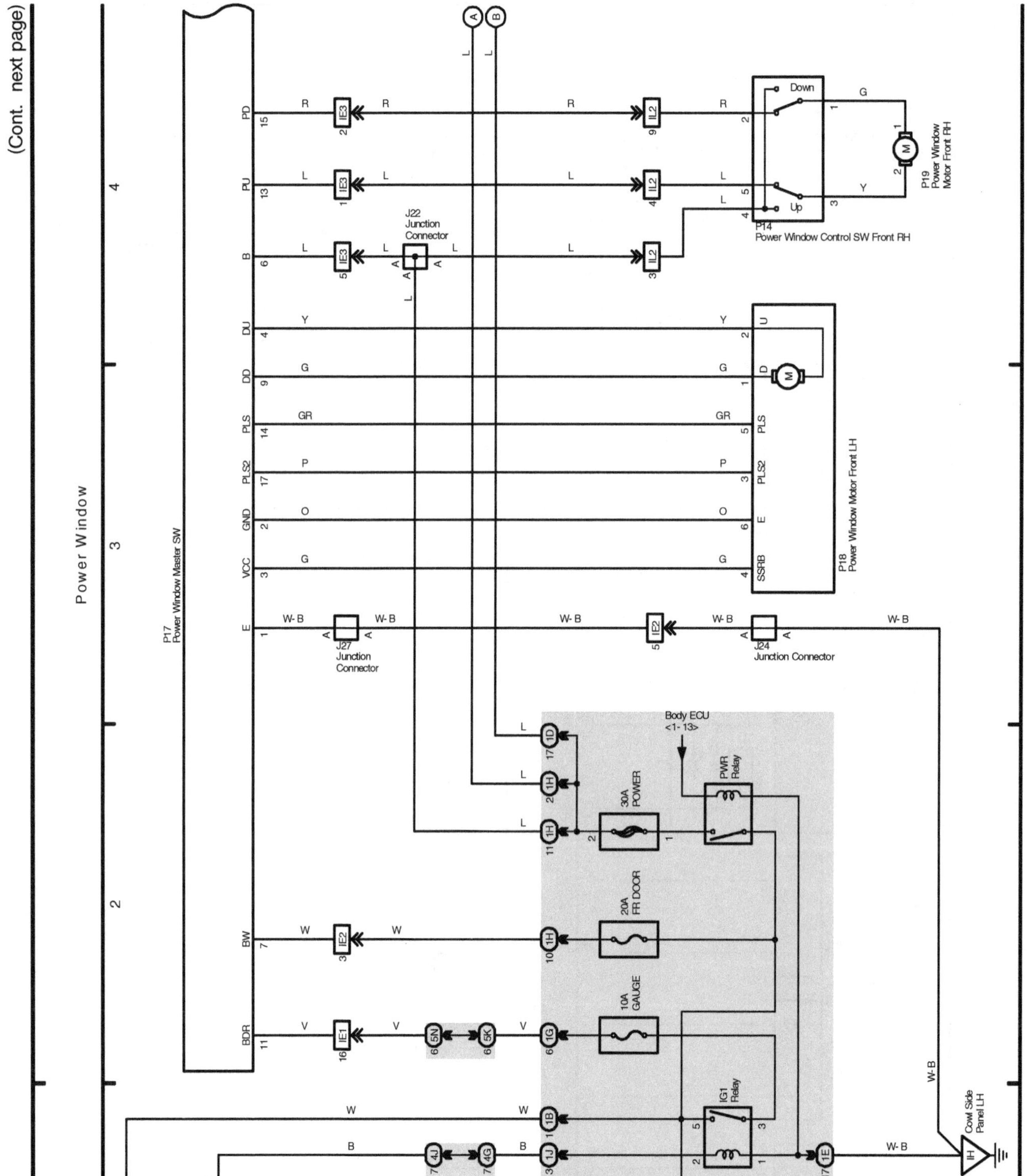
(Cont. next page)
12 PRIUS
Power Window
Power Source
P17 Power Window Master SW
PD
PU
B
DU
DD
PLS
PLS2
GND
VCC
E
BW
BDR
J22 Junction Connector
J27 Junction Connector
J24 Junction Connector
P14 Power Window Control SW Front RH
Down
Up
P19 Power Window Motor Front RH
P18 Power Window Motor Front LH
SSRB
Body ECU <1- 13>
PWR Relay
30A POWER
20A FR DOOR
10A GAUGE
IG1 Relay
7. 5A AM1
Cowl Side Panel LH
P 6 Power Source Control ECU
IG1D
AM1
SSW1
SSW2
Multiplex Communication System (Power Train Control) System<3- 18>
100A DC/DC
F15 Fusible Link Block
120A MAIN
Battery

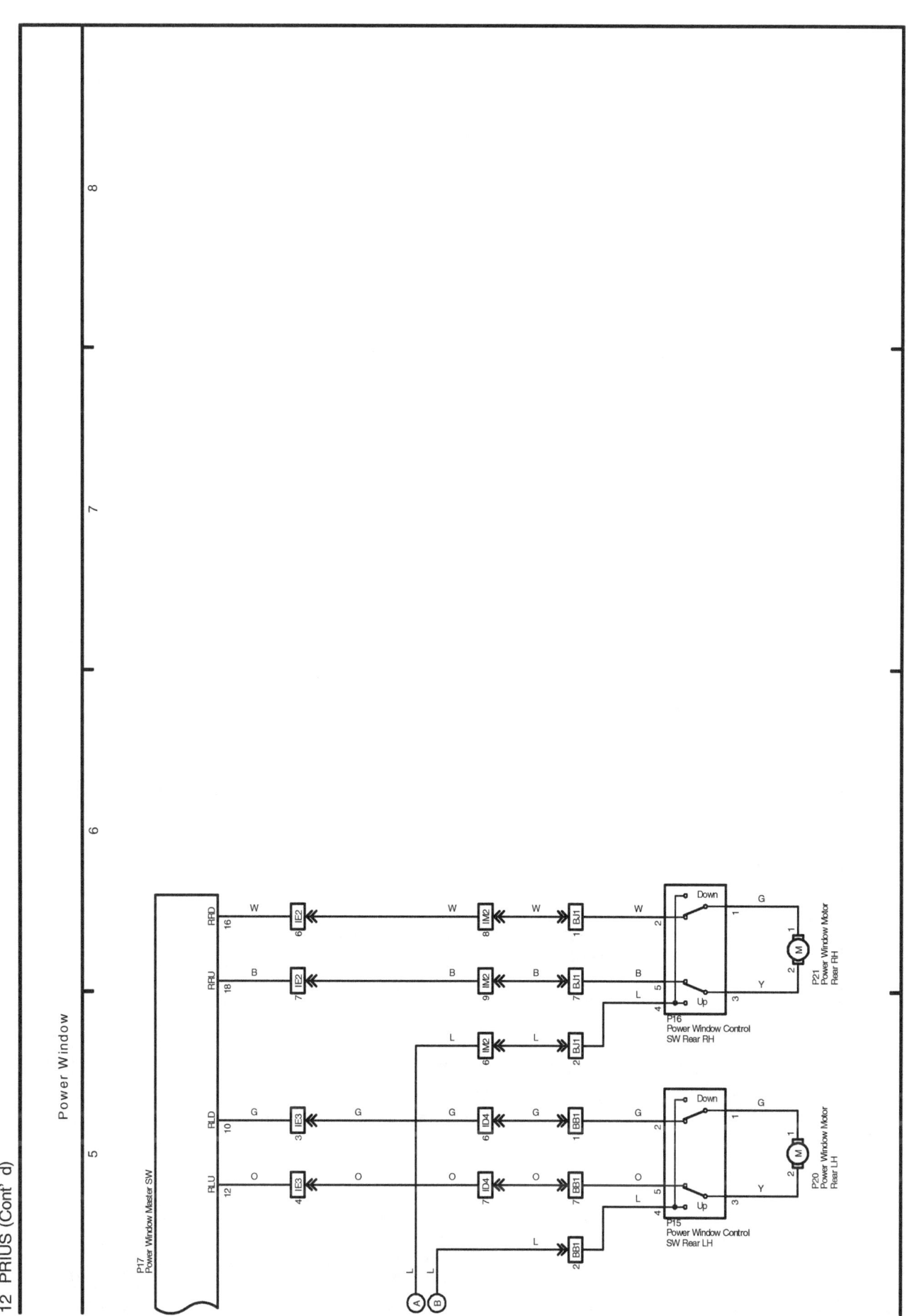

12 PRIUS (Cont' d)

Power Window

P17 Power Window Master SW

RRD 16	W	
RRU 18	B	
RLD 10	G	
RLU 12	O	

P16 Power Window Control SW Rear RH

P21 Power Window Motor Rear RH

P15 Power Window Control SW Rear LH

P20 Power Window Motor Rear LH

13

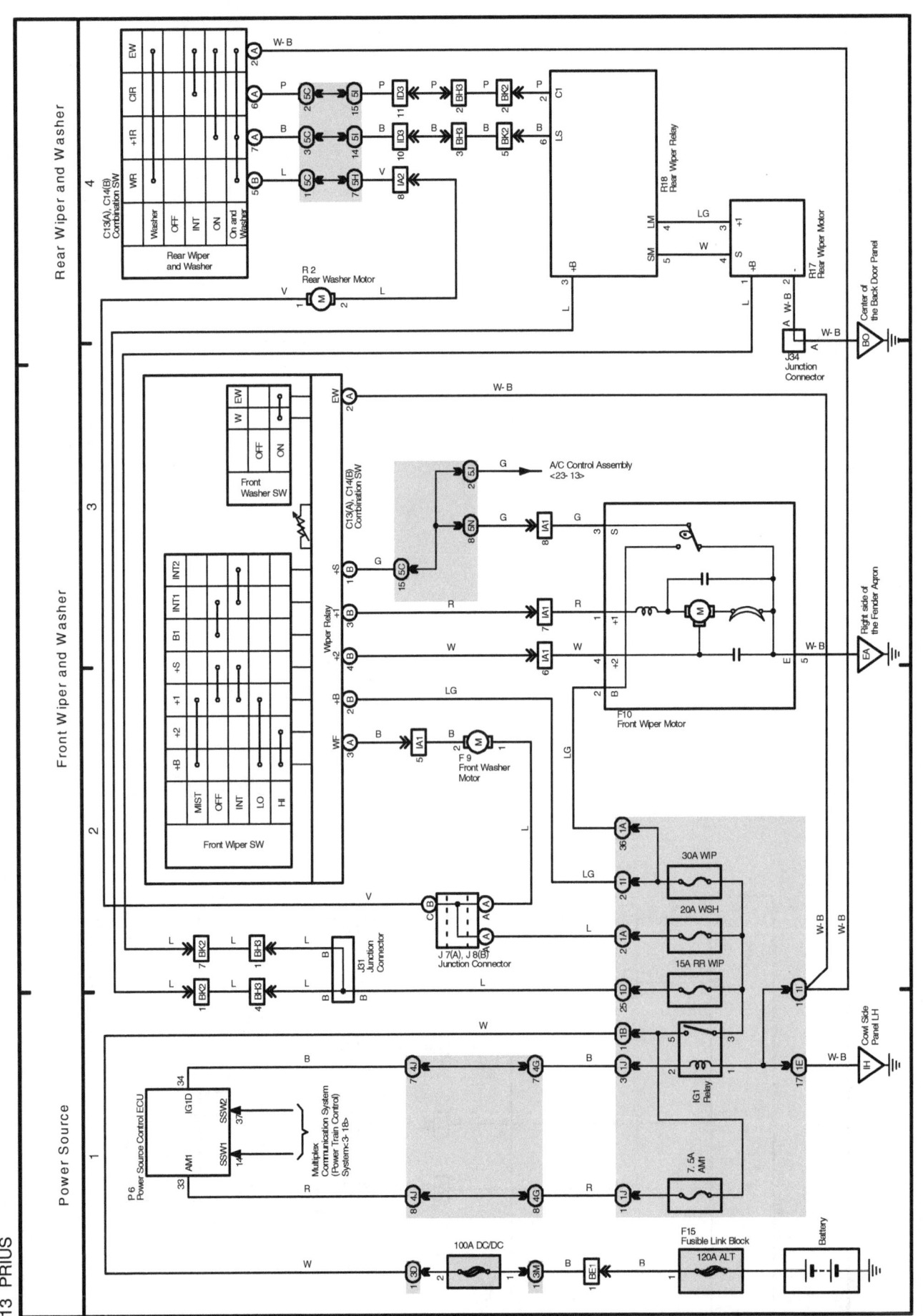

Model Year 2004

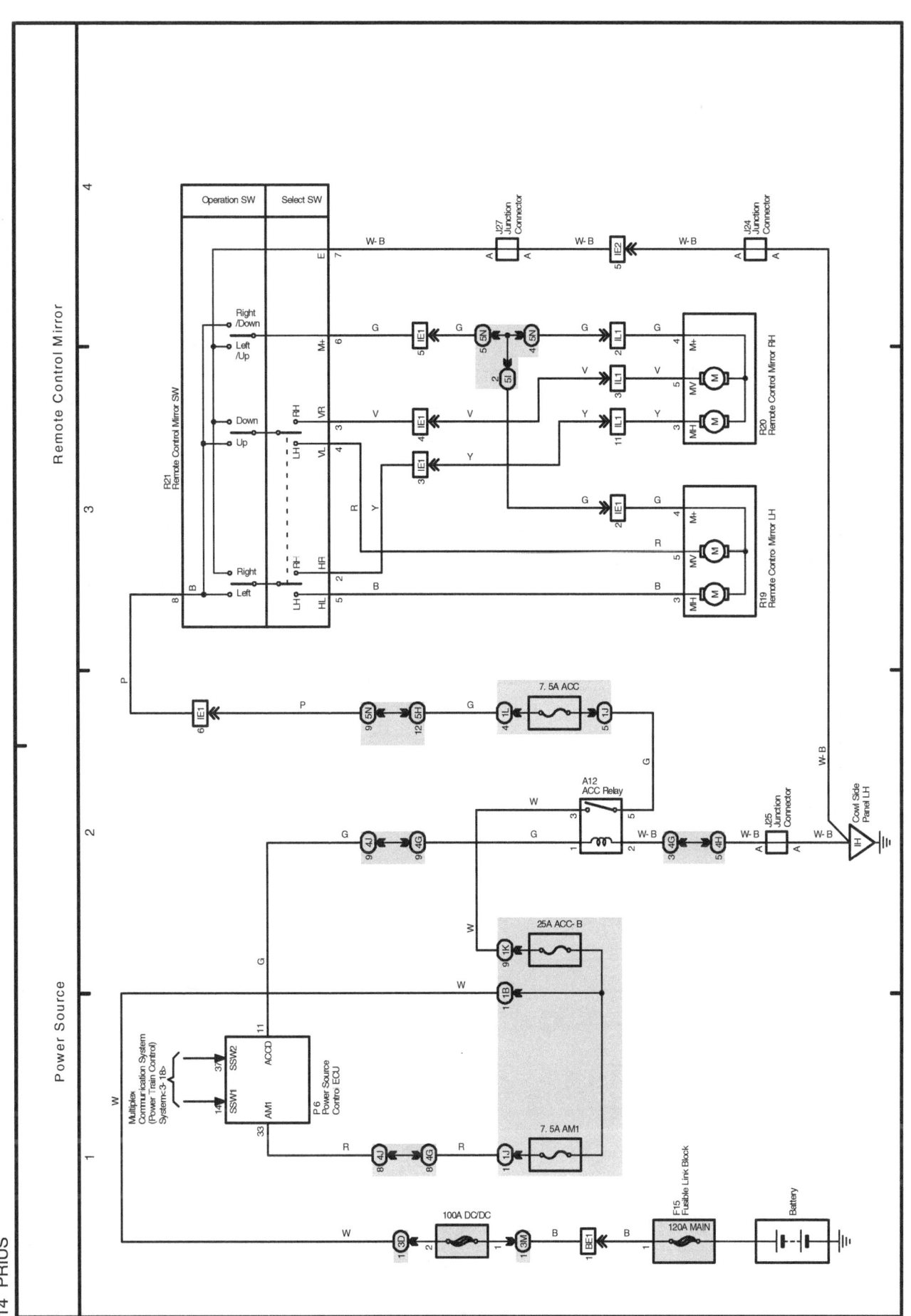

13

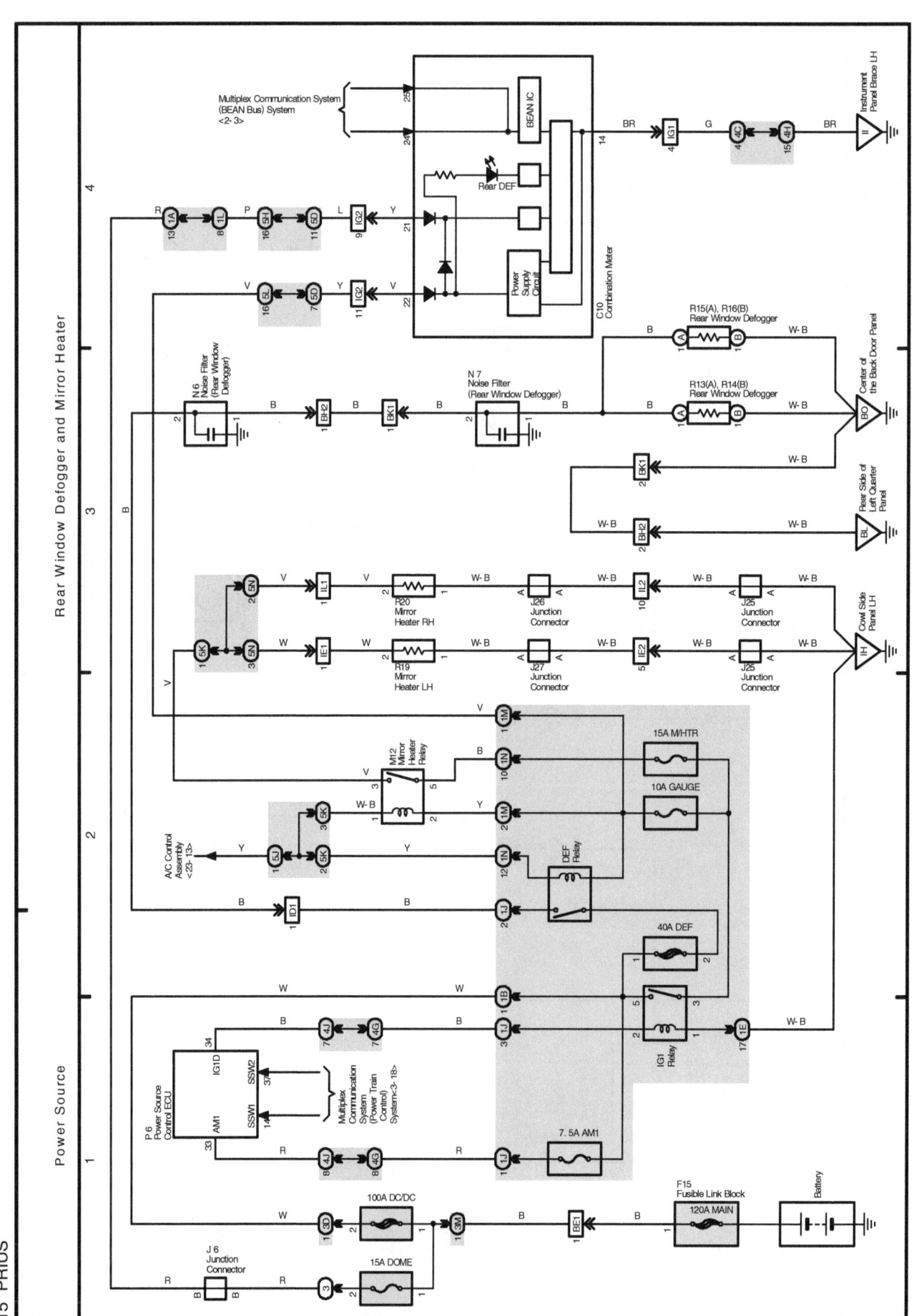

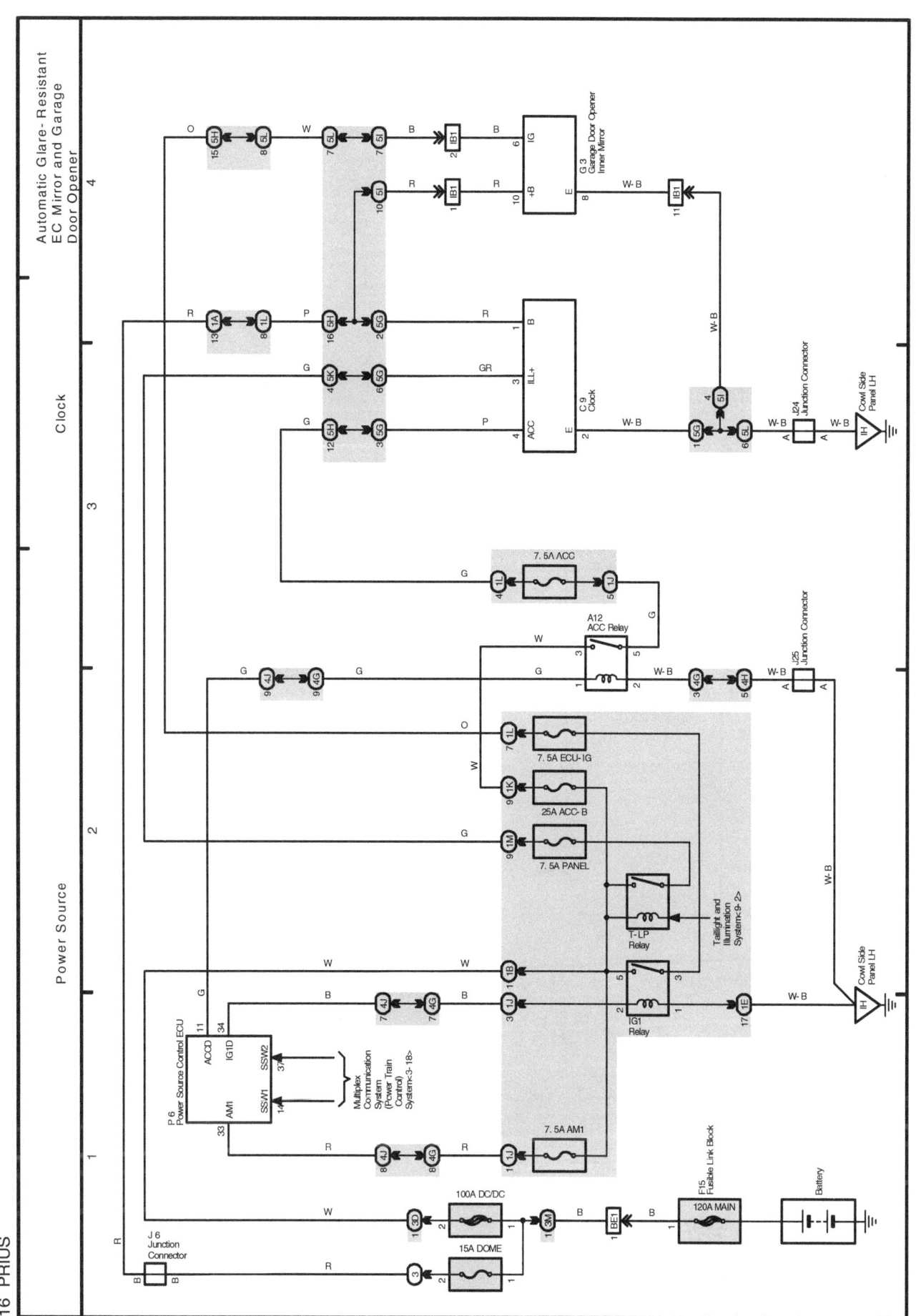

Model Year 2004

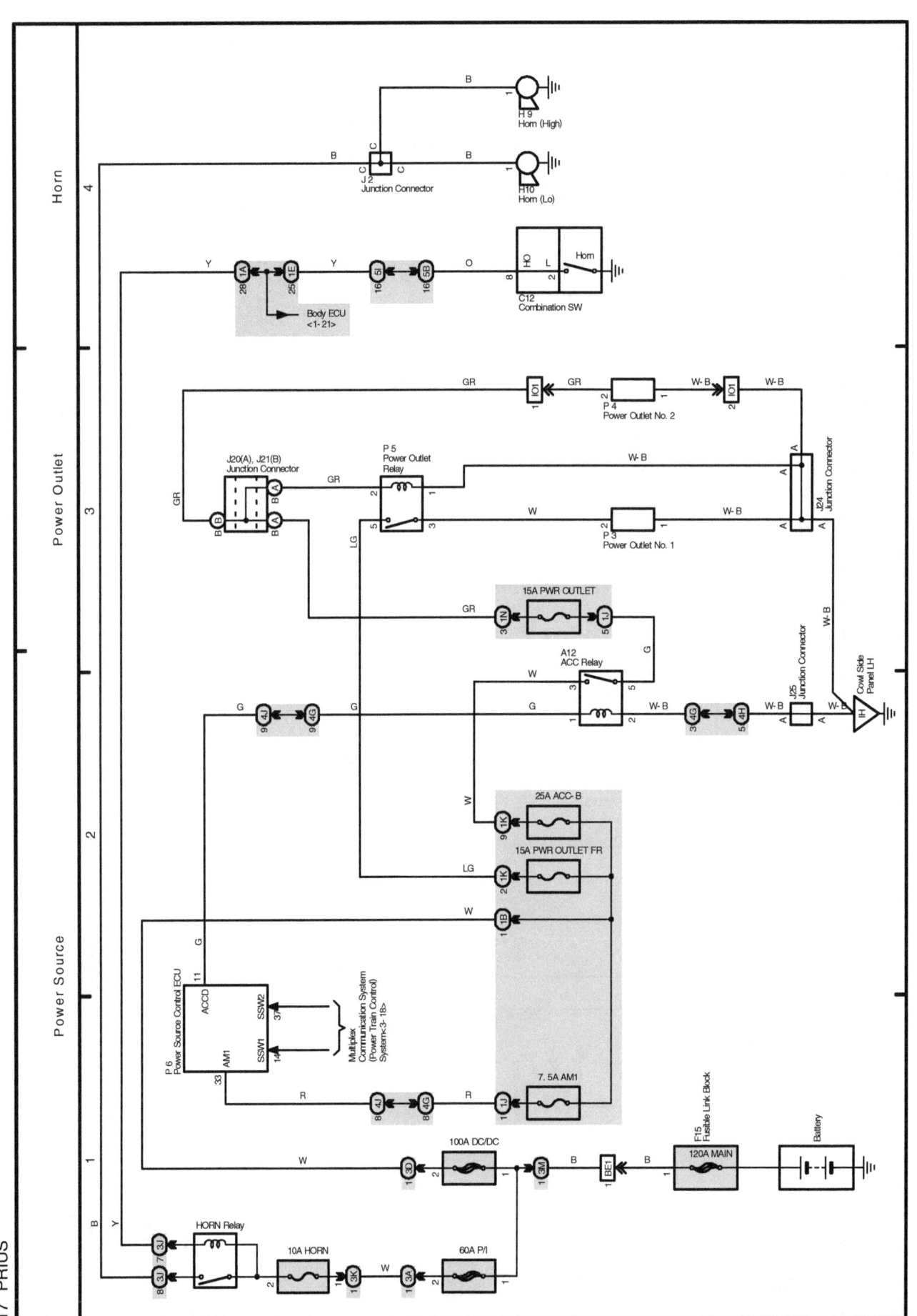

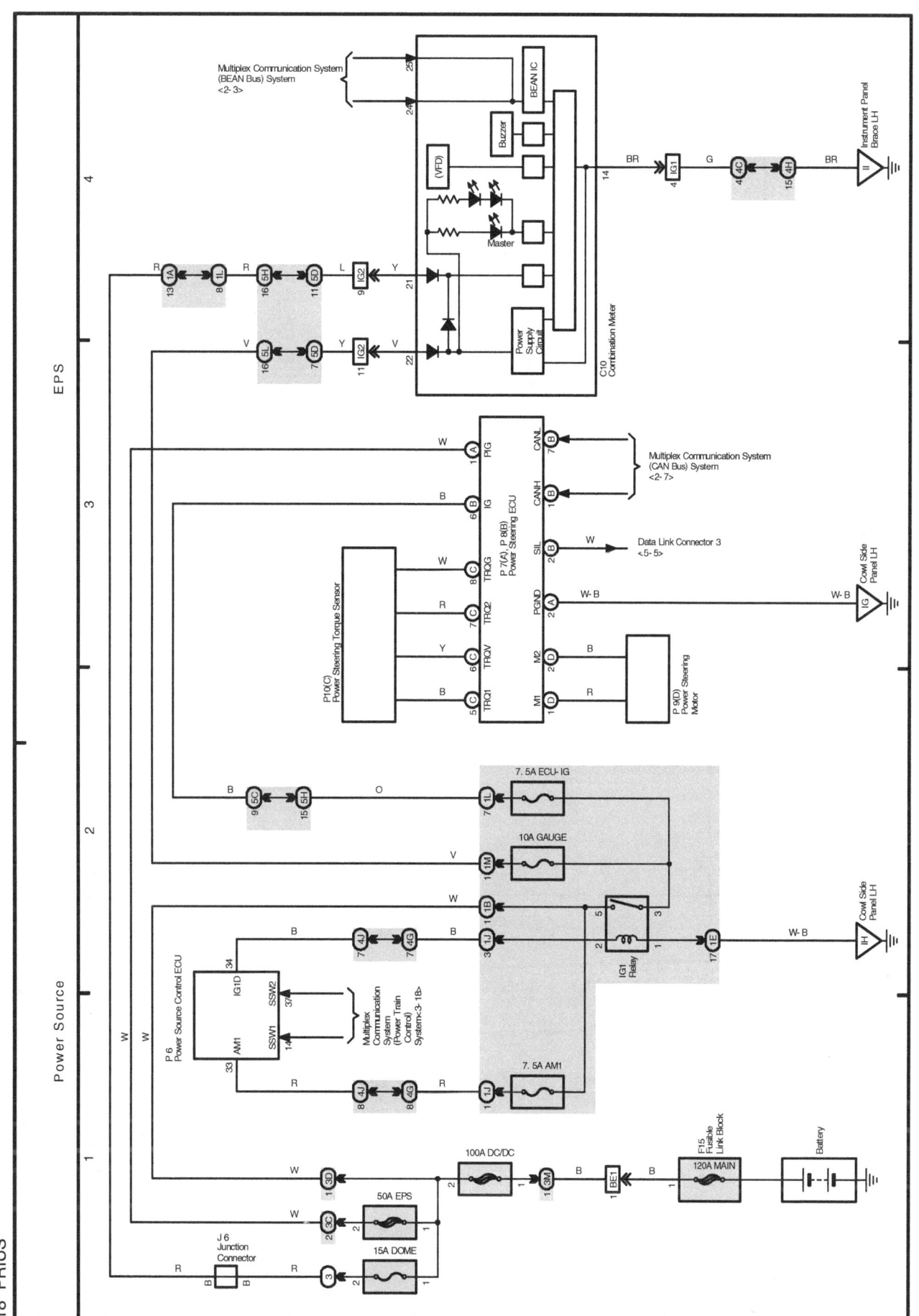

13

Model Year 2004

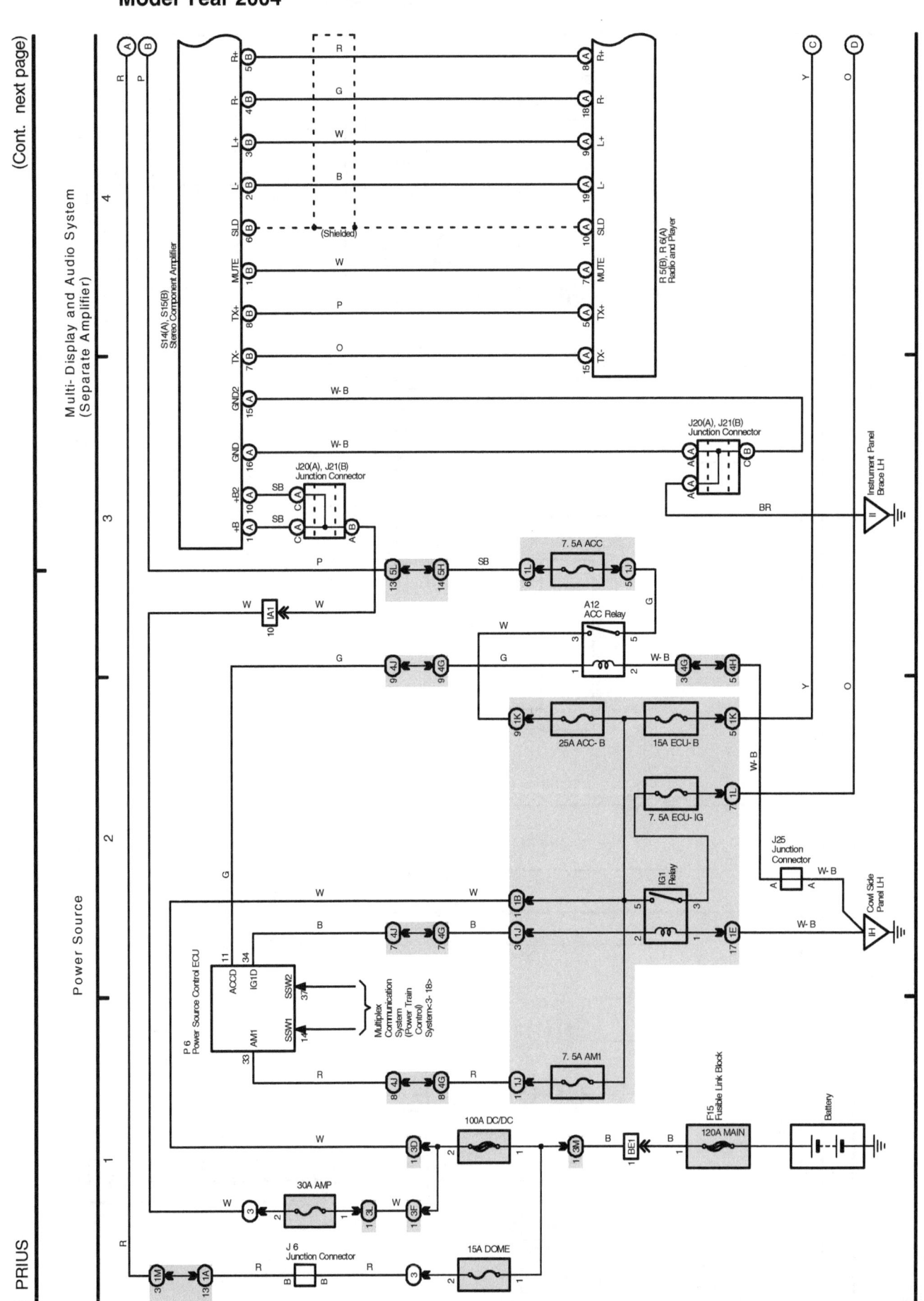

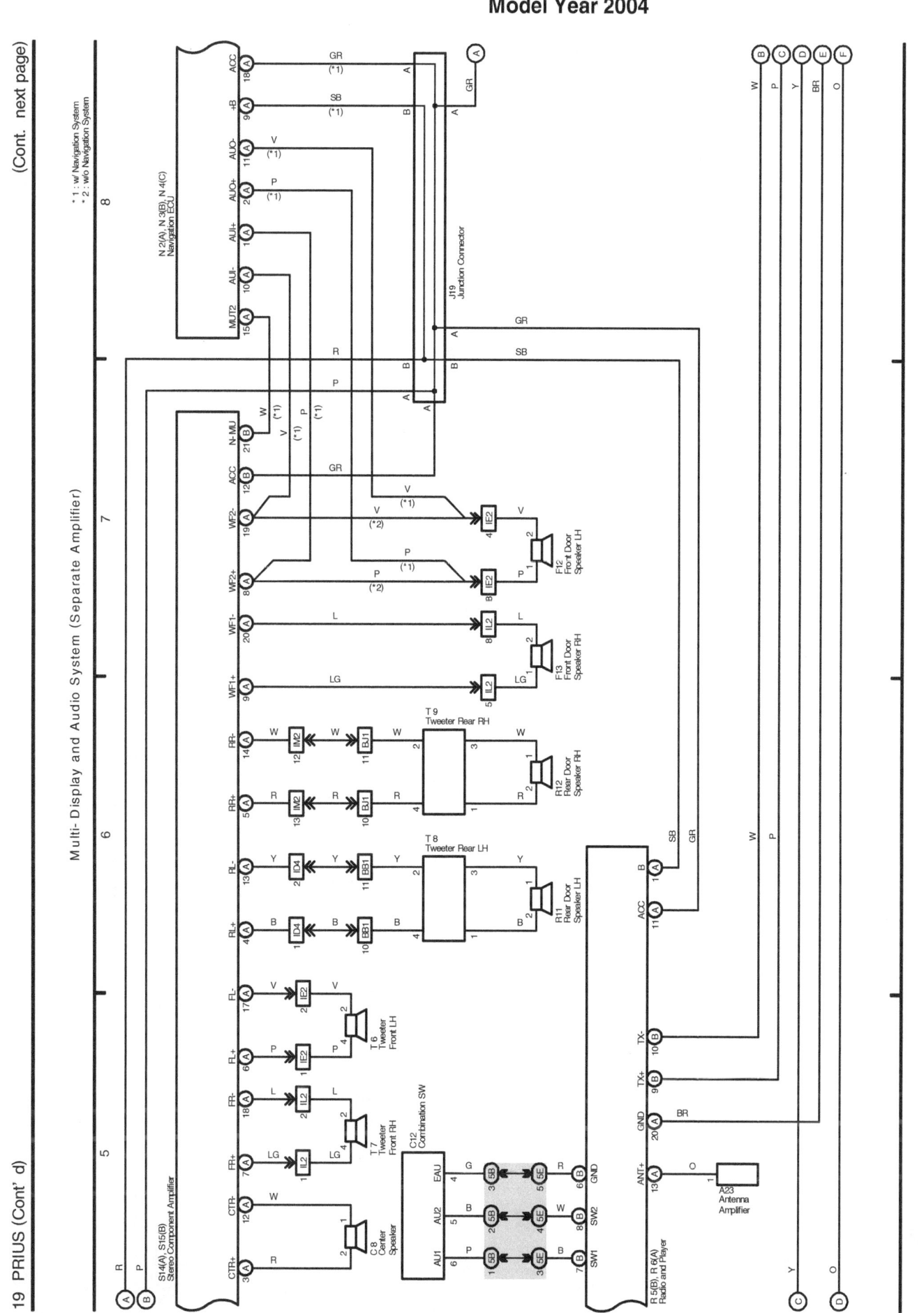

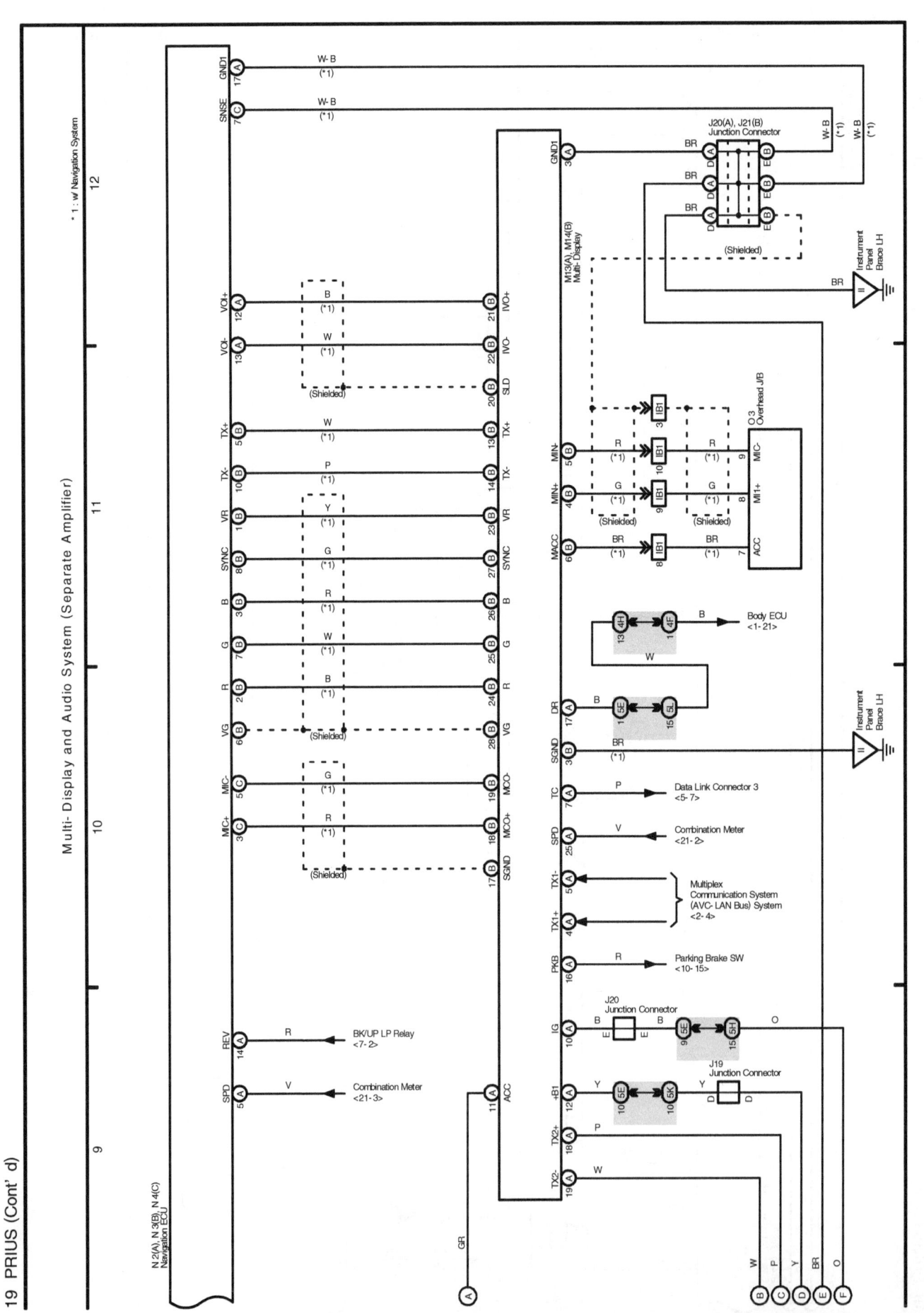

Model Year 2004

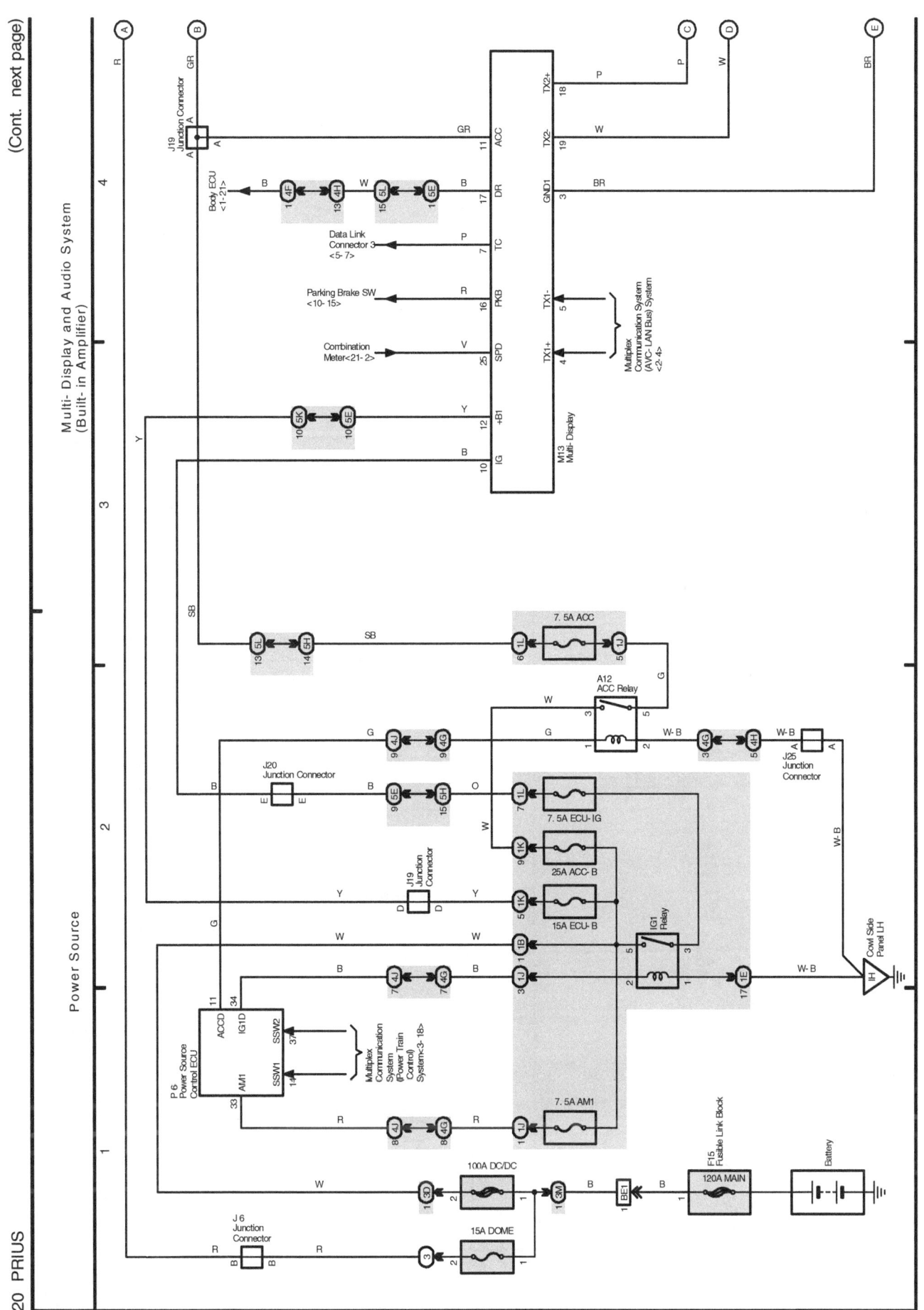

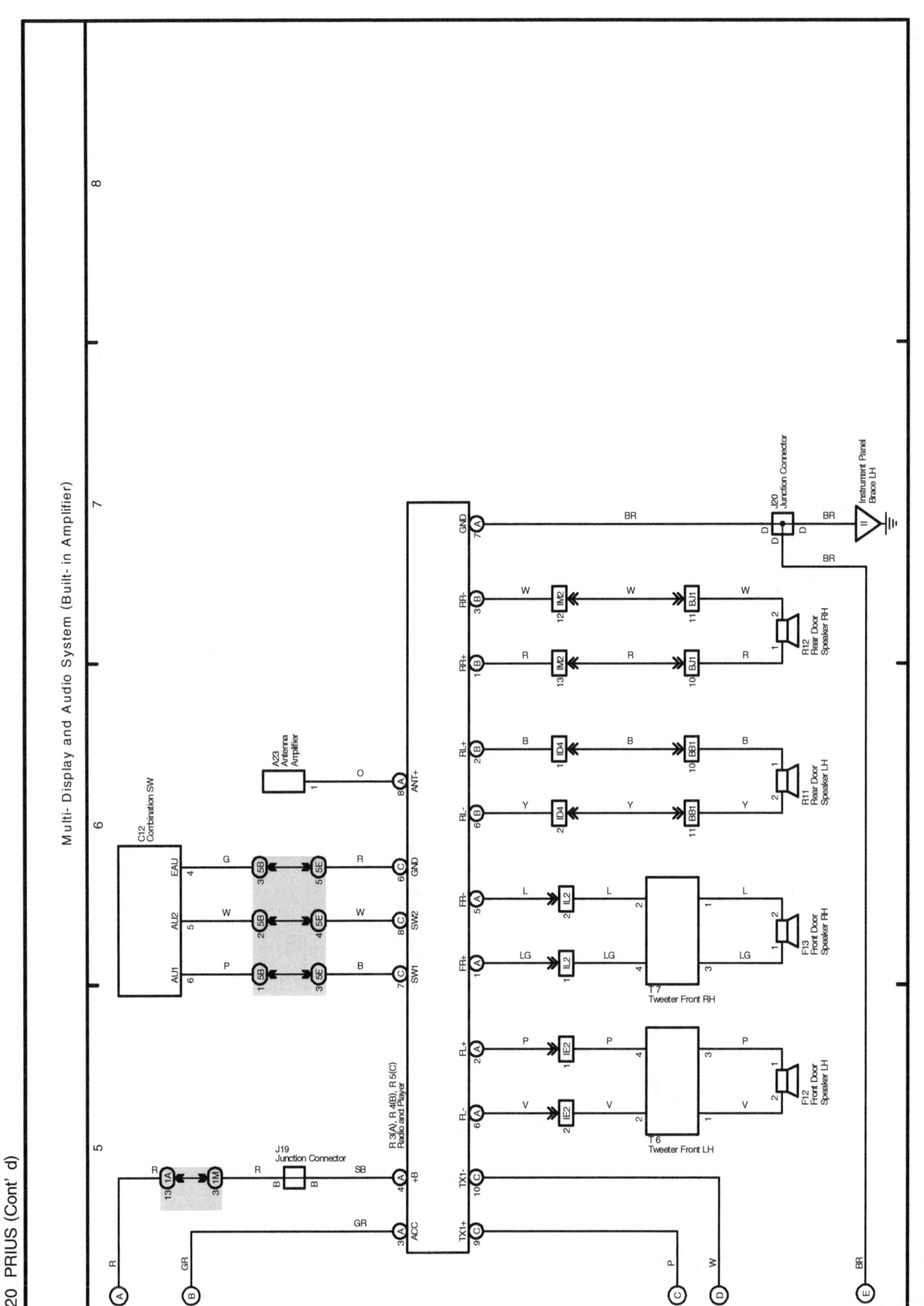

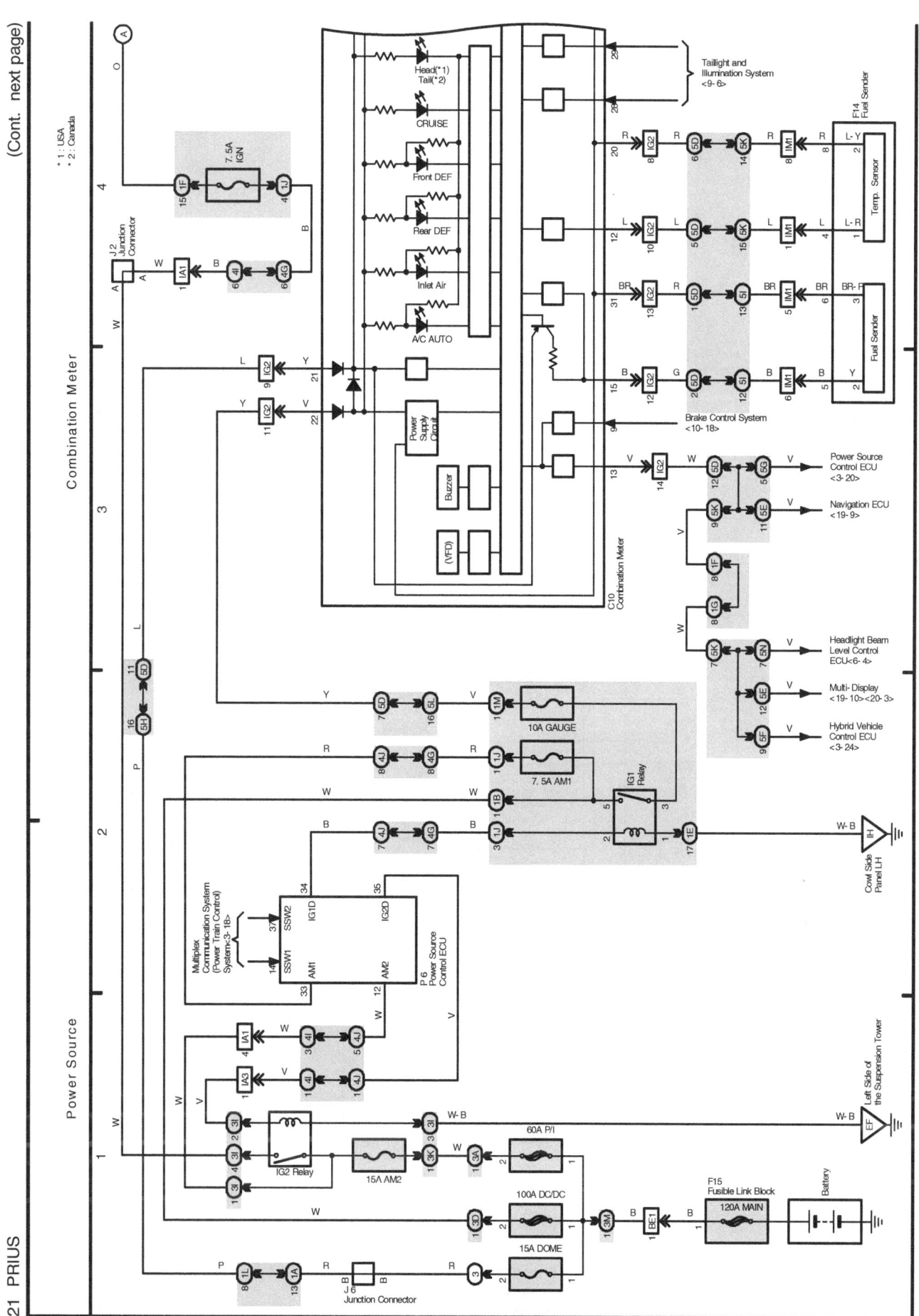

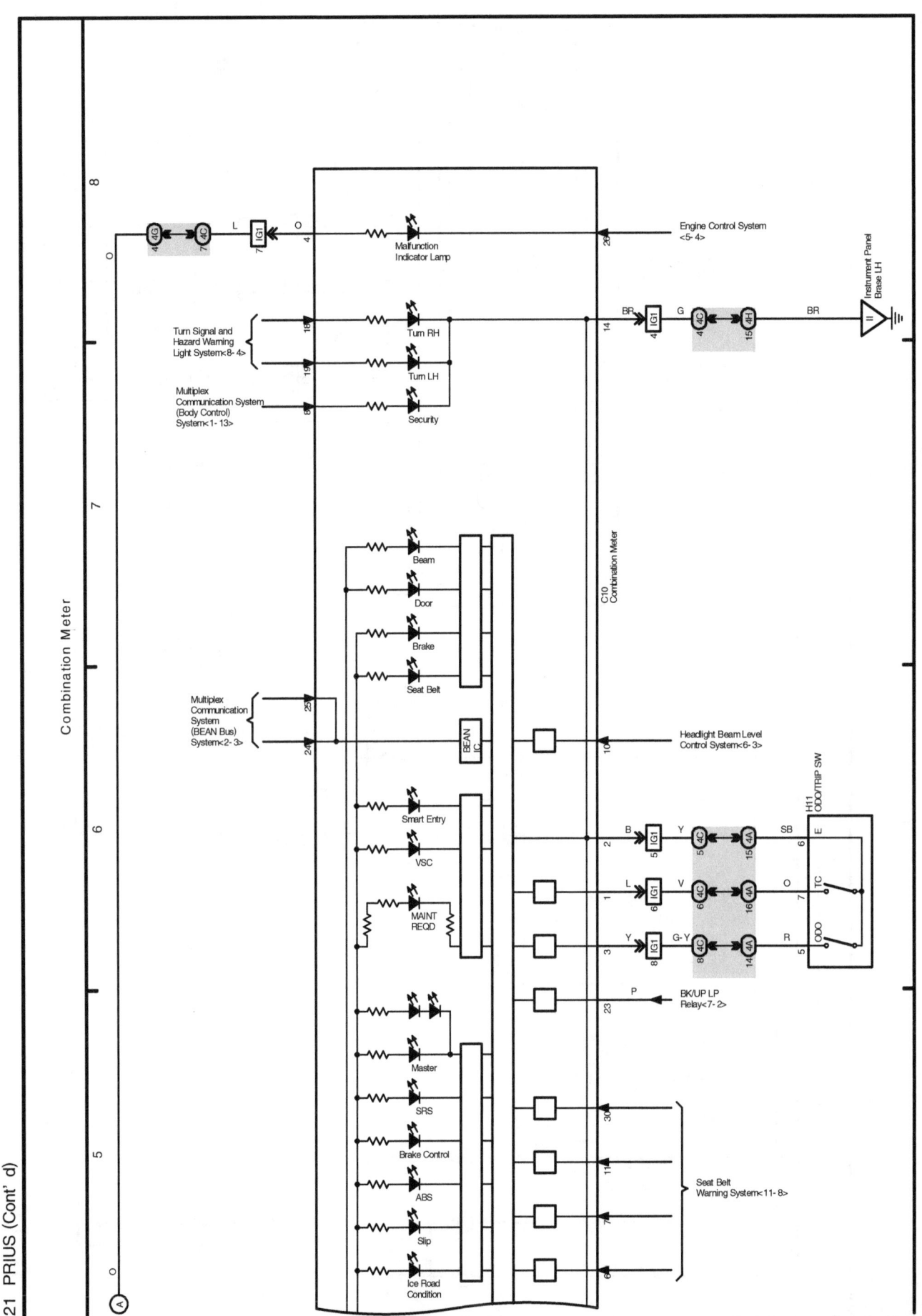

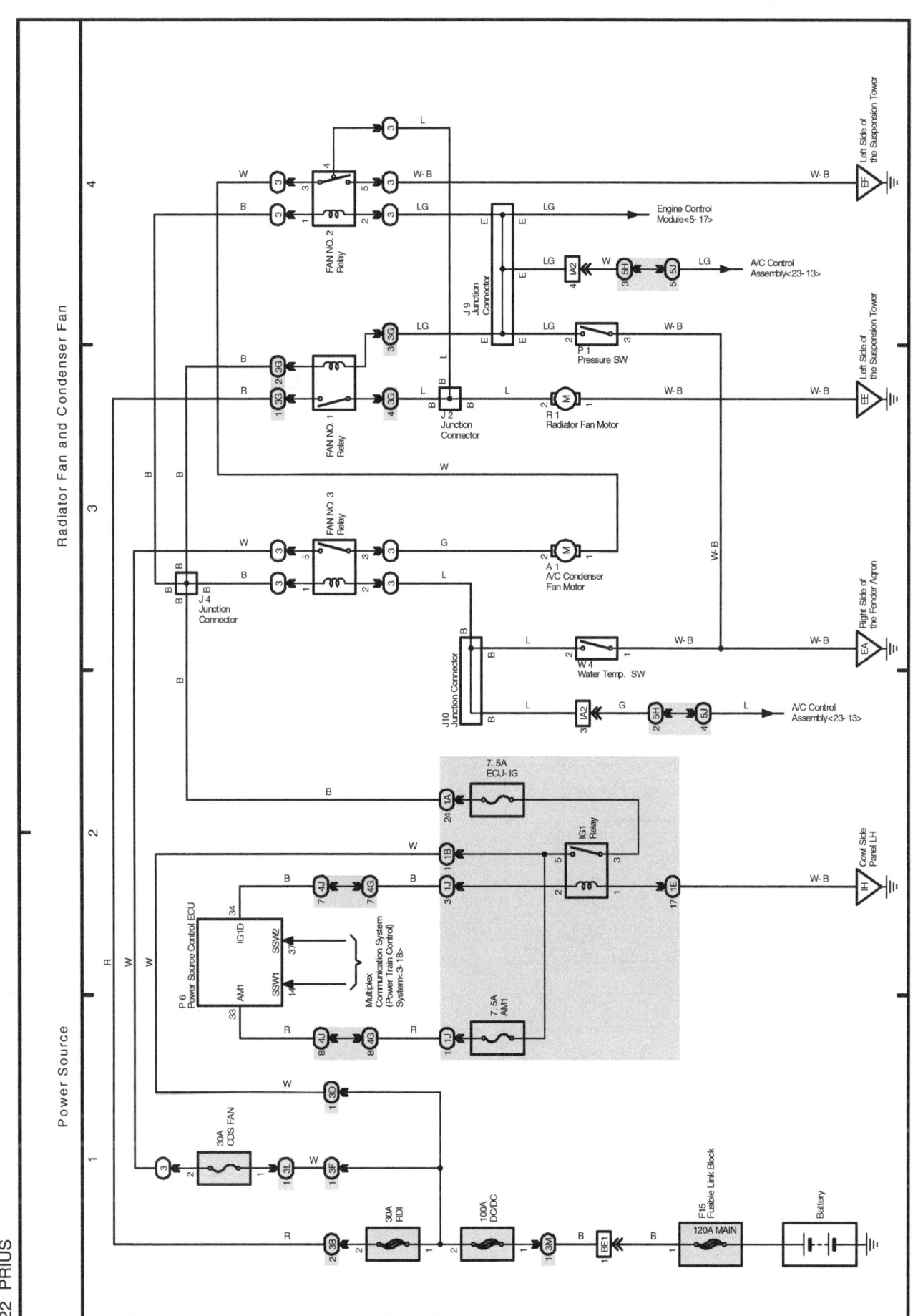

Model Year 2004

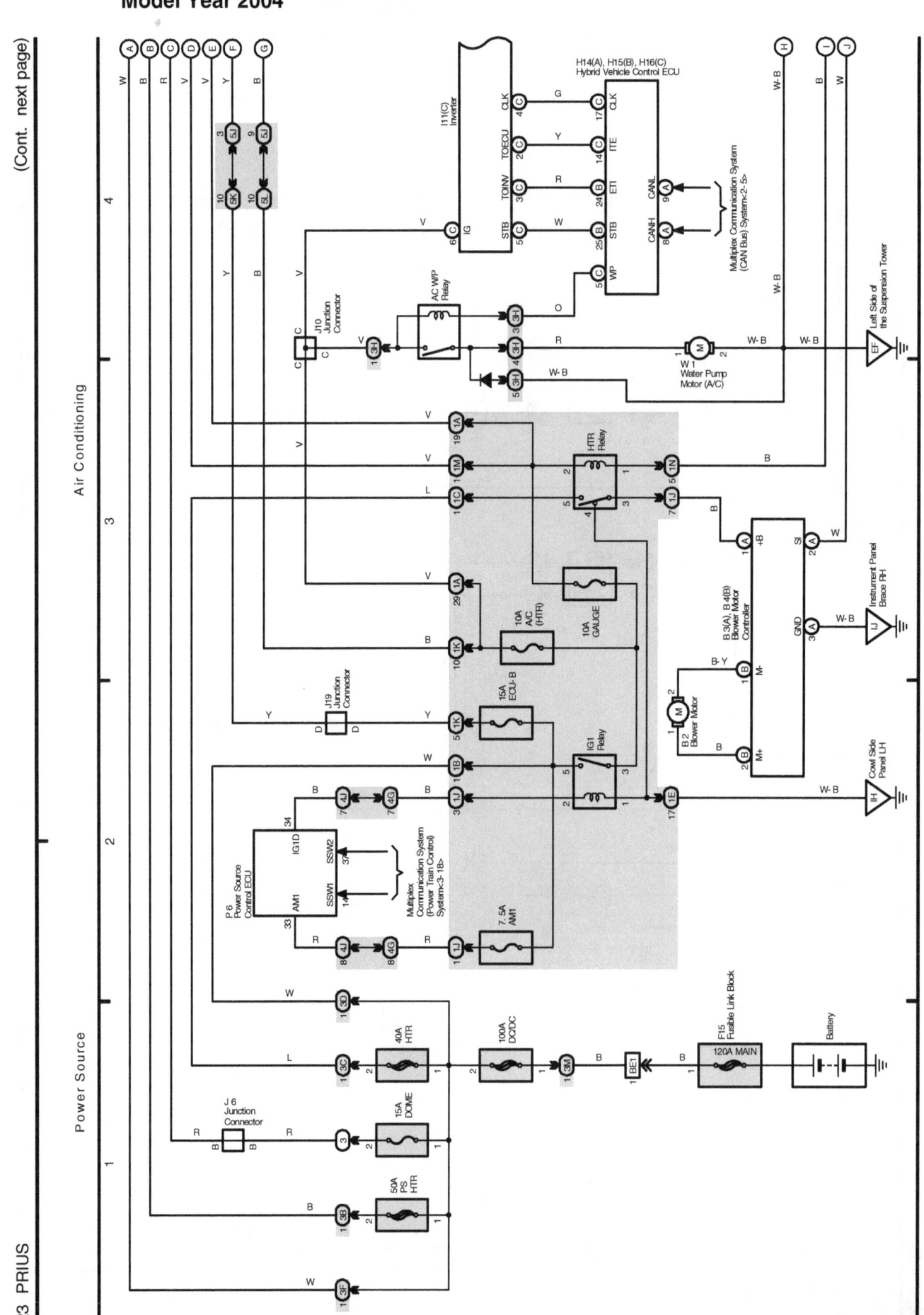

(Cont. next page)

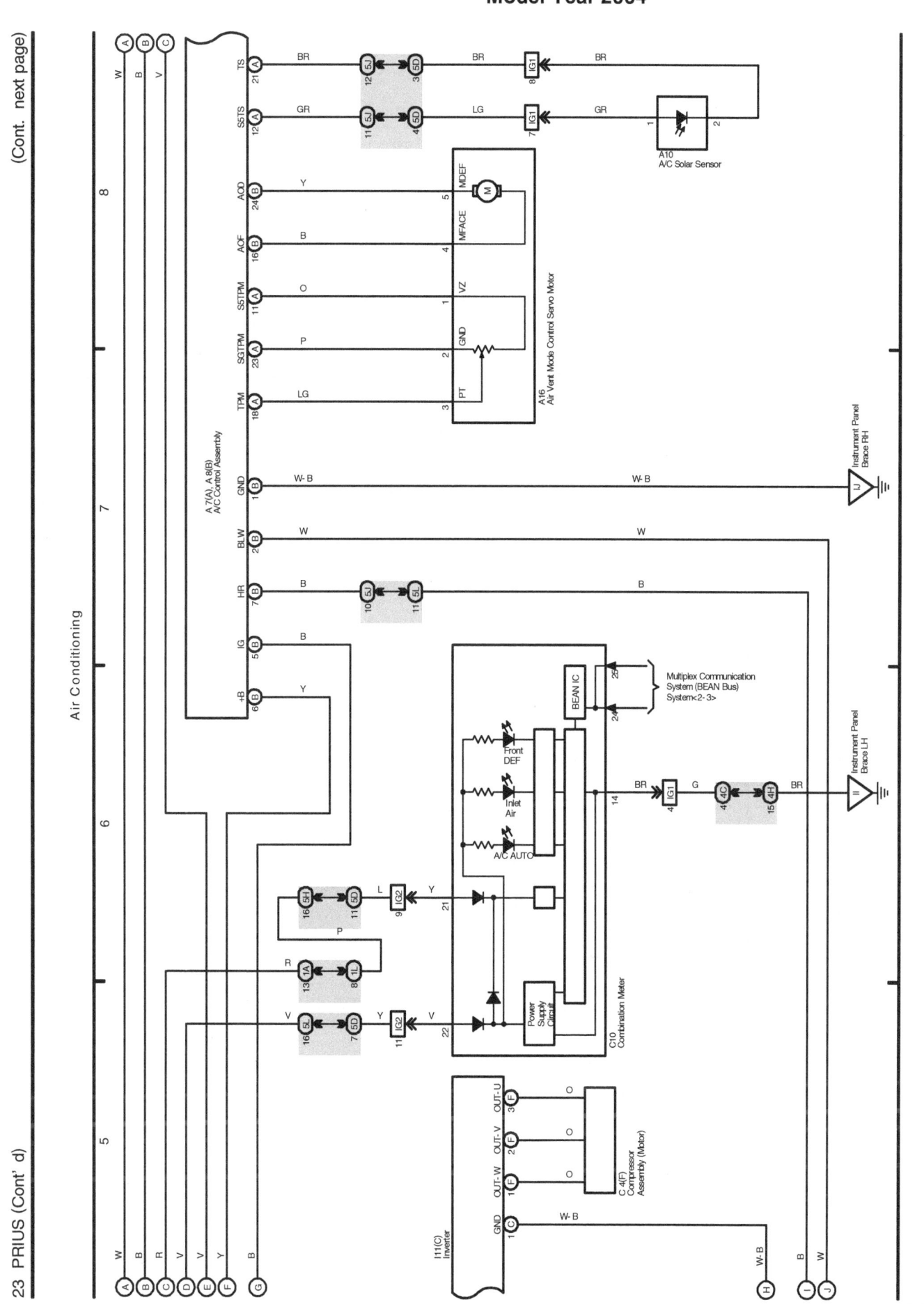

Air Conditioning

A 7(A), A 8(B)
A/C Control Assembly

A10
A/C Solar Sensor

A16
Air Vent Mode Control Servo Motor

Instrument Panel
Brace RH

Instrument Panel
Brace LH

Multiplex Communication
System (BEAN Bus)
System<2- 3>

BEAN IC

Front
DEF

Inlet
Air

A/C AUTO

Power
Supply
Circuit

C10
Combination Meter

I11(C)
Inverter

C 4(F)
Compressor
Assembly (Motor)

23 PRIUS (Cont' d)

(Cont. next page)

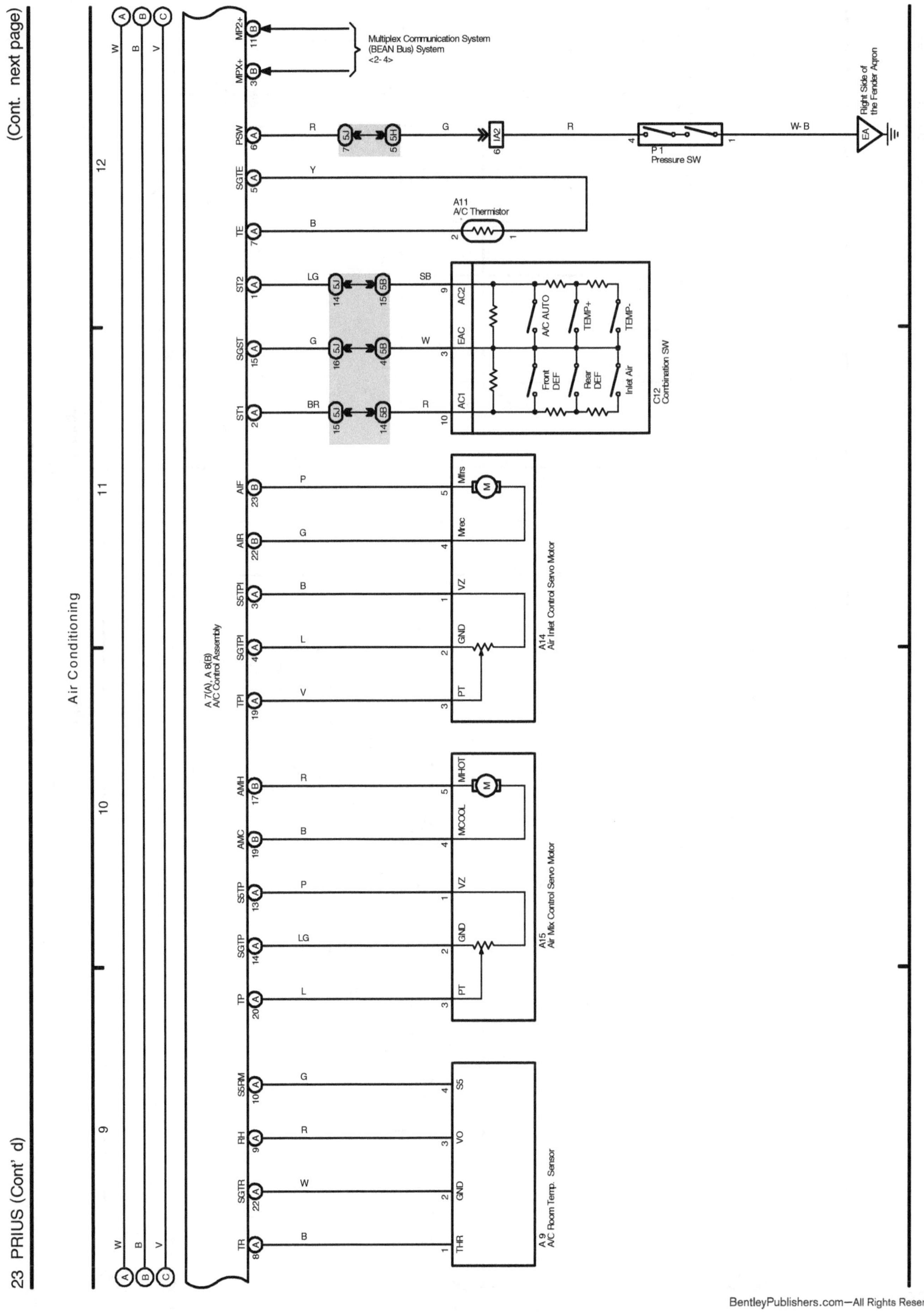

23 PRIUS (Cont' d)

Air Conditioning

Multiplex Communication System
(BEAN Bus) System
<2- 4>

A11
A/C Thermistor

C12
Combination SW

A/C AUTO   TEMP+   TEMP-
Front DEF   Rear DEF   Inlet Air
AC2   EAC   AC1

A7(A), A 8(B)
A/C Control Assembly

A14
Air Inlet Control Servo Motor

A15
Air Mix Control Servo Motor

A9
A/C Room Temp. Sensor

P 1
Pressure SW

Right Side of
the Fender Apron

Air Conditioning

30A PTC HTR1

30A PTC HTR2

PTC HTR 1 Relay

PTC HTR 2 Relay

PS HTR Relay

J6 Junction Connector

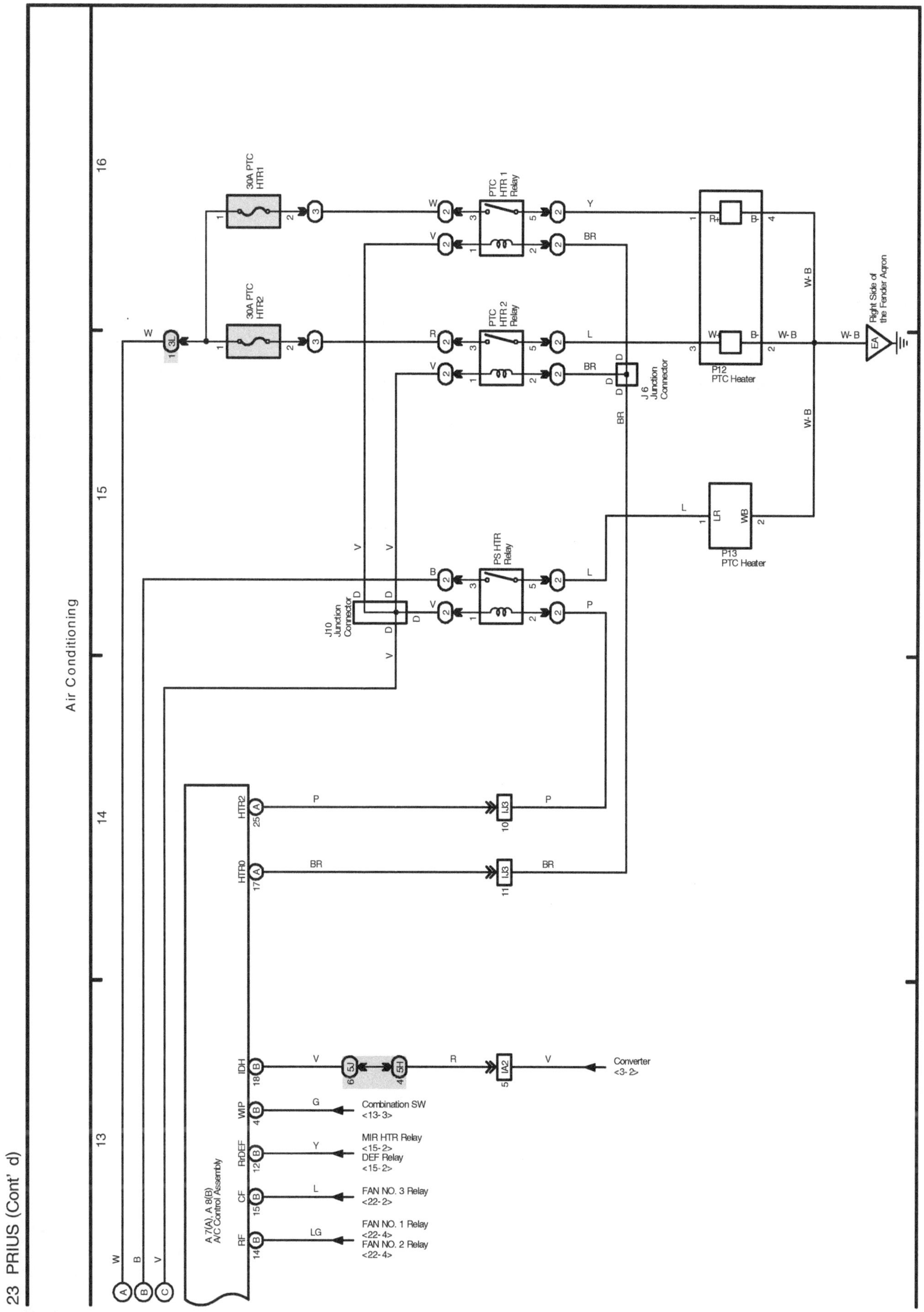

J10 Junction Connector

P12 PTC Heater

P13 PTC Heater

Right Side of the Fender Apron

J3

A2

J10

Converter
<3-2>

HTR2
25

HTR0
17

IDH
18

WIP
4

RrDEF
12

CF
15

RF
14

A 7(A), A 8(B)
A/C Control Assembly

Combination SW
<13-3>

MIR HTR Relay
<15-2>
DEF Relay
<15-2>

FAN NO. 3 Relay
<22-2>

FAN NO. 1 Relay
<22-4>
FAN NO. 2 Relay
<22-4>

23 PRIUS (Cont'd)

Component	Page

MODEL YEAR 2007

2007 electrical wiring diagrams index

Component	Page

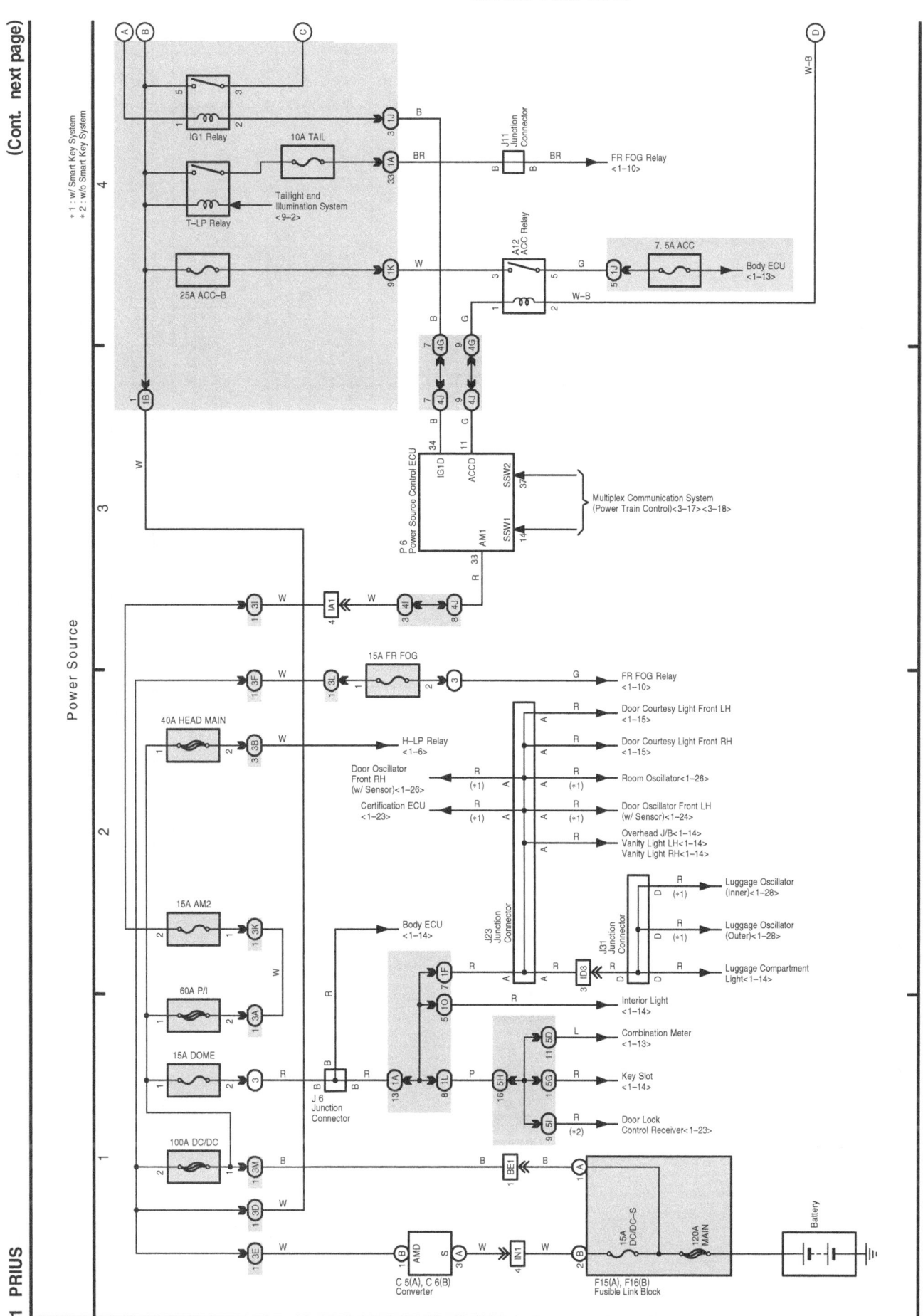

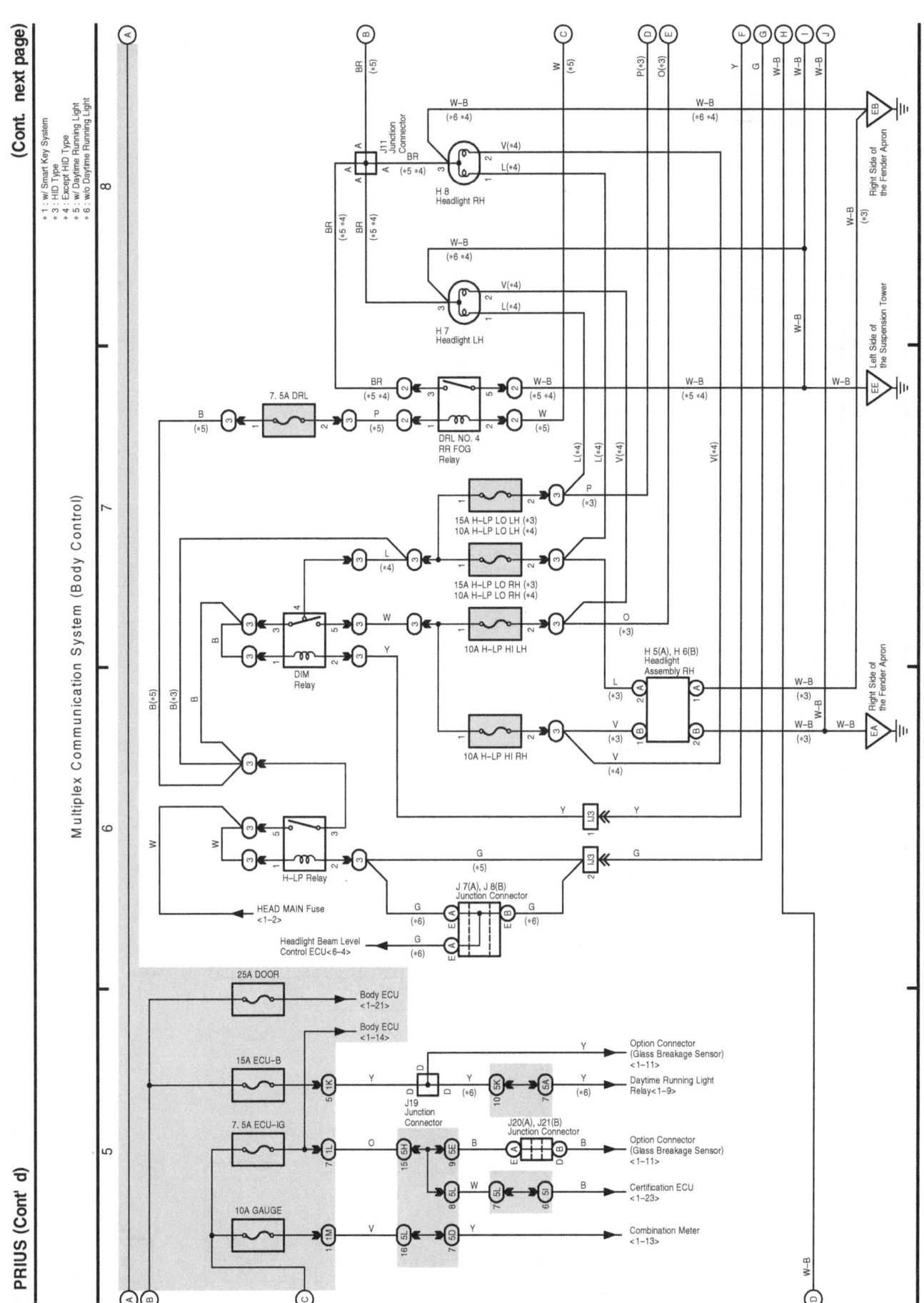

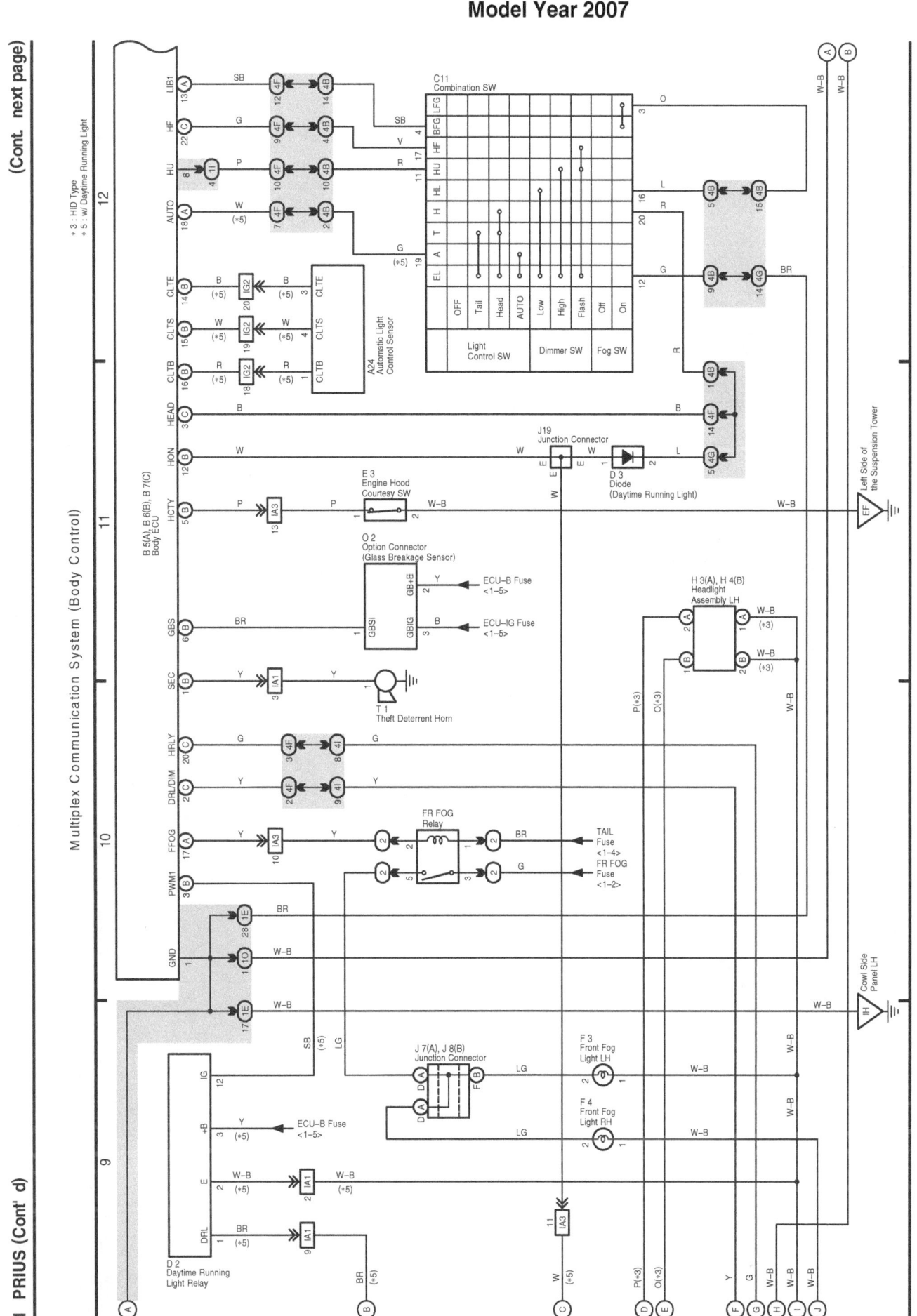

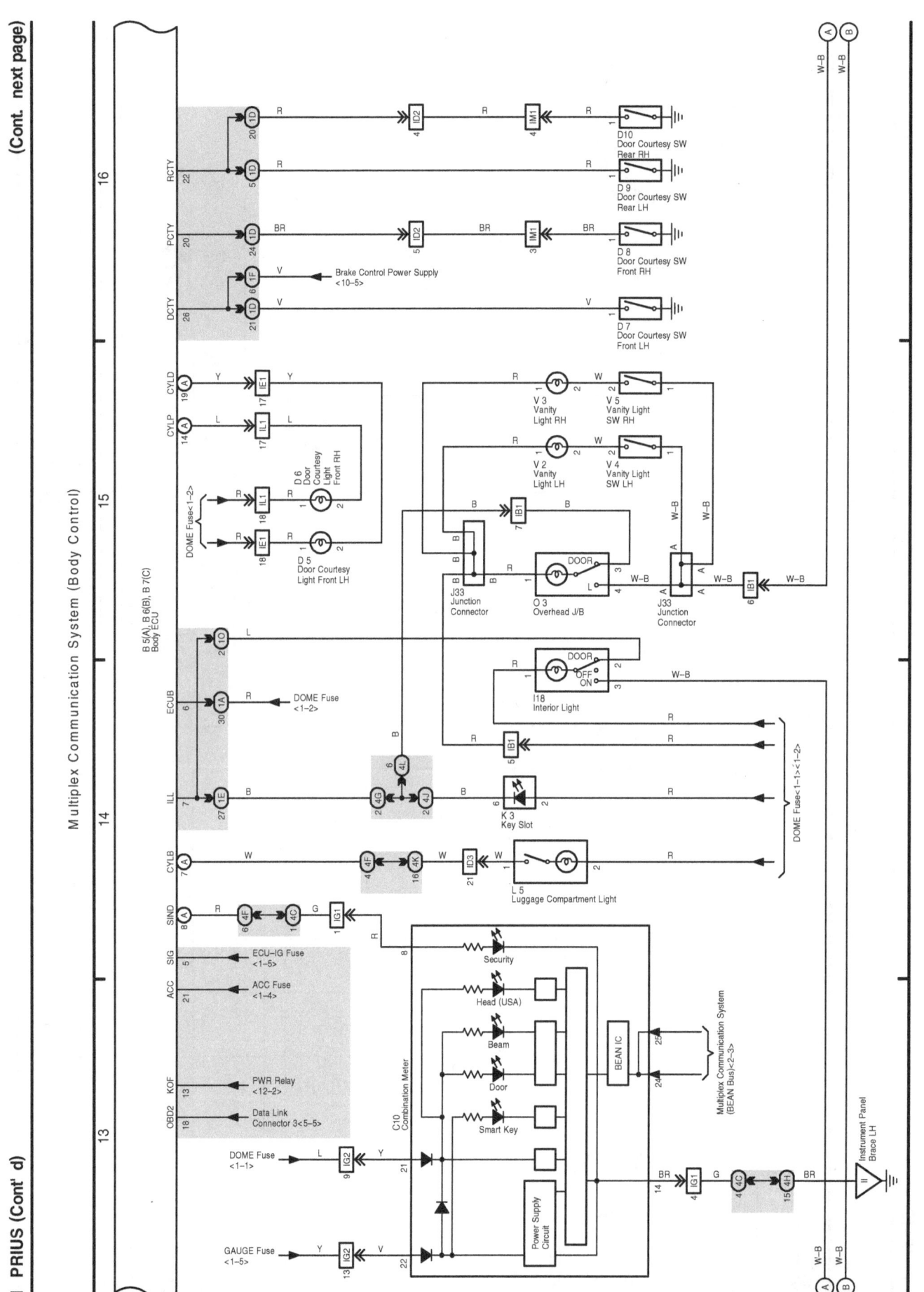

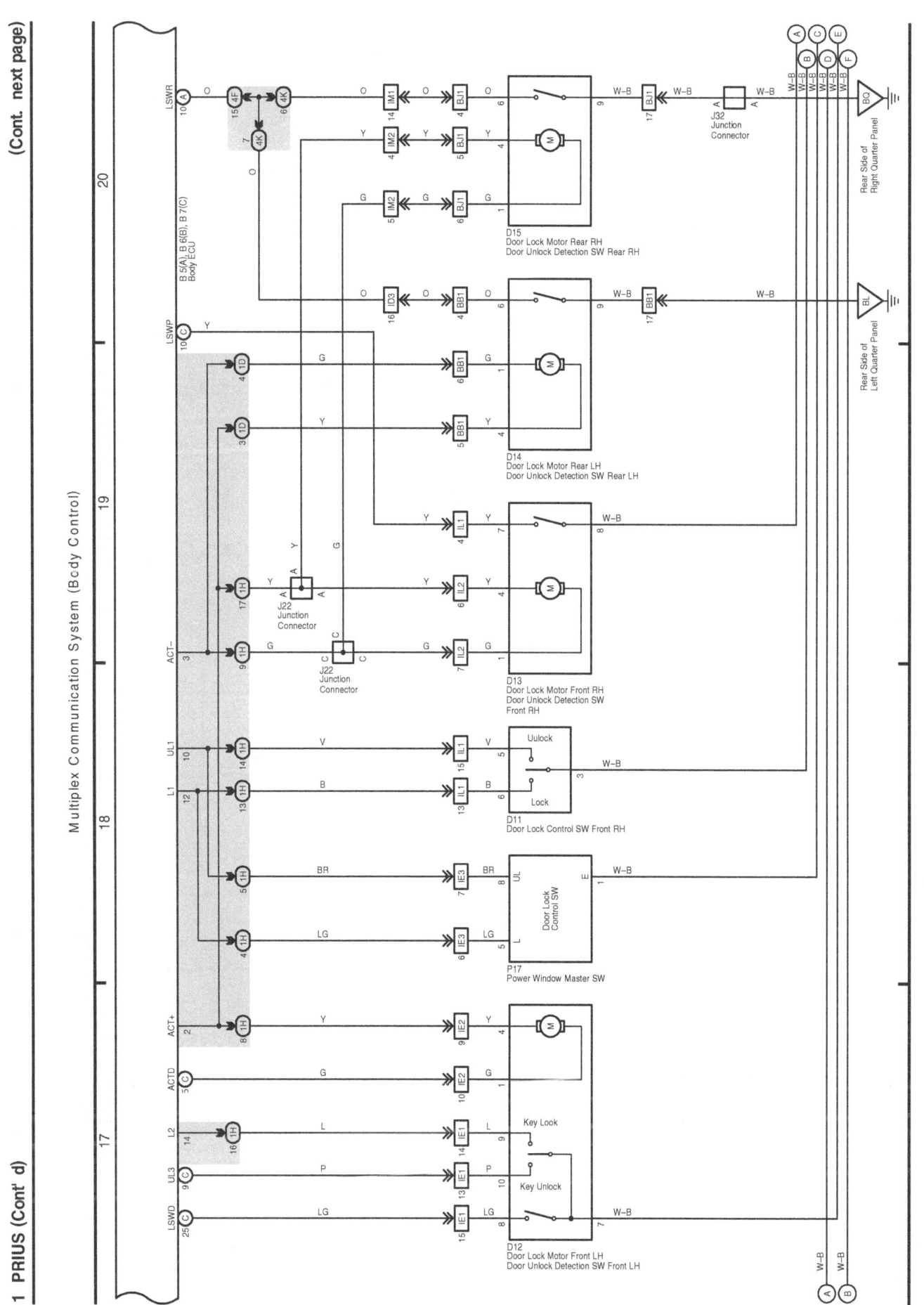

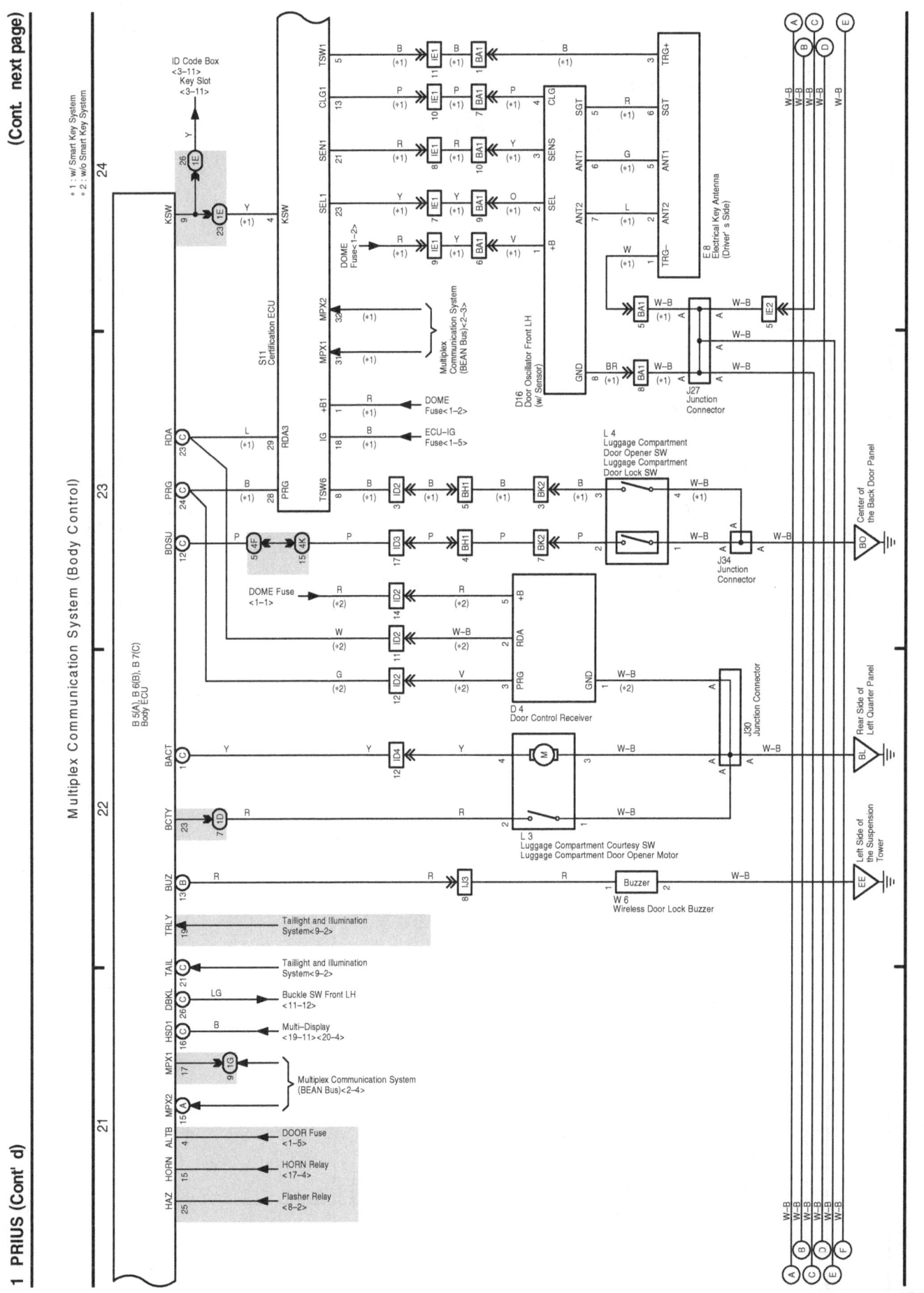

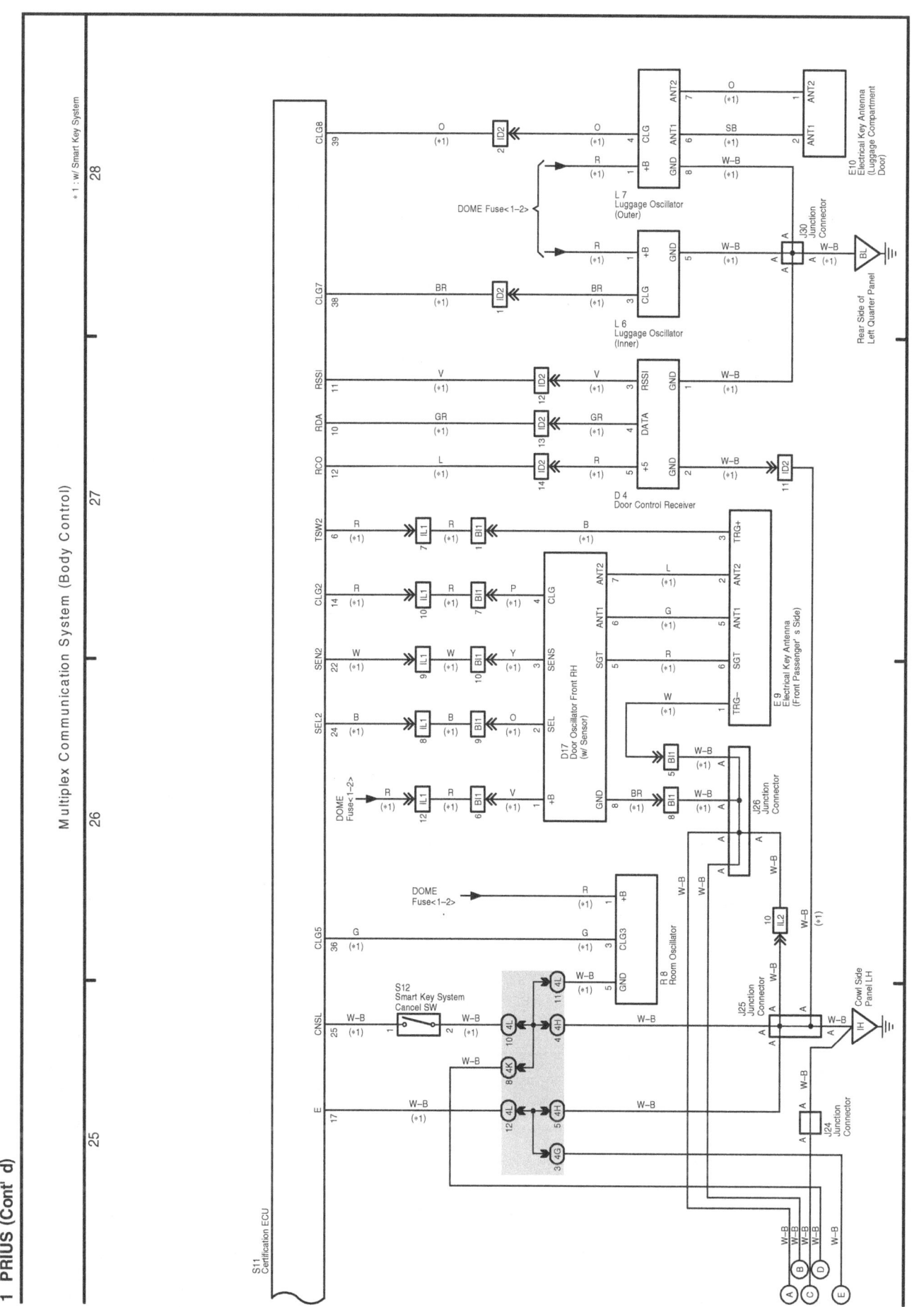

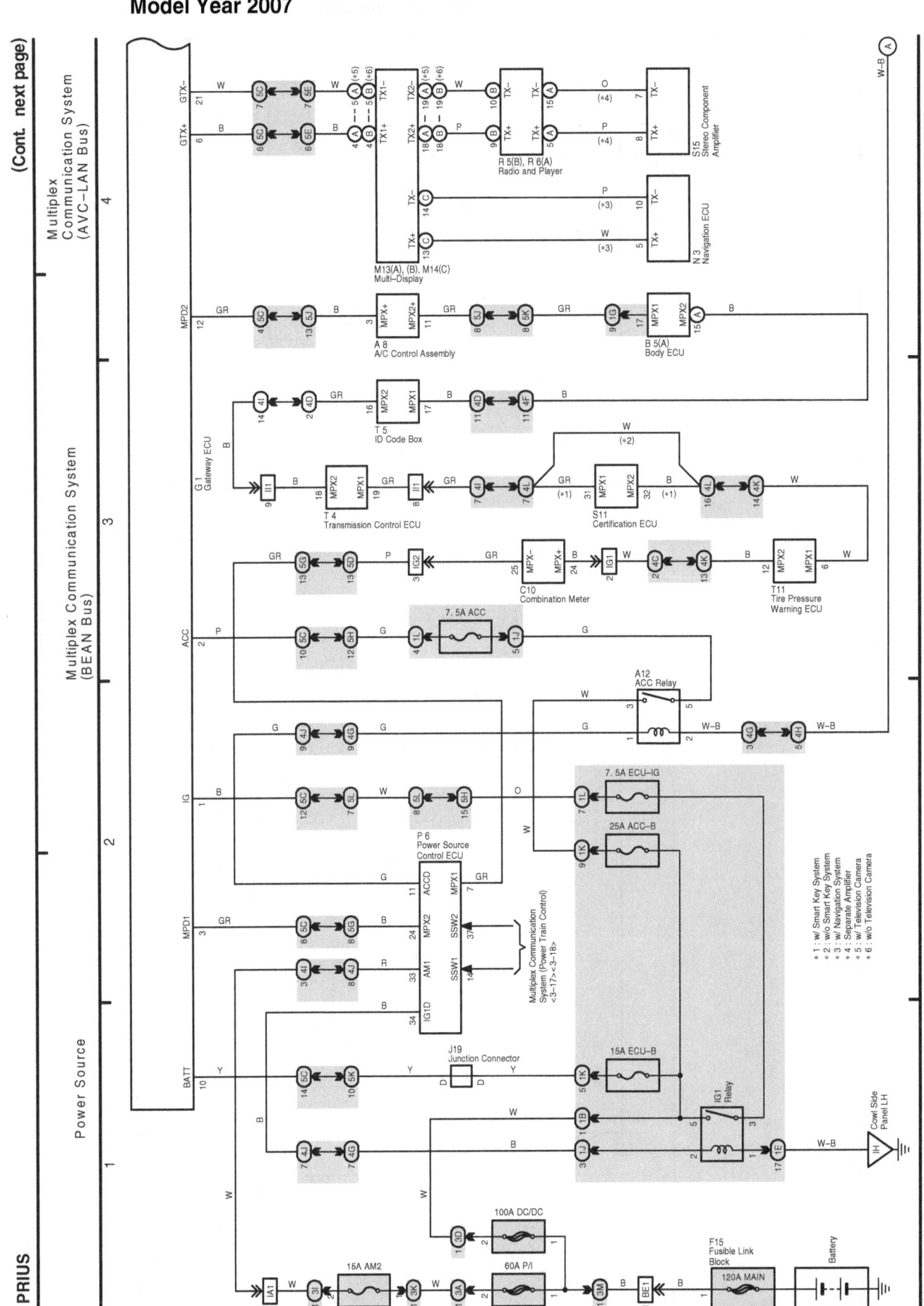

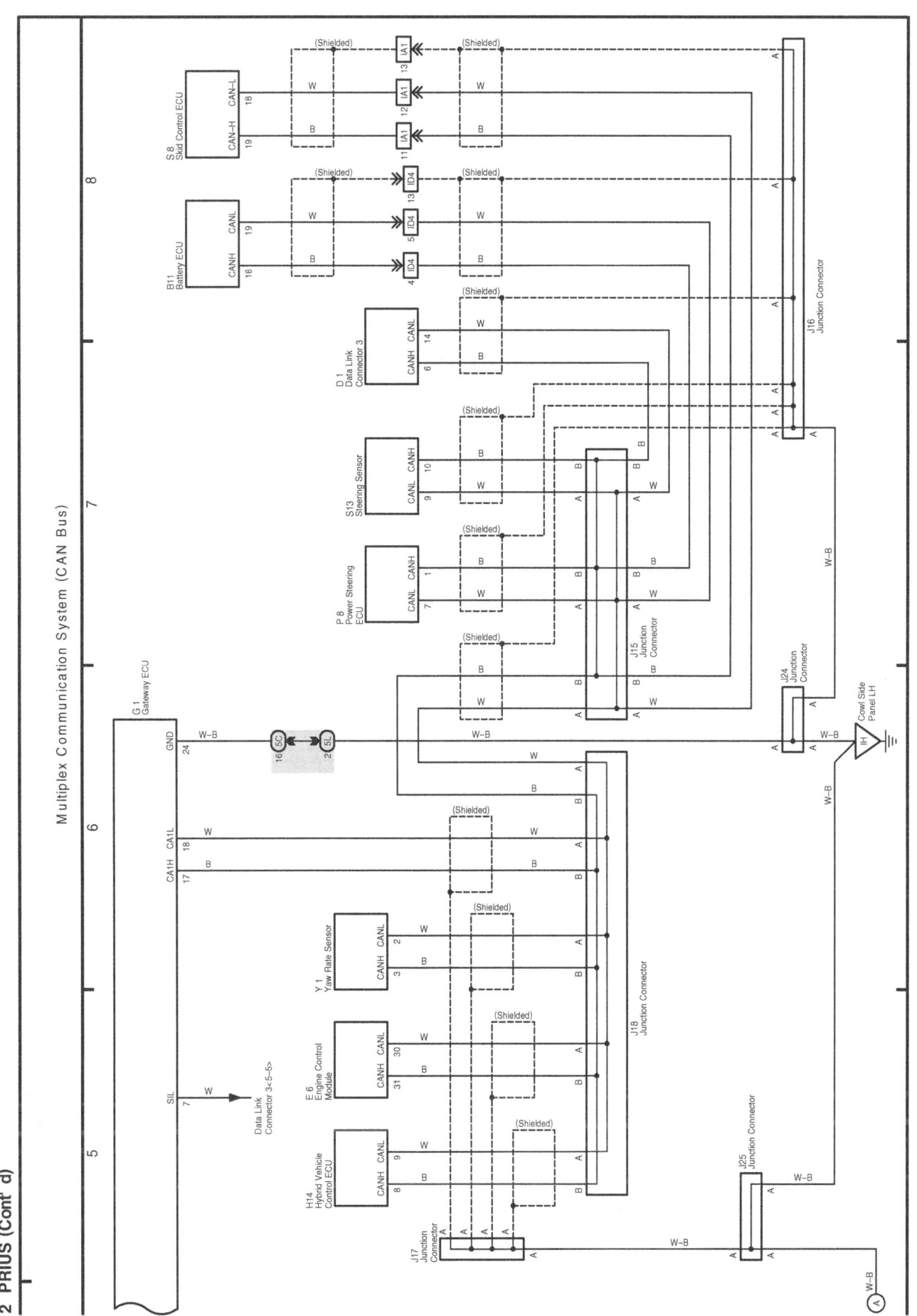

Model Year 2007

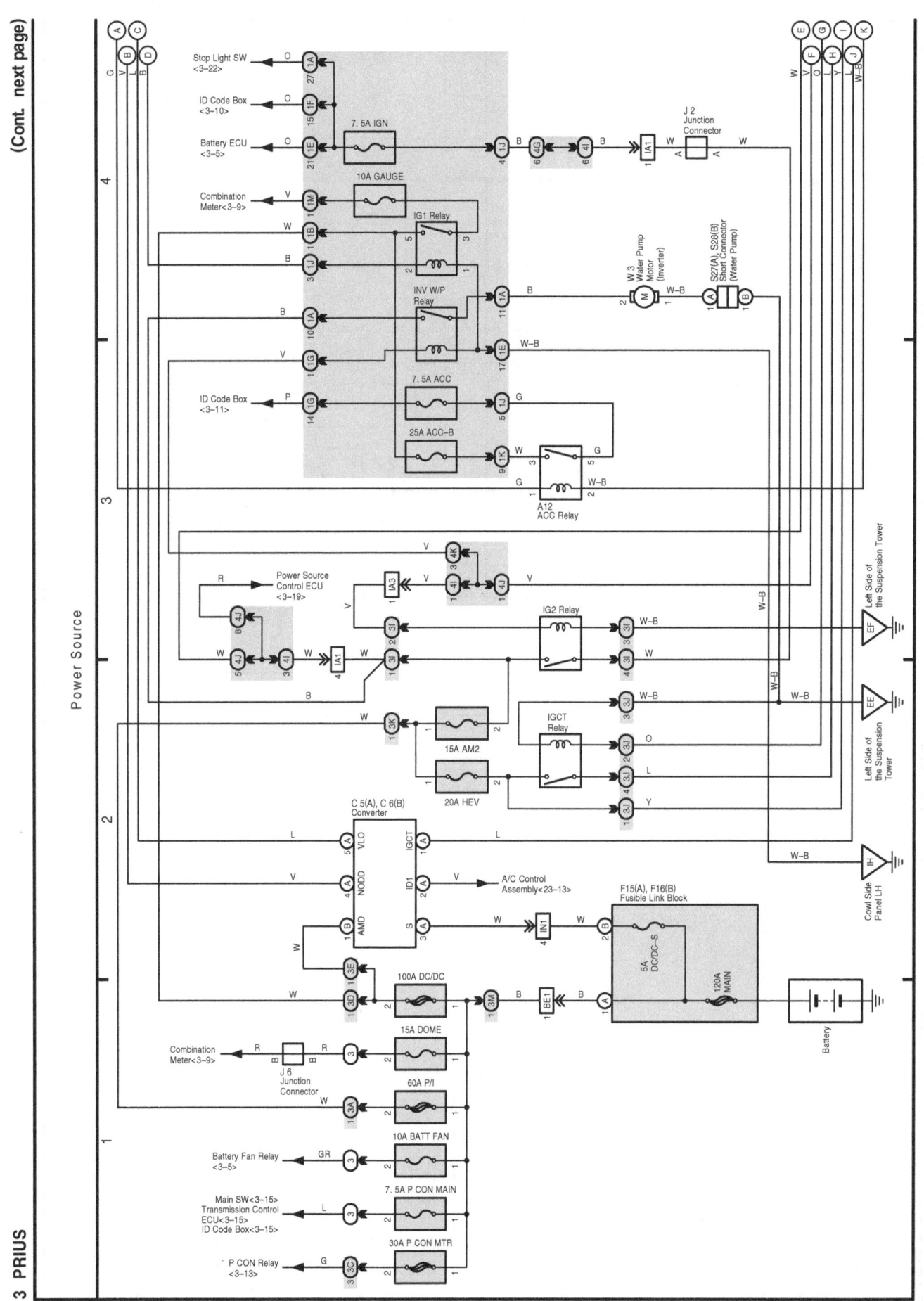

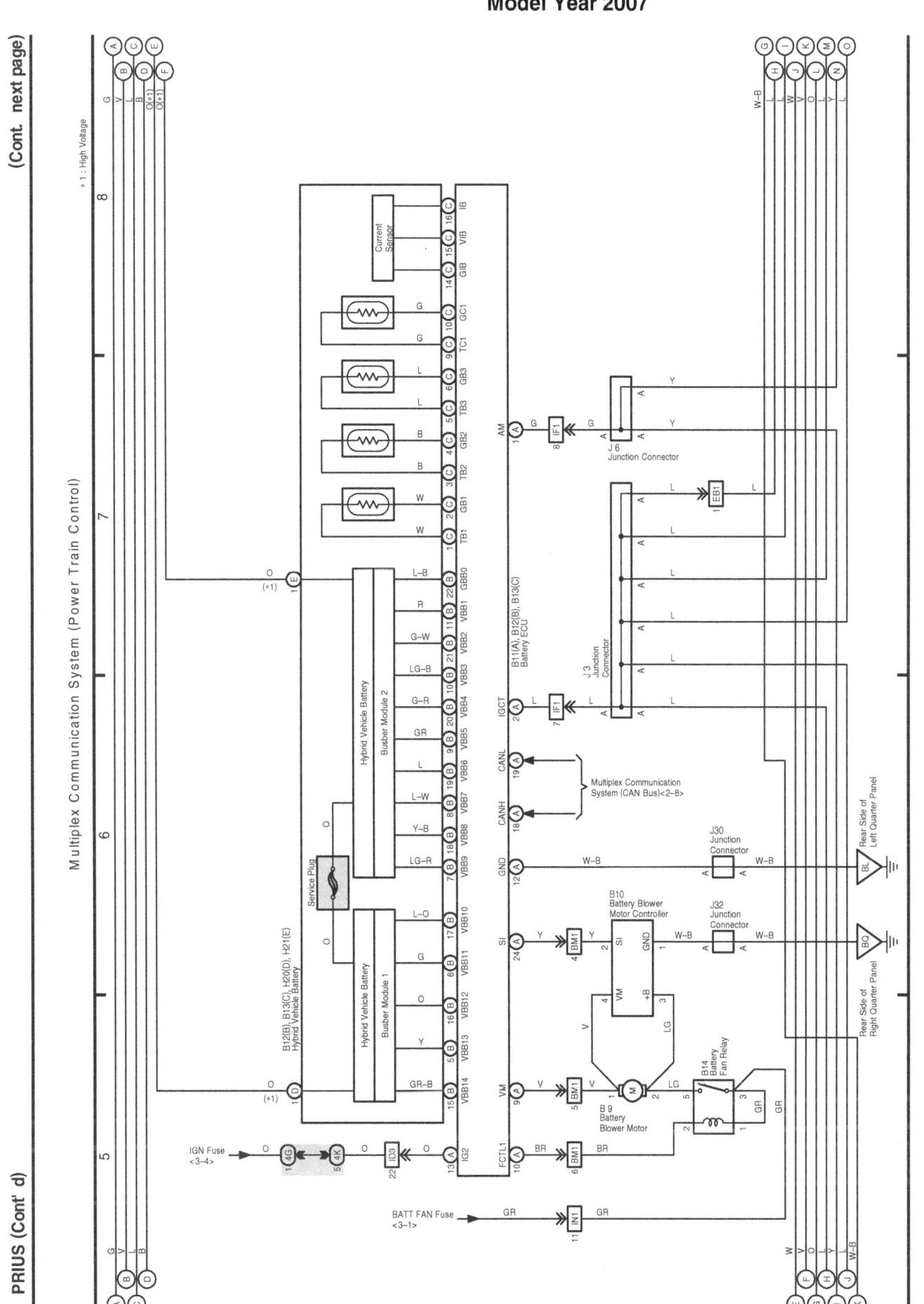

Model Year 2007

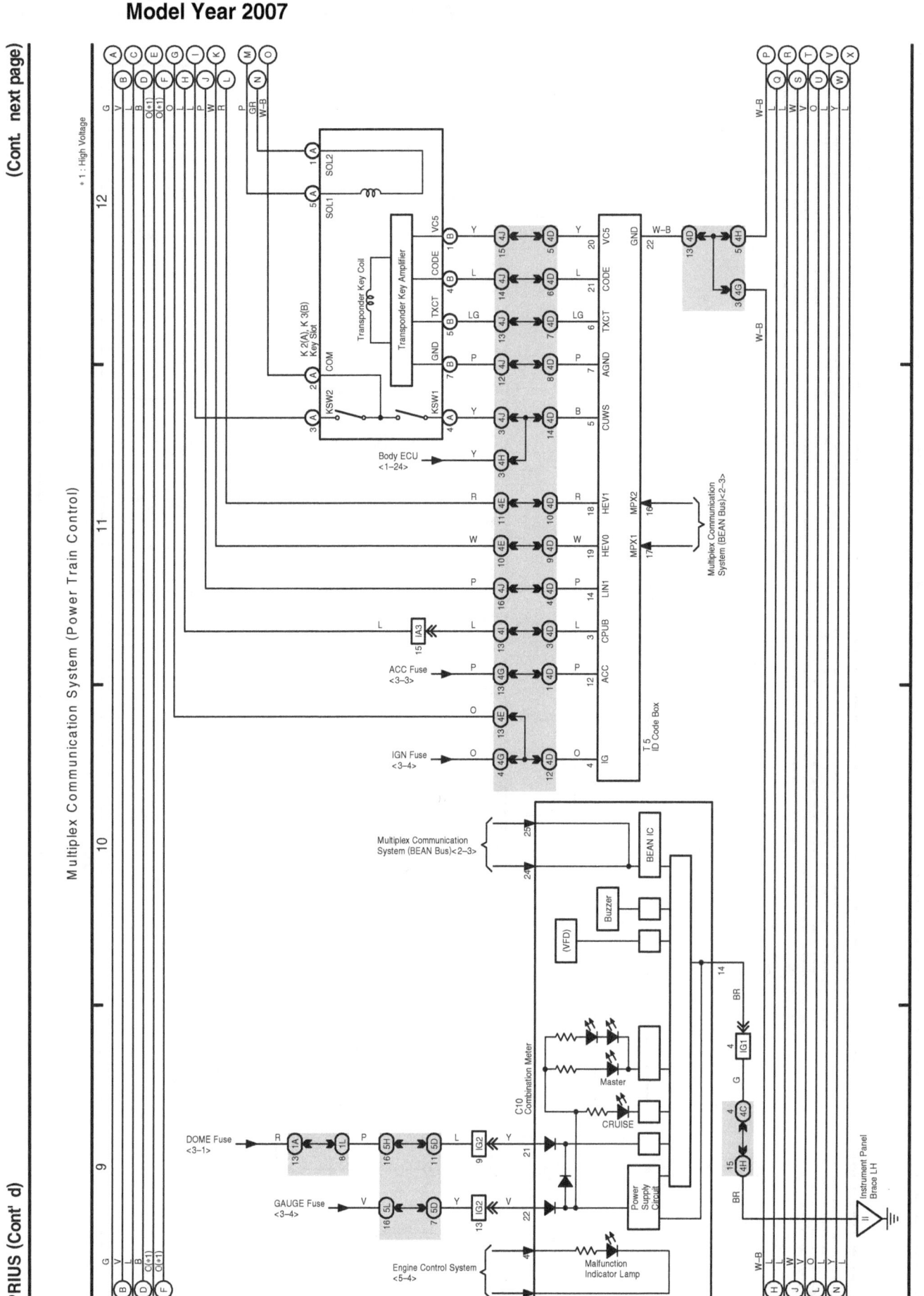

(Cont. next page)

3 PRIUS (Cont'd)

Multiplex Communication System (Power Train Control)

* 1 : High Voltage

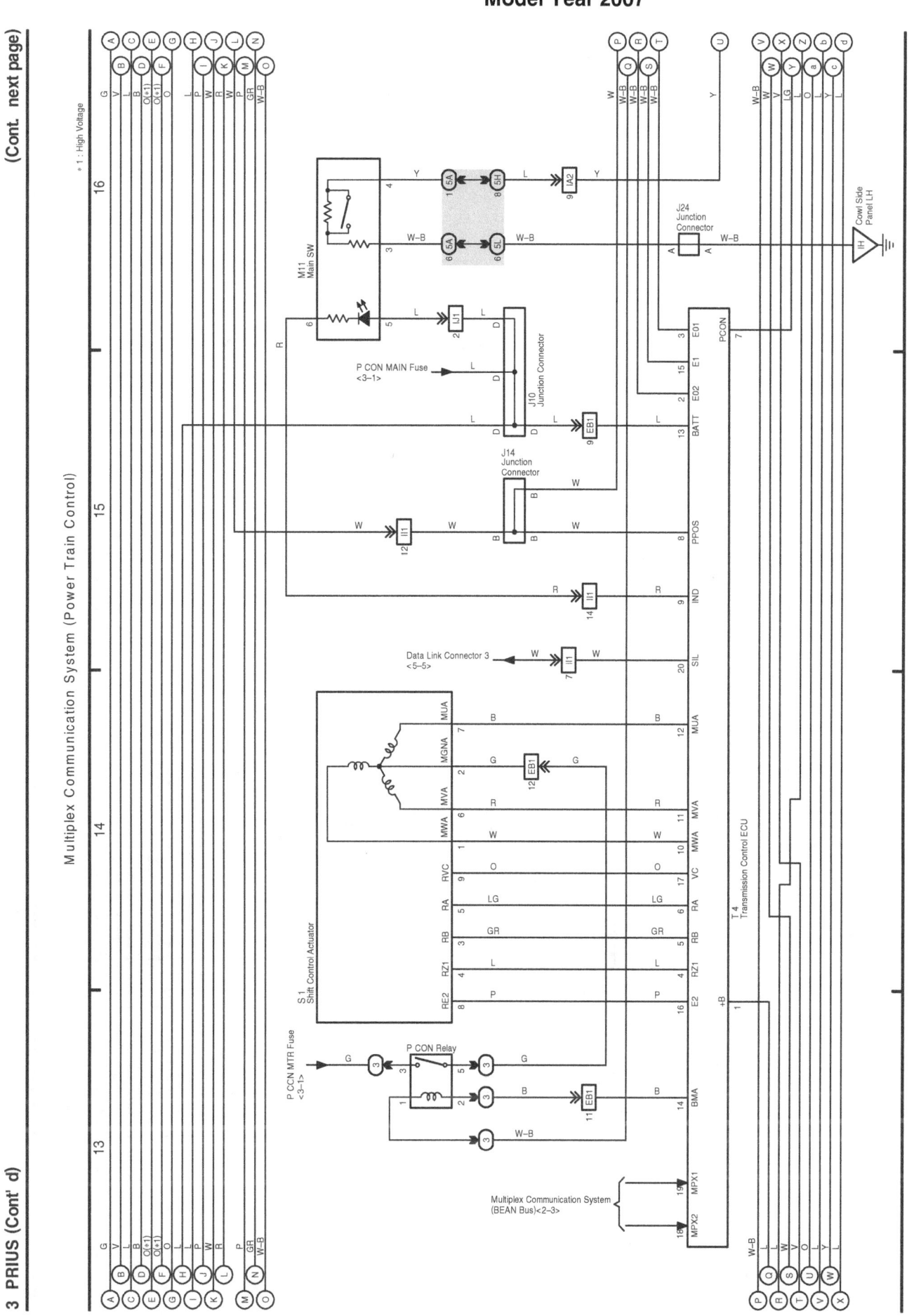

Model Year 2007

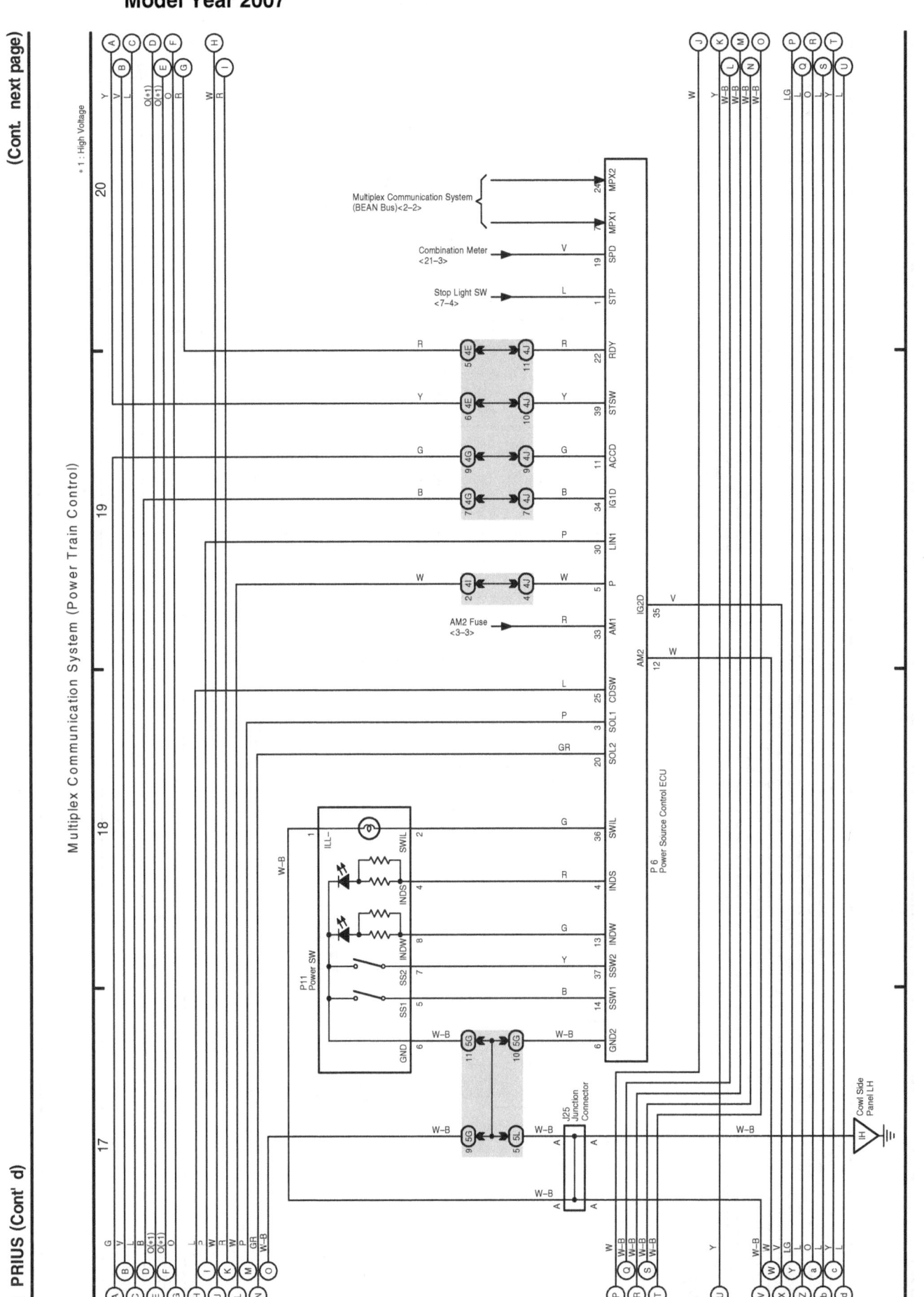

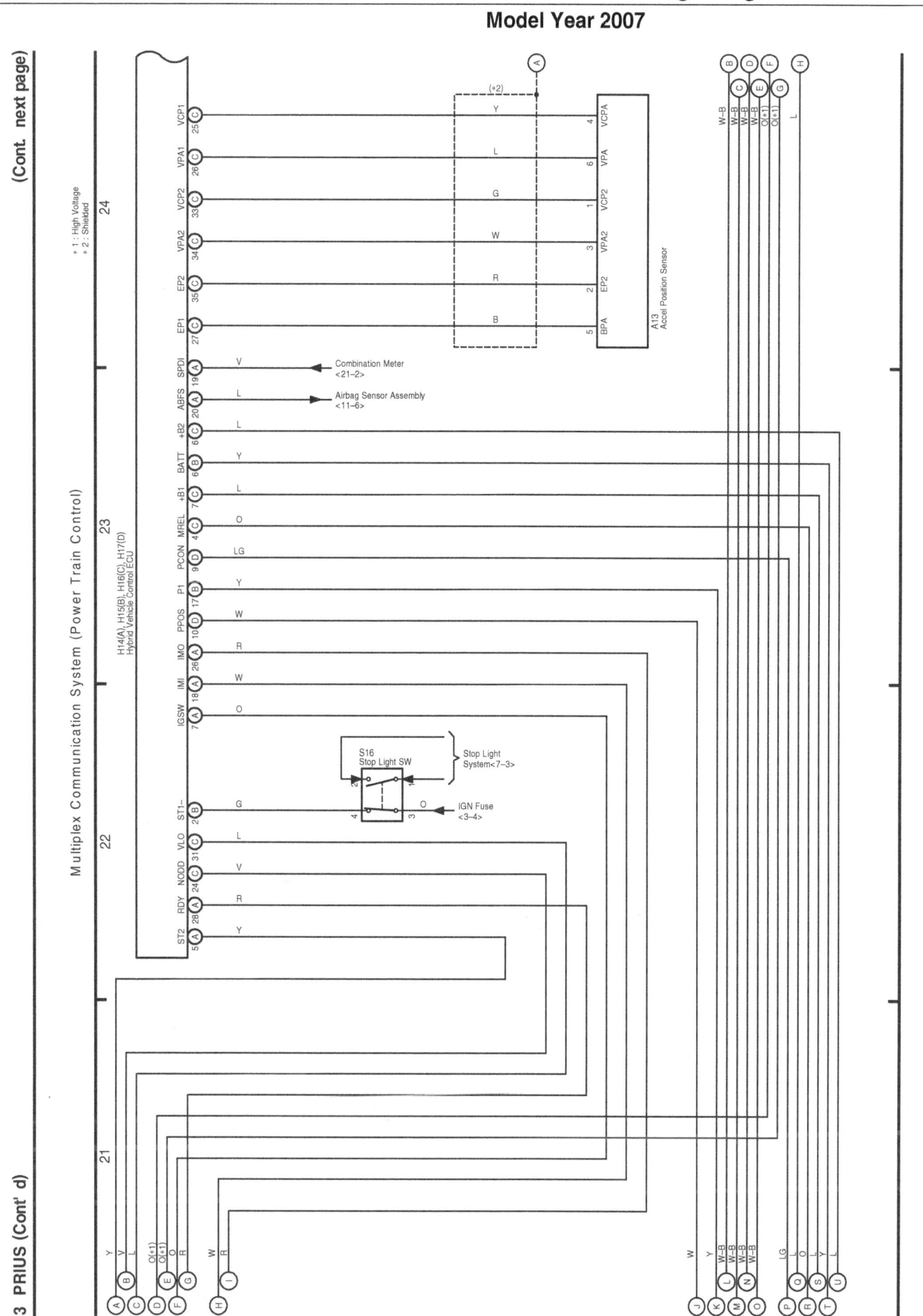

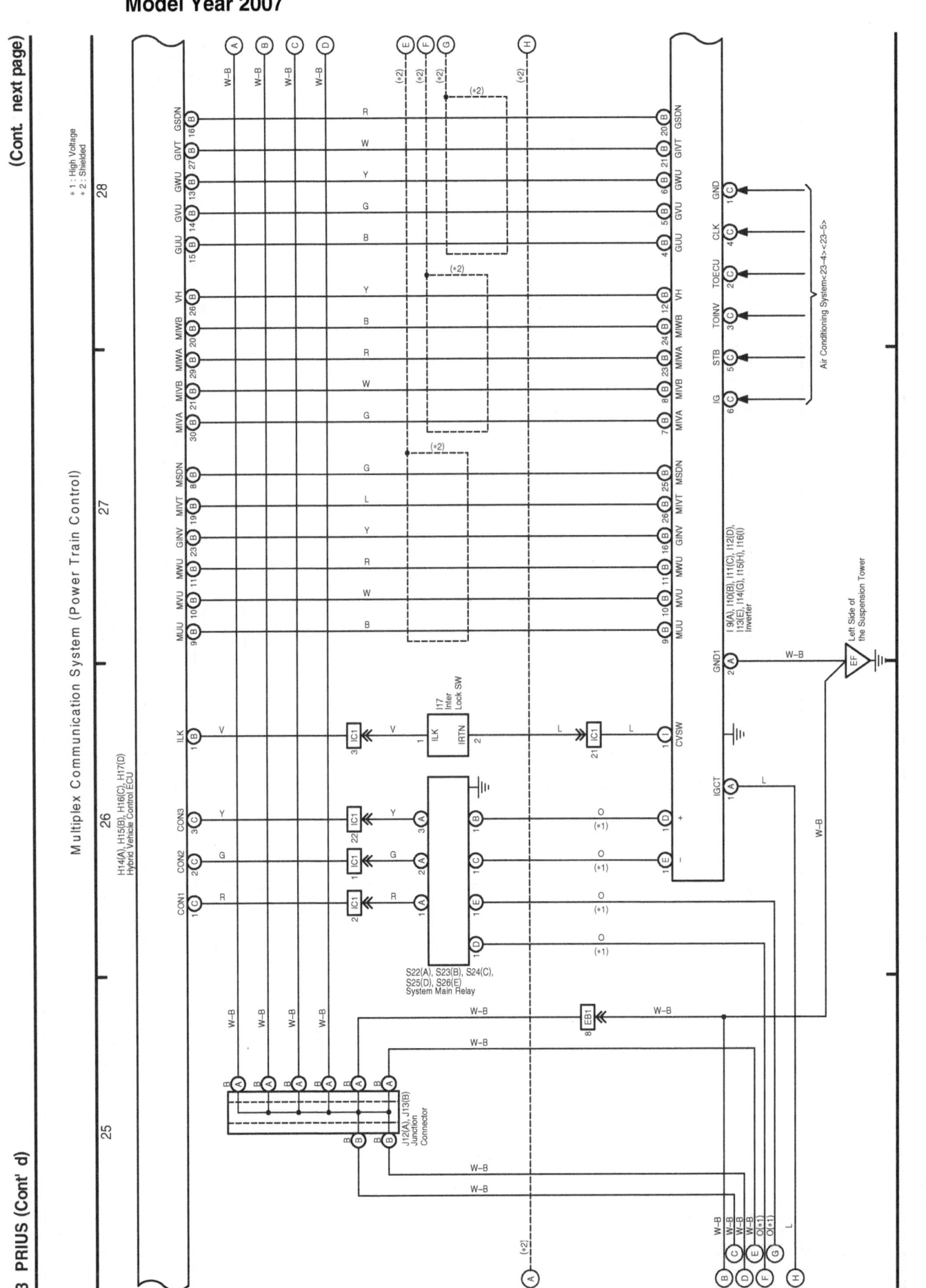

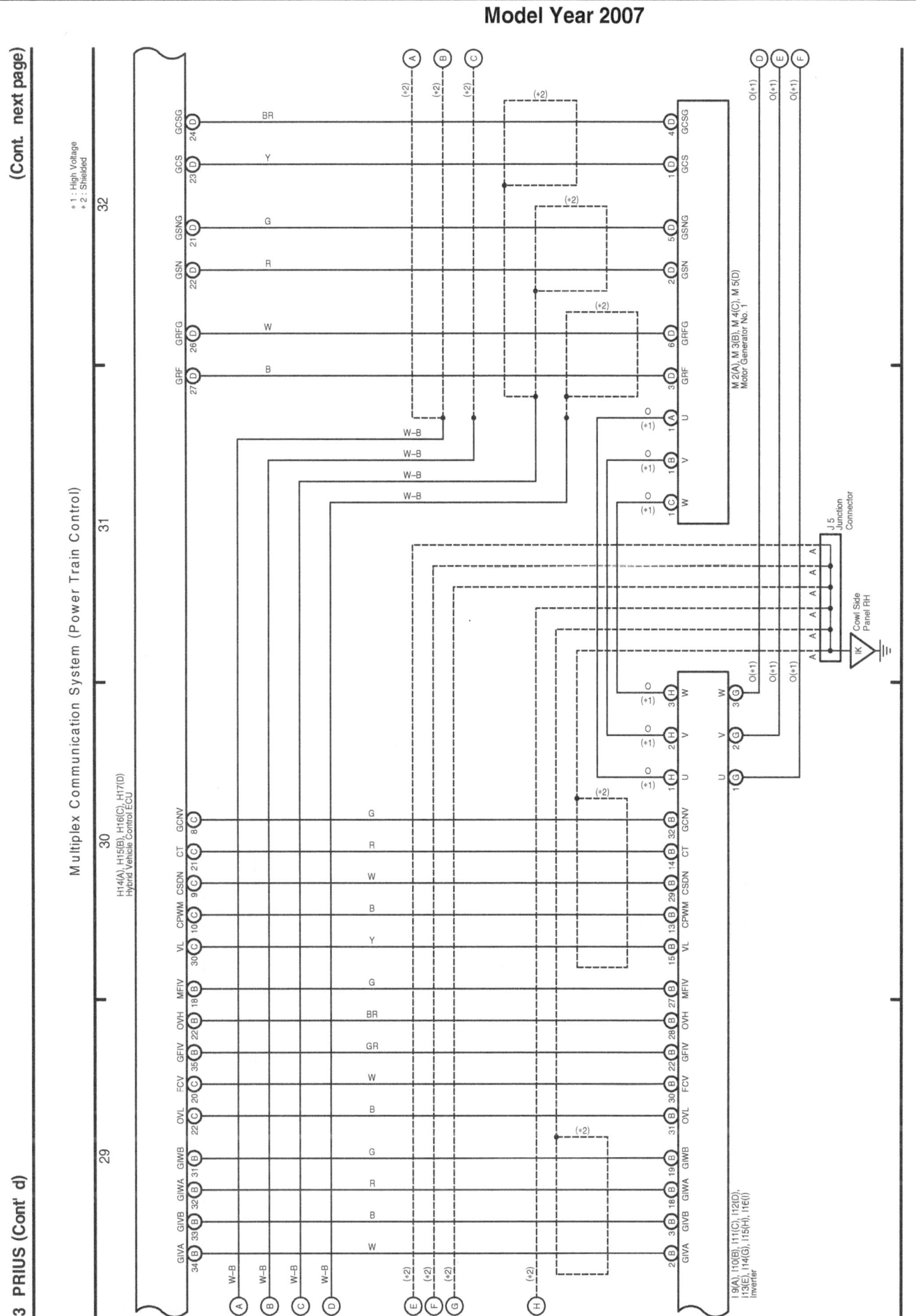

(Cont. next page)

3 PRIUS (Cont' d)

* 1 : High Voltage
* 2 : Shielded

Model Year 2007

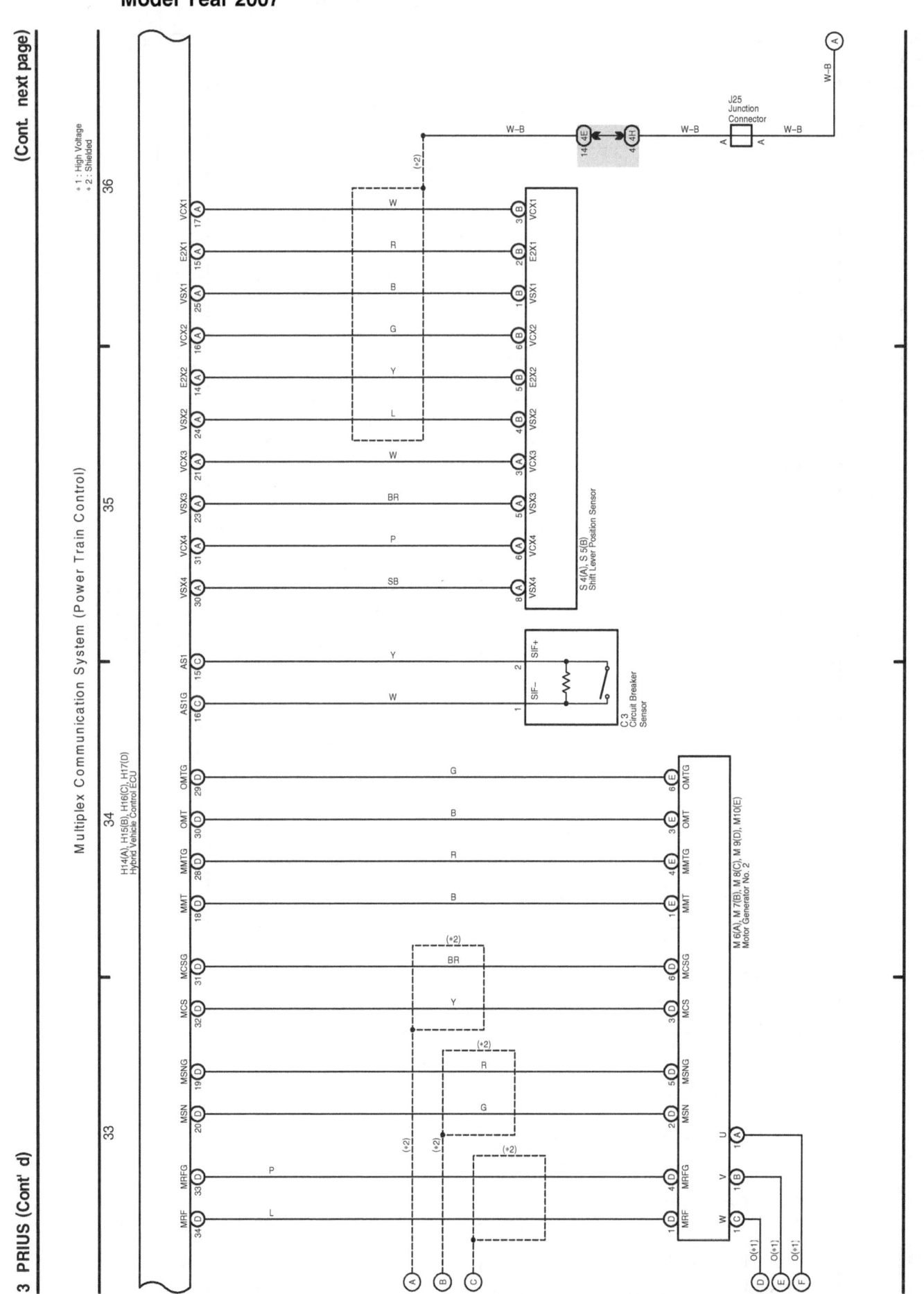

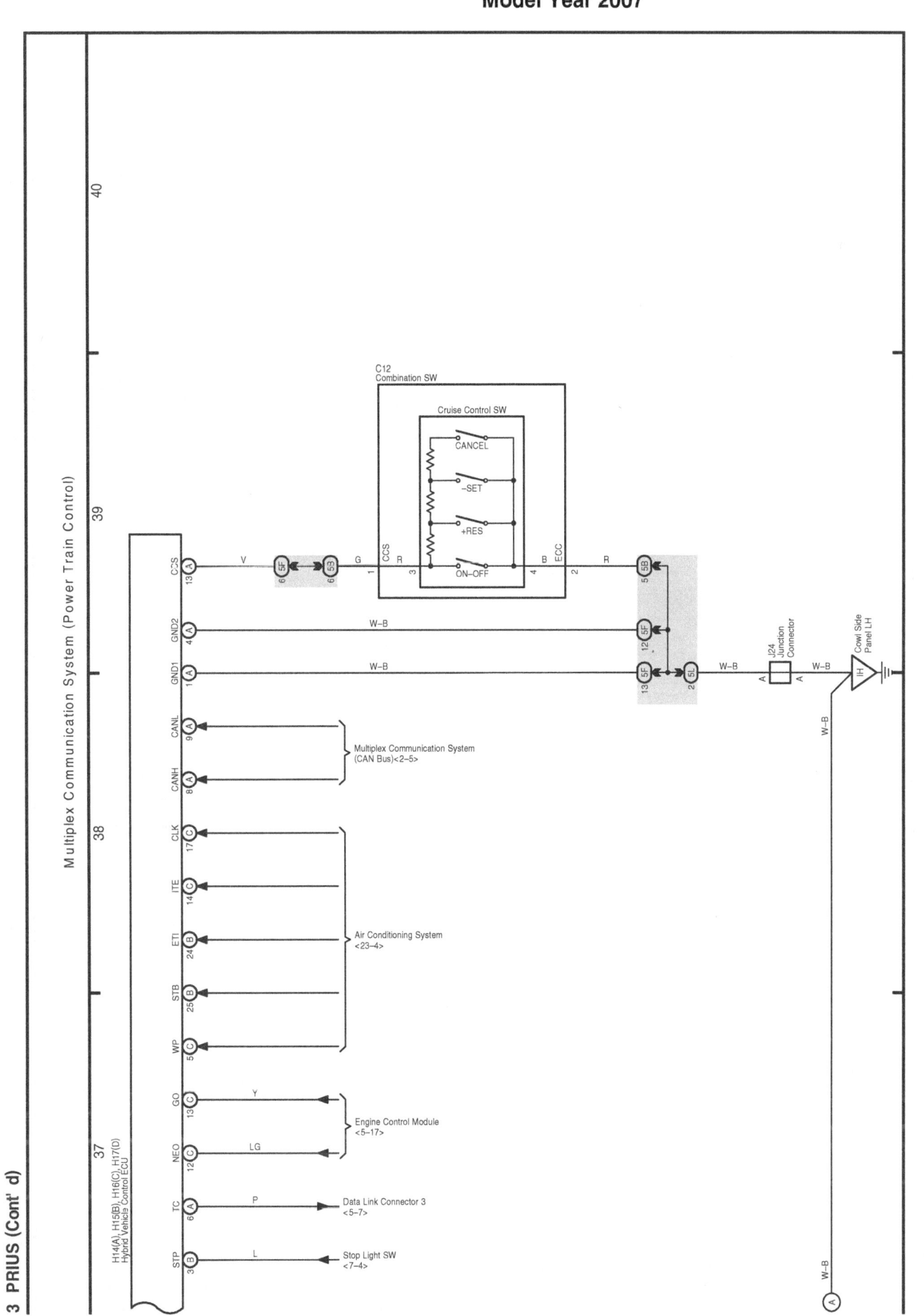

3 PRIUS (Cont' d)

Multiplex Communication System (Power Train Control)

40

39

38

37

H14(A), H15(B), H16(C), H17(D)
Hybrid Vehicle Control ECU

C12
Combination SW

Cruise Control SW

CANCEL

–SET

+RES

ON–OFF

CCS

CCS 13 Ⓐ   V   6 5F   6 5J   G   1   3   R   4   B ECC   2   R   5 5B

GND2 4 Ⓐ   W–B   12 5F

GND1 1 Ⓐ   W–B   13 5F   2 5L   W–B   A   J24
Junction
Connector   A   W–B   IH   Cowl Side
Panel LH

CANL 9 Ⓐ
CANH 8 Ⓐ   Multiplex Communication System
(CAN Bus)<2–5>

CLK 17 Ⓒ
ITE 14 Ⓒ
ETI 24 Ⓑ   Air Conditioning System
<23–4>
STB 25 Ⓑ
WP 5 Ⓒ

GO 13 Ⓒ   Y
NEO 12 Ⓒ   LG   Engine Control Module
<5–17>

TC 6 Ⓐ   P   Data Link Connector 3
<5–7>

STP 3 Ⓑ   L   Stop Light SW
<7–4>

W–B   A

13

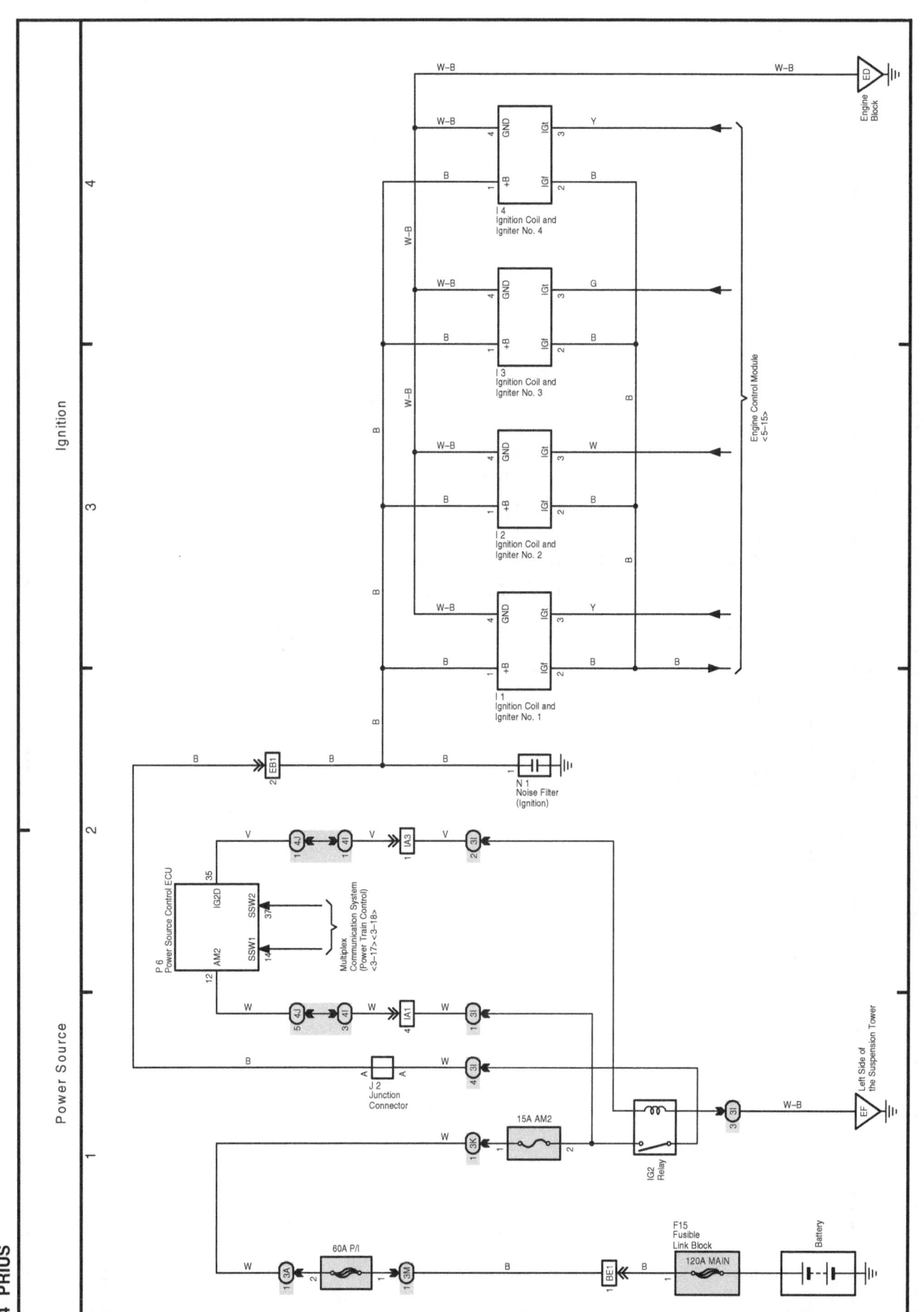

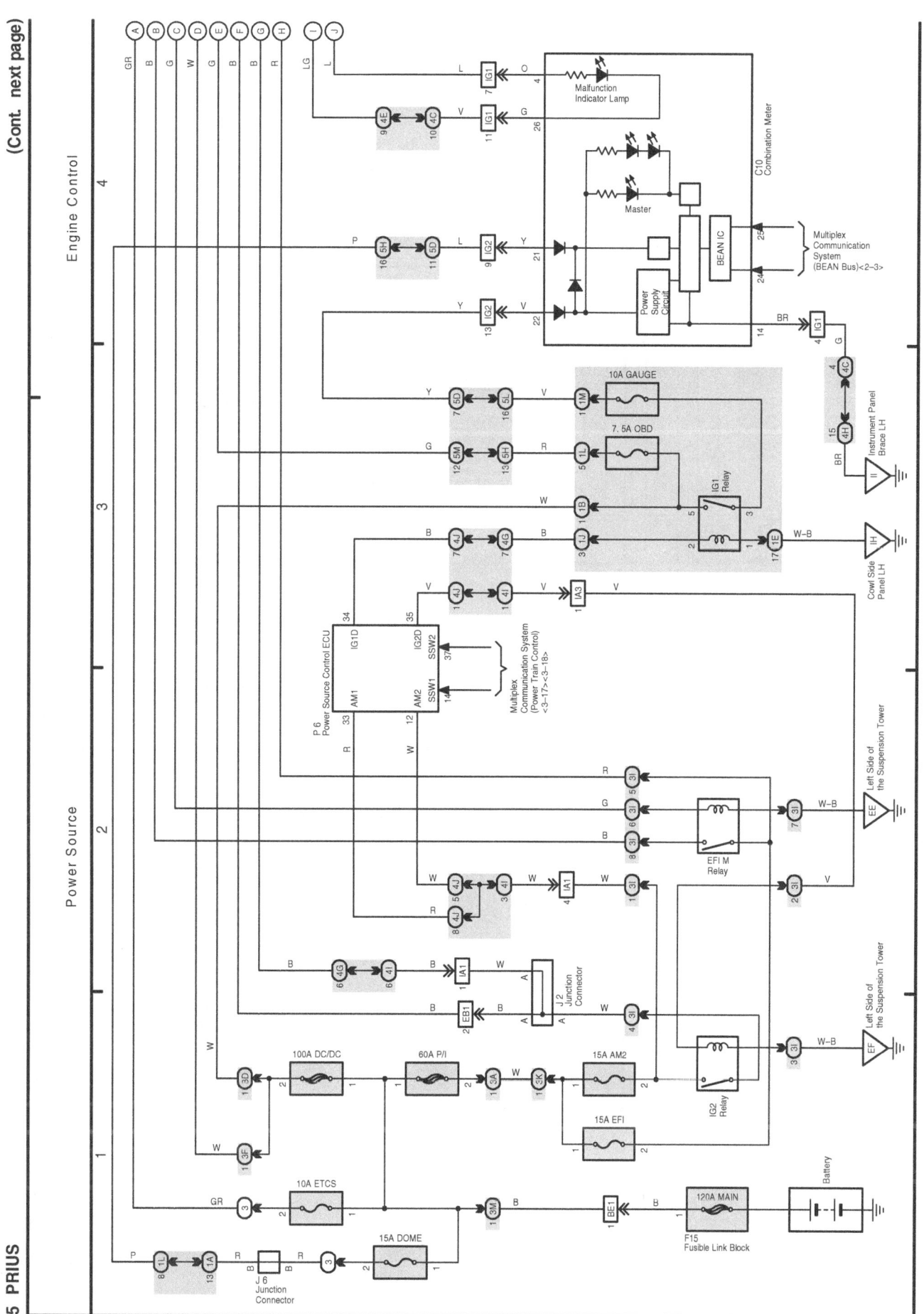

Model Year 2007

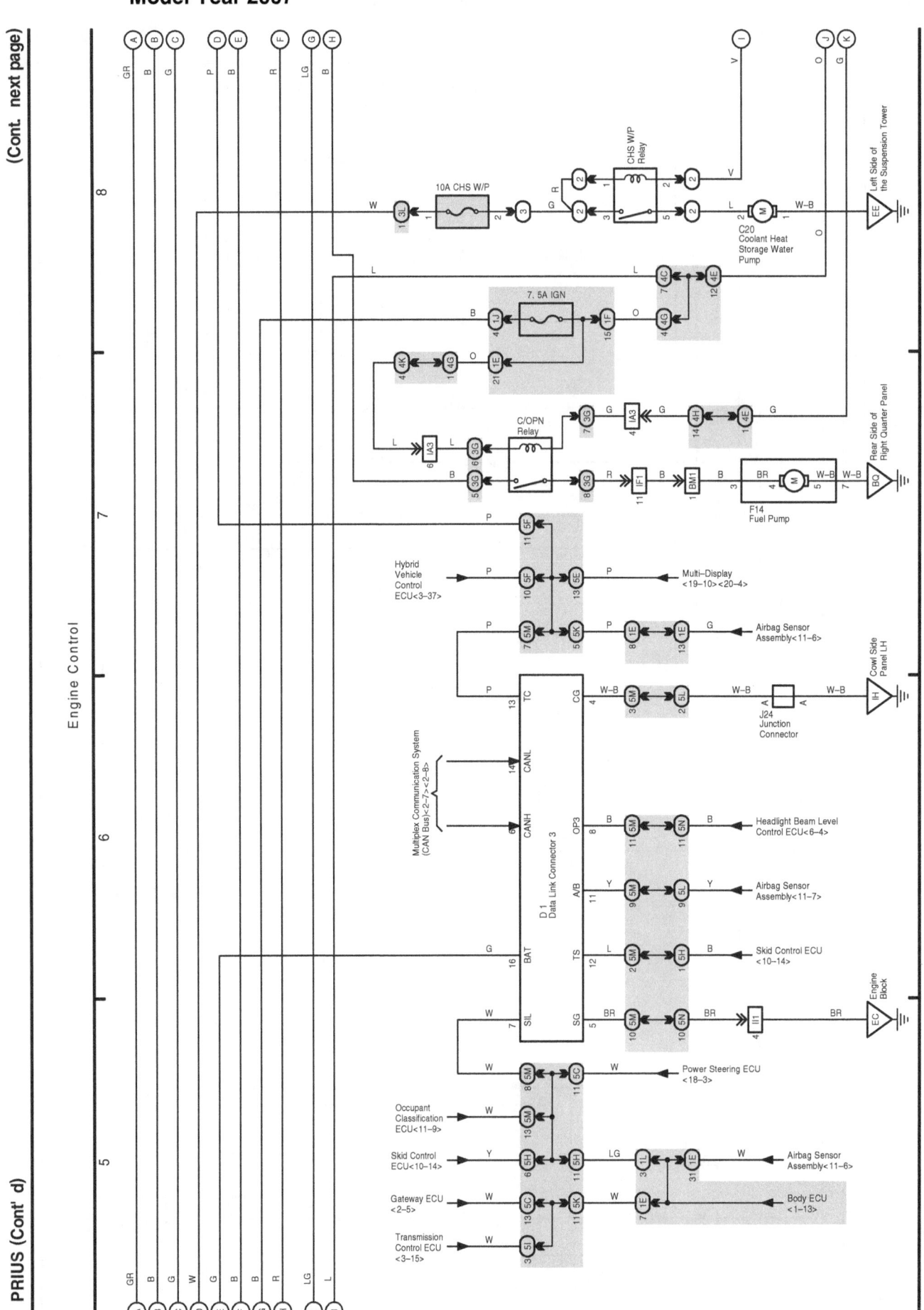

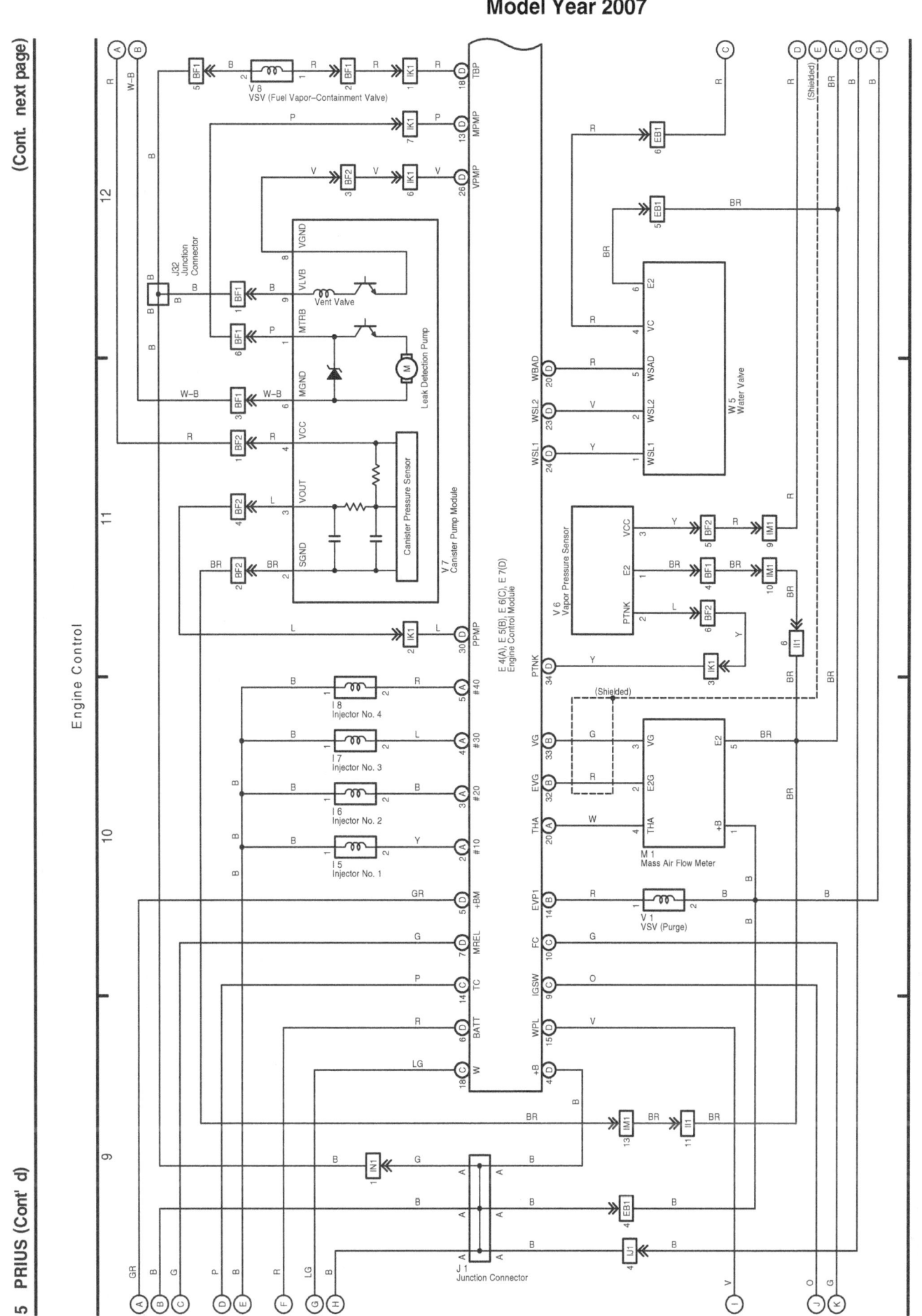

5 PRIUS (Cont' d)

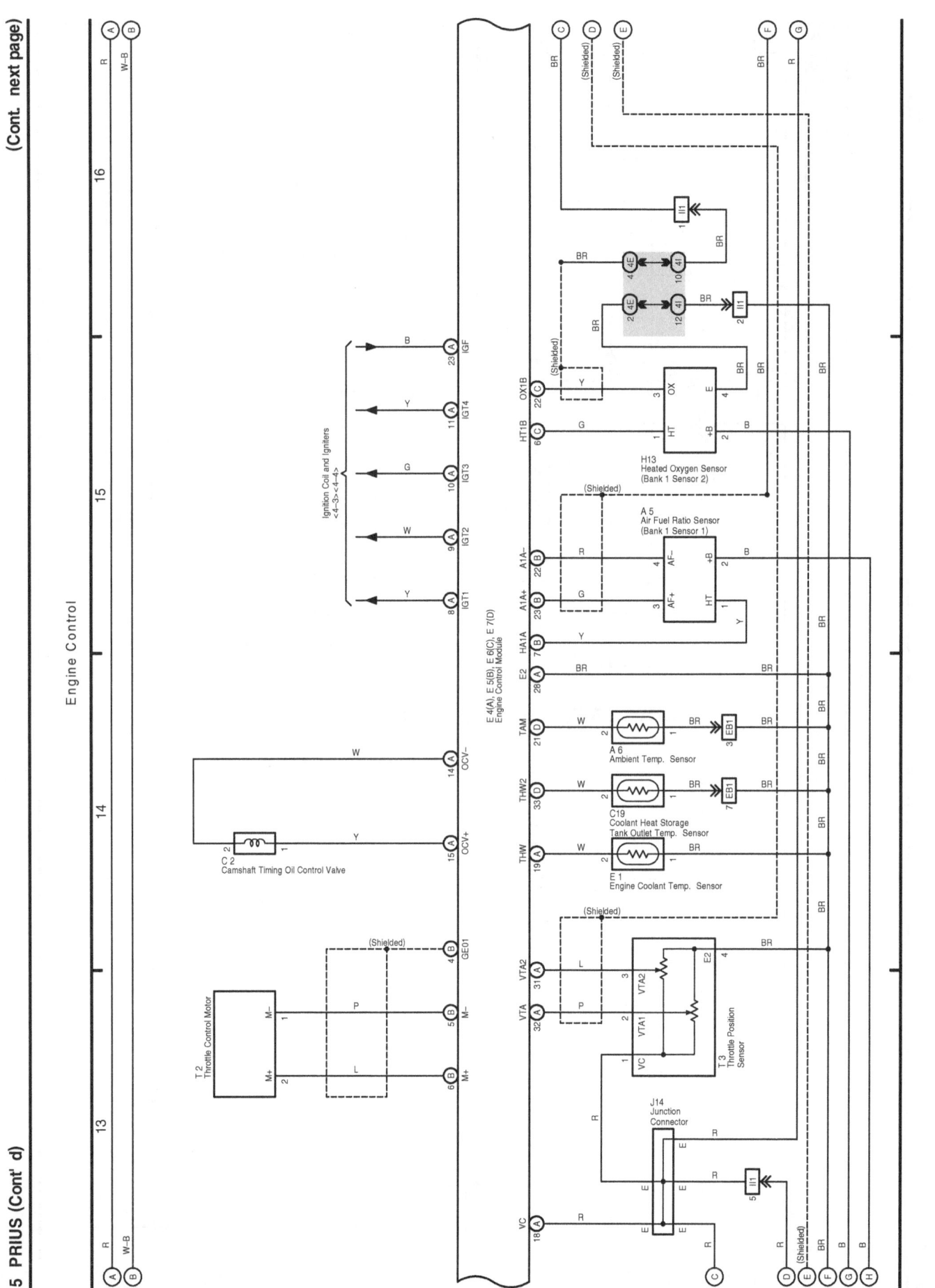

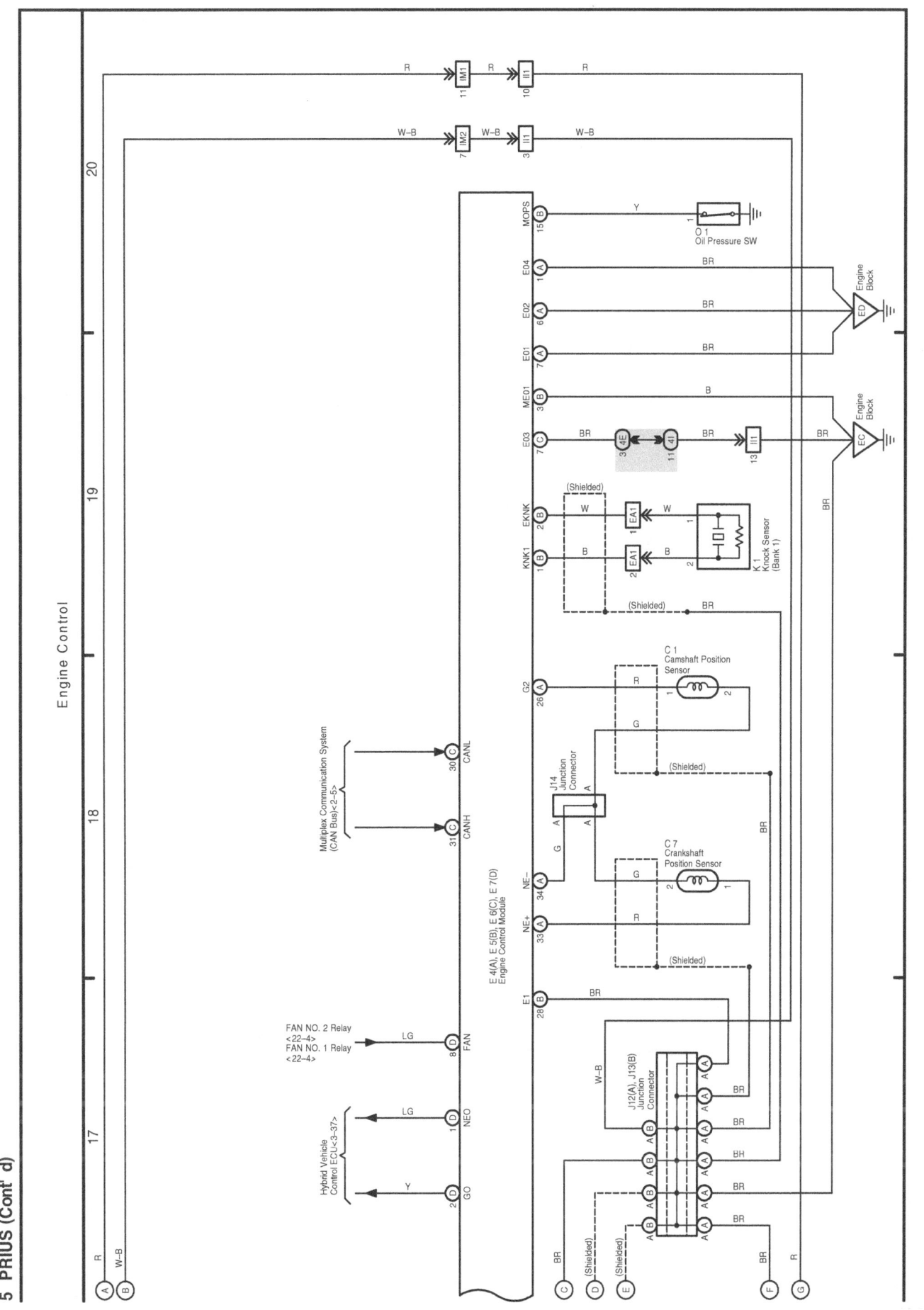

5 PRIUS (Cont'd)

Engine Control

Model Year 2007

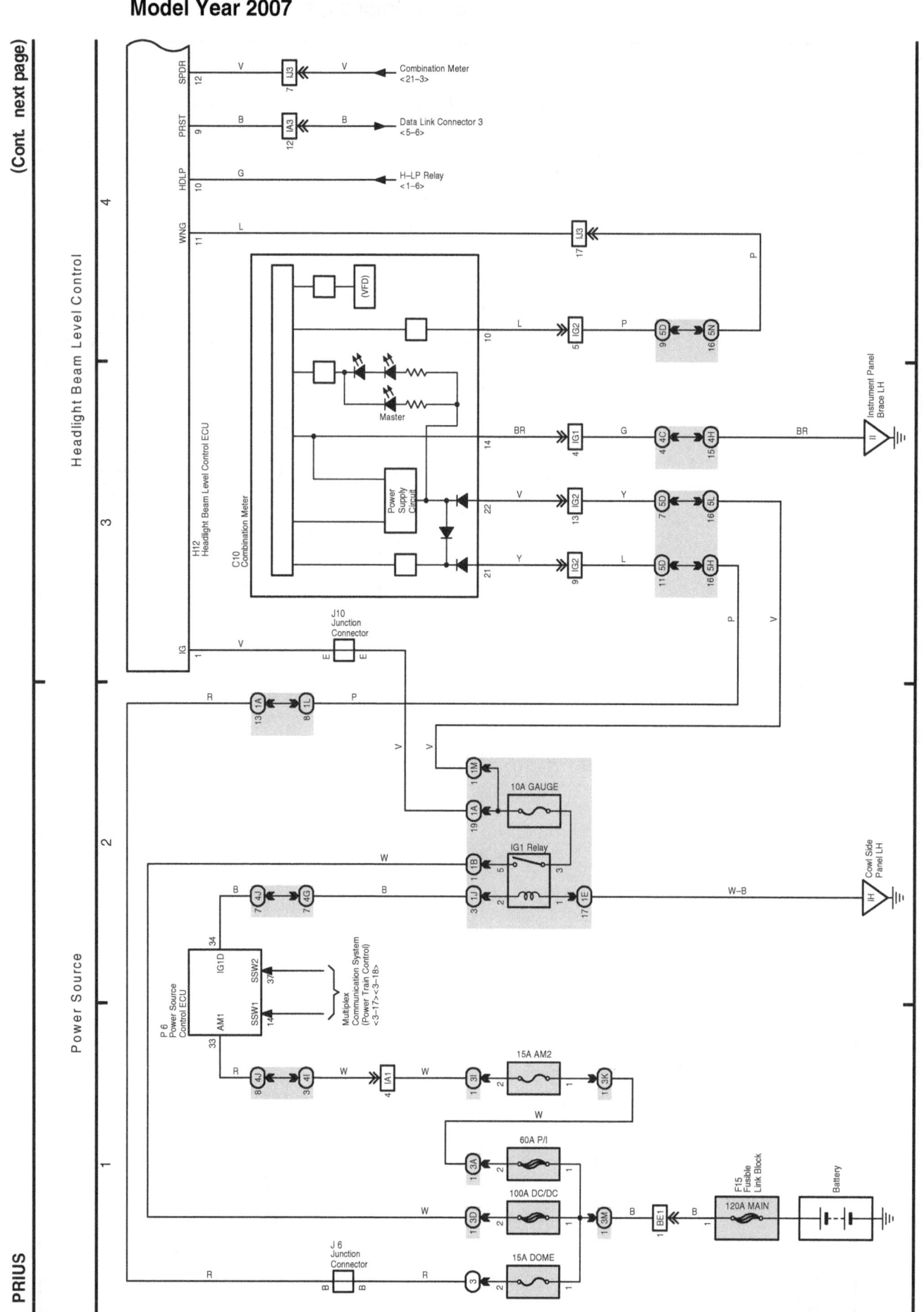

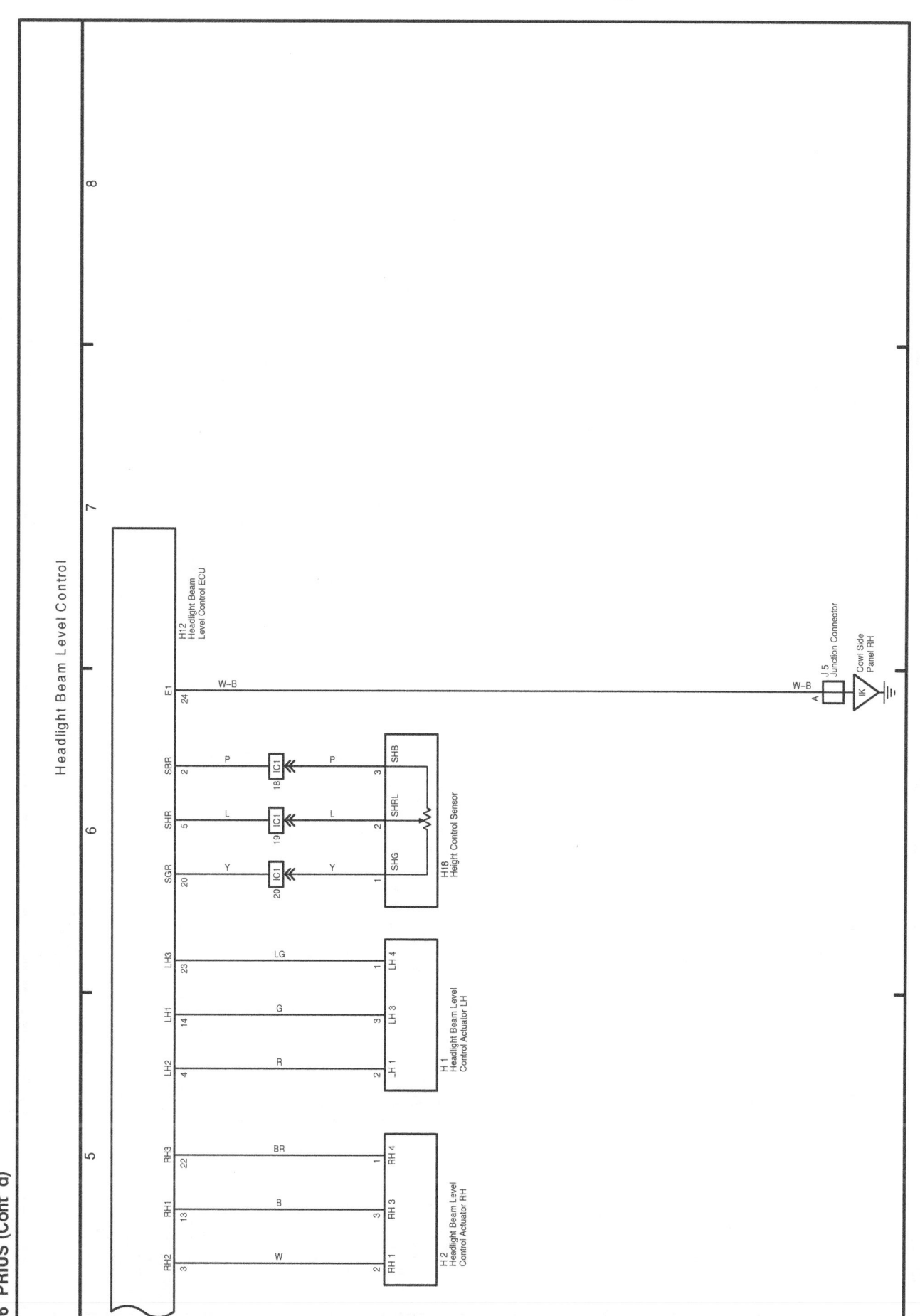

Headlight Beam Level Control

H12 Headlight Beam Level Control ECU

| E1 | 24 | W–B | | | W–B | A | J 5 Junction Connector | 1K | Cowl Side Panel RH |

SBR	2	P	18 IC1	P	3	SHB
SHR	5	L	19 IC1	L	2	SHRL
SGR	20	Y	20 IC1	Y	1	SHG

H18 Height Control Sensor

LH3	23	LG	1	LH 4
LH1	14	G	3	LH 3
LH2	4	R	2	LH 1

H 1 Headlight Beam Level Control Actuator LH

RH3	22	BR	1	RH 4
RH1	13	B	3	RH 3
RH2	3	W	2	RH 1

H 2 Headlight Beam Level Control Actuator RH

6 PRIUS (Cont' d)

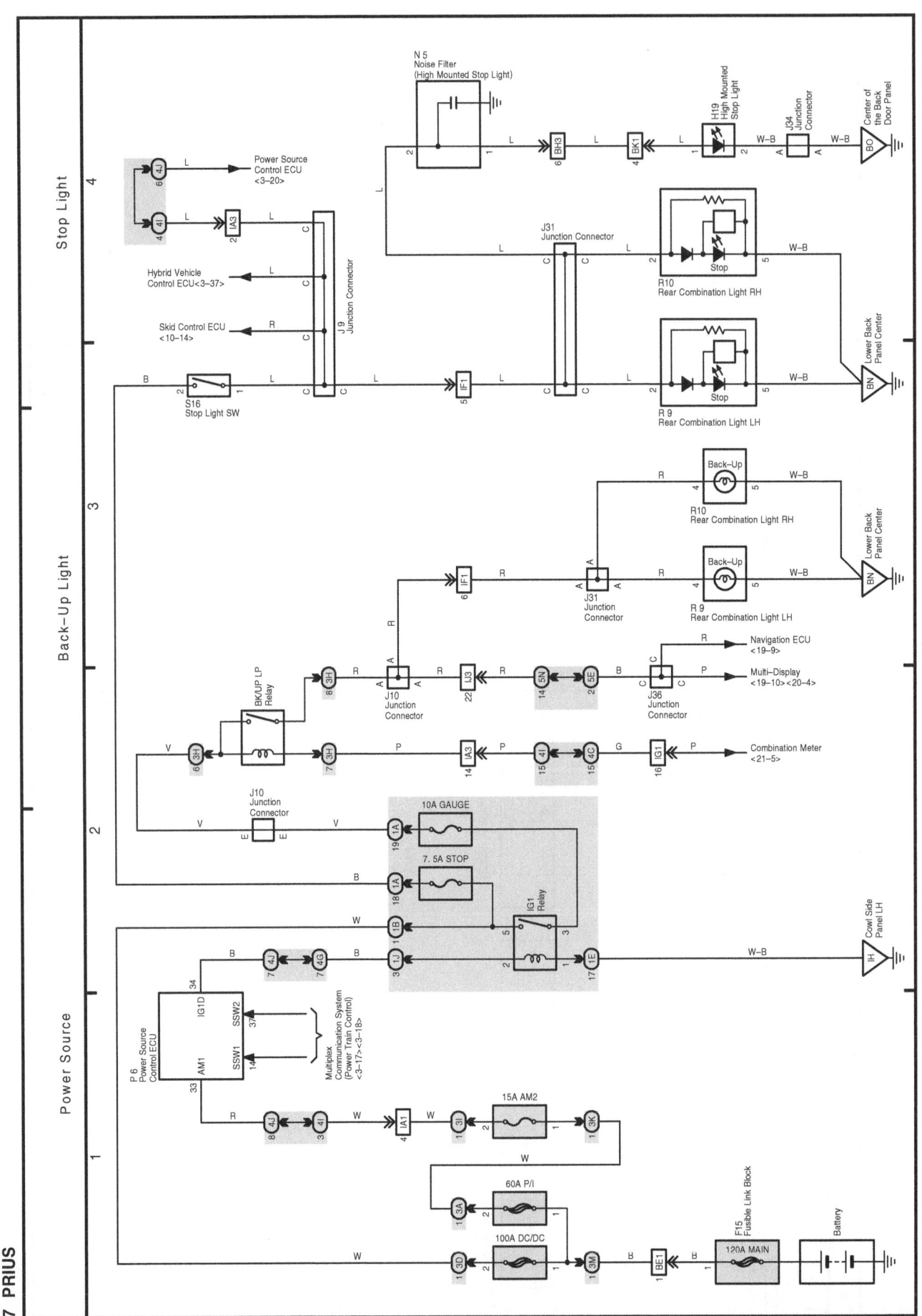

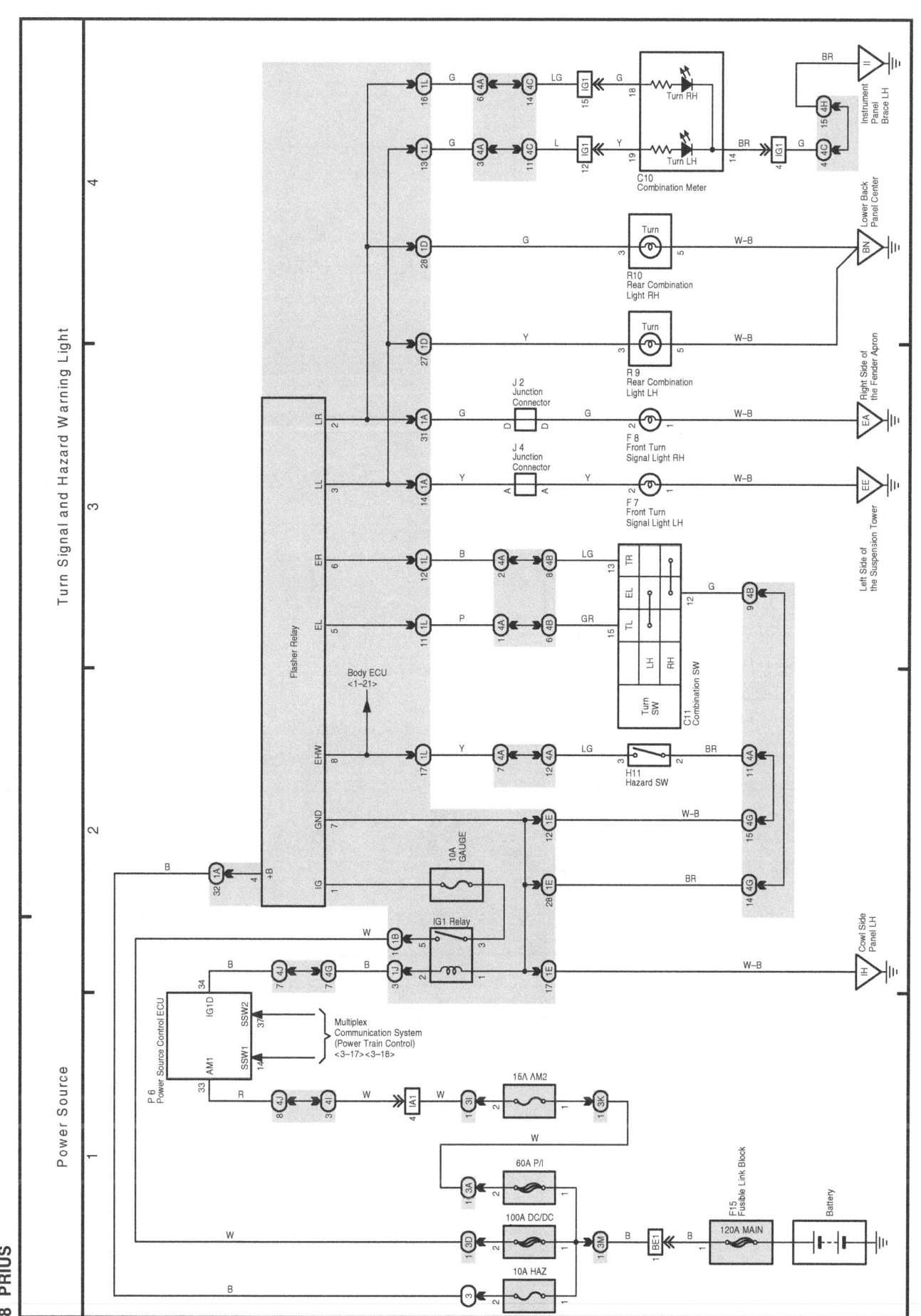

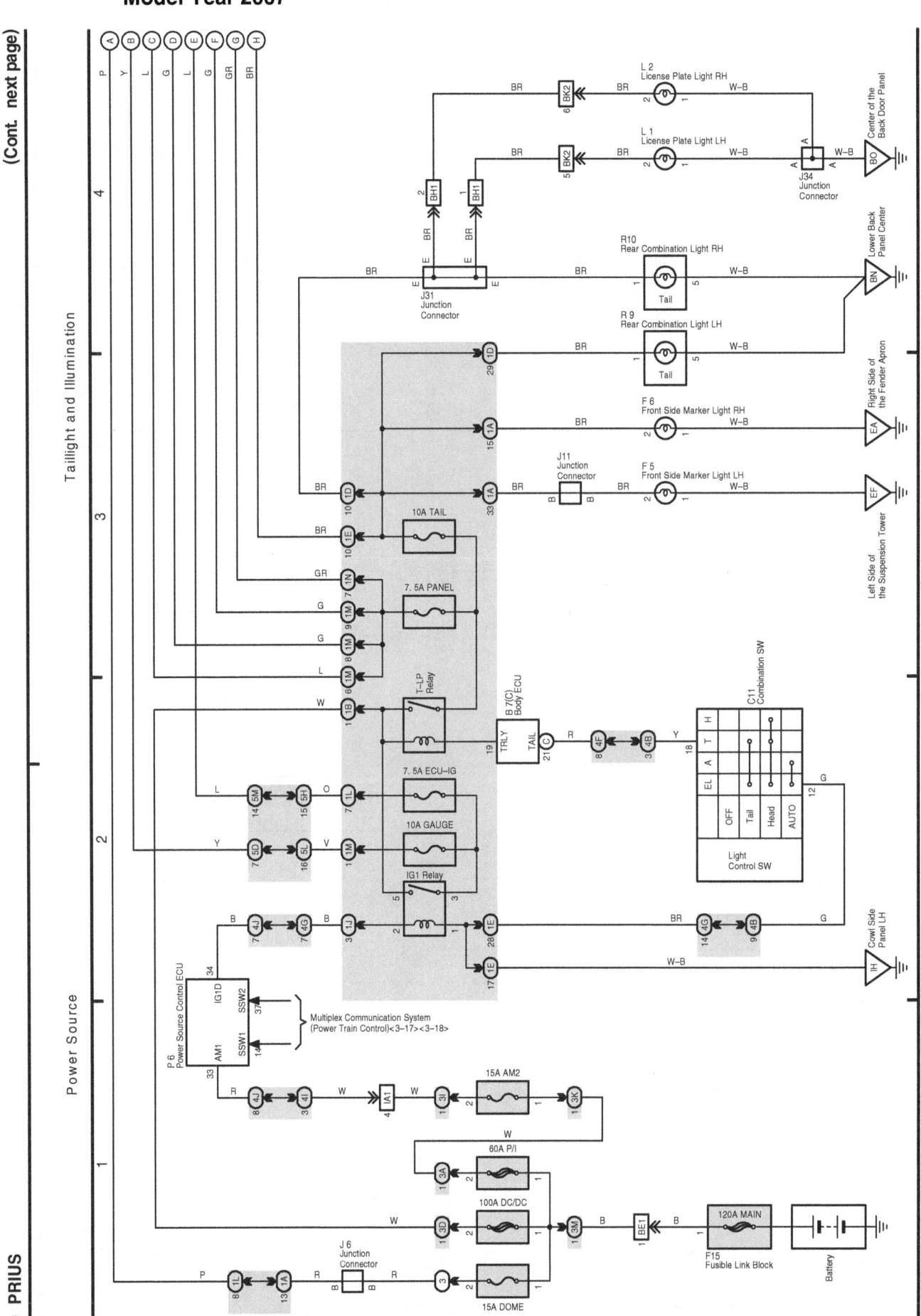

Taillight and Illumination

Power Source

(Cont. next page)

9 PRIUS

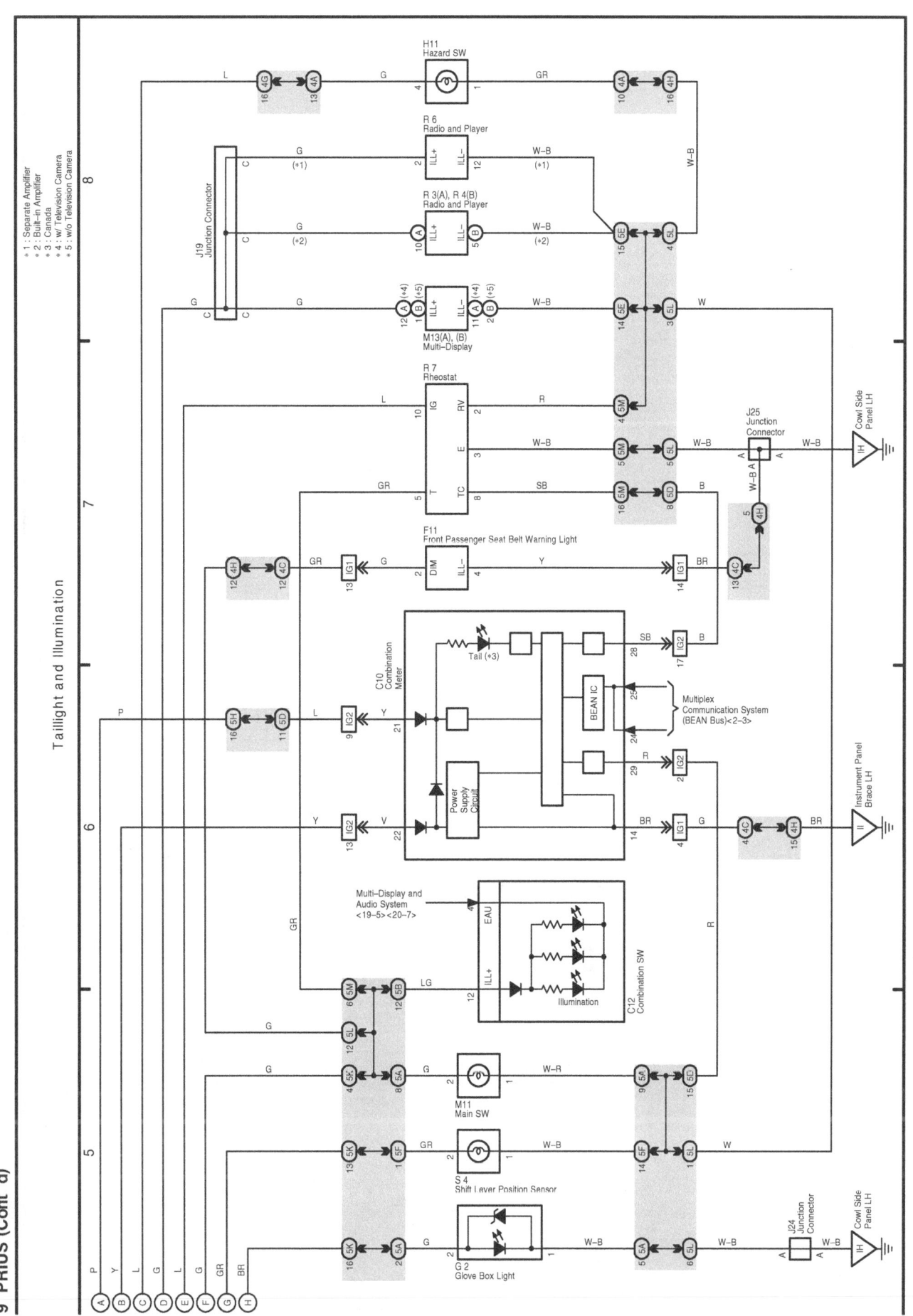

Taillight and Illumination

9 PRIUS (Cont'd)

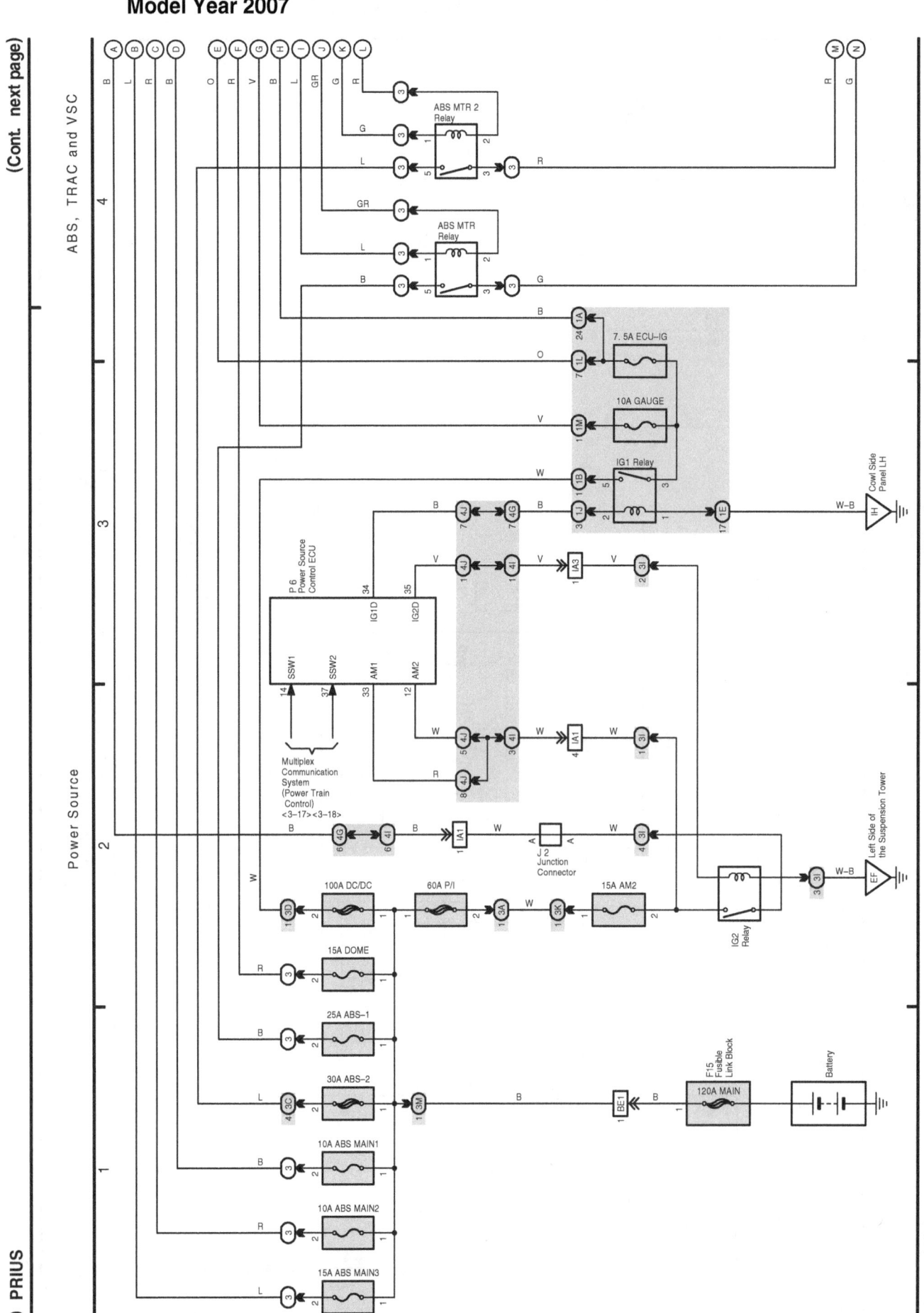

10 PRIUS

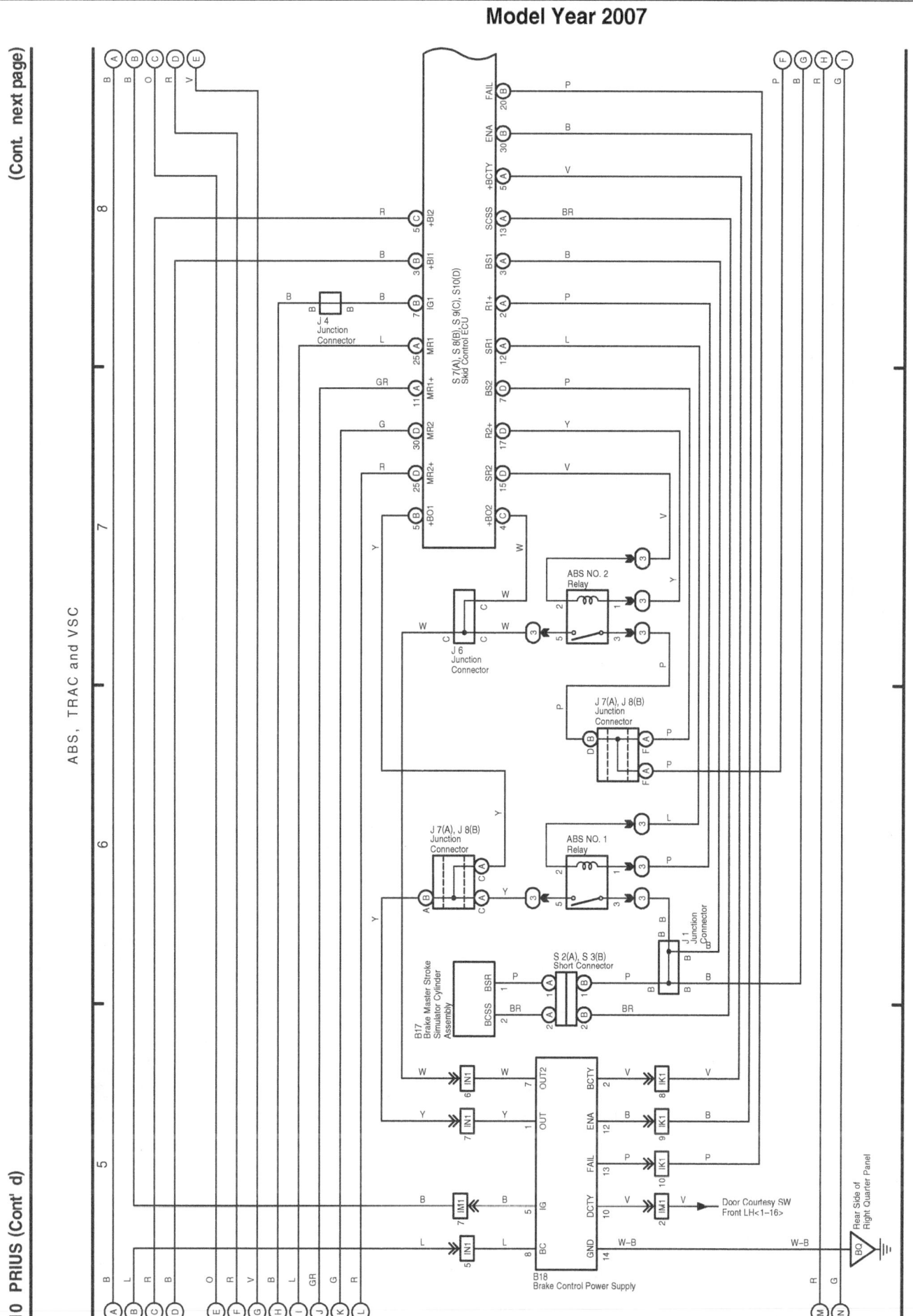

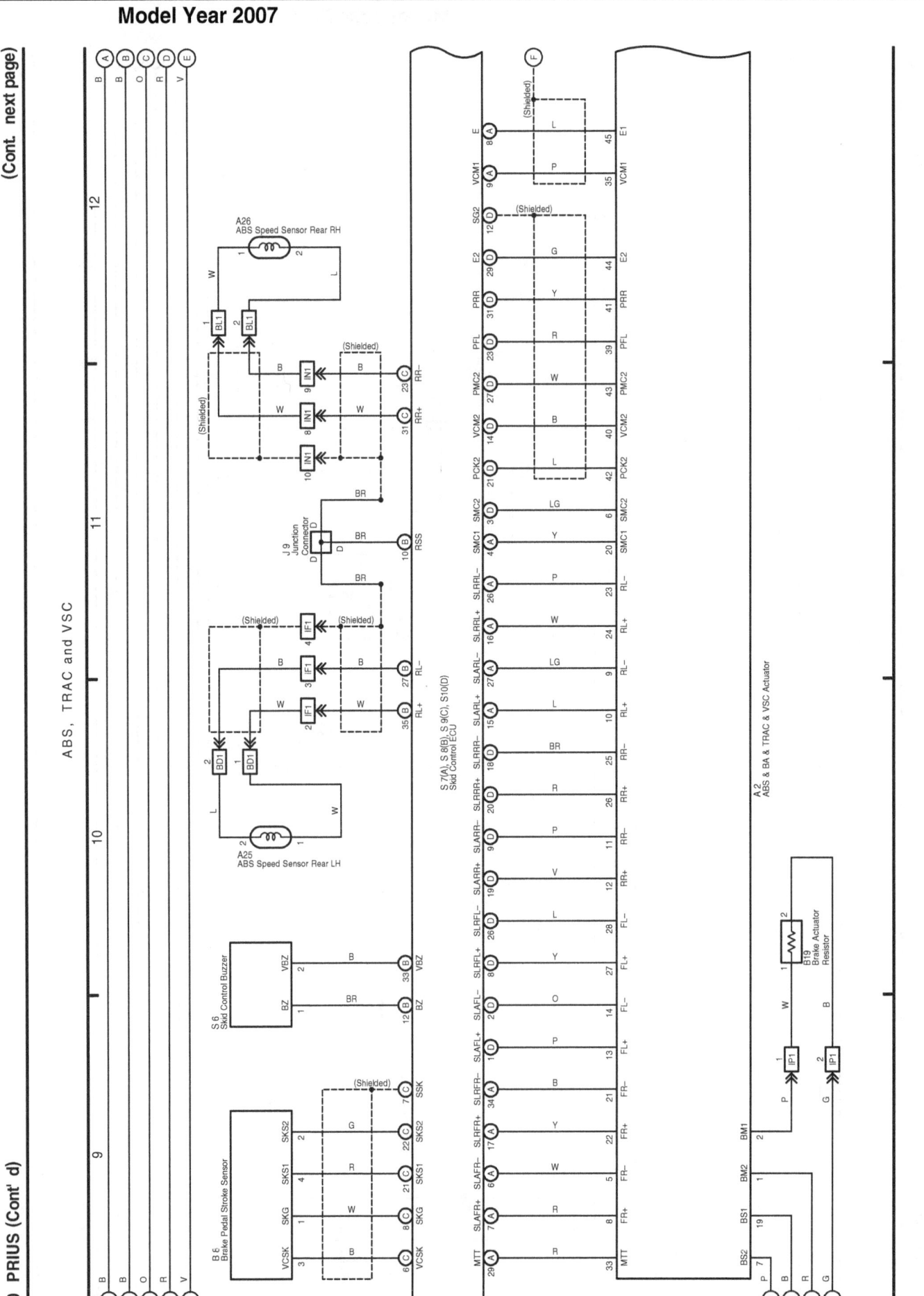

Model Year 2007

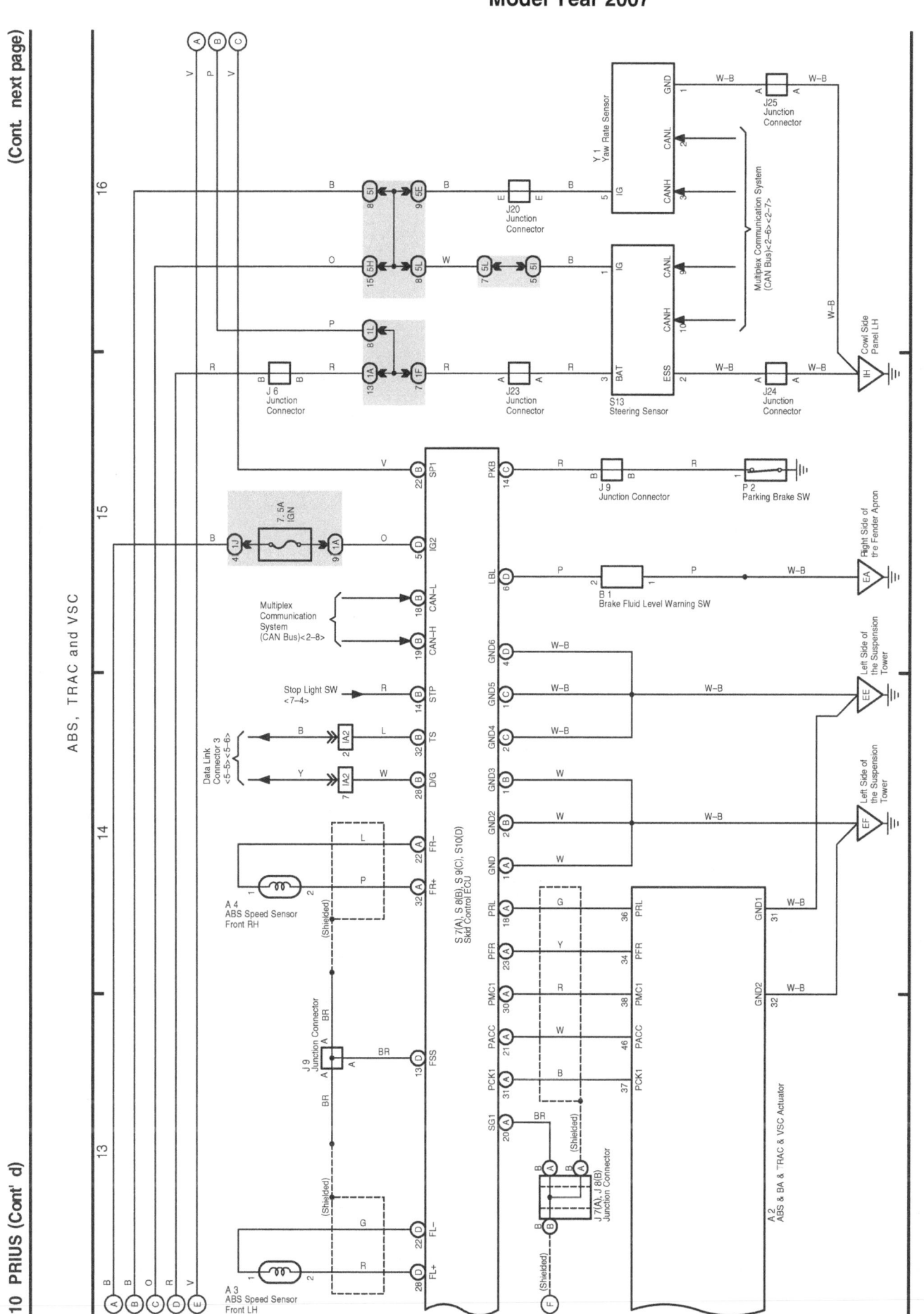

Model Year 2007

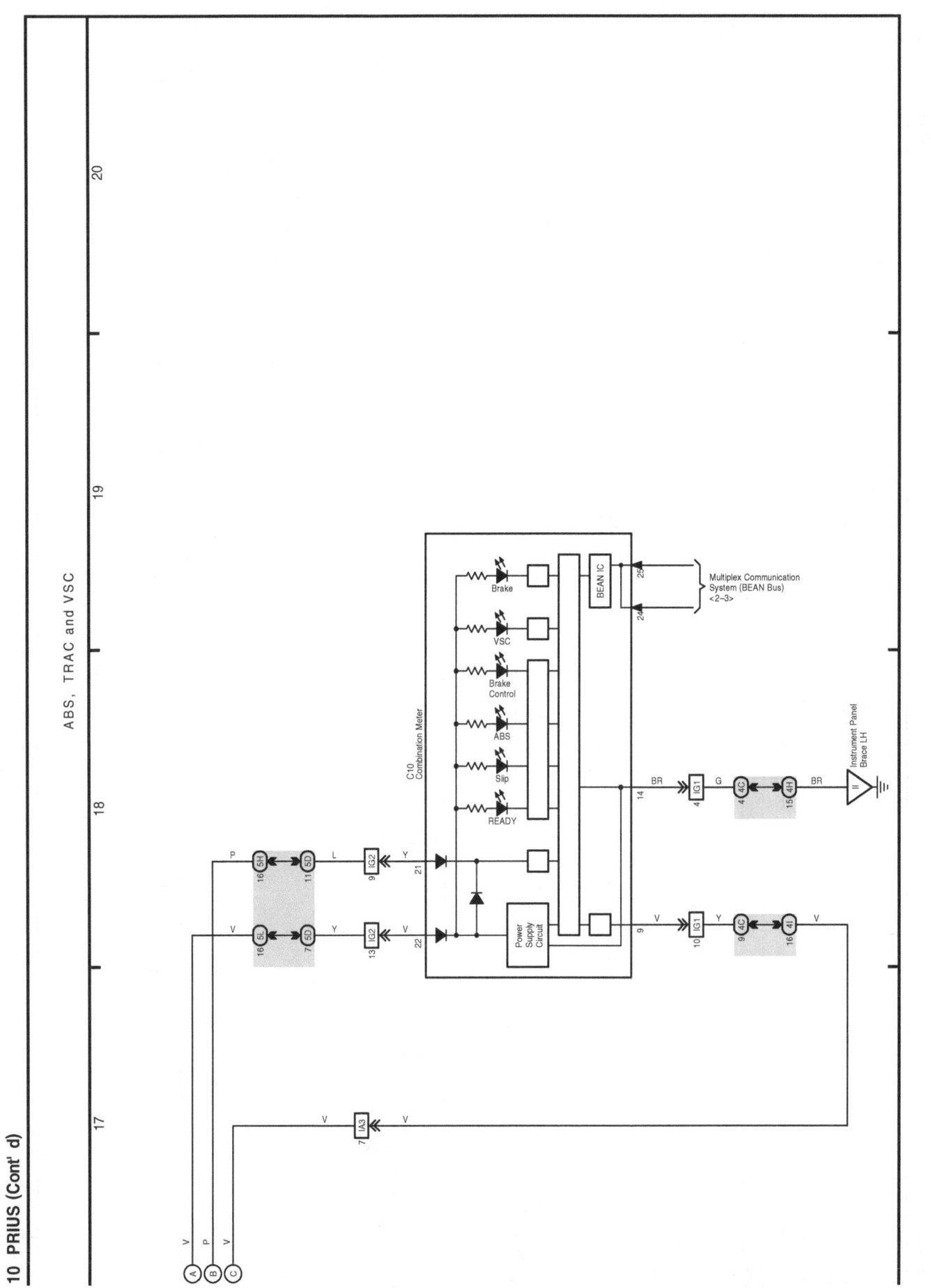

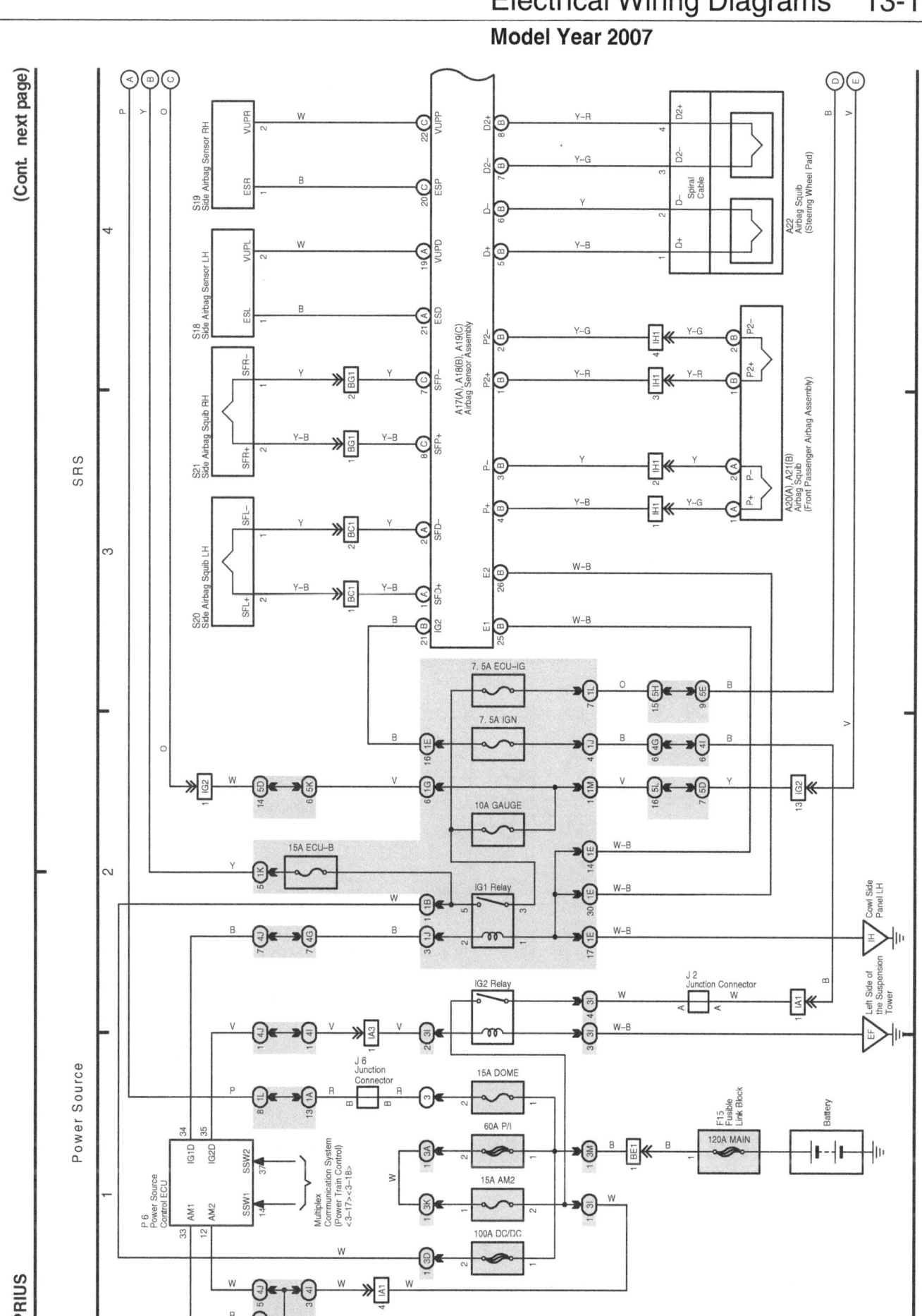

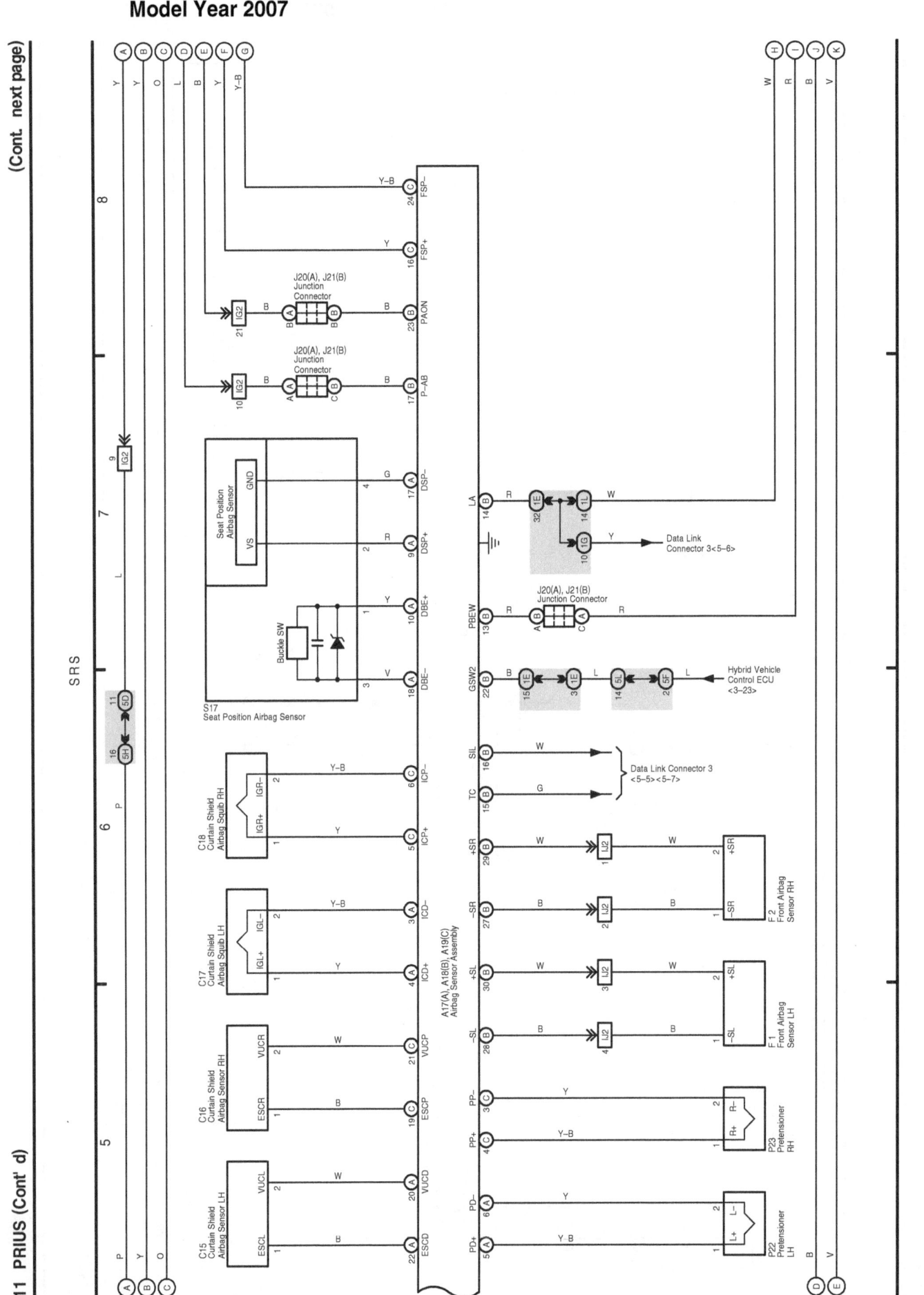

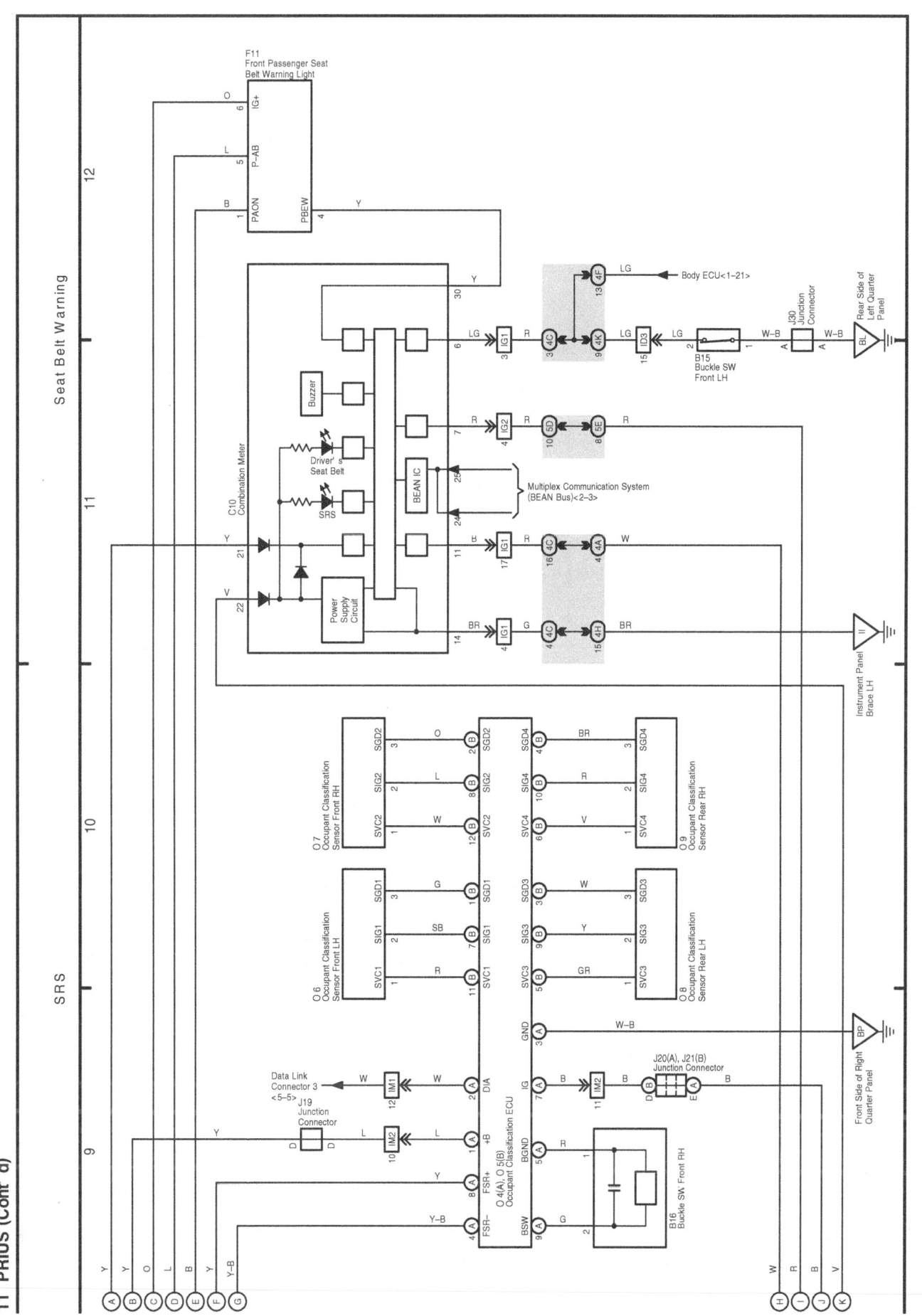

11 PRIUS (Cont'd)

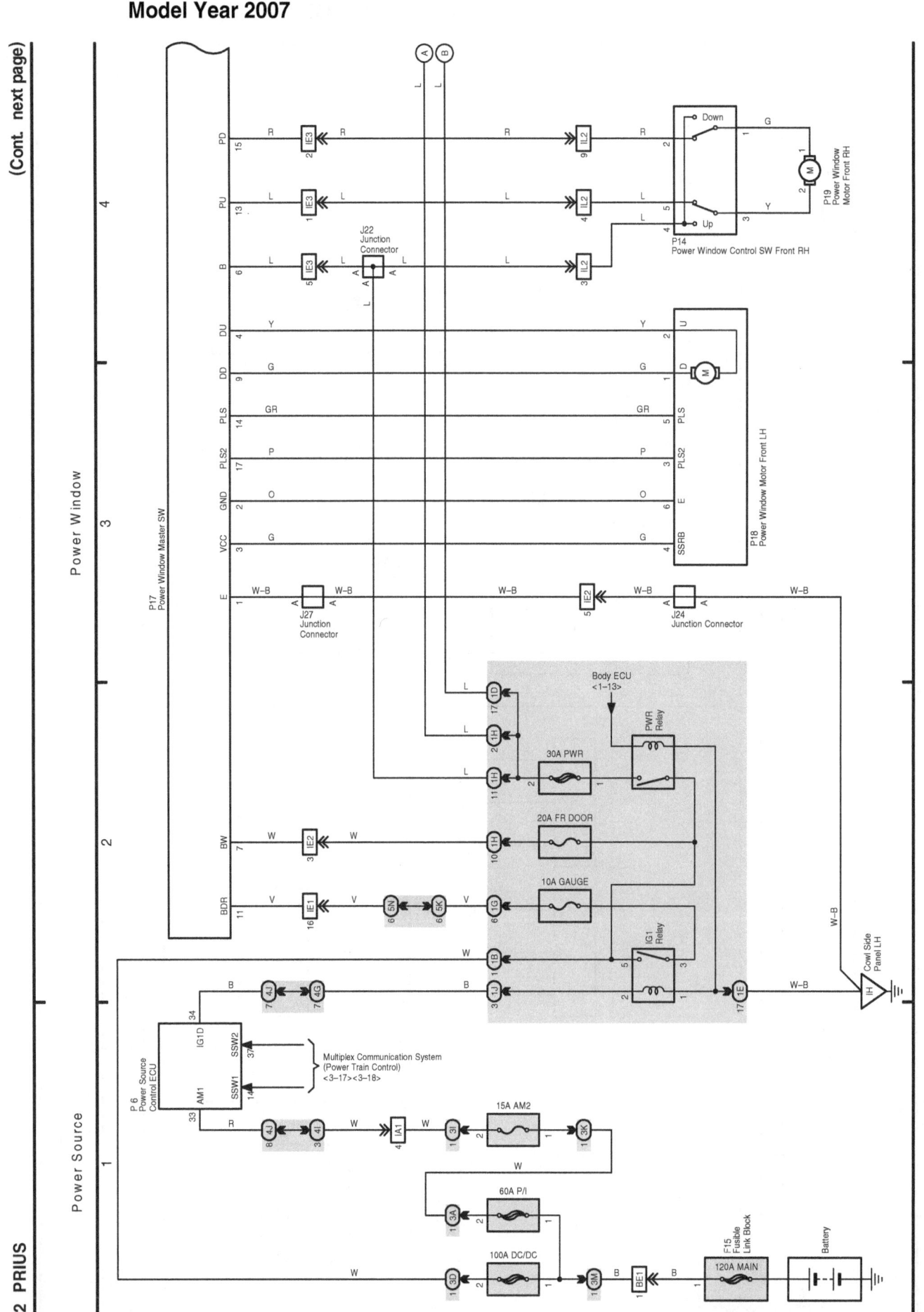

Power Window

13

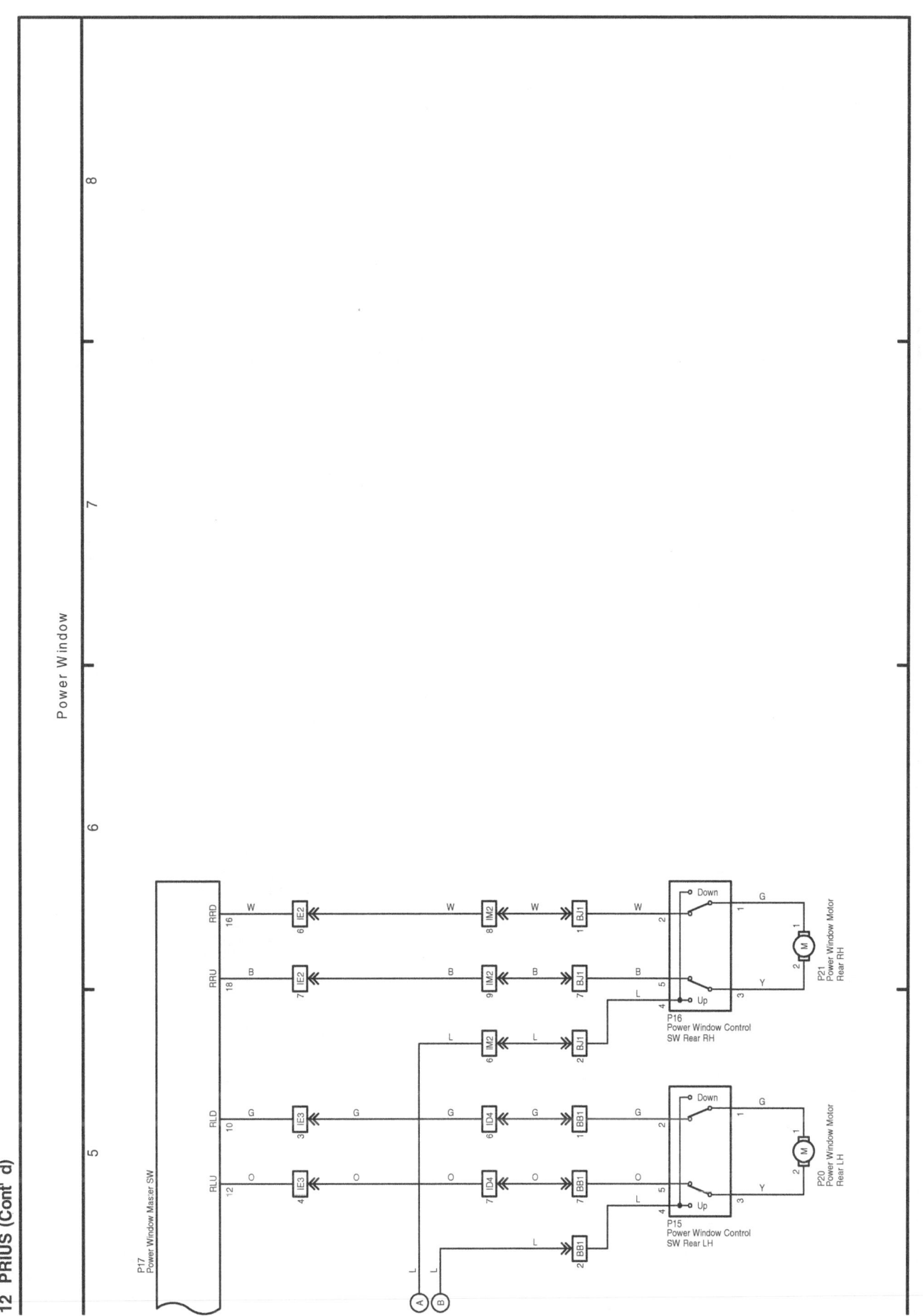

Model Year 2007

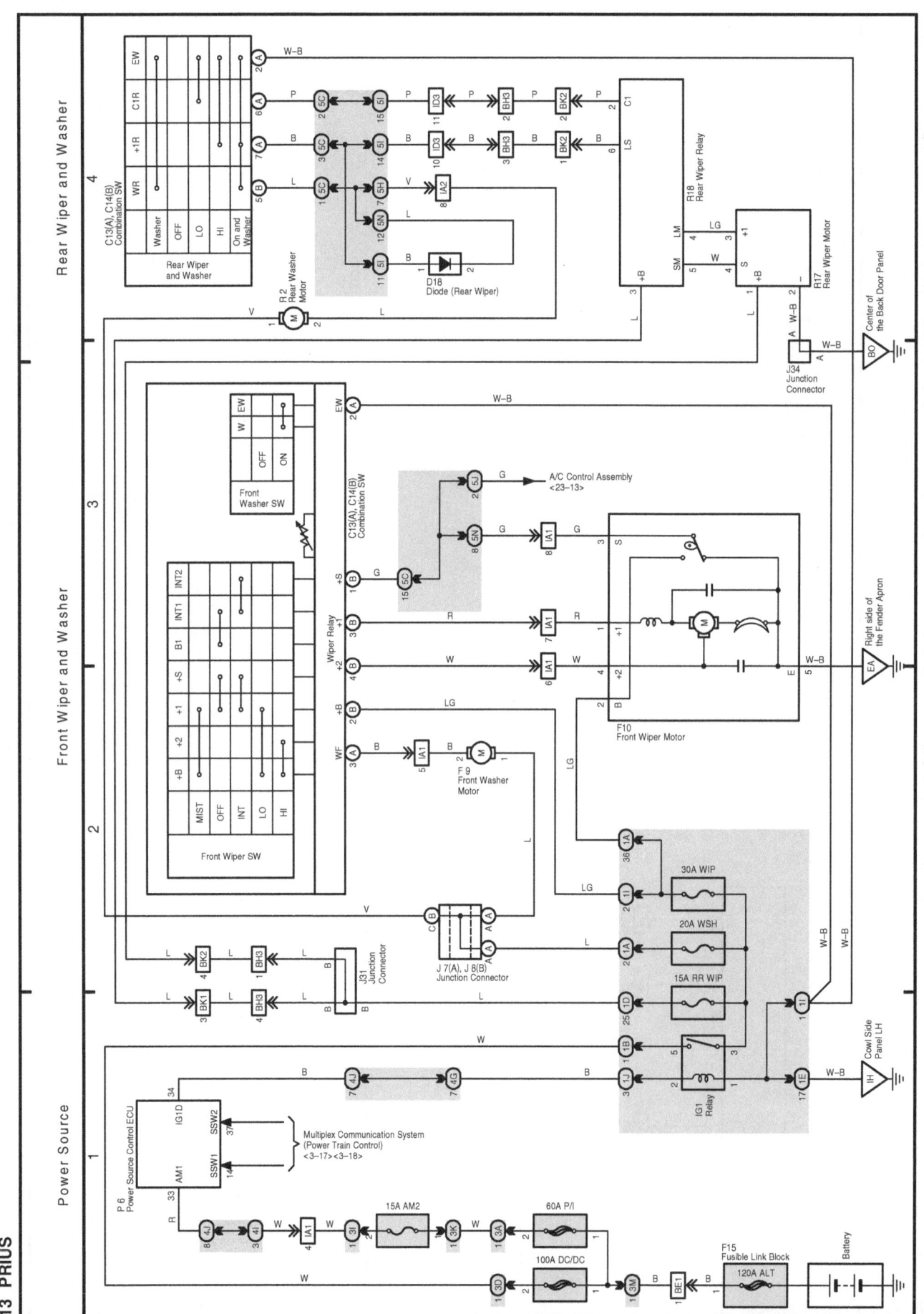

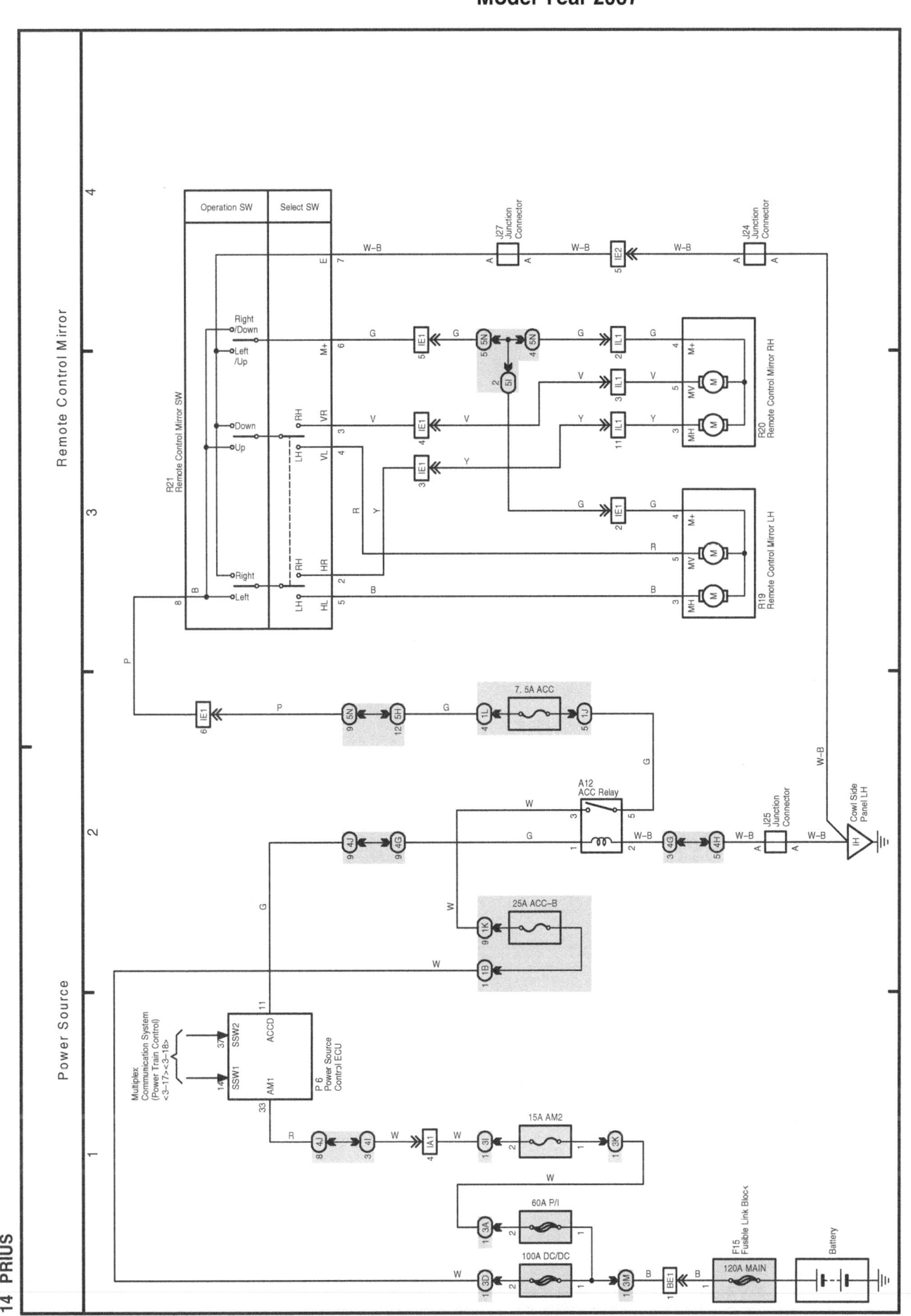

Model Year 2007

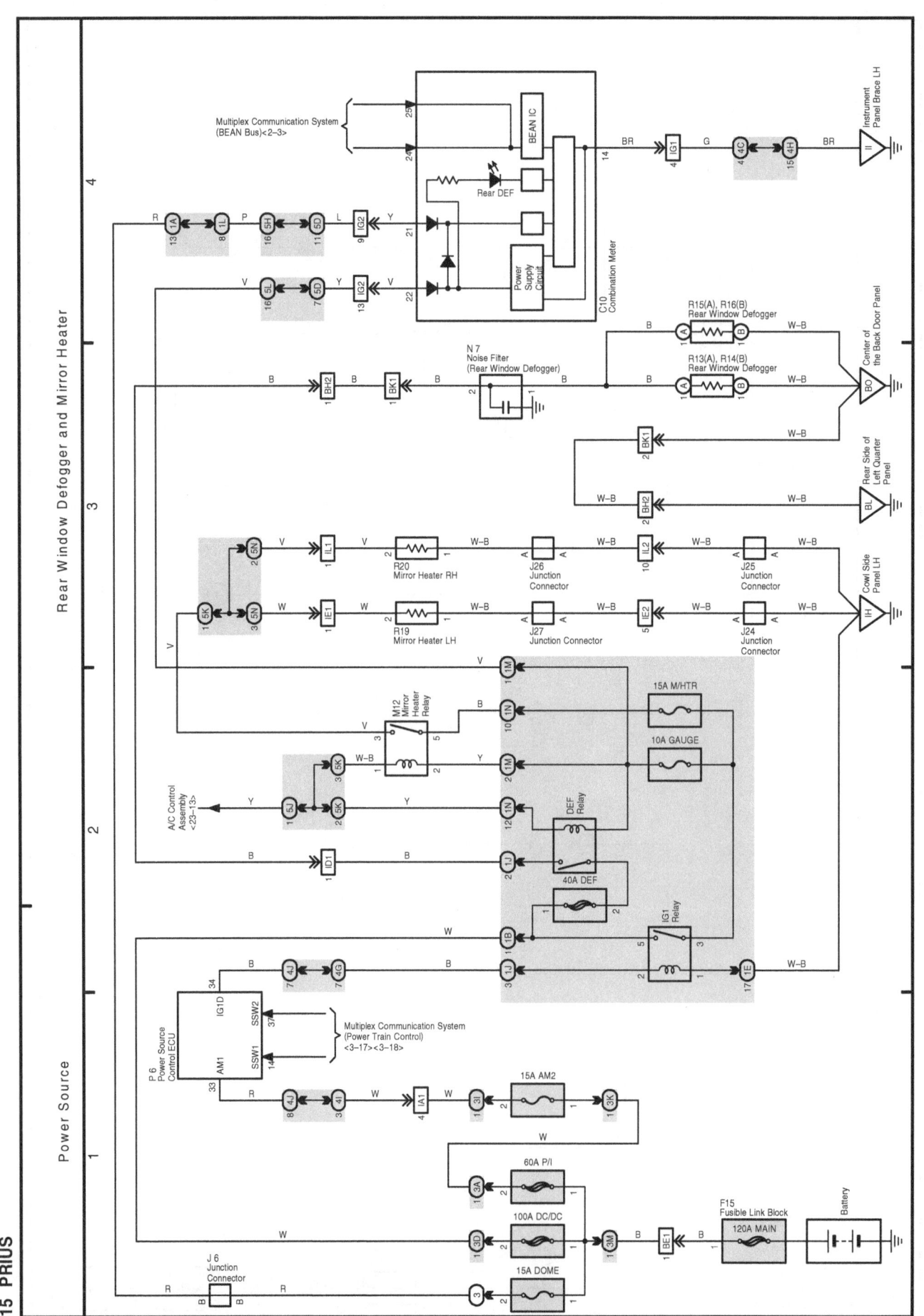

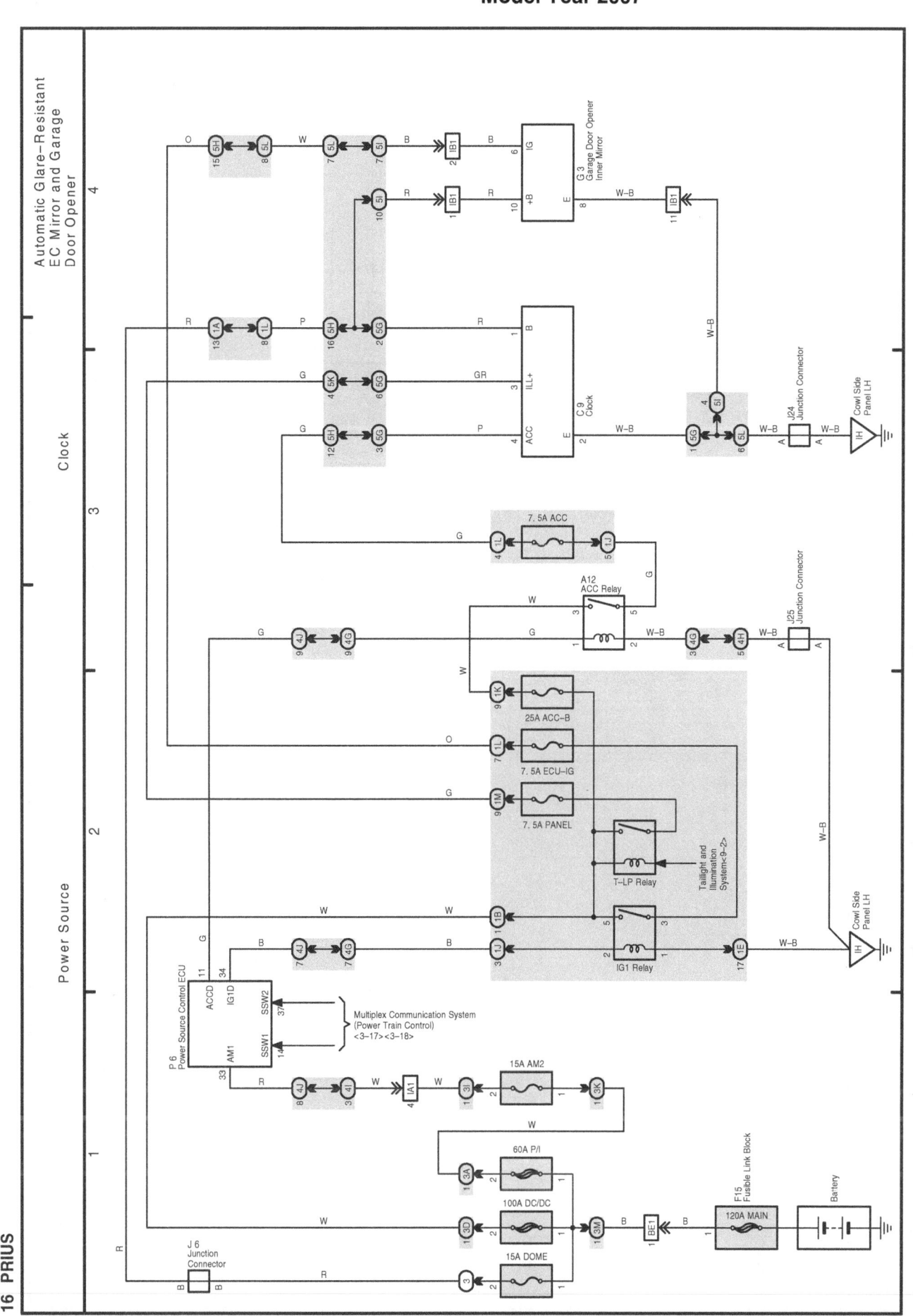

13

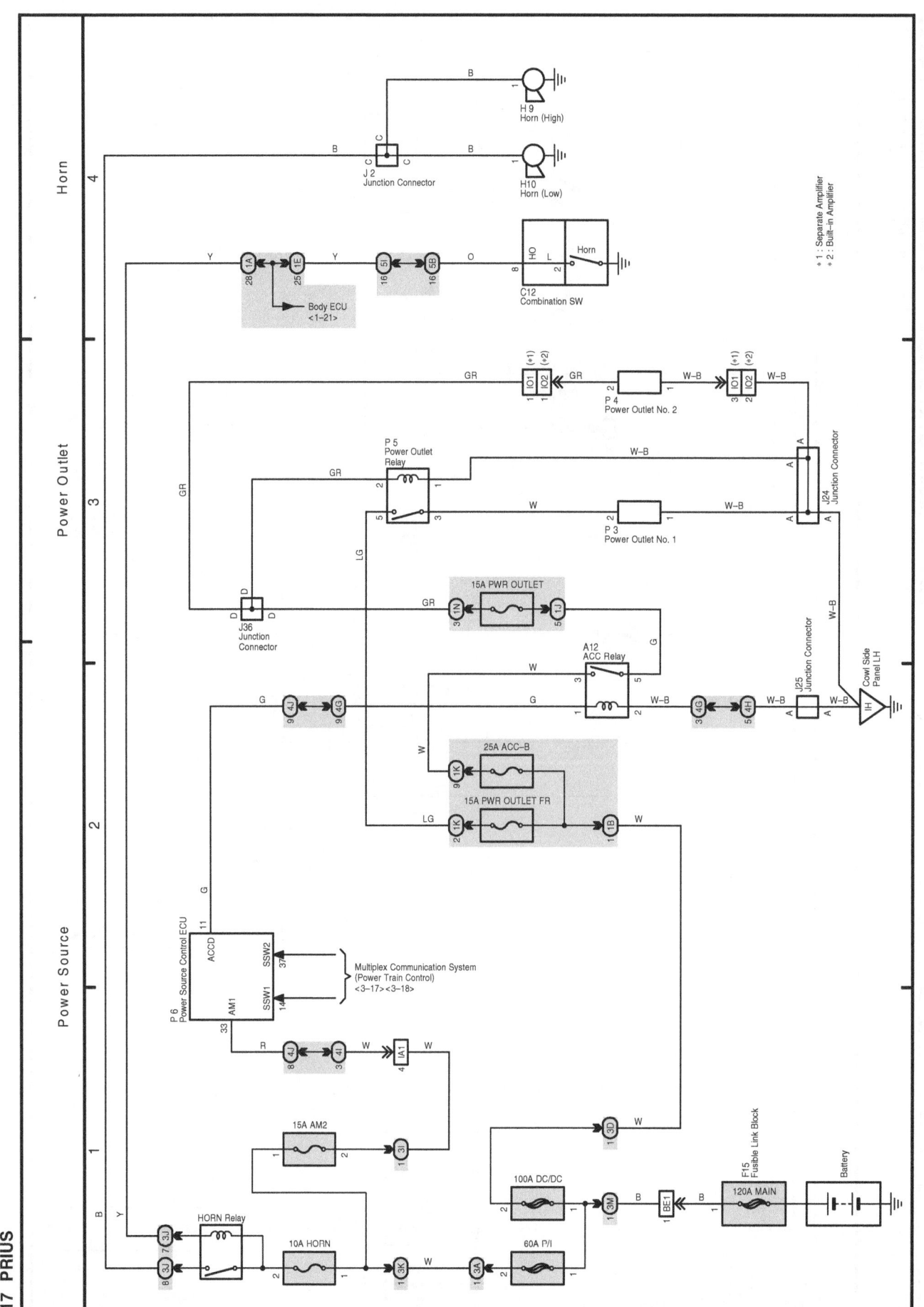

17 PRIUS

Model Year 2007

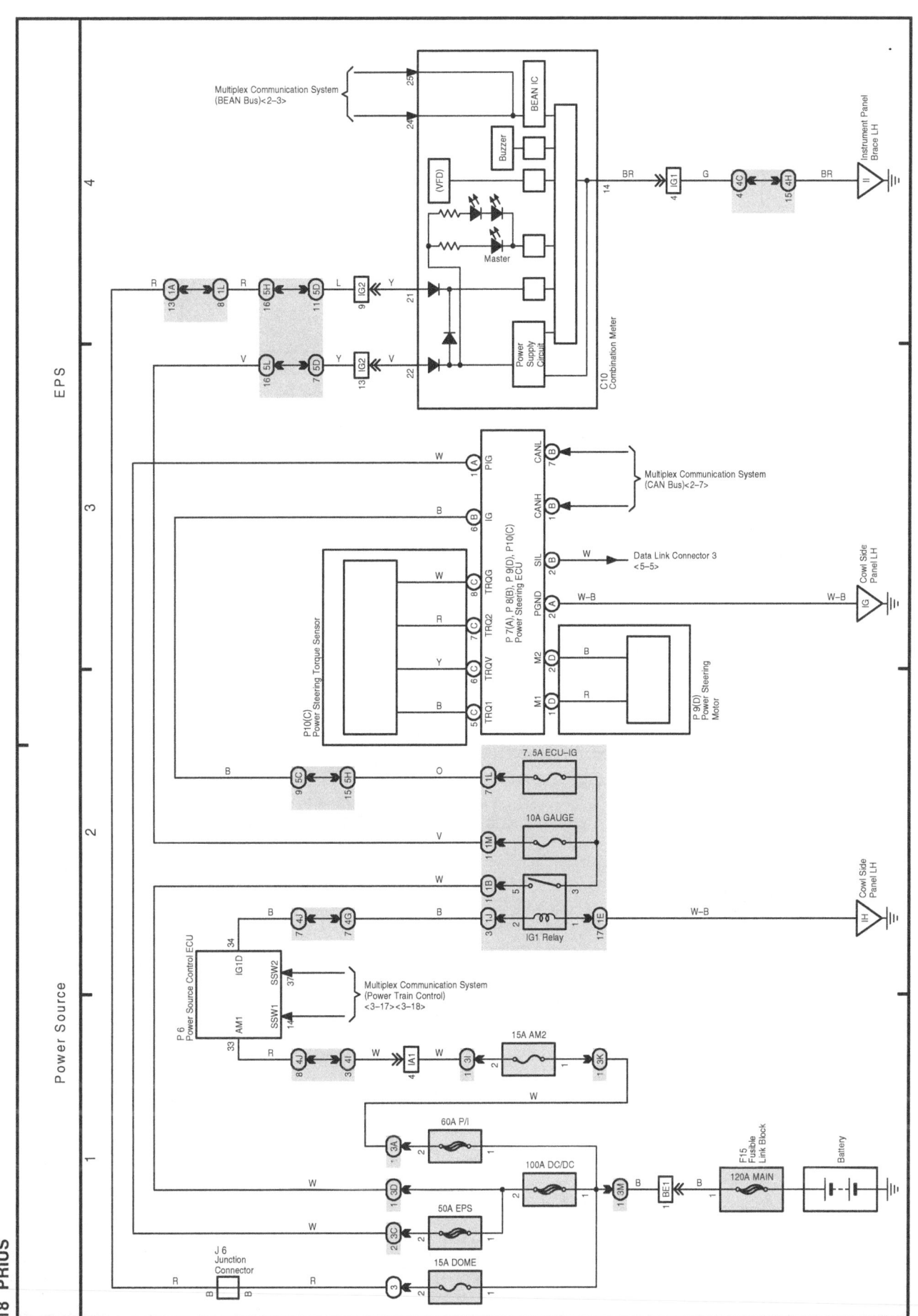

Model Year 2007

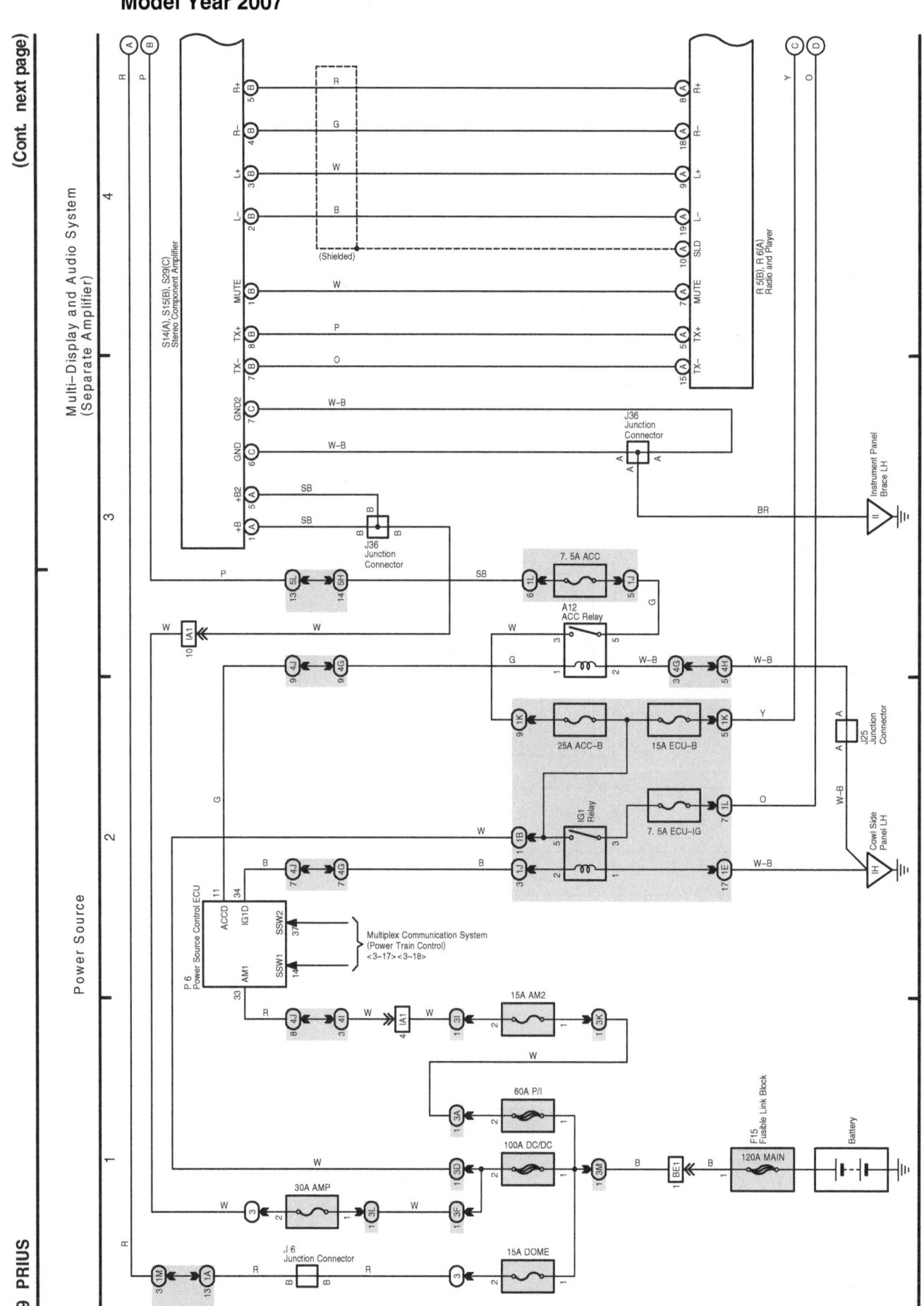

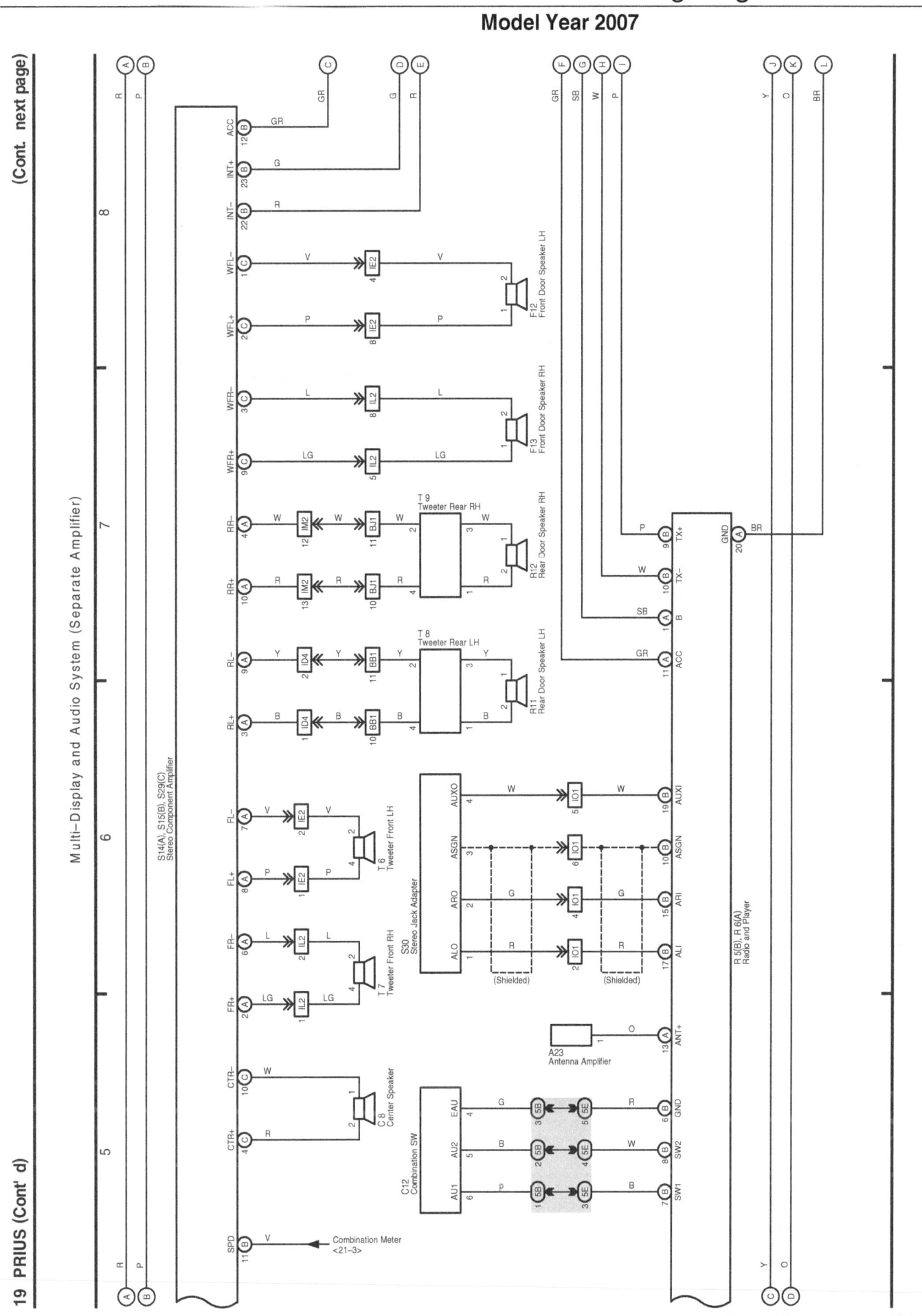

Model Year 2007

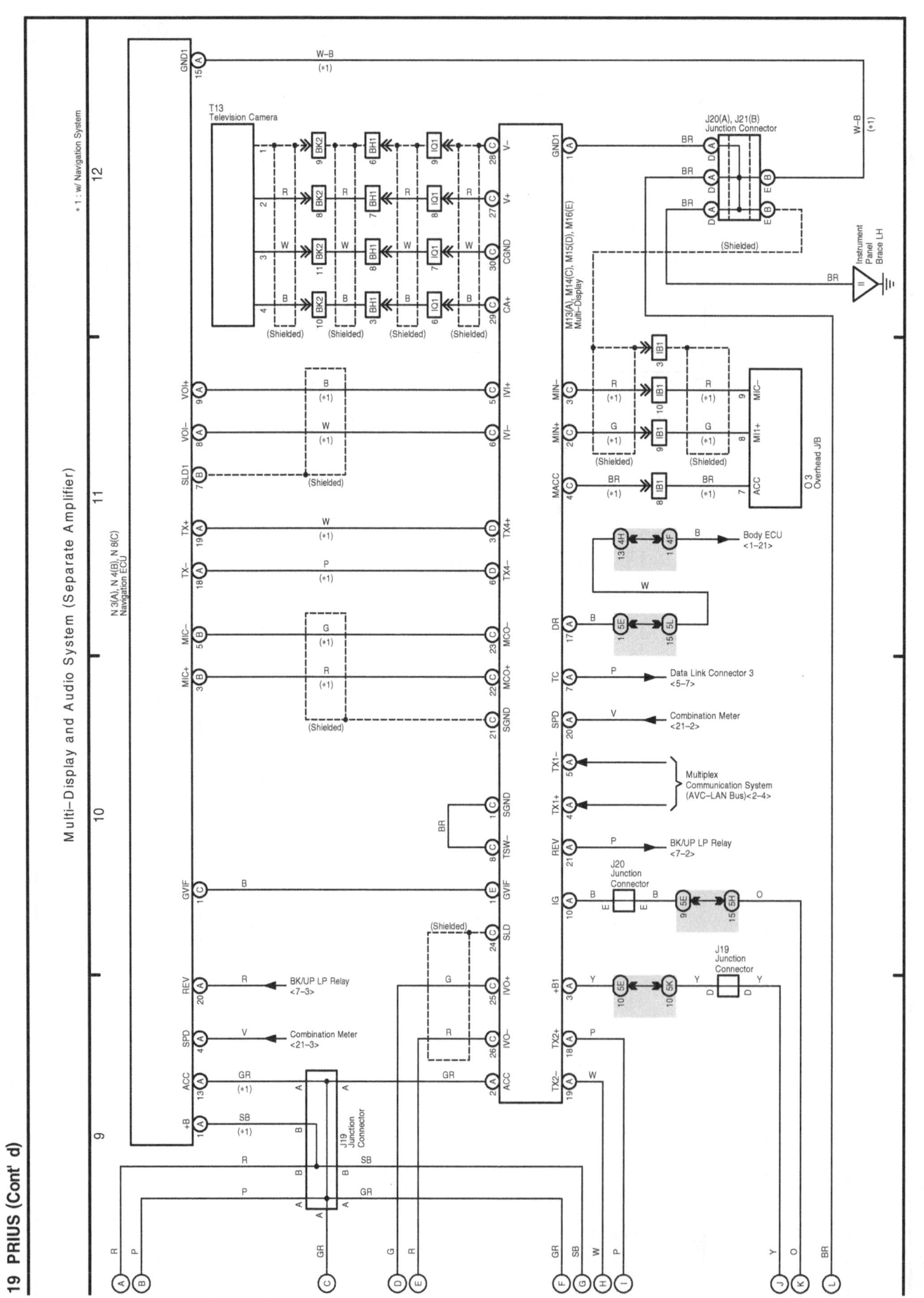

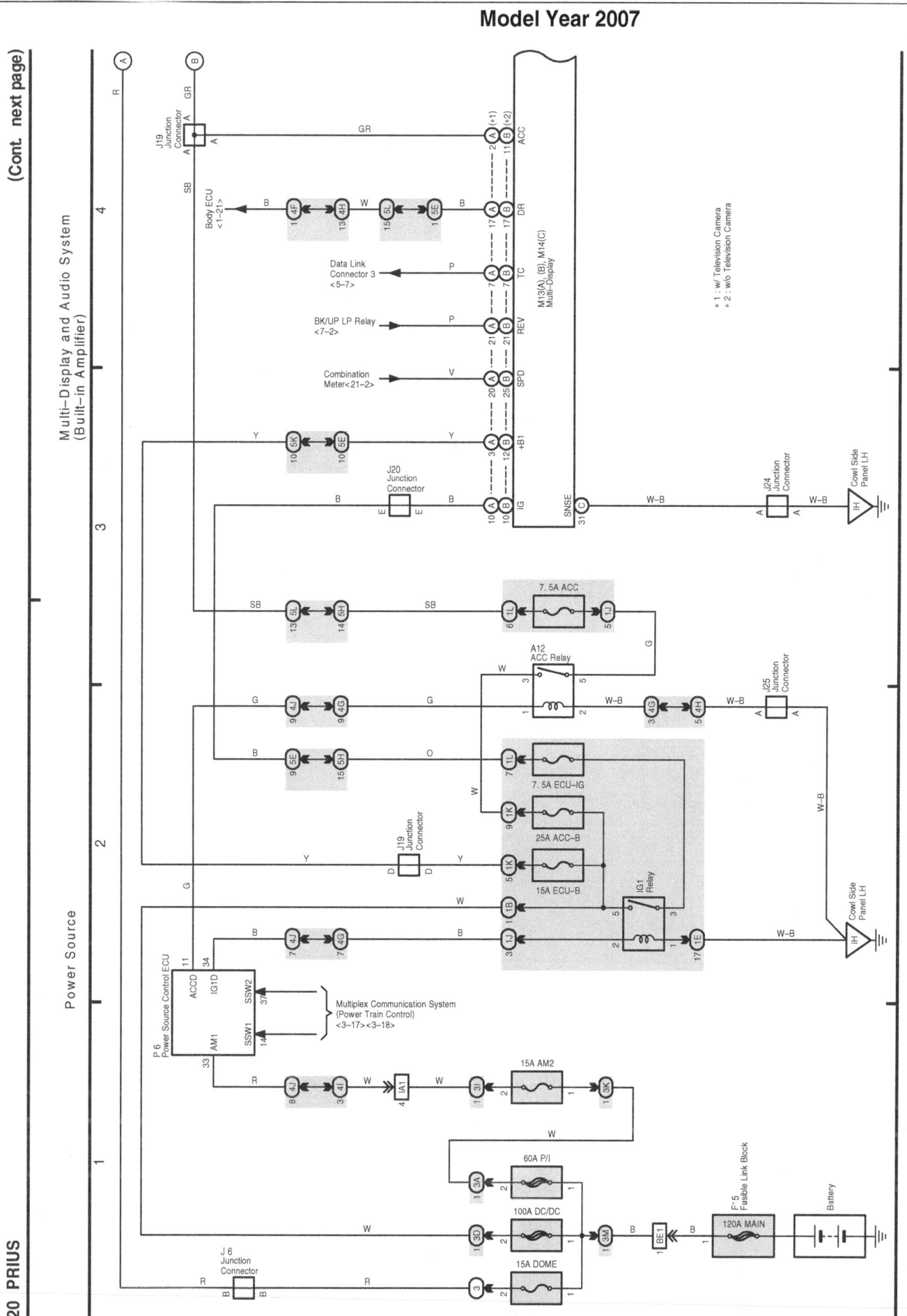

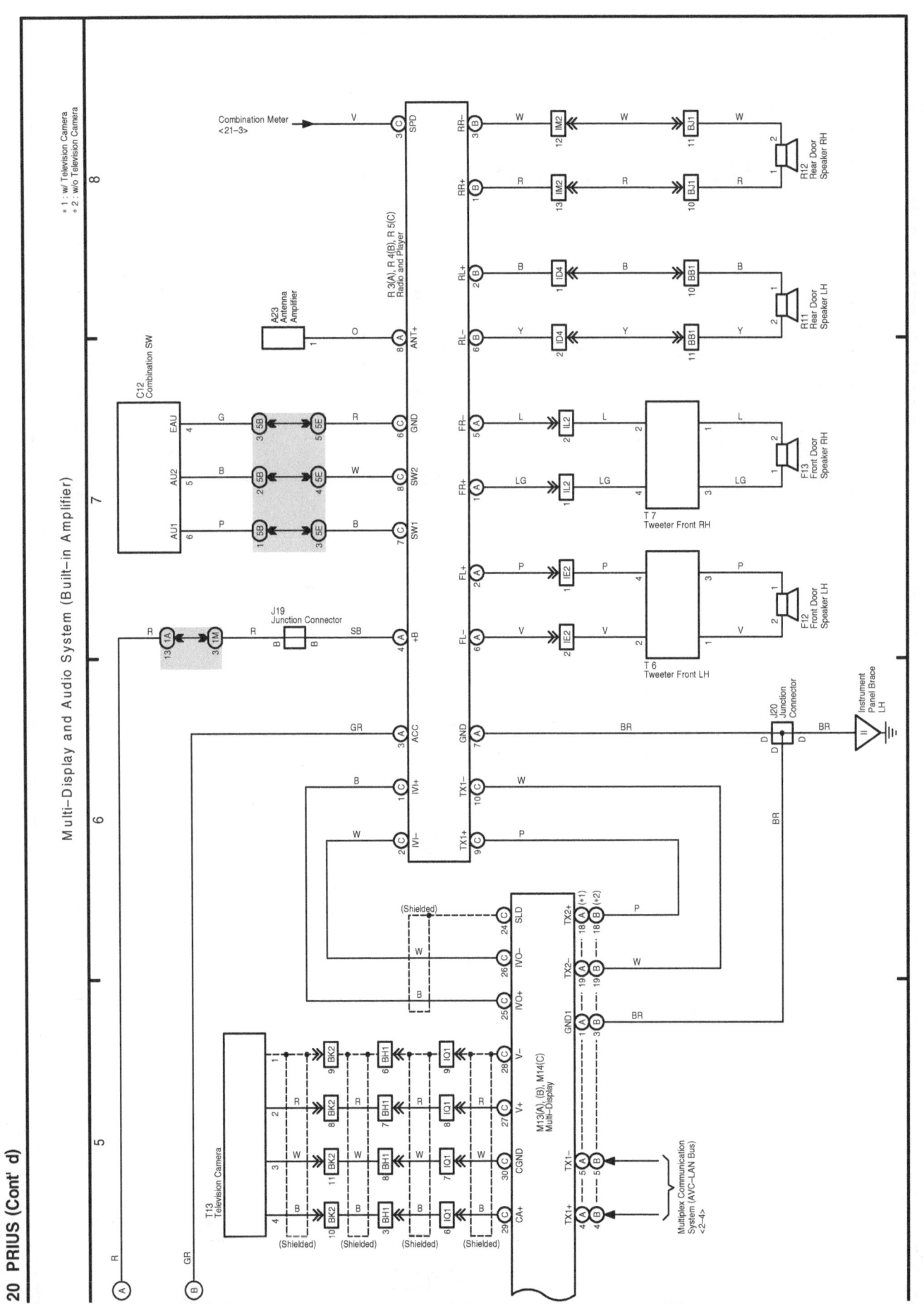

Multi-Display and Audio System (Built-in Amplifier)

20 PRIUS (Cont'd)

Model Year 2007

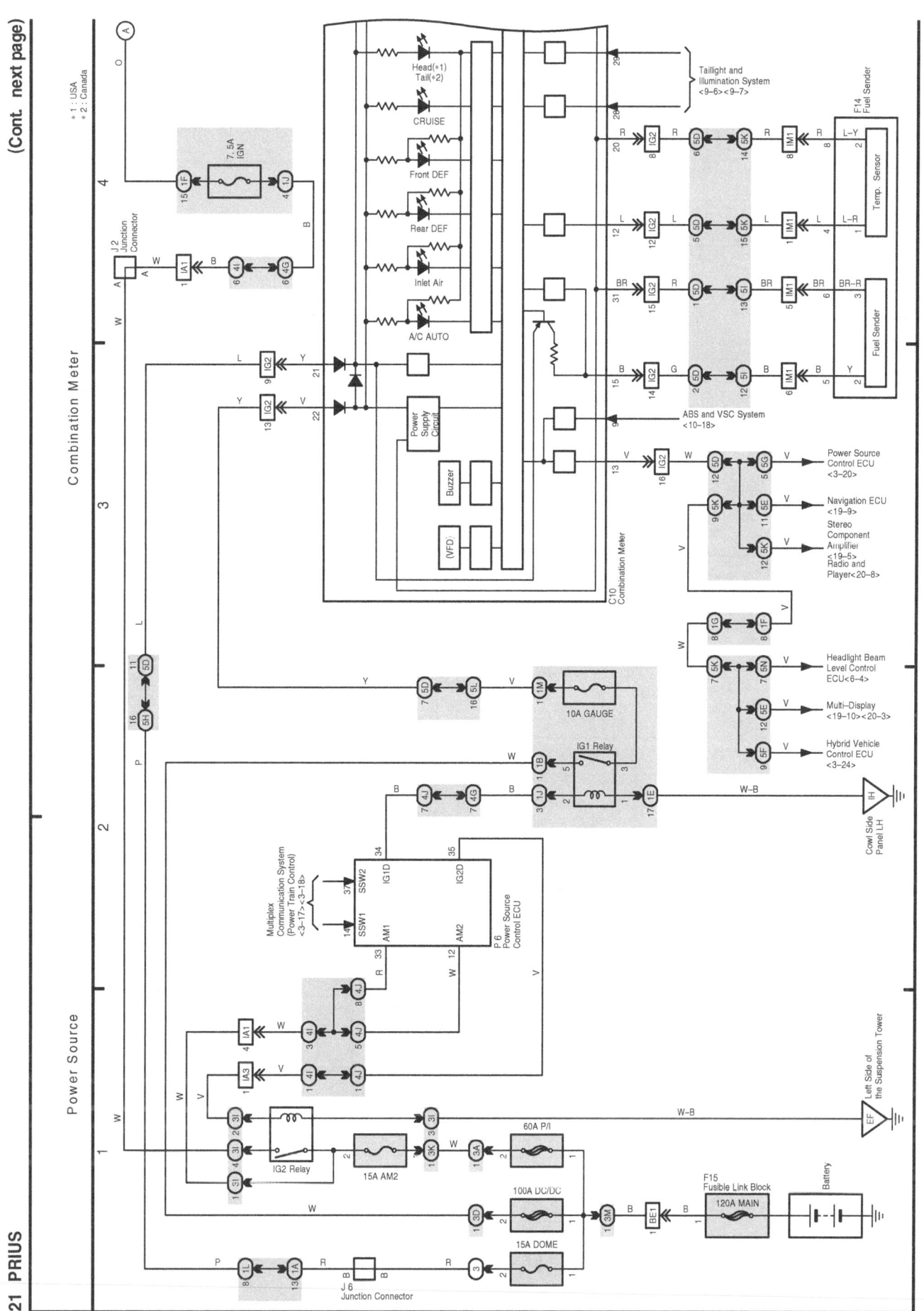

21 PRIUS

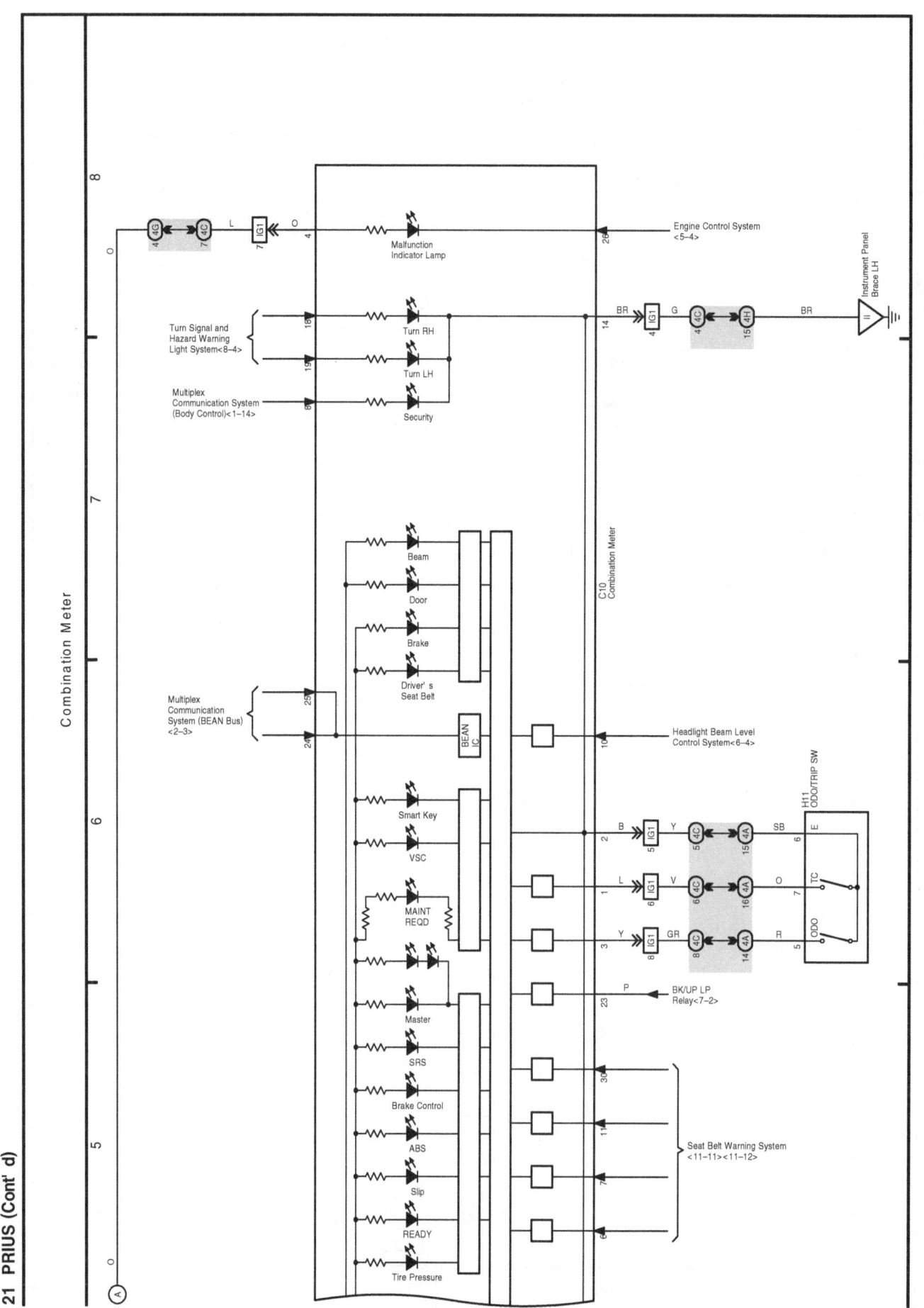

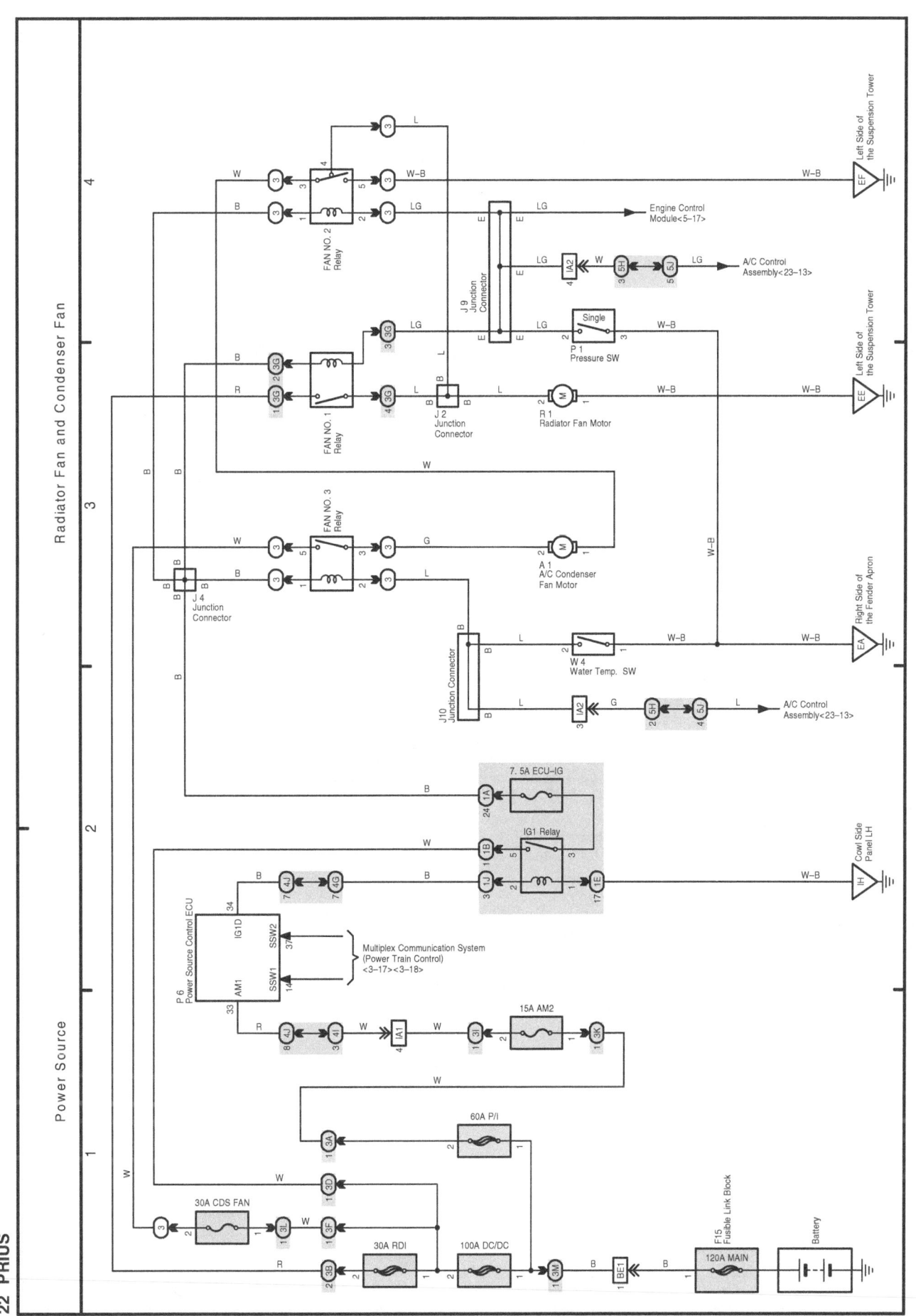

Model Year 2007

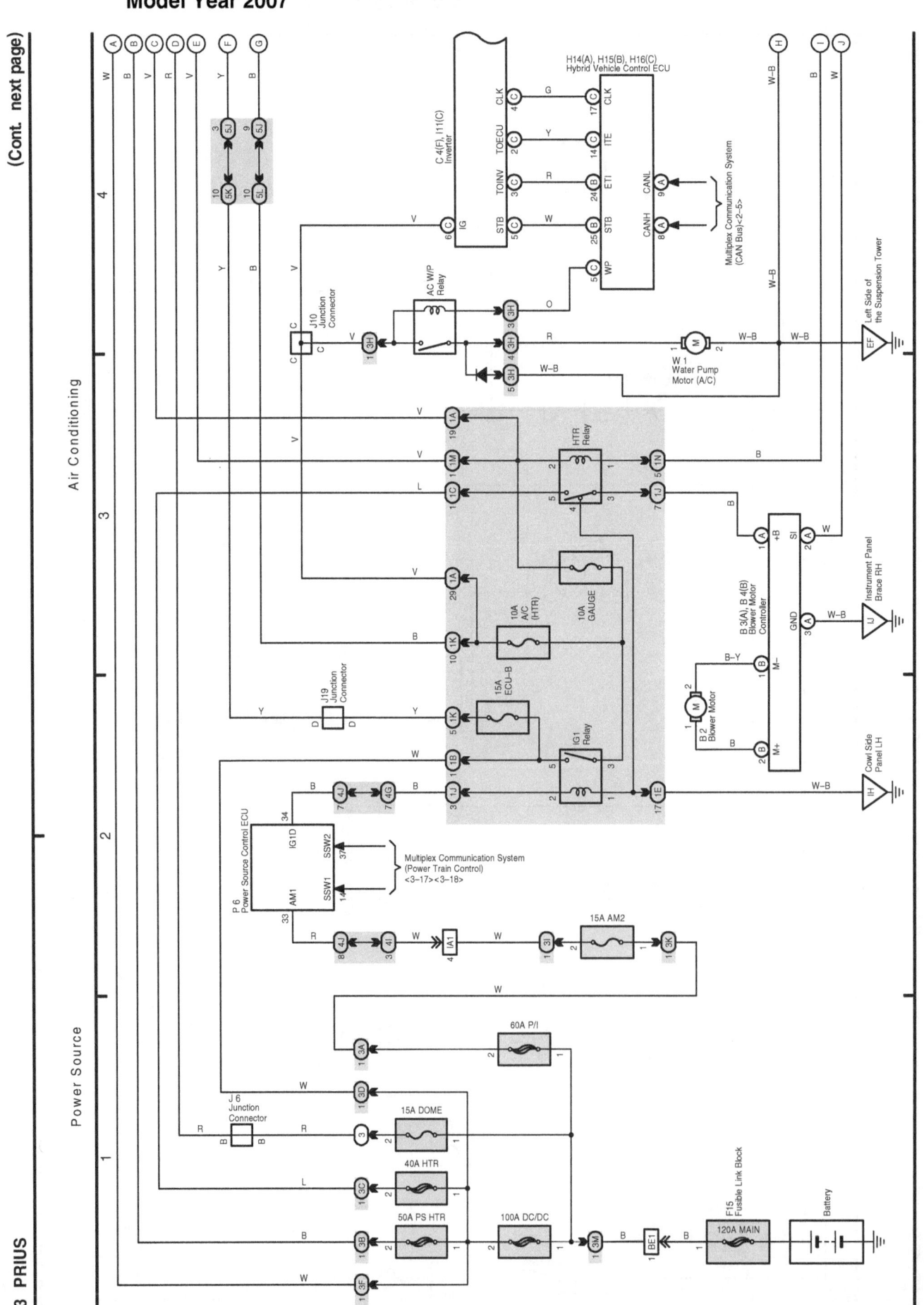

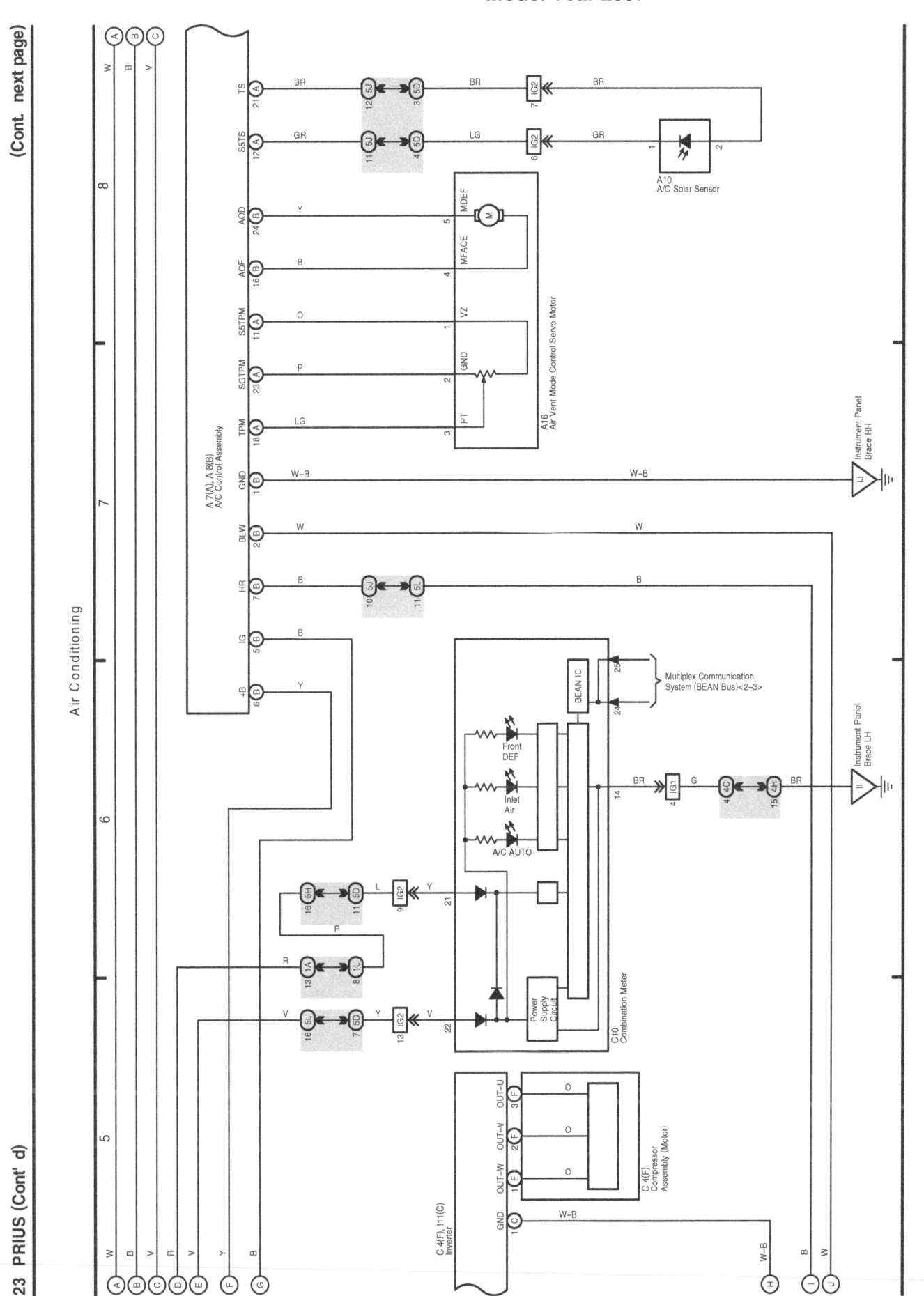

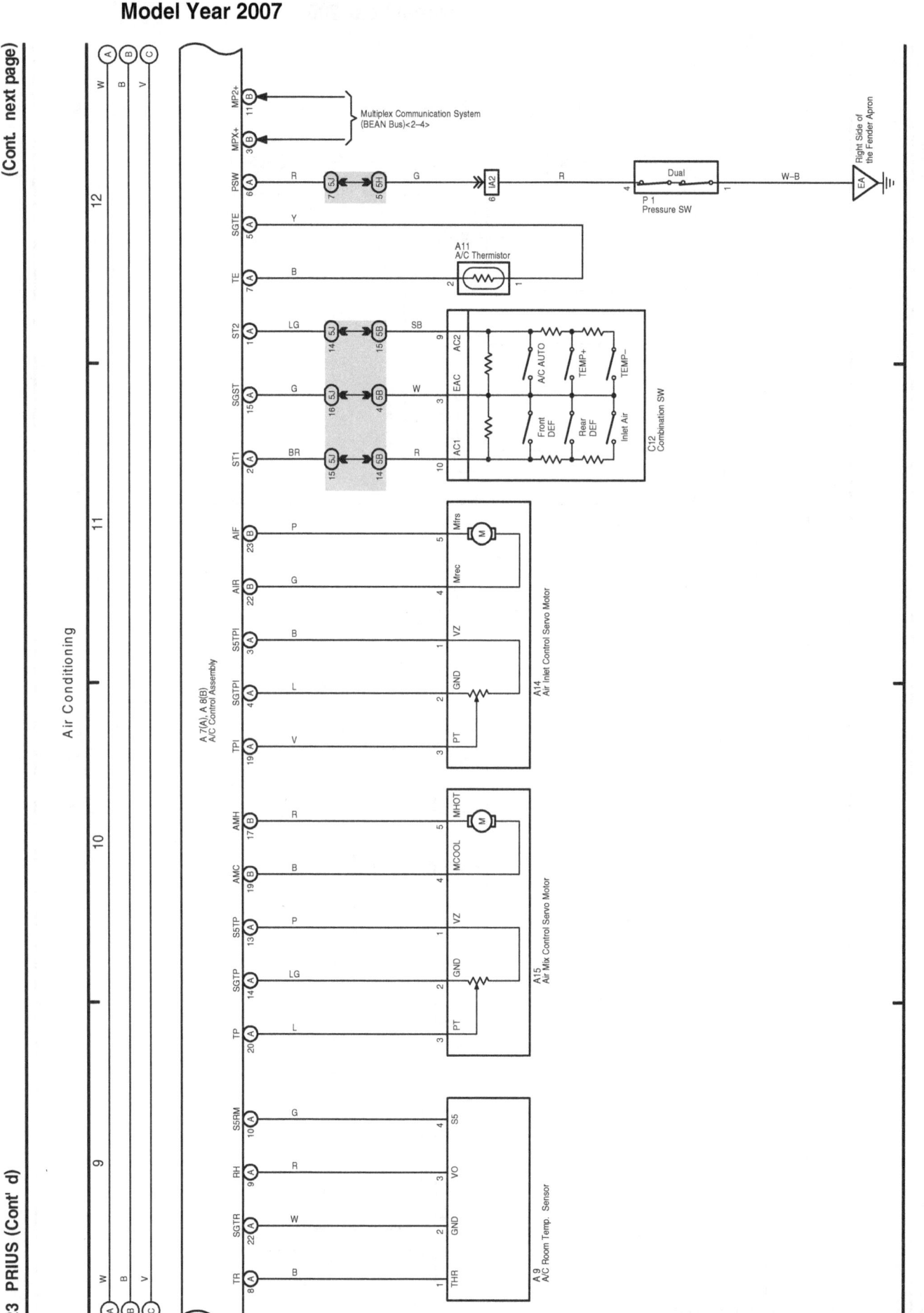

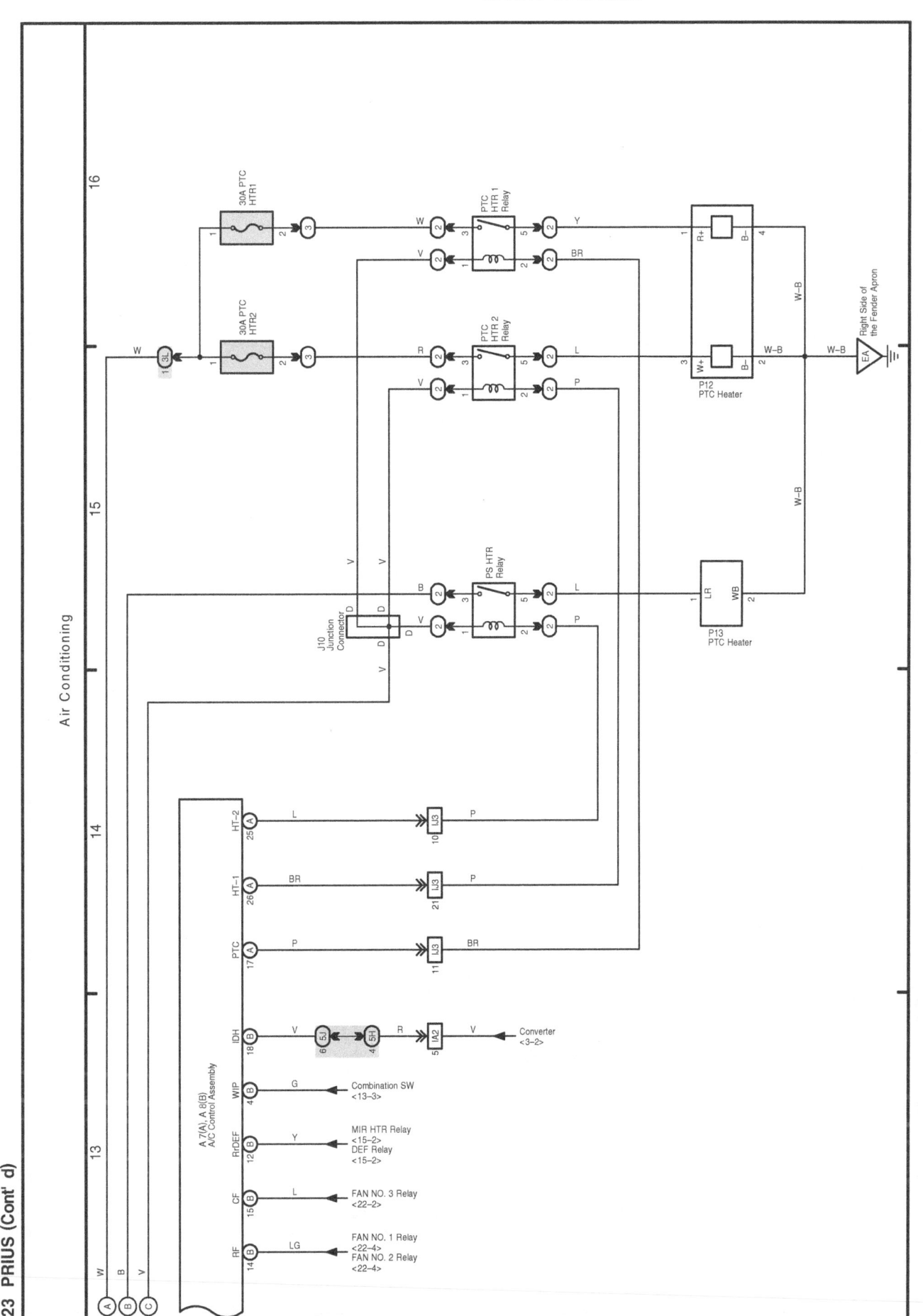

Model Year 2007

(Cont. next page)

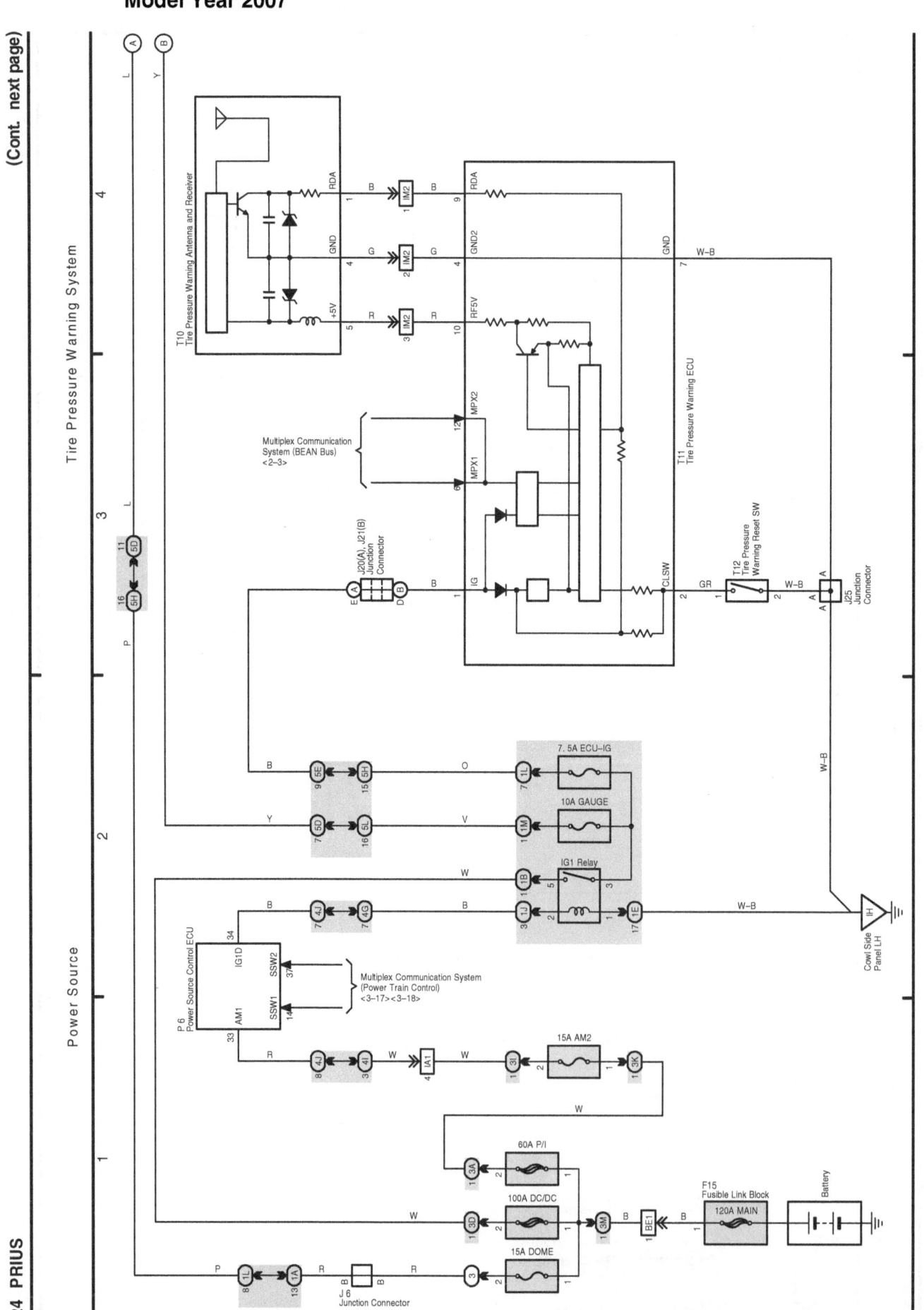

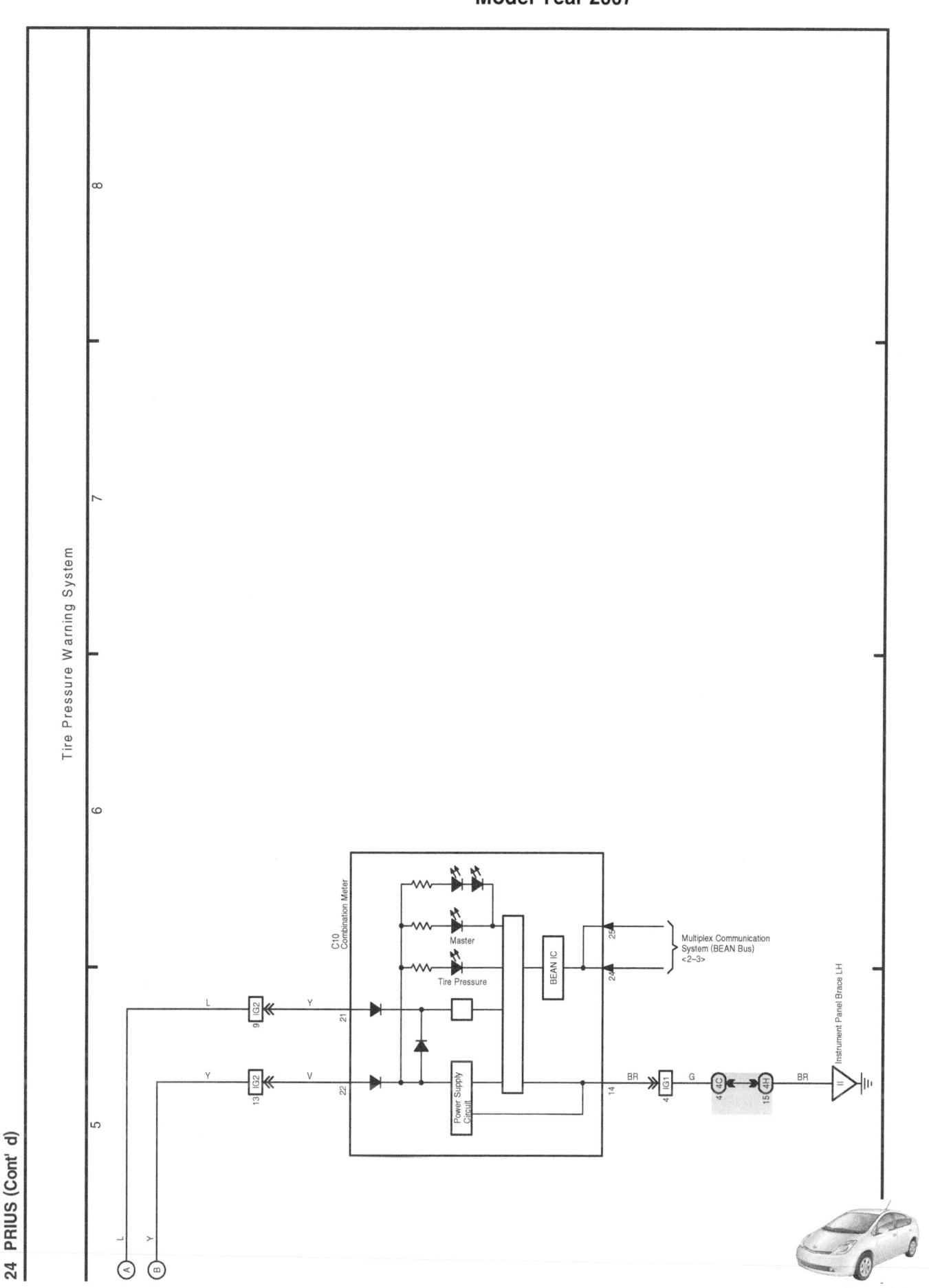

24 PRIUS (Cont'd)

Tire Pressure Warning System

C10 Combination Meter

Master

Tire Pressure

BEAN IC

Multiplex Communication System (BEAN Bus) <2–3>

Power Supply Circuit

Instrument Panel Brace LH

13

14
Toyota Pocket Reference Guide

14

GENERAL

This chapter contains a copy the 2005 Toyota Prius Pocket Reference Guide. The pocket reference guide is normally included with the purchase of a new Toyota Prius. It contains a brief description of Prius features and an overview of fundamental Prius operations. It is not intended as a substitute for the Prius Owner's Manual.

NOTE—
- *This 2005 Prius Pocket Reference Guide is courtesy of Toyota Motor Sales (TMS) USA, Inc. No review of its inclusion in this manual by TMS is expressed or implied. For the most up-to-date information visit* **http://techinfo.toyota.com**.

Prius safety precautions

In addition to the safety warnings given here, always read and observe the **Warnings**, **Cautions** and safety procedures in **3 Safety** before working on vehicle. Orange-colored cables carry lethal high voltage. Use extreme care when working near high voltage cables and components.

WARNING—
- *Risk of electrocution! Avoid touching orange-colored high voltage wiring and high voltage components unless you are certain that high voltage is not present.*
- *The Prius hybrid system has voltages as high as 500 volts. Voltages over 60 volts DC and 25 volts AC are a shock hazard.*

The Prius engine may start at any time if the hybrid system is in **READY** mode. See **3 Safety** for instructions on turning off the hybrid system.

WARNING—
- *Be sure hybrid system is OFF when servicing vehicle (READY indicator not illuminated). Failure to switch the hybrid system OFF could result in engine start at any time.*

2005 Prius

This *Pocket Reference Guide* is a summary guide for basic vehicle operations. It contains brief descriptions of fundamental operations so you can locate and use the vehicle's main equipment quickly and easily.

The *Pocket Reference Guide* is not intended as a substitute for the *Owner's Manual* located in the vehicle's glove box. We strongly encourage you to review the *Owner's Manual* and supplementary manuals so you will have a better understanding of the vehicle's capabilities and limitations.

Your dealership and the entire staff of Toyota Motor Sales, U.S.A., Inc., wish you many years of satisfied driving in your new Prius.

! A word about safe vehicle operations

This *Pocket Reference Guide* is not a full guide to Prius operations. Every Prius owner should review the *Owner's Manual* that accompanies this vehicle.

Pay special attention to the boxed information highlighted in yellow throughout the *Owner's Manual*. Each box contains safe operating instructions to help you avoid injury or equipment malfunction.

All information in this *Pocket Reference Guide* is current at the time of printing. Toyota reserves the right to make changes at any time without notice.

TABLE OF CONTENTS

[1] *Programmable by consumer. For dealer-programmable features, please visit your Toyota dealer.*

[2] *HomeLink® is a registered trademark of Johnson Controls, Inc.*

BASIC VEHICLE OPERATION

OVERVIEW

FEATURES/OPERATIONS

SAFETY AND EMERGENCY FEATURES

14

BASIC VEHICLE OPERATION

Key fob

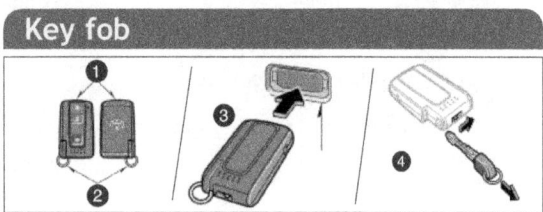

❶ **Master key** Ignition key & wireless remote.
❷ **Mechanical key** Fits into master key and can be removed to manually lock/unlock driver's door only.
❸ **Ignition key slot** When inserting, push completely in. When removing, gently pull, it will be pushed out by a spring. **DO NOT FORCE THE KEY**; if it cannot be removed, push it all the way in again, then pull it out.
❹ **To remove or replace mechanical key** Slide the lock knob in the direction of the arrow.

Turning the Hybrid System on

Pressing down on the brake pedal

❶ Insert key*.
❷ Depress the brake pedal, and push the "POWER" button briefly and firmly.
❸ The "READY" light will blink. After a few seconds, when the light remains on and a beep sounds, you may begin driving.

Without pressing down on the brake pedal

The brake pedal must be depressed to turn the Hybrid System on. If the brake pedal is not depressed, pressing "POWER" will change the operation mode in succession from:

ACC	Accessories such as radio will operate.
↓	
-IG-ON	Ignition is on, Hybrid System is not engaged.
↓	
OFF	All systems OFF.

*It is not necessary to insert the ignition key (key fob) if smart key system is installed and activated.

2

Shifting

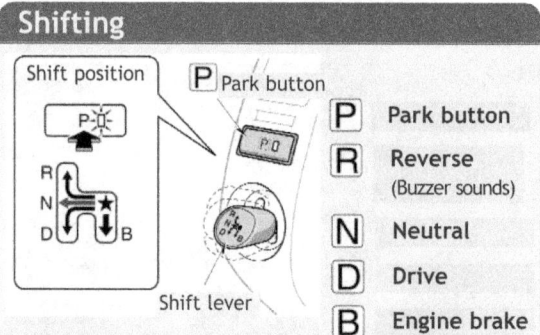

P	Park button
R	Reverse (Buzzer sounds)
N	Neutral
D	Drive
B	Engine brake

Brake pedal must be depressed when shifting to or from the **P** Park position.
NOTE: The shift lever will always return to its original position after shifting. **ALWAYS CONFIRM SHIFT POSITION BY CHECKING INDICATOR SYMBOLS ON THE INSTRUMENT CLUSTER.**

Parking & turning off the Hybrid System

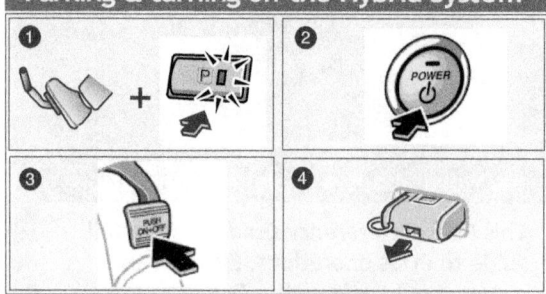

❶ While depressing brake pedal, push **P** Park button above the shift lever, when the vehicle is at a complete stop.
❷ Push the "POWER" button to turn off the system.
❸ Fully depress the parking brake.
❹ Remove the key fob.
WARNING: If the "POWER" button is held for longer than 3 seconds while the vehicle is moving, the Hybrid System will shut off.

Information

In instances when the engine starts, and/or on a short trip after the engine is stopped, the motor water pump may continue operating for a short time. This is not a concern, but a standard operation of the vehicle to ensure optimum performance.

3

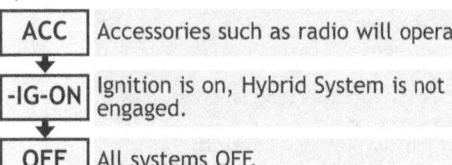

BASIC VEHICLE OPERATION

OVERVIEW

FEATURES / OPERATIONS

SAFETY AND EMERGENCY FEATURES

OVERVIEW

Instrument panel

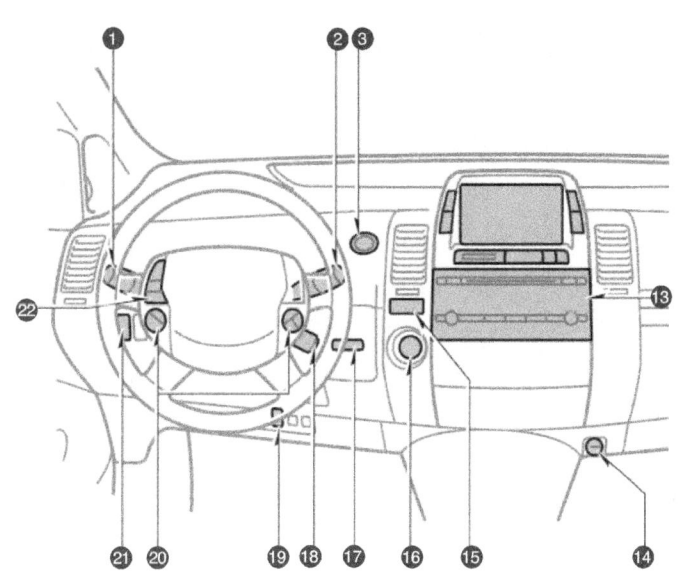

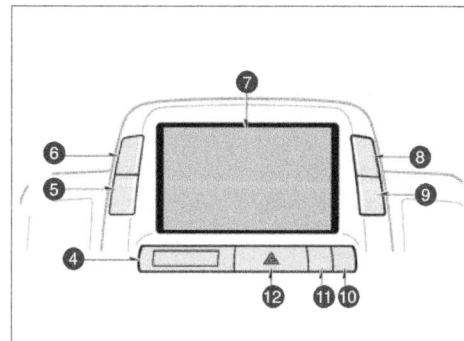

With navigation system[1]

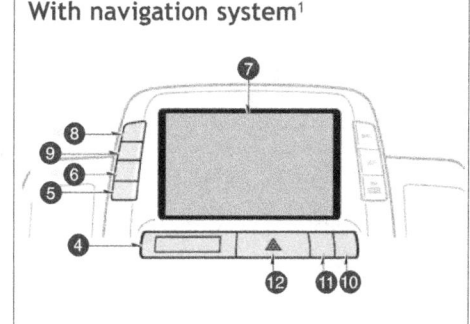

❶ Headlight, turn signal and front fog light* controls
❷ Wiper and washer controls
❸ "POWER" button
❹ Clock
❺ "AUDIO" switch (Multi-information display control switch)
❻ "CLIMATE" switch (Multi-information display control switch)
❼ Multi-information display
❽ "DISPLAY" switch (Multi-information display control switch)
❾ "INFO" switch (Multi-information display control switch)
❿ Km/h or MPH button
⓫ Trip meter reset button
⓬ Emergency flasher switch

⓭ Audio
⓮ 12V Power outlet
⓯ P Park button
⓰ Electronic shift lever
⓱ Ignition key (key fob) slot
⓲ Cruise control lever
⓳ Smart key system cancel switch*
⓴ Climate steering wheel switches
㉑ Dimmer control wheel
㉒ Audio steering wheel switches

*If installed

[1] *For details, refer to the Navigation System Owner's Manual.*

BASIC VEHICLE OPERATION

OVERVIEW

FEATURES/OPERATIONS

SAFETY AND EMERGENCY FEATURES

14

OVERVIEW

Instrument cluster

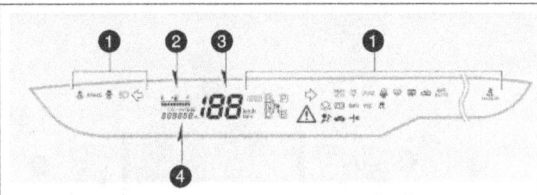

1 Service reminder indicators and indicator lights
2 Fuel gauge
3 Speedometer
4 Odometer and two trip meters

Indicator symbols

 Brake system warning light[1]

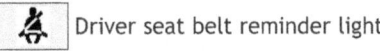 Driver seat belt reminder light[1]

 Front passenger seat belt reminder light[1]

Battery warning light[2]

Malfunction indicator light[1]

Low engine oil pressure warning light[2]

Low fuel level indicator light[1]

Master warning light[1]

High coolant temperature warning light[2]

ABS   Anti-lock Brake System warning light[1]

⚠CAUTION

When the Anti-lock Brake System (ABS) function is in action, you may feel the brake pedal pulsating and hear a noise. In this situation, to let the Anti-lock Brake System work for you, just hold the brake pedal down more firmly. Do not pump the brake as this will result in reduced braking performance.

Open door warning light[1]

Airbag SRS warning light[1]

VSC   Vehicle Stability Control warning light[1]

MAINT REQD   Engine oil replacement reminder light[1]

MAIN   Hybrid vehicle battery warning light[2]

PS   Electric power steering system warning light[2]

Smart Entry and Start warning light[5]

Turn signal indicator light

Headlight high beam indicator light

Headlight indicator light

Tail light indicator light

Slip indicator light

Automatic head light leveling system warning light[2]

CRUISE   Cruise control indicator light[3]

Hybrid System warning light[2]

Running mode position indicator light[4]

READY   Driving ready light

A/C AUTO   Automatic air conditioner indicator light

Recirculate mode indicator light

Windshield air flow indicator light

Rear window and outside rear view mirror defoggers indicator light

Low temperature indicator light

Hybrid vehicle immobilizer / Theft deterrent system indicator light

---

[1] For details, refer to "Service reminder indicators and warning buzzers-- Instrument cluster" Section 2-5, 2005 Owner's Manual.

[2] For details, refer to "Service reminder indicators and warning buzzers-- Multi-information display" Section 2-5, 2005 Owner's Manual.

[3] If this light falshes, see "Cruise control" Section 2-6, 2005 Owner's Manual.

[4] For details, refer to "Hybrid transaxle" Section 2-6, 2005 Owner's Manual.

[5] For details, refer to "Smart entry and start system" Section 2-1, 2005 Owner's Manual.

BASIC VEHICLE OPERATION

OVERVIEW

FEATURES/OPERATIONS

SAFETY AND EMERGENCY FEATURES

OVERVIEW

Fuel tank door opener and cap

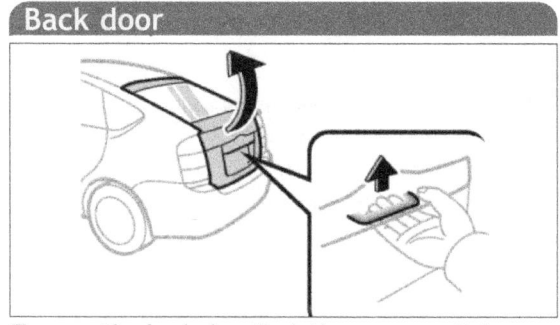

❶ **To open the fuel tank door from driver side** Pull up on the opener.

❷ **To remove the fuel tank cap** Turn the cap counterclockwise 90 degrees, then turn it an additional 30 degrees. Pause slightly before removing it.

❸ **The removed cap can be stored on the fuel tank door.**

❹ **To replace the fuel tank cap** Turn clockwise until a click is heard. If not tightened enough, Check Engine "🔧" indicator may illuminate.

NOTE: MAINTAIN GASOLINE IN THE TANK AT ALL TIMES. SERIOUS DAMAGE TO THE HYBRID SYSTEM CAN OCCUR IF THE VEHICLE RUNS OUT OF GAS.

Back door

To open the back door Push the opener switch under the handle, and raise the door.

8

Hood release lever

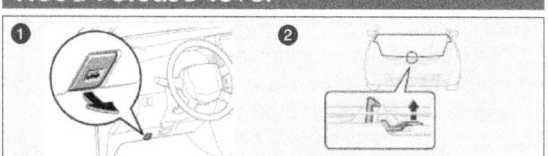

❶ **To release the hood** Pull the lever inside vehicle.
❷ **To open the hood** Insert finger through the opening between the hood and grill. Pull up on the catch lever inside the compartment and lift the hood.

Engine compartment

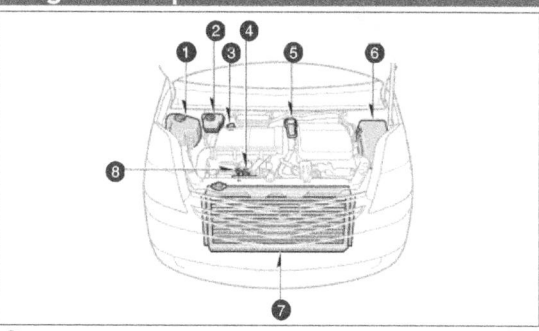

❶ Windshield washer fluid tank
❷ Brake fluid reservoir
❸ Engine oil filler cap
❹ Engine coolant reservoir
❺ Inverter reservoir tank
❻ Fuse block/Jumpstart access points
❼ Radiator and A/C condenser
❽ Engine oil level dipstick

Note: Regularly scheduled maintenance, including oil changes, will help extend the life of your vehicle and maintain performance. Please refer to the "Owner's Warranty Information Booklet," "Scheduled Maintenance Guide" or "Owner's Manual Supplement."

9

BASIC VEHICLE OPERATION

OVERVIEW

FEATURES/OPERATIONS

SAFETY AND EMERGENCY FEATURES

14

FEATURES/OPERATIONS

Hybrid Synergy Drive System

The Hybrid Synergy Drive System utilizes a computer controlled gasoline engine and electric motor to provide the most efficient combination of power for the vehicle. To conserve energy, when the brakes are applied, braking force generates electricity which is then sent to the battery. In addition, the engine shuts off when the vehicle is stopped. The benefits are better fuel economy, reduced vehicle emissions and improved performance.

Note: Fuel consumption and energy information of the Hybrid System are shown on the multi-information display.

Tips for improved fuel economy

❶ Ensure tire pressures are maintained at levels specified in the *Owner's Manual*.
❷ Link trips, if possible, to reduce engine cold starts.
❸ Avoid driving at speeds that are higher than necessary, especially on the highway.
❹ When possible, avoid sudden stops to maximize regenerative braking energy.
❺ Minimize use of the air conditioning.

⚠CAUTION

- The vehicle has both high voltage DC and AC systems as well as a 12-volt system. DC and AC high voltage are both very dangerous and can cause death, severe burns, electric shock or other serious injuries.
- In order to avoid personal injuries, do not touch, remove or replace high voltage cables which are colored orange, and/or their connectors, high voltage parts such as the inverter unit, hybrid vehicle battery, etc.

Refer to the *Owner's Manual* for more details.

Starting the Hybrid System

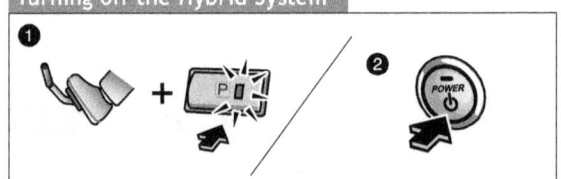

❶ Insert key*.
❷ Depress the brake pedal, and push the "POWER" button briefly and firmly.
❸ The "READY" light will blink. After a few seconds, when the light remains on and a beep sounds, you may begin driving.

*It is not necessary to insert the ignition key (key fob) if smart key system is installed and activated.

Without pressing down on the brake pedal

The brake pedal must be depressed to turn the Hybrid System on. If the brake pedal is not depressed, pressing "POWER" will change the operation mode in succession from:

ACC	Accessories such as the radio will operate.

↓

-IG-ON	Ignition is on, Hybrid System is not engaged.

↓

OFF	All systems OFF.

Turning off the Hybrid System

❶ Depress the brake pedal, then push the P Park button above the shifter.
❷ Push the "POWER" button to turn off the system.

Refer to the *Owner's Manual* for more details.

BASIC VEHICLE OPERATION

OVERVIEW

FEATURES/OPERATIONS

SAFETY AND EMERGENCY FEATURES

Key fob

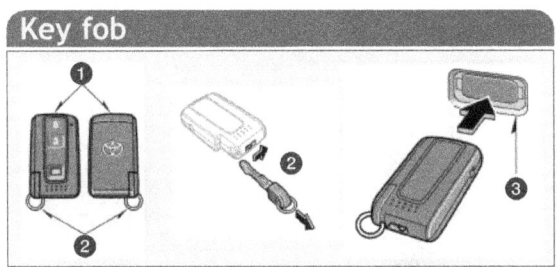

1. **Master key** Ignition key and wireless remote.
2. **Mechanical key** Can be removed to manually lock/unlock the driver's door only.
3. **Ignition key (key fob) slot**

Using a mechanical key

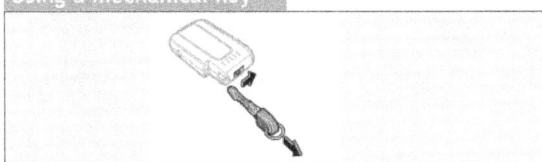

To use the mechanical key Slide the lock knob and pull out.

Keyless entry

Locking operation | Unlocking operation

1. **To lock** Push " 🔒."
2. **To unlock driver door** Push " 🔓 " once.
   To unlock all the doors Push " 🔓 " twice.

NOTE: After unlocking, if a door is not opened within thirty (30) seconds, all doors will relock for safety.

Alarm operation

3. **To activate alarm with remote** Push "🔊."
Refer to the *Owner's Manual* for more details.

12

Smart key system (if installed)

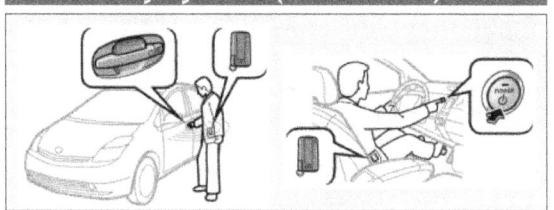

By carrying a smart key, the vehicle can be locked, unlocked and the Hybrid System engaged without handling the key.

Locking operation | Unlocking operation

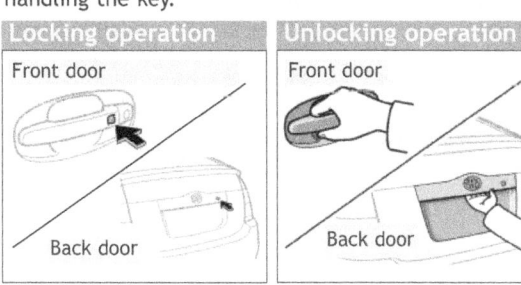

To lock the doors Push the lock button on the outside door handle (with all doors closed, and the Hybrid System turned off).

To unlock the doors With the key within 3 feet of the door, take hold of the door handle.

NOTE: After unlocking, if a door is not opened within thirty (30) seconds, all doors will relock for safety. Refer to your Owner's Manual, and page 14 of this guide for smart key unlocking programmable options.

Smart key system cancel switch

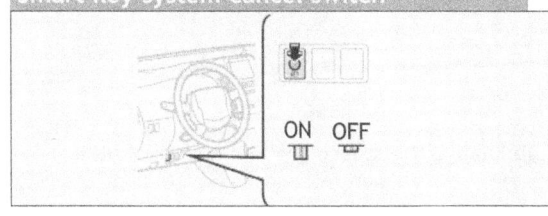

To disable smart key system Push the cancel switch located below the steering wheel.

NOTE: To conserve battery power, turn the smart key system "OFF" when not using the vehicle for prolonged periods of time. For more battery saving information, refer to the *Owner's Manual* for more details.

13

FEATURES/OPERATIONS

Smart key unlock functions- Programmable (if installed)

The smart key unlocking function can be programmed to operate in 3 different modes when smart key is activated. In all modes, grasping the passenger door handle will unlock all doors.
Driver side door only Grasp driver side handle to unlock driver side door only.
All doors All doors will unlock by grasping driver side, or back door handle.
Driver side and back door To open driver side door or back door independently, grasp the handle.

Refer to the *Owner's Manual* for more information on this feature, and how to change modes.

Parking brake

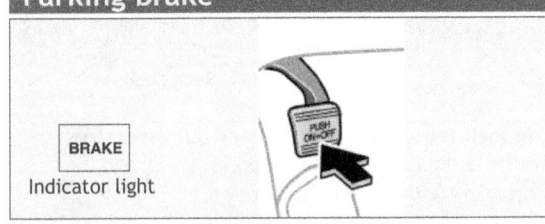

Indicator light

To set Depress the pedal.
To release Depress again.

Tilt steering wheel

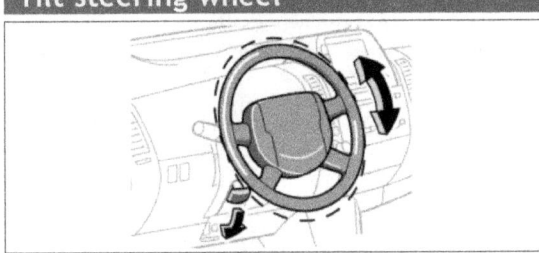

To change the steering wheel angle Hold the steering wheel, push the lock release lever down, tilt to desired angle, and return the lever to its locked position.
Note: Do not attempt to adjust while the vehicle is in motion.

Hybrid transaxle

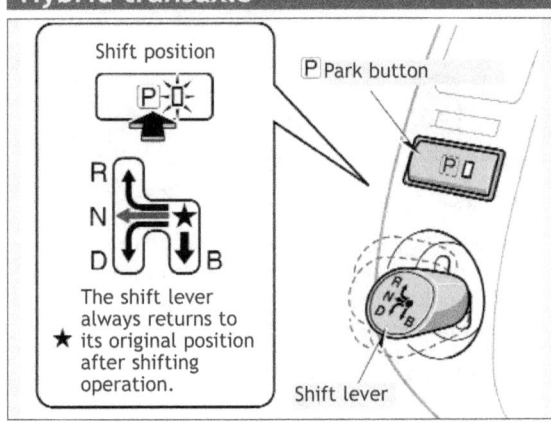

Shift position

P Park button

R
N
D   B

The shift lever always returns to ★ its original position after shifting operation.

Shift lever

The shift position is displayed on the instrument cluster.

P Park button
D,B,N ➡ P:Push the P Park button, when the vehicle is completely stopped.

R Reverse (Buzzer sounds)
P ➡ R:Shift the lever while depressing the brake pedal.
D,B,N ➡ R:Shift the lever when the vehicle is completely stopped.

N Neutral
D,B,P ➡ N:Shift the lever and hold until the "N" Neutral indicator is displayed. From P to N, you must depress the brake pedal.

D Driving
P ➡ D: Shift the lever while depressing the brake pedal.
R ➡ D: Shift the lever when the vehicle is completely stopped.
B,N ➡ D: Shift the lever.

B Engine brake Increases engine braking
Shift the lever only from "D" to "B" or vice versa

Shifting the lever improperly will cause the rejection function to operate. A beep will sound and the hybrid transaxle cannot be shifted.

14

15

FEATURES/OPERATIONS

BASIC VEHICLE OPERATION

OVERVIEW

FEATURES/OPERATIONS

SAFETY AND EMERGENCY FEATURES

14

Lights & turn signals

Headlights

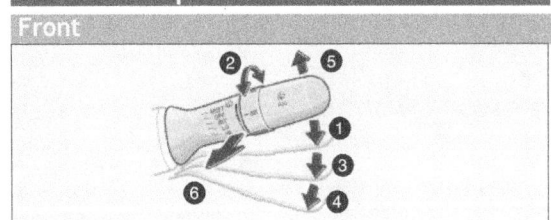

High beam indicator

Headlight indicator

❶ **Parking, tail, license plate, side marker and instrument panel lights** Twist the lever knob to position 1.
❷ **Headlights and all of the above** Twist the lever knob to position 2.
❸ **AUTO*** Twist the lever knob to position 3.
-Daytime running light system Automatically turns on the headlights at a reduced intensity.
❹ **High beams** Push the lever forward.
❺ **Low beams**
❻ **High beam flasher** Pull the lever toward you.
Note: Automatic light cutoff system*
Automatically turns off lights when the driver's door is opened with the hybrid system off.

*if installed

Turn signals

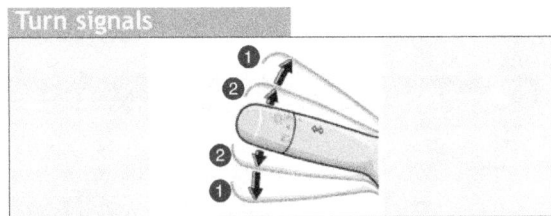

❶ **Right or left turn** Push the lever up or down.
❷ **Lane change** Move the lever up or down to position 2 and hold.

Front fog lights (if installed)

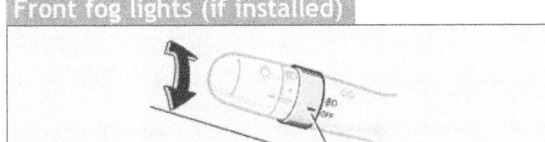

To turn on/off the fog lights Twist the band.

Window wiper & washer

Front

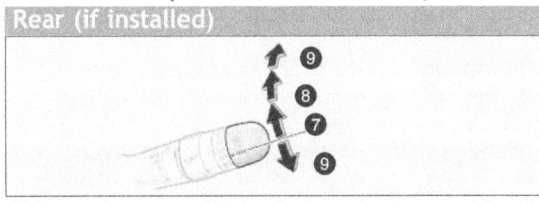

❶ **Intermittent speed** Push the lever down to position 1.
❷ **Interval adjuster** Twist the band to adjust the intermittent speed.
❸ **Slow speed** Push the lever down to position 3.
❹ **Fast speed** Push the lever down to position 4.
❺ **Single wipe** Push the lever up to position 5.
❻ **Wash and wipe** Pull the lever toward you.

Rear (if installed)

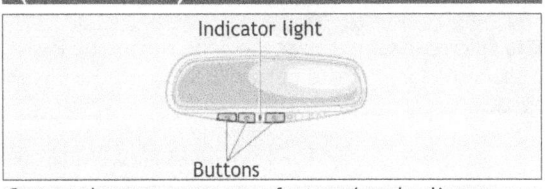

❼ **Rear slow speed** Twist the lever knob to position 7.
❽ **Rear high speed** Twist the lever knob to position 8.
❾ **Rear wash and wipe** Twist the lever knob upward or downward to position 9.

Garage door opener (HomeLink®) (if installed)

Indicator light

Buttons

Garage door openers manufactured under license from HomeLink®* can be programmed to operate garage doors, estate gates, security lighting, etc.

Refer to the *Owner's Manual* for more details. For programming assistance, contact the Toyota Customer Experience Center at 1-800-331-4331, or visit http://www.homelink.com

*HomeLink® is a registered trademark of Johnson Controls, Inc.

FEATURES/OPERATIONS

Seat adjustments-Front

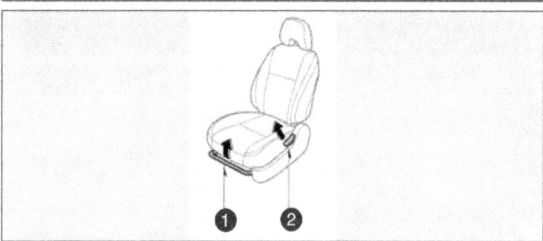

❶ Position lever
❷ Seatback angle lever

Seats-Head restraints

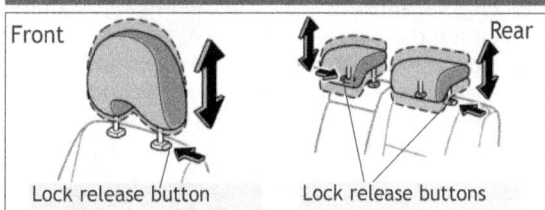

Front   Rear

Lock release button   Lock release buttons

To raise Pull up the head restraint.
To lower Push down the head restraint while pressing the lock release button.

Seat adjustments-Rear

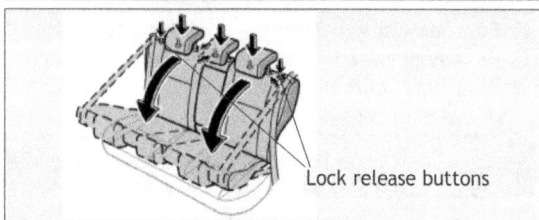

Lock release buttons

To fold rear seats Lower the head restraints. Push down the lock release button and fold the seatback down.

Power outlets

Instrument panel (12V)   Center console box (12V)

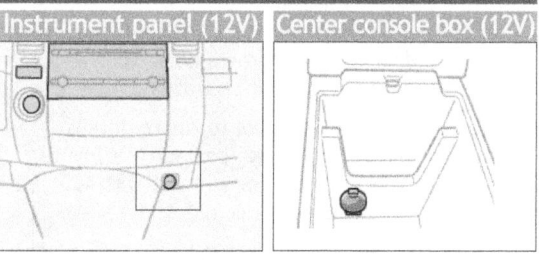

Windows

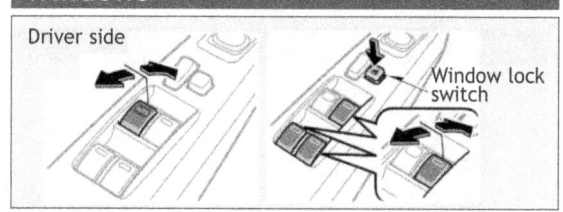

Driver side

Window lock switch

Window operation

To open or close Push down or pull up on the switch.
Automatic operation (driver side only) Push the switch completely down or pull it completely up and release to fully open or close. To stop window midway, lightly push the switch in the opposite direction.

Window lock switch

Push the switch to deactivate the passenger windows.

Luggage storage box

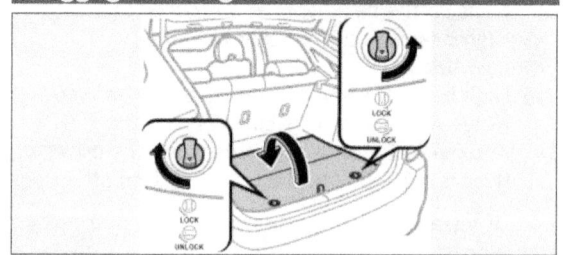

To open Turn the knobs to the "UNLOCK" position and open the lid.

Cup and Bottle holders

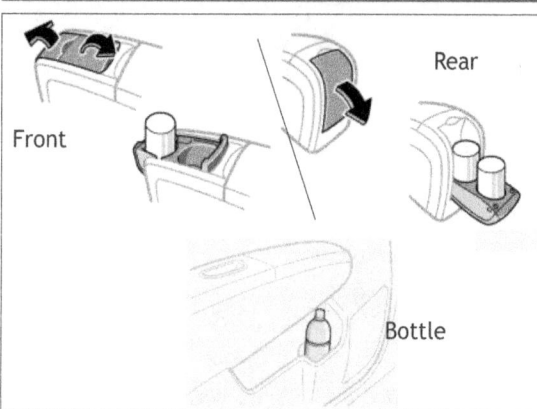

Rear

Front

Bottle

18

19

FEATURES/OPERATIONS

Air conditioning/Heating

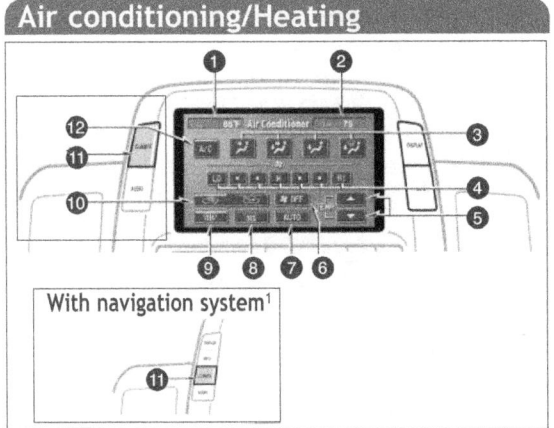

With navigation system[1]

1. Outside temperature display
2. Passenger compartment temperature display
3. Air flow control icons (See "To select air flow vents" below)
4. Fan speed control icons
5. Temperature selector icons
6. "OFF" icon Air conditioning OFF button.
7. "AUTO" icon Touch to turn automatic air conditioning ON/OFF.
8. Rear window and outside rear view mirror defogger icon
9. Windshield air flow icon
10. Air intake selector icon Push to select fresh or recirculated air. To clear windshield quickly, " " will automatically set to fresh air.
11. "CLIMATE" button Push to display the air conditioning operation screen.
12. Air conditioning on-off icon

To select air flow vents

Touch one of the following:

13. Instrument panel vents
14. Floor and panel vents
15. Floor vents
16. Floor and windshield vents

[1] For details, refer to the "Navigation System Owner's Manual."

20

Steering wheel switches

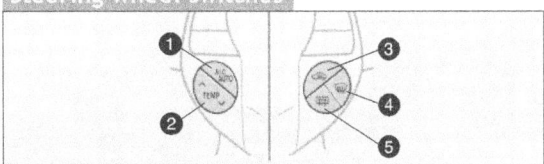

1. "AC AUTO"
2. Temperature
3. Air intake selector Push to select fresh or recirculated air.
4. Windshield vent
5. Rear window and outside rear view mirror defoggers

Cruise control

Turning system on/off   Setting a speed

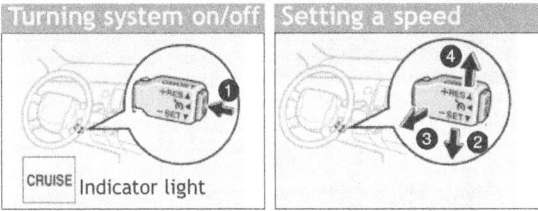

CRUISE Indicator light

1. To turn the system "ON" or "OFF" Push the button.
2. To set a speed Bring the vehicle to the desired speed. Push the lever down toward "- SET."
3. To cancel the set speed Pull the lever to "CANCEL." The set speed may also be cancelled by depressing the brake pedal.
4. To resume set speed after cancel Push the lever up toward "+ RES." Note that if vehicle speed falls below 25 mph, the set speed will not be resumed.

NOTE: To raise set speed, push up toward "+RES." To lower set speed, push down toward "-SET."

Refer to the *Owner's Manual* for more details.

Light Control-Instrument panel

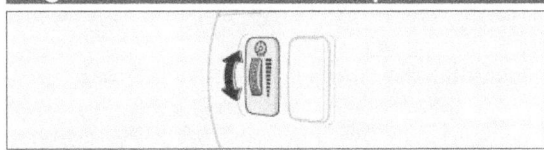

To adjust the brightness of the instrument panel Rotate the wheel up to increase, or down to decrease the brightness of the instrument panel lights.

21

FEATURES/OPERATIONS

Audio

Type 1

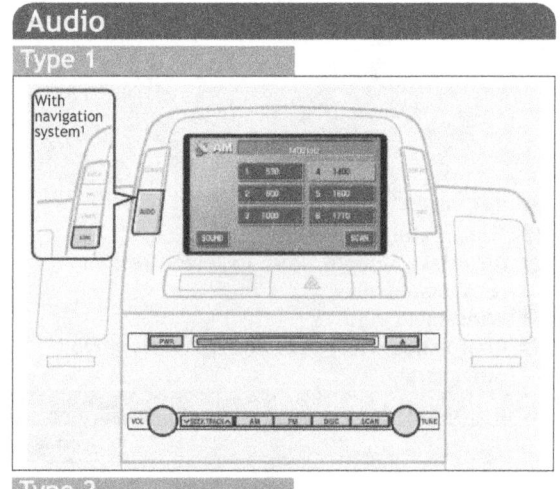

Type 2

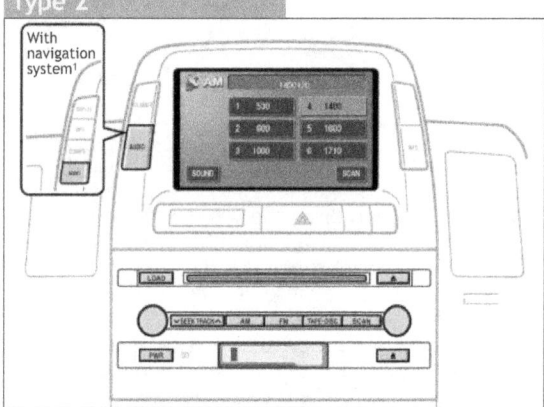

Audio operation screen

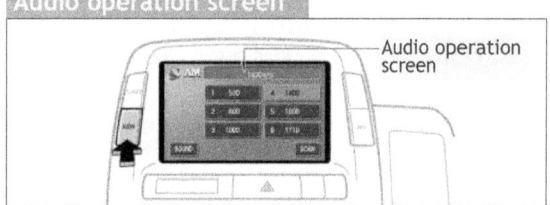

Audio operation screen

To display the screen Push "AUDIO" button.

---

[1] For details, refer to the "Navigation System Owner's Manual."

22

BASIC OPERATION

To turn on the audio system Push "PWR," "AM," "FM," "DISC," or "TAPE·DISC."
To turn off the system Push "PWR."
To adjust the volume Turn "VOL."
To adjust tone and balance Touch the "SOUND" icon on the screen to display the menu.

RADIO

To select a station Push either side of "SEEK TRACK."
To scan for stations Push "SCAN." Push again to hold selection.
To select the band Push "AM" or "FM".
-**To preset a station** Tune in the desired station and touch a station selector icon (1-6) until you hear a beep.
-**To select a preset station** Touch desired station selector icon (1-6) on the display.

CASSETTE TAPE PLAYER

To play Insert a cassette tape.
To fast forward Touch "▶▶" icon on the display.
To rewind Touch "◀◀" icon on the display.
To select a direction Touch "◀I▶" icon on the display.
To eject a cassette tape Push "▲."

CD PLAYER

To play Insert a compact disc.
To select a track Push either side of "SEEK TRACK."
To scan tracks on a disc Touch "SCAN" icon on the display. Push again to hold selection.
To eject a compact disc Push "▲."
Type 2 only is equipped with ···
  CD Changer
  -**To load one disc** Push "LOAD" and insert 1 disc.
  -**To load multiple discs** Push and hold "LOAD" until you hear a beep. Insert one disc. Shutter will close and then re-open for next disc.

Refer to the *Owner's Manual* for more details.

23

FEATURES/OPERATIONS

Audio continued

Steering wheel switches

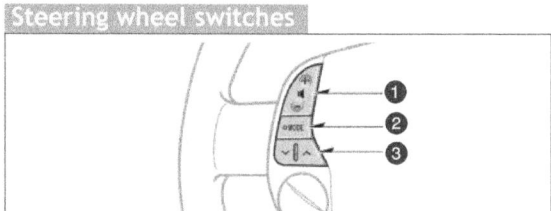

❶ **Volume control switch**
❷ **"MODE" switch** Push to select an audio mode.
❸ **" ∧ ∨ " switch**
In **radio mode** Push to select a preset station; push and hold to seek a station.
In **tape mode** Push to skip up or down to next/previous track; push and hold to fast forward or reverse.
In **CD mode** Push to skip up or down to next/previous track.

Refer to the *Owner's Manual* for more details.

Clock

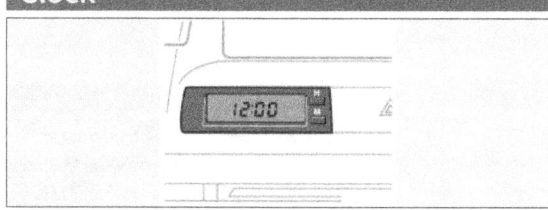

To reset the hour Push the "H" button.
To reset the minutes Push the "M" button.

Refer to the *Owner's Manual* for more details.

SAFETY AND EMERGENCY FEATURES

Door locks-Power

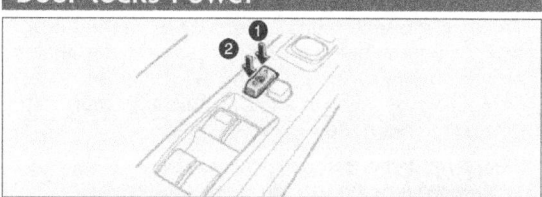

❶ **To lock** Push down on the front of the switch.
❷ **To unlock** Push down on the back of the switch.

Doors-Child safety locks

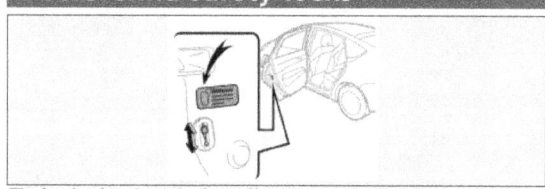

To lock the inside handle Move the lever to "LOCK," allowing the door to be opened only from the outside.

Seat belts

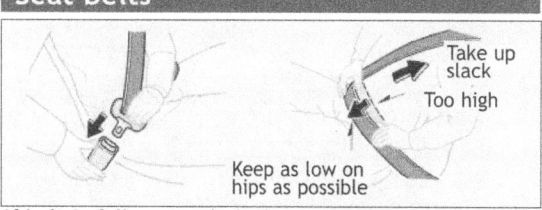

If belt is fully extended, then retracted even slightly, it cannot be re-extended beyond that point, unless fully retracted again. This feature is used to help hold child restraint systems securely.

To find out more information about seat belts, and how to install a child restraint system, refer to the *Owner's Manual*.

Seat belts-Shoulder belt anchor

To raise Slide the anchor upward.
To lower Squeeze the lock release button and slide the anchor downward.

BASIC VEHICLE OPERATION

OVERVIEW

FEATURES/OPERATIONS

SAFETY AND EMERGENCY FEATURES

14

SAFETY AND EMERGENCY FEATURES

Airbag-Supplemental Restraint System

The Airbag Supplemental Restraint System (SRS) front, side and side curtain* airbags are designed to provide further protection for the driver and outboard passenger in addition to the primary safety protection provided by the seat belts.

Please read the following caution boxes, and refer to the *Owner's Manual* for more details.

*If installed

⚠CAUTION

- The driver and front passenger airbag Supplemental Restraint System (SRS) is designed only as a supplement to the primary protection of the seat belt systems of the driver and front passenger. The front seat occupants are particularly susceptible to injury if they do not wear their seat belts; when sudden braking or a collision occurs, they may be thrown forward. To obtain maximum protection in an accident, the driver and all passengers in the vehicle should always wear their seat belts when driving because serious injuries or death can result to unrestrained occupants. For instructions and precautions concerning the seat belt system, see "Seat belts" in the *Owner's Manual*.
- Toyota strongly urges the use of a proper child restraint system on the rear seat that conforms to the size of the child. According to accident statistics, a child is safer when properly restrained in the rear seat than in the front seat.
- Never use a rear-facing child restraint system in the front seat. The force of the rapid inflation of the passenger airbag can cause severe injury or death to a child.
- Unless it is unavoidable, do not install a forward-facing child restraint system on the front seat. If you must install a forward-facing child restraint system on the front seat, move the seat as far back as possible.
- Make sure you have complied with all installation instructions provided by the child restraint manufacturer and the system is properly secured.
- The Toyota driver, front passenger, front seat-mounted side airbags and side curtain airbags are Supplemental Restraint Systems (SRS). The driver and front passenger airbags are designed to deploy in severe (usually frontal) collisions where the magnitude and duration of the forward deceleration of the vehicle exceeds the design threshold level. In all other accidents, the airbags will not inflate.
- To decrease the risk of injury from a deploying airbag, always wear seatbelts, sit upright in the middle of the seat as far back as possible from the airbag modules and do not lean against the door.
- Do not put objects in front of an airbag or around the seatback. Do not use rearward-facing child seats in any front passenger seat. The force of a deploying airbag SRS may cause serious injury or death.

Please see your *Owner's Manual* for further instructions.

Emergency flashers

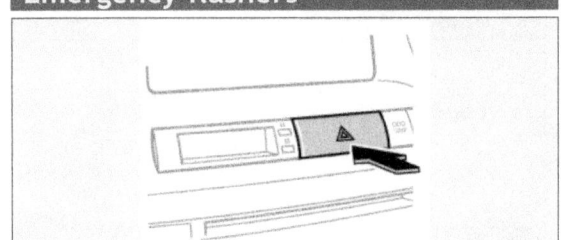

To turn the emergency flashers ON/OFF Push the button.

VSC (Vehicle Stability Control)[1] (if installed)

Helps provide comprehensive control of the Anti-lock Brakes, Brake-Assist[2], Traction Control, engine control and other systems. This system helps maintain control of the vehicle under adverse conditions.

Rear Air Vent

NOTE: The air vent on the right side of the rear seatback is designed to assist in cooling the hybrid vehicle battery. **DO NOT BLOCK OR COVER THIS VENT**, *as it may cause overheating, resulting in reduced performance.*

[1] *Vehicle Stability Control (VSC) is an electronic system designed to help the driver maintain vehicle control under adverse conditions. It is not a substitute for safe driving practices. Factors including speed, road conditions and driver steering input can all affect whether VSC will be effective in preventing loss of control.*
[2] *Brake-Assist is designed to help the driver take full advantage of the benefits of ABS (Anti-lock Brake System). It is not a substitute for safe driving practices. Braking effectiveness also depends on proper brake-system maintenance and tire and road conditions.*

SAFETY AND EMERGENCY FEATURES

Jump starting
Jump start terminal

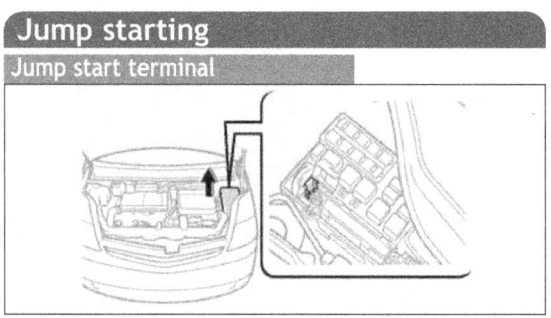

The jump start terminal is in the fuse box. To access the terminal, open the fuse block cover and the jump start terminal cover.

Connecting jumper cables

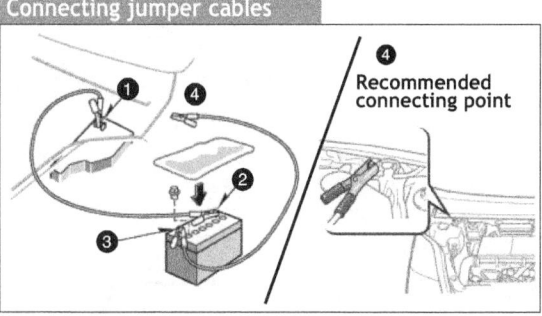

Recommended connecting point

❶ Connect positive (red) jumper cable to the jump start terminal.
❷ Connect positive (red) jumper cable to the positive (+) terminal on the booster battery.
❸ Connect negative (black) jumper cable to the negative (-) terminal on the booster battery.
❹ Connect negative (black) jumper cable to the recommended connecting point of the vehicle with the discharged battery.
❺ Depress brake pedal, and press "POWER" button to start the vehicle.

Refer to the *Owner's Manual* for more details.

Spare tire & tools
Tool location

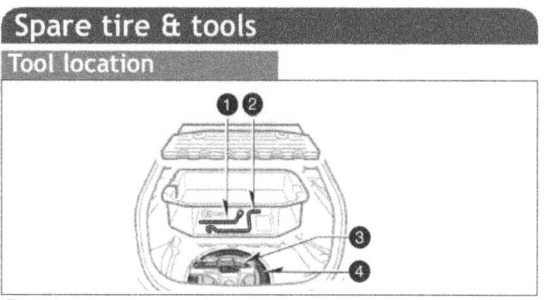

❶ Wheel nut wrench
❷ Jack handle
❸ Jack
❹ Spare tire

Removing the spare tire

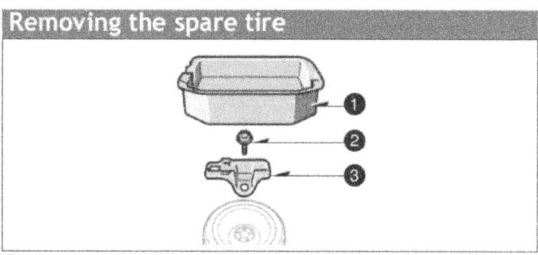

❶ Remove the luggage storage box.
❷ Loosen the bolt and remove it.
❸ Remove the jack box.

Refer to the *Owner's Manual* for jack positioning and tire changing procedures.

BASIC VEHICLE OPERATION

OVERVIEW

FEATURES/OPERATIONS

SAFETY AND EMERGENCY FEATURES

14

If you have any questions or comments please contact the Toyota Customer Experience Center at 1-800-331-4331, or visit our informative, interactive Web site at http://www.toyota.com

15

Toyota Emergency Response Guide

GENERAL

This chapter contains a copy the 2004 Toyota Prius Emergency Response Guide. The emergency response guide was published to educate and assist emergency and first responders in the safe handling of Prius hybrid technology.

NOTE—
* *Emergency Response Guides for select Toyota alternative fuel vehicles may be viewed at* **http://techinfo.toyota.com**.

NOTE—

- *This 2004 Toyota Prius Emergency Response Guide is courtesy of Toyota Motor Sales (TMS) USA, Inc. No review of its inclusion in this manual by TMS is expressed or implied. For the most up-to-date information visit* **http://techinfo.toyota.com**.

Prius safety precautions

In addition to the safety warnings given here, always read and observe the **Warnings**, **Cautions** and safety procedures in **3 Safety** before working on vehicle. Orange-colored cables carry lethal high voltage. Use extreme care when working near high voltage cables and components.

WARNING—

- *Risk of electrocution! Avoid touching orange-colored high voltage wiring and high voltage components unless you are certain that high voltage is not present.*

- *The Prius hybrid system has voltages as high as 500 volts. Voltages over 60 volts DC and 25 volts AC are a shock hazard.*

The Prius engine may start at any time if the hybrid system is in **READY** mode. See **3 Safety** for instructions on turning off the hybrid system.

WARNING—

- *Be sure hybrid system is OFF when servicing vehicle (READY indicator not illuminated). Failure to switch the hybrid system OFF could result in engine start at any time.*

HYBRID SYNERGY DRIVE

TOYOTA PRIUS

2004 Model

2nd Generation

Emergency Response Guide

04PRIUSERG REV – (1/22/04)

15

Foreword

In May 2000, Toyota released the 1st generation Toyota Prius gasoline-electric hybrid vehicle in North America. Approximately 50,000 1st generation Prius were sold in the 2001 - 2003 model years. To educate and assist emergency responders in the safe handling of the 1st generation Prius hybrid technology, Toyota published the Prius Emergency Response Guide (M/N 00400-ERG02-0U).

With the release of the 2nd generation Prius in October 2003, this new 2004 model year Toyota Prius Emergency Response Guide was published for emergency responders. While many features from the 1st generation model are similar, emergency responders should recognize and understand the new, updated features of the 2nd generation Prius covered in this guide.

2nd Generation Prius New Features:

- Complete model change with a new exterior and interior design.
- Adoption of *Hybrid Synergy Drive* as the name for the Toyota Gasoline - Electric Hybrid System.
- *Hybrid Synergy Drive* includes a boost converter in the inverter assembly that boosts to 500-Volts the available voltage to the electric motor.
- The boost converter allows a reduction in the high voltage hybrid vehicle battery pack to 201-Volts.
- Addition of a high voltage 201-Volt motor driven air conditioning compressor.
- New electronic automatic transmission gearshift selector.
- Elimination of the conventional ignition switch with the new standard electronic key system and optional smart entry and start electronic key.
- Frontal airbags, optional side airbags for front occupants, and optional curtain shield airbags for front and rear occupants.

High voltage electrical safety remains an important factor in the emergency handling of the Prius *Hybrid Synergy Drive* system. It is important to recognize and understand the disabling procedures and warnings throughout the guide.

Additional topics contained in the guide include:

- Toyota Prius identification.
- Major *Hybrid Synergy Drive* component locations and descriptions.
- Extrication, fire, recovery, and additional emergency response information.
- Roadside assistance information.

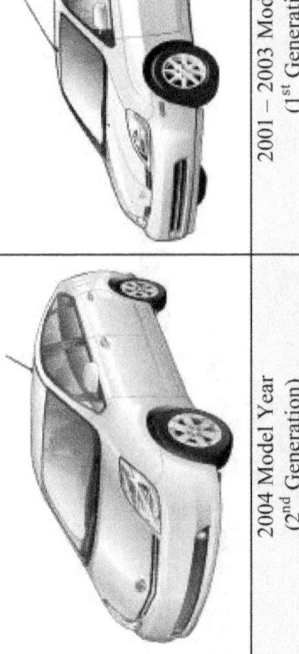

2004 Model Year (2nd Generation)	2001 – 2003 Model Years (1st Generation)

By following the information in this guide, emergency responders should be able to mitigate a rescue involving the 2nd generation Prius hybrid vehicle safely.

Note:
Emergency Response Guides for select Toyota alternative fuel vehicles may be viewed at *http://techinfo.toyota.com*.

-i-

Table of Contents

15

About the Prius

The Toyota Prius continues into its 2nd generation as a gasoline-electric hybrid vehicle. The gasoline-electric hybrid system has been renamed *Hybrid Synergy Drive*. *Hybrid Synergy Drive* means the vehicle contains a gasoline engine and an electric motor for power. Two energy sources are stored on board the vehicle:

1. Gasoline stored in the fuel tank for the gasoline engine.
2. Electricity stored in a high voltage Hybrid Vehicle (HV) battery pack for the electric motor.

The result of combining these two power sources is increased fuel economy and reduced emissions. The gasoline engine also powers an electric generator to recharge the battery pack; unlike a pure all electric vehicle, the Prius never needs to be recharged from an external electric power source.

Depending on the driving conditions one or both sources are used to power the vehicle. The following illustration demonstrates how the Prius operates in various driving modes.

❶ On light acceleration at low speeds, the vehicle is powered by the electric motor. The gasoline engine is shut off.

❷ During normal driving the vehicle is powered mainly by the gasoline engine. The gasoline engine is also used to recharge the battery pack.

❸ During full acceleration, such as climbing a hill, both the gasoline engine and the electric motor power the vehicle.

❹ During deceleration, such as braking, the vehicle regenerates the kinetic energy from the front wheels to produce electricity that recharges the battery pack.

❺ While the vehicle is stopped, the gasoline engine and electric motor are off, however the vehicle remains on and operational.

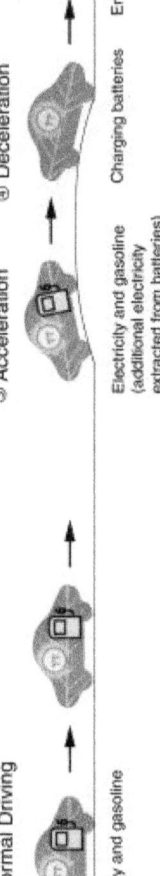

① Starting — Electricity
② Normal Driving — Electricity and gasoline
③ Acceleration — Electricity and gasoline (additional electricity extracted from batteries)
④ Deceleration — Charging batteries
⑤ Stopping — Engine automatically stopped

-1-

Prius Identification

In appearance, the 2004 Prius is a 5-door hatchback. Exterior, interior, and engine compartment illustrations are provided to assist in identification.

The alphanumeric 17 character Vehicle Identification Number (VIN) is provided in the front windshield cowl and driver door post.

Example VIN: <u>JTDKB20U840020208</u>
(A Prius is identified by the first 6 alphanumeric characters **JTDKB2**)

Exterior
1 **TOYOTA** **PRIUS** [logo] logos on rear hatchback door.
2 Gasoline fuel filler door located on driver side rear quarter panel.

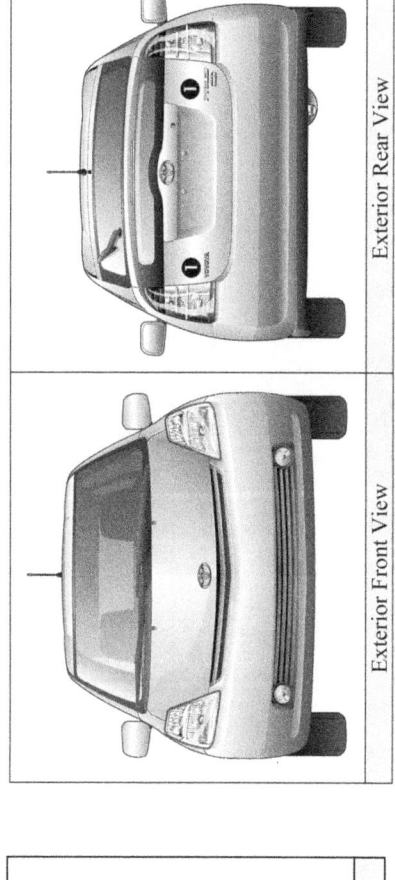

Exterior Front View

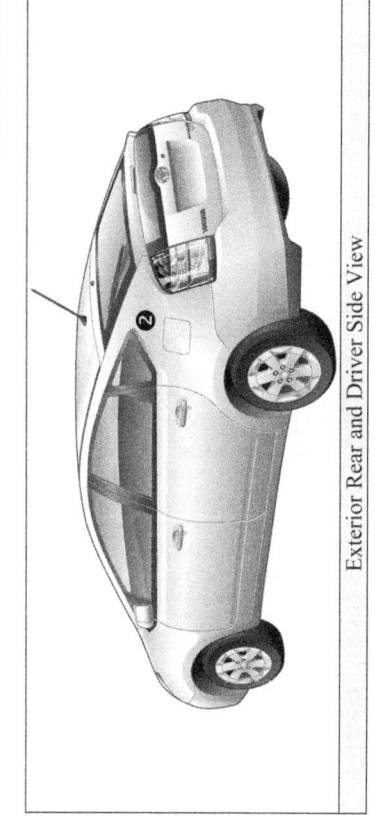

Exterior Rear View

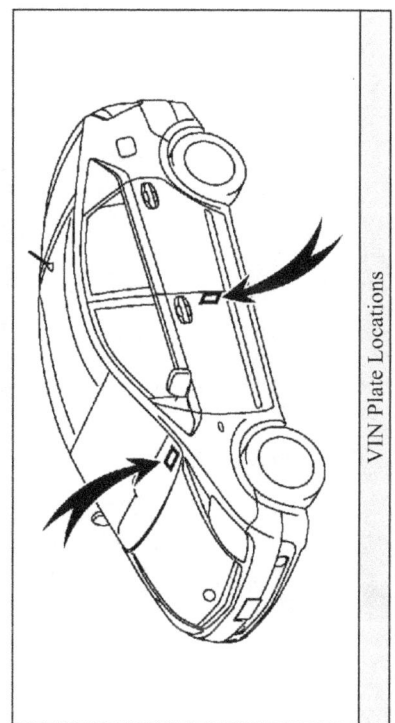

VIN Plate Locations

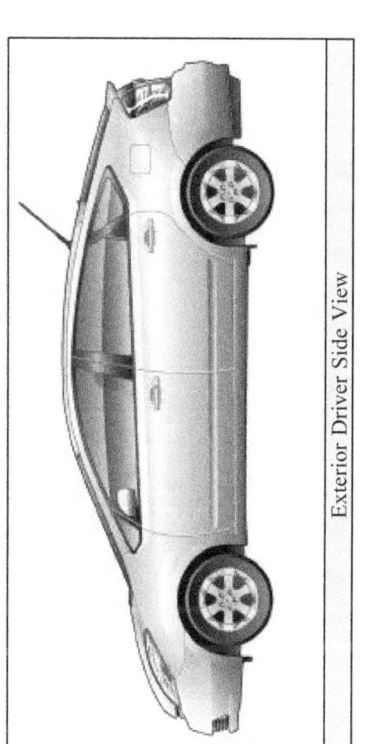

Exterior Rear and Driver Side View

Exterior Driver Side View

15

Prius Identification (Continued)

Interior

3 Dashboard mounted automatic transmission gearshift selector.

4 Instrument cluster (speedometer, fuel gauge, **READY** light, warning lights) located in center dash and near the base of the windshield.

5 LCD monitor (fuel consumption, energy monitor, radio controls, A/C controls) located above the center dash.

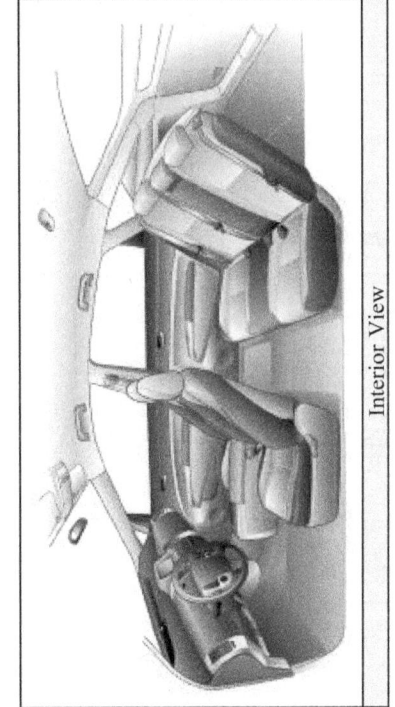

Interior View

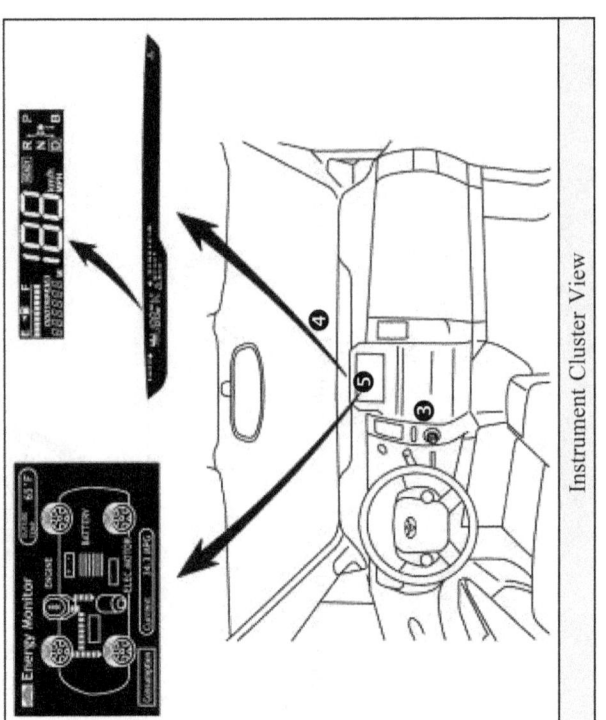

Instrument Cluster View

Engine Compartment

6 1.5 liter aluminum alloy gasoline engine.

7 High voltage inverter/converter assembly with the logos on the cover.

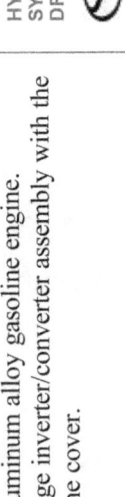

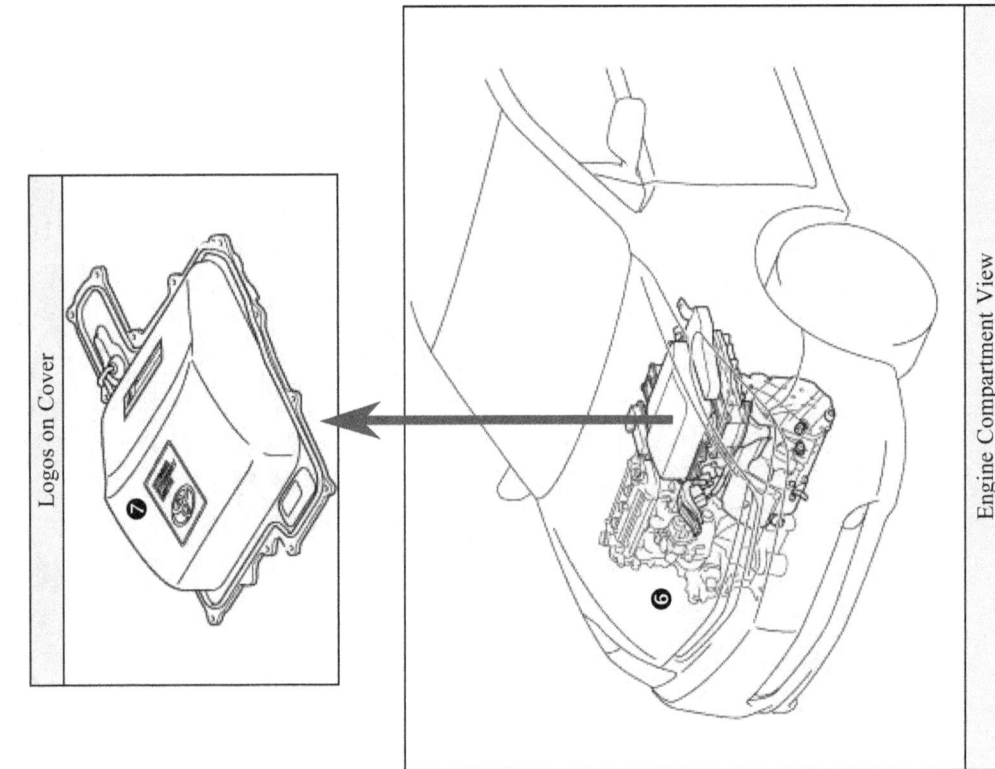

Logos on Cover

Engine Compartment View

-3-

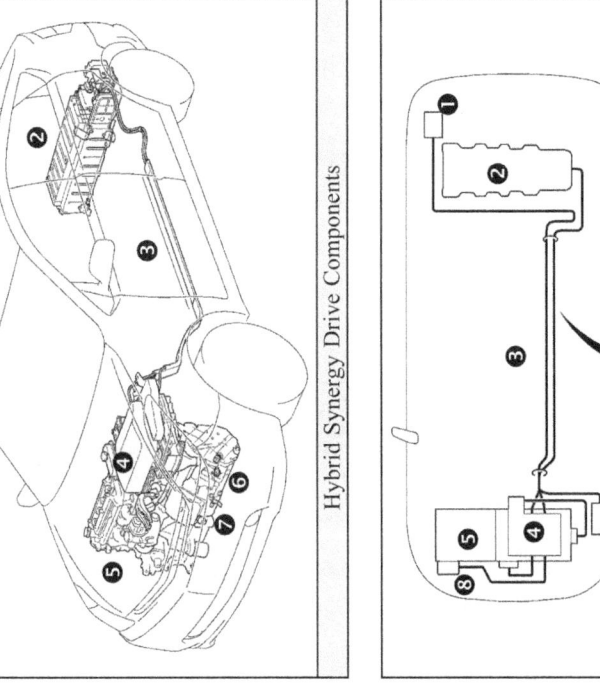
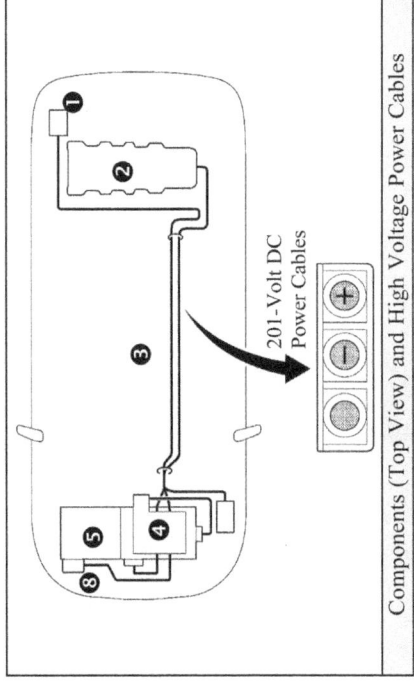
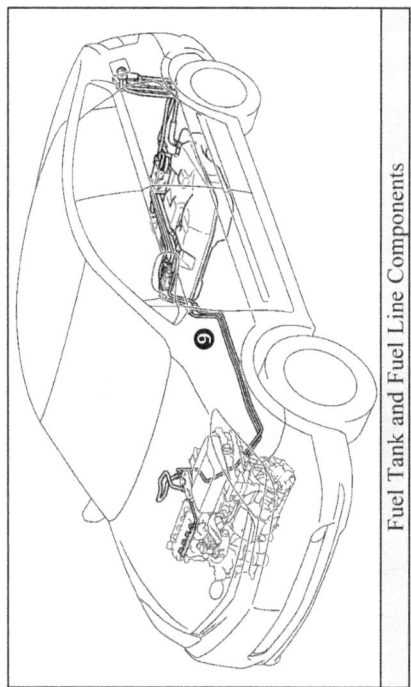

Hybrid Synergy Drive Components

201-Volt DC Power Cables

Components (Top View) and High Voltage Power Cables

Fuel Tank and Fuel Line Components

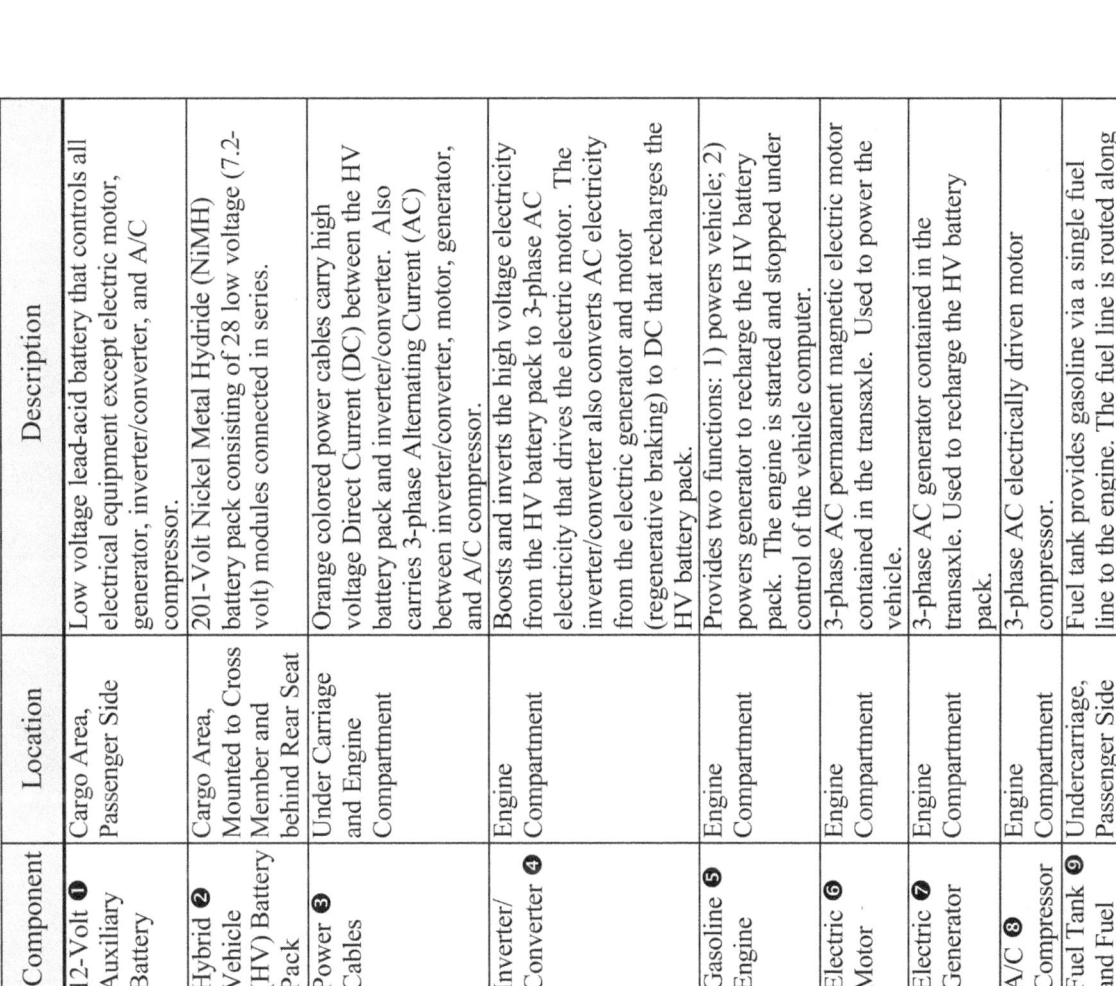

Hybrid Synergy Drive Component Locations & Descriptions

Component	Location	Description
12-Volt Auxiliary Battery ❶	Cargo Area, Passenger Side	Low voltage lead-acid battery that controls all electrical equipment except electric motor, generator, inverter/converter, and A/C compressor.
Hybrid Vehicle (HV) Battery Pack ❷	Cargo Area, Mounted to Cross Member and behind Rear Seat	201-Volt Nickel Metal Hydride (NiMH) battery pack consisting of 28 low voltage (7.2-volt) modules connected in series.
Power Cables ❸	Under Carriage and Engine Compartment	Orange colored power cables carry high voltage Direct Current (DC) between the HV battery pack and inverter/converter. Also carries 3-phase Alternating Current (AC) between inverter/converter, motor, generator, and A/C compressor.
Inverter/ Converter ❹	Engine Compartment	Boosts and inverts the high voltage electricity from the HV battery pack to 3-phase AC electricity that drives the electric motor. The inverter/converter also converts AC electricity from the electric generator and motor (regenerative braking) to DC that recharges the HV battery pack.
Gasoline Engine ❺	Engine Compartment	Provides two functions: 1) powers vehicle; 2) powers generator to recharge the HV battery pack. The engine is started and stopped under control of the vehicle computer.
Electric Motor ❻	Engine Compartment	3-phase AC permanent magnetic electric motor contained in the transaxle. Used to power the vehicle.
Electric Generator ❼	Engine Compartment	3-phase AC generator contained in the transaxle. Used to recharge the HV battery pack.
A/C Compressor ❽	Engine Compartment	3-phase AC electrically driven motor compressor.
Fuel Tank and Fuel Lines ❾	Undercarriage, Passenger Side	Fuel tank provides gasoline via a single fuel line to the engine. The fuel line is routed along passenger side under the floor pan.

15

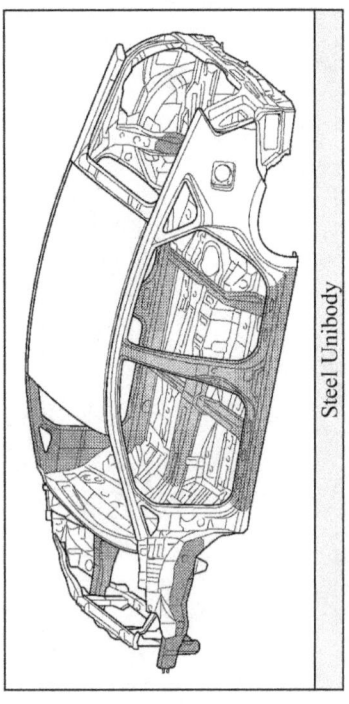

Steel Unibody

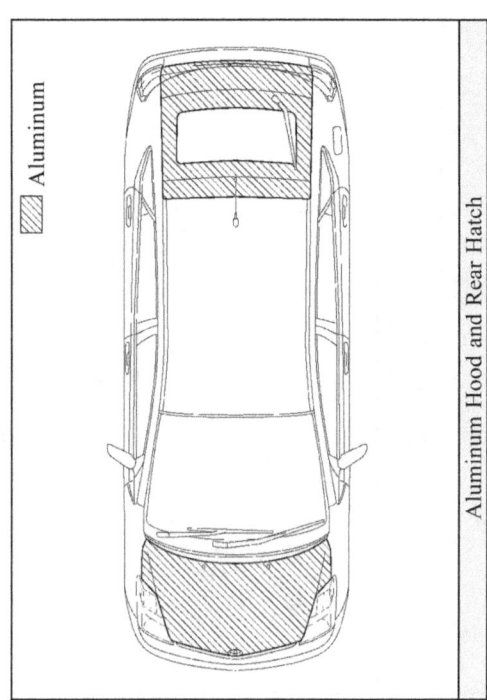

Aluminum

Aluminum Hood and Rear Hatch

-5-

Hybrid Synergy Drive Component Locations & Descriptions (Continued)

Key Specifications:

Gasoline Engine:	76 hp, 1.5 liter Aluminum Alloy Engine
Electric Motor:	67 hp, Permanent Magnet Motor
Transmission:	Automatic Only
HV Battery:	201-Volt Sealed NiMH
Curb Weight:	2,890 lbs
Fuel Tank:	11.9 gals
Miles Per Gallon:	60/51 mpg (City/Hwy)
Liters/100 km:	4.0/4.2 L/100 km (City/Hwy)
Frame Material:	Steel unibody
Body Material:	Steel panels except aluminum hood and rear hatch.

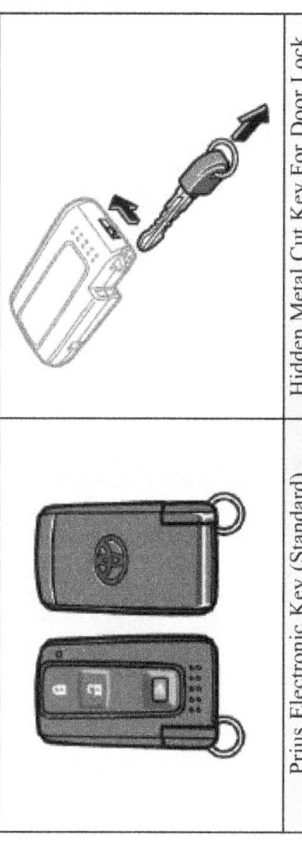

	Prius Electronic Key (Standard)	Hidden Metal Cut Key For Door Lock

	Electronic Key Slot	Power Button with Status Indicator Light

Ignition Mode	Power Button Indicator Light
Off	Off
Accessory	Green
Ignition-On	Amber
Vehicle Started (READY-On)	Off
Malfunction	Blinking Amber

Electronic Key

The 2004 Prius introduces a new electronic key as standard equipment.

Electronic key features:
* Wireless transmitter to lock/unlock the doors.
* Electronic key for starting.
* Hidden metal cut key to lock/unlock the doors from the driver exterior door lock.

Door (Lock/Unlock)
Two methods are available to lock/unlock the doors.

1. Pushing wireless electronic key lock/unlock buttons.

2. Inserting the hidden metal cut key in driver door lock and turning clockwise once unlocks the driver door, twice unlocks all doors. To lock all doors turn the key counter-clockwise once. Only the driver door contains an exterior door lock.

Vehicle Starting/Stopping
The electronic key has replaced the conventional metal cut key, and an electronic key slot and power button have replaced the ignition switch.

* A standard electronic key as shown in the illustration is inserted into the electronic key slot.

* The electronic key slot does not rotate like a conventional ignition switch. Instead, a power button with an integral status indicator light is provided above the electronic key slot to cycle through the various ignition modes. With the brake pedal released, the first push of the power button operates the accessory mode, the second push operates the ignition-on mode, and the third push turns the ignition off again.

Ignition Mode Sequence (Brake pedal released):

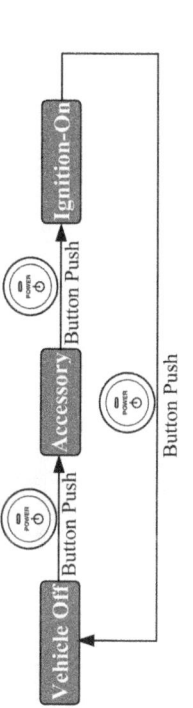

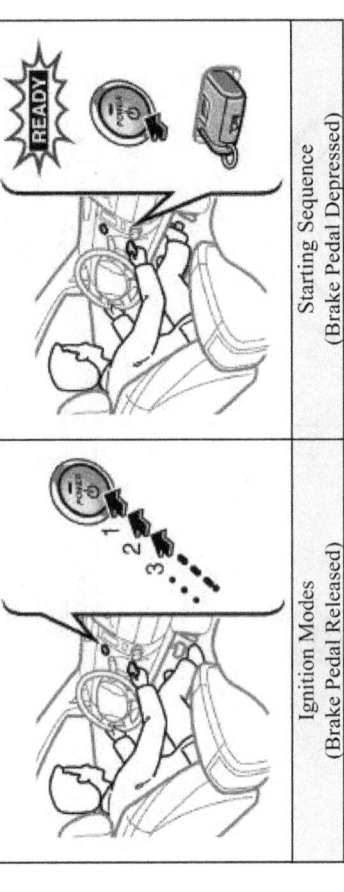

Ignition Modes
(Brake Pedal Released)

Starting Sequence
(Brake Pedal Depressed)

Electronic Key (Continued)

Vehicle Starting/Stopping (Continued)

- Starting the vehicle takes priority over all other ignition modes and is accomplished by depressing the brake pedal and pushing the power button once. To verify the vehicle has started, the power button status indicator light is off and the **READY** light is illuminated in the instrument cluster.

- Once the vehicle has started and is on and operational (READY-on), the vehicle is shut off by bringing the vehicle to a complete stop and then depressing the power button once.

- The key slot prevents the electronic key from being removed while the vehicle is on and operational (READY-on) or in the ignition-on mode.

-7-

Smart Entry & Start Electronic Key (Optional Equipment)

The Prius may be equipped with an optional *smart entry and start electronic key* that appears similar in function and design to the standard electronic key. However, the smart key contains a transceiver that communicates bi-directionally enabling the vehicle to recognize the smart key in close proximity to the vehicle. The system can lock or unlock doors without pushing smart key buttons and start the hybrid system without inserting the smart key into the electronic key slot.

Smart key features:
- Passive (remote) function to lock/unlock the doors and start the vehicle.
- Wireless transmitter to lock/unlock the doors.
- Electronic key for starting.
- Hidden metal cut key to lock/unlock the doors from the driver door lock.

Door (Lock/Unlock)
Three methods are available to lock/unlock the doors.

1. Pushing wireless smart key lock/unlock buttons.

2. Touching the sensor on the backside of either exterior front door handle, with the smart key in close proximity to the vehicle, unlocks the doors. Pushing the black button on the front door handle locks the doors.

3. Inserting the metal cut key in driver door lock and turning clockwise once unlocks the driver door, twice unlocks all doors. To lock all doors turn the key counter-clockwise once. Only the driver door contains an exterior door lock.

Vehicle Starting/Stopping
The ignition modes and starting sequence are the same as the standard electronic key except the smart key does not have to be inserted into the electronic key slot.

- The optional smart key as shown in the illustrations may be inserted into the electronic key slot or kept in close proximity to the vehicle.

- With brake pedal released, the first push of the power button operates the accessory mode, the second push operates the ignition-on mode, and the third push turns the ignition off again.

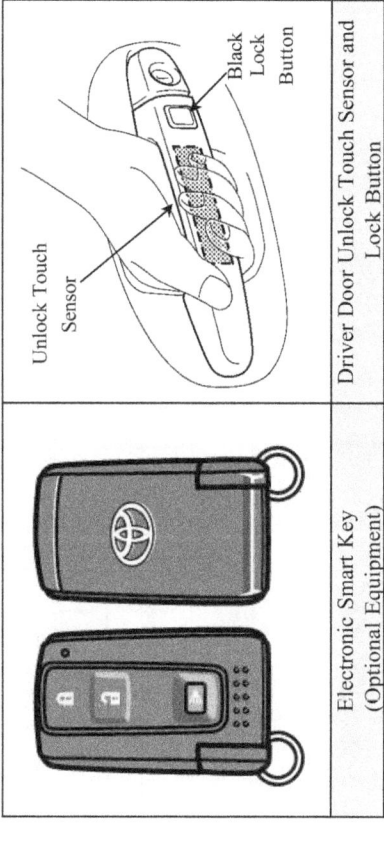

Unlock Touch Sensor

Black Lock Button

Electronic Smart Key (Optional Equipment)

Driver Door Unlock Touch Sensor and Lock Button

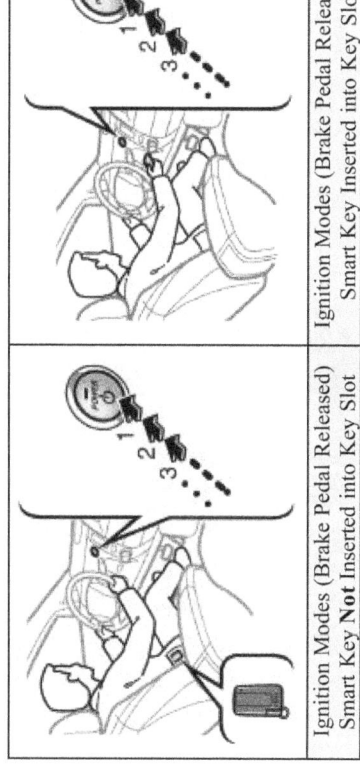

Ignition Modes (Brake Pedal Released) Smart Key **Not** Inserted into Key Slot

Ignition Modes (Brake Pedal Released) Smart Key Inserted into Key Slot

-8-

15

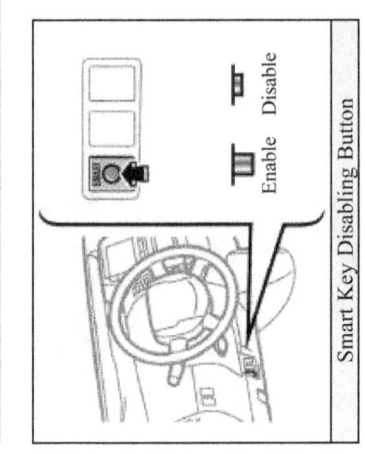

Ignition Mode	Power Button Indicator Light
Off	Off
Accessory	Green
Ignition-On	Amber
Vehicle Started (READY-On)	Off
Malfunction	Blinking Amber

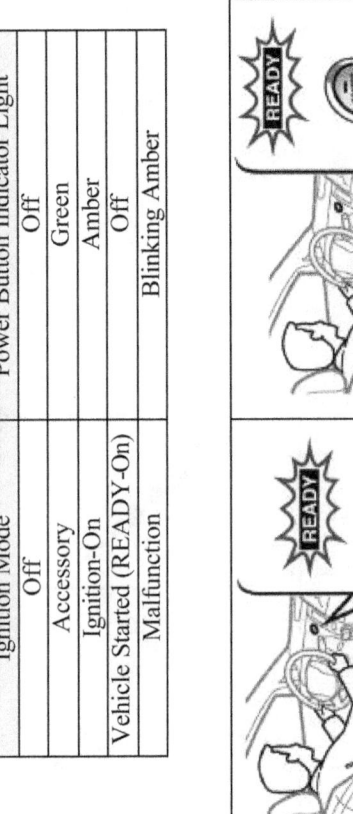

Starting Sequence (Brake Pedal Depressed)
Smart Key **Not** Inserted into Key Slot

Starting Sequence (Brake Pedal Depressed)
Smart Key Inserted into Key Slot

Enable   Disable

Smart Key Disabling Button

Smart Entry & Start Electronic Key (Optional Equipment) (Continued)

Vehicle Starting/Stopping (Continued)

Ignition Mode Sequence (Brake pedal released):

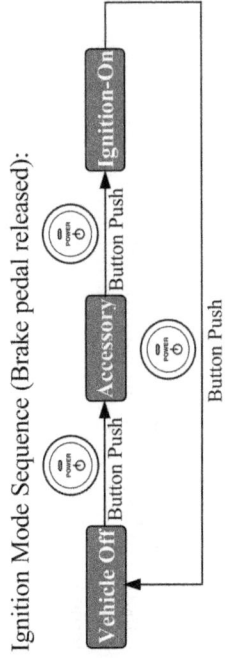

Vehicle Off → Button Push → Accessory → Button Push → Ignition-On

Button Push

- Starting the vehicle takes priority over all other ignition modes and is accomplished by depressing the brake pedal and pushing the power button once. To verify the vehicle has started, the power button status indicator light is off and the **READY** light is illuminated in the instrument cluster.

- Once the vehicle has started and is on and operational (READY-on), the vehicle is shut off by bringing the vehicle to a complete stop and then depressing the power button once.

- Vehicles equipped with the optional smart key have a disabling button located beneath the steering column as shown in the illustration. When disabled, the smart key must be inserted into the key slot to enable the ignition modes or start the vehicle.

- The key slot prevents the electronic key from being removed while the vehicle is on and operational (READY-on) or in the ignition-on mode.

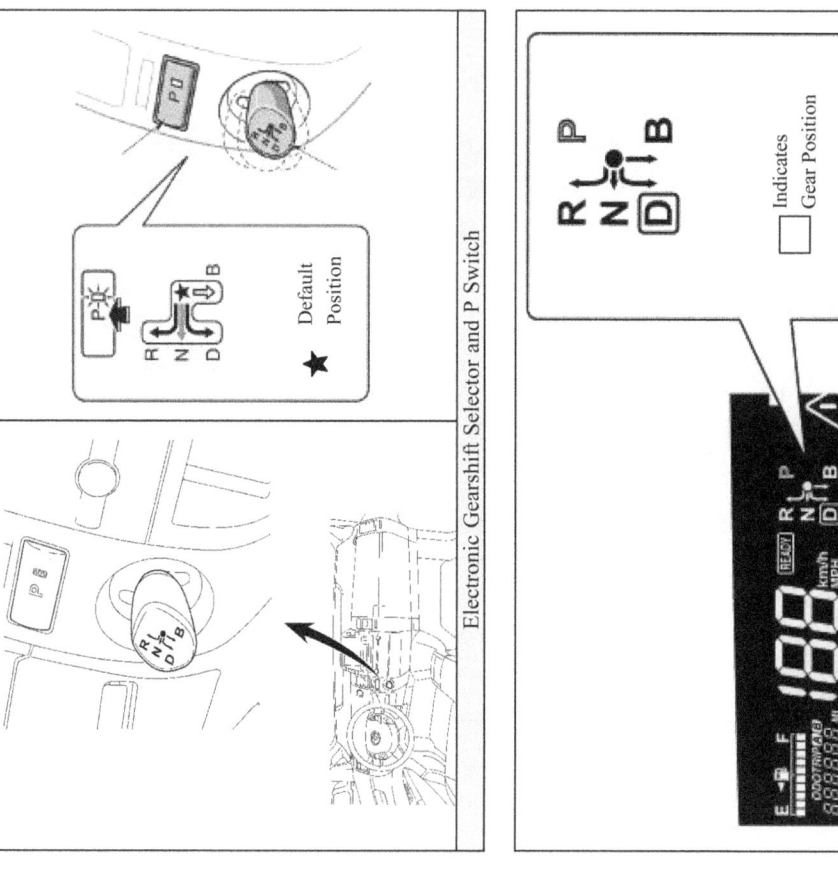

Electronic Gearshift Selector and P Switch

Gearshift Position Identified in the Instrument Cluster.

Electronic Gearshift Selector

The Prius electronic gearshift selector is a newly developed momentary select shift-by-wire system that engages the transaxle in **R**everse, **N**eutral, **D**rive, or engine **B**rake modes.

- These modes may only be engaged while the vehicle is on and operational (READY-on), except for Neutral which may also be engaged while in the ignition-on mode. After selecting the gear position R, N, D, or B the transaxle remains in that position, identified on the instrument cluster, but the shift selector returns to a default position.

- Unlike a conventional vehicle, the electronic shift selector does not contain a park position. Instead, a separate **P** switch located above the shift selector engages the park position.

- When the vehicle is stopped, regardless of shift selector position, the electro-mechanical parking pawl is engaged to lock the transaxle into park by either depressing the **P** switch or pushing the power button to shut off the vehicle.

- Being electronic, the gearshift selector and the park systems depend on the low voltage 12-Volt auxiliary battery for power. If the 12-Volt auxiliary battery is discharged or disconnected, the vehicle cannot be started and cannot be shifted out of park.

-10-

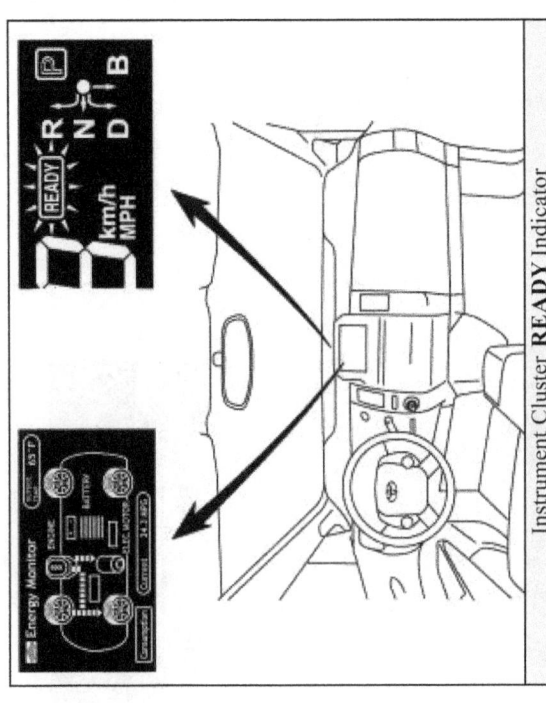

Instrument Cluster **READY** Indicator

Hybrid Synergy Drive Operation

Once the **READY** indicator is illuminated in the instrument cluster, the vehicle may be driven. However, the gasoline engine does not idle like a typical automobile and will start and stop automatically. It is important to recognize and understand the **READY** indicator provided in the instrument cluster. When lit, it informs the driver the vehicle is on and operational even though the gasoline engine may be off and the engine compartment is silent.

Vehicle Operation

• With the Prius, the gasoline engine may stop and start at any time while the **READY** indicator is on.

• Never assume the vehicle is shut off just because the engine is off. Always look for the **READY** indicator status. The vehicle is shut off when the **READY** indicator is off.

• The vehicle may be powered by:
   1. The electric motor only.
   2. The gasoline engine only.
   3. A combination of both the electric motor and the gasoline engine.

• The vehicle computer determines the mode in which the vehicle operates to improve fuel economy and reduce emissions. The driver cannot manually select the mode.

Hybrid Vehicle (HV) Battery Pack and Auxiliary Battery

The Prius contains a high voltage, Hybrid Vehicle (HV) battery pack and a low voltage auxiliary battery. The HV battery pack contains non-spillable, sealed Nickel Metal Hydride (NiMH) battery modules and the auxiliary battery is a typical automotive lead-acid type.

HV Battery Pack

- The HV battery pack is enclosed in a metal case and is rigidly mounted to the cargo area floor pan cross member behind the rear seat. The metal case is isolated from high voltage and concealed by a cover in the cargo area.

- The HV battery pack consists of 28 low voltage (7.2-Volt) NiMH battery modules connected in series to produce approximately 201-Volts. Each NiMH battery module is non-spillable and sealed in a plastic case.

- The electrolyte used in the NiMH battery module is an alkaline of potassium and sodium hydroxide. The electrolyte is absorbed into the battery cell plates and will form a gel that will not normally leak, even in a collision.

- In the unlikely event the battery pack is overcharged, the modules vent gases directly outside the vehicle through a vent hose connected to each NiMH battery module.

HV Battery Pack	
Battery pack voltage	201-Volts
Number of NiMH battery modules in the pack	28
Battery pack weight	86 lbs/39 kg
NiMH battery module voltage	7.2-Volts
NiMH battery module dimensions	11 x 3/4 x 4 inches 27.9 x 1.9 x 10.1 cm
NiMH battery module weight	2.2 lbs/1 kg

Components Powered by the HV Battery Pack

- Electric Motor
- Electric Generator
- Inverter/Converter
- Power Cables
- A/C Compressor

HV Battery Pack Recycling

- The HV battery pack is recyclable. Contact the nearest Toyota dealer, or:

  United States: (800) 331-4331
  Canada: (888) Toyota 8 [(888)-869-6828]

Auxiliary Battery

- The Prius also contains a lead-acid 12-Volt battery. This 12-Volt auxiliary battery powers the vehicle electrical system similar to a conventional vehicle. As with other conventional vehicles, the auxiliary battery is grounded to the metal chassis of the vehicle.

- The auxiliary battery is located in the passenger side rear cargo area. It also contains a hose to vent gases outside the vehicle if overcharged.

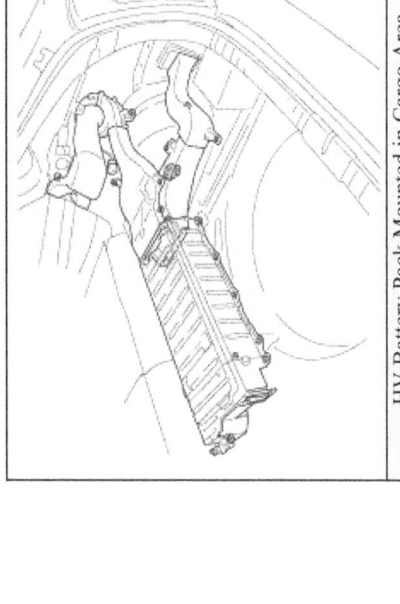

201-Volt HV Battery Pack

12-Volt Auxiliary Battery in Rear Cargo Area (Passenger Side)

HV Battery Pack Mounted in Cargo Area

15

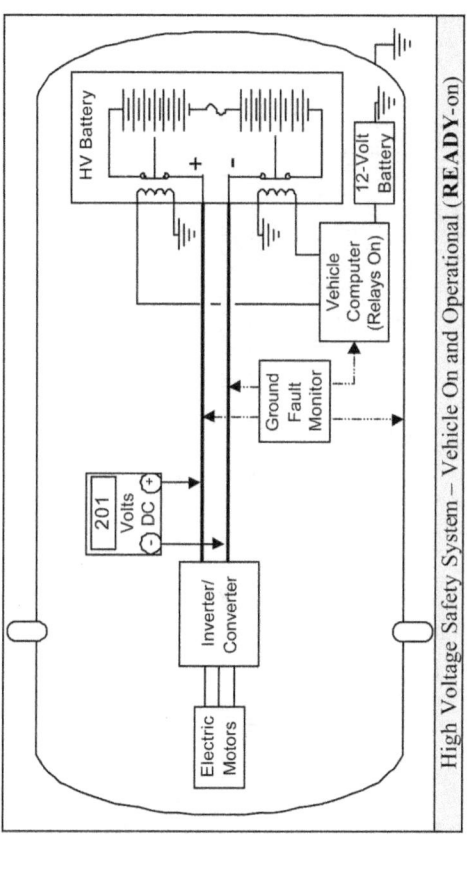

High Voltage Safety System – Vehicle Shut Off (**READY**-off)

High Voltage Safety System – Vehicle On and Operational (**READY**-on)

High Voltage Safety

The HV battery pack powers the high voltage electrical system with DC electricity. Positive and negative high voltage power cables are routed from the battery pack, under the vehicle floor pan, to the inverter/converter. The inverter/converter contains a circuit that boosts the HV battery voltage from 201 to 500-Volts DC. The inverter creates 3-phase AC to power the motors in the engine compartment. Sets of 3 power cables are routed from the inverter to each high voltage motor (electric motor, electric generator, and A/C compressor). Occupants in the vehicle and emergency responders are separated from high voltage electricity by the following systems:

High Voltage Safety System

- A high voltage fuse ❶ provides short circuit protection in the HV battery pack.

- Positive and negative high voltage power cables ❷ connected to the HV battery pack are controlled by 12-Volt normally open relays ❸. When the vehicle is shut off, the relays stop electricity flow from the HV battery pack.

WARNING:

- *Power remains in the high voltage electrical system for 5 minutes after the HV battery pack is shut off.*

- *Never touch, cut, or open any orange high voltage power cable or high voltage component.*

- Both positive and negative power cables ❷ are isolated from the metal chassis, so there is no possibility of shock by touching the metal chassis.

- A ground fault monitor ❹ continuously monitors for high voltage leakage to the metal chassis while the vehicle is running. If a malfunction is detected, the vehicle computer ❺ will illuminate the master warning light ⚠ in the instrument cluster and the hybrid warning light 🚗 in the LCD display.

- The HV battery pack relays will automatically open to stop electricity flow in a collision sufficient to activate the SRS airbags.

SRS Airbags and Seat Belt Pretensioners

Standard Equipment

- Electronic frontal impact sensors (2) are mounted in the engine compartment ❶.
- Front seat belt pretensioners are mounted near the base of the B-pillar ❷.
- Frontal dual stage airbag for the driver ❸ is mounted in the steering wheel hub.
- Frontal dual stage airbag for the front passenger ❹ is integrated into the dashboard and deploys through the top of the dashboard.
- SRS computer ❺ is mounted on the floor pan underneath the center console. It also contains an impact sensor.

Optional Side Impact Airbag Package

- Front electronic side impact sensors (2) are mounted near the base of the B-pillars ❻.
- Rear electronic side impact sensors (2) are mounted near the base of the C-pillars ❼.
- Front seat side impact airbags ❽ are mounted in the front seats.
- Curtain shield side impact airbags ❾ are mounted along the outer edge inside the roof rails.

WARNING:

- *The SRS computer is equipped with a back up source that powers the SRS airbags up to 90 seconds after disabling the vehicle.*
- *The front seat side airbags and the curtain shield side airbags may deploy independent of each other.*

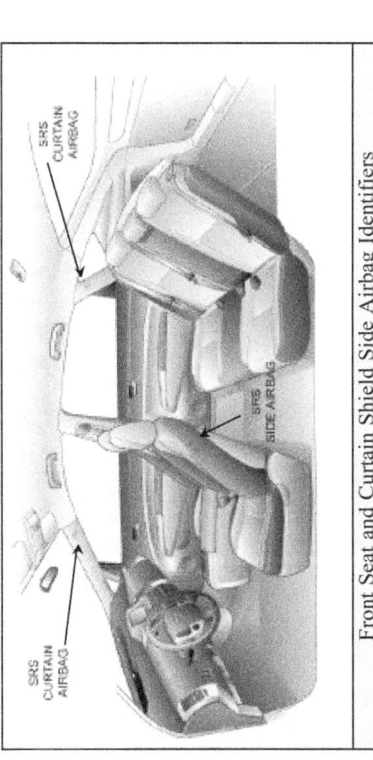

Frontal, Optional Front Seat Side, and Optional Curtain Shield Side Airbags.

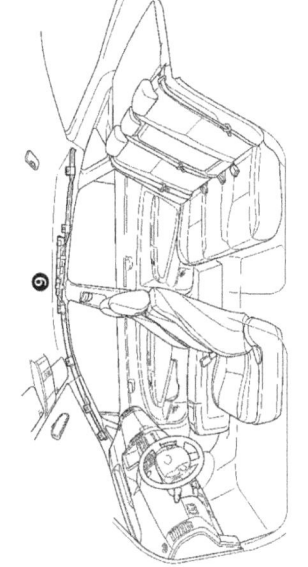

Front Seat and Curtain Shield Side Airbag Identifiers

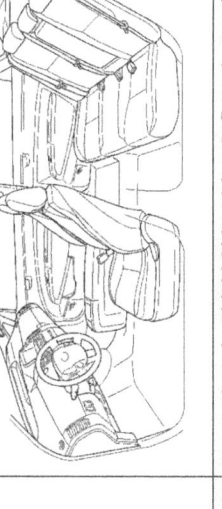

Curtain Shield Side Airbag Inflator in Roof Rail

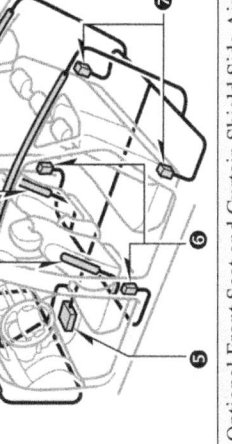

Optional Front Seat and Curtain Shield Side Airbags

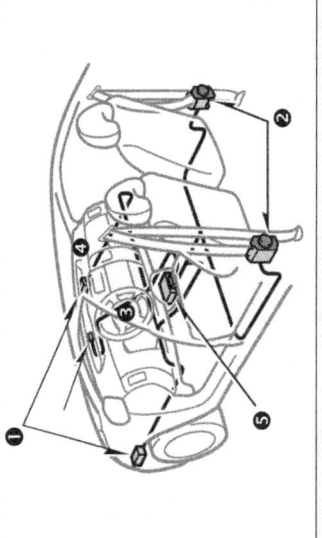

Standard Frontal Airbags and Seat Belt Pretensioners

-14-

15

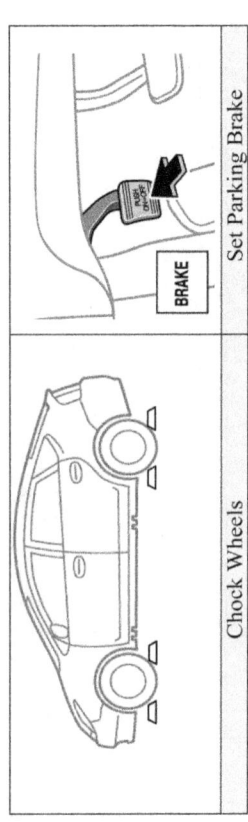

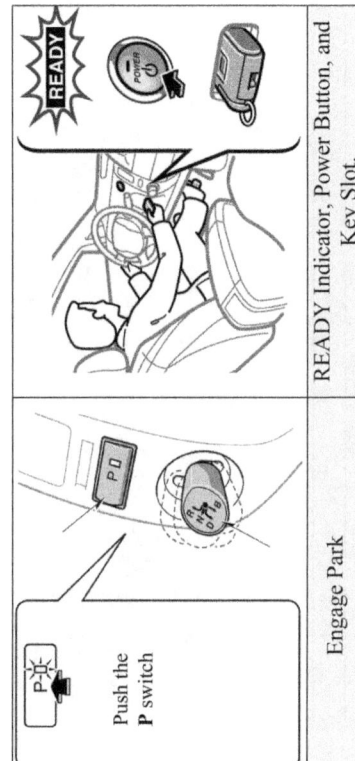

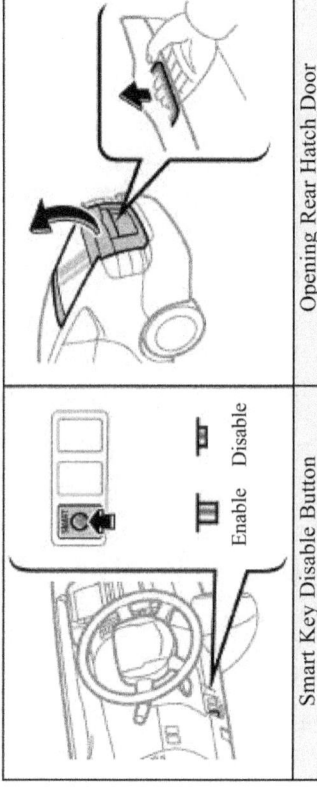

Emergency Response

On arrival, emergency responders should follow their standard operating procedures for vehicle incidents. Emergencies involving the Prius may be handled like other automobiles except as noted in these guidelines for Extrication, Fire, Overhaul, Recovery, Spills, First Aid, and Submersion.

WARNING:
- *Never assume the Prius is shut off simply because it is silent.*
- *Always observe the instrument cluster for the **READY** indicator status to verify whether the vehicle is on or shut off.*

Extrication

- Immobilize Vehicle

  Chock wheels and set the parking brake.

  Push the **P** switch to engage park.

- Disable Vehicle

  Performing either of the two procedures will shut the vehicle off and disable the HV battery pack, SRS airbags, and gasoline fuel pump.

Procedure #1

1. Confirm the status of **READY** indicator in the instrument cluster.
2. If the **READY** indicator is illuminated, the vehicle is on and operational. Shut off the vehicle by pushing the power button once.
3. The vehicle is already shut off if the instrument cluster lights and the **READY** indicator are **not** illuminated. Do **not** push the power button the vehicle may start.
4. Remove the electronic key from the key slot.
5. If equipped, disable the smart key button underneath the steering column.
6. Keep the electronic key at least 16 feet (5 meters) away from the vehicle.
7. If the electronic key cannot be removed from the key slot or if the electronic key cannot be found, disconnect the 12-Volt auxiliary battery in the rear cargo area.

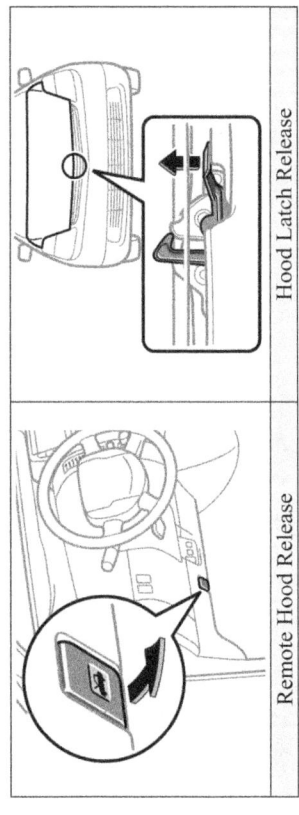
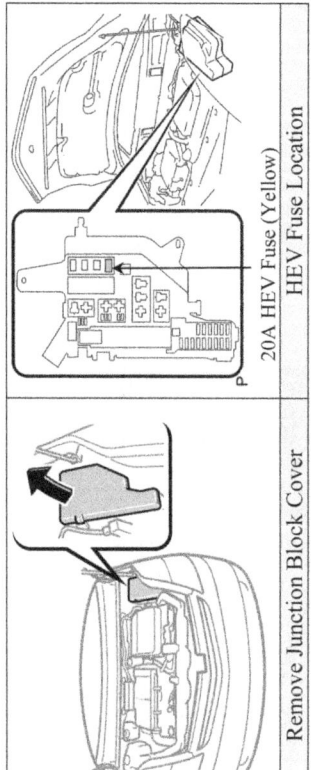

12-Volt Auxiliary Battery

Access to 12-Volt Auxiliary Battery

Hood Latch Release

Remote Hood Release

HEV Fuse Location

20A HEV Fuse (Yellow)

Remove Junction Block Cover

Emergency Response (Continued)

Extrication (Continued)

Alternate Procedure (power button inaccessible)

Procedure #2

1. Disconnect the 12-Volt auxiliary battery in the rear cargo area.
2. Remove the HEV fuse (20A yellow colored) in the engine compartment junction block as illustrated. When in doubt, pull all four fuses in the fuse block.

WARNING:

- *After disabling the vehicle, power is maintained for **90 seconds** in the SRS system and **5 minutes** in the high voltage electrical system.*
- *If either of the disabling procedures above cannot be performed, proceed with caution as there is no assurance that the high voltage electrical system, SRS, or fuel pump are disabled.*
- ***Never** touch, cut, or open any orange high voltage power cable or high voltage component.*

15

Emergency Response (Continued)

Extrication (Continued)

- **Stabilize Vehicle**
  Crib at (4) points directly under the front and rear pillars.
  Do not place cribbing under the high voltage power cables, exhaust system, or fuel system.

- **Access Patients**
  Glass Removal
  Use normal glass removal procedures as required.

  SRS Awareness
  Responders need to be cautious when working in close proximity to undeployed airbags and seat belt pretensioners. Deployed front dual stage airbags automatically ignite both stages within a fraction of a second.

  Door Removal/Displacement
  Doors can be removed by conventional rescue tools such as hand, electric, and hydraulic. In certain situations, it may be easier to pry back the body to expose and unbolt the hinges.

  Roof Removal
  The vehicle may contain optional curtain shield airbags. If equipped and undeployed, it is not recommend to remove or to displace the roof. Optional curtain shield airbags may be identified as illustrated.

  Dash Displacement
  The vehicle may contain optional curtain shield airbags. When equipped, do not remove or displace the roof during a dash displacement to avoid cutting into the airbags or inflators. As an alternative, dash displacement may be performed by using a Modified Dash Roll.

  If not equipped with the optional curtain shield airbags, displace the dash by using a conventional dash roll, Modified Dash Roll, or jacking the dash.

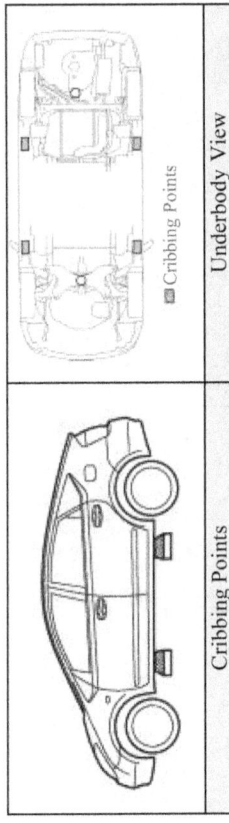

Cribbing Points

Underbody View

Cribbing Points

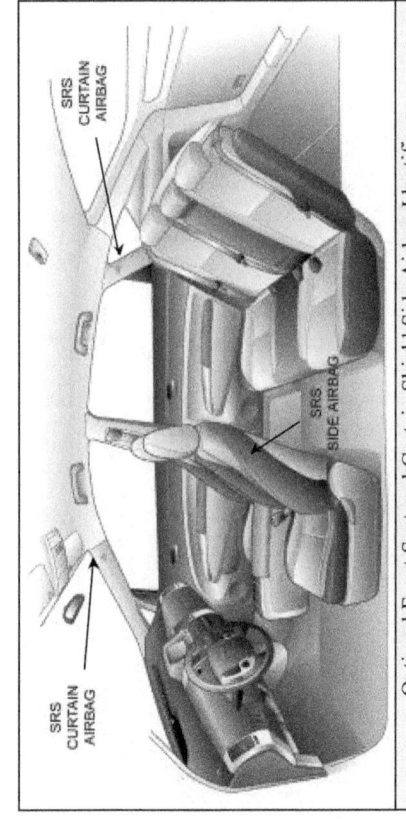

SRS CURTAIN AIRBAG

SRS CURTAIN AIRBAG

SRS SIDE AIRBAG

Optional Front Seat and Curtain Shield Side Airbag Identifiers

-17-

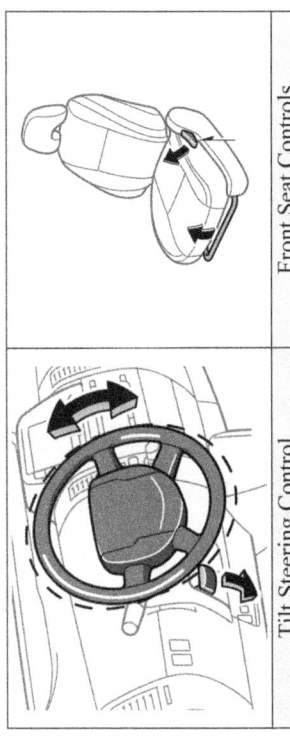

Front Seat Controls

Tilt Steering Control

Emergency Response (Continued)

Extrication (Continued)

Rescue Lift Air Bags
Responders should not place cribbing or rescue lift airbags under the high voltage power cables, exhaust system, or fuel system.

Repositioning Steering Wheel and Seat
Tilt steering and seat controls are shown in the illustration

Fire

Approach and extinguish a fire using proper vehicle fire fighting practices as recommended by NFPA, IFSTA, or the National Fire Academy (USA).

- Extinguishing Agent
  Water has been proven to be a suitable extinguishing agent.

- Initial Fire Attack
  Perform a fast, aggressive fire attack.
  Divert the runoff from entering watershed areas.

  Attack teams may not be able to identify a Prius until the fire has been knocked down and overhaul operations have commenced.

- Fire in the HV Battery Pack
  Should a fire occur in the NiMH HV battery pack, the incident commander will have to decide whether to pursue an offensive or defensive attack.

WARNING:

- *Potassium hydroxide and sodium hydroxide are key ingredients in the NiMH battery module electrolyte.*
- *The modules are contained within a metal case and access is limited to a small opening on the top.*
- *The cover should **Never** be breached or removed under any circumstances, including fire. Doing so may result in severe electrical burns, shock or electrocution.*

-18-

15

Emergency Response (Continued)

Fire (Continued)

When allowed to burn themselves out, the Prius NiMH battery modules burn rapidly and can quickly be reduced to ashes except for the metal alloy cell plates.

Offensive Fire Attack

Flooding the HV battery pack, located in the cargo area, with copious amounts of water at a safe distance will effectively control the HV battery pack fire by cooling the adjacent NiMH battery modules to a point below their ignition temperature. The remaining modules on fire, if not extinguished by the water, will burn themselves out.

Defensive Fire Attack

If the decision has been made to fight the fire using a defensive attack, the fire attack crew should pull back a safe distance and allow the NiMH battery modules to burn themselves out. During this defensive operation, fire crews may utilize a water stream or fog pattern to protect exposures or to control the path of smoke.

Overhaul

During overhaul, if not already done, immobilize and disable the vehicle. See illustrations on page 15.

- Immobilize Vehicle

  Chock wheels and set the parking brake. Push the **P** switch to engage park.

- Disable Vehicle

  Performing either of the two procedures will shut the vehicle off and disable the HV battery pack, SRS airbags, and gasoline fuel pump.

Procedure #1

1. Confirm the status of **READY** indicator in the instrument cluster.
2. If the **READY** indicator is illuminated, the vehicle is on and operational. Shut off the vehicle by pushing the power button once.

3. The vehicle is already shut off if the instrument cluster lights and the **READY** indicator are **not** illuminated. Do **not** push the power button the vehicle may start.
4. Remove the electronic key from the key slot.
5. If equipped, disable the smart key button underneath the steering column.
6. Keep the electronic key at least 16 feet (5 meters) away from the vehicle.
7. If the electronic key cannot be removed from the key slot or if the electronic key cannot be found, disconnect the 12-Volt auxiliary battery in the rear cargo area.

Alternate Procedure (power button inaccessible)

Procedure #2

1. Disconnect the 12-Volt auxiliary battery in the rear cargo area.
2. Remove the HEV fuse (20A yellow colored) in the engine compartment junction block as illustrated on page 16. When in doubt, pull all four fuses in the fuse block.

WARNING:

- *After disabling the vehicle, power is maintained for **90 seconds** in the SRS system and **5 minutes** in the high voltage electrical system.*
- *If either of the disabling steps above cannot be performed, proceed with caution as there is no assurance that the high voltage electrical system, SRS, or fuel pump are disabled.*
- ***Never** touch, cut, or open any orange high voltage power cable or high voltage component..*

Recovery/Recycling NiMH HV Battery Pack

Clean up of the HV battery pack can be accomplished by the vehicle recovery crew without further concern from runoff or spill. For information regarding recycling of the HV battery pack, contact the nearest Toyota dealer, or:

United States: (800) 331-4331
Canada: (888) Toyota 8 [(888)-869-6828]

Emergency Response (Continued)

Spills

The Prius contains the same common automotive fluids used in other Toyota vehicles, with the exception of NiMH electrolyte used in the HV battery pack. The NiMH battery electrolyte is a caustic alkaline (pH 13.5) that is damaging to human tissues. The electrolyte, however, is absorbed in the cell plates and will not normally spill or leak out even if a battery module is cracked. A catastrophic crash that would breach both the metal battery pack case and the plastic battery module would be a rare occurrence.

Similar to using baking soda to neutralize a lead-acid battery electrolyte spill, a dilute boric acid solution or vinegar is used to neutralize a NiMH battery electrolyte spill.

During an emergency, Toyota Material Safety Data Sheets (MSDS) may be requested by contacting:

    United States: CHEMTREC at (800) 424-9300
    Canada: CANUTEC at *666 or (613) 996-6666 (collect)

- Handle NiMH Electrolyte Spills Using The Following Personal Protective Equipment (PPE):
  Splash shield or safety goggles. Fold down helmet shields are not acceptable for acid or electrolyte spills.
  Rubber, latex or Nitrile gloves.
  Apron suitable for alkaline.
  Rubber boots.

- Neutralize NiMH Electrolyte
  Use a boric acid solution or vinegar.
  Boric acid solution - 800 grams boric acid to 20 liters water or 5.5 ounces boric acid to 1 gallon of water.

First Aid

Emergency responders may not be familiar with a NiMH electrolyte exposure when rendering aid to a patient. Exposure to the electrolyte is unlikely except in a catastrophic crash or through improper handling. Utilize the following guidelines during an exposure.

WARNING:
The NiMH battery electrolyte is a caustic alkaline (pH 13.5) that is damaging to human tissue.

- Wear Personal Protective Equipment (PPE)
  Splash shield or safety goggles. Fold down helmet shields are not acceptable for acid or electrolyte spills.
  Rubber, latex or Nitrile gloves.
  Apron suitable for alkaline.
  Rubber boots.

- Absorption
  Perform gross decontamination by removing affected clothing and properly disposing of the garments.
  Rinse the affected areas with water for 20 minutes.
  Transport to the nearest emergency medical care facility.

- Inhalation Non-Fire Situations
  No toxic gases are emitted under normal conditions.

- Inhalation Fire Situations
  Toxic gases are given off as the by-product of combustion. All responders in the Hot Zone should wear the proper PPE for fire fighting including SCBA.
  Remove patient from the hazardous environment to a safe area and administer oxygen.
  Transport to the nearest emergency medical care facility.

- Ingestion
  Do not induce vomiting.
  Allow patient to drink large quantities of water to dilute electrolyte (Never give water to an unconscious person).
  If vomiting occurs spontaneously, keep patients head lowered and forward to reduce the risk of aspiration.
  Transport to the nearest emergency medical care facility.

-20-

15

-21-

Emergency Response (Continued)

<u>Submersion</u>

Handle a Prius that is fully or partially submerged in water by disabling the HV battery pack, SRS airbags, and gasoline fuel pump.

- Remove vehicle from the water.

- Drain water from the vehicle if possible.

- Follow the immobilizing and disabling procedures on page 15.

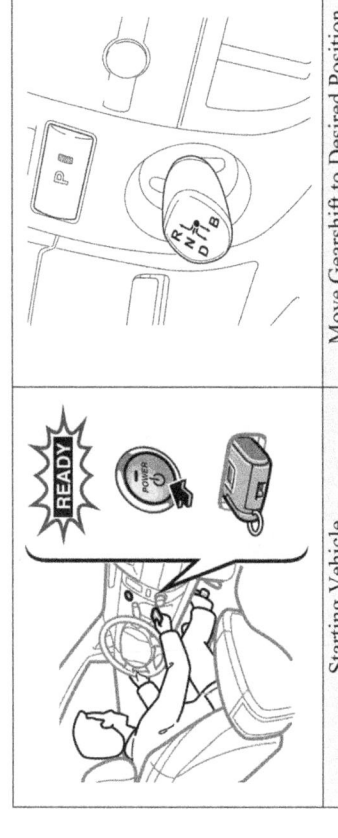

Move Gearshift to Desired Position

Starting Vehicle

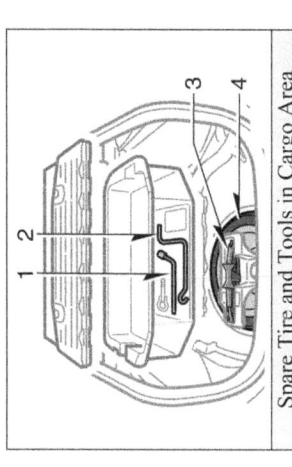

Spare Tire and Tools in Cargo Area

Roadside Assistance

The Prius utilizes an electronic gearshift selector and an electronic **P** switch for park. If the 12-Volt auxiliary battery is discharged or disconnected, the vehicle cannot be started nor can it be shifted out of park. If discharged, the 12-Volt auxiliary battery can be jump started to allow vehicle starting and shifting out of park. Most other roadside assistance operations may be handled like conventional Toyota vehicles.

Toyota Roadside Assistance is available during the basic warranty period by contacting:

United States: (877) 304-6495
Canada: (888) TOYOTA 8 [(888) 869-6828]

Towing
The Prius is a front wheel drive vehicle and it **must** be towed with the front wheels off the ground. Failure to do so may cause serious damage to Hybrid Synergy Drive components.

Vehicle Operation
Refer to the Electronic Key section page 6 for vehicle starting/stopping and page 15 for vehicle disabling information.

• The vehicle may be shifted out of park into Neutral only in the ignition-on and READY-on modes.

• If the 12-Volt auxiliary battery is discharged, the vehicle will not start and shifting out of park is not possible. There is no manual override except to jump start the vehicle.

Spare Tire
The spare tire, jack, and tools are provided in the cargo area as illustrated. The spare tire is for temporary use only (do not exceed 50 mph/80 kph).

15

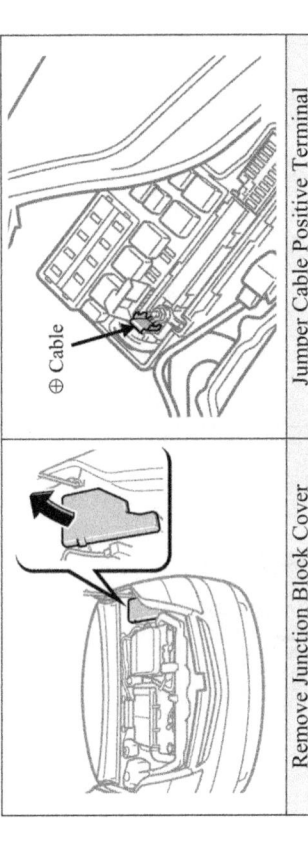

Remove Junction Block Cover | Jumper Cable Positive Terminal

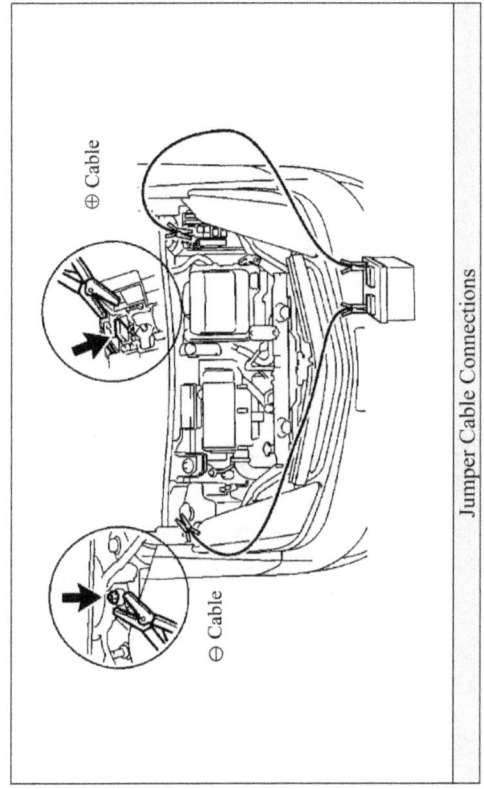

Jumper Cable Connections

Roadside Assistance (Continued)

Jump Starting

The 12-Volt auxiliary battery may be jump started if the vehicle does not start and the instrument cluster gauges are dim or off after depressing the brake pedal and pushing the power button.

The 12-Volt auxiliary battery is located in the cargo area. The rear hatch door will not unlock or open if the auxiliary battery is discharged. Instead, an accessible remote 12-Volt auxiliary battery positive terminal is provided in the engine compartment junction block, as illustrated, for jump starting.

- Remove the junction block cover and connect the positive jumper cable to the positive terminal in the junction block.

- Connect the negative terminal to the ground nut.

- The high voltage HV battery pack cannot be jump started.

Immobilizer & Anti-Theft Alarm

The vehicle comes standard with an electronic key immobilizer system. An anti-theft alarm is optional equipment.

- The vehicle may only be started with a learned immobilizer coded electronic key.

- To disable the optional alarm use the unlock button on the electronic key, unlock the driver door with the hidden metal cut key, or engage the ignition-on mode.

WARNING

*Your common sense, good judgement and general alertness are crucial to safe and successful service work. Before attempting any work on your Toyota, be sure to read the **Warnings**, **Cautions** and safety procedures in **3 Safety** and the copyright page at the front of the manual. Review these warnings and cautions each time you prepare to work on your car. Please also read any warnings and cautions that accompany the procedures in the manual.*

Filters
air 5-10
cabin air 9-7
oil 5-7

Fire
15-23

First aid
15-25

Foglight
10-18

Freeze-frame data
11-11

Front suspension
8-30

Fuel system
2-9

Fuel tank
2-9, 6-18
cap gasket 6-17
door opener 14-7

Fuses
driver side 12-9
engine compartment 12-5

Fusible links
12-13

G

Garage door opener
14-11

Glove compartment
9-7

Grounds
12-24

H

Hazard warning switch
10-24, 14-16

Headlight
10-10
switch 10-25
see also Lights

Heat storage tank
2-16

Heating
14-13

High voltage system
2-26
air-conditioning inverter 2-28
boost converter 2-27
DC-DC converter 2-29
disabling 3-12
HV battery 2-30, 15-17
cooling system 2-33
DTC table 11-51
ECU 2-32
neutralizing spills 3-19, 15-25
recycling 15-24
inverter 2-26
safety 3-4, 15-18
service plug 2-31
removing 3-12
switching OFF 3-10
system main relay (SMR) 2-33
testing 3-16
warnings and cautions 3-2

Hood release
14-7

Horn
10-9
button 8-52

Hybrid
1-6
control system DTC table 11-54
coolant 7-3
ECU 2-34
operating modes 1-11
parallel 1-6
series 1-6
synergy drive 1-7, 2-2, 14-8, 15-16
transaxle 2-18, 14-10

I

Identification
15-7
date of manufacture 4-13
tire pressure sensor 8-61
VIN vi, 4-13

Ignition system
coil 5-15
spark plugs 5-16

I/M
11-7

Immobilizer
15-28
DTC table 11-40

Information codes (INFs)
11-10

Injector
2-9

Inspection mode
11-3

Instruments
14-5
lighting 14-13

Intake manifold
2-7

Interior
1-17
lights 10-21

Inverter
1-9, 2-26
coolant 7-3
cooling system 2-26

J

Jack stands
4-16

Jacking
4-4, 4-6

Jump starting
3-20, 14-17

K

Key
14-4, 14-9, 15-11

Keyless entry
14-9

L

Level sensor (xenon headlights)
8-42, 10-16

License plate light
10-21

Lifting
4-4

Lights
10-10 14-11
DTC table 11-73
see also Headlight

Lock
9-12

Luggage storage box
3-13, 14-12

4 INDEX

S

Safety
3-1, 15-18
equipment 3-6

Scan tool
11-12

Seat
front 9-22
adjustment 14-12
headrest 14-12
rear 9-25, 14-12

Seat belt
14-15
front 9-22
pretensioner 15-19
rear 9-25

Security
alarm 15-28
immobilizer 15-28

Serpentine belt
5-12

Service
advice 4-8
schedules 4-18

Service plug
2-31
removing 3-12

Shiftting the Prius
valet instruction 2-50

Shift control
2-25, 14-4, 14-10, 15-15
DTC table 11-87

Shock absorber
front 8-30
rear 8-43

Short circuits
13-11

Side bolster airbag
9-22

Skid control
2-42

Smart key
14-9, 15-13

Sound system
14-14
DTC table 11-20
speaker 9-12, 9-14

Spare tire
14-17, 15-27

Spark plugs
5-16

Speakers
9-12, 9-14

Specifications, fluid
brake fluid 8-24
engine coolant 5-30
engine oil 5-6
transaxle coolant 7-3
transaxle lubricant 7-11

Speed sensor (resolver)
2-23

Spring
front 8-30
rear 8-43

SRS (supplemental restraint system)
14-16, 15-19
DTC table 11-89

Stabilizer bar
rear 8-42

Starting the Prius
valet instruction 2-50

Starting system
DTC table 11-85

Static damage
12-2

Steering
1-16, 2-39
column 10-25
joints & boots 8-34
torque sensor 8-55
wheel 8-53, 14-10
see also EPS (electric power steering)

Steering column switches
10-25

Stop light switch
10-22

Strut
front 8-30

Supplemental restraint system (SRS)
14-16
DTC table 11-89

Suspension
1-15
front 8-30
rear 8-42
troubleshooting 8-31

Switches
back-up light 10-22
brake light 10-22
door switches 10-23
hazard warning 10-24
headlight dimmer 10-25
horn 8-52
light 10-25
mirror 10-23
steering column stalk 10-25
turn signal 10-25
window 10-13
wiper / washer 10-25

System main relay (SMR)
2-33

T

Tailgate
14-7

Taillights
10-20

Technical data
1-3, 2-4

Thermostat
5-42

Throttle
2-7

THS II
1-7

Tie rod
8-34

Tightening torques
4-10

Timing chain
5-24

Tire pressure warning system (TPWS)
2-47, 8-57
DTC table 11-96
initialization 8-60
registering sensors 8-61
warning light 11-15
warning system 8-57

Tires
8-56

TIS (Toyota technical information system)
4-17

Tools
4-14, 14-17

6 INDEX

Selected Books and Repair Information From Bentley Publishers

Engineering

Physics for Gearheads *Randy Beikmann* ISBN 978-0-8376-1615-5

Mechanical Ignition Handbook: The Hack Mechanic Guide to Vintage Ignition Systems *Rob Siegel* ISBN 978-0-8376-1767-1

The Hack Mechanic Guide to European Automotive Electrical Systems *Rob Siegel* ISBN 978-0-8376-1751-0

Supercharged! Design, Testing and Installation of Supercharger Systems *Corky Bell* ISBN 978-0-8376-0168-7

Bosch Fuel Injection and Engine Management *Charles O. Probst, SAE* ISBN 978-0-8376-0300-1

Bosch Automotive Handbook Updated 9th Edition *Robert Bosch, GmbH* ISBN 978-0-8376-1732-9

Motorsports

Alex Zanardi: My Sweetest Victory *Alex Zanardi and Gianluca Gasparini* ISBN 978-0-8376-1249-2

The Unfair Advantage *Mark Donohue and Paul van Valkenburgh* ISBN 978-0-8376-0069-7

Equations of Motion - Adventure, Risk and Innovation *William F. Milliken* ISBN 978-0-8376-1570-7

Audi Repair Manuals

Audi A4 Service Manual: 2002-2008, 1.8L Turbo, 2.0L Turbo, 3.0L, 3.2L *Bentley Publishers* ISBN 978-0-8376-1574-5

Audi A4 Service Manual: 1996-2001, 1.8L Turbo, 2.8L *Bentley Publishers* ISBN 978-0-8376-1675-9

Audi TT Service Manual: 2000-2006, 1.8L turbo, 3.2 L *Bentley Publishers* ISBN 978-0-8376-1625-4

Audi A6 Service Manual: 1998-2004 *Bentley Publishers* ISBN 978-0-8376-1670-4

BMW

Memoirs of a Hack Mechanic *Rob Siegel* ISBN 978-0-8376-1720-6

BMW X3 (E83) Service Manual: 2004-2010 *Bentley Publishers* ISBN 978-0-8376-1731-2

BMW X5 (E53) Service Manual: 2000-2006 *Bentley Publishers* ISBN 978-0-8376-1643-8

BMW 4 Series (F32, F33, F36) Service Manual: 2014-2016 *Bentley Publishers* ISBN 978-0-8376-1765-7

BMW 3 Series (F30, F31, F34) Service Manual: 2012-2015 *Bentley Publishers* ISBN 978-0-8376-1752-7

BMW 3 Series (E90, E91, E92, E93) Service Manual: 2006-2011 *Bentley Publishers* ISBN 978-0-8376-1723-7

BMW 3 Series (E46) Service Manual: 1999-2005 *Bentley Publishers* ISBN 978-0-8376-1657-5

Porsche

Porsche 911 (996) Service Manual: 1999-2005 *Bentley Publishers* ISBN 978-0-8376-1710-7

Porsche 911 (993) Service Manual: 1995-1998 *Bentley Publishers* ISBN 978-0-8376-1719-0

Porsche Boxster. Boxster S (986) Service Manual: 1997-2004 *Bentley Publishers* ISBN 978-0-8376-1645-2

Porsche 911 Carrera Service Manual: 1984-1989 *Bentley Publishers* ISBN 978-0-8376-1696-4

Porsche 911 (964): Enthusiast's Companion *Bentley Publishers* ISBN 978-0-8376-0293-6

Porsche: Excellence Was Expected *Karl Ludvigsen* ISBN 978-0-8376-0235-6

Ferdinand Porsche – Genesis of Genius *Karl Ludvigsen* ISBN 978-0-8376-1557-8

Porsche – Origin of the Species *Karl Ludvigsen* ISBN 978-0-8376-1331-4

Volkswagen

Volkswagen Rabbit, GTI Service Manual: 2006-2009 *Bentley Publishers* ISBN 978-0-8376-1664-3

Volkswagen Jetta, Golf, GTI Service Manual: 1999-2005 *Bentley Publishers* ISBN 978-0-8376-1678-0

Volkswagen Jetta Service Manual: 2005-2010 *Bentley Publishers* ISBN 978-0-8376-1616-2

Volkswagen Passat Service Manual: 1998-2005 *Bentley Publishers* ISBN 978-0-8376-1669-8

Volkswagen Jetta, Golf, GTI: 1993-1999, Cabrio: 1995-2002 Service Manual *Bentley Publishers* ISBN 978-0-8376-1660-5

MINI Repair Manuals

MINI Cooper Service Manual: 2007-2013 *Bentley Publishers* ISBN 978-0-8376-1730-5

MINI Cooper Service Manual: 2002-2006 *Bentley Publishers* ISBN 978-0-8376-1639-1

MINI Cooper Diagnosis Without Guesswork: 2002-2006 *Bentley Publishers* ISBN 978-0-8376-1571-4

Mercedes-Benz

Mercedes-Benz C-Class (W202) Service Manual 1994-2000 *Bentley Publishers* ISBN 978-0-8376-1692-6

Mercedes Benz E-Class (W124) Owner's Bible: 1986-1995 *Bentley Publishers* ISBN 978-0-8376-0230-1

BentleyPublishers® Automotive Reference

Bentley Publishers has published service manuals and automobile books since 1950. For more information, please contact Bentley Publishers at 1734 Massachusetts Avenue, Cambridge, MA 02138 USA, or visit our web site at **BentleyPublishers.com**